Geometry
Concepts and Skills

Ron Larson
Laurie Boswell
Lee Stiff

McDougal Littell
A HOUGHTON MIFFLIN COMPANY
Evanston, Illinois • Boston • Dallas

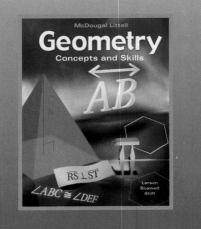

About Geometry: Concepts and Skills

This book has been written so that all students can understand geometry. The course focuses on the key topics that provide a strong foundation in the essentials of geometry. Lesson concepts are presented in a clear, straightforward manner, supported by frequent worked-out examples. The page format makes it easy for students to follow the flow of a lesson, and the vocabulary and visual tips in the margins help students learn how to read the text and diagrams. Checkpoint questions within lessons give students a way to check their understanding as they go along. The exercises for each lesson provide many opportunities to practice and maintain skills, as well as to apply concepts to real-world problems.

ISBN: 0-618-50157-6   23456789–DWO–08 07 06 05

Internet Web Site: http://www.classzone.com

About the Authors

RON LARSON is a professor of mathematics at Penn State University at Erie, where he has taught since receiving his Ph.D. in mathematics from the University of Colorado in 1970. He is the author of a broad range of instructional materials for middle school, high school, and college. Dr. Larson has been an innovative writer of multimedia approaches to mathematics, and his Calculus and Precalculus texts are both available in interactive form on the Internet.

LAURIE BOSWELL is a mathematics teacher at Profile Junior-Senior High School in Bethlehem, New Hampshire. A recipient of the 1986 Presidential Award for Excellence in Mathematics Teaching, she is also the 1992 Tandy Technology Scholar and the 1991 recipient of the Richard Balomenos Mathematics Education Service Award from the New Hampshire Association of Teachers of Mathematics. She has had leadership positions in state and NCTM committees.

LEE STIFF is a professor of mathematics education in the College of Education of North Carolina State University at Raleigh and has taught mathematics at the high school and middle school levels. He has served on the NCTM Board of Directors and was elected President of NCTM for the years 2000–2002. He is the 1992 recipient of the W. W. Rankin Award for Excellence in Mathematics Education presented by the North Carolina Council of Teachers of Mathematics.

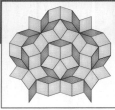

CONSULTANT FOR CURRICULUM AND INSTRUCTIONAL DESIGN

Patrick Hopfensperger
Mathematics Teacher
Homestead High School
Mequon, WI

REVIEWERS

Isidro Castillo
Mathematics Teacher
Huntington Park High School
Los Angeles, CA

Grace O. Dike
Assistant Principal (Mathematics)
Norman Thomas High School
New York, NY

Carol Forman
Mathematics Teacher
Catoctin High School
Thurmont, MD

Ellen Thomas Lawrence
Mathematics Teacher
Francis Scott Key High School
Union Bridge, MD

Evie Raffanti
Mathematics Teacher
Niles West High School
Skokie, IL

Alice Smith Rau
Mathematics Teacher
Francis Scott Key High School
Union Bridge, MD

Emma Wilkinson
Mathematics Teacher
Brunswick High School
Brunswick, OH

TEACHER PANEL

William Anderson
Mathematics Teacher
Clay High School
Oregon, OH

Pat Cameron
Mathematics Teacher
Pickerington High School
Pickerington, OH

Randall Hahn
Mathematics Teacher
Canton South High School
Canton, OH

Rita Kegg
Mathematics Teacher
Mentor High School
Mentor, OH

Alan Novy
Mathematics Teacher
Valley Forge High School
Parma Heights, OH

Robert Seitz
Mathematics Teacher
Collingwood High School
Cleveland, OH

Marsha Smith
Mathematics Teacher
Xenia High School
Xenia, OH

Kim Snyder
Mathematics Teacher
Strongsville High School
Strongsville, OH

Doug Weygandt
Mathematics Teacher
Hilliard Davidson High School
Hilliard, OH

Chapter 1 Basics of Geometry

▶ **CHAPTER STUDY GUIDE**   **2**

STUDENT HELP

Visualize It! *2, 15, 16, 23, 24, 29, 30, 36, 37*
Study Tip *8, 49*
Vocabulary Tip *34*
Reading Tip *9, 22*
Skills Review *28, 32, 49*
Test Tip *47*

APPLICATION HIGHLIGHTS

Chemistry *6*
Braille *7*
Moon Phases *12*
3-Wheeled Car *19*
Sculpture *26*
Perspective *27*
Shark Teeth *28*
Runways *40*

INTERNET

4, 6, 7, 10, 12, 18, 24, 32, 39, 40

1.1 Finding and Describing Patterns   **3**

1.2 Inductive Reasoning   **8**

1.3 Points, Lines, and Planes   **14**
QUIZ 1, *20*

1.4 Sketching Intersections   **22**
▶ ACTIVITY: *Exploring Intersections, 21*

1.5 Segments and Their Measures   **28**

1.6 Angles and Their Measures   **35**
▶ ACTIVITY: *Kinds of Angles, 34*
QUIZ 2, *41*

REVIEW AND ASSESSMENT

Chapter Readiness Quiz, *2*
Quizzes, *20, 41*
Standardized Test Practice, *7, 13, 20, 27, 33, 40*
Chapter Summary and Review, *42*
Chapter Test, *46*
Chapter Standardized Test, *47*
Brain Games, *48*
Algebra Review, *49*

Getting Ready

Pre-Course Test   **xx**
A diagnostic test on key skills from earlier courses, referenced to the Skills Review (pp. 653–674)

Pre-Course Practice   **xxii**
Additional practice on the skills in the Pre-Course Test, also referenced to the Skills Review

Chapter 2 Segments and Angles

▶ **CHAPTER STUDY GUIDE**   **52**

2.1   **Segment Bisectors**   **53**

2.2   **Angle Bisectors**   **61**
    ▶ **ACTIVITY:** *Folding Angle Bisectors, 60*

2.3   **Complementary and Supplementary Angles**   **67**
    QUIZ 1, *73*

2.4   **Vertical Angles**   **75**
    ▶ **ACTIVITY:** *Angles and Intersecting Lines, 74*

2.5   **If-Then Statements and Deductive Reasoning**   **82**

2.6   **Properties of Equality and Congruence**   **88**
    QUIZ 2, *94*

    Project: *Drawing in Perspective*   **102**

STUDENT HELP

Visualize It! *52, 61, 62, 67, 69, 75, 76*
Study Tip *54, 68, 77, 82, 90, 101*
Vocabulary Tip *53, 58, 74, 82*
Reading Tip *55*
Skills Review *55*
Test Tip *99*

APPLICATION HIGHLIGHTS

Strike Zone *58*
Paper Airplanes *65*
Lasers *65*
Bridges *71*
Beach Chairs *72*
Flags *79*
Drafting Table *80*
Advertising *86*

INTERNET

57, 63, 65, 71, 72, 79, 80, 84, 86, 90

REVIEW AND ASSESSMENT

Chapter Readiness Quiz, *52*
Quizzes, *73, 94*
Standardized Test Practice, *59, 66, 73, 81, 87, 93*
Chapter Summary and Review, *95*
Chapter Test, *98*
Chapter Standardized Test, *99*
Brain Games, *100*
Algebra Review, *101*

Chapter 3

Parallel and Perpendicular Lines

▶ **CHAPTER STUDY GUIDE**   **106**

3.1   Relationships Between Lines   **108**
  ▶ ACTIVITY: *Lines in Space, 107*

3.2   Theorems About Perpendicular Lines   **114**
  QUIZ 1, *120*

3.3   Angles Formed by Transversals   **121**

3.4   Parallel Lines and Transversals   **128**
  ▶ ACTIVITY: *Parallel Lines and Angles, 126*
  QUIZ 2, *135*

3.5   Showing Lines are Parallel   **136**

3.6   Using Perpendicular and Parallel Lines   **143**
  ▶ TECHNOLOGY: *Parallel Lines and Slope, 150*

3.7   Translations   **152**
  QUIZ 3, *159*

STUDENT HELP

Visualize It! *106, 107, 108, 112, 121, 128, 129, 131*
Study Tip *114, 167*
Vocabulary Tip *152*
Reading Tip *153, 154*
Skills Review *150*
Test Tip *165*

APPLICATION HIGHLIGHTS

Furniture *111*
Orienteering *119*
Auto Racing *122*
Bicycles *124*
Rainbows *133*
Kiteboarding *141*
Guitar *148*
Chess *157*

INTERNET

118, 133, 134, 137, 148, 153

REVIEW AND ASSESSMENT

Chapter Readiness Quiz, *106*
Quizzes, *120, 135, 159*
Standardized Test Practice, *113, 119, 125, 134, 142, 149, 158*
Chapter Summary and Review, *160*
Chapter Test, *164*
Chapter Standardized Test, *165*
Brain Games, *166*
Algebra Review, *167*
Cumulative Practice, Chapters 1–3, *168*

Chapter 4 Triangle Relationships

▶ **CHAPTER STUDY GUIDE**   **172**

4.1 Classifying Triangles   **173**

4.2 Angle Measures of Triangles   **179**
QUIZ 1, *184*

4.3 Isosceles and Equilateral Triangles   **185**

4.4 The Pythagorean Theorem and the Distance Formula   **192**
▶ ACTIVITY: *Areas and Right Triangles, 191*
QUIZ 2, *198*

4.5 The Converse of the Pythagorean Theorem   **200**
▶ TECHNOLOGY: *Side Lengths of Triangles, 199*

4.6 Medians of a Triangle   **207**
▶ ACTIVITY: *Intersecting Medians, 206*

4.7 Triangle Inequalities   **212**
QUIZ 3, *218*

Project: *Balancing Shapes*   **228**

REVIEW AND ASSESSMENT

Chapter Readiness Quiz, *172*
Quizzes, *184, 198, 218*
Standardized Test Practice, *178, 184, 190, 198, 205, 211, 217*
Chapter Summary and Review, *219*
Chapter Test, *224*
Chapter Standardized Test, *225*
Brain Games, *226*
Algebra Review, *227*

STUDENT HELP

Visualize It! *172, 177, 178, 181, 183, 186, 217*
Study Tip *194, 201*
Vocabulary Tip *173, 175, 185*
Reading Tip *179*
Skills Review *192, 206*
Test Tip *225*

APPLICATION HIGHLIGHTS

Basketball *177*
Water Resources *183*
Architecture *186*
Rock Climbing *189*
Support Beam *196*
Campus Pathways *197*
Garden *200*
Kitchen Design *215*

INTERNET

174, 180, 183, 189, 196, 197, 202, 208, 211, 213

Chapter 5 Congruent Triangles

▶ **CHAPTER STUDY GUIDE**   **232**

5.1 Congruence and Triangles   **233**

5.2 Proving Triangles are Congruent: SSS and SAS   **241**
▶ ACTIVITY: *Congruent Triangles, 240*
QUIZ 1, *249*

5.3 Proving Triangles are Congruent: ASA and AAS   **250**

5.4 Hypotenuse-Leg Congruence Theorem: HL   **257**
QUIZ 2, *263*
▶ TECHNOLOGY: *Investigating Congruence, 264*

5.5 Using Congruent Triangles   **265**

5.6 Angle Bisectors and Perpendicular Bisectors   **273**
▶ ACTIVITY: *Investigating Bisectors, 272*

5.7 Reflections and Symmetry   **282**
▶ ACTIVITY: *Investigating Reflections, 281*
QUIZ 3, *290*

REVIEW AND ASSESSMENT

Chapter Readiness Quiz, *232*
Quizzes, *249, 263, 290*
Standardized Test Practice, *239, 248, 256, 262, 271, 280, 289*
Chapter Summary and Review, *291*
Chapter Test, *296*
Chapter Standardized Test, *297*
Brain Games, *298*
Algebra Review, *299*

STUDENT HELP

Visualize It! *232, 235, 242, 250, 252, 266, 282, 284*
Study Tip *234, 235, 243, 244, 248, 251, 252, 259, 264, 270, 273*
Vocabulary Tip *257*
Skills Review *240, 287*
Test Tip *297*

APPLICATION HIGHLIGHTS

Sculpture *239*
Quilting *247*
Origami *255*
Skateboard Ramp *257*
Stage Lighting *262*
Facilities Planning *275*
Soccer *278*
Kaleidoscopes *285*

INTERNET

238, 244, 247, 255, 258, 261, 267, 270, 275, 277, 278, 283, 285, 288

Chapter 6 Quadrilaterals

▶ **CHAPTER STUDY GUIDE**   **302**

6.1   **Polygons**   **303**

6.2   **Properties of Parallelograms**   **310**
    ▶ ACTIVITY: *Investigating Parallelograms, 309*

6.3   **Showing Quadrilaterals are Parallelograms**   **316**
    QUIZ 1, *323*
    ▶ TECHNOLOGY: *Making Parallelograms, 324*

6.4   **Rhombuses, Rectangles, and Squares**   **325**

6.5   **Trapezoids**   **332**
    ▶ TECHNOLOGY: *Midsegment of a Trapezoid, 331*

6.6   **Reasoning About Special Quadrilaterals**   **337**
    QUIZ 2, *341*

    Project: *Creating Tessellations*   **352**

REVIEW AND ASSESSMENT

Chapter Readiness Quiz, *302*
Quizzes, *323, 341*
Standardized Test Practice, *308, 315, 322, 330, 336, 341*
Chapter Summary and Review, *342*
Chapter Test, *346*
Chapter Standardized Test, *347*
Brain Games, *348*
Algebra Review, *349*
Cumulative Practice, Chapters 1–6, *350*

STUDENT HELP

Visualize It! *302, 309, 311, 314, 332*
Study Tip *304, 305, 316, 324, 326, 337, 349*
Vocabulary Tip *303, 331, 333*
Skills Review *322*
Test Tip *347*

APPLICATION HIGHLIGHTS

Street Signs *303*
Plants *307*
Truck Lift *310*
Scissors Lift *314*
Bicycle Gears *321*
Pool Table *322*
Making a Chair *329*
Gem Cutting *340*

INTERNET

307, 315, 317, 321, 326, 329, 336, 338, 340

Chapter 7 Similarity

STUDENT HELP

Visualize It! *356, 359, 373, 381, 384, 394*
Study Tip *357, 367, 374, 380, 394, 395*
Vocabulary Tip *365*
Skills Review *358*
Test Tip *405*

APPLICATION HIGHLIGHTS

Batting Average *357*
Map Scale *360*
Mural *370*
Aspect Ratio *371*
Hockey *374*
A-Frame *383*
Fractals *391*
Flashlight Image *397*

INTERNET

360, 363, 366, 370, 376, 377, 383, 387, 391, 397

▶ **CHAPTER STUDY GUIDE**   **356**

7.1 Ratio and Proportion   **357**

7.2 Similar Polygons   **365**
   ▶ **ACTIVITY:** *Conjectures About Similarity, 364*

7.3 Showing Triangles are Similar: AA   **372**
   QUIZ 1, *378*

7.4 Showing Triangles are Similar: SSS and SAS   **379**

7.5 Proportions and Similar Triangles   **386**

7.6 Dilations   **393**
   QUIZ 2, *398*
   ▶ **TECHNOLOGY:** *Dilations Using Coordinates, 399*

REVIEW AND ASSESSMENT

Chapter Readiness Quiz, *356*
Quizzes, *378, 398*
Standardized Test Practice, *363, 371, 377, 385, 392, 397*
Chapter Summary and Review, *400*
Chapter Test, *404*
Chapter Standardized Test, *405*
Brain Games, *406*
Algebra Review, *407*

Chapter 8 Polygons and Area

▶ **CHAPTER STUDY GUIDE** — 410

8.1 Classifying Polygons — 411

8.2 Angles in Polygons — 417
  ▶ ACTIVITY: *Angle Sum of Polygons, 416*
  QUIZ 1, *423*

8.3 Area of Squares and Rectangles — 424

8.4 Area of Triangles — 431
  ▶ ACTIVITY: *Finding Area of Triangles, 430*
  QUIZ 2, *437*
  ▶ TECHNOLOGY: *Area of Similar Triangles, 438*

8.5 Area of Parallelograms — 439

8.6 Area of Trapezoids — 446

8.7 Circumference and Area of Circles — 452
  ▶ ACTIVITY: *Finding Area of Circles, 451*
  QUIZ 3, *459*

Project: *Designing a Park* — 468

REVIEW AND ASSESSMENT

Chapter Readiness Quiz, *410*
Quizzes, *423, 437, 459*
Standardized Test Practice, *415, 423, 429, 437, 445, 450, 458*
Chapter Summary and Review, *460*
Chapter Test, *464*
Chapter Standardized Test, *465*
Brain Games, *466*
Algebra Review, *467*

STUDENT HELP

Visualize It! *410, 419, 426, 428, 432, 450, 454*
Study Tip *447, 452*
Vocabulary Tip *451, 454*
Skills Review *418*
Test Tip *465*

APPLICATION HIGHLIGHTS

Web Site Icons *414*
Home Plate *422*
Outdoor Bench *422*
Judo *428*
Maize Maze *429*
Basaltic Columns *436*
Covered Bridge *449*
Landscaping *457*

INTERNET

412, 421, 425, 436, 441, 449, 457

Chapter 9
Surface Area and Volume

▶ **CHAPTER STUDY GUIDE**   **472**

9.1   **Solid Figures**   **473**

9.2   **Surface Area of Prisms and Cylinders**   **483**
  ▶ **ACTIVITY:** *Investigating Surface Area, 481*

9.3   **Surface Area of Pyramids and Cones**   **491**
  QUIZ 1, *499*

9.4   **Volume of Prisms and Cylinders**   **500**

9.5   **Volume of Pyramids and Cones**   **510**
  ▶ **ACTIVITY:** *Investigating Volume, 508*

9.6   **Surface Area and Volume of Spheres**   **517**
  QUIZ 2, *523*

REVIEW AND ASSESSMENT

Chapter Readiness Quiz, *472*
Quizzes, *499, 523*
Standardized Test Practice, *480, 490, 498, 507, 516, 522*
Chapter Summary and Review, *524*
Chapter Test, *528*
Chapter Standardized Test, *529*
Brain Games, *530*
Algebra Review, *531*
Cumulative Practice, Chapters 1–9, *532*

STUDENT HELP

Visualize It! *472, 474, 484, 485, 491, 517*
Study Tip *474, 475, 478, 483, 484, 492, 501, 510, 515*
Vocabulary Tip *473*
Reading Tip *500*
Skills Review *492*
Test Tip *529*

APPLICATION HIGHLIGHTS

Rainforest Pyramid *491*
Veterinary Medicine *497*
Lampshades *498*
Swimming Pools *505*
Aquariums *505*
Pet Feeder *515*
Volcanoes *516*
Planetarium *522*

INTERNET

486, 494, 497, 504, 506, 514, 515, 518, 521, 522

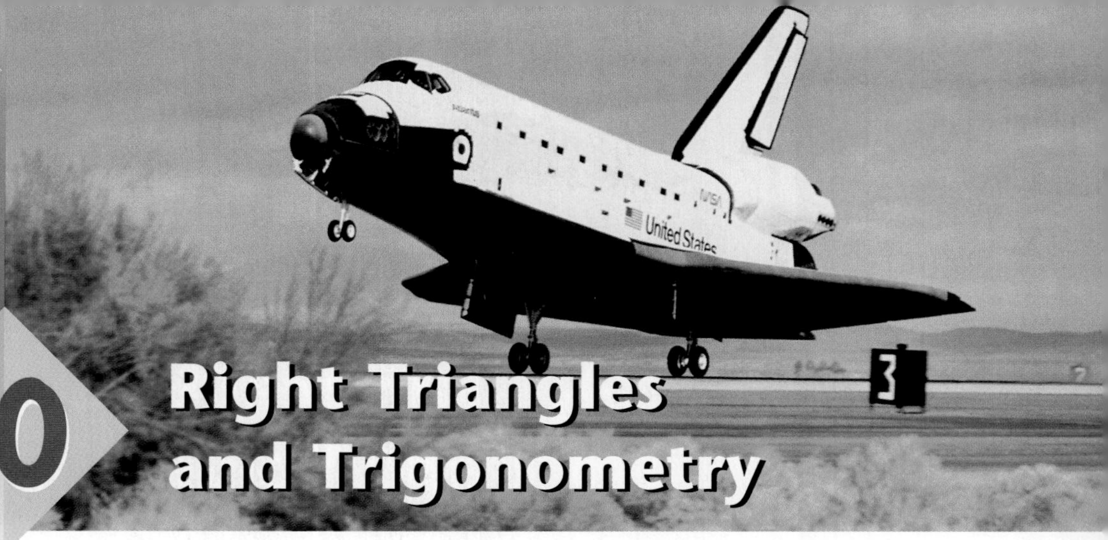

Chapter 10 — Right Triangles and Trigonometry

STUDENT HELP

Visualize It! *536, 549, 565, 571*
Study Tip *537, 538, 559, 571*
Reading Tip *543, 557, 569*
Skills Review *538*
Test Tip *581*

APPLICATION HIGHLIGHTS

Jewelry *546*
Tipping Platform *553*
Fitness *553*
Tree Height *559*
Water Slide *561*
Surveying *562*
Ramps *573*
Space Shuttle *574*

INTERNET

540, 543, 551, 553, 559, 561, 567, 570, 574

▶ **CHAPTER STUDY GUIDE** — **536**

10.1 **Simplifying Square Roots** — **537**

10.2 **45°-45°-90° Triangles** — **542**

10.3 **30°-60°-90° Triangles** — **549**
   ▶ ACTIVITY: *Special Right Triangles, 548*
   QUIZ 1, *555*

10.4 **Tangent Ratio** — **557**
   ▶ ACTIVITY: *Right Triangle Ratio, 556*

10.5 **Sine and Cosine Ratios** — **563**

10.6 **Solving Right Triangles** — **569**
   QUIZ 2, *575*

   Project: *Indirect Measurement* — **584**

REVIEW AND ASSESSMENT

Chapter Readiness Quiz, *536*
Quizzes, *555, 575*
Standardized Test Practice, *541, 547, 554, 562, 568, 574*
Chapter Summary and Review, *576*
Chapter Test, *580*
Chapter Standardized Test, *581*
Brain Games, *582*
Algebra Review, *583*

Chapter 11 Circles

STUDENT HELP

Visualize It! *588, 592, 602, 605, 616, 618, 633, 637*
Study Tip *589, 603, 609, 631*
Vocabulary Tip *590, 595, 597*
Skills Review *597, 603, 628*
Test Tip *647*

APPLICATION HIGHLIGHTS

GPS Device *599*
Fireworks *600*
Time Zones *605*
Archaeology *609*
Rescue Beacon *612*
Cell Phones *631*
Wheel Hubs *636*
Graphic Design *638*

INTERNET

590, 599, 606, 609, 612, 614, 618, 621, 630, 635, 638

▶ **CHAPTER STUDY GUIDE**   **588**

11.1 **Parts of a Circle**   **589**

11.2 **Properties of Tangents**   **595**
   ▶ ACTIVITY: *Tangents and Circles, 594*

11.3 **Arcs and Central Angles**   **601**
   QUIZ 1, *607*

11.4 **Arcs and Chords**   **608**

11.5 **Inscribed Angles and Polygons**   **614**
   ▶ ACTIVITY: *Exploring Inscribed Angles, 613*

11.6 **Properties of Chords**   **620**
   QUIZ 2, *625*
   ▶ TECHNOLOGY: *Intersecting Secants, 626*

11.7 **Equations of Circles**   **627**

11.8 **Rotations**   **633**
   QUIZ 3, *639*
   ▶ TECHNOLOGY: *Reflections and Rotations, 640*

REVIEW AND ASSESSMENT

Chapter Readiness Quiz, *588*
Quizzes, *607, 625, 639*
Standardized Test Practice, *593, 600, 607, 612, 619, 625, 632, 638*
Chapter Summary and Review, *641*
Chapter Test, *646*
Chapter Standardized Test, *647*
Brain Games, *648*
Cumulative Practice, Chapters 1–11, *649*

Contents of
Student Resources

Skills Review Handbook — 653

Problem Solving	653	The Coordinate Plane	664
Decimals	655	Slope of a Line	665
Fraction Concepts	656	Graphing Linear Equations	666
Fractions and Decimals	657	Slope-Intercept Form	667
Adding and Subtracting Fractions	658	Powers and Square Roots	668
		Evaluating Expressions	670
Multiplying and Dividing Fractions	659	The Distributive Property	671
Ratio and Proportion	660	One-Step Equations	672
		Multi-Step Equations	673
Inequalities and Absolute Value	662	Using Formulas	674
Integers	663		

Extra Practice for Chapters 1–11 — 675

End-of-Course Test — 697

Tables — 701

Symbols	701	Squares and Square Roots	704
Properties and Formulas	702	Trigonometric Ratios	705

Postulates and Theorems — 706

Appendices — 711

Glossary — 719

English-to-Spanish Glossary — 732

Index — 747

Selected Answers — SA1

Getting Ready
A Guide to Student Help

Each chapter begins with a Study Guide

CHAPTER PREVIEW .... gives an overview of what you will be learning.

KEY WORDS .... lists important new words in the chapter.

READINESS QUIZ .... checks your understanding of words and skills that you will use in the chapter, and tells you where to go for review.

VISUAL STRATEGY .... suggests a visual way to make your learning easier.

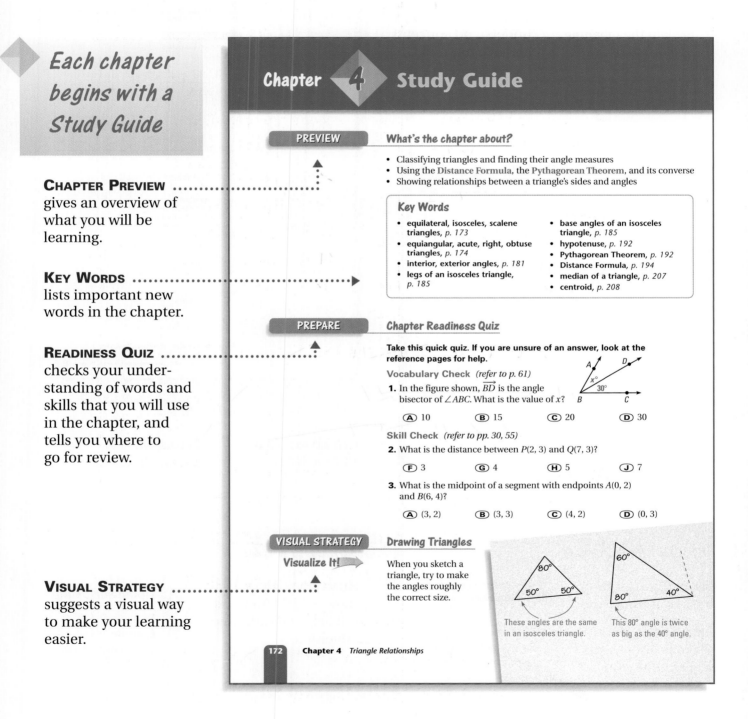

Chapter **4** **Study Guide**

PREVIEW   What's the chapter about?

- Classifying triangles and finding their angle measures
- Using the Distance Formula, the Pythagorean Theorem, and its converse
- Showing relationships between a triangle's sides and angles

Key Words

- equilateral, isosceles, scalene triangles, *p. 173*
- equiangular, acute, right, obtuse triangles, *p. 174*
- interior, exterior angles, *p. 181*
- legs of an isosceles triangle, *p. 185*
- base angles of an isosceles triangle, *p. 185*
- hypotenuse, *p. 192*
- Pythagorean Theorem, *p. 192*
- Distance Formula, *p. 194*
- median of a triangle, *p. 207*
- centroid, *p. 208*

PREPARE   Chapter Readiness Quiz

Take this quick quiz. If you are unsure of an answer, look at the reference pages for help.

Vocabulary Check *(refer to p. 61)*

1. In the figure shown, $\overrightarrow{BD}$ is the angle bisector of $\angle ABC$. What is the value of x?

  A 10   **B** 15   **C** 20   **D** 30

Skill Check *(refer to pp. 30, 55)*

2. What is the distance between $P(2, 3)$ and $Q(7, 3)$?

  F 3   **G** 4   **H** 5   **J** 7

3. What is the midpoint of a segment with endpoints $A(0, 2)$ and $B(6, 4)$?

  A (3, 2)   **B** (3, 3)   **C** (4, 2)   **D** (0, 3)

VISUAL STRATEGY   Drawing Triangles

Visualize It!   When you sketch a triangle, try to make the angles roughly the correct size.

These angles are the same in an isosceles triangle.

This 80° angle is twice as big as the 40° angle.

172   **Chapter 4**   *Triangle Relationships*

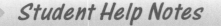

Student Help Notes

VOCABULARY TIPS explain the meaning and origin of words.

STUDY TIPS help you understand concepts and avoid errors.

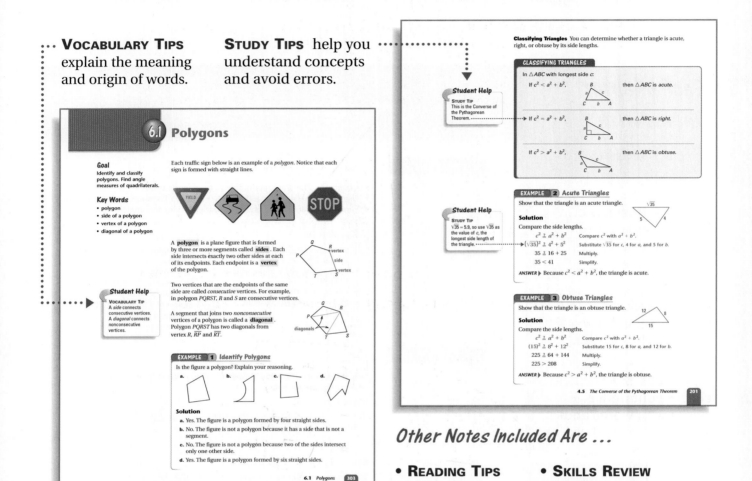

Classifying Triangles You can determine whether a triangle is acute, right, or obtuse by its side lengths.

CLASSIFYING TRIANGLES

In $\triangle ABC$ with longest side c:

If $c^2 < a^2 + b^2$, then $\triangle ABC$ is *acute*.

Student Help
STUDY TIP
This is the Converse of the Pythagorean Theorem.

If $c^2 = a^2 + b^2$, then $\triangle ABC$ is *right*.

If $c^2 > a^2 + b^2$, then $\triangle ABC$ is *obtuse*.

EXAMPLE 2 Acute Triangles

Show that the triangle is an acute triangle.

Student Help
STUDY TIP
$\sqrt{35} \approx 5.9$, so use $\sqrt{35}$ as the value of c, the longest side length of the triangle.

Solution
Compare the side lengths.

$$c^2 \stackrel{?}{<} a^2 + b^2 \quad \text{Compare } c^2 \text{ with } a^2 + b^2.$$
$$(\sqrt{35})^2 \stackrel{?}{<} 4^2 + 5^2 \quad \text{Substitute } \sqrt{35} \text{ for } c, 4 \text{ for } a, \text{ and } 5 \text{ for } b.$$
$$35 \stackrel{?}{<} 16 + 25 \quad \text{Multiply.}$$
$$35 < 41 \quad \text{Simplify.}$$

ANSWER Because $c^2 < a^2 + b^2$, the triangle is acute.

EXAMPLE 3 Obtuse Triangles

Show that the triangle is an obtuse triangle.

Solution
Compare the side lengths.

$$c^2 \stackrel{?}{>} a^2 + b^2 \quad \text{Compare } c^2 \text{ with } a^2 + b^2.$$
$$(15)^2 \stackrel{?}{>} 8^2 + 12^2 \quad \text{Substitute } 15 \text{ for } c, 8 \text{ for } a, \text{ and } 12 \text{ for } b.$$
$$225 \stackrel{?}{>} 64 + 144 \quad \text{Multiply.}$$
$$225 > 208 \quad \text{Simplify.}$$

ANSWER Because $c^2 > a^2 + b^2$, the triangle is obtuse.

4.5 The Converse of the Pythagorean Theorem **201**

6.1 Polygons

Goal
Identify and classify polygons. Find angle measures of quadrilaterals.

Key Words
• polygon
• side of a polygon
• vertex of a polygon
• diagonal of a polygon

Each traffic sign below is an example of a *polygon*. Notice that each sign is formed with straight lines.

A **polygon** is a plane figure that is formed by three or more segments called **sides**. Each side intersects exactly two other sides at each of its endpoints. Each endpoint is a **vertex** of the polygon.

Two vertices that are the endpoints of the same side are called *consecutive* vertices. For example, in polygon *PQRST*, *R* and *S* are consecutive vertices.

Student Help
VOCABULARY TIP
A *side* connects consecutive vertices. A *diagonal* connects nonconsecutive vertices.

A segment that joins two *nonconsecutive* vertices of a polygon is called a **diagonal**. Polygon *PQRST* has two diagonals from vertex *R*, $\overline{RP}$ and $\overline{RT}$.

EXAMPLE 1 Identify Polygons

Is the figure a polygon? Explain your reasoning.

a.   b.   c.   d.

Solution
a. Yes. The figure is a polygon formed by four straight sides.
b. No. The figure is not a polygon because it has a side that is not a segment.
c. No. The figure is not a polygon because two of the sides intersect only one other side.
d. Yes. The figure is a polygon formed by six straight sides.

6.1 Polygons **303**

Other Notes Included Are ...

• **READING TIPS**
• **LOOK BACK**

• **SKILLS REVIEW**
• **EXTRA PRACTICE**

Internet References

MORE EXAMPLES are at classzone.com.

HOMEWORK HELP for some exercises is at classzone.com.

Student Help
CLASSZONE.COM

MORE EXAMPLES
More examples at classzone.com

Homework Help

HOMEWORK HELP chart shows which examples will help you with which exercises.

Homework Help

Example 1: Exs. 11–16
Example 2: Exs. 17–41
Example 3: Exs. 42–47

Visualizing Geometry

VISUAL PRESENTATIONS of lessons use photographs and diagrams to develop concepts. Color is used in text and diagrams to assist learning.

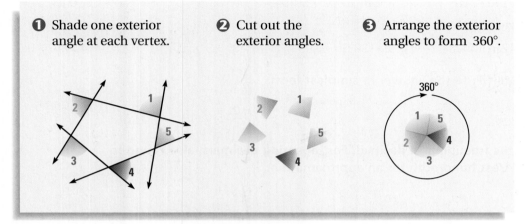

❶ Shade one exterior angle at each vertex.

❷ Cut out the exterior angles.

❸ Arrange the exterior angles to form 360°.

VISUALIZE IT! NOTES illustrate concepts and provide helpful hints for remembering ideas.

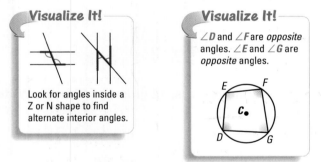

Visualize It!

Look for angles inside a Z or N shape to find alternate interior angles.

Visualize It!

∠D and ∠F are *opposite* angles. ∠E and ∠G are *opposite* angles.

VISUALIZE IT! EXERCISES ask you to make sketches that match descriptions, analyze diagrams, and draw conclusions from them.

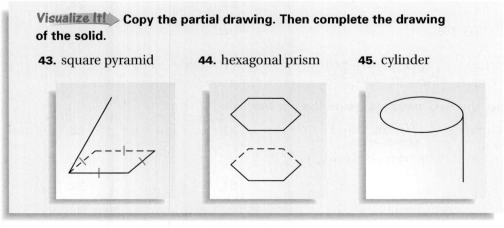

Visualize It! Copy the partial drawing. Then complete the drawing of the solid.

43. square pyramid

44. hexagonal prism

45. cylinder

Getting Ready
Pre-Course Test

DECIMALS AND FRACTIONS

Skills Review pp. 655–659

Evaluate.

1. $5.125 + 0.78$ **2.** $130.5 - 1.09$ **3.** 3.9×2.4 **4.** $9.6 \div 0.02$

Evaluate. Write the answer in simplest form.

5. $\dfrac{1}{8} + \dfrac{5}{8}$ **6.** $\dfrac{3}{4} - \dfrac{1}{2}$ **7.** $\dfrac{4}{5} \times \dfrac{3}{10}$ **8.** $\dfrac{7}{8} \div \dfrac{1}{2}$

Write the fraction as a decimal. For repeating decimals, also round to the nearest hundredth for an approximation.

9. $\dfrac{2}{5}$ **10.** $\dfrac{5}{8}$ **11.** $\dfrac{1}{3}$ **12.** $\dfrac{1}{6}$

Write the decimal as a fraction in simplest form.

13. 0.25 **14.** 0.375 **15.** 0.51 **16.** $0.\overline{6}$

RATIO AND PROPORTION

Skills Review pp. 660–661

There are 22 students in a geometry class, 12 girls and 10 boys. Write each ratio in simplest form.

17. boys : girls   **18.** girls : boys

19. boys : students   **20.** girls : students

Solve the proportion.

21. $\dfrac{x}{5} = \dfrac{16}{20}$ **22.** $\dfrac{9}{x} = \dfrac{12}{21}$ **23.** $\dfrac{3}{4} = \dfrac{x}{30}$ **24.** $\dfrac{5}{2} = \dfrac{4}{x}$

INEQUALITIES AND ABSOLUTE VALUE

Skills Review p. 662

Compare the two numbers. Write the answer using <, >, or =.

25. -4 and -8 **26.** 6 and -6 **27.** -1.5 and -1.9 **28.** 3.08 and 3.17

Evaluate.

29. $|-5|$ **30.** $|-17|$ **31.** $|3|$ **32.** $|9.9|$

INTEGERS

Skills Review
p. 663

Evaluate.

33. $-3 + 16$ **34.** $-8 - 4$ **35.** $(-5)(-9)$ **36.** $100 \div (-4)$

THE COORDINATE PLANE; SLOPE OF A LINE

Skills Review
pp. 664–665

Plot the points in a coordinate plane.

37. $A(3, 1)$ **38.** $B(2, -4)$ **39.** $C(-1, 5)$ **40.** $D(0, -2)$

Find the slope of the line that passes through the points.

41. $(-3, -2)$ and $(0, 0)$ **42.** $(-2, 1)$ and $(5, 1)$ **43.** $(0, 4)$ and $(6, -2)$

POWERS AND SQUARE ROOTS

Skills Review
pp. 668–669

Simplify.

44. $(-3)^3$ **45.** 2^4 **46.** $\sqrt{81}$ **47.** $\sqrt{64}$

48. $\sqrt{50}$ **49.** $\sqrt{72}$ **50.** $\dfrac{4}{\sqrt{2}}$ **51.** $\sqrt{\dfrac{1}{9}}$

EVALUATING EXPRESSIONS; THE DISTRIBUTIVE PROPERTY

Skills Review
pp. 670–671

Evaluate the expression when $n = -1$.

52. $2n^2 - 5$ **53.** $n + 90$ **54.** $n(n - 4)$ **55.** $(10 - n)^2$

Use the distributive property to rewrite the expression without parentheses.

56. $-8(x + 3)$ **57.** $a(a - 7)$ **58.** $(y - 6)(5)$ **59.** $(12 + z)z$

SOLVING EQUATIONS

Skills Review
pp. 672–673

Solve the equation.

60. $x + 11 = 4$ **61.** $17 = m - 16$ **62.** $12 - x = 15$ **63.** $-8y = -2$

64. $\dfrac{x}{2} = -9$ **65.** $3a - 1 = 8$ **66.** $24 = \dfrac{5}{8}x + 4$ **67.** $16z - 9 = 7z$

DECIMALS AND FRACTIONS

Skills Review pp. 655–659

Evaluate.

1. $0.67 + 1.045$ **2.** $8.5 + 1.52$ **3.** $13.7 + 0.03$ **4.** $\$4.19 + \$10.50$

5. $0.45 - 0.08$ **6.** $120 - 58.5$ **7.** $16.8 - 3.72$ **8.** $\$20 - \$1.99 - \$5$

9. 3.4×6.1 **10.** 0.02×10 **11.** 8.4×1.05 **12.** $\$15 \times 0.06$

13. $33.5 \div 0.01$ **14.** $0.418 \div 2$ **15.** $15 \div 1.5$ **16.** $56.44 \div 8.3$

Write two fractions equivalent to the given fraction.

17. $\frac{2}{3}$ **18.** $\frac{1}{5}$ **19.** $\frac{10}{20}$ **20.** $\frac{9}{12}$ **21.** $\frac{4}{7}$

Find the reciprocal of the number.

22. $\frac{3}{8}$ **23.** 9 **24.** $\frac{1}{4}$ **25.** $\frac{5}{2}$ **26.** 1

Add or subtract. Write the answer in simplest form.

27. $\frac{1}{4} + \frac{3}{4}$ **28.** $\frac{5}{12} + \frac{5}{12}$ **29.** $\frac{5}{9} - \frac{2}{9}$ **30.** $\frac{6}{7} - \frac{1}{7}$

31. $\frac{2}{5} + \frac{1}{15}$ **32.** $\frac{5}{6} - \frac{2}{9}$ **33.** $\frac{7}{8} - \frac{3}{4}$ **34.** $\frac{2}{3} - \frac{1}{2}$

Multiply or divide. Write the answer in simplest form.

35. $\frac{3}{4} \times \frac{1}{4}$ **36.** $\frac{1}{2} \times \frac{4}{5}$ **37.** $15 \times \frac{3}{8}$ **38.** $\frac{5}{8} \times \frac{2}{3}$

39. $\frac{3}{10} \div \frac{3}{5}$ **40.** $\frac{7}{12} \div \frac{1}{3}$ **41.** $20 \div \frac{2}{3}$ **42.** $\frac{7}{10} \div 8$

Write the fraction as a decimal. For repeating decimals, also round to the nearest hundredth for an approximation.

43. $\frac{1}{2}$ **44.** $\frac{2}{3}$ **45.** $\frac{4}{9}$ **46.** $\frac{3}{8}$ **47.** $\frac{3}{4}$

Write the decimal as a fraction in simplest form.

48. 0.13 **49.** 0.05 **50.** 0.625 **51.** 0.3 **52.** $0.\overline{8}$

RATIO AND PROPORTION

Skills Review
pp. 660–661

There are 27 students in a geometry class, 15 boys and 12 girls. Write each ratio in simplest form.

1. boys : girls   **2.** girls : boys   **3.** girls : students   **4.** boys : students

Simplify the ratio.

5. $\dfrac{1 \text{ ft}}{4 \text{ in.}}$ **6.** $\dfrac{20 \text{ ft}}{5 \text{ yd}}$ **7.** $\dfrac{85 \text{ cm}}{1 \text{ m}}$ **8.** $\dfrac{2 \text{ kg}}{500 \text{ g}}$

Solve the proportion.

9. $\dfrac{x}{3} = \dfrac{20}{21}$ **10.** $\dfrac{18}{x} = \dfrac{9}{4}$ **11.** $\dfrac{5}{8} = \dfrac{x}{2}$ **12.** $\dfrac{9}{14} = \dfrac{9}{x}$

13. $\dfrac{5}{x} = \dfrac{2}{10}$ **14.** $\dfrac{9}{10} = \dfrac{x}{4}$ **15.** $\dfrac{x}{10} = \dfrac{9}{50}$ **16.** $\dfrac{24}{36} = \dfrac{6}{x}$

INEQUALITIES AND ABSOLUTE VALUE

Skills Review
p. 662

Compare the two numbers. Write the answer using <, >, or =.

1. -8 and -10 **2.** 934 and 943   **3.** 0 and -5 **4.** -8 and 8

5. $\dfrac{1}{4}$ and 0.25   **6.** $\dfrac{1}{9}$ and $\dfrac{1}{7}$ **7.** 8.65 and 8.74   **8.** -0.5 and -0.55

Write the numbers in order from least to greatest.

9. $4, -6, -9, 0, 3$ **10.** $3.06, 3.16, 3.6, 3.1, 3.61$

11. $8652, 8562, 8256, 8265, 8526$ **12.** $-2.4, -1.6, -0.8, -1.9, -2.0$

Evaluate.

13. $|9|$ **14.** $|-16|$ **15.** $|-1|$ **16.** $|0|$ **17.** $|2.5|$ **18.** $|-4|$

INTEGERS

Skills Review
p. 663

Evaluate.

1. $-7 + (-5)$ **2.** $8 + (-2)$ **3.** $-10 + 6$ **4.** $20 + (-5) + 2$

5. $-6 - 5$ **6.** $19 - 24$ **7.** $-1 - (-6)$ **8.** $12 - (-9)$

9. $8(-7)$ **10.** $-1(20)$ **11.** $-8(-4)$ **12.** $-5(5)(6)$

13. $48 \div (-4)$ **14.** $-8 \div (-1)$ **15.** $-75 \div 25$ **16.** $-81 \div (-27)$

THE COORDINATE PLANE

Skills Review
p. 664

Give the coordinates of each point.

1. A **2.** B **3.** C

4. D **5.** E **6.** F

7. G **8.** H **9.** J

Plot the points in a coordinate plane.

10. $K(4, 1)$ **11.** $L(-3, -3)$ **12.** $M(0, 2)$

13. $N(-3, 4)$ **14.** $P(2, -1)$ **15.** $Q(-1, 0)$

SLOPE OF A LINE

Skills Review
p. 665

Find the slope of the line that passes through the points.

1. $(-3, -1)$ and $(0, 0)$ **2.** $(4, 2)$ and $(1, 7)$ **3.** $(-3, 2)$ and $(6, 2)$

4. $(-1, 2)$ and $(1, -2)$ **5.** $(-2, -5)$ and $(2, -3)$ **6.** $(2, 6)$ and $(4, 4)$

Plot the points and draw a line that passes through them. Determine whether the slope is *positive*, *negative*, *zero*, or *undefined*.

7. $(4, -1)$ and $(-2, -1)$ **8.** $(0, 0)$ and $(3, -2)$ **9.** $(-1, 4)$ and $(-1, 3)$

10. $(0, -2)$ and $(0, 5)$ **11.** $(2, 1)$ and $(-5, 1)$ **12.** $(2, 2)$ and $(4, 5)$

POWERS AND SQUARE ROOTS

Skills Review
pp. 668–669

Evaluate.

1. 5^3 **2.** $(-2)^3$ **3.** $(-4)^2$ **4.** 100^2 **5.** $(-1)^4$

Find all square roots of the number or write *no real square roots*.

6. 81   **7.** 16   **8.** -4 **9.** -100 **10.** 36

Evaluate. Give the exact value if possible. Otherwise, approximate to the nearest tenth.

11. $\sqrt{25}$ **12.** $\sqrt{9}$ **13.** $\sqrt{10}$ **14.** $\sqrt{21}$ **15.** $\sqrt{49}$

Simplify.

16. $\sqrt{20}$ **17.** $\sqrt{600}$ **18.** $\sqrt{75}$ **19.** $\sqrt{63}$ **20.** $\sqrt{52}$

21. $\sqrt{\dfrac{4}{81}}$ **22.** $\sqrt{\dfrac{1}{4}}$ **23.** $\dfrac{1}{\sqrt{2}}$ **24.** $\dfrac{5}{\sqrt{3}}$ **25.** $\dfrac{10}{\sqrt{5}}$

EVALUATING EXPRESSIONS

Skills Review
p. 670

Evaluate the expression.

1. $12 - 8 \cdot 2 + 4$ **2.** $20 - 3^2 - 5$ **3.** $7^2 \cdot 2 + 2$ **4.** $(8 + 19) \div (4 - 1)$

5. $19 + 16 \div 4$ **6.** $3(8 - 2)^2$ **7.** $(-7)(5 - 2 \cdot 3)$ **8.** $8 \cdot 4 - 5^2$

Evaluate the expression when $n = -4$.

9. $2n^2$ **10.** $(-5n)^2$ **11.** $n(n + 6)$ **12.** $90 - n$

13. $-8n + 10$ **14.** $11 + 6n$ **15.** $(-n)^3$ **16.** $n^2 - 100$

THE DISTRIBUTIVE PROPERTY

Skills Review
p. 671

Use the distributive property to rewrite the expression.

1. $3(y - 5)$ **2.** $(4a - 1)6$ **3.** $-2(3x + 3)$ **4.** $(10 + z)z$

5. $2(x + y)$ **6.** $(c + 8)(-5)$ **7.** $x(x - 4)$ **8.** $6x(x - 1)$

Simplify the expression.

9. $5x + 8 - 9x$ **10.** $-12y - y + 2$ **11.** $4 + z + z - 5$ **12.** $x^2 + 2x - 6x - 12$

13. $2(x - 5) + 13$ **14.** $4y - (y + 6)$ **15.** $18 - (9 - x)$ **16.** $a(a + 2) - 5(a - 3)$

SOLVING EQUATIONS

Skills Review
pp. 672–673

Solve the equation.

1. $x - 4 = 18$ **2.** $10 = m + 7$ **3.** $x + 2 = -5$ **4.** $y - 8 = -6$

5. $4a = -24$ **6.** $-x = 9$ **7.** $6m - 5 = 1$ **8.** $2n + 3 = 11$

9. $5a + 7 = 4a$ **10.** $8 - 7x = x$ **11.** $10 - 2x = 2x$ **12.** $2n - 1 = 5n + 8$

13. $\dfrac{n}{5} = 7$ **14.** $-\dfrac{2}{3}z = 22$ **15.** $\dfrac{x}{8} - 2 = -13$ **16.** $8 = \dfrac{1}{2}x + 6$

USING FORMULAS

Skills Review
p. 674

Use the formulas for a rectangle with length ℓ and width w.

1. A rectangle is 8 cm long and 6 cm wide. Find the perimeter.

2. Find the area of a rectangle with length 14 ft and width 5 ft.

3. Find the length of a rectangle with area 56 m² and width 8 m.

4. A rectangle has perimeter 20 in. and length 3 in. Find the width.

Area = ℓw
Perimeter = $2\ell + 2w$

Basics of Geometry

How are runways named?

Runways are named based on the angles they form with due north, measured in a clockwise direction. These angles are called *bearings*. To determine the runway number, the bearing is divided by 10.

The plane in the diagram has a bearing of 50°.

$50 \div 10 = 5$

It is on runway 5.

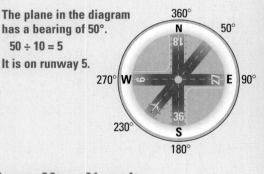

Learn More About It

You will learn more about airport runways in Exercises 40–44 on p. 40.

Who uses
Basics of Geometry?

SURVEYOR
Surveyors use angles to determine boundaries for roads, cell phone towers, and buildings. They also help determine safe speed limits on roads. (p. 39)

SCIENTIST
Scientists make observations, look for patterns, and use previous experiences to develop conjectures that can be tested. (p. 9)

How will you use these ideas?

- Understand how the Braille alphabet works. (p. 7)
- Predict when a full moon will occur. (p. 12)
- Understand why all tires of a three-wheeled car always touch the ground. (p. 19)
- Sketch intersecting lines in a perspective drawing. (p. 27)
- Use angle measures to locate cities by longitude. (p. 40)

Chapter 1

PREVIEW

What's the chapter about?

- Making predictions and **conjectures** based on patterns
- Sketching **points**, **lines**, **planes**, and their intersections
- Measuring **segments** and **angles**

Key Words

- conjecture, *p. 8*
- inductive reasoning, *p. 8*
- counterexample, *p. 10*
- point, line, plane, *p. 14*
- postulate, *p. 14*
- segment, *p. 16*
- ray, *p. 16*
- distance, length, *p. 28*

- congruent segments, *p. 30*
- sides of an angle, *p. 35*
- vertex of an angle, *p. 35*
- measure of an angle, *p. 36*
- congruent angles, *p. 36*
- acute, right, obtuse, and straight angle, *p. 36*

PREPARE

Chapter Readiness Quiz

Take this quick quiz. If you are unsure of an answer, look at the reference pages for help.

Skill Check *(refer to pp. 655, 662, 663, 668)*

1. Evaluate $102.9 - 34.7$.

    (A) 68.2   **(B)** 72.2   **(C)** 78.2   **(D)** 137.6

2. Evaluate $|-4|$.

    (F) -4 **(G)** -2 **(H)** 2   **(J)** 4

3. Evaluate $-6 + (-5)$.

    (A) -11 **(B)** -1 **(C)** 1   **(D)** 11

4. Evaluate $5^2 + (-1)^2$.

    (F) 8   **(G)** 16   **(H)** 24   **(J)** 26

VISUAL STRATEGY

Learning Vocabulary

Visualize It! ➡

Important words in this book are in **bold and highlighted** type. Keep a section in your notebook for definitions. Draw sketches near them to help you.

Vocabulary

acute angle: an angle with a measure between 0° and 90°

35°

1.1

Finding and Describing Patterns

Goal
Find patterns and use them to make predictions.

Key Words
- pattern
- prediction

In the bracelet shown at the right, the beads and knots follow a pattern. You can repeat the pattern to make the bracelet longer.

EXAMPLE 1 Describe a Visual Pattern

Describe a pattern in the figures.

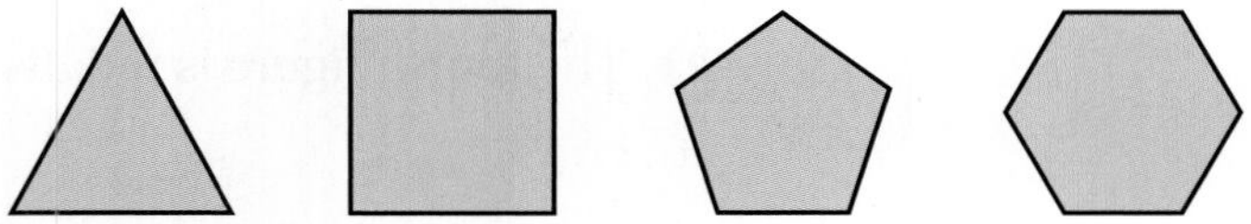

Solution

The figures have 3 sides, 4 sides, 5 sides, and 6 sides.

ANSWER ▶ The number of sides increases by one.

EXAMPLE 2 Describe a Number Pattern

Describe a pattern in the numbers.

a. 3, 6, 9, 12, 15, 18, . . .

b. 1, 4, 9, 16, 25, 36, . . .

Solution

a. Each number after the first is 3 more than the previous one.

b. The numbers are squares of consecutive numbers.

1	4	9	16	25	36
1^2	2^2	3^2	4^2	5^2	6^2

Checkpoint ✓ **Describe a Visual or Number Pattern**

Describe a pattern.

1.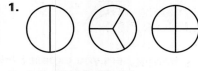

2.

3. 4, 8, 12, 16, 20, 24, . . .

4. 35, 30, 25, 20, 15, 10, . . .

Student Help
CLASSZONE.COM

MORE EXAMPLES
More examples at classzone.com

EXAMPLE 3 Make a Prediction

Sketch the next figure you expect in the pattern.

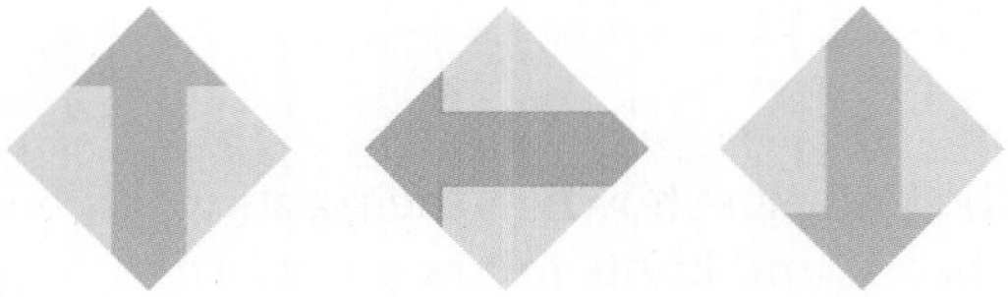

Solution

The arrow's color changes back and forth between green and red. The arrow makes a quarter turn each time.

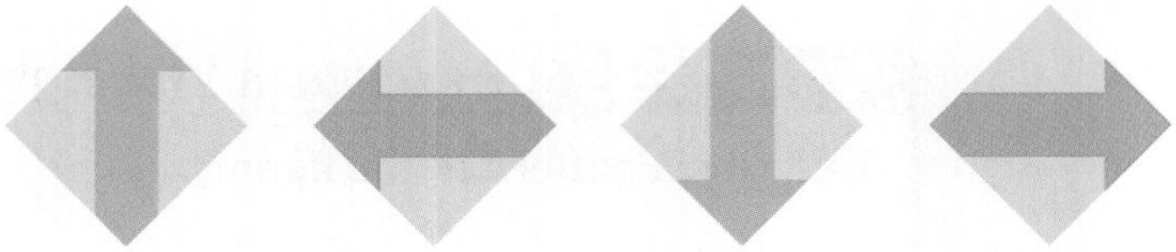

ANSWER ▶ The fourth figure is red. Its arrow points to the right.

EXAMPLE 4 Make a Prediction

Sketch the next figure you expect in the pattern.

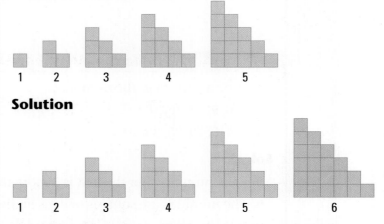

Solution

ANSWER ▶ The sixth figure has six squares in the bottom row.

Checkpoint ✓ Make a Prediction

Sketch the next two figures you expect in the pattern.

5.

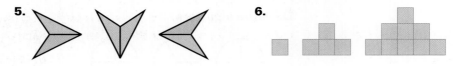

6.

Write the next two numbers you expect in the pattern.

7. $-2, -5, -8, -11, \ldots$

8. $4, 10, 16, 22, \ldots$

Guided Practice

Skill Check **Sketch the next figure you expect in the pattern.**

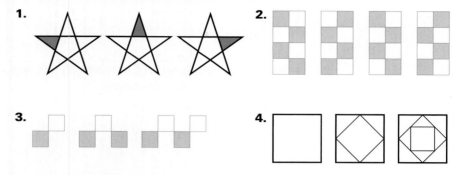

Describe a pattern in the numbers. Write the next two numbers you expect in the pattern.

5. 3, 11, 19, 27, . . .   **6.** 2, 6, 18, 54, . . .   **7.** 7.0, 7.5, 8.0, 8.5, . . .

8. 13, 7, 1, −5, . . .   **9.** 256, 64, 16, 4, . . .   **10.** 3, 0, −3, 0, 3, 0, . . .

Practice and Applications

Extra Practice
See p. 675.

Describing Visual Patterns **Sketch the next figure you expect in the pattern.**

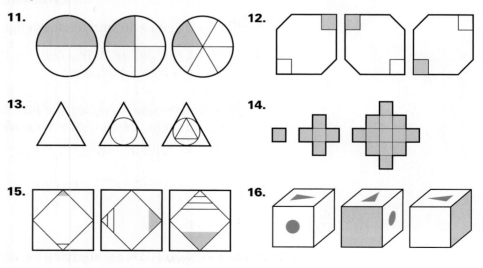

Homework Help

Example 1: Exs. 11–16
Example 2: Exs. 17–25
Example 3: Exs. 26–32
Example 4: Exs. 26–32

Describing Number Patterns **Describe a pattern in the numbers. Write the next number you expect in the pattern.**

17. 4, 9, 14, 19, . . .   **18.** 2, −7, −16, −25, . . .

19. 320, 80, 20, 5, . . .   **20.** 2.5, 5, 10, 20, . . .

21. 1, 3, 6, 10, 15, . . .   **22.** 5, 7, 11, 17, 25, . . .

xy Using Algebra Find a pattern in the coordinates of the points. Then write the coordinates of another point in the pattern.

23.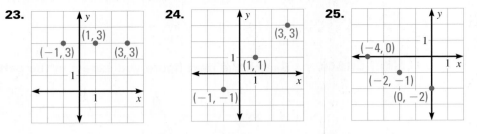

24.

25.

Making Predictions In Exercises 26–30, use the staircase pattern from Example 4 shown below.

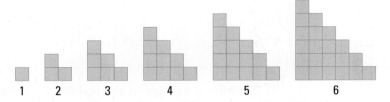

26. Find the distance around each figure. Organize your results in a table like the one shown.

Figure	1	2	3	4	5	6
Distance	4	8	?	?	?	?

27. Use your table to describe a pattern in the distances.

28. Write a variable expression for the distance around the *n*th figure.

29. Predict the distance around the tenth figure.

30. ⚖ **You be the Judge** Will a figure in this pattern have a distance of 60? If so, which one?

31. Science Connection Diagrams for four molecules are shown. Draw a diagram for the next two molecules in the pattern.

LABORATORY TECHNOLOGISTS study microscopic cells, such as bacteria. The doubling period for a population of bacteria may be as short as 20 minutes.

32. Bacteria Growth You are studying bacteria in biology class. The table shows the number of bacteria after *n* doubling periods. Predict the number of bacteria after 8 doubling periods.

n (doubling periods)	0	1	2	3	4	5
Billions of bacteria	3	6	12	24	48	96

33. Braille System The Braille alphabet uses raised dots that can be read by touch. Describe a pattern that links the first ten letters and the next ten letters. Complete the missing letters.

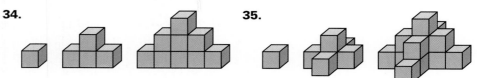

A B C D E F G H I J

K L M N O P Q R S T

Visualizing Patterns The first three objects in a pattern are shown. How many blocks are in the next object?

34.

35.

Standardized Test Practice

36. Multiple Choice What is the next number you expect?

55, 110, 165, 220, . . .

(A) 255   (B) 265   (C) 275   (D) 440

37. Multiple Choice What is the next number you expect?

1, 5, 13, 25, . . .

(F) 33   (G) 38   (H) 41   (J) 169

Mixed Review

Problem Solving Draw a diagram to solve. *(Skills Review, p. 653)*

38. Robert, Susan, and Todd are standing in a line. How many ways can they be arranged?

39. A table is two feet longer than it is wide. What are five possible areas for the table?

Algebra Skills

Adding Decimals Find the sum. *(Skills Review, p. 655)*

40. $9.3 + 0.2$ **41.** $2.4 + 8.9$ **42.** $10.5 + 5.5$

43. $0.71 + 0.33$ **44.** $5.64 + 12.75$ **45.** $34.08 + 11.16$

Plotting Points Plot the points in a coordinate plane.
(Skills Review, p. 664)

46. $A(5, 2)$ **47.** $B(6, 1)$ **48.** $C(3, -8)$ **49.** $D(4, -1)$

50. $E(-2, 7)$ **51.** $F(-5, 2)$ **52.** $G(-2, -6)$ **53.** $H(-4, -3)$

1.2 Inductive Reasoning

Goal
Use inductive reasoning to make conjectures.

Key Words
- conjecture
- inductive reasoning
- counterexample

Scientists and mathematicians look for patterns and try to draw conclusions from them. A **conjecture** is an unproven statement that is based on a pattern or observation. Looking for patterns and making conjectures is part of a process called **inductive reasoning**.

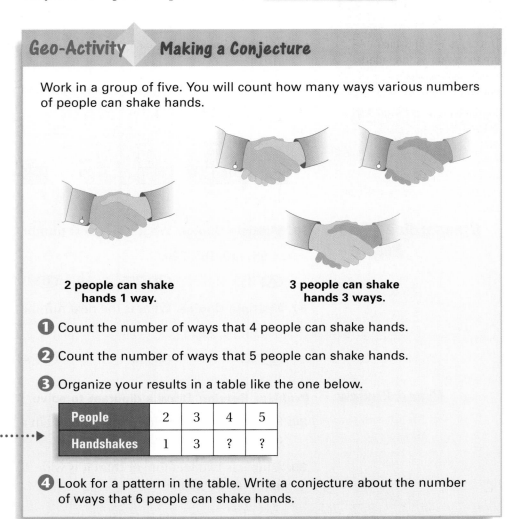

Geo-Activity — Making a Conjecture

Work in a group of five. You will count how many ways various numbers of people can shake hands.

2 people can shake hands 1 way.

3 people can shake hands 3 ways.

➊ Count the number of ways that 4 people can shake hands.

➋ Count the number of ways that 5 people can shake hands.

➌ Organize your results in a table like the one below.

People	2	3	4	5
Handshakes	1	3	?	?

➍ Look for a pattern in the table. Write a conjecture about the number of ways that 6 people can shake hands.

Student Help

STUDY TIP
Copy this table in your notebook and complete it. Do not write in your textbook.

Much of the reasoning in geometry consists of three stages.

➊ *Look for a Pattern* Look at several examples. Use diagrams and tables to help discover a pattern.

➋ *Make a Conjecture* Use the examples to make a general conjecture. Modify it, if necessary.

➌ *Verify the Conjecture* Use logical reasoning to verify that the conjecture is true in all cases. (You will do this in later chapters.)

EXAMPLE 1 Make a Conjecture

Complete the conjecture.

Conjecture: The sum of any two odd numbers is __?__.

Solution

Begin by writing several examples.

$$1 + 1 = 2 \qquad 5 + 1 = 6 \qquad 3 + 7 = 10$$
$$3 + 13 = 16 \qquad 21 + 9 = 30 \qquad 101 + 235 = 336$$

Each sum is even. You can make the following conjecture.

ANSWER ▶ The sum of any two odd numbers is *even*.

EXAMPLE 2 Make a Conjecture

Complete the conjecture.

Conjecture: The sum of the first n odd positive integers is __?__.

Solution

List some examples and look for a pattern.

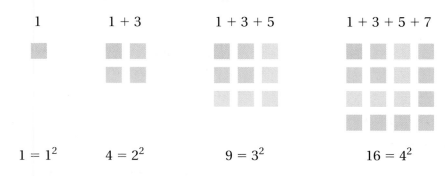

1	1 + 3	1 + 3 + 5	1 + 3 + 5 + 7

$$1 = 1^2 \qquad 4 = 2^2 \qquad 9 = 3^2 \qquad 16 = 4^2$$

ANSWER ▶ The sum of the first n odd positive integers is n^2.

Checkpoint ✓ Make a Conjecture

Complete the conjecture based on the pattern in the examples.

1. ***Conjecture:*** The product of any two odd numbers is __?__.

    EXAMPLES

$$1 \times 1 = 1 \qquad 3 \times 5 = 15 \qquad 3 \times 11 = 33$$
$$7 \times 9 = 63 \qquad 11 \times 11 = 121 \qquad 1 \times 15 = 15$$

2. ***Conjecture:*** The product of the numbers $(n - 1)$ and $(n + 1)$ is __?__.

    EXAMPLES

$$1 \cdot 3 = 2^2 - 1 \qquad 3 \cdot 5 = 4^2 - 1 \qquad 5 \cdot 7 = 6^2 - 1$$
$$7 \cdot 9 = 8^2 - 1 \qquad 9 \cdot 11 = 10^2 - 1 \qquad 11 \cdot 13 = 12^2 - 1$$

Counterexamples Just because something is true for several examples does not *prove* that it is true in general. To prove a conjecture is true, you need to prove it is true in all cases.

A conjecture is considered false if it is *not always* true. To prove a conjecture is false, you need to find only one *counterexample*. A **counterexample** is an example that shows a conjecture is false.

EXAMPLE 3 Find a Counterexample

Show the conjecture is false by finding a counterexample.

Conjecture: The sum of two numbers is always greater than the larger of the two numbers.

Solution

Here is a counterexample. Let the two numbers be 0 and 3.

The sum is $0 + 3 = 3$, but 3 is not greater than 3.

ANSWER ▶ The conjecture is false.

EXAMPLE 4 Find a Counterexample

Show the conjecture is false by finding a counterexample.

Conjecture: All shapes with four sides the same length are squares.

Solution

Here are some counterexamples.

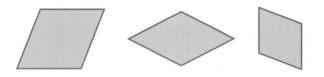

These shapes have four sides the same length, but they are not squares.

ANSWER ▶ The conjecture is false.

Checkpoint ✓ *Find a Counterexample*

Show the conjecture is false by finding a counterexample.

3. If the product of two numbers is even, the numbers must be even.

4. If a shape has two sides the same length, it must be a rectangle.

Guided Practice

Vocabulary Check

1. Explain what a *conjecture* is.

2. How can you prove that a conjecture is false?

Skill Check

Complete the conjecture with *odd* or *even*.

3. *Conjecture:* The difference of any two odd numbers is __?__ .

4. *Conjecture:* The sum of an odd number and an even number is __?__ .

Show the conjecture is false by finding a counterexample.

5. Any number divisible by 2 is divisible by 4.

6. The difference of two numbers is less than the greater number.

7. A circle can always be drawn around a four-sided shape so that it touches all four corners of the shape.

Practice and Applications

Extra Practice
See p. 675.

8. Rectangular Numbers The dot patterns form rectangles with a length that is one more than the width. Draw the next two figures to find the next two "rectangular" numbers.

2   6   12   20

9. Triangular Numbers The dot patterns form triangles. Draw the next two figures to find the next two "triangular" numbers.

1   3   6   10

Homework Help

Example 1: Exs. 8–16
Example 2: Exs. 8–16
Example 3: Exs. 17–19
Example 4: Exs. 17–19

Technology Use a calculator to explore the pattern. Write a conjecture based on what you observe.

10. $101 \times 25 = $ __?__
$101 \times 34 = $ __?__
$101 \times 49 = $ __?__

11. $11 \times 11 = $ __?__
$111 \times 111 = $ __?__
$1111 \times 1111 = $ __?__

12. $3 \times 4 = $ __?__
$33 \times 34 = $ __?__
$333 \times 334 = $ __?__

Student Help

CLASSZONE.COM

HOMEWORK HELP
Extra help with problem
solving in Exs. 13–14 is
at classzone.com

Making Conjectures Complete the conjecture based on the pattern
you observe.

13. *Conjecture:* The product of an odd number and an even number
is __?__.

$3 \cdot 6 = 18$	$22 \cdot 13 = 286$	$43 \cdot 102 = 4386$
$5 \cdot 12 = 60$	$-5 \cdot 2 = -10$	$254 \cdot 63 = 16{,}002$
$14 \cdot 9 = 126$	$-11 \cdot (-4) = 44$	

14. *Conjecture:* The sum of three consecutive integers is always three
times __?__.

$3 + 4 + 5 = 3 \cdot 4$	$6 + 7 + 8 = 3 \cdot 7$	$9 + 10 + 11 = 3 \cdot 10$
$4 + 5 + 6 = 3 \cdot 5$	$7 + 8 + 9 = 3 \cdot 8$	$10 + 11 + 12 = 3 \cdot 11$
$5 + 6 + 7 = 3 \cdot 6$	$8 + 9 + 10 = 3 \cdot 9$	$11 + 12 + 13 = 3 \cdot 12$

15. Counting Diagonals In the shapes below, the *diagonals* are
shown in **blue**. Write a conjecture about the number of diagonals
of the next two shapes.

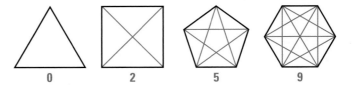

      0   2   5   9

16. Moon Phases A full moon occurs when the moon is on the
opposite side of Earth from the sun. During a full moon, the
moon appears as a complete circle. Suppose that one year, full
moons occur on these dates:

July 21 Thursday   August 19 Friday   September 18 Sunday   October 17 Monday   November 16 Wednesday   December 15 Thursday

Determine how many days are between these full moons and
predict when the next full moon occurs.

Error Analysis Show the conjecture is false by finding a
counterexample.

17. *Conjecture:* If the product of two numbers is positive, then the
two numbers must both be positive.

18. *Conjecture:* All rectangles with a perimeter of 20 feet have the
same area. *Note:* Perimeter = 2(length + width).

19. *Conjecture:* If two sides of a triangle are the same length, then the
third side must be shorter than either of those sides.

Link to
Science

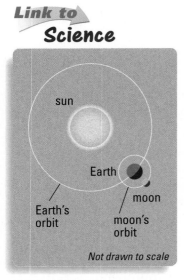

sun

Earth

moon

Earth's
orbit

moon's
orbit

Not drawn to scale

FULL MOONS happen when
Earth is between the moon
and the sun.

Application Links
CLASSZONE.COM

20. Telephone Keypad Write a conjecture about the letters you expect on the next telephone key. Look at a telephone to see whether your conjecture is correct.

21. Challenge Prove the conjecture below by writing a variable statement and using algebra.

Conjecture: The sum of five consecutive integers is always divisible by five.

$$x + (x + 1) + (x + 2) + (x + 3) + (x + 4) = \underline{\quad?\quad}$$

Standardized Test Practice

22. Multiple Choice Which of the following is a counterexample of the conjecture below?

Conjecture: The product of two positive numbers is always greater than either number.

ⓐ 2, 2   ⓑ $\frac{1}{2}$, 2   ⓒ 3, 10   ⓓ 2, −1

23. Multiple Choice You fold a large piece of paper in half four times, then unfold it. If you cut along the fold lines, how many identical rectangles will you make?

ⓕ 4   ⓖ 8   ⓗ 16   ⓙ 32

Mixed Review

Describing Patterns Sketch the next figure you expect in the pattern. *(Lesson 1.1)*

24. V \/\ \/\/

25. 1 Z | 2 | Y X 3

Algebra Skills

Using Integers Evaluate. *(Skills Review, p. 663)*

26. $8 + (-3)$ **27.** $-2 + 9$ **28.** $9 - (-1)$ **29.** $-7 - 3$

30. $3(-5)$ **31.** $(-2)(-7)$ **32.** $20 \div (-5)$ **33.** $(-8) \div (-2)$

Evaluating Expressions Evaluate the expression when $x = 3$. *(Skills Review, p. 670)*

34. $x + 7$ **35.** $5 - x$ **36.** $x - 9$ **37.** $2x + 5$

38. $x^2 + 6$ **39.** $x^2 - 4x$ **40.** $3x^2$ **41.** $2x^3$

1.3 Points, Lines, and Planes

Goal
Use postulates and undefined terms.

Key Words
- undefined term
- point, line, plane
- postulate
- collinear, coplanar
- segment
- ray
- endpoint

The legs of the tripod touch the table at three *points*. The legs suggest *lines*, and the table surface suggests a *plane*.

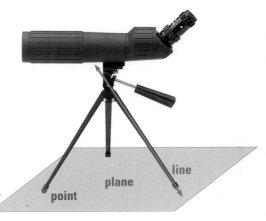

Geometry depends on a common understanding of terms such as *point*, *line*, and *plane*. Because these terms cannot be mathematically defined using other known words, they are called **undefined terms** .

A **point** has no dimension. It is represented by a small dot.

point A   • A

A **line** has one dimension. It extends without end in two directions. It is represented by a line with two arrowheads.

line ℓ or BC

A **plane** has two dimensions. It is represented by a shape that looks like a floor or wall. You have to imagine that it extends without end.

plane M or plane DEF

You need two points to describe a line, and you need three points to describe a plane, because the geometry in this book follows the two *postulates* given below. **Postulates** are statements that are accepted without further justification.

POSTULATES 1 and 2

Postulate 1 Two Points Determine a Line

Words Through any two points there is exactly one line.

Symbols Line *n* passes through points *P* and *Q*.

Postulate 2 Three Points Determine a Plane

Words Through any three points not on a line there is exactly one plane.

Symbols Plane *T* passes through points *A*, *B*, and *C*.

EXAMPLE **1** **Name Points, Lines, and Planes**

Use the diagram at the right.

   a. Name three points.

   b. Name two lines.

   c. Name two planes.

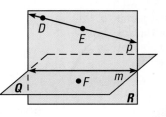

Solution

   a. *D*, *E*, and *F* are points.

   b. Line *m* and line *p*

   c. *Q* and *R* are planes.

Collinear points are points that lie on the same line.

Coplanar points are points that lie on the same plane.

Coplanar lines are lines that lie on the same plane.

Visualize It!

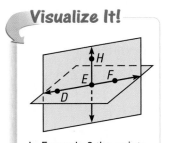

In Example 2 the points *D*, *E*, *F*, and *H* are also coplanar. The plane containing them is shown in green above.

EXAMPLE **2** **Name Collinear and Coplanar Points**

Use the diagram at the right.

   a. Name three points that are collinear.

   b. Name four points that are coplanar.

   c. Name three points that are not collinear.

Solution

   a. Points *D*, *E*, and *F* lie on the same line. So, they are collinear.

   b. Points *D*, *E*, *F*, and *G* lie on the same plane, so they are coplanar.

   c. Points *H*, *E*, and *G* do not lie on the same line. There are many other correct answers.

Checkpoint ✓ *Name Points, Lines, and Planes*

Use the diagram at the right.

   1. Name two lines.

   2. Name two planes.

   3. Name three points that are collinear.

   4. Name three points that are not collinear.

   5. Name four points that are coplanar.

   6. Name two lines that are coplanar.

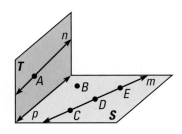

The line $\overleftrightarrow{AB}$ passes through A and B.

The **segment** $\overline{AB}$ consists of the **endpoints** A and B, and all points on $\overleftrightarrow{AB}$ that are between A and B.

The **ray** $\overrightarrow{AB}$ consists of the endpoint A and all points on $\overleftrightarrow{AB}$ that lie on the same side of A as B.

SUMMARY	LINES, SEGMENTS, and RAYS	
Word	**Symbol**	**Diagram**
line	$\overleftrightarrow{AB}$ or $\overleftrightarrow{BA}$	
segment	$\overline{AB}$ or $\overline{BA}$	
ray	$\overrightarrow{AB}$	
	$\overrightarrow{BA}$	

Note that $\overleftrightarrow{AB}$ is the same as $\overleftrightarrow{BA}$. Also, $\overline{AB}$ is the same as $\overline{BA}$. However, $\overrightarrow{AB}$ is not the same as $\overrightarrow{BA}$. The two rays have different endpoints and extend in different directions.

EXAMPLE **3** **Draw Lines, Segments, and Rays**

Draw three noncollinear points, J, K, and L. Then draw $\overleftrightarrow{JK}$, $\overline{KL}$, and $\overrightarrow{LJ}$.

Solution

❶ *Draw J, K, and L.*   ❷ *Draw $\overleftrightarrow{JK}$.*   ❸ *Draw $\overline{KL}$.*   ❹ *Draw $\overrightarrow{LJ}$.*

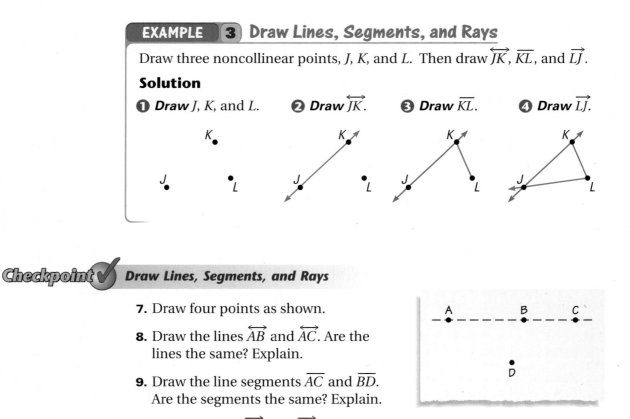

Checkpoint ✓ **Draw Lines, Segments, and Rays**

7. Draw four points as shown.

8. Draw the lines $\overleftrightarrow{AB}$ and $\overleftrightarrow{AC}$. Are the lines the same? Explain.

9. Draw the line segments $\overline{AC}$ and $\overline{BD}$. Are the segments the same? Explain.

10. Draw the rays $\overrightarrow{CA}$ and $\overrightarrow{CB}$. Are the rays the same? Explain.

Guided Practice

Vocabulary Check

1. Write in words how you would say each of these symbols aloud: $\overleftrightarrow{PQ}$, $\overline{PQ}$, $\overrightarrow{PQ}$, and $\overleftrightarrow{QP}$.

2. Explain the difference between $\overrightarrow{PQ}$ and $\overrightarrow{QP}$. *The letters are switch*

Skill Check

Decide whether the statement is *true* or *false*.

3. Points A, B, and C are collinear.

4. Points A, B, and C are coplanar.

5. Points B, C, and D are coplanar.

6. Point C lies on $\overleftrightarrow{AB}$.

7. $\overleftrightarrow{AB}$ lies on plane ABC.

8. $\overleftrightarrow{DE}$ lies on plane ABC.

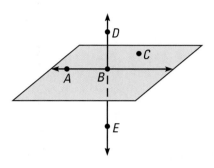

Sketch a line that contains point *S* between points *R* and *T*. Decide whether the statement is *true* or *false*.

9. $\overleftrightarrow{RS}$ is the same as $\overleftrightarrow{RT}$.

10. $\overrightarrow{ST}$ is the same as $\overrightarrow{TS}$.

11. $\overrightarrow{ST}$ is the same as $\overrightarrow{RT}$.

12. $\overrightarrow{RS}$ is the same as $\overrightarrow{RT}$.

13. $\overline{RS}$ is the same as $\overline{ST}$.

14. $\overline{ST}$ is the same as $\overline{TS}$.

Practice and Applications

Extra Practice

See p. 675.

Naming Points, Lines, and Planes Use the diagram at the right.

15. Name four points.

16. Name two lines.

17. Name the plane that contains A, B, and C.

18. Name the plane that contains A, D, and E.

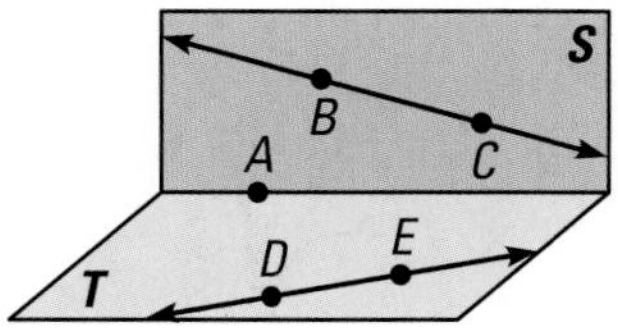

Evaluating Statements Decide whether the statement is *true* or *false*.

19. A lies on line ℓ.

20. A, B, and C are collinear.

21. B lies on line ℓ.

22. A, B, and C are coplanar.

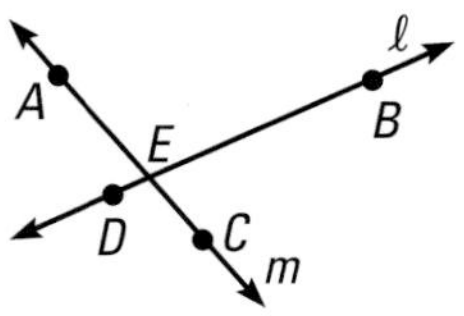

Homework Help

Example 1: Exs. 15–18
Example 2: Exs. 19–62
Example 3: Exs. 63–65

23. C lies on line m.

24. D, E, and B are collinear.

25. D lies on line m.

26. D, E, and B are coplanar.

Naming Collinear Points Name a point that is collinear with the given points.

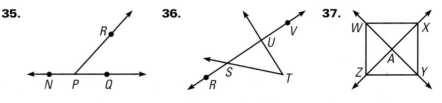

27. *F* and *H*

28. *G* and *K*

29. *K* and *L*

30. *M* and *J*

31. *J* and *N*

32. *K* and *H*

33. *H* and *G*

34. *J* and *F*

Naming Noncollinear Points Name three points that are not collinear.

35.

36.

37.

Naming Coplanar Points Name a point that is coplanar with the given points.

38. *A*, *B*, and *C*

39. *D*, *C*, and *F*

40. *G*, *A*, and *D*

41. *E*, *F*, and *G*

42. *A*, *B*, and *H*

43. *B*, *C*, and *F*

44. *A*, *B*, and *F*

45. *B*, *C*, and *G*

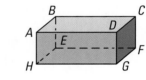

Naming Noncoplanar Points Name all the points that are *not* coplanar with the given points.

46. *N*, *K*, and *L*

47. *S*, *P*, and *M*

48. *P*, *Q*, and *N*

49. *R*, *S*, and *L*

50. *P*, *Q*, and *R*

51. *R*, *K*, and *N*

52. *P*, *S*, and *K*

53. *Q*, *K*, and *L*

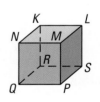

Game Board In Exercises 54–57, use the game board.

54. Name four collinear points.

55. Name three points that are not collinear.

56. Name four segments that contain point *R*.

57. $\overleftrightarrow{AD}$ divides the board in half. $\overleftrightarrow{QT}$ also divides the board in half. Name the other lines that divide the board in half.

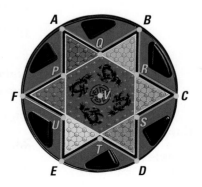

You be the Judge In Exercises 58–62, use the diagram of the indoor tennis court.

58. Name two points that are collinear with *P*.

59. Name three points that are coplanar with *P*.

60. Name two planes that contain *J*.

61. Name two planes that do not contain *J*.

62. Are the points *K* and *N* coplanar with points *J* and *Q*? Explain.

Visualize It! Sketch the lines, segments, and rays. If you have geometry software, try creating your sketch using it.

63. Draw four points *J*, *K*, *L*, and *M*, no three of which are collinear. Sketch $\overleftrightarrow{JK}$, $\overline{KL}$, $\overleftrightarrow{LM}$, and $\overrightarrow{MJ}$.

64. Draw two points, *A* and *B*. Sketch $\overrightarrow{AB}$. Add a point *C* on the ray so *B* is between *A* and *C*.

65. Draw three noncollinear points *F*, *G*, and *H*. Sketch $\overline{FG}$ and add a point *J* on $\overline{FG}$. Then sketch $\overrightarrow{JH}$.

Three-Wheeled Car In Exercises 66–69, refer to the photograph of the three-wheeled car.

66. A four-wheeled car is driving slowly over uneven ground. Is it possible that only three wheels will be touching the ground at a given time?

67. Is it possible to draw four points that do not lie on a plane?

68. A three-wheeled car is driving slowly over uneven ground. Is it possible that only two wheels will be touching the ground at a given time?

69. Is it possible to draw three points that do not lie on a plane?

70. Multiple Choice Which of the statements is *false*?

Ⓐ *F*, *G*, and *H* are collinear.

Ⓑ *C*, *D*, *K*, and *L* are coplanar.

Ⓒ *L* lies on $\overleftrightarrow{AB}$.

Ⓓ $\overrightarrow{DE}$ contains $\overline{CE}$.

Mixed Review

Describing Number Patterns Predict the next number. *(Lesson 1.1)*

71. 6, 17, 28, 39, . . .   **72.** 9, 4, −1, −6, . . .

73. 4, 20, 100, 500, . . .   **74.** 0, 5, 15, 30, 50, . . .

Algebra Skills

Fractions Write the fraction as a decimal. For repeating decimals, round to the nearest hundredth. *(Skills Review, p. 657)*

75. $\frac{1}{2}$ **76.** $\frac{3}{4}$ **77.** $\frac{3}{5}$ **78.** $\frac{4}{10}$

79. $\frac{2}{3}$ **80.** $\frac{4}{3}$ **81.** $\frac{7}{9}$ **82.** $\frac{11}{2}$

Quiz 1

Sketch the next figure you expect in the pattern. *(Lesson 1.1)*

1. **2.**

Find a counterexample to prove that the statement is false. *(Lesson 1.2)*

3. If a number is divisible by 10, then it is divisible by 20.

4. Two sides of a triangle can never have the same length.

5. The sum of two numbers is always greater than either number.

6. If you fold a square piece of paper in half, then unfold it and cut along the fold, you will always create two rectangles of the same size.

Sketch the figure. *(Lesson 1.3)*

7. Draw three noncollinear points *P*, *Q*, and *R*. Sketch $\overrightarrow{QP}$. Add a point *T* on the ray so that *P* is between *Q* and *T*. Then sketch $\overleftrightarrow{RT}$.

8. Draw four points, *V*, *X*, *Y*, and *Z*, no three of which are collinear. Sketch $\overleftrightarrow{VY}$, $\overleftrightarrow{XZ}$, and $\overleftrightarrow{YZ}$.

Question

When planes meet, what points do they have in common?

Materials
- three index cards
- scissors

Explore

❶ Label two index cards as shown. Cut each card along the dotted line.

❷ Slide two cards together. Answer Exercises 1–4.

❸ Label and cut a third card as shown. Cut another slot in plane *M* and slide the cards together. Answer Exercises 5–7.

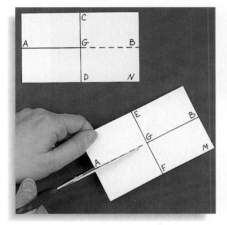

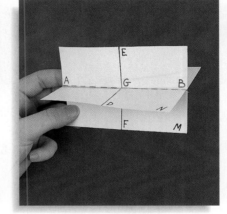

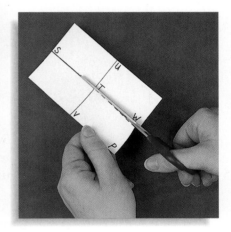

Think About It

Student Help

LOOK BACK
The index cards stand for planes, but you must imagine the planes extend without end. See p. 14.

1. Where do $\overleftrightarrow{AB}$ and $\overleftrightarrow{CD}$ meet? Where do $\overleftrightarrow{AB}$ and $\overleftrightarrow{EF}$ meet?

2. When the cards are together, where do $\overleftrightarrow{CD}$ and $\overleftrightarrow{EF}$ meet?

3. Where do planes *M* and *N* meet?

4. Are $\overleftrightarrow{CD}$ and $\overleftrightarrow{EF}$ coplanar? Explain.

5. Where do $\overleftrightarrow{EF}$ and $\overleftrightarrow{UV}$ meet?

6. Where do planes *M* and *P* meet?

7. Do planes *N* and *P* meet?

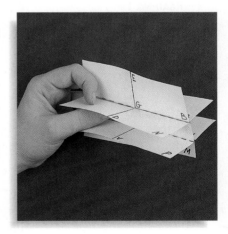

Sketching Intersections

Goal

Sketch simple figures and their intersections.

Key Words

- intersect
- intersection

The photograph shows the intersection of two streets in Seattle. The intersection is the part where the two streets cross each other.

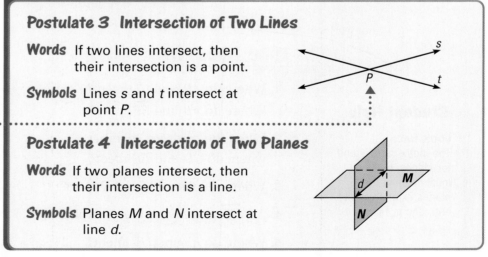

In geometry, figures **intersect** if they have any points in common.

The **intersection** of two or more figures is the point or points that the figures have in common.

Student Help

READING TIP
The letter *P* names the point of intersection even though no dot is drawn there. ⋯⋯⋯

POSTULATES 3 and 4

Postulate 3 Intersection of Two Lines

Words If two lines intersect, then their intersection is a point.

Symbols Lines *s* and *t* intersect at point *P*.

Postulate 4 Intersection of Two Planes

Words If two planes intersect, then their intersection is a line.

Symbols Planes *M* and *N* intersect at line *d*.

Postulates 3 and 4 are written as *if-then statements*. You will learn more about if-then statements in Lesson 2.5.

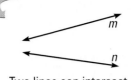

Two lines can intersect even if a diagram does not show where they intersect. The lines above intersect at a point that is not shown.

EXAMPLE 1 **Name Intersections of Lines**

Use the diagram at the right.

a. Name the intersection of $\overleftrightarrow{AC}$ and $\overleftrightarrow{BE}$.

b. Name the intersection of $\overleftrightarrow{BE}$ and $\overleftrightarrow{DF}$.

c. Name the intersection of $\overleftrightarrow{AC}$ and $\overleftrightarrow{DF}$.

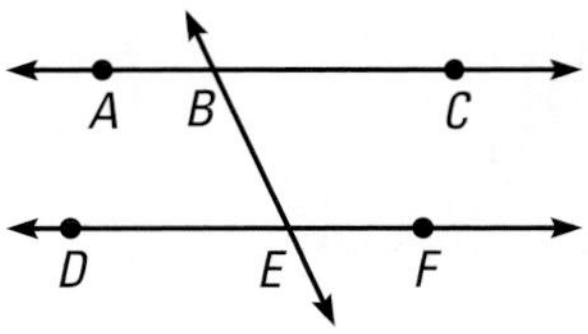

Solution

a. $\overleftrightarrow{AC}$ and $\overleftrightarrow{BE}$ intersect at point B.

b. $\overleftrightarrow{BE}$ and $\overleftrightarrow{DF}$ intersect at point E.

c. $\overleftrightarrow{AC}$ and $\overleftrightarrow{DF}$ do not appear to intersect.

EXAMPLE 2 **Name Intersections of Planes**

Use the diagram at the right.

a. Name the intersection of planes S and R.

b. Name the intersection of planes R and T.

c. Name the intersection of planes T and S.

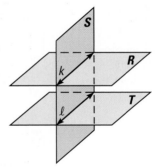

Solution

a. Planes S and R intersect at line k.

b. Planes R and T do not appear to intersect.

c. Planes T and S intersect at line ℓ.

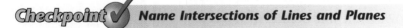

Checkpoint ✓ **Name Intersections of Lines and Planes**

Use the diagram at the right.

1. Name the intersection of $\overleftrightarrow{PS}$ and $\overleftrightarrow{QR}$.

2. Name the intersection of $\overleftrightarrow{TV}$ and $\overleftrightarrow{QU}$.

3. Name the intersection of $\overleftrightarrow{PS}$ and $\overleftrightarrow{UV}$.

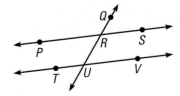

Use the diagram at the right.

4. Name the intersection of planes X and Y.

5. Name the intersection of planes Y and Z.

6. Name the intersection of planes Z and X.

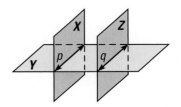

When you sketch lines and planes that intersect, you can use dashed lines, colored pencils, and shading to create a three-dimensional look.

EXAMPLE 3 Sketch Intersections of Lines and Planes

Sketch a plane. Then sketch each of the following.

   a. a line that is in the plane

   b. a line that does not intersect the plane

   c. a line that intersects the plane at a point

Solution

a. Draw the plane. Then draw a line in the plane.

b. Draw the plane. Then draw a line above or below the plane.

c. Draw the plane. Then draw a line that intersects the plane.

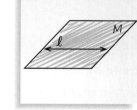
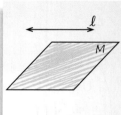
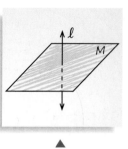

Visualize It!

Use dashed lines to show where a line is hidden by a plane.

EXAMPLE 4 Sketch Intersections of Planes

Sketch two planes that intersect in a line.

Solution

❶ *Draw* one plane as if you are looking straight at it. Shade the plane.

❷ *Draw* a second plane that is horizontal. Shade this plane a different color.

❸ *Draw* the line of intersection. Use dashed lines to show where one plane is hidden.

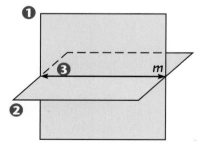

Checkpoint ✓ Sketch Intersecting Lines and Planes

   7. Sketch three lines that lie in a plane.

   8. Sketch two lines that intersect a plane at the same point.

   9. Sketch two planes that do not intersect.

Guided Practice

Vocabulary Check   **1.** Describe what an *intersection* is.

Skill Check   **Decide whether the statement is *true* or *false*.**

2. $\overleftrightarrow{BD}$ and $\overleftrightarrow{DC}$ intersect at point D.

3. $\overleftrightarrow{AB}$ and $\overleftrightarrow{BD}$ intersect at point A.

4. $\overleftrightarrow{BD}$ intersects plane M at point B.

5. $\overleftrightarrow{AB}$ and $\overleftrightarrow{DC}$ do not appear to intersect.

6. $\overleftrightarrow{BD}$ is the intersection of planes M and N.

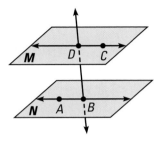

Practice and Applications

Extra Practice

See p. 676.

Everyday Intersections What kind of geometric intersection does the photograph suggest?

7.   **8.**   **9.**

Naming Intersections of Lines In Exercises 10–15, use the diagram at the right.

10. Name the intersection of $\overleftrightarrow{PQ}$ and $\overleftrightarrow{TS}$.

11. Name the intersection of $\overleftrightarrow{QS}$ and $\overleftrightarrow{PT}$.

12. Name the intersection of $\overleftrightarrow{SQ}$ and $\overleftrightarrow{TR}$.

13. Name the intersection of $\overleftrightarrow{RS}$ and $\overleftrightarrow{PT}$.

14. Name the intersection of $\overleftrightarrow{RP}$ and $\overleftrightarrow{PT}$.

15. Name the intersection of $\overleftrightarrow{RS}$ and $\overleftrightarrow{ST}$.

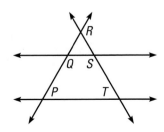

Homework Help

Example 1: Exs. 10–15, 22–24
Example 2: Exs. 16–21, 25–27
Example 3: Exs. 28–32
Example 4: Exs. 28–32

Naming Intersections of Planes Name the intersection of the given planes, or write *no intersection*.

16. *P* and *Q*
17. *Q* and *R*
18. *P* and *R*
19. *P* and *S*
20. *Q* and *S*
21. *R* and *S*

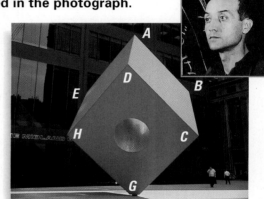

Completing Sentences Fill in the blank with the appropriate response based on the points labeled in the photograph.

22. $\overleftrightarrow{AB}$ and $\overleftrightarrow{BC}$ intersect at __?__.

23. $\overleftrightarrow{AD}$ and $\overleftrightarrow{AE}$ intersect at __?__.

24. $\overleftrightarrow{HG}$ and $\overleftrightarrow{DH}$ intersect at __?__.

25. Plane *ABC* and plane *DCG* intersect at __?__.

26. Plane *GHD* and plane *DHE* intersect at __?__.

27. Plane *EAD* and plane *BCD* intersect at __?__.

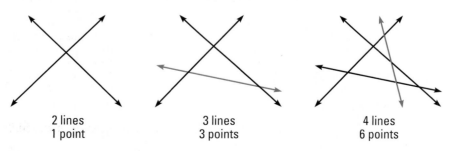
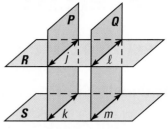

Red Cube, *1968, red painted steel, by sculptor Isamu Noguchi (above), 1904–1988. It is located on Broadway in New York City.*

Visualize It! Sketch the figure described.

28. Two lines that lie in a plane but do not intersect.

29. Three lines that intersect in a point.

30. Two planes that do not intersect.

31. Three planes that do not intersect.

32. Two lines that intersect and another line that does not intersect either one.

33. **Challenge** In the diagrams below, every line intersects all the other lines, but only two lines pass through each intersection point.

2 lines
1 point

3 lines
3 points

4 lines
6 points

Draw 5 lines that intersect in this way. Is there a pattern to the number of intersection points in the diagrams?

34. Multi-Step Problem In *perspective drawing*, lines that do not intersect in real life are represented by lines that intersect on the horizon line at a point called a *vanishing point*.

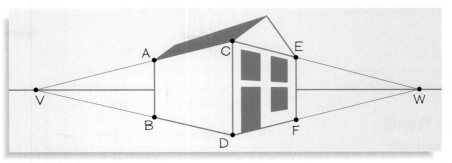

a. Name two lines that intersect at vanishing point *V*. Name two lines that intersect at vanishing point *W*.

b. Trace the diagram. Draw $\overleftrightarrow{EV}$ and $\overleftrightarrow{AW}$. Label their intersection as point *G*.

c. Draw $\overleftrightarrow{FV}$ and $\overleftrightarrow{BW}$. Label their intersection as point *H*.

d. Use dashed lines to draw the hidden edges of the house: $\overline{GH}$, $\overline{AG}$, $\overline{BH}$, $\overline{EG}$, and $\overline{FH}$.

Mixed Review

Using Algebra **Find a pattern in the coordinates of the points. Then write the coordinates of another point in the pattern.** *(Lesson 1.1)*

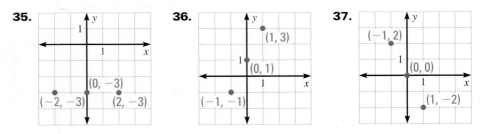

35. **36.** **37.**

Naming Points **Use the diagram shown.** *(Lesson 1.3)*

38. Name three collinear points.

39. Name three noncollinear points.

40. Are all the points coplanar? Explain.

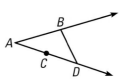

Algebra Skills

Subtracting Decimals **Find the difference.** *(Skills Review, p. 655)*

41. $13.8 - 2.4$ **42.** $10.6 - 4.4$ **43.** $7.5 - 3.8$

44. $9.68 - 5.22$ **45.** $24.72 - 16.15$ **46.** $5 - 1.29$

Finding Absolute Values **Evaluate.** *(Skills Review, p. 662)*

47. $|-7|$ **48.** $|-3|$ **49.** $|0|$ **50.** $|4|$

51. $|5 - 3|$ **52.** $|12 - 7|$ **53.** $|3 - 5|$ **54.** $|7 - 12|$

1.5 Segments and Their Measures

Goal
Measure segments.
Add segment lengths.

Key Words
- coordinate
- distance
- length
- between
- congruent segments

The points on a line can be matched one to one with the real numbers. The real number that corresponds to a point is the **coordinate** of the point.

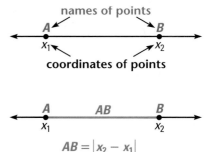

names of points

coordinates of points

In the diagram, x_1 and x_2 are coordinates. The small numbers are *subscripts*. The coordinates are read as "x sub 1" and "x sub 2."

$$AB = |x_2 - x_1|$$

The **distance** between points A and B is written as AB. It is the absolute value of the difference of the coordinates of A and B. AB is also called the **length** of $\overline{AB}$.

EXAMPLE 1 Find the Distance Between Two Points

Measure the total length of the shark's tooth to the nearest $\frac{1}{8}$ inch. Then measure the length of the exposed part.

Solution

Use a ruler to measure in inches.

❶ Align the zero mark of the ruler with one end of the shark's tooth.

❷ Find the length of the shark's tooth, AC.
$$AC = \left|2\frac{1}{4} - 0\right| = 2\frac{1}{4}$$

❸ Find the length of the exposed part, BC.
$$BC = \left|2\frac{1}{4} - \frac{7}{8}\right| = 1\frac{3}{8}$$

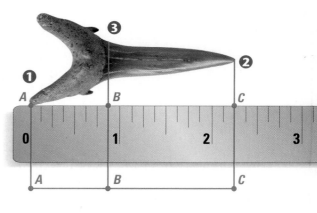

Student Help

SKILLS REVIEW
For help with absolute value, see p. 662.

ANSWER ▶ The length of the shark's tooth is $2\frac{1}{4}$ inches. The length of the exposed part is $1\frac{3}{8}$ inches.

Checkpoint ✓ Find the Distance Between Two Points

Measure the length of the segment to the nearest $\frac{1}{8}$ inch.

1. A————————————B

2. C————————————D

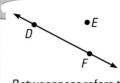
When three points lie on a line, one of them is **between** the other two. In the diagram of Postulate 5 below, *B* is between *A* and *C*.

POSTULATE 5

Segment Addition Postulate

Words and Symbols

If *B* is between *A* and *C*, then $AC = AB + BC$.

If $AC = AB + BC$, then *B* is between *A* and *C*.

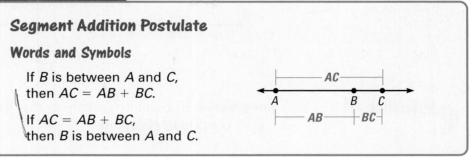

EXAMPLE 2 Find a Distance by Adding

Use the map to find the distance from Athens to Albany.

Solution

Because the three cities lie on a line, you can use the Segment Addition Postulate.

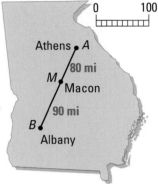

$AM = 80$ miles	Use map.
$MB = 90$ miles	Use map.
$AB = AM + MB$	Segment Addition Postulate
$\quad = 80 + 90$	Substitute.
$\quad = 170$	Add.

ANSWER ▶ The distance from Athens to Albany is 170 miles.

Note that in Example 2, if the cities were not collinear, you would not be able to use the Segment Addition Postulate.

 Using Algebra

EXAMPLE 3 Find a Distance by Subtracting

Use the diagram to find *EF*.

Solution

$DF = DE + EF$	Segment Addition Postulate
$16 = 10 + EF$	Substitute 16 for *DF* and 10 for *DE*.
$16 - 10 = 10 + EF - 10$	Subtract 10 from each side.
$6 = EF$	Simplify.

Find the length.

3. Find *AC*.

4. Find *ST*.

Congruence In geometry, segments that have the same length are called **congruent segments** .

Use short tick marks to indicate congruent segments.

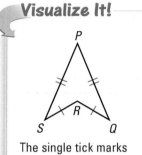

The single tick marks show that $\overline{SR} \cong \overline{QR}$. The double tick marks show that $\overline{SP} \cong \overline{QP}$.

WORDS

The length *AB* **is equal to** the length *CD*.

Segment $\overline{AB}$ **is congruent to** segment $\overline{CD}$.

SYMBOLS

$AB = CD$

$\overline{AB} \cong \overline{CD}$

The symbol for indicating congruence is ≅.

EXAMPLE 4 **Decide Whether Segments are Congruent**

Are the segments shown in the coordinate plane congruent?

Solution

For a horizontal segment, subtract the *x*-coordinates.

$$DE = |1 - (-3)| = |4| = 4$$

For a vertical segment, subtract the *y*-coordinates.

$$FG = |-3 - 1| = |-4| = 4$$

ANSWER ▶ $\overline{DE}$ and $\overline{FG}$ have the same length. So, $\overline{DE} \cong \overline{FG}$.

Plot the points in a coordinate plane. Then decide whether $\overline{AB}$ and $\overline{CD}$ are congruent.

5. $A(-2, 3)$, $B(3, 3)$, $C(-3, 4)$, $D(-3, -1)$

6. $A(0, 5)$, $B(0, -1)$, $C(5, 0)$, $D(-1, 0)$

Guided Practice

Vocabulary Check

1. Is the distance between *M* and *N* the same as the length of $\overline{MN}$?

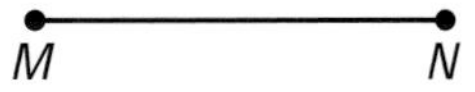

M ——————— N

Skill Check

2. Measure the length of the line segment in Exercise 1 to the nearest millimeter.

Find the length.

3. Find *DF*.

4. Find *QR*.

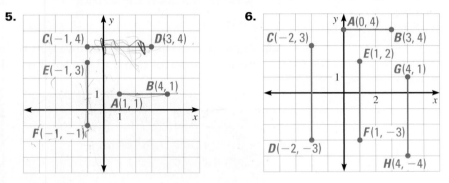

Determine which segments in the coordinate plane are congruent.

5.

6.

Practice and Applications

Extra Practice

See p. 676.

Measurement Measure the length of the segment to the nearest millimeter.

7. **8.** **9.**

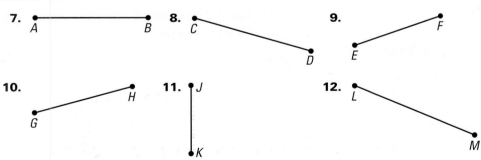

10. **11.** **12.**

Homework Help

Example 1: Exs. 7–12
Example 2: Exs. 13–23
Example 3: Exs. 24–26
Example 4: Exs. 27–30

Visualize It! Draw a sketch of the three collinear points. Then write the Segment Addition Postulate for the points.

13. *E* is between *D* and *F*.

14. *H* is between *G* and *J*.

15. *M* is between *N* and *P*.

16. *R* is between *Q* and *S*.

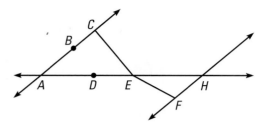

You be the Judge Use the diagram to determine whether the statement is *true* or *false*.

17. *B* is between *A* and *C*.

18. *E* is between *C* and *F*.

19. *E* is between *D* and *H*.

20. *D* is between *A* and *H*.

21. *C* is between *B* and *E*.

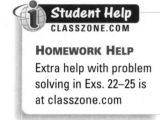

Student Help

CLASSZONE.COM

HOMEWORK HELP
Extra help with problem solving in Exs. 22–25 is at classzone.com

Segment Addition Postulate Find the length.

22. Find *PR*.

23. Find *SU*.

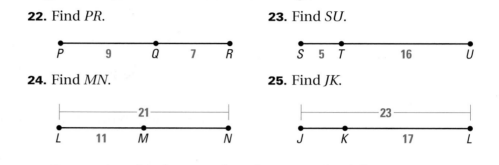

24. Find *MN*.

25. Find *JK*.

26. **Fishing** Use the photograph to determine the difference in length between the two fish and the total length of both fish.

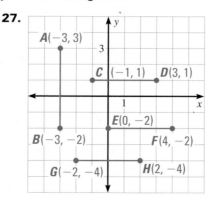

Coral Grouper

Trout

inches

Congruent Segments Determine which segments in the coordinate plane are congruent.

Student Help

SKILLS REVIEW
For help plotting points in a coordinate plane, see p. 664.

27.

28.

Technology Plot the points in a coordinate plane. Decide whether $\overline{PQ}$ and $\overline{RS}$ are congruent. You may use geometry software.

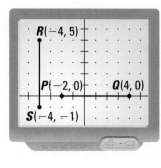

29. $P(-2, 0)$
$Q(4, 0)$
$R(-4, 5)$
$S(-4, -1)$

30. $P(2, -1)$
$Q(2, 3)$
$R(-3, -5)$
$S(2, -5)$

xy **Using Algebra** Write a variable expression for the length.

31. Write an expression for AC.

32. Write an expression for QR.

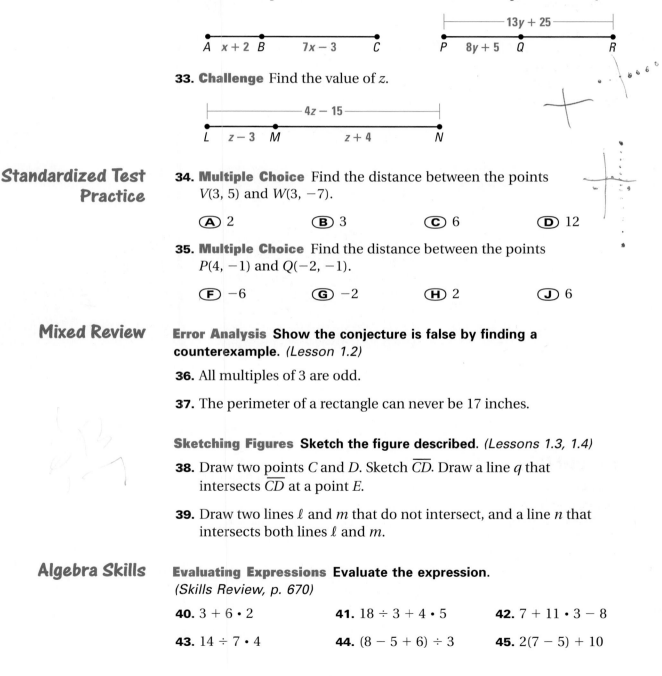

33. Challenge Find the value of z.

Standardized Test Practice

34. Multiple Choice Find the distance between the points $V(3, 5)$ and $W(3, -7)$.

(A) 2   (B) 3   (C) 6   (D) 12

35. Multiple Choice Find the distance between the points $P(4, -1)$ and $Q(-2, -1)$.

(F) -6 (G) -2 (H) 2   (J) 6

Mixed Review

Error Analysis Show the conjecture is false by finding a counterexample. *(Lesson 1.2)*

36. All multiples of 3 are odd.

37. The perimeter of a rectangle can never be 17 inches.

Sketching Figures Sketch the figure described. *(Lessons 1.3, 1.4)*

38. Draw two points C and D. Sketch $\overline{CD}$. Draw a line q that intersects $\overline{CD}$ at a point E.

39. Draw two lines ℓ and m that do not intersect, and a line n that intersects both lines ℓ and m.

Algebra Skills

Evaluating Expressions Evaluate the expression. *(Skills Review, p. 670)*

40. $3 + 6 \cdot 2$

41. $18 \div 3 + 4 \cdot 5$

42. $7 + 11 \cdot 3 - 8$

43. $14 \div 7 \cdot 4$

44. $(8 - 5 + 6) \div 3$

45. $2(7 - 5) + 10$

Question

How do you classify angles based on their angle measures?

Materials

- paper
- scissors
- protractor

Explore

1 Tear a large corner off two pieces of paper. These are called *right angles.*

2 Cut each right angle into two smaller angles. Angles smaller than a right angle are called *acute angles.*

3 Arrange three angles to form an angle larger than a right angle. Angles larger than a right angle are called *obtuse angles.*

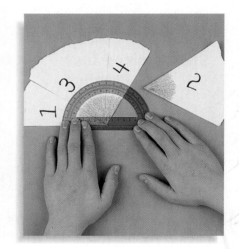

Think About It

Student Help

VOCABULARY TIP
The word *acute* means "sharp" and the word *obtuse* means "blunt." These meanings may help you remember the geometric terms.

1. Stack your angles on top of each other to compare their sizes. Arrange the angles from smallest to largest.

2. Choose two angles and place them next to each other to form a larger angle. Use a protractor to estimate the measure of the angle they form. Is the angle *acute*, *right*, or *obtuse*?

3. Choose three angles and place them next to each other to form a larger angle. Use a protractor to estimate the measure of the angle they form. Is the angle *acute*, *right*, or *obtuse*?

4. Arrange the four angles to form a *straight angle*, an angle with a measure of 180°.

1.6 Angles and Their Measures

Goal

Measure and classify angles. Add angle measures.

Key Words

- angle
- sides and vertex of an angle
- measure of an angle
- degree
- congruent angles
- acute, right, obtuse, and straight angle

An **angle** consists of two rays that have the same endpoint.

The rays are the **sides** of the angle.

The endpoint is the **vertex** of the angle.

In the photograph at the right, the sides of ∠*BAC* are $\overrightarrow{AB}$ and $\overrightarrow{AC}$. The vertex of ∠*BAC* is point *A*.

You can also write ∠*BAC* as ∠*CAB*. Notice that the middle letter in the name of the angle is always the vertex of the angle.

You can write simply ∠*A* if there are no other angles that have this vertex.

Mountaineers approaching Gasherbrum II, Karakorum Range, Himalayas.

EXAMPLE 1 Name Angles

Name the angles in the figure.

Solution

There are three different angles.

 ∠*PQS* or ∠*SQP*

 ∠*SQR* or ∠*RQS*

 ∠*PQR* or ∠*RQP*

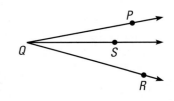

You should not name any of these angles as ∠*Q*, because all three angles have *Q* as their vertex. The name ∠*Q* would not distinguish one angle from the others.

Checkpoint ✓ Name Angles

Name the angles in the figure.

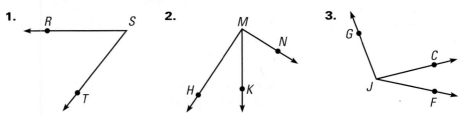

The **measure** of an angle is written in units called **degrees** (°). The measure of ∠A is denoted by m∠A.

EXAMPLE 2 **Measure Angles**

Use a protractor to approximate the measure of ∠BAC.

Solution

❶ Place the center of the protractor over the vertex point A.

❷ Align the protractor with one side of the angle.

❸ The second side of the angle crosses the protractor at the 50° mark. So, m∠BAC = 50°.

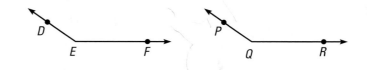

Two angles are **congruent angles** if they have the same measure. In the diagram below, the two angles have the same measure, so ∠DEF is congruent to ∠PQR. You can write ∠DEF ≅ ∠PQR.

Student Help

VISUAL STRATEGY
Add these words to the vocabulary pages in your notebook, as shown on p. 2.

Angles are classified as **acute**, **right**, **obtuse**, or **straight**, according to their measures. Angles have measures greater than 0° and less than or equal to 180°.

Visualize It!

90°

A small corner mark in an angle means that the angle is a right angle.

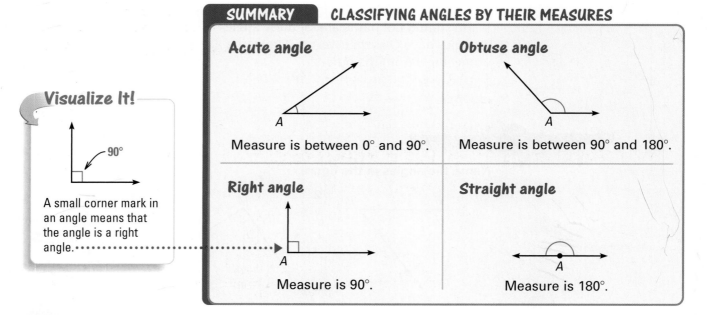

SUMMARY   **CLASSIFYING ANGLES BY THEIR MEASURES**

Acute angle

A

Measure is between 0° and 90°.

Obtuse angle

A

Measure is between 90° and 180°.

Right angle

A

Measure is 90°.

Straight angle

A

Measure is 180°.

EXAMPLE 3 Classify Angles

Classify each angle.

    a. $m\angle A = 130°$ **b.** $m\angle B = 90°$ **c.** $m\angle C = 45°$

Solution

    a. $\angle A$ is *obtuse* because its measure is greater than 90°.

    b. $\angle B$ is *right* because its measure is 90°.

    c. $\angle C$ is *acute* because its measure is less than 90°.

POSTULATE 6

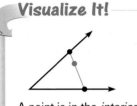

Visualize It!

A point is in the *interior* of an angle if it is between points that lie on each side of the angle.

Angle Addition Postulate

Words If P is in the interior of $\angle RST$, then the measure of $\angle RST$ is the sum of the measures of $\angle RSP$ and $\angle PST$.

Symbols If P is in the interior of $\angle RST$, then $m\angle RSP + m\angle PST = m\angle RST$.

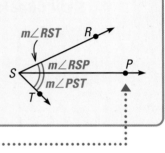

EXAMPLE 4 Add Angle Measures

Find the measure of $\angle PTM$.

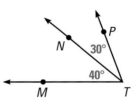

Solution

$$m\angle PTM = m\angle PTN + m\angle NTM \qquad \text{Angle Addition Postulate}$$

$$= 30° + 40° \qquad \text{Substitute 30° for } m\angle PTN \text{ and 40° for } m\angle NTM.$$

$$= 70° \qquad \text{Add angle measures.}$$

ANSWER ▶ The measure of $\angle PTM$ is 70°.

Checkpoint ✓ **Add and Subtract Angle Measures**

Find the measure of $\angle ABC$.

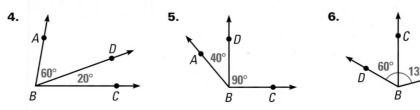

4.   **5.**   **6.**

Guided Practice

Vocabulary Check   Match the angle with its classification.

A. acute   **B.** obtuse   **C.** right   **D.** straight

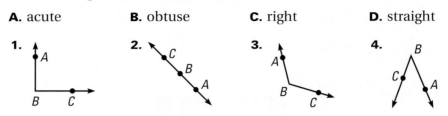

1.   **2.**   **3.**   **4.**

Skill Check   Name the vertex and the sides of the angle. Then estimate the measure of the angle.

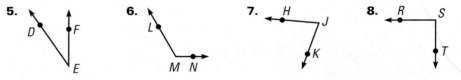

5.   **6.**   **7.**   **8.**

Classify the angle as *acute*, *right*, *obtuse*, or *straight*.

9. $m\angle A = 180°$ **10.** $m\angle B = 34°$ **11.** $m\angle C = 100°$ **12.** $m\angle D = 9°$

Use the diagram at the right to answer the questions. Explain your answers.

13. Is $\angle DEF \cong \angle FEG$?

14. Is $\angle DEG \cong \angle HEG$?

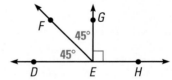

Practice and Applications

Extra Practice

See p. 676.

Naming Parts of an Angle Name the vertex and the sides of the angle.

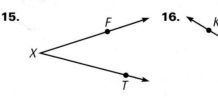

15.   **16.** 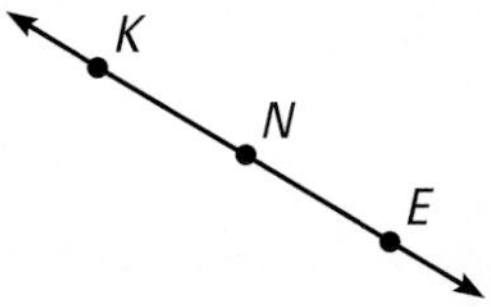   **17.**

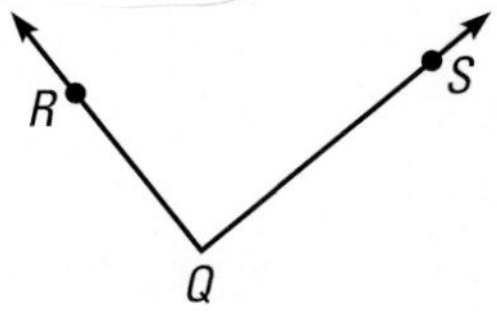

Homework Help

Example 1: Exs. 15–20
Example 2: Exs. 21–23
Example 3: Exs. 24–26, 30–33
Example 4: Exs. 27–29

Naming Angles Write two names for the angle.

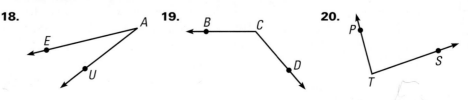

18.   **19.**   **20.**

Measuring Angles Copy the angle and use a protractor to measure it to the nearest degree. Extend the sides of the angle if necessary.

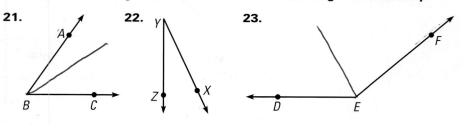

21.   **22.**   **23.**

Classifying Angles State whether the angle appears to be *acute*, *right*, *obtuse*, or *straight*. Then estimate its measure.

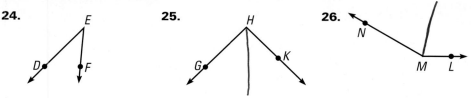

24.   **25.**   **26.**

Angle Addition Postulate Find the measure of the angle.

27. $m\angle ABC = $ ___?___   **28.** $m\angle DEF = $ ___?___   **29.** $m\angle PQR = $ ___?___

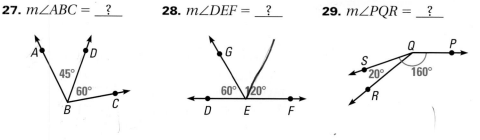

| **EXAMPLE** | **Angles on the Coordinate Plane** |

Plot the points $A(3, 0)$, $B(0, 0)$, $C(-2, 2)$ and sketch $\angle ABC$. Classify the angle.

Solution

Plot the points. Use a protractor to estimate the angle measure.

This angle has a measure of 135°.

So, $\angle ABC$ is obtuse.

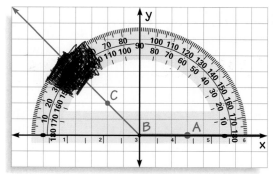

Visualize It! In Exercises 30–33, use the example above as a model. Plot the points and sketch $\angle ABC$. Classify the angle.

30. $A(3, 0)$, $B(0, 0)$, $C(0, 3)$ **31.** $A(3, 0)$, $B(0, 0)$, $C(4, -4)$

32. $A(-3, 0)$, $B(0, 0)$, $C(2, -2)$ **33.** $A(0, 4)$, $B(0, 0)$, $C(2, 2)$

Geography For each city, estimate the measure of ∠*BOA*, where *B* is on the 0° longitude line, *O* is the North Pole, and *A* is the city.

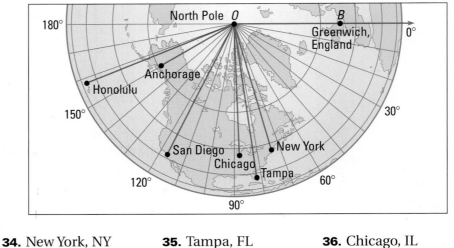

34. New York, NY   **35.** Tampa, FL   **36.** Chicago, IL

37. San Diego, CA   **38.** Honolulu, HI   **39.** Anchorage, AK

Airport Runways In Exercises 40–44, use the diagram of Ronald Reagan Washington National Airport and the information about runway numbering on the page facing page 1.

An airport runway number is its *bearing* (the angle measured clockwise from due north) divided by 10. Because a full circle contains 360°, runway numbers range from 1 to 36.

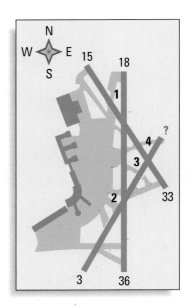

40. Find *m*∠1.   **41.** Find *m*∠2.

42. Find *m*∠3.   **43.** Find *m*∠4.

44. What is the number of the unlabeled runway?

Student Help

LOOK BACK
For an example of runway numbers, see the page facing p. 1.

Standardized Test Practice

45. Multi-Step Problem Fold a piece of paper in half three times and label it as shown.

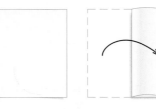

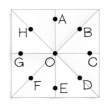

a. Name eight congruent acute angles.

b. Name eight right angles.

c. Name eight congruent obtuse angles.

Naming Rays **Name the ray described.** *(Lesson 1.3)*

46. Name a ray that contains *M*.

47. Name a ray that has *N* as an endpoint.

48. Name two rays that intersect at *P*.

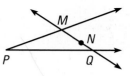

Betweenness **Draw a sketch of the three collinear points. Then write the Segment Addition Postulate for the points.** *(Lesson 1.5)*

49. *Y* is between *X* and *Z*.   **50.** *Q* is between *P* and *R*.

51. *B* is between *A* and *C*.   **52.** *K* is between *J* and *L*.

Algebra Skills   **One-Step Equations** **Solve the equation.** *(Skills Review p. 672)*

53. $x + 3 = 15$ **54.** $y + 4 = 2$ **55.** $z - 7 = 9$ **56.** $w - 5 = -2$

57. $2p = 24$ **58.** $-9 = 3q$ **59.** $5r = 125$ **60.** $-12 = 6s$

Quiz 2

In Exercises 1–3, use the photo shown at the right. *(Lesson 1.4)*

1. Name two lines that do not appear to intersect.

2. Name two lines that intersect at *B*.

3. Name two lines that intersect at *E*.

Judi Brown competing at the Summer Olympics.

Plot the points in a coordinate plane. Decide whether $\overline{AB}$ **and** $\overline{CD}$ **are congruent.** *(Lesson 1.5)*

4. *A*(0, 0), *B*(5, 0), *C*(2, 4), *D*(2, −1)   **5.** *A*(−3, 2), *B*(3, 2), *C*(6, 0), *D*(−6, 0)

Classify the angle as *acute, right, obtuse,* **or** *straight.* *(Lesson 1.6)*

6. $m\angle Z = 90°$ **7.** $m\angle Y = 126°$ **8.** $m\angle X = 180°$

9. $m\angle W = 35°$ **10.** $m\angle V = 5°$ **11.** $m\angle U = 45°$

Use the Angle Addition Postulate to find the measure of the angle. *(Lesson 1.6)*

12. Find $m\angle JKL$.   **13.** Find $m\angle WXY$.   **14.** Find $m\angle VUW$.

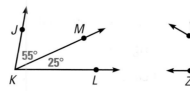
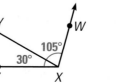
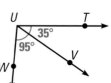

VOCABULARY

- **conjecture**, *p. 8*
- **inductive reasoning**, *p. 8*
- **counterexample**, *p. 10*
- **undefined term**, *p. 14*
- **point**, *p. 14*
- **line**, *p. 14*
- **plane**, *p. 14*
- **postulate**, *p. 14*
- **collinear points**, *p. 15*
- **coplanar points**, *p. 15*
- **coplanar lines**, *p. 15*

- **segment**, *p. 16*
- **endpoint**, *p. 16*
- **ray**, *p. 16*
- **intersect**, *p. 22*
- **intersection**, *p. 22*
- **coordinate**, *p. 28*
- **distance**, *p. 28*
- **length**, *p. 28*
- **between**, *p. 29*
- **congruent segments**, *p. 30*

- **angle**, *p. 35*
- **sides of an angle**, *p. 35*
- **vertex of an angle**, *p. 35*
- **measure of an angle**, *p. 36*
- **degrees**, *p. 36*
- **congruent angles**, *p. 36*
- **acute angle**, *p. 36*
- **right angle**, *p. 36*
- **obtuse angle**, *p. 36*
- **straight angle**, *p. 36*

VOCABULARY REVIEW

Fill in the blank.

1. __?__ are lines that lie in the same plane.

2. A(n) __?__ consists of two __?__ that have the same endpoint.

3. A(n) __?__ is an unproven statement that is based on a pattern or observation.

4. The endpoint of the rays that form an angle is called its __?__.

5. Two or more figures __?__ if they have points in common.

6. An angle that has a measure between 0° and 90° is called a(n) __?__ angle.

7. Points on the same line are __?__ points.

8. An angle that has a measure of 180° is called a(n) __?__ angle.

9. Two angles that have the same measure are called __?__ angles.

10. A(n) __?__ is an example that shows a conjecture is false.

11. An angle that has a measure between 90° and 180° is called a(n) __?__ angle.

12. Two segments that have the same length are called __?__ segments.

1.1 FINDING AND DESCRIBING PATTERNS

Examples on pp. 3–4

EXAMPLE **Describe a pattern in the numbers $-7, 0, 7, 14, \ldots$.**
Write the next two numbers you expect in the pattern.

Each number is 7 more than the previous number.
The next two numbers are 21 and 28.

Describe a pattern in the numbers. Write the next two numbers you expect in the pattern.

13. $5, 14, 23, 32, \ldots$ **14.** $6, 18, 54, 162, \ldots$ **15.** $100, 90, 80, 70, \ldots$

Sketch the next figure you expect in the pattern.

16.

17.

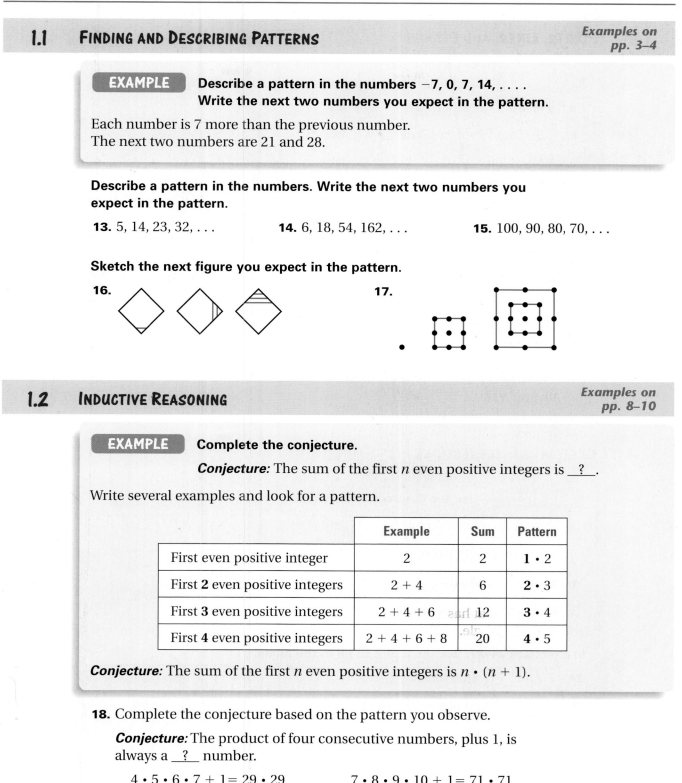

1.2 INDUCTIVE REASONING

Examples on pp. 8–10

EXAMPLE **Complete the conjecture.**

Conjecture: The sum of the first n even positive integers is __?__.

Write several examples and look for a pattern.

	Example	Sum	Pattern
First even positive integer	2	2	**1 · 2**
First **2** even positive integers	2 + 4	6	**2 · 3**
First **3** even positive integers	2 + 4 + 6	12	**3 · 4**
First **4** even positive integers	2 + 4 + 6 + 8	20	**4 · 5**

Conjecture: The sum of the first n even positive integers is $n \cdot (n + 1)$.

18. Complete the conjecture based on the pattern you observe.

Conjecture: The product of four consecutive numbers, plus 1, is always a __?__ number.

$4 \cdot 5 \cdot 6 \cdot 7 + 1 = 29 \cdot 29$ $7 \cdot 8 \cdot 9 \cdot 10 + 1 = 71 \cdot 71$

$5 \cdot 6 \cdot 7 \cdot 8 + 1 = 41 \cdot 41$ $6 \cdot 7 \cdot 8 \cdot 9 + 1 = 55 \cdot 55$

19. Show the conjecture is false by finding a counterexample.

Conjecture: The cube of a number is always greater than the number.

1.3   POINTS, LINES, AND PLANES

Examples on pp. 14–16

EXAMPLES   Decide whether the statement is *true* or *false*.

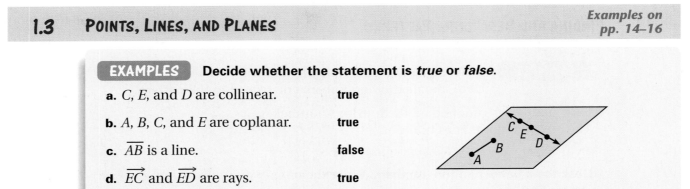

a. *C*, *E*, and *D* are collinear.   **true**

b. *A*, *B*, *C*, and *E* are coplanar.   **true**

c. $\overline{AB}$ is a line.   **false**

d. $\overrightarrow{EC}$ and $\overrightarrow{ED}$ are rays.   **true**

In Exercises 20–22, use the diagram at the right to decide whether the statement is *true* or *false*.

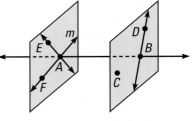

20. Point *A* lies on line *m*.

21. Point *E* lies on line *m*.

22. Points *B*, *C*, and *D* are collinear.

23. Draw four points *J*, *K*, *L*, and *M*, no three of which are collinear. Sketch $\overline{LK}$ and add a point *N* on that line segment. Then sketch $\overrightarrow{NJ}$ and $\overrightarrow{NM}$.

1.4   SKETCHING INTERSECTIONS

Examples on pp. 22–24

EXAMPLES   Use the diagram at the right.

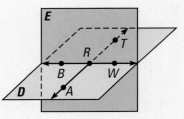

a. Name the intersection of lines $\overleftrightarrow{AT}$ and $\overleftrightarrow{BW}$.

Lines $\overleftrightarrow{AT}$ and $\overleftrightarrow{BW}$ intersect at point *R*.

b. Name the intersection of planes *D* and *E*.

Planes *D* and *E* intersect at $\overleftrightarrow{BW}$.

In Exercises 24–27, use the figure to fill in the blank.

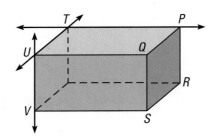

24. $\overleftrightarrow{TU}$ and $\overleftrightarrow{VU}$ intersect at ___?___.

25. Plane *PQR* and plane *UVS* intersect at ___?___.

26. Plane *RSV* and plane *QUV* intersect at ___?___.

27. Plane *QSV* and plane *TUV* intersect at ___?___.

Visualize It! Sketch the figure described.

28. Two lines that are not coplanar and do not intersect

29. A plane and two lines that intersect the plane at one point

1.5 SEGMENTS AND THEIR MEASURES

Examples on pp. 28–30

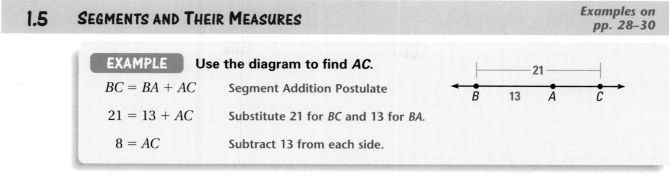

> **EXAMPLE** **Use the diagram to find AC.**
>
> $BC = BA + AC$ Segment Addition Postulate
>
> $21 = 13 + AC$ Substitute 21 for BC and 13 for BA.
>
> $8 = AC$ Subtract 13 from each side.

Find the length.

30. Find AC.

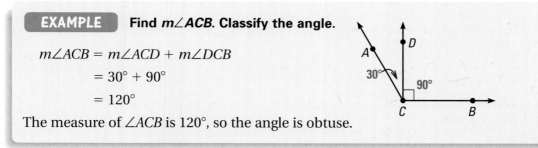

31. Find RS.

Plot the points. Decide whether $\overline{PQ}$ and $\overline{QR}$ are congruent.

32. $P(2, 3)$, $Q(2, -5)$, $R(9, -5)$ **33.** $P(-5, 4)$, $Q(1, 4)$, $R(1, -2)$

1.6 ANGLES AND THEIR MEASURES

Examples on pp. 35–37

> **EXAMPLE** **Find $m\angle ACB$. Classify the angle.**
>
> $m\angle ACB = m\angle ACD + m\angle DCB$
>
> $= 30° + 90°$
>
> $= 120°$
>
> The measure of $\angle ACB$ is 120°, so the angle is obtuse.

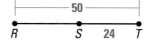

Copy the angle, extend its sides, and use a protractor to measure it to the nearest degree. Then classify it as *acute*, *right*, *obtuse*, or *straight*.

34.

35.

36.

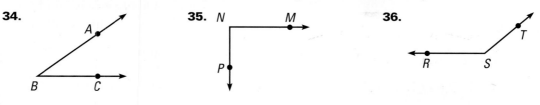

Find the measure of the angle.

37. $m\angle DEF = $ ____?____   **38.** $m\angle HJL = $ ____?____   **39.** $m\angle QNM = $ ____?____

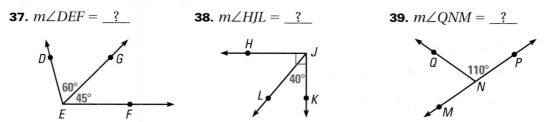

Describe a pattern in the numbers. Write the next two numbers you expect in the pattern.

1. 10, 17, 24, . . .

2. −29, −12, 5, . . .

3. 1, 5, 13, 25, . . .

4. 2.8, 3.4, 4, 4.6, . . .

5. Complete the conjecture based on the pattern you observe.

    Conjecture: The product of any two even numbers is __?__.

$$2 \cdot 4 = 8 \qquad\qquad -4 \cdot 10 = -40$$
$$4 \cdot 6 = 24 \qquad\qquad 12 \cdot 26 = 312$$
$$6 \cdot 8 = 48 \qquad\qquad -104 \cdot (-88) = 9152$$

The first five figures in a pattern are shown. Each square in the grid is 1 unit × 1 unit.

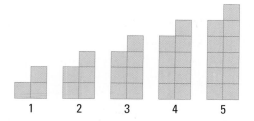

6. Make a table that shows the distance around each figure at each stage.

7. Describe the pattern of the distances and use it to predict the distance around the figure at stage 10.

In Exercises 8–11, use the diagram below.

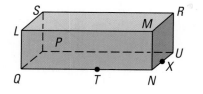

8. Name three collinear points.

9. Name four noncoplanar points.

10. Name the intersection of $\overleftrightarrow{QT}$ and $\overleftrightarrow{UN}$.

11. Name the intersection of plane *LMN* and plane *QLS*.

In Exercises 12 and 13, find the length.

12. Find *PR*.

13. Find *AB*.

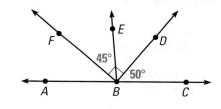

Plot the points in a coordinate plane. Then decide whether $\overline{AB}$ and $\overline{CD}$ are congruent.

14. $A(1, 3)$, $B(1, -2)$, $C(-2, 2)$, $D(3, 2)$

15. $A(0, 4)$, $B(0, -2)$, $C(5, -1)$, $D(1, -1)$

In Exercises 16–20, use the diagram below.

16. Name two congruent angles.

17. Find $m\angle ABF$.

18. Find $m\angle CBF$.

19. Find $m\angle EBA$.

20. Name an acute angle, an obtuse angle, a straight angle, and a right angle.

21. In the figure of the gymnast below, $m\angle ABD = 25°$ and $m\angle DBC = 35°$. Find the measures of $\angle ABC$ and $\angle CBE$.

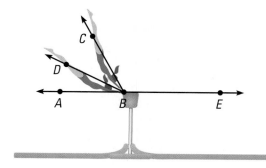

Chapter 1 Standardized Test

Test Tip Most standardized tests are based on concepts and skills taught in school. The best way to prepare is to keep up with your regular studies.

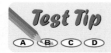

1. What is the next number you expect in the sequence?

4488; 44,088; 440,088; 4,400,088

Ⓐ 400,008 Ⓑ 40,000,088

Ⓒ 44,000,088 Ⓓ 440,000,088

2. Which statement is a counterexample to the conjecture that the square of any integer is greater than the integer?

Ⓕ 4^2 is greater than 4.

Ⓖ $(-3)^2$ is greater than 3.

Ⓗ 0^2 is not greater than 0.

Ⓙ 200^2 is not greater than 200.

3. Which of the following statements is *false*?

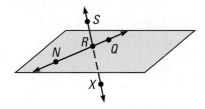

Ⓐ *R* is between *N* and *Q*.

Ⓑ *N*, *R*, and *Q* are coplanar.

Ⓒ *X*, *N*, and *R* are collinear.

Ⓓ *S*, *R*, and *X* are collinear.

4. Which of the points lies on $\overrightarrow{SR}$?

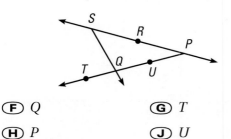

Ⓕ *Q* Ⓖ *T*

Ⓗ *P* Ⓙ *U*

5. Multi-Step Problem Use the figure below.

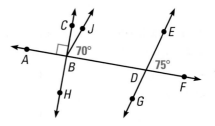

a. Name four collinear points.

b. Name the following types of angles: acute, obtuse, straight, and right.

c. Find $m\angle ABH$, $m\angle GDF$, and $m\angle ABJ$.

6. Which of the line segments in the coordinate plane are congruent?

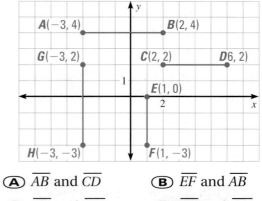

Ⓐ $\overline{AB}$ and $\overline{CD}$ Ⓑ $\overline{EF}$ and $\overline{AB}$

Ⓒ $\overline{CD}$ and $\overline{GH}$ Ⓓ $\overline{AB}$ and $\overline{GH}$

7. In the diagram, what is the value of *PQ*?

Ⓕ 4 Ⓖ 6

Ⓗ 8 Ⓙ 9

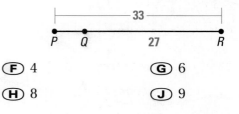

BraiN GaMes

Geometry Scavenger Hunt

Object of the Game To be the first team to complete the scavenger hunt.

How to Play With members of your team, search your classroom for items that fit the given description. Keep a list of objects you find. The team that finds the most items in a given time wins.

Another Way to Play The team that finds the most items that fit each category wins a point for that category. The team with the most points wins.

Or, create your own list of items to find and swap it with the list created by another team.

SCAVENGER HUNT

1. a plane
2. two planes that intersect
3. a right angle
4. a 3 inch segment
5. a 45° angle
6. a 9 inch segment
7. a pair of congruent angles that are not right angles
8. an obtuse angle
9. two planes that do not intersect
10. a pair of adjacent angles

To evaluate an expression involving variables, substitute a value for each variable, and then simplify using the order of operations.

EXAMPLE 1   Evaluate Expressions

Evaluate $4x + 9y$ when $x = 3$ and $y = -5$.

Solution

$4x + 9y$	Write original expression.
$4(3) + 9(-5)$	Substitute 3 for x and -5 for y.
$12 + (-45)$	Multiply.
-33	Add.

Student Help

SKILLS REVIEW
For help using the order of operations, see p. 670.

Try These

Evaluate the expression when $x = 2$, $y = 7$, and $z = -3$.

1. $3x + 4y$ **2.** $2x + 2y$ **3.** $6x + y$ **4.** $5x + 7y$

5. $14x - 4y$ **6.** $y - 2x$ **7.** $5x - 3y$ **8.** $11y - 4x$

9. $3y + 2z$ **10.** $x - 4z$ **11.** $x + y + z$ **12.** $-2x + 5z$

EXAMPLE 2   Solve Two-Step Equations

Solve the equation $2x - 5 = 7$.

Solution

$2x - 5 = 7$	Write original equation.
$2x - 5 + 5 = 7 + 5$	Add 5 to each side.
$2x = 12$	Simplify.
$\dfrac{2x}{2} = \dfrac{12}{2}$	Divide each side by 2.
$x = 6$	Simplify.

Student Help

STUDY TIP
To check that the solution is correct, substitute 6 for x in the original equation and evaluate.

$2(x) - 5 = 7$

$2(6) - 5 = 7$

$12 - 5 = 7$ ✓

Try These

Solve the equation.

13. $3x - 2 = 13$ **14.** $\dfrac{n}{8} + 2 = 4$ **15.** $4 + 5w = 24$ **16.** $6p - 1 = 17$

17. $10 + \dfrac{y}{3} = 7$ **18.** $4z + 11 = 15$ **19.** $9 = -2t - 5$ **20.** $1 = \dfrac{b}{4} - 6$

Chapter 2

Segments and Angles

How is a strike zone determined?

In baseball, the *strike zone* is the area above home plate where a ball is considered a strike. The location of the strike zone is based on each player's height and batting stance.

The midpoint between the top of the batter's shoulders and the top of the batter's belt determines the top of the strike zone.

Learn More About It

You will learn more about strike zones in Exercises 36 and 37 on p. 58.

Who uses Segments and Angles?

KITE DESIGNER
Kite designers use geometric principles in designing and making kites. A kite's struts often bisect the angles they support. (p. 62)

ERGONOMIST
Ergonomists design offices, furniture, and equipment to improve the safety and comfort of workers. For example, drafting tables are angled so that people using them can work without injuring their backs. (p. 80)

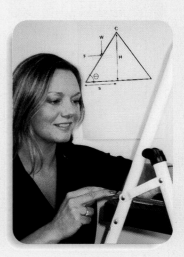

How will you use these ideas?

• Determine the strike zone for different batting stances. (p. 58)
• Describe angle relationships in a paper airplane pattern. (p. 65)
• Predict the angle of reflection of a laser. (p. 65)
• Learn about angle relationships found in the Alamillo Bridge in Spain. (p. 71)
• Interpret the meaning of advertising slogans. (p. 86)

What's the chapter about?

- Analyzing **segment bisectors** and **angle bisectors**
- Identifying **complementary angles**, **supplementary angles**, **vertical angles**, and **linear pairs**
- Using properties of equality and congruence

> ### Key Words
>
> - **midpoint**, *p. 53*
> - **segment bisector**, *p. 53*
> - **bisect**, *p. 53*
> - **angle bisector**, *p. 61*
> - **complementary angles**, *p. 67*
> - **supplementary angles**, *p. 67*
>
> - **adjacent angles**, *p. 68*
> - **theorem**, *p. 69*
> - **vertical angles**, *p. 75*
> - **linear pair**, *p. 75*
> - **if-then statement**, *p. 82*
> - **deductive reasoning**, *p. 83*

PREPARE

Chapter Readiness Quiz

Take this quick quiz. If you are unsure of an answer, look at the reference pages for help.

Vocabulary Check *(refer to p. 36)*

1. Suppose $m\angle ABC = 100°$. What type of angle is $\angle ABC$?

    A acute   **B** right   **C** obtuse   **D** straight

Skill Check *(refer to pp. 37, 672)*

2. In the diagram, $m\angle PQR = 165°$ and $m\angle PQS = 22°$. What is $m\angle SQR$?

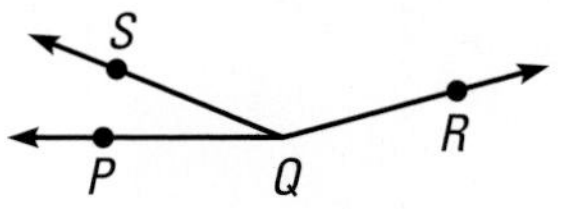

    F 121°   **G** 143°   **H** 153°   **J** 158°

3. Which of the following is a solution of the equation $4x = -20$?

    A -80 **B** -16 **C** -5 **D** 5

VISUAL STRATEGY

Picturing Theorems

Visualize It!

In this chapter, you will learn the first of many *theorems*.

To help you visualize a theorem, draw an example that uses specific measures.

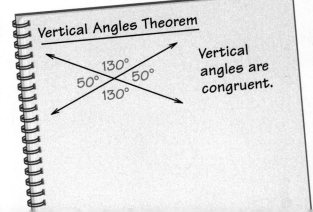

Vertical Angles Theorem

Vertical angles are congruent.

2.1 Segment Bisectors

Goal

Bisect a segment. Find the coordinates of the midpoint of a segment.

Key Words

• midpoint
• segment bisector
• bisect

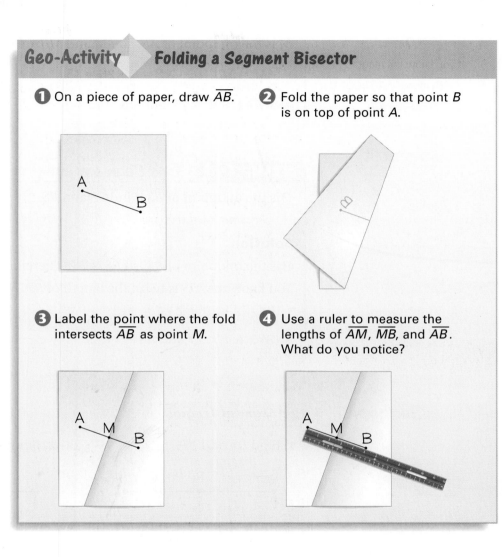

Geo-Activity   **Folding a Segment Bisector**

1 On a piece of paper, draw $\overline{AB}$.

A

B

2 Fold the paper so that point B is on top of point A.

3 Label the point where the fold intersects $\overline{AB}$ as point M.

A   M   B

4 Use a ruler to measure the lengths of $\overline{AM}$, $\overline{MB}$, and $\overline{AB}$. What do you notice?

A   M   B

In the Geo-Activity, M is called the *midpoint* of $\overline{AB}$. The **midpoint** of a segment is the point on the segment that divides it into two congruent segments.

A **segment bisector** is a segment, ray, line, or plane that intersects a segment at its midpoint. To **bisect** a segment means to divide the segment into two congruent segments.

Student Help

VOCABULARY TIP
Bi- means "two," and *-sect* means "to cut." So, *bisect* means "to cut in two."

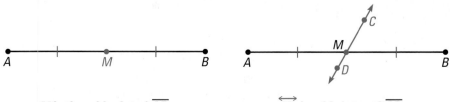

M is the midpoint of $\overline{AB}$. $\overleftrightarrow{CD}$ **is a bisector of $\overline{AB}$.**

2.1 *Segment Bisectors*   **53**

STUDY TIP
The midpoint of a segment divides the segment in half.

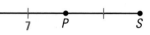

If you know the length of $\overline{AB}$, multiply AB by $\frac{1}{2}$ to find AM and MB.

EXAMPLE 1 Find Segment Lengths

M is the midpoint of $\overline{AB}$. Find AM and MB.

Solution

M is the midpoint of $\overline{AB}$, so AM and MB are each half the length of $\overline{AB}$.

$$AM = MB = \frac{1}{2} \cdot AB = \frac{1}{2} \cdot 26 = 13$$

ANSWER ▶ $AM = 13$ and $MB = 13$.

EXAMPLE 2 Find Segment Lengths

P is the midpoint of $\overline{RS}$. Find PS and RS.

Solution

P is the midpoint of $\overline{RS}$, so $PS = RP$. Therefore, $PS = 7$.
You know that RS is twice the length of $\overline{RP}$.

$$RS = 2 \cdot RP = 2 \cdot 7 = 14$$

ANSWER ▶ $PS = 7$ and $RS = 14$.

Checkpoint ✓ Find Segment Lengths

1. Find DE and EF.

2. Find NP and MP.

Using Algebra

EXAMPLE 3 Use Algebra with Segment Lengths

Line ℓ is a segment bisector of $\overline{AB}$.
Find the value of x.

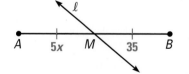

Solution

$AM = MB$	Line ℓ bisects $\overline{AB}$ at point M.
$5x = 35$	Substitute $5x$ for AM and 35 for MB.
$\dfrac{5x}{5} = \dfrac{35}{5}$	Divide each side by 5.
$x = 7$	Simplify.

CHECK ✓ Check your solution by substituting 7 for x.

$$5x = 5(7) = 35$$

Midpoints If you know the coordinates of the endpoints of a line segment in a coordinate plane, you can find the coordinates of the midpoint of the segment using the Midpoint Formula.

Student Help

READING TIP
The numbers 1 and 2 in x_1 and y_2 are called *subscripts*. You read x_1 as "x sub 1" and y_2 as "y sub 2."

THE MIDPOINT FORMULA

Words The coordinates of the midpoint of a segment are the averages of the x-coordinates and the y-coordinates of the endpoints.

Symbols The midpoint of the segment joining $A(x_1, y_1)$ and $B(x_2, y_2)$ is $M\left(\dfrac{x_1 + x_2}{2}, \dfrac{y_1 + y_2}{2}\right)$.

EXAMPLE 4 Use the Midpoint Formula

Find the coordinates of the midpoint of $\overline{AB}$.

a. $A(1, 2), B(7, 4)$ **b.** $A(-2, 3), B(5, -1)$

Solution

First make a sketch. Then use the Midpoint Formula.

Student Help

SKILLS REVIEW
For help plotting points in a coordinate plane, see p. 664.

a.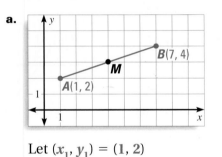

b.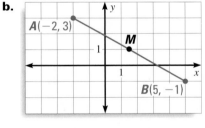

Let $(x_1, y_1) = (1, 2)$ and $(x_2, y_2) = (7, 4)$.

$$M = \left(\frac{x_1 + x_2}{2}, \frac{y_1 + y_2}{2}\right)$$

$$= \left(\frac{1 + 7}{2}, \frac{2 + 4}{2}\right)$$

$$= (4, 3)$$

Let $(x_1, y_1) = (-2, 3)$ and $(x_2, y_2) = (5, -1)$.

$$M = \left(\frac{x_1 + x_2}{2}, \frac{y_1 + y_2}{2}\right)$$

$$= \left(\frac{-2 + 5}{2}, \frac{3 + (-1)}{2}\right)$$

$$= \left(\frac{3}{2}, 1\right)$$

Checkpoint ✓ **Use the Midpoint Formula**

Sketch $\overline{PQ}$. Then find the coordinates of its midpoint.

3. $P(2, 5), Q(4, 3)$ **4.** $P(0, -2), Q(4, 0)$ **5.** $P(-1, 2), Q(-4, 1)$

Guided Practice

Vocabulary Check

1. In the diagram shown at the right, name the *midpoint* and a *segment bisector* of $\overline{AB}$.

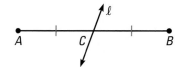

Skill Check

M is the midpoint of the segment. Find the segment lengths.

2. Find *RM* and *MS*.

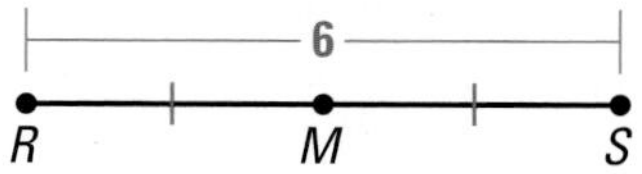

3. Find *FM* and *MG*.

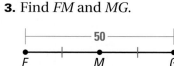

4. Find *MQ* and *PQ*.

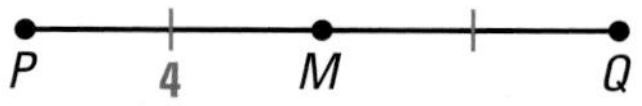

5. Find *YM* and *YZ*.

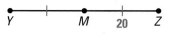

M is the midpoint of $\overline{JK}$. Find the value of the variable.

6.

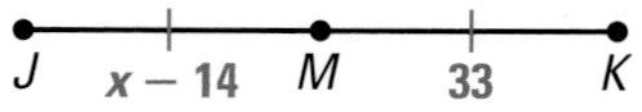

7.

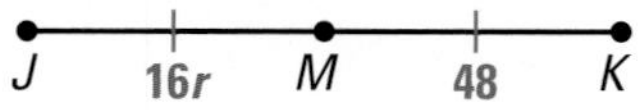

Find the coordinates of the midpoint of $\overline{PR}$.

8. **9.** **10.**

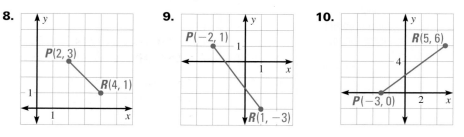

Practice and Applications

Extra Practice

See p. 677.

Recognizing Midpoints In Exercises 11–14, determine whether *M* is the midpoint of $\overline{AB}$. Explain your reasoning.

11. **12.**

13. **14.**

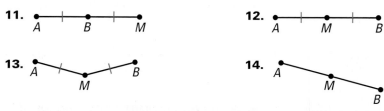

15. Visualize It! Sketch a line segment, $\overline{PQ}$, that is bisected by line ℓ at point *R*.

Homework Help

Example 1: Exs. 16–19
Example 2: Exs. 20–23
Example 3: Exs. 26–29
Example 4: Exs. 30–35

Finding Segment Lengths *M* is the midpoint of the segment. Find the segment lengths.

16. Find *KM* and *ML*.

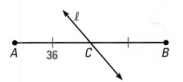

38

K   M   L

17. Find *DM* and *ME*.

82

D   M   E

18. Find *YM* and *MZ*.

17

Y   M   Z

19. Find *AM* and *MB*.

2.7

A   M   B

Finding Segment Lengths Line ℓ bisects the segment. Find the segment lengths.

20. Find *CB* and *AB*.

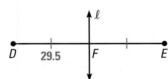

A   36   C   B

ℓ

21. Find *MP* and *MN*.

M   P   15   N

ℓ

22. Find *FE* and *DE*.

D   29.5   F   E

ℓ

23. Find *UT* and *ST*.

S   3.6   U   T

ℓ

Biking The Minuteman Bikeway is a 10.5 mile bike path that runs from Arlington to Bedford, Massachusetts.

24. Caitlin and Laurie begin at opposite ends of the Minuteman Bikeway and meet at the halfway point on the path. How far does each rider bike?

25. Caitlin starts on the path 4.3 miles from the Arlington end. Laurie starts on the path 3 miles from the Bedford end. How far will each rider bike before reaching the halfway point on the path?

Using Algebra Find the value of the variable.

26.

A   6p   M   72   B

27.

A   19   M   q + 7   B

28.

A   r − 3   M   15   B

29.

A   4   M   2s + 6   B

Student Help
CLASSZONE.COM

HOMEWORK HELP
Extra help with problem solving in Exs. 30–35 is at classzone.com

Midpoint Formula Find the coordinates of the midpoint of $\overline{PQ}$.

30. $P(0, 0), Q(4, 6)$
31. $P(3, 8), Q(7, 6)$
32. $P(-5, 6), Q(9, 7)$

33. $P(-12, 0), Q(6, 1)$
34. $P(-4, 4), Q(4, 0)$
35. $P(3, 2), Q(-7, -4)$

Student Help

LOOK BACK
For more about
baseball, see p. 50.

Strike Zone **In Exercises 36 and 37, use the information below.**
In baseball, the *strike zone* is the region a baseball needs to pass
through for the umpire to declare it a strike if the batter does not
swing. The top of the strike zone is a horizontal plane passing through
the midpoint of the top of the batter's shoulders and the top of the
uniform pants when the player is in a batting stance.

▶ Source: Major League Baseball

36. Find the coordinate of *T*.   **37.** Find the coordinate of *T*.

Student Help

VOCABULARY TIP
Lines of *latitude* run
parallel to the Equator.
Lines of *longitude* run
north-south.

EXAMPLE **Latitude-Longitude Coordinates**

Find the coordinates of
the place halfway between
San Francisco (**37.8°N, 122.4°W**)
and Los Angeles (**34.1°N, 118.2°W**).

Solution

$$M = \left(\frac{x_1 + x_2}{2}, \frac{y_1 + y_2}{2} \right)$$

$$= \left(\frac{37.8° + 34.1°}{2}, \frac{122.4° + 118.2°}{2} \right)$$

$$= (35.95°N, 120.3°W)$$

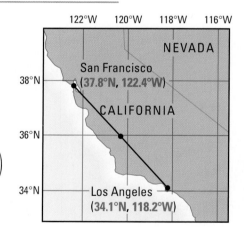

ANSWER ▶ The place halfway between San Francisco and Los Angeles
has coordinates (35.95°N, 120.3°W).

Latitude-Longitude Coordinates **Find the coordinates of the place
halfway between the two cities in California.**

38. Fresno: (36.7°N, 119.8°W)   **39.** Bishop: (37.4°N, 118.4°W)
Napa: (38.3°N, 122.3°W)   Los Angeles: (34.1°N, 118.2°W)

40. San Francisco: (37.8°N, 122.4°W)   **41.** Santa Barbara: (34.4°N, 119.7°W)
Palo Alto: (37.4°N, 122.1°W)   Oakland: (37.8°N, 122.3°W)

42. Using Midpoints In the diagram below, B is the midpoint of $\overline{AC}$, $AB = 9$, and $AD = 25$. Find CD.

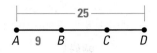

43. Challenge The midpoint of $\overline{AB}$ is $M(7, 5)$. The coordinates of point A are $(4, 1)$. Find the coordinates of point B. Explain.

44. Multiple Choice T is the midpoint of $\overline{QR}$. What is the value of x?

(A) 17   (B) 22

(C) 29.5   (D) 88

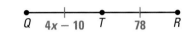

45. Multiple Choice What is the midpoint of the segment joining $(2, 7)$ and $(-6, 2)$?

(F) $\left(-2, \dfrac{9}{2}\right)$ (G) $(-4, 9)$ (H) $(-2, 4)$ (J) $\left(\dfrac{9}{2}, -2\right)$

Evaluating Statements Use the diagram at the right to determine whether the statement is *true* or *false*. (Lessons 1.3, 1.5)

46. Point A lies on line m.

47. Point E lies on line ℓ.

48. Points B, E, and C are collinear.

49. Lines ℓ and m intersect at point E.

50. Point E is between points B and C.

51. Point F is between points A and B.

Classifying Angles Name the vertex and sides of the angle. Then state whether it appears to be *acute*, *right*, *obtuse*, or *straight*. (Lesson 1.6)

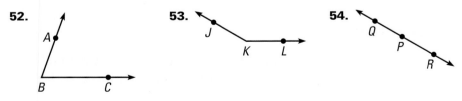

52.   **53.**   **54.**

Evaluating Expressions Evaluate the expression. (Skills Review, p. 670)

55. $2 \cdot 15 + 40$ **56.** $120 - 35 \cdot 3$ **57.** $\dfrac{1}{2} \cdot 50 + 145$

58. $\dfrac{5}{4} \cdot 16 - 20$ **59.** $6 + 3 \cdot 5 - 2$ **60.** $11 \cdot 4 + 7 - 20$

61. $12 \cdot 2 - 3 \cdot 4$ **62.** $5 - 10 \cdot 6 + 1$ **63.** $2 - (3 + 4) \cdot 5$

Activity 2.2 Folding Angle Bisectors

Question

How can you bisect an angle?

Materials

- protractor
- straightedge

Explore

1 On a piece of paper, use a straightedge to draw an acute angle. Label the angle $\angle ABC$.

2 Fold the paper so $\overrightarrow{BC}$ is on top of $\overrightarrow{BA}$.

3 Draw a point D on the fold inside $\angle ABC$. Then use a protractor to measure $\angle ABD$, $\angle DBC$, and $\angle ABC$.

Student Help

LOOK BACK
For help using a protractor, see p. 36.

Think About It

1. What do you notice about the angles you measured in Step 3?

2. Repeat Steps 1 through 3 with an obtuse angle. Compare your results with the results from Exercise 1.

3. Copy and complete:

a. $m\angle ABD = \underline{\ ?\ } \cdot m\angle ABC$ **b.** $m\angle DBC = \underline{\ ?\ } \cdot m\angle ABC$

c. $m\angle ABC = \underline{\ ?\ } \cdot m\angle ABD$ **d.** $m\angle ABC = \underline{\ ?\ } \cdot m\angle DBC$

4. Extension Is it possible to fold congruent angles from a straight angle? Explain your reasoning.

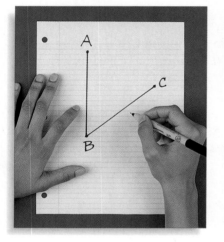

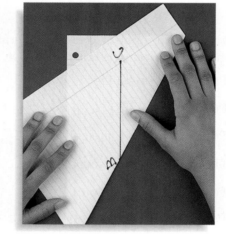

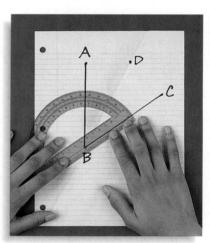

Angle Bisectors

Goal
Bisect an angle.

Key Words
• angle bisector

An **angle bisector** is a ray that divides an angle into two angles that are congruent. In the photograph of the hang glider, $\overrightarrow{BD}$ bisects $\angle ABC$ because it divides the angle into two congruent angles.

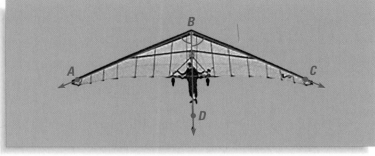

$$\angle ABD \cong \angle DBC$$

If $\overrightarrow{BD}$ bisects $\angle ABC$, then the measures of $\angle ABD$ and $\angle DBC$ are *half* the measure of $\angle ABC$. Also, the measure of $\angle ABC$ is *twice* the measure of $\angle ABD$ or $\angle DBC$.

Visualize It!
In this book, an arc that crosses two or more angles identifies the measure of the entire angle it crosses. • • • • • • • • • • • •

EXAMPLE 1 Find Angle Measures

$\overrightarrow{BD}$ bisects $\angle ABC$, and $m\angle ABC = 110°$. Find $m\angle ABD$ and $m\angle DBC$.

Solution

$$m\angle ABD = \frac{1}{2}(m\angle ABC) \qquad \overrightarrow{BD} \text{ bisects } \angle ABC.$$

$$= \frac{1}{2}(110°) \qquad \text{Substitute } 110° \text{ for } m\angle ABC.$$

$$= 55° \qquad \text{Simplify.}$$

$\angle ABD$ and $\angle DBC$ are congruent, so $m\angle DBC = m\angle ABD$.

ANSWER So, $m\angle ABD = 55°$, and $m\angle DBC = 55°$.

Checkpoint ✓ Find Angle Measures

$\overrightarrow{HK}$ bisects $\angle GHJ$. Find $m\angle GHK$ and $m\angle KHJ$.

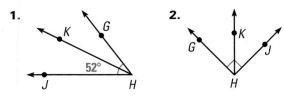

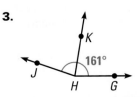

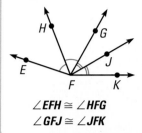
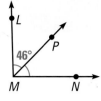

EXAMPLE 2 Find Angle Measures and Classify an Angle

$\overrightarrow{MP}$ bisects $\angle LMN$, and $m\angle LMP = 46°$.

a. Find $m\angle PMN$ and $m\angle LMN$.

b. Determine whether $\angle LMN$ is *acute*, *right*, *obtuse*, or *straight*. Explain.

Solution

a. $\overrightarrow{MP}$ bisects $\angle LMN$, so $m\angle LMP = m\angle PMN$.
You know that $m\angle LMP = 46°$. Therefore, $m\angle PMN = 46°$.

The measure of $\angle LMN$ is twice the measure of $\angle LMP$.

$$m\angle LMN = 2(m\angle LMP) = 2(46°) = 92°$$

So, $m\angle PMN = 46°$, and $m\angle LMN = 92°$.

b. $\angle LMN$ is obtuse because its measure is between 90° and 180°.

Checkpoint ✓ Find Angle Measures and Classify an Angle

$\overrightarrow{QS}$ bisects $\angle PQR$. Find $m\angle SQP$ and $m\angle PQR$. Then determine whether $\angle PQR$ is *acute, right, obtuse,* or *straight*.

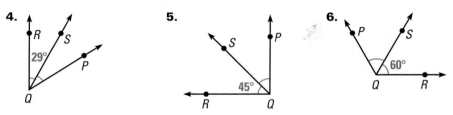

4.   5.   6.

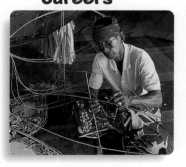
EXAMPLE 3 Use Angle Bisectors

In the kite, $\angle DAB$ is bisected by $\overrightarrow{AC}$, and $\angle BCD$ is bisected by $\overrightarrow{CA}$. Find $m\angle DAB$ and $m\angle BCD$.

Solution

$m\angle DAB = 2(m\angle BAC)$ $\overrightarrow{AC}$ bisects $\angle DAB$.

$\quad\quad\quad = 2(45°)$ Substitute 45° for $m\angle BAC$.

$\quad\quad\quad = 90°$ Simplify.

$m\angle BCD = 2(m\angle ACB)$ $\overrightarrow{CA}$ bisects $\angle BCD$.

$\quad\quad\quad = 2(27°)$ Substitute 27° for $m\angle ACB$.

$\quad\quad\quad = 54°$ Simplify.

ANSWER ▶ The measure of $\angle DAB$ is 90°, and the measure of $\angle BCD$ is 54°.

7. $\overrightarrow{KM}$ bisects $\angle JKL$.
Find $m\angle JKM$ and $m\angle MKL$.

8. $\overrightarrow{UV}$ bisects $\angle WUT$.
Find $m\angle WUV$ and $m\angle WUT$.

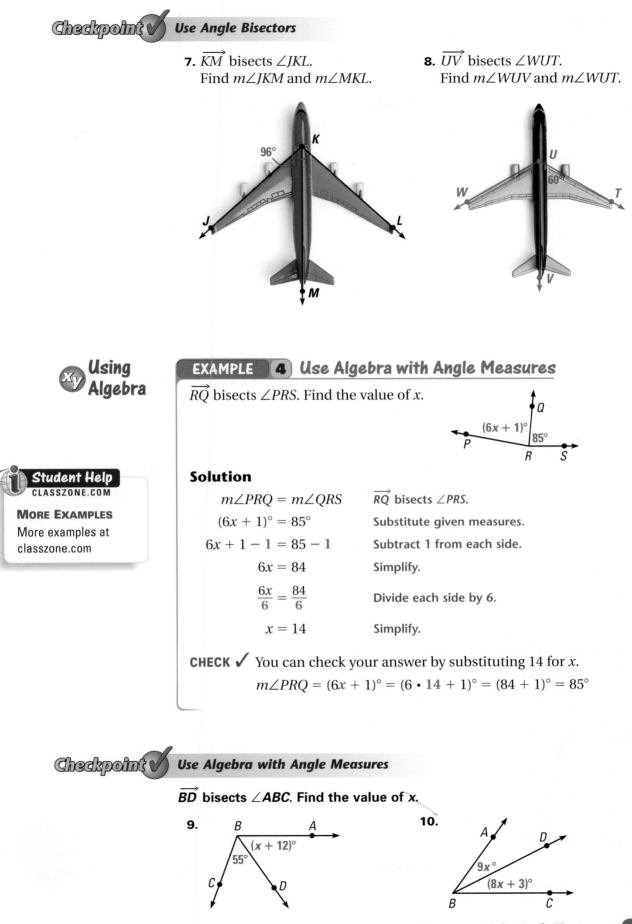

96°

K

J

L

M

U

60°

W

T

V

Using Algebra

xy

EXAMPLE 4 Use Algebra with Angle Measures

$\overrightarrow{RQ}$ bisects $\angle PRS$. Find the value of x.

$(6x + 1)°$

Q

85°

P

R

S

Solution

$m\angle PRQ = m\angle QRS$	$\overrightarrow{RQ}$ bisects $\angle PRS$.
$(6x + 1)° = 85°$	Substitute given measures.
$6x + 1 - \mathbf{1} = 85 - \mathbf{1}$	Subtract 1 from each side.
$6x = 84$	Simplify.
$\dfrac{6x}{6} = \dfrac{84}{6}$	Divide each side by 6.
$x = 14$	Simplify.

CHECK ✓ You can check your answer by substituting 14 for x.

$m\angle PRQ = (6x + 1)° = (6 \cdot \mathbf{14} + 1)° = (84 + 1)° = 85°$

Student Help
CLASSZONE.COM

MORE EXAMPLES
More examples at
classzone.com

Checkpoint ✓ **Use Algebra with Angle Measures**

$\overrightarrow{BD}$ **bisects** $\angle ABC$. **Find the value of** x.

9.

B

A

$(x + 12)°$

55°

C

D

10.

A

D

$9x°$

$(8x + 3)°$

B

C

Guided Practice

Vocabulary Check

1. What kind of geometric figure is an *angle bisector*?

Skill Check

$\overrightarrow{BD}$ bisects ∠*ABC*. Find the angle measure.

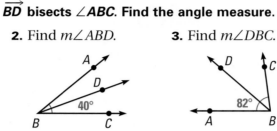

2. Find *m*∠*ABD*.

3. Find *m*∠*DBC*.

4. Find *m*∠*DBC*.

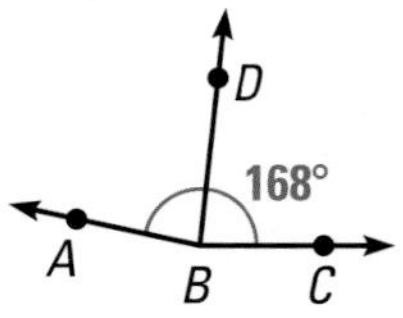

5. Find *m*∠*ABC*.

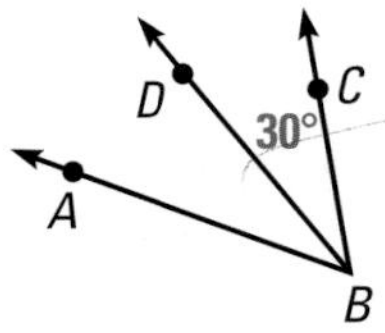

6. Find *m*∠*CBA*.

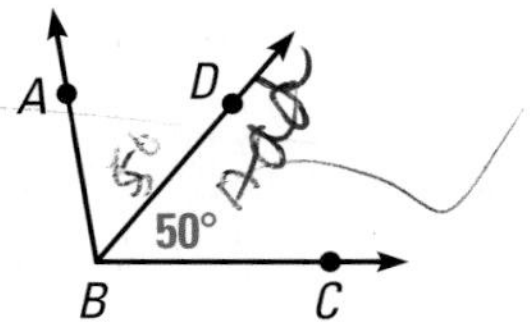

7. Find *m*∠*ABC*.

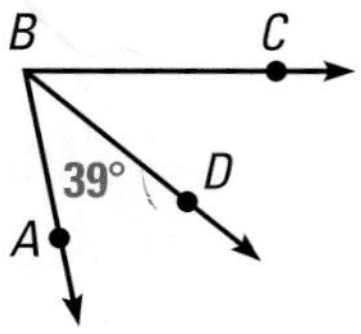

Practice and Applications

Extra Practice

See p. 677.

Finding Angle Measures $\overrightarrow{QS}$ bisects ∠*PQR*. Find *m*∠*PQS* and *m*∠*SQR*.

8.

9.

10.

11.

12.

13.

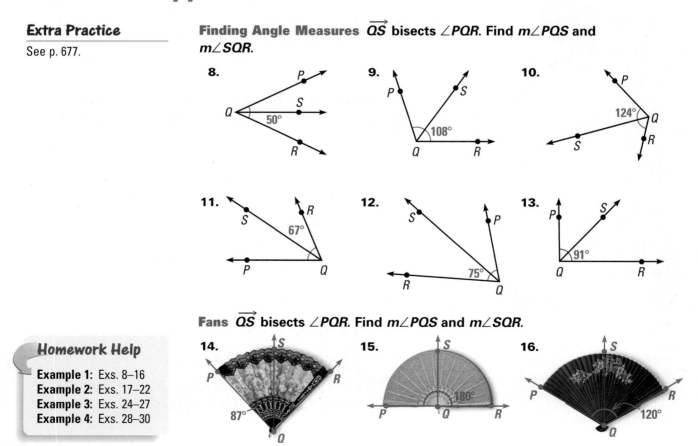

Fans $\overrightarrow{QS}$ bisects ∠*PQR*. Find *m*∠*PQS* and *m*∠*SQR*.

14.

15.

16.

Homework Help

Example 1: Exs. 8–16
Example 2: Exs. 17–22
Example 3: Exs. 24–27
Example 4: Exs. 28–30

Finding Angle Measures $\vec{BD}$ bisects $\angle ABC$. Find $m\angle ABD$ and $m\angle ABC$. Then determine whether $\angle ABC$ is *acute, right, obtuse,* or *straight*.

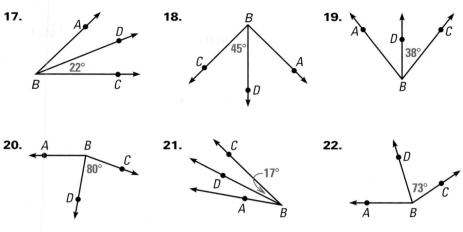

17.

18.

19.

20.

21.

22.

23. Paper Airplanes The diagram at the right represents an unfolded piece of paper used to make a paper airplane like the one shown below. Using the diagram, name the angles that are bisected by $\vec{AK}$.

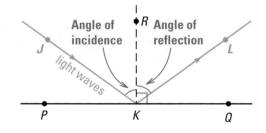

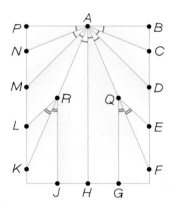

Lasers In Exercises 24–27, use the diagram below. When light is reflected by a smooth surface, the angle of incidence is equal to the angle of reflection.

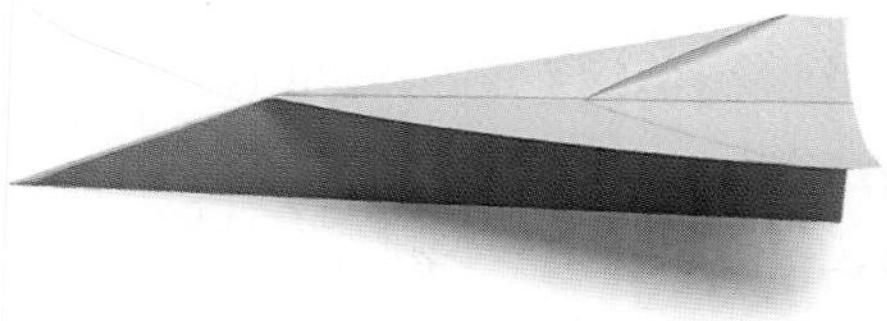

Angle of incidence   •R Angle of reflection

light waves

P   K   Q

24. Name an angle bisector in the diagram.

25. If the angle of reflection is $67°$, what is the angle of incidence?

26. If $m\angle JKL = 109°$, what is the angle of reflection?

27. **You be the Judge** Can you determine whether $\angle JKP$ is congruent to $\angle LKQ$ in the diagram above? Explain your reasoning.

Using Algebra $\overrightarrow{KM}$ bisects $\angle JKL$. Find the value of the variable.

28.
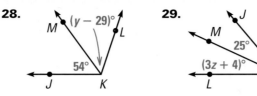

29.

30.
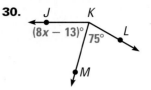

31. Technology Use geometry software to draw $\triangle ABC$. Construct the angle bisector of $\angle BAC$. Then find the midpoint of $\overline{BC}$. Drag any of the points. Does the angle bisector *always* pass through the midpoint of the opposite side? Does it *ever* pass through the midpoint?

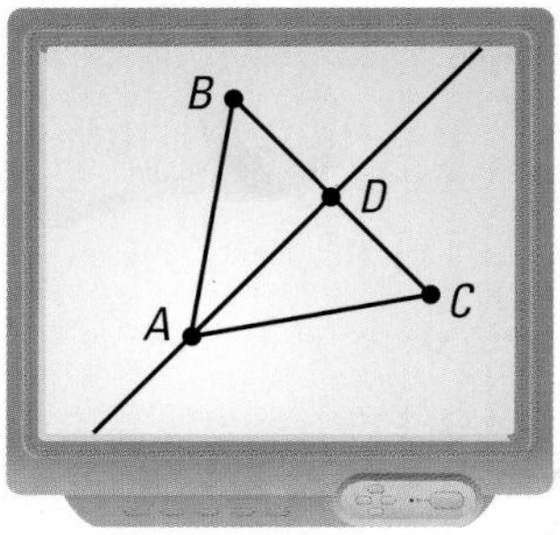

32. Challenge $\overrightarrow{BD}$ bisects $\angle ABE$ and $\overrightarrow{BF}$ bisects $\angle EBC$. Use the diagram shown to find $m\angle DBF$.

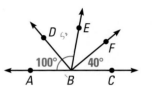

Standardized Test Practice

33. Multiple Choice In the diagram below, $\overrightarrow{BD}$ bisects $\angle ABC$ and $m\angle ABC = 23°$. What is $m\angle ABD$?

   Ⓐ 11.5°   **Ⓑ** 12.5°

   Ⓒ 23°   **Ⓓ** 46°

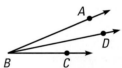

Mixed Review

Describing Number Patterns Describe a pattern in the numbers. Write the next number you expect in the pattern. *(Lesson 1.1)*

34. 1, 9, 17, 25, . . .   **35.** −13, −8, −3, 2, . . .

36. 5.6, 5.16, 5.116, 5.1116, . . .   **37.** 60, 30, 15, 7.5, . . .

Classifying Angles Use the diagram below to classify the angle as *acute, right, obtuse,* or *straight*. *(Lesson 1.6)*

38. $\angle EBC$ **39.** $\angle ABE$

40. $\angle DBC$ **41.** $\angle ABC$

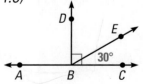

Algebra Skills

Solving Equations Solve the equation. *(Skills Review, p. 673)*

42. $2x - 15 = 9$ **43.** $3a + 12 = 48$ **44.** $10 - 3y = 52$

45. $5m - 11 = -46$ **46.** $-2z + 4 = 8$ **47.** $3 = -n + 23$

2.3 Complementary and Supplementary Angles

Goal
Find measures of complementary and supplementary angles.

Key Words
- complementary angles
- supplementary angles
- adjacent angles
- theorem

Two angles are **complementary angles** if the sum of their measures is 90°. Each angle is the **complement** of the other.

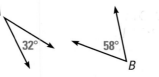

∠A and ∠B are complementary angles.
$m\angle A + m\angle B = 32° + 58° = 90°$

Two angles are **supplementary angles** if the sum of their measures is 180°. Each angle is the **supplement** of the other.

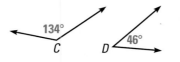

∠C and ∠D are supplementary angles.
$m\angle C + m\angle D = 134° + 46° = 180°$

EXAMPLE 1 Identify Complements and Supplements

Determine whether the angles are *complementary*, *supplementary*, or *neither*.

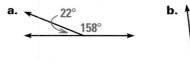

a. 22° 158°   **b.** 15° 85°   **c.** 55° 35°

Solution

a. Because 22° + 158° = 180°, the angles are supplementary.

b. Because 15° + 85° = 100°, the angles are neither complementary nor supplementary.

c. Because 55° + 35° = 90°, the angles are complementary.

Visualize It!

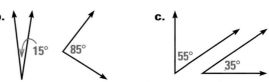

2 ∠1 and ∠2 are complementary.

∠3 and ∠4 are supplementary.

Complementary angles make up the **C**orner of a piece of paper. **S**upplementary angles make up the **S**ide of a piece of paper.

Checkpoint ✓ Identify Complements and Supplements

Determine whether the angles are *complementary*, *supplementary*, or *neither*.

1. 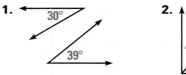 30° 39°

2.  41° 49°

3. 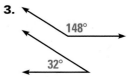 148° 32°

2.3 Complementary and Supplementary Angles **67**

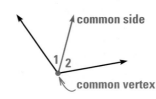
Student Help

STUDY TIP
You can use numbers to refer to angles. Make sure that you do not confuse angle names with angle measures.

Two angles are **adjacent angles** if they share a common vertex and side, but have no common interior points.

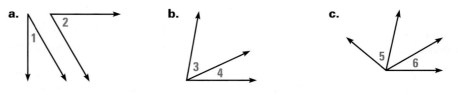

∠1 and ∠2 are adjacent angles.

EXAMPLE 2 Identify Adjacent Angles

Tell whether the numbered angles are *adjacent* or *nonadjacent*.

a.   b.   c.

Solution

  a. Because the angles do not share a common vertex or side, ∠1 and ∠2 are nonadjacent.

  b. Because the angles share a common vertex and side, and they do not have any common interior points, ∠3 and ∠4 are adjacent.

  c. Although ∠5 and ∠6 share a common vertex, they do not share a common side. Therefore, ∠5 and ∠6 are nonadjacent.

EXAMPLE 3 Measures of Complements and Supplements

  a. ∠A is a complement of ∠C, and m∠A = 47°. Find m∠C.
  b. ∠P is a supplement of ∠R, and m∠R = 36°. Find m∠P.

Solution

  a. ∠A and ∠C are complements, so their sum is 90°.

$$m\angle A + m\angle C = 90°$$
$$47° + m\angle C = 90°$$
$$47° + m\angle C - 47° = 90° - 47°$$
$$m\angle C = 43°$$

  b. ∠P and ∠R are supplements, so their sum is 180°.

$$m\angle P + m\angle R = 180°$$
$$m\angle P + 36° = 180°$$
$$m\angle P + 36° - 36° = 180° - 36°$$
$$m\angle P = 144°$$

Checkpoint ✓ Measures of Complements and Supplements

  4. ∠B is a complement of ∠D, and m∠D = 79°. Find m∠B.

  5. ∠G is a supplement of ∠H, and m∠G = 115°. Find m∠H.

A **theorem** is a true statement that follows from other true statements. The two theorems that follow are about complementary and supplementary angles.

Student Help

VISUAL STRATEGY
Draw examples of these theorems with specific measures, as shown on p. 52.

THEOREMS 2.1 and 2.2

2.1 Congruent Complements Theorem

Words If two angles are complementary to the same angle, then they are congruent.

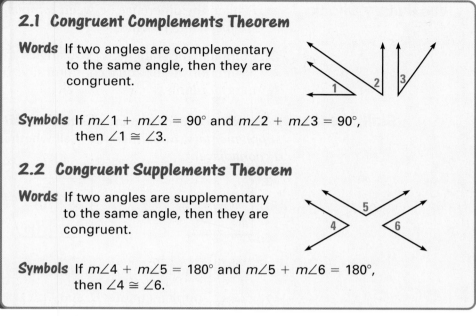

Symbols If $m\angle 1 + m\angle 2 = 90°$ and $m\angle 2 + m\angle 3 = 90°$, then $\angle 1 \cong \angle 3$.

2.2 Congruent Supplements Theorem

Words If two angles are supplementary to the same angle, then they are congruent.

Symbols If $m\angle 4 + m\angle 5 = 180°$ and $m\angle 5 + m\angle 6 = 180°$, then $\angle 4 \cong \angle 6$.

You can use theorems in your reasoning about geometry, as shown in Example 4.

EXAMPLE 4 **Use a Theorem**

$\angle 7$ and $\angle 8$ are supplementary, and $\angle 8$ and $\angle 9$ are supplementary. Name a pair of congruent angles. Explain your reasoning.

Solution

$\angle 7$ and $\angle 9$ are both supplementary to $\angle 8$. So, by the Congruent Supplements Theorem, $\angle 7 \cong \angle 9$.

Checkpoint **Use a Theorem**

6. In the diagram, $m\angle 10 + m\angle 11 = 90°$, and $m\angle 11 + m\angle 12 = 90°$.

Name a pair of congruent angles. Explain your reasoning.

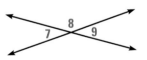

Guided Practice

Vocabulary Check

1. Explain the difference between *complementary angles* and *supplementary angles*.

2. Complete the statement: Two angles are __?__ if they share a common vertex and a common side, but have no common interior points.

Skill Check

In Exercises 3–5, determine whether the angles are *complementary*, *supplementary*, or *neither*. Also tell whether the angles are *adjacent* or *nonadjacent*.

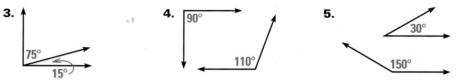

3. 75° 15°
4. 90° 110°
5. 30° 150°

6. ∠A is a complement of ∠B, and m∠A = 10°. Find m∠B.

7. ∠C is a supplement of ∠D, and m∠D = 109°. Find m∠C.

Practice and Applications

Extra Practice

See p. 677.

Identifying Angles Determine whether the angles are *complementary*, *supplementary*, or *neither*. Also tell whether the angles are *adjacent* or *nonadjacent*.

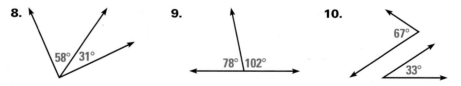

8. 58° 31°
9. 78° 102°
10. 67° 33°

Identifying Angles Determine whether the two angles shown on the clock faces are *complementary*, *supplementary*, or *neither*.

11.

12.

13.

14.

Homework Help

Example 1: Exs. 8–14, 30–32
Example 2: Exs. 8–10
Example 3: Exs. 15–28 33, 34
Example 4: Exs. 38–42

Finding Complements Find the measure of a complement of the angle given.

15. 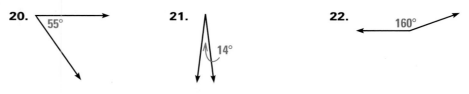 41°

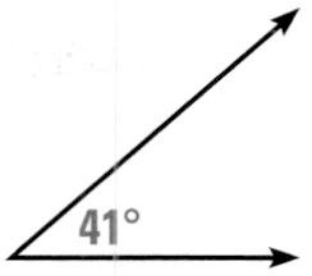

16. 86°

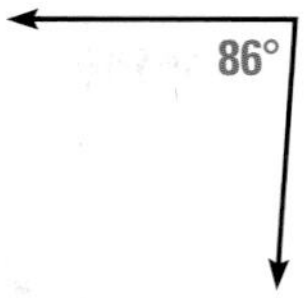

17. 24°

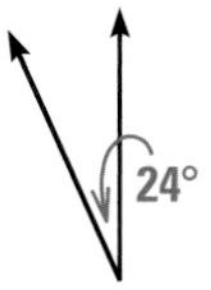

18. ∠K is a complement of ∠L, and m∠K = 74°. Find m∠L.

19. ∠P is a complement of ∠Q, and m∠P = 9°. Find m∠Q.

Finding Supplements Find the measure of a supplement of the angle given.

20. 55°

21. 14°

22. 160°

23. ∠A is a supplement of ∠B, and m∠A = 96°. Find m∠B.

24. ∠P is a supplement of ∠Q, and m∠P = 7°. Find m∠Q.

Finding Complements and Supplements Find the measures of a complement and a supplement of the angle.

25. m∠A = 39°   **26.** m∠B = 89°   **27.** m∠C = 54°

28. Bridges The Alamillo Bridge in Seville, Spain, was designed by Santiago Calatrava. In the bridge, m∠1 = 58°, and m∠2 = 24°. Find the measures of the supplements of both ∠1 and ∠2.

Naming Angles In the diagram, ∠QPR is a right angle.

29. Name a straight angle.

30. Name two congruent supplementary angles.

31. Name two supplementary angles that are not congruent.

32. Name two complementary angles.

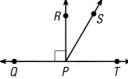

Beach Chairs **Adjustable beach chairs form angles that are supplementary. Find the value of *x*.**

33.

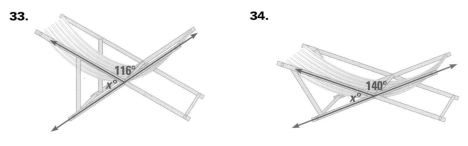

34.

Student Help
CLASSZONE.COM

HOMEWORK HELP
Extra help with problem solving in Exs. 35–37 is at classzone.com

Using Algebra **$\angle ABD$ and $\angle DBC$ are complementary angles. Find the value of the variable.**

35.

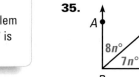

36.

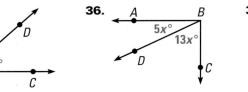

37.

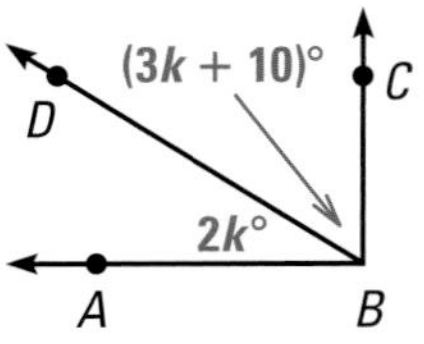

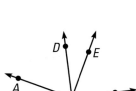

38. Complementary Angles $\angle ABD$ and $\angle DBE$ are complements, and $\angle CBE$ and $\angle DBE$ are complements. Can you show that $\angle ABD \cong \angle CBE$? Explain.

39. Technology Use geometry software to draw two intersecting lines. Measure three of the four angles formed. Drag the points and observe the angle measures. What theorem does this illustrate?

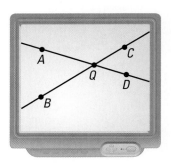

Complements and Supplements **Find the angle measure described.**

40. $\angle 1$ and $\angle 2$ are both supplementary to $\angle 3$, and $m\angle 1 = 43°$. Find the measure of $\angle 2$.

41. $\angle 4$ and $\angle 6$ are both complementary to $\angle 5$, and $m\angle 5 = 85°$. Find the measure of $\angle 4$.

42. $\angle P$ is supplementary to $\angle Q$, $\angle R$ is supplementary to $\angle P$, and $m\angle Q = 60°$. Find the measure of $\angle R$.

43. Challenge $\angle C$ and $\angle D$ are supplementary angles. The measure of $\angle D$ is eight times the measure of $\angle C$. Find $m\angle C$ and $m\angle D$.

44. Multiple Choice What is the measure of a complement of a 27° angle?

   (A) 53°   (B) 63°   (C) 117°   (D) 163°

45. Multiple Choice $\angle 1$ and $\angle 2$ are supplementary. Suppose that $m\angle 1 = 60°$ and $m\angle 2 = (2x + 20)°$. What is the value of x?

   (F) 5   (G) 10   (H) 50   (J) 100

Mixed Review

Segment Addition Postulate Find the length. *(Lesson 1.5)*

46. Find *FH*.   **47.** Find *KL*.

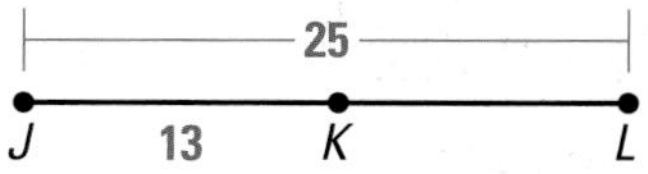

   F   4.5   G   8.2   H   25   J   13   K   L

Midpoint Formula Find the coordinates of the midpoint of $\overline{AB}$. *(Lesson 2.1)*

48. $A(0, 0)$, $B(8, 2)$ **49.** $A(-6, 0)$, $B(2, 4)$ **50.** $A(4, 1)$, $B(10, 3)$

51. $A(-2, 5)$, $B(-2, 7)$ **52.** $A(3, -8)$, $B(-1, 0)$ **53.** $A(-5, -9)$, $B(11, 5)$

Algebra Skills

Evaluating Decimals Evaluate. *(Skills Review, p. 655)*

54. $2.58 + 8.04$ **55.** $5.17 - 1.96$ **56.** 1.4×3.1

57. 0.61×0.38 **58.** $11.2 \div 1.4$ **59.** $2 \times 5.4 \times 3.9$

Quiz 1

1. In the diagram, K is the midpoint of $\overline{JL}$. Find *KL* and *JL*. *(Lesson 2.1)*

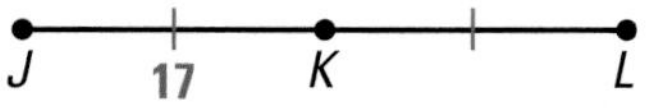

      J   17   K   L

Find the coordinates of the midpoint of $\overline{AB}$. *(Lesson 2.1)*

2. $A(1, 3)$, $B(7, -1)$ **3.** $A(-4, -2)$, $B(6, 4)$ **4.** $A(-5, 3)$, $B(3, -3)$

In Exercises 5–7, $\overrightarrow{KM}$ bisects $\angle JKL$. Find the angle measure. *(Lesson 2.2)*

5. Find $m\angle JKM$.   **6.** Find $m\angle JKL$.   **7.** Find $m\angle JKL$.

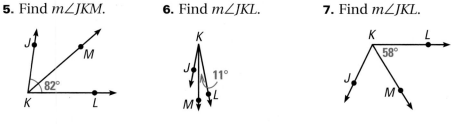

8. $\angle F$ is a supplement of $\angle G$, and $m\angle F = 101°$. Find $m\angle G$. *(Lesson 2.3)*

9. The measure of $\angle D$ is 83°. Find the measure of a complement and a supplement of $\angle D$. *(Lesson 2.3)*

Activity 2.4 Angles and Intersecting Lines

Question

What is the relationship between the angles formed by two intersecting lines?

Materials

- straightedge
- protractor

Explore

1. On a piece of paper, draw line ℓ using a straightedge. Label two points A and B on the line.

2. Draw line m so that it intersects line ℓ. Label the point of intersection E. Label two points C and D on line m as shown below.

3. Use a protractor to measure the four angles formed by the intersecting lines. Record the angle measures.

Think About It

Student Help

VOCABULARY TIP
Recall from Lesson 2.3 that *adjacent angles* share a common vertex and a common side.

∠1 and ∠2 are adjacent angles.

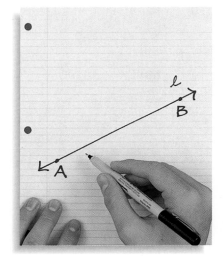

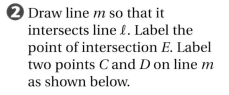

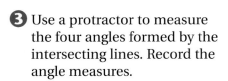

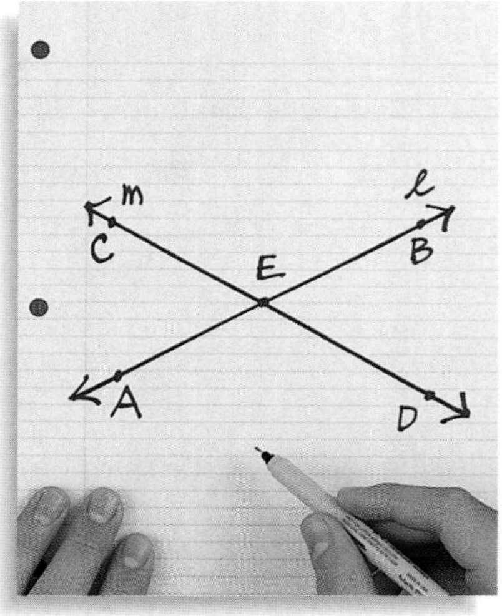

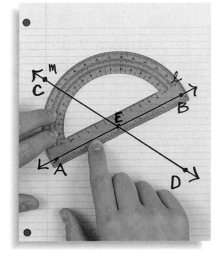

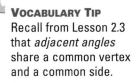

1. What do you notice about the *nonadjacent angles* you measured in Step 3?

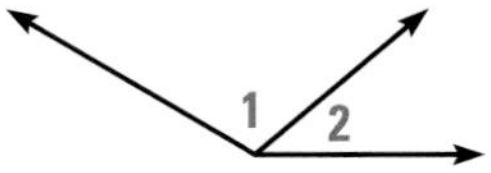

2. Find the sum of the measures of any two *adjacent angles* in Step 3. What do you notice?

3. Repeat Steps 1–3 using two different lines. What do you notice about the measures of adjacent angles and nonadjacent angles?

4. **Extension** Draw a third line, n, that goes through point E. Use a protractor to measure the six angles formed by the intersecting lines. Record your results. What do you notice about the angle measures?

2.4 Vertical Angles

Goal
Find the measures of angles formed by intersecting lines.

Key Words
• vertical angles
• linear pair

Two angles are **vertical angles** if they are not adjacent and their sides are formed by two intersecting lines. The scissors show two sets of vertical angles.

∠1 and ∠3 are vertical angles.
∠2 and ∠4 are vertical angles.

Two adjacent angles are a **linear pair** if their noncommon sides are on the same line.

∠5 and ∠6 are a linear pair.

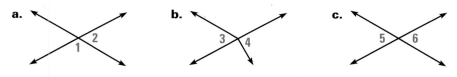

Visualize It!

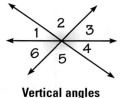

You can use colored pencils to help you see pairs of vertical angles.

Vertical angles
∠1 and ∠4
∠2 and ∠5
∠3 and ∠6

EXAMPLE **1** **Identify Vertical Angles and Linear Pairs**

Determine whether the labeled angles are *vertical angles*, a *linear pair*, or *neither*.

a.   b.   c.

Solution

a. ∠1 and ∠2 are a linear pair because they are adjacent and their noncommon sides are on the same line.

b. ∠3 and ∠4 are neither vertical angles nor a linear pair.

c. ∠5 and ∠6 are vertical angles because they are not adjacent and their sides are formed by two intersecting lines.

POSTULATE 7

Linear Pair Postulate

Words If two angles form a linear pair, then they are supplementary.

Symbols $m\angle 1 + m\angle 2 = 180°$

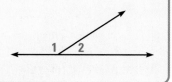

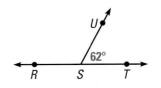

EXAMPLE 2 Use the Linear Pair Postulate

Find the measure of ∠RSU.

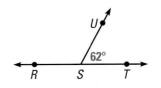

Solution

∠RSU and ∠UST are a linear pair. By the Linear Pair Postulate, they are supplementary. To find m∠RSU, subtract m∠UST from 180°.

m∠RSU = 180° − m∠UST = 180° − 62° = 118°

Student Help

VISUAL STRATEGY
Draw an example of this theorem with specific measures, as shown on p. 52.

THEOREM 2.3

Vertical Angles Theorem

Words Vertical angles are congruent.

Symbols ∠1 ≅ ∠3 and ∠2 ≅ ∠4.

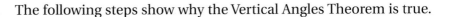

The following steps show why the Vertical Angles Theorem is true.

❶ ∠1 and ∠2 are a linear pair, so ∠1 and ∠2 are supplementary.

❷ ∠2 and ∠3 are a linear pair, so ∠2 and ∠3 are supplementary.

Student Help

LOOK BACK
To review the Congruent Supplements Theorem, see p. 69. ·········▶

❸ ∠1 and ∠3 are supplementary to the same angle, so ∠1 is congruent to ∠3 by the Congruent Supplements Theorem.

EXAMPLE 3 Use the Vertical Angles Theorem

Find the measure of ∠CED.

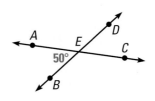

Solution

∠AEB and ∠CED are vertical angles. By the Vertical Angles Theorem, ∠CED ≅ ∠AEB, so m∠CED = m∠AEB = 50°.

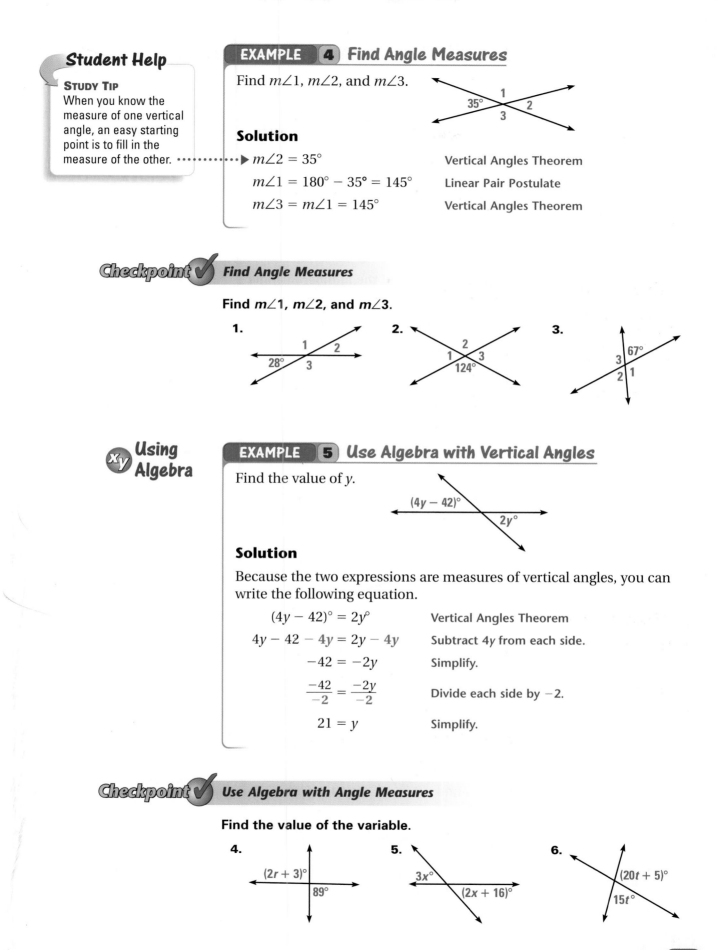

STUDY TIP
When you know the measure of one vertical angle, an easy starting point is to fill in the measure of the other. ·········▶

EXAMPLE 4 Find Angle Measures

Find $m\angle 1$, $m\angle 2$, and $m\angle 3$.

Solution

▶ $m\angle 2 = 35°$ Vertical Angles Theorem

$m\angle 1 = 180° - 35° = 145°$ Linear Pair Postulate

$m\angle 3 = m\angle 1 = 145°$ Vertical Angles Theorem

Checkpoint ✓ *Find Angle Measures*

Find $m\angle 1$, $m\angle 2$, and $m\angle 3$.

1.

2.

3.

Using Algebra *xy*

EXAMPLE 5 Use Algebra with Vertical Angles

Find the value of y.

$(4y - 42)°$

$2y°$

Solution

Because the two expressions are measures of vertical angles, you can write the following equation.

$(4y - 42)° = 2y°$ Vertical Angles Theorem

$4y - 42 - 4y = 2y - 4y$ Subtract 4y from each side.

$-42 = -2y$ Simplify.

$\dfrac{-42}{-2} = \dfrac{-2y}{-2}$ Divide each side by -2.

$21 = y$ Simplify.

Checkpoint ✓ *Use Algebra with Angle Measures*

Find the value of the variable.

4.

$(2r + 3)°$

$89°$

5.

$3x°$

$(2x + 16)°$

6.

$(20t + 5)°$

$15t°$

Guided Practice

Vocabulary Check   **Complete the statement.**

1. Two adjacent angles whose noncommon sides are on the same line are called __?__.

2. Two angles are called __?__ if they are not adjacent and their sides are formed by two intersecting lines.

Skill Check   **Find the measure of the numbered angle.**

3.
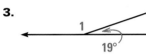

4.

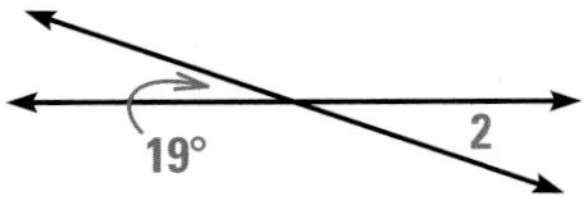

Find $m\angle 1$, $m\angle 2$, and $m\angle 3$.

5.
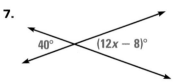

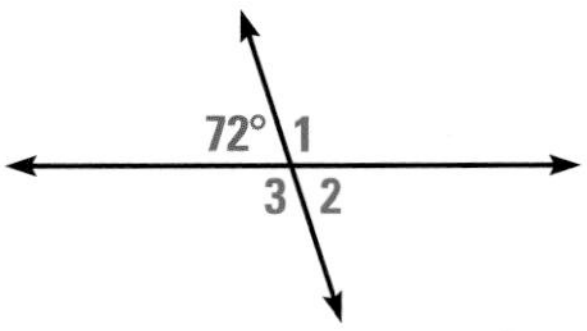

6.
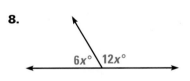

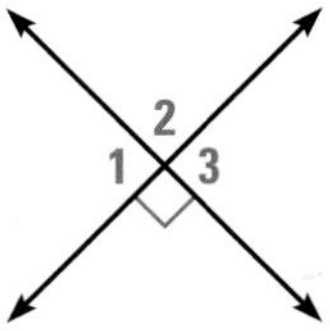

Find the value of x.

7.

8.

Practice and Applications

Extra Practice

See p. 678.

Vertical Angles and Linear Pairs Determine whether the angles are *vertical angles*, a *linear pair*, or *neither*.

9. $\angle 5$ and $\angle 6$

10. $\angle 5$ and $\angle 9$

11. $\angle 5$ and $\angle 8$

12. $\angle 6$ and $\angle 9$

13. $\angle 8$ and $\angle 9$

14. $\angle 5$ and $\angle 7$

Homework Help

Example 1: Exs. 9–14
Example 2: Exs. 15–19
Example 3: Exs. 20–22
Example 4: Exs. 28–37
Example 5: Exs. 51–56

Using the Linear Pair Postulate Find the measure of $\angle 1$.

15.

16.

17.

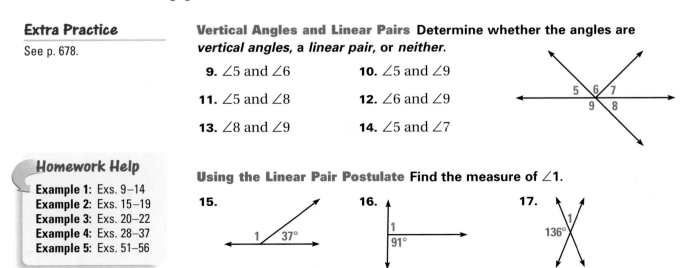

Linear Pairs Find the measure of the angle described.

18. $\angle 1$ and $\angle 2$ are a linear pair, and $m\angle 1 = 51°$. Find $m\angle 2$.

19. $\angle 3$ and $\angle 4$ are a linear pair, and $m\angle 4 = 124°$. Find $m\angle 3$.

Using the Vertical Angles Theorem Find the measure of $\angle 1$.

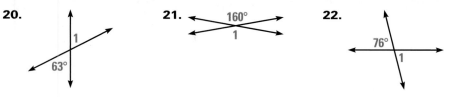

20.   **21.**   **22.**

Evaluating Statements Use the figure below to decide whether the statement is *true* or *false*.

23. If $m\angle 1 = 40°$, then $m\angle 2 = 140°$.

24. If $m\angle 4 = 130°$, then $m\angle 2 = 50°$.

25. $\angle 1$ and $\angle 4$ are a linear pair.

26. $m\angle 1 + m\angle 4 = m\angle 3 + m\angle 2$

27. $\angle 1$ and $\angle 4$ are vertical angles.

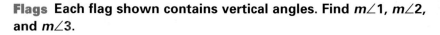

Student Help

CLASSZONE.COM

HOMEWORK HELP
Extra help with problem solving in Exs. 28–33 is at classzone.com

Finding Angle Measures Find $m\angle 1$, $m\angle 2$, and $m\angle 3$.

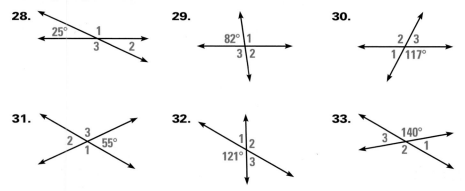

28.   **29.**   **30.**

31.   **32.**   **33.**

Flags Each flag shown contains vertical angles. Find $m\angle 1$, $m\angle 2$, and $m\angle 3$.

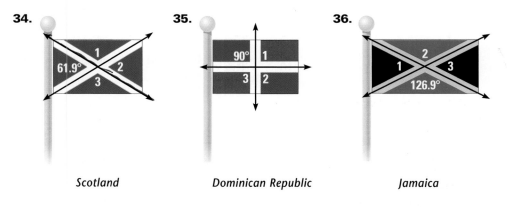

34.   **35.**   **36.**

Scotland   Dominican Republic   Jamaica

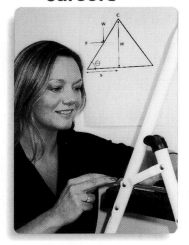

37. Drafting Table The legs of the drafting table form vertical angles. Find the measures of $\angle 1$, $\angle 2$, and $\angle 3$.

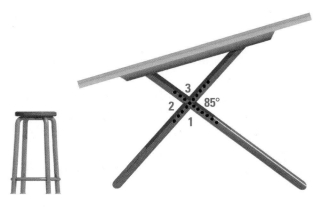

Finding Angle Measures Find $m\angle 1$, $m\angle 2$, $m\angle 3$, and $m\angle 4$.

38.

39.

40.

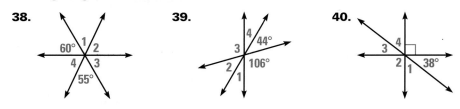

Vertical Angles Use the diagram to complete the statement.

41. $\angle BGC \cong$ ___?___

42. $\angle AGB \cong$ ___?___

43. $\angle AGC \cong$ ___?___

44. $\angle CGE \cong$ ___?___

45. $m\angle AGF =$ ___?___ °

46. $m\angle DGE =$ ___?___ °

47. $m\angle CGE =$ ___?___ °

48. $m\angle BGC =$ ___?___ °

49. $m\angle DGF =$ ___?___ °

50. $m\angle AGD =$ ___?___ °

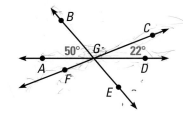

Using Algebra Find the value of the variable.

51.

52.

53.

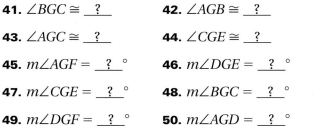

Using Algebra Find the value of the variable. Then use substitution to find $m\angle ABC$.

54.

55.

56.

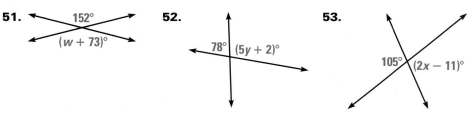

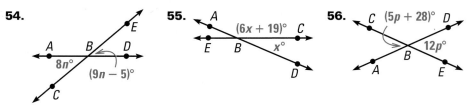

57. Challenge Find the values of x and y in the diagram below.

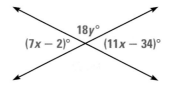

$18y°$
$(7x - 2)°$ $(11x - 34)°$

58. Visualize It! Sketch and label four angles so that $\angle 1$ and $\angle 2$ are acute vertical angles, $\angle 3$ is a right angle adjacent to $\angle 2$, and $\angle 1$ and $\angle 4$ form a linear pair.

Standardized Test Practice

59. Multi-Step Problem Use the diagram below.

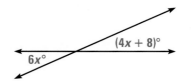

$(4x + 8)°$
$6x°$

a. Use the Vertical Angles Theorem to write an equation.

b. Solve your equation to find the value of x.

c. Find the measures of the acute angles formed by the lines.

d. Find the measures of the obtuse angles formed by the lines.

Mixed Review

Describing Number Patterns Describe a pattern in the numbers. Write the next number you expect in the pattern. *(Lesson 1.1)*

60. 4, 11, 18, 25, . . . **61.** 3, 15, 75, 375, . . .

62. 32, 16, 8, 4, . . . **63.** 404, 414, 424, 434, . . .

Congruent Segments Determine which segments in the coordinate plane are congruent. *(Lesson 1.5)*

64.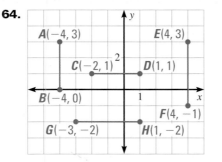

65.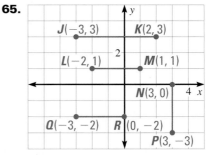

Algebra Skills

Simplifying Expressions Simplify the expression. *(Skills Review, p. 671)*

66. $-16x + 9x$ **67.** $7 + a - 2a$ **68.** $-8z^2 + 5z^2 - 4$

69. $6b^2 + 6b - b^2$ **70.** $-4(t - 3) - 4t$ **71.** $3w^2 - 1 - w^2 + 5$

2.5 If-Then Statements and Deductive Reasoning

Goal
Use if-then statements.
Apply laws of logic.

Key Words
- if-then statement
- hypothesis
- conclusion
- deductive reasoning

An **if-then statement** has two parts. The "if" part contains the **hypothesis** . The "then" part contains the **conclusion** .

Student Help

VOCABULARY TIP
If-then statements are also called *conditional statements*.

The following sentence is an example of an if-then statement:

hypothesis

If the team wins the semi-final,

then the team will play in the championship.

conclusion

EXAMPLE 1 Identify the Hypothesis and Conclusion

Identify the hypothesis and the conclusion of the if-then statement.

If I pass the driving test, then I will get my driver's license.

Solution

I pass the driving test is the hypothesis.

I will get my driver's license is the conclusion.

EXAMPLE 2 Write If-Then Statements

Rewrite the statement as an if-then statement.

a. Every game on my computer is fun to play.

b. I will buy the CD if it costs less than $15.

Solution

a. If a game is on my computer, then it is fun to play.

Student Help

STUDY TIP
Example 2, part (b), shows that the conclusion of a statement is not always the last part. ·········▶

b. If the CD costs less than $15, then I will buy it.

Deductive reasoning uses facts, definitions, accepted properties, and the laws of logic to make a logical argument. This form of reasoning differs from *inductive reasoning*, in which previous examples and patterns are used to form a conjecture.

LAWS OF LOGIC

Law of Detachment

If the hypothesis of a true if-then statement is true, then the conclusion is also true.

Law of Syllogism

If statement p, then statement q. ⟶ If these statements are true,
If statement q, then statement r.

If statement p, then statement r. ⟵ then this statement is true.

EXAMPLE 3 Use the Law of Detachment

What can you conclude from the following true statements?

If you wash the cotton T-shirt in hot water, then it will shrink.

You wash the cotton T-shirt in hot water.

Solution

The hypothesis (you wash the cotton T-shirt in hot water) of a true if-then statement is true. By the Law of Detachment, the conclusion must be true.

ANSWER ▶ You can conclude that the cotton T-shirt shrinks.

Checkpoint ✓ **If-Then Statements and the Law of Detachment**

Rewrite the statement as an if-then statement. Then underline the hypothesis and circle the conclusion.

1. All teachers at East High School have taught for at least 5 years.

2. An angle is obtuse if its measure is 170°.

What can you conclude from the given true statements?

3. If x has a value of 7, then $2x - 3$ has a value of 11. The value of x is 7.

4. If you study at least two hours for the test, then you will pass the test. You study three hours for the test.

EXAMPLE 4 **Use the Law of Detachment**

Which argument is correct? Explain your reasoning.

Argument 1: If two angles are vertical angles, then they are congruent. ∠1 and ∠2 are congruent. So, ∠1 and ∠2 are vertical angles.

Argument 2: If two angles are vertical angles, then they are congruent. ∠1 and ∠2 are vertical angles. So, ∠1 and ∠2 are congruent.

Solution

Argument 2 is correct. The hypothesis (two angles are vertical angles) is true, which implies that the conclusion (they are congruent) is true.

You can use the following counterexample to show that Argument 1 is false. In the diagram at the right, ∠1 ≅ ∠2, but they are not vertical angles.

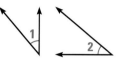

Checkpoint ✓ **Use the Law of Detachment**

5. Which argument is correct? Explain your reasoning.

Argument 1: If two angles form a linear pair, then they are supplementary. ∠3 and ∠4 form a linear pair. So, ∠3 and ∠4 are supplementary.

Argument 2: If two angles form a linear pair, then they are supplementary. ∠3 and ∠4 are supplementary. So, ∠3 and ∠4 form a linear pair.

EXAMPLE 5 **Use the Law of Syllogism**

Write the statement that follows from the pair of true statements.

If the daily high temperature is 32°F or less, then the water in the pipe is frozen.

If the water in the pipe is frozen, then the pipe will break.

Solution

Use the Law of Syllogism.

If the daily high temperature is 32°F or less, then the pipe will break.

Checkpoint ✓ **Use the Law of Syllogism**

6. Write the statement that follows from the pair of true statements.

If the ball is thrown at the window, it will hit the window.

If the ball hits the window, then the window will break.

Guided Practice

Vocabulary Check   **Complete the statement.**

   1. The "if" part of an if-then statement contains the __?__.

   2. The "then" part of an if-then statement contains the __?__.

Skill Check   **In Exercises 3 and 4, rewrite the statement as an if-then statement.**

   3. Adjacent angles share a common side.

   4. You will be late to school if you miss the bus.

   5. What can you conclude from the following true statements?

      If the endpoints of a segment have coordinates $(-1, -2)$ and $(5, 2)$, then the midpoint of the segment is at $(2, 0)$.

      The endpoints of $\overline{AB}$ are $A(-1, -2)$ and $B(5, 2)$.

   6. Use the Law of Syllogism to write the if-then statement that follows from the pair of true statements.

      If the perimeter of a square is 20 feet, then the length of a side of the square is 5 feet.

      If the length of a side of a square is 5 feet, then the area is 25 square feet.

Practice and Applications

Extra Practice

See p. 678.

Parts of an If-Then Statement **Identify the hypothesis and the conclusion of the if-then statement.**

   7. If the car is running, then the key is in the ignition.

   8. If the measure of an angle is 60°, then the angle is acute.

Writing If-Then Statements **Rewrite the statement as an if-then statement. Then underline the hypothesis and circle the conclusion.**

   9. A number divisible by 6 is also divisible by 3 and 2.

   10. Eagles are fish-eating birds.

   11. A shape has four sides if it is a square.

   12. Two angles are supplementary if they form a linear pair.

Homework Help

Example 1: Exs. 7–12,
20, 21, 24–27
Example 2: Exs. 9–12,
20, 21, 24–27
Example 3: Exs. 13–15
Example 4: Ex. 16
Example 5: Exs. 17–19

Using the Law of Detachment In Exercises 13–15, what can you conclude from the given true statements?

13. If two planes intersect, then their intersection is a line. Two planes are intersecting.

14. If x has a value of 4, then $2x$ has a value of 8. The value of x is 4.

15. If Central High School wins the championship, then the school will celebrate. Central High School wins the championship.

16.  **You be the Judge** Which argument is correct? Explain your reasoning.

Argument 1: If two angles measure 40° and 50°, then the angles are complementary. The measure of ∠1 is 40° and the measure of ∠2 is 50°. So, ∠1 and ∠2 are complementary.

Argument 2: If two angles measure 40° and 50°, then the angles are complementary. ∠1 and ∠2 are complementary. So, $m\angle 1 = 40°$ and $m\angle 2 = 50°$.

Using the Law of Syllogism Write the if-then statement that follows from the pair of true statements.

17. If the sun is shining, then it is a beautiful day.

If it is a beautiful day, then we will have a picnic.

18. If the stereo is on, then the volume is loud.

If the volume is loud, then the neighbors will complain.

19. If Todd goes to the movies, then Gabriela will go to the movies.

If Chris goes to the movies, then Todd will go to the movies.

Advertising Use the following advertising slogan: "Want a great selection of used cars? Come and see Bargain Bob's Used Cars!"

20. Rewrite the slogan as an if-then statement. Then underline the hypothesis and circle the conclusion.

21. Find an advertising slogan that can be written as an if-then statement. Then repeat Exercise 20 using the slogan.

Logical Reasoning Select the word or phrase that makes the concluding statement true.

22. The Oak Terrace apartment building does not allow dogs. Serena lives at Oak Terrace. So, Serena (*must, may, must not*) keep a dog.

23. The Kolob Arch is the world's widest natural arch. The world's widest natural arch is in Zion National Park. So, the Kolob Arch (*is, may be, is not*) in Zion National Park.

Quotes of Wisdom Rewrite the statement as an if-then statement. Then underline the hypothesis and circle the conclusion.

24.
> If you tell the truth, you don't have to remember anything.
> Mark Twain

25.
> You have to expect things of yourself before you can do them.
> Michael Jordan

26.
> If one is lucky, a solitary fantasy can totally transform one million realities.
> Maya Angelou

27.
> Whoever is happy will make others happy too.
> Anne Frank

Standardized Test Practice

28. Multiple Choice What is the *conclusion* of the following if-then statement?

If the storm passes, then our plane will take off.

- **A** The storm passes.
- **B** Our plane will take off.
- **C** Then our plane will take off.
- **D** None of these

Mixed Review

Classifying Angles Classify the angle as *acute, right, obtuse,* or *straight.* (Lesson 1.6)

29. $m\angle A = 20°$ **30.** $m\angle B = 154°$ **31.** $m\angle C = 90°$

32. $m\angle D = 7°$ **33.** $m\angle E = 180°$ **34.** $m\angle F = 89°$

Midpoint Formula Find the coordinates of the midpoint of $\overline{AB}$. (Lesson 2.1)

35. $A(0, 0), B(-2, 6)$ **36.** $A(2, 3), B(8, 5)$ **37.** $A(0, -8), B(6, 6)$

Algebra Skills

Solving Equations Solve the equation. (Skills Review, p. 673)

38. $4y - 2 = 4$ **39.** $6 = -2t + 1$ **40.** $4x = -5 + x$

41. $w + 4 = 3w$ **42.** $12x + 33 = 9x$ **43.** $14b - 17 = -3b$

2.6 Properties of Equality and Congruence

Goal
Use properties of equality and congruence.

Key Words
• Reflexive Property
• Symmetric Property
• Transitive Property

Reflexive Property

Jean is the same height as Jean.

Symmetric Property

If Jean is the same height as Pedro, **then** Pedro is the same height as Jean.

Transitive Property

If Jean is the same height as Pedro **and** Pedro is the same height as Chris, **then** Jean is the same height as Chris.

The photos above illustrate the *Reflexive, Symmetric,* and *Transitive Properties* of Equality. You can use these properties in geometry with statements about equality and congruence.

Student Help

> **LOOK BACK**
> To review the difference between equality and congruence, see p. 30.

PROPERTIES OF EQUALITY AND CONGRUENCE

Reflexive Property

Equality $AB = AB$
$m\angle A = m\angle A$

Congruence $\overline{AB} \cong \overline{AB}$
$\angle A \cong \angle A$

Symmetric Property

Equality
If $AB = CD$, then $CD = AB$.
If $m\angle A = m\angle B$, then $m\angle B = m\angle A$.

Congruence
If $\overline{AB} \cong \overline{CD}$, then $\overline{CD} \cong \overline{AB}$.
If $\angle A \cong \angle B$, then $\angle B \cong \angle A$.

Transitive Property

Equality
If $AB = CD$ and $CD = EF$,
then $AB = EF$.

If $m\angle A = m\angle B$ and $m\angle B = m\angle C$,
then $m\angle A = m\angle C$.

Congruence
If $\overline{AB} \cong \overline{CD}$ and $\overline{CD} \cong \overline{EF}$,
then $\overline{AB} \cong \overline{EF}$.

If $\angle A \cong \angle B$ and $\angle B \cong \angle C$,
then $\angle A \cong \angle C$.

EXAMPLE 1 **Name Properties of Equality and Congruence**

Name the property that the statement illustrates.

  a. If $\overline{GH} \cong \overline{JK}$, then $\overline{JK} \cong \overline{GH}$.

  b. $DE = DE$

  c. If $\angle P \cong \angle Q$ and $\angle Q \cong \angle R$, then $\angle P \cong \angle R$.

Solution

  a. Symmetric Property of Congruence

  b. Reflexive Property of Equality

  c. Transitive Property of Congruence

Checkpoint ✓ **Name Properties of Equality and Congruence**

Name the property that the statement illustrates.

  1. If $DF = FG$ and $FG = GH$, then $DF = GH$.

  2. $\angle P \cong \angle P$

  3. If $m\angle S = m\angle T$, then $m\angle T = m\angle S$.

Logical Reasoning In geometry, you are often asked to explain why statements are true. Reasons can include definitions, theorems, postulates, or properties.

EXAMPLE 2 **Use Properties of Equality**

In the diagram, N is the midpoint of $\overline{MP}$, and P is the midpoint of $\overline{NQ}$. Show that $MN = PQ$.

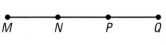

Solution

$MN = NP$	Definition of midpoint
$NP = PQ$	Definition of midpoint
$MN = PQ$	Transitive Property of Equality

Checkpoint ✓ **Use Properties of Equality and Congruence**

  4. $\angle 1$ and $\angle 2$ are vertical angles, and $\angle 2 \cong \angle 3$. Show that $\angle 1 \cong \angle 3$.

$\angle 1 \cong \angle 2$	__?__ Theorem
$\angle 2 \cong \angle 3$	Given
$\angle 1 \cong \angle 3$	__?__ Property of Congruence

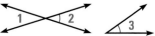

Student Help

STUDY TIP
In geometry, you can use properties of equality that you learned in algebra.

PROPERTIES OF EQUALITY

Addition Property

Adding the same number to each side of an equation produces an equivalent equation.

Example

$$x - 3 = 7$$
$$x - 3 + 3 = 7 + 3$$

Subtraction Property

Subtracting the same number from each side of an equation produces an equivalent equation.

Example

$$y + 5 = 11$$
$$y + 5 - 5 = 11 - 5$$

Multiplication Property

Multiplying each side of an equation by the same nonzero number produces an equivalent equation.

Example

$$\frac{1}{4}z = 6$$
$$\frac{1}{4}z \cdot 4 = 6 \cdot 4$$

Division Property

Dividing each side of an equation by the same nonzero number produces an equivalent equation.

Example

$$8x = 16$$
$$\frac{8x}{8} = \frac{16}{8}$$

Substitution Property

Substituting a number for a variable in an equation produces an equivalent equation.

Example

$$x = 7$$
$$2x + 4 = 2(7) + 4$$

Student Help
CLASSZONE.COM

MORE EXAMPLES
More examples at classzone.com

EXAMPLE 3 Justify the Congruent Supplements Theorem

$\angle 1$ and $\angle 2$ are both supplementary to $\angle 3$. Show that $\angle 1 \cong \angle 2$.

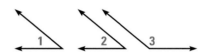

Solution

$m\angle 1 + m\angle 3 = 180°$	Definition of supplementary angles
$m\angle 2 + m\angle 3 = 180°$	Definition of supplementary angles
$m\angle 1 + m\angle 3 = m\angle 2 + m\angle 3$	Substitution Property of Equality
$m\angle 1 = m\angle 2$	Subtraction Property of Equality
$\angle 1 \cong \angle 2$	Definition of congruent angles

Checkpoint *Use Properties of Equality and Congruence*

5. In the diagram, M is the midpoint of $\overline{AB}$. Show that $AB = 2 \cdot AM$.

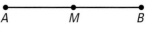

$MB = AM$	Definition of __?__
$AB = AM + MB$	__?__ Postulate
$AB = AM + AM$	__?__ Property of Equality
$AB = 2 \cdot AM$	Distributive property

2.6 Exercises

Guided Practice

Vocabulary Check

Match the statement with the property it illustrates.

1. $m\angle DEF = m\angle DEF$

A. Symmetric Property of Equality

2. If $\overline{PQ} \cong \overline{ST}$, then $\overline{ST} \cong \overline{PQ}$.

B. Reflexive Property of Equality

3. $\overline{XY} \cong \overline{XY}$

C. Transitive Property of Equality

4. If $\angle J \cong \angle K$ and $\angle K \cong \angle L$, then $\angle J \cong \angle L$.

D. Reflexive Property of Congruence

5. If $PQ = QR$ and $QR = RS$, then $PQ = RS$.

E. Symmetric Property of Congruence

6. If $m\angle X = m\angle Y$, then $m\angle Y = m\angle X$.

F. Transitive Property of Congruence

Skill Check

Name the property that the statement illustrates.

7. $\angle ABC \cong \angle ABC$

8. If $m\angle B = m\angle D$ and $m\angle D = m\angle F$, then $m\angle B = m\angle F$.

9. If $\overline{GH} \cong \overline{JK}$, then $\overline{JK} \cong \overline{GH}$.

Practice and Applications

Extra Practice

See p. 678

Completing Statements Use the property to complete the statement.

10. *Reflexive Property of Equality:* $JK = $ __?__

11. *Symmetric Property of Equality:* If $m\angle P = m\angle Q$, then __?__ $=$ __?__.

12. *Transitive Property of Equality:* If $AB = BC$ and $BC = CD$, then __?__ $=$ __?__.

13. *Reflexive Property of Congruence:* __?__ $\cong \angle GHJ$

14. *Symmetric Property of Congruence:* If __?__ $\cong$ __?__, then $\angle XYZ \cong \angle ABC$.

15. *Transitive Property of Congruence:* If $\overline{GH} \cong \overline{IJ}$ and __?__ $\cong$ __?__, then $\overline{GH} \cong \overline{PQ}$.

Naming Properties **Name the property that the statement illustrates.**

16. If $AB = CD$, then $AB + EF = CD + EF$.

17. If $m\angle C = 90°$, then $2(m\angle C) + 15° = 2(90°) + 15°$.

18. If $XY = YZ$, then $3 \cdot XY = 3 \cdot YZ$.

Homework Help

Example 1: Exs. 10–18
Example 2: Exs. 19–24
Example 3: Exs. 19–24

19. Using Properties In the diagram, $m\angle 1 + m\angle 2 = 132°$, and $m\angle 2 = 105°$. Complete the argument to show that $m\angle 1 = 27°$.

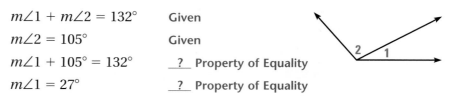

$m\angle 1 + m\angle 2 = 132°$	Given
$m\angle 2 = 105°$	Given
$m\angle 1 + 105° = 132°$	__?__ Property of Equality
$m\angle 1 = 27°$	__?__ Property of Equality

20. Using Properties of Congruence In the diagram, $\overline{AB} \cong \overline{FG}$, and $\overleftrightarrow{BF}$ bisects $\overline{AC}$ and $\overline{DG}$. Complete the argument to show that $\overline{BC} \cong \overline{DF}$.

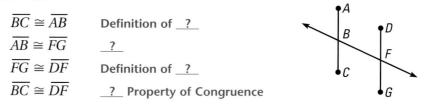

$\overline{BC} \cong \overline{AB}$	Definition of __?__
$\overline{AB} \cong \overline{FG}$	__?__
$\overline{FG} \cong \overline{DF}$	Definition of __?__
$\overline{BC} \cong \overline{DF}$	__?__ Property of Congruence

21. Unscramble the Steps In the diagram below, $PQ = RS$. Copy the diagram and arrange the statements and reasons in order to make a logical argument to show that $PR = QS$.

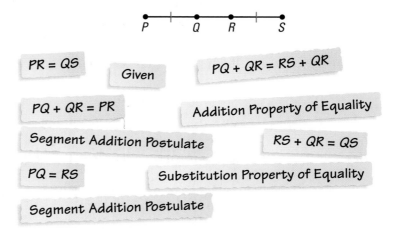

PR = QS

Given

PQ + QR = RS + QR

PQ + QR = PR

Addition Property of Equality

Segment Addition Postulate

RS + QR = QS

PQ = RS

Substitution Property of Equality

Segment Addition Postulate

22. Using Properties of Equality In the diagram at the right, $m\angle WPY = m\angle XPZ$. Complete the argument to show that $m\angle WPX = m\angle YPZ$.

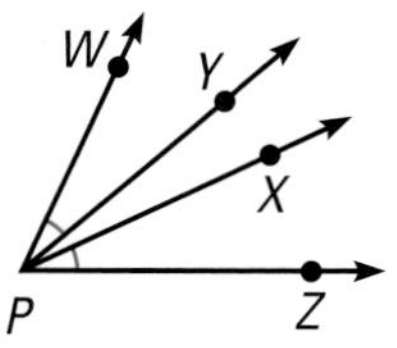

$m\angle WPY = m\angle XPZ$	Given
$m\angle WPX = m\angle WPY + m\angle YPX$	__?__
$m\angle YPZ = m\angle YPX + m\angle XPZ$	__?__
$m\angle WPY + m\angle YPX = m\angle YPX + m\angle XPZ$	__?__
$m\angle WPX = m\angle YPZ$	__?__

Student Help

LOOK BACK
To review the Congruent
Complements Theorem,
see p. 69.

23. Congruent Complements Theorem Show that the Congruent Complements Theorem is true. Use Example 3 on page 90 as a model. Provide a reason for each step.

In the diagram, ∠1 is complementary to ∠2, and ∠3 is complementary to ∠2. Show that ∠1 ≅ ∠3.

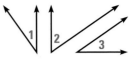

24. Error Analysis In the diagram, $\overline{SR} \cong \overline{CB}$ and $\overline{AC} \cong \overline{QR}$. Explain what is wrong with the student's argument.

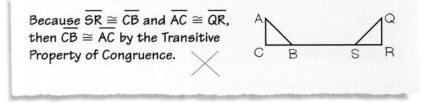

Because $\overline{SR} \cong \overline{CB}$ and $\overline{AC} \cong \overline{QR}$, then $\overline{CB} \cong \overline{AC}$ by the Transitive Property of Congruence.

Using Algebra Find the value of the variable using the given information. Provide a reason for each step.

25. $AB = BC$, $BC = CD$

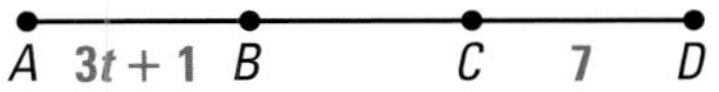

A 3t + 1 B   C   7   D

26. $QR = RS$, $ST = RS$

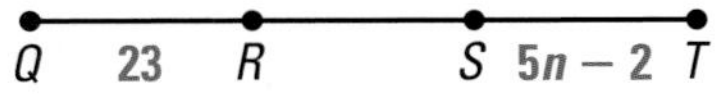

Q   23   R   S 5n − 2 T

27. Challenge Fold two corners of a piece of paper so their edges match as shown at the right.

What do you notice about the angle formed by the fold lines?

Show that the angle measure is always the same. Provide a reason for each step.

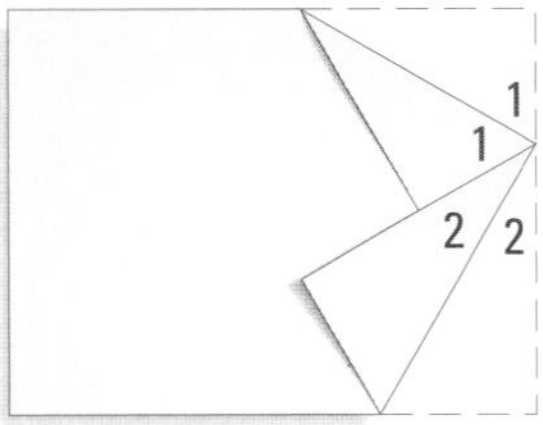

Standardized Test Practice

28. Multiple Choice Which statement illustrates the Symmetric Property of Congruence?

Ⓐ If $\overline{AD} \cong \overline{BC}$, then $\overline{DA} \cong \overline{CB}$.

Ⓑ If $\overline{WX} \cong \overline{XY}$ and $\overline{XY} \cong \overline{YZ}$, then $\overline{WX} \cong \overline{YZ}$.

Ⓒ If $\overline{AB} \cong \overline{GH}$, then $\overline{GH} \cong \overline{AB}$.

Ⓓ $\overline{AB} \cong \overline{BA}$

29. Multiple Choice In the figure below, $\overline{QT} \cong \overline{TS}$ and $\overline{RS} \cong \overline{TS}$. What is the value of x?

Ⓕ 4   Ⓖ 12

Ⓗ 16   Ⓙ 32

7x + 4   6x + 8

Naming Collinear Points Use the diagram to name a point that is collinear with the given points. *(Lesson 1.3)*

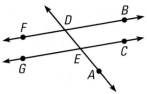

30. G and E **31.** F and B

32. A and D **33.** B and D

Sketching Intersections Sketch the figure described. *(Lesson 1.4)*

34. Three lines that do not intersect but lie in the same plane.

35. Two lines that intersect at one point, and another line that intersects both of those lines at different points.

Algebra Skills

Plotting Points Plot the point in a coordinate plane. *(Skills Review, p. 664)*

36. $(5, 2)$ **37.** $(0, -7)$ **38.** $(1, -4)$ **39.** $(-8, -3)$

40. $(-6, 7)$ **41.** $(10, 2)$ **42.** $(-1, 1)$ **43.** $(9, -4)$

Quiz 2

Find the measures of the numbered angles. *(Lesson 2.4)*

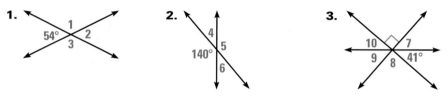

In Exercises 4 and 5, rewrite the statement as an if-then statement. *(Lesson 2.5)*

4. A square is a four-sided figure.   **5.** The value of x^2 is 25 if $x = 5$.

6. Use the Law of Syllogism to write the statement that follows from the pair of true statements. *(Lesson 2.5)*

If we charter a boat, then we will go deep sea fishing.

If we go deep sea fishing, then we will be gone all day.

7. In the diagram, $\overrightarrow{KM}$ bisects $\angle JKN$, and $\overrightarrow{KN}$ bisects $\angle MKL$. Complete the argument to show that $m\angle JKM = m\angle NKL$. *(Lesson 2.6)*

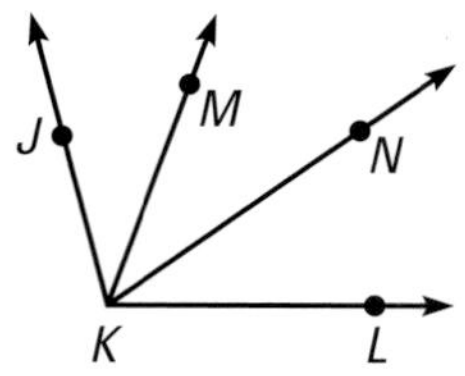

$m\angle JKM = m\angle MKN$ Definition of __?__

$m\angle MKN = m\angle NKL$ Definition of __?__

$m\angle JKM = m\angle NKL$ __?__ Property of Equality

VOCABULARY

- **midpoint**, *p. 53*
- **segment bisector**, *p. 53*
- **bisect**, *p. 53*
- **angle bisector**, *p. 61*
- **complementary angles**, *p. 67*
- **complement of an angle**, *p. 67*

- **supplementary angles**, *p. 67*
- **supplement of an angle**, *p. 67*
- **adjacent angles**, *p. 68*
- **theorem**, *p. 69*
- **vertical angles**, *p. 75*

- **linear pair**, *p. 75*
- **if-then statement**, *p. 82*
- **hypothesis**, *p. 82*
- **conclusion**, *p. 82*
- **deductive reasoning**, *p. 83*

VOCABULARY REVIEW

Fill in the blank.

1. Two angles are __?__ if the sum of their measures is 180°.

2. A(n) __?__ is a ray that divides an angle into two congruent angles.

3. A(n) __?__ is a segment, ray, line, or plane that intersects a segment at its midpoint.

4. __?__ angles are nonadjacent angles whose sides are formed by two intersecting lines.

5. Two angles are __?__ if they have a common vertex and side, but no common interior points.

6. Two angles are __?__ if the sum of their measures is 90°.

2.1 SEGMENT BISECTORS

Examples on pp. 53–55

EXAMPLE *M* is the midpoint of $\overline{AB}$. Find *MB* and *AB*.

M is the midpoint of $\overline{AB}$, so $AM = MB$. Therefore, $MB = AM = 14$.

The length of $\overline{AB}$ is twice the length of $\overline{AM}$.

$AB = 2 \cdot AM = 2 \cdot 14 = 28$

ANSWER ▶ $MB = 14$ and $AB = 28$.

7. *R* is the midpoint of $\overline{PQ}$. Find *PR* and *PQ*.

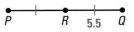

Find the coordinates of the midpoint of $\overline{FG}$.

8. $F(4, 1)$, $G(10, 9)$ **9.** $F(4, -4)$, $G(0, 7)$ **10.** $F(-3, 1)$, $G(-6, -5)$

2.2 ANGLE BISECTORS

Examples on pp. 61–63

> **EXAMPLE** In the diagram, $\overrightarrow{XY}$ bisects $\angle WXZ$. Find $m\angle WXY$ and $m\angle YXZ$.
>
> $m\angle WXY = \frac{1}{2}(m\angle WXZ) = \frac{1}{2}(120°) = 60°$
>
> You know that $\angle WXY \cong \angle YXZ$, so $m\angle YXZ = 60°$ also.

$\overrightarrow{BD}$ bisects $\angle ABC$. Find the angle measure.

11. Find $m\angle ABC$.   **12.** Find $m\angle ABD$.   **13.** Find $m\angle DBC$.

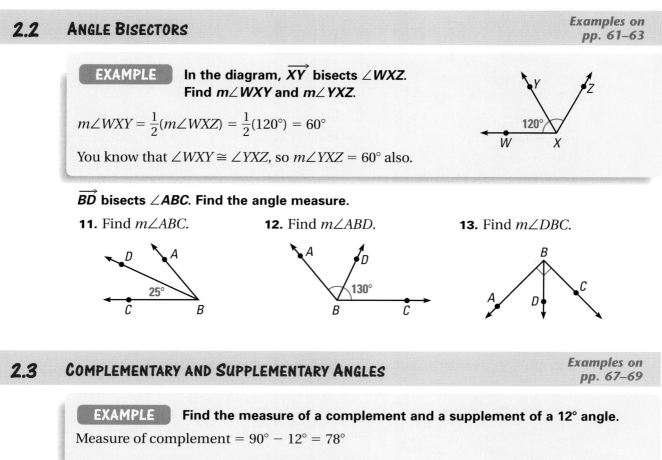

2.3 COMPLEMENTARY AND SUPPLEMENTARY ANGLES

Examples on pp. 67–69

> **EXAMPLE** Find the measure of a complement and a supplement of a 12° angle.
>
> Measure of complement = 90° − 12° = 78°
>
> Measure of supplement = 180° − 12° = 168°

14. Find the measure of a complement and a supplement of a 79° angle.

2.4 VERTICAL ANGLES

Examples on pp. 75–77

> **EXAMPLE** Find $m\angle 1$, $m\angle 2$, and $m\angle 3$. 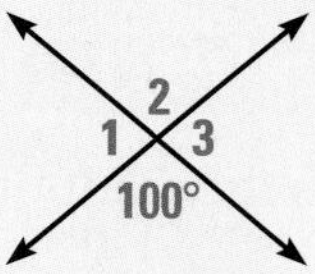
>
> $m\angle 2 = 100°$
>
> $m\angle 1 = 180° - m\angle 2 = 180° - 100° = 80°$
>
> $m\angle 3 = m\angle 1 = 80°$

Find $m\angle 1$, $m\angle 2$, and $m\angle 3$.

15.   **16.**   **17.**   **18.**

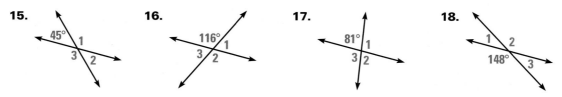

2.5 IF-THEN STATEMENTS AND DEDUCTIVE REASONING

Examples on pp. 82–84

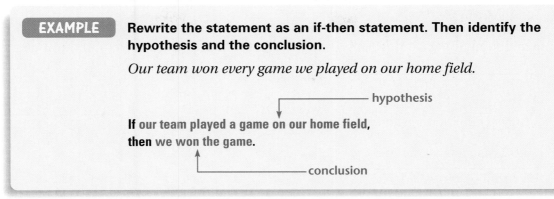

EXAMPLE Rewrite the statement as an if-then statement. Then identify the hypothesis and the conclusion.

Our team won every game we played on our home field.

hypothesis

If our team played a game on our home field, **then** we won the game.

conclusion

In Exercises 19 and 20, write the statement as an if-then statement. Then underline the hypothesis and circle the conclusion.

19. Every computer in the store is on sale.

20. I'll go to the mall if you come with me.

21. Use the Law of Syllogism to write the if-then statement that follows from the pair of true statements.

If Mike goes to the concert, then Jon will go to the concert.

If Jon goes to the concert, then Jeannine will go to the concert.

2.6 PROPERTIES OF EQUALITY AND CONGRUENCE

Examples on pp. 88–90

EXAMPLES Name the property that the statement illustrates.

Statement	Property
a. $\angle T \cong \angle T$	**a.** Reflexive Property of Congruence
b. If $AC = XY$ and $XY = TU$, then $AC = TU$.	**b.** Transitive Property of Equality
c. If $m\angle C = m\angle F$, then $m\angle F = m\angle C$.	**c.** Symmetric Property of Equality

Match the statement with the property it illustrates.

22. If $m\angle 2 = m\angle 3$, then $m\angle 3 = m\angle 2$.　　**A.** Addition Property of Equality

23. If $m\angle S = 45°$, then $m\angle S + 35° = 80°$.　　**B.** Transitive Property of Equality

24. If $AE = EG$ and $EG = JK$, then $AE = JK$.　　**C.** Multiplication Property of Equality

25. If $m\angle K = 9°$, then $3(m\angle K) = 27°$.　　**D.** Substitution Property of Equality

26. If $AB = 12$, then $2 \cdot AB + 3 = 2(12) + 3$.　　**E.** Symmetric Property of Equality

1. R is the midpoint of $\overline{PQ}$. Find RQ and PQ.

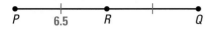

2. Line ℓ bisects $\overline{FG}$. Find the value of r.

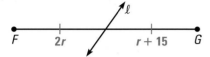

In Exercises 3 and 4, find the coordinates of the midpoint of $\overline{AB}$.

3. $A(0, 9)$, $B(4, -3)$ **4.** $A(-3, 5)$, $B(-7, -2)$

5. $\overrightarrow{BD}$ bisects $\angle ABC$. Find $m\angle ABD$ and $m\angle DBC$.

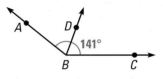

6. $\overrightarrow{KM}$ bisects $\angle JKL$. Find the value of x.

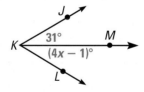

7. $\angle D$ is a supplement of $\angle E$, and $m\angle D = 29°$. Find $m\angle E$.

8. $\angle F$ is a complement of $\angle G$, and $m\angle G = 76°$. Find $m\angle F$.

9. $\angle 4$ and $\angle 5$ are a linear pair, and $m\angle 4 = 61°$. Find $m\angle 5$.

10. Find $m\angle 1$, $m\angle 2$, and $m\angle 3$.

11. Use the diagram to find the angle measures.

  a. $m\angle AHB$

  b. $m\angle FHE$

  c. $m\angle AHF$

  d. $m\angle CHD$

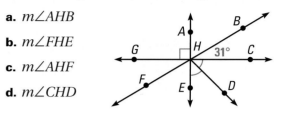

Write the statement as an if-then statement.

12. A 60° angle is an acute angle.

13. Meg will be happy if it snows tomorrow.

In Exercises 14–16, name the property that the statement illustrates.

14. $m\angle 2 = m\angle 2$

15. If $\angle 5 \cong \angle 6$, then $\angle 6 \cong \angle 5$.

16. If $AB = CD$ and $CD = FG$, then $AB = FG$.

17. Write the if-then statement that follows from the pair of true statements.

If I am in Boston, then I am in Massachusetts.

If I am in Massachusetts, then I am in New England.

18. In the diagram below, $m\angle RPQ = m\angle RPS$. Complete the argument to show that $m\angle SPQ = 2(m\angle RPQ)$.

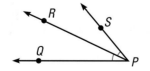

$m\angle RPQ = m\angle RPS$	Given
$m\angle SPQ = m\angle RPQ + m\angle RPS$	?
$m\angle SPQ = m\angle RPQ + m\angle RPQ$	?
$m\angle SPQ = 2(m\angle RPQ)$	Distributive property

Test Tip If you are unsure of an answer, try to eliminate some of the choices so you can make an educated guess.

1. S is the midpoint of $\overline{RT}$, and $RS = 23$. What is RT?

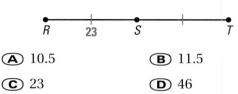

(A) 10.5   (B) 11.5

(C) 23   (D) 46

2. What are the coordinates of the midpoint of the segment joining $(4, -5)$ and $(-2, -1)$?

(F) $(2, -6)$ (G) $(1, -2)$

(H) $(1, -3)$ (J) $(-8, 5)$

3. $\overrightarrow{SU}$ bisects $\angle RST$. What is the value of x?

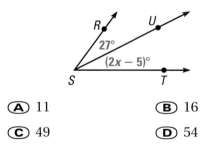

(A) 11   (B) 16

(C) 49   (D) 54

4. If $\angle 5$ and $\angle 6$ are both supplementary to $\angle 7$, and $m\angle 5 = 17°$, what is $m\angle 6$?

(F) 17°   (G) 73°

(H) 163°   (J) 180°

5. Use the diagram to determine which of the following statements is *false*.

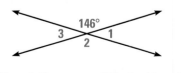

(A) $m\angle 1 = 34°$ (B) $m\angle 2 = 146°$

(C) $\angle 1 \cong \angle 2$ (D) $\angle 1 \cong \angle 3$

6. What is the *conclusion* of the following statement?

If today is Saturday, then tomorrow is Sunday.

(F) Today is Saturday.

(G) Today is Sunday.

(H) Tomorrow is Saturday.

(J) Tomorrow is Sunday.

7. Which property is illustrated by the following statement?

If $\angle 1 \cong \angle 2$, then $\angle 2 \cong \angle 1$.

(A) Symmetric Property of Equality

(B) Symmetric Property of Congruence

(C) Transitive Property of Equality

(D) Transitive Property of Congruence

8. Multi-Step Problem Use the diagram below.

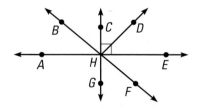

a. Name two pairs of complementary angles.

b. Name two pairs of supplementary angles.

c. Name two sets of linear pairs.

d. Name two pairs of vertical angles.

e. Complete the statements.

If $m\angle BHC = 50°$, then $m\angle AHB = \underline{\ ?\ }°$.

If $m\angle CHE = 90°$, then $m\angle AHG = \underline{\ ?\ }°$.

If $m\angle BHE = 140°$, then $m\angle AHF = \underline{\ ?\ }°$.

BraiN GaMes

Logic Puzzle

Object of the Game To use deductive reasoning to correctly determine the type and name of each student's pet.

How to Play Keep track of the clues by recording the pieces of information in a grid like the one shown. Put an X in the boxes that you can eliminate, and put a check in the boxes that you are sure of. Clue 1 of the puzzle is done for you.

	Alex	Carole	Mark	Sean	Tamara
Buddy					
Fang					
Merlin					
Prince					
Stripe					
Dog					X
Cat	X	X	X	X	✓
Fish					X
Guinea Pig					X
Rabbit					X

Tamara has a cat, so no one else has a cat, and Tamara does not have any other pets.

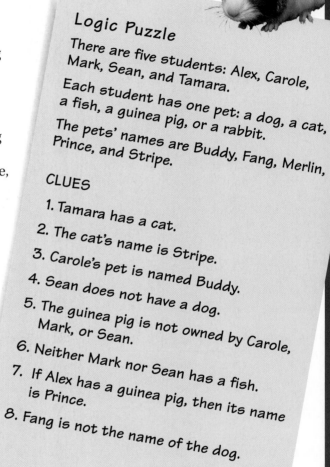

Logic Puzzle

There are five students: Alex, Carole, Mark, Sean, and Tamara.

Each student has one pet: a dog, a cat, a fish, a guinea pig, or a rabbit.

The pets' names are Buddy, Fang, Merlin, Prince, and Stripe.

CLUES

1. Tamara has a cat.
2. The cat's name is Stripe.
3. Carole's pet is named Buddy.
4. Sean does not have a dog.
5. The guinea pig is not owned by Carole, Mark, or Sean.
6. Neither Mark nor Sean has a fish.
7. If Alex has a guinea pig, then its name is Prince.
8. Fang is not the name of the dog.

Like terms are terms in an expression that have the same variable raised to the same power. Constant terms, such as 2 and -5, are also considered like terms.

EXAMPLE 1 Combine Like Terms

Simplify the expression $6x - 2y + 10x + 7y$.

Solution

$$
\begin{aligned}
6x - 2y + 10x + 7y &= 6x + 10x - 2y + 7y && \text{Group like terms.} \\
&= (6 + 10)x + (-2 + 7)y && \text{Distributive prop.} \\
&= 16x + 5y && \text{Simplify within parentheses.}
\end{aligned}
$$

Try These

Simplify the expression.

1. $7p + 15p$ **2.** $r - 3r$ **3.** $3q + 6q - 2q$

4. $2t + 4t + 7$ **5.** $8x + 3 - 5x$ **6.** $-9c - 3b + 15c$

7. $11y + 16z + 24z + 8y$ **8.** $18f - 13g - 14f - g$

EXAMPLE 2 Solve Equations With Variables on Both Sides

Solve the equation $4x - 7 = 3x + 1$.

Solution

$$
\begin{aligned}
4x - 7 &= 3x + 1 && \text{Write original equation.} \\
4x - 3x - 7 &= 3x - 3x + 1 && \text{Subtract } 3x \text{ from each side.} \\
x - 7 &= 1 && \text{Simplify.} \\
x - 7 + 7 &= 1 + 7 && \text{Add 7 to each side.} \\
x &= 8 && \text{Simplify.}
\end{aligned}
$$

Student Help

> **STUDY TIP**
> Remember to check your solution by substituting the value of the variable into the original equation.

Try These

Solve the equation.

9. $4w = 3w + 10$ **10.** $6y = 11 - 5y$ **11.** $10p - 12 = 8p$

12. $q + 14 = -6q$ **13.** $2t + 5 = t - 9$ **14.** $5x - 1 = 3x + 7$

15. $6a - 13 = 4a + 9$ **16.** $3r - 2 = 7r + 18$ **17.** $12d - 7d = 2d + 6$

Drawing in Perspective

Objective

Draw objects in one-point perspective.

The photograph at the right shows one-point perspective. Lines appear to meet at a *vanishing point* at eye level, along a *horizon line*.

Materials

- paper
- pencil
- straightedge
- magazines

Drawing

❶ Draw a rectangle. Draw a horizon line first. Then pick a vanishing point.

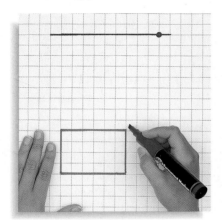

❷ Connect corners of the rectangle to the vanishing point.

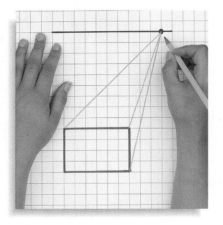

❸ Draw segments to complete a box. Erase the guide lines you used.

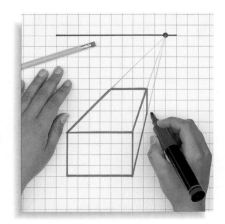

Investigation

1. Use the photograph at the top of this page. What happens to the trees as they approach the vanishing point? Do objects appear smaller or larger as they get farther away?

2. Draw three different boxes of various sizes, using the same vanishing point.

3. Place three textbooks or cereal boxes in a row on a table. Move your chair away from the table and to the left. Draw the objects. Include the vanishing point on your drawing.

Present Your Results

Make a folder of photographs and drawings
that show perspective.

▶ Find photographs in newspapers or magazines that show
perspective.

▶ Draw horizon lines and vanishing points on the
photographs. Also draw some lines that meet at the
vanishing point.

▶ Include the drawings you made in the Investigation.

▶ Write a few sentences about how the photographs and
drawings demonstrate perspective.

Extension

Draw a landscape scene or street scene of your
choice in one-point perspective. For example,
find a straight street with buildings or a view
of walkways in a park.

Parallel and Perpendicular Lines

Will the boats' paths ever cross?

If a sailboat heads directly into the wind, the sails flap and are useless. One solution is for boats to sail at an angle to the wind, as shown in the diagram.

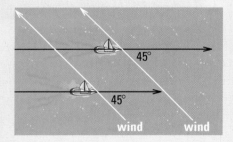

During a race, sailboats often head into the wind at the same angle and they appear to be racing in *parallel* paths—paths that never cross.

Learn More About It

You will learn more about paths of sailboats in Exercise 25 on p. 149.

Who uses Parallel and Perpendicular Lines?

PHYSICAL THERAPIST
Physical therapists use angles to measure the range of motion of elbows, knees, and other joints. These measurements help the therapist evaluate people's injuries. (p. 134)

BICYCLE DESIGNER
The angles in a bike frame influence the position of the rider. Georgena Terry builds bicycles whose designs feature a frame geometry more suitable for women. (p. 124)

How will you use these ideas?

- Understand how escalators work. (p. 112)
- Learn how a compass and map are used in orienteering. (p. 119)
- See how surfing and kite flying are combined in the sport of kiteboarding. (p. 141)
- Understand how the strings of a guitar are related to the frets. (p. 148)

Chapter 3

PREVIEW

What's the chapter about?

- Identifying relationships between lines
- Using properties of **parallel** and **perpendicular lines**
- Showing that two lines are parallel

> #### Key Words
>
> - parallel lines, *p. 108*
> - perpendicular lines, *p. 108*
> - skew lines, *p. 108*
> - parallel planes, *p. 109*
> - transversal, *p. 121*
>
> - corresponding angles, *p. 121*
> - alternate interior angles, *p. 121*
> - alternate exterior angles, *p. 121*
> - same-side interior angles, *p. 121*
> - converse, *p. 136*

PREPARE

Chapter Readiness Quiz

Take this quick quiz. If you are unsure of an answer, look at the reference pages for help.

Vocabulary Check *(refer to p. 75)*

1. Name a pair of vertical angles.

(A) ∠1 and ∠4   (B) ∠2 and ∠4

(C) ∠2 and ∠3   (D) ∠3 and ∠4

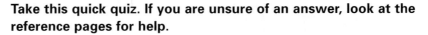

Skill Check *(refer to pp. 75, 673)*

2. The measure of ∠7 is 68°, and ∠7 and ∠8 form a linear pair. What is the measure of ∠8?

(F) 22°   (G) 68°   (H) 112°   (J) 80°

3. Which of the following is a solution of the equation $5x + 9 = 6x - 11$?

(A) $\frac{11}{20}$ (B) 2   (C) 11   (D) 20

VISUAL STRATEGY

Reading and Drawing Diagrams

Visualize It! ➡

Use dashed lines to show parts of a figure that are hidden behind other parts. The dashed line shows that line *n* is not in plane *S*.

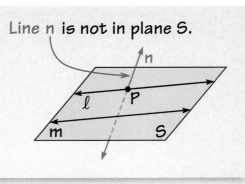

Line *n* is not in plane *S*.

Question

How are lines related in space?

Materials

• pencil
• straightedge
• lined paper

Explore

❶ Use a straightedge to draw two identical rectangles.

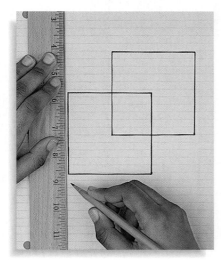

❷ Connect the corresponding corners of the rectangles.

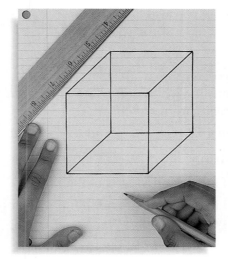

❸ Erase parts of "hidden" lines to form dashed lines.

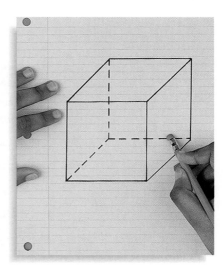

Think About It

Visualize It!

Shading your sketch will help make it look three-dimensional.

Using your sketch from the steps above, label the corners as shown. Then extend $\overline{AD}$ and $\overline{CG}$.

1. Will $\overleftrightarrow{AD}$ and $\overleftrightarrow{CG}$ ever intersect in space? Lines that intersect on the page do not necessarily intersect in space.

2. Determine whether the following pairs of lines will intersect in space.

    a. $\overleftrightarrow{BC}$ and $\overleftrightarrow{AE}$ **b.** $\overleftrightarrow{GH}$ and $\overleftrightarrow{DH}$

    c. $\overleftrightarrow{CD}$ and $\overleftrightarrow{DH}$ **d.** $\overleftrightarrow{AB}$ and $\overleftrightarrow{EH}$

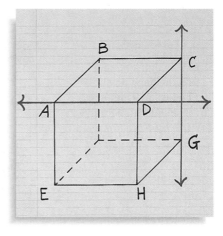

Relationships Between Lines

Goal
Identify relationships between lines.

Key Words
- parallel lines
- perpendicular lines
- skew lines
- parallel planes
- line perpendicular to a plane

Two lines are **parallel lines** if they lie in the same plane and do not intersect. On the building, lines *r* and *s* are parallel lines. You can write this as $r \parallel s$. Triangles (▸) are used to indicate that the lines are parallel.

Two lines are **perpendicular lines** if they intersect to form a right angle. Lines *s* and *t* are perpendicular lines. You can write this as $s \perp t$.

EXAMPLE **1** **Identify Parallel and Perpendicular Lines**

Determine whether the lines are *parallel*, *perpendicular*, or *neither*.

   a. *n* and *m*   **b.** *p* and *q*   **c.** *n* and *p*

Solution

   a. Lines *n* and *m* are parallel.

   b. Lines *p* and *q* are neither parallel nor perpendicular.

   c. Lines *n* and *p* are perpendicular.

Two lines are **skew lines** if they do not lie in the same plane. Skew lines never intersect. In the diagram, lines *c* and *b* are skew lines.

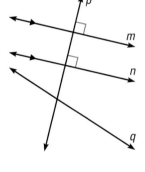

Visualize It!
Lines that intersect on the page do not necessarily intersect in space, such as lines *f* and *g*.

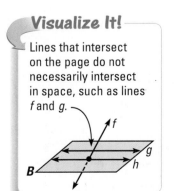

EXAMPLE **2** **Identify Skew Lines**

Determine whether the lines are skew.

   a. *f* and *h*

   b. *f* and *g*

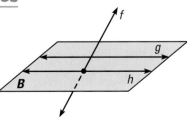

Solution

   a. Lines *f* and *h* are not skew lines because they intersect.

   b. Lines *f* and *g* are skew lines.

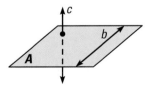

Checkpoint ✓ Identify Relationships Between Lines

Use the diagram.

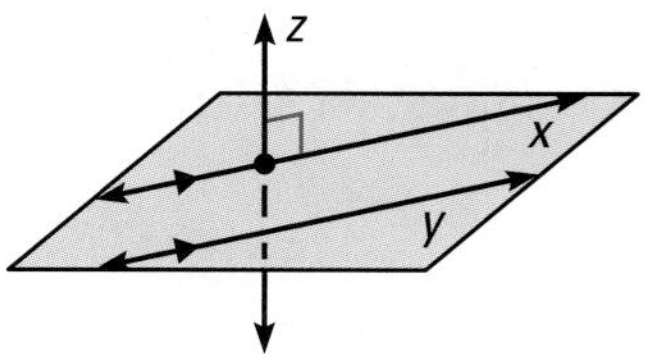

1. Name a pair of parallel lines.
2. Name a pair of perpendicular lines.
3. Name a pair of skew lines.

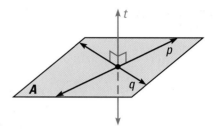

Two planes are **parallel planes** if they do not intersect. A **line perpendicular to a plane** is a line that intersects a plane in a point and that is perpendicular to every line in the plane that intersects it.

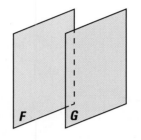

Plane *F* **is parallel to** plane *G*.

Line *t* **is perpendicular to** plane *A*.

EXAMPLE 3 Identify Relationships in Space

a. Name a plane that appears parallel to plane *B*.

b. Name a line that appears perpendicular to plane *B*.

Solution

a. Plane *C* appears parallel to plane *B*.

b. Line ℓ appears perpendicular to plane *B*.

Checkpoint ✓ Identify Relationships in Space

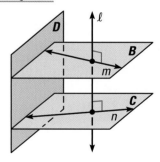

Think of each segment in the diagram as part of a line.

4. Name a line that is skew to $\overleftrightarrow{VW}$.
5. Name a plane that appears parallel to plane *VWX*.
6. Name a line that is perpendicular to plane *VWX*.

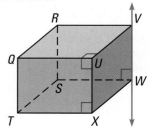

3.1 Exercises

Guided Practice

Vocabulary Check

1. How are *skew lines* and *parallel lines* alike? How are they different?

Skill Check

Fill in the blank with ∥ or ⊥ to make the statement true.

2. Line *k* __?__ line *m*.

3. Line *m* __?__ line *ℓ*.

4. Line *ℓ* __?__ line *j*.

5. Line *k* __?__ line *j*.

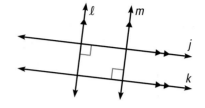

Match the photo with the corresponding description of the chopsticks.

A. skew   **B.** parallel   **C.** intersecting

6. 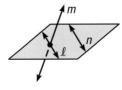   **7.** 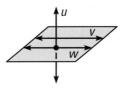   **8.**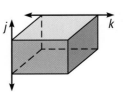

Practice and Applications

Extra Practice

See p. 679.

Line Relationships Determine whether the lines are *parallel*, *perpendicular*, or *neither*.

9. *a* and *c*   **10.** *q* and *s*   **11.** *y* and *z*

Skew Lines Determine whether the lines are skew. Explain.

12. *u* and *w*   **13.** *m* and *n*   **14.** *j* and *k*

Homework Help

Example 1: Exs. 9–11
Example 2: Exs. 12–14
Example 3: Exs. 15–19,
          21–24

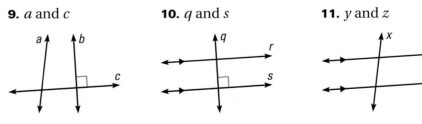
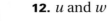

Identifying Relationships **In Exercises 15–19, think of each segment in the diagram as part of a line. Fill in the blank with *parallel, perpendicular,* or *skew*.**

15. $\overleftrightarrow{DE}$, $\overleftrightarrow{AB}$, and $\overleftrightarrow{GC}$ appear to be __?__.

16. $\overleftrightarrow{DE}$ and $\overleftrightarrow{BE}$ are __?__.

17. $\overleftrightarrow{BE}$ and $\overleftrightarrow{GC}$ are __?__ .

18. $\overleftrightarrow{BE}$ is __?__ to plane *DEF*.

19. Plane *GAD* and plane *CBE* appear to be __?__.

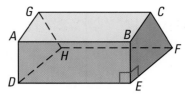

20. Tightrope Walking Philippe Petit sometimes uses a long pole to help him balance on the tightrope. Are the rope and the pole at the left *intersecting, perpendicular, parallel,* or *skew*?

Link to Balance

PHILIPPE PETIT, the French highwire artist, walked more than 2000 feet up an inclined cable to the Eiffel Tower. The photo above is from a performance in New York City.

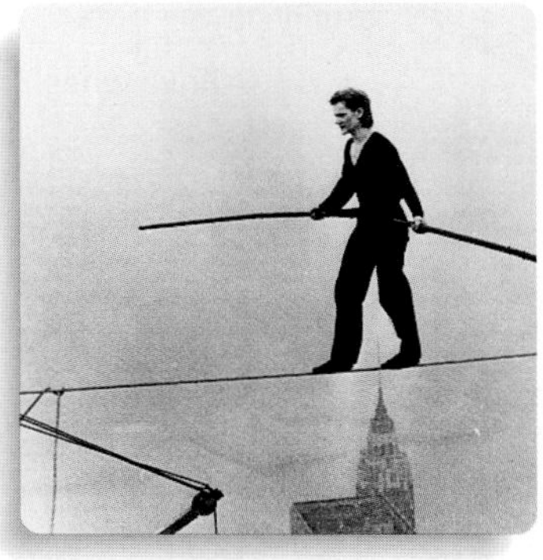

Relationships in Space **Think of each segment in the diagram below as part of a line. There may be more than one correct answer.**

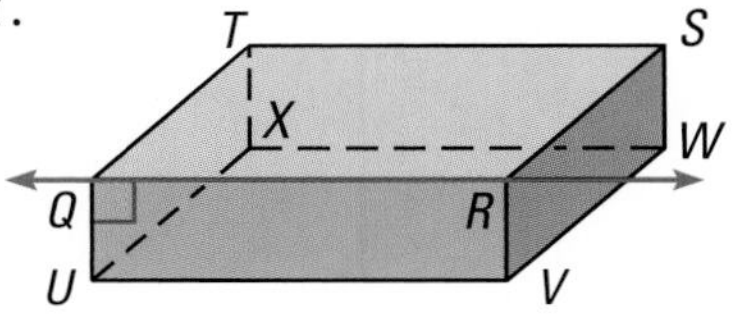

21. Name a line that appears parallel to $\overleftrightarrow{QR}$.

22. Name a line perpendicular to $\overleftrightarrow{QR}$.

23. Name a line skew to $\overleftrightarrow{QR}$.

24. Name a plane that appears parallel to plane *QRS*.

Visualize It! **Sketch a figure that fits the description.**

25. Three lines that are parallel

26. A line that is perpendicular to two parallel lines

27. Two planes that intersect

28. A line that is perpendicular to two parallel planes

29. A line that is perpendicular to two skew lines (*Hint*: Start by sketching a figure like the one above in Exercises 21–24.)

Furniture Design **In Exercises 30–33, use the photo of the chair designed by Mario Botta shown at the right.**

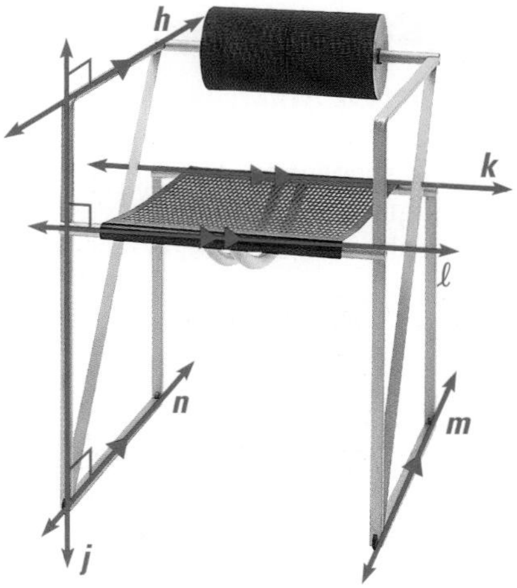

30. Name two pairs of parallel lines.

31. What kind of lines are *h* and *m*?

32. Name two lines that are skew.

33. How many lines shown on the chair are perpendicular to *j*?

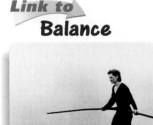

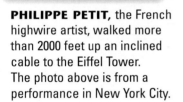

Escalators In Exercises 34 and 35, use the following information.
When a step on an up-escalator
reaches the top, it flips over and
goes back down to the bottom.
On each step, let plane *A* be the
plane you stand on.

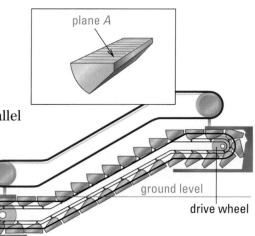

plane *A*

ground level

drive wheel

34. As each step moves around the
escalator, is plane *A* always parallel
to the ground level? Explain.

35. When a person is standing
on plane *A*, is it parallel to
ground level? Explain.

EXAMPLE *Sketch a Prism*

A *prism* is a three-dimensional figure with two identical faces,
called *bases*, that lie in parallel planes as shown below.

a. Sketch a prism with bases that have
six sides. Label the prism.

b. Name two edges that appear parallel.

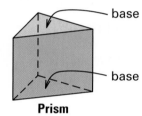

base

base

Prism

Solution

a. To draw the prism, follow these steps.

❶ *Sketch* two identical bases in
parallel planes. In this case,
the bases have six sides.

❷ *Connect* the bases and make
hidden edges dashed. Label
the prism.

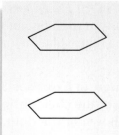

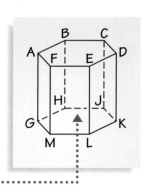

Student Help

VISUAL STRATEGY
Use dashed lines
to show parts of a
figure that are hidden
behind other parts. ••••••

b. Edges $\overline{AG}$ and $\overline{DK}$ appear parallel.

**Prisms Sketch a prism with bases that have the given number of
sides. Label the prism. Name two edges that appear parallel.**

36. Three sides   **37.** Four sides   **38.** Five sides

Challenge Fill in the blank with *always*, *sometimes*, or *never*.

39. Two skew lines are __?__ parallel.

40. Two perpendicular lines __?__ intersect.

41. Two skew lines are __?__ coplanar.

42. Multiple Choice Two lines are __?__ lines if they do not lie in the same plane and they do not intersect.

    (A) perpendicular   **(B)** parallel

    (C) coplanar   **(D)** skew

43. Multiple Choice Use the diagram below to determine which of the following statements is *false*. Think of each segment in the diagram as part of a line.

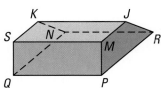

    (F) $\overleftrightarrow{QP}$ and $\overleftrightarrow{MP}$ are not parallel.

    (G) $\overleftrightarrow{MP}$ and $\overleftrightarrow{NR}$ are skew.

    (H) $\overleftrightarrow{JM}$ and $\overleftrightarrow{KS}$ are perpendicular.

    (J) Plane *KJM* and plane *QPM* are not parallel.

If-Then Statements Identify the hypothesis and the conclusion of the if-then statement. *(Lesson 2.5)*

44. If the band plays, then each member gets $50.

45. If $m\angle 5 = 120°$, then $\angle 5$ is obtuse.

46. If there is a sale, then the store will be crowded.

47. If we can get tickets, then we'll go to the movies.

Properties of Congruence Use the property to complete the statement. *(Lesson 2.6)*

48. *Reflexive Property of Congruence:* __?__ $\cong \angle XYZ$

49. *Symmetric Property of Congruence:* If $\angle 1 \cong \angle 2$, then __?__ $\cong$ __?__ .

50. *Transitive Property of Congruence:* If $\overline{AB} \cong \overline{EF}$ and $\overline{EF} \cong \overline{ST}$, then __?__ $\cong$ __?__ .

Reciprocals Find the reciprocal. *(Skills Review, p. 656)*

51. 26   **52.** -7 **53.** 10   **54.** $\dfrac{3}{8}$

Integers Evaluate. *(Skills Review, p. 663)*

55. $18 + (-3)$ **56.** $-4 \div 2$ **57.** $17 + (-6)$ **58.** $16 - (-5)$

59. $-5 + 31$ **60.** $24 - 28$ **61.** $(-8)(-10)$ **62.** $-25 - 19$

3.2

Theorems About Perpendicular Lines

Goal
Use theorems about perpendicular lines.

Key Words
- complementary angles p. 67
- perpendicular lines p. 108

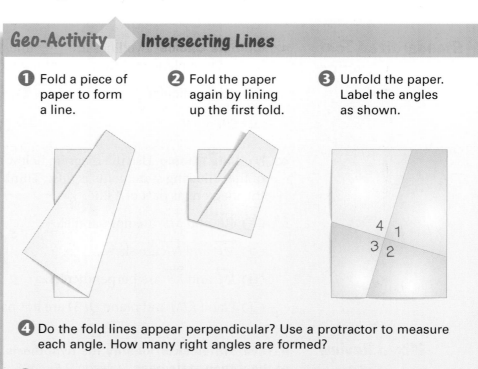

Geo-Activity ▸ **Intersecting Lines**

① Fold a piece of paper to form a line.

② Fold the paper again by lining up the first fold.

③ Unfold the paper. Label the angles as shown.

④ Do the fold lines appear perpendicular? Use a protractor to measure each angle. How many right angles are formed?

⑤ Write one or more conjectures about perpendicular lines.

The Geo-Activity above suggests the following theorems about perpendicular lines.

Student Help

STUDY TIP

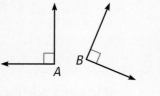

Theorem 3.2 tells you that if one right angle is marked on a pair of intersecting lines, then the other three angles are also right angles.

THEOREMS 3.1 and 3.2

Theorem 3.1

Words All right angles are congruent.

Symbols If $m\angle A = 90°$ and $m\angle B = 90°$, then $\angle A \cong \angle B$.

Theorem 3.2

Words If two lines are perpendicular, then they intersect to form four right angles.

Symbols If $n \perp m$, then $m\angle 1 = 90°$, $m\angle 2 = 90°$, $m\angle 3 = 90°$, and $m\angle 4 = 90°$.

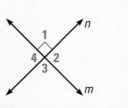

EXAMPLE **1** **Perpendicular Lines and Reasoning**

In the diagram, $r \perp s$ and $r \perp t$. Determine whether enough information is given to conclude that the statement is true. Explain your reasoning.

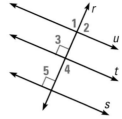

a. $\angle 3 \cong \angle 5$

b. $\angle 4 \cong \angle 5$

c. $\angle 2 \cong \angle 3$

Solution

a. Yes, enough information is given. Both angles are right angles. By Theorem 3.1, they are congruent.

b. Yes, enough information is given. Lines r and t are perpendicular. So, by Theorem 3.2, $\angle 4$ is a right angle. By Theorem 3.1, all right angles are congruent.

c. Not enough information is given to conclude that $\angle 2 \cong \angle 3$.

Checkpoint ✓ **Perpendicular Lines and Reasoning**

In the diagram, $g \perp e$ and $g \perp f$. Determine whether enough information is given to conclude that the statement is true. Explain.

1. $\angle 6 \cong \angle 10$ **2.** $\angle 7 \cong \angle 10$

3. $\angle 6 \cong \angle 8$ **4.** $\angle 7 \cong \angle 11$

5. $\angle 7 \cong \angle 9$ **6.** $\angle 6 \cong \angle 11$

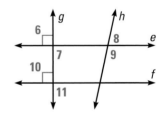

Student Help

LOOK BACK
Theorems 3.3 and 3.4 refer to *adjacent angles.* For the definition of adjacent angles, see p. 68.

THEOREMS 3.3 and 3.4

Theorem 3.3

Words If two lines intersect to form adjacent congruent angles, then the lines are perpendicular.

Symbols If $\angle 1 \cong \angle 2$, then $\overleftrightarrow{AC} \perp \overleftrightarrow{BD}$.

Theorem 3.4

Words If two sides of adjacent acute angles are perpendicular, then the angles are complementary.

Symbols If $\overrightarrow{EF} \perp \overrightarrow{EH}$, then $m\angle 3 + m\angle 4 = 90°$.

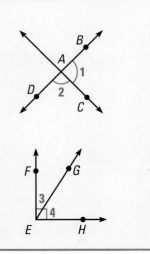

HELICOPTERS Main rotors of a helicopter may have two to eight blades. The blades create the helicopter's lift power.

EXAMPLE 2 Use Theorems About Perpendicular Lines

In the helicopter at the right, are ∠AXB and ∠CXB right angles? Explain.

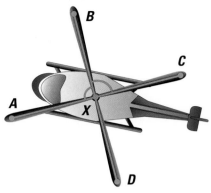

Solution

If two lines intersect to form adjacent congruent angles, as $\overline{AC}$ and $\overline{BD}$ do, then the lines are perpendicular (Theorem 3.3). So, $\overline{AC} \perp \overline{BD}$.

Because $\overline{AC}$ and $\overline{BD}$ are perpendicular, they form four right angles (Theorem 3.2). So, ∠AXB and ∠CXB are right angles.

EXAMPLE 3 Use Algebra with Perpendicular Lines

In the diagram at the right, $\overrightarrow{EF} \perp \overrightarrow{EH}$ and $m\angle GEH = 30°$. Find the value of y.

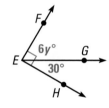

Solution

∠FEG and ∠GEH are adjacent acute angles and $\overrightarrow{EF} \perp \overrightarrow{EH}$. So, ∠FEG and ∠GEH are complementary (Theorem 3.4).

$6y° + 30° = 90°$ $m\angle FEG + m\angle GEH = 90°$

$6y = 60$ Subtract 30 from each side.

$y = 10$ Divide each side by 6.

ANSWER ▶ The value of y is 10.

Checkpoint ✓ **Use Algebra with Perpendicular Lines**

Find the value of the variable. Explain your reasoning.

7. ∠EFG ≅ ∠HFG   **8.** $\overrightarrow{AB} \perp \overrightarrow{AD}$ 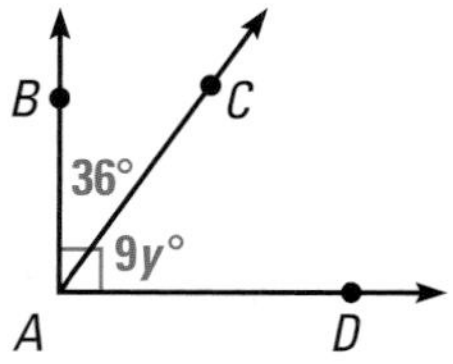   **9.** $\overrightarrow{KJ} \perp \overrightarrow{KL}$, ∠JKM ≅ ∠MKL

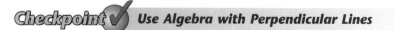

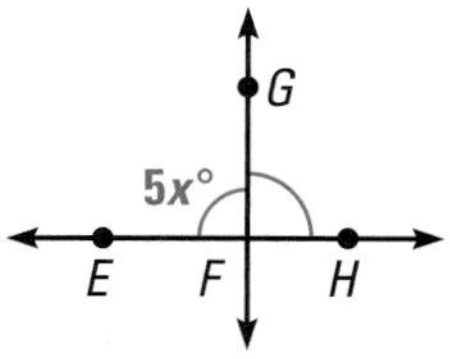

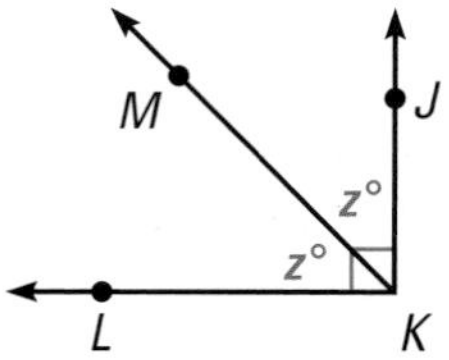

3.2 Exercises

Guided Practice

Vocabulary Check

1. Complete the statement: If two lines intersect to form adjacent congruent angles, then the lines are __?__.

Skill Check

Write the theorem that justifies the statement about the diagram.

2. ∠5 and ∠6 are right angles.

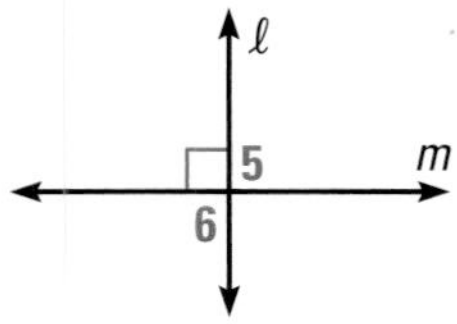

3. $j \perp k$

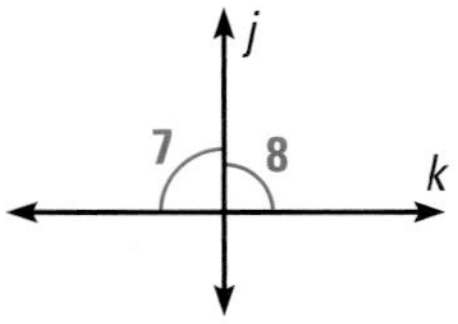

4. $m\angle 9 + m\angle 10 = 90°$

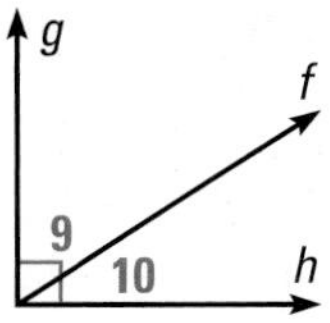

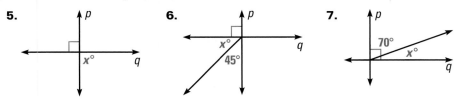

In Exercises 5–7, $p \perp q$. Write an equation to find the value of x. (Do not solve the equation.)

5.

6.

7.

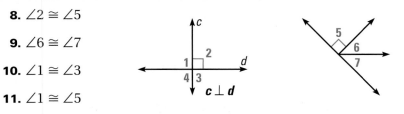

Practice and Applications

Extra Practice

See p. 679.

Perpendicular Lines and Reasoning Determine whether enough information is given to conclude that the statement is true. Explain.

8. ∠2 ≅ ∠5

9. ∠6 ≅ ∠7

10. ∠1 ≅ ∠3

11. ∠1 ≅ ∠5

Logical Reasoning What can you conclude about ∠1 and ∠2 using the given information?

12. $\overrightarrow{BA} \perp \overleftrightarrow{BC}$

13. $n \perp m$

14. $h \perp k$

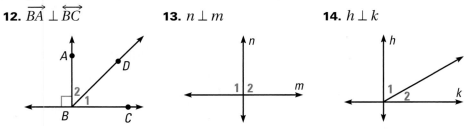

Homework Help

Example 1: Exs. 8–11
Example 2: Exs. 12–14
Example 3: Exs. 17–22

Error Analysis Students were asked to set up an equation to find the value of *x*, given that $v \perp w$. Describe and correct any errors.

15.

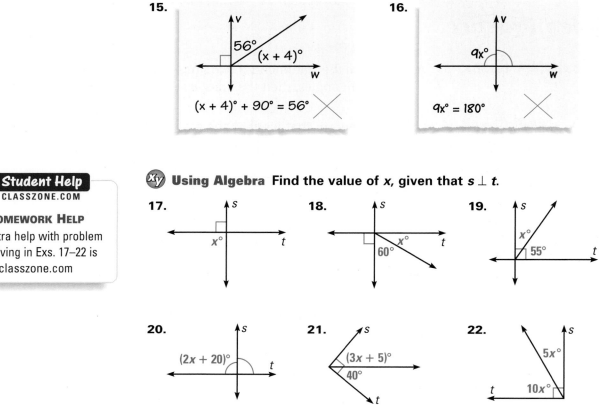

$(x + 4)° + 90° = 56°$ ✗

16.

$9x° = 180°$ ✗

Student Help

CLASSZONE.COM

HOMEWORK HELP

Extra help with problem solving in Exs. 17–22 is at classzone.com

Using Algebra Find the value of *x*, given that $s \perp t$.

17.

18.

19.

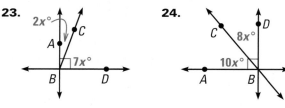

20.

21.

22.

Angle Measures Find the value of *x*, given that $\overleftrightarrow{AB} \perp \overleftrightarrow{BD}$. Then use the value of *x* to find $m\angle CBD$.

23.

24.

25.

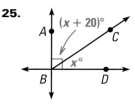

26. Window Repair You are fixing a window frame. You fit two strips of wood together to make the crosspieces. For the glass panes to fit, each angle formed by the crosspieces must be a right angle. Do you need to measure all four angles to be sure they are all right angles? Explain.

27. **You be the Judge** In the diagram shown, ∠1 and ∠3 are congruent and complementary. Can you conclude that $\overrightarrow{BA} \perp \overrightarrow{BC}$? Explain your reasoning.

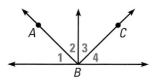

ORIENTEERING
The students above are part of an in-school orienteering training program at Clark Montessori High School in Cincinnati, Ohio.

Sports In orienteering, a compass and a map are used to navigate through a wilderness area. Suppose you are in an orienteering event and you are traveling at 40° east of magnetic north, as shown below.

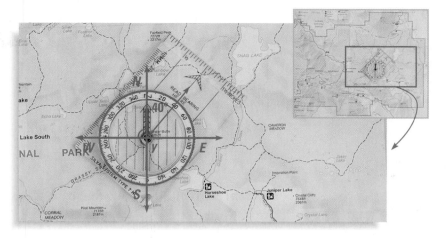

28. What can you conclude, given that ∠NYW and ∠SYW are congruent? Explain.

29. How many degrees do you need to turn to travel due east?

30. How many degrees do you need to turn to travel due south from the position shown on the compass?

Origami Origami is the Japanese art of folding pieces of paper into objects. The folds on the paper shown below are the basis for many objects. On the paper, $\overline{BF} \perp \overline{HD}$.

31. Are ∠DJE and ∠EJF complementary? Explain your reasoning.

32. If $m\angle BJC = m\angle CJD$, what are their measures?

33. Is there enough information to conclude that ∠AJG is a right angle? Explain your reasoning.

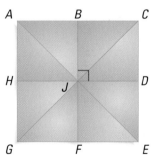

Multiple Choice In Exercises 34 and 35, use the diagram below.

34. Which of the following is true if $g \perp h$?

    (A) $m\angle 1 + m\angle 2 > 180°$

    (B) $m\angle 1 + m\angle 2 < 180°$

    (C) $m\angle 1 + m\angle 2 = 180°$

    (D) None of these

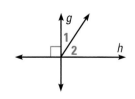

35. If $g \perp h$ and $m\angle 1 = 40°$, what is $m\angle 2$?

    (F) 40°   **(G)** 50°   **(H)** 60°   **(J)** 140°

Mixed Review

Classifying Angles State whether the angle appears to be *acute*, *right*, *obtuse*, or *straight*. Then estimate its measure. *(Lesson 1.6)*

36. 37. 38.

Finding Complements and Supplements Find the measure of the angle. *(Lesson 2.3)*

39. ∠A is a complement of ∠B, and $m\angle A = 37°$. Find $m\angle B$.

40. ∠C is a supplement of ∠D, and $m\angle C = 56°$. Find $m\angle D$.

Vertical Angles Find the value of *x*. *(Lesson 2.4)*

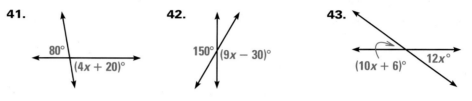

41. 80° $(4x + 20)°$

42. 150° $(9x - 30)°$

43. $(10x + 6)°$ $12x°$

Algebra Skills

Decimals Evaluate. *(Skills Review, p. 655)*

44. $13.6 + 9.8$ **45.** $14 - 2.21$ **46.** 7.4×5.9

47. $79.2 \div 9$ **48.** $100 - 4.5 - 26.1$ **49.** 30×11.1

Quiz 1

Think of each segment on the shopping bag as part of a line. There may be more than one correct answer. *(Lesson 3.1)*

1. Name two lines perpendicular to $\overleftrightarrow{FG}$.

2. Name a line skew to $\overleftrightarrow{BF}$.

3. Name a line that appears parallel to $\overleftrightarrow{AD}$.

4. Name a line perpendicular to plane *HGC*.

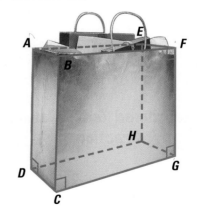

Find the value of the variable, given that $p \perp q$. *(Lesson 3.2)*

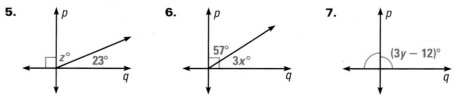

5. $z°$ 23°

6. 57° $3x°$

7. $(3y - 12)°$

3.3 Angles Formed by Transversals

Goal

Identify angles formed by transversals.

Key Words

- transversal
- corresponding angles
- alternate interior angles
- alternate exterior angles
- same-side interior angles

A **transversal** is a line that intersects two or more coplanar lines at different points. For instance, in the diagram below, the blue line t is a transversal.

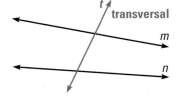

The angles formed by two lines and a transversal have special names.

Two angles are **corresponding angles** if they occupy corresponding positions.

The following pairs of angles are corresponding angles:

$\angle 1$ and $\angle 5$ $\angle 2$ and $\angle 6$

$\angle 3$ and $\angle 7$ $\angle 4$ and $\angle 8$

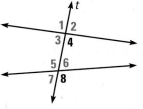

Two angles are **alternate interior angles** if they lie between the two lines on the opposite sides of the transversal.

The following pairs of angles are alternate interior angles:

$\angle 3$ and $\angle 6$

$\angle 4$ and $\angle 5$

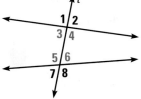

Two angles are **alternate exterior angles** if they lie outside the two lines on the opposite sides of the transversal.

The following pairs of angles are alternate exterior angles:

$\angle 1$ and $\angle 8$

$\angle 2$ and $\angle 7$

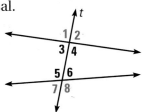

Two angles are **same-side interior angles** if they lie between the two lines on the same side of the transversal.

The following pairs of angles are same-side interior angles:

$\angle 3$ and $\angle 5$

$\angle 4$ and $\angle 6$

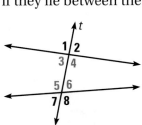

Visualize It!

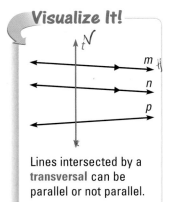

Lines intersected by a **transversal** can be parallel or not parallel.

EXAMPLE 1 **Describe Angles Formed by Transversals**

Describe the relationship between the angles.

a. ∠1 and ∠2   **b.** ∠3 and ∠4   **c.** ∠5 and ∠6

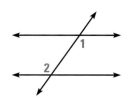 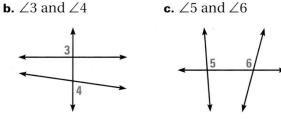

Solution

a. alternate interior angles

b. alternate exterior angles

c. same-side interior angles

Link to
Auto Racing

RACE CAR DESIGN
To maximize the speed of a race car, the angles of the front and rear wings can be adjusted.

EXAMPLE 2 **Identify Angles Formed by Transversals**

List all pairs of angles that fit the description.

a. corresponding

b. alternate exterior

c. alternate interior

d. same-side interior

Solution

a. corresponding:

∠1 and ∠5   ∠2 and ∠6

∠3 and ∠7   ∠4 and ∠8

b. alternate exterior:

∠1 and ∠8   ∠3 and ∠6

c. alternate interior:

∠2 and ∠7   ∠4 and ∠5

d. same-side interior:

∠2 and ∠5   ∠4 and ∠7

Top view of car

Checkpoint ✓ *Describe Angles Formed by Transversals*

Describe the relationship between the angles.

1. ∠2 and ∠7   **2.** ∠3 and ∠5

3. ∠1 and ∠5   **4.** ∠4 and ∠5

5. ∠4 and ∠8   **6.** ∠4 and ∠6

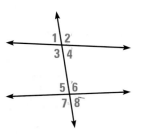

3.3 Exercises

Guided Practice

Vocabulary Check

1. Sketch two lines and a *transversal*. Shade a pair of *alternate interior angles*.

Skill Check

Match the diagram with the description of the angles.

A. alternate interior   **B.** corresponding   **C.** same-side interior

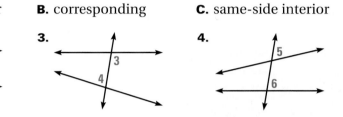

2.

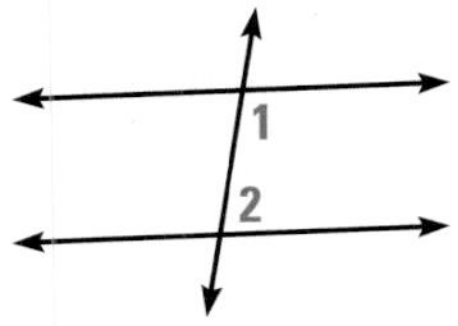

3.

4.

In Exercises 5–8, use the diagram shown below. The transversal is shown in blue.

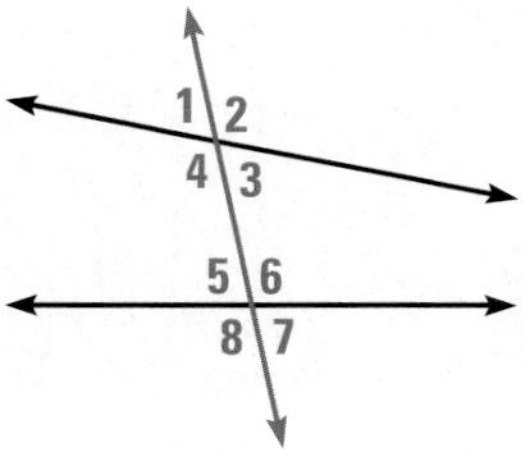

5. Name a pair of corresponding angles.

6. Name a pair of alternate interior angles.

7. Name a pair of alternate exterior angles.

8. Name a pair of same-side interior angles.

Practice and Applications

Extra Practice

See p. 679.

Describing Angles Describe the relationship between ∠1 and ∠2. The transversal is shown in blue.

9.

10.

11.

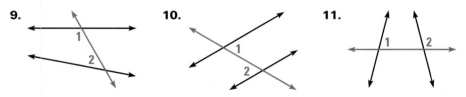

Identifying Angles Use the diagram shown. There is more than one correct answer.

Homework Help

Example 1: Exs. 9–11, 16–28
Example 2: Exs. 12–15, 29–32

12. Name a pair of corresponding angles.

13. Name a pair of alternate interior angles.

14. Name a pair of alternate exterior angles.

15. Name a pair of same-side interior angles.

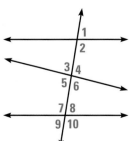

3.3 *Angles Formed by Transversals*   **123**

Describing Angles In Exercises 16–21, complete the statement using *corresponding, alternate interior, alternate exterior,* or *same-side interior.*

16. ∠6 and ∠7 are __?__ angles.

17. ∠1 and ∠6 are __?__ angles.

18. ∠2 and ∠4 are __?__ angles.

19. ∠2 and ∠6 are __?__ angles.

20. ∠4 and ∠8 are __?__ angles.

21. ∠4 and ∠7 are __?__ angles.

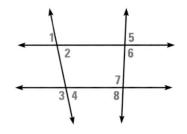

22. Bicycles In the bicycle shown, what is the relationship between ∠7 and ∠8?

Classifying Angles Use the diagram below to describe the relationship between the pair of angles.

23. ∠BCA and ∠DGJ

24. ∠DGJ and ∠FDE

25. ∠FDE and ∠KHL

26. ∠DGJ and ∠GJH

27. ∠CGH and ∠GJH

28. ∠BCA and ∠CGH

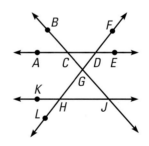

Easels Use the diagram of the easel at the right. An easel is used to display or support an artist's canvas.

29. Name two pairs of alternate exterior angles.

30. Name two pairs of same-side interior angles.

31. Name two pairs of alternate interior angles.

32. Name three pairs of corresponding angles.

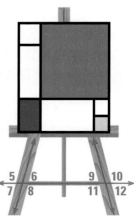

33. Challenge Sketch two lines and a transversal. Label angles 1, 2, 3, and 4 so that ∠1 and ∠2 are corresponding angles, ∠3 and ∠4 are corresponding angles, and ∠1 and ∠4 are same-side interior angles.

34. Multiple Choice In the diagram below, ∠1 and ∠3 are __?__ angles.

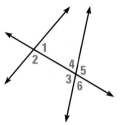

   (A) corresponding

   (B) alternate interior

   (C) alternate exterior

   (D) same-side interior

35. Multiple Choice In the diagram above, a pair of corresponding angles are __?__.

   (F) ∠1 and ∠6   (G) ∠3 and ∠5

   (H) ∠1 and ∠2   (J) None of these

Mixed Review

Line Relationships Think of each segment in the diagram as part of a line. Fill in the blank. There may be more than one correct answer. *(Lesson 3.1)*

36. $\overleftrightarrow{AD}$ and __?__ are perpendicular.

37. $\overleftrightarrow{DC}$ and __?__ appear to be parallel.

38. $\overleftrightarrow{EH}$ and __?__ are skew.

39. Plane *EFG* and plane __?__ appear to be parallel.

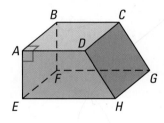

Perpendicular Lines Find the value of *x*, given that ℓ ⊥ *k*. *(Lesson 3.2)*

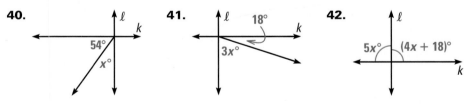

40. 54°, x°

41. 18°, 3x°

42. 5x°, (4x + 18)°

Algebra Skills

Ratios Simplify the ratio. *(Skills Review, p. 660)*

43. $\dfrac{32 \text{ ft}}{80 \text{ ft}}$ **44.** $\dfrac{6 \text{ yd}}{24 \text{ ft}}$ **45.** $\dfrac{7 \text{ ft}}{84 \text{ in.}}$ **46.** $\dfrac{10 \text{ mi}}{800 \text{ ft}}$

Evaluating Expressions Evaluate the expression when *y* = 4. *(Skills Review, p. 670)*

47. $y(y + 9)$ **48.** $y^2 - 2y$ **49.** $(y - 1)(y + 1)$

Parallel Lines and Angles

Question

What are the relationships among the angles formed when two parallel lines are cut by a transversal?

Materials

• lined paper
• straightedge
• protractor

Explore

1 On a piece of lined paper, trace over two of the lines with a pen or pencil. Label one of the parallel lines *j* and label the other *k*.

2 Draw a transversal intersecting the parallel lines. Label the transversal *t*. Label the angles as shown.

3 Use a protractor to measure all eight angles formed by the lines. Record the angle measures on a piece of paper.

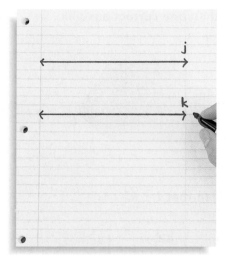

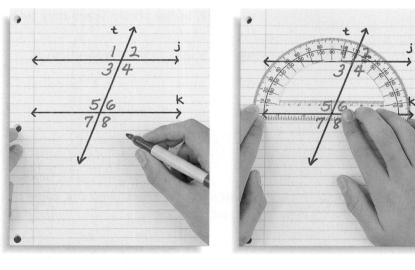

Student Help

LOOK BACK
To review definitions of corresponding, alternate interior, alternate exterior, and same-side interior angles, see p. 121.

Think About It

1. Name a pair of corresponding angles. What are their measures?

2. Name a pair of alternate interior angles. What are their measures?

3. Name a pair of alternate exterior angles. What are their measures?

4. Name a pair of same-side interior angles. What are their measures?

Explore

④ Draw two parallel lines *j* and *k*, and a transversal *s*. Label the angles as shown.

⑤ Use a protractor to measure all eight angles. Record the angle measures on a piece of paper.

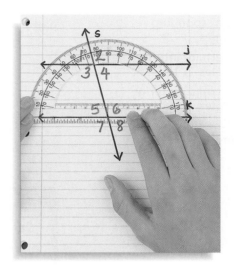

⑥ Make a table like the one shown. In the angle column, list pairs of corresponding angles. Then use your list of angle measures to complete the table.

⑦ Make a conjecture about the measures of pairs of corresponding angles when two parallel lines are cut by a transversal.

	Angle	Measure
Pair 1	∠1	?
	∠5	?
Pair 2	∠2	?
	∠6	?

Think About It

5. Repeat Steps 6 and 7 above for pairs of alternate interior angles.

6. Repeat Steps 6 and 7 above for pairs of alternate exterior angles.

7. Repeat Steps 6 and 7 above for pairs of same-side interior angles.

8. In the photo for Step 4 above, suppose ∠2 is a right angle. Is line *s* perpendicular to line *k*? Explain your reasoning.

Parallel Lines and Transversals

Goal

Find the congruent angles formed when a transversal cuts parallel lines.

Key Words

- transversal p. 121
- corresponding angles p. 121
- alternate interior angles p. 121
- alternate exterior angles p. 121
- same-side interior angles p. 121

In the photograph of the tennis court, the angle the sideline makes with the service line is the same as the angle it makes with the base line.

This photograph illustrates a postulate about angles and parallel lines.

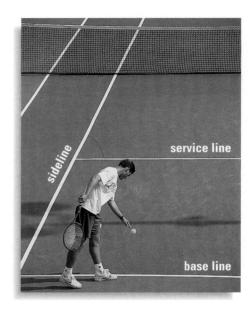

POSTULATE 8

Corresponding Angles Postulate

Words If two parallel lines are cut by a transversal, then corresponding angles are congruent.

Symbols If $j \parallel k$, then the following are true:

$$\angle 1 \cong \angle 5 \qquad \angle 2 \cong \angle 6$$
$$\angle 3 \cong \angle 7 \qquad \angle 4 \cong \angle 8$$

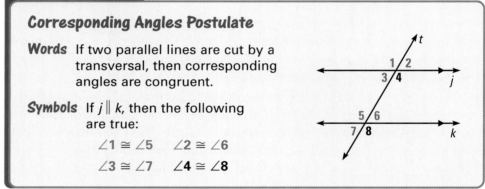

Visualize It!

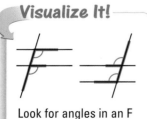

Look for angles in an F shape to help you find corresponding angles.

EXAMPLE 1 Find Measures of Corresponding Angles

Find the measure of the numbered angle.

a.

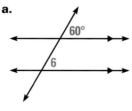

b.

c.

Solution

a. $m\angle 6 = 60°$ **b.** $m\angle 5 = 135°$ **c.** $m\angle 2 = 90°$

Find the measure of the numbered angle.

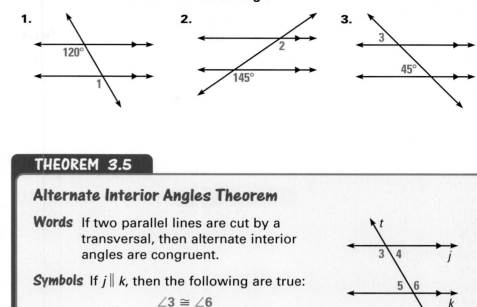

THEOREM 3.5

Alternate Interior Angles Theorem

Words If two parallel lines are cut by a transversal, then alternate interior angles are congruent.

Symbols If $j \parallel k$, then the following are true:

$$\angle 3 \cong \angle 6$$
$$\angle 4 \cong \angle 5$$

Visualize It!

Look for angles inside a Z or N shape to find alternate interior angles.

EXAMPLE 2 **Find Measures of Alternate Interior Angles**

Find the measure of $\angle PQR$.

a.   **b.**   **c.**

Solution

a. $m\angle PQR = 35°$ b. $m\angle PQR = 120°$ c. $m\angle PQR = 70°$

Find the measure of the numbered angle.

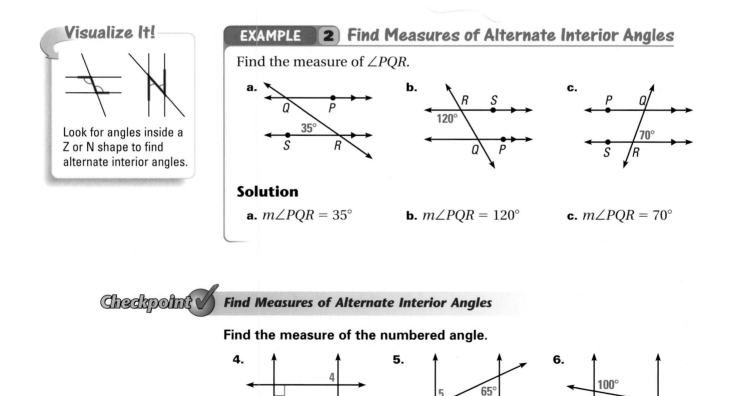

THEOREM 3.6

Alternate Exterior Angles Theorem

Words If two parallel lines are cut by a transversal, then alternate exterior angles are congruent.

Symbols If $j \parallel k$, then the following are true:

$$\angle 1 \cong \angle 8$$
$$\angle 2 \cong \angle 7$$

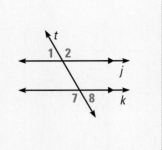

| EXAMPLE | **3** | **Find Measures of Alternate Exterior Angles** |

Find the measures of $\angle 1$ and $\angle 2$.

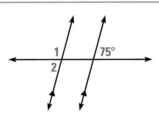

Student Help

LOOK BACK
To review linear pairs,
see p. 75. ·····················

Solution

The measure of $\angle 2$ is 75° because alternate exterior angles are congruent. The measure of $\angle 2$ can be used to find the measure of $\angle 1$.

$$m\angle 1 + m\angle 2 = 180° \qquad \text{Linear Pair Postulate}$$
$$m\angle 1 + 75° = 180° \qquad \text{Substitute } 75° \text{ for } m\angle 2.$$
$$m\angle 1 + 75° - 75° = 180° - 75° \qquad \text{Subtract } 75° \text{ from each side.}$$
$$m\angle 1 = 105° \qquad \text{Simplify.}$$

Checkpoint ✓ **Use Angle Relationships**

Find the measure of the numbered angle.

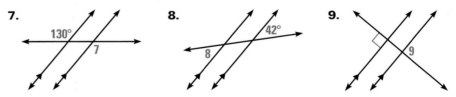

7.   **8.**   **9.**

Use the diagram below. Tell whether the angles are *congruent* or *not congruent*. Explain.

10. $\angle 1$ and $\angle 8$ **11.** $\angle 3$ and $\angle 4$

12. $\angle 4$ and $\angle 2$ **13.** $\angle 2$ and $\angle 7$

14. $\angle 3$ and $\angle 7$ **15.** $\angle 3$ and $\angle 8$

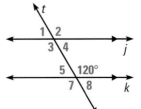

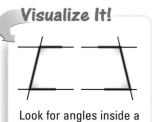

Look for angles inside a C shape to find same-side interior angles.

THEOREM 3.7

Same-Side Interior Angles Theorem

Words If two parallel lines are cut by a transversal, then same-side interior angles are supplementary.

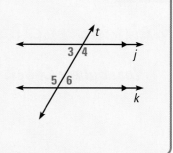

Symbols If $j \parallel k$, then the following are true:

$$m\angle 3 + m\angle 5 = 180°$$
$$m\angle 4 + m\angle 6 = 180°$$

EXAMPLE 4 **Find Measures of Same-Side Interior Angles**

Find the measure of the numbered angle.

a.

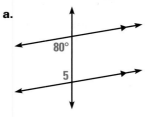

b.

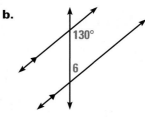

Solution

a. $m\angle 5 + 80° = 180°$

$\quad\quad m\angle 5 = 100°$

b. $m\angle 6 + 130° = 180°$

$\quad\quad\quad m\angle 6 = 50°$

Using Algebra

EXAMPLE 5 **Use Algebra with Angle Relationships**

Find the value of x.

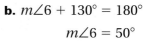

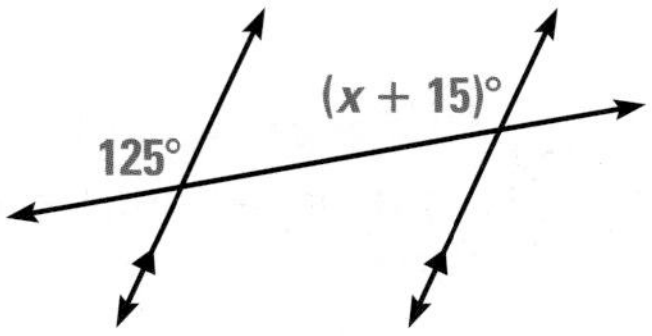

Solution

$(x + 15)° = 125°$ Corresponding Angles Postulate

$\quad\quad\quad x = 110$ Subtract 15 from each side.

Checkpoint **Use Algebra with Angle Relationships**

Find the value of **x**.

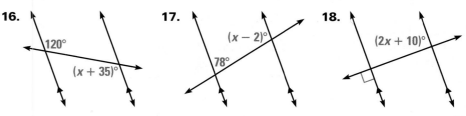

16. $120°$ $(x + 35)°$

17. $(x - 2)°$ $78°$

18. $(2x + 10)°$

3.4 Exercises

Guided Practice

Vocabulary Check

Tell whether the angles are *corresponding angles, alternate interior angles, alternate exterior angles, same-side interior angles,* or *none of these*.

1. ∠1 and ∠5   **2.** ∠5 and ∠4

3. ∠2 and ∠8   **4.** ∠6 and ∠2

5. ∠3 and ∠6   **6.** ∠7 and ∠3

7. ∠4 and ∠7   **8.** ∠8 and ∠3

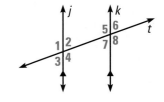

Skill Check

What postulate or theorem justifies the statement?

9. ∠10 ≅ ∠15

10. ∠12 ≅ ∠13

11. $m\angle 11 + m\angle 13 = 180°$

12. ∠9 ≅ ∠13

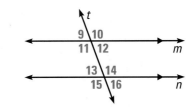

13. Logical Reasoning Two parallel lines are cut by a transversal so that one of the angles formed is a right angle. What can you say about the measures of all the other angles? Explain.

Practice and Applications

Extra Practice

See p. 679.

Visualize It! Draw two parallel lines. Use a protractor to draw a transversal so that one of the angles has the given measure. Measure all the angles and write the angle measures on your drawing.

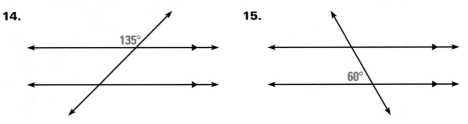

14. 135°

15. 60°

Homework Help

Example 1: Exs. 16–18
Example 2: Exs. 19–21, 25
Example 3: Exs. 22–24
Example 4: Exs. 29–31
Example 5: Exs. 32–37

Corresponding Angles Find the measure of the numbered angle.

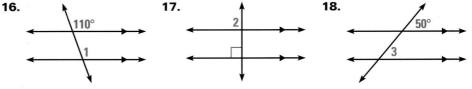

16. 110° 1

17. 2

18. 50° 3

Alternate Interior Angles Find the measure of the numbered angle.

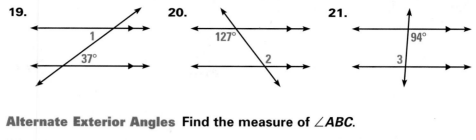

19.

20.

21.

Alternate Exterior Angles Find the measure of ∠ABC.

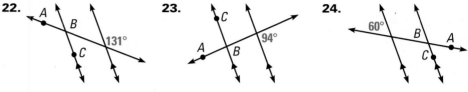

22.

23.

24.

25. **Rainbows** When sunlight enters a drop of rain, different colors leave the drop at different angles. For red light, $m\angle 2 = 42°$. What is $m\angle 1$? Explain.

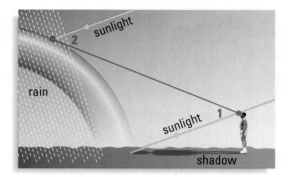

Logical Reasoning Find $m\angle 1$ and $m\angle 2$. Explain your reasoning.

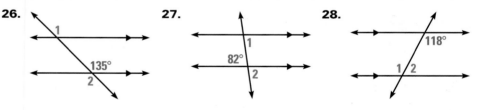

26.

27.

28.

Same-Side Interior Angles Find the measure of the numbered angle.

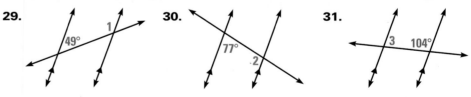

29.

30.

31.

ⓧⓨ Using Algebra Find the value of *y*.

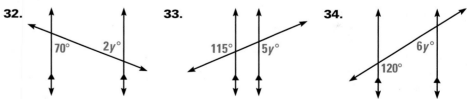

32.

33.

34.

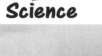

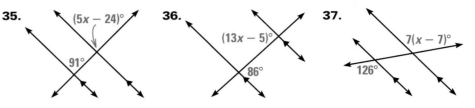

Using Algebra Find the value of *x*.

35. (5x − 24)° 91°

36. (13x − 5)° 86°

37. 7(x − 7)° 126°

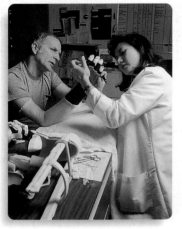
38. Physical Therapy Sports physicians and physical therapists use a
tool called a *goniometer* to measure range of motion.

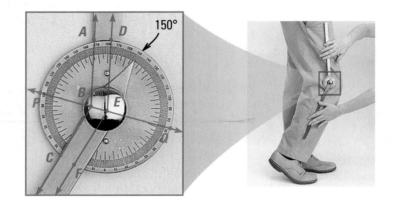

In the diagram, $\overrightarrow{BA} \parallel \overrightarrow{ED}$ and $\overrightarrow{BC} \parallel \overrightarrow{EF}$. Use the blue transversal
to explain why $\angle ABC \cong \angle DEF$.

Error Analysis A student has written some angle measures
incorrectly. Copy the diagram and correct the errors.

39. 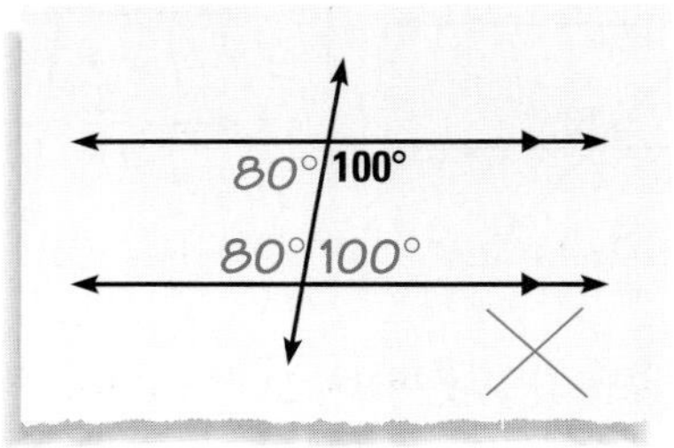 80° 100° 80° 100°

40. 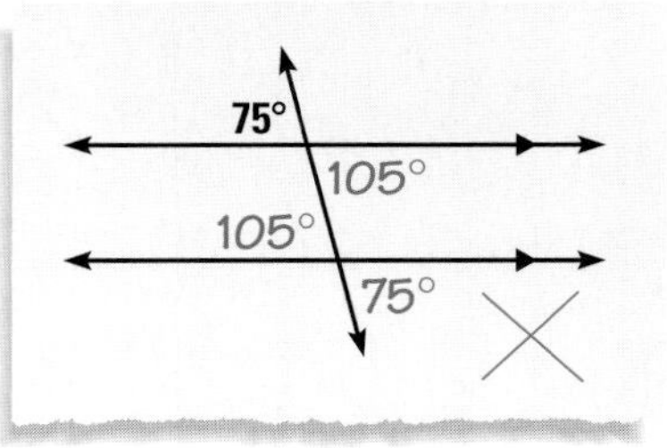 75° 105° 105° 75°

41. Multiple Choice Which statement is *false*?

Ⓐ $m\angle 2 + m\angle 5 = 180°$

Ⓑ $m\angle 5 + m\angle 6 = 180°$

Ⓒ $m\angle 6 + m\angle 7 = 180°$

Ⓓ $m\angle 3 + m\angle 8 = 180°$

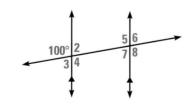

42. Multiple Choice Which statement about the diagram above
is *true*?

Ⓕ $\angle 2 \cong \angle 4$　　Ⓖ $\angle 5 \cong \angle 7$　　Ⓗ $\angle 3 \cong \angle 8$　　Ⓙ $\angle 6 \cong \angle 3$

Mixed Review

Identifying Line Relationships Fill in the blank with *parallel*, *perpendicular*, or *skew*. (Lesson 3.1)

43. Line j and line k are __?__.

44. Line j and line m are __?__.

45. Line k and line m are __?__.

46. Line m appears __?__ to plane B.

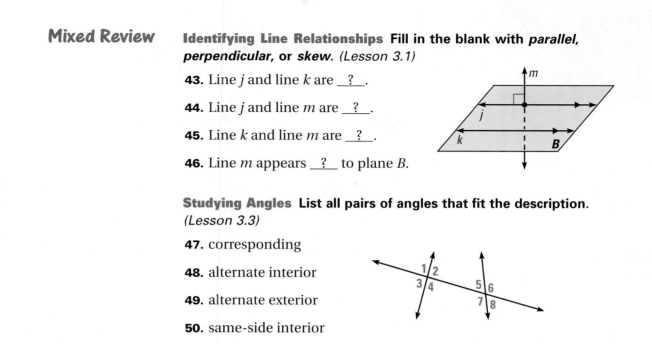

Studying Angles List all pairs of angles that fit the description. (Lesson 3.3)

47. corresponding

48. alternate interior

49. alternate exterior

50. same-side interior

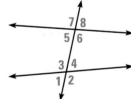

Algebra Skills

xy **Solving Equations** Solve the equation. (Skills Review, p. 673)

51. $3y - 4 = 20$ **52.** $4 - 6p = 2p - 3$ **53.** $75 + 7x = 2x$

54. $14r + 81 = -r$ **55.** $12s - 5 = 7s$ **56.** $5(z + 3) = 12$

Quiz 2

Use the diagram to describe the relationship between the pair of angles. (Lesson 3.3)

1. $\angle 1$ and $\angle 8$ **2.** $\angle 4$ and $\angle 6$

3. $\angle 6$ and $\angle 2$ **4.** $\angle 2$ and $\angle 7$

5. $\angle 4$ and $\angle 5$ **6.** $\angle 3$ and $\angle 6$

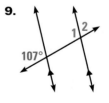

Find the measures of $\angle 1$ and $\angle 2$. (Lesson 3.4)

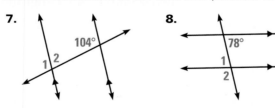

7.   **8.**   **9.**

Find the value of x. (Lesson 3.4)

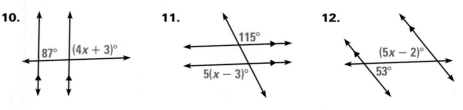

10.   **11.**   **12.**

3.5 Showing Lines are Parallel

Goal
Show that two lines are parallel.

Key Words
- converse
- hypothesis p. 82
- conclusion p. 82

Suppose two lines are cut by a transversal and a pair of corresponding angles are congruent. Are the two lines parallel? This question asks whether the *converse* of the Corresponding Angles Postulate is true.

The **converse** of an if-then statement is the statement formed by switching the hypothesis and the conclusion. Here is an example.

Statement:
  If **you live in Sacramento**, then **you live in California**.

Converse:
  If **you live in California**, then **you live in Sacramento**.

The converse of a true statement may or may not be true. As shown on the map at the right, if you live in California, you don't necessarily live in Sacramento; you could live in Fresno or San Diego.

OREGON

IDAHO

Sacramento

NEVADA

UT

Fresno

CALIFORNIA

ARIZO

San Diego

EXAMPLE 1 Write the Converse of an If-Then Statement

Statement: If two segments are congruent, then the two segments have the same length.

a. Write the converse of the true statement above.

b. Determine whether the converse is true.

Solution

a. *Converse:* If two segments have the same length, then the two segments are congruent.

b. The converse is a true statement.

Checkpoint ✓ Write the Converse of an If-Then Statement

Write the converse of the true statement. Then determine whether the converse is true.

1. If two angles have the same measure, then the two angles are congruent.

2. If $\angle 3$ and $\angle 4$ are complementary, then $m\angle 3 + m\angle 4 = 90°$.

3. If $\angle 1$ and $\angle 2$ are right angles, then $\angle 1 \cong \angle 2$.

Converse of a Postulate Postulate 9 below is the converse of Postulate 8, the Corresponding Angles Postulate, which you learned in Lesson 3.4.

POSTULATE 9

Corresponding Angles Converse

Words If two lines are cut by a transversal so that corresponding angles are congruent, then the lines are parallel.

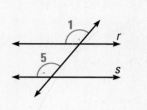

Symbols If ∠1 ≅ ∠5, then r ∥ s.

EXAMPLE 2 Apply Corresponding Angles Converse

Is enough information given to conclude that $\overleftrightarrow{BD} \parallel \overleftrightarrow{EG}$? Explain.

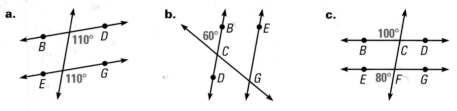

Solution

a. Yes. The two marked angles are corresponding and congruent. There is enough information to use the Corresponding Angles Converse to conclude that $\overleftrightarrow{BD} \parallel \overleftrightarrow{EG}$.

b. No. You are not given any information about the angles formed where $\overleftrightarrow{EG}$ intersects $\overleftrightarrow{CG}$.

c. Yes. You can conclude that $m\angle EFC = 100°$. So, there is enough information to use the Corresponding Angles Converse to conclude that $\overleftrightarrow{BD} \parallel \overleftrightarrow{EG}$.

Checkpoint ✓ **Apply Corresponding Angles Converse**

Is enough information given to conclude that $\overleftrightarrow{RT} \parallel \overleftrightarrow{XZ}$? Explain.

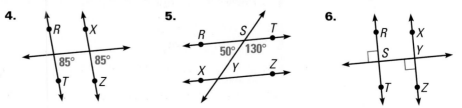

LOOK BACK
To review the Alternate Interior Angles Theorem and the Alternate Exterior Angles Theorem, see pp. 129–130.

THEOREMS 3.8 and 3.9

3.8 Alternate Interior Angles Converse

Words If two lines are cut by a transversal so that alternate interior angles are congruent, then the lines are parallel.

Symbols If $\angle 4 \cong \angle 5$, then $r \parallel s$.

3.9 Alternate Exterior Angles Converse

Words If two lines are cut by a transversal so that alternate exterior angles are congruent, then the lines are parallel.

Symbols If $\angle 1 \cong \angle 8$, then $r \parallel s$.

EXAMPLE 3 Identify Parallel Lines

Does the diagram give enough information to conclude that $m \parallel n$?

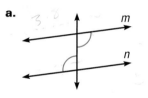
a.

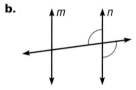
b.

Solution

a. Yes. The angle congruence marks on the diagram allow you to conclude that $m \parallel n$ by the Alternate Interior Angles Converse.

b. No. Not enough information is given to conclude that $m \parallel n$.

Checkpoint *Identify Parallel Lines*

7. Does the diagram give enough information to conclude that $c \parallel d$? Explain.

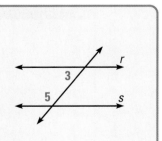

THEOREM 3.10

Same-Side Interior Angles Converse

Words If two lines are cut by a transversal so that same-side interior angles are supplementary, then the lines are parallel.

Symbols If $m\angle 3 + m\angle 5 = 180°$, then $r \parallel s$.

Using Algebra

EXAMPLE **4** **Use Same-Side Interior Angles Converse**

Find the value of x so that $j \parallel k$.

Solution

Lines j and k are parallel if the marked angles are supplementary.

$$5x° + 115° = 180° \quad \text{Supplementary angles}$$
$$5x = 65 \quad \text{Subtract 115 from each side.}$$
$$x = 13 \quad \text{Divide each side by 5.}$$

ANSWER ▶ So, if $x = 13$, then $j \parallel k$.

U.S. Navy Blue Angels

Checkpoint ✓ **Use Same-Side Interior Angles Converse**

Find the value of **x** so that **v ∥ w**.

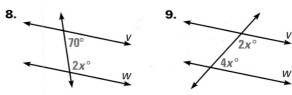

8. 70° ... 2x°

9. 2x° ... 4x°

10. (x + 22)°

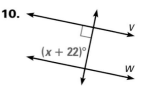

3.5 Exercises

Guided Practice

Vocabulary Check

1. Describe how to form the *converse* of an if-then statement.

2. Give an example of an if-then statement and its *converse*.

Skill Check

Match the theorem or postulate used to explain why $p \parallel q$ with the diagram.

3. Same-Side Interior Angles Converse

4. Alternate Interior Angles Converse

5. Corresponding Angles Converse

A. 62° ... 62°

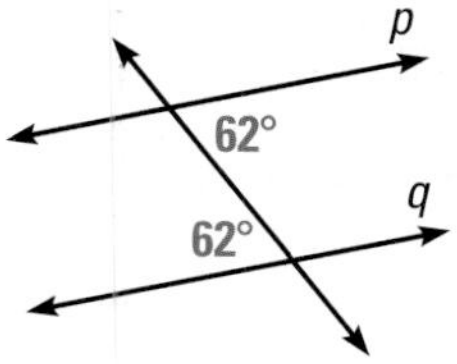

B. 105° ... 105°

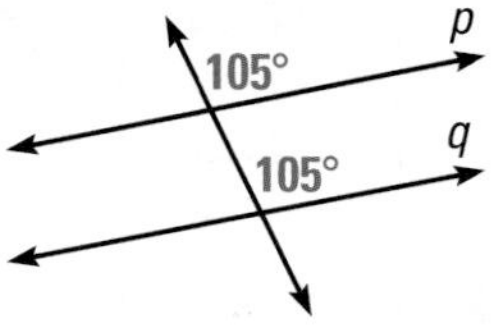

C. 123° ... 57°

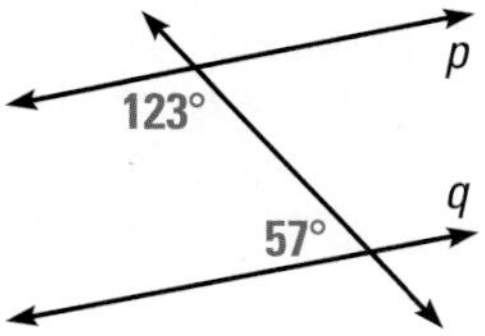

Practice and Applications

Extra Practice

See p. 680.

Writing Converses In Exercises 6–9, write the converse of the true statement. Then determine whether the converse is true.

6. If two lines never intersect in a plane, then the lines are parallel.

7. If ∠1 and ∠2 are supplementary, then $m∠1 + m∠2 = 180°$.

8. If ∠A measures 38°, then ∠A is acute.

9. If ∠B measures 123°, then ∠B is obtuse.

Identifying Parallel Lines Determine whether enough information is given to conclude that $m \parallel n$. Explain.

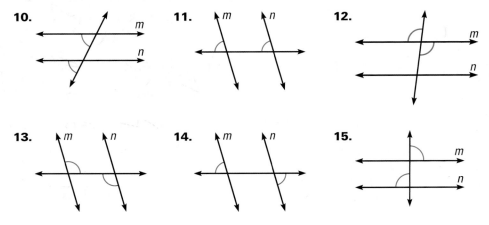

10.　　**11.**　　**12.**

13.　　**14.**　　**15.**

Visualize It! Sketch the described figure.

16. Draw two parallel lines and a transversal with ∠3 and ∠4 as congruent corresponding angles so that $m∠3 = m∠4 = 60°$.

17. Draw two parallel lines and a transversal with ∠5 and ∠6 as same-side interior angles so that $m∠5 = 45°$.

Logical Reasoning Are $\overleftrightarrow{AC}$ and $\overleftrightarrow{DF}$ parallel? Explain.

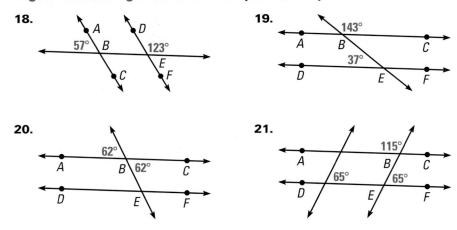

18.　　**19.**

Homework Help

Example 1: Exs. 6–9
Example 2: Exs. 10–15
Example 3: Exs. 10–15
Example 4: Exs. 24–29

20.　　**21.**

22. 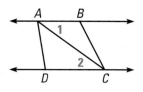 **You be the Judge** In the diagram, $\angle 1 \cong \angle 2$. One of your classmates states that if $\angle 1 \cong \angle 2$, then $\overleftrightarrow{AB} \parallel \overleftrightarrow{DC}$. Is your classmate right? Explain your reasoning.

23. Kiteboarding The lines on the photo of the kiteboarder below show the angles formed between the control bar and the kite lines. Find the value of x so that $n \parallel m$.

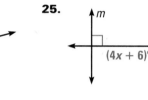 **Using Algebra** Find the value of x so that $m \parallel n$.

24.

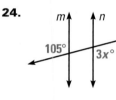

25.

26.

27.

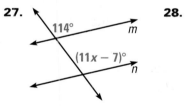

28.

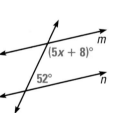

29.

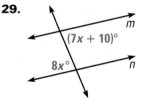

30. Technology Use geometry software to draw two parallel segments and a transversal. Choose a pair of alternate interior angles and construct their angle bisectors. Make a conjecture about the bisectors. Describe how to show that your conjecture is true.

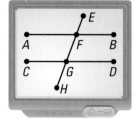

Logical Reasoning Name two parallel lines. Explain your reasoning.

31.

32.

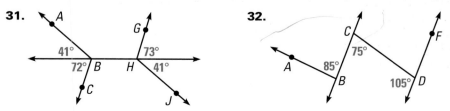

33. Building Stairs One way to build
stairs is to attach triangular blocks
to an angled support, as shown at
the right. The sides of the angled
support are parallel. If the support
makes a 32° angle with the floor,
what must $m\angle 1$ be so the top of the
step will be parallel to the floor?

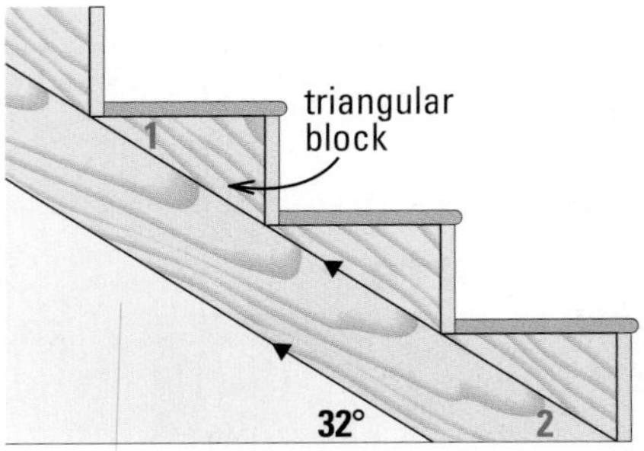

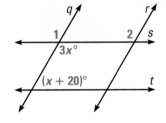

triangular
block

32°

34. Challenge Using the diagram shown, find the
measures of $\angle 1$ and $\angle 4$ so that $f \parallel g$.

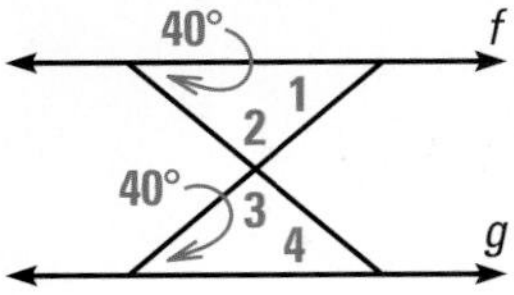

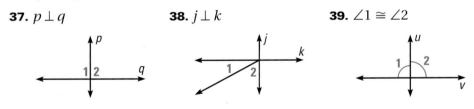

40°

40°

f

g

1
2
3
4

Multiple Choice In Exercises 35 and 36, use the diagram below.

35. If $\angle 1 \cong \angle 2$, which statement is true?

(A) $r \parallel s$

(B) $q \parallel r$

(C) $s \parallel t$

(D) None of these

36. Find the value of x so that $s \parallel t$.

(F) 10

(G) 40

(H) 50

(J) 60

q r

1 2 s

$3x°$

$(x + 20)°$ t

Mixed Review

**Perpendicular Lines What can you conclude about $\angle 1$ and $\angle 2$
using the given information?** *(Lesson 3.2)*

37. $p \perp q$

38. $j \perp k$

39. $\angle 1 \cong \angle 2$

p

1 2 q

j

k

1 2

u

1 2

v

Angle Measures In the diagram below, $m \parallel n$. *(Lessons 3.3, 3.4)*

40. What kind of angles are $\angle 1$ and $\angle 5$?

41. What kind of angles are $\angle 1$ and $\angle 2$?

42. What is the measure of $\angle 4$?

43. What is the measure of $\angle 2$?

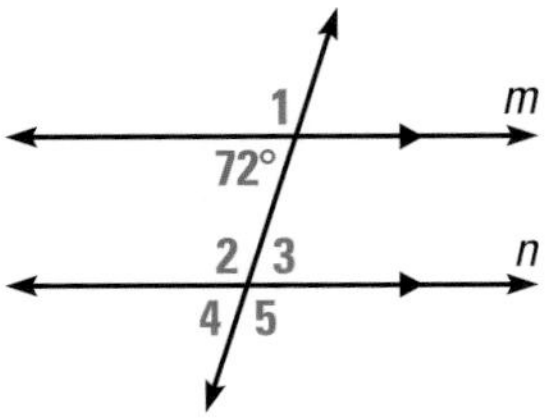

1 m

$72°$

2 3 n

4 5

Algebra Skills

**Evaluating Fractions Add or subtract. Write the answer in simplest
form.** *(Skills Review, p. 658)*

44. $\dfrac{3}{8} + \dfrac{7}{8}$

45. $\dfrac{9}{11} - \dfrac{2}{11}$

46. $\dfrac{7}{12} + \dfrac{5}{12}$

47. $\dfrac{8}{9} - \dfrac{2}{9}$

3.6 Using Perpendicular and Parallel Lines

Goal

Construct parallel and perpendicular lines. Use properties of parallel and perpendicular lines.

Key Words

• construction

A **construction** is a geometric drawing that uses a limited set of tools, usually a compass and a straightedge (a ruler without marks).

compass   **straightedge**

Geo-Activity — Constructing a Perpendicular to a Line

Use the following steps to construct a perpendicular to a line in two different cases:

	Line perpendicular to a line through a point *not* on the line.	Line perpendicular to a line through a point *on* the line.
① Place the compass at point *P* and draw an arc that intersects line ℓ twice. Label the intersections *A* and *B*.	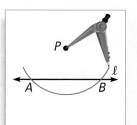	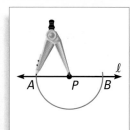
② Open your compass wider. Draw an arc with center *A*. Using the same radius, draw an arc with center *B*. Label the intersection of the arcs *Q*.	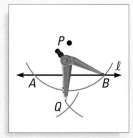	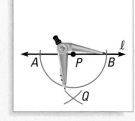
③ Use a straightedge to draw $\overleftrightarrow{PQ}$. $\overleftrightarrow{PQ} \perp \ell$.	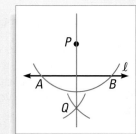	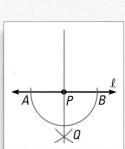

EXAMPLE 1 Construct Parallel Lines

Construct a line that passes through point *P* and is parallel to line *ℓ*.

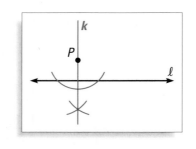

Solution

① ***Construct*** a line perpendicular to *ℓ* through *P* using the construction on the previous page. Label the line *k*.

② ***Construct*** a line perpendicular to *k* through *P* using the construction on the previous page. Label the line *j*. Line *j* is parallel to line *ℓ*.

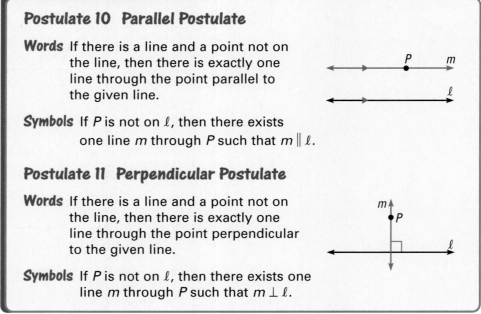

Checkpoint ✔ **Construct Parallel Lines**

1. Draw a line *c* and a point *A* not on the line. Construct a line *d* that passes through point *A* and is parallel to line *c*.

POSTULATES 10 and 11

Postulate 10 Parallel Postulate

Words If there is a line and a point not on the line, then there is exactly one line through the point parallel to the given line.

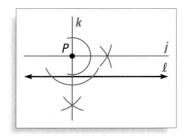

Symbols If *P* is not on *ℓ*, then there exists one line *m* through *P* such that *m* ∥ *ℓ*.

Postulate 11 Perpendicular Postulate

Words If there is a line and a point not on the line, then there is exactly one line through the point perpendicular to the given line.

Symbols If *P* is not on *ℓ*, then there exists one line *m* through *P* such that *m* ⊥ *ℓ*.

THEOREMS 3.11 and 3.12

Theorem 3.11

Words If two lines are parallel to the same line, then they are parallel to each other.

Symbols If $q \parallel r$ and $r \parallel s$, then $q \parallel s$.

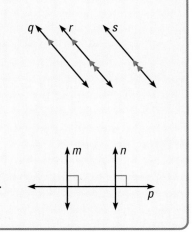

Theorem 3.12

Words In a plane, if two lines are perpendicular to the same line, then they are parallel to each other.

Symbols If $m \perp p$ and $n \perp p$, then $m \parallel n$.

Link to
History

CLIFF DWELLINGS were built mostly between 1000 and 1300 by Native Americans. The cliff dwellings above and at the right are preserved at Bandelier National Monument in New Mexico.

EXAMPLE 2 Use Properties of Parallel Lines

Ladders were used to move from level to level of cliff dwellings, as shown at right. Each rung on the ladder is parallel to the rung immediately below it. Explain why $\ell \parallel p$.

Solution

You are given that $\ell \parallel m$ and $m \parallel n$. By Theorem 3.11, $\ell \parallel n$. Since $\ell \parallel n$ and $n \parallel p$, it follows that $\ell \parallel p$.

EXAMPLE 3 Use Properties of Parallel Lines

Find the value of x that makes $\overleftrightarrow{AB} \parallel \overleftrightarrow{CD}$.

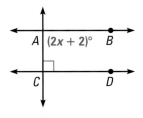

Solution

By Theorem 3.12, $\overleftrightarrow{AB}$ and $\overleftrightarrow{CD}$ will be parallel if $\overleftrightarrow{AB}$ and $\overleftrightarrow{CD}$ are both perpendicular to $\overleftrightarrow{AC}$. For this to be true $\angle BAC$ must measure 90°.

$(2x + 2)° = 90°$ *$m\angle BAC$ must be 90°.*

$2x = 88$ Subtract 2 from each side.

$x = 44$ Divide each side by 2.

ANSWER ▶ If $x = 44$, then $\overleftrightarrow{AB} \parallel \overleftrightarrow{CD}$.

2. Use the information in the diagram to explain why $a \parallel c$.

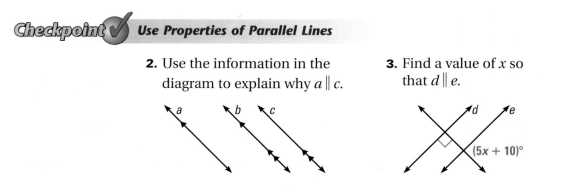

3. Find a value of x so that $d \parallel e$.

You have now studied six ways to show that two lines are parallel.

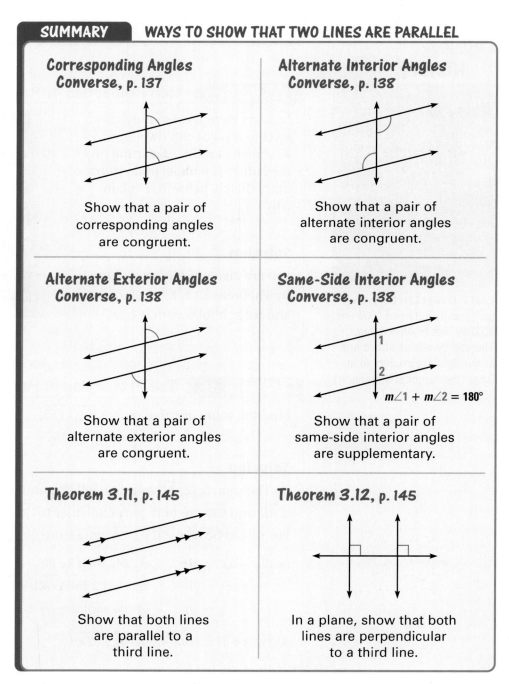

SUMMARY   **WAYS TO SHOW THAT TWO LINES ARE PARALLEL**

Corresponding Angles Converse, p. 137

Show that a pair of corresponding angles are congruent.

Alternate Interior Angles Converse, p. 138

Show that a pair of alternate interior angles are congruent.

Alternate Exterior Angles Converse, p. 138

Show that a pair of alternate exterior angles are congruent.

Same-Side Interior Angles Converse, p. 138

$m\angle 1 + m\angle 2 = 180°$

Show that a pair of same-side interior angles are supplementary.

Theorem 3.11, p. 145

Show that both lines are parallel to a third line.

Theorem 3.12, p. 145

In a plane, show that both lines are perpendicular to a third line.

3.6 Exercises

Guided Practice

Vocabulary Check **1.** What are the two basic tools used for a *construction*?

Skill Check **Using the given information, state the theorem that you can use to conclude that *r* ∥ *s*.**

2. $r \parallel t, t \parallel s$　　　　　　　　　　　**3.** $r \perp t, t \perp s$

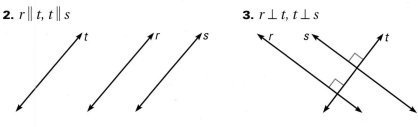

Practice and Applications

Extra Practice
See p. 680.

Logical Reasoning Using the given information, state the postulate or theorem that allows you to conclude that *j* ∥ *k*.

4. $j \parallel n, k \parallel n$　　　　　**5.** $j \perp n, k \perp n$　　　　　**6.** $\angle 1 \cong \angle 2$

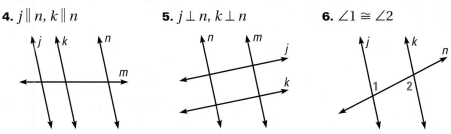

Showing Lines are Parallel Explain how you would show that *c* ∥ *d*. State any theorems or postulates that you would use.

7.　　　　　　　**8.**　　　　　　　**9.**

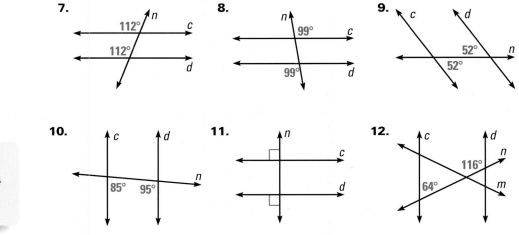

Homework Help

Example 1: Exs. 22–24
Example 2: Exs. 4–12
Example 3: Exs. 19–21

Naming Parallel Lines In Exercises 13–16, determine which lines, if any, must be parallel. Explain your reasoning.

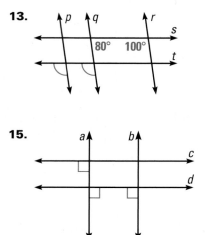

13.

14.

15.

16.

17. **Guitars** In the photo of the guitar at the right, each fret is parallel to the fret beside it. Explain why the 8th fret is parallel to the 10th fret.

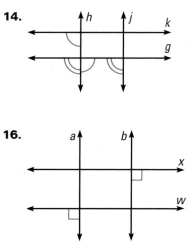

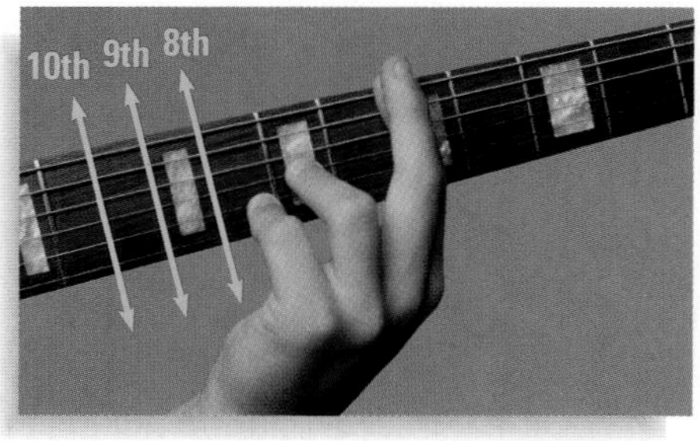

18. **Visualize It!** Make a diagonal fold on a piece of lined notebook paper. Explain how to use the angles formed to show that the lines on the paper are parallel.

Using Algebra Find the value of x so that $g \parallel h$.

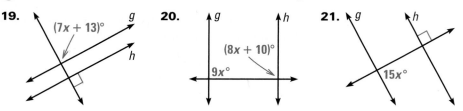

19.

$(7x + 13)°$

20.

$(8x + 10)°$

$9x°$

21.

$15x°$

Constructions In Exercises 22–24, use a compass and a straightedge to construct the lines.

22. Draw a horizontal line ℓ and choose a point P on line ℓ. Construct a line m perpendicular to line ℓ through point P.

23. Draw a vertical line ℓ and choose a point P to the right of line ℓ. Construct a line m perpendicular to line ℓ through point P.

24. Draw a horizontal line ℓ and choose a point P above line ℓ. Construct a line m parallel to line ℓ through point P.

Student Help

LOOK BACK
For an example of boats sailing at an angle to the wind, see p. 104.

25. Sailing If the wind is constant, will the boats' paths ever cross? Explain.

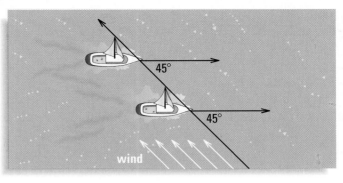

26. Challenge Theorem 3.12 applies only to lines in a plane. Draw a diagram of a three-dimensional example of two lines that are perpendicular to the same line but are not parallel to each other.

Standardized Test Practice

27. Multiple Choice Find the value of x so that $m \parallel n$.

   Ⓐ 20   Ⓑ 25

   Ⓒ 40   Ⓓ 90

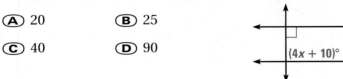

28. Multi-Step Problem Use the information given in the diagram at the right.

  a. Explain why $\overline{AB} \parallel \overline{CD}$.

  b. Explain why $\overline{CD} \parallel \overline{EF}$.

  c. What is $m\angle 1$? How do you know?

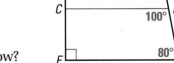

Mixed Review

Points, Lines and Planes Decide whether the statement is *true* or *false*. *(Lesson 1.3)*

29. N lies on $\overleftrightarrow{MK}$.

30. J, K, and M are collinear.

31. K lies in plane JML.

32. J lies on $\overrightarrow{KL}$.

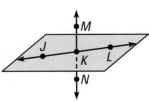

Plotting Points Plot the point in a coordinate plane. *(Skills Review, p. 664)*

33. $A(2, 3)$ **34.** $B(-1, 6)$ **35.** $C(-4, 7)$ **36.** $D(-2, -5)$

Algebra Skills

Expressions Evaluate the expression. *(Skills Review, p. 670)*

37. $-5 \cdot 6 - 10 \div 5$ **38.** $-8 + 33 - 14$ **39.** $24 \div (9 + 3)$

40. $4(8 - 3)^2 - 12$ **41.** $48 - 3^2 \cdot 5 - 6^2$ **42.** $[(1 - 8)^2 + 7] \div 8$

3.6 Parallel Lines and Slope

Question

How is slope used to show that two lines are parallel?

Explore

❶ Draw and label two segments and a transversal. Label the points of intersection.

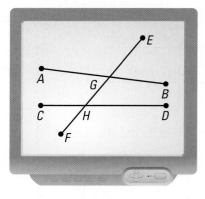

❷ Measure a pair of corresponding angles.

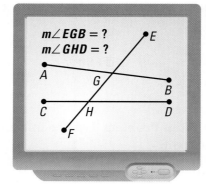

❸ Drag point *B* until the two angles measured in Step 2 are congruent.

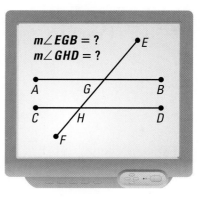

Student Help

SKILLS REVIEW
To review the slope of a line, see p. 665

Think About It

1. Are $\overline{AB}$ and $\overline{CD}$ in Step 3 parallel? What theorem does this illustrate?

   In algebra, you learned that the *slope* of a non-vertical line is the ratio of the vertical change (the rise) over the horizontal change (the run). The slope of a line can be positive or negative.

2. Measure the slopes of $\overline{AB}$ and $\overline{CD}$ in Step 3. What do you notice about the slopes?

3. Drag point *B* to a different position. Drag point *D* so that the slopes of $\overline{AB}$ and $\overline{CD}$ are equal. What are the measures of the pair of corresponding angles?

4. Make a conjecture about the slopes of parallel lines.

Explore

④ Draw a non-horizontal segment $\overline{AB}$. Construct and label two points, C and D, on $\overline{AB}$.

⑤ Construct two lines perpendicular to $\overline{AB}$ through points C and D.

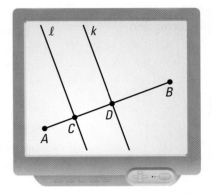

Think About It

5. What theorem allows you to conclude that the lines constructed in Step 5 are parallel?

6. Measure the slopes of the lines constructed in Step 5. Explain how to use the slopes to verify that the lines are parallel.

7. Measure the slope of $\overline{AB}$. Multiply the slope of $\overline{AB}$ by the slope of one of the other lines. What is the result?

8. Drag point B. What happens to the calculation made in Exercise 7 as the slopes of the lines change?

9. **Extension** Construct and label point E on $\overline{AB}$. Construct line m parallel to line k through point E. What theorem allows you to conclude that lines ℓ and m are parallel? Compare the slopes of the lines to verify that they are parallel.

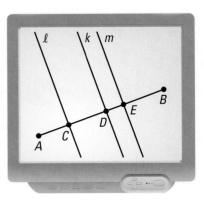

3.7 Translations

Goal
Identify and use translations.

Key Words
- translation
- image
- transformation

In 1996, New York City's Empire Theater was slid 170 feet up 42nd Street to a new location.

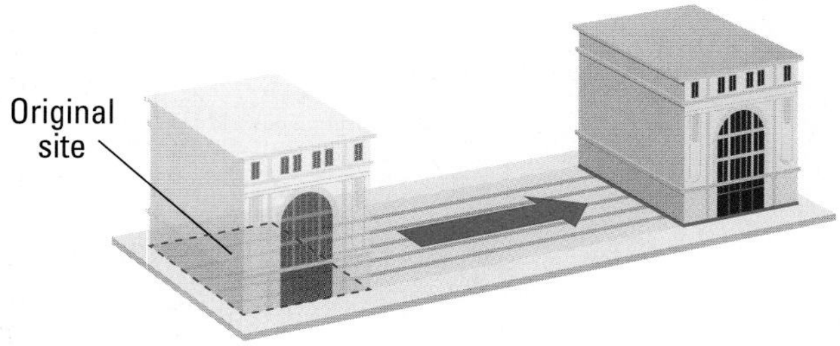

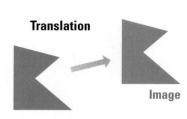

Original site

A slide is also called a **translation** . The new figure after the translation is the **image** . In this book, the original figure is given in blue and its image in red, as shown at the right.

Translation

Image

A translation is one kind of **transformation** . A transformation is an operation that *maps,* or moves, a figure an image. You will study other transformations in Lessons 5.7, 7.6, and 11.8.

Student Help

VOCABULARY TIP
Use the following relationship to help you remember that a translation is a slide:

translation
slide

EXAMPLE 1 **Compare a Figure and Its Image**

Decide whether the red figure is a translation of the blue figure.

a.   b.   c.

Solution

a. Yes, this is a translation.

b. No, this is *not* a translation. The image is a mirror image of the original figure.

c. No, this is *not* a translation. The original figure is rotated.

Checkpoint ✓ **Compare a Figure and Its Image**

Decide whether the red figure is a translation of the blue figure.

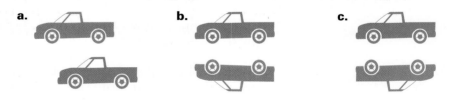

1.   2.    3.

Labeling Translations When labeling points on the image, write the prime symbol (') next to the letter used in the original figure, as shown at the right.

In a translation, segments connecting points in the original figure to their corresponding points in the image are congruent and parallel. For example, $\overline{AA'}$ and $\overline{BB'}$ at the right are congruent and parallel.

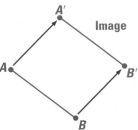

Image

EXAMPLE 2 Describe Translations

Describe the translation of the segment.

Solution

Point *P* is moved 4 units to the right and 2 units down to get to point *P'*. So, every point on $\overline{PQ}$ moves 4 units to the right and 2 units down.

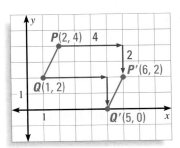

Translations in a coordinate plane can also be described using the following coordinate notation:

$$(x, y) \rightarrow (x + a, y + b)$$

Each point shifts *a* units horizontally (right or left) and *b* units vertically (up or down). When moving right or up, *add* the number of units. When moving left or down, *subtract* the number of units. Here are some examples:

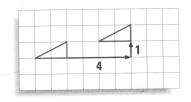   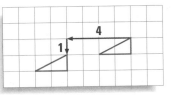

$(x, y) \rightarrow (x + 4, y + 1)$ $(x, y) \rightarrow (x - 4, y - 1)$

EXAMPLE 3 Use Coordinate Notation

Describe the translation using coordinate notation.

Solution

Each point is moved 3 units to the left and 4 units up.

ANSWER The translation can be described using the notation $(x, y) \rightarrow (x - 3, y + 4)$.

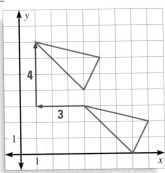

Checkpoint ✓ Describe Translations

Describe the translation using words and coordinate notation.

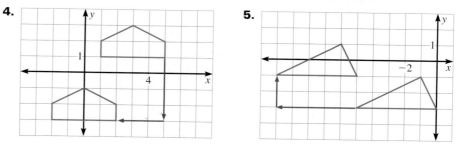

4.

5.

EXAMPLE 4 Draw Translated Figures

Draw the triangle given by points $A(-2, 5)$, $B(0, 7)$, and $C(3, 7)$. Then draw the image of the triangle after the translation given by $(x, y) \rightarrow (x + 2, y - 3)$.

Solution

First, sketch $\triangle ABC$ as shown. To find points A', B', and C', start at points A, B, and C, and slide each point 2 units to the right and 3 units down.

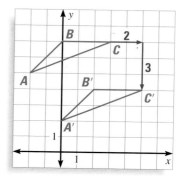

$\triangle ABC$	$\triangle A'B'C'$
$A(-2, 5)$	$A'(0, 2)$
$B(0, 7)$	$B'(2, 4)$
$C(3, 7)$	$C'(5, 4)$

Notice that each x-value of $\triangle A'B'C'$ is 2 units more than the corresponding x-value of $\triangle ABC$ and each y-value of $\triangle A'B'C'$ is 3 units less than the corresponding y-value of $\triangle ABC$.

> **Student Help**
>
> **READING TIP**
> In this book, shapes are named by listing in order the labels at their corners. For example, the blue triangle in Example 4 is named $\triangle ABC$.

Checkpoint ✓ Draw Translated Figures

Draw the image of the figure after the given translation.

6. $(x, y) \rightarrow (x + 3, y - 2)$

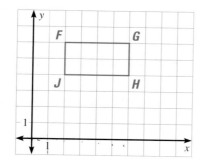

7. $(x, y) \rightarrow (x - 3, y + 4)$

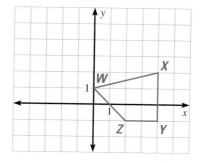

3.7 Exercises

Guided Practice

Vocabulary Check

1. What is a *translation*?

2. Complete the statement: A translation shows a blue triangle and a red triangle. The blue triangle is the original figure and the red triangle is the __?__.

Skill Check

Window Frames **Decide whether "opening the window" is a translation of the moving part.**

3. Double hung

4. Casement

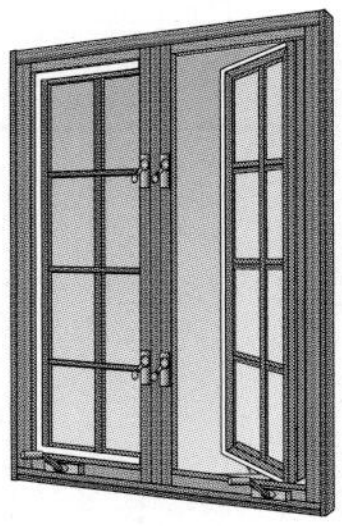

5. Sliding

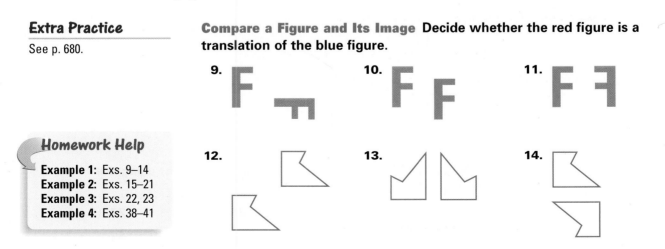

Decide whether the statement is *true* or *false*. Explain.

6. The red figure is a translation of the blue figure.

7. To move from △*ABC* to △*A'B'C'*, shift 3 units to the right and 2 units up.

8. The translation from △*ABC* to △*A'B'C'* is given by $(x, y) \rightarrow (x - 3, y - 2)$.

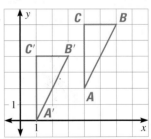

Practice and Applications

Extra Practice

See p. 680.

Compare a Figure and Its Image **Decide whether the red figure is a translation of the blue figure.**

9.

10.

11.

Homework Help

Example 1: Exs. 9–14
Example 2: Exs. 15–21
Example 3: Exs. 22, 23
Example 4: Exs. 38–41

12.

13.

14.

Matching Translations Match the description of the translation with its diagram.

15. 4 units right and 3 units up
16. 6 units right and 2 units down
17. 7 units left and 1 unit up
18. 5 units right and 2 units down

A.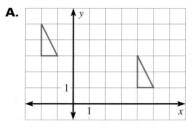

B.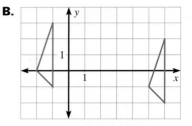

C.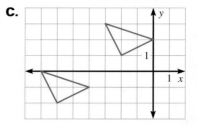

D.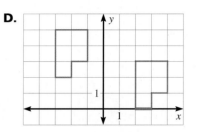

Describing Translations Describe the translation using words.

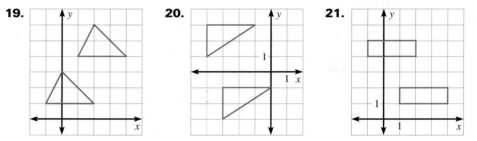

19. **20.** **21.**

Coordinate Notation Describe the translation using coordinate notation.

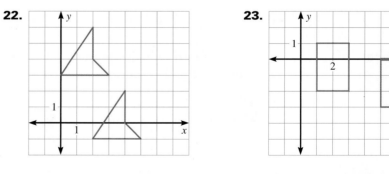

22. **23.**

A Point and Its Image Find the image of the point using the translation $(x, y) \rightarrow (x + 4, y - 3)$.

24. $(2, 5)$　　　**25.** $(-3, 7)$　　　**26.** $(-1, -4)$　　　**27.** $(4, -6)$

28. $(0, 0)$　　　**29.** $(-4, 3)$　　　**30.** $(3, -4)$　　　**31.** $(-1, -1)$

Finding an Image Find the coordinates of *P′*, *Q′*, *R′*, and *S′* using the given translation.

32. $(x, y) \rightarrow (x + 1, y - 4)$

33. $(x, y) \rightarrow (x - 3, y + 2)$

34. $(x, y) \rightarrow (x + 5, y - 5)$

35. $(x, y) \rightarrow (x, y - 3)$

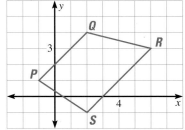

Chess In chess, six different kinds of pieces are moved according to individual rules. The board below shows some moves for the Knight (the piece shaped like a horse).

36. Describe the translation used by the White Knight to capture the Black Pawn.

37. Assume that the White Knight has taken the place of the Black Pawn. Describe the translation used by the Black Knight to move to capture the White Knight at its new location.

Drawing Translated Figures Draw the image of the figure after the given translation.

38. $(x, y) \rightarrow (x + 2, y + 1)$

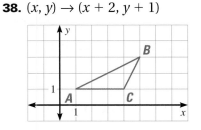

39. $(x, y) \rightarrow (x + 4, y - 5)$

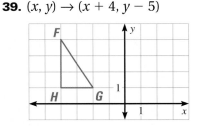

40. $(x, y) \rightarrow (x - 5, y + 3)$

41. $(x, y) \rightarrow (x - 3, y + 8)$

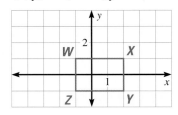

Use Points on an Image A point on an image and the translation are given. Find the corresponding point on the original figure.

42. Point on image: $(0, 3)$; translation: $(x, y) \rightarrow (x - 3, y + 2)$

43. Point on image: $(-2, 4)$; translation: $(x, y) \rightarrow (x + 5, y - 1)$

44. Point on image: $(6, -1)$; translation: $(x, y) \rightarrow (x + 3, y + 7)$

45. 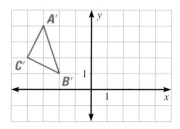 **You be the Judge** The figure on the grid shown at the right is the image after the translation $(x, y) \rightarrow (x - 6, y + 4)$. One of your classmates tells you that C on the original figure is $(2, -2)$. Do you agree? Explain your reasoning.

Technology In Exercises 46 and 47, use geometry software to complete the steps below.

❶ Draw a triangle and translate it.

❷ Construct $\overline{JJ'}$ and $\overline{KK'}$.

46. If two lines have the same slope, then they are parallel. Measure the slopes of $\overline{JJ'}$ and $\overline{KK'}$. Are $\overline{JJ'}$ and $\overline{KK'}$ parallel?

47. What should $m\angle KJJ' + m\angle K'KJ$ be? Measure the angles and check your answer.

48. Challenge Point C is located at $(1, 3)$. The translation that shifts C to C' is given by $(x, y) \rightarrow (x + 5, y - 4)$. The translation that shifts C' to C'' is given by $(x, y) \rightarrow (x - 1, y + 8)$. Give the coordinate notation that describes the translation directly from C to C''. (*Hint*: Start by plotting C, C', and C''.)

Standardized Test Practice

Multiple Choice In Exercises 49 and 50, use the diagram below.

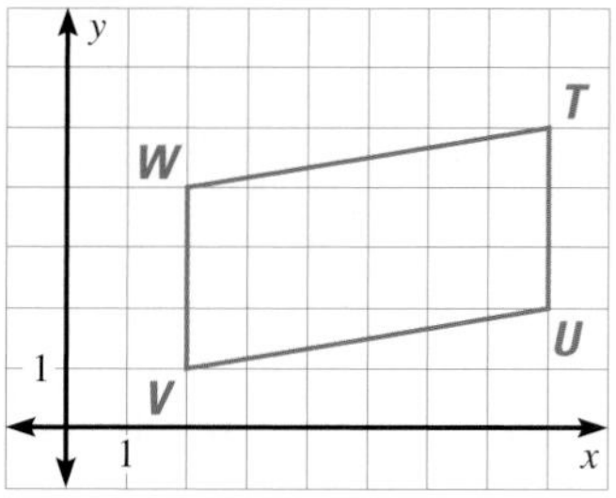

49. Find the coordinates of T' using the translation $(x, y) \rightarrow (x - 5, y + 2)$.

  (A) $(3, 7)$ (B) $(10, 0)$

  (C) $(3, 5)$ (D) $(-5, 7)$

50. Find the coordinates of W' using the translation $(x, y) \rightarrow (x + 3, y - 3)$.

  (F) $(5, 1)$ (G) $(-1, 7)$

  (H) $(5, 7)$ (J) $(-1, 1)$

Mixed Review

Classifying Angles State whether the angle appears to be *acute*, *right*, *obtuse*, or *straight*. Then estimate its measure. *(Lesson 1.6)*

51.   **52.**   **53.**

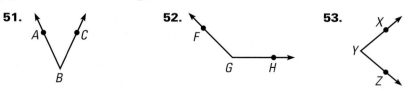

Algebra Skills

Problem Solving Use problem solving strategies to answer the question. *(Skills Review, p. 653)*

54. Your telephone company charges $.15 per minute for all long distance calls. This month you paid $12.60 for long distance calls. How many minutes did you spend on long distance calls?

55. You just bought a CD single that has four tracks. In how many different orders can the songs be played?

Ordering Numbers Write the numbers in order from least to greatest. *(Skills Review, p. 662)*

56. $-0.4, 0.5, 0, 1.0, -0.1, 0.9$

57. $3.4, -1.2, 0.7, -1.5, 0, 1.1, -4$

58. $6.7, 7.6, -0.77, 6.6, -0.7, -6.7$

59. $-6.12, 6.3, -6.8, -6.1, 6, 6.09$

Quiz 3

Determine whether enough information is given to conclude that
$m \parallel n$. **Explain.** *(Lesson 3.5)*

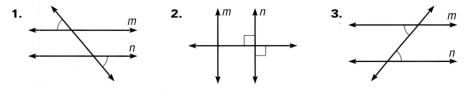

In Exercises 4–6, explain how you would show that $p \parallel q$. State any
theorems or postulates that you would use. *(Lesson 3.6)*

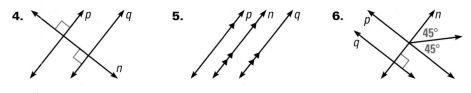

7. Draw a vertical line ℓ and construct a line m perpendicular to it through a point P to the left of line ℓ. *(Lesson 3.6)*

In Exercises 8 and 9, describe the translation of the figure using
coordinate notation. *(Lesson 3.7)*

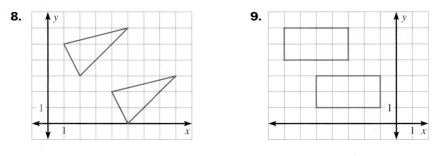

Chapter 3 Summary and Review

VOCABULARY

- **parallel lines,** *p. 108*
- **perpendicular lines,** *p. 108*
- **skew lines,** *p. 108*
- **parallel planes,** *p. 109*
- **line perpendicular to a plane,** *p. 109*
- **transversal,** *p. 121*
- **corresponding angles,** *p. 121*
- **alternate interior angles,** *p. 121*
- **alternate exterior angles,** *p. 121*
- **same-side interior angles,** *p. 121*
- **converse,** *p. 136*
- **construction,** *p. 143*
- **translation,** *p. 152*
- **image,** *p. 152*
- **transformation,** *p. 152*

VOCABULARY REVIEW

Fill in the blank.

1. Two lines are __?__ if they lie in the same plane and do not intersect.
2. A(n) __?__ is a line that intersects two or more coplanar lines at different points.
3. Two lines are __?__ if they intersect to form a right angle.
4. Two angles are __?__ if they lie outside two lines on opposite sides of a transversal.
5. A(n) __?__ is a geometric drawing that uses a limited set of tools, usually a compass and a straightedge.
6. Two planes that do not intersect are called __?__.

3.1 RELATIONSHIPS BETWEEN LINES

Examples on pp. 108–109

EXAMPLES **Name of a pair of parallel lines, perpendicular lines, and skew lines.**

Lines r and s are parallel.

Lines q and r are perpendicular.

Lines q and s are skew.

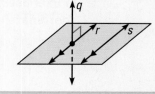

In the diagram at the right, think of each segment as part of a line. Fill in the blank with *parallel, perpendicular,* or *skew*.

7. $\overleftrightarrow{FJ}$ and $\overleftrightarrow{GH}$ appear to be __?__.
8. $\overleftrightarrow{KN}$ and $\overleftrightarrow{JN}$ are __?__.
9. $\overleftrightarrow{FK}$ and $\overleftrightarrow{HJ}$ are __?__.
10. $\overleftrightarrow{JN}$ and $\overleftrightarrow{MN}$ are __?__.

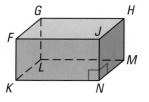

3.2 THEOREMS ABOUT PERPENDICULAR LINES

Examples on pp. 114–116

EXAMPLES In the diagram, $a \perp b$ and $a \perp d$. **Give the theorem that supports the statement.**

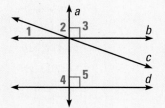

a. $\angle 3 \cong \angle 5$

All right angles are congruent. So, $\angle 3 \cong \angle 5$. (Theorem 3.1)

b. $m\angle 4 = 90°$

If two lines are perpendicular, they intersect to form four right angles. So, $m\angle 4 = 90°$. (Theorem 3.2)

c. $\angle 1$ and $\angle 2$ are complementary.

If two sides of adjacent acute angles are perpendicular, then the angles are complementary. So, $\angle 1$ and $\angle 2$ are complementary. (Theorem 3.4)

Determine whether enough information is given to conclude that the statement is true. Explain.

11. $m\angle 11 = 90°$

12. $m\angle 9 + m\angle 10 = 90°$

13. $h \perp j$

14. $\angle 9 \cong \angle 10$

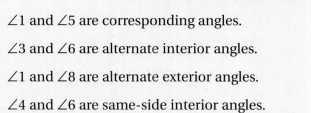

$f \perp g$

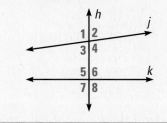

3.3 ANGLES FORMED BY TRANSVERSALS

Examples on pp. 121–122

EXAMPLE Name a pair of corresponding angles, alternate interior angles, alternate exterior angles, and same-side interior angles.

$\angle 1$ and $\angle 5$ are corresponding angles.

$\angle 3$ and $\angle 6$ are alternate interior angles.

$\angle 1$ and $\angle 8$ are alternate exterior angles.

$\angle 4$ and $\angle 6$ are same-side interior angles.

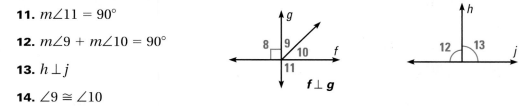

Complete the statement using *corresponding*, *alternate interior*, *alternate exterior*, or *same-side interior*.

15. $\angle 8$ and $\angle 12$ are __?__ angles.

16. $\angle 9$ and $\angle 14$ are __?__ angles.

17. $\angle 10$ and $\angle 12$ are __?__ angles.

18. $\angle 11$ and $\angle 12$ are __?__ angles.

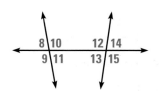

3.4 PARALLEL LINES AND TRANSVERSALS

Examples on pp. 128–131

EXAMPLE In the diagram, $b \parallel c$. Name three pairs of congruent angles and one pair of supplementary angles.

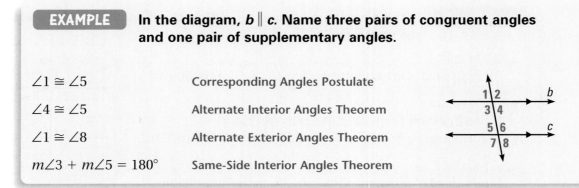

$\angle 1 \cong \angle 5$	Corresponding Angles Postulate
$\angle 4 \cong \angle 5$	Alternate Interior Angles Theorem
$\angle 1 \cong \angle 8$	Alternate Exterior Angles Theorem
$m\angle 3 + m\angle 5 = 180°$	Same-Side Interior Angles Theorem

Find the measure of the numbered angle.

19.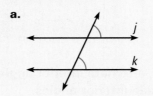

20.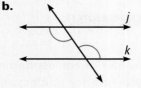

21.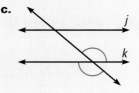

3.5 SHOWING LINES ARE PARALLEL

Examples on pp. 136–139

EXAMPLES Is enough information given to conclude that $j \parallel k$? Explain.

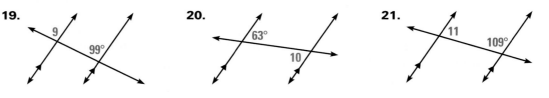

a. Yes. Lines j and k are parallel by the Corresponding Angles Converse.

b. Yes. Lines j and k are parallel by the Alternate Interior Angles Converse.

c. No. Not enough information is given.

Find the value of x so that $r \parallel s$.

22. 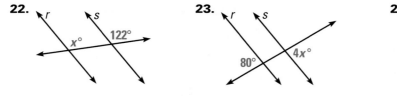 **23.** **24.**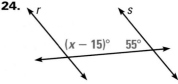

3.6 USING PERPENDICULAR AND PARALLEL LINES

Examples on pp. 143–146

EXAMPLE In the diagram, $j \perp t$, $m \perp t$, and $m \parallel n$. Explain why $j \parallel n$.

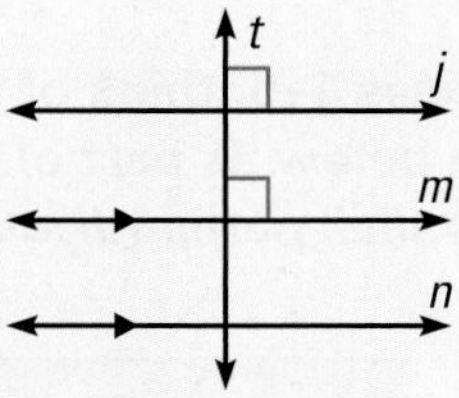

Because j and m lie in the same plane and are both perpendicular to t, $j \parallel m$. (Theorem 3.12)

Because $j \parallel m$ and $m \parallel n$, $j \parallel n$. (Theorem 3.11)

Using the given information, state the postulate or theorem that allows you to conclude that $p \parallel q$.

25. $p \parallel r, q \parallel r$ **26.** $p \perp s, q \perp s$ **27.** $\angle 1 \cong \angle 2$

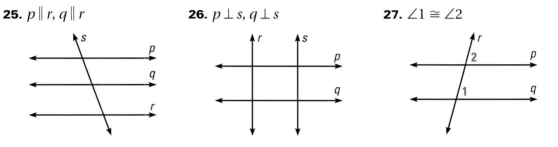

3.7 TRANSLATIONS

Examples on pp. 152–154

EXAMPLE Describe the translation using coordinate notation.

Each point is moved 4 units to the left and 2 units down. So, the translation can be described using the notation $(x, y) \rightarrow (x - 4, y - 2)$.

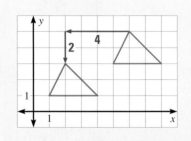

Decide whether the red figure is a translation of the blue figure.

28.   **29.**   **30.**

In Exercises 31 and 32, use the translation at the right. The original figure is blue and the image is red.

31. Describe the translation using words.

32. Describe the translation using coordinate notation.

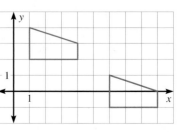

In Exercises 1–5, think of each segment in the diagram below as part of a line. Fill in the blank with *parallel, perpendicular,* or *skew*.

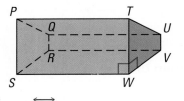

1. $\overleftrightarrow{PT}$ and $\overleftrightarrow{UV}$ are __?__.

2. $\overleftrightarrow{TW}$ and $\overleftrightarrow{WV}$ are __?__.

3. $\overleftrightarrow{PT}$ and $\overleftrightarrow{SW}$ appear __?__.

4. Plane *PQR* and plane *TUV* appear __?__.

5. $\overleftrightarrow{TW}$ is __?__ to plane *SWV*.

6. What can you conclude about $\angle FGJ$ and $\angle JGH$, given that $\overrightarrow{FG} \perp \overleftrightarrow{GH}$?

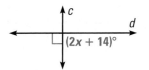

7. Find the value of *x* given that $c \perp d$.

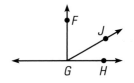

In Exercises 8–13, identify the relationship between the angles in the diagram below.

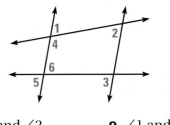

8. $\angle 1$ and $\angle 2$

9. $\angle 1$ and $\angle 6$

10. $\angle 2$ and $\angle 3$

11. $\angle 1$ and $\angle 5$

12. $\angle 4$ and $\angle 2$

13. $\angle 5$ and $\angle 3$

14. Find $m\angle 1$, $m\angle 2$, and $m\angle 3$. Explain your reasoning.

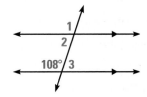

In Exercises 15 and 16, find the value of *y* so that $m \parallel n$.

15.

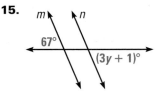

16.

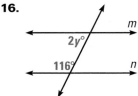

17. A carpenter wants to cut two boards to fit snugly together. The carpenter's squares are aligned along $\overline{EF}$, as shown. Are $\overline{AB}$ and $\overline{CD}$ parallel? State the theorem that justifies your answer.

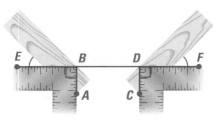

18. Describe the translation using words and coordinate notation.

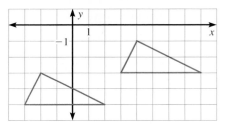

Test Tip
ⒶⒷ Ⓒ Ⓓ

Do not worry about how much time you have left or how others are doing. Concentrate on your own work.

---

1. Two lines are __?__ lines if they lie in the same plane and do not intersect.

Ⓐ intersecting   Ⓑ parallel

Ⓒ perpendicular   Ⓓ skew

2. If two lines form adjacent congruent angles, then the lines are __?__.

Ⓕ parallel   Ⓖ perpendicular

Ⓗ skew   Ⓙ collinear

3. Find the value of *x*, given that $p \perp q$.

Ⓐ 16

Ⓑ 50

Ⓒ 90

Ⓓ 106

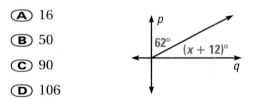

4. Which angles are alternate interior angles?

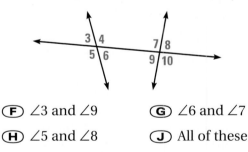

Ⓕ ∠3 and ∠9   Ⓖ ∠6 and ∠7

Ⓗ ∠5 and ∠8   Ⓙ All of these

5. If $a \parallel b$, which angles are congruent?

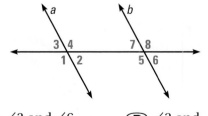

Ⓐ ∠3 and ∠6   Ⓑ ∠3 and ∠8

Ⓒ ∠2 and ∠5   Ⓓ None of these

6. Find the value of *y* so that $m \parallel n$.

Ⓕ 35

Ⓖ 55

Ⓗ 110

Ⓙ 180

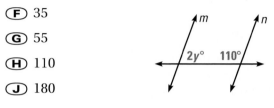

7. Multi-Step Problem Use the diagram below.

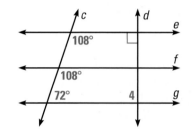

a. Explain why $e \parallel f$.

b. Explain why $f \parallel g$.

c. Explain why $e \parallel g$.

d. What is $m\angle 4$? Explain.

8. Choose the coordinate notation that describes the translation from $\triangle ABC$ to $\triangle A'B'C'$.

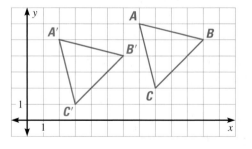

Ⓐ $(x, y) \rightarrow (x + 5, y + 1)$

Ⓑ $(x, y) \rightarrow (x + 5, y - 1)$

Ⓒ $(x, y) \rightarrow (x - 5, y + 1)$

Ⓓ $(x, y) \rightarrow (x - 5, y - 1)$

BraiN
GaMes

What's the Angle?

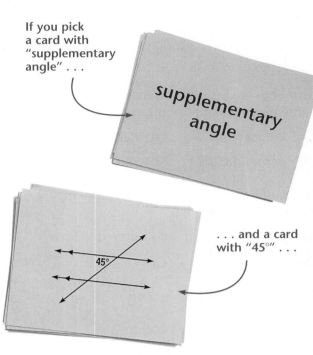

If you pick a card with "supplementary angle" . . .

supplementary angle

. . . and a card with "45°" . . .

45°

. . . your answer will be 135°.

Materials
• 6 description cards
• 26 diagram cards

Object of the Game
To correctly give the measures of angles.

Set Up
Shuffle each stack of cards. Place the description cards face down in one pile and the diagram cards face down in another pile.

How to Play

Step 1 ▶ Each player takes a turn selecting one card from each pile.

Step 2 ▶ The player calculates the measure of the angle given on the description card. If a pair of cards has no answer, say so.

Step 3 ▶ The other players determine if the answer is correct. If the answer is correct, record a point for that person. Then place each card at the bottom of its pile.

Step 4 ▶ After a set amount of time, complete the round so every player gets an equal number of turns. The player with the most points wins.

Another Way to Play
Each player has one minute to calculate as many angle measures as possible. The other players check each answer at the end of the minute. After each player has a turn, the player with the most correct answers wins.

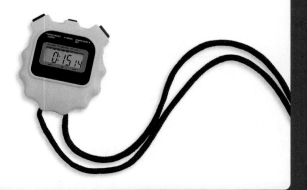

You must reverse the inequality sign when you multiply or divide each side of an inequality by a negative number.

EXAMPLE 1   Solve Inequalities

Solve the inequality.

a. $6x + 11 > 29$ **b.** $7 - 4y \le y + 12$

Solution

a. $6x + 11 > 29$

$\qquad 6x > 18$

$\qquad x > 3$ Divide by 6.

b. $7 - 4y \le y + 12$

$\qquad 7 - 5y \le 12$

$\qquad -5y \le 5$

$\qquad\qquad y \ge -1$ Divide by -5.

Student Help

STUDY TIP
Both sides of the inequality have been divided by a negative number, -5, so change "$\le$" to "$\ge$."

Try These

Solve the inequality.

1. $x - 3 > 12$ **2.** $8q + 1 < 25$ **3.** $-3z + 8 \ge 20$

4. $16 - 9c \le -2$ **5.** $10 - 2p \le -4p + 4$ **6.** $5k - 6 > 3k + 16$

If $b^2 = a$, then b is a *square root* of a. Every positive number has one positive and one negative square root. The radical symbol $\sqrt{}$ indicates the positive square root.

EXAMPLE 2   Evaluate Squares and Square Roots

Evaluate the expression.

a. 7^2 **b.** $(-8)^2$ **c.** $(\sqrt{3})^2$ **d.** $\sqrt{36}$

Solution

a. $7^2 = 7 \cdot 7 = 49$ **b.** $(-8)^2 = (-8)(-8) = 64$

c. $(\sqrt{3})^2 = 3$ **d.** $\sqrt{36} = \sqrt{6^2} = 6$

Try These

Evaluate the expression.

7. 4^2 **8.** 14^2 **9.** $(-3)^2$ **10.** $(-11)^2$

11. $(\sqrt{5})^2$ **12.** $(\sqrt{10})^2$ **13.** $\sqrt{81}$ **14.** $\sqrt{400}$

1. Describe a pattern in the numbers 10, 12, 15, 19, 24, ... Then write the next number you expect in the pattern. (Lesson 1.1)

2. Show that the conjecture is false by finding a counterexample.

   Conjecture: The square of a number is always greater than the number. (Lesson 1.2)

In the diagram, $\overleftrightarrow{AB}$, $\overleftrightarrow{AC}$, and $\overleftrightarrow{BC}$ lie in plane *M*. (Lessons 1.3, 1.4)

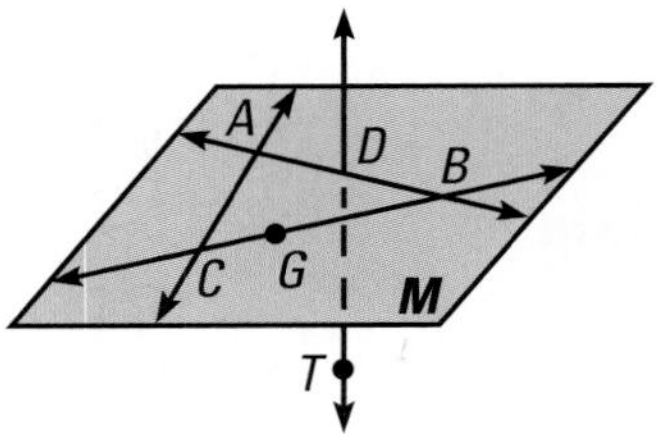

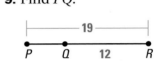

3. Name a point that is collinear with points *A* and *D*.

4. Name a point that is not coplanar with *A*, *B*, and *C*.

5. Name the intersection of $\overleftrightarrow{AD}$ and $\overleftrightarrow{CG}$.

6. Name two lines that do not appear to intersect.

Find the length. (Lesson 1.5)

7. Find *DE*.

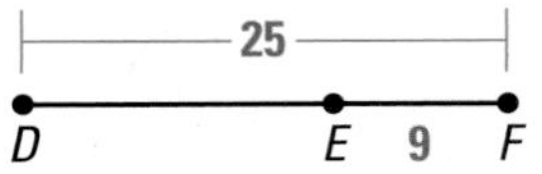

8. Find *MN*.

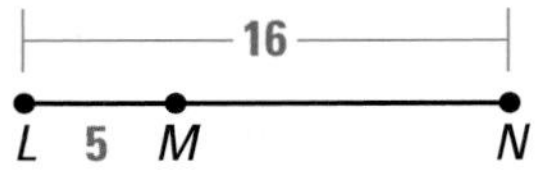

9. Find *PQ*.

In Exercises 10 and 11, plot the points in a coordinate plane and sketch ∠*ABC*. Classify the angle as *acute, right,* or *obtuse*. (Lesson 1.6)

10. $A(-6, 6)$, $B(-2, 2)$, $C(4, 2)$

11. $A(2, 1)$, $B(4, 7)$, $C(10, 5)$

12. Line ℓ bisects $\overline{AB}$. Find *AC* and *AB*. (Lesson 2.1)

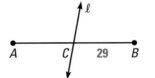

13. $\overrightarrow{KM}$ bisects ∠*JKL*. Find the value of *x*. (Lesson 2.2)

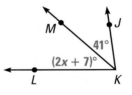

Find the value of the variable. (Lessons 2.3, 2.4)

14.

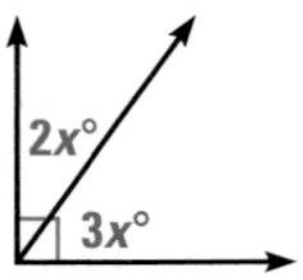

15.

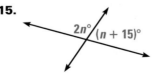

16.

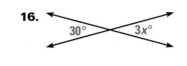

17. Rewrite the statement as an if-then statement. Then underline the hypothesis and circle the conclusion. (Lesson 2.5)

   Statement: Intersecting lines are coplanar lines.

Name the property that the statement illustrates. (Lesson 2.6)

18. If $\overline{XY} \cong \overline{YZ}$, then $\overline{YZ} \cong \overline{XY}$.

19. If $m\angle P = m\angle Q$ and $m\angle Q = m\angle R$, then $m\angle P = m\angle R$.

20. If $AB = CD$, then $AB - 2 = CD - 2$.

Sketch a figure that fits the description. (Lesson 3.1)

21. Line k is perpendicular to line j and line h is parallel to line k.

22. Line w lies in plane D and line v is skew to line w.

In Exercises 23–26, use the diagram at the right. (Lessons 3.3–3.5)

23. Name four pairs of corresponding angles.

24. If $\overleftrightarrow{AC} \parallel \overleftrightarrow{DE}$ and $m\angle 2 = 55°$, find the measure of $\angle 6$.

25. If $\overleftrightarrow{BD} \parallel \overleftrightarrow{CF}$ and $m\angle 2 = 55°$, find the measure of $\angle 4$.

26. If $m\angle 3 + m\angle 6 = 180°$, which lines are parallel? Explain.

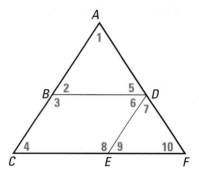

Is enough information given to conclude that $m \parallel n$? Explain.
(Lesson 3.5)

27.

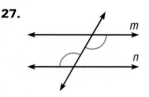

28.

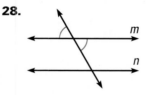

29.

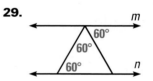

Construction In Exercises 30–32, use the diagram at the right.
The diagram shows two posts that support a raised deck.
The posts have two parallel braces, as shown. (Lessons 3.4, 3.6)

30. If $m\angle 1 = 35°$, find $m\angle 2$.

31. If $m\angle 3 = 40°$, what other angle has a measure of 40°?

32. Given that each post is perpendicular to the deck, explain
how to show that the posts are parallel to each other.

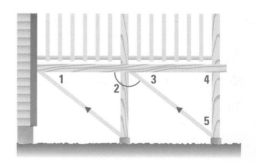

33. A segment has endpoints $A(-2, -3)$ and $B(2, 0)$. Graph $\overline{AB}$
and its image after the translation $(x, y) \rightarrow (x - 4, y + 1)$. (Lesson 3.7)

4 Triangle Relationships

How is it supported?

A skyway 41 stories above the ground connects the Petronas Towers in Malaysia. The skyway is supported by beams that make a triangular shape. The rigid structure of a triangle is very strong.

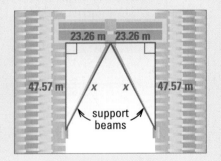

The spires of the Petronas Towers make the building taller than Chicago's Sears Tower. However, the Sears Tower has more floors: 110 compared to the 88 in the Petronas Towers.

Learn More About It

You will learn more about the Petronas Towers in Exercise 26 on p. 196.

Who uses Triangle Relationships?

WATER RESOURCE MANAGER
Water resource managers gather information like rainfall data and water usage to study the effects of water on the environment. They use triangular structures to minimize erosion. (p. 183)

ROCK CLIMBER
The climber is using a method of rock climbing called *top roping*. When the red and blue ropes shown are the same length, the angles they form at the top of the rock have the same measure. (p. 189)

How will you use these ideas?

- Learn more about basketball plays. (p. 177)
- Understand how triangular structures are used to prevent erosion. (p. 183)
- See how rock climbers use a safety rope. (p. 189)
- Analyze tile patterns. (p. 190)
- Investigate a baseball's path during a double play. (p. 205)

What's the chapter about?

- Classifying triangles and finding their angle measures
- Using the **Distance Formula**, the **Pythagorean Theorem**, and its converse
- Showing relationships between a triangle's sides and angles

---

Key Words

- equilateral, isosceles, scalene triangles, *p. 173*
- equiangular, acute, right, obtuse triangles, *p. 174*
- interior, exterior angles, *p. 181*
- legs of an isosceles triangle, *p. 185*

- base angles of an isosceles triangle, *p. 185*
- hypotenuse, *p. 192*
- **Pythagorean Theorem**, *p. 192*
- **Distance Formula**, *p. 194*
- median of a triangle, *p. 207*
- centroid, *p. 208*

Chapter Readiness Quiz

Take this quick quiz. If you are unsure of an answer, look at the reference pages for help.

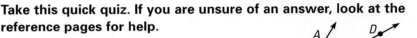

Vocabulary Check *(refer to p. 61)*

1. In the figure shown, $\overrightarrow{BD}$ is the angle bisector of $\angle ABC$. What is the value of x?

   A 10   **B** 15   **C** 20   **D** 30

Skill Check *(refer to pp. 30, 55)*

2. What is the distance between $P(2, 3)$ and $Q(7, 3)$?

   F 3   **G** 4   **H** 5   **J** 7

3. What is the midpoint of a segment with endpoints $A(0, 2)$ and $B(6, 4)$?

   A (3, 2)   **B** (3, 3)   **C** (4, 2)   **D** (0, 3)

Drawing Triangles

Visualize It! ➡

When you sketch a triangle, try to make the angles roughly the correct size.

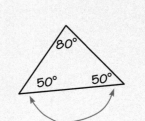

These angles are the same in an isosceles triangle.

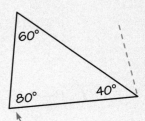

This 80° angle is twice as big as the 40° angle.

4.1 Classifying Triangles

Goal
Classify triangles by their sides and by their angles.

Key Words
- equilateral, isosceles, scalene triangles
- equiangular, acute, right, obtuse triangles
- vertex

A **triangle** is a figure formed by three segments joining three noncollinear points. A triangle can be classified by its sides and by its angles.

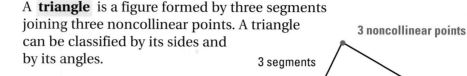

3 noncollinear points

3 segments

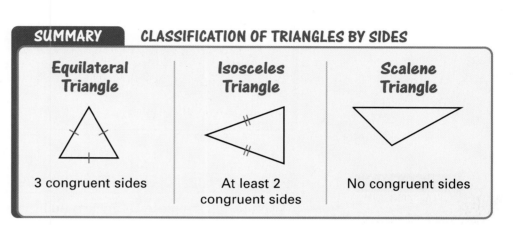

SUMMARY   **CLASSIFICATION OF TRIANGLES BY SIDES**

Equilateral Triangle	Isosceles Triangle	Scalene Triangle
3 congruent sides	At least 2 congruent sides	No congruent sides

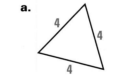

EXAMPLE 1 Classify Triangles by Sides

Classify the triangle by its sides.

a.

b.

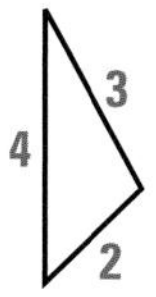

c.

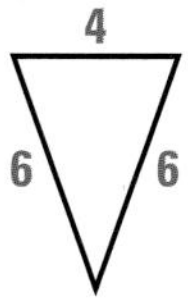

Student Help

VOCABULARY TIP
Equi- means "equal," and *-lateral* means "side." So, *equilateral* means equal sides.

Solution

a. Because this triangle has 3 congruent sides, it is equilateral.

b. Because this triangle has no congruent sides, it is scalene.

c. Because this triangle has 2 congruent sides, it is isosceles.

 Checkpoint ✓ **Classify Triangles by Sides**

Classify the triangle by its sides.

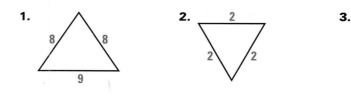

1.

2.

3.

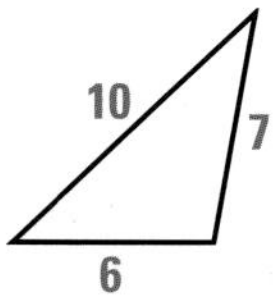

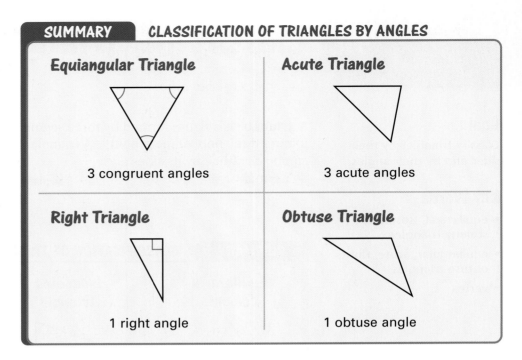

SUMMARY — CLASSIFICATION OF TRIANGLES BY ANGLES

Equiangular Triangle

3 congruent angles

Acute Triangle

3 acute angles

Right Triangle

1 right angle

Obtuse Triangle

1 obtuse angle

Student Help CLASSZONE.COM

MORE EXAMPLES
More examples at classzone.com

EXAMPLE 2 Classify Triangles by Angles and Sides

Classify the triangle by its angles and by its sides.

a.

70°
40°
70°

b.

3
5
4

c.

40°
6.4
9
95°
45°
5.8

Solution

a. Because this triangle has 3 angles with measures less than 90° and 2 congruent sides, it is an *acute isosceles triangle.*

b. Because this triangle has a right angle and no congruent sides, it is a *right scalene triangle.*

c. Because this triangle has one angle greater than 90° and no congruent sides, it is an *obtuse scalene triangle.*

Checkpoint ✓ Classify Triangles by Angles and Sides

Classify the triangle by its angles and by its sides.

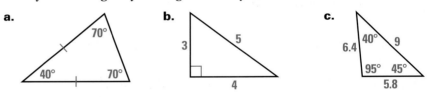

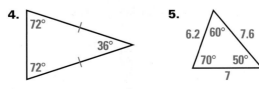

4.

72°
36°
72°

5.

6.2
60°
7.6
70°
50°
7

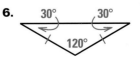

6.

30°
30°
120°

Student Help

> **VOCABULARY TIP**
> The plural of *vertex* is *vertices*.

A **vertex** of a triangle is a point that joins two sides of the triangle. The side across from an angle is the *opposite* side.

Point *B* is a vertex.

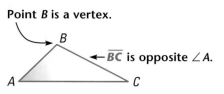

$\overline{BC}$ is opposite $\angle A$.

EXAMPLE 3 **Identify the Parts of a Triangle**

Name the side that is opposite the angle.

a. $\angle A$ **b.** $\angle B$ **c.** $\angle C$

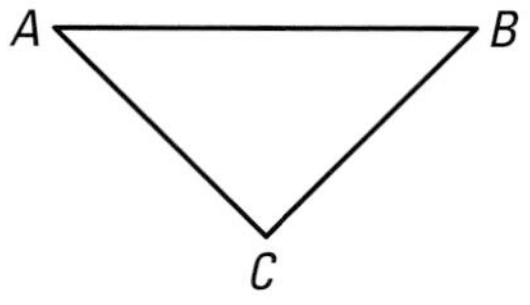

Solution

a. $\overline{BC}$ is the side that is opposite $\angle A$.

b. $\overline{AC}$ is the side that is opposite $\angle B$.

c. $\overline{AB}$ is the side that is opposite $\angle C$.

4.1 Exercises

Guided Practice

Vocabulary Check

1. What is the difference between an *obtuse triangle* and an *acute triangle*?

In Exercises 2–4, use the diagram.

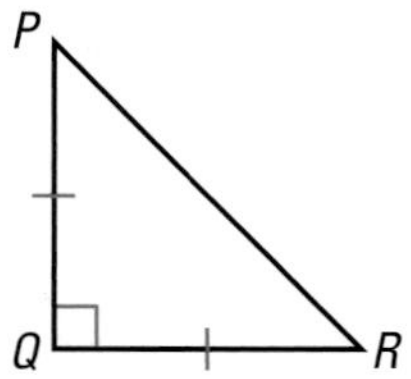

2. Name the side *opposite* $\angle P$.

3. Name the side *opposite* $\angle Q$.

4. Classify the triangle by its sides.

Skill Check

Classify the triangle by its sides.

5.

6.

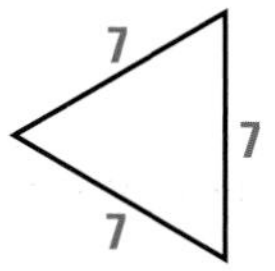

7.

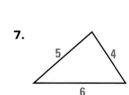

Classify the triangle by its angles.

8. 70° 40° 70°

9.

10.

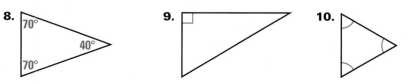

Practice and Applications

Extra Practice
See p. 681.

Classifying Triangles Classify the triangle by its sides.

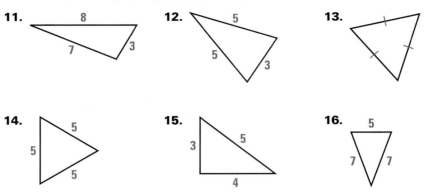

11.

12.

13.

14.

15.

16.

Classifying Triangles Classify the triangle by its angles.

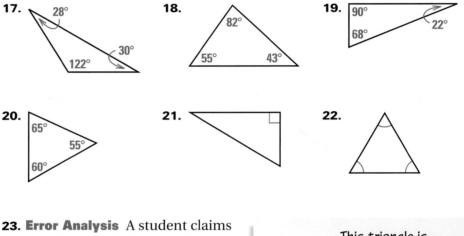

17.

18.

19.

20.

21.

22.

23. Error Analysis A student claims that the triangle is both obtuse and acute because it has an obtuse angle and an acute angle. What is wrong with his reasoning?

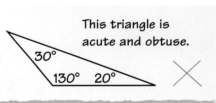

This triangle is acute and obtuse.

30°
130° 20°

Classifying Triangles Classify the triangle by its angles and by its sides.

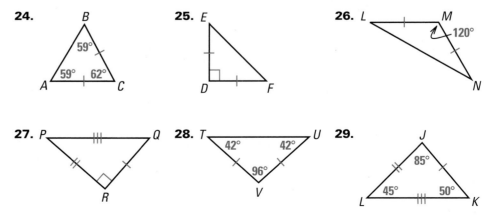

24.

25.

26.

27.

28.

29.

Homework Help

Example 1: Exs. 11–16
Example 2: Exs. 17–41
Example 3: Exs. 42–47

Student Help

VISUAL STRATEGY
In Exs. 30–36 draw a sketch with side lengths or angle measures that are roughly correct, as shown on p. 172.

EXAMPLE Classify Triangles

Classify the triangle described.

a. Side lengths: 6, 8, 9

b. Angle measures: 50°, 60°, 70°

Solution

You may want to sketch the triangle.

a.

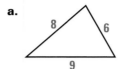

Because the triangle has three sides with different lengths, the triangle is scalene.

b.

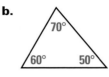

Because the triangle has three angles with measures less than 90°, the triangle is acute.

Matching Triangles **In Exercises 30–36, use the example above to match the triangle description with the most specific name.**

30. Side lengths: 2 cm, 3 cm, 4 cm

31. Side lengths: 3 cm, 2 cm, 3 cm

32. Side lengths: 4 cm, 4 cm, 4 cm

33. Angle measures: 60°, 60°, 60°

34. Angle measures: 30°, 60°, 90°

35. Angle measures: 20°, 145°, 15°

36. Angle measures: 50°, 55°, 75°

A. Equilateral

B. Scalene

C. Obtuse

D. Equiangular

E. Isosceles

F. Acute

G. Right

Link to Sports

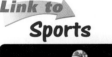

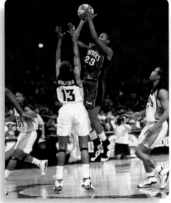

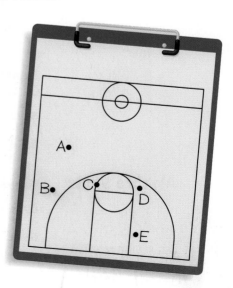

BASKETBALL The triangle offense is used by many professional teams. Players are usually spaced 15 feet to 18 feet apart from each other. This provides many options for passing so a player can make a basket.

Basketball **The diagram shows the position and spacing of five basketball players running the "triangle offense."**

37. What type of triangle is formed by players A, B, and C?

38. What type of triangle is formed by players C, D, and E?

39. What type of triangle is formed by players B, D, and E?

40. Which three players appear to form an obtuse triangle?

41. Which three players appear to form a scalene triangle?

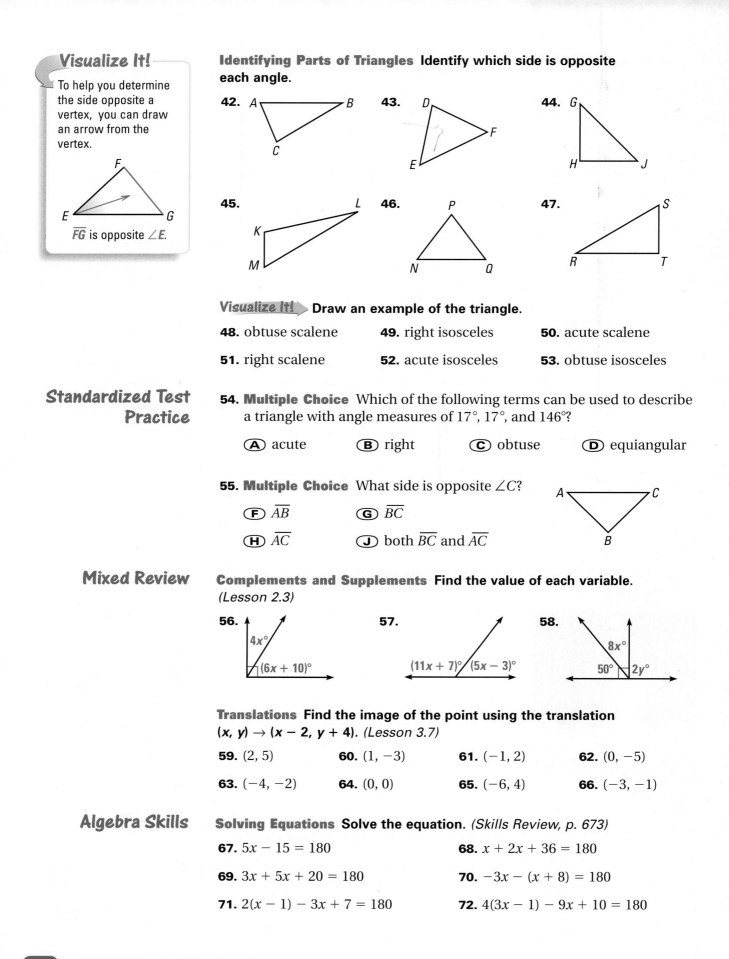

Visualize It!

To help you determine the side opposite a vertex, you can draw an arrow from the vertex.

$\overline{FG}$ is opposite $\angle E$.

Identifying Parts of Triangles Identify which side is opposite each angle.

42.

43.

44.

45.

46.

47.

Visualize It! Draw an example of the triangle.

48. obtuse scalene
49. right isosceles
50. acute scalene

51. right scalene
52. acute isosceles
53. obtuse isosceles

Standardized Test Practice

54. Multiple Choice Which of the following terms can be used to describe a triangle with angle measures of $17°$, $17°$, and $146°$?

(A) acute   **(B)** right   **(C)** obtuse   **(D)** equiangular

55. Multiple Choice What side is opposite $\angle C$?

(F) $\overline{AB}$ **(G)** $\overline{BC}$

(H) $\overline{AC}$ **(J)** both $\overline{BC}$ and $\overline{AC}$

Mixed Review

Complements and Supplements Find the value of each variable. *(Lesson 2.3)*

56.

57.

58.

Translations Find the image of the point using the translation $(x, y) \rightarrow (x - 2, y + 4)$. *(Lesson 3.7)*

59. $(2, 5)$ **60.** $(1, -3)$ **61.** $(-1, 2)$ **62.** $(0, -5)$

63. $(-4, -2)$ **64.** $(0, 0)$ **65.** $(-6, 4)$ **66.** $(-3, -1)$

Algebra Skills

Solving Equations Solve the equation. *(Skills Review, p. 673)*

67. $5x - 15 = 180$

68. $x + 2x + 36 = 180$

69. $3x + 5x + 20 = 180$

70. $-3x - (x + 8) = 180$

71. $2(x - 1) - 3x + 7 = 180$

72. $4(3x - 1) - 9x + 10 = 180$

Angle Measures of Triangles

Goal
Find angle measures in triangles.

Key Words
- corollary
- interior angles
- exterior angles

The diagram below shows that when you tear off the corners of any triangle, you can place the angles together to form a straight angle.

THEOREM 4.1

Triangle Sum Theorem

Words The sum of the measures of the angles of a triangle is 180°.

Symbols In $\triangle ABC$, $m\angle A + m\angle B + m\angle C = 180°$.

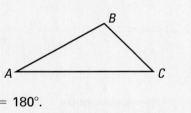

Student Help

READING TIP
Triangles are named by their vertices. $\triangle ABC$ is read "triangle ABC."

EXAMPLE 1 Find an Angle Measure

Given $m\angle A = 43°$ and $m\angle B = 85°$, find $m\angle C$.

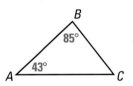

Solution

$m\angle A + m\angle B + m\angle C = 180°$	Triangle Sum Theorem
$43° + 85° + m\angle C = 180°$	Substitute 43° for $m\angle A$ and 85° for $m\angle B$.
$128° + m\angle C = 180°$	Simplify.
$128° + m\angle C - 128° = 180° - 128°$	Subtract 128° from each side.
$m\angle C = 52°$	Simplify.

ANSWER ▶ $\angle C$ has a measure of 52°.

CHECK ✓ Check your solution by substituting 52° for $m\angle C$.
$43° + 85° + 52° = 180°$

A **corollary** to a theorem is a statement that can be proved easily using the theorem. The corollary below follows from the Triangle Sum Theorem.

Student Help

LOOK BACK
For the definition of complementary angles, see p. 67.

COROLLARY

Corollary to the Triangle Sum Theorem

Words The acute angles of a right triangle are complementary.

Symbols In $\triangle ABC$, if $m\angle C = 90°$, then $m\angle A + m\angle B = 90°$.

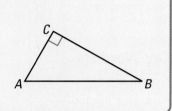

EXAMPLE 2 **Find Angle Measures**

$\triangle ABC$ and $\triangle ABD$ are right triangles. Suppose $m\angle ABD = 35°$.

   a. Find $m\angle DAB$.   **b.** Find $m\angle BCD$.

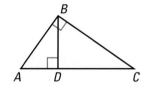

Student Help

CLASSZONE.COM

MORE EXAMPLES
More examples at classzone.com

Solution

a. $m\angle DAB + m\angle ABD = 90°$ Corollary to the Triangle Sum Theorem

        $m\angle DAB + 35° = 90°$ Substitute 35° for $m\angle ABD$.

  $m\angle DAB + 35° - 35° = 90° - 35°$ Subtract 35° from each side.

             $m\angle DAB = 55°$ Simplify.

b. $m\angle DAB + m\angle BCD = 90°$ Corollary to the Triangle Sum Theorem

        $55° + m\angle BCD = 90°$ Substitute 55° for $m\angle DAB$.

            $m\angle BCD = 35°$ Subtract 55° from each side.

Checkpoint ✔ *Find an Angle Measure*

1. Find $m\angle A$.   **2.** Find $m\angle B$.   **3.** Find $m\angle C$.

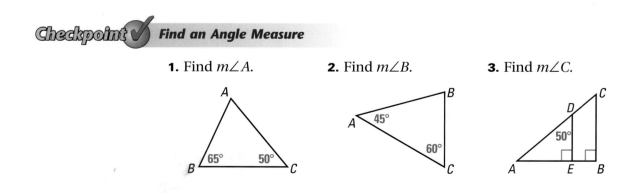

When the sides of a triangle are extended, other angles are formed. The three original angles are the **interior angles**.

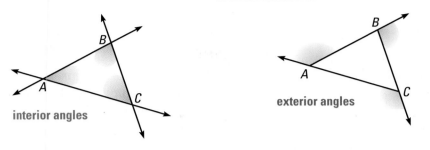

interior angles

exterior angles

The angles that are adjacent to the interior angles are the **exterior angles**. It is common to show only *one* exterior angle at each vertex.

Visualize It!

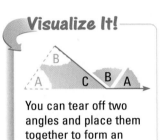

You can tear off two angles and place them together to form an exterior angle.

THEOREM 4.2

Exterior Angle Theorem

Words The measure of an exterior angle of a triangle is equal to the sum of the measures of the two nonadjacent interior angles.

Symbols $m\angle 1 = m\angle A + m\angle B$

EXAMPLE 3 Find an Angle Measure

Given $m\angle A = 58°$ and $m\angle C = 72°$, find $m\angle 1$.

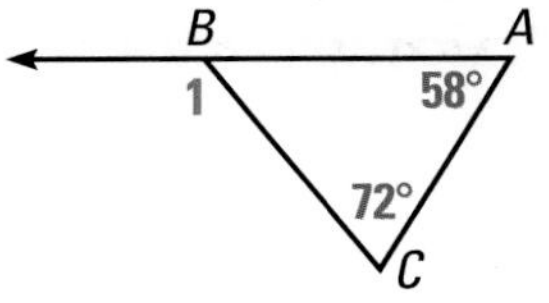

Solution

$m\angle 1 = m\angle A + m\angle C$ Exterior Angle Theorem

$\qquad = 58° + 72°$ Substitute 58° for $m\angle A$ and 72° for $m\angle C$.

$\qquad = 130°$ Simplify.

ANSWER ▶ $\angle 1$ has a measure of 130°.

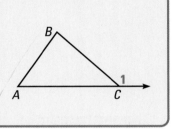

Checkpoint ✓ **Find an Angle Measure**

4. Find $m\angle 2$.   **5.** Find $m\angle 3$.   **6.** Find $m\angle 4$.

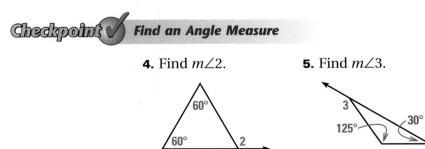

4.2 Exercises

Guided Practice

Vocabulary Check

1. Copy △*ABC* and label its *interior* angles 1, 2, and 3. Then draw three of its *exterior* angles and label the angles 4, 5, and 6.

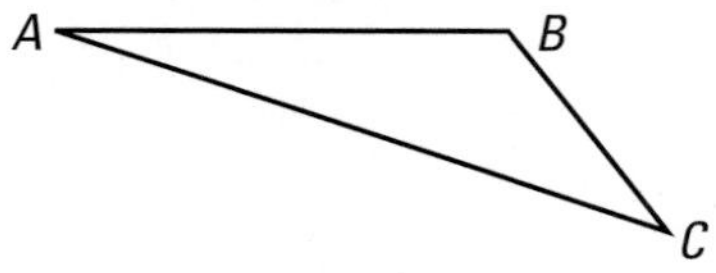

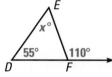

Skill Check

2. Use the diagram to determine which equation can be used to find *m∠DEF*.

A. $55° + x° = 110°$ **B.** $55° + 110° = x°$

C. $55° - x° = 110°$ **D.** $55° - 110° = x°$

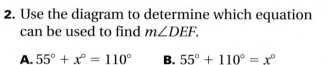

Find the value of x.

3.   **4.**   **5.**

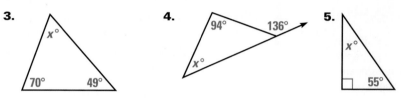

Practice and Applications

Extra Practice
See p. 681.

Finding Angle Measures Find the measure of ∠1.

6.   **7.**   **8.**

9.   **10.**   **11.**

Homework Help

Example 1: Exs. 6–11, 15–21, 23, 24
Example 2: Exs. 6–11, 15–21
Example 3: Exs. 12–14, 18–22

Exterior Angles Find the measure of ∠2.

12.   **13.**   **14.**

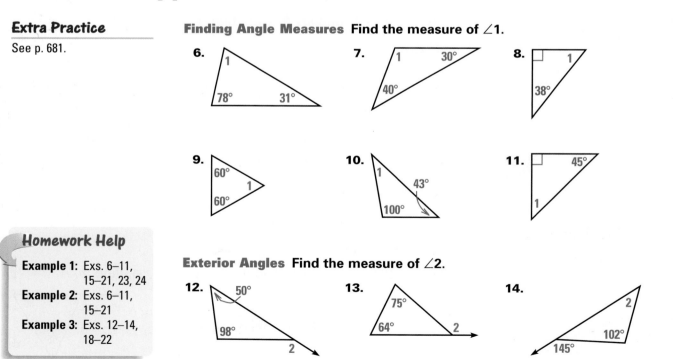

Water Resources In Exercises 15–17, use the diagram.
A structure built with rocks is used to redirect the flow of water in a stream and increase the rate of the water's flow. Its shape is a right triangle.

15. Identify the side opposite ∠MNL.

16. If the measure of the upstream angle is 37°, what is the measure of the downstream angle?

17. It is generally recommended that the upstream angle should be between 30° and 45°. Give a range of angle measures for the downstream angle.

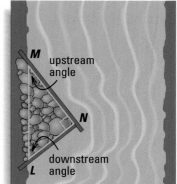

Using Algebra Find the value of each variable.

18.

19.

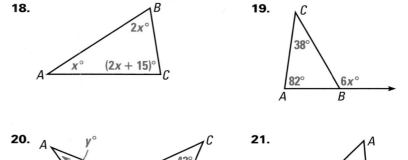

20.

21.

22. Technology Use geometry software to complete the steps below.

① Draw A, B, C and $\triangle ABC$.

② Draw $\overleftrightarrow{AB}$ and a point P on it as shown.

③ Find $m\angle PBC$.

④ Find $m\angle BAC + m\angle BCA$.

⑤ Move point C.

What do you notice? What theorem does this demonstrate?

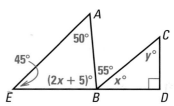

23. Angle Measures in a Triangle The measure of one interior angle of a triangle is 26°. The other interior angles are congruent. Find their measures.

24. 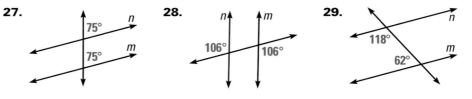 **Using Algebra** In $\triangle PQR$, the measure of $\angle P$ is 36°. The measure of $\angle Q$ is five times the measure of $\angle R$. Find $m\angle Q$ and $m\angle R$.

Standardized Test Practice

25. Multiple Choice Find the value of x.

Ⓐ 8   Ⓑ 13

Ⓒ 16   Ⓓ 29

$(2x - 3)°$ 23°   128°

26. Multiple Choice Suppose a triangle has interior angle measures of 50°, 60°, and 70°. Which of the following is *not* an exterior angle measure?

Ⓕ 100°   Ⓖ 110°   Ⓗ 120°   Ⓙ 130°

Mixed Review

Showing Lines are Parallel Explain how you would show that $m \parallel n$. State any theorems or postulates that you would use. (Lesson 3.5)

27.   **28.**   **29.**

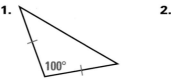   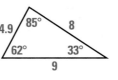 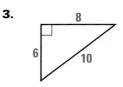

Algebra Skills

Comparing Numbers Compare the two numbers. Write the answer using <, >, or =. (Skills Review, p. 662)

30. 1015 and 1051   **31.** 3.5 and 3.06   **32.** 8.09 and 8.1

33. 1.75 and 1.57   **34.** 0 and 0.5   **35.** 2.055 and 2.1

Quiz 1

Classify the triangle by its angles and by its sides. (Lesson 4.1)

1.   **2.**   **3.**

100°   4.9 / 85° / 8 / 62° / 33° / 9   8 / 6 / 10

Find the measure of $\angle 1$. (Lesson 4.2)

4.   **5.**   **6.**

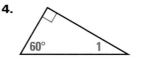 60° / 1   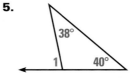 38° / 1 / 40°   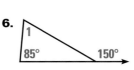 1 / 85° / 150°

4.3 Isosceles and Equilateral Triangles

Goal

Use properties of isosceles and equilateral triangles.

Key Words

- **legs of an isosceles triangle**
- **base of an isosceles triangle**
- **base angles**

Geo-Activity — Properties of Isosceles Triangles

1 Fold a sheet of paper in half. Use a straightedge to draw a line from the fold to the bottom edge. Cut along the line to form an isosceles triangle.

2 Unfold and label the angles as shown. Use a protractor to measure $\angle H$ and $\angle K$. What do you notice?

3 Repeat Steps 1 and 2 for different isosceles triangles. What can you say about $\angle H$ and $\angle K$ in the different triangles?

Student Help

VOCABULARY TIP
Isos- means "equal," and *-sceles* means "leg." So, *isosceles* means equal legs.

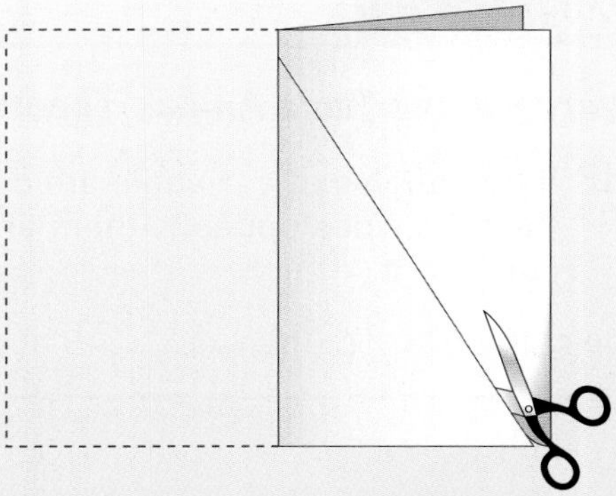

The Geo-Activity shows that two angles of an isosceles triangle are always congruent. These angles are opposite the congruent sides.

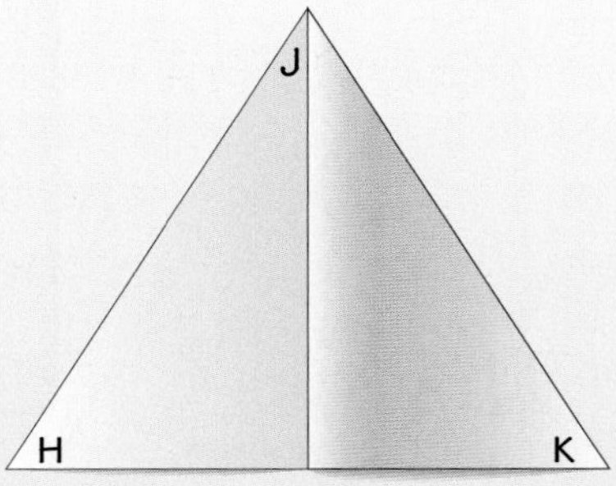

The congruent sides of an isosceles triangle are called **legs**.

The other side is called the **base**.

The two angles at the base of the triangle are called the **base angles**.

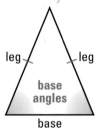

Isosceles Triangle

THEOREM 4.3

Base Angles Theorem

Words If two sides of a triangle are congruent, then the angles opposite them are congruent.

Symbols If $\overline{AB} \cong \overline{AC}$, then $\angle C \cong \angle B$.

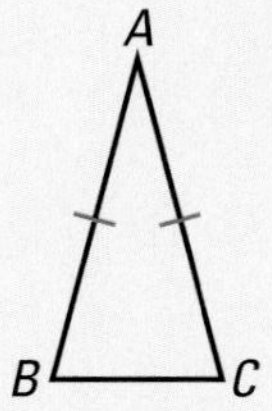

EXAMPLE 1 Use the Base Angles Theorem

Find the measure of ∠L.

Solution

Angle L is a base angle of an isosceles triangle. From the Base Angles Theorem, ∠L and ∠N have the same measure.

ANSWER ▶ The measure of ∠L is 52°.

Rock and Roll Hall of Fame, Cleveland, Ohio

THEOREM 4.4

Converse of the Base Angles Theorem

Words If two angles of a triangle are congruent, then the sides opposite them are congruent.

Symbols If ∠B ≅ ∠C, then $\overline{AC} \cong \overline{AB}$.

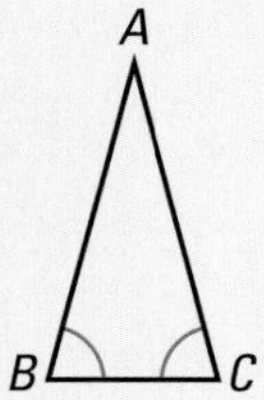

Visualize It!

Base angles don't have to be on the bottom of an isosceles triangle.

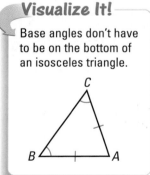

EXAMPLE 2 Use the Converse of the Base Angles Theorem

Find the value of x.

Solution

By the Converse of the Base Angles Theorem, the legs have the same length.

$DE = DF$ Converse of the Base Angles Theorem

$x + 3 = 12$ Substitute x + 3 for DE and 12 for DF.

$x = 9$ Subtract 3 from each side.

ANSWER ▶ The value of x is 9.

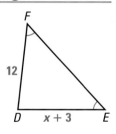

Checkpoint ✓ Use Isosceles Triangle Theorems

Find the value of y.

1. 50°, y°
2. y, 9
3. 16, y + 4

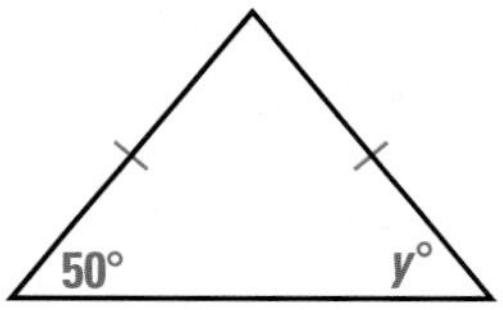

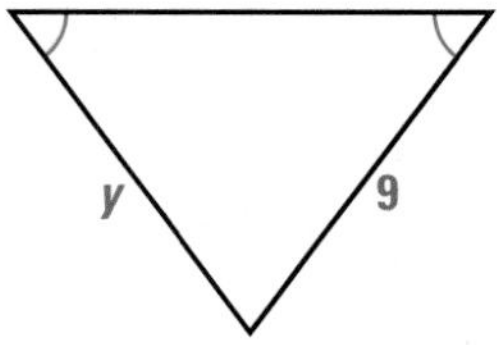

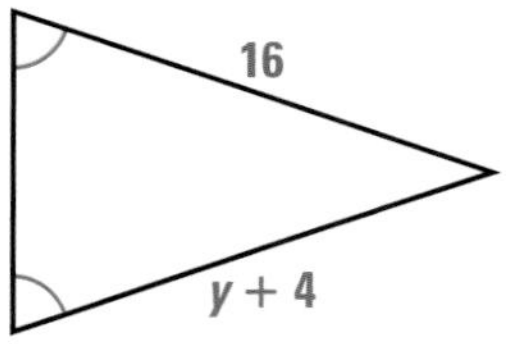

Student Help

LOOK BACK
For the definition of equilateral triangle, see p. 173.

THEOREMS 4.5 and 4.6

4.5 Equilateral Theorem

Words If a triangle is equilateral, then it is equiangular.

Symbols If $\overline{AB} \cong \overline{AC} \cong \overline{BC}$, then $\angle A \cong \angle B \cong \angle C$.

4.6 Equiangular Theorem

Words If a triangle is equiangular, then it is equilateral.

Symbols If $\angle B \cong \angle C \cong \angle A$, then $\overline{AB} \cong \overline{AC} \cong \overline{BC}$.

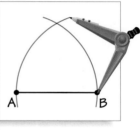

Constructing an Equilateral Triangle You can construct an equilateral triangle using a straightedge and compass.

❶ Draw $\overline{AB}$. Draw an arc with center A that passes through B.

❷ Draw an arc with center B that passes through A.

❸ The intersection of the arcs is point C. $\triangle ABC$ is equilateral.

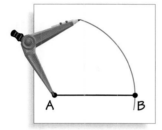

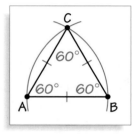

By the Triangle Sum Theorem, the measures of the three congruent angles in an equilateral triangle must add up to 180°. So, each angle in an equilateral triangle measures 60°.

 Using Algebra

EXAMPLE 3 **Find the Side Length of an Equiangular Triangle**

Find the length of each side of the equiangular triangle.

Solution

The angle marks show that $\triangle QRT$ is equiangular. So, $\triangle QRT$ is also equilateral.

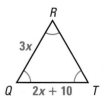

$3x = 2x + 10$ Sides of an equilateral $\triangle$ are congruent.

$x = 10$ Subtract 2x from each side.

$3(10) = 30$ Substitute 10 for x.

ANSWER ▸ Each side of $\triangle QRT$ is 30.

Guided Practice

Vocabulary Check

1. What is the difference between *equilateral* and *equiangular*?

Skill Check

Tell which sides and angles of the triangle are congruent.

2.

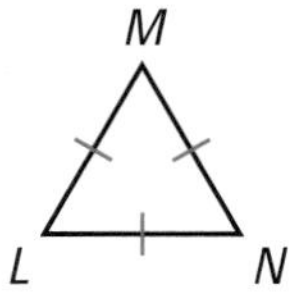

M

L ___ N

3.

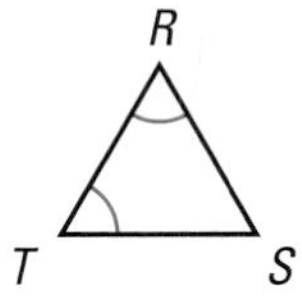

R

T ___ S

4.

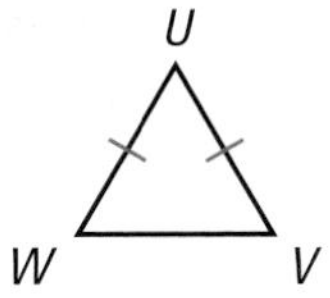

U

W ___ V

Find the value of x. Tell what theorem(s) you used.

5.

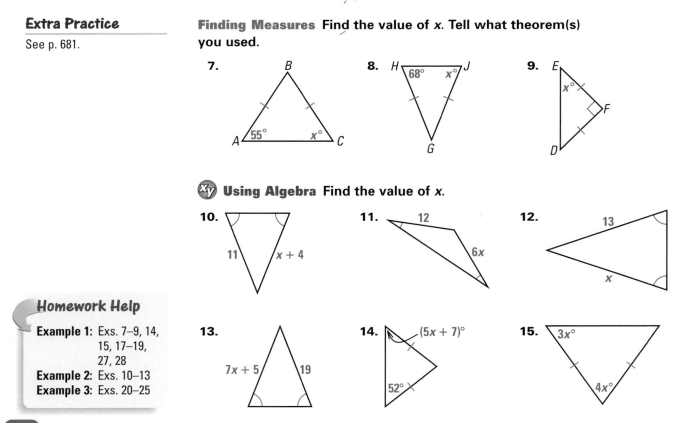

x°   50°

6.

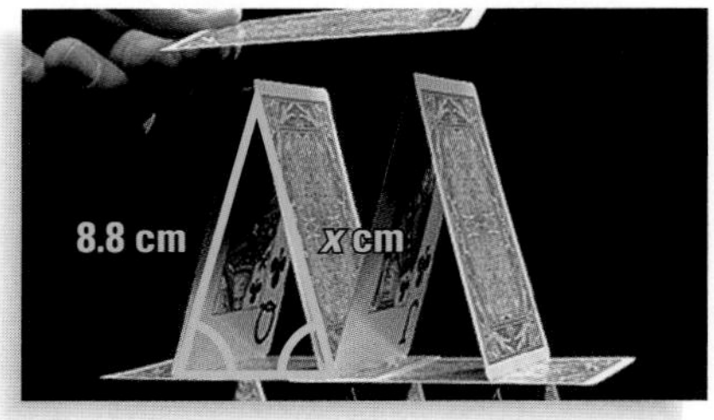

8.8 cm   x cm

Practice and Applications

Extra Practice

See p. 681.

Finding Measures Find the value of x. Tell what theorem(s) you used.

7.

B

A 55°   x° C

8.

H 68°   x° J

G

9.

E

x°

F

D

Using Algebra Find the value of x.

10.

11   x + 4

11.

12

6x

12.

13

x

Homework Help

Example 1: Exs. 7–9, 14,
15, 17–19,
27, 28
Example 2: Exs. 10–13
Example 3: Exs. 20–25

13.

7x + 5   19

14.

(5x + 7)°

52°

15.

3x°

4x°

16. ⚖️ **You be the Judge** Someone in your class tells you that all equilateral triangles are isosceles triangles. Do you agree? Use theorems or definitions to support your answer.

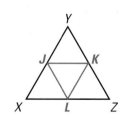

Student Help

CLASSZONE.COM

HOMEWORK HELP
Extra help with problem solving in Exs. 17–19 is at classzone.com

ˣʸ **Using Algebra** Find the measure of ∠A.

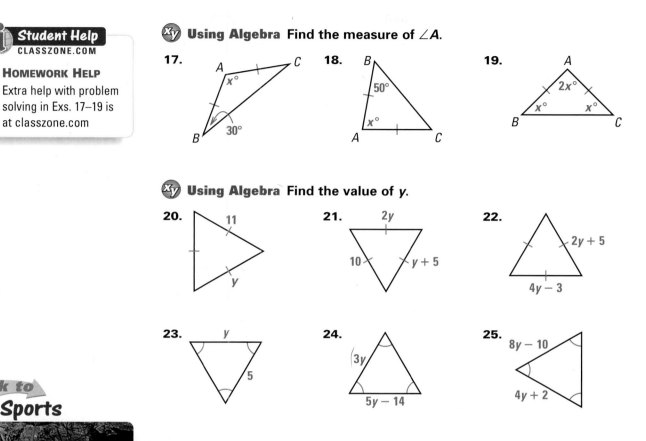

17.

18.

19.

ˣʸ **Using Algebra** Find the value of y.

20. 11, y

21. 2y, 10, y + 5

22. 2y + 5, 4y − 3

23. y, 5

24. 3y, 5y − 14

25. 8y − 10, 4y + 2

Link to Sports

26. Challenge In the diagram at the right, △XYZ is equilateral and the following pairs of segments are parallel: $\overline{XY}$ and $\overline{LK}$; $\overline{ZY}$ and $\overline{LJ}$; $\overline{XZ}$ and $\overline{JK}$. Describe a plan for showing that △JKL must be equilateral.

ROCK CLIMBING The climber is using a method of rock climbing called *top roping*. If the climber slips, the anchors catch the fall.

Application Links

CLASSZONE.COM

Rock Climbing In one type of rock climbing, climbers tie themselves to a rope that is supported by anchors. The diagram shows a red and a blue anchor in a horizontal slit in a rock face.

27. If the red anchor is longer than the blue anchor, are the base angles congruent?

28. If a climber adjusts the anchors so they are the same length, do you think that the base angles will be congruent? Why or why not?

Tiles In Exercises 29–31, use the diagram at the left. In the diagram, $\overline{VX} \cong \overline{WX} \cong \overline{YX} \cong \overline{ZX}$.

29. Copy the diagram. Use what you know about side lengths to mark your diagram.

30. Explain why $\angle XWV \cong \angle XVW$.

31. Name four isosceles triangles.

32. Technology Use geometry software to complete the steps.

  ❶ Construct circle A.

  ❷ Draw points B and C on the circle.

  ❸ Connect the points to form $\triangle ABC$.

Is $\triangle ABC$ isosceles? Measure the sides of the triangle to check your answer.

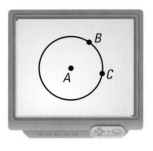

Standardized Test Practice

Multiple Choice In Exercises 33 and 34, use the diagram below.

33. What is the measure of $\angle EFD$?

  (A) $55°$ (B) $65°$

  (C) $125°$ (D) $180°$

34. What is the measure of $\angle DEF$?

  (F) $50°$ (G) $70°$

  (H) $125°$ (J) $180°$

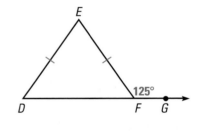

Mixed Review

Angle Bisectors $\overrightarrow{BE}$ is the angle bisector. Find $m\angle DBC$ and $m\angle ABC$. *(Lesson 2.2)*

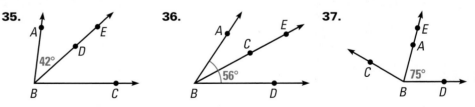

35. **36.** **37.**

Vertical Angles Find the value of the variable. *(Lesson 2.4)*

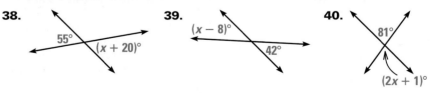

38. **39.** **40.**

Algebra Skills

Evaluating Square Roots Evaluate. *(Skills Review, p. 668)*

41. $\sqrt{49}$ **42.** $\sqrt{121}$ **43.** $\sqrt{1}$ **44.** $\sqrt{400}$

Activity 4.4 Areas and Right Triangles

Question

What is the relationship among the lengths of the sides of a right triangle?

Materials

- graph paper
- straightedge

Explore

1 On a piece of graph paper, draw a right triangle with legs that are three units each.

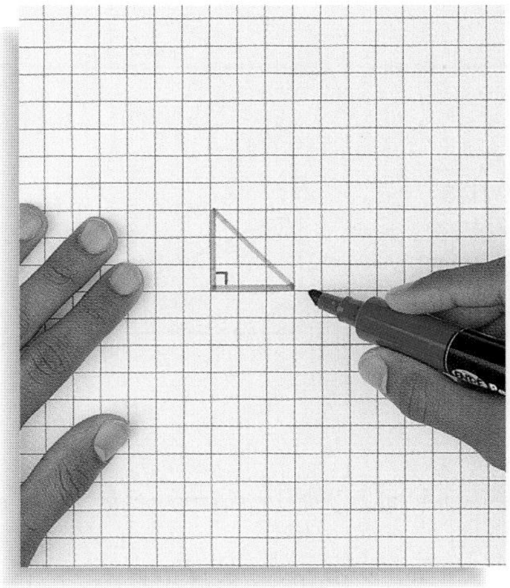

2 Draw a square from each side of the triangle as shown below.

3 Find the area of each square by counting each grid. Count 2 triangles as one whole square.

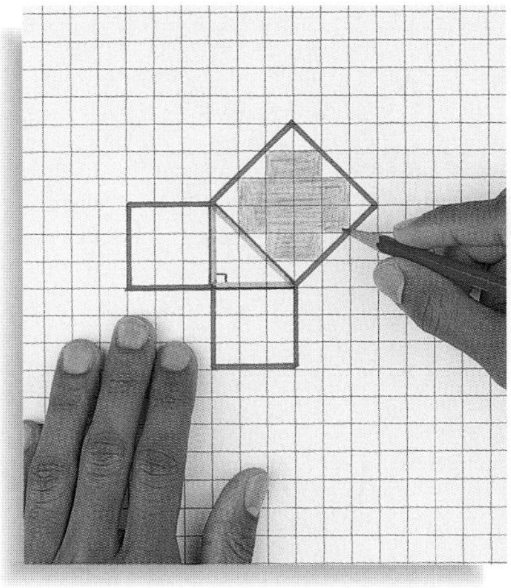

Think About It

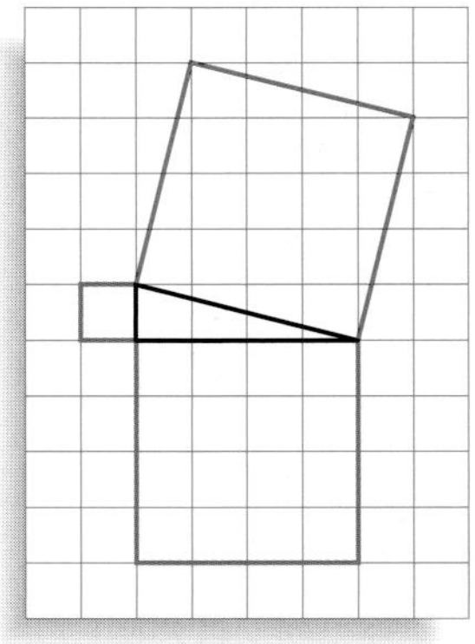

1. Is the sum of the areas of the squares from the two legs equal to the area of the square from the hypotenuse?

2. Draw another right triangle with legs that are 4 units each. Repeat Steps 1–3 and Exercise 1. Do you get the same result?

3. **Extension** Look at the right triangle shown at the left with legs of lengths 1 and 4. Show that the area of the square from the hypotenuse is 17.

4. **Extension** Make a conjecture about the sum of the areas of the squares from two legs and the area of the square from the hypotenuse.

4.4 # The Pythagorean Theorem and the Distance Formula

Goal
Use the Pythagorean Theorem and the Distance Formula.

Key Words
• leg
• hypotenuse
• Pythagorean Theorem
• Distance Formula

The photo shows part of twin skyscrapers in Malaysia that are connected by a skywalk. The skywalk is supported by a set of beams.

In a right triangle, the sides that form the right angle are called **legs**. The side opposite the right angle is called the **hypotenuse**.

In Exercise 26 you will find the length of the support beam using the Pythagorean Theorem.

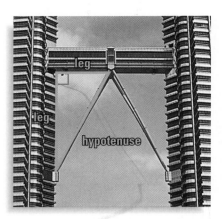

THEOREM 4.7

The Pythagorean Theorem

Words In a right triangle, the square of the length of the hypotenuse is equal to the sum of the squares of the lengths of the legs.

$$(\text{hypotenuse})^2 = (\text{leg})^2 + (\text{leg})^2$$

Symbols If $m\angle C = 90°$, then $c^2 = a^2 + b^2$.

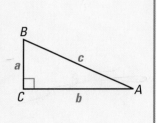

EXAMPLE 1 Find the Length of the Hypotenuse

Find the length of the hypotenuse.

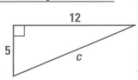

Solution

$(\textbf{hypotenuse})^2 = (\textbf{leg})^2 + (\textbf{leg})^2$	Pythagorean Theorem
$c^2 = 5^2 + 12^2$	Substitute.
$c^2 = 25 + 144$	Multiply.
$c^2 = 169$	Add.
$\sqrt{c^2} = \sqrt{169}$	Find the positive square root.
$c = 13$	Solve for c.

ANSWER ▶ The length of the hypotenuse is 13.

Student Help

SKILLS REVIEW
To review square roots, see p. 669.

EXAMPLE 2 **Find the Length of a Leg**

Find the unknown side length.

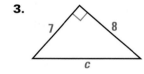

Solution

$(\text{hypotenuse})^2 = (\text{leg})^2 + (\text{leg})^2$	Pythagorean Theorem
$14^2 = 7^2 + b^2$	Substitute.
$196 = 49 + b^2$	Multiply.
$196 - 49 = 49 + b^2 - 49$	Subtract 49 from each side.
$147 = b^2$	Simplify.
$\sqrt{147} = \sqrt{b^2}$	Find the positive square root.
$12.1 \approx b$	Approximate with a calculator.

ANSWER ▶ The side length is about 12.1.

Checkpoint ✓ **Find the Lengths of the Hypotenuse and Legs**

Find the unknown side length.

1.

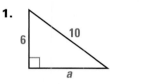

2.

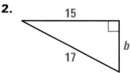

3.

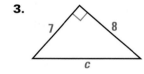

EXAMPLE 3 **Find the Length of a Segment**

Find the distance between the points
$A(1, 2)$ and $B(4, 6)$.

Student Help

LOOK BACK
To review finding
distances on a
coordinate plane,
see p. 30.

Solution

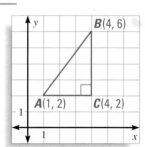

Draw a right triangle with hypotenuse $\overline{AB}$.
▶ $BC = 6 - 2 = 4$ and $CA = 4 - 1 = 3$. Use the
Pythagorean Theorem.

$(\text{hypotenuse})^2 = (\text{leg})^2 + (\text{leg})^2$	
$(AB)^2 = 3^2 + 4^2$	Substitute.
$(AB)^2 = 9 + 16$	Multiply.
$(AB)^2 = 25$	Add.
$\sqrt{(AB)^2} = \sqrt{25}$	Find the positive square root.
$AB = 5$	Simplify.

Distance Formula Using the steps shown in Example 3, the Pythagorean Theorem can be used to develop the **Distance Formula**, which gives the distance between two points in a coordinate plane.

THE DISTANCE FORMULA

If $A(x_1, y_1)$ and $B(x_2, y_2)$ are points in a coordinate plane, then the distance between A and B is

$$AB = \sqrt{(x_2 - x_1)^2 + (y_2 - y_1)^2}.$$

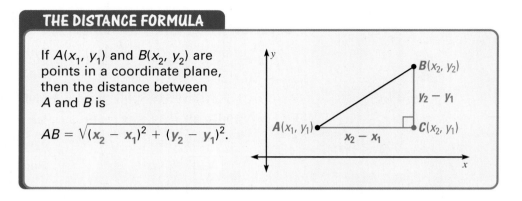

EXAMPLE 4 **Use the Distance Formula**

Find the distance between $D(1, 2)$ and $E(3, -2)$.

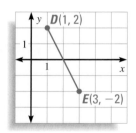

Solution

Begin by plotting the points in a coordinate plane.

$x_1 = 1$, $y_1 = 2$, $x_2 = 3$, and $y_2 = -2$.

Student Help

STUDY TIP
$\sqrt{4 + 16} \neq \sqrt{4} + \sqrt{16}$.
The square root of a sum does *not* equal the sum of the square roots. You must add 4 and 16 *before* taking the square root. ·····▶

$$DE = \sqrt{(x_2 - x_1)^2 + (y_2 - y_1)^2}$$ The Distance Formula

$$= \sqrt{(3 - 1)^2 + (-2 - 2)^2}$$ Substitute.

$$= \sqrt{2^2 + (-4)^2}$$ Simplify.

$$= \sqrt{4 + 16}$$ Multiply.

$$= \sqrt{20}$$ Add.

$$\approx 4.5$$ Approximate with a calculator.

ANSWER ▶ The distance between D and E is about 4.5 units.

Checkpoint ✓ **Use the Distance Formula**

Find the distance between the points.

4.

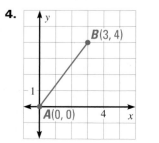

5.

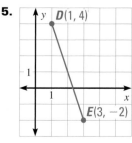

6.

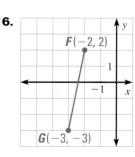

4.4 Exercises

Guided Practice

Vocabulary Check

1. Sketch a right triangle and label its vertices. Then use your triangle to state the Pythagorean Theorem.

Skill Check

Find the unknown side length. Round your answer to the nearest tenth, if necessary.

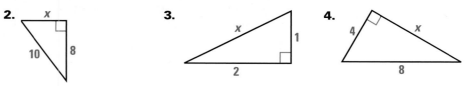

2.   x, 10, 8

3.   x, 1, 2

4.   4, x, 8

Find the distance between the points. Round your answer to the nearest tenth, if necessary.

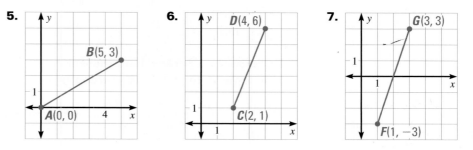

5. *B*(5, 3), *A*(0, 0)

6. *D*(4, 6), *C*(2, 1)

7. *G*(3, 3), *F*(1, −3)

Practice and Applications

Extra Practice

See p. 681.

Finding a Hypotenuse Find the length of the hypotenuse.

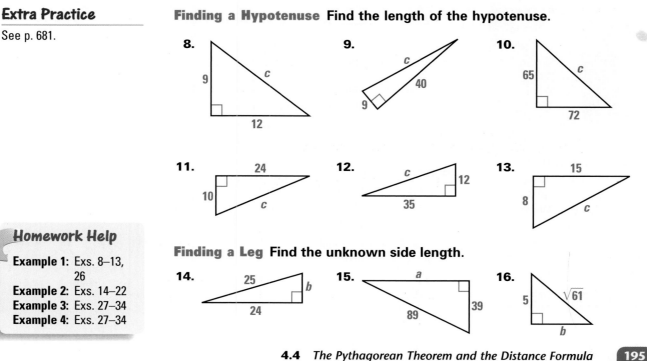

8. 9, c, 12

9. c, 40, 9

10. 65, c, 72

11. 24, 10, c

12. c, 12, 35

13. 15, 8, c

Homework Help

Example 1: Exs. 8–13, 26
Example 2: Exs. 14–22
Example 3: Exs. 27–34
Example 4: Exs. 27–34

Finding a Leg Find the unknown side length.

14. 25, 24, b

15. a, 39, 89

16. 5, $\sqrt{61}$, b

Pythagorean Triples

A *Pythagorean triple* is a set of three positive integers a, b, and c that satisfy the equation $c^2 = a^2 + b^2$. For example, the integers 3, 4, and 5 form a Pythagorean triple because $5^2 = 3^2 + 4^2$.

Find the length of the hypotenuse of the right triangle. Tell whether the side lengths form a Pythagorean triple.

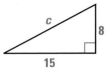

Solution

$$(\text{hypotenuse})^2 = (\text{leg})^2 + (\text{leg})^2 \qquad \text{Pythagorean Theorem}$$
$$c^2 = 8^2 + 15^2 \qquad \text{Substitute 8 and 15 for the legs.}$$
$$c^2 = 64 + 225 \qquad \text{Multiply.}$$
$$c^2 = 289 \qquad \text{Add.}$$
$$c = 17 \qquad \text{Find the positive square root.}$$

ANSWER ▶ Because the side lengths 8, 15, and 17 are integers, they form a Pythagorean triple.

Pythagorean Triples **Find the unknown side length. Tell whether the side lengths form a Pythagorean triple.**

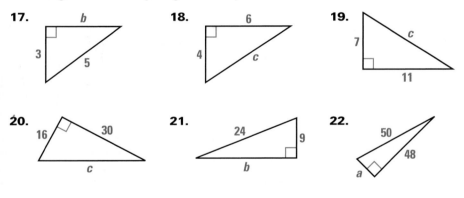

17.

18.

19.

20.

21.

22.

Visualize It! **Tell whether the side lengths form a Pythagorean triple. If so, draw a right triangle with the side lengths.**

23. 21, 29, 20

24. 25, 7, 24

25. 5, 12, 14

26. Support Beam The skyscrapers shown on page 170 are connected by a skywalk with support beams. Use the diagram to find the approximate length of each support beam.

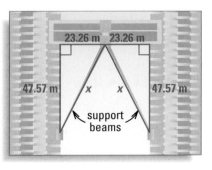

Link to
Architecture

PETRONAS TOWERS
These 1483 foot buildings tower over the city of Kuala Lumpur, Malaysia. When the Petronas Towers were designed by Cesar Pelli in 1991, they were the tallest buildings in the world.

Application Links
CLASSZONE.COM

Distance Formula Find the distance between the points. Round your answer to the nearest tenth.

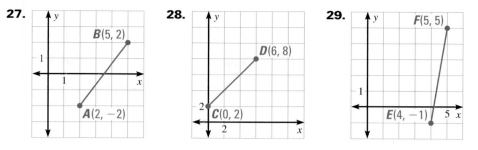

27. B(5, 2) A(2, −2)

28. D(6, 8) C(0, 2)

29. F(5, 5) E(4, −1)

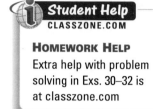
Congruence Graph *P*, *Q*, and *R*. Then use the Distance Formula to decide whether $\overline{PQ} \cong \overline{QR}$.

30. P(4, −4)
Q(1, −6)
R(−1, −3)

31. P(−1, −6)
Q(−8, 5)
R(3, −2)

32. P(5, 1)
Q(−5, −7)
R(−3, 6)

Sum of Distances In Exercises 33 and 34, use the map below. Sidewalks around the edge of a campus quadrangle connect the buildings. Students sometimes take shortcuts by walking across the grass along the pathways shown. The coordinate system shown is measured in yards.

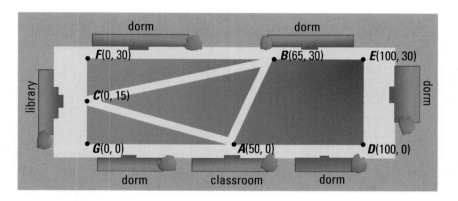

33. Find the distances from *A* to *B*, from *B* to *C*, and from *C* to *A* if you have to walk around the quadrangle along the sidewalks.

34. Find the distances from *A* to *B*, from *B* to *C*, and from *C* to *A* if you are able to walk across the grass along the pathways.

Challenge Find the value of *x*. Use a calculator, and round your answer to the nearest tenth.

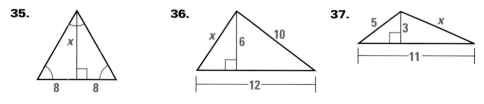

35. x, 8, 8

36. x, 6, 10, 12

37. 5, 3, x, 11

38. Multiple Choice What is the distance from $(3, 5)$ to $(-1, -4)$?

(A) $\sqrt{5}$ (B) $\sqrt{17}$ (C) $2\sqrt{13}$ (D) $\sqrt{97}$

39. Multiple Choice Which of the following is the length of the hypotenuse of a right triangle with legs of lengths 33 and 56?

(F) 65   (G) 72.9   (H) 85.8   (J) 89

Mixed Review

Finding Absolute Values Evaluate. *(Skills Review, p. 662)*

40. $|-7|$ **41.** $|1.05|$ **42.** $|0|$ **43.** $|-0.02|$

Solving Inequalities Solve the inequality. *(Algebra Review, p. 167)*

44. $x + 5 < 8$ **45.** $10 + x \geq 12$ **46.** $4x \geq 28$ **47.** $6x + 11 \leq 11$

Algebra Skills

Fractions and Decimals Write the decimal as a fraction in simplest form. *(Skills Review, p. 657)*

48. 0.4   **49.** 0.08   **50.** 0.54   **51.** 0.12

52. 0.250   **53.** 0.173   **54.** $0.\overline{3}$ **55.** $0.\overline{1}$

Quiz 2

Find the value of x. *(Lesson 4.3)*

1.   13 $3x - 5$

2. $55°$ $(2x + 1)°$

3. $x + 5$ $4x - 16$

In Exercises 4–6, find the distance between the points. *(Lesson 4.4)*

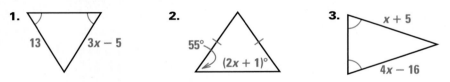

4. $A(-2, 3)$, $B(3, 0)$

5. $A(-3, -1)$, $B(1, -2)$

6. $B(1, 2)$, $A(-1, -1)$

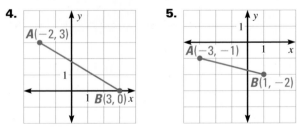
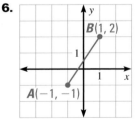

7. A device used to measure windspeed is attached to the top of a pole. Support wires are attached to the pole 5 feet above the ground. Each support wire is 6 feet long. About how far from the base of the pole is each wire attached to the ground? *(Lesson 4.4)*

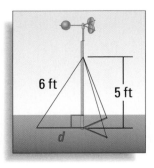

6 ft   5 ft d

Question

What is the relationship between the side lengths of a triangle and its angle measures?

Explore

① Draw A, B, C, and $\triangle ABC$.

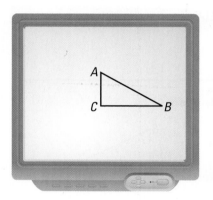

② Measure AB, BC, and CA. Calculate $(AB)^2$ and $(BC)^2 + (CA)^2$.

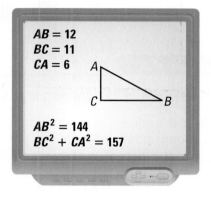

$AB = 12$
$BC = 11$
$CA = 6$

$AB^2 = 144$
$BC^2 + CA^2 = 157$

③ Measure $\angle ACB$.

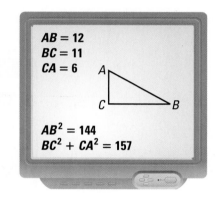

$AB = 12$
$BC = 11$
$CA = 6$

$AB^2 = 144$
$BC^2 + CA^2 = 157$

Think About It

Copy the table below and record the values as you work Exercises 1–3.

	AB	BC	CA	$(AB)^2$	$(BC)^2 + (CA)^2$	$m\angle ACB$
Triangle 1	?	?	?	?	?	?
Triangle 2	?	?	?	?	?	?
Triangle 3	?	?	?	?	?	?

1. Drag point A or B until $(AB)^2 = (BC)^2 + (CA)^2$. What do you notice about $m\angle ACB$?

2. Drag point A or B until $(AB)^2 > (BC)^2 + (CA)^2$. What do you notice about $m\angle ACB$?

3. Drag point A or B until $(AB)^2 < (BC)^2 + (CA)^2$. What do you notice about $m\angle ACB$?

4. Can you create an acute triangle in which $(AB)^2 > (BC)^2 + (CA)^2$?

4.5 The Converse of the Pythagorean Theorem

Goal

Use the Converse of Pythagorean Theorem. Use side lengths to classify triangles.

Key Words

• converse p. 136

A gardener can use the Converse of the Pythagorean Theorem to make sure that the corners of a garden bed form right angles.

In the photograph, a triangle with side lengths 3 feet, 4 feet, and 5 feet ensures that the angle at one corner is a right angle.

THEOREM 4.8

The Converse of the Pythagorean Theorem

Words If the square of the length of the longest side of a triangle is equal to the sum of the squares of the lengths of the other two sides, then the triangle is a right triangle.

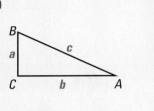

Symbols If $c^2 = a^2 + b^2$, then $\triangle ABC$ is a right triangle.

Student Help

LOOK BACK
For the definition of converse, see p. 136.

EXAMPLE 1 Verify a Right Triangle

Is $\triangle ABC$ a right triangle?

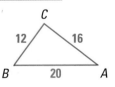

Solution

Let c represent the length of the longest side of the triangle. Check to see whether the side lengths satisfy the equation $c^2 = a^2 + b^2$.

$$c^2 \stackrel{?}{=} a^2 + b^2 \qquad \text{Compare } c^2 \text{ with } a^2 + b^2.$$

$$20^2 \stackrel{?}{=} 12^2 + 16^2 \qquad \text{Substitute 20 for } c, \text{ 12 for } a, \text{ and 16 for } b.$$

$$400 \stackrel{?}{=} 144 + 256 \qquad \text{Multiply.}$$

$$400 = 400 \qquad \text{Simplify.}$$

ANSWER ▶ It is true that $c^2 = a^2 + b^2$. So, $\triangle ABC$ is a right triangle.

Classifying Triangles You can determine whether a triangle is acute, right, or obtuse by its side lengths.

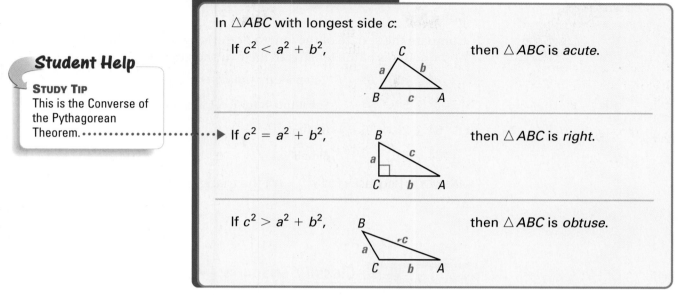

CLASSIFYING TRIANGLES

In $\triangle ABC$ with longest side c:

If $c^2 < a^2 + b^2$, then $\triangle ABC$ is *acute*.

If $c^2 = a^2 + b^2$, then $\triangle ABC$ is *right*.

If $c^2 > a^2 + b^2$, then $\triangle ABC$ is *obtuse*.

Student Help

STUDY TIP
This is the Converse of the Pythagorean Theorem.

EXAMPLE **2** Acute Triangles

Show that the triangle is an acute triangle.

Student Help

STUDY TIP
$\sqrt{35} \approx 5.9$, so use $\sqrt{35}$ as the value of c, the longest side length of the triangle.

Solution
Compare the side lengths.

$$c^2 \stackrel{?}{=} a^2 + b^2 \qquad \text{Compare } c^2 \text{ with } a^2 + b^2.$$
$$(\sqrt{35})^2 \stackrel{?}{=} 4^2 + 5^2 \qquad \text{Substitute } \sqrt{35} \text{ for } c, 4 \text{ for } a, \text{ and } 5 \text{ for } b.$$
$$35 \stackrel{?}{=} 16 + 25 \qquad \text{Multiply.}$$
$$35 < 41 \qquad \text{Simplify.}$$

ANSWER ▶ Because $c^2 < a^2 + b^2$, the triangle is acute.

EXAMPLE **3** Obtuse Triangles

Show that the triangle is an obtuse triangle.

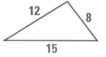

Solution
Compare the side lengths.

$$c^2 \stackrel{?}{=} a^2 + b^2 \qquad \text{Compare } c^2 \text{ with } a^2 + b^2.$$
$$(15)^2 \stackrel{?}{=} 8^2 + 12^2 \qquad \text{Substitute } 15 \text{ for } c, 8 \text{ for } a, \text{ and } 12 \text{ for } b.$$
$$225 \stackrel{?}{=} 64 + 144 \qquad \text{Multiply.}$$
$$225 > 208 \qquad \text{Simplify.}$$

ANSWER ▶ Because $c^2 > a^2 + b^2$, the triangle is obtuse.

EXAMPLE 4 **Classify Triangles**

Classify the triangle as *acute*, *right*, or *obtuse*.

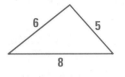

Solution

Compare the square of the length of the longest side with the sum of the squares of the lengths of the two shorter sides.

$c^2 \overset{?}{=} a^2 + b^2$ Compare c^2 with $a^2 + b^2$.

$8^2 \overset{?}{=} 5^2 + 6^2$ Substitute 8 for c, 5 for a, and 6 for b.

$64 \overset{?}{=} 25 + 36$ Multiply.

$64 > 61$ Simplify.

ANSWER ▶ Because $c^2 > a^2 + b^2$, the triangle is obtuse.

EXAMPLE 5 **Classify Triangles**

Classify the triangle with the given side lengths as *acute*, *right*, or *obtuse*.

  a. 4, 6, 7   **b.** 12, 35, 37

Solution

a.	**b.**
$c^2 \overset{?}{=} a^2 + b^2$	$c^2 \overset{?}{=} a^2 + b^2$
$7^2 \overset{?}{=} 4^2 + 6^2$	$37^2 \overset{?}{=} 12^2 + 35^2$
$49 \overset{?}{=} 16 + 36$	$1369 \overset{?}{=} 144 + 1225$
$49 < 52$	$1369 = 1369$
The triangle is acute.	The triangle is right.

Checkpoint ✓ **Classify Triangles**

Classify the triangle as *acute*, *right*, or *obtuse*. Explain.

1.   **2.**   **3.**

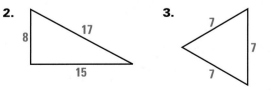

Use the side lengths to classify the triangle as *acute*, *right*, or *obtuse*.

4. 7, 24, 24   **5.** 7, 24, 25   **6.** 7, 24, 26

4.5 Exercises

Guided Practice

Vocabulary Check
1. Write the Converse of the Pythagorean Theorem in your own words.

Skill Check
Determine whether the triangle is *acute*, *right*, or *obtuse*.

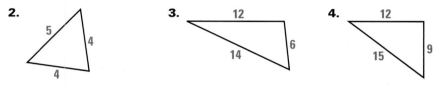

2.

3. 12 14 6

4. 12 15 9

Match the side lengths of a triangle with the best description.

5. 2, 10, 11   **A.** right

6. 8, 5, 7   **B.** acute

7. 5, 5, 5   **C.** obtuse

8. 6, 8, 10   **D.** equiangular

Practice and Applications

Extra Practice

See p. 682.

Verifying Right Triangles Show that the triangle is a right triangle.

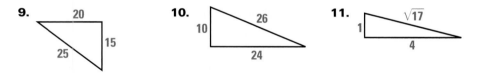

9. 20 25 15

10. 10 26 24

11. $\sqrt{17}$ 1 4

Verifying Acute Triangles Show that the triangle is an acute triangle.

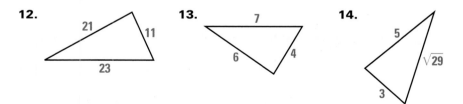

12. 21 11 23

13. 7 6 4

14. 5 $\sqrt{29}$ 3

Homework Help

Example 1: Exs. 9–11, 24
Example 2: Exs. 12–14
Example 3: Exs. 15–17
Example 4: Exs. 18–23, 37–38
Example 5: Exs. 25–36

Verifying Obtuse Triangles Show that the triangle is an obtuse triangle.

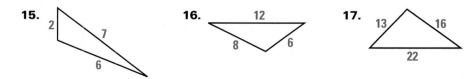

15. 2 7 6

16. 12 8 6

17. 13 16 22

Classifying Triangles Classify the triangle as *acute*, *right*, or *obtuse*.

18.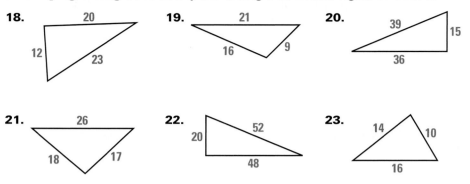

19.

20.

21.

22.

23.

EARLY MATHEMATICS
This photograph shows part
of a Babylonian clay tablet
made around 350 B.C. The
tablet contains a table of
numbers.

24. Early Mathematics The Babylonian tablet shown at the left contains
several sets of triangle side lengths, suggesting that the Babylonians
may have been aware of the relationships among the side lengths
of right triangles. The side lengths in the table below show several
sets of numbers from the tablet. Use a calculator to verify that each
set of side lengths satisfies the Pythagorean Theorem.

a	b	c
120	119	169
4,800	4,601	6,649
13,500	12,709	18,541

Classifying Triangles Classify the triangle with the given side
lengths as *acute*, *right*, or *obtuse*.

25. 20, 99, 101

26. 21, 28, 35

27. 26, 10, 17

28. 7, 10, 11

29. 4, $\sqrt{67}$, 9

30. $\sqrt{13}$, 6, 7

31. 468, 595, 757

32. 10, 11, 14

33. 4, 5, 5

34. 17, 144, 145

35. 10, 49, 50

36. $\sqrt{5}$, 5, 5.5

Air Travel In Exercises 37 and 38, use the map below.

37. Use the distances given on the
map to tell whether the triangle
formed by the three cities is a
right triangle.

38. Cincinnati is directly west of
Washington, D.C. Is Tallahassee
directly south of Cincinnati?
Explain your answer.

39. 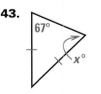 **You be the Judge** A classmate tells you if you find three side lengths that form a right triangle and double each of them, the sides will form an obtuse triangle. Is your classmate correct? Explain.

Challenge Graph points *P*, *Q*, and *R*. Connect the points to form △*PQR*. Decide whether △*PQR* is *acute*, *right*, or *obtuse*.

40. $P(-3, 4)$, $Q(5, 0)$, $R(-6, -2)$ **41.** $P(-1, 2)$, $Q(4, 1)$, $R(0, -1)$

Standardized Test Practice

42. Multi-Step Problem A double play occurs in baseball when two outs are made on a single play. In the diagram shown, the ball is hit to the player at point *A*. A double play is made when the player at point *A* throws the ball to the player at point *B* who in turn throws it to the player at point *C*.

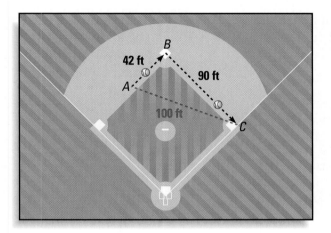

a. Use the diagram to determine what kind of triangle is formed by points *A*, *B*, and *C*.

b. What kind of triangle is formed by points *A*, *B*, and *C* if the distance between points *A* and *C* is 99 feet?

c. Critical Thinking Find values for *AB* and *AC* that would make △*ABC* in the diagram a right triangle if *BC* = 90 feet.

Mixed Review   **Finding Measures** Find the value of *x*. *(Lesson 4.3)*

43.
67°
$x°$

44.
8   3x − 4

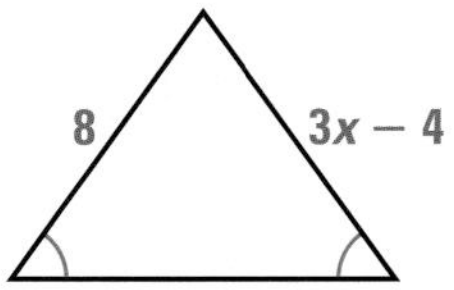

45.
$5x°$
$2x°$

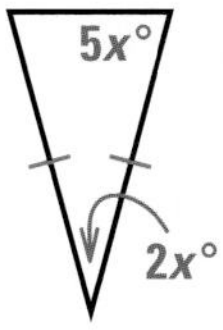

Algebra Skills   **Multiplying Fractions** Multiply. Write the answer as a fraction or a mixed number in simplest form. *(Skills Review, p. 659)*

46. $\frac{1}{2} \times \frac{4}{5}$ **47.** $\frac{3}{8} \times \frac{3}{4}$ **48.** $\frac{3}{11} \times \frac{11}{12}$ **49.** $\frac{3}{5} \times \frac{5}{9}$

50. $\frac{3}{4} \times 6$ **51.** $8 \times 1\frac{3}{4}$ **52.** $1\frac{1}{3} \times \frac{4}{9}$ **53.** $5\frac{1}{4} \times \frac{2}{3}$

Activity 4.6 Intersecting Medians

Question

What is the relationship between segments formed by the intersection of the medians of a triangle?

Materials

- straightedge
- scissors
- ruler

Explore

1 On a piece of paper, draw a triangle and cut it out.

2 Find the midpoint of each side by folding each side, vertex to vertex, and pinching the paper at the middle.

3 Draw a segment from each midpoint to the vertex of the opposite angle. These segments are called *medians*.

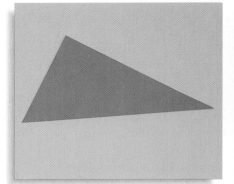

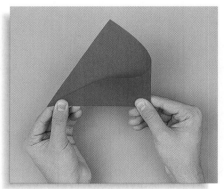

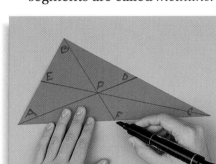

Think About It

1. Label the triangle as shown above. Copy and complete the table.

Length of median	$AD = ?$	$BF = ?$	$CE = ?$
Length of segment from *P* to vertex	$AP = ?$	$BP = ?$	$CP = ?$
Median length multiplied by $\frac{2}{3}$	$\frac{2}{3}AD = ?$	$\frac{2}{3}BF = ?$	$\frac{2}{3}CE = ?$

Student Help

SKILLS REVIEW
For help with multiplying fractions, see p. 659.

2. Is there a relationship between the distance from P to a vertex and the distance from that vertex to the midpoint of the opposite side?

3. Extension Repeat Steps 1 through 3 with triangles of different shapes and sizes and complete a table like the one in Exercise 1. Do your results differ? Explain.

Medians of a Triangle

Goal

Identify medians in triangles.

Key Words

• median of a triangle
• centroid

A cardboard triangle will balance on the end of a pencil if the pencil is placed at a particular point on the triangle. Finding balancing points of objects is important in engineering, construction, and science.

A **median of a triangle** is a segment from a vertex to the midpoint of the opposite side.

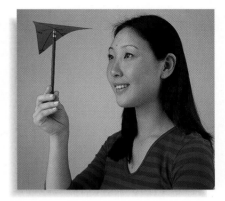

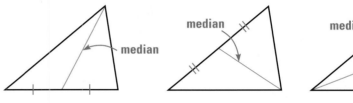

EXAMPLE 1 Draw a Median

In △STR, draw a median from S to its opposite side.

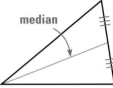

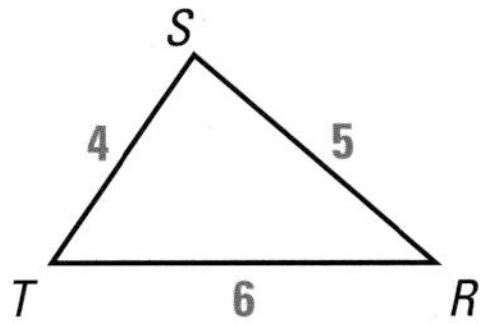

Solution

The side opposite ∠S is $\overline{TR}$.

Find the midpoint of $\overline{TR}$, and label it P. Then draw a segment from point S to point P. $\overline{SP}$ is a median of △STR.

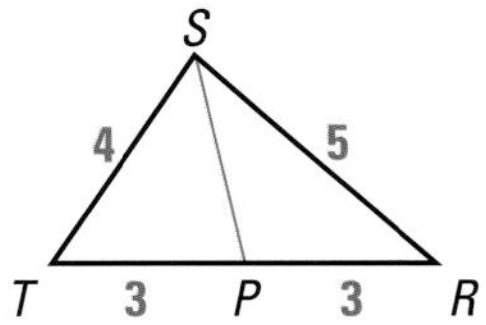

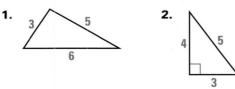 **Draw a Median**

Copy the triangle and draw a median.

1.

2.

3.

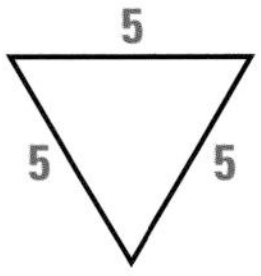

The following theorem tells you that the three medians of a triangle intersect at one point. This point is called the **centroid** of the triangle.

THEOREM 4.9

Intersection of Medians of a Triangle

Words The medians of a triangle intersect at the centroid, a point that is two thirds of the distance from each vertex to the midpoint of the opposite side.

Symbols If P is the centroid of $\triangle ABC$, then

$AP = \frac{2}{3}AD$, $BP = \frac{2}{3}BF$, and $CP = \frac{2}{3}CE$.

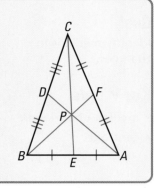

Student Help
CLASSZONE.COM

MORE EXAMPLES
More examples at classzone.com

EXAMPLE 2 Use the Centroid of a Triangle

E is the centroid of $\triangle ABC$ and $DA = 27$. Find EA and DE.

Solution

Using Theorem 4.9, you know that

$$EA = \frac{2}{3}DA = \frac{2}{3}(27) = 18.$$

Now use the Segment Addition Postulate to find ED.

$DA = DE + EA$	Segment Addition Postulate
$27 = DE + 18$	Substitute 27 for DA and 18 for EA.
$27 - 18 = DE + 18 - 18$	Subtract 18 from each side.
$9 = DE$	Simplify.

ANSWER $\overline{EA}$ has a length of 18 and $\overline{DE}$ has a length of 9.

EXAMPLE 3 Use the Centroid of a Triangle

P is the centroid of $\triangle QRS$ and $RP = 10$. Find the length of $\overline{RT}$.

Solution

$RP = \frac{2}{3}RT$	Use Theorem 4.9.
$10 = \frac{2}{3}RT$	Substitute 10 for RP.
$\frac{3}{2}(10) = \frac{3}{2}\left(\frac{2}{3}RT\right)$	Multiply each side by $\frac{3}{2}$.
$15 = RT$	Simplify.

ANSWER The median $\overline{RT}$ has a length of 15.

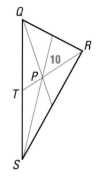

The centroid of the triangle is shown. Find the lengths.

4. Find *BE* and *ED*, given *BD* = 24.

5. Find *JG* and *KG*, given *JK* = 4.

6. Find *PQ* and *PN*, given *QN* = 20.

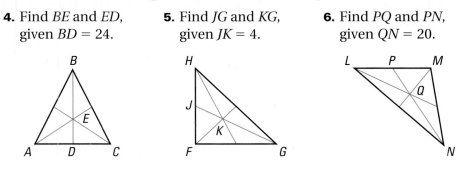

4.6 Exercises

Guided Practice

Vocabulary Check

In Exercises 1 and 2, complete the statement.

1. The segment from a vertex of a triangle to the midpoint of the opposite side is a(n) __?__.

2. The __?__ is the point where the three medians intersect.

3. Copy △*ABC*, then draw the median from point *A* to $\overline{BC}$.

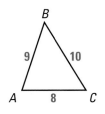

Skill Check

$\overline{BD}$ **is a median of** △***ABC***. **Find the length of** $\overline{AD}$.

4.

5.

6.

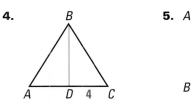

7. *T* is the centroid of △*PQR* and *PS* = 33. Find *PT* and *ST*.

8. *E* is the centroid of △*ABC* and *BE* = 12. Find *BD* and *ED*.

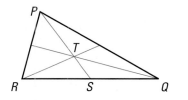

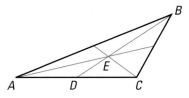

Practice and Applications

Extra Practice

See p. 682.

In Exercises 9 and 10, copy the triangle and draw the three medians of the triangle.

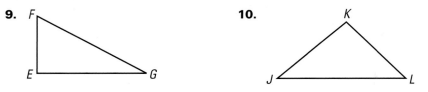

9.   **10.**

Using a Centroid *P* is the centroid of △*LMN*. Find *PN* and *QP*.

11. $QN = 9$ **12.** $QN = 21$ **13.** $QN = 30$

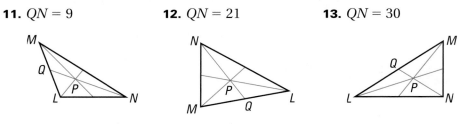

Using a Centroid *D* is the centroid of △*ABC*. Find *CD* and *CE*.

14. $DE = 5$ **15.** $DE = 11$ **16.** $DE = 9$

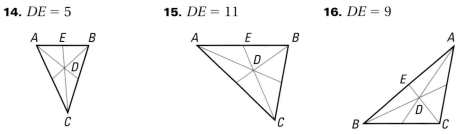

17. Error Analysis *D* is the centroid of △*ABC*. Your friend wants to find *DE*. The median $AE = 18$. Find and correct the error. Explain your reasoning.

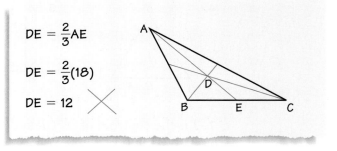

$$DE = \frac{2}{3}AE$$

$$DE = \frac{2}{3}(18)$$

$$DE = 12 \quad \times$$

Homework Help

Example 1: Exs. 9, 10, 18
Example 2: Exs. 11–13, 17
Example 3: Exs. 14–16

18. Finding a Centroid Draw a triangle and find the midpoint of each side. Then draw the three medians of your triangle. Label the centroid *P*.

Student Help
CLASSZONE.COM

HOMEWORK HELP
Extra help with problem solving in Exs. 19–21 is at classzone.com

Using Algebra **Copy the graph shown.**

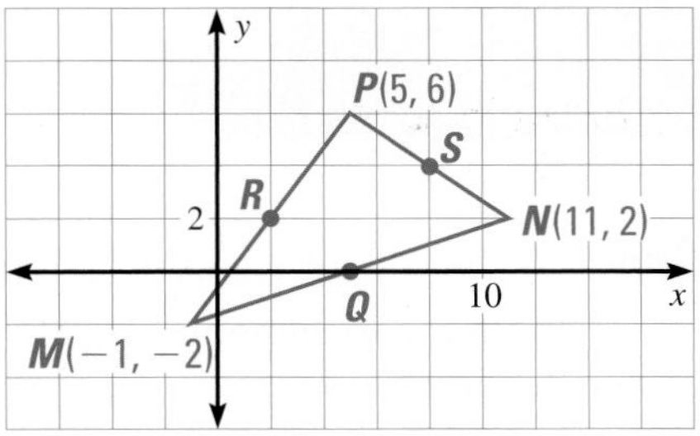

19. Find the coordinates of Q, R, and S, the midpoints of the sides of the triangle.

20. Find the length of each median.

21. Find the coordinates of the centroid. Label this point as T.

Standardized Test Practice

22. Multiple Choice In the figure shown, N is the centroid of $\triangle JKL$ and $KM = 36$. What is the length of $\overline{MN}$?

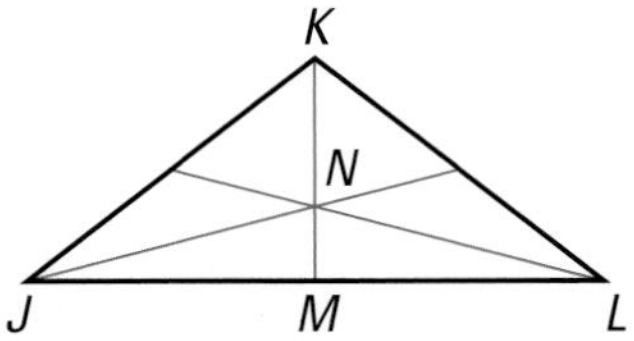

Ⓐ 9 Ⓑ 12

Ⓒ 16 Ⓓ 24

23. Multiple Choice In the figure shown, P is the centroid of $\triangle RST$ and $PT = 12$. What is the length of $\overline{VT}$?

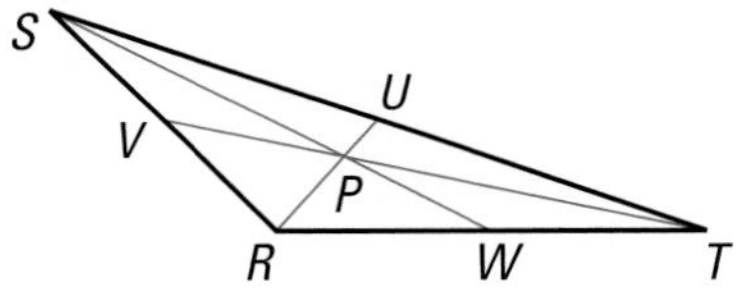

Ⓕ 8 Ⓖ 18

Ⓗ 24 Ⓙ 36

Mixed Review

Finding Angle Measures in a Triangle **Find $m\angle 1$.** *(Lesson 4.2)*

24.
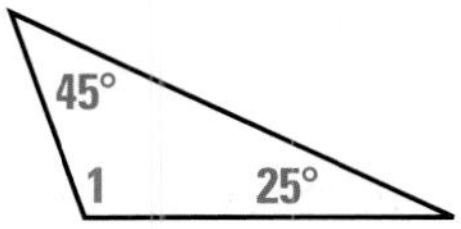

25.
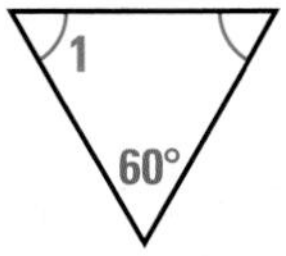

26.
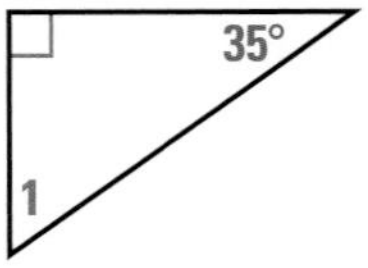

27.
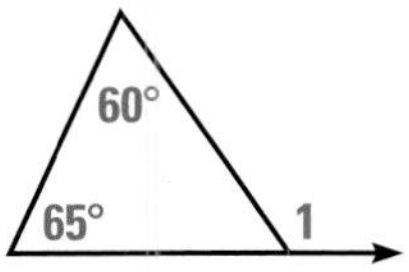

28.
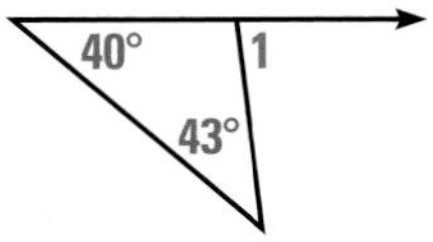

29.
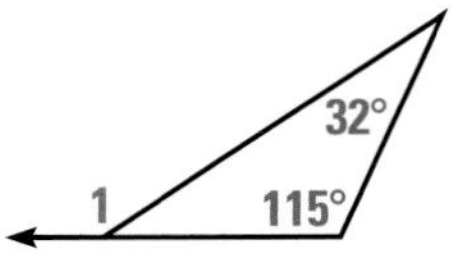

Algebra Skills

Writing Equivalent Fractions **Write two fractions equivalent to the given fraction.** *(Skills Review, p. 656)*

30. $\frac{1}{2}$ **31.** $\frac{1}{5}$ **32.** $\frac{3}{4}$ **33.** $\frac{8}{14}$

34. $\frac{12}{26}$ **35.** $\frac{2}{20}$ **36.** $\frac{8}{36}$ **37.** $\frac{10}{45}$

38. $\frac{14}{35}$ **39.** $\frac{18}{24}$ **40.** $\frac{20}{30}$ **41.** $\frac{24}{33}$

4.7 Triangle Inequalities

Goal

Use triangle measurements to decide which side is longest and which angle is largest.

The diagrams below show a relationship between the longest and shortest sides of a triangle and the largest and smallest angles.

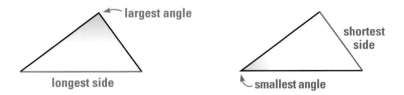

largest angle

longest side

shortest side

smallest angle

THEOREMS 4.10 and 4.11

Theorem 4.10

Words If one side of a triangle is longer than another side, then the angle opposite the longer side is larger than the angle opposite the shorter side.

Symbols If $BC > AB$, then $m\angle A > m\angle C$.

Theorem 4.11

Words If one angle of a triangle is larger than another angle, then the side opposite the larger angle is longer than the side opposite the smaller angle.

Symbols If $m\angle D > m\angle E$, then $EF > DF$.

EXAMPLE 1 Order Angle Measures

Name the angles from largest to smallest.

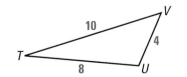

Solution

$TV > TU$, so $m\angle U > m\angle V$. Also, $TU > UV$, so $m\angle V > m\angle T$.

ANSWER ▶ The order of the angles from largest to smallest is $\angle U, \angle V, \angle T$.

EXAMPLE 2 **Order Side Lengths**

Name the sides from longest to shortest.

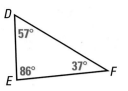

Solution

$m\angle E > m\angle D$, so $DF > FE$. Also, $m\angle D > m\angle F$, so $FE > DE$.

ANSWER ▶ The order of the sides from longest to shortest is $\overline{DF}$, $\overline{FE}$, $\overline{DE}$.

Checkpoint ✓ **Order Angle Measures and Side Lengths**

Name the angles from largest to smallest.

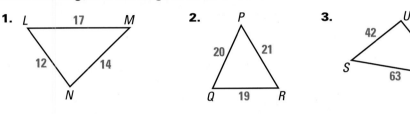

Name the sides from longest to shortest.

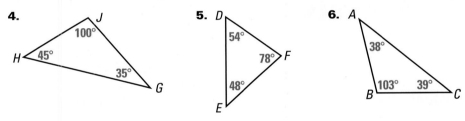

Segments of a Triangle Not every group of three segments can be used to form a triangle. The lengths of the segments must have the following relationship.

THEOREM 4.12

Triangle Inequality

Words The sum of the lengths of any two sides of a triangle is greater than the length of the third side.

Symbols

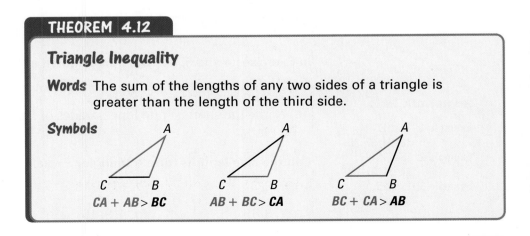

$CA + AB > BC$ $AB + BC > CA$ $BC + CA > AB$

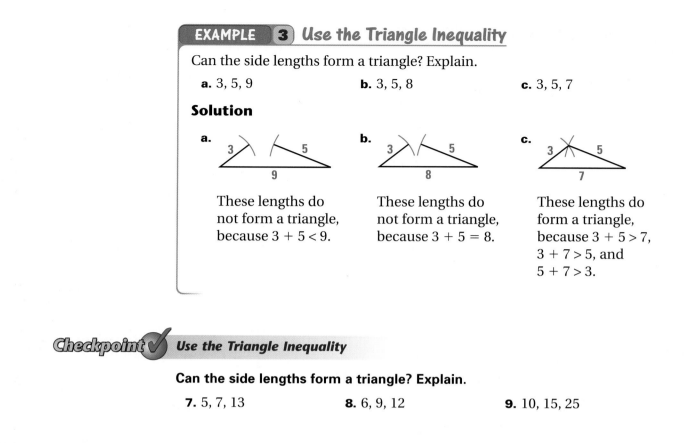

EXAMPLE 3 Use the Triangle Inequality

Can the side lengths form a triangle? Explain.

a. 3, 5, 9   **b.** 3, 5, 8   **c.** 3, 5, 7

Solution

a. These lengths do not form a triangle, because $3 + 5 < 9$.

b. These lengths do not form a triangle, because $3 + 5 = 8$.

c. These lengths do form a triangle, because $3 + 5 > 7$, $3 + 7 > 5$, and $5 + 7 > 3$.

Checkpoint ✓ Use the Triangle Inequality

Can the side lengths form a triangle? Explain.

7. 5, 7, 13   **8.** 6, 9, 12   **9.** 10, 15, 25

4.7 Exercises

Guided Practice

Vocabulary Check

1. Complete the statement: The symbol ">" means __?__ , and the symbol "<" means __?__ .

Skill Check

2. Name the smallest angle of $\triangle ABC$.

3. Name the longest side of $\triangle ABC$.

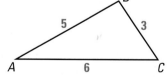

In Exercises 4 and 5, use the figure shown at the right.

4. Name the smallest and largest angles of $\triangle DEF$.

5. Name the shortest and longest sides of $\triangle DEF$.

Can the side lengths form a triangle? Explain.

6. 1, 2, 3   **7.** 6, 10, 15   **8.** 12, 16, 30

9. 7, 8, 13   **10.** 4, 9, 16   **11.** 5, 5, 10

Practice and Applications

Extra Practice

See p. 682.

Comparing Angle Measures **Name the smallest and largest angles of the triangle.**

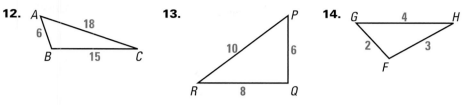

12.

A
18
6
B
15
C

13.

P
10
6
R
8
Q

14.

G
4
H
2
3
F

Comparing Side Lengths **Name the shortest and longest sides of the triangle.**

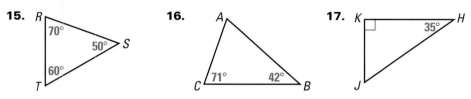

15.

R
70°
50°
S
60°
T

16.

A
C
71°
42°
B

17.

K
35°
H
J

Ordering Angles **Name the angles from largest to smallest.**

18.

L
10
M
14
8
K

19.

P
18
12
N
24
Q

20.

T
9
6
R
5
S

21.

B
15
13
A
10
C

22.

X
7
Y
16
20
W

23.

E
29
40
D
38
F

Link to Kitchen Design

KITCHEN TRIANGLES
For ease of movement among appliances, the perimeter of an ideal kitchen triangle should be less than 22 feet and more than 15 feet.

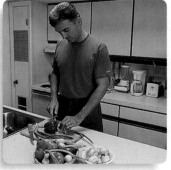

Design **In Exercises 24 and 25, use the following information.**
The term "kitchen triangle" refers to the imaginary triangle formed by the refrigerator, the sink, and the stove. The distances shown are measured in feet.

STOVE
4 ft
82°
6.4 ft
60°
38°
5.6 ft
SINK
REFRIGERATOR

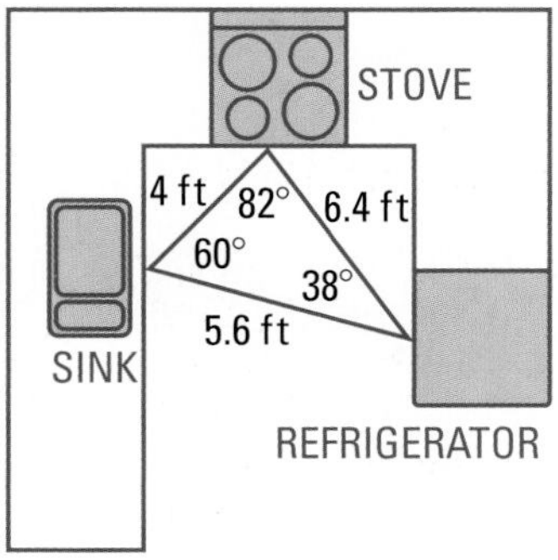

24. What is wrong with the labels on the kitchen triangle?

25. Can a kitchen triangle have the following side lengths: 9 feet, 3 feet, and 5 feet? Explain why or why not.

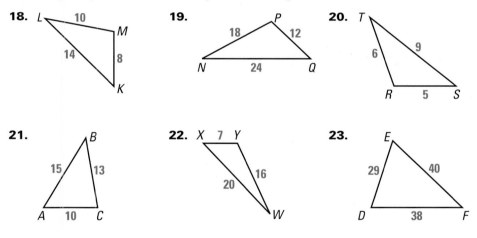

Ordering Sides Name the sides from longest to shortest.

26.
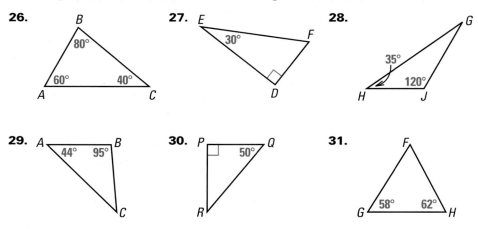

27. E

28. G

29. A

30. P

31.

Error Analysis Explain why the side lengths given with the triangles are not correct.

32.
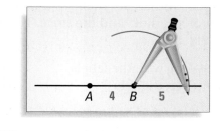

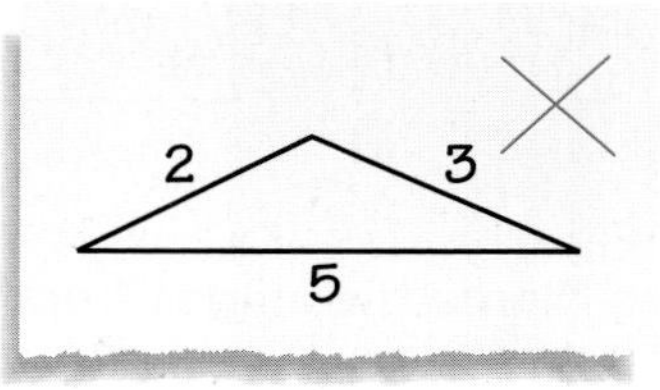

33.
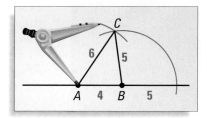

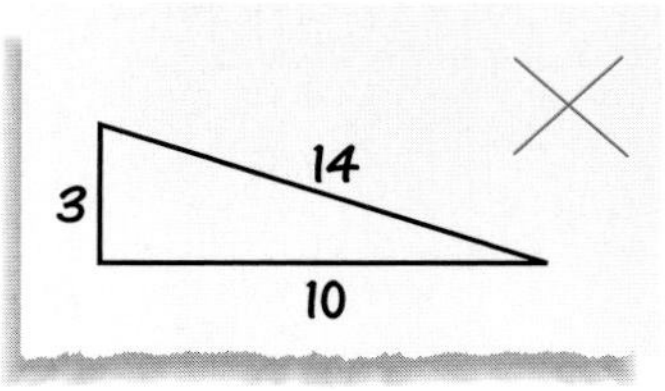

EXAMPLE   *Use the Triangle Inequality*

Is it possible to draw a triangle that has side lengths of 4, 5, and 6? If so, draw the triangle.

Solution

Yes, these side lengths satisfy the Triangle Inequality: $4 + 5 > 6$, $5 + 6 > 4$, and $4 + 6 > 5$. So, it is possible to draw the triangle, as shown below.

❶ Mark $\overline{AB}$ of length 4 cm on a line. Then draw an arc of radius 5 cm with center at B.

❷ Draw an arc of radius 6 cm with center at A. Mark the intersection of the two arcs as C. △ABC has side lengths of 4 cm, 5 cm, and 6 cm.

Using the Triangle Inequality Determine whether it is possible to draw a triangle with the given side lengths. If so, draw the triangle.

34. 4, 7, 10   **35.** 10, 12, 22   **36.** 17, 9, 30

Visualize It! Sketch a triangle and label it with the given angle measures and side lengths.

37. Angles: 59°, 46°, 75°
Sides: 13 cm, 9.7 cm, 11.5 cm

38. Angles: 135°, 15°, 30°
Sides: 7.1 cm, 2.6 cm, 5 cm

39. Taking a Shortcut Suppose you are walking south on the sidewalk of Pine Street. When you reach Pleasant Street, you cut across the empty lot to go to the corner of Oak Hill Avenue and Union Street. Explain why this route is shorter than staying on the sidewalks.

40. **You be the Judge** Suppose you are camping. You decide to hike 4.6 miles northwest and then turn and hike 1.8 miles east. Your friend tells you that you are about one and a half miles from camp. Is your friend right? Explain why or why not.

Logical Reasoning In Exercises 41–43, use the figure shown and the given information.
By adjusting the length of the boom lines from A to B, the operator of the crane shown can raise and lower the boom. Suppose the mast $\overline{AC}$ is 50 feet long and the boom $\overline{BC}$ is 100 feet long.

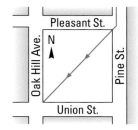

41. Is the boom *raised* or *lowered* when the boom lines are shortened?

42. *AB* must be less than ___?___ feet.

43. As the boom is raised or lowered, is $\angle ACB$ ever larger than $\angle BAC$? Explain.

44. Multi-Step Problem You are given an 18-inch piece of wire. You want to bend the wire to form a triangle so that the length of each side is a whole number.

   a. Sketch four possible isosceles triangles and label each side length.

   b. Sketch a possible acute scalene triangle.

   c. Sketch a possible obtuse scalene triangle.

   d. List three combinations of segment lengths with a sum of 18 that will not produce triangles.

Mixed Review

Identifying Parts of a Triangle In Exercises 45–48, use the figure shown to complete the statement. *(Lessons 4.1, 4.3, 4.4)*

45. __?__ is the hypotenuse of △RST.

46. In △RST, $\overline{RT}$ is the side __?__ ∠RST.

47. The legs of △RST are __?__ and __?__.

48. __?__ is the base of △RST.

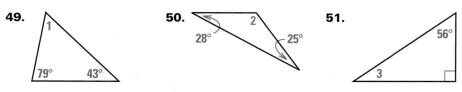

Finding Measures Find the measure of the numbered angle. *(Lesson 4.2)*

49.   **50.**   **51.**

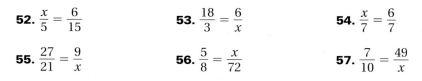

Algebra Skills

Solving Proportions Solve the proportion. *(Skills Review, p. 660)*

52. $\dfrac{x}{5} = \dfrac{6}{15}$ **53.** $\dfrac{18}{3} = \dfrac{6}{x}$ **54.** $\dfrac{x}{7} = \dfrac{6}{7}$

55. $\dfrac{27}{21} = \dfrac{9}{x}$ **56.** $\dfrac{5}{8} = \dfrac{x}{72}$ **57.** $\dfrac{7}{10} = \dfrac{49}{x}$

Quiz 3

Use the side lengths to classify the triangle as *acute, right,* or *obtuse.* *(Lesson 4.5)*

1. 6, 11, 14   **2.** 15, 7, 16   **3.** 18, 80, 82

N is the centroid of △*JKL*. Find *KN* and *MN*. *(Lesson 4.6)*

4. *KM* = 6   **5.** *KM* = 39   **6.** *KM* = 60

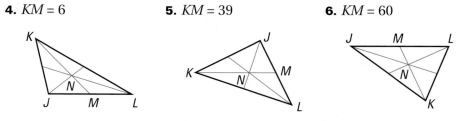

Name the sides from longest to shortest. *(Lesson 4.7)*

7.   **8.**   **9.**

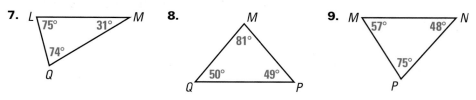

Chapter 4 Summary and Review

VOCABULARY

- **triangle,** *p. 173*
- **equilateral triangle,** *p. 173*
- **isosceles triangle,** *p. 173*
- **scalene triangle,** *p. 173*
- **equiangular triangle,** *p. 174*
- **acute triangle,** *p. 174*
- **right triangle,** *p. 174*
- **obtuse triangle,** *p. 174*
- **vertex,** *p. 175*
- **corollary,** *p. 180*
- **interior angle,** *p. 181*
- **exterior angle,** *p. 181*
- **legs of an isosceles triangle,** *p. 185*
- **base of an isosceles triangle,** *p. 185*
- **base angles of an isosceles triangle,** *p. 185*
- **legs of a right triangle,** *p. 192*
- **hypotenuse,** *p. 192*
- **Pythagorean Theorem,** *p. 192*
- **Distance Formula,** *p. 194*
- **median of a triangle,** *p. 207*
- **centroid,** *p. 208*

VOCABULARY REVIEW

Fill in the blank.

1. A(n) __?__ is a figure formed by three segments joining three noncollinear points.

2. The side opposite the right angle is the __?__ of a right triangle.

3. A(n) __?__ to a theorem is a statement that can be proved easily using the theorem.

4. The congruent sides of an isosceles triangle are called __?__, and the third side is called the __?__.

5. A point that joins two sides of a triangle is called a(n) __?__.

6. A segment from a vertex of a triangle to the midpoint of its opposite side is called a(n) __?__.

7. The point at which the medians of a triangle intersect is called the __?__ of a triangle.

4.1 CLASSIFYING TRIANGLES

Examples on pp. 173–175

EXAMPLES Classify the triangle by its angles and by its sides.

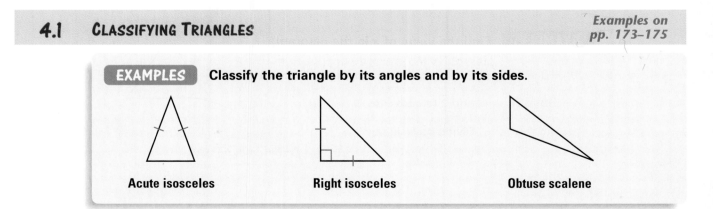

Acute isosceles   Right isosceles   Obtuse scalene

Classify the triangle by its sides.

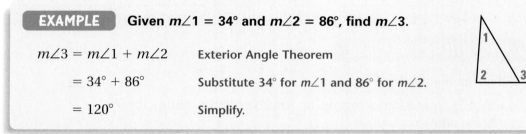

8.

9.

10.

11. What kind of triangle has angle measures of 30°, 60°, and 90°?

12. What kind of triangle has angle measures of 84°, 55°, and 41°?

13. What kind of triangle has side lengths of 4 feet, 8 feet, and 8 feet?

4.2   ANGLE MEASURES OF TRIANGLES   *Examples on*
                                                          pp. 179–181

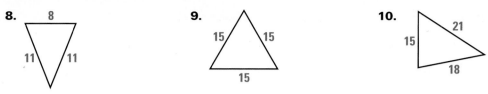

> **EXAMPLE**   **Given $m\angle 1 = 34°$ and $m\angle 2 = 86°$, find $m\angle 3$.**
>
> $m\angle 3 = m\angle 1 + m\angle 2$ Exterior Angle Theorem
>
> $\quad\quad = 34° + 86°$ Substitute 34° for $m\angle 1$ and 86° for $m\angle 2$.
>
> $\quad\quad = 120°$ Simplify.

Find $m\angle 1$.

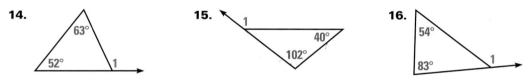

14.

15.

16.

17. The measure of one interior angle of a triangle is 16°. The other
interior angles are congruent. Find their measures.

18. The measure of one of the interior angles of a right triangle is 31°.
Find the measures of the other interior angles.

4.3   ISOSCELES AND EQUILATERAL TRIANGLES   *Examples on*
                                                          pp. 185–187

> **EXAMPLE**   **Find the value of *x* in the diagram.**
>
> $3x - 2 = 16$ Converse of the Base Angles Theorem
>
> $3x = 18$ Add 2 to each side.
>
> $x = 6$ Divide each side by 3.

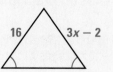

Find the value of *x*.

19.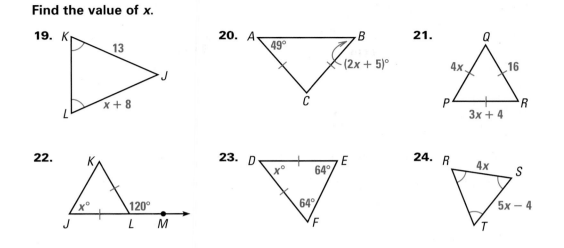

20.

21.

22.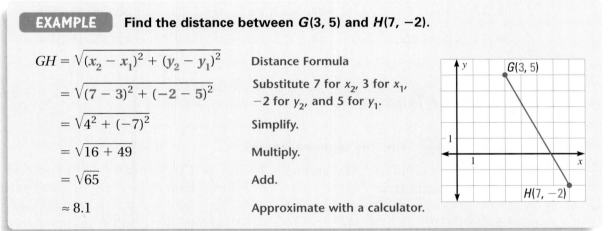

23.

24.

4.4 THE PYTHAGOREAN THEOREM AND THE DISTANCE FORMULA

Examples on pp. 192–194

EXAMPLE Find the distance between *G*(3, 5) and *H*(7, −2).

$$GH = \sqrt{(x_2 - x_1)^2 + (y_2 - y_1)^2}$$ Distance Formula

$$= \sqrt{(7 - 3)^2 + (-2 - 5)^2}$$ Substitute 7 for x_2, 3 for x_1, −2 for y_2, and 5 for y_1.

$$= \sqrt{4^2 + (-7)^2}$$ Simplify.

$$= \sqrt{16 + 49}$$ Multiply.

$$= \sqrt{65}$$ Add.

$$\approx 8.1$$ Approximate with a calculator.

Find the unknown side length. Use a calculator to round your answer to the nearest tenth, if necessary.

25.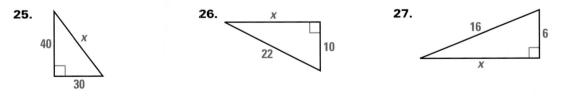

26.

27.

Find the distance between the two points. Use a calculator to round your answer to the nearest tenth, if necessary.

28. *A*(0, 0)
    B(−3, 4)

29. *A*(2, 5)
    B(6, −4)

30. *A*(−8, 7)
    B(3, 7)

31. *A*(−4, −1)
    B(0, 6)

32. *A*(−2, −1)
    B(−6, −7)

33. *A*(8, −3)
    B(−2, 4)

34. *A*(9, 1)
    B(−3, −6)

35. *A*(5, 4)
    B(0, 6)

4.5 THE CONVERSE OF THE PYTHAGOREAN THEOREM

Examples on pp. 200–202

EXAMPLE Classify the triangle as *acute*, *right*, or *obtuse*.

Compare the square of the length of the longest side with the sum of the squares of the lengths of the two shorter sides.

$c^2 \stackrel{?}{=} a^2 + b^2$ Compare c^2 with $a^2 + b^2$.

$21^2 \stackrel{?}{=} 17^2 + 13^2$ Substitute 21 for c, 17 for a, and 13 for b.

$441 \stackrel{?}{=} 289 + 169$ Multiply.

$441 < 458$ Simplify.

$c^2 < a^2 + b^2$, so the triangle is acute.

Use the side lengths to classify the triangle as *acute*, *right*, or *obtuse*.

36. 12, 9, 15   **37.** 7, 11, 16   **38.** 18, 19, 22

39. 18, 42, 44   **40.** 10, 3, 12   **41.** 15, 21, 31

4.6 MEDIANS OF A TRIANGLE

Examples on pp. 207–209

EXAMPLES Find the segment lengths.

a. D is the centroid of $\triangle ABC$ and $AE = 12$. Find AD and ED.

$AD = \frac{2}{3}AE$

$\quad = \frac{2}{3}(12) = 8$

$AE = AD + ED$

$12 = 8 + ED$

$4 = ED$

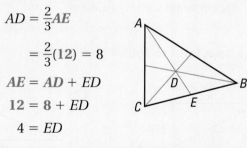

b. T is the centroid of $\triangle QRS$ and $RT = 18$. Find RU.

$RT = \frac{2}{3}RU$

$18 = \frac{2}{3}RU$

$\frac{3}{2}(18) = RU$

$27 = RU$

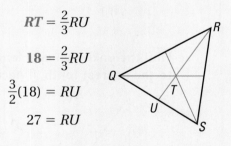

P is the centroid of $\triangle JKL$. Find *KP* and *PM*.

42. $KM = 18$ **43.** $KM = 42$ **44.** $KM = 120$

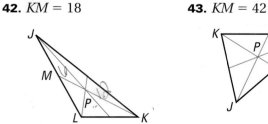

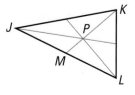

D is the centroid of △ABC. Find CE and DE.

45. $CD = 8$ **46.** $CD = 16$ **47.** $CD = 28$

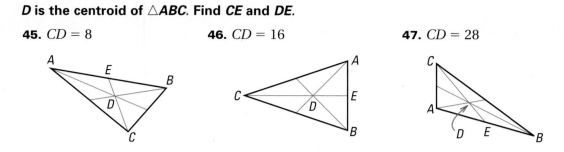

4.7 TRIANGLE INEQUALITIES

Examples on pp. 212–214

> **EXAMPLE**   **Name the sides of the triangle shown from longest to shortest.**
>
> By Theorem 4.11, if one angle of a triangle is larger than another angle, then the side opposite the larger angle is longer than the side opposite the smaller angle.
>
> So, because $m\angle F > m\angle G > m\angle H$, $GH > FH > GF$. The sides from longest to shortest are $\overline{GH}$, $\overline{FH}$, and $\overline{GF}$.

Name the angles from largest to smallest.

48.   **49.**   **50.**

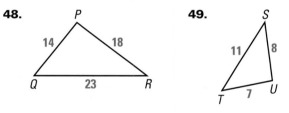 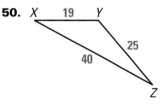

Name the sides from longest to shortest.

51.   **52.**   **53.**

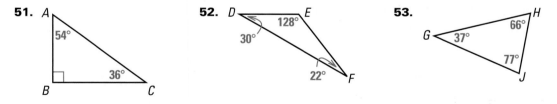

Determine whether it is possible to draw a triangle with the given side lengths. Explain your reasoning.

54. 10, 11, 20   **55.** 21, 23, 25   **56.** 3, 10, 15

57. 6, 6, 12   **58.** 13, 14, 15   **59.** 2, 3, 4

60. 4, 5, 9   **61.** 11, 11, 20   **62.** 14, 20, 38

Identify a triangle in the diagram that fits the given description.

1. obtuse

2. acute

3. equilateral

4. isosceles

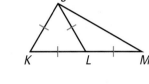

In Exercises 5–7, find the value of x.

5.

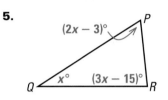

6.

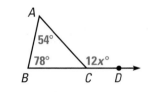

7.

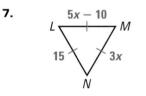

8. Find the length of the hypotenuse in the triangle shown. Use a calculator to round your answer to the nearest tenth.

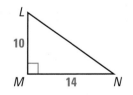

Plot the points and find the distance between them.

9. $P(0, 0), Q(-6, -8)$

10. $P(2, 4), Q(-2, 6)$

11. Is the triangle shown below acute, right, or obtuse?

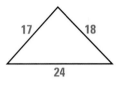

In Exercises 12 and 13, classify the triangle with the given side lengths as *acute*, *right*, or *obtuse*.

12. 6, 9, 13   13. 12, 14, 20

14. D is the centroid of $\triangle ABC$. Find DC and DE if $EC = 33$.

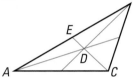

15. Name the sides from longest to shortest.

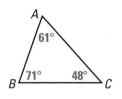

16. Find the measures of all numbered angles in the figure below.

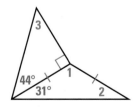

Determine whether the side lengths can form a triangle.

17. 5, 8, 18   18. 20, 24, 40

19. 7, 7, 14   20. 31, 45, 50

Test Tip
ⒶⒷⒸⒹ
Put a mark next to questions you skip so that you will remember to come back to them later.

1. Classify the triangle by its angles and by its sides.

Ⓐ acute scalene

Ⓑ obtuse isosceles

Ⓒ acute equilateral

Ⓓ right isosceles

2. What is $m\angle BCD$?

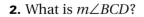

Ⓕ 35°   Ⓖ 90°

Ⓗ 125°   Ⓙ 180°

3. A triangle has two sides that have lengths of 14 feet and 22 feet. Which of the following lengths could *not* represent the length of the third side?

Ⓐ 8 ft   Ⓑ 12 ft

Ⓒ 14 ft   Ⓓ 20 ft

4. Which of the following is the correct order of the side lengths of the triangle from longest to shortest?

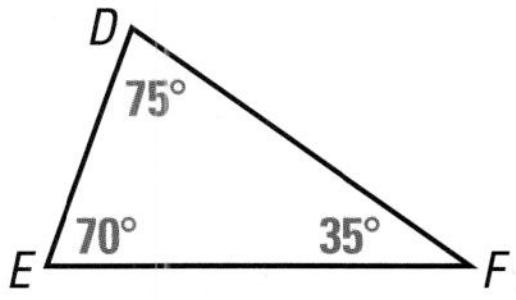

Ⓕ EF, DF, DE

Ⓖ DF, EF, DE

Ⓗ DE, DF, EF

Ⓙ EF, DE, DF

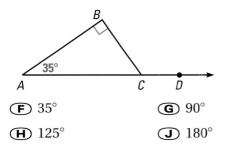

5. What is the distance between the points $J(3, 5)$ and $K(8, -2)$?

Ⓐ $\sqrt{34}$ Ⓑ 8.5

Ⓒ $\sqrt{74}$ Ⓓ 18

6. Classify the triangle.

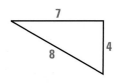

Ⓕ right

Ⓖ acute

Ⓗ equiangular

Ⓙ obtuse

7. In the triangle shown, what is the value of x?

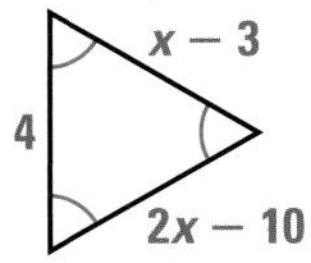

Ⓐ 4

Ⓑ 7

Ⓒ 8

Ⓓ 14

Multi-Step Problem In Exercises 8–10, use the figure shown.

8. What is the sum of x and y?

9. Which measure is greater, $x°$ or $y°$?

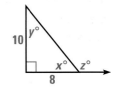

10. Which of the following is true?

Ⓕ $z = 90$ Ⓖ $z > 90$

Ⓗ $z < 90$ Ⓙ $z = y$

BraiN GaMes

Picture it

interior angle

Vertex

isosceles triangle

Materials
- 21 index cards or pieces of paper per team
- timer or watch

Object of the Game In one minute, teams guess as many vocabulary words as possible that a team member sketches.

Set Up Each team writes vocabulary words from Chapter 4 on index cards or pieces of paper. Use the vocabulary list on page 219. Place the cards in a pile with the vocabulary words facing down.

How to Play

Step 1 ▶ Each team chooses a player to sketch.

Step 2 ▶ The person who is sketching, looks at the word on the top card, without anyone else seeing it. A one minute timer is set. The sketcher draws a picture of the word on the other side of the card.

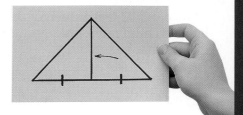

Step 3 ▶ When a team member guesses correctly, the sketcher goes to the next card.

Step 4 ▶ At the end of the minute, each card is checked to see if the word was drawn correctly. Record a point for each correct card.

Step 5 ▶ Play continues until each team member has had a turn to sketch. The team with the most points wins.

Another Way to Play Extend each turn to three minutes. Instead of just saying the vocabulary word, team members also have to write the definition on the card.

A *ratio* is a comparison of a number a and a nonzero number b using division.

EXAMPLE 1 Simplify Ratios

a. $\dfrac{8 \text{ male students}}{14 \text{ female students}}$ **b.** $\dfrac{16 \text{ inches}}{3 \text{ feet}}$

Solution

a. $\dfrac{8 \text{ male students}}{14 \text{ female students}} = \dfrac{8 \div 2}{14 \div 2} = \dfrac{4}{7}$

b. Use the fact that 1 foot = 12 inches to convert 3 feet to inches.

$\dfrac{16 \text{ inches}}{3 \text{ feet}} = \dfrac{16 \text{ inches}}{3 \times 12 \text{ inches}} = \dfrac{16 \text{ inches}}{36 \text{ inches}} = \dfrac{16 \div 4}{36 \div 4} = \dfrac{4}{9}$

Try These

Simplify the ratio.

1. $\dfrac{9 \text{ hours}}{24 \text{ hours}}$ **2.** $\dfrac{10 \text{ inches}}{2 \text{ feet}}$ **3.** $\dfrac{40 \text{ minutes}}{4 \text{ hours}}$ **4.** $\dfrac{6 \text{ pounds}}{20 \text{ ounces}}$

If a and b are two quantities that have different kinds of units of measure, then $\dfrac{a}{b}$ is a *rate of a per b*. A rate with 1 as its denominator is a *unit rate*. For example, $2 per pound $\left(\dfrac{\$2}{1 \text{ lb}} \right)$ is a unit rate.

EXAMPLE 2 Find Unit Rates

Suppose you travel 336 miles using 12 gallons of gasoline. Find the unit rate in miles per gallon.

Solution

$\text{Rate} = \dfrac{336 \text{ miles}}{12 \text{ gallons}} = \dfrac{336 \text{ miles} \div 12}{12 \text{ gallons} \div 12} = \dfrac{28 \text{ miles}}{1 \text{ gallon}} = 28 \text{ miles/gallon}$

Try These

Find the unit rate.

5. You work 56 hours in 8 days. **6.** You travel 60 miles in 2 hours.

7. You earn $38 in 4 hours. **8.** You pay $5.88 for 12 bagels.

Balancing Shapes

Objective

Find the balance points of triangles and other shapes.

Materials

- cardboard
- straightedge
- scissors
- paper punch
- string
- paper clip

How to Find a Balance Point

❶ Draw a large triangle on cardboard and cut it out. Punch holes in the triangle near the vertices.

❷ Tie a weight and a paper clip to the two ends of a string. Hang your triangle from the paper clip. Mark the vertical line the string makes on the triangle.

❸ Repeat Step 2 with the other holes you made. Then balance the triangle on a pencil. The balance point should be close to where the lines intersect.

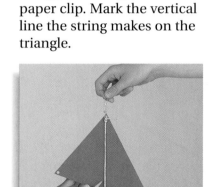

Investigation

1. Use the steps above to find the balance point of a right triangle, an equilateral triangle, and a scalene triangle. What are the lines you drew on the cardboard called? What is the balance point of a triangle called?

2. Cut out shapes like the ones below. Use the steps above to find their balance points. Then analyze the lines you drew. Make a conjecture about the balance points in relation to the diagonals.

square   rectangle   parallelogram

3. Cut out and find the balance points of other shapes, such as those shown below. Is the balance point at the intersection of the diagonals?

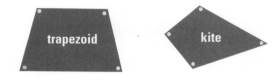

trapezoid

kite

4. Cut out some shapes of your own choice. Find the balance points.

Present Your Results

Write a report about balancing shapes.

▶ Include your answers to Exercises 1–4.

▶ Explain how to find the balance points of various shapes.

Create a mobile of the shapes you cut out.

▶ For each shape, tie a knot in a string. Thread the string through a hole at the balance point until the string stops at the knot.

▶ Hang all your shapes from one string, or hang them from different strings and tie the strings to a coat hanger.

▶ Be creative! Color or decorate the shapes.

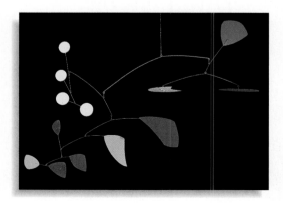

Extension

Research the American sculptor Alexander Calder (1898–1976), creator of the first mobiles.

This mobile includes horizontal red and yellow plates that hang from their balancing points.

5

Congruent Triangles

Where should a goalie stand?

A soccer goalie instinctively imagines a triangle formed by the goal posts and the ball. The best position to stand allows the goalie to reach each side of the triangle in the same amount of time.

As the ball moves and the shape of the triangle changes, the goalie's best position also changes.

Learn More About It

You will learn more about soccer in Exercises 21 and 22 on p. 278.

Who uses Congruent Triangles?

FACILITIES PLANNER
Facilities planners help businesses determine the best locations for new buildings. They can help companies save money and run more efficiently. (p. 275)

TYPE DESIGNER
Type designers design fonts that appear in books, magazines, newspapers, and other materials. Erik Spiekermann has designed many fonts that are widely used today. (p. 288)

How will you use these ideas?

- See how triangles are used in sculptures. (p. 239)
- Investigate origami patterns. (p. 255)
- Identify triangles in skateboard ramps. (p. 257)
- Analyze lighting for a stage production. (p. 262)
- Look for patterns in string designs. (p. 269)
- Find out how kaleidoscope patterns are created. (p. 285)

Chapter 5 Study Guide

PREVIEW — What's the chapter about?

- Identifying corresponding parts of **congruent triangles**
- Showing triangles are congruent
- Using **angle bisectors** and **perpendicular bisectors**
- Using **reflections** and line symmetry

Key Words

- **corresponding parts,** *p. 233*
- **congruent figures,** *p. 233*
- **proof,** *p. 243*
- **distance from a point to a line,** *p. 273*
- **equidistant,** *p. 273*
- **perpendicular bisector,** *p. 274*
- **reflection,** *p. 282*
- **line of symmetry,** *p. 284*

PREPARE — Chapter Readiness Quiz

Take this quick quiz. If you are unsure of an answer, look at the reference pages for help.

Vocabulary Check *(refer to p. 192)*

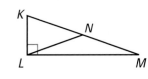

1. Which segment in the figure is the *hypotenuse*?

(A) $\overline{KL}$ (B) $\overline{LN}$ (C) $\overline{NM}$ (D) $\overline{KM}$

Skill Check *(refer to pp. 61, 128)*

2. If $m\angle FGH = 100°$ and $\overrightarrow{GJ}$ bisects $\angle FGH$, what is $m\angle FGJ$?

(F) 25° (G) 50° (H) 90° (J) 100°

3. Use the diagram at the right to determine which of the following statements is true.

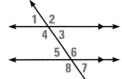

(A) $\angle 7 \cong \angle 2$ (B) $\angle 5 \cong \angle 2$

(C) $\angle 1 \cong \angle 8$ (D) $\angle 3 \cong \angle 7$

VISUAL STRATEGY — Studying Triangles

Visualize It!

When working with overlapping triangles, you may find it helpful to draw the triangles separately.

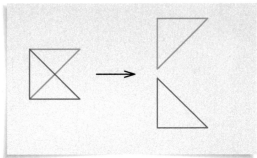

5.1 Congruence and Triangles

Goal

Identify congruent triangles and corresponding parts.

Key Words

• corresponding parts
• congruent figures

The houses below are located in San Francisco, California. The two triangles outlined on the houses have the same size and shape.

Suppose △ABC slides over to fit on △DEF. When the vertices are matched this way, ∠A and ∠D are *corresponding angles* and $\overline{AC}$ and $\overline{DF}$ are *corresponding sides*.

Corresponding angles and corresponding sides are examples of **corresponding parts**.

Figures are **congruent** if all pairs of corresponding angles are congruent and all pairs of corresponding sides are congruent.

Congruent

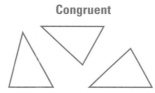

Same size and shape

Not congruent

Different sizes or shapes

EXAMPLE 1 List Corresponding Parts

Given that △JKL ≅ △RST, list all corresponding congruent parts.

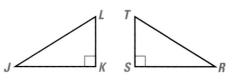

Solution

The order of the letters in the names of the triangles shows which parts correspond.

Corresponding Angles	Corresponding Sides
△JKL ≅ △RST, so ∠J ≅ ∠R.	△JKL ≅ △RST, so $\overline{JK} \cong \overline{RS}$.
△JKL ≅ △RST, so ∠K ≅ ∠S.	△JKL ≅ △RST, so $\overline{KL} \cong \overline{ST}$.
△JKL ≅ △RST, so ∠L ≅ ∠T.	△JKL ≅ △RST, so $\overline{JL} \cong \overline{RT}$.

Student Help

LOOK BACK
To review vertices of a triangle, see p. 175.

5.1 Congruence and Triangles   **233**

EXAMPLE **2** Write a Congruence Statement

The two triangles are congruent.

a. Identify all corresponding congruent parts.

b. Write a congruence statement.

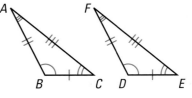

Student Help

STUDY TIP
To name the triangles in Example 2, you can start at any vertex.

$\triangle ACB \cong \triangle FED$

$\triangle BCA \cong \triangle DEF$

$\triangle CAB \cong \triangle EFD$

Be sure the letters are listed in corresponding order. ·····

Solution

a. Corresponding Angles

$\angle A \cong \angle F$

$\angle B \cong \angle D$

$\angle C \cong \angle E$

Corresponding Sides

$\overline{AB} \cong \overline{FD}$

$\overline{BC} \cong \overline{DE}$

$\overline{AC} \cong \overline{FE}$

b. List the letters in the triangle names so that the corresponding angles match. One possible congruence statement is

▶ $\triangle ABC \cong \triangle FDE$.

EXAMPLE **3** Use Properties of Congruent Triangles

In the diagram, $\triangle PQR \cong \triangle XYZ$.

a. Find the length of $\overline{XZ}$.

b. Find $m\angle Q$.

Solution

a. Because $\overline{XZ} \cong \overline{PR}$, you know that $XZ = PR = 10$.

b. Because $\angle Q \cong \angle Y$, you know that $m\angle Q = m\angle Y = 95°$.

Checkpoint ✓ **Name Corresponding Parts and Congruent Triangles**

1. Given $\triangle STU \cong \triangle YXZ$, list all corresponding congruent parts.

2. Given $\triangle ABC \cong \triangle DEF$, find the length of $\overline{DF}$ and $m\angle B$.

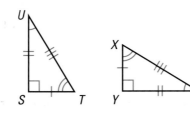

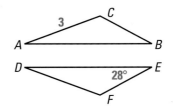

3. Which congruence statement is correct? Why?

A. $\triangle JKL \cong \triangle MNP$

B. $\triangle JKL \cong \triangle NMP$

C. $\triangle JKL \cong \triangle NPM$

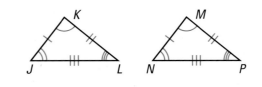

EXAMPLE 4 **Determine Whether Triangles are Congruent**

Use the two triangles at the right.

a. Identify all corresponding congruent parts.

b. Determine whether the triangles are congruent. If they are congruent, write a congruence statement.

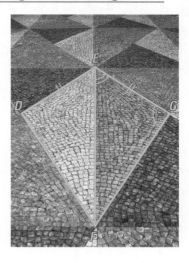

Student Help

STUDY TIP
Since $\overline{EF}$ is a shared side of both triangles, you know that $\overline{EF} \cong \overline{EF}$ by the Reflexive Property of Congruence.

Solution

a.

Corresponding Angles	Corresponding Sides
$\angle D \cong \angle G$	$\overline{DE} \cong \overline{GE}$
$\angle DEF \cong \angle GEF$	$\overline{DF} \cong \overline{GF}$
$\angle DFE \cong \angle GFE$	$\overline{EF} \cong \overline{EF}$

b. All three sets of corresponding angles are congruent and all three sets of corresponding sides are congruent, so the two triangles are congruent. A congruence statement is $\triangle DEF \cong \triangle GEF$.

EXAMPLE 5 **Determine Whether Triangles are Congruent**

In the figure, $\overline{HG} \parallel \overline{LK}$. Determine whether the triangles are congruent. If so, write a congruence statement.

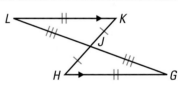

Visualize It!

Remember that when parallel lines are cut by a transversal, the alternate interior angles are congruent.

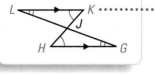

Solution

Start by labeling any information you can conclude from the figure. You can list the following angles congruent.

$\angle HJG \cong \angle KJL$	Vertical angles are congruent.
$\angle H \cong \angle K$	Alternate Interior Angles Theorem
$\angle G \cong \angle L$	Alternate Interior Angles Theorem

The congruent sides are marked on the diagram, so $\overline{HJ} \cong \overline{KJ}$, $\overline{HG} \cong \overline{KL}$, and $\overline{JG} \cong \overline{JL}$. Since all corresponding parts are congruent, $\triangle HJG \cong \triangle KJL$.

Checkpoint ✓ **Determine Whether Triangles are Congruent**

4. In the figure, $\overline{XY} \parallel \overline{ZW}$. Determine whether the two triangles are congruent. If they are, write a congruence statement.

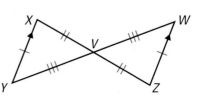

5.1 Exercises

Guided Practice

Vocabulary Check

Determine whether the angles or sides are *corresponding angles*, *corresponding sides*, or *neither*.

1. ∠C and ∠L   **2.** $\overline{AC}$ and $\overline{JK}$

3. $\overline{BC}$ and $\overline{KL}$ **4.** ∠B and ∠L

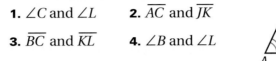

Skill Check

Given that △**XYZ** ≅ △**EFD**, determine the congruent side or angle that corresponds to the side or angle.

5. ∠Y   **6.** ∠D   **7.** $\overline{XZ}$ **8.** $\overline{FD}$

In Exercises 9–12, find the missing length or angle measure, given that △**LMN** ≅ △**PQR**.

9. $m\angle P = \underline{\ ?\ }$ **10.** $m\angle M = \underline{\ ?\ }$

11. $QR = \underline{\ ?\ }$ **12.** $LN = \underline{\ ?\ }$

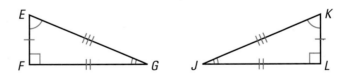

13. Determine whether the triangles are congruent. If they are, write a congruence statement.

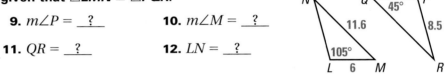

Practice and Applications

Extra Practice

See p. 683.

Corresponding Parts Determine whether the angles or sides are *corresponding angles*, *corresponding sides*, or *neither*.

14. ∠M and ∠S   **15.** ∠L and ∠R

16. $\overline{MN}$ and $\overline{ST}$ **17.** $\overline{LM}$ and $\overline{TS}$

18. $\overline{RT}$ and $\overline{LN}$ **19.** ∠N and ∠R

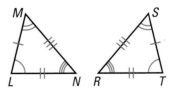

Homework Help

Example 1: Exs. 14–19, 21–24
Example 2: Exs. 21–36
Example 3: Exs. 37–40
Example 4: Exs. 42–47
Example 5: Exs. 42–47

20. Congruent Triangles Determine which of the following is a correct congruence statement for the triangles in Exercises 14–19. There is only one correct answer.

A. △LNM ≅ △RTS   **B.** △NML ≅ △RST   **C.** △MNL ≅ △STR

Identifying Congruent Parts In the diagram, △**LMN** ≅ △**PQR**.
Complete the statement with the corresponding congruent part.

21. ∠R ≅ ___?___

22. $\overline{LN}$ ≅ ___?___

23. ∠RPQ ≅ ___?___

24. $\overline{QP}$ ≅ ___?___

25. △MNL ≅ ___?___

26. △PRQ ≅ ___?___

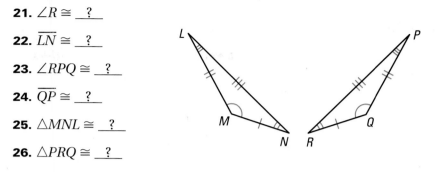

Naming Congruent Triangles Determine whether the congruence
statement correctly describes the congruent triangles shown
in the necklace.

27. △FGH ≅ △NML

28. △GFH ≅ △NLM

29. △GHF ≅ △MLN

30. △HFG ≅ △LNM

31. △HGF ≅ △LNM

32. △FHG ≅ △LNM

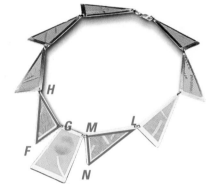

Writing Congruent Statements In Exercises 33 and 34, the
triangles are congruent. Identify all pairs of corresponding
congruent parts. Then write a congruence statement.

33.   **34.**

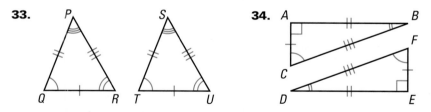

Marking Triangles In Exercises 35 and 36, △**ABC** ≅ △**DEF**. Draw
the triangles on your paper. Then mark every angle and side of
the triangles to show the corresponding congruent parts.

35.   **36.**

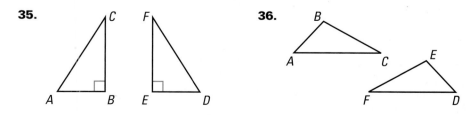

Using Congruent Triangles In Exercises 37–40, △ABC ≅ △DEF.

37. Find the length of $\overline{DF}$ and m∠B.

38. Find the length of $\overline{AB}$ and m∠F.

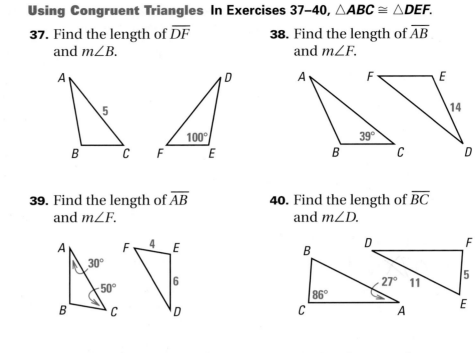

39. Find the length of $\overline{AB}$ and m∠F.

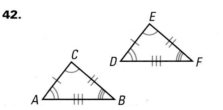

40. Find the length of $\overline{BC}$ and m∠D.

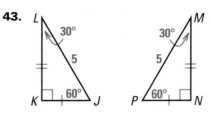

41. Writing Congruence Statements Given that △FGH ≅ △TSR, determine which congruence statement *does not* describe the triangles.

    A. △HGF ≅ △RST   **B.** △FHG ≅ △TRS   **C.** △GFH ≅ △SRT

Congruent Triangles Determine whether the triangles are congruent. If so, write a congruence statement.

42.

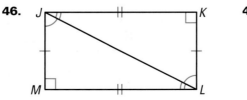

43.

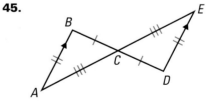

44.

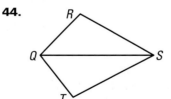

45.

46.

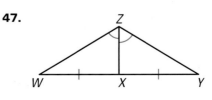

47.

Link to Art

SCULPTURE This sculpture by George Rickey, which is displayed in the Albany International Airport, uses supported triangles made from stainless steel.

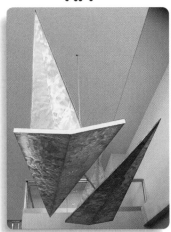

Sculpture The diagram below represents a view of the base of the sculpture *Four Triangles Hanging*.

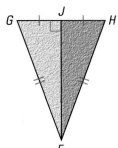

48. Explain how you know that $\angle GJF \cong \angle HJF$.

49. Explain how you know that $\angle JGF \cong \angle JHF$.

50. Do you have enough information to show that $\triangle GFJ \cong \triangle HFJ$? Explain your reasoning.

Error Analysis In Exercises 51 and 52, refer to Jillian's work and the diagram below.

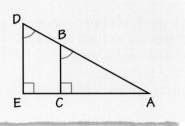

Jillian

$\angle ABC \cong \angle ADE$

$\angle ACB \cong \angle AED$

$\angle BAC \cong \angle DAE$

✗ The corresponding angles are congruent so $\triangle ABC \cong \triangle ADE$.

51. How does Jillian know that $\angle BAC \cong \angle DAE$?

52. Is $\triangle ABC \cong \triangle ADE$? Explain your reasoning.

Standardized Test Practice

53. Multiple Choice Which congruence statement *does not* describe the triangles at the right?

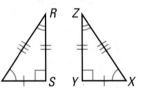

Ⓐ $\triangle TSR \cong \triangle XYZ$ Ⓑ $\triangle RST \cong \triangle XYZ$

Ⓒ $\triangle STR \cong \triangle YXZ$ Ⓓ $\triangle TRS \cong \triangle XZY$

Mixed Review

Naming Properties Name the property that the statement illustrates. *(Lesson 2.6)*

54. $m\angle J = m\angle J$

55. $\overline{PQ} \cong \overline{QP}$

56. If $\angle PQR \cong \angle FGH$, then $\angle FGH \cong \angle PQR$.

57. If $AB = CD$ and $CD = FG$, then $AB = FG$.

Classifying Triangles Classify the triangle with the given side lengths as *acute, right,* or *obtuse*. *(Lesson 4.5)*

58. 5, 2, 6

59. 5, 9, 10

60. 14, 5, 12

Algebra Skills

Evaluating Decimals Evaluate. *(Skills Review, p. 655)*

61. $4.15 + 7.8$

62. $12.64 - 8.92$

63. $14 + 5.33$

64. $0.91 - 0.17$

65. $1.476 + 6.2 + 9.4$

66. $10.872 - 7.65$

Activity 5.2 Congruent Triangles

Question

Can you determine that two triangles are congruent without listing all of the corresponding congruent sides and angles?

Materials
- two pencils
- protractor
- straightedge

Explore

1 On a piece of paper, place two pencils so their erasers are at the center of a protractor. Arrange the pencils to form a 45° angle.

2 Mark two vertices of a triangle by pressing the pencil points to the paper. Mark the center of the protractor as the third vertex.

3 Remove the pencils and protractor and draw the sides of the triangle.

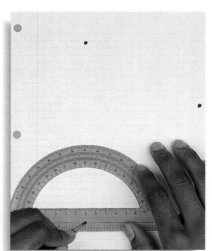

4 Repeat Steps 1–3 using the same pencils. Try to make a triangle that has a 45° angle but is *not* congruent to the one you made.

Think About It

Student Help

LOOK BACK
For help with using a protractor, see p. 36.

1. What do you notice about the triangles you made?

2. Based on this activity, if you know that two sides of a triangle are congruent to two sides of another triangle, what other information do you need to know to show that the triangles are congruent?

5.2 Proving Triangles are Congruent: SSS and SAS

Goal

Show triangles are congruent using SSS and SAS.

Key Words

• proof

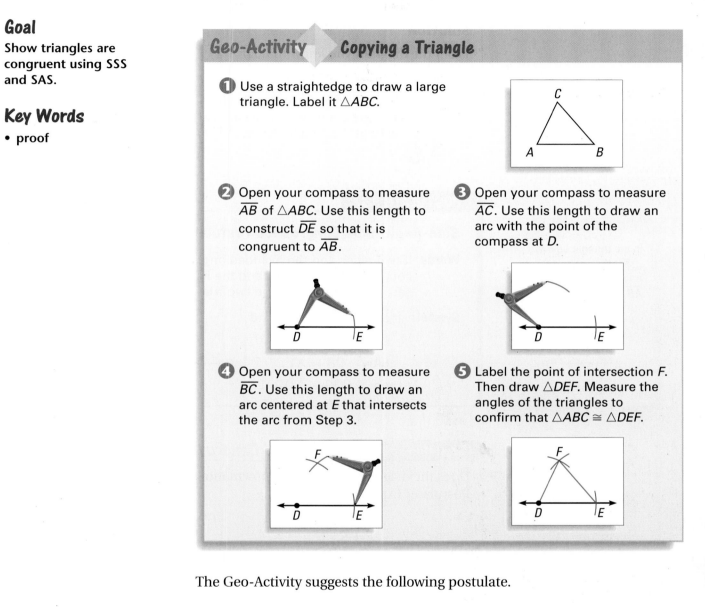

Geo-Activity ▷ **Copying a Triangle**

① Use a straightedge to draw a large triangle. Label it △ABC.

② Open your compass to measure $\overline{AB}$ of △ABC. Use this length to construct $\overline{DE}$ so that it is congruent to $\overline{AB}$.

③ Open your compass to measure $\overline{AC}$. Use this length to draw an arc with the point of the compass at D.

④ Open your compass to measure $\overline{BC}$. Use this length to draw an arc centered at E that intersects the arc from Step 3.

⑤ Label the point of intersection F. Then draw △DEF. Measure the angles of the triangles to confirm that △ABC ≅ △DEF.

The Geo-Activity suggests the following postulate.

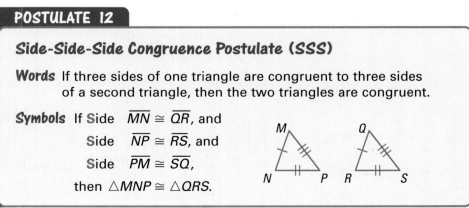

POSTULATE 12

Side-Side-Side Congruence Postulate (SSS)

Words If three sides of one triangle are congruent to three sides of a second triangle, then the two triangles are congruent.

Symbols If **Side** $\overline{MN} \cong \overline{QR}$, and

Side $\overline{NP} \cong \overline{RS}$, and

Side $\overline{PM} \cong \overline{SQ}$,

then △MNP ≅ △QRS.

EXAMPLE 1 Use the SSS Congruence Postulate

Does the diagram give enough information to show that the triangles are congruent? Explain.

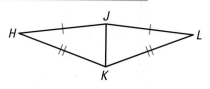

Solution

From the diagram you know that $\overline{HJ} \cong \overline{LJ}$ and $\overline{HK} \cong \overline{LK}$.

By the Reflexive Property, you know that $\overline{JK} \cong \overline{JK}$.

ANSWER ▶ Yes, enough information is given. Because corresponding sides are congruent, you can use the SSS Congruence Postulate to conclude that $\triangle HJK \cong \triangle LJK$.

Visualize It!

In the triangle below, $\angle B$ is the *included angle* between sides $\overline{AB}$ and $\overline{BC}$.

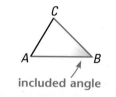

included angle

POSTULATE 13

Side-Angle-Side Congruence Postulate (SAS)

Words If two sides and the included angle of one triangle are congruent to two sides and the included angle of a second triangle, then the two triangles are congruent.

Symbols If Side $\overline{PQ} \cong \overline{WX}$, and

Angle $\angle Q \cong \angle X$, and

Side $\overline{QR} \cong \overline{XY}$,

then $\triangle PQR \cong \triangle WXY$.

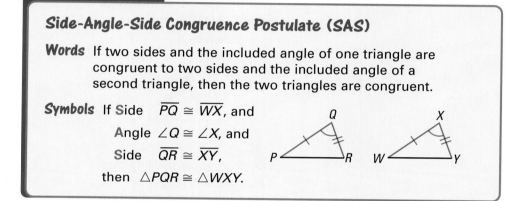

EXAMPLE 2 Use the SAS Congruence Postulate

Does the diagram give enough information to use the SAS Congruence Postulate? Explain your reasoning.

a.

b.

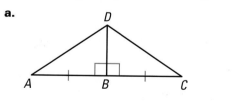

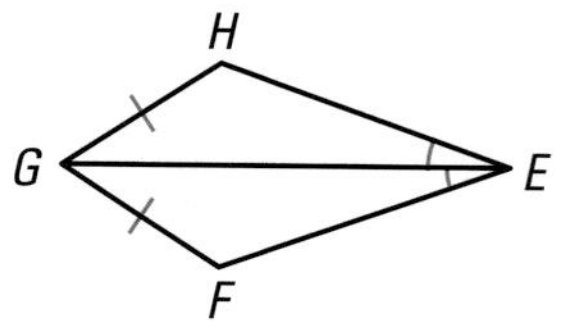

Solution

a. From the diagram, you know that $\overline{AB} \cong \overline{CB}$ and $\overline{DB} \cong \overline{DB}$.

The angle included between $\overline{AB}$ and $\overline{DB}$ is $\angle ABD$.

The angle included between $\overline{CB}$ and $\overline{DB}$ is $\angle CBD$.

Because the included angles are congruent, you can use the SAS Congruence Postulate to conclude that $\triangle ABD \cong \triangle CBD$.

b. You know that $\overline{GF} \cong \overline{GH}$ and $\overline{GE} \cong \overline{GE}$. However, the congruent angles are not included between the congruent sides, so you cannot use the SAS Congruence Postulate.

242 **Chapter 5** *Congruent Triangles*

Writing Proofs A **proof** is a convincing argument that shows why a statement is true. A *two-column proof* has numbered statements and reasons that show the logical order of the argument. Each statement has a reason listed to its right.

HOW TO WRITE A PROOF

- List the given information first.

- Use information from the diagram.

- Give a reason for every statement.

- Use given information, definitions, postulates, and theorems as reasons.

- List statements in order. If a statement relies on another statement, list it later than the statement it relies on.

- End the proof with the statement you are trying to prove.

EXAMPLE 3 Write a Proof

Write a two-column proof that shows $\triangle JKL \cong \triangle NML$.

Given $\overline{JL} \cong \overline{NL}$
L is the midpoint of $\overline{KM}$.

Prove $\triangle JKL \cong \triangle NML$

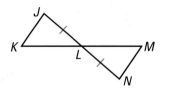

Solution

The proof can be set up in two columns. The proof begins with the given information and ends with the statement you are trying to prove.

Statements	Reasons	
S 1. $\overline{JL} \cong \overline{NL}$	**1.** Given	These are the given statements.
2. L is the midpoint of $\overline{KM}$.	**2.** Given	
A 3. $\angle JLK \cong \angle NLM$	**3.** Vertical Angles Theorem	This information is from the diagram.
S 4. $\overline{KL} \cong \overline{ML}$	**4.** Definition of midpoint	Statement 4 follows from Statement 2.
5. $\triangle JKL \cong \triangle NML$	**5.** SAS Congruence Postulate	Statement 5 follows from the congruences of Statements 1, 3, and 4.

Student Help

STUDY TIP
You can remind yourself about side and angle congruences by writing letters as shown.

EXAMPLE 4 **Prove Triangles are Congruent**

You are making a model of the window shown in the photo. You know that $\overline{DR} \perp \overline{AG}$ and $\overline{RA} \cong \overline{RG}$. Write a proof to show that $\triangle DRA \cong \triangle DRG$.

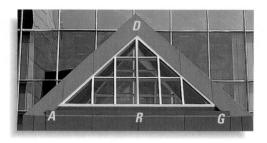

Solution

❶ Make a diagram and label it with the given information.

❷ Write the given information and the statement you need to prove.

Given ▸ $\overline{DR} \perp \overline{AG}$, $\overline{RA} \cong \overline{RG}$

Prove ▸ $\triangle DRA \cong \triangle DRG$

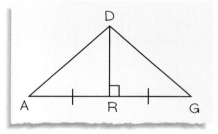

❸ Write a two-column proof. List the given statements first.

Student Help

STUDY TIP
Think about what you can say given that $\overline{DR} \perp \overline{AG}$. ⋯⋯⋯

Then think about what other information you can deduce from the diagram. ⋯⋯⋯

Statements	Reasons
1. $\overline{RA} \cong \overline{RG}$	1. Given
2. $\overline{DR} \perp \overline{AG}$	2. Given
3. $\angle DRA$ and $\angle DRG$ are right angles.	3. $\perp$ lines form right angles.
4. $\angle DRA \cong \angle DRG$	4. Right angles are congruent.
5. $\overline{DR} \cong \overline{DR}$	5. Reflexive Property of Congruence
6. $\triangle DRA \cong \triangle DRG$	6. SAS Congruence Postulate

Checkpoint ✓ **Prove Triangles are Congruent**

1. Fill in the missing statements and reasons.

Given ▸ $\overline{CB} \cong \overline{CE}$, $\overline{AC} \cong \overline{DC}$

Prove ▸ $\triangle BCA \cong \triangle ECD$

Statements	Reasons
1. $\overline{CB} \cong \overline{CE}$	1. _____?_____
2. _____?_____	2. Given
3. $\angle BCA \cong \angle ECD$	3. _____?_____
4. $\triangle BCA \cong \triangle ECD$	4. _____?_____

5.2 Exercises

Guided Practice

Vocabulary Check

Use △*JKL* to name the angle included between the two sides.

1. $\overline{JK}$ and $\overline{KM}$

2. $\overline{JK}$ and $\overline{MJ}$

3. $\overline{KL}$ and $\overline{JL}$

4. $\overline{KM}$ and $\overline{LM}$

5. $\overline{LK}$ and $\overline{KM}$

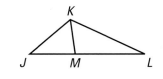

Skill Check

Decide whether enough information is given to show that the triangles are congruent. If so, tell which congruence postulate you would use.

6. △*ABC*, △*DEC*   7. △*FGH*, △*JKH*   8. △*PQR*, △*SRQ*

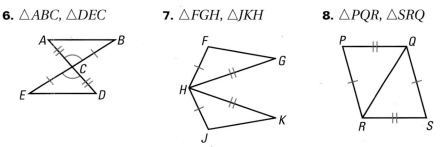

Practice and Applications

Extra Practice

See p. 683.

Naming Included Angles Use the diagram shown to name the angle included between the two sides.

9. $\overline{AB}$ and $\overline{BD}$ 10. $\overline{CD}$ and $\overline{BC}$

11. $\overline{AC}$ and $\overline{CB}$ 12. $\overline{BA}$ and $\overline{AD}$

13. $\overline{DC}$ and $\overline{BD}$ 14. $\overline{BD}$ and $\overline{BC}$

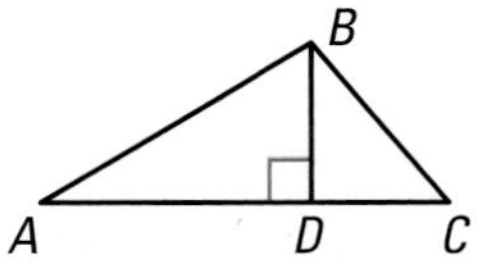

Using SSS Decide whether enough information is given to use the SSS Congruence Postulate. Explain your reasoning.

15.   16.   17.

Homework Help

Example 1: Exs. 15–17, 21–31
Example 2: Exs. 18–31
Example 3: Exs. 34–36
Example 4: Exs. 34–36

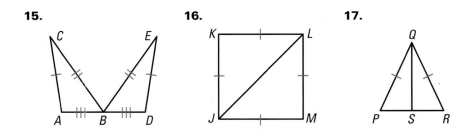

Using SAS Congruence Decide whether enough information is given to use the SAS Congruence Postulate. Explain your reasoning.

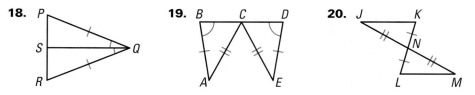

18. P, S, Q, R

19. B, C, D, A, E

20. J, K, N, L, M

You be the Judge Decide whether enough information is given to show that the triangles are congruent. If so, tell which congruence postulate you would use.

21. B, A, C, F, D, E

22. G, H, K, J

23. M, N, Q, P

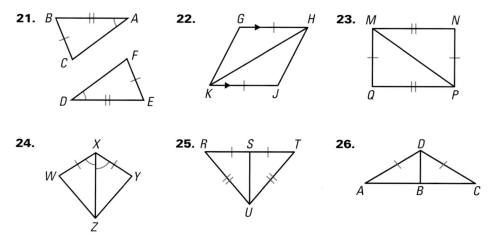

24. X, W, Y, Z

25. R, S, T, U

26. D, A, B, C

Textiles In Exercises 27 and 28, use the photo of the Navajo rug. In the triangles on the rug, $\overline{BC} \cong \overline{DE}$ and $\overline{AC} \cong \overline{CE}$.

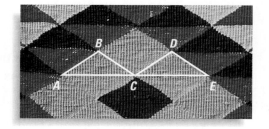

27. What additional information is needed to use the SSS Congruence Postulate to show that $\triangle ABC \cong \triangle CDE$?

28. What additional information is needed to use the SAS Congruence Postulate to show that $\triangle ABC \cong \triangle CDE$?

Missing Information Determine what single piece of information you need to know in order to use either the SSS or SAS Congruence Postulate to show that the triangles are congruent.

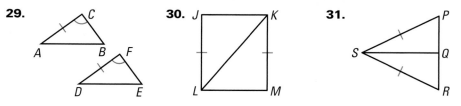

29. C, A, B, F, D, E

30. J, K, L, M

31. P, S, Q, R

Quilting Use the labels on the diagrams to explain how you know that the triangles are congruent.

32. *WXYZ* is a square.

33. $\overline{AB} \parallel \overline{CD}$

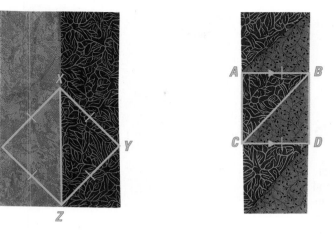

Reasoning In Exercises 34 and 35, fill in the missing statements and reasons.

34. Given ▶ $\overline{EF} \cong \overline{GH}$
$\overline{FG} \cong \overline{HE}$

Prove ▶ $\triangle EFG \cong \triangle GHE$

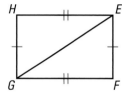

Statements	Reasons
1. $\overline{EF} \cong \overline{GH}$	**1.** Given
2. $\overline{FG} \cong \overline{HE}$	**2.** _____?_____
3. $\overline{GE} \cong \overline{GE}$	**3.** _____?_____
4. $\triangle EFG \cong \triangle GHE$	**4.** _____?_____

35. Given ▶ $\overline{SP} \cong \overline{TP}$
$\overline{PQ}$ bisects $\angle SPT$.

Prove ▶ $\triangle SPQ \cong \triangle TPQ$

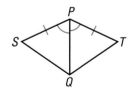

Statements	Reasons
1. $\overline{SP} \cong \overline{TP}$	**1.** Given
2. $\overline{PQ}$ bisects $\angle SPT$.	**2.** _____?_____
3. $\angle SPQ \cong \angle TPQ$	**3.** _____?_____
4. _____?_____	**4.** Reflexive Prop. of Cong.
5. $\triangle SPQ \cong \triangle TPQ$	**5.** _____?_____

36. Reasoning Fill in the missing statements and reasons.

Given ▶ $\overline{AC} \cong \overline{BC}$

M is the midpoint of $\overline{AB}$.

Prove ▶ $\triangle ACM \cong \triangle BCM$

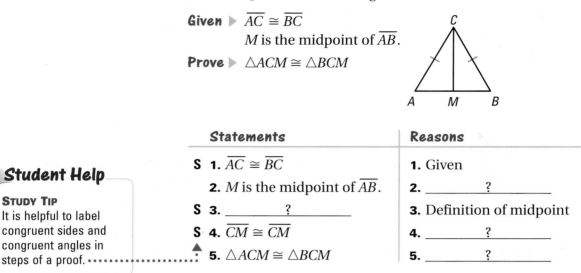

Student Help

STUDY TIP
It is helpful to label congruent sides and congruent angles in steps of a proof. ·······

Statements	Reasons
S 1. $\overline{AC} \cong \overline{BC}$	1. Given
2. M is the midpoint of $\overline{AB}$.	2. _____?_____
S 3. _____?_____	3. Definition of midpoint
S 4. $\overline{CM} \cong \overline{CM}$	4. _____?_____
▲ **5.** $\triangle ACM \cong \triangle BCM$	5. _____?_____

37. Error Analysis Using the diagram below, Maria was asked whether it can be shown that $\triangle ABC \cong \triangle DEF$. Explain her error.

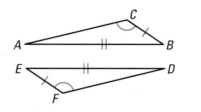

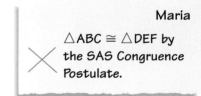

Maria
$\triangle ABC \cong \triangle DEF$ by the SAS Congruence Postulate.

Challenge Write a proof to show that the triangles are congruent.

38. $\triangle ABD$ and $\triangle CBD$ are equilateral.

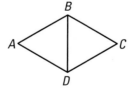

39. $\overline{XZ} \cong \overline{YZ}$, and $\overline{ZM}$ bisects $\angle YZX$.

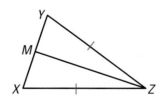

Standardized Test Practice

40. Multiple Choice In $\triangle RST$ and $\triangle ABC$, $\overline{RS} \cong \overline{AB}$, $\overline{ST} \cong \overline{BC}$, and $\overline{TR} \cong \overline{CA}$. Which angle is congruent to $\angle T$?

ⓐ $\angle A$ ⓑ $\angle R$ ⓒ $\angle C$ ⓓ $\angle B$

41. Multiple Choice In the diagram below, $\triangle DEF$ is equilateral and G is the midpoint of $\overline{DE}$. Which of the statements is *not* true?

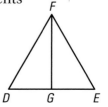

ⓕ $\overline{DF} \cong \overline{EF}$ ⓖ $\overline{DG} \cong \overline{DF}$

ⓗ $\overline{DG} \cong \overline{EG}$ ⓙ $\triangle DFG \cong \triangle EFG$

Mixed Review

Classifying Angles **Use the diagram to determine whether the angles are *corresponding, alternate interior, alternate exterior,* or *same-side interior* angles.** *(Lesson 3.3)*

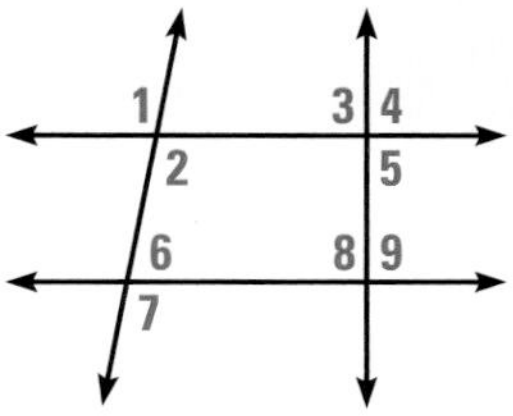

42. $\angle 1$ and $\angle 5$

43. $\angle 2$ and $\angle 6$

44. $\angle 7$ and $\angle 2$

45. $\angle 5$ and $\angle 8$

46. $\angle 9$ and $\angle 4$

47. $\angle 5$ and $\angle 9$

Using the Triangle Inequality **Determine whether it is possible to draw a triangle with the given side lengths.** *(Lesson 4.7)*

48. 14, 8, 25

49. 20, 10, 28

50. 16, 14, 30

Algebra Skills

Evaluating Square Roots **Evaluate. Give the exact value if possible. If not, approximate to the nearest tenth.** *(Skills Review, p. 669)*

51. $\sqrt{3}$

52. $\sqrt{12}$

53. $\sqrt{40}$

54. $\sqrt{159}$

55. $\sqrt{14.76}$

56. $\sqrt{0.87}$

57. $\sqrt{1.12}$

58. $\sqrt{40.85}$

Quiz 1

In the diagram, $\triangle ABC \cong \triangle QPR$. Complete the statement with the corresponding congruent part. *(Lesson 5.1)*

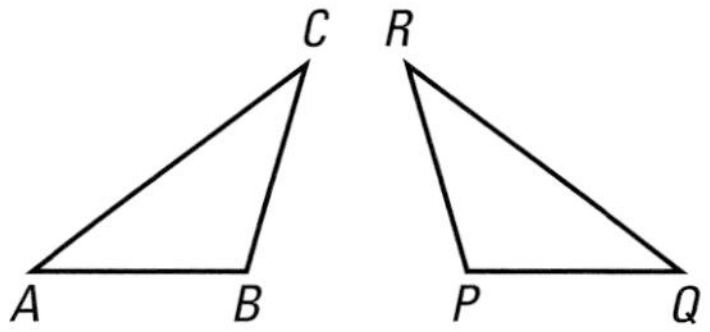

1. $\angle R \cong$ __?__

2. $\overline{AB} \cong$ __?__

3. $\triangle BAC \cong$ __?__

4. $\triangle RPQ \cong$ __?__

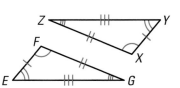

5. Write a congruence statement for the congruent triangles shown at the right. *(Lesson 5.1)*

Decide whether enough information is given to show that the triangles are congruent. If so, tell which congruence postulate you would use. Explain your reasoning. *(Lesson 5.2)*

6.

7.

8.

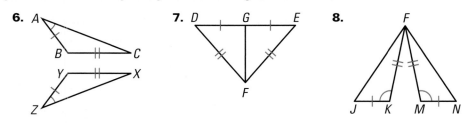

5.3 Proving Triangles are Congruent: ASA and AAS

Goal

Show triangles are congruent using ASA and AAS.

Key Words

• vertical angles p. 75
• alternate interior angles p. 121

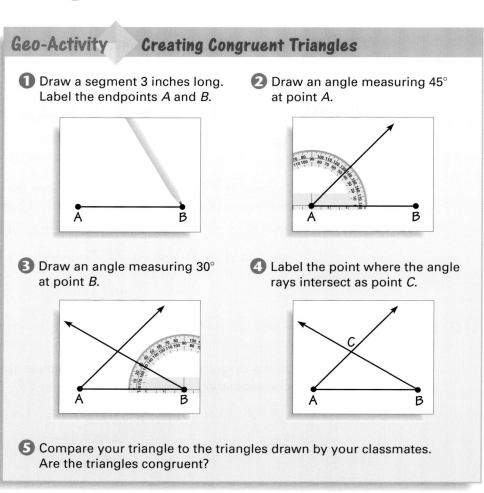

Geo-Activity Creating Congruent Triangles

1 Draw a segment 3 inches long. Label the endpoints A and B.

2 Draw an angle measuring 45° at point A.

3 Draw an angle measuring 30° at point B.

4 Label the point where the angle rays intersect as point C.

5 Compare your triangle to the triangles drawn by your classmates. Are the triangles congruent?

The Geo-Activity above suggests the following postulate.

Visualize It!

In this triangle, $\overline{AC}$ is the *included side* between ∠A and ∠C.

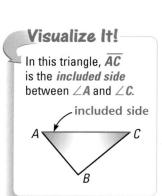

included side

POSTULATE 14

Angle-Side-Angle Congruence Postulate (ASA)

Words If two angles and the included side of one triangle are congruent to two angles and the included side of a second triangle, then the two triangles are congruent.

Symbols If Angle ∠A ≅ ∠D, and
             Side $\overline{AC} ≅ \overline{DF}$, and
             Angle ∠C ≅ ∠F,
             then △ABC ≅ △DEF.

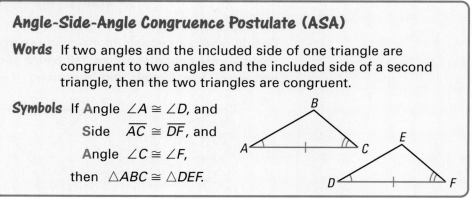

EXAMPLE 1 **Determine When To Use ASA Congruence**

Based on the diagram, can you use the ASA Congruence Postulate to show that the triangles are congruent? Explain your reasoning.

a.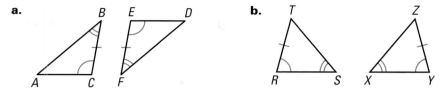

b.

Student Help

STUDY TIP
You can use the ASA Congruence Postulate because $\overline{BC}$ and $\overline{FE}$ are *included* between the congruent angles. ········▶

Solution

a. You are given that $\angle C \cong \angle E$, $\angle B \cong \angle F$, and $\overline{BC} \cong \overline{FE}$.

▶ You can use the ASA Congruence Postulate to show that $\triangle ABC \cong \triangle DFE$.

b. You are given that $\angle R \cong \angle Y$ and $\angle S \cong \angle X$.

You know that $\overline{RT} \cong \overline{YZ}$, but these sides are not included between the congruent angles, so you cannot use the ASA Congruence Postulate.

THEOREM 5.1

Angle-Angle-Side Congruence Theorem (AAS)

Words If two angles and a non-included side of one triangle are congruent to two angles and the corresponding non-included side of a second triangle, then the two triangles are congruent.

Symbols If Angle $\angle A \cong \angle D$, and

Angle $\angle C \cong \angle F$, and

Side $\overline{BC} \cong \overline{EF}$,

then $\triangle ABC \cong \triangle DEF$.

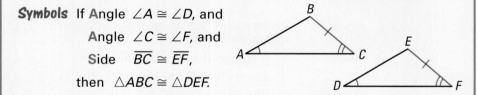

EXAMPLE 2 **Determine What Information is Missing**

What additional congruence is needed to show that $\triangle JKL \cong \triangle NML$ by the AAS Congruence Theorem?

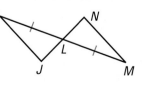

Solution

You are given $\overline{KL} \cong \overline{ML}$.

Because $\angle KLJ$ and $\angle MLN$ are vertical angles, $\angle KLJ \cong \angle MLN$.

The angles that make $\overline{KL}$ and $\overline{ML}$ the non-included sides are $\angle J$ and $\angle N$, so you need to know that $\angle J \cong \angle N$.

EXAMPLE 3 Decide Whether Triangles are Congruent

Does the diagram give enough information to show that the triangles are congruent? If so, state the postulate or theorem you would use.

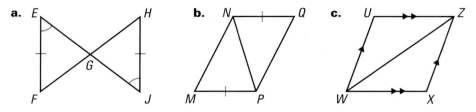

a. E   H
         G
    F   J

b. N   Q
    M   P

c. U   Z
    W   X

Solution

a. $\overline{EF} \cong \overline{JH}$ Given

     $\angle E \cong \angle J$ Given

     $\angle FGE \cong \angle HGJ$ Vertical Angles Theorem

Use the AAS Congruence Theorem to conclude that $\triangle EFG \cong \triangle JHG$.

b. Based on the diagram, you know only that $\overline{MP} \cong \overline{QN}$ and $\overline{NP} \cong \overline{NP}$. You cannot conclude that the triangles are congruent.

c. $\angle UZW \cong \angle XWZ$ Alternate Interior Angles Theorem

     $\overline{WZ} \cong \overline{WZ}$ Reflexive Prop. of Congruence

     $\angle UWZ \cong \angle XZW$ Alternate Interior Angles Theorem

Use the ASA Congruence Postulate to conclude that $\triangle WUZ \cong \triangle ZXW$.

EXAMPLE 4 Prove Triangles are Congruent

A step in the Cat's Cradle string game creates the triangles shown. Prove that $\triangle ABD \cong \triangle EBC$.

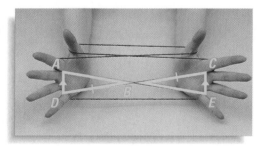

Solution

Given ▶ $\overline{BD} \cong \overline{BC}$, $\overline{AD} \parallel \overline{EC}$

Prove ▶ $\triangle ABD \cong \triangle EBC$

Statements	Reasons
1. $\overline{BD} \cong \overline{BC}$	**1.** Given
2. $\overline{AD} \parallel \overline{EC}$	**2.** Given
3. $\angle D \cong \angle C$	**3.** Alternate Interior Angles Theorem
4. $\angle ABD \cong \angle EBC$	**4.** Vertical Angles Theorem
5. $\triangle ABD \cong \triangle EBC$	**5.** ASA Congruence Postulate

---

Student Help

STUDY TIP
The sides of *MNQP* look parallel but this information is not marked, so you cannot conclude that any angles are congruent.

Visualize It!

Because $\angle A$ and $\angle E$ are also alternate interior angles, you can show that $\triangle ABD \cong \triangle EBC$ by the AAS Congruence Theorem.

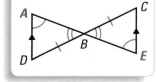

---

1. Complete the statement: You can use the ASA Congruence Postulate when the congruent sides are __?__ between the corresponding congruent angles.

Does the diagram give enough information to show that the triangles are congruent? If so, state the postulate or theorem you would use.

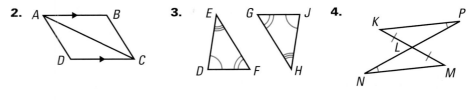

2.   **3.**   **4.**

5.3 Exercises

Guided Practice

Vocabulary Check

Tell whether the side is *included* or *not included* between the given angles.

1. $\overline{FG}$ is __?__ between $\angle F$ and $\angle G$.

2. $\overline{GH}$ is __?__ between $\angle F$ and $\angle G$.

3. $\overline{FH}$ is __?__ between $\angle H$ and $\angle G$.

4. $\overline{HG}$ is __?__ between $\angle H$ and $\angle G$.

Skill Check

What congruence do you need to know in order to use the indicated postulate or theorem to conclude that the triangles are congruent?

5. ASA Congruence Postulate

6. AAS Congruence Theorem

Does the diagram give enough information to show that the triangles are congruent? If so, state the postulate or theorem you would use.

7. $\triangle RST$ and $\triangle TQR$

8. $\triangle JKL$ and $\triangle NML$

9. $\triangle ABC$ and $\triangle DEF$

Practice and Applications

Extra Practice

See p. 683.

Recognizing Included Sides Tell whether the side is *included* or *not included* between the given angles.

10. $\overline{AB}$ is ___?___ between $\angle B$ and $\angle BCA$.

11. $\overline{AC}$ is ___?___ between $\angle BAC$ and $\angle BCA$.

12. $\overline{AC}$ is ___?___ between $\angle DAC$ and $\angle D$.

13. $\overline{BC}$ is ___?___ between $\angle CAB$ and $\angle B$.

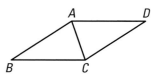

Choosing ASA or AAS Tell which postulate or theorem you would use to show that the triangles are congruent. Explain your reasoning.

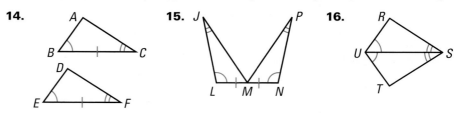

14.

15.

16.

Showing Triangles are Congruent Does the diagram give enough information to show that the triangles are congruent? If so, state the postulate or theorem you would use. Explain your reasoning.

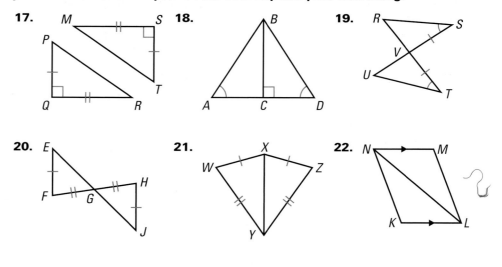

17.

18.

19.

20.

21.

22.

23. Sea Plane In the sea plane at the right, $\angle L$ and $\angle R$ are right angles, $\overline{KL} \cong \overline{QR}$, and $\angle J \cong \angle P$.

What postulate or theorem allows you to conclude that $\triangle JKL \cong \triangle PQR$?

Homework Help

Example 1: Exs. 14–22
Example 2: Exs. 24–30
Example 3: Exs. 17–22
Example 4: Exs. 34, 35

Missing Information Determine what congruence is needed in order to use the indicated postulate or theorem to show that the triangles are congruent.

24. ASA Congruence Postulate

25. AAS Congruence Theorem

26. ASA Congruence Postulate

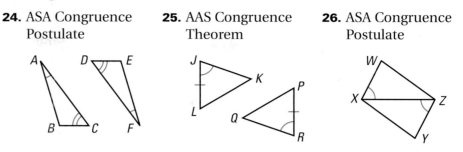

ORIGAMI is the Japanese art of folding paper into objects. The seal shown in the photograph was folded from a single piece of square paper.

Origami The triangles below show a step in folding an origami seal. State the third congruence needed to prove that △ABC ≅ △ABD using the indicated postulate or theorem.

27. Given ▶ ∠CBA ≅ ∠DBA, $\overline{BA} \cong \overline{BA}$
Use the AAS Congruence Theorem.

28. Given ▶ ∠C ≅ ∠D, $\overline{AC} \cong \overline{AD}$
Use the ASA Congruence Postulate.

29. Given ▶ ∠C ≅ ∠D, ∠CAB ≅ ∠DAB
Use the ASA Congruence Postulate.

30. Given ▶ ∠C ≅ ∠D, $\overline{AC} \cong \overline{AD}$
Use the SAS Congruence Postulate.

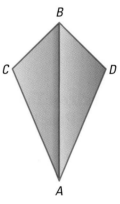

Visualize It! ▶ Use the given information to make a sketch of △PQR and △STU. Mark the triangles with the given information.

31. ∠Q ≅ ∠T
∠R ≅ ∠U
$\overline{QR} \cong \overline{TU}$

32. ∠P ≅ ∠S
∠R ≅ ∠U
$\overline{PQ} \cong \overline{ST}$

33. ∠Q ≅ ∠T
∠S ≅ ∠P
$\overline{QR} \cong \overline{TU}$

34. Logical Reasoning Fill in the missing statements and reasons.

Given ▶ $\overline{GF} \cong \overline{GL}$
$\overline{FH} \parallel \overline{LK}$

Prove ▶ △FGH ≅ △LGK

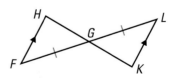

Statements	Reasons
1. $\overline{GF} \cong \overline{GL}$	**1.** Given
2. $\overline{FH} \parallel \overline{LK}$	**2.** _____?_____
3. ∠F ≅ ∠L	**3.** _____?_____
4. _____?_____	**4.** Vertical Angles Theorem
5. △FGH ≅ △LGK	**5.** _____?_____

35. Logical Reasoning Fill in the missing statements and reasons.

Given ▸ $\overline{BC} \cong \overline{EC}$
$\overline{AB} \perp \overline{AD}$
$\overline{DE} \perp \overline{AD}$

Prove ▸ $\triangle ABC \cong \triangle DEC$

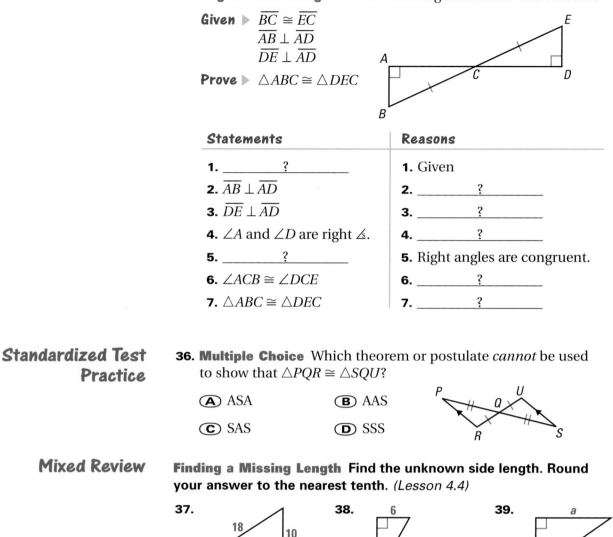

Statements	Reasons
1. _____?_____	1. Given
2. $\overline{AB} \perp \overline{AD}$	2. _____?_____
3. $\overline{DE} \perp \overline{AD}$	3. _____?_____
4. $\angle A$ and $\angle D$ are right $\angle$s.	4. _____?_____
5. _____?_____	5. Right angles are congruent.
6. $\angle ACB \cong \angle DCE$	6. _____?_____
7. $\triangle ABC \cong \triangle DEC$	7. _____?_____

Standardized Test Practice

36. Multiple Choice Which theorem or postulate *cannot* be used to show that $\triangle PQR \cong \triangle SQU$?

Ⓐ ASA   Ⓑ AAS

Ⓒ SAS   Ⓓ SSS

Mixed Review

Finding a Missing Length Find the unknown side length. Round your answer to the nearest tenth. *(Lesson 4.4)*

37.

38.

39.

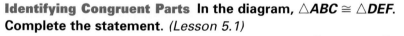

Identifying Congruent Parts In the diagram, $\triangle ABC \cong \triangle DEF$. Complete the statement. *(Lesson 5.1)*

40. $\angle C \cong$ __?__

41. $\overline{BA} \cong$ __?__

42. $\angle D \cong$ __?__

43. $\overline{EF} \cong$ __?__

44. $\angle B \cong$ __?__

45. $\overline{CB} \cong$ __?__

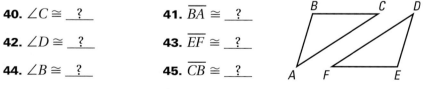

Algebra Skills

Fraction Operations Divide. Write your answer in simplest form. *(Skills Review, p. 659)*

46. $\dfrac{1}{2} \div 6$ **47.** $\dfrac{4}{5} \div 4$ **48.** $\dfrac{1}{6} \div \dfrac{2}{3}$ **49.** $\dfrac{5}{8} \div \dfrac{5}{16}$

50. $\dfrac{7}{9} \div \dfrac{2}{7}$ **51.** $\dfrac{3}{10} \div \dfrac{12}{25}$ **52.** $8 \div \dfrac{3}{4}$ **53.** $\dfrac{4}{11} \div 12$

5.4 Hypotenuse-Leg Congruence Theorem: HL

Goal

Use the HL Congruence Theorem and summarize congruence postulates and theorems.

Key Words

• hypotenuse p. 192
• leg of a right triangle p. 192

The triangles that make up the skateboard ramp below are right triangles.

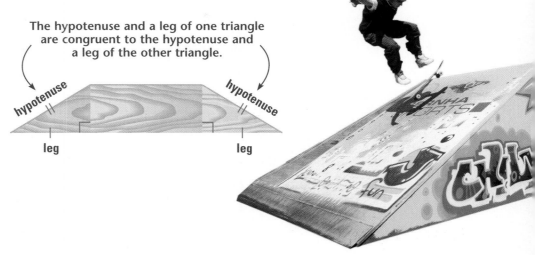

The hypotenuse and a leg of one triangle are congruent to the hypotenuse and a leg of the other triangle.

hypotenuse   hypotenuse

leg   leg

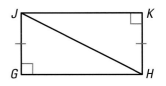

Student Help

VOCABULARY TIP
Remember that the longest side of a right triangle is called the hypotenuse.

hypotenuse   leg

leg

THEOREM 5.2

Hypotenuse-Leg Congruence Theorem (HL)

Words If the hypotenuse and a leg of a right triangle are congruent to the hypotenuse and a leg of a second right triangle, then the two triangles are congruent.

Symbols If △*ABC* and △*DEF* are right triangles, and

H $\overline{AC} \cong \overline{DF}$, and

L $\overline{BC} \cong \overline{EF}$,

then △*ABC* ≅ △*DEF*.

EXAMPLE **1** **Determine When To Use HL**

Is it possible to show that △*JGH* ≅ △*HKJ* using the HL Congruence Theorem? Explain your reasoning.

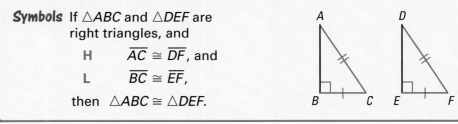

Solution

In the diagram, you are given that △*JGH* and △*HKJ* are right triangles.

By the Reflexive Property, you know $\overline{JH} \cong \overline{JH}$ (hypotenuse) and you are given that $\overline{JG} \cong \overline{HK}$ (leg). You can use the HL Congruence Theorem to show that △*JGH* ≅ △*HKJ*.

EXAMPLE 2 Use the HL Congruence Theorem

Use the diagram to prove that $\triangle PRQ \cong \triangle PRS$.

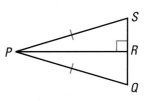

Solution

Given ▶ $\overline{PR} \perp \overline{SQ}$
$\overline{PQ} \cong \overline{PS}$

Prove ▶ $\triangle PRQ \cong \triangle PRS$

Statements	Reasons
1. $\overline{PR} \perp \overline{SQ}$	1. Given
2. $\angle PRQ$ and $\angle PRS$ are right $\angle$s.	2. $\perp$ lines form right angles.
3. $\triangle PRQ$ and $\triangle PRS$ are right triangles.	3. Definition of right triangle
H 4. $\overline{PQ} \cong \overline{PS}$	4. Given
L 5. $\overline{PR} \cong \overline{PR}$	5. Reflexive Prop. of Congruence
6. $\triangle PRQ \cong \triangle PRS$	6. HL Congruence Theorem

---

SUMMARY   TRIANGLE CONGRUENCE POSTULATES AND THEOREMS

You have studied five ways to prove that $\triangle ABC \cong \triangle DEF$.

SSS
Side $\overline{AB} \cong \overline{DE}$
Side $\overline{AC} \cong \overline{DF}$
Side $\overline{BC} \cong \overline{EF}$

SAS
Side $\overline{AB} \cong \overline{DE}$
Angle $\angle B \cong \angle E$
Side $\overline{BC} \cong \overline{EF}$

ASA
Angle $\angle A \cong \angle D$
Side $\overline{AB} \cong \overline{DE}$
Angle $\angle B \cong \angle E$

AAS
Angle $\angle A \cong \angle D$
Angle $\angle B \cong \angle E$
Side $\overline{BC} \cong \overline{EF}$

HL
$\triangle ABC$ and $\triangle DEF$ are right triangles.
Hypotenuse $\overline{AB} \cong \overline{DE}$
Leg $\overline{BC} \cong \overline{EF}$

EXAMPLE **3** Decide Whether Triangles are Congruent

Does the diagram give enough information to show that the triangles are congruent? If so, state the postulate or theorem you would use.

a.
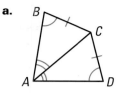

b.
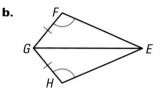

STUDY TIP
There is no SSA Congruence Theorem or Postulate, so you cannot conclude that the triangles in Example 3(b) are congruent.

Solution

a. From the diagram, you know that $\angle BAC \cong \angle DAC$, $\angle B \cong \angle D$, and $\overline{BC} \cong \overline{DC}$. You can use the AAS Congruence Theorem to show that $\triangle BAC \cong \triangle DAC$.

b. From the diagram, you know that $\overline{FG} \cong \overline{HG}$, $\overline{EG} \cong \overline{EG}$, and $\angle EFG \cong \angle EHG$. Because the congruent angles are not included between the congruent sides, you cannot show that $\triangle FGE \cong \triangle HGE$.

EXAMPLE **4** Prove Triangles are Congruent

Use the information in the diagram to prove that $\triangle RST \cong \triangle UVW$.

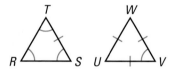

Solution

Statements	Reasons
A 1. $\angle S \cong \angle V$	**1.** Given
S 2. $\overline{ST} \cong \overline{VW}$	**2.** Given
3. $\triangle UVW$ is equilateral.	**3.** Definition of equilateral triangle
4. $\angle V \cong \angle W$	**4.** Equilateral triangles are equiangular.
5. $\angle T \cong \angle V$	**5.** Given
A 6. $\angle T \cong \angle W$	**6.** Transitive Prop. of Congruence
7. $\triangle RST \cong \triangle UVW$	**7.** ASA Congruence Postulate

Checkpoint ✓ **Decide Whether Triangles are Congruent**

Does the diagram give enough information to show that the triangles are congruent? If so, state the postulate or theorem you would use.

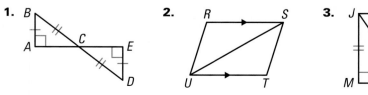

Guided Practice

Vocabulary Check

Tell whether the segment is a *leg* or the *hypotenuse* of the right triangle.

1. $\overline{AC}$

2. $\overline{BC}$

3. $\overline{AB}$

4. $\overline{KL}$

5. $\overline{KJ}$

6. $\overline{JL}$

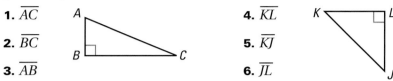

Skill Check

Determine whether you are given enough information to show that the triangles are congruent. Explain your answer.

7.   8.   9.

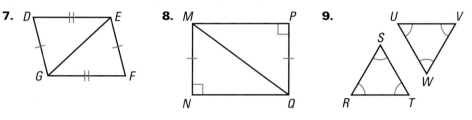

Practice and Applications

Extra Practice

See p. 683.

HL Congruence Theorem Determine whether you can use the HL Congruence Theorem to show that the triangles are congruent. Explain your reasoning.

10.   11.   12.

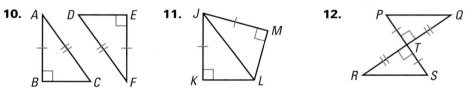

Landscaping To support a tree, you attach wires from the trunk of the tree to stakes in the ground as shown below.

13. What information do you need to know in order to use the HL Congruence Theorem to show that $\triangle JKL \cong \triangle MKL$?

Homework Help

Example 1: Exs. 10–13, 24, 29–31
Example 2: Ex. 32
Example 3: Exs. 13–24, 29–31
Example 4: Ex. 32

14. Suppose K is the midpoint of $\overline{JM}$. Name a theorem or postulate you could use to show that $\triangle JKL \cong \triangle MKL$. Explain your reasoning.

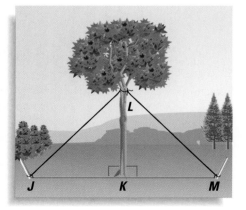

You be the Judge Decide whether enough information is given to show that the triangles are congruent. If so, state the theorem or postulate you would use. Explain your reasoning.

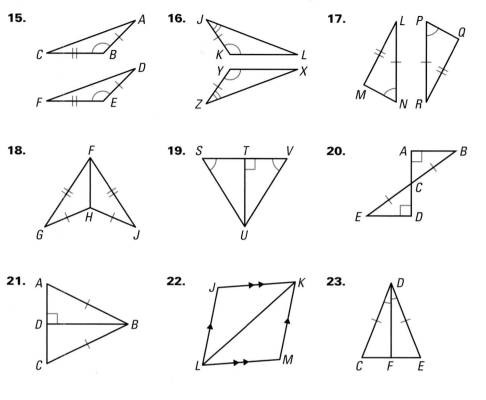

15.

16.

17.

18.

19.

20.

21.

22.

23.

24. **Logical Reasoning** Three students are given the diagram shown at the right and asked which congruence postulate or theorem can be used to show that △ABC ≅ △CDA. Explain why all three answers are correct.

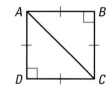

Meghan

△ABC ≅ △CDA by the SSS Congruence Postulate.

Keith

△ABC ≅ △CDA by the SAS Congruence Postulate.

Angie

△ABC ≅ △CDA by the Hypotenuse-Leg Congruence Theorem.

Student Help
CLASSZONE.COM

HOMEWORK HELP
Extra help with problem solving in Exs. 25–28 is at classzone.com

Visualize It! Use the given information to sketch △*LMN* and △*STU*. Mark the triangles with the given information.

25. ∠*LNM* and ∠*TUS* are right angles. $\overline{LM} \cong \overline{TS}$, $\overline{TU} \cong \overline{LN}$

26. $\overline{LM} \perp \overline{MN}$, $\overline{ST} \perp \overline{TU}$, $\overline{LM} \cong \overline{ST}$, $\overline{LN} \cong \overline{SU}$

27. $\overline{LM} \perp \overline{MN}$, $\overline{ST} \perp \overline{TU}$, $\overline{LM} \cong \overline{NM} \cong \overline{UT} \cong \overline{ST}$

28. $\overline{ML} \perp \overline{LN}$, $\overline{TS} \perp \overline{SU}$, $\overline{LN} \cong \overline{SU}$, $\overline{MN} \cong \overline{TU}$

Missing Information What congruence is needed to show that the triangles are congruent? Using that congruence, tell which theorem or postulate you would use to show that the triangles are congruent.

29.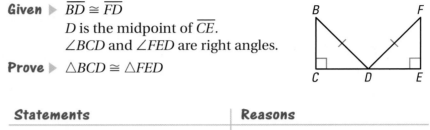

30.

31.

32. Logical Reasoning Fill in the missing statements and reasons.

Given $\overline{BD} \cong \overline{FD}$
   D is the midpoint of $\overline{CE}$.
   $\angle BCD$ and $\angle FED$ are right angles.

Prove $\triangle BCD \cong \triangle FED$

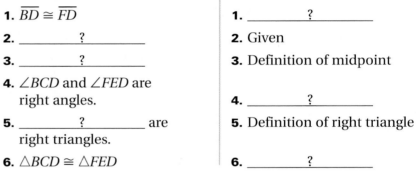

Statements	Reasons
1. $\overline{BD} \cong \overline{FD}$	**1.** _____?_____
2. _____?_____	**2.** Given
3. _____?_____	**3.** Definition of midpoint
4. $\angle BCD$ and $\angle FED$ are right angles.	**4.** _____?_____
5. _____?_____ are right triangles.	**5.** Definition of right triangle
6. $\triangle BCD \cong \triangle FED$	**6.** _____?_____

Standardized Test Practice

33. Multi-Step Problem The diagram below is a plan showing the light created by two spotlights. Both spotlights are the same distance from the stage.

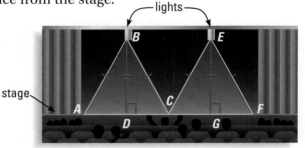

a. Show that $\triangle ABD \cong \triangle CBD$. Tell what theorem or postulate you use and explain your reasoning.

b. Is there another way to show that $\triangle ABD \cong \triangle CBD$? If so, tell how. Explain your reasoning.

c. Are all four right triangles in the diagram congruent? Explain your reasoning.

Parallel Lines Find $m\angle 1$ and $m\angle 2$. Explain your reasoning. *(Lesson 3.4)*

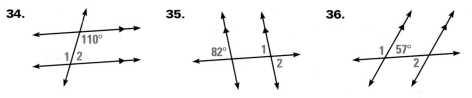

34. **35.** **36.**

Showing Congruence Decide whether enough information is given to show that the triangles are congruent. If so, state the theorem or postulate you would use. Explain your reasoning. *(Lessons 5.2, 5.3)*

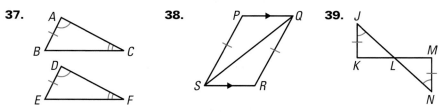

37. **38.** **39.**

Evaluating Expressions Evaluate. *(Skills Review, p. 670)*

40. $2 \cdot 4 + 5$ **41.** $10 - 5 \cdot 2$ **42.** $3 + 4^2 - 11$

43. $7 \cdot 2 + 6 \cdot 3$ **44.** $3 \cdot 5 - 2 \cdot 7$ **45.** $5^2 - 10 \cdot 2$

Quiz 2

Tell whether the theorem or postulate can be used to show that $\triangle LMN \cong \triangle QMP$. *(Lessons 5.3, 5.4)*

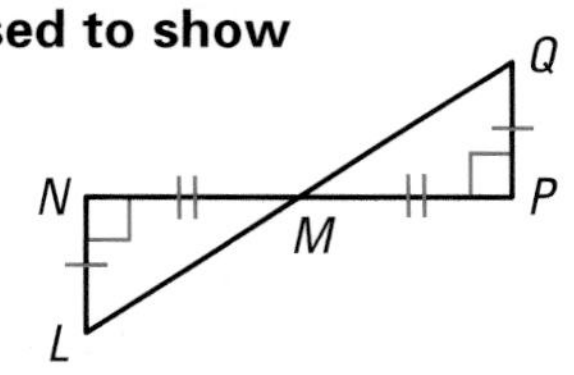

1. ASA   **2.** AAS

3. HL   **4.** SSS

Tell whether enough information is given to show that the triangles are congruent. If so, tell which theorem or postulate you would use. Explain your reasoning. *(Lessons 5.3, 5.4)*

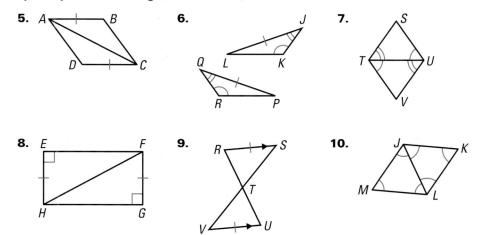

5.   **6.**   **7.**

8.   **9.**   **10.**

5.4 *Hypotenuse-Leg Congruence Theorem: HL*   **263**

5.4 Investigating Congruence

Question

Is there a side-side-angle congruence postulate or theorem?

Explore

❶ Draw a segment and label it $\overline{AB}$. Draw a point not on $\overline{AB}$ and label this point E. Construct $\overleftrightarrow{AE}$.

❷ Draw a circle centered at point B that intersects $\overleftrightarrow{AE}$ in two points as shown. Label the intersection points G and H.

❸ Draw $\overline{BG}$ and $\overline{BH}$. Hide the circle.

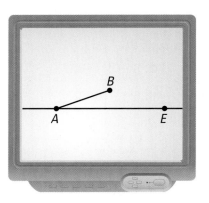

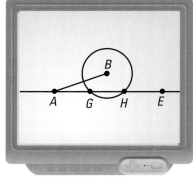

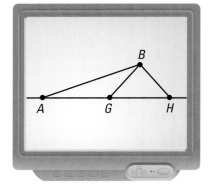

Think About It

1. Find the measures of the segments and angles listed in the tables.

Segments	$\overline{AB}$	$\overline{AG}$	$\overline{BG}$	$\overline{BH}$	$\overline{AH}$
	?	?	?	?	?

Angles	$\angle ABG$	$\angle BAG$	$\angle AGB$	$\angle ABH$	$\angle BAH$	$\angle AHB$
	?	?	?	?	?	?

Student Help

VISUAL STRATEGY
Drawing overlapping triangles separately makes it easier to see the triangles. An example is on p. 232.

2. List the sides of $\triangle ABG$ that are congruent to the sides of $\triangle ABH$.

3. List the angles of $\triangle ABG$ that are congruent to the angles of $\triangle ABH$.

4. Do you think that $\triangle ABH \cong \triangle ABG$? Explain your reasoning.

5. Sketch $\triangle ABG$ and $\triangle ABH$ separately on a piece of paper. Mark the corresponding congruences on the triangles.

6. Explain why there is no side-side-angle congruence postulate.

5.5 Using Congruent Triangles

Goal
Show corresponding parts of congruent triangles are congruent.

Key Words
- corresponding parts
  p. 233

If you know that two triangles are congruent, you can use the definition of congruent triangles from Lesson 5.1 to conclude that the corresponding parts are congruent.

If you know $\triangle ABC \cong \triangle DEF$, then you can conclude:

Corresponding Sides	Corresponding Angles
$\overline{AB} \cong \overline{DE}$	$\angle A \cong \angle D$
$\overline{BC} \cong \overline{EF}$	$\angle B \cong \angle E$
$\overline{AC} \cong \overline{DF}$	$\angle C \cong \angle F$

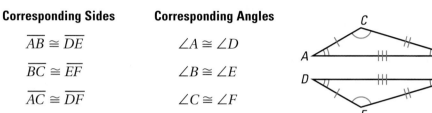

EXAMPLE 1 Use Corresponding Parts

In the diagram, $\overline{AB}$ and $\overline{CD}$ bisect each other at M. Prove that $\angle A \cong \angle B$.

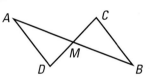

Solution

❶ First sketch the diagram and label any congruent segments and congruent angles.

❷ Because $\angle A$ and $\angle B$ are corresponding angles in $\triangle ADM$ and $\triangle BCM$, show that $\triangle ADM \cong \triangle BCM$ to prove that $\angle A \cong \angle B$.

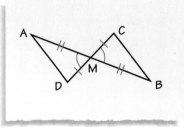

Statements	Reasons
1. $\overline{AB}$ and $\overline{CD}$ bisect each other at M.	1. Given
2. $\overline{MA} \cong \overline{MB}$	2. Definition of segment bisector
3. $\angle AMD \cong \angle BMC$	3. Vertical Angles Theorem
4. $\overline{MD} \cong \overline{MC}$	4. Definition of segment bisector
5. $\triangle ADM \cong \triangle BCM$	5. SAS Congruence Postulate
6. $\angle A \cong \angle B$	6. Corresponding parts of congruent triangles are congruent.

Student Help

LOOK BACK
For the definition of congruent figures, see p. 233.

Diagrams often show overlapping triangles. It is usually helpful to visualize or redraw the triangles so that they do not overlap.

Original diagram

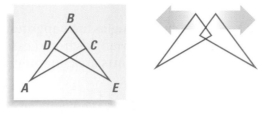

△**ABC** and △**EBD** overlap.

Redrawn diagram

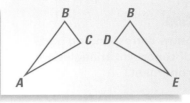

△**ABC** and △**EBD** do not overlap.

EXAMPLE **2** **Visualize Overlapping Triangles**

Sketch the overlapping triangles separately. Mark all congruent angles and sides. Then tell what theorem or postulate you can use to show △*JGH* ≅ △*KHG*.

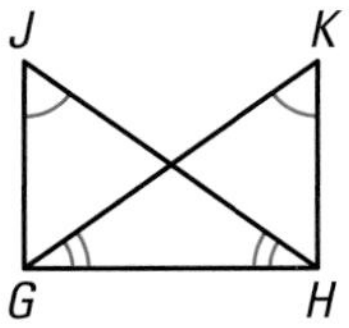

Student Help

VISUAL STRATEGY
Drawing overlapping triangles separately makes it easier to see the triangles and correctly mark congruent sides and angles, as shown on p. 232.

Solution

❶ Sketch the triangles separately and mark any given information.

Think of △*JGH* moving to the left and △*KHG* moving to the right.

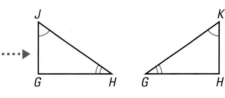

Mark ∠*GJH* ≅ ∠*HKG* and ∠*JHG* ≅ ∠*KGH*.

❷ Look at the original diagram for shared sides, shared angles, or any other information you can conclude.

In the original diagram, $\overline{GH}$ and $\overline{HG}$ are the same side, so $\overline{GH} \cong \overline{HG}$.

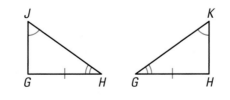

Add congruence marks to $\overline{GH}$ in each triangle.

❸ You can use the AAS Congruence Theorem to show that △*JGH* ≅ △*KHG*.

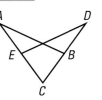

Student Help

CLASSZONE.COM

MORE EXAMPLES
More examples at classzone.com

EXAMPLE **3** *Use Overlapping Triangles*

Write a proof that shows $\overline{AB} \cong \overline{DE}$.

Given ▶ $\angle ABC \cong \angle DEC$
$\overline{CB} \cong \overline{CE}$

Prove ▶ $\overline{AB} \cong \overline{DE}$

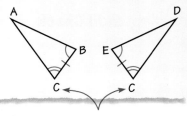

Solution

❶ Sketch the triangles separately. Then label the given information and any other information you can conclude from the diagram.

In the original diagram, $\angle C$ is the same in both triangles ($\angle BCA \cong \angle ECD$).

Mark $\angle C \cong \angle C$.

❷ Show $\triangle ABC \cong \triangle DEC$ to prove that $\overline{AB} \cong \overline{DE}$.

Statements	Reasons
1. $\angle ABC \cong \angle DEC$	1. Given
2. $\overline{CB} \cong \overline{CE}$	2. Given
3. $\angle C \cong \angle C$	3. Reflexive Prop. of Congruence
4. $\triangle ABC \cong \triangle DEC$	4. ASA Congruence Postulate
5. $\overline{AB} \cong \overline{DE}$	5. Corresponding parts of congruent triangles are congruent.

Checkpoint ✓ *Use Overlapping Triangles*

1. Tell which triangle congruence theorem or postulate you would use to show that $\overline{AB} \cong \overline{CD}$.

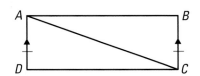

Redraw the triangles separately and label all congruences. Explain how to show that the triangles or corresponding parts are congruent.

2. Given $\overline{KJ} \cong \overline{KL}$ and $\angle J \cong \angle L$, show $\overline{NJ} \cong \overline{ML}$.

3. Given $\angle SPR \cong \angle QRP$ and $\angle Q \cong \angle S$, show $\triangle PQR \cong \triangle RSP$.

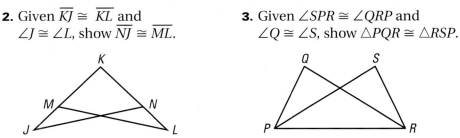

Guided Practice

Vocabulary Check

1. In the diagram, △ABC ≅ △DEF. Why can you conclude that ∠CBA ≅ ∠FED?

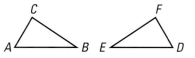

Skill Check

2. Visualize It! Tell which diagram correctly represents all the congruences in the original figure.

Original figure   **A.**   **B.**

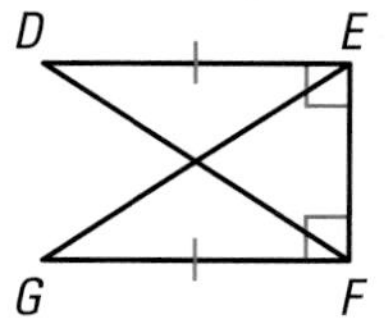

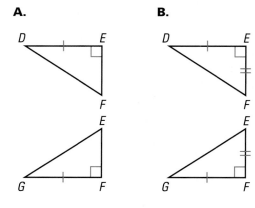

Explain how to show that the statement is true.

3. ∠STU ≅ ∠UVS   **4.** $\overline{AB} \cong \overline{DC}$ **5.** ∠J ≅ ∠M

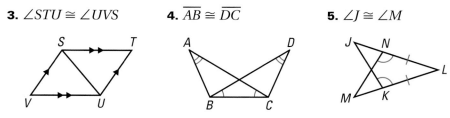

Practice and Applications

Extra Practice

See p. 684.

6. Showing Congruence In the diagram, △JKL ≅ △PQR. Why can you conclude that ∠K ≅ ∠Q?

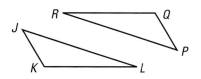

Finding Congruent Parts Tell which triangles you need to show are congruent in order to show that the statement is true.

7. ∠A ≅ ∠D   **8.** ∠J ≅ ∠N   **9.** $\overline{DE} \cong \overline{BA}$

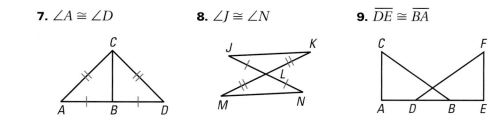

Homework Help

Example 1: Exs. 15, 16, 19
Example 2: Exs. 10–13
Example 3: Exs. 14–20

Visualize It! **Sketch the overlapping triangles separately. Mark all congruent angles and sides. Then tell what theorem or postulate you can use to show that the triangles are congruent.**

10. $\overline{BC} \cong \overline{DA}$, $\angle ADB \cong \angle CBD$

11. $\angle E \cong \angle H$, $\overline{EF} \cong \overline{HJ}$

Link to Crafts

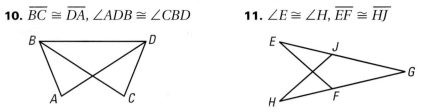

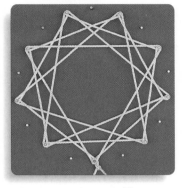

STRING DESIGNS The shape and size of a string design is determined by how many points along a circle are used to create the design.

String Designs **What theorem or postulate can you use to show that the triangles in the string design are congruent? Explain your reasoning.**

12. $\triangle ABC \cong \triangle DEF$

13. $\triangle GHJ \cong \triangle KHM$

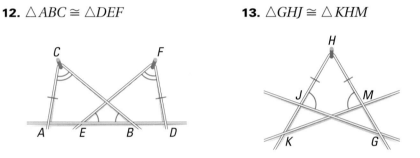

14. Logical Reasoning Fill in the missing statements and reasons.

Given ▸ $\overline{AB} \cong \overline{AE}$

$\angle ACB \cong \angle ADE$

Prove ▸ $\angle B \cong \angle E$

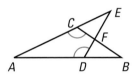

Statements	Reasons
1. $\overline{AB} \cong \overline{AE}$	1. ____?____
2. ____?____	2. Given
3. ____?____	3. Reflexive Prop. of Congruence
4. $\triangle ABC \cong \triangle AED$	4. ____?____
5. $\angle B \cong \angle E$	5. ____?____

Finding Congruent Parts **Use the information in the diagram to prove that the statement is true.**

15. $\angle A \cong \angle C$

16. $\overline{JK} \cong \overline{NM}$

17. $\overline{QT} \cong \overline{SR}$

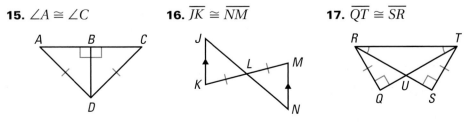

Student Help
CLASSZONE.COM

HOMEWORK HELP
Extra help with problem solving in Ex. 18 is at classzone.com

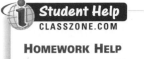

18. Argyle Patterns In the argyle pattern shown below, $\overline{UV} \cong \overline{VW} \cong \overline{XY} \cong \overline{YZ}$ and $\angle UVW \cong \angle XYZ$. Prove that $\overline{WU} \cong \overline{ZX}$.

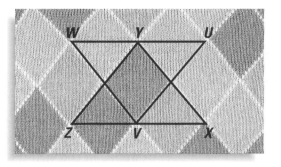

Logical Reasoning In Exercises 19 and 20, fill in the missing statements and reasons.

19. Given ▶ $\overline{BD}$ and $\overline{AE}$ bisect each other at C.

Prove ▶ $\angle A \cong \angle E$

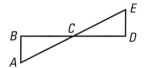

Statements	Reasons
1. $\overline{BD}$ and $\overline{AE}$ bisect each other at C.	**1.** ___?___
2. $\overline{BC} \cong \overline{DC}$	**2.** ___?___
3. ___?___	**3.** Def. of segment bisector
4. $\angle BCA \cong \angle DCE$	**4.** ___?___
5. $\triangle ABC \cong \triangle EDC$	**5.** ___?___
6. $\angle A \cong \angle E$	**6.** ___?___

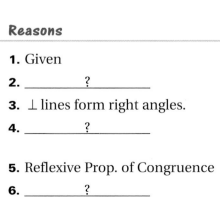

Student Help

STUDY TIP
If you get stuck, remember that you know the given information and what you are trying to prove. You can fill those in first, then go back to the other steps.

20. Given ▶ $\overline{JK} \perp \overline{LK}$, $\overline{ML} \perp \overline{KL}$
$\overline{JL} \cong \overline{MK}$

Prove ▶ $\overline{JK} \cong \overline{ML}$

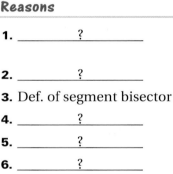

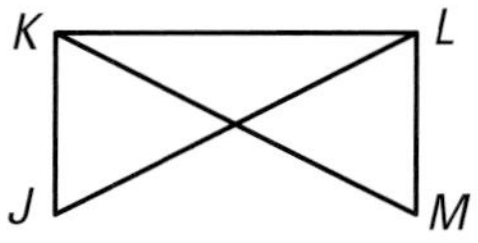

Statements	Reasons
1. ___?___	**1.** Given
2. $\overline{JK} \perp \overline{LK}$, $\overline{ML} \perp \overline{KL}$	**2.** ___?___
3. ___?___	**3.** $\perp$ lines form right angles.
4. $\triangle JKL$ and $\triangle MLK$ are right triangles.	**4.** ___?___
5. ___?___	**5.** Reflexive Prop. of Congruence
6. $\triangle JKL \cong \triangle MLK$	**6.** ___?___
7. ___?___	**7.** ___?___

21. Challenge In the figure at the right, $\overline{LK} \parallel \overline{PN}$, $\angle LJK \cong \angle PMN$, and $\overline{JM} \cong \overline{ML} \cong \overline{LP}$. What theorem or postulate can be used to show that $\triangle JKL \cong \triangle MNP$? Explain.

Standardized Test Practice

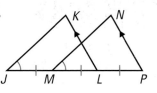

22. Multiple Choice In the diagram, suppose that $\overline{AD} \cong \overline{CB}$ and $\angle BCA \cong \angle DAC$. Which triangles can you use to prove that $\angle EBA \cong \angle EDC$?

Ⓐ $\triangle ABC$ and $\triangle CDA$

Ⓑ $\triangle ABE$ and $\triangle CDE$

Ⓒ $\triangle DEB$ and $\triangle AEC$

Ⓓ Not enough information

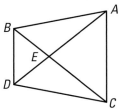

23. Multiple Choice In the diagram, suppose that $\overline{AE} \cong \overline{CE}$ and $\overline{BE} \cong \overline{DE}$. Which triangles can you use to prove that $\overline{AB} \cong \overline{CD}$?

Ⓕ $\triangle ABC$ and $\triangle CDA$

Ⓖ $\triangle ABE$ and $\triangle CDE$

Ⓗ $\triangle DEB$ and $\triangle AEC$

Ⓙ Not enough information

Mixed Review

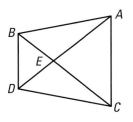

Angle Bisectors In the diagram, $\overrightarrow{BD}$ bisects $\angle ABC$. Find the value of x. *(Lesson 2.2)*

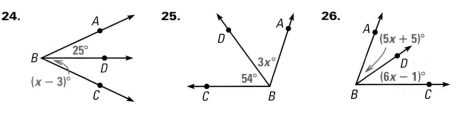

24.

25.

26.

Perpendicular Lines Find the value of x, given that $p \perp q$. *(Lesson 3.2)*

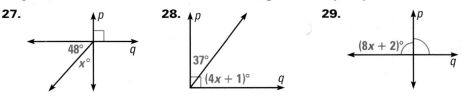

27.

28.

29.

Algebra Skills

Solving Equations Solve the equation. *(Skills Review, p. 673)*

30. $x + 5 = 8$ **31.** $7x = -63$ **32.** $4x - 9 = 23$

33. $11 + 3x = 32$ **34.** $5x - 3x + 10 = 24$ **35.** $x + 2x - 8 = 19$

Question

What is true about any point on the perpendicular bisector of a segment?

Materials
- ruler
- protractor

Explore

1 On a piece of paper, draw $\overline{AB}$. Fold the paper so that point B lies directly on point A.

2 Draw a line along the crease in the paper. Label the point where the line intersects $\overline{AB}$ as point M.

3 Label another point on the line you made in Step 2 as point C. Draw $\overline{CA}$ and $\overline{CB}$.

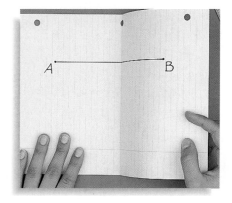

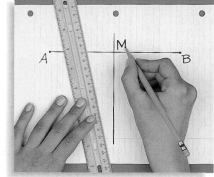

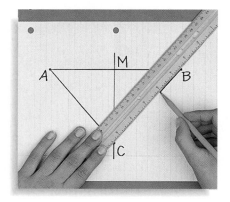

4 Copy and complete the table at right.

Segment or angle	$\overline{MA}$	$\overline{MB}$	$\angle CMA$	$\angle CMB$
Measure	?	?	?	?

Think About It

Student Help

LOOK BACK
To review segment bisectors, see p. 53.

1. Line $\overleftrightarrow{CM}$ is called the *perpendicular bisector* of $\overline{AB}$. Why do you think this describes $\overleftrightarrow{CM}$?

2. Choose three other points on $\overleftrightarrow{CM}$. Label the points D, E, and F. Copy and complete the table below. What do you notice?

Point C	Point D	Point E	Point F
$CA = ?$	$DA = ?$	$EA = ?$	$FA = ?$
$CB = ?$	$DB = ?$	$EB = ?$	$FB = ?$

3. Reasoning What is true about any point on the perpendicular bisector of a segment?

Angle Bisectors and Perpendicular Bisectors

Goal

Use angle bisectors and perpendicular bisectors.

Key Words

- distance from a point to a line
- equidistant
- angle bisector p. 61
- perpendicular bisector

The **distance from a point to a line** is measured by the length of the perpendicular segment from the point to the line.

When a point is the same distance from one line as it is from another line, the point is **equidistant** from the two lines.

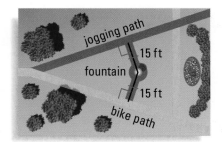

The fountain is equidistant from the jogging path and the bike path.

THEOREM 5.3

Angle Bisector Theorem

Words If a point is on the bisector of an angle, then it is equidistant from the two sides of the angle.

If 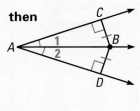 **then**

Symbols If $m\angle 1 = m\angle 2$, then $\overline{BC} \cong \overline{BD}$.

EXAMPLE 1 Use the Angle Bisector Theorem

Prove that $\triangle TWU \cong \triangle VWU$.

Given ▶ $\overrightarrow{UW}$ bisects $\angle TUV$.
$\triangle UTW$ and $\triangle UVW$ are right triangles.

Prove ▶ $\triangle TWU \cong \triangle VWU$.

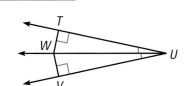

Solution

Statements	Reasons
1. $\overrightarrow{UW}$ bisects $\angle TUV$.	1. Given
2. $\triangle UTW$ and $\triangle UVW$ are right triangles.	2. Given
H 3. $\overline{WU} \cong \overline{WU}$	3. Reflexive Prop. of Congruence
L 4. $\overline{WV} \cong \overline{WT}$	4. Angle Bisector Theorem
5. $\triangle TWU \cong \triangle VWU$	5. HL Congruence Theorem

Student Help

STUDY TIP
You can also show that the triangles in Example 1 are congruent by the AAS Congruence Theorem.

5.6 *Angle Bisectors and Perpendicular Bisectors*

Perpendicular Bisectors A segment, ray, or line that is perpendicular to a segment at its midpoint is called a **perpendicular bisector** .

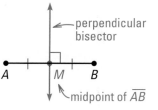

perpendicular bisector

midpoint of $\overline{AB}$

THEOREM 5.4

Perpendicular Bisector Theorem

Words If a point is on the perpendicular bisector of a segment, then it is equidistant from the endpoints of the segment.

Symbols If C is on the perpendicular bisector of $\overline{AB}$, then $\overline{CA} \cong \overline{CB}$.

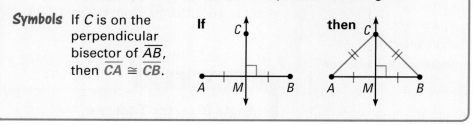

Using Algebra

EXAMPLE 2 Use Perpendicular Bisectors

Use the diagram to find AB.

Solution

In the diagram, $\overleftrightarrow{AC}$ is the perpendicular bisector of $\overline{DB}$.

$8x = 5x + 12$	By the Perpendicular Bisector Theorem, $AB = AD$.
$3x = 12$	Subtract $5x$ from each side.
$\dfrac{3x}{3} = \dfrac{12}{3}$	Divide each side by 3.
$x = 4$	Simplify.

You are asked to find AB, not just the value of x.

ANSWER ▶ $AB = 8x = 8 \cdot 4 = 32$

Checkpoint ✓ **Use Angle Bisectors and Perpendicular Bisectors**

1. Find FH.　　**2.** Find MK.　　**3.** Find EF.

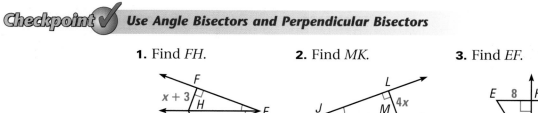

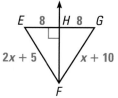

EXAMPLE 3 **Use the Perpendicular Bisector Theorem**

In the diagram, $\overleftrightarrow{MN}$ is the perpendicular bisector of $\overline{ST}$. Prove that $\triangle MST$ is isosceles.

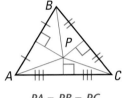

Solution

To prove that $\triangle MST$ is isosceles, show that $MS = MT$.

Statements	Reasons
1. $\overleftrightarrow{MN}$ is the $\perp$ bisector of $\overline{ST}$.	**1.** Given
2. $MS = MT$	**2.** Perpendicular Bisector Theorem
3. $\triangle MST$ is isosceles.	**3.** Def. of isosceles triangle

Intersecting Bisectors One consequence of the Perpendicular Bisector Theorem is that the perpendicular bisectors of a triangle intersect at a point that is equidistant from the vertices of the triangle.

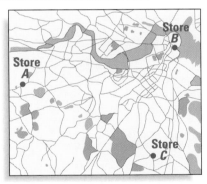

$PA = PB = PC$

EXAMPLE 4 **Use Intersecting Bisectors of a Triangle**

A company plans to build a warehouse that is equidistant from each of its three stores, A, B, and C. Where should the warehouse be built?

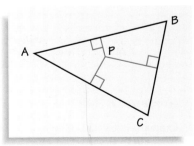

Solution

Think of the stores as the vertices of a triangle. The point where the perpendicular bisectors intersect will be equidistant from each store.

❶ Trace the location of the stores on a piece of paper. Connect the points of the locations to form $\triangle ABC$.

❷ Draw the perpendicular bisectors of $\overline{AB}$, $\overline{BC}$, and $\overline{CA}$. Label the intersection of the bisectors P.

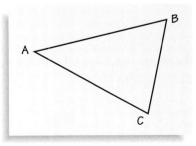

ANSWER ▸ Because P is equidistant from each vertex of $\triangle ABC$, the warehouse should be built near location P.

Guided Practice

Vocabulary Check   **Complete the statement.**

1. If a point is on the bisector of an angle, then it is __?__ from the two sides of the angle.

2. If D is on the __?__ of $\overline{AB}$, then D is equidistant from A and B.

Skill Check   **Use the information in the diagram to find the measure.**

3. Find AD.

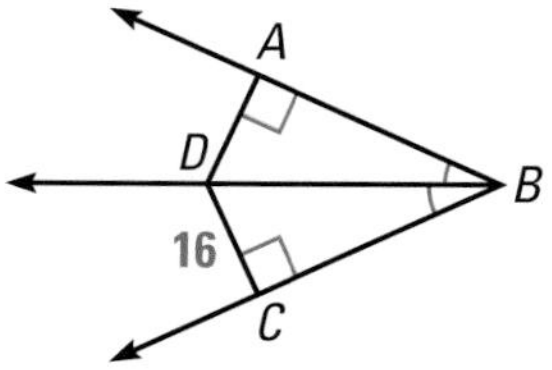

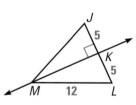

4. Find EF.

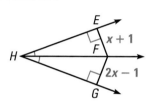

5. Find JM.

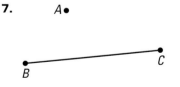

6. Find QR.

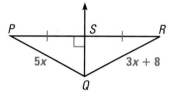

Practice and Applications

Extra Practice

See p. 684.

Visualize It! Copy each diagram on a piece of paper. Then draw a segment that represents the distance from **A** to $\overline{BC}$.

7.

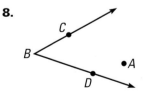

8.

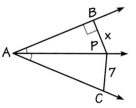

9. **Error Analysis** Explain why Paige cannot make this conclusion, given the diagram shown.

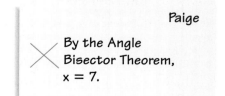

Paige

By the Angle Bisector Theorem, $x = 7$.

Homework Help

Example 1: Exs. 32, 33
Example 2: Exs. 10–12
         14–19
Example 3: Exs. 32, 33
Example 4: Exs. 23–29

Using Algebra Find the value of *x*.

10.

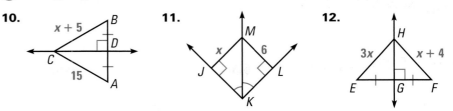

11.

12.

13. Roof Trusses In the diagram of the roof truss shown below, you are given that $\overline{AB}$ bisects $\angle CAD$ and that $\angle ACB$ and $\angle ADB$ are right angles. What can you say about $\overline{BC}$ and $\overline{BD}$? Why?

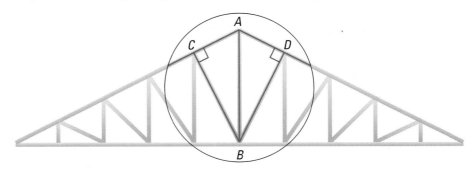

Using Bisectors Use the diagram to find the indicated measure(s).

14. Find $m\angle JKM$.

15. Find SV.

16. Find HG.

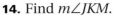

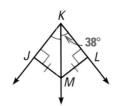

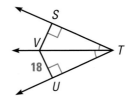

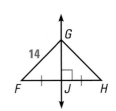

17. Find LK.

18. Find PQ.

19. Find AD and BC.

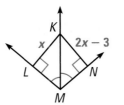

Link to
Careers

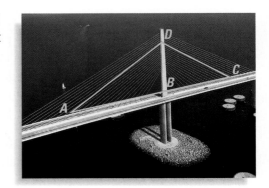

CIVIL ENGINEERS plan and build large construction projects, such as bridges, canals, and tunnels.

Career Links
CLASSZONE.COM

20. Bridges In the photo, the road is perpendicular to the support beam and $\overline{AB} \cong \overline{CB}$.

What theorem allows you to conclude that $\overline{AD} \cong \overline{CD}$? Explain.

5.6 *Angle Bisectors and Perpendicular Bisectors*

277

Soccer One way a goalie can determine a good defensive position is to imagine a triangle formed by the goal posts and the ball.

21. When the ball is far from the goal, the goalie most likely stands on line ℓ. How is ℓ related to the goal line ($\overleftrightarrow{AC}$)?

22. As the ball moves closer, the goalie moves from line ℓ to other places in front of the goal. How should $\overrightarrow{BG}$ relate to $\angle ABC$? Explain.

Using Perpendicular Bisectors Use the information in the diagram.

23. Find CG and AG.   **24.** Find VR and VQ.   **25.** Name all congruent segments.

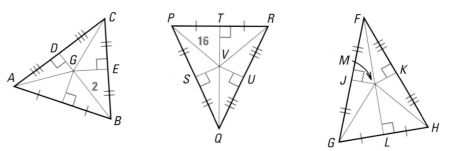

Student Help
CLASSZONE.COM

HOMEWORK HELP
Extra help with problem
solving in Exs. 26–29 is
at classzone.com

Analyzing a Map In Exercises 26–29, use the map shown and the following information.

A city planner is trying to decide whether a new household at point X should be covered by fire station A, B, or C.

26. Trace the points A, B, C, and X on a piece of paper and draw the segments $\overline{AB}$, $\overline{BC}$, and $\overline{CA}$.

27. Draw the perpendicular bisectors of $\overline{AB}$, $\overline{BC}$, and $\overline{CA}$. Check that they meet at a point.

28. The perpendicular bisectors divide the town into three regions.
Shade the region closest to fire station A red.
Shade the region closest to fire station B blue.
Shade the region closest to fire station C gray.

29. Writing In an emergency at household X, which fire station should respond? Explain your choice.

Technology In Exercises 30 and 31, use geometry drawing software to complete the steps below.

❶ Draw $\overline{AB}$. Find the midpoint of $\overline{AB}$ and label it C.

❷ Construct the perpendicular bisector of $\overline{AB}$ through C.

❸ Construct point D along the perpendicular bisector. Construct $\overline{DA}$ and $\overline{DB}$.

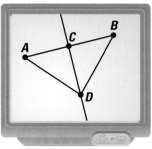

30. What is the relationship between $\overline{DA}$ and $\overline{DB}$? Measure $\overline{DA}$ and $\overline{DB}$ to verify your answer.

31. Move D to another point along the perpendicular bisector. Will the relationship between $\overline{DA}$ and $\overline{DB}$ stay the same? Why?

32. **Proving the Perpendicular Bisector Theorem** Fill in the missing statements and reasons.

Given ▷ $\overleftrightarrow{AD}$ is the perpendicular bisector of $\overline{BC}$.

Prove ▷ $AB = AC$

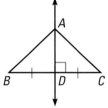

Statements	Reasons
1. $\overleftrightarrow{AD}$ is the perpendicular bisector of $\overline{BC}$.	1. _____?_____
2. $\overline{DB} \cong \overline{DC}$	2. _____?_____
3. _____?_____	3. ⊥ lines form right angles.
4. _____?_____	4. Right angles are congruent.
5. _____?_____	5. Reflexive Prop. of Congruence
6. $\triangle ADB \cong \triangle ADC$	6. _____?_____
7. $\overline{AB} \cong \overline{AC}$	7. _____?_____
8. _____?_____	8. Def. of congruent segments

Student Help

LOOK BACK
For help with writing proofs, see p. 243.

33. **Challenge** Use the diagram and the information below to prove the Angle Bisector Theorem.

Given ▷ D is on the bisector of $\angle BAC$. $\overline{DB} \perp \overrightarrow{AB}$, $\overline{DC} \perp \overrightarrow{AC}$

Prove ▷ $\overline{DB} \cong \overline{DC}$

Hint: First prove that $\triangle ADB \cong \triangle ADC$.

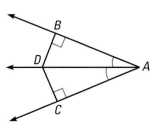

5.6 *Angle Bisectors and Perpendicular Bisectors*

34. Multiple Choice In the figure at the right, what is *SR*?

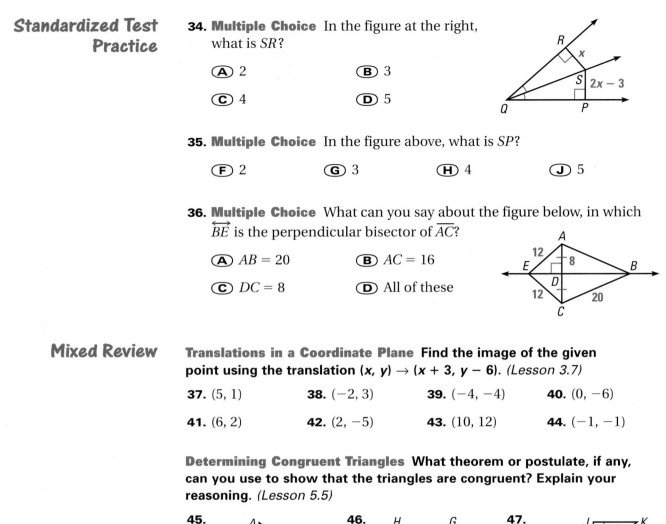

  A 2   **B** 3

  C 4   **D** 5

35. Multiple Choice In the figure above, what is *SP*?

  F 2   **G** 3   **H** 4   **J** 5

36. Multiple Choice What can you say about the figure below, in which $\overleftrightarrow{BE}$ is the perpendicular bisector of $\overline{AC}$?

  A $AB = 20$ **B** $AC = 16$

  C $DC = 8$ **D** All of these

Mixed Review

Translations in a Coordinate Plane Find the image of the given point using the translation $(x, y) \rightarrow (x + 3, y - 6)$. *(Lesson 3.7)*

37. $(5, 1)$ **38.** $(-2, 3)$ **39.** $(-4, -4)$ **40.** $(0, -6)$

41. $(6, 2)$ **42.** $(2, -5)$ **43.** $(10, 12)$ **44.** $(-1, -1)$

Determining Congruent Triangles What theorem or postulate, if any, can you use to show that the triangles are congruent? Explain your reasoning. *(Lesson 5.5)*

45.   **46.**   **47.**

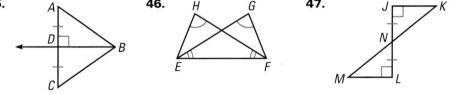

Algebra Skills

Ordering Numbers Write the numbers in order from least to greatest. *(Skills Review, p. 662)*

48. $3, -3, 0.3, -0.3, 0.6, 0$ **49.** $-0.25, 1, -0.75, 4, -1.25, 0.25$

50. $-0.4, 0.1, 0, 4.0, -0.1, -4$ **51.** $-3.3, 3.1, 3.8, -3.9, -3, 3.5$

52. $0.55, -1, 1.1, 1, 0.5, -0.1, 0$ **53.** $3.2, 1, 2.1, 3.25, -2.5, 5$

Solving Equations Solve the equation. *(Skills Review, p. 673)*

54. $4x + 3 = 11$ **55.** $2y - 9 = -11$ **56.** $5d - 35 = 90$

57. $4a + 9a = 39$ **58.** $x + 2 = 3x - 4$ **59.** $4r - 2 = 5r + 6$

60. $q = 2q - 9$ **61.** $2z + 5 = 4z - 1$ **62.** $10t + 10 = 12t$

Activity ◆ 5.7 ◆ Investigating Reflections

Question

What happens when a figure is reflected in a line?

Materials
- ruler
- protractor

Explore

① Fold a piece of paper in half. Open the paper. Draw a triangle on one side of the fold line and label the vertices *X*, *Y*, and *Z*.

② Fold the paper on the fold line and trace *X*, *Y*, and *Z* on the back of the paper. Open the paper, copy the points to the front, and label them *X'*, *Y'*, and *Z'*.

③ Draw △*X'Y'Z'*. Then draw $\overline{XX'}$, $\overline{ZZ'}$, and $\overline{YY'}$. Label the points where $\overline{XX'}$, $\overline{ZZ'}$ and $\overline{YY'}$ intersect the fold line as *A*, *B*, and *C*, as shown.

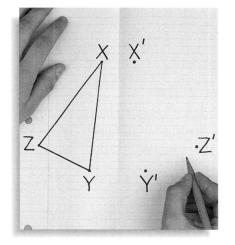

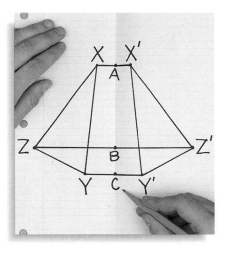

Student Help

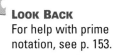

LOOK BACK
For help with prime notation, see p. 153.

Think About It

1. Copy and complete the table.

Segment	XA	AX'	ZB	BZ'	YC	CY'
Measure	?	?	?	?	?	?

2. Compare *XA* and *AX'*. Compare *ZB* and *BZ'*. Compare *YC* and *CY'*. What do you notice about these segments?

3. Copy and complete the table of angle measures. What do you notice about the angles?

Angle	∠*XAB*	∠*ZBA*	∠*YCB*
Measure	?	?	?

4. How does the fold line relate to $\overline{XX'}$, $\overline{YY'}$, and $\overline{ZZ'}$?

5.7 Reflections and Symmetry

Goal

Identify and use reflections and lines of symmetry.

Key Words

- image p. 152
- reflection
- line of symmetry

A **reflection** is a transformation that creates a mirror image. The original figure is reflected in a line that is called the *line of reflection*.

PROPERTIES OF REFLECTIONS

❶ The reflected image is congruent to the original figure.

❷ The orientation of the reflected image is reversed.

❸ The line of reflection is the perpendicular bisector of the segments joining the corresponding points.

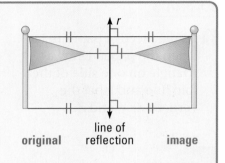

original   line of reflection   image

EXAMPLE 1 Identify Reflections

Tell whether the red triangle is the reflection of the blue triangle in line *m*.

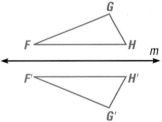

Solution

Check to see if all three properties of a reflection are met.

❶ Is the image congruent to the original figure? Yes. ✔

❷ Is the orientation of the image reversed? Yes. ✔

△*FGH* has a clockwise orientation.

△*F'G'H'* has a counterclockwise orientation.

❸ Is *m* the perpendicular bisector of the segments connecting the corresponding points? Yes. ✔

Visualize It!

clockwise orientation

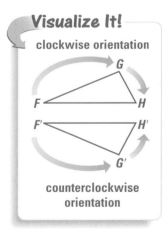

counterclockwise orientation

To check, draw a diagram and connect the corresponding endpoints.

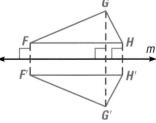

ANSWER ▶ Because all three properties are met, the red triangle is the reflection of the blue triangle in line *m*.

EXAMPLE 2 Identify Reflections

Tell whether the red triangle is the reflection of the blue triangle in line *m*.

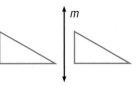

Solution

Check to see if all three properties of a reflection are met.

❶ Is the image congruent to the original figure? Yes. ✔

❷ Is the orientation of the image reversed? No.

ANSWER ▶ The red triangle is *not* a reflection of the blue triangle.

Student Help

VOCABULARY TIP
Use the following relationship to help you remember that a reflection is a flip:

reflection
flip

EXAMPLE 3 Reflections in a Coordinate Plane

a. Which segment is the reflection of $\overline{AB}$ in the *x*-axis? Which point corresponds to *A*? to *B*?

b. Which segment is the reflection of $\overline{AB}$ in the *y*-axis? Which point corresponds to *A*? to *B*?

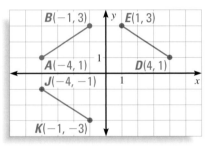

Solution

a. The *x*-axis is the perpendicular bisector of $\overline{AJ}$ and $\overline{BK}$, so the reflection of $\overline{AB}$ in the *x*-axis is $\overline{JK}$.

$A(-4, 1) \rightarrow J(-4, -1)$ *A is reflected onto J.*

$B(-1, 3) \rightarrow K(-1, -3)$ *B is reflected onto K.*

b. The *y*-axis is the perpendicular bisector of $\overline{AD}$ and $\overline{BE}$, so the reflection of $\overline{AB}$ in the *y*-axis is $\overline{DE}$.

$A(-4, 1) \rightarrow D(4, 1)$ *A is reflected onto D.*

$B(-1, 3) \rightarrow E(1, 3)$ *B is reflected onto E.*

Checkpoint ✓ **Identify Reflections**

Tell whether the red figure is a reflection of the blue figure. If the red figure is a reflection, name the line of reflection.

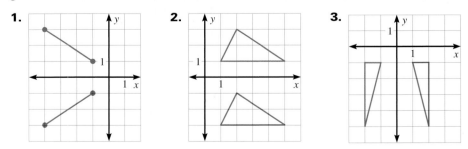

Symmetry In the photo, the mirror's edge creates a *line of symmetry*. A figure in the plane has a **line of symmetry** if the figure can be reflected onto itself by a reflection in the line.

A line of symmetry is a line of reflection.

Visualize It!

You may want to draw a shape on paper, cut it out, and then fold it to find the lines of symmetry.

EXAMPLE **4** **Determine Lines of Symmetry**

Determine the number of lines of symmetry in a square.

Solution

Think about how many different ways you can fold a square so that the edges of the figure match up perfectly.

vertical fold   **horizontal fold**   **diagonal fold**   **diagonal fold**

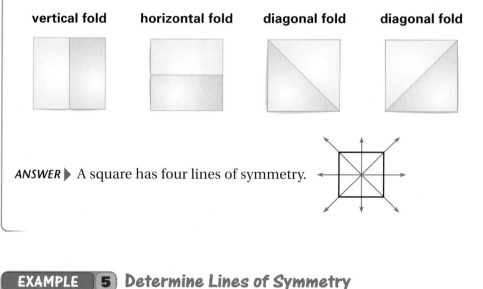

ANSWER ▶ A square has four lines of symmetry.

EXAMPLE **5** **Determine Lines of Symmetry**

Determine the number of lines of symmetry in each figure.

a. 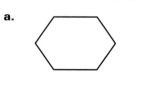   **b.** 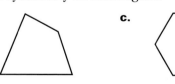   **c.**

Solution

a. 2 lines of symmetry   **b.** no lines of symmetry   **c.** 6 lines of symmetry

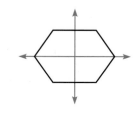   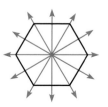

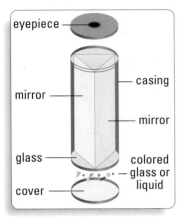

eyepiece

mirror

casing

mirror

glass

colored glass or liquid

cover

KALEIDOSCOPES The parts of a kaleidoscope are shown above.

Application Links
CLASSZONE.COM

EXAMPLE 6 Use Lines of Symmetry

Mirrors are used to create images seen through a kaleidoscope. The angle between the mirrors is $\angle A$.

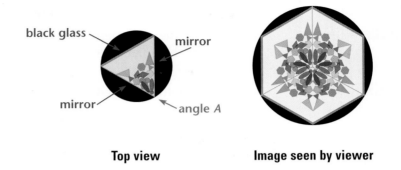

black glass

mirror

mirror

angle A

Top view

Image seen by viewer

Find the angle measure used to create the kaleidoscope design. Use the equation $m\angle A = \dfrac{180°}{n}$, where n is the number of lines of symmetry in the pattern.

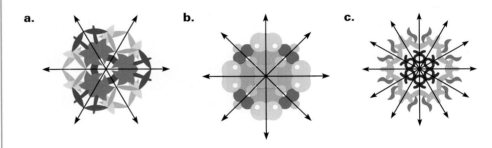

a.

b.

c.

Solution

a. The design has 3 lines of symmetry. So, in the formula, $n = 3$.

$$m\angle A = \frac{180°}{n} = \frac{180°}{3} = 60°$$

b. The design has 4 lines of symmetry. So, in the formula, $n = 4$.

$$m\angle A = \frac{180°}{n} = \frac{180°}{4} = 45°$$

c. The design has 6 lines of symmetry. So, in the formula, $n = 6$.

$$m\angle A = \frac{180°}{n} = \frac{180°}{6} = 30°$$

Checkpoint ✓ *Determine Lines of Symmetry*

Determine the number of lines of symmetry in the figure.

4.

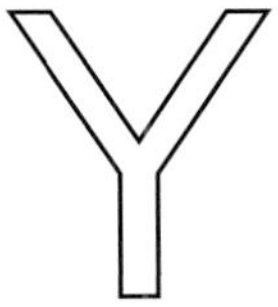

5.

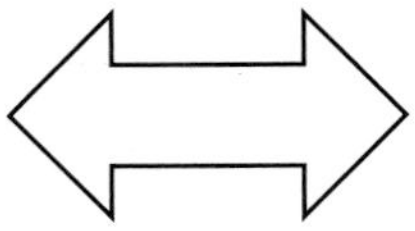

6.

Guided Practice

Vocabulary Check

1. Complete the statement: A figure in the plane has a(n) __?__ if the figure can be reflected onto itself by a(n) __?__ in the line.

Skill Check

Determine whether the red figure is a reflection of the blue figure.

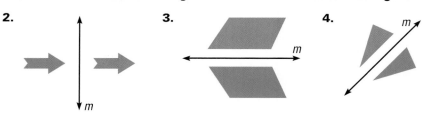

2.   3.   4.

Flowers **Determine the number of lines of symmetry in the flower.**

5.   6.   7.

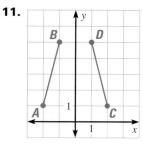

Practice and Applications

Extra Practice

See p. 684.

Identifying Reflections **Determine whether the figure in red is a reflection of the figure in blue. Explain why or why not.**

8.   9.   10.

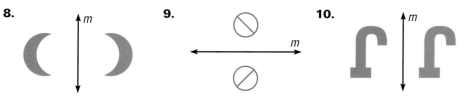

Reflections in a Coordinate Plane **Tell whether the grid shows a reflection in the *x-axis*, the *y-axis*, or *neither*.**

Homework Help

Example 1: Exs. 8–10
Example 2: Exs. 8–10
Example 3: Exs. 11–16
Example 4: Exs. 21–29
Example 5: Exs. 21–29
Example 6: Exs. 37–39

11.   12.   13.

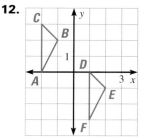

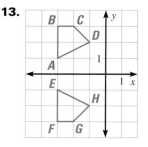

Student Help

SKILLS REVIEW
To review coordinates,
see p. 664.

Reflections in a Coordinate Plane In Exercises 14–16, use the diagram at the right.

14. Which segment is the reflection of $\overline{AB}$ in the x-axis? Which point corresponds to A? to B?

15. Which segment is the reflection of $\overline{AB}$ in the y-axis? Which point corresponds to A? to B?

16. Compare the coordinates for $\overline{AB}$ with the coordinates for its reflection in the x-axis. How are the coordinates alike? How are they different?

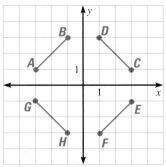

Visualize It! Trace the figure and draw its reflection in line k.

17.

18.

19.

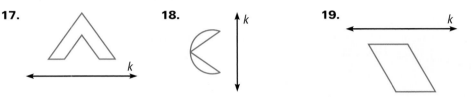

20. **Paper Folding** Follow these steps.

   ❶ Fold a piece of paper in half, twice.

   ❷ Draw a triangle and cut it out.

   ❸ Unfold the paper and label the sections.

   Which of the triangles are reflections of the triangle in section A? Explain.

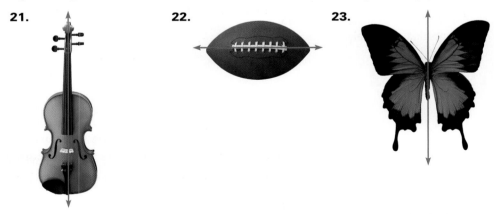

Symmetry Decide whether the line shown is a line of symmetry.

21.

22.

23.

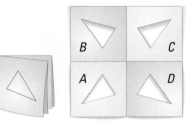

Lines of Symmetry Determine the number of lines of symmetry.

24.

25.

26.

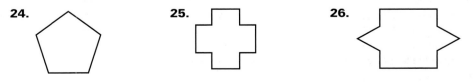

You be the Judge **Determine whether all lines of symmetry are shown. If not, sketch the figure and draw all the lines of symmetry.**

27.

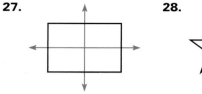

28.

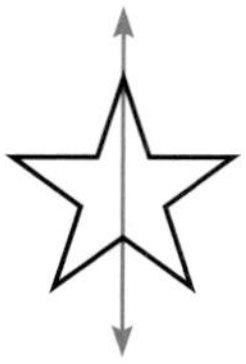

29.

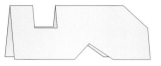

30. **Visualize It!** A piece of paper is folded in half and some cuts are made as shown. Sketch the figure that represents the piece of paper unfolded.

Link to Careers

TYPE DESIGNERS design fonts that appear in books, magazines, newspapers, and other materials that we read every day. Erik Spiekermann, shown above, has designed many fonts that are widely used today.

Career Links CLASSZONE.COM

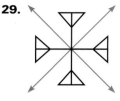

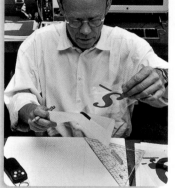

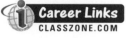

Type Design **In Exercises 31 and 32, use the lowercase letters of the alphabet shown below.**

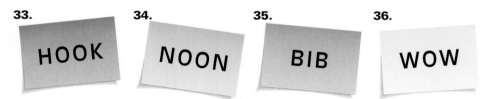

a b c d e f g h i j k l m
n o p q r s t u v w x y z

31. Which letters are reflections of other letters?

32. Draw each letter that has at least one line of symmetry and sketch its line(s) of symmetry. Which letters have one line of symmetry? Which letters have two lines of symmetry?

Word Reflections **Determine if the entire word has any lines of symmetry. If so, write the word and draw the line(s) of symmetry.**

33. HOOK

34. NOON

35. BIB

36. WOW

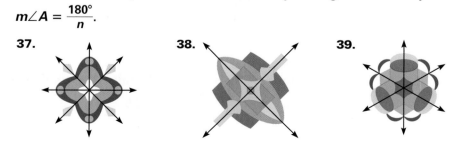

Kaleidoscope Designs **Find the measure of the angle between the mirrors ($\angle A$) that produces the kaleidoscope design. Use the equation $m\angle A = \frac{180°}{n}$.**

37.

38.

39.

Using Algebra

EXAMPLE   *Show Triangles are Congruent*

Show that $\triangle ABC \cong \triangle JKL$.

Solution

Show that the corresponding sides are congruent.

For sides on a horizontal grid line, subtract the *x*-coordinates.

$$CA = |5 - 1| = 4$$
$$LJ = |5 - 1| = 4$$

For sides on a vertical grid line, subtract the y-coordinates.

$$BC = |4 - 2| = 2$$
$$KL = |-4 - (-2)| = |-2| = 2$$

For any other sides, use the distance formula.

$$AB = \sqrt{(5 - 1)^2 + (4 - 2)^2} = \sqrt{4^2 + 2^2} = \sqrt{20}$$
$$JK = \sqrt{(5 - 1)^2 + ((-4 - (-2))^2} = \sqrt{4^2 + (-2)^2} = \sqrt{20}$$

By the SSS Congruence Postulate, $\triangle ABC \cong \triangle JKL$.

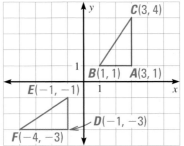

Student Help

LOOK BACK
For help with the distance formula, see p. 194.

Showing Triangles are Congruent In Exercises 40 and 41, refer to the example above. Show that $\triangle ABC \cong \triangle DEF$.

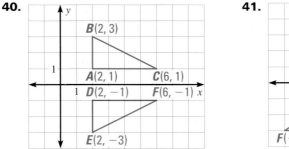

40.

41.

Standardized Test Practice

42. Multiple Choice Which triangle shows the image when $\triangle XYZ$ is reflected in the *y*-axis?

Ⓐ $\triangle DEF$ Ⓑ $\triangle JKL$

Ⓒ $\triangle PQR$ Ⓓ None of these

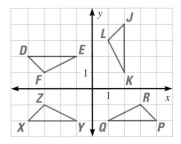

43. Multiple Choice How many lines of symmetry does the figure at the right have?

Ⓕ 0   Ⓖ 1

Ⓗ 2   Ⓙ 3

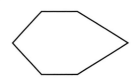

Mixed Review

Showing Lines are Parallel Find the value of *x* so that *p* ∥ *q*.
(Lesson 3.5)

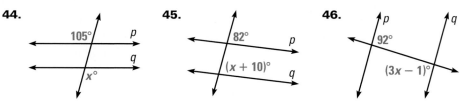

44. **45.** **46.**

Finding Angle Measures Find the measure of ∠1. *(Lesson 4.2)*

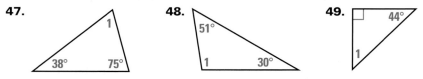

47. **48.** **49.**

Algebra Skills

Comparing Numbers Compare the two numbers. Write the answer using >, <, or =. *(Skills Review, p. 662)*

50. 2348 and 2384 **51.** −5 and −7 **52.** 19.1 and 19.01

53. −11.2 and −11.238 **54.** 0.065 and 0.056 **55.** 1.011 and 1.11

Quiz 3

1. Sketch the overlapping triangles separately. Mark all congruent angles and sides.

Which postulate or theorem can you use to show that the triangles are congruent? *(Lesson 5.5)*

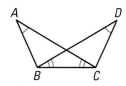

Use the diagram to find the indicated measure(s). *(Lesson 5.6)*

2. Find *DC*. **3.** Find *ML* and *JK*. **4.** Find *AB*.

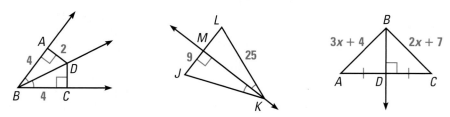

Determine the number of lines of symmetry in the figure. *(Lesson 5.7)*

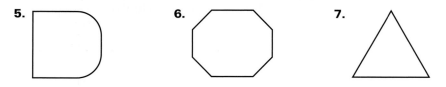

5. **6.** **7.**

VOCABULARY

- **corresponding parts,** *p. 233*
- **congruent figures,** *p. 233*
- **proof,** *p. 243*
- **distance from a point to a line,** *p. 273*
- **equidistant,** *p. 273*
- **perpendicular bisector,** *p. 274*
- **reflection,** *p. 282*
- **line of symmetry,** *p. 284*

VOCABULARY REVIEW

Fill in the blank.

1. When two figures are __?__, their corresponding sides and their corresponding angles are congruent.

2. A(n) __?__ is a convincing argument that shows why a statement is true.

3. If a point is on the __?__ of a segment, then it is equidistant from the endpoints of the segment.

4. If a point is on the angle bisector of an angle, then it is __?__ from the two sides of the angle.

5. A(n) __?__ is a transformation that creates a mirror image.

5.1 CONGRUENCE AND TRIANGLES

Examples on pp. 233–235

> **EXAMPLE** In the diagram, △**ABC** ≅ △**RST**. Identify all corresponding congruent parts.
>
> **Corresponding angles**
>
> ∠A ≅ ∠R
> ∠B ≅ ∠S
> ∠C ≅ ∠T
>
> **Corresponding sides**
>
> $\overline{AB} \cong \overline{RS}$
> $\overline{AC} \cong \overline{RT}$
> $\overline{BC} \cong \overline{ST}$

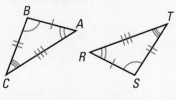

Use the triangles shown at the right to determine whether the given angles or sides represent *corresponding angles*, *corresponding sides*, or *neither*.

6. ∠J and ∠R
7. $\overline{KL}$ and $\overline{QR}$
8. ∠K and ∠Q
9. $\overline{PQ}$ and $\overline{LJ}$
10. $\overline{JK}$ and $\overline{PR}$
11. ∠R and ∠L

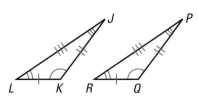

5.2   PROVING TRIANGLES ARE CONGRUENT: SSS AND SAS

Examples on pp. 241–244

EXAMPLES   Tell which congruence postulate you would use to show that the triangles are congruent.

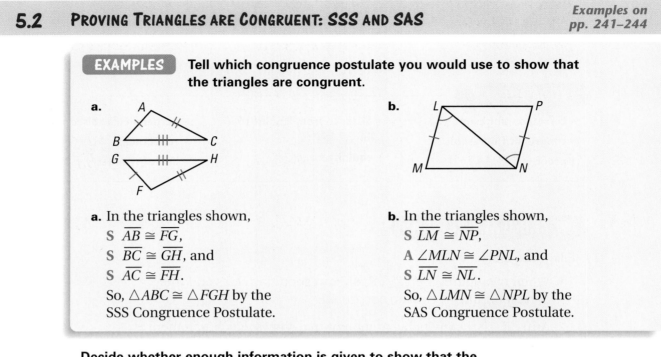

a. In the triangles shown,
   S $\overline{AB} \cong \overline{FG}$,
   S $\overline{BC} \cong \overline{GH}$, and
   S $\overline{AC} \cong \overline{FH}$.
   So, $\triangle ABC \cong \triangle FGH$ by the SSS Congruence Postulate.

b. In the triangles shown,
   S $\overline{LM} \cong \overline{NP}$,
   A $\angle MLN \cong \angle PNL$, and
   S $\overline{LN} \cong \overline{NL}$.
   So, $\triangle LMN \cong \triangle NPL$ by the SAS Congruence Postulate.

Decide whether enough information is given to show that the triangles are congruent. If so, tell which congruence postulate you would use.

12. 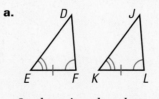   **13.** 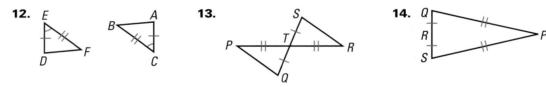   **14.**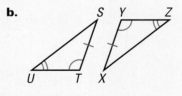

5.3   PROVING TRIANGLES ARE CONGRUENT: ASA AND AAS

Examples on pp. 250–253

EXAMPLES   Tell which congruence postulate or theorem you would use to show that the triangles are congruent.

a. In the triangles shown,
   A $\angle E \cong \angle K$,
   S $\overline{EF} \cong \overline{KL}$, and
   A $\angle F \cong \angle L$.
   So, $\triangle DEF \cong \triangle JKL$ by the ASA Congruence Postulate.

b. In the triangles shown,
   A $\angle U \cong \angle Z$,
   A $\angle T \cong \angle Y$, and
   S $\overline{ST} \cong \overline{XY}$.
   So, $\triangle STU \cong \triangle XYZ$ by the AAS Congruence Theorem.

Determine what information is needed to use the indicated postulate or theorem to show that the triangles are congruent.

15. AAS Congruence Theorem

16. ASA Congruence Postulate

17. ASA Congruence Postulate

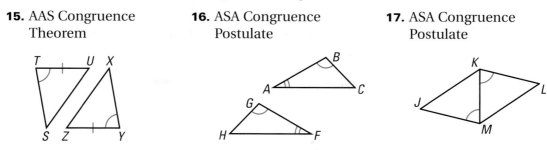

5.4   HYPOTENUSE-LEG CONGRUENCE THEOREM: HL

Examples on pp. 257–259

EXAMPLE   **Prove that △*ABC* ≅ △*BFD*.**

Given ▸ $\overline{CB} \perp \overline{AF}$, $\overline{DF} \perp \overline{AF}$

B is the midpoint of $\overline{AF}$.

$\overline{AC} \cong \overline{BD}$

Prove ▸ △*ABC* ≅ △*BFD*

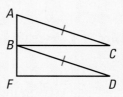

Show that the triangles are right triangles, the hypotenuses are congruent, and that corresponding legs are congruent.

Statements	Reasons
1. $\overline{CB} \perp \overline{AF}$, $\overline{DF} \perp \overline{AF}$, and *B* is the midpoint of $\overline{AF}$.	**1.** Given
2. ∠*CBA* and ∠*DFB* are right angles.	**2.** ⊥ lines form right angles.
3. △*ABC* and △*BFD* are right triangles.	**3.** Definition of right triangle
H 4. $\overline{AC} \cong \overline{BD}$	**4.** Given
L 5. $\overline{AB} \cong \overline{BF}$	**5.** Definition of midpoint
6. △*ABC* ≅ △*BFD*	**6.** HL Congruence Theorem

18. Use the information given in the diagram to fill in the missing statements and reasons to prove that △*UZV* ≅ △*XYW*.

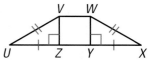

Statements	Reasons
1. ∠*UZV* and ∠*XYW* are right angles.	**1.** _____?_____
2. △*UZV* and △*XYW* are right triangles.	**2.** _____?_____
3. _____?_____	**3.** Given
4. $\overline{UZ} \cong \overline{XY}$	**4.** _____?_____
5. _____?_____	**5.** HL Congruence Theorem

5.5 USING CONGRUENT TRIANGLES

Examples on
pp. 265–267

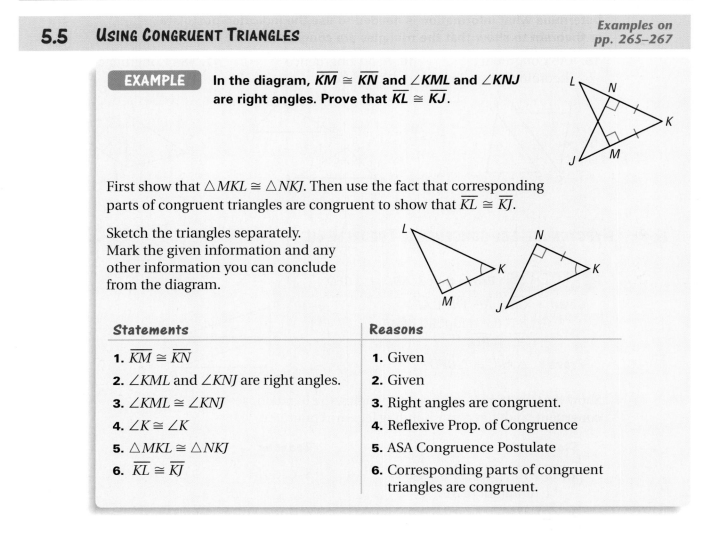

EXAMPLE In the diagram, $\overline{KM} \cong \overline{KN}$ and $\angle KML$ and $\angle KNJ$ are right angles. Prove that $\overline{KL} \cong \overline{KJ}$.

First show that $\triangle MKL \cong \triangle NKJ$. Then use the fact that corresponding parts of congruent triangles are congruent to show that $\overline{KL} \cong \overline{KJ}$.

Sketch the triangles separately. Mark the given information and any other information you can conclude from the diagram.

Statements	Reasons
1. $\overline{KM} \cong \overline{KN}$	1. Given
2. $\angle KML$ and $\angle KNJ$ are right angles.	2. Given
3. $\angle KML \cong \angle KNJ$	3. Right angles are congruent.
4. $\angle K \cong \angle K$	4. Reflexive Prop. of Congruence
5. $\triangle MKL \cong \triangle NKJ$	5. ASA Congruence Postulate
6. $\overline{KL} \cong \overline{KJ}$	6. Corresponding parts of congruent triangles are congruent.

Sketch the overlapping triangles separately. Use the given information to mark all congruences. Then tell what theorem or postulate you can use to show that the triangles are congruent.

19. $\overline{AC} \cong \overline{BD}$ **20.** $\overline{MN} \cong \overline{KL}$ **21.** $\overline{PR} \cong \overline{TR}$

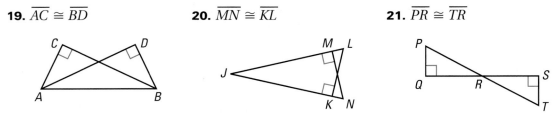

22. Use the diagram and the information given in Exercise 19 above to prove that $\angle CBA \cong \angle DAB$.

23. Use the diagram and the information given in Exercise 20 above to prove that $\overline{JM} \cong \overline{JK}$.

24. Use the diagram and the information given in Exercise 21 above to prove that $\overline{QR} \cong \overline{SR}$.

5.6 ANGLE BISECTORS AND PERPENDICULAR BISECTORS

Examples on pp. 273–275

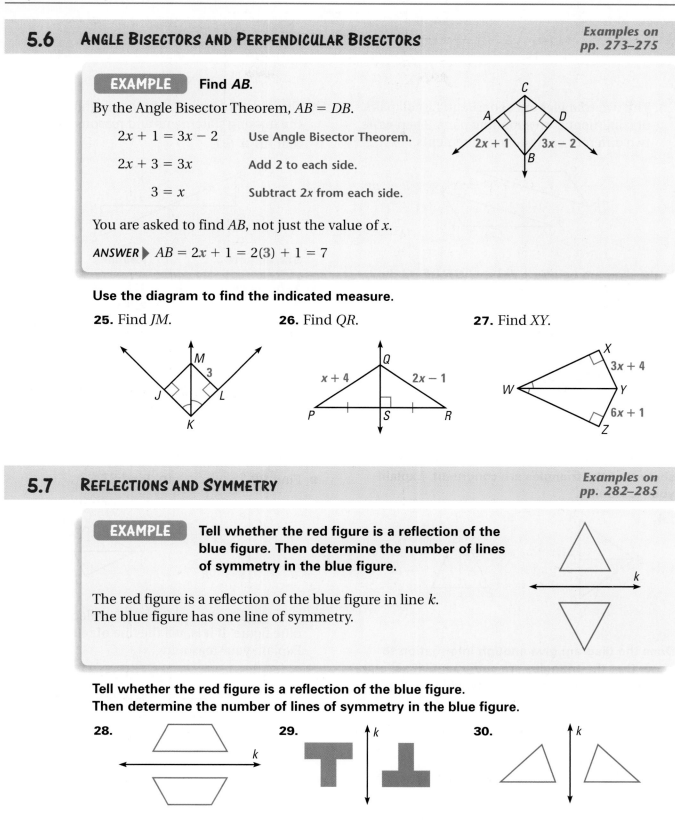

EXAMPLE **Find AB.**

By the Angle Bisector Theorem, $AB = DB$.

$2x + 1 = 3x - 2$ Use Angle Bisector Theorem.

$2x + 3 = 3x$ Add 2 to each side.

$3 = x$ Subtract $2x$ from each side.

You are asked to find AB, not just the value of x.

ANSWER ▶ $AB = 2x + 1 = 2(3) + 1 = 7$

Use the diagram to find the indicated measure.

25. Find JM.

26. Find QR.

27. Find XY.

5.7 REFLECTIONS AND SYMMETRY

Examples on pp. 282–285

EXAMPLE **Tell whether the red figure is a reflection of the blue figure. Then determine the number of lines of symmetry in the blue figure.**

The red figure is a reflection of the blue figure in line k.
The blue figure has one line of symmetry.

Tell whether the red figure is a reflection of the blue figure. Then determine the number of lines of symmetry in the blue figure.

28.

29.

30.

31. Draw a six-sided figure that has two lines of symmetry.

1. The two triangles are congruent. List all pairs of congruent corresponding parts. Then write two different congruence statements.

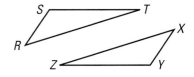

In the diagram below, △JKL ≅ △STU. Find the indicated measure.

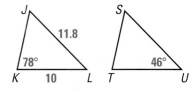

2. Find $m\angle L$.   **3.** Find TU.

Tell which postulate or theorem you would use to show that the triangles are congruent. Explain your reasoning.

4.   **5.**

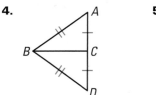 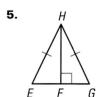

Does the diagram give enough information to show that the triangles are congruent? If so, state the postulate or theorem you would use. Explain your reasoning.

6.   **7.**

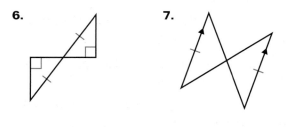

8. Given the information in the diagram, fill in the missing statements and reasons to show that $\overline{AB} \cong \overline{ED}$.

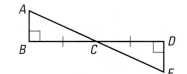

Statements	Reasons
1. $\overline{BC} \cong \overline{DC}$	1. _____?_____
2. _____?_____	2. Given
3. _____?_____	3. Right angles are congruent.
4. $\angle ACB \cong \angle ECD$	4. _____?_____
5. $\triangle ABC \cong \triangle EDC$	5. _____?_____
6. $\overline{AB} \cong \overline{ED}$	6. _____?_____

Find the indicated measure.

9. Find PR.   **10.** Find ST.

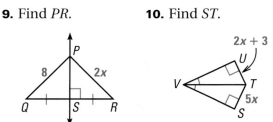

11. Tell whether the red figure is a reflection of the blue figure. If it is, tell the line of reflection. Explain your reasoning.

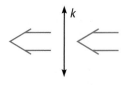

Determine the number of lines of symmetry.

12.   **13.**

Chapter 5 Standardized Test

Test Tip Draw your own sketches that show the information given in a problem. This may help you see a way to approach a problem.

1. Given that $\triangle ABC \cong \triangle FHG$, tell which of the following statements is true.

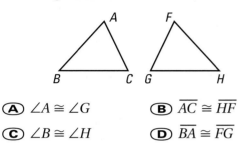

Ⓐ $\angle A \cong \angle G$ Ⓑ $\overline{AC} \cong \overline{HF}$

Ⓒ $\angle B \cong \angle H$ Ⓓ $\overline{BA} \cong \overline{FG}$

2. Based on the diagram, which theorem or postulate *cannot* be used to show that $\triangle JKL \cong \triangle NML$?

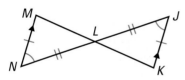

Ⓕ ASA Congruence Postulate

Ⓖ AAS Congruence Theorem

Ⓗ SAS Congruence Postulate

Ⓙ HL Congruence Theorem

3. In the diagram, $\overline{AD} \cong \overline{BC}$, $\overline{AC} \cong \overline{BD}$, and $\angle A \cong \angle B$. Decide which of the postulates or theorems listed below can be used to show that $\triangle ADC \cong \triangle BCD$.

I. SAS **II.** HL **III.** SSS

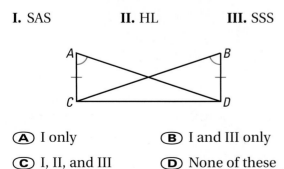

Ⓐ I only Ⓑ I and III only

Ⓒ I, II, and III Ⓓ None of these

4. What is the value of x?

Ⓕ 3

Ⓖ 4

Ⓗ 9

Ⓙ 12

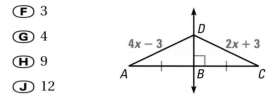

5. In the diagram above, what is AD?

Ⓐ 3 Ⓑ 4 Ⓒ 9 Ⓓ 12

6. How many lines of symmetry are in the equilateral triangle below?

Ⓕ 0

Ⓖ 1

Ⓗ 2

Ⓙ 3

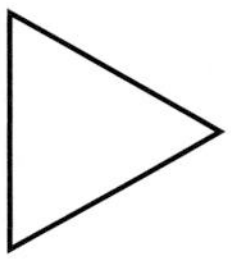

Multi-Step Problem In Exercises 7–9, use the diagram below.

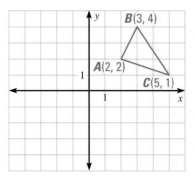

7. Sketch the reflection of the triangle in the x-axis. Label the triangle $\triangle A'B'C'$.

8. What are the coordinates of the point of the reflection that correspond to A? to B? to C?

9. How do the coordinates of $\triangle ABC$ relate to the coordinates of the reflected triangle?

BraiN GaMes

Mirror Reflections

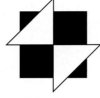
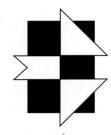

original image   target image

Materials

- mirror
- original and target images

Object of the Game   To find target images made from the original image using a mirror.

How to Play   There are 5 target images next to each original image. Try to create the target images.

Step 1 ▶ Place a mirror anywhere on the original image and look at the image made by the reflection. Does it match any of the target images?

Step 2 ▶ Move the mirror over the image and at different angles trying to duplicate one of the target images.

Step 3 ▶ When you create one of the target images, draw a line where you placed the mirror and label the line with the letter of the target image.

Players receive a point for each target image they find. The player with the most points after a set amount of time wins.

Another Way to Play   Create your own original image and target images. Challenge a classmate to find your target images.

To find whether a point lies on a line, substitute the x- and y-values into the equation of the line and see whether the equation is true.

EXAMPLE 1 **Points on a Line**

Determine whether the point lies on the line whose equation is $2x + y = 5$.

  a. $(2, 1)$ **b.** $(-1, 3)$

Solution

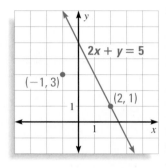

a.

$$2x + y = 5$$
$$2(2) + 1 \stackrel{?}{=} 5$$
$$4 + 1 \stackrel{?}{=} 5$$
$$5 = 5 \checkmark$$

$(2, 1)$ lies on the line.

b.

$$2x + y = 5$$
$$2(-1) + 3 \stackrel{?}{=} 5$$
$$-2 + 3 \stackrel{?}{=} 5$$
$$1 \neq 5$$

$(-1, 3)$ does not lie on the line.

Try These

Determine whether the point lies on the line whose equation is given.

  1. $3x + 2y = 13$; $(3, 2)$ **2.** $5x - 4y = 4$; $(0, -1)$

  3. $y = 3x - 8$; $(-4, 4)$ **4.** $-x + 6y = -2$; $(4, 1)$

  5. $x - 7y = 5$; $(-5, 0)$ **6.** $2x - 4y = -2$; $(-1, -1)$

EXAMPLE 2 **Find Slope**

Find the slope of the line that passes through the points $(-3, 1)$ and $(3, -2)$.

Solution

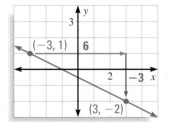

Let $(x_1, y_1) = (-3, 1)$ and $(x_2, y_2) = (3, -2)$.

$$\text{slope} = \frac{y_2 - y_1}{x_2 - x_1} = \frac{-2 - 1}{3 - (-3)} = \frac{-3}{6} = -\frac{1}{2}$$

Try These

Find the slope of the line that passes through the points.

  7. $(3, 1)$ and $(8, 7)$ **8.** $(3, 4)$ and $(3, -5)$ **9.** $(6, -6)$ and $(-1, 1)$

  10. $(-5, 1)$ and $(-2, 8)$ **11.** $(-1, 4)$ and $(4, 4)$ **12.** $(-2, -4)$ and $(2, 6)$

How do photographers reach high places?

Scissors lifts can lift photographers, movie crews, and other people who need to reach high places.

The design of the lift ensures that as the platform is raised or lowered it is always parallel to the ground.

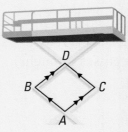

Learn More About It

You will learn more about scissors lifts in Exercises 34–37 on p. 314.

Who uses Quadrilaterals?

FURNITURE DESIGNER
Furniture designers use geometry and trigonometry to create designs for furniture that is structurally sound and visually interesting. (p. 329)

GEMOLOGIST
Gemologists consider the color and clarity of a gem, as well as the cut, when evaluating its value. After cutting, the facets of some gems are rectangles and trapezoids. (p. 340)

How will you use these ideas?

- Discover plant roots and stems that resemble polygons. (p. 307)
- See how photographers take overhead photos. (p. 314)
- Find out how the derailleur of a bicycle uses quadrilaterals. (p. 321)
- Predict the path of a ball on a pool table. (p. 322)
- Learn how gems are cut to enhance their sparkle. (p. 340)

What's the chapter about?

- Classifying **polygons** and finding angle measures of quadrilaterals
- Using properties of **parallelograms**, **rhombuses**, **rectangles**, **squares**, and **trapezoids**
- Identifying special quadrilaterals

> ### Key Words
>
> - **polygon**, *p. 303*
> - **diagonal of a polygon**, *p. 303*
> - **parallelogram**, *p. 310*
> - **rhombus**, *p. 325*
> - **rectangle**, *p. 325*
>
> - **square**, *p. 325*
> - **trapezoid**, *p. 332*
> - **isosceles trapezoid**, *p. 332*
> - **midsegment of a trapezoid**, *p. 333*

Chapter Readiness Quiz

Take this quick quiz. If you are unsure of an answer, look at the reference pages for help.

Vocabulary Check *(refer to p. 173)*

1. What type of triangle is $\triangle FGH$?

   (A) scalene   **(B)** equilateral

   (C) isosceles   **(D)** None of these

Skill Check *(refer to pp. 131, 180)*

2. What is the measure of $\angle 4$?

   (F) 45°   **(G)** 55°

   (H) 65°   **(J)** 125°

3. In $\triangle JKL$, $m\angle J = 55°$ and $m\angle K = 90°$. What is $m\angle L$?

   (A) 15°   **(B)** 25°   **(C)** 35°   **(D)** 45°

Drawing Quadrilaterals

Visualize It! ➡

You can used lined paper to help you draw quadrilaterals that have at least one pair of opposite sides parallel.

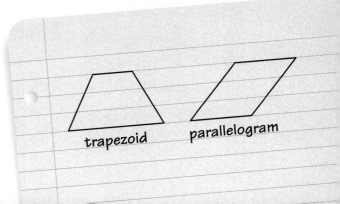

trapezoid   parallelogram

Polygons

Goal

Identify and classify polygons. Find angle measures of quadrilaterals.

Key Words

- polygon
- side of a polygon
- vertex of a polygon
- diagonal of a polygon

Each traffic sign below is an example of a *polygon*. Notice that each sign is formed with straight lines.

A **polygon** is a plane figure that is formed by three or more segments called **sides**. Each side intersects exactly two other sides at each of its endpoints. Each endpoint is a **vertex** of the polygon.

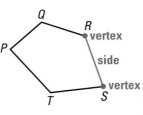

Two vertices that are the endpoints of the same side are called *consecutive* vertices. For example, in polygon *PQRST*, *R* and *S* are consecutive vertices.

A segment that joins two *nonconsecutive* vertices of a polygon is called a **diagonal**. Polygon *PQRST* has two diagonals from vertex *R*, $\overline{RP}$ and $\overline{RT}$.

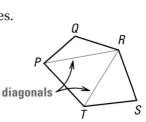

Student Help

VOCABULARY TIP
A *side* connects consecutive vertices. A *diagonal* connects nonconsecutive vertices.

EXAMPLE 1 **Identify Polygons**

Is the figure a polygon? Explain your reasoning.

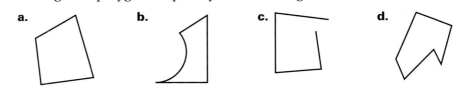

a.   b.   c.   d.

Solution

a. Yes. The figure is a polygon formed by four straight sides.

b. No. The figure is not a polygon because it has a side that is not a segment.

c. No. The figure is not a polygon because two of the sides intersect only one other side.

d. Yes. The figure is a polygon formed by six straight sides.

Classifying Polygons You can classify polygons by the number of sides they have. Some special types of polygons are listed below.

TYPES OF POLYGONS

Triangle	3 sides 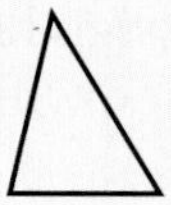	**Hexagon**	6 sides 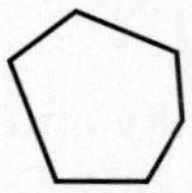
Quadrilateral	4 sides 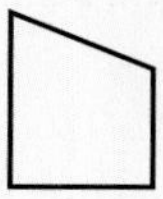	**Heptagon**	7 sides 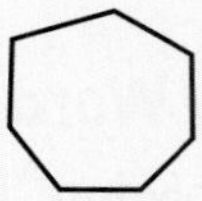
Pentagon	5 sides 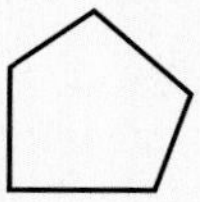	**Octagon**	8 sides 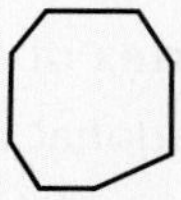

EXAMPLE 2 **Classify Polygons**

Decide whether the figure is a polygon. If so, tell what type. If not, explain why.

a. 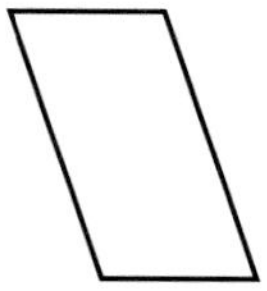   b. 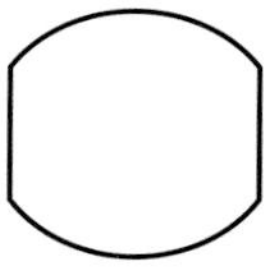   c. 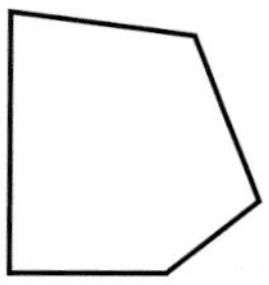   d.

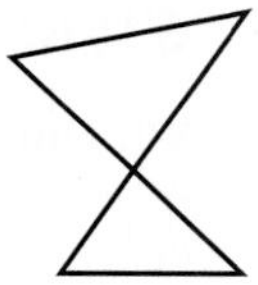

Solution

a. The figure is a polygon with four sides, so it is a quadrilateral.

b. The figure is not a polygon because it has some sides that are not segments.

c. The figure is a polygon with five sides, so it is a pentagon.

d. The figure is not a polygon because some of the sides intersect more than two other sides.

Checkpoint ✓ *Identify and Classify Polygons*

Decide whether the figure is a polygon. If so, tell what type. If not, explain why.

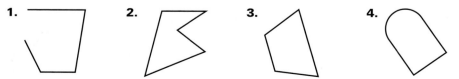

1.   **2.**   **3.**   **4.**

Quadrilaterals A diagonal of a quadrilateral divides it into two triangles, each with angle measures that add up to 180°. So, the sum of the measures of the interior angles of a quadrilateral is 2 × 180°, or 360°.

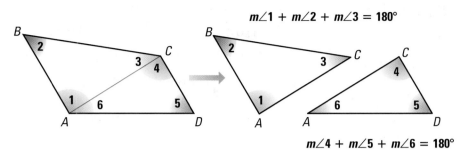

$m\angle1 + m\angle2 + m\angle3 = 180°$

$m\angle4 + m\angle5 + m\angle6 = 180°$

THEOREM 6.1

Quadrilateral Interior Angles Theorem

Words The sum of the measures of the interior angles of a quadrilateral is 360°.

Symbols $m\angle1 + m\angle2 + m\angle3 + m\angle4 = 360°$

Student Help

STUDY TIP
Name a polygon by listing its vertices *consecutively* in either direction. Two names for the quadrilateral in Example 3 are *PQRS* and *RQPS*.

EXAMPLE **3** **Find Angle Measures of Quadrilaterals**

Find the measure of ∠S.

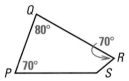

Solution

Use the fact that the sum of the measures of the interior angles of a quadrilateral is 360°.

$m\angle P + m\angle Q + m\angle R + m\angle S = 360°$ — Quadrilateral Interior Angles Theorem

$70° + 80° + 70° + m\angle S = 360°$ — Substitute angle measures.

$220° + m\angle S = 360°$ — Simplify.

$m\angle S = 140°$ — Subtract 220° from each side.

ANSWER ▶ The measure of ∠S is 140°.

Checkpoint ✓ **Find Angle Measures of Quadrilaterals**

Find the measure of ∠A.

5.

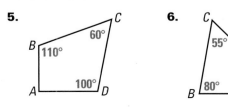

6.

7.

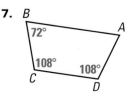

Guided Practice

Vocabulary Check

1. What type of polygon has 8 sides? 15 sides?

2. Use the diagram of the pentagon shown at the right. Name all of the *diagonals* from vertex *D*.

Skill Check

Is the figure a polygon? Explain your reasoning.

3.   **4.**   **5.**

Find the measure of ∠*A*.

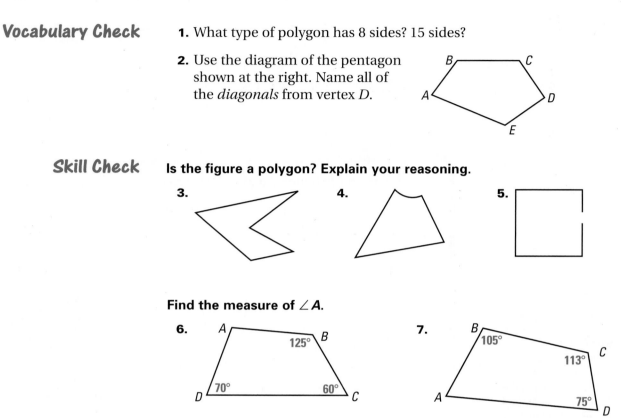

6.   **7.**

Practice and Applications

Extra Practice

See p. 685.

Classifying Polygons Decide whether the figure is a polygon. If so, tell what type. If not, explain why.

8.   **9.**   **10.**

11. Logical Reasoning What is the fewest number of sides a polygon can have? Explain your answer, then name the polygon.

Homework Help

Example 1: Exs. 8–10
Example 2: Exs. 8–10, 21, 24–27
Example 3: Exs. 15–20, 28

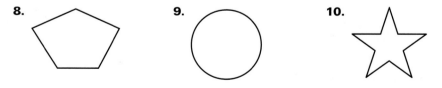 **Visualize It!** Sketch the figure(s) described.

12. Two different pentagons

13. A hexagon with three diagonals drawn from a single vertex

14. A quadrilateral with two obtuse angles

Finding Angle Measures Find the measure of ∠A.

15.
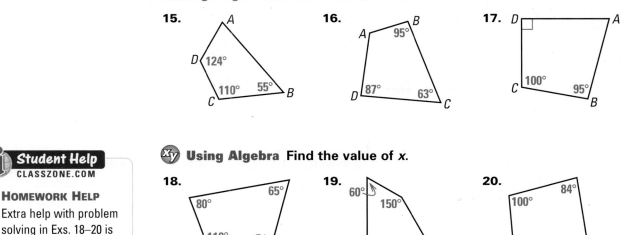

16.

17.

Student Help

CLASSZONE.COM

HOMEWORK HELP
Extra help with problem solving in Exs. 18–20 is at classzone.com

Using Algebra Find the value of *x*.

18.

19.

20.

Parachutes Some gym classes play games using parachutes that look like the polygon below.

21. Tell how many sides the polygon has and what type of polygon it is.

22. Polygon *LMNPQRST* is one name for the polygon. State two other names using the vertices.

23. Name all of the diagonals that have vertex *M* as an endpoint. Not all of the diagonals are shown.

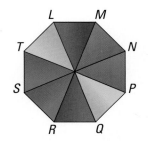

Link to Plants

CARAMBOLA, or star fruit, has a cross section shaped like a five-pointed star.

Plants Use the following information.
Cross sections of roots and stems often resemble polygons. Next to each cross section is the polygon it resembles. Tell how many sides each polygon has and tell what type of polygon it is.

▶ Source: *The History and Folklore of North American Wildflowers*

24. Virginia Snakeroot

25. Caraway
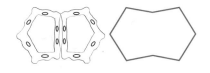

26. Fennel

27. Poison Hemlock
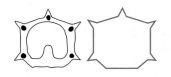

28. Technology Use geometry software to draw a quadrilateral. Measure each interior angle and calculate the sum. What happens to the sum as you drag the vertices of the quadrilateral?

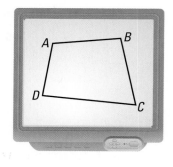

29. Multi-Step Problem Envelope manufacturers fold a specially-shaped piece of paper to make an envelope, as shown below.

a. How many sides are formed by the outer edges of the paper before it is folded? Name the type of polygon.

b. Tell how many sides are formed by the outer edges of the paper in Steps 2–4. Name the type of polygon formed after each step.

c. If the four angles of the red quadrilateral in Step 4 are congruent, then what is the measure of each angle?

Mixed Review

Line Relationships Determine whether the lines are *parallel, perpendicular,* or *neither*. (Lesson 3.1)

30. $\overleftrightarrow{AB}$ and $\overleftrightarrow{CE}$

31. $\overleftrightarrow{AC}$ and $\overleftrightarrow{BE}$

32. $\overleftrightarrow{AB}$ and $\overleftrightarrow{AC}$

33. $\overleftrightarrow{AC}$ and $\overleftrightarrow{CE}$

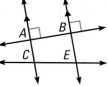

Finding Angle Measures Find the measure of the numbered angle. (Lesson 3.4)

34.

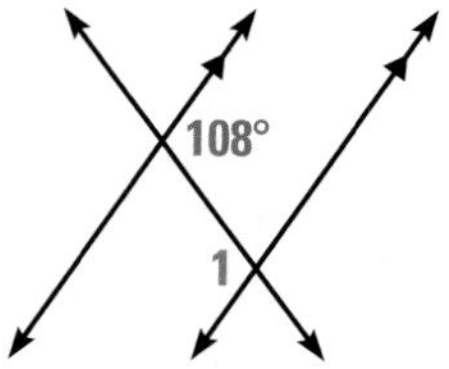

108°

1

35.

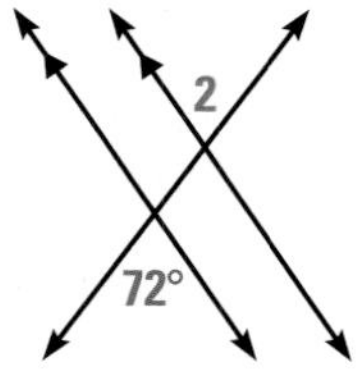

2

72°

36.

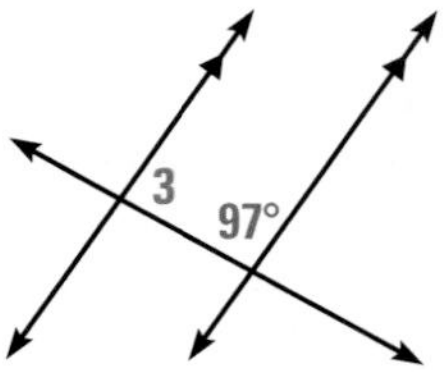

3

97°

Algebra Skills

Distributive Property Use the distributive property to rewrite the expression without parentheses. (Skills Review, p. 671)

37. $4(x + 3)$

38. $(x - 1)6$

39. $-2(x - 7)$

40. $-5(2x + 3)$

41. $-3(5x - 2)$

42. $(4x - 4)x$

Question

What are some of the properties of a parallelogram?

Materials
- lined paper
- tracing paper
- ruler
- protractor

Explore

1 Place a piece of tracing paper on top of a piece of lined paper. Trace two lines of the lined paper.

2 Turn the tracing paper so that the lines on the lined paper intersect the lines you drew. Trace two more lines to form a quadrilateral.

3 Use a ruler to measure the length of each side of the quadrilateral. Then use a protractor to measure each angle of the quadrilateral.

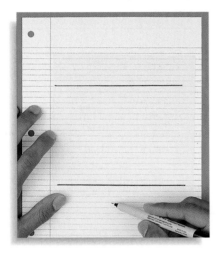

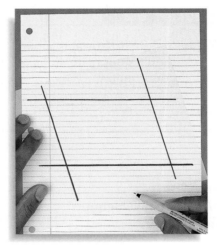

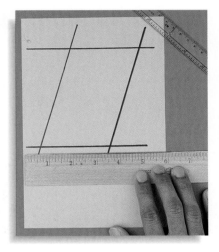

Visualize It!

B, C
A, D

In *ABCD*, $\overline{AB}$ and $\overline{DC}$ are opposite sides, and $\overline{AD}$ and $\overline{BC}$ are opposite sides.

Think About It

1. The figure you drew is called a *parallelogram*. Why do you think this type of quadrilateral is called a parallelogram?

2. What do you notice about the lengths of the opposite sides of the figure you drew?

3. What do you notice about the measures of the opposite angles of the figure you drew?

4. Based on your results from Exercises 2 and 3, complete the statements.

   a. The opposite sides of a parallelogram are __?__.

   b. The opposite angles of a parallelogram are __?__.

Properties of Parallelograms

6.2

Goal
Use properties of parallelograms.

Key Words
• parallelogram

Parallelogram lifts, like the one shown in the photograph, are used to raise heavy-duty vehicles.

A **parallelogram** is a quadrilateral with both pairs of opposite sides parallel.

The symbol $\square PQRS$ is read "parallelogram $PQRS$."

In $\square PQRS$, $\overline{PQ} \parallel \overline{SR}$ and $\overline{QR} \parallel \overline{PS}$.

THEOREM 6.2

Words If a quadrilateral is a parallelogram, then its opposite sides are congruent.

Symbols In $\square PQRS$, $\overline{PQ} \cong \overline{SR}$ and $\overline{QR} \cong \overline{PS}$.

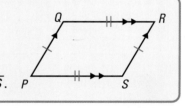

EXAMPLE 1 Find Side Lengths of Parallelograms

$FGHJ$ is a parallelogram. Find JH and FJ.

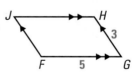

Solution

$JH = FG$	Opposite sides of a $\square$ are congruent.
$= 5$	Substitute 5 for FG.
$FJ = GH$	Opposite sides of a $\square$ are congruent.
$= 3$	Substitute 3 for GH.

ANSWER ▶ In $\square FGHJ$, $JH = 5$ and $FJ = 3$.

Checkpoint ✓ *Find Side Lengths of Parallelograms*

1. $ABCD$ is a parallelogram. Find AB and AD.

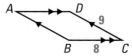

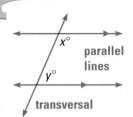

Consecutive angles of a parallelogram are like same-side interior angles. By Theorem 3.7, they are supplementary.

THEOREMS 6.3 and 6.4

Theorem 6.3

Words If a quadrilateral is a parallelogram, then its opposite angles are congruent.

Symbols In □*PQRS*, ∠*P* ≅ ∠*R* and ∠*Q* ≅ ∠*S*.

Theorem 6.4

Words If a quadrilateral is a parallelogram, then its consecutive angles are supplementary.

Symbols In □*PQRS*, $x° + y° = 180°$.

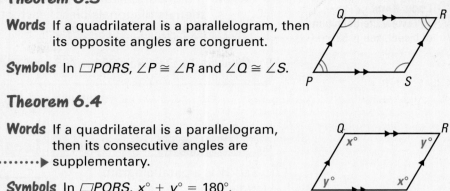

EXAMPLE 2 Find Angle Measures of Parallelograms

PQRS is a parallelogram. Find the missing angle measures.

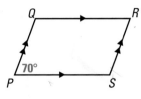

Solution

❶ By Theorem 6.3, the opposite angles of a parallelogram are congruent, so $m∠R = m∠P = 70°$.

❷ By Theorem 6.4, the consecutive angles of a parallelogram are supplementary.

$m∠Q + m∠P = 180°$ Consecutive angles of a □ are supplementary.

$m∠Q + 70° = 180°$ Substitute 70° for *m∠P*.

$m∠Q = 110°$ Subtract 70° from each side.

❸ By Theorem 6.3, the opposite angles of a parallelogram are congruent, so $m∠S = m∠Q = 110°$.

ANSWER The measure of ∠*R* is 70°, the measure of ∠*Q* is 110°, and the measure of ∠*S* is 110°.

Checkpoint ✓ Find Angle Measures of Parallelograms

ABCD is a parallelogram. Find the missing angle measures.

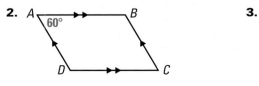

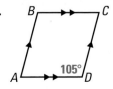

6.2 *Properties of Parallelograms*   **311**

Student Help

LOOK BACK
To review the definition of bisect, see p. 53.

THEOREM 6.5

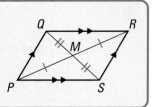

Words If a quadrilateral is a parallelogram, then its diagonals bisect each other.

Symbols In □*PQRS*, $\overline{QM} \cong \overline{MS}$ and $\overline{PM} \cong \overline{MR}$.

EXAMPLE 3 Find Segment Lengths

TUVW is a parallelogram.
Find *TX*.

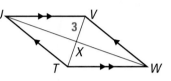

Solution

$TX = XV$	Diagonals of a □ bisect each other.
$= 3$	Substitute 3 for *XV*.

SUMMARY   PROPERTIES OF PARALLELOGRAMS

Definition of parallelogram, p. 310

If a quadrilateral is a parallelogram, then both pairs of opposite sides are parallel.

Theorem 6.2, p. 310

If a quadrilateral is a parallelogram, then its opposite sides are congruent.

Theorem 6.3, p. 311

If a quadrilateral is a parallelogram, then its opposite angles are congruent.

Theorem 6.4, p. 311

If a quadrilateral is a parallelogram, then its consecutive angles are supplementary.

$x° + y° = 180°$

Theorem 6.5, p. 312

If a quadrilateral is a parallelogram, then its diagonals bisect each other.

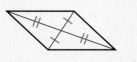

6.2 Exercises

Guided Practice

Vocabulary Check

1. Complete the statement: A(n) _?_ is a quadrilateral with both pairs of opposite sides parallel.

Skill Check

Decide whether the figure is a parallelogram. If it is not, explain why.

2.

3.

Complete the statement. Give a reason for your answer.

4. $\overline{JK} \cong$ _?_

5. $\angle MLK \cong$ _?_

6. $\angle JKL \cong$ _?_

7. $\overline{JN} \cong$ _?_

8. $\angle MNL \cong$ _?_

9. $\overline{NM} \cong$ _?_

Find the measure in the parallelogram.

10. Find $m\angle C$.

11. Find HK.

12. Find $m\angle Y$.

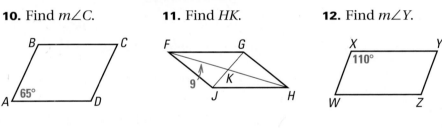

Practice and Applications

Extra Practice

See p. 685.

Congruent Segments Match the segment in $\square PQRS$ with a congruent one. Give a reason for your answer.

13. $\overline{PT}$ **A.** $\overline{RS}$

14. $\overline{QR}$ **B.** $\overline{RT}$

15. $\overline{QT}$ **C.** $\overline{PS}$

16. $\overline{PQ}$ **D.** $\overline{ST}$

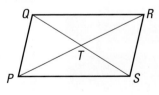

Homework Help

Example 1: Exs. 13–16, 22–24

Example 2: Exs. 17–20, 25–27

Example 3: Exs. 13–16, 28–30

Congruent Angles Match the angle in $\square VWXY$ with a congruent one. Give a reason for your answer.

17. $\angle VZY$ **E.** $\angle WZX$

18. $\angle WVY$ **F.** $\angle VWX$

19. $\angle WXZ$ **G.** $\angle YVZ$

20. $\angle VYX$ **H.** $\angle YXW$

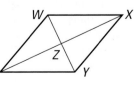

Student Help

VISUAL STRATEGY
In Ex. 21, use lined paper to help you sketch a parallelogram, as shown on on p. 302.

21. ***You be the Judge*** *EFGH* is a parallelogram. Is $\overline{EF}$ parallel to $\overline{HG}$ or $\overline{GF}$? Explain your answer.

Finding Side Lengths ***EFGH*** **is a parallelogram. Find *EF* and *FG*.**

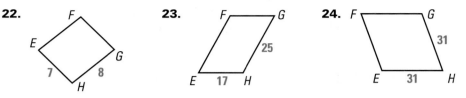

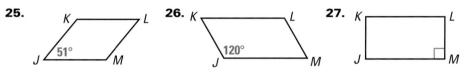

22.

23.

24.

Finding Angle Measures ***JKLM*** **is a parallelogram. Find the missing angle measures.**

25.

26.

27.

Finding Segment Lengths ***ABCD*** **is a parallelogram. Find *DE*.**

28.

29.

30.

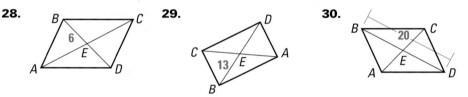

Link to Photography

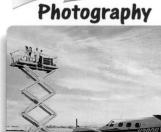

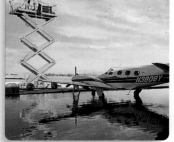

SCISSORS LIFT
Photographers can use scissors lifts for overhead shots. The crossing beams of the lift form parallelograms that raise and lower the platform. For more about scissors lifts, see p. 300.

Using Algebra **Find the values of *x* and *y* in the parallelogram.**

31.

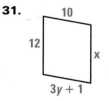

32.

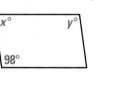

33.

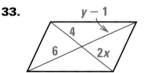

Scissors Lift **Use the diagram of the scissors lift below.**

34. What is $m\angle B$ when $m\angle A$ is 120°?

35. Suppose you decrease $m\angle A$. What happens to $m\angle B$?

36. Suppose you decrease $m\angle A$. What happens to AD?

37. Suppose you decrease $m\angle A$. What happens to the overall height of the scissors lift?

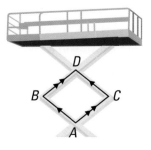

Student Help

CLASSZONE.COM

HOMEWORK HELP
Extra help with problem
solving in Exs. 38–41 is
at classzone.com

Staircases In the diagram below, the red quadrilateral and the blue
quadrilateral are parallelograms.

38. Which angle in the red parallelogram is
congruent to ∠1?

39. Which angles in the blue parallelogram
are supplementary to ∠6?

40. Which postulate can be used to prove
that ∠1 ≅ ∠5?

41. Challenge Is the red parallelogram
congruent to the blue parallelogram?
Explain your reasoning.

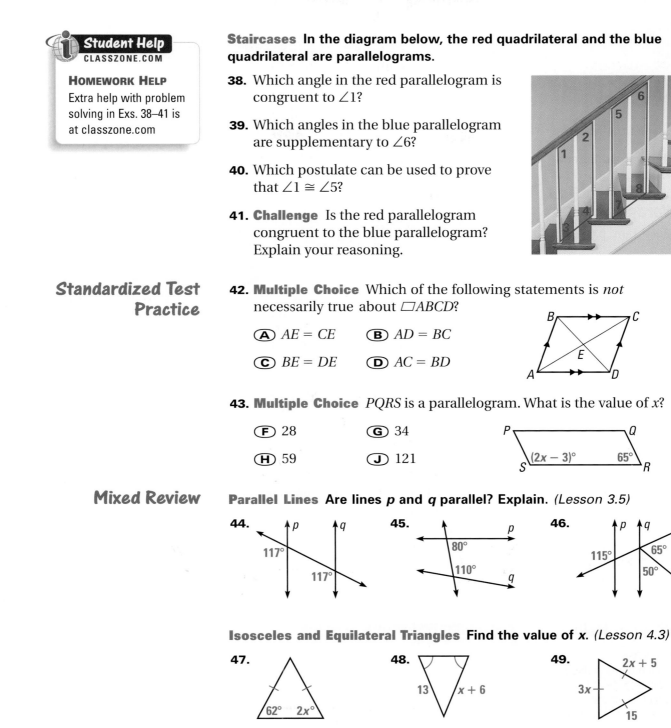

**Standardized Test
Practice**

42. Multiple Choice Which of the following statements is *not*
necessarily true about □*ABCD*?

A $AE = CE$ **B** $AD = BC$

C $BE = DE$ **D** $AC = BD$

43. Multiple Choice *PQRS* is a parallelogram. What is the value of *x*?

F 28   **G** 34

H 59   **J** 121

Mixed Review

Parallel Lines Are lines *p* and *q* parallel? Explain. *(Lesson 3.5)*

44.
117°
117°

45.
80°
110°

46.
115° 65°
50°

Isosceles and Equilateral Triangles Find the value of *x*. *(Lesson 4.3)*

47.
62° 2x°

48.
13 x + 6

49.
2x + 5
3x
15

Algebra Skills

**Finding Slope Find the slope of the line that passes through the
points.** *(Skills Review, p. 665)*

50. (1, 3) and (6, 5)

51. (3, −8) and (7, 4)

52. (2, 1) and (−1, 0)

53. (−4, 2) and (5, −1)

54. (6, −2) and (12, 14)

55. (0, −3) and (−5, −6)

6.3 Showing Quadrilaterals are Parallelograms

Goal
Show that a quadrilateral is a parallelogram.

Key Words
• parallelogram p. 310

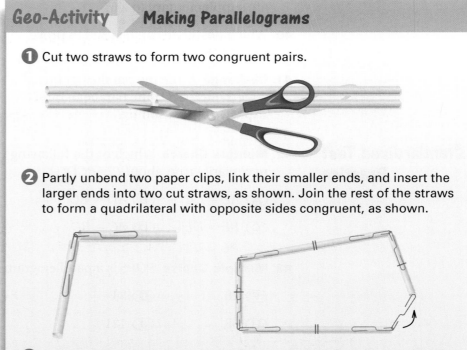

Geo-Activity — **Making Parallelograms**

1 Cut two straws to form two congruent pairs.

2 Partly unbend two paper clips, link their smaller ends, and insert the larger ends into two cut straws, as shown. Join the rest of the straws to form a quadrilateral with opposite sides congruent, as shown.

3 Change the angles of your quadrilateral. Is your quadrilateral always a parallelogram?

The Geo-Activity above describes one way to show that a quadrilateral is a parallelogram.

Student Help

STUDY TIP
The theorems in this lesson are the converses of the theorems in Lesson 6.2.

THEOREMS 6.6 and 6.7

Theorem 6.6

Words If both pairs of opposite sides of a quadrilateral are congruent, then the quadrilateral is a parallelogram.

Symbols If $\overline{PQ} \cong \overline{SR}$ and $\overline{QR} \cong \overline{PS}$, then $PQRS$ is a parallelogram.

Theorem 6.7

Words If both pairs of opposite angles of a quadrilateral are congruent, then the quadrilateral is a parallelogram.

Symbols If $\angle P \cong \angle R$ and $\angle Q \cong \angle S$, then $PQRS$ is a parallelogram.

Student Help
CLASSZONE.COM

More Examples
More examples at classzone.com

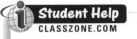

EXAMPLE 1 Use Opposite Sides

Tell whether the quadrilateral is a parallelogram. Explain your reasoning.

Solution

The quadrilateral is not a parallelogram. It has two pairs of congruent sides, but opposite sides are not congruent.

EXAMPLE 2 Use Opposite Angles

Tell whether the quadrilateral is a parallelogram. Explain your reasoning.

Solution

The quadrilateral is a parallelogram because both pairs of opposite angles are congruent.

Checkpoint Use Opposite Sides and Opposite Angles

In Exercises 1 and 2, tell whether the quadrilateral is a parallelogram. Explain your reasoning.

1.

2.

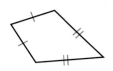

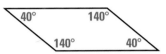

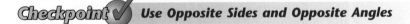

3. In quadrilateral $WXYZ$, $WX = 15$, $YZ = 20$, $XY = 15$, and $ZW = 20$. Is $WXYZ$ a parallelogram? Explain your reasoning.

THEOREM 6.8

Words If an angle of a quadrilateral is supplementary to both of its consecutive angles, then the quadrilateral is a parallelogram.

Symbols If $m\angle P + m\angle Q = 180°$ and $m\angle Q + m\angle R = 180°$, then $PQRS$ is a parallelogram.

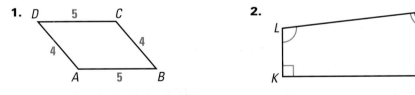

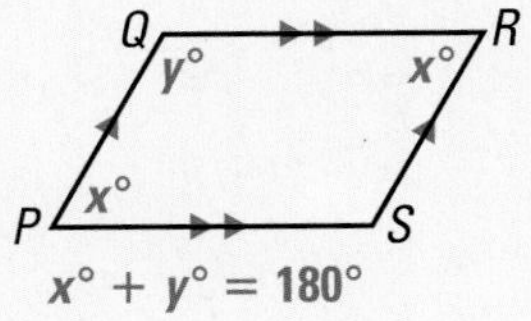

EXAMPLE 3 Use Consecutive Angles

Tell whether the quadrilateral is a parallelogram. Explain your reasoning.

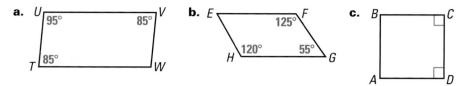

a. U 95° 85° V / T 85° W

b. E 125° F / H 120° 55° G

c. B C / A D

Solution

a. $\angle U$ is supplementary to $\angle T$ and $\angle V$ ($85° + 95° = 180°$). So, by Theorem 6.8, *TUVW* is a parallelogram.

b. $\angle G$ is supplementary to $\angle F$ ($55° + 125° = 180°$), but $\angle G$ is *not* supplementary to $\angle H$ ($55° + 120° \neq 180°$). So, *EFGH* is *not* a parallelogram.

c. $\angle D$ is supplementary to $\angle C$ ($90° + 90° = 180°$), but you are not given any information about $\angle A$ or $\angle B$. Therefore, you cannot conclude that *ABCD* is a parallelogram.

THEOREM 6.9

Words If the diagonals of a quadrilateral bisect each other, then the quadrilateral is a parallelogram.

Symbols If $\overline{QM} \cong \overline{MS}$ and $\overline{PM} \cong \overline{MR}$, then *PQRS* is a parallelogram.

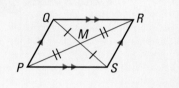

EXAMPLE 4 Use Diagonals

Tell whether the quadrilateral is a parallelogram. Explain your reasoning.

a. J K / 19 18 / 18 19 / M L

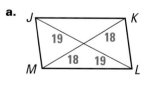

b. P Q / 2 3 / 4 3 / S R

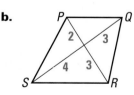

Solution

a. The diagonals of *JKLM* bisect each other. So, by Theorem 6.9, *JKLM* is a parallelogram.

b. The diagonals of *PQRS* do not bisect each other. So, *PQRS* is *not* a parallelogram.

Tell whether the quadrilateral is a parallelogram. Explain your reasoning.

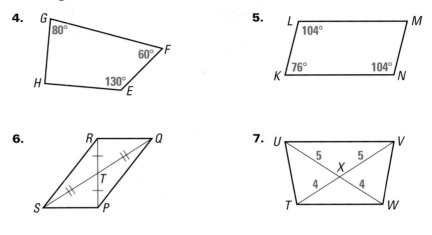

4.

G 80°

F 60°

H 130° E

5.

L 104° M

K 76° 104° N

6.

R Q

T

S P

7.

U 5 5 V

X

T 4 4 W

You have learned five ways to show that a quadrilateral is a parallelogram.

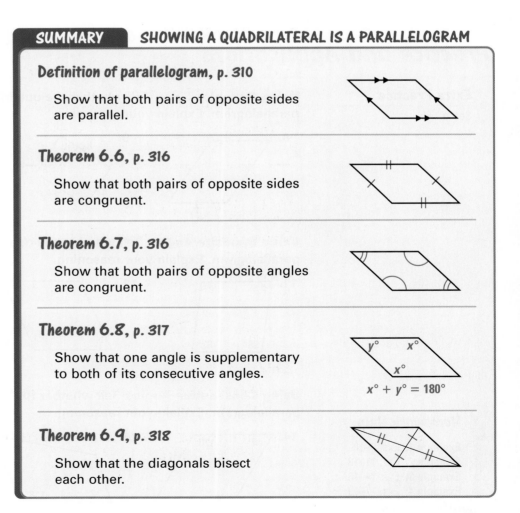

SUMMARY   **SHOWING A QUADRILATERAL IS A PARALLELOGRAM**

Definition of parallelogram, p. 310

Show that both pairs of opposite sides are parallel.

Theorem 6.6, p. 316

Show that both pairs of opposite sides are congruent.

Theorem 6.7, p. 316

Show that both pairs of opposite angles are congruent.

Theorem 6.8, p. 317

Show that one angle is supplementary to both of its consecutive angles.

$y°$ $x°$

$x°$

$x° + y° = 180°$

Theorem 6.9, p. 318

Show that the diagonals bisect each other.

6.3 Exercises

Guided Practice

Vocabulary Check

In Exercises 1–3, name all the sides or angles of ▱EFGH that match the description.

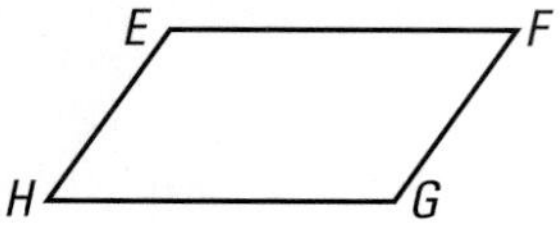

1. Opposite sides are parallel.

2. Opposite angles are congruent.

3. Consecutive angles are supplementary.

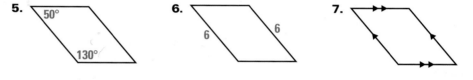

4. Explain why every parallelogram is a quadrilateral, but not every quadrilateral is a parallelogram.

Skill Check

Decide whether you are given enough information to show that the quadrilateral is a parallelogram. Explain your reasoning.

5.

6.

7.

Practice and Applications

Extra Practice

See p. 685.

Using Opposite Sides Tell whether the quadrilateral is a parallelogram. Explain your reasoning.

8.

9.

10.

Using Opposite Angles Tell whether the quadrilateral is a parallelogram. Explain your reasoning.

11.

12.

13.

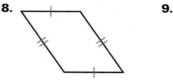
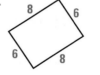
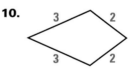

Using Consecutive Angles Tell whether the quadrilateral is a parallelogram. Explain your reasoning.

14.

15.

16.

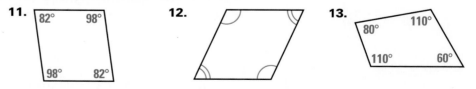
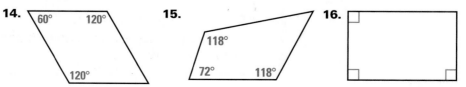

Homework Help

Example 1: Exs. 8–10
Example 2: Exs. 11–13
Example 3: Exs. 14–16
Example 4: Exs. 17–19

Using Diagonals Tell whether the quadrilateral is a parallelogram. Explain your reasoning.

17.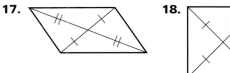

18.

19.

Link to
Bicycles

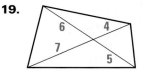

DERAILLEURS (named from the French word meaning "to derail") move the chain to change gears.

Application Links
CLASSZONE.COM

20. **Bicycle Gears** When you change gears on a bicycle, the derailleur moves the chain to the new gear. For the derailleur at the right, $AB = 1.8$ cm, $BC = 3.6$ cm, $CD = 1.8$ cm, and $DA = 3.6$ cm. Explain why $\overline{AB}$ and $\overline{CD}$ are always parallel when the derailleur moves.

21. **Error Analysis** What is wrong with the student's argument below?

A quadrilateral that has one pair of sides congruent and the other pair of sides parallel is always a parallelogram.

22. **You be the Judge** Three of the interior angles of a quadrilateral have measures of 75°, 75°, and 105°. Is this enough information to conclude that the quadrilateral is a parallelogram? Explain your answer.

23. **Visualize It!** Explain why the following method of drawing a parallelogram works. State a theorem to support your answer.

❶ Use a ruler to draw a segment and its midpoint.

❷ Draw another segment so the midpoints coincide.

❸ Connect the endpoints of the segments.

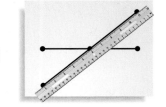

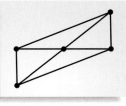

24. **Challenge** If one pair of opposite sides of a quadrilateral is both congruent and parallel, is the quadrilateral a parallelogram? Explain your reasoning.

Student Help

SKILLS REVIEW
To review the formula for finding slope, see p. 665.

EXAMPLE Coordinate Geometry

Use the slopes of the segments in the diagram to determine if the quadrilateral is a parallelogram.

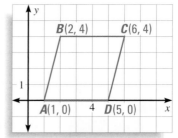

Solution

Lines and line segments are parallel if they have the same slope.

Slope of $\overline{AB}$: $\frac{4-0}{2-1} = \frac{4}{1} = 4$

Slope of $\overline{DC}$: $\frac{4-0}{6-5} = \frac{4}{1} = 4$

Slope of $\overline{BC}$: $\frac{4-4}{6-2} = \frac{0}{4} = 0$

Slope of $\overline{AD}$: $\frac{0-0}{5-1} = \frac{0}{4} = 0$

ANSWER ▶ The slopes of $\overline{AB}$ and $\overline{DC}$ are the same, so $\overline{AB} \parallel \overline{DC}$. The slopes of $\overline{BC}$ and $\overline{AD}$ are the same, so $\overline{AD} \parallel \overline{BC}$. Both pairs of opposite sides are parallel, so *ABCD* is a parallelogram.

Coordinate Geometry Use the slopes of the segments in the diagram to determine if the quadrilateral is a parallelogram.

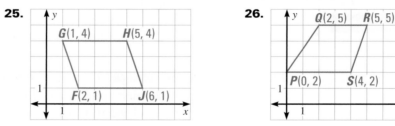

25.

26.

Standardized Test Practice

27. Multi-Step Problem Suppose you shoot a pool ball as shown below and it rolls back to where it started. The ball bounces off each wall at the same angle at which it hits the wall.

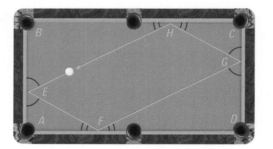

a. The ball hits the first wall at an angle of 63°. So $m\angle AEF = m\angle BEH = 63°$. Explain why $m\angle AFE = 27°$.

b. Explain why $m\angle FGD = 63°$.

c. What is $m\angle GHC$? $m\angle EHB$?

d. Find the measure of each interior angle of *EFGH*. What kind of quadrilateral is *EFGH*? How do you know?

Finding Angle Measures Find the measure of ∠A. *(Lesson 6.1)*

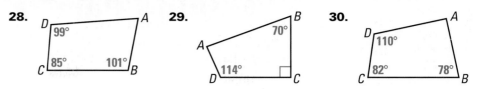

28.

29.

30.

Finding Measures Find the measure in □*JKLM*. *(Lesson 6.2)*

31. Find $m\angle K$.   **32.** Find $m\angle J$.

33. Find ML.   **34.** Find KL.

Evaluating Expressions Evaluate the expression for the given value of the variable. *(Skills Review, p. 670)*

35. $2x + 7$ when $x = 5$ **36.** $4y - 3$ when $y = 2$

37. $13 + 3m$ when $m = 3$ **38.** $1 - b$ when $b = -10$

39. $5 - 2a$ when $a = -6$ **40.** $8c - 5$ when $c = -4$

41. $12x + x^2$ when $x = -1$ **42.** $\frac{3}{4}q^2 - 2$ when $q = 4$

43. $5n^3 - 4n$ when $n = 2$ **44.** $15p + p^2$ when $p = -3$

Quiz 1

Decide whether the figure is a polygon. If so, tell what type. If not, explain why. *(Lesson 6.1)*

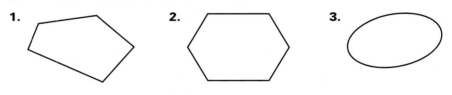

1.   **2.**   **3.**

Find the values of the variables in the parallelogram. *(Lesson 6.2)*

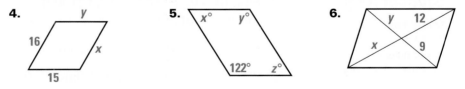

4.   **5.**   **6.**

Tell whether the quadrilateral is a parallelogram. Explain your reasoning. *(Lesson 6.3)*

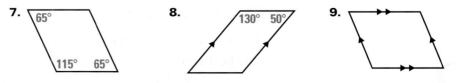

7.   **8.**   **9.**

Question

How can you use the angle measures in a quadrilateral to show that it is a parallelogram?

Explore

❶ Draw quadrilateral *ABCD*.

❷ Measure the angles of the quadrilateral.

❸ Drag the vertices until $m\angle A = m\angle C$ and $m\angle B = m\angle D$.

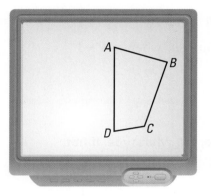

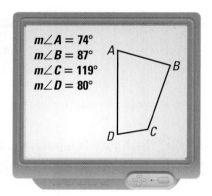

$m\angle A = 74°$
$m\angle B = 87°$
$m\angle C = 119°$
$m\angle D = 80°$

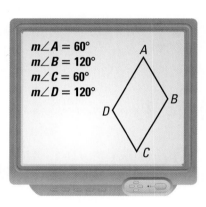

$m\angle A = 60°$
$m\angle B = 120°$
$m\angle C = 60°$
$m\angle D = 120°$

Think About It

Student Help

STUDY TIP
Recall that parallel lines and parallel segments have the same slope.

1. Find the slopes of $\overline{AB}$, $\overline{BC}$, $\overline{CD}$, and $\overline{DA}$. What do you notice about the slopes of opposite sides?

2. What do the slopes tell you about the sides of the quadrilateral?

3. What kind of figure is quadrilateral *ABCD*? Use your results from Exercise 2 to help you.

4. What theorem does this exploration illustrate?

5. **Extension** Draw quadrilateral *EFGH*. Draw segments $\overline{EG}$ and $\overline{FH}$. Construct a point *I* at the intersection of $\overline{EG}$ and $\overline{FH}$. Measure $\overline{EI}$, $\overline{IG}$, $\overline{FI}$, and $\overline{IH}$. Drag any of the vertices of *EFGH* so that $EI = IG$ and $FI = IH$. What do you notice? What theorem does this illustrate?

6.4 Rhombuses, Rectangles, and Squares

Goal
Use properties of special types of parallelograms.

Key Words
- rhombus
- rectangle
- square

In this lesson you will study three special types of parallelograms.

A **rhombus** is a parallelogram with **four congruent sides**.

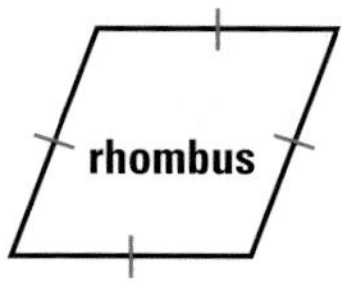

A **rectangle** is a parallelogram with **four right angles**.

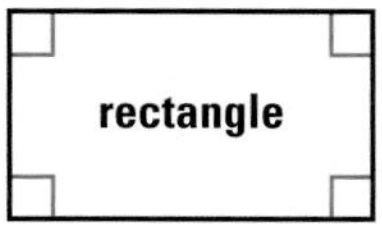

A **square** is a parallelogram with **four congruent sides** and **four right angles**.

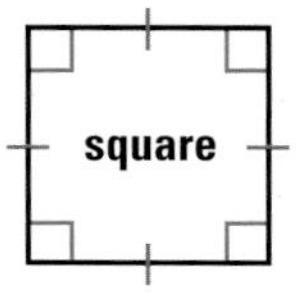

EXAMPLE 1 *Use Properties of Special Parallelograms*

In the diagram, *ABCD* is a rectangle.

a. Find *AD* and *AB*.

b. Find *m∠A*, *m∠B*, *m∠C*, and *m∠D*.

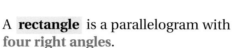

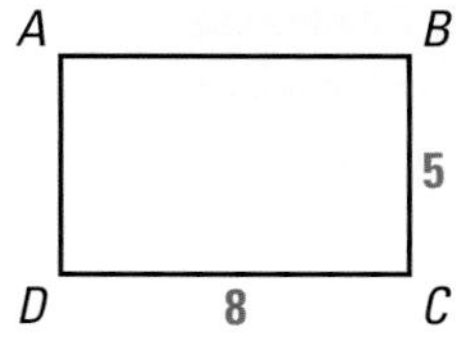

Solution

a. By definition, a rectangle is a parallelogram, so *ABCD* is a parallelogram. Because opposite sides of a parallelogram are congruent, *AD* = *BC* = 5 and *AB* = *DC* = 8.

b. By definition, a rectangle has four right angles, so *m∠A* = *m∠B* = *m∠C* = *m∠D* = 90°.

Checkpoint ✓ *Use Properties of Special Parallelograms*

1. In the diagram, *PQRS* is a rhombus. Find *QR*, *RS*, and *SP*.

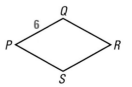

STUDY TIP
The corollaries allow
you to show that a
quadrilateral is a
rhombus, rectangle, or
square without first
showing that it is a
parallelogram.

COROLLARIES

Rhombus Corollary

Words If a quadrilateral has four congruent sides, then it is a rhombus.

Symbols If $\overline{AB} \cong \overline{BC} \cong \overline{CD} \cong \overline{AD}$, then $ABCD$ is a rhombus.

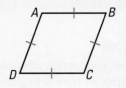

Rectangle Corollary

Words If a quadrilateral has four right angles, then it is a rectangle.

Symbols If $m\angle A = m\angle B = m\angle C = m\angle D = 90°$, then $ABCD$ is a rectangle.

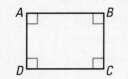

Square Corollary

Words If a quadrilateral has four congruent sides and four right angles, then it is a square.

Symbols If $\overline{AB} \cong \overline{BC} \cong \overline{CD} \cong \overline{AD}$ and $m\angle A = m\angle B = m\angle C = m\angle D = 90°$, then $ABCD$ is a square.

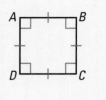

EXAMPLE 2 Identify Special Quadrilaterals

Use the information in the diagram
to name the special quadrilateral.

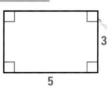

Solution

The quadrilateral has four right angles. So, by the Rectangle Corollary,
the quadrilateral is a rectangle.

Because all of the sides are not the same length, you know that the
quadrilateral is not a square.

Checkpoint ✓ Identify Special Quadrilaterals

Use the information in the diagram to name the special quadrilateral.

2.

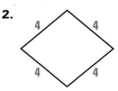

3.

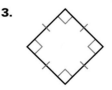

THEOREM 6.10

Words The diagonals of a rhombus are perpendicular.

Symbols In rhombus *ABCD*, $\overline{AC} \perp \overline{BD}$.

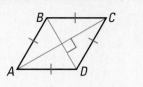

EXAMPLE 3 Use Diagonals of a Rhombus

ABCD is a rhombus. Find the value of *x*.

Solution

By Theorem 6.10, the diagonals of a rhombus are perpendicular. Therefore, $\angle BEC$ is a right angle, so $\triangle BEC$ is a right triangle.

By the Corollary to the Triangle Sum Theorem, the acute angles of a right triangle are complementary. So, $x = 90 - 60 = 30$.

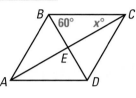

Student Help

LOOK BACK
To review the Corollary to the Triangle Sum Theorem, see p. 180.

THEOREM 6.11

Words The diagonals of a rectangle are congruent.

Symbols In rectangle *ABCD*, $\overline{AC} \cong \overline{BD}$.

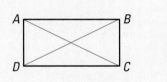

Link to Carpentry

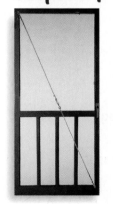

DOORS If a screen door is not rectangular, you can use a piece of hardware called a *turnbuckle* to shorten the longer diagonal until the door is rectangular.

EXAMPLE 4 Use Diagonals of a Rectangle

a. You nail four pieces of wood together to build a four-sided frame, as shown. What is the shape of the frame?

b. The diagonals measure 7 ft 4 in. and 7 ft 2 in. Is the frame a rectangle?

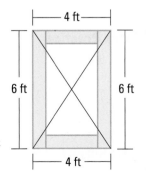

Solution

a. The frame is a parallelogram because both pairs of opposite sides are congruent.

b. The frame is not a rectangle because the diagonals are not congruent.

Checkpoint ✓ Use Diagonals

Find the value of *x*.

4. rhombus *ABCD*

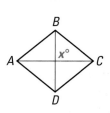

5. rectangle *EFGH*

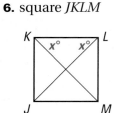

6. square *JKLM*

6.4 Exercises

Guided Practice

Vocabulary Check

1. What is the name for a parallelogram with four congruent sides?

Skill Check

List all of the properties that must be true for the quadrilateral.

2. Parallelogram

3. Rectangle

4. Rhombus

5. Square

A. All sides are congruent.

B. All angles are congruent.

C. The diagonals are congruent.

D. Opposite angles are congruent.

6. *PQRS* is a rectangle. The length of $\overline{QS}$ is 12. Find *PR* and *PT*.

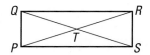

Practice and Applications

Extra Practice

See p. 686.

Using Properties **Find the measures.**

7. rhombus *ABCD*

8. rectangle *EFGH*

9. square *WXYZ*

Homework Help

Example 1: Exs. 7–9
Example 2: Exs. 10–12
Example 3: Ex. 22
Example 4: Ex. 13

$AB = \underline{}$

$BC = \underline{}$

$AD = \underline{}$

$m\angle E = \underline{}°$

$m\angle F = \underline{}°$

$m\angle G = \underline{}°$

$m\angle W = \underline{}°$

$YZ = \underline{}$

$XY = \underline{}$

Using Corollaries Use the information in the diagram to name the
special quadrilateral.

10.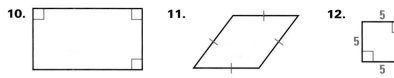

11.

12.

13. **Making a Chair** If you
measure the diagonals of the
chair frame as shown and find
that they are congruent, can
you conclude that the frame is
rectangular? If not, what other
information do you need?
Explain your reasoning.

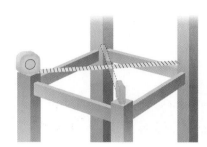

Sorting Quadrilaterals In Exercises 14–17, list each quadrilateral for
which the statement is true.

parallelogram   rectangle   rhombus   square

14. It has four right angles.

15. Opposite sides are congruent.

16. Diagonals bisect each other.

17. Diagonals are perpendicular.

Using
Algebra

| EXAMPLE | **Use Properties of Quadrilaterals** |

PQRS is a rectangle.
Find the value of *x*.

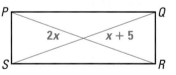

Solution

$PR = SQ$ Diagonals of a rectangle are congruent.

$2x = x + 5$ Substitute $2x$ for *PR* and $x + 5$ for *SQ*.

$x = 5$ Subtract *x* from each side.

Using Algebra Find the value of *x*.

18. rhombus *KLMN*

19. square *ABCD*

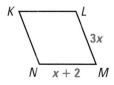

20. rectangle *EFGH*

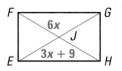

21. Logical Reasoning In ▱*JKLM*, ∠*J* is a right angle. Explain why ▱*JKLM* is a rectangle.

22. Using Theorems Find the value of *x* in rhombus *QRST*.

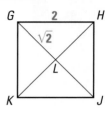

Challenge *GHJK* is a square with diagonals intersecting at *L*. Given that *GH* = 2 and *GL* = √2, complete the statement.

23. *HK* = __?__

24. *m*∠*KLJ* = __?__

25. *m*∠*HJG* = __?__

26. Perimeter of △*HJK* = __?__

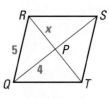

Standardized Test Practice

27. Multiple Choice In ▱*KLMN*, *KL* = *LM*. What is *m*∠*N*?

Ⓐ 30°   Ⓑ 45°

Ⓒ 90°   Ⓓ Cannot be determined

28. Multiple Choice In rhombus *ABCD*, *AB* = 7*x* − 3 and *CD* = 25. What is the value of *x*?

Ⓕ 3   Ⓖ 4

Ⓗ 7   Ⓙ 25

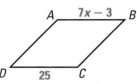

Mixed Review

Finding Angle Measures Find the measure of the numbered angle. (*Lesson 3.4*)

29.   **30.**   **31.**

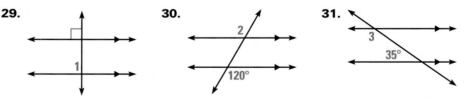

Algebra Skills

Finding Ratios Find the ratio of the length to the width for the rectangle. Write the ratio in simplest form. (*Skills Review, p. 660*)

32.   **33.**   **34.**

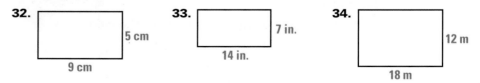

Question

What are some properties of the midsegment of a trapezoid?

Explore

❶ Draw $\overleftrightarrow{AB}$. Draw a point C not on $\overleftrightarrow{AB}$ and construct a line parallel to $\overleftrightarrow{AB}$ through point C.

❷ Construct a point D on the new line and draw $\overline{AD}$ and $\overline{BC}$, as shown below.

❸ Construct the midpoints of $\overline{AD}$ and $\overline{BC}$. Label the points E and F. Draw $\overline{EF}$.

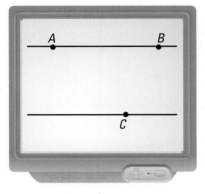

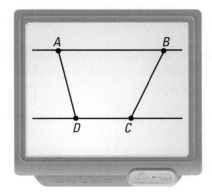

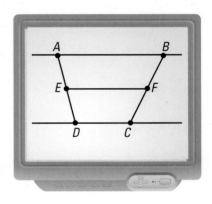

Think About It

1. Measure the distances AB, DC, and EF.

2. Calculate $\dfrac{(AB + DC)}{2}$.

3. Drag points A, B, C, and D. Do not allow $\overline{AD}$ to cross $\overline{BC}$.

What do you notice about EF and $\dfrac{(AB + DC)}{2}$?

4. Measure the slopes of $\overleftrightarrow{AB}$, $\overleftrightarrow{DC}$, and $\overline{EF}$. What do you notice? What do the slopes tell you about $\overleftrightarrow{AB}$, $\overleftrightarrow{DC}$, and $\overline{EF}$?

5. Extension Drag the points so that $\overline{AD}$ crosses $\overline{BC}$. *ABCD* is no longer a polygon. Write an expression for EF in terms of AB and DC.

6.5 Trapezoids

Goal
Use properties of trapezoids.

Key Words
- trapezoid
- bases, legs, and base angles of a trapezoid
- isosceles trapezoid
- midsegment of a trapezoid

A **trapezoid** is a quadrilateral with exactly one pair of parallel sides. The parallel sides are the **bases**. The nonparallel sides are the **legs**.

A trapezoid has two pairs of **base angles**. In trapezoid $ABCD$, $\angle C$ and $\angle D$ are one pair of base angles. $\angle A$ and $\angle B$ are the other pair.

If the legs of a trapezoid are congruent, then the trapezoid is an **isosceles trapezoid**.

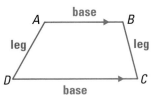

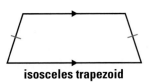
isosceles trapezoid

THEOREMS 6.12 and 6.13

Theorem 6.12

Words If a trapezoid is isosceles, then each pair of base angles are congruent.

Symbols In the isosceles trapezoid $ABCD$, $\angle A \cong \angle B$ and $\angle C \cong \angle D$.

Theorem 6.13

Words If a trapezoid has a pair of congruent base angles, then it is isosceles.

Symbols In trapezoid $ABCD$, if $\angle C \cong \angle D$ then $ABCD$ is isosceles.

EXAMPLE 1 Find Angle Measures of Trapezoids

$PQRS$ is an isosceles trapezoid. Find the missing angle measures.

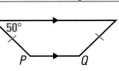

Solution

❶ $PQRS$ is an isosceles trapezoid and $\angle R$ and $\angle S$ are a pair of base angles. So, $m\angle R = m\angle S = 50°$.

❷ Because $\angle S$ and $\angle P$ are same-side interior angles formed by parallel lines, they are supplementary. So, $m\angle P = 180° - 50° = 130°$.

❸ Because $\angle Q$ and $\angle P$ are a pair of base angles of an isosceles trapezoid, $m\angle Q = m\angle P = 130°$.

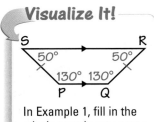

Visualize It!

In Example 1, fill in the missing angle measures as you find them.

Checkpoint ✓ Find Angle Measures of Trapezoids

ABCD is an isosceles trapezoid. Find the missing angle measures.

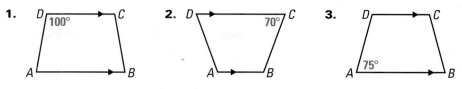

1.

2.

3.

Student Help

VOCABULARY TIP
The midsegment of a trapezoid is sometimes called the *median* of a trapezoid.

Midsegments The **midsegment of a trapezoid** is the segment that connects the midpoints of its legs. The midsegment of a trapezoid is parallel to the bases.

The length of the midsegment of a trapezoid is half the sum of the lengths of the bases.

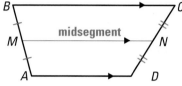

$$MN = \frac{1}{2}(AD + BC)$$

EXAMPLE 2 Midsegment of a Trapezoid

Find the length of the midsegment $\overline{DG}$ of trapezoid *CEFH*.

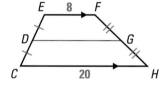

Solution

Use the formula for the midsegment of a trapezoid.

$DG = \frac{1}{2}(EF + CH)$	Formula for midsegment of a trapezoid
$= \frac{1}{2}(8 + 20)$	Substitute 8 for *EF* and 20 for *CH*.
$= \frac{1}{2}(28)$	Add.
$= 14$	Multiply.

ANSWER ▶ The length of the midsegment $\overline{DG}$ is 14.

Checkpoint ✓ Midsegment of a Trapezoid

Find the length of the midsegment $\overline{MN}$ of the trapezoid.

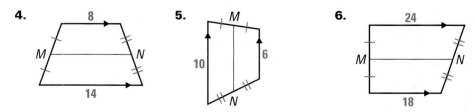

4.

5.

6.

6.5 Exercises

Guided Practice

Vocabulary Check

1. Name the *bases* of trapezoid *ABCD*.

2. Name the *legs* of trapezoid *ABCD*.

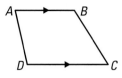

Skill Check

Decide whether the quadrilateral is a *trapezoid*, an *isosceles trapezoid*, or *neither*.

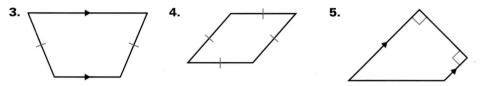

3.   **4.**   **5.**

Find the length of the midsegment.

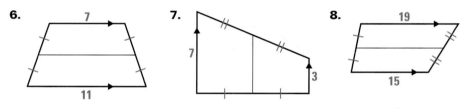

6.   **7.**   **8.**

Practice and Applications

Extra Practice

See p. 686.

Parts of a Trapezoid Match the parts of trapezoid *PQRS* with the correct description.

9. $\overline{QR}$ and $\overline{PS}$ **A.** legs

10. $\angle Q$ and $\angle S$ **B.** base angles

11. $\angle R$ and $\angle Q$ **C.** opposite angles

12. $\overline{MN}$ **D.** bases

13. $\overline{PQ}$ and $\overline{RS}$ **E.** midsegment

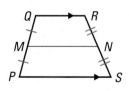

Finding Angle Measures *JKLM* is an isosceles trapezoid. Find the missing angle measures.

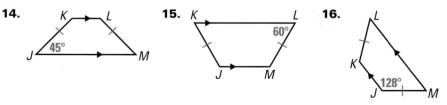

14.   **15.**   **16.**

Homework Help

Example 1: Exs. 14–19
Example 2: Exs. 20–26

Finding Angle Measure *QRST* is a trapezoid. Find the missing angle measures.

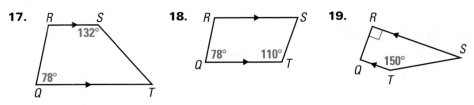

17. R   S
        132°

     78°
     Q   T

18. R →   S
     78°   110°
     Q →   T

19. R
           ←
         150°   S
     Q ←
         T

Finding Midsegments Find the length of the midsegment $\overline{MN}$ of the trapezoid.

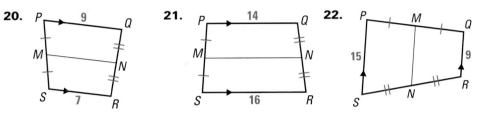

20. P → 9   Q
     M   N
     S → 7 R

21. P → 14 Q
     M   N
     S → 16 R

22. P   M   Q
     15   9
     S   N   R

(xy) **Using Algebra** Find the value of *x*.

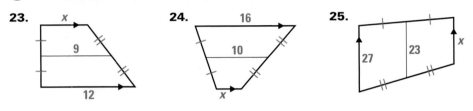

23.   x
        9
        12

24.   16
       10
        x

25.
     27 23 x

Link to
Cake Design

CAKE DESIGNERS form and sculpt shapes and figures onto cakes by using tools such as icing bags, handmade paper cones, or cutters.

26. **Cake Design** The top layer of the cake in the diagram at the right has a diameter of 10 inches. The bottom layer has a diameter of 22 inches. What is the diameter of the middle layer?

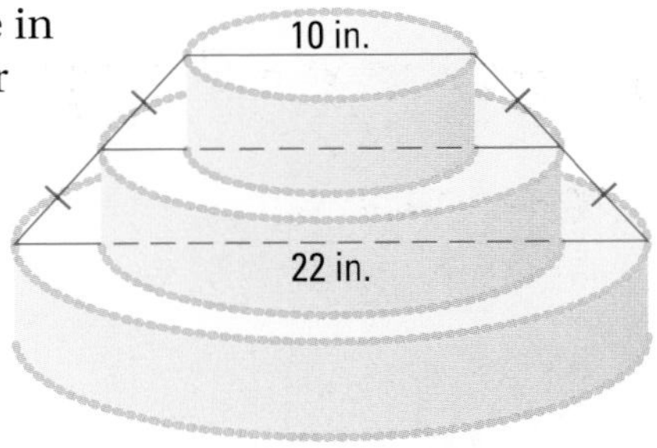

10 in.

22 in.

Coordinate Geometry The vertices of a trapezoid are *A*(2, 6), *B*(8, 6), *C*(8, 2), and *D*(4, 2).

27. Plot the vertices on a coordinate plane. Connect them to form trapezoid *ABCD*.

28. Name the bases of trapezoid *ABCD*.

29. Name the legs of trapezoid *ABCD*.

30. Find the coordinates of the midpoint of each leg. Then plot these points on the coordinate plane you drew in Exercise 27. What is the line segment that connects these two points called?

Student Help
CLASSZONE.COM

HOMEWORK HELP
Extra help with problem solving in Exs. 31–33 is at classzone.com

Visualize It! **In Exercises 31–33, use the figures shown below.** The figure on the left is a trapezoid with midsegment of length m. The figure on the right is formed by cutting the trapezoid along its midsegment and rearranging the two pieces.

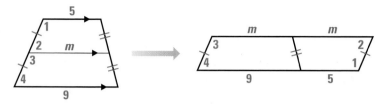

31. Which theorem or postulate from Chapter 3 can you use to show that $\angle 1 \cong \angle 3$ and $\angle 2 \cong \angle 4$ in the figure on the left?

32. What kind of quadrilateral is on the right? Explain your answer.

33. Challenge How does the diagram help you see that the length of the midsegment is half the sum of the lengths of the bases?

Standardized Test Practice

34. Multiple Choice In the trapezoid at the right, what is the value of x?

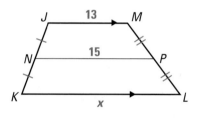

(A) 13 (B) 15

(C) 17 (D) 28

35. Multiple Choice Which of the following must a trapezoid have?

(F) congruent bases

(G) diagonals that bisect each other

(H) exactly one pair of parallel sides

(J) a pair of congruent opposite angles

Mixed Review

Logical Reasoning Tell whether the quadrilateral is a parallelogram. Explain your reasoning. *(Lesson 6.3)*

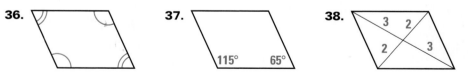

36.

37.

38.

Algebra Skills

Multiplying Multiply. Write the answer in simplest form. *(Skills Review, p. 659)*

39. $\frac{1}{2} \times 20$ **40.** $52 \times \frac{1}{4}$ **41.** $136 \times \frac{1}{8}$ **42.** $\frac{3}{4} \times 60$

43. $\frac{2}{3} \times \frac{3}{7}$ **44.** $\frac{7}{8} \times \frac{2}{14}$ **45.** $\frac{5}{6} \times \frac{1}{3}$ **46.** $\frac{4}{21} \times \frac{7}{16}$

6.6 **Reasoning About Special Quadrilaterals**

Goal

Identify special quadrilaterals based on limited information.

Key Words

- parallelogram p. 310
- rectangle p. 325
- rhombus p. 325
- square p. 325
- trapezoid p. 332
- isosceles trapezoid p. 332

In this chapter, you have studied six special types of quadrilaterals. The diagram below shows how these quadrilaterals are related. Each shape is a special example of the shape(s) listed above it.

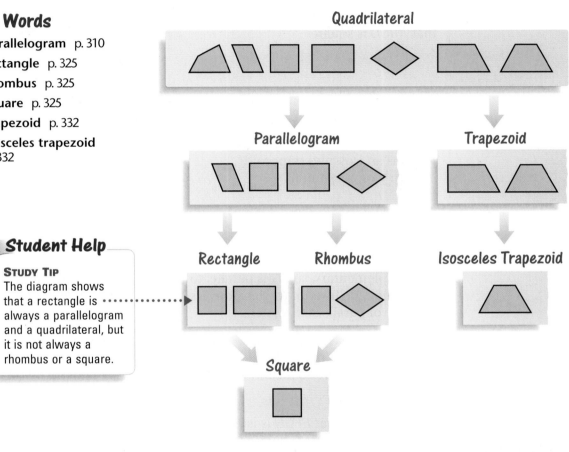

Student Help

STUDY TIP
The diagram shows that a rectangle is always a parallelogram and a quadrilateral, but it is not always a rhombus or a square.

EXAMPLE **1** **Use Properties of Quadrilaterals**

Determine whether the quadrilateral is a trapezoid, parallelogram, rectangle, rhombus, or square.

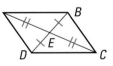

Solution

The diagram shows $\overline{CE} \cong \overline{EA}$ and $\overline{DE} \cong \overline{EB}$, so the diagonals of the quadrilateral bisect each other. By Theorem 6.9, you can conclude that the quadrilateral is a parallelogram.

You *cannot* conclude that *ABCD* is a rectangle, rhombus, or square because no information about the sides or angles is given.

EXAMPLE **2** **Identify a Rhombus**

Are you given enough information in the diagram to conclude that *ABCD* is a square? Explain your reasoning.

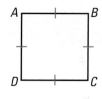

Solution

The diagram shows that all four sides are congruent. Therefore, you know that it is a rhombus. The diagram does not give any information about the angle measures, so you cannot conclude that *ABCD* is square.

EXAMPLE **3** **Identify a Trapezoid**

Are you given enough information in the diagram to conclude that *EFGH* is an isosceles trapezoid? Explain your reasoning.

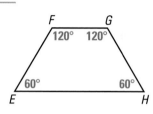

Solution

❶ *First* show that *EFGH* is a trapezoid. ∠*E* and ∠*F* are supplementary, so $\overline{FG}$ is parallel to $\overline{EH}$ by Theorem 3.10, the Same-Side Interior Angles Converse. So, *EFGH* has *at least* one pair of parallel sides.

To show that *EFGH* is a trapezoid, you must show that it has *only one* pair of parallel sides. The opposite angles of *EFGH* are not congruent, so it cannot be a parallelogram. Therefore, *EFGH* is a trapezoid.

❷ *Next* show that *EFGH* is isosceles. Because the base angles are congruent, *EFGH* is an isosceles trapezoid by Theorem 6.13.

Checkpoint ✓ **Identify Quadrilaterals**

Are you given enough information to conclude that the figure is the given type of special quadrilateral? Explain your reasoning.

1. A square?

2. A rhombus?

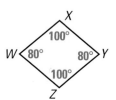

3. A trapezoid?

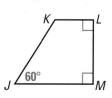

6.6 Exercises

Guided Practice

Skill Check Copy the chart. Put a ✓ mark in the box if the shape *always* has the given property.

	Property	▱	Rectangle	Rhombus	Square	Trapezoid
1.	Both pairs of opp. sides are ∥.	?	?	?	?	?
2.	Exactly 1 pair of opp. sides are ∥.	?	?	?	?	?
3.	Diagonals are perpendicular.	?	?	?	?	?
4.	Diagonals are congruent.	?	?	?	?	?

Practice and Applications

Extra Practice

See p. 686.

Properties of Quadrilaterals Copy the chart. Put a ✓ mark in the box if the shape *always* has the given property.

	Property	▱	Rectangle	Rhombus	Square	Trapezoid
5.	Both pairs of opp. sides are congruent.	?	?	?	?	?
6.	Diagonals bisect each other.	?	?	?	?	?
7.	Both pairs of opp. angles are congruent.	?	?	?	?	?
8.	All sides are congruent.	?	?	?	?	?

Using Properties of Quadrilaterals Determine whether the quadrilateral is a trapezoid, parallelogram, rectangle, rhombus, or square.

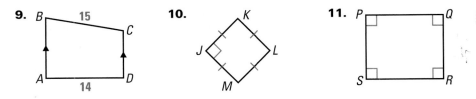

9.

10.

11.

Homework Help

Example 1: Exs. 9–11, 18, 19
Example 2: Exs. 12–17
Example 3: Exs. 12–17

Identifying Quadrilaterals Are you given enough information to conclude that the figure is the given type of special quadrilateral? Explain your reasoning.

12. A rhombus?

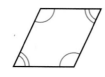

13. A trapezoid?

14. An isosceles trapezoid?

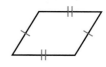

15. A rectangle?

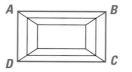

16. A square?

17. A parallelogram?

Gem Cutting Use the diagrams and the following information.
There are different ways of cutting a gem to enhance its beauty. One of the cuts used for gems is called the *step cut*. Each face of a cut gem is called a *facet*.

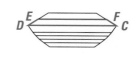

18. In *ABCD*, ∠*A*, ∠*B*, ∠*C*, and ∠*D* are all right angles. What shape is *ABCD*?

19. $\overline{EF}$ is parallel to $\overline{DC}$; $\overline{ED}$ and $\overline{FC}$ are congruent, but not parallel. What shape is the facet labeled *EFCD*?

Using a Venn Diagram In Exercises 20–23, use the Venn diagram to decide whether the following statements are *true* or *false*.

20. All rectangles are squares.

21. All squares are rectangles.

22. All squares are rhombuses.

23. All rhombuses are parallelograms.

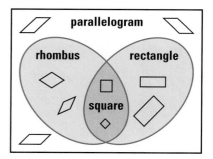

24. Technology Use geometry software to draw a triangle. Construct the midpoint of each side and connect the midpoints as shown. What type of quadrilateral is *BEFD*? Explain.

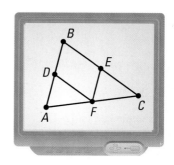

25. Challenge What type of quadrilateral is *PQRS*, with vertices *P*(2, 5), *Q*(5, 5), *R*(6, 2), and *S*(1, 2)?

Standardized Test Practice

26. Multiple Choice Which of the following statements is *never* true?

  (A) A rectangle is a square.

  (B) A parallelogram is a trapezoid.

  (C) A rhombus is a parallelogram.

  (D) A parallelogram is a rectangle.

Mixed Review

Solving Proportions Solve the proportion. *(Skills Review, p. 660)*

27. $\dfrac{x}{3} = \dfrac{4}{12}$ **28.** $\dfrac{4}{7} = \dfrac{x}{21}$ **29.** $\dfrac{10}{x} = \dfrac{5}{8}$ **30.** $\dfrac{3}{10} = \dfrac{24}{x}$

31. $\dfrac{x}{24} = \dfrac{5}{12}$ **32.** $\dfrac{3}{5} = \dfrac{x}{20}$ **33.** $\dfrac{8}{x} = \dfrac{1}{2}$ **34.** $\dfrac{3}{7} = \dfrac{21}{x}$

Algebra Skills

Writing Decimals Write the fraction as a decimal. For repeating decimals, also round to the nearest hundredth for an approximation. *(Skills Review, p. 657)*

35. $\dfrac{1}{5}$ **36.** $\dfrac{3}{8}$ **37.** $\dfrac{5}{6}$ **38.** $\dfrac{7}{20}$

Quiz 2

Find the value of x. *(Lesson 6.4)*

  1. rhombus *ABCD*   **2.** rectangle *FGHJ*   **3.** square *PQRS*

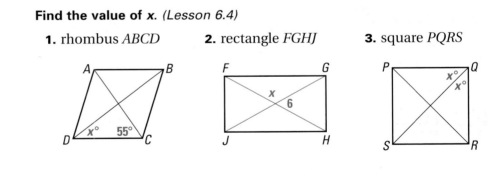

What kind of special quadrilateral is the red shape? *(Lesson 6.5)*

  4. 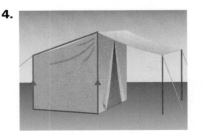   **5.**

6. Which kinds of quadrilaterals can you form with four straws of the same length? You must attach the straws at their ends and cannot bend any of them. *(Lesson 6.6)*

VOCABULARY

- **polygon,** *p. 303*
- **side of a polygon,** *p. 303*
- **vertex of a polygon,** *p. 303*
- **diagonal of a polygon,** *p. 303*
- **parallelogram,** *p. 310*

- **rhombus,** *p. 325*
- **rectangle,** *p. 325*
- **square,** *p. 325*
- **trapezoid,** *p. 332*
- **bases of a trapezoid,** *p. 332*

- **legs of a trapezoid,** *p. 332*
- **base angles of a trapezoid,** *p. 332*
- **isosceles trapezoid,** *p. 332*
- **midsegment of a trapezoid,** *p. 333*

VOCABULARY REVIEW

Fill in each blank.

1. A(n) __?__ is a quadrilateral with both pairs of opposite sides parallel.

2. A(n) __?__ is a plane figure that is formed by three or more segments called sides.

3. A(n) __?__ is a parallelogram with four congruent sides.

4. A(n) __?__ is a parallelogram with four right angles.

5. A parallelogram with four congruent sides and four right angles is a(n) __?__.

6. A(n) __?__ is a quadrilateral with exactly one pair of sides parallel.

7. Each endpoint of the sides of a polygon is called a(n) __?__.

8. A segment that joins two nonconsecutive vertices of a polygon is called a(n) __?__.

9. The nonparallel sides of a trapezoid are called its __?__ and the parallel sides are called its __?__.

6.1 POLYGONS

Examples on pp. 303–305

EXAMPLE **Decide whether the figure is a polygon. If so, tell what type. If not, explain why.**

The figure is a polygon because it has straight sides and each side intersects exactly two other sides at each of its endpoints.

The polygon has five sides, so it is a pentagon.

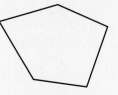

Decide whether the figure is a polygon. If so, tell what type. If not, explain why.

10.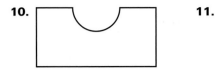

11.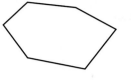

12.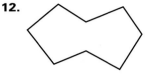

Sketch the figure(s) described.

13. Two different heptagons

14. A quadrilateral with one right angle

6.2 PROPERTIES OF PARALLELOGRAMS

Examples on pp. 310–312

EXAMPLES *ABCD* is a parallelogram. Find the measure.

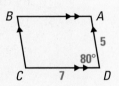

a. Find *AB* and *BC*.

By Theorem 6.2, the opposite sides of a parallelogram are congruent. So, *AB* = *DC* = 7, and *BC* = *AD* = 5.

b. Find *m∠A*.

By Theorem 6.4, the consecutive angles of a parallelogram are supplementary.

$m\angle A + m\angle D = 180°$ **Consec. ∠s of a ▱ are supplementary.**

$m\angle A + 80° = 180°$ **Substitute 80° for *m∠D*.**

$m\angle A = 100°$ **Subtract 80° from each side.**

Find the measures in the parallelogram.

15. Find *BC* and *DC*.

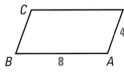

16. Find *m∠F* and *m∠G*.

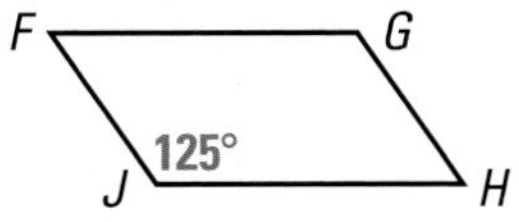

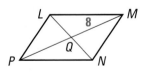

17. Find *PQ* and *PM*.

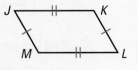

6.3 SHOWING QUADRILATERALS ARE PARALLELOGRAMS

Examples on pp. 316–319

EXAMPLE Tell whether *JKLM* is a parallelogram. Explain your reasoning.

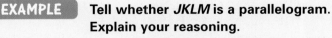

By Theorem 6.6, *JKLM* is a parallelogram because both pairs of opposite sides are congruent.

Tell whether the quadrilateral is a parallelogram. Explain your reasoning.

18.

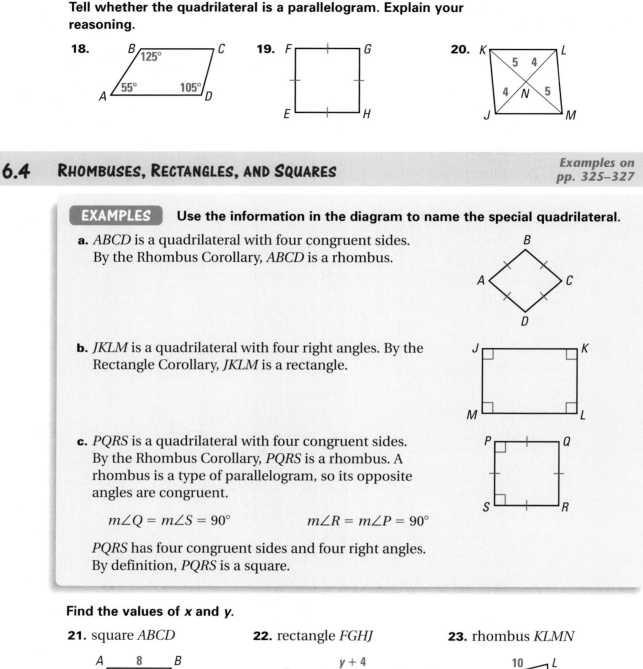

19. F ⊢ G

20. K

6.4 RHOMBUSES, RECTANGLES, AND SQUARES

Examples on pp. 325–327

> **EXAMPLES** Use the information in the diagram to name the special quadrilateral.
>
> **a.** *ABCD* is a quadrilateral with four congruent sides. By the Rhombus Corollary, *ABCD* is a rhombus.
>
> **b.** *JKLM* is a quadrilateral with four right angles. By the Rectangle Corollary, *JKLM* is a rectangle.
>
> **c.** *PQRS* is a quadrilateral with four congruent sides. By the Rhombus Corollary, *PQRS* is a rhombus. A rhombus is a type of parallelogram, so its opposite angles are congruent.
>
> $m\angle Q = m\angle S = 90°$ $m\angle R = m\angle P = 90°$
>
> *PQRS* has four congruent sides and four right angles. By definition, *PQRS* is a square.

Find the values of x and y.

21. square *ABCD*

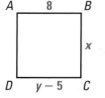

22. rectangle *FGHJ*

23. rhombus *KLMN*

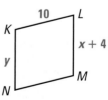

Tell whether the statement is *true* or *false*.

24. All rhombuses are squares.

25. All rectangles are parallelograms.

26. All rhombuses are rectangles.

27. All squares are parallelograms.

6.5 TRAPEZOIDS

Examples on pp. 332–333

EXAMPLES *ABCD* is an isosceles trapezoid. Find the measure.

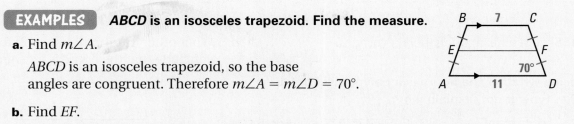

a. Find $m\angle A$.

ABCD is an isosceles trapezoid, so the base angles are congruent. Therefore $m\angle A = m\angle D = 70°$.

b. Find *EF*.

The length of the midsegment $\overline{EF}$ is half the sum of the bases.

$$EF = \frac{1}{2}(BC + AD) = \frac{1}{2}(7 + 11) = \frac{1}{2}(18) = 9$$

Find the measure in the trapezoid.

28. Find $m\angle P$.

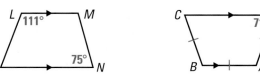

29. Find $m\angle C$.

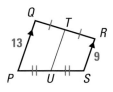

30. Find *TU*.

6.6 REASONING ABOUT SPECIAL QUADRILATERALS

Examples on pp. 337–338

EXAMPLE Are you given enough information in the diagram to conclude that *FGHJ* is a trapezoid? Explain your reasoning.

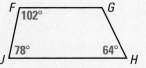

Because $m\angle F + m\angle J = 102° + 78° = 180°$, $\angle F$ and $\angle J$ are supplementary. The same-side interior angles are supplementary. So, by Theorem 3.10, $\overline{FG} \parallel \overline{JH}$.

Because $m\angle J + m\angle H = 78° + 64° = 142°$, $\angle J$ and $\angle H$ are *not* supplementary, so $\overline{FJ}$ is *not* parallel to $\overline{GH}$.

FGHJ has *exactly* one pair of parallel sides, so it is a trapezoid.

Are you given enough information to conclude that the figure is the given type of special quadrilateral? Explain your reasoning.

31. A rhombus?

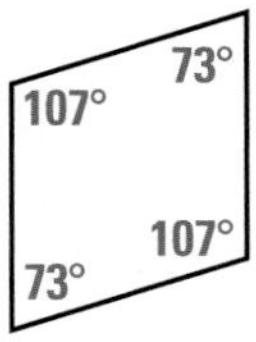

32. A trapezoid?

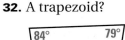

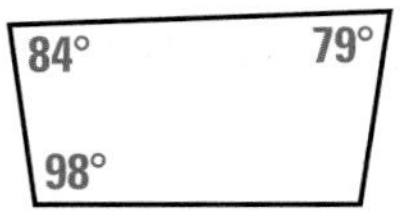

33. A rectangle?

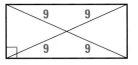

1. Sketch a hexagon. Label its vertices.

Decide whether the figure is a polygon. If so, tell what type. If not, explain why.

2.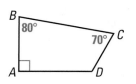

3.

4. Find $m\angle D$.

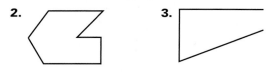

In ▱ABCD, find the values of x and y.

5.

6.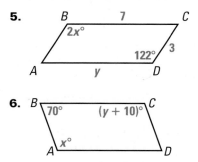

Tell whether the quadrilateral is a parallelogram. Explain your reasoning.

7.

8.

9.

10.
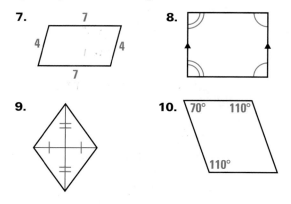

11. What other information do you need to conclude that the figure is a rectangle?

12. In rhombus *JKLM*, find the values of a and b.

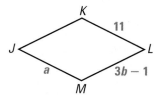

13. *PQRS* is a trapezoid. Find $m\angle S$ and $m\angle Q$.

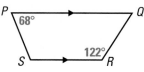

14. Find the length of the midsegment of trapezoid *STUV*.

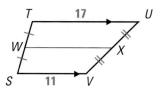

Determine whether the quadrilateral is a trapezoid, parallelogram, rectangle, rhombus, or square.

15.

16.
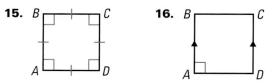

17. Are you given enough information in the diagram to conclude that *EFGH* is a rectangle? Explain your reasoning.

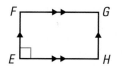

Test Tip
Ⓐ Ⓑ Ⓒ Ⓓ

Diagrams may not be drawn to scale. Use only information that is given or marked on diagrams.

1. What type of polygon is shown below?

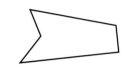

Ⓐ pentagon   Ⓑ hexagon

Ⓒ heptagon   Ⓓ octagon

2. Find the value of x.

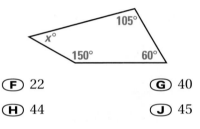

Ⓕ 22   Ⓖ 40

Ⓗ 44   Ⓙ 45

3. The diagonals of a parallelogram __?__.

Ⓐ are congruent   Ⓑ are perpendicular

Ⓒ bisect each other   Ⓓ are parallel

4. *FGHJ* is a rectangle. What is *FG*?

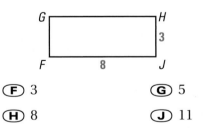

Ⓕ 3   Ⓖ 5

Ⓗ 8   Ⓙ 11

5. *ABCD* is a trapezoid. Which of the following statements is true?

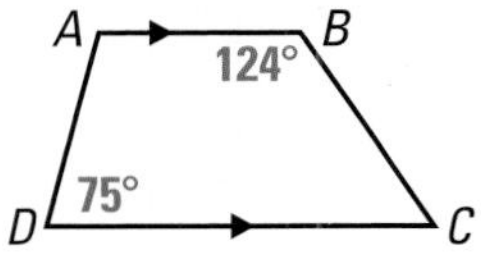

Ⓐ $m\angle C = 56°$

Ⓑ $m\angle A = 75°$

Ⓒ $\angle A$ and $\angle C$ are supplementary.

Ⓓ $\angle C$ and $\angle D$ are supplementary.

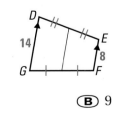

6. Which of the following terms could *not* be used to describe the figure below?

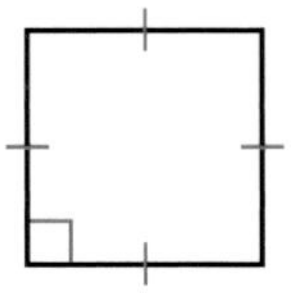

Ⓕ parallelogram   Ⓖ rhombus

Ⓗ square   Ⓙ trapezoid

7. *WXYZ* is an isosceles trapezoid. What are the values of x and y?

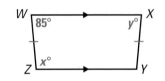

Ⓐ $x = 85, y = 95$ Ⓑ $x = 100, y = 85$

Ⓒ $x = 105, y = 85$ Ⓓ $x = 95, y = 85$

8. *STUV* is a rhombus. What are the values of x and y?

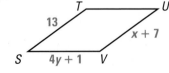

Ⓕ $x = 3, y = 3$ Ⓖ $x = 3, y = 6$

Ⓗ $x = 6, y = 3$ Ⓙ $x = 6, y = 4$

9. What is the length of the midsegment of trapezoid *DEFG*?

Ⓐ 8   Ⓑ 9

Ⓒ 10   Ⓓ 11

BraiN GaMes

Polyominoes

Materials
- graph paper
- scissors

Object of the Game To be the team to find the most number of ways to connect five squares edge to edge.

Set Up Cut squares out of graph paper.

How to Play

Step 1 ▶ Arrange 5 squares edge to edge in as many ways as possible. Do not include any congruent figures. If a figure is a rotation or a reflection of one of the other figures, it is a congruent figure.

Step 2 ▶ Draw a picture of each figure on graph paper.

Step 3 ▶ Work until your teacher tells you time is up. Each team receives a point for each figure it finds. A team loses a point if they have congruent figures or they have a figure in which the squares are not arranged edge to edge.

Another Way to Play After you have found all of the possible figures, cut out the drawings and arrange them so that they fit together as a large rectangle.

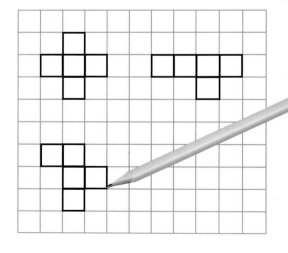

A *proportion* is an equation that states that two ratios are equal. A property that is helpful when solving a proportion is the *cross product property*.

$$\text{If } \frac{a}{b} = \frac{c}{d}, \text{ then } ad = bc.$$

EXAMPLE **Solve Proportions**

Solve the proportion.

a. $\dfrac{x}{18} = \dfrac{5}{6}$ **b.** $\dfrac{3}{8} = \dfrac{y+2}{32}$

Solution

a. $\dfrac{x}{18} = \dfrac{5}{6}$ Write original proportion.

$x \cdot 6 = 18 \cdot 5$ Cross product property

$6x = 90$ Multiply.

$\dfrac{6x}{6} = \dfrac{90}{6}$ Divide each side by 6.

$x = 15$ Simplify.

b. $\dfrac{3}{8} = \dfrac{y+2}{32}$ Write original proportion.

$3 \cdot 32 = 8(y + 2)$ Cross product property

$96 = 8y + 16$ Multiply and distribute.

$80 = 8y$ Subtract 16 from each side.

$\dfrac{80}{8} = \dfrac{8y}{8}$ Divide each side by 8.

$10 = y$ Simplify.

Student Help

STUDY TIP
Check your solutions by substituting the value of the variable into the original equation.

Try These

Solve the proportion.

1. $\dfrac{3}{4} = \dfrac{t}{40}$ **2.** $\dfrac{4}{9} = \dfrac{x}{63}$ **3.** $\dfrac{2}{5} = \dfrac{6}{w}$ **4.** $\dfrac{5}{b} = \dfrac{8}{15}$

5. $\dfrac{7}{2} = \dfrac{7}{y}$ **6.** $\dfrac{35}{x} = \dfrac{5}{14}$ **7.** $\dfrac{d}{4} = \dfrac{11}{14}$ **8.** $\dfrac{54}{h} = \dfrac{9}{10}$

9. $\dfrac{3z}{10} = \dfrac{7}{20}$ **10.** $\dfrac{4}{7} = \dfrac{c+2}{21}$ **11.** $\dfrac{8}{15} = \dfrac{40}{r+1}$ **12.** $\dfrac{1}{6} = \dfrac{4}{v+5}$

1. Describe the pattern in the numbers 2, 11, 20, 29, ... Then write the next two numbers you expect in the pattern. **(Lesson 1.1)**

2. Plot the points $A(-4, 0)$, $B(5, 0)$, $C(3, 6)$, and $D(3, -2)$ in a coordinate plane. Then decide whether $\overline{AB}$ and $\overline{CD}$ are congruent. **(Lesson 1.5)**

Find the coordinates of the midpoint of $\overline{FG}$. **(Lesson 2.1)**

3. $F(-2, 5)$, $G(0, -7)$

4. $F(1, 4)$, $G(7, -2)$

5. $F(-4, -2)$, $G(6, 4)$

$\overrightarrow{BD}$ **bisects** $\angle ABC$. **Find the value of x. Then determine whether** $\angle ABC$ **is** *acute, right, obtuse,* **or** *straight.* **(Lesson 2.2)**

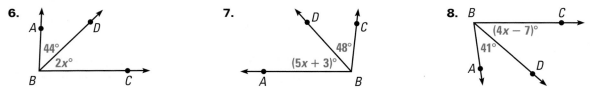

6. 44°, 2x°

7. 48°, (5x + 3)°

8. (4x − 7)°, 41°

9. $\angle P$ is a complement of $\angle Q$, and $m\angle P = 28°$. Find $m\angle Q$. **(Lesson 2.3)**

10. $\angle Y$ is a supplement of $\angle Z$, and $m\angle Y = 146°$. Find $m\angle Z$. **(Lesson 2.3)**

Use the diagram below to complete the statement using *corresponding, alternate interior, alternate exterior, same-side interior,* **or** *vertical.* **(Lessons 2.4, 3.3)**

11. $\angle 1$ and $\angle 4$ are __?__ angles.

12. $\angle 3$ and $\angle 5$ are __?__ angles.

13. $\angle 1$ and $\angle 7$ are __?__ angles.

14. $\angle 4$ and $\angle 6$ are __?__ angles.

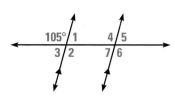

Use the diagram above to find the measure of the angle. **(Lesson 3.4)**

15. $m\angle 4 = $ __?__ °

16. $m\angle 7 = $ __?__ °

17. $m\angle 5 = $ __?__ °

18. $m\angle 2 = $ __?__ °

Find the value of x. **(Lessons 4.2, 4.3)**

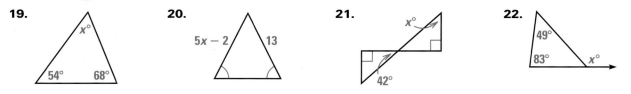

19. x°, 54°, 68°

20. 5x − 2, 13

21. x°, 42°

22. 49°, 83°, x°

Find the distance between *A* and *B*. (Lesson 4.4)

23. $A(1, 4)$, $B(-3, 1)$ **24.** $A(-2, 1)$, $B(3, 13)$ **25.** $A(3, -4)$, $B(9, 4)$

Can the side lengths form a triangle? Explain. (Lesson 4.7)

26. 6, 7, 8   **27.** 3, 6, 12   **28.** 4, 10, 14

Does the diagram give enough information to show that the triangles are congruent? If so, state the theorem or postulate you would use.
(Lessons 5.2, 5.3, 5.4)

29. $\triangle ABC$ and $\triangle DEC$ **30.** $\triangle FJG$ and $\triangle HJG$ **31.** $\triangle KPL$ and $\triangle NPM$ **32.** $\triangle QRS$ and $\triangle QTS$

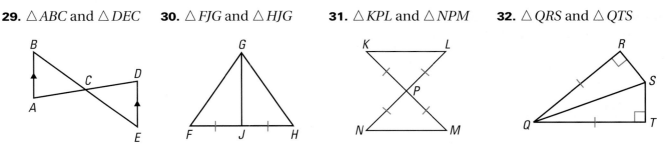

33. Sketch a square. How many lines of symmetry does a square have?
(Lessons 5.7, 6.4)

Find the values of *x* and *y*. (Lesson 6.2)

34.   **35.**   **36.**

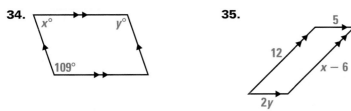 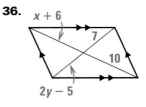

37. In quadrilateral *EFGH*, $m\angle E = 90°$, $m\angle F = 90°$, and $m\angle G = 67°$. What special kind of quadrilateral must *EFGH* be? Explain your reasoning. (Lesson 6.6)

Billboard Supports The two ten-foot posts that support a vertical billboard form an angle of 115° with level ground, as shown.

38. What theorem or postulate could you use to show that $\triangle ABC$ is congruent to $\triangle DEF$? (Lesson 5.3)

39. Are $\overleftrightarrow{AB}$ and $\overleftrightarrow{DE}$ parallel? Explain. (Lesson 3.6)

40. What type of quadrilateral must *ADEB* be? Explain your reasoning. (Lesson 6.6)

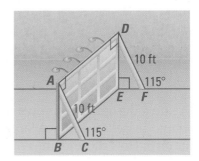

Chapters 5-6 Project

Creating Tessellations

Objective

Use regular tessellations to create geometric designs.

A tessellation, or tiling, of a plane is a collection of tiles that fill the plane with no gaps or overlaps. You can tessellate a plane with squares, triangles, or hexagons. You can use these tessellations to create other geometric designs that tessellate.

Materials

- square, triangle, and hexagon grid paper
- straightedge
- colored pencils or markers

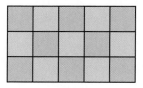

squares

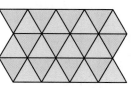

triangles

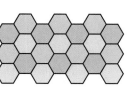

hexagons

Drawing

1. Choose a basic shape that tessellates. Draw lines of symmetry.

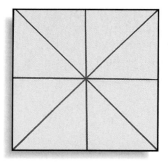

2. Draw a design that has symmetry.

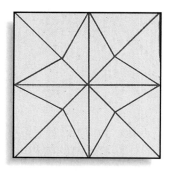

3. Color the design.

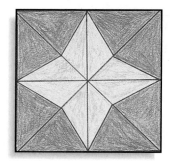

Investigation

1. The design in Step 3 is copied four times to tessellate an area. What type of polygon is in the center?
2. Create a design of your own using a square as the basic shape. Tessellate an area large enough to see the overall pattern. How did the lines of symmetry you drew help you create a design?

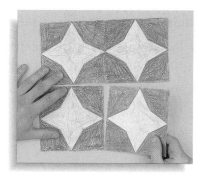

Investigation

3. Create a design of your own using a triangle as the basic shape. Tessellate a large enough area to see an overall pattern. What shapes do you see before and after your design is tessellated?

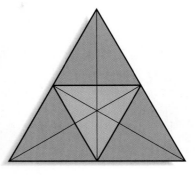

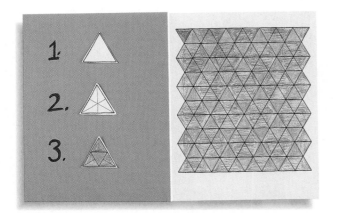

Present Your Results

Write a report to present your results.

▶ Make a book of designs that tessellate.

▶ Include the designs you copied and created in the Investigation and any additional designs you create.

▶ On one page show the steps for creating the design using one basic shape. On another page show the result when this design is tessellated.

Extension

Think of a way in which you would like to use a design that tessellates. Examples include designs in fabric, upholstery, car seat covers, bracelets, belts, wallpaper, and flooring. Then create a design and show how you would use it.

Chapter 7 Similarity

How does a drawing become a mural?

Murals are often created by enlarging an original drawing. People use projection machines, grids, and other methods to make sure that all parts of a mural are in proportion to the original drawing.

original figure

enlarged figure

Learn More About It

You will learn more about enlarging drawings in Exercise 21 on p. 370.

Who uses Similarity?

MAP MAKER
Map makers analyze photographs, satellite images, and other data to create maps. Maps may be designed for travel, tourism, weather forecasting, and geological exploration. (p. 360)

ARTIST
Painters, photographers, and sculptors use proportions to enlarge and reduce the size of an original art piece. Proportions are also used to draw human figures and make perspective drawings. (p. 370)

How will you use these ideas?

- Estimate distances on a map. (p. 360)
- Compare the dimensions of television screens. (p. 371)
- Analyze a hockey pass. (p. 374)
- Calculate the height of a flag pole. (p. 377)
- See how similarity appears in fractals. (p. 391)

PREVIEW

What's the chapter about?

- Using **ratios** and **proportions**
- Identifying **similar polygons** and showing that triangles are similar
- Identifying and drawing **dilations**

Key Words

- ratio of *a* to *b*, *p. 357*
- proportion, *p. 359*
- similar polygons, *p. 365*

- scale factor, *p. 366*
- midsegment of a triangle, *p. 389*
- dilation, *p. 393*

PREPARE

Chapter Readiness Quiz

Take this quick quiz. If you are unsure of an answer, look at the reference pages for help.

Vocabulary Check *(refer to pp. 234, 241)*

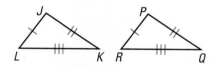

1. Which *congruence statement* is correct for the triangles at the right?

   (A) $\triangle LKJ \cong \triangle QRP$ **(B)** $\triangle JLK \cong \triangle PQR$

   (C) $\triangle LJK \cong \triangle RPQ$ **(D)** $\triangle KLJ \cong \triangle QPR$

Skill Check *(refer to pp. 333, 656)*

2. What is the value of *x*?

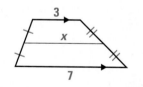

   (F) 4   **(G)** 5

   (H) 5.5   **(J)** 6

3. Which of the following fractions can be simplified to $\frac{2}{7}$?

   (A) $\frac{8}{18}$ **(B)** $\frac{6}{21}$ **(C)** $\frac{12}{28}$ **(D)** $\frac{18}{33}$

VISUAL STRATEGY

Separating Triangles

Visualize It! ➡

To help you see triangle relationships more clearly, sketch overlapping triangles separately and label them with their measures.

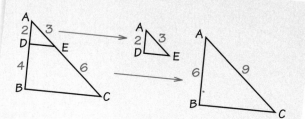

Ratio and Proportion

Goal
Use ratios and proportions.

Key Words
- ratio of *a* to *b*
- proportion
- means
- extremes

In 2000, Nomar Garciaparra of the Boston Red Sox won the American League batting title for the second straight year, with a *batting average* of .372. He was at bat 529 times and had 197 hits. A baseball player's batting average is calculated using a *ratio*.

$$\frac{\text{hits}}{\text{times at bat}} = \frac{197}{529} \approx 0.372$$

A **ratio** is a comparison of a number *a* and a nonzero number *b* using division.

The ratio of *a* to *b* can be written in three ways: as the fraction $\frac{a}{b}$ (or an equivalent decimal), as *a* : *b*, or as "*a* to *b*." A ratio is usually written in simplest form.

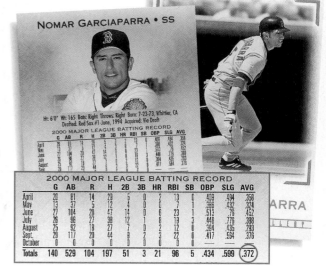

NOMAR GARCIAPARRA • SS

Ht: 6'0" Wt: 165 Bats: Right Throws: Right Born: 7-23-73, Whittier, CA
Drafted: Red Sox #1-June, 1994 Acquired: Via Draft

2000 MAJOR LEAGUE BATTING RECORD

	G	AB	R	H	2B	3B	HR	RBI	SB	OBP	SLG	AVG
April	20	81	14	29	5	0	2	13	0	.409	.494	.358
May	13	37	5	12	4	0	0	7	1	.366	.432	.324
June	27	104	20	47	14	0	6	23	1	.513	.76	.452
July	26	96	27	38	12	1	8	19	3	.446	.779	.398
August	25	92	18	27	7	0	2	12	0	.364	.435	.293
Sept.	29	117	20	44	8	2	3	22	0	.417	.564	.376
October	0	0	0	0	0	0	0	0	0	—	—	—
Totals	140	529	104	197	51	3	21	96	5	.434	.599	.372

EXAMPLE 1 Simplify Ratios

Simplify the ratio.

a. 60 cm : 200 cm

b. $\dfrac{3 \text{ ft}}{18 \text{ in.}}$

Solution

a. 60 cm : 200 cm can be written as the fraction $\dfrac{60 \text{ cm}}{200 \text{ cm}}$.

$$\frac{60 \text{ cm}}{200 \text{ cm}} = \frac{60 \div 20}{200 \div 20}$$ Divide numerator and denominator by their greatest common factor, 20.

$$= \frac{3}{10}$$ Simplify. $\frac{3}{10}$ is read as "3 to 10."

b. $\dfrac{3 \text{ ft}}{18 \text{ in.}} = \dfrac{3 \cdot 12 \text{ in.}}{18 \text{ in.}}$ Substitute 12 in. for 1 ft.

$$= \frac{36 \text{ in.}}{18 \text{ in.}}$$ Multiply.

$$= \frac{36 \div 18}{18 \div 18}$$ Divide numerator and denominator by their greatest common factor, 18.

$$= \frac{2}{1}$$ Simplify. $\frac{2}{1}$ is read as "2 to 1."

Student Help

STUDY TIP
Before you simplify a ratio, make sure that the quantities in the numerator and denominator are measured in the same units.

EXAMPLE 2 Use Ratios

In the diagram, $AB : BC$ is $4 : 1$ and $AC = 30$. Find AB and BC.

Solution

Let $x = BC$. Because the ratio of AB to BC is 4 to 1, you know that $AB = 4x$.

$AB + BC = AC$	Segment Addition Postulate
$4x + x = 30$	Substitute $4x$ for AB, x for BC, and 30 for AC.
$5x = 30$	Add like terms.
$x = 6$	Divide each side by 5.

To find AB and BC, substitute 6 for x.

$$AB = 4x = 4 \cdot 6 = 24 \qquad\qquad BC = x = 6$$

ANSWER ▶ So, $AB = 24$ and $BC = 6$.

EXAMPLE 3 Use Ratios

The perimeter of a rectangle is 80 feet. The ratio of the length to the width is $7 : 3$. Find the length and the width of the rectangle.

Solution

The ratio of length to width is 7 to 3. You can let the length $\ell = 7x$ and the width $w = 3x$.

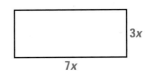

Student Help

SKILLS REVIEW
To review the formula for the perimeter of a rectangle, see p. 674.

$2\ell + 2w = P$	Formula for the perimeter of a rectangle
$2(7x) + 2(3x) = 80$	Substitute $7x$ for ℓ, $3x$ for w, and 80 for P.
$14x + 6x = 80$	Multiply.
$20x = 80$	Add like terms.
$x = 4$	Divide each side by 20.

To find the length and width of the rectangle, substitute 4 for x.

$$\ell = 7x = 7 \cdot 4 = 28 \qquad\qquad w = 3x = 3 \cdot 4 = 12$$

ANSWER ▶ The length is 28 feet, and the width is 12 feet.

Checkpoint ✓ Use Ratios

1. In the diagram, $EF : FG$ is $2 : 1$ and $EG = 24$. Find EF and FG.

2. The perimeter of a rectangle is 84 feet. The ratio of the length to the width is $4 : 3$. Find the length and the width of the rectangle.

means

$$a : b = c : d$$

extremes

The **means** are the inner terms, *b* and *c*, and the **extremes** are the outer terms, *a* and *d*.

Solving Proportions An equation that states that two ratios are equal is called a **proportion** .

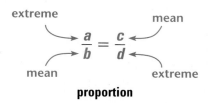

extreme

mean

$$\frac{a}{b} = \frac{c}{d}$$

mean

extreme

proportion

The numbers *b* and *c* are the **means** of the proportion. The numbers *a* and *d* are the **extremes** of the proportion. You can solve a proportion using the *cross product property*.

CROSS PRODUCT PROPERTY

Words In a proportion, the product of the extremes is equal to the product of the means.

$$ad = bc$$

$$\frac{a}{b} \times \frac{c}{d}$$

Symbols If $\frac{a}{b} = \frac{c}{d}$, then $ad = bc$.

Using Algebra

EXAMPLE 4 Solve a Proportion

Solve the proportion $\frac{5}{3} = \frac{y + 2}{6}$.

Solution

$\dfrac{5}{3} = \dfrac{y + 2}{6}$	Write original proportion.
$5 \cdot 6 = 3(y + 2)$	Cross product property
$30 = 3y + 6$	Multiply and use distributive property.
$30 - 6 = 3y + 6 - 6$	Subtract 6 from each side.
$24 = 3y$	Simplify.
$\dfrac{24}{3} = \dfrac{3y}{3}$	Divide each side by 3.
$8 = y$	Simplify.

CHECK ✓ Check your solution by substituting 8 for *y*.

$$\frac{y + 2}{6} = \frac{8 + 2}{6} = \frac{10}{6} = \frac{5}{3}$$

Checkpoint ✓ **Solve a Proportion**

Solve the proportion.

3. $\dfrac{3}{x} = \dfrac{6}{8}$ **4.** $\dfrac{5}{3} = \dfrac{15}{y}$ **5.** $\dfrac{m + 2}{5} = \dfrac{14}{10}$

EXAMPLE **5** **Write and Solve a Proportion**

Use the map of Texas to estimate the distance between Dallas and Houston.

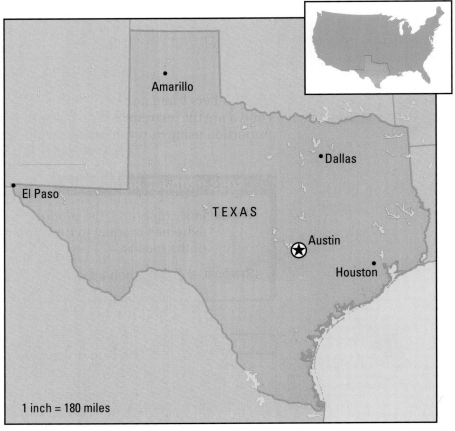

1 inch = 180 miles

Solution

From the scale on the map, you know that 1 inch represents 180 miles.

On the map, the distance between Dallas and Houston is $1\frac{1}{4}$ inches, which can be written as 1.25 inches.

Let x represent the actual distance between Dallas and Houston. You can write the following proportion.

$$\frac{1 \text{ in.}}{180 \text{ mi}} = \frac{1.25 \text{ in.}}{x \text{ mi}} \qquad \text{Write a proportion.}$$

$$1 \cdot x = 180 \cdot 1.25 \qquad \text{Cross product property}$$

$$x = 225 \qquad \text{Simplify.}$$

ANSWER ▶ The distance between Dallas and Houston is about 225 miles.

Checkpoint ✓ **Write and Solve a Proportion**

Use the map of Texas and a ruler to estimate the distance between the two cities.

6. El Paso and Amarillo   **7.** Houston and Austin

Guided Practice

Vocabulary Check

1. Give an example of a *ratio*.

2. Identify the *means* and the *extremes* of the proportion $\frac{a}{b} = \frac{3}{4}$.

Skill Check

In Exercises 3–6, simplify the ratio.

3. $\frac{12 \text{ m}}{10 \text{ m}}$

4. $\frac{21 \text{ pencils}}{35 \text{ pencils}}$

5. $\frac{2 \text{ years}}{8 \text{ months}}$

6. $\frac{2 \text{ yd}}{16 \text{ ft}}$

7. In the diagram, $FG : GH = 4 : 3$ and $FH = 56$. Find FG and GH.

8. The perimeter of a rectangle is 27. The ratio of the length to the width is $2 : 1$. Find the length and width of the rectangle.

Solve the proportion.

9. $\frac{x}{2} = \frac{5}{10}$

10. $\frac{3}{t} = \frac{12}{20}$

11. $\frac{8}{5} = \frac{24}{y}$

12. $\frac{x+1}{3} = \frac{14}{21}$

Practice and Applications

Extra Practice
See p. 687.

Writing Ratios A track team won 8 meets and lost 2. Find the ratio.

13. wins to losses

14. wins to the number of track meets

15. losses to wins

16. losses to the number of track meets

Simplifying Ratios Simplify the ratio.

17. $\frac{16 \text{ lb}}{2 \text{ lb}}$

18. $\frac{14 \text{ in.}}{42 \text{ in.}}$

19. $\frac{35 \text{ mi}}{12 \text{ mi}}$

20. $\frac{6 \text{ days}}{4 \text{ weeks}}$

21. $\frac{3 \text{ ft}}{12 \text{ in.}}$

22. $\frac{6 \text{ yd}}{10 \text{ ft}}$

23. $\frac{60 \text{ cm}}{1 \text{ m}}$

24. $\frac{400 \text{ m}}{0.5 \text{ km}}$

Homework Help

Example 1: Exs. 13–31
Example 2: Exs. 32–34
Example 3: Exs. 35–37
Example 4: Exs. 38–45
Example 5: Exs. 47–53

Finding Ratios Find the ratio of the length to the width of the rectangle. Then simplify the ratio.

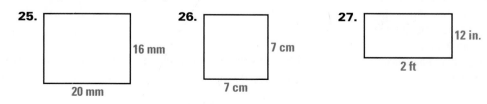

25. 16 mm 20 mm

26. 7 cm 7 cm

27. 12 in. 2 ft

Finding Ratios Use the number line to find the ratio of the segment lengths.

28. $AB:CD$ **29.** $BD:CF$ **30.** $BF:AD$ **31.** $CF:AB$

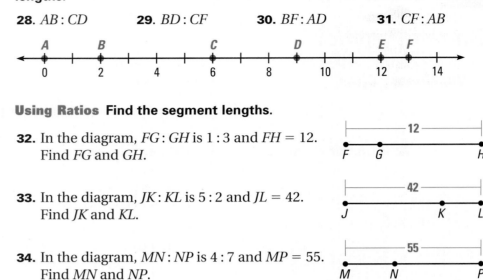

Using Ratios Find the segment lengths.

32. In the diagram, $FG:GH$ is $1:3$ and $FH=12$. Find FG and GH.

33. In the diagram, $JK:KL$ is $5:2$ and $JL=42$. Find JK and KL.

34. In the diagram, $MN:NP$ is $4:7$ and $MP=55$. Find MN and NP.

Using Ratios Sketch the rectangle described and label its sides using Example 3 as a model. Then find the length and the width of the rectangle.

35. The perimeter of a rectangle is 110 inches. The ratio of the length to the width is $4:1$.

36. The perimeter of a rectangle is 84 feet. The ratio of the width to the length is $2:5$.

37. The perimeter of a rectangle is 132 meters. The ratio of the length to the width is $8:3$.

Using Algebra In Exercises 38–45, solve the proportion.

38. $\dfrac{1}{2}=\dfrac{x}{22}$ **39.** $\dfrac{6}{a}=\dfrac{2}{5}$ **40.** $\dfrac{9}{4}=\dfrac{36}{z}$ **41.** $\dfrac{b}{35}=\dfrac{8}{5}$

42. $\dfrac{r+7}{60}=\dfrac{4}{15}$ **43.** $\dfrac{s-1}{6}=\dfrac{1}{2}$ **44.** $\dfrac{5}{3}=\dfrac{t+8}{18}$ **45.** $\dfrac{12}{5x-3}=\dfrac{6}{11}$

46. Challenge Solve the proportion $\dfrac{x}{4}=\dfrac{25}{x}$.

Babe Ruth's Bat A sculpture of Babe Ruth's 35-inch bat is 120 feet long. Round your answers to the nearest tenth of an inch.

47. How long is the sculpture in inches?

48. The diameter of the sculpture near the base is 9 feet. Estimate the corresponding diameter of Babe Ruth's bat.

49. The diameter of the handle of the sculpture is 3.5 feet. Estimate the diameter of the handle of Babe Ruth's bat.

Link to
Sculpture

BABE RUTH'S BAT
A free-standing sculpture patterned after Babe Ruth's bat stands outside a sports museum in Louisville, Kentucky.

Student Help

CLASSZONE.COM

HOMEWORK HELP

Extra help with problem solving in Exs. 50–53 is at classzone.com

Using a Map Use the map of North Carolina and a ruler to estimate the distance between the two cities.

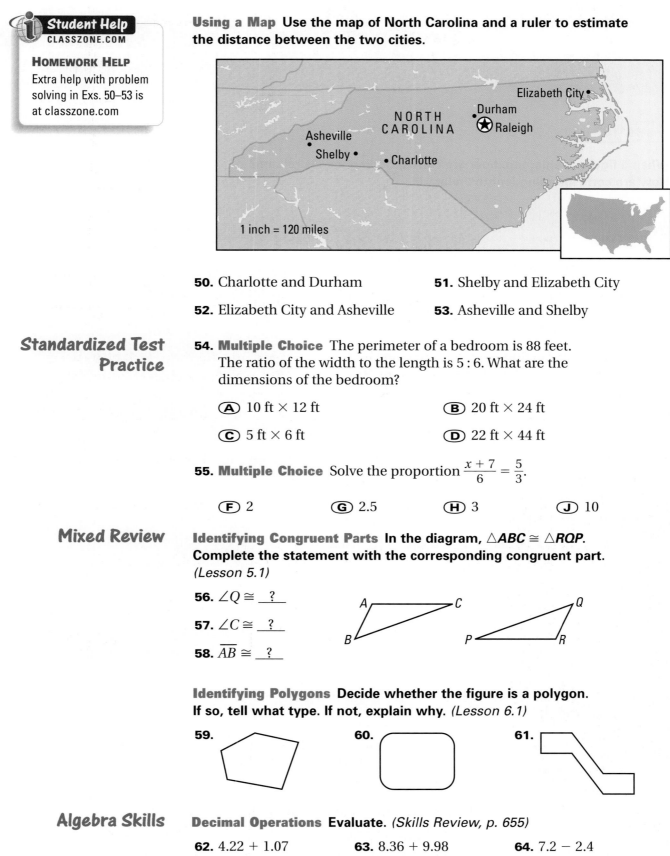

1 inch = 120 miles

50. Charlotte and Durham

51. Shelby and Elizabeth City

52. Elizabeth City and Asheville

53. Asheville and Shelby

Standardized Test Practice

54. Multiple Choice The perimeter of a bedroom is 88 feet. The ratio of the width to the length is 5 : 6. What are the dimensions of the bedroom?

(A) 10 ft × 12 ft (B) 20 ft × 24 ft

(C) 5 ft × 6 ft (D) 22 ft × 44 ft

55. Multiple Choice Solve the proportion $\frac{x+7}{6} = \frac{5}{3}$.

(F) 2 (G) 2.5 (H) 3 (J) 10

Mixed Review

Identifying Congruent Parts In the diagram, $\triangle ABC \cong \triangle RQP$. Complete the statement with the corresponding congruent part. *(Lesson 5.1)*

56. $\angle Q \cong$ _?_

57. $\angle C \cong$ _?_

58. $\overline{AB} \cong$ _?_

Identifying Polygons Decide whether the figure is a polygon. If so, tell what type. If not, explain why. *(Lesson 6.1)*

59. **60.** **61.**

Algebra Skills

Decimal Operations Evaluate. *(Skills Review, p. 655)*

62. $4.22 + 1.07$ **63.** $8.36 + 9.98$ **64.** $7.2 - 2.4$

65. 3.5×5.6 **66.** $7.35 \div 0.15$ **67.** $15.12 \div 1.26$

Activity 7.2 Conjectures About Similarity

Question

When a figure is enlarged, how are corresponding angles related?
How are corresponding lengths related?

Materials

- ruler
- calculator
- protractor

Explore

Photo 1 is an enlargement of Photo 2.

1 Use a ruler to find the length of $\overline{AB}$ in each photo.
Then use a calculator to find the ratio of AB in
Photo 1 to AB in Photo 2. Round to the nearest tenth.

2 Use a protractor to find $m\angle 1$ in each photo.
Then find the ratio of $m\angle 1$ in Photo 1 to $m\angle 1$
in Photo 2.

3 Continue finding measurements in the photos
and record your results in a table like the one
shown below.

Photo 1

Measurement	Photo 1	Photo 2	Ratio
AB	6 cm	5 cm	1.2
AF	?	?	?
CD	?	?	?
$m\angle 1$	?	?	?
$m\angle 2$	?	?	?

Photo 2

Student Help

LOOK BACK
For help measuring
segments and angles,
see pp. 28 and 36.

Think About It

1. Make a conjecture about the relationship between corresponding
   lengths when a figure is enlarged.

2. Make a conjecture about the relationship between corresponding
   angles when a figure is enlarged.

3. Suppose an angle in Photo 2 has a measure of 35°. What is the
   measure of the corresponding angle in Photo 1?

4. **Extension** Suppose a segment in Photo 1 is 5 centimeters long.
   What is the measure of the corresponding segment in Photo 2?

7.2 Similar Polygons

Goal

Identify similar polygons.

Key Words

- similar polygons
- scale factor

In geometry, two figures that have the same shape are called *similar*.

Two polygons are **similar polygons** if corresponding angles are congruent and corresponding side lengths are proportional.

In the diagram, *ABCD* is similar to *EFGH*. The symbol ~ indicates similarity. So, you can write *ABCD* ~ *EFGH*. When you refer to similar polygons, list their corresponding vertices in the same order.

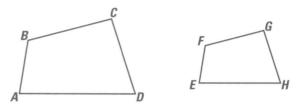

ABCD ~ EFGH

Corresponding Angles	Ratios of Corresponding Sides
$\angle A \cong \angle E$	$\dfrac{EF}{AB} = \dfrac{FG}{BC} = \dfrac{GH}{CD} = \dfrac{HE}{DA}$
$\angle B \cong \angle F$	
$\angle C \cong \angle G$	
$\angle D \cong \angle H$	

Student Help

VOCABULARY TIP
$\triangle PRQ \sim \triangle STU$ is called a *similarity statement.*

EXAMPLE 1 Use Similarity Statements

$\triangle PRQ \sim \triangle STU$.

a. List all pairs of congruent angles.

b. Write the ratios of the corresponding sides in a statement of proportionality.

c. Check that the ratios of corresponding sides are equal.

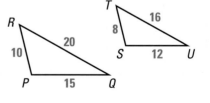

Solution

a. $\angle P \cong \angle S$, $\angle R \cong \angle T$, and $\angle Q \cong \angle U$.

b. $\dfrac{ST}{PR} = \dfrac{TU}{RQ} = \dfrac{US}{QP}$

c. $\dfrac{ST}{PR} = \dfrac{8}{10} = \dfrac{4}{5}$, $\dfrac{TU}{RQ} = \dfrac{16}{20} = \dfrac{4}{5}$, and $\dfrac{US}{QP} = \dfrac{12}{15} = \dfrac{4}{5}$.

The ratios of corresponding sides are all equal to $\dfrac{4}{5}$.

Scale Factor If two polygons are similar, then the ratio of the lengths of two corresponding sides is called the **scale factor** .

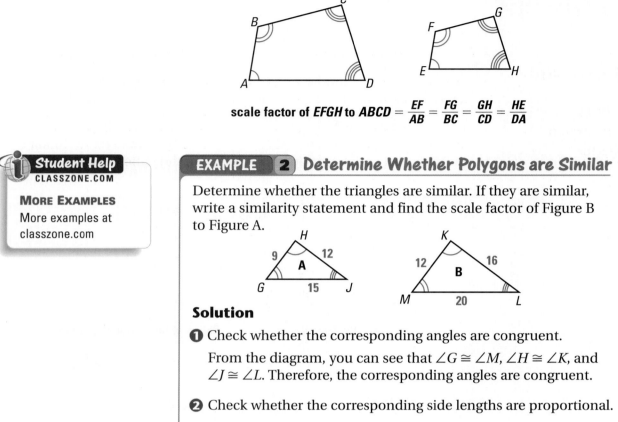

scale factor of *EFGH* to *ABCD* = $\dfrac{EF}{AB}$ = $\dfrac{FG}{BC}$ = $\dfrac{GH}{CD}$ = $\dfrac{HE}{DA}$

Student Help
CLASSZONE.COM

MORE EXAMPLES
More examples at classzone.com

EXAMPLE 2 Determine Whether Polygons are Similar

Determine whether the triangles are similar. If they are similar, write a similarity statement and find the scale factor of Figure B to Figure A.

Solution

❶ Check whether the corresponding angles are congruent.

From the diagram, you can see that $\angle G \cong \angle M$, $\angle H \cong \angle K$, and $\angle J \cong \angle L$. Therefore, the corresponding angles are congruent.

❷ Check whether the corresponding side lengths are proportional.

$$\frac{MK}{GH} = \frac{12}{9} = \frac{12 \div 3}{9 \div 3} = \frac{4}{3}$$

$$\frac{KL}{HJ} = \frac{16}{12} = \frac{16 \div 4}{12 \div 4} = \frac{4}{3}$$

All three ratios are equal, so the corresponding side lengths are proportional.

$$\frac{LM}{JG} = \frac{20}{15} = \frac{20 \div 5}{15 \div 5} = \frac{4}{3}$$

ANSWER ▶ By definition, the triangles are similar. $\triangle GHJ \sim \triangle MKL$.

The scale factor of Figure A is $\dfrac{4}{3}$.

Checkpoint ✓ *Determine Whether Polygons are Similar*

Determine whether the polygons are similar. If they are similar, write a similarity statement and find the scale factor of Figure B to Figure A.

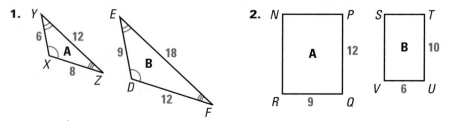

EXAMPLE 3 Use Similar Polygons

$\triangle RST \sim \triangle GHJ$.
Find the value of x.

Student Help

STUDY TIP
You can find x using other proportions that include TR. Another proportion you can use is $\dfrac{ST}{HJ} = \dfrac{TR}{JG}$.

Solution

Because the triangles are similar, the corresponding side lengths are proportional. To find the value of x, you can use the following proportion.

$\dfrac{GH}{RS} = \dfrac{JG}{TR}$ Write proportion.

$\dfrac{15}{10} = \dfrac{9}{x}$ Substitute 15 for GH, 10 for RS, 9 for JG, and x for TR.

$15 \cdot x = 10 \cdot 9$ Cross product property

$15x = 90$ Multiply.

$\dfrac{15x}{15} = \dfrac{90}{15}$ Divide each side by 15.

$x = 6$ Simplify.

EXAMPLE 4 Perimeters of Similar Polygons

The outlines of a pool and the patio around the pool are similar rectangles.

a. Find the ratio of the length of the patio to the length of the pool.

b. Find the ratio of the perimeter of the patio to the perimeter of the pool.

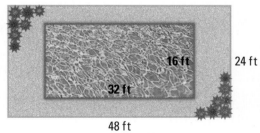

Solution

a. The ratio of the length of the patio to the length of the pool is

$$\frac{\text{length of patio}}{\text{length of pool}} = \frac{48 \text{ feet}}{32 \text{ feet}} = \frac{48 \div 16}{32 \div 16} = \frac{3}{2}.$$

b. The perimeter of the patio is $2(24) + 2(48) = 144$ feet.

The perimeter of the pool is $2(16) + 2(32) = 96$ feet.

The ratio of the perimeter of the patio to the perimeter of the pool is

$$\frac{\text{perimeter of patio}}{\text{perimeter of pool}} = \frac{144 \text{ feet}}{96 \text{ feet}} = \frac{144 \div 48}{96 \div 48} = \frac{3}{2}.$$

In Example 4 on the previous page, notice that the ratio of the perimeters of the similar figures is equal to the ratio of the side lengths. This observation is generalized in the following theorem.

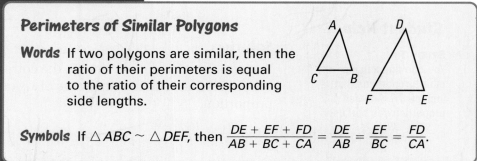

THEOREM 7.1

Perimeters of Similar Polygons

Words If two polygons are similar, then the ratio of their perimeters is equal to the ratio of their corresponding side lengths.

Symbols If $\triangle ABC \sim \triangle DEF$, then $\dfrac{DE + EF + FD}{AB + BC + CA} = \dfrac{DE}{AB} = \dfrac{EF}{BC} = \dfrac{FD}{CA}$.

Checkpoint ✓ *Use Similar Polygons*

In the diagram, $\triangle PQR \sim \triangle STU$.

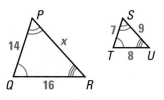

3. Find the value of x.

4. Find the ratio of the perimeter of $\triangle STU$ to the perimeter of $\triangle PQR$.

7.2 Exercises

Guided Practice

Vocabulary Check

1. If two triangles are *congruent*, must they be *similar*? Explain.

2. If two triangles are *similar*, must they be *congruent*? Explain.

Skill Check

In Exercises 3–6, $\triangle ABC \sim \triangle LMN$.

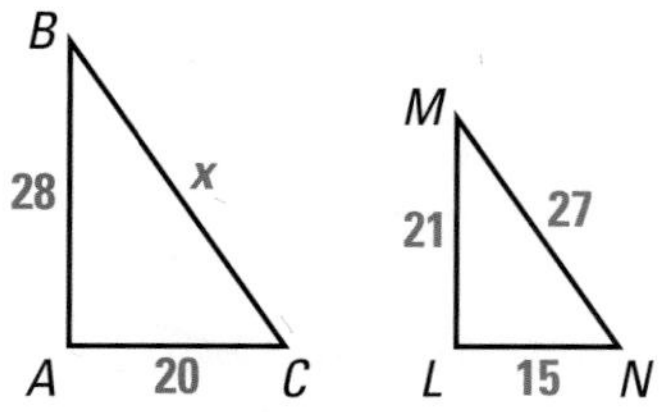

3. List all pairs of congruent angles.

4. Write the ratios of the corresponding sides in a statement of proportionality.

5. Find the scale factor of $\triangle LMN$ to $\triangle ABC$.

6. Find the value of x.

7. Are the two rectangles shown at the right similar? Explain your reasoning.

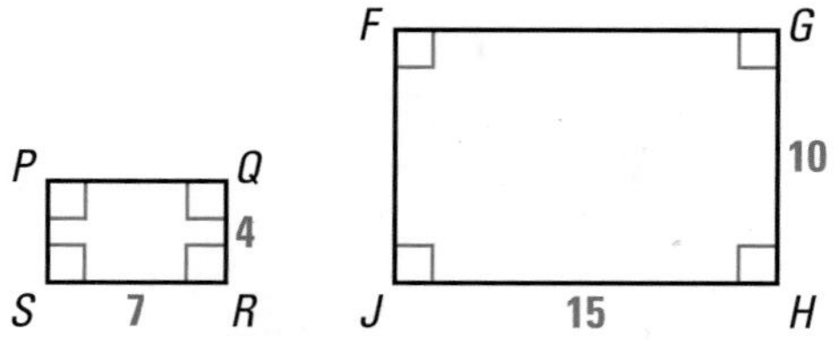

Practice and Applications

Extra Practice
See p. 687.

Using Similarity Statements List all pairs of congruent angles. Then write the ratios of the corresponding sides in a statement of proportionality.

8. △PQR ~ △DEF

9. ABCDE ~ QRSTU

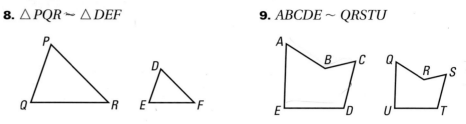

10. Error Analysis △FGH ~ △JKL. A student was asked to list all pairs of congruent angles and write the ratios of the corresponding sides in a statement of proportionality. Copy the diagram and correct the student's errors.

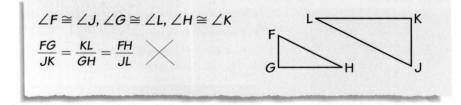

∠F ≅ ∠J, ∠G ≅ ∠L, ∠H ≅ ∠K

$$\frac{FG}{JK} = \frac{KL}{GH} = \frac{FH}{JL}$$

Determining Similarity Determine whether the polygons are similar. If they are similar, write a similarity statement and find the scale factor of Figure B to Figure A.

11.

12.

13.

14.

15.

16.

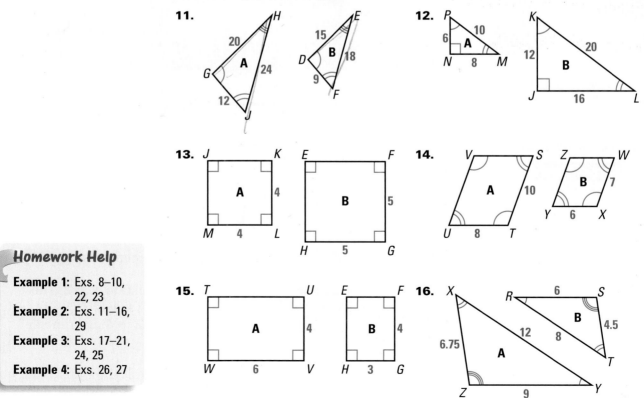

Homework Help

Example 1: Exs. 8–10, 22, 23
Example 2: Exs. 11–16, 29
Example 3: Exs. 17–21, 24, 25
Example 4: Exs. 26, 27

Using Similar Polygons The two polygons are similar. Find the values of *x* and *y*.

17.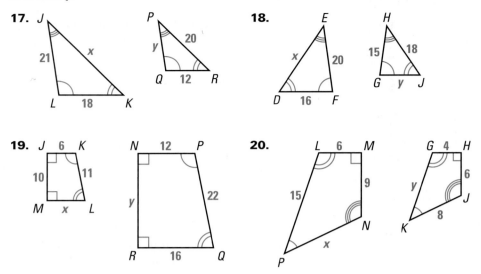

18.

19.

20.

21. **Mural** Alejandro Romero created the mural, *Chicago Federation of Labor*, by enlarging the 56 in. by 21 in. sketch shown below. Romero used a scale factor of about 3.5. What are the dimensions of the mural in inches? In feet?

Using Similar Polygons In Exercises 22–26, use the diagram below, where *FGHJ* ~ *KLMN*.

22. Find $m\angle N$.

23. Find $m\angle F$.

24. Find the value of *x*.

25. Find the value of *y*.

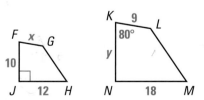

26. Find the ratio of the perimeter of *KLMN* to the perimeter of *FGHJ*.

27. **Perimeters of Similar Polygons** $\triangle QRS$ is similar to $\triangle XYZ$. The ratio of one side of $\triangle XYZ$ to the corresponding side of $\triangle QRS$ is 6 : 7. What is the ratio of the perimeter of $\triangle XYZ$ to the perimeter of $\triangle QRS$?

28. **Challenge** $\triangle JKL$ is similar to $\triangle STU$. The ratio of *ST* to *JK* is 5 to 2. The perimeter of $\triangle STU$ is 35 feet. Find the perimeter of $\triangle JKL$.

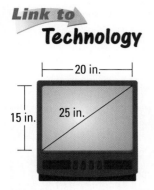
29. Television Screens The *aspect ratio* of a television screen is the length-to-width ratio of the screen. A standard definition television has an aspect ratio of 4 : 3. A high definition projection television has an aspect ratio of 16 : 9. Are the television screens similar rectangles?

EXAMPLE *Logical Reasoning*

Are two isosceles trapezoids *always, sometimes,* or *never* similar?

Solution

It is possible to sketch two similar isosceles trapezoids.

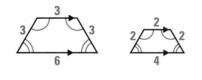

It is also possible to sketch two isosceles trapezoids that are *not* similar.

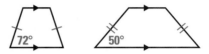

ANSWER ▶ Therefore, two isosceles trapezoids are sometimes similar.

Logical Reasoning **Are the polygons *always, sometimes,* or *never* similar?**

30. Two isosceles triangles

31. Two rhombuses

32. Two equilateral triangles

33. A right and an isosceles triangle

Standardized Test Practice

34. Multiple Choice $\triangle DEF \sim \triangle MNP$. Which statement may be *false*?

(A) $\angle E \cong \angle N$

(B) $\angle P \cong \angle D$

(C) $\dfrac{MN}{DE} = \dfrac{NP}{EF}$

(D) $\dfrac{MN}{DE} = \dfrac{PM}{FD}$

Mixed Review

Showing Triangles are Congruent Does the diagram give enough information to show that the triangles are congruent? If so, state the postulate or theorem you would use. *(Lessons 5.3, 5.4)*

35. **36.** **37.**

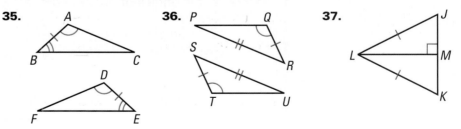

Algebra Skills

Writing Equivalent Fractions Write two equivalent fractions.
(Skills Review, p. 656)

38. $\dfrac{1}{3}$ **39.** $\dfrac{2}{5}$ **40.** $\dfrac{4}{7}$ **41.** $\dfrac{9}{4}$

Goal

Show that two triangles are similar using the AA Similarity Postulate.

Key Words

• similar polygons p. 365

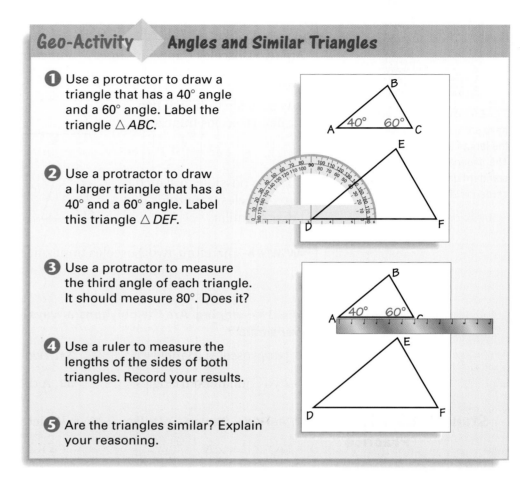

Geo-Activity **Angles and Similar Triangles**

① Use a protractor to draw a triangle that has a 40° angle and a 60° angle. Label the triangle △ABC.

② Use a protractor to draw a larger triangle that has a 40° and a 60° angle. Label this triangle △DEF.

③ Use a protractor to measure the third angle of each triangle. It should measure 80°. Does it?

④ Use a ruler to measure the lengths of the sides of both triangles. Record your results.

⑤ Are the triangles similar? Explain your reasoning.

POSTULATE 15

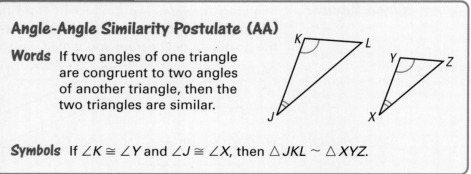

Angle-Angle Similarity Postulate (AA)

Words If two angles of one triangle are congruent to two angles of another triangle, then the two triangles are similar.

Symbols If ∠K ≅ ∠Y and ∠J ≅ ∠X, then △JKL ∼ △XYZ.

This postulate allows you to say that two triangles are similar if you know that two pairs of angles are congruent. In other words, you don't need to compare all of the side lengths and angle measures to show that two triangles are similar.

Visualize It!

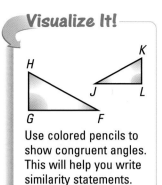

Use colored pencils to show congruent angles. This will help you write similarity statements.

EXAMPLE **1** **Use the AA Similarity Postulate**

Determine whether the triangles are similar. If they are similar, write a similarity statement. Explain your reasoning.

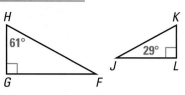

Solution

If two pairs of angles are congruent, then the triangles are similar.

❶ $\angle G \cong \angle L$ because they are both marked as right angles.

❷ Find $m\angle F$ to determine whether $\angle F$ is congruent to $\angle J$.

$$m\angle F + 90° + 61° = 180° \qquad \text{Triangle Sum Theorem}$$
$$m\angle F + 151° = 180° \qquad \text{Add.}$$
$$m\angle F = 29° \qquad \text{Subtract 151° from each side.}$$

Both $\angle F$ and $\angle J$ measure 29°, so $\angle F \cong \angle J$.

ANSWER ▶ By the AA Similarity Postulate, $\triangle FGH \sim \triangle JLK$.

EXAMPLE **2** **Use the AA Similarity Postulate**

Are you given enough information to show that $\triangle RST$ is similar to $\triangle RUV$? Explain your reasoning.

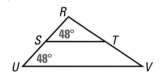

Student Help

VISUAL STRATEGY
Redraw overlapping triangles as two separate triangles, as shown on p. 356. ⋯⋯⋯⋯⋯▶

Solution

Redraw the diagram as two triangles: $\triangle RUV$ and $\triangle RST$.

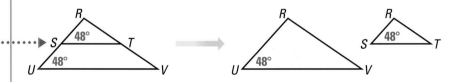

From the diagram, you know that both $\angle RST$ and $\angle RUV$ measure 48°, so $\angle RST \cong \angle RUV$. Also, $\angle R \cong \angle R$ by the Reflexive Property of Congruence. By the AA Similarity Postulate, $\triangle RST \sim \triangle RUV$.

Checkpoint ✓ *Use the AA Similarity Postulate*

Determine whether the triangles are similar. If they are similar, write a similarity statement.

1.

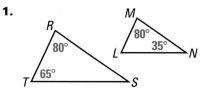

2.

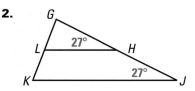

Using Algebra

EXAMPLE 3 Use Similar Triangles

A hockey player passes the puck to a teammate by bouncing the puck off the wall of the rink, as shown below. According to the laws of physics, the angles that the path of the puck makes with the wall are congruent. How far from the wall will the teammate pick up the pass?

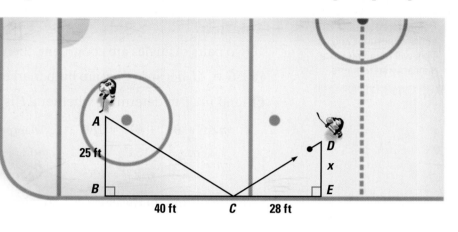

25 ft

40 ft   C   28 ft

Student Help

> **STUDY TIP**
> In problems like Example 3, you must show that the triangles are similar before you can write and solve the proportion. ·············

Solution

From the diagram, you know that $\angle B \cong \angle E$. From the laws of physics given in the problem, $\angle ACB \cong \angle DCE$. Therefore, $\triangle ABC \sim \triangle DEC$ by the AA Similarity Postulate.

$\dfrac{DE}{AB} = \dfrac{EC}{BC}$ Write a proportion.

$\dfrac{x}{25} = \dfrac{28}{40}$ Substitute x for DE, 25 for AB, 28 for EC, and 40 for BC.

$x \cdot 40 = 25 \cdot 28$ Cross product property

$40x = 700$ Multiply.

$\dfrac{40x}{40} = \dfrac{700}{40}$ Divide each side by 40.

$x = 17.5$ Simplify.

ANSWER ▶ The teammate will pick up the pass 17.5 feet from the wall.

Checkpoint ✓ **Use Similar Triangles**

Write a similarity statement for the triangles. Then find the value of the variable.

3.

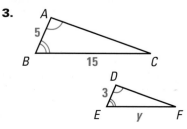

4.

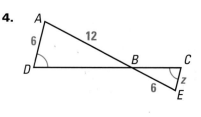

Guided Practice

Vocabulary Check

1. Complete the statement: If two angles of one triangle are congruent to two angles of another triangle, then __?__.

Skill Check

Determine whether the triangles are similar. If they are similar, write a similarity statement. Explain your reasoning.

2.

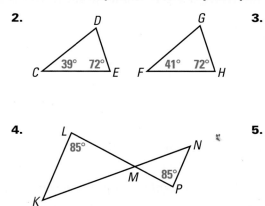

3.

4.

5.

6. Write a similarity statement for the triangles. Then find the value of *x*.

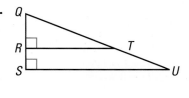

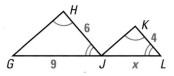

Practice and Applications

Extra Practice

See p. 687.

Using the AA Similarity Postulate Determine whether the triangles are similar. If they are similar, write a similarity statement.

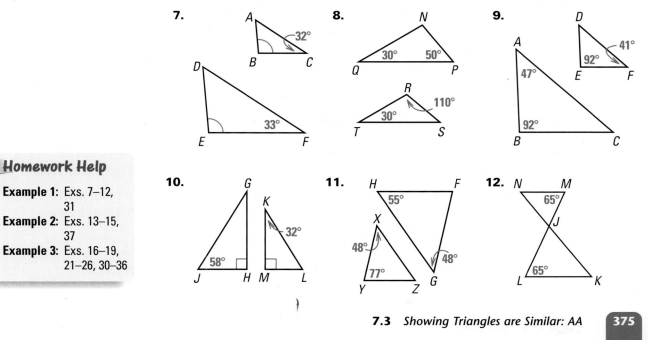

7.

8.

9.

Homework Help

Example 1: Exs. 7–12, 31

Example 2: Exs. 13–15, 37

Example 3: Exs. 16–19, 21–26, 30–36

10.

11.

12.

Using the AA Similarity Postulate Determine whether you can show that the triangles are similar. If they are similar, write a similarity statement. Explain your reasoning.

13.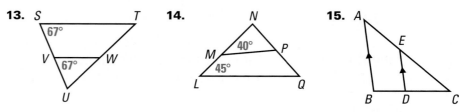

14.

15.

Similar Triangles Use the diagram to complete the statement.

16. $\triangle PQR \sim$ ___?___

17. $\dfrac{LM}{PQ} = \dfrac{?}{QR}$

18. $\dfrac{12}{y} = \dfrac{15}{?}$

19. $y =$ ___?___

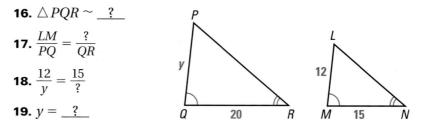

20. The scale factor of $\triangle LMN$ to $\triangle PQR$ is ___?___.

Student Help

CLASSZONE.COM

HOMEWORK HELP

Extra help with problem solving in Exs. 21–26 is at classzone.com

Using Similar Triangles Find the value of the variable.

21.

22.

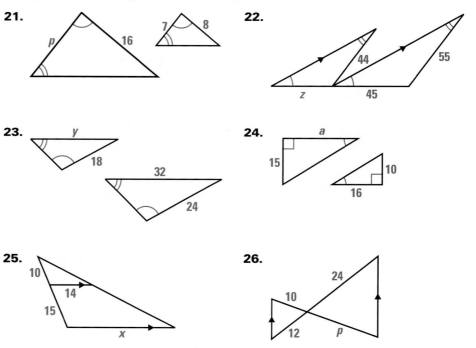

23.

24.

25.

26.

Logical Reasoning Decide whether the statement is *true* or *false*.

27. If an acute angle of a right triangle is congruent to an acute angle of another right triangle, then the triangles are similar.

28. Some equilateral triangles are not similar.

29. All isosceles triangles with a 40° vertex angle are similar.

Link to
Public Art

UNISPHERE The Unisphere at Flushing Meadow Park in New York is a stainless steel model of Earth. The Unisphere was built for the 1964–65 World's Fair.

Application Links
CLASSZONE.COM

30. Unisphere To estimate the height of the Unisphere, you place a mirror on the ground and stand where you can see the top of the model in the mirror, as shown in the diagram. Write and solve a proportion to estimate the height of the Unisphere.

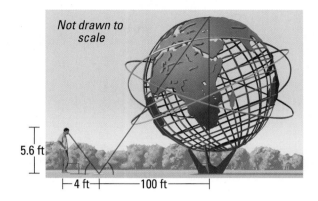

Not drawn to scale

5.6 ft

├─4 ft─┤ ├───100 ft───┤

Challenge *ABCD* is a trapezoid, *AB* = 8, *AE* = 6, *EC* = 15, and *DE* = 10. Complete the statement.

31. $\triangle ABE \sim$ ___?___

32. $\dfrac{AB}{?} = \dfrac{AE}{?} = \dfrac{BE}{?}$

33. $\dfrac{6}{?} = \dfrac{8}{?}$

34. $\dfrac{15}{?} = \dfrac{10}{?}$

35. $x =$ ___?___

36. $y =$ ___?___

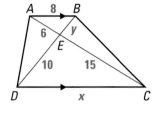

37. **You be the Judge** Meredith claims that the triangles shown at the right are similar. Brian thinks that they are not similar. Who is right? Explain your reasoning.

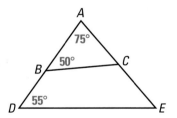

Standardized Test Practice

38. Multi-Step Problem Julia uses the shadow of a flagpole to estimate its height. She stands so that the tip of her shadow coincides with the tip of the flagpole's shadow as shown.

a. Explain why the two overlapping triangles in the diagram are similar.

b. Using the similar triangles, write a proportion that models the situation.

c. Solve the proportion to calculate the height of the flagpole.

5 ft

7 ft   28 ft

Mixed Review

Congruent Triangles In the diagram, $\triangle FGH \cong \triangle RST$. Complete the statement. *(Lesson 5.1)*

39. $m\angle F = $ _?_ °   **40.** $m\angle T = $ _?_ °

41. $\overline{GH} \cong $ _?_   **42.** $\triangle TSR \cong $ _?_

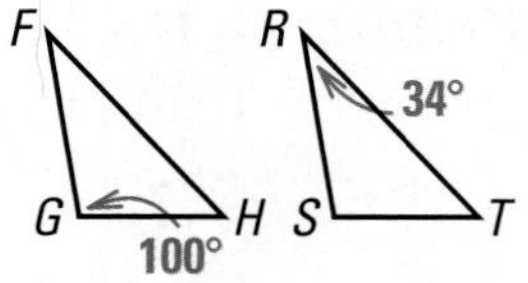

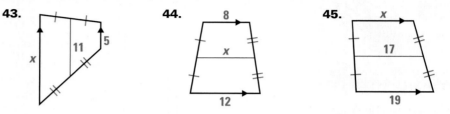

Trapezoid Midsegments Find the value of *x*. *(Lesson 6.5)*

43.   **44.**   **45.**

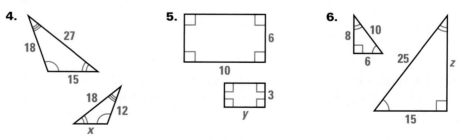

Algebra Skills

Plotting Points Plot the points in a coordinate plane. *(Skills Review, p. 664)*

46. $A(-4, 5)$ **47.** $B(-1, -3)$ **48.** $C(0, 7)$ **49.** $D(2, -6)$

50. $F(7, 2)$ **51.** $G(-8, -1)$ **52.** $J(7, -7)$ **53.** $K(-3, 3)$

Quiz 1

Solve the proportion. *(Lesson 7.1)*

1. $\dfrac{x}{16} = \dfrac{3}{4}$ **2.** $\dfrac{5}{8} = \dfrac{25}{y}$ **3.** $\dfrac{11}{2} = \dfrac{z+3}{6}$

The two polygons are similar. Find the value of the variable. *(Lesson 7.2)*

4.   **5.**   **6.**

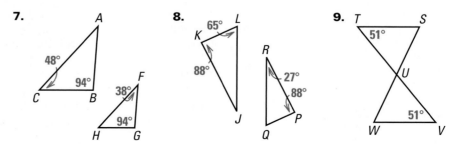

Determine whether the triangles are similar. If they are similar, write a similarity statement. Explain your reasoning. *(Lesson 7.3)*

7.   **8.**   **9.**

7.4 Showing Triangles are Similar: SSS and SAS

Goal

Show that two triangles are similar using the SSS and SAS Similarity Theorems.

Key Words

- similar polygons p. 365

The triangles in the Navajo rug look similar. To show that they are similar, you can use the definition of similar polygons or the AA Similarity Postulate.

In this lesson, you will learn two new methods to show that two triangles are similar.

THEOREM 7.2

Side-Side-Side Similarity Theorem (SSS)

Words If the corresponding sides of two triangles are proportional, then the triangles are similar.

Symbols If $\dfrac{FG}{AB} = \dfrac{GH}{BC} = \dfrac{HF}{CA}$, then $\triangle ABC \sim \triangle FGH$.

EXAMPLE 1 Use the SSS Similarity Theorem

Determine whether the triangles are similar. If they are similar, write a similarity statement and find the scale factor of Triangle B to Triangle A.

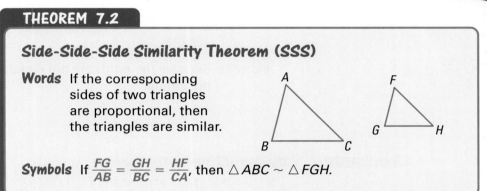

Solution

Find the ratios of the corresponding sides.

$$\frac{SU}{PR} = \frac{6}{12} = \frac{6 \div 6}{12 \div 6} = \frac{1}{2}$$

$$\frac{UT}{RQ} = \frac{5}{10} = \frac{5 \div 5}{10 \div 5} = \frac{1}{2}$$

$$\frac{TS}{QP} = \frac{4}{8} = \frac{4 \div 4}{8 \div 4} = \frac{1}{2}$$

All three ratios are equal. So, the corresponding sides of the triangles are proportional.

ANSWER ▶ By the SSS Similarity Theorem, $\triangle PQR \sim \triangle STU$.

The scale factor of Triangle B to Triangle A is $\frac{1}{2}$.

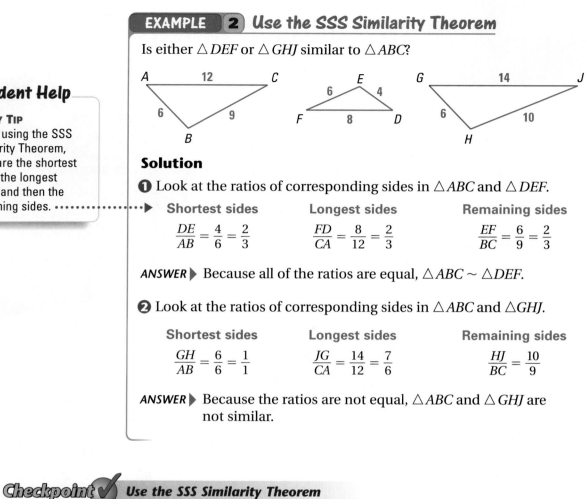

EXAMPLE 2 Use the SSS Similarity Theorem

Is either △DEF or △GHJ similar to △ABC?

Student Help

STUDY TIP
When using the SSS Similarity Theorem, compare the shortest sides, the longest sides, and then the remaining sides. ••••••••••••

Solution

❶ Look at the ratios of corresponding sides in △ABC and △DEF.

Shortest sides	Longest sides	Remaining sides
$\dfrac{DE}{AB} = \dfrac{4}{6} = \dfrac{2}{3}$	$\dfrac{FD}{CA} = \dfrac{8}{12} = \dfrac{2}{3}$	$\dfrac{EF}{BC} = \dfrac{6}{9} = \dfrac{2}{3}$

ANSWER ▶ Because all of the ratios are equal, △ABC ~ △DEF.

❷ Look at the ratios of corresponding sides in △ABC and △GHJ.

Shortest sides	Longest sides	Remaining sides
$\dfrac{GH}{AB} = \dfrac{6}{6} = \dfrac{1}{1}$	$\dfrac{JG}{CA} = \dfrac{14}{12} = \dfrac{7}{6}$	$\dfrac{HJ}{BC} = \dfrac{10}{9}$

ANSWER ▶ Because the ratios are not equal, △ABC and △GHJ are not similar.

Checkpoint ✓ Use the SSS Similarity Theorem

Determine whether the triangles are similar. If they are similar, write a similarity statement.

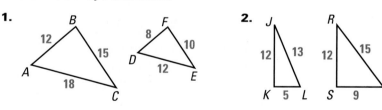

1.

2.

Student Help

LOOK BACK
To review included angles, see p. 242.

THEOREM 7.3

Side-Angle-Side Similarity Theorem (SAS)

Words If an angle of one triangle is congruent to an angle of a second triangle and the lengths of the sides that include these angles are proportional, then the triangles are similar.

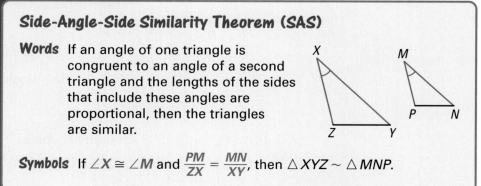

Symbols If $\angle X \cong \angle M$ and $\dfrac{PM}{ZX} = \dfrac{MN}{XY}$, then △XYZ ~ △MNP.

EXAMPLE 3 Use the SAS Similarity Theorem

Determine whether the triangles are similar. If they are similar, write a similarity statement.

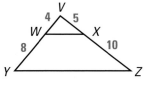

Solution

$\angle C$ and $\angle F$ both measure $61°$, so $\angle C \cong \angle F$.

Compare the ratios of the side lengths that include $\angle C$ and $\angle F$.

Shorter sides $\dfrac{DF}{AC} = \dfrac{5}{3}$ **Longer sides** $\dfrac{FE}{CB} = \dfrac{10}{6} = \dfrac{5}{3}$

The lengths of the sides that include $\angle C$ and $\angle F$ are proportional.

ANSWER ▶ By the SAS Similarity Theorem, $\triangle ABC \sim \triangle DEF$.

EXAMPLE 4 Similarity in Overlapping Triangles

Show that $\triangle VYZ \sim \triangle VWX$.

Student Help

VISUAL STRATEGY
Redraw overlapping triangles as two separate triangles, as shown on p. 356. ·········▶

Solution

Separate the triangles, $\triangle VYZ$ and $\triangle VWX$, and label the side lengths.

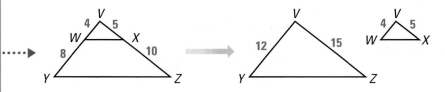

$\angle V \cong \angle V$ by the Reflexive Property of Congruence.

Shorter sides

$\dfrac{VW}{VY} = \dfrac{4}{4+8} = \dfrac{4}{12} = \dfrac{1}{3}$

Longer sides

$\dfrac{XV}{ZV} = \dfrac{5}{5+10} = \dfrac{5}{15} = \dfrac{1}{3}$

The lengths of the sides that include $\angle V$ are proportional.

ANSWER ▶ By the SAS Similarity Theorem, $\triangle VYZ \sim \triangle VWX$.

Checkpoint ✓ Use the SAS Similarity Theorem

Determine whether the triangles are similar. If they are similar, write a similarity statement. Explain your reasoning.

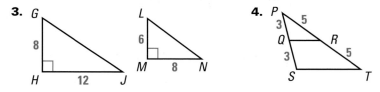

7.4 Exercises

Guided Practice

Vocabulary Check

1. If two sides of a triangle are proportional to two sides of another triangle, can you conclude that the triangles are similar?

Skill Check

In Exercises 2 and 3, determine whether the triangles are similar. If they are similar, write a similarity statement.

2.
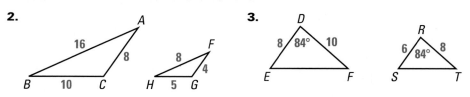

3.

4. Is either △ *LMN* or △ *XYZ* similar to △ *ABC*? Explain.

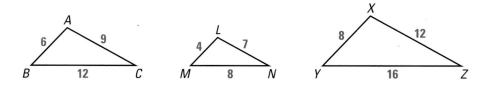

Practice and Applications

Extra Practice

See p. 688.

SSS Similarity Theorem Determine whether the two triangles are similar. If they are similar, write a similarity statement and find the scale factor of Triangle B to Triangle A.

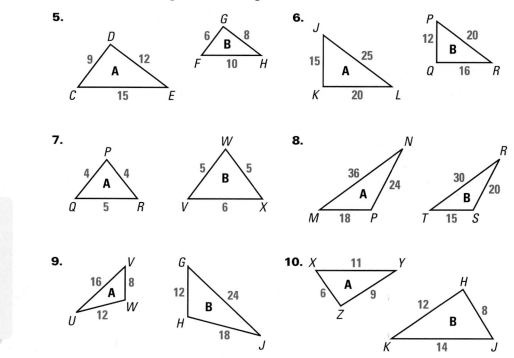

Homework Help

Example 1: Exs. 5–10, 21–26
Example 2: Exs. 11–13
Example 3: Exs. 14–18, 21–26
Example 4: Exs. 19, 20, 26–29

SSS Similarity Theorem Is either △ *RST* or △ *XYZ* similar to △ *ABC*? Explain your reasoning.

11.

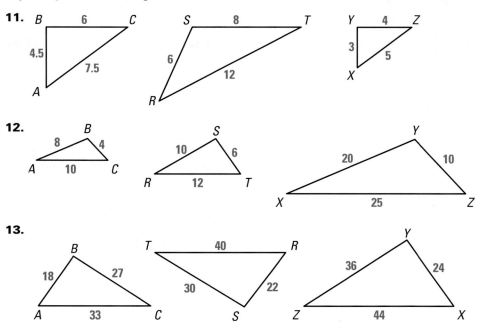

12.

13.

14. A-Frame Building Suppose you are constructing an A-frame home that is modeled after a ski lodge. The ski lodge and home are shown below. Are the triangles similar? Explain your reasoning.

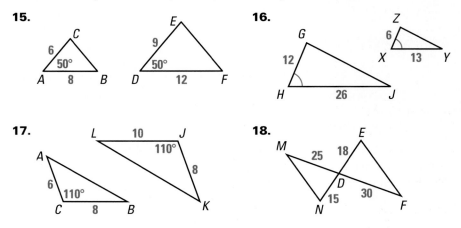

Student Help
CLASSZONE.COM

HOMEWORK HELP
Extra help with problem solving in Exs. 15–18 is at classzone.com

SAS Similarity Theorem Determine whether the two triangles are similar. If they are similar, write a similarity statement.

15.

16.

17.

18.

Overlapping Triangles Show that the overlapping triangles are similar. Then write a similarity statement.

19.

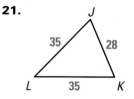

20.

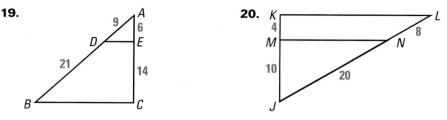

Determining Similarity Determine whether the triangles are similar. If they are similar, state the similarity and the postulate or theorem that justifies your answer.

21.

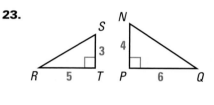

22.

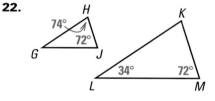

23.

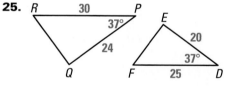

24.

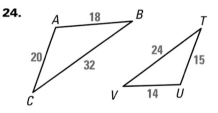

25.

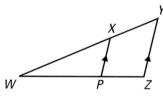

26.

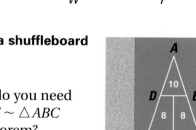

Shuffleboard In the portion of a shuffleboard court shown, $\dfrac{AD}{AB} = \dfrac{DE}{BC}$.

27. What piece of information do you need in order to show that $\triangle ADE \sim \triangle ABC$ using the SSS Similarity Theorem?

28. What piece of information do you need in order to show that $\triangle ADE \sim \triangle ABC$ using the SAS Similarity Theorem?

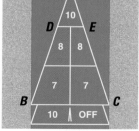

29. **You be the Judge** Jon claims that $\triangle SUV$ is similar to $\triangle SRT$ when $x = 6$. Dave believes that the triangles are similar when $x = 5$. Who is right? Explain your reasoning.

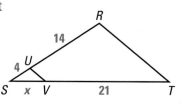

Technology In Exercises 30 and 31, use geometry software to complete the steps below.

❶ Draw △ABC.

❷ Construct a line perpendicular to $\overline{AB}$ through C. Label the intersection D.

❸ Measure $\overline{CA}$, $\overline{CD}$, $\overline{CB}$, and $\overline{BD}$.

❹ Calculate the ratios $\frac{CA}{CD}$ and $\frac{CB}{BD}$.

❺ Drag point C until $\frac{CA}{CD} = \frac{CB}{BD}$.

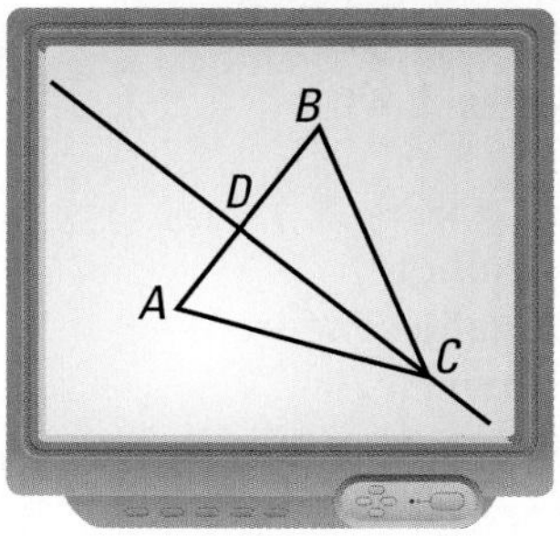

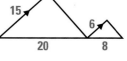

30. For what measure of ∠ACB are △ABC and △CBD similar?

31. What theorem supports your answer to Exercise 30?

Standardized Test Practice

32. Multiple Choice Which method can be used to show that the two triangles at the right are similar?

Ⓐ AA   Ⓑ SSS

Ⓒ SAS   Ⓓ Cannot be shown

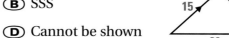

33. Multiple Choice In the diagram, △MNP ~ △RST. Find the value of x.

Ⓕ 20   Ⓖ 24

Ⓗ 30   Ⓙ 32

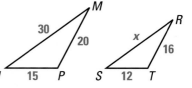

Mixed Review

Using Bisectors In the diagram below, $\overrightarrow{TV}$ bisects ∠STU. *(Lesson 5.6)*

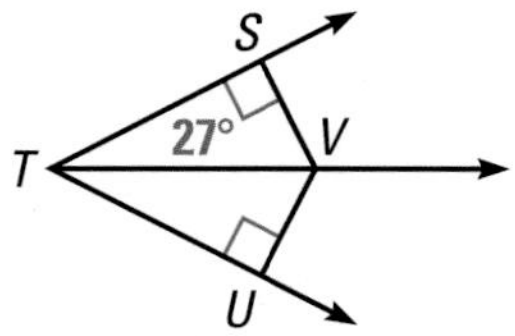

34. $\overline{ST} \cong$?

35. ∠VTU ≅ ?

36. m∠STU = ?

37. Is ∠TVS congruent to ∠TVU? Explain your reasoning.

Solving Proportions Solve the proportion. *(Lesson 7.1)*

38. $\frac{b}{12} = \frac{5}{6}$ **39.** $\frac{24}{y} = \frac{4}{9}$ **40.** $\frac{5}{8} = \frac{c}{56}$ **41.** $\frac{5}{2} = \frac{60}{a}$

Algebra Skills

Writing Decimals as Fractions Write the decimal as a fraction in simplest form. *(Skills Review, p. 657)*

42. 0.4   **43.** 0.25   **44.** 0.64   **45.** 0.88

46. 0.26   **47.** 0.55   **48.** 0.7   **49.** 0.34

7.5 Proportions and Similar Triangles

Goal

Use the Triangle Proportionality Theorem and its converse.

Key Words

• midsegment of a triangle

Geo-Activity — Investigating Proportional Segments

1 Draw a triangle. Label its vertices *A*, *B*, and *C*. Make sure that each side is at least 4 cm. Draw a point on $\overline{AB}$. Label the point *D*.

2 Draw a line through *D* parallel to $\overline{AC}$. Label the intersection of the line and $\overline{BC}$ as point *E*.

3 Measure $\overline{BD}$, $\overline{DA}$, $\overline{BE}$, and $\overline{EC}$ in centimeters. Then calculate the ratios $\dfrac{BD}{DA}$ and $\dfrac{BE}{EC}$.

4 Make a conjecture about the ratios of segment lengths of a triangle's sides when the triangle is cut by a line parallel to the triangle's third side.

Proportionality Suppose that a point *P* lies on $\overline{GH}$ and a point *Q* lies on $\overline{JK}$. If $\dfrac{GP}{PH} = \dfrac{JQ}{QK}$, then we say that $\overline{GH}$ and $\overline{JK}$ are *divided proportionally*.

In the Geo-Activity above, $\overline{DE}$ divides $\overline{AB}$ and $\overline{CB}$ proportionally.

THEOREM 7.4

Triangle Proportionality Theorem

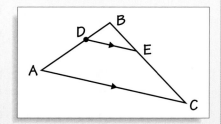

Words If a line parallel to one side of a triangle intersects the other two sides, then it divides the two sides proportionally.

Symbols In △ *QRS*, if $\overline{TU} \parallel \overline{QS}$, then $\dfrac{RT}{TQ} = \dfrac{RU}{US}$.

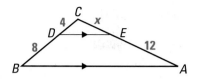

EXAMPLE 1 Find Segment Lengths

Find the value of x.

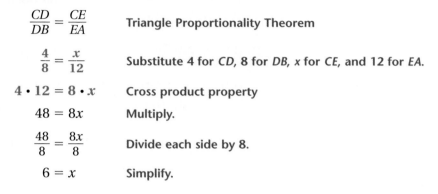

Solution

$\dfrac{CD}{DB} = \dfrac{CE}{EA}$ **Triangle Proportionality Theorem**

$\dfrac{4}{8} = \dfrac{x}{12}$ **Substitute 4 for *CD*, 8 for *DB*, *x* for *CE*, and 12 for *EA*.**

$4 \cdot 12 = 8 \cdot x$ **Cross product property**

$48 = 8x$ **Multiply.**

$\dfrac{48}{8} = \dfrac{8x}{8}$ **Divide each side by 8.**

$6 = x$ **Simplify.**

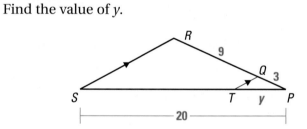

Student Help
CLASSZONE.COM

MORE EXAMPLES
More examples at
classzone.com

EXAMPLE 2 Find Segment Lengths

Find the value of y.

Solution

You know that $PS = 20$ and $PT = y$. By the Segment Addition Postulate, $TS = 20 - y$.

$\dfrac{PQ}{QR} = \dfrac{PT}{TS}$ **Triangle Proportionality Theorem**

$\dfrac{3}{9} = \dfrac{y}{20 - y}$ **Substitute 3 for *PQ*, 9 for *QR*, *y* for *PT*, and (20 − *y*) for *TS*.**

$3(20 - y) = 9 \cdot y$ **Cross product property**

$60 - 3y = 9y$ **Distributive property**

$60 - 3y + 3y = 9y + 3y$ **Add 3*y* to each side.**

$60 = 12y$ **Simplify.**

$\dfrac{60}{12} = \dfrac{12y}{12}$ **Divide each side by 12.**

$5 = y$ **Simplify.**

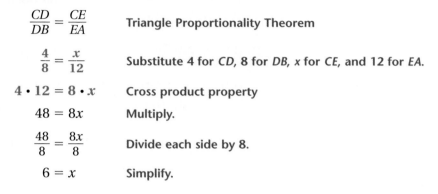

Converse of the Triangle Proportionality Theorem

Words If a line divides two sides of a triangle proportionally, then it is parallel to the third side.

Symbols In $\triangle QRS$, if $\dfrac{RT}{TQ} = \dfrac{RU}{US}$, then $\overline{TU} \parallel \overline{QS}$.

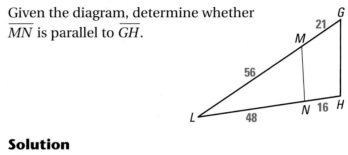

EXAMPLE 3 Determine Parallels

Given the diagram, determine whether $\overline{MN}$ is parallel to $\overline{GH}$.

Solution

Find and simplify the ratios of the two sides divided by $\overline{MN}$.

$$\frac{LM}{MG} = \frac{56}{21} = \frac{8}{3} \qquad\qquad \frac{LN}{NH} = \frac{48}{16} = \frac{3}{1}$$

ANSWER ▶ Because $\dfrac{8}{3} \neq \dfrac{3}{1}$, $\overline{MN}$ is not parallel to $\overline{GH}$.

Checkpoint ✓ **Find Segment Lengths and Determine Parallels**

Find the value of the variable.

1.
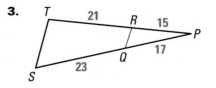

2.

Given the diagram, determine whether $\overline{QR}$ is parallel to $\overline{ST}$. Explain.

3.
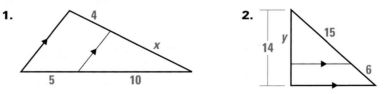

4.
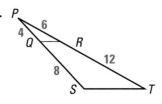

A **midsegment of a triangle** is a segment that connects the midpoints of two sides of a triangle. The following theorem about midsegments is a special case of the Triangle Proportionality Theorem.

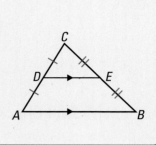
EXAMPLE 4 **Use the Midsegment Theorem**

Find the length of $\overline{QS}$.

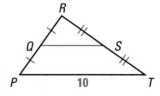

Solution

From the marks on the diagram, you know S is the midpoint of $\overline{RT}$, and Q is the midpoint of $\overline{RP}$. Therefore, $\overline{QS}$ is a midsegment of $\triangle PRT$. Use the Midsegment Theorem to write the following equation.

$$QS = \frac{1}{2}PT = \frac{1}{2}(10) = 5$$

ANSWER ▶ The length of $\overline{QS}$ is 5.

Checkpoint ✓ **Use the Midsegment Theorem**

Find the value of the variable.

5.

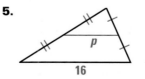

6.

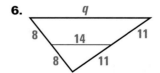

7. Use the Midsegment Theorem to find the perimeter of $\triangle ABC$.

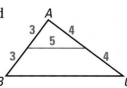

Guided Practice

Vocabulary Check

Complete the statement.

1. The __?__ Theorem states that if a line divides two sides of a triangle proportionally, then it is __?__ to the third side.

2. A __?__ of a triangle is a segment that connects the midpoints of two sides of a triangle.

Skill Check

Copy and complete the proportion using the diagram below.

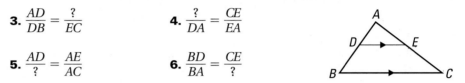

3. $\dfrac{AD}{DB} = \dfrac{?}{EC}$

4. $\dfrac{?}{DA} = \dfrac{CE}{EA}$

5. $\dfrac{AD}{?} = \dfrac{AE}{AC}$

6. $\dfrac{BD}{BA} = \dfrac{CE}{?}$

Find the value of the variable.

7.

8.

9.

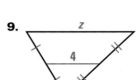

Practice and Applications

Extra Practice

See p. 688.

⟨xy⟩ Using Algebra Solve the proportion.

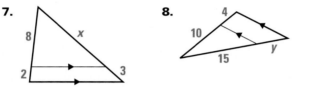

10. $\dfrac{2}{3} = \dfrac{m}{36}$

11. $\dfrac{t}{2} = \dfrac{5}{12}$

12. $\dfrac{21}{y} = \dfrac{7}{18}$

13. $\dfrac{27}{r} = \dfrac{3}{4}$

Finding Segment Lengths Find the value of the variable.

14.

15.

16.

Homework Help

Example 1: Exs. 14–19
Example 2: Exs. 14–19
Example 3: Exs. 20–23
Example 4: Exs. 24–29,
                33–37

17.

18.

19.

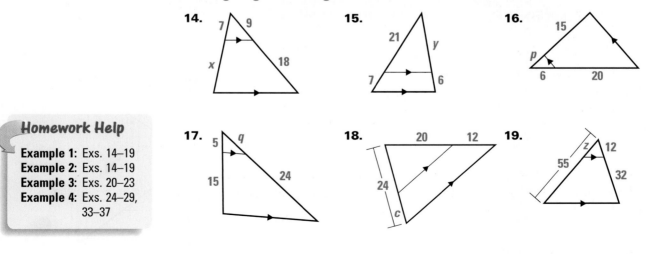

Determining Parallels Given the diagram, determine whether $\overline{QS}$ is parallel to $\overline{PT}$.

20.

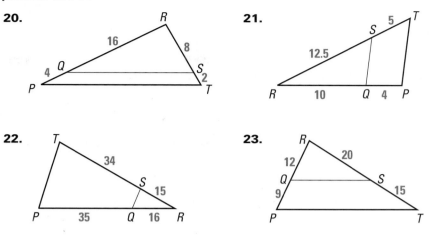

21.

22.

23.

Using the Midsegment Theorem Find the value of the variable.

24.

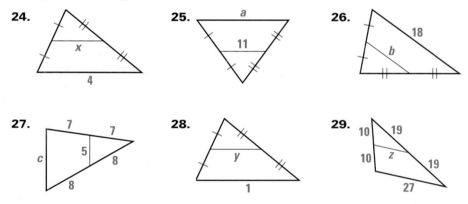

25.

26.

27.

28.

29.

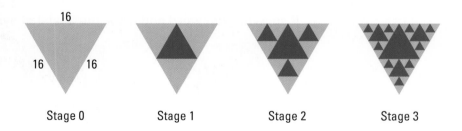

Visualize It! The design below approximates a fractal. Begin with an equilateral triangle. Shade the triangle formed by the three midsegments. Continue the process for each unshaded triangle.

Stage 0   Stage 1   Stage 2   Stage 3

30. Find the perimeter of the dark blue triangle in Stage 1.

31. Challenge Find the total perimeter of all the dark blue triangles in Stage 2.

32. Challenge Find the total perimeter of all the dark blue triangles in Stage 3.

Link to
Fractals

FRACTALS are shapes that look the same at many levels of magnification. Take a small part of the image above and you will see that it looks similar to the whole image.

Application Links
CLASSZONE.COM

Midsegment Theorem Use the diagram below to complete
the statement.

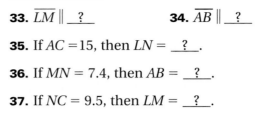

33. $\overline{LM} \parallel$ ___?___

34. $\overline{AB} \parallel$ ___?___

35. If $AC = 15$, then $LN =$ ___?___.

36. If $MN = 7.4$, then $AB =$ ___?___.

37. If $NC = 9.5$, then $LM =$ ___?___.

Technology In Exercises 38 and 39, use geometry software to
complete the steps below.

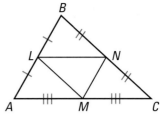

① Draw $\triangle ABC$.

② Construct the angle bisector of $\angle A$.

③ Construct the intersection of the
angle bisector and $\overline{BC}$. Label it D.

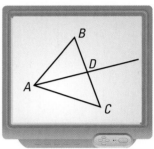

④ Measure $\overline{DC}$, $\overline{AC}$, $\overline{DB}$, and $\overline{AB}$. Then
calculate the ratios $\dfrac{DC}{AC}$ and $\dfrac{DB}{AB}$.

38. Drag one or more of the triangle's vertices. What do you notice
about the ratios as the shape changes?

39. Complete the conjecture: If a ray bisects an angle of a triangle,
then it divides the opposite side into segments whose lengths are
___?___ to the lengths of the other two sides.

Standardized Test Practice

40. Multiple Choice What is the value of x?

(**A**) 21   (**B**) 24

(**C**) 32   (**D**) 42

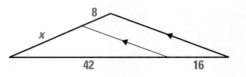

Mixed Review

Reflections Determine if the entire word has any lines of symmetry.
If so, write the word and draw the line(s) of symmetry. *(Lesson 5.7)*

41.   **42.**   **43.**

Algebra Skills

Finding Slope Find the slope of the line that passes through the
points. *(Skills Review, p. 665)*

44. $(0, 2)$ and $(4, 8)$ **45.** $(1, 2)$ and $(3, 4)$ **46.** $(5, 2)$ and $(5, 3)$

47. $(-5, 6)$ and $(1, 2)$ **48.** $(-4, 4)$ and $(2, 0)$ **49.** $(3, 7)$ and $(-1, -3)$

50. $(5, 3)$ and $(-1, 1)$ **51.** $(0, -4)$ and $(3, 5)$ **52.** $(-3, 2)$ and $(6, -5)$

7.6 Dilations

Goal
Identify and draw dilations.

Key Words
- dilation
- reduction
- enlargement

Geo-Activity   **Drawing a Dilation**

1 Draw a triangle. Label it △*PQR*. Choose a point *C* outside the triangle.

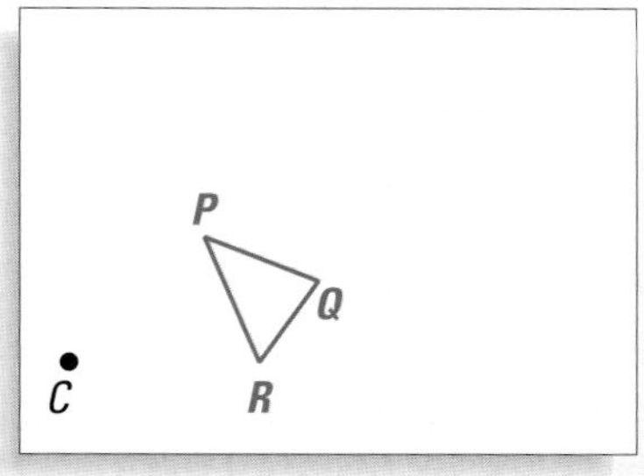

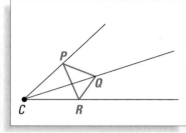

2 Use a straightedge to draw lines from *C* through *P*, *Q*, and *R*.

3 Measure $\overline{CP}$ and locate a point *P′* on $\overrightarrow{CP}$ such that *CP′* = 2 · *CP*. Locate *Q′* and *R′* the same way.

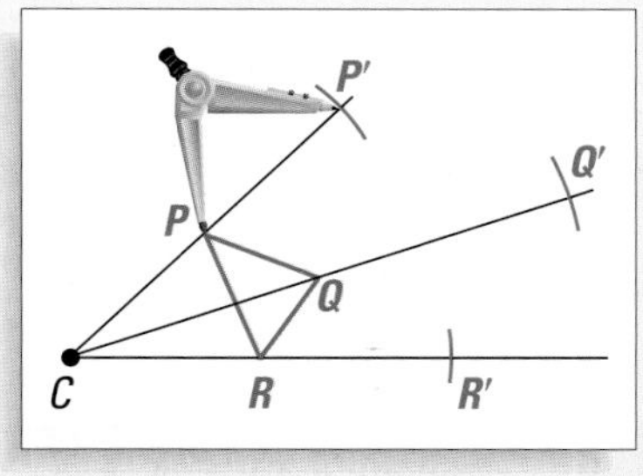

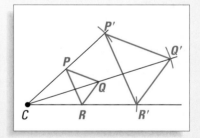

4 Connect the points *P′*, *Q′*, and *R′* to form △*P′Q′R′*.

5 Calculate the ratios $\frac{P'R'}{PR}$, $\frac{R'Q'}{RQ}$, and $\frac{Q'P'}{QP}$. Then show that △*PQR* is similar to △*P′Q′R′*.

6 What is the scale factor of △*P′Q′R′* to △*PQR*? How does it compare to the ratio $\frac{CP'}{CP}$?

Student Help

LOOK BACK
To review other types of transformations, see pp. 152 and 282.

A **dilation** is a transformation with center *C* and scale factor *k* that maps each point *P* to an image point *P′* so that *P′* lies on $\overrightarrow{CP}$ and *CP′* = *k* · *CP*.

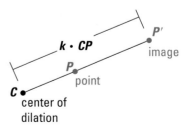

As you saw in the Geo-Activity above, a dilation maps a figure onto a similar figure, called the image.

Types of Dilations If the image is smaller than the original figure, then the dilation is a **reduction**. If the image is larger than the original figure, then the dilation is an **enlargement**.

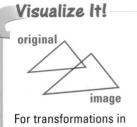
EXAMPLE 1 Identify Dilations

Tell whether the dilation is a *reduction* or an *enlargement*.

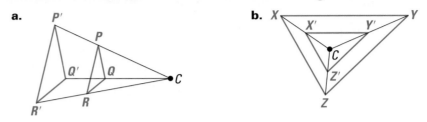

a.

b.

Solution

  a. The dilation is an enlargement because the image ($\triangle P'Q'R'$) is larger than the original figure ($\triangle PQR$).

  b. The dilation is a reduction because the image ($\triangle X'Y'Z'$) is smaller than the original figure ($\triangle XYZ$).

Scale Factor The *scale factor* of a dilation is the ratio of CP' to CP. This is also equal to the scale factor of $\triangle P'Q'R'$ to $\triangle PQR$.

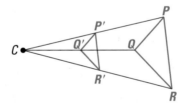

$$\text{scale factor} = k = \frac{CP'}{CP} = \frac{P'Q'}{PQ}$$

EXAMPLE 2 Find Scale Factors

Find the scale factor of the dilation.

a.

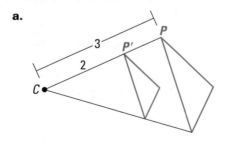

b.

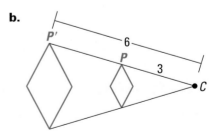

Solution

Find the ratio of CP' to CP.

  a. scale factor $= \dfrac{CP'}{CP} = \dfrac{2}{3}$

  b. scale factor $= \dfrac{CP'}{CP} = \dfrac{6}{3} = 2$

Tell whether the dilation is a *reduction* or an *enlargement*. Then find the scale factor of the dilation.

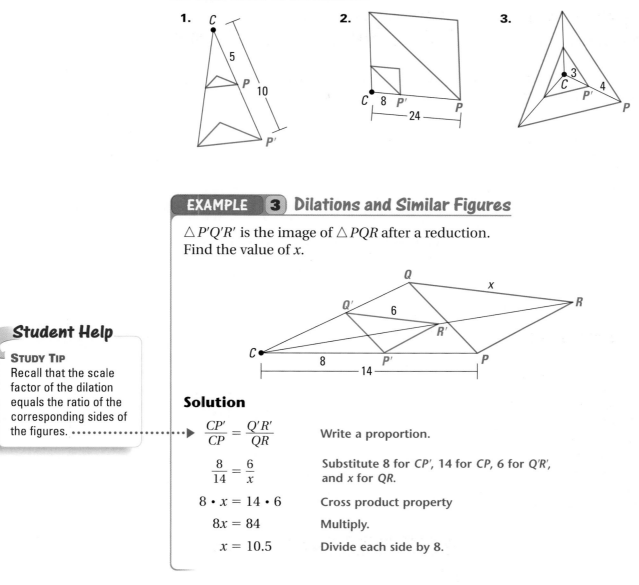

1.

2.

3.

EXAMPLE 3 Dilations and Similar Figures

$\triangle P'Q'R'$ is the image of $\triangle PQR$ after a reduction. Find the value of x.

Student Help

> **STUDY TIP**
> Recall that the scale factor of the dilation equals the ratio of the corresponding sides of the figures. ·······

Solution

$\dfrac{CP'}{CP} = \dfrac{Q'R'}{QR}$ Write a proportion.

$\dfrac{8}{14} = \dfrac{6}{x}$ Substitute 8 for *CP'*, 14 for *CP*, 6 for *Q'R'*, and *x* for *QR*.

$8 \cdot x = 14 \cdot 6$ Cross product property

$8x = 84$ Multiply.

$x = 10.5$ Divide each side by 8.

Checkpoint ✓ **Dilations and Similar Figures**

The red figure is the image of the blue figure after a dilation. Find the value of the variable.

4.

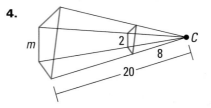

5.

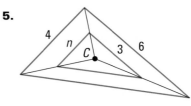

Guided Practice

Vocabulary Check

1. Complete: In a *dilation*, every image is __?__ to the original figure.

Skill Check

2. **Error Analysis** Katie found the scale factor of the dilation shown to be $\frac{1}{2}$. What did Katie do wrong?

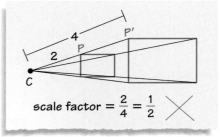

scale factor $= \frac{2}{4} = \frac{1}{2}$ ✗

3. Is the dilation shown a reduction or an enlargement? How do you know?

Tell whether the dilation is a *reduction* or an *enlargement*.

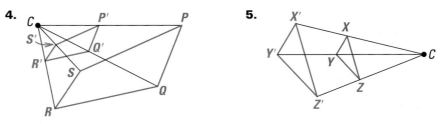

4.

5.

Practice and Applications

Extra Practice

See p. 688.

Identifying Dilations **Tell whether the dilation is a *reduction* or an *enlargement*. Then find its scale factor.**

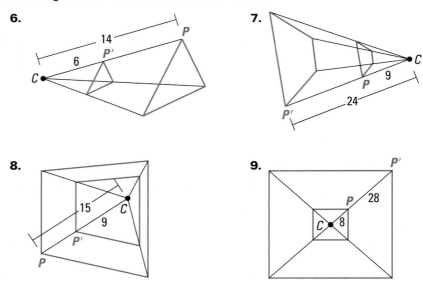

6.

7.

8.

9.

Homework Help

Example 1: Exs. 6–9,
            11–14
Example 2: Exs. 6–9, 15
Example 3: Exs. 11–14,
            16

10. **Visualize It!** Sketch quadrilateral *EFGH*. Then sketch a dilation of *EFGH* with center *C* and scale factor 3.

Dilations and Similar Figures The red figure is the image of the blue figure after a dilation. Tell whether the dilation is a *reduction* or an *enlargement*. Then find the value of the variable.

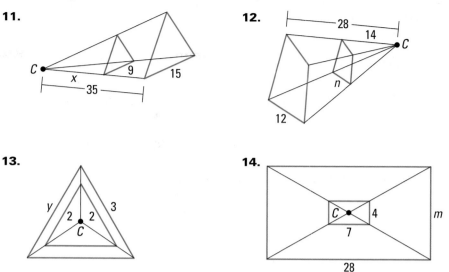

11.

C x 9 15 35

12.

28 14 C n 12

13.

y 2 2 3 C

14.

C 4 m 7 28

Student Help
CLASSZONE.COM

HOMEWORK HELP
Extra help with problem solving in Exs. 15–16 is at classzone.com

Flashlight Image In Exercises 15 and 16, use the following information and the diagram below.

The flashlight in the photograph below has a removable clear cap with a picture of a bug on it. When the flashlight is on, the bug is projected onto a wall. This situation models a dilation.

15. What is the scale factor of the dilation?

16. Write and solve a proportion to find the height of the bug projected onto the wall.

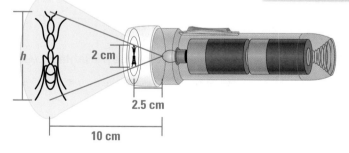

h 2 cm 2.5 cm 10 cm

Standardized Test Practice

17. Multiple Choice The length of a side of $J'K'L'M'$ is what percent of the length of the corresponding side of $JKLM$?

Ⓐ 3%

Ⓑ 12%

Ⓒ $33\frac{1}{3}\%$

Ⓓ 300%

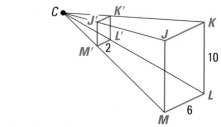

C K' J' L' M' 2 J K 10 L 6 M

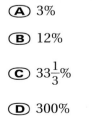

Finding Angle Measures Find the measure of $\angle 1$. *(Lesson 4.2)*

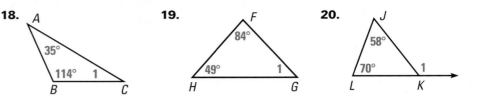

18.

19.

20.

Solving Proportions Solve the proportion. *(Lesson 7.1)*

21. $\dfrac{d}{7} = \dfrac{12}{28}$

22. $\dfrac{35}{10} = \dfrac{7}{x + 1}$

23. $\dfrac{9}{2} = \dfrac{t + 3}{12}$

Algebra Skills

Evaluating Expressions Evaluate the expression when $x = -3$.
(Skills Review, p. 670)

24. $x^2 + 8$

25. $-4x - 9$

26. $(x + 2)(x - 5)$

27. $11 - \dfrac{15}{x}$

28. $2x^3$

29. $4x^2 + 3x - 1$

Quiz 2

Determine whether the triangles are similar. If they are similar,
write a similarity statement. *(Lesson 7.4)*

1.

2.

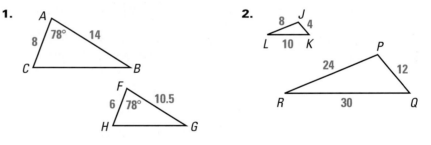

Find the value of the variable. *(Lesson 7.5)*

3.

4.

5.

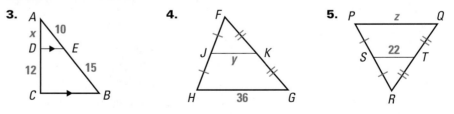

Tell whether the dilation is a *reduction* or an *enlargement*.
Then find its scale factor. *(Lesson 7.6)*

6.

7.

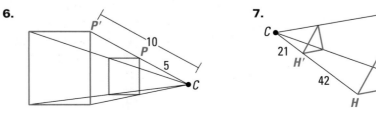

7.6 Dilations Using Coordinates

Question

In a dilation in a coordinate plane, how are the coordinates of the original figure and its image related?

Explore

1 Create a set of axes. Draw a triangle, △*CDE*.

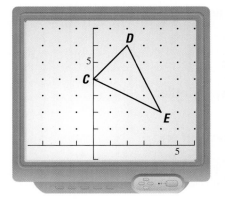

2 Dilate △*CDE* with center (0, 0) using a scale factor of 0.5. This creates △*C′D′E′*.

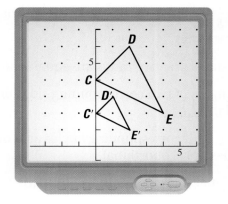

3 Find the coordinates of points *C*, *C′*, *D*, *D′*, *E*, and *E′*.

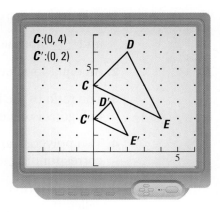

Think About It

1. Drag any of the vertices. Compare the *x*- and *y*-coordinates of each vertex of △*CDE* with the *x*- and *y*-coordinates of the corresponding vertex of △*C′D′E′*.

2. Repeat Steps 1–3 and Exercise 1 several times using different scale factors. Make a conjecture about the relationship between the scale factor of the dilation and the coordinates of the vertices of the original figure and the image.

3. △*XYZ* is shown at the right. Suppose you dilate △*XYZ* using the origin as the center of dilation and a scale factor of 3.

Use your conjecture from Exercise 2 to predict the coordinates of the vertices of the image. Check your results using the geometry software.

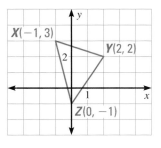

VOCABULARY

- **ratio of *a* to *b*,** *p. 357*
- **proportion,** *p. 359*
- **means of a proportion,** *p. 359*
- **extremes of a proportion,** *p. 359*
- **similar polygons,** *p. 365*
- **scale factor,** *p. 366*
- **midsegment of a triangle,** *p. 389*
- **dilation,** *p. 393*
- **reduction,** *p. 394*
- **enlargement,** *p. 394*

VOCABULARY REVIEW

Fill in each blank.

1. In the proportion $\dfrac{f}{g} = \dfrac{h}{j}$, __?__ and __?__ are the means, and __?__ and __?__ are the extremes.

2. An equation that states that two ratios are equal is a(n) __?__.

3. The ratio of the lengths of two corresponding sides of two similar polygons is called the __?__.

4. Two polygons are __?__ if corresponding angles are congruent and corresponding sides are proportional.

5. A segment that connects the midpoints of two sides of a triangle is called the __?__.

6. A(n) __?__ is a transformation that maps a figure onto a similar figure.

7. If the image of a dilation is larger than the original figure, then the dilation is a(n) __?__.

7.1 RATIO AND PROPORTION

Examples on pp. 357–360

EXAMPLE Solve the proportion $\dfrac{2}{5} = \dfrac{4}{x+6}$.

$\dfrac{2}{5} = \dfrac{4}{x+6}$	Write original proportion.
$2(x+6) = 5 \cdot 4$	Cross product property
$2x + 12 = 20$	Use distributive property and multiply.
$2x = 8$	Subtract 12 from each side.
$x = 4$	Divide each side by 2.

Solve the proportion.

8. $\dfrac{y}{18} = \dfrac{1}{3}$ **9.** $\dfrac{4}{7} = \dfrac{24}{s}$ **10.** $\dfrac{2}{3} = \dfrac{z-6}{15}$ **11.** $\dfrac{x+4}{40} = \dfrac{3}{5}$

7.2   **SIMILAR POLYGONS**   *Examples on pp. 365–368*

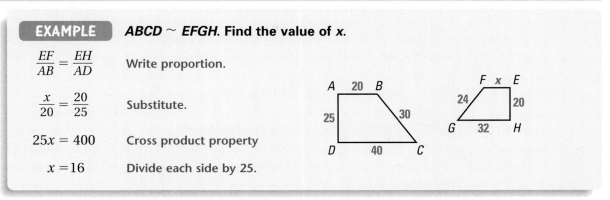

EXAMPLE   *ABCD* ~ *EFGH*. Find the value of *x*.

$\dfrac{EF}{AB} = \dfrac{EH}{AD}$ Write proportion.

$\dfrac{x}{20} = \dfrac{20}{25}$ Substitute.

$25x = 400$ Cross product property

$x = 16$ Divide each side by 25.

The polygons are similar. Find the value of the variable.

12. **13.** **14.**

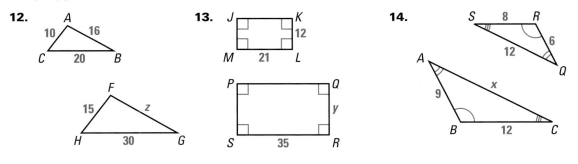

7.3   **SHOWING TRIANGLES ARE SIMILAR: AA**   *Examples on pp. 372–374*

EXAMPLE   **Determine whether the triangles below are similar. If they are similar, write a similarity statement.**

$\angle A \cong \angle D$ because they both measure $55°$, and $\angle B \cong \angle E$ because they are both right angles.

Therefore, by the AA Similarity Postulate, the triangles are similar. $\triangle ABC \sim \triangle DEF$.

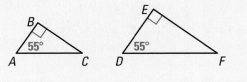

Determine whether the triangles are similar. If they are similar, write a similarity statement.

15. **16.** **17.**

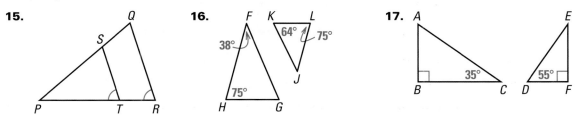

7.4 SHOWING TRIANGLES ARE SIMILAR: SSS AND SAS

Examples on pp. 379–381

EXAMPLE Determine whether the triangles at the right are similar. If they are similar, write a similarity statement.

$\angle ACB \cong \angle ECD$, because vertical angles are congruent.

To apply the SAS Similarity Theorem, compare the ratios of the corresponding sides that include $\angle ACB$ and $\angle ECD$.

Shorter sides $\dfrac{CE}{AC} = \dfrac{10}{16} = \dfrac{5}{8}$ **Longer sides** $\dfrac{CD}{BC} = \dfrac{15}{21} = \dfrac{5}{7}$

ANSWER ▶ The ratios of the corresponding sides that include $\angle ACB$ and $\angle DCE$ are not equal. Therefore, the triangles are not similar.

Determine whether the triangles are similar. If they are similar, write a similarity statement.

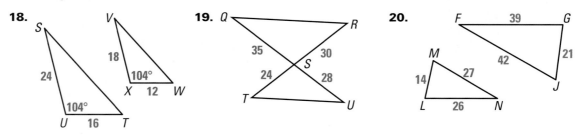

18.   **19.**   **20.**

7.5 PROPORTIONS AND SIMILAR TRIANGLES

Examples on pp. 386–389

EXAMPLE Find the value of *x.*

Because $\overline{NM}$ is parallel to $\overline{KL}$, you can use the Triangle Proportionality Theorem to find the value of *x*.

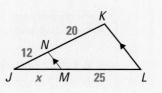

$\dfrac{JN}{NK} = \dfrac{JM}{ML}$ Triangle Proportionality Theorem

$\dfrac{12}{20} = \dfrac{x}{25}$ Substitute.

$12 \cdot 25 = 20 \cdot x$ Cross product property

$300 = 20x$ Multiply.

$15 = x$ Divide each side by 20.

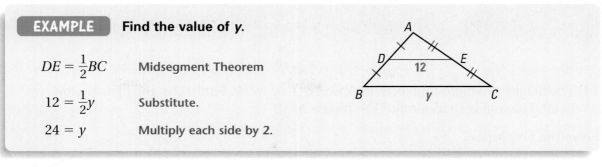

EXAMPLE   Find the value of *y*.

$DE = \frac{1}{2}BC$ Midsegment Theorem

$12 = \frac{1}{2}y$ Substitute.

$24 = y$ Multiply each side by 2.

Find the value of the variable.

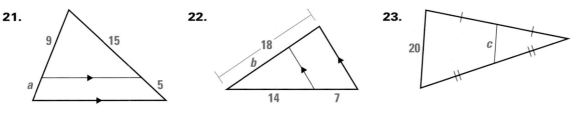

21.   9   15   *a*   5

22.   18   *b*   14   7

23.   20   *c*

7.6   DILATIONS

Examples on pp. 393–395

EXAMPLES   Tell whether the dilation is a *reduction* or an *enlargement*. Then find the scale factor of the dilation.

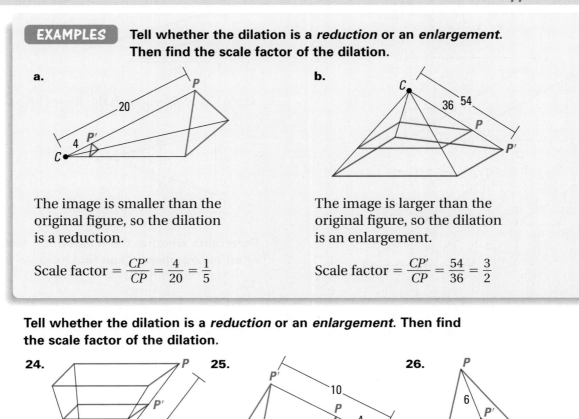

a.   20   *P*   4   *P'*   *C*

The image is smaller than the original figure, so the dilation is a reduction.

Scale factor = $\dfrac{CP'}{CP} = \dfrac{4}{20} = \dfrac{1}{5}$

b.   *C*   36   54   *P*   *P'*

The image is larger than the original figure, so the dilation is an enlargement.

Scale factor = $\dfrac{CP'}{CP} = \dfrac{54}{36} = \dfrac{3}{2}$

Tell whether the dilation is a *reduction* or an *enlargement*. Then find the scale factor of the dilation.

24.   *P*   *P'*   8   12   *C*

25.   *P'*   10   *P*   4   *C*

26.   *P*   6   *P'*   5   *C*

1. The height-to-length ratio of a brick wall is 3 : 20. The wall is 40 feet long. How high is it?

Solve the proportion.

2. $\dfrac{2}{9} = \dfrac{x}{27}$

3. $\dfrac{x-3}{35} = \dfrac{4}{7}$

Determine whether the polygons are similar. If they are similar, write a similarity statement.

4.

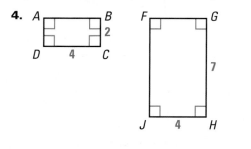

5.

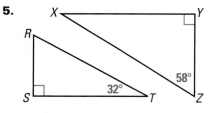

6.

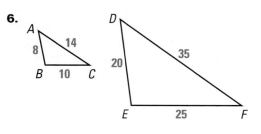

7.

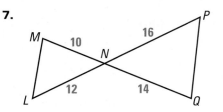

8. *QRST* is similar to *WXYZ*. The ratio of *QR* to *WX* is 3 : 7. What is the ratio of the perimeter of *QRST* to the perimeter of *WXYZ*?

9. Find *TQ* in the figure below.

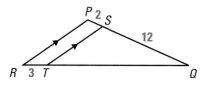

In Exercises 10 and 11, find the value of the variable.

10.

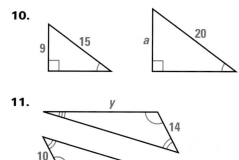

11.

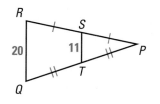

12. What is wrong with the figure below?

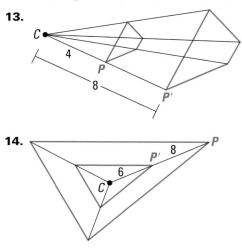

Determine whether the dilation is a *reduction* or an *enlargement*. Then find its scale factor.

13.

14.

1. Simplify the ratio $\frac{16 \text{ ft}}{4 \text{ yd}}$.

   (A) $\frac{1}{4}$ **(B)** $\frac{4}{3}$ **(C)** $\frac{4}{1}$ **(D)** $\frac{3}{4}$

2. $\triangle ABC$ is similar to $\triangle DEF$. What are the values of x and y?

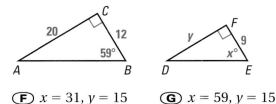

   (F) $x = 31$, $y = 15$ **(G)** $x = 59$, $y = 15$

   (H) $x = 59$, $y = 16$ **(J)** $x = 31$, $y = 12$

3. Which of the following statements is *false*?

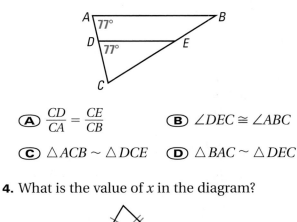

   (A) $\frac{CD}{CA} = \frac{CE}{CB}$ **(B)** $\angle DEC \cong \angle ABC$

   (C) $\triangle ACB \sim \triangle DCE$ **(D)** $\triangle BAC \sim \triangle DEC$

4. What is the value of x in the diagram?

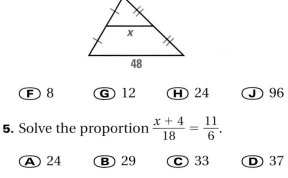

   (F) 8   **(G)** 12   **(H)** 24   **(J)** 96

5. Solve the proportion $\frac{x + 4}{18} = \frac{11}{6}$.

   (A) 24   **(B)** 29   **(C)** 33   **(D)** 37

6. You want to enlarge a drawing of a car that is 4 inches long. Your enlargement will be 12 inches long. What is the scale factor of the enlargement to the drawing?

   (F) 3 to 1   **(G)** 4 to 1

   (H) 1 to 3   **(J)** 1 to 4

7. Determine whether the dilation is a reduction or enlargement. Then find its scale factor.

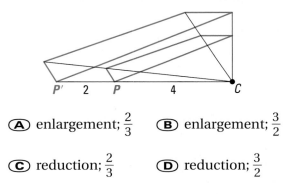

   (A) enlargement; $\frac{2}{3}$ **(B)** enlargement; $\frac{3}{2}$

   (C) reduction; $\frac{2}{3}$ **(D)** reduction; $\frac{3}{2}$

8. Multi-Step Problem The Greek mathematician Thales calculated the height of the Great Pyramid in Egypt by placing a rod at the tip of the pyramid's shadow and using similar triangles as shown.

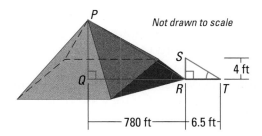

Not drawn to scale

   a. Explain why $\triangle PQR$ is similar to $\triangle SRT$.

   b. Find the scale factor of $\triangle PQR$ to $\triangle SRT$.

   c. Find the height of the Great Pyramid.

BraiN GaMes

Tangrams

Materials
- 7 tangram pieces
- scissors
- ruler

Object of the Game To find as many ways as possible to use some or all of the tangram pieces to make shapes that are similar to individual pieces.

Set Up If your tangram pieces are printed on paper, carefully cut them out.

How to Play

Step 1 ▶ Look at the smallest triangle. Find tangram pieces that are similar to the triangle.

Step 2 ▶ Use more than one piece to make triangles that are similar to the original triangle. Trace each figure to record your answers.

Step 3 ▶ Look at the parallelogram. Use more than one piece to make parallelograms that are similar to the original parallelogram. Trace each figure to record your answers.

Step 4 ▶ Measure the sides of the figures to check if they are similar to the original figure.

Another Way to Play Use more than one piece to create a figure then try to create figures similar to it.

When simplifying radical expressions, you can use the *Product Property of Radicals*, which states that $\sqrt{ab} = \sqrt{a} \cdot \sqrt{b}$, where $a \geq 0$ and $b \geq 0$.

EXAMPLE 1   Simplify Radical Expressions

Simplify the expression $\sqrt{20}$.

Solution

Look for perfect square factors to remove from the radicand.

$$\sqrt{20} = \sqrt{4 \cdot 5} \qquad \text{Factor using perfect square factor.}$$
$$= \sqrt{4} \cdot \sqrt{5} \qquad \text{Product Property of Radicals}$$
$$= 2\sqrt{5} \qquad \text{Simplify: } \sqrt{4} = 2.$$

Try These

Simplify the expression.

1. $\sqrt{12}$ 2. $\sqrt{63}$ 3. $\sqrt{44}$ 4. $\sqrt{125}$

5. $\sqrt{150}$ 6. $\sqrt{80}$ 7. $\sqrt{48}$ 8. $\sqrt{72}$

EXAMPLE 2   Use Formulas

Solve for ℓ in the formula for the perimeter of a rectangle, $P = 2\ell + 2w$.

Solution

$$P = 2\ell + 2w \qquad \text{Write the formula.}$$
$$P - 2w = 2\ell \qquad \text{Subtract } 2w \text{ from each side.}$$
$$\frac{P - 2w}{2} = \ell \qquad \text{Divide each side by 2.}$$

ANSWER ▸ The formula, when solved for ℓ, is $\ell = \dfrac{P - 2w}{2}$.

Try These

Solve for the indicated variable in the formula.

9. Solve for h: $A = bh$ 10. Solve for B: $V = \dfrac{1}{3}Bh$

11. Solve for P: $S = 2B + Ph$ 12. Solve for b_2: $A = \dfrac{1}{2}(b_1 + b_2)h$

Polygons and Area

Where do hexagons appear in nature?

Basaltic columns are geological formations that result from rapidly cooling lava. Most basaltic columns are hexagonal (six-sided) shapes.

The Giant's Causeway on the Irish coast features hexagonal columns that reach a height of 82 feet.

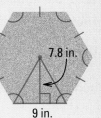

7.8 in.

9 in.

Learn More About It

You will learn more about rock formations in Exercise 31 on p. 436.

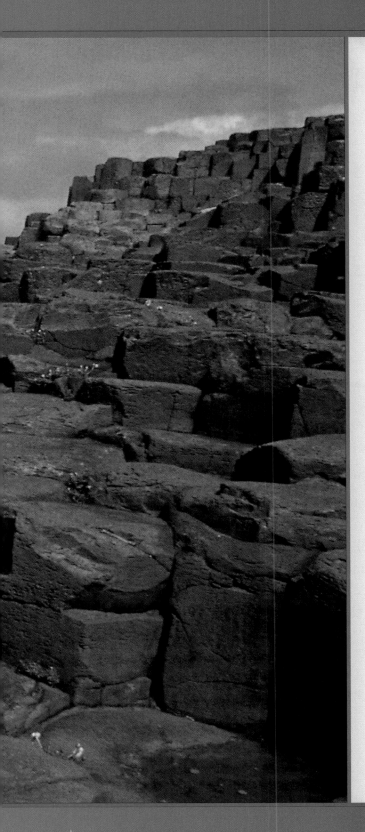

Who uses Polygons and Area?

FLOORING INSTALLER
Flooring installers are hired by flooring contractors to install, repair, or replace floor coverings, such as carpet and hardwood. (p. 414)

LANDSCAPE ARCHITECT
Landscape architects use engineering knowledge and creativity to design outdoor environments, such as parks, gardens, and recreational areas. (p. 457)

How will you use these ideas?

- Measure the angles of home plate on a baseball field. (p. 422)
- Find the area of a judo mat. (p. 428)
- Estimate the cost of planting a cornfield maze. (p. 429)
- See how cranberries are harvested. (p. 456)
- Determine the area covered by a lawn sprinkler. (p. 457)

Chapter 8

PREVIEW

What's the chapter about?

- Finding measures of **interior** and **exterior angles** of polygons
- Finding the **area** of squares, rectangles, triangles, parallelograms, and trapezoids
- Finding the **circumference** and **area** of circles

Key Words

- **convex**, *p. 411*
- **concave**, *p. 411*
- **equilateral**, *p. 412*
- **equiangular**, *p. 412*
- **regular**, *p. 412*

- **area**, *p. 424*
- **radius**, *p. 452*
- **diameter**, *p. 452*
- **circumference**, *p. 452*
- **sector**, *p. 454*

PREPARE

Chapter Readiness Quiz

Take this quick quiz. If you are unsure of an answer, look at the reference pages for help.

Vocabulary Check *(refer to p. 325)*

1. Which term does *not* describe the polygon below?

 (A) rhombus **(B)** quadrilateral

 (C) rectangle **(D)** parallelogram

Skill Check *(refer to p. 305)*

2. What is the sum of the measures of the interior angles of a quadrilateral?

 (F) 90° **(G)** 180° **(H)** 360° **(J)** 540°

VISUAL STRATEGY

Breaking Polygons into Parts

Visualize It! ➡️ You can break a complex polygon into simpler parts whose areas you know.

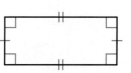

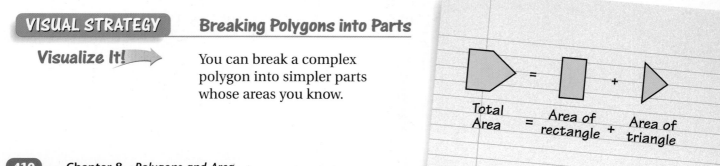

Total Area = Area of rectangle + Area of triangle

8.1 Classifying Polygons

Goal
Describe polygons.

Key Words
- convex
- concave
- equilateral
- equiangular
- regular

The Iranian tile pattern at the right shows several polygons. These polygons can be classified as *convex* or *concave*.

A polygon is **convex** if no line that contains a side of the polygon passes through the interior of the polygon. A polygon that is not convex is called **concave**.

Convex polygon

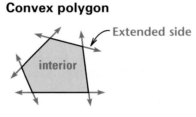

None of the extended sides pass through the interior.

Concave polygon

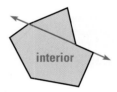

At least one extended side passes through the interior.

EXAMPLE 1 **Identify Convex and Concave Polygons**

Decide whether the polygon is *convex* or *concave*.

a.

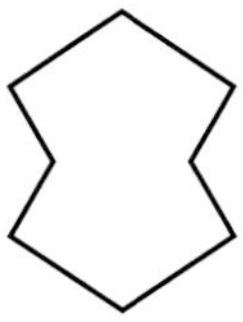

b.

Solution

a. At least one extended side passes through the interior. So, the polygon is concave.

b. None of the extended sides pass through the interior. So, the polygon is convex.

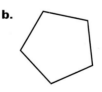

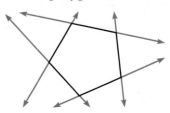

A polygon is **equilateral** if all of its sides are congruent. A polygon is **equiangular** if all of its interior angles are congruent. A polygon is **regular** if it is both equilateral and equiangular.

Equilateral

All sides are congruent.

Equiangular

All angles are congruent.

Regular Polygons

All sides are congruent and all angles are congruent.

Student Help

CLASSZONE.COM

MORE EXAMPLES
More examples at classzone.com

EXAMPLE 2 **Identify Regular Polygons**

Decide whether the polygon is regular. Explain your answer.

a. 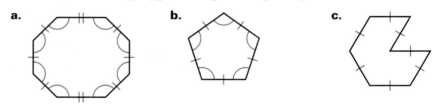 b. c.

Solution

a. Although the polygon is equiangular, it is not equilateral. So, the polygon is not regular.

b. Because the polygon is both equilateral and equiangular, it is regular.

c. Although the polygon is equilateral, it is not equiangular. So, the polygon is not regular.

Checkpoint ✓ **Describe Polygons**

Decide whether the polygon is *convex* or *concave*. Then decide whether the polygon is regular. Explain your answer.

1. 2. 3.

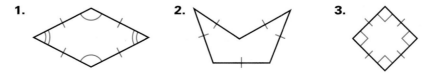

Guided Practice

Vocabulary Check

1. Sketch a *concave* polygon.

2. Describe the difference between an *equilateral* polygon and an *equiangular* polygon.

3. What is a *regular* polygon?

Skill Check

Decide whether the polygon shown in black is *convex* or *concave*.

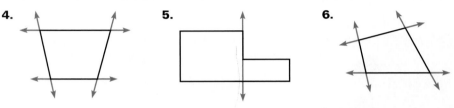

4. **5.** **6.**

Match the polygon with the description.

A. concave   **B.** equilateral   **C.** convex equiangular

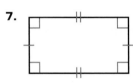 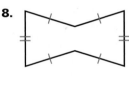 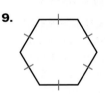

7. **8.** **9.**

Practice and Applications

Extra Practice

See p. 689.

Convex and Concave Polygons Decide whether the polygon is *convex* or *concave*.

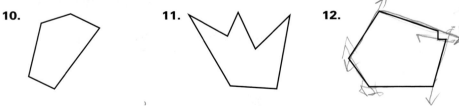

10. **11.** **12.**

Equilateral and Equiangular Polygons Decide whether the polygon is *equilateral*, *equiangular*, or *neither*.

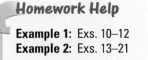

Homework Help

Example 1: Exs. 10–12
Example 2: Exs. 13–21

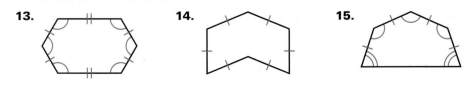

13. **14.** **15.**

Regular Polygons Decide whether the polygon is regular. Explain your answer.

16.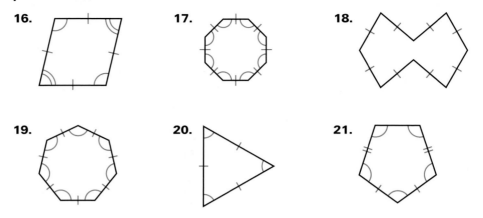

17.

18.

19.

20.

21.

Link to
Careers

FLOORING INSTALLERS are hired by flooring contractors to install, repair, or replace floor coverings such as carpet and hardwood.

Flooring Decide whether the polygon outlined in red in the floor pattern is *convex* or *concave*.

22.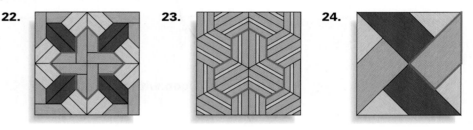

23.

24.

Web site Icons Use the polygons outlined on the website icons shown below.

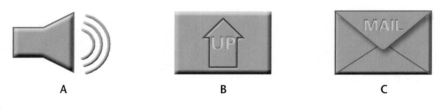

A   B   C

25. Which polygons are convex? Which polygons are concave?

26. Do any of the polygons appear to be regular? Explain.

Logical Reasoning Answer the question about the polygon.

27. Is the triangle equiangular? Explain.

60°
60°

28. Is the parallelogram equilateral? Explain.

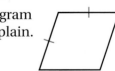

Student Help

LOOK BACK
To review the names given to polygons, see p. 304. For example, a *pentagon* has five sides.

Visualize It! Decide whether it is possible to sketch a polygon that fits the description. If so, sketch it.

29. A concave pentagon

30. A convex quadrilateral

31. A polygon that is equilateral but not equiangular

32. A polygon that is equiangular but not equilateral

Finding Perimeters In Exercises 33–35, the polygons are equilateral. Find the perimeter of the polygon.

33. 3 in.

34. 7 cm

35. 4 ft

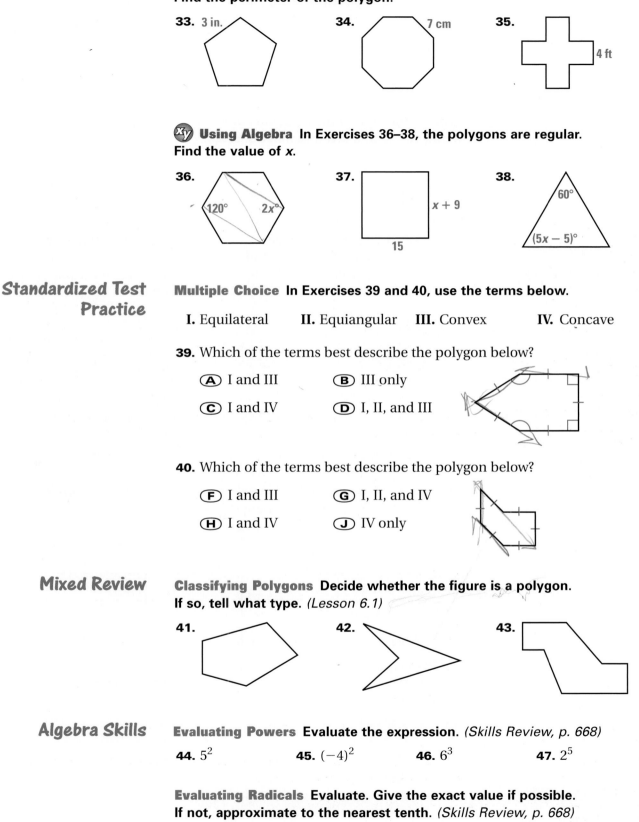

Using Algebra In Exercises 36–38, the polygons are regular. Find the value of *x*.

36. 120° 2*x*°

37. *x* + 9   15

38. 60° (5*x* − 5)°

Standardized Test Practice

Multiple Choice In Exercises 39 and 40, use the terms below.

I. Equilateral   II. Equiangular   III. Convex   IV. Concave

39. Which of the terms best describe the polygon below?

(A) I and III   (B) III only

(C) I and IV   (D) I, II, and III

40. Which of the terms best describe the polygon below?

(F) I and III   (G) I, II, and IV

(H) I and IV   (J) IV only

Mixed Review

Classifying Polygons Decide whether the figure is a polygon. If so, tell what type. *(Lesson 6.1)*

41.

42.

43.

Algebra Skills

Evaluating Powers Evaluate the expression. *(Skills Review, p. 668)*

44. 5^2 **45.** $(-4)^2$ **46.** 6^3 **47.** 2^5

Evaluating Radicals Evaluate. Give the exact value if possible. If not, approximate to the nearest tenth. *(Skills Review, p. 668)*

48. $\sqrt{36}$ **49.** $\sqrt{1}$ **50.** $\sqrt{169}$ **51.** $\sqrt{5}$

Activity 8.2 Angle Sum of Polygons

Question

What is the sum of the measures of the interior angles of a polygon with a given number of sides?

Materials

- paper
- pencil
- straightedge

Explore

1 Using your straightedge, draw convex polygons with three sides, four sides, five sides, and six sides. A pentagon has been drawn below.

2 In each polygon, pick a vertex and draw the diagonals from that one vertex. Notice that this divides the pentagon into three triangles.

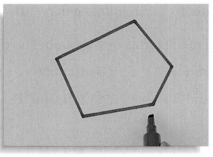

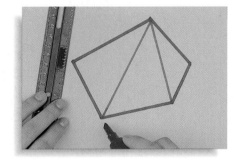

3 Copy and complete the table below. Use the fact that the sum of the measures of the interior angles of a triangle is 180°.

Polygon	Number of sides	Number of triangles	Sum of measures of interior angles
Triangle	3	1	$1 \cdot 180° = 180°$
Quadrilateral	?	?	?
Pentagon	?	?	?
Hexagon	?	?	?

Think About It

1. Look for a pattern in the last column of the table. What is the sum of the measures of the interior angles of a heptagon (7-sided polygon)? of an octagon (8-sided polygon)? Put the answers in your table.

2. Write an expression for the sum of the measures of the interior angles of any convex polygon with n sides.

8.2 Angles in Polygons

Goal
Find the measures of interior and exterior angles of polygons.

Key Words
- interior angle p. 181
- exterior angle p. 181

The definitions for interior angles and exterior angles can be extended to include angles formed in any polygon. In the diagrams shown below, interior angles are red, and exterior angles are blue.

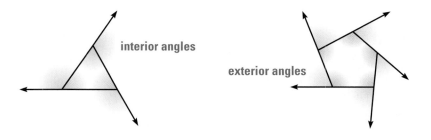

Activity 8.2 suggests the *Polygon Interior Angles Theorem* shown below.

THEOREM 8.1

Polygon Interior Angles Theorem

Words The sum of the measures of the interior angles of a convex polygon with n sides is $(n - 2) \cdot 180°$.

Symbols $m\angle 1 + m\angle 2 + \cdots + m\angle n = (n - 2) \cdot 180°$

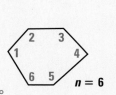

EXAMPLE 1 Use the Polygon Interior Angles Theorem

Find the sum of the measures of the interior angles of a convex heptagon.

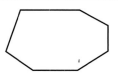

Solution
A heptagon has 7 sides. Use the Polygon Interior Angles Theorem and substitute 7 for n.

$(n - 2) \cdot 180° = (7 - 2) \cdot 180°$ Substitute 7 for n.

$= 5 \cdot 180°$ Simplify.

$= 900°$ Multiply.

ANSWER ▶ The sum of the measures of the interior angles of a convex heptagon is 900°.

EXAMPLE 2 Find the Measure of an Interior Angle

Find the measure of ∠A in the diagram.

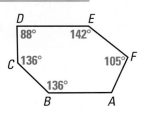

Solution

The polygon has 6 sides, so the sum of the measures of the interior angles is:

$(n - 2) \cdot 180° = (6 - 2) \cdot 180° = 4 \cdot 180° = 720°$.

Add the measures of the interior angles and set the sum equal to 720°.

$$136° + 136° + 88° + 142° + 105° + m\angle A = 720° \quad \text{The sum is 720°.}$$

$$607° + m\angle A = 720° \quad \text{Simplify.}$$

$$m\angle A = 113° \quad \text{Subtract 607°.}$$

ANSWER ▶ The measure of ∠A is 113°.

Student Help

SKILLS REVIEW
To review solving an equation, see p. 671.

EXAMPLE 3 Interior Angles of a Regular Polygon

Find the measure of an interior angle of a regular octagon.

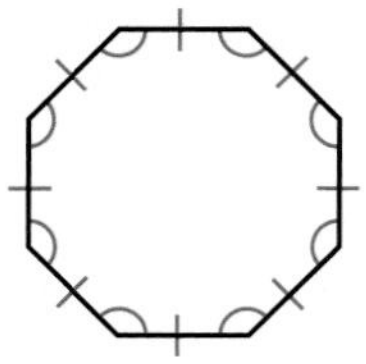

Solution

The sum of the measures of the interior angles of any octagon is:

$(n - 2) \cdot 180° = (8 - 2) \cdot 180° = 6 \cdot 180° = 1080°$.

Because the octagon is regular, each angle has the same measure. So, divide 1080° by 8 to find the measure of one interior angle.

$$\frac{1080°}{8} = 135°$$

ANSWER ▶ The measure of an interior angle of a regular octagon is 135°.

Checkpoint ✓ Find Measures of Interior Angles

In Exercises 1–3, find the measure of ∠G.

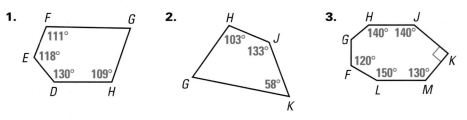

1.

2.

3.

4. Find the measure of an interior angle of a regular polygon with twelve sides.

Exterior Angles The diagrams below show that the sum of the measures of the exterior angles of the convex polygon is 360°.

❶ Shade one exterior angle at each vertex.

❷ Cut out the exterior angles.

❸ Arrange the exterior angles to form 360°.

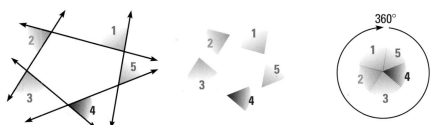

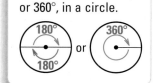

Visualize It!

A circle contains two straight angles. So, there are 180° + 180°, or 360°, in a circle.

The sum of the measures of the exterior angles of a convex polygon does not depend on the number of sides that the polygon has.

THEOREM 8.2

Polygon Exterior Angles Theorem

Words The sum of the measures of the exterior angles of a convex polygon, one angle at each vertex, is 360°.

Symbols $m\angle 1 + m\angle 2 + \cdots + m\angle n = 360°$

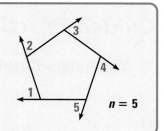

$n = 5$

Using Algebra

EXAMPLE 4 **Find the Measure of an Exterior Angle**

Find the value of x.

Solution

Using the Polygon Exterior Angles Theorem, set the sum of the measures of the exterior angles equal to 360°.

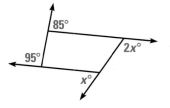

$95° + 85° + 2x° + x° = 360°$ Polygon Exterior Angles Theorem

$180 + 3x = 360$ Combine like terms.

$3x = 180$ Subtract 180 from each side.

$x = 60$ Divide each side by 3.

ANSWER ▶ The value of x is 60.

Find the value of *x*.

5.
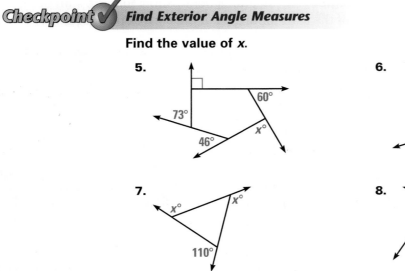

6.
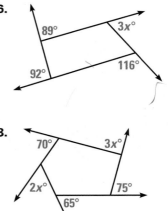

7.

8.

8.2 Exercises

Guided Practice

Vocabulary Check

1. Name an *interior angle* and an *exterior angle* of polygon *ABCDE* shown at the right.

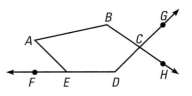

Skill Check

2. Write the formula that is used to find the sum of the measures of the interior angles of any convex polygon with *n* sides.

3. Use your answer from Exercise 2 to find the sum of the measures of the interior angles of a convex polygon with 9 sides.

Write an equation to find the measure of ∠1. Do not solve the equation.

4.
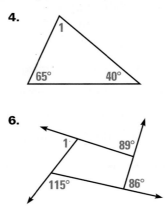

5.

6.
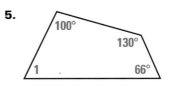

7.
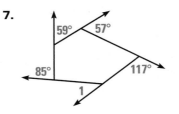

Practice and Applications

Extra Practice

See p. 689.

Sum of Interior Angle Measures **Find the sum of the measures of the interior angles of the convex polygon.**

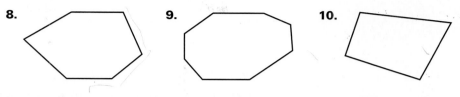

8.

9.

10.

Polygons with *n* Sides **Find the sum of the measures of the interior angles of the convex polygon with *n* sides.**

11. $n = 10$

12. $n = 15$

13. $n = 20$

14. $n = 30$

15. $n = 52$

16. $n = 100$

Interior Angle Measures **Find the measure of $\angle A$.**

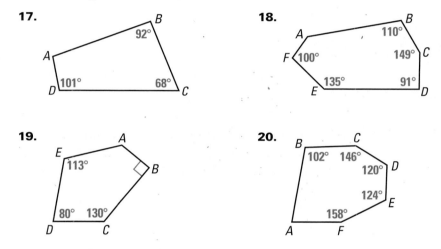

17.

18.

19.

20.

Student Help
CLASSZONE.COM

HOMEWORK HELP
Extra help with problem solving in Exs. 21–23 is at classzone.com

Interior Angles of Regular Polygons **Find the measure of an interior angle of the regular polygon.**

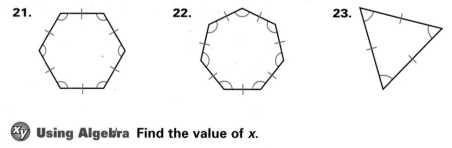

21.

22.

23.

Using Algebra **Find the value of *x*.**

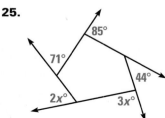

24.

25.

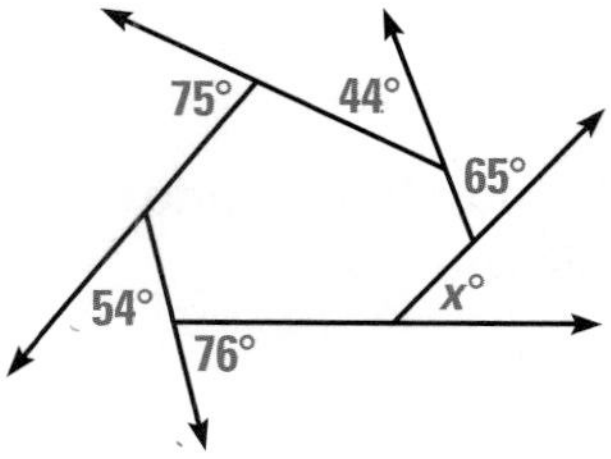

Homework Help

Example 1: Exs. 8–16
Example 2: Exs. 17–20
Example 3: Exs. 21–23
Example 4: Exs. 24, 25

BASEBALL Home plate is used to find the placement of the foul lines on the playing field.

Baseball **A home plate for a baseball field is a pentagon as shown.**

26. Is the polygon regular? Explain why or why not.

27. What is the sum of the interior angles?

28. Find the measures of $\angle C$ and $\angle E$.

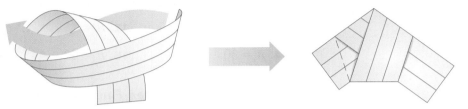

Visualize It! **Cut a strip of lined paper and tie it into an overhand knot as shown. Gently flatten the knot to form a pentagon. The pentagon should be regular.**

29. Find the measure of an interior angle of a regular pentagon.

30. Measure the interior angles of your knot with a protractor. Use your answer to Exercise 29 to determine whether your pentagon is regular.

Logical Reasoning **Select the word that makes the statement true.**

31. The sum of the measures of the exterior angles of a convex polygon, one at each vertex, is (*always, sometimes, never*) 360°.

32. The sum of the measures of the interior angles of a convex octagon is (*always, sometimes, never*) 1440°.

33. The measures of the exterior angles of a convex polygon are (*always, sometimes, never*) equal.

34. **Outdoor Furniture** You are constructing a regular hexagonal wooden bench like the one shown. On the bench, $\angle 1 \cong \angle 2$. Find the measures of $\angle 1$ and $\angle 2$ so that you know what angle to use to cut the pieces of wood.

Challenge **Find the number of sides of the regular polygon with the given exterior angle measure.**

35. 60°   **36.** 20°   **37.** 72°   **38.** 10°

Multiple Choice In Exercises 39 and 40, use the diagram below.

39. What is the value of *x*?

    A 18   **B** 78

    C 117   **D** 198

40. What is the measure of ∠*P*?

    F 39°   **G** 78°   **H** 156°   **J** 234°

Mixed Review

Using a Centroid *E* is the centroid of △*ABC*. Find *BE* and *ED*. (*Lesson 4.6*)

41. *BD* = 6   **42.** *BD* = 33   **43.** *BD* = 52

Algebra Skills

Absolute Value Evaluate. (*Skills Review, p. 662*)

44. $|-5|$ **45.** $|11|$ **46.** $|-48|$ **47.** $|0|$

48. $|13.2|$ **49.** $|-2|$ **50.** $|-0.001|$ **51.** $|-1.11|$

Quiz 1

Decide whether the polygon is regular. Explain your answer. (*Lesson 8.1*)

1.   **2.**   **3.**

Find the measure of ∠1. (*Lesson 8.2*)

4.   **5.**   **6.**

7.   **8.**

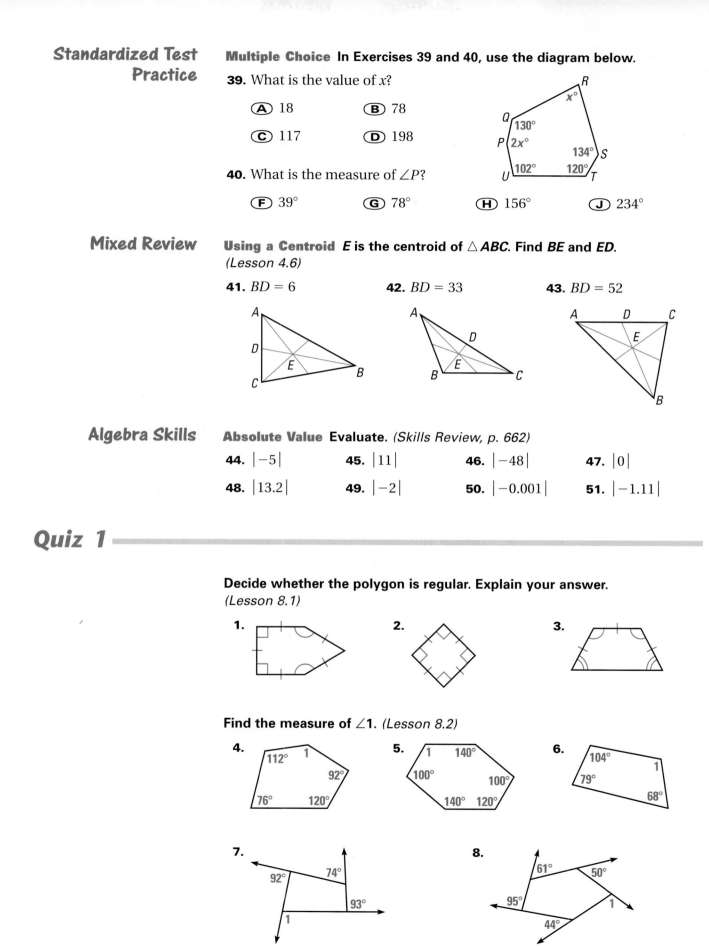

8.3 Area of Squares and Rectangles

Goal

Find the area of squares and rectangles.

Key Words

- area
- square p. 325
- rectangle p. 325

Can you tell which of the rectangles below covers more surface?

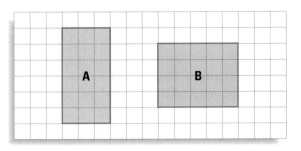

Rectangle A is made up of 18 squares while rectangle B is made up of 20 squares. So, rectangle B covers more *area*. The amount of surface covered by a figure is its **area**.

Area is measured in square units such as square inches (in.²) and square meters (m²).

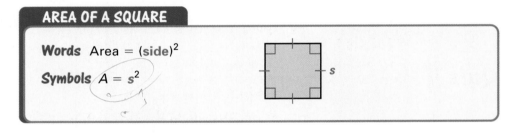

AREA OF A SQUARE

Words Area = (side)²

Symbols $A = s^2$

EXAMPLE 1 Find the Area of a Square

Find the area of the square.

9 ft

Solution

Use the formula for the area of a square and substitute 9 for *s*.

$A = s^2$ Formula for the area of a square

$= 9^2$ Substitute 9 for *s*.

$= 81$ Simplify.

ANSWER ▶ The area of the square is 81 square feet.

AREA OF A RECTANGLE

Words Area = (base)(height)

Symbols $A = bh$

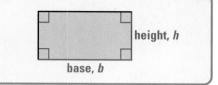

height, h

base, b

EXAMPLE 2 **Find the Area of a Rectangle**

Find the area of the rectangular pool.

Solution

Use the formula for the area of a rectangle. Substitute 24 for b and 16 for h.

$A = bh$ Formula for the area of a rectangle

$= 24 \cdot 16$ Substitute 24 for b and 16 for h.

$= 384$ Multiply.

16 ft

24 ft

ANSWER ▶ The area of the pool is 384 square feet.

 Using Algebra

EXAMPLE 3 **Find the Height of a Rectangle**

The rectangle has an area of 54 square inches. Find its height.

$A = 54$ in.^{2} h

9 in.

Solution

Use the formula for the area of a rectangle and substitute 54 for A and 9 for b.

$A = bh$ Formula for the area of a rectangle

$54 = 9h$ Substitute 54 for A and 9 for b.

$6 = h$ Divide each side by 9.

ANSWER ▶ The height of the rectangle is 6 inches.

Checkpoint ✓ **Area of Squares and Rectangles**

Find the area of the quadrilateral.

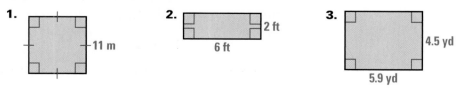

1. 11 m

2. 2 ft   6 ft

3. 4.5 yd   5.9 yd

4. A rectangle has an area of 52 square meters and a height of 4 meters. Find the length of its base.

To find the area of a complex polygon, divide the polygon into smaller regions whose areas you can find.

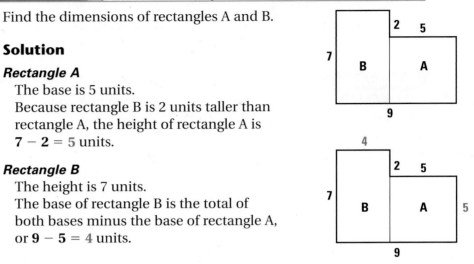

EXAMPLE 4 *Divide a Complex Polygon into Rectangles*

Find the dimensions of rectangles A and B.

Solution

Rectangle A
The base is 5 units.
Because rectangle B is 2 units taller than rectangle A, the height of rectangle A is
$7 - 2 = 5$ units.

Rectangle B
The height is 7 units.
The base of rectangle B is the total of both bases minus the base of rectangle A, or $9 - 5 = 4$ units.

EXAMPLE 5 *Find the Area of a Complex Polygon*

Find the area of the polygon made up of rectangles.

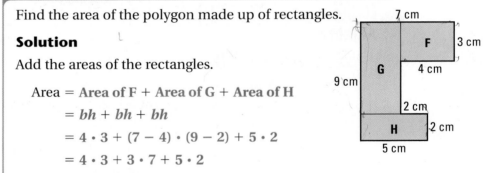

Solution

Add the areas of the rectangles.

Area = **Area of F + Area of G + Area of H**

$= bh + bh + bh$

$= 4 \cdot 3 + (7 - 4) \cdot (9 - 2) + 5 \cdot 2$

$= 4 \cdot 3 + 3 \cdot 7 + 5 \cdot 2$

$= 12 + 21 + 10$

$= 43$

ANSWER ▶ The total area of the polygon is 43 square centimeters.

Checkpoint ✓ *Polygons Made Up of Rectangles*

Find the area of the polygon made up of rectangles.

5.

6.

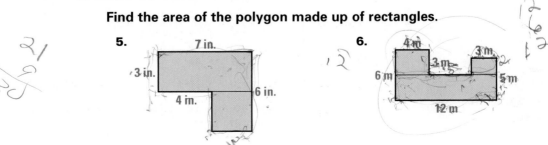

8.3 Exercises

Guided Practice

Vocabulary Check

1. What kind of quadrilateral has opposite sides parallel, opposite sides congruent, and four right angles?

Skill Check

Match the figure with the corresponding area equation.

A. $A = x^2$ **B.** $A = 2x^2$ **C.** $A = 4x^2$

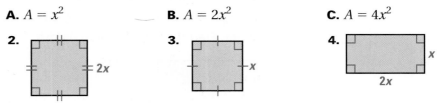

2.   2x

3.   x

4.   x   2x

Determine whether the statement about the diagram is *true* or *false*. Explain your answer.

5. To find the area of the entire polygon, add the areas of the three rectangles.

6. The height of rectangle A is 1 unit.

7. The height of rectangle C is 5 units.

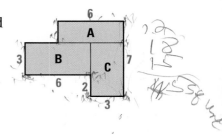

Practice and Applications

Extra Practice

See p. 689.

Area of a Square Find the area of the square.

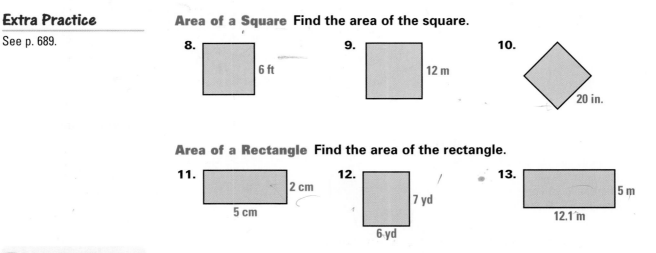

8.   6 ft

9.   12 m

10.   20 in.

Area of a Rectangle Find the area of the rectangle.

11.   2 cm   5 cm

12.   7 yd   6 yd

13.   5 m   12.1 m

Homework Help

Example 1: Exs. 8–10, 14
Example 2: Exs. 11–13, 15, 16
Example 3: Exs. 20–22
Example 4: Exs. 24–26
Example 5: Exs. 27–30

Visualize It! Sketch the figure and find its area.

14. A square with side lengths of 2.2 centimeters

15. A rectangle with a base of 4 meters and a height of 11 meters

16. A rectangle with a base of 13 feet and a height of 8 feet

Judo The dimensions of the squares on a judo mat are given in the diagram.

17. Find the area of the entire mat.

18. Find the area of the contest area.

19. Find the area of the contest area including the danger area.

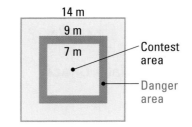

14 m
9 m
7 m
Contest area
Danger area

xy Using Algebra In Exercises 20–22, *A* gives the area of the rectangle. Find the missing side length.

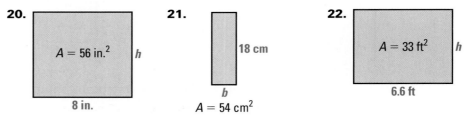

20.

$A = 56$ in.^{2} *h*

8 in.

21.

18 cm

b

$A = 54$ cm^2

22.

$A = 33$ ft^2 *h*

6.6 ft

23. *You be the Judge* The perimeter of a square is 28 feet. Can you conclude that the area of the square is 49 square feet? Explain.

Dividing a Polygon Find the dimensions of the rectangle.

24. Rectangle A

25. Rectangle B

26. Rectangle C

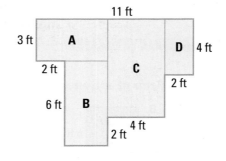

11 ft

3 ft   A

2 ft

6 ft   B

D   4 ft

C

2 ft

4 ft
2 ft

Visualize It!

In Exs. 27–30, the polygons can be divided into rectangles in different ways. For example, Ex. 27 can be divided as follows:

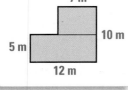

7 m
5 m
10 m
12 m

Area of Complex Polygons Find the area of the polygon made up of rectangles.

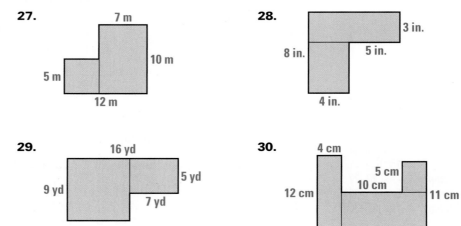

27.

7 m

5 m
10 m

12 m

28.

3 in.

8 in.   5 in.

4 in.

29.

16 yd

9 yd
5 yd

7 yd

30.

4 cm

5 cm
10 cm

12 cm

11 cm

18 cm

Maize Maze Brett Herbst transforms cornfields into mazes. His maze in Utah, shown at the right, is in the shape of Utah.

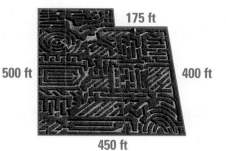

31. What is the area covered by the maze, which is made up of two rectangles?

32. How many acres does the maze cover? (1 acre = 43,560 square feet)

33. Suppose corn seed costs $34 per acre and fertilizer costs $57 per acre. How much will it cost to seed and fertilize a field with the same dimensions as the maze?

Standardized Test Practice

34. Multi-Step Problem The polygon below is made up of rectangles.

a. Write an expression for the area of the polygon.

b. Suppose the area is 65 square units. Find the value of x.

c. Using your results from part (b), sketch the figure and label all of its dimensions.

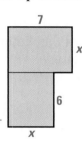

Mixed Review

Congruent Parts Use the diagram of parallelogram *ABCD*. Match the segment or angle with a congruent one. Give a reason for your answer. *(Lesson 6.2)*

35. $\overline{CE}$

36. $\overline{CD}$

37. $\angle ABD$

38. $\angle CBA$

A. $\overline{AB}$

B. $\angle ADC$

C. $\overline{AE}$

D. $\angle CDB$

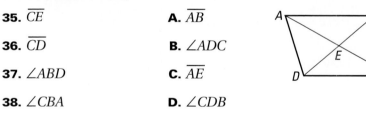

Determining Similarity Determine whether the triangles are similar. If so, state the similarity and the postulate or theorem that justifies your answer. *(Lesson 7.4)*

39.

40.

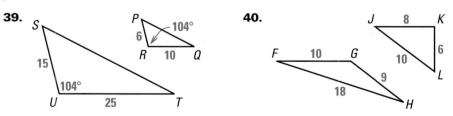

Algebra Skills

Comparing Numbers Compare the two numbers. Write the answer using <, >, or =. *(Skills Review, p. 662)*

41. 8 and −18

42. 2459 and 2495

43. −10 and 0

44. −1.12 and −1.01

45. 2.44 and 2.044

46. −0.75 and −0.7

Question

How do you find the area of a triangle?

┌─ **Materials** ─
• grid paper
• colored pencils
  or markers
• scissors
└

Explore

1 Draw a triangle on grid paper. Then draw a rectangle that encloses the triangle. Write down the dimensions of the rectangle.

2 Cut out the rectangle. Then cut the triangles out of the rectangle.

3 Try to cover the large triangle with the two smaller triangles.

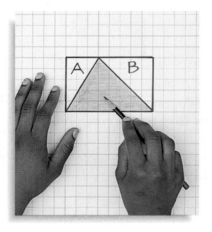

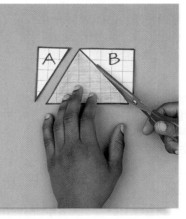

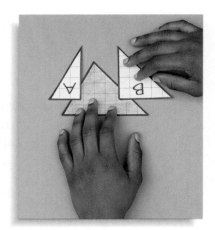

Think About It

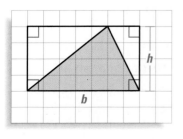

1. Do the two smaller triangles cover the same area as the large triangle?

2. How is the area of the large triangle related to the area of the original rectangle?

3. Use the dimensions of the rectangle in Step 1 to find the area of the rectangle. Then use your answer to find the area of the large triangle.

4. Use the diagram at the left to write a rule for finding the area of a triangle given its base b and its height h.

5. Find the area of a triangle with a base of 14 feet and a height of 6 feet.

Area of Triangles

Goal
Find the area of triangles.

Key Words
• height of a triangle
• base of a triangle

The amount of material needed to make the sail at the right is determined by the area of the triangular sail.

The *height* and *base* of a triangle are used to find its area.

The **height of a triangle** is the perpendicular segment from a vertex to the line containing the opposite side. The opposite side is called the **base of the triangle** . The terms *height* and *base* are also used to represent the segment lengths.

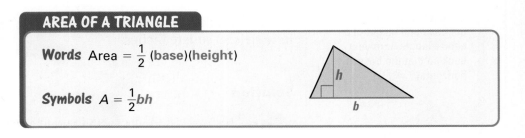

In a right triangle, a leg is a height.　　**A height can be inside the triangle.**　　**A height can be outside the triangle.**

As shown in Activity 8.4, the area of a triangle is found using a base and its corresponding height.

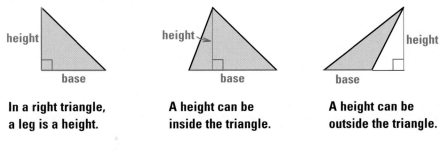

AREA OF A TRIANGLE

Words Area = $\frac{1}{2}$ (base)(height)

Symbols $A = \frac{1}{2}bh$

Triangles with the Same Area Triangles can have the same area without necessarily being congruent. For example, all of the triangles below have the same area but they are not congruent.

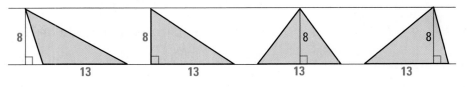

EXAMPLE 1 Find the Area of a Right Triangle

Find the area of the right triangle.

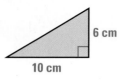

6 cm
10 cm

Solution

Use the formula for the area of a triangle. Substitute 10 for b and 6 for h.

$A = \frac{1}{2}bh$	Formula for the area of a triangle
$= \frac{1}{2}(10)(6)$	Substitute 10 for b and 6 for h.
$= 30$	Simplify.

ANSWER ▶ The triangle has an area of 30 square centimeters.

EXAMPLE 2 Find the Area of a Triangle

Find the area of the triangle.

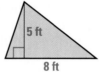

5 ft
8 ft

Solution

$A = \frac{1}{2}bh$	Formula for the area of a triangle
$= \frac{1}{2}(8)(5)$	Substitute 8 for b and 5 for h.
$= 20$	Simplify.

ANSWER ▶ The triangle has an area of 20 square feet.

Visualize It!

To help you determine the base and height of a tilted triangle, turn your book so that the base is horizontal.

h
13 in.

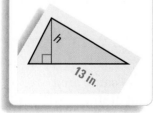

EXAMPLE 3 Find the Height of a Triangle

Find the height of the triangle, given that its area is 39 square inches.

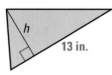

h
13 in.

Solution

$A = \frac{1}{2}bh$	Formula for the area of a triangle
$39 = \frac{1}{2}(13)h$	Substitute 39 for A and 13 for b.
$78 = 13h$	Multiply each side by 2.
$6 = h$	Divide each side by 13.

ANSWER ▶ The triangle has a height of 6 inches.

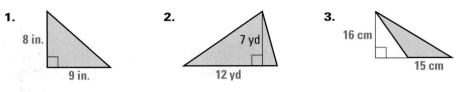

In Exercises 1–3, find the area of the triangle.

1. 8 in. 9 in.

2. 7 yd 12 yd

3. 16 cm 15 cm

4. A triangle has an area of 84 square inches and a height of 14 inches. Find the base.

EXAMPLE **4** **Areas of Similar Triangles**

a. Find the ratio of the areas of the similar triangles.

b. Find the scale factor of $\triangle ABC$ to $\triangle DEF$ and compare it to the ratio of their areas.

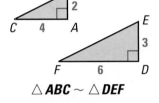

$\triangle ABC \sim \triangle DEF$

Solution

a. Area of $\triangle ABC = \frac{1}{2}bh = \frac{1}{2}(4)(2) = 4$ square units

Area of $\triangle DEF = \frac{1}{2}bh = \frac{1}{2}(6)(3) = 9$ square units

Ratio of areas $= \dfrac{\text{Area of } \triangle ABC}{\text{Area of } \triangle DEF} = \dfrac{4}{9}$

Student Help

LOOK BACK
To review scale factor,
see p. 366.

b. The scale factor of $\triangle ABC$ to $\triangle DEF$ is $\frac{2}{3}$.

The ratio of the areas is the square of the scale factor: $\dfrac{2^2}{3^2} = \dfrac{4}{9}$.

The relationship in Example 4 is generalized for all similar polygons in the following theorem.

THEOREM 8.3

Areas of Similar Polygons

Words If two polygons are similar with a scale factor of $\frac{a}{b}$, then the ratio of their areas is $\frac{a^2}{b^2}$.

Symbols If $ABCD \sim EFGH$ with a scale factor of $\frac{a}{b}$, then $\dfrac{\text{Area of } ABCD}{\text{Area of } EFGH} = \dfrac{a^2}{b^2}$.

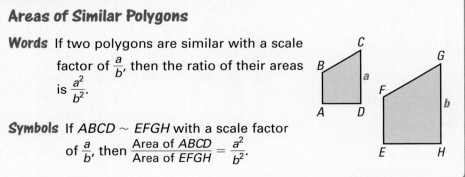

8.4 Exercises

Guided Practice

Vocabulary Check

1. What are the measures of the base and the height of the shaded triangle at the right?

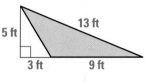

5 ft   13 ft
3 ft   9 ft

Skill Check

The triangle has a horizontal base of 15 units and a height of 7 units. Sketch the triangle and label its base and its height.

2. 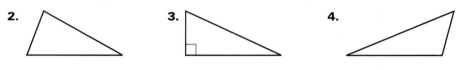   3.   4.

Practice and Applications

Extra Practice

See p. 690.

Area of a Right Triangle Find the area of the right triangle.

5.   6. 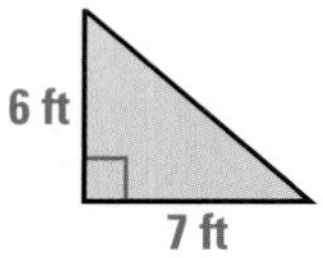   7.

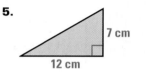

7 cm
12 cm

6 ft
7 ft

3 yd   5 yd

Finding Area In Exercises 8–13, find the area of the triangle.

8. 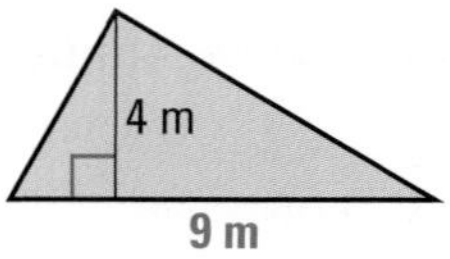   9. 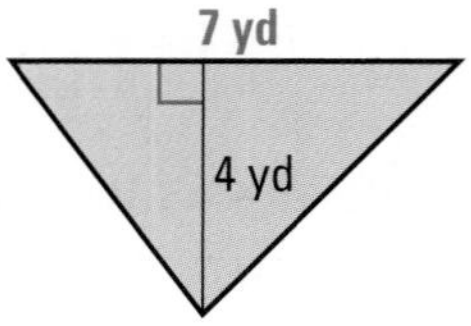   10.

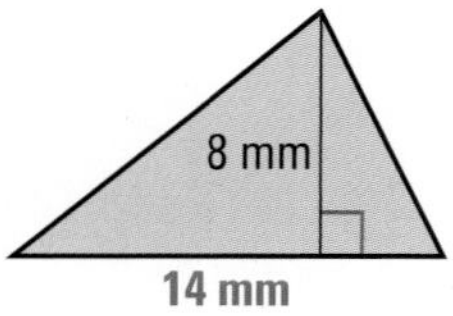

4 m
9 m

7 yd
4 yd

8 mm
14 mm

11. 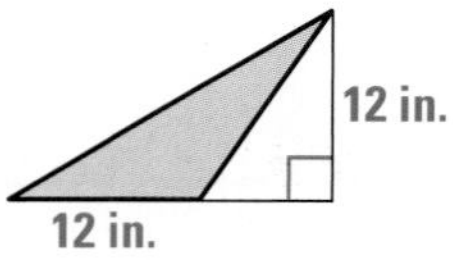   12. 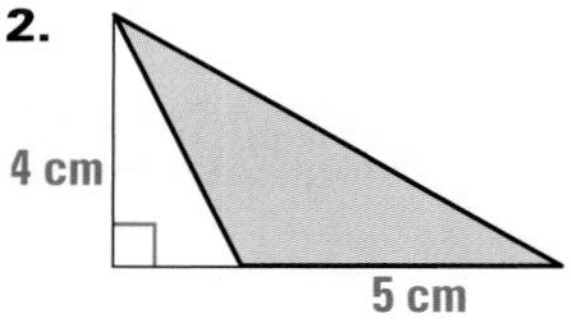   13.

12 in.
12 in.

4 cm
5 cm

9 ft   14 ft

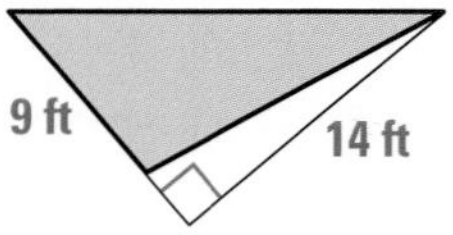

14. **You be the Judge** In the triangle at the right, Trisha says the base is 15 and the height is 4. Luis says that the base is 5 and the height is 12. Who is right? Explain your reasoning.

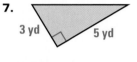

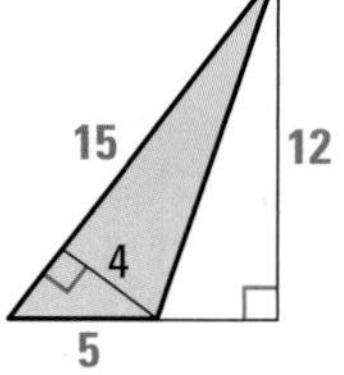

15   12
4
5

Homework Help

Example 1: Exs. 5–7
Example 2: Exs. 8–13
Example 3: Exs. 16–20
Example 4: Exs. 26, 27

15. Visualize It! Draw three different triangles that each have an area of 24 square units.

Using Algebra In Exercises 16–18, *A* gives the area of the triangle. Find the missing measure.

16. $A = 22$ ft^2

17. $A = 63$ cm^2

18. $A = 80$ m^2

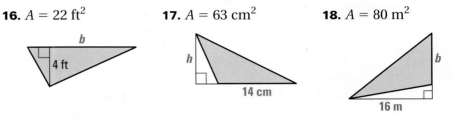

19. Finding the Height A triangle has an area of 78 square inches and a base of 13 inches. Find the height.

20. Finding the Base A triangle has an area of 135 square meters and a height of 9 meters. Find the base.

Tiles In Exercises 21 and 22, use the diagram of the tile pattern.

21. Find the area of one triangular tile.

22. The tiles are being used to make a rectangular border that is 4 inches high and 48 inches long. How many tiles are needed for the border? (*Hint:* Start by finding the area of the border.)

Complex Polygons Find the area of the polygon by using the triangles and rectangles shown.

23.

24.

25.

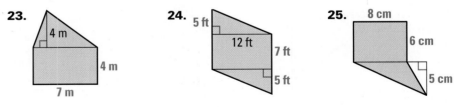

Areas of Similar Triangles In Exercises 26 and 27, the triangles are similar. Find the scale factor of $\triangle PQR$ to $\triangle XYZ$. Then find the ratio of their areas.

26.

27.

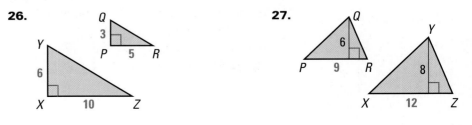

Area of a Regular Octagon In Exercises 28–30, use the regular octagon at the right.

28. Find the area of $\triangle GXF$ in the octagon.

29. Copy the diagram. To form congruent triangles, connect the following pairs of vertices: A and E, B and F, C and G, D and H. How many triangles are formed?

30. What is the area of the octagon? Explain.

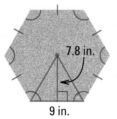

31. Rock Formations Many basaltic columns are hexagonal. The top of one of these columns is a regular hexagon as shown below. Find its area. (Another photograph of basaltic columns is on page 408.)

7.8 in.

9 in.

| EXAMPLE | *Using the Pythagorean Theorem* |

Find the area of the triangle.

13   5 b

Solution

First, find the base. Use the Pythagorean Theorem to find the value of b.

$(\text{hypotenuse})^2 = (\text{leg})^2 + (\text{leg})^2$	Pythagorean Theorem
$(13)^2 = (5)^2 + (b)^2$	Substitute.
$169 = 25 + b^2$	Simplify.
$144 = b^2$	Subtract 25 from each side.
$12 = b$	Find the positive square root.

Use 12 as the base in the formula for the area of a triangle.

$A = \frac{1}{2}bh = \frac{1}{2}(12)(5) = 30$ square units

Using the Pythagorean Theorem Find the area of the triangle.

32.   **33.**   **34.**

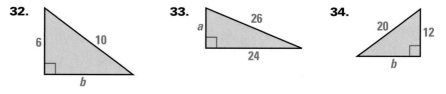

Standardized Test Practice

35. Multiple Choice Given that the area of the triangle is 99 square meters, what is the height of the triangle?

(A) 4.5 m   (B) 9 m

(C) 11 m   (D) 22 m

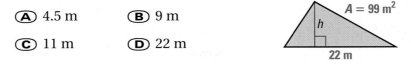

$A = 99\ m^2$

h

22 m

Mixed Review

Trapezoids Find the value of *x* in the trapezoid. *(Lesson 6.5)*

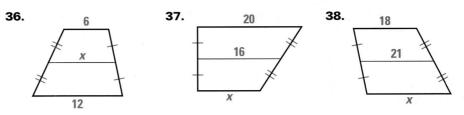

36. 6 x 12

37. 20 16 x

38. 18 21 x

Algebra Skills

Naming Coordinates Give the coordinates of the point.
(Skills Review, p. 664)

39. *A*   **40.** *B*

41. *C*   **42.** *D*

43. *E*   **44.** *F*

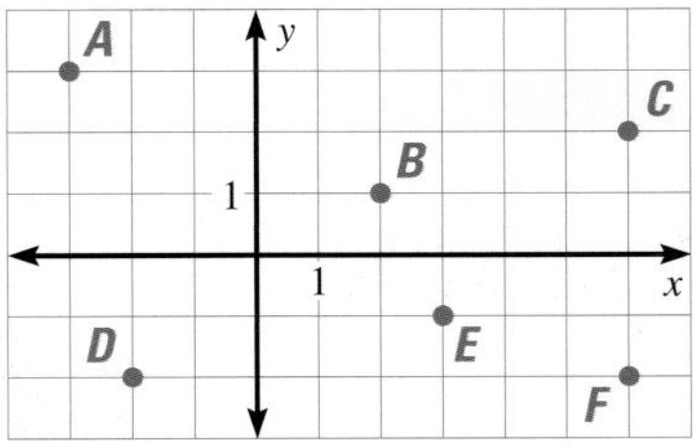

Quiz 2

Find the area of the polygon. *(Lessons 8.3, 8.4)*

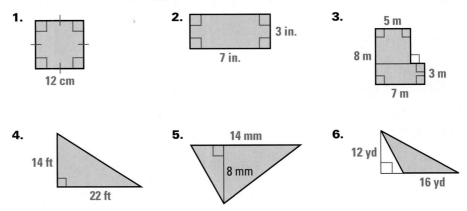

1. 12 cm

2. 3 in. 7 in.

3. 5 m 8 m 3 m 7 m

4. 14 ft 22 ft

5. 14 mm 8 mm

6. 12 yd 16 yd

In Exercises 7–9, *A* gives the area of the polygon. Find the missing measure. *(Lessons 8.3, 8.4)*

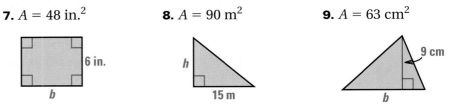

7. $A = 48\ in.^2$ 6 in. b

8. $A = 90\ m^2$ h 15 m

9. $A = 63\ cm^2$ 9 cm b

8.4 Area of Similar Triangles

Question

How are the areas of similar triangles related to the scale factor of the triangles?

Explore

1 Draw a triangle. Construct point *D* outside the triangle.

2 Dilate the triangle by a scale factor of 3 using *D* as the center.

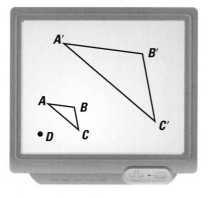

3 Construct the interior of each triangle. Measure the area of each triangle.

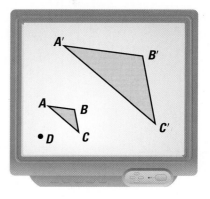

Think About It

Student Help

LOOK BACK
To review the definition of scale factor, see p. 366.

1. Divide the area of △*A'B'C'* by the area of △*ABC*. How is the ratio of the areas related to the scale factor?

2. What happens to the ratio of the areas as you drag point *A*?

3. What theorem does this exploration illustrate?

Extension Use geometry software to draw a triangle. Construct the interior of the triangle.

4. What is the area of the triangle?

5. The scale factor of this triangle to a larger triangle is 2.7. What is the area of the larger triangle?

6. To check your answer to Exercise 5, dilate the original triangle by a scale factor of 2.7 and measure the area of the larger triangle.

8.5 Area of Parallelograms

Goal

Find the area of parallelograms.

Key Words

- base of a parallelogram
- height of a parallelogram
- parallelogram p. 310
- rhombus p. 325

Geo-Activity ▸ Exploring the Area of a Parallelogram

1 Use a straightedge to draw a line through one of the vertices of an index card.

2 Cut out the triangle. Tape the triangle to the opposite side to form a parallelogram.

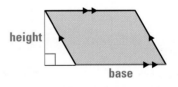

3 How does the area of the parallelogram compare to the area of the rectangular index card? How do their bases compare? How do their heights compare?

4 Write a conjecture about the formula for the area of a parallelogram.

Either pair of parallel sides of a parallelogram are called the **bases of a parallelogram** .

The shortest distance between the bases of a parallelogram is called the **height of a parallelogram** . The segment that represents the height is perpendicular to the bases.

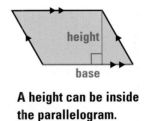

A height can be inside the parallelogram.

A height can be outside the parallelogram.

As the Geo-Activity suggests, the area of a parallelogram is found using a base and its corresponding height.

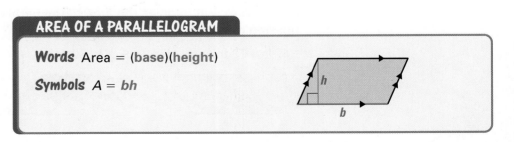

AREA OF A PARALLELOGRAM

Words Area = (base)(height)

Symbols $A = bh$

EXAMPLE 1 **Find the Area of a Parallelogram**

Find the area of the parallelogram.

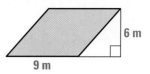

Solution

Use the formula for the area of a parallelogram. Substitute 9 for b and 6 for h.

$A = bh$ Formula for the area of a parallelogram

  $= (9)(6)$ Substitute 9 for b and 6 for h.

  $= 54$ Multiply.

ANSWER ▸ The parallelogram has an area of 54 square meters.

 Using Algebra

EXAMPLE 2 **Find the Height of a Parallelogram**

Find the height of the parallelogram given that its area is 78 square feet.

$A = 78 \text{ ft}^2$

Solution

$A = bh$ Formula for the area of a parallelogram

$78 = 12h$ Substitute 78 for A and 12 for b.

$6.5 = h$ Divide each side by 12.

ANSWER ▸ The parallelogram has a height of 6.5 feet.

Checkpoint ✔ **Area of Parallelograms**

Find the area of the parallelogram.

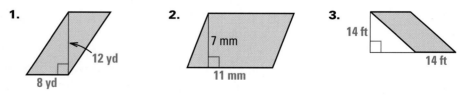

1. 12 yd, 8 yd

2. 7 mm, 11 mm

3. 14 ft, 14 ft

In Exercises 4–6, A gives the area of the parallelogram. Find the missing measure.

4. $A = 72 \text{ in.}^2$ **5.** $A = 30 \text{ m}^2$ **6.** $A = 28 \text{ cm}^2$

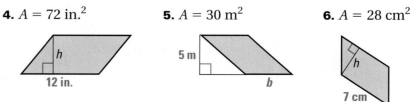

AREA OF A RHOMBUS

Words Area = $\frac{1}{2}$(product of diagonals)

Symbols $A = \frac{1}{2}d_1 d_2$

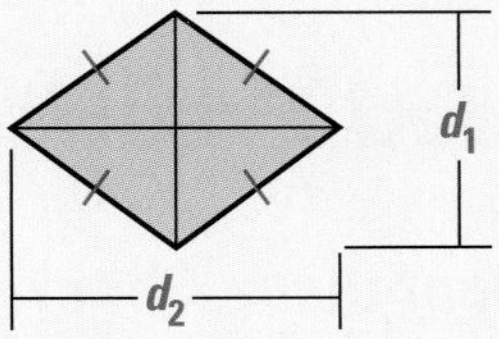

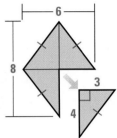

Area of a Rhombus The formula for the area of a rhombus can be justified using the area of a triangle. A specific case is given below.

The diagonals divide a rhombus into four congruent right triangles. So, the area of the rhombus is 4 times the area of one of the right triangles.

Area of 1 triangle = $\frac{1}{2}bh = \frac{1}{2}(3)(4) = 6$ square units

Area of 4 triangles = $4(6) = 24$ square units

Notice that $\frac{1}{2}d_1 d_2$, or $\frac{1}{2}(6)(8)$, also equals 24 square units.

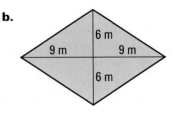

Student Help
CLASSZONE.COM

MORE EXAMPLES
More examples at classzone.com

EXAMPLE 3 **Find the Area of a Rhombus**

Find the area of the rhombus.

a.
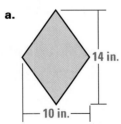

b.
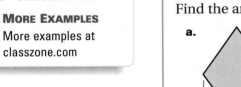

Solution

a. $A = \frac{1}{2}d_1 d_2$

   $= \frac{1}{2}(14)(10)$

   $= 70$

The area of the rhombus is 70 square inches.

Solution

b. $A = \frac{1}{2}d_1 d_2$

   $= \frac{1}{2}(6 + 6)(9 + 9)$

   $= \frac{1}{2}(12)(18)$

   $= 108$

The area of the rhombus is 108 square meters.

Guided Practice

Vocabulary Check

1. The parallelogram at the right has a base of 7 units and a height of 4 units. Sketch the parallelogram and label its base and height.

Skill Check

Match the quadrilateral with the corresponding area equation.

A. $A = \frac{1}{2}(6)(10)$ **B.** $A = (13)(6)$ **C.** $A = (10)(6)$

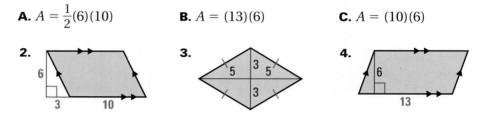

2.   **3.**   **4.**

Find the measures of the diagonals of the rhombus.

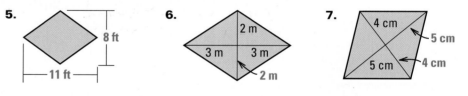

5.   **6.**   **7.**

Practice and Applications

Extra Practice

See p. 690.

Area of Parallelograms **Find the area of the parallelogram.**

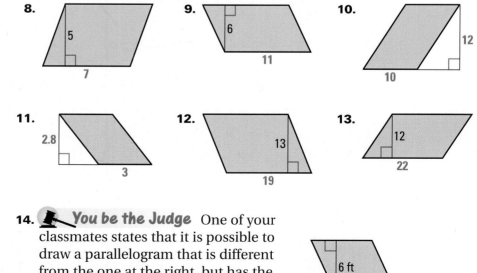

8.   **9.**   **10.**

11.   **12.**   **13.**

Homework Help

Example 1: Exs. 8–13
Example 2: Exs. 18–22
Example 3: Exs. 23–28

14. **You be the Judge** One of your classmates states that it is possible to draw a parallelogram that is different from the one at the right, but has the same area. Do you agree or disagree? Explain your reasoning.

6 ft

7 ft

15. Stained Glass The piece of stained glass at the right is made up of eight congruent parallelograms. Each parallelogram has a base of 8 centimeters and a height of 3 centimeters. Find the area of the entire piece.

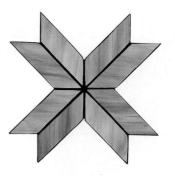

Error Analysis In Exercises 16 and 17, students were asked to find the area of the parallelogram. Describe and correct any errors.

16.

$$A = bh$$
$$= (7)(5)$$
$$= 35$$

17.

$$A = \frac{1}{2}bh$$
$$= \frac{1}{2}(14)(11)$$
$$= 77$$

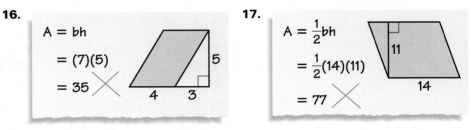

Using Algebra In Exercises 18–20, *A* gives the area of the parallelogram. Find the missing measure.

18. $A = 88$ cm^2

19. $A = 30$ in.^{2}

20. $A = 39$ ft^2

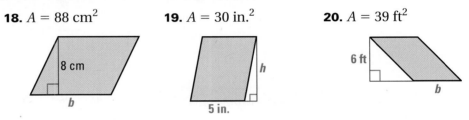

21. A parallelogram has a base of 13 meters and an area of 104 square meters. Find the height.

22. A parallelogram has a height of 12 feet and an area of 132 square feet. Find the base.

Area of Rhombuses Find the area of the rhombus.

23.

24.

25.

26.

27.

28.

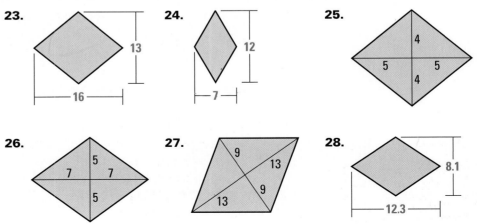

Penrose Rhombuses The rhombuses shown below are named after the British physicist Roger Penrose. He found that these rhombuses can be used to cover a surface without any gaps and without having to repeat the same pattern. An example is shown below.

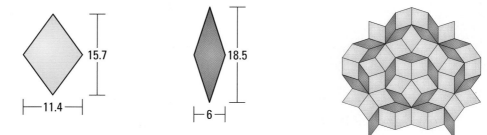

29. Find the area of the yellow rhombus.

30. Find the area of the red rhombus.

31. The pattern above contains 32 yellow and 21 red rhombuses. Find its area.

Area of Complex Polygons Find the area of the entire polygon by adding the areas of the smaller polygons.

32.   **33.**   **34.**

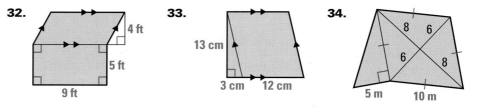

EXAMPLE | **Area on the Coordinate Plane**

Find the area of the parallelogram.

Solution

Count the squares to find the base and the height. The base is 4 units and the height is 5 units.

$A = bh$ — Formula for area of a parallelogram

$= (4)(5)$ — Substitute 4 for b and 5 for h.

$= 20$ — Multiply.

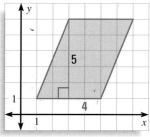

Area on the Coordinate Plane Find the area of the parallelogram.

35.   **36.**   **37.**

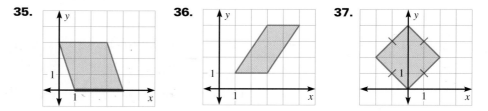

Challenge Find the area of the given quadrilateral.

38. Parallelogram *ABCD*

39. Rhombus *FGHJ*

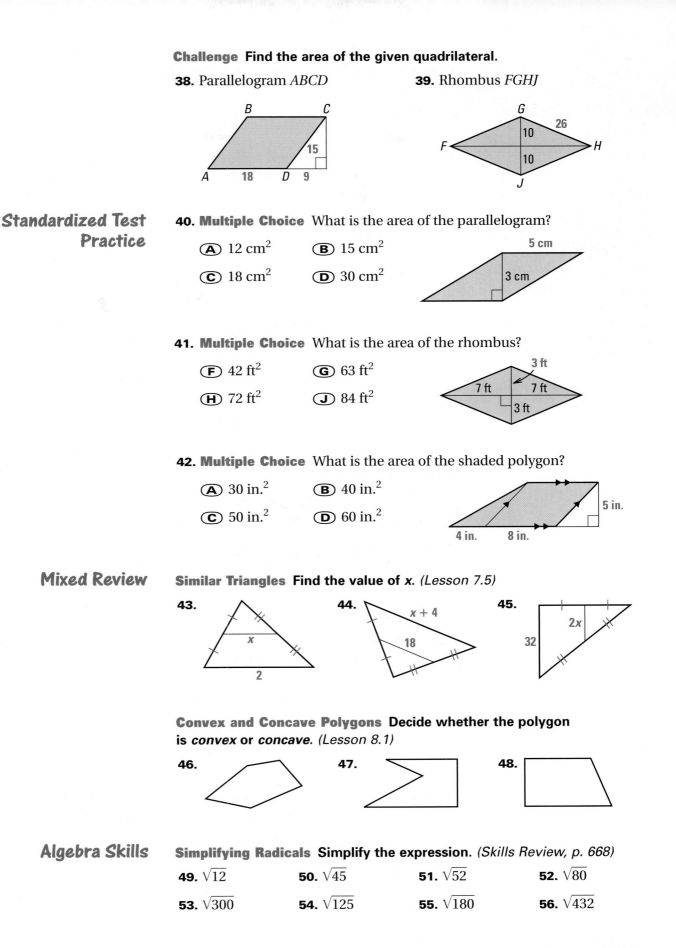

40. Multiple Choice What is the area of the parallelogram?

(A) 12 cm²   (B) 15 cm²

(C) 18 cm²   (D) 30 cm²

41. Multiple Choice What is the area of the rhombus?

(F) 42 ft²   (G) 63 ft²

(H) 72 ft²   (J) 84 ft²

42. Multiple Choice What is the area of the shaded polygon?

(A) 30 in.²   (B) 40 in.²

(C) 50 in.²   (D) 60 in.²

Mixed Review

Similar Triangles Find the value of *x*. *(Lesson 7.5)*

43.   **44.**   **45.**

Convex and Concave Polygons Decide whether the polygon is *convex* or *concave*. *(Lesson 8.1)*

46.   **47.**   **48.**

Algebra Skills

Simplifying Radicals Simplify the expression. *(Skills Review, p. 668)*

49. $\sqrt{12}$ **50.** $\sqrt{45}$ **51.** $\sqrt{52}$ **52.** $\sqrt{80}$

53. $\sqrt{300}$ **54.** $\sqrt{125}$ **55.** $\sqrt{180}$ **56.** $\sqrt{432}$

8.6 # Area of Trapezoids

Goal
Find the area of trapezoids.

Key Words
- trapezoid p. 332
- base of a trapezoid p. 332
- height of a trapezoid

Recall that the parallel sides of a trapezoid are called the *bases* of the trapezoid, with lengths denoted by b_1 and b_2.

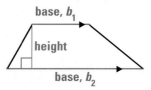

The shortest distance between the bases is the **height of the trapezoid** .

Suppose that two congruent trapezoids with bases b_1 and b_2 and height h are arranged to form a parallelogram as shown.

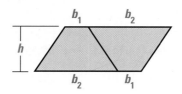

Student Help

LOOK BACK
To review more about trapezoids, see p. 332.

The area of the parallelogram is $h(b_1 + b_2)$. Because the two trapezoids are congruent, the area of one of the trapezoids is half the area of the parallelogram.

AREA OF A TRAPEZOID

Words Area $= \frac{1}{2}$(height)(sum of bases)

Symbols $A = \frac{1}{2}h(b_1 + b_2)$

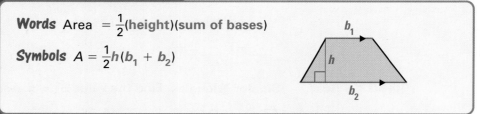

EXAMPLE ❶ **Find the Area of a Trapezoid**

Find the area of the trapezoid.

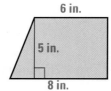

Solution

$A = \frac{1}{2}h(b_1 + b_2)$ Formula for the area of a trapezoid

$= \frac{1}{2}(5)(6 + 8)$ Substitute 5 for h, 6 for b_1, and 8 for b_2.

$= \frac{1}{2}(5)(14)$ Simplify within parentheses.

$= 35$ Simplify.

ANSWER ▶ The area of the trapezoid is 35 square inches.

Find the area of the trapezoid.

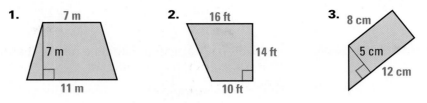

1. 7 m / 7 m / 11 m

2. 16 ft / 14 ft / 10 ft

3. 8 cm / 5 cm / 12 cm

EXAMPLE **2** **Use the Area of a Trapezoid**

Find the value of b_2 given that the area of the trapezoid is 96 square meters.

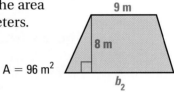

9 m / 8 m / $A = 96\ m^2$ / b_2

Solution

$$A = \frac{1}{2}h(b_1 + b_2)$$ Formula for the area of a trapezoid

▶ $$96 = \frac{1}{2}(8)(9 + b_2)$$ Substitute 96 for A, 8 for h, and 9 for b_1.

$$192 = 8(9 + b_2)$$ Multiply each side by 2.

$$192 = 72 + 8b_2$$ Use the distributive property.

$$120 = 8b_2$$ Subtract 72 from each side.

$$15 = b_2$$ Divide each side by 8.

ANSWER ▶ The value of b_2 is 15 meters.

A gives the area of the trapezoid. Find the missing measure.

4. $A = 77\ ft^2$

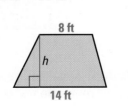

8 ft / h / 14 ft

5. $A = 39\ cm^2$

b_1 / 6 cm / 8 cm

6. $A = 84\ in.^2$

13 in. / 8 in. / b_2

7. A trapezoid has an area of 294 square yards. Its height is 14 yards and the length of one base is 30 yards. Find the length of the other base.

8.6 Exercises

Guided Practice

Vocabulary Check

1. Sketch a trapezoid. Label its height h and its bases b_1 and b_2.

Skill Check

Find the height and the lengths of the bases of the trapezoid.

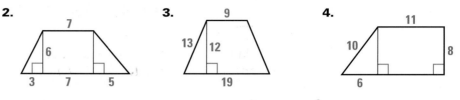

2.

3. 9

4. 11

Match the trapezoid with the equation used to find the height.

A. $A = \frac{1}{2}h(5 + 13)$ **B.** $A = \frac{1}{2}h(8 + 13)$ **C.** $A = \frac{1}{2}h(5 + 8)$

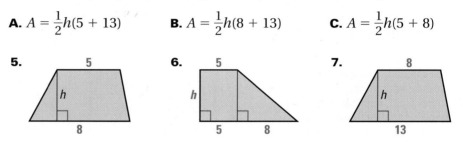

5. 5
h
8

6. 5
h
5   8

7. 8
h
13

Practice and Applications

Extra Practice
See p. 690.

Area of a Trapezoid Find the area of the trapezoid.

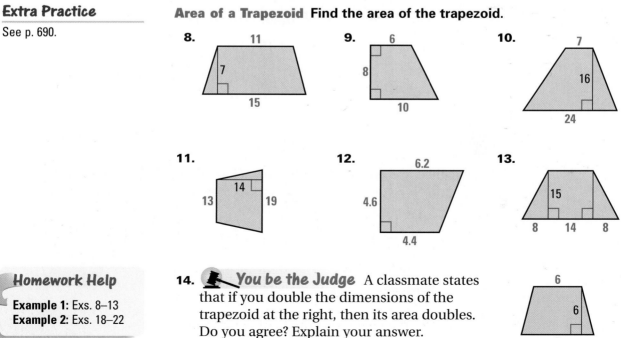

8. 11
7
15

9. 6
8
10

10. 7
16
24

11. 14
13   19

12. 6.2
4.6
4.4

13. 15
8   14   8

Homework Help

Example 1: Exs. 8–13
Example 2: Exs. 18–22

14. **You be the Judge** A classmate states that if you double the dimensions of the trapezoid at the right, then its area doubles. Do you agree? Explain your answer.

6
6
9

15. Visualize It! Draw three different trapezoids with a height of 5 units and bases of 3 units and 7 units. Then find the areas of the trapezoids. What do you notice?

Student Help

LOOK BACK
To review the midsegment of a trapezoid, see p. 333.

Technology In Exercises 16 and 17, use geometry software.

❶ Draw a trapezoid.

❷ Draw the midsegment.

16. Find the length of the midsegment and the height of the trapezoid. Multiply the two measures.

17. Find the area of the trapezoid. How does the area compare to your answer for Exercise 16?

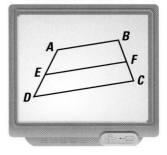

Using Algebra In Exercises 18–20, *A* gives the area of the trapezoid. Find the missing measure.

18. $A = 135$ cm^2 **19.** $A = 132$ in.^{2} **20.** $A = 198$ m^2

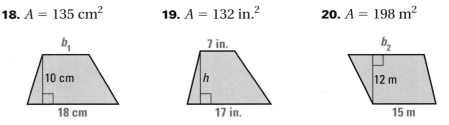

21. A trapezoid has an area of 50 square units. The lengths of the bases are 10 units and 15 units. Find the height.

22. A trapezoid has an area of 24 square units. The height is 3 units and the length of one of the bases is 5 units. Find the length of the other base.

Student Help
CLASSZONE.COM

HOMEWORK HELP
Extra help with problem solving in Exs. 21–22 is at classzone.com

Bridges In Exercises 23–25, use the following information.
The roof on the bridge below, consists of four sides: two congruent trapezoids and two congruent triangles.

Doe River Covered Bridge in Elizabethton, Tennessee

23. Find the combined area of the two trapezoids.

24. Use the diagram at the right to find the combined area of the two triangles.

25. What is the area of the entire roof?

Detail of roof

8.6 *Area of Trapezoids* **449**

Student Help

VISUAL STRATEGY
To find the area of a complex polygon, you can add the areas of the simpler shapes that make up the polygon, as shown on p. 410.

Windows Find the area of the window.

26.
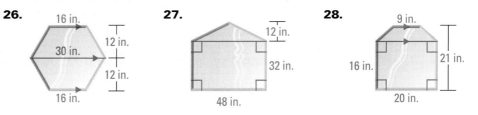

27.

28.

Using the Pythagorean Theorem Find the height using the Pythagorean Theorem and a calculator. Then find the area of the trapezoid.

29.
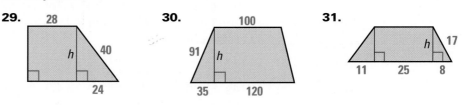

30.

31.

Standardized Test Practice

32. **Multiple Choice** What is the area of the trapezoid?

   Ⓐ 25 in.^{2} Ⓑ 42 in.^{2}

   Ⓒ 68 in.^{2} Ⓓ 84 in.^{2}

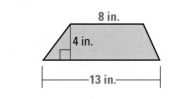

33. **Multiple Choice** What is the area of the trapezoid?

   Ⓕ 88 ft^2 Ⓖ 128 ft^2

   Ⓗ 152 ft^2 Ⓙ 176 ft^2

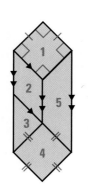

Mixed Review

Finding Area Match the region with a formula for its area. Use each formula exactly once. *(Lessons 8.3–8.6)*

34. Region 1   **A.** $A = s^2$

35. Region 2   **B.** $A = \frac{1}{2}d_1d_2$

36. Region 3   **C.** $A = \frac{1}{2}bh$

37. Region 4   **D.** $A = \frac{1}{2}h(b_1 + b_2)$

38. Region 5   **E.** $A = bh$

Algebra Skills

Fraction Operations Add or subtract. Write the answer as a fraction in simplest form. *(Skills Review, p. 658)*

39. $\frac{3}{8} + \frac{5}{8}$ 40. $\frac{5}{9} - \frac{2}{9}$ 41. $\frac{3}{4} + \frac{1}{12}$ 42. $\frac{4}{7} - \frac{1}{5}$

Question

How do you find the area of a circle using the radius?

Materials
- compass
- straightedge
- scissors

Explore

1 Use a compass to draw a circle on a piece of paper. Cut the circle out. Fold the circle in half, four times.

2 Cut the circle along the fold lines to divide the circle into 16 equal wedges.

3 Arrange the wedges to form a shape resembling a parallelogram. The base and height of the parallelogram are labeled.

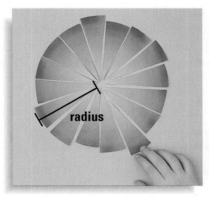

radius

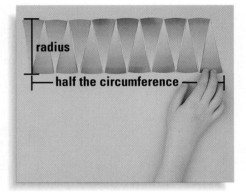

radius

half the circumference

Think About It

Student Help

VOCABULARY TIP
The *circumference* is the distance around a circle.

1. The area of the parallelogram in Step 3 can be used to approximate the area of the original circle. Write a verbal expression for the area of the parallelogram.

2. The ratio of the circumference *C* to the diameter *d* of a circle is denoted by the Greek letter π (or *pi*), which is approximately equal to 3.14. So, $C = \pi d$. Because the diameter is twice the radius *r* of the circle,

$$C = \pi d = \pi(2r) = 2\pi r.$$

Use the fact that $C = 2\pi r$ to write your verbal expression from Exercise 1 using variables. Simplify the expression.

3. Find the area of the circle at the right. Use 3.14 as an approximation for π.

4

8.7 Circumference and Area of Circles

Goal
Find the circumference and area of circles.

Key Words
- circle
- center
- radius
- diameter
- circumference
- central angle
- sector

A **circle** is the set of all points in a plane that are the same distance from a given point, called the **center** of the circle. A circle with center P is called "circle P," or $\odot P$.

The distance from the center to a point on the circle is the **radius**. The plural of radius is *radii*.

The distance across the circle, through the center, is the **diameter**. The diameter d is twice the radius r. So, $d = 2r$.

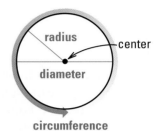

The **circumference** of a circle is the distance around the circle.

For any circle, the ratio of the circumference to its diameter is denoted by the Greek letter π, or *pi*. The number π is 3.14159 . . . , which is an irrational number. This means that π neither terminates nor repeats. So, an approximation of 3.14 is used for π.

CIRCUMFERENCE OF A CIRCLE

Words Circumference = π(diameter)
= 2π(radius)

Symbols $C = \pi d$ or $C = 2\pi r$

EXAMPLE 1 Find the Circumference of a Circle

Find the circumference of the circle.

Solution

$C = 2\pi r$	Formula for the circumference
$= 2\pi(4)$	Substitute 4 for r.
$= 8\pi$	Simplify.
$\approx 8(3.14)$	Use 3.14 as an approximation for π.
$= 25.12$	Multiply.

ANSWER ▶ The circumference is about 25 inches.

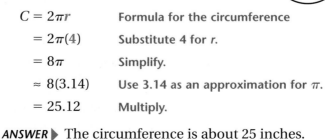

Student Help

STUDY TIP
When simplifying an expression involving π, substitute 3.14 for π. You can also use the π key on your calculator, as in Examples 2 and 3.

Find the circumference of the circle. Round your answer to the nearest whole number.

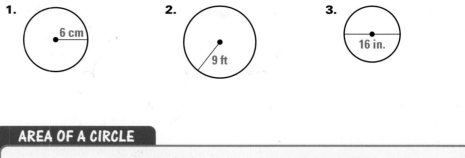

1. 6 cm

2. 9 ft

3. 16 in.

AREA OF A CIRCLE

Words Area = π(radius)^2

Symbols $A = \pi r^2$

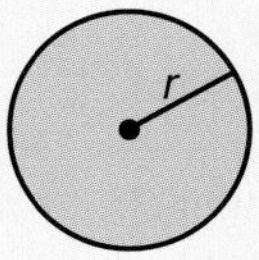

r

EXAMPLE **2** **Find the Area of a Circle**

Find the area of the circle.

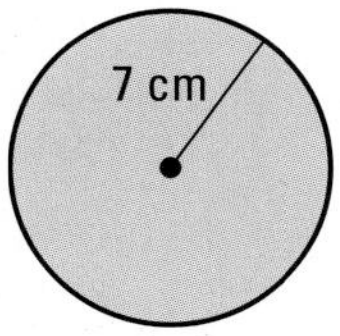

7 cm

Student Help

KEYSTROKE HELP
If your calculator has π written above a key, use the following keystrokes to simplify 49π:

49 ✕ 2nd π

Solution

$$A = \pi r^2 \qquad \text{Formula for the area of a circle}$$
$$= \pi(7)^2 \qquad \text{Substitute 7 for } r.$$
$$= 49\pi \qquad \text{Simplify.}$$
$$\approx 153.94 \qquad \text{Use a calculator.}$$

ANSWER ▶ The area is about 154 square centimeters.

EXAMPLE **3** **Use the Area of a Circle**

Find the radius of a circle with an area of 380 square feet.

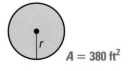

r

$A = 380$ ft^2

Solution

$$A = \pi r^2 \qquad \text{Formula for the area of a circle}$$
$$380 = \pi r^2 \qquad \text{Substitute 380 for } A.$$
$$120.96 \approx r^2 \qquad \text{Divide each side by } \pi. \text{ Use a calculator.}$$
$$11 \approx r \qquad \text{Take the positive square root.}$$

ANSWER ▶ The radius is about 11 feet.

Find the area of the circle. Round your answer to the nearest whole number.

4.

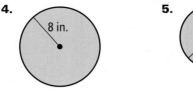

8 in.

5.

3 cm

6.

•12 ft

Student Help

VOCABULARY TIP
The term *radius* is also used to name a segment that connects the center of a circle to a point on the circle. Two such radii are used to determine a *sector* of a circle.

Central Angles An angle whose vertex is the center of a circle is a **central angle** of the circle.

A region of a circle determined by two radii and a part of the circle is called a **sector** of the circle.

Because a sector is a portion of a circle, the following proportion can be used to find the area of a sector.

$$\frac{Area\ of\ sector}{Area\ of\ entire\ circle} = \frac{Measure\ of\ central\ angle}{Measure\ of\ entire\ circle}$$

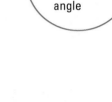

sector

central angle

EXAMPLE **4** **Find the Area of a Sector**

Find the area of the blue sector.

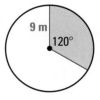

9 m

120°

Solution

❶ First find the area of the circle.

$$A = \pi r^2 = \pi(9)^2 \approx 254.47$$

The area of the circle is about 254 square meters.

❷ Then find the area of the sector. Let *x* equal the area of the sector.

$$\frac{Area\ of\ sector}{Area\ of\ entire\ circle} = \frac{Measure\ of\ central\ angle}{Measure\ of\ entire\ circle}$$

Visualize It!

A circle contains two straight angles. So, there are 180° + 180°, or 360°, in a circle.

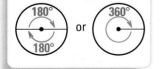

180°
180°
or
360°

$$\frac{x}{254} = \frac{120°}{360°} \qquad \text{Substitute.}$$

$$360x = 254 \cdot 120 \qquad \text{Cross product property}$$

$$360x = 30,480 \qquad \text{Simplify.}$$

$$\frac{360x}{360} = \frac{30,480}{360} \qquad \text{Divide each side by 360.}$$

$$x \approx 84.67 \qquad \text{Simplify.}$$

ANSWER ▶ The area of the sector is about 85 square meters.

Checkpoint ✓ Find the Area of a Sector

In Exercises 7 and 8, A represents the area of the entire circle and x represents the area of the blue sector. Complete the proportion used to find x. Do not solve the proportion.

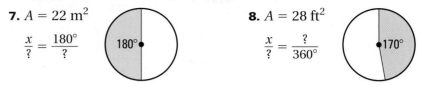

7. $A = 22 \text{ m}^2$

$\frac{x}{?} = \frac{180°}{?}$

180°

8. $A = 28 \text{ ft}^2$

$\frac{x}{?} = \frac{?}{360°}$

170°

Find the area of the blue sector. Round your answer to the nearest whole number.

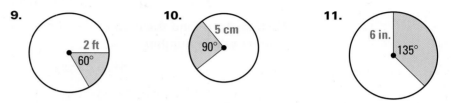

9.

2 ft
60°

10.

5 cm
90°

11.

6 in.
135°

8.7 Exercises

Guided Practice

Vocabulary Check

1. Sketch a circle. Sketch and label a *radius* and a *diameter* of the circle.

2. Describe how to find the *circumference* of a circle given its radius.

Skill Check

Copy and complete the table below.

	Radius, r	Diameter, d
3.	?	14 in.
4.	11 cm	?
5.	3.5 m	?
6.	?	1 ft

r
d

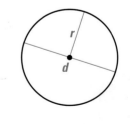

Write an equation for the area A or the circumference C by filling in the missing number.

7. $C = 2\pi$?

8

8. $A =$? $(3)^2$

3

9. $A = \pi($? $)^2$

14

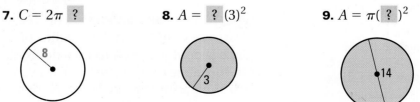

Practice and Applications

Extra Practice

See p. 690.

Finding Circumference Find the circumference of the circle. Round your answer to the nearest whole number.

10.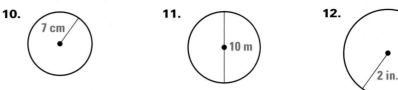
7 cm

11.
10 m

12.
2 in.

13. A circle with a radius of 13 yards

14. A circle with a diameter of 15 meters

Finding Area Find the area of the circle. Round your answer to the nearest whole number.

15.
4 ft

16.
1 cm

17.
6 in.

18.
9 m

19.
16 ft

20.
19 yd

21. Cranberries To harvest cranberries, the field is flooded so that the berries float. What area of cranberries can be gathered into a circular region with a radius of 5.5 meters?

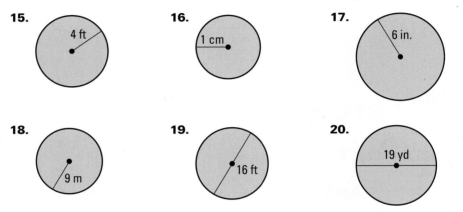

22. Error Analysis A student was asked to find the area of the circle below. Describe any errors.

$$A = \pi r^2$$
$$\approx (3.14)(12)^2$$
$$= 452.16$$

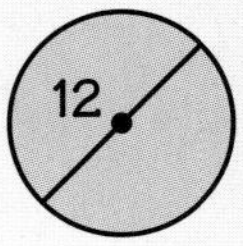

12

Homework Help

Example 1: Exs. 10–14
Example 2: Exs. 15–20
Example 3: Exs. 24–29
Example 4: Exs. 31–35

23. **You be the Judge** One of your classmates states that if the radius of a circle is doubled, then its area doubles. Do you agree or disagree? Explain your reasoning using the circles at the right.

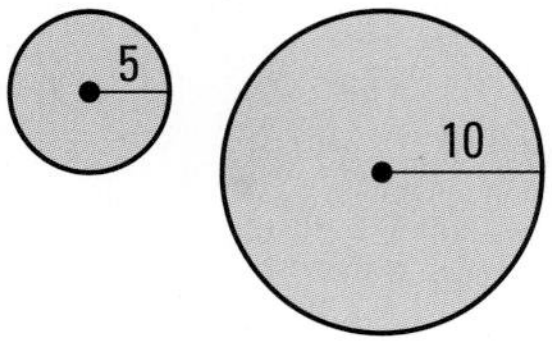

5

10

 Using Algebra Use the area A of the circle to find the radius r. Round your answer to the nearest whole number.

24. $A = 13$ in.^{2}

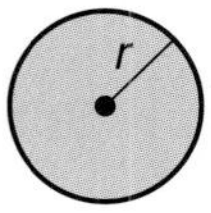

25. $A = 531$ m^2

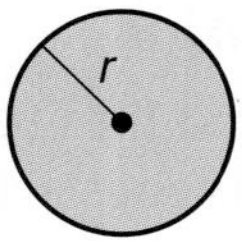

26. $A = 154$ ft^2

27. A circle has an area of 50 square units. What is its radius?

28. A circle has an area of 452 square units. What is its diameter?

29. A circle has an area of 28 square units. What is its diameter?

30. Challenge The circle at the right has an area of 78.5 square yards. What is its circumference?

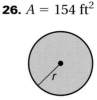

$A = 78.5$ yd^2

Sectors and Proportions In Exercises 31 and 32, A represents the area of the entire circle and x represents the area of the blue sector. Complete the proportion used to find x. Do not solve the proportion.

31. $A = 12$ ft^2

$$\frac{x}{?} = \frac{?}{360°}$$

32. $A = 198$ yd^2

$$\frac{x}{?} = \frac{100°}{?}$$

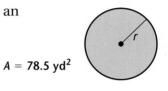

Area of Sectors Find the area of the blue sector. Start by finding the area of the circle. Round your answer to the nearest whole number.

33.

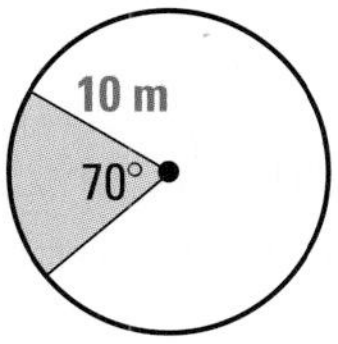

34.

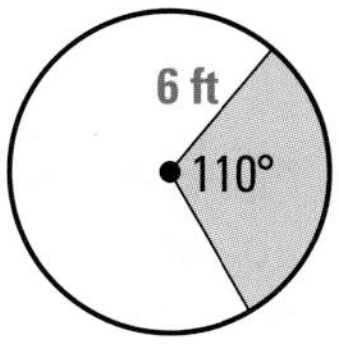

35.

Landscaping The diagram shows the area of a lawn covered by a water sprinkler. Round your answer to the nearest whole number.

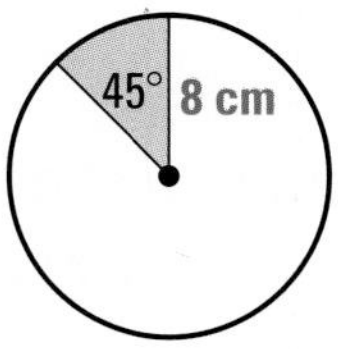

36. What is the area of the lawn that is covered by the sprinkler?

37. Suppose the water pressure is weakened so that the radius is 12 feet. What is the area of lawn that will be covered?

15 ft   145°

Find the area of the shaded region.

Solution

❶ First find the area of the outer region, which is a square.

Area of square = s^2 = $(12)^2$ = **144 ft²**

❷ Then find the area of the inner region, which is a circle. The diameter of the circle is 12 feet, so the radius is 6 feet.

Area of circle = $\pi r^2 \approx \pi(6)^2 \approx$ **113 ft²**

❸ Finally, subtract the area of the circle from the area of the square.

Area of shaded region = Area of square − Area of circle

$$\approx 144 - 113$$

$$= 31$$

ANSWER ▶ The area of the shaded region is about 31 square feet.

Finding Complex Areas Use the method in the example above to find the area of the shaded region. Round your answer to the nearest whole number.

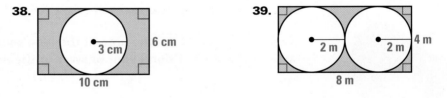

38. 6 cm 3 cm 10 cm

39. 2 m 2 m 4 m 8 m

Standardized Test Practice

40. Multi-Step Problem Earth has a radius of about 3960 miles at the equator. Suppose a cable is wrapped around Earth at the equator, as shown in the diagram.

a. Find the length of the cable by finding the circumference of Earth. (Assume that Earth is perfectly round. Use 3.14 for π.)

b. Suppose 10 miles is added to the cable length in part (a). Use this length as the circumference of a new circle. Find the radius of the larger circle. (Use 3.14 for π.)

c. Suppose you are standing at the equator. How far are you from the cable in part (b)?

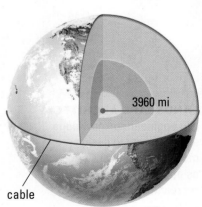

cable

3960 mi

Mixed Review

Identifying Quadrilaterals Use the information in the diagram to name the special quadrilateral. *(Lesson 6.6)*

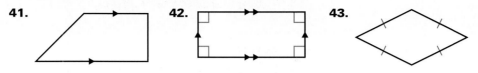

41.

42.

43.

Squares and Rectangles Find the area of the polygon. *(Lesson 8.3)*

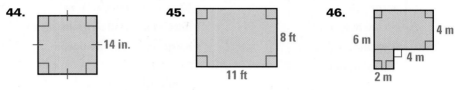

44.

14 in.

45.

8 ft

11 ft

46.

6 m   4 m

4 m

2 m

Algebra Skills

Integers Evaluate the expression. *(Skills Review, p. 663)*

47. $-4 + 7$

48. $-5 - (-5)$

49. $(-4)(-11)$

50. $12 - (-12)$

51. $33 \div (-3)$

52. $14 + (-3) + 4$

53. $-6 - 10$

54. $(-5)(-13)$

55. $22 - (-9)$

Quiz 3

Find the area of the figure. In Exercises 5 and 6, round your answer to the nearest whole numbers. *(Lessons 8.5–8.7)*

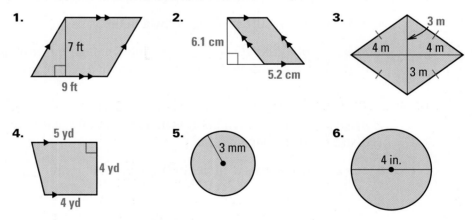

1.   7 ft   9 ft

2.   6.1 cm   5.2 cm

3.   3 m   4 m   4 m   3 m

4.   5 yd   4 yd   4 yd

5.   3 mm

6.   4 in.

In Exercises 7–9, *A* gives the area of the figure. Find the missing measure. In Exercise 9, round your answer to the nearest whole number. *(Lessons 8.5–8.7)*

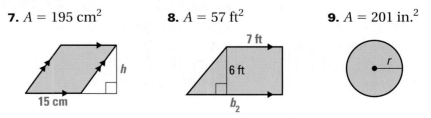

7. $A = 195 \text{ cm}^2$

15 cm   h

8. $A = 57 \text{ ft}^2$

7 ft   6 ft b_2

9. $A = 201 \text{ in.}^2$

r

VOCABULARY

- **convex**, *p. 411*
- **concave**, *p. 411*
- **equilateral**, *p. 412*
- **equiangular**, *p. 412*
- **regular**, *p. 412*
- **area**, *p. 424*
- **height of a triangle**, *p. 431*

- **base of a triangle**, *p. 431*
- **base of a parallelogram**, *p. 439*
- **height of a parallelogram**, *p. 439*
- **height of a trapezoid**, *p. 446*
- **circle**, *p. 452*

- **center of a circle**, *p. 452*
- **radius**, *p. 452*
- **diameter**, *p. 452*
- **circumference**, *p. 452*
- **central angle**, *p. 454*
- **sector**, *p. 454*

VOCABULARY REVIEW

Fill in the blank.

1. A polygon is __?__ if no line that contains a side of the polygon passes through the interior of the polygon.

2. A polygon is __?__ if all of its interior angles are congruent.

3. If a polygon is equilateral and equiangular, then it is __?__.

4. The amount of surface covered by a figure is its __?__.

5. The __?__ of a triangle is the perpendicular segment from a vertex to the line containing the opposite side of the triangle.

6. Either pair of parallel sides of a parallelogram are called the __?__.

7. A(n) __?__ is the set of all points in a plane that are the same distance from a given point.

8. The distance across a circle through its center is the __?__.

8.1 CLASSIFYING POLYGONS

Examples on pp. 411–412

EXAMPLE   **Decide whether the polygon is regular. Explain your answer.**

Although the polygon is equilateral, it is not equiangular. So, the polygon is not regular.

Decide whether the polygon is regular. Explain your answer.

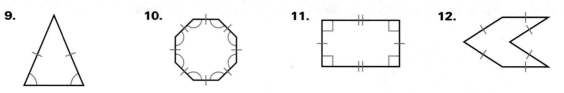

9.   10.   11.   12.

8.2   ANGLES IN POLYGONS

Examples on pp. 417–420

EXAMPLE   **Find the measure of ∠A in the diagram.**

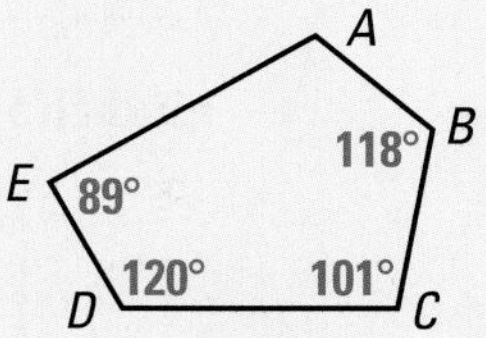

The polygon has 5 sides, so the sum of the measures of the interior angles is:

$$(n - 2) \cdot 180° = (5 - 2) \cdot 180° = 3 \cdot 180° = 540°.$$

Add the measures of the interior angles and set the sum equal to 540°.

$$89° + 120° + 101° + 118° + m\angle A = 540° \qquad \text{The sum is } 540°.$$

$$428° + m\angle A = 540° \qquad \text{Simplify.}$$

$$m\angle A = 112° \qquad \text{Subtract } 428° \text{ from each side.}$$

Find the measure of ∠1.

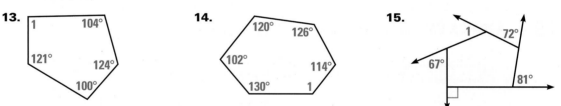

13.   14.   15.

8.3   AREA OF SQUARES AND RECTANGLES

Examples on pp. 424–426

EXAMPLE   **Find the area of the rectangle.**

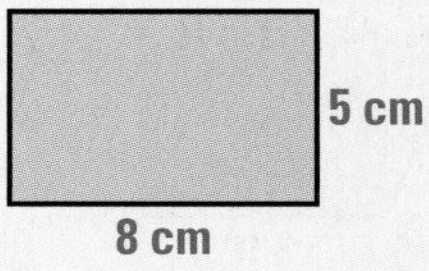

$$A = bh \qquad \text{Formula for the area of a rectangle}$$

$$= (8)(5) \qquad \text{Substitute 8 for } b \text{ and 5 for } h.$$

$$= 40 \text{ cm}^2 \qquad \text{Multiply.}$$

5 cm

8 cm

Find the area of the polygon.

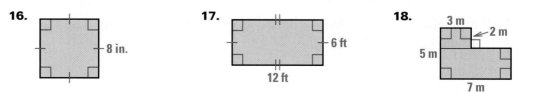

16.   17.   18.

8.4 AREA OF TRIANGLES

Examples on pp. 431–433

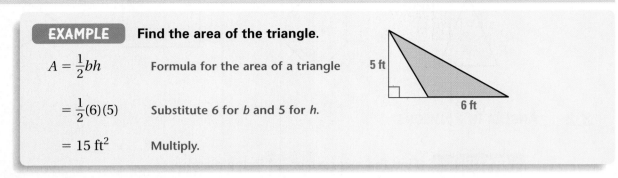

EXAMPLE Find the area of the triangle.

$A = \frac{1}{2}bh$ Formula for the area of a triangle

$= \frac{1}{2}(6)(5)$ Substitute 6 for *b* and 5 for *h*.

$= 15 \text{ ft}^2$ Multiply.

Find the area of the triangle.

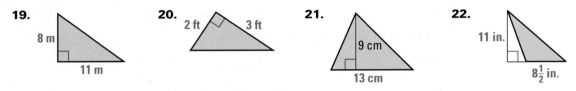

19.

20.

21.

22.

23. A triangle has an area of 117 square feet and a height of 9 feet. Find the base.

24. A triangle has an area of 81 square meters and a base of 18 meters. Find the height.

8.5 AREA OF PARALLELOGRAMS

Examples on pp. 439–441

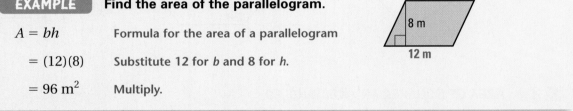

EXAMPLE Find the area of the parallelogram.

$A = bh$ Formula for the area of a parallelogram

$= (12)(8)$ Substitute 12 for *b* and 8 for *h*.

$= 96 \text{ m}^2$ Multiply.

Find the area of the parallelogram.

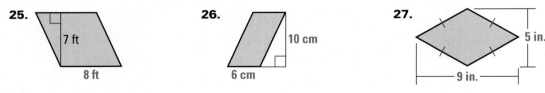

25.

26.

27.

28. A parallelogram has an area of 135 square inches and a base of 15 inches. Find the height.

29. A parallelogram has an area of 121 square meters and a height of 11 meters. Find the base.

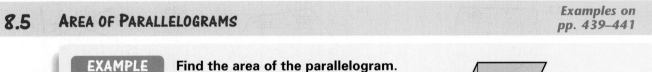

8.6 AREA OF TRAPEZOIDS

Examples on pp. 446–447

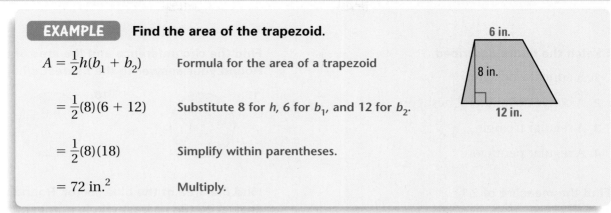

EXAMPLE Find the area of the trapezoid.

$A = \frac{1}{2}h(b_1 + b_2)$ Formula for the area of a trapezoid

$= \frac{1}{2}(8)(6 + 12)$ Substitute 8 for h, 6 for b_1, and 12 for b_2.

$= \frac{1}{2}(8)(18)$ Simplify within parentheses.

$= 72$ in.^{2} Multiply.

Find the area of the trapezoid.

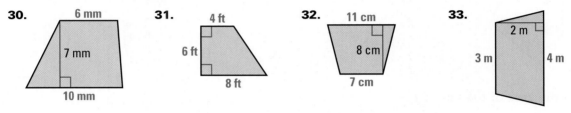

30. 6 mm / 7 mm / 10 mm

31. 4 ft / 6 ft / 8 ft

32. 11 cm / 8 cm / 7 cm

33. 2 m / 3 m / 4 m

34. A trapezoid has an area of 100 square yards. The lengths of the bases are 9 yards and 11 yards. Find the height.

8.7 CIRCUMFERENCE AND AREA OF CIRCLES

Examples on pp. 452–455

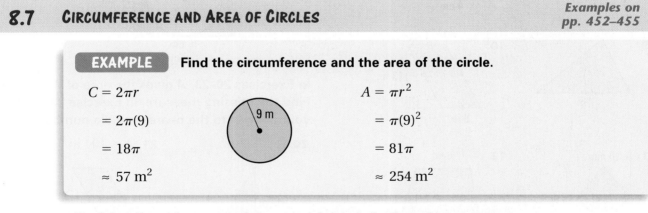

EXAMPLE Find the circumference and the area of the circle.

$C = 2\pi r$

$= 2\pi(9)$

$= 18\pi$

≈ 57 m^2

$A = \pi r^2$

$= \pi(9)^2$

$= 81\pi$

≈ 254 m^2

Find the circumference and the area of the circle. Round your answer to the nearest whole number.

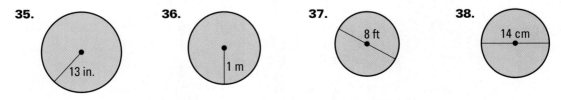

35. 13 in.

36. 1 m

37. 8 ft

38. 14 cm

39. A circle has a circumference of 50 square feet. Find the radius.

40. A circle has an area of 380 square centimeters. Find the radius.

Chapter 8 Chapter Test

Sketch the figure described.

1. A concave octagon
2. A convex equilateral hexagon
3. A regular triangle
4. A regular pentagon

Find the measure of ∠1.

5.
1
120°
136°
111°
129°
100°

6.
65°
62°
1
50°

Find the area of the polygon.

7.
7 ft

8.
5 cm
4 cm

9.
4 m
7 m

10.
13 in.
8 in.

11.
10 mm
12 mm

12.
6 yd
6 yd
9 yd

13.
4 m
9 m
3 m
7 m

14.
3 ft
5 ft
4 ft
6 ft

Find the circumference and the area of the circle. Round your answer to the nearest whole number.

15.
2 in.

16.
6 m

Find the area of the blue sector. Round your answer to the nearest whole number.

17.
5 ft
130°

18.
60°
8 mm

19. Find the area of the shaded region. Round your answer to the nearest whole number.

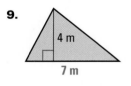

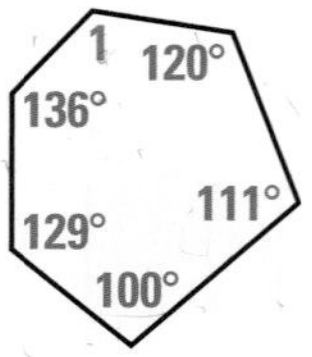

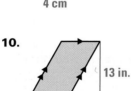

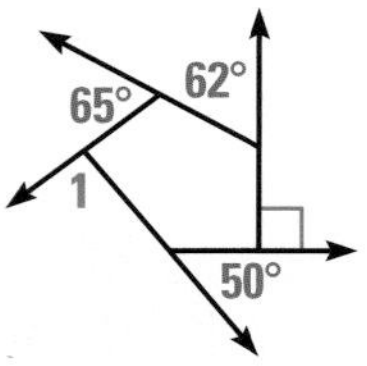

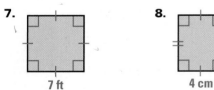

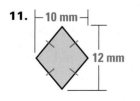

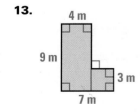

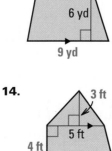

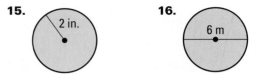

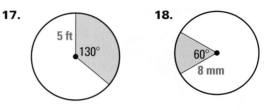

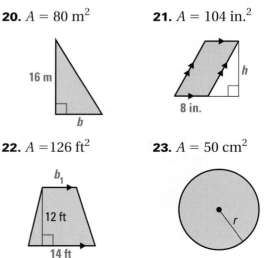

6 cm
12 cm
16 cm

In Exercises 20–23, *A* gives the area of the figure. Find the missing measure. In Exercise 23, round your answer to the nearest whole number.

20. $A = 80\text{ m}^2$

16 m
b

21. $A = 104\text{ in.}^2$

h
8 in.

22. $A = 126\text{ ft}^2$

b1
12 ft
14 ft

23. $A = 50\text{ cm}^2$

r

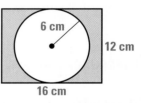

1. What is the measure of ∠C?

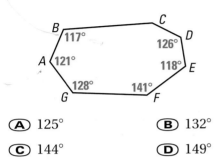

(A) 125°   (B) 132°

(C) 144°   (D) 149°

2. What is the value of x?

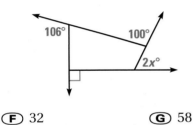

(F) 32   (G) 58

(H) 64   (J) 138

3. What is the area of the polygon made up of rectangles?

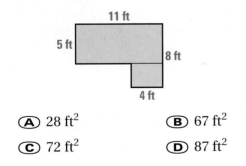

(A) 28 ft²   (B) 67 ft²

(C) 72 ft²   (D) 87 ft²

4. A triangle has an area of 54 square inches. What is the base of the triangle, given that its height is 9 inches?

(F) 6 in.   (G) 8 in.

(H) 10 in.   (J) 12 in.

5. What is the area of the polygon?

(A) 78 cm²

(B) 84 cm²

(C) 120 cm²

(D) 156 cm²

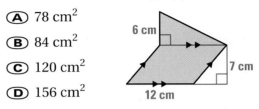

6. What is the area of the rhombus?

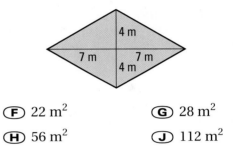

(F) 22 m²   (G) 28 m²

(H) 56 m²   (J) 112 m²

7. What is the area of the trapezoid?

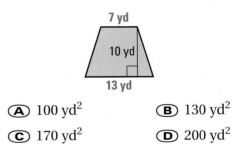

(A) 100 yd²   (B) 130 yd²

(C) 170 yd²   (D) 200 yd²

Multi-Step Problem In Exercises 8–10, use the diagram below.

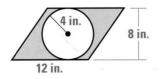

8. Find the area of the parallelogram.

9. Find the area of the circle. Round your answer to the nearest whole number.

10. Find the area of the shaded region.

BraiN GaMes

Sum of Parts

Materials
- 3 puzzles
- scissors
- pen or pencil

Object of the Game To be the first team to solve all three of the puzzles.

Set Up For each puzzle, carefully cut out the smaller pieces.

How to Play

Step 1 ▶ Use the 12 small rhombuses to completely cover the hexagon.

Step 2 ▶ Use the 8 trapezoids to completely cover the hexagon.

Step 3 ▶ Use the 6 small concave hexagons to completely cover the hexagon.

Another Way to Play Create your own puzzles by copying the hexagon and cutting it into smaller pieces. Challenge members of your team to solve your puzzle.

An expression like 7^3 is called a *power*. The *exponent* 3 represents the number of times the *base* 7 is used as a factor: $7^3 = 7 \cdot 7 \cdot 7 = 343$.

EXAMPLE 1 Evaluate Powers

Evaluate the expression.

a. 8^2 **b.** $(-5)^3$ **c.** $(-3)^1$ **d.** 2^5

Solution

a. $8^2 = 8 \cdot 8 = 64$ **b.** $(-5)^3 = (-5) \cdot (-5) \cdot (-5) = -125$

c. $(-3)^1 = -3$ **d.** $2^5 = 2 \cdot 2 \cdot 2 \cdot 2 \cdot 2 = 32$

Try These

Evaluate the expression.

1. 2^4 **2.** 9^3 **3.** $(-3)^5$ **4.** $(-1)^4$ **5.** 10^3 **6.** 3^6

To solve percent problems, use the equation $a = p \cdot b$, where a is the number being compared to the base, p is the percent, and b is the base number.

EXAMPLE 2 Use Percents

a. What is 36% of 150?   **b.** 24 is what percent of 80?

Solution

a. $a = p \cdot b$

$a = (36\%) \cdot 150$

$a = 0.36 \cdot 150$

$a = 54$

ANSWER ▶ 36% of 150 is 54.

b. $a = p \cdot b$

$24 = p \cdot 80$

$\dfrac{24}{80} = \dfrac{80p}{80}$

$0.3 = p$

$30\% = p$

ANSWER ▶ 24 is 30% of 80.

Try These

7. What is 60% of 85?   **8.** What is 4% of 200?

9. 18 is what percent of 40?   **10.** 48 is what percent of 300?

Designing a Park

Objective

Materials
- paper
- ruler
- poster board

Use similarity and area in park design.

Suppose your town has decided to plan a new park, and you are in charge of designing it. To present ideas for approval, you'll need to have a scale drawing of the park and all of its parts. The area set aside for the park is 800 feet wide and 1000 feet long.

Investigation

1 Make a scale drawing of the outline of the park on a poster, showing the park as a rectangle that is 8 inches wide and 10 inches long. What is the scale factor for the drawing?

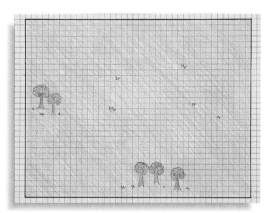

2 The town wants a playing field to be 200 feet wide and 400 feet long. What are the field's dimensions on your scale drawing? What is the actual area? the area on your scale drawing?

3 You set aside a place for dogs to play. You sketch the Free Run Meadow as a 2 inch by 2 inch square on the poster. What is the Meadow area on the scale drawing? What will its actual area be?

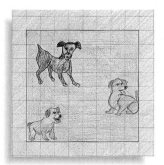

4 The Parks Department decides to have a circular pool, with radius of 50 feet. What is the approximate area covered by the pool? What is the length of the radius on your scale drawing?

5 Use your answers in Steps 1–4 to copy and complete the table.

	Actual Dimensions	Actual Area	Dimensions on Scale Drawing	Area on Scale Drawing
Entire Park	?	?	?	?
Playing Field	?	?	?	?
Free Run Meadow	?	?	?	?
Pool	?	?	?	?

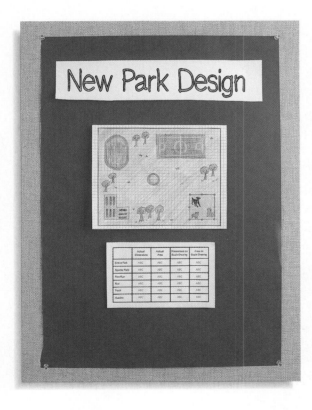

Present Your Results

Make a poster that displays your scale drawing and completed table.

▶ Include at least two other areas you want in the park, such as a community garden, a running track, or a soccer field.

▶ Expand your table to include these new areas.

Extension

Design another special park for your city, such as a playground or a picnic area. Find dimensions for swings, picnic tables, etc., and present a scale drawing of your plan.

Chapter 9 Surface Area and Volume

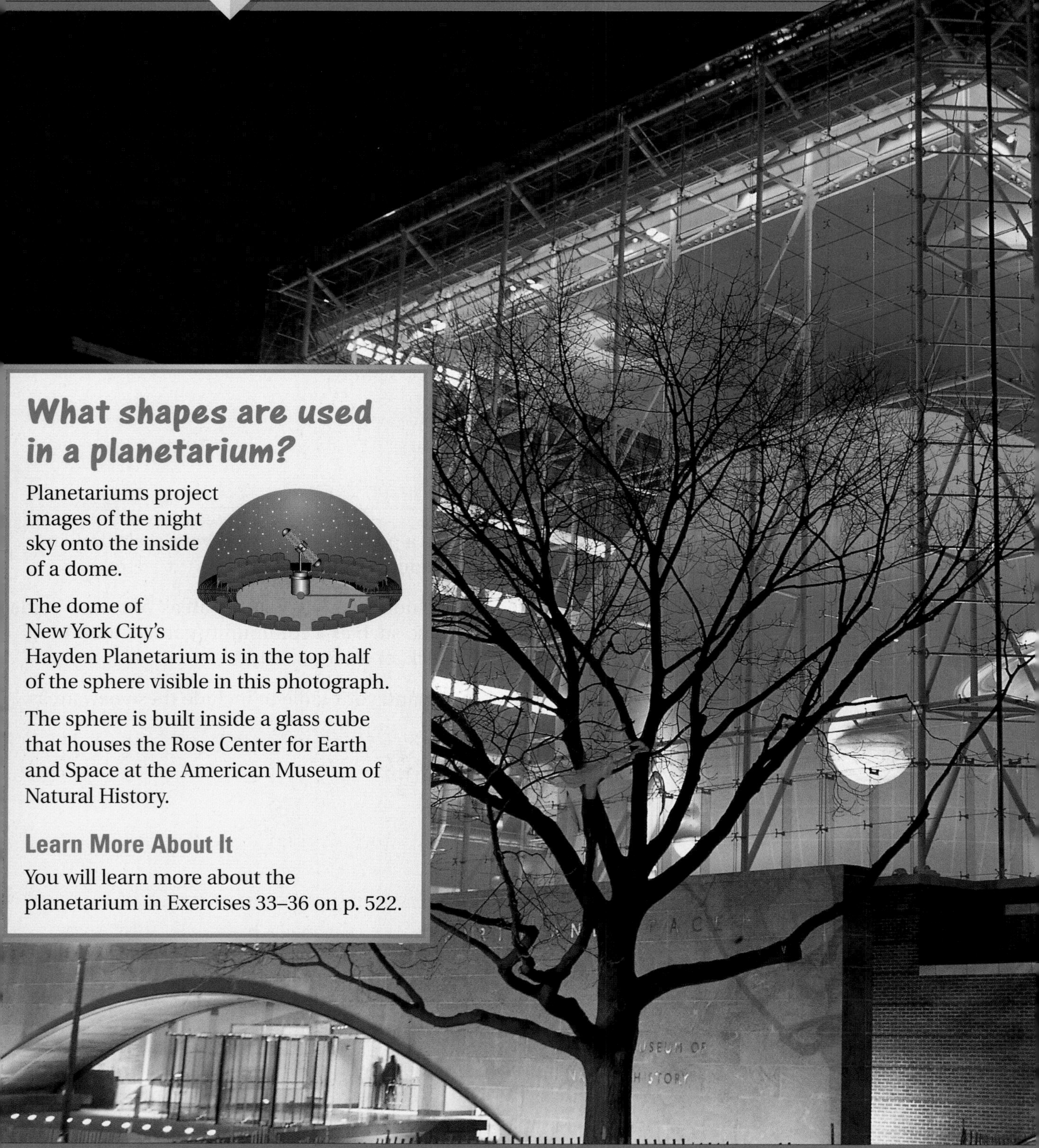

What shapes are used in a planetarium?

Planetariums project images of the night sky onto the inside of a dome.

The dome of New York City's Hayden Planetarium is in the top half of the sphere visible in this photograph.

The sphere is built inside a glass cube that houses the Rose Center for Earth and Space at the American Museum of Natural History.

Learn More About It

You will learn more about the planetarium in Exercises 33–36 on p. 522.

Who uses Surface Area and Volume?

VETERINARIAN
Veterinarians provide treatment for sick and injured animals. They also offer preventive care for healthy animals. (p. 497)

AQUARIUM DIVER
Aquarium divers take care of fish and plants in an aquarium. They monitor the volume of water in a tank and insure that the tank is not overcrowded. (p. 505)

How will you use these ideas?

- Analyze the shape of the first music recordings. (p. 489)
- Determine the amount of material needed to make various objects. (p. 497)
- Compare the volumes of swimming pools. (p. 505)
- Calculate the amount of food in a pet feeder. (p. 515)
- Find the amount of glass in the cube of the Rose Center for Earth and Space. (p. 522)

What's the chapter about?

- Identifying and naming **solids**
- Finding the **surface area** of solids
- Finding the **volume** of solids

Key Words

- **solid,** *p. 473*
- **base,** *p. 473*
- **face,** *p. 474*
- **surface area,** *p. 483*

- **lateral area,** *p. 484*
- **height, slant height,** *p. 491*
- **volume,** *p. 500*
- **hemisphere,** *p. 517*

Chapter Readiness Quiz

Take this quick quiz. If you are unsure of an answer, look at the reference pages for help.

Skill Check *(refer to pp. 192, 431, 453)*

1. What is the length of the hypotenuse in the triangle shown?

  (A) 13   **(B)** 17
  (C) 19   **(D)** 169

2. What is the area of the triangle shown above?

  (F) 15 units^2 **(G)** 30 units^2 **(H)** 60 units^2 **(J)** 120 units^2

3. What is the approximate area of the circle?

  (A) 18.8 in.^{2} **(B)** 37.7 in.^{2}
  (C) 113 in.^{2} **(D)** 226 in.^{2}

6 in.

Drawing Three Dimensional Figures

Visualize It! ➡ Here is a helpful method for drawing three dimensional figures.

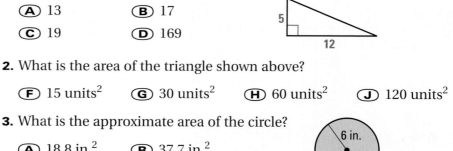

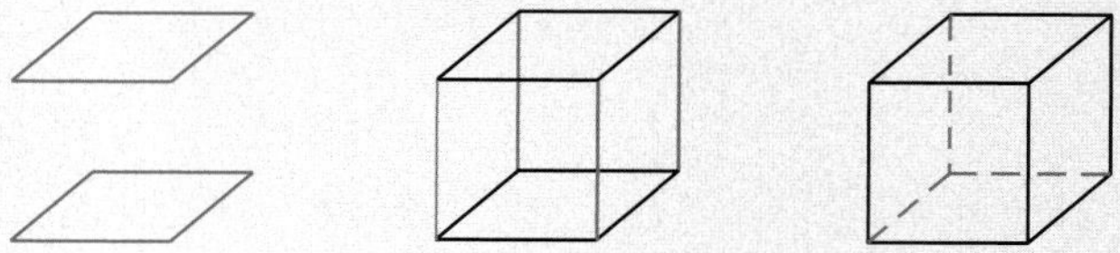

Draw the bases.   Connect the bases using vertical lines.   Erase so that hidden edges are dashed lines.

Solid Figures

Goal

Identify and name solid figures.

Key Words

- solid
- polyhedron
- base
- face
- edge

The three-dimensional shapes on this page are examples of *solid figures*, or **solids**. When a solid is formed by polygons, it is called a **polyhedron**.

Polyhedra Prisms and pyramids are examples of polyhedra. To name a prism or pyramid, use the shape of the *base*.

Rectangular prism

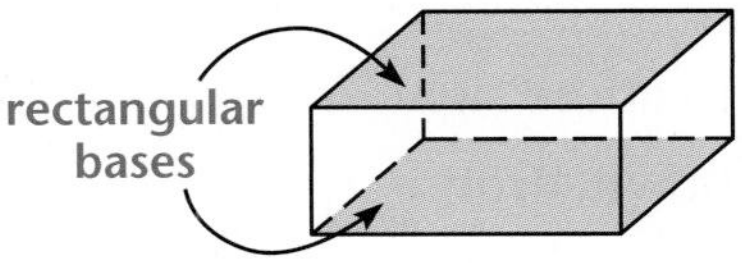

Triangular pyramid

The two **bases** of a prism are congruent polygons in parallel planes.

The **base** of a pyramid is a polygon.

Not Polyhedra Solids with curved surfaces, like the cylinder, cone, and sphere shown below, are not polyhedra.

Cylinder

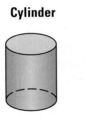

Cone

Sphere

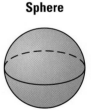

Student Help

VOCABULARY TIP
Poly- means "many" and *-hedron* is Greek for "side" or "face." A polyhedron is a figure with many faces. The plural of polyhedron is *polyhedra*.

EXAMPLE 1 Identify and Name Polyhedra

Tell whether the solid is a polyhedron. If so, identify the shape of the bases. Then name the solid.

a.
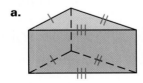

b.
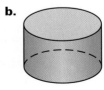

Solution

a. The solid is formed by polygons so it is a polyhedron. The bases are congruent triangles in parallel planes. This figure is a triangular prism.

b. A cylinder has a curved surface, so it is not a polyhedron.

Student Help

STUDY TIP
In this book, all of the solids are *right solids*. This means that the segment representing the ***height*** is perpendicular to the base(s).

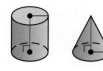

Parts of a Polyhedron To avoid confusion, the word *side* is not used when describing polyhedra. Instead, the plane surfaces are called **faces** and the segments joining the vertices are called **edges**.

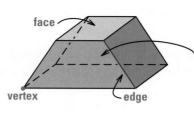

face
The trapezoidal faces of this polyhedron are the bases.
vertex
edge

EXAMPLE 2 Find Faces and Edges

Use the diagram at the right.

a. Name the polyhedron.

b. Count the number of faces and edges.

c. List any congruent faces and congruent edges.

V
U
T
P
S
Q
R

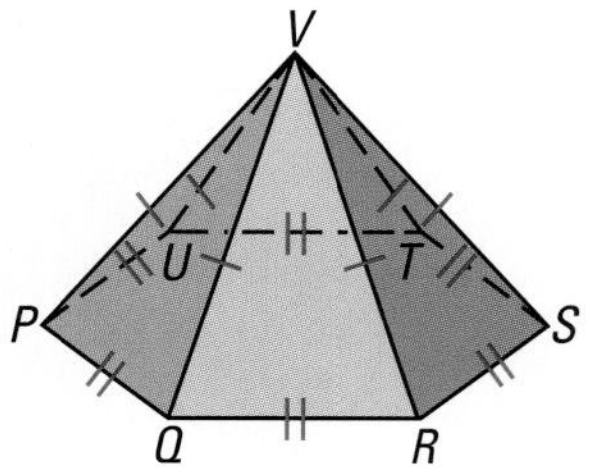

Solution

a. The polyhedron is a hexagonal pyramid.

b. The polyhedron has 7 faces and 12 edges.

c. Using the markings on the diagram, you can conclude the following:

Congruent faces

$\triangle PQV \cong \triangle QRV \cong \triangle RSV \cong \triangle STV \cong \triangle TUV \cong \triangle UPV$

Congruent edges

$\overline{PQ} \cong \overline{QR} \cong \overline{RS} \cong \overline{ST} \cong \overline{TU} \cong \overline{UP}$
$\overline{PV} \cong \overline{QV} \cong \overline{RV} \cong \overline{SV} \cong \overline{TV} \cong \overline{UV}$

Student Help

VISUAL STRATEGY
For more help drawing three dimensional figures, see p. 472.

EXAMPLE 3 Sketch a Polyhedron

Sketch a triangular prism.

Solution

1 Draw the triangular bases.

2 Connect the corresponding vertices of the bases with vertical lines.

3 Partially erase the hidden lines to create dashed lines. Shade the prism.

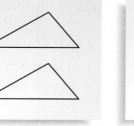

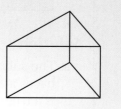

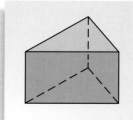

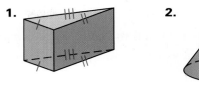
Tell whether the solid is a polyhedron. If so, identify the shape of the base(s). Then name the solid.

1. **2.** **3.**

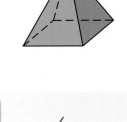

4. Copy the partial drawing of a triangular pyramid. Then complete the drawing of the pyramid.

Student Help

STUDY TIP
In this book, the faces of a pyramid, not including the base, are congruent isosceles triangles, unless otherwise noted.

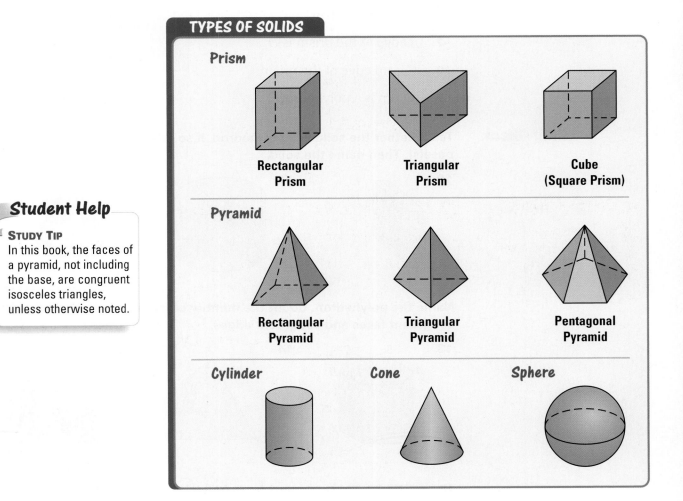

TYPES OF SOLIDS

Prism

Rectangular Prism | Triangular Prism | Cube (Square Prism)

Pyramid

Rectangular Pyramid | Triangular Pyramid | Pentagonal Pyramid

Cylinder | Cone | Sphere

Guided Practice

Vocabulary Check

In Exercises 1–3, match the solid with its name.

A. prism   **B.** pyramid   **C.** cylinder

1. 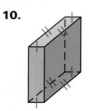   **2.**   **3.**

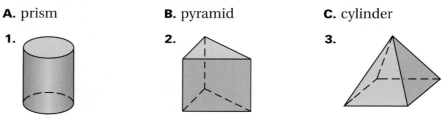

In Exercises 4–9, tell whether the statement is *true* or *false*. Refer to the prism below, if necessary.

4. *CDHG* is a face of the prism.

5. A prism has only one base.

6. *ABCD* and *EFGH* are possible bases of the prism.

7. An edge of the prism is *H*.

8. $\overline{GC}$ is an edge of the prism.

9. A prism is a polyhedron.

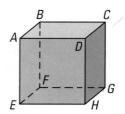

Skill Check

Tell whether the solid is a polyhedron. If so, identify the shape of the base(s). Then name the solid.

10. 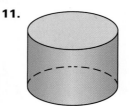   **11.** 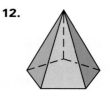   **12.**

Name the polyhedron. Count the number of faces and edges. List any congruent faces and congruent edges.

13.   **14.**   **15.**

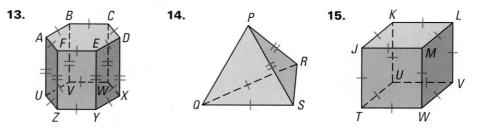

16. Visualize It! How many faces and edges does a box of cereal have?

Practice and Applications

Extra Practice

See p. 691.

Name Bases and Solids Tell whether the solid is a polyhedron. If so, identify the shape of the base(s). Then name the solid.

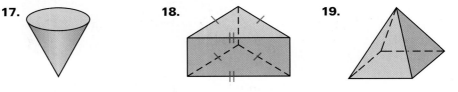

17.

18.

19.

Logical Reasoning Tell whether the statement is *true* or *false*.

20. A rectangular pyramid has two bases.

21. A triangular prism has two bases.

22. The bases of a prism are congruent polygons.

23. A cone has two bases.

24. A sphere is a polyhedron.

Identify Solids Match the solid with its name.

A. cone   **B.** pyramid   **C.** cylinder

D. rectangular prism   **E.** cube   **F.** sphere

25.

26.

27.

28.

29.

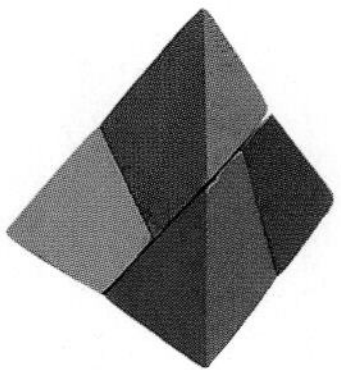

30.

Error Analysis Julie incorrectly identified the solid below as a pyramid with a square base.

Homework Help

Example 1: Exs. 17–19,
25–35
Example 2: Exs. 36–38
Example 3: Exs. 43–51

31. Correctly identify the solid.

32. What would you say to Julie to help her tell the difference between this solid and a pyramid?

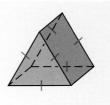

Identify Polyhedra Tell whether the solid is a polyhedron. If so, identify the shape of the base(s). Then name the solid.

33.

34.

35.

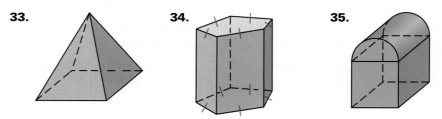

Counting Faces and Edges Name the polyhedron. Then count the number of faces and edges. List any congruent faces and congruent edges.

36.

37.

38.

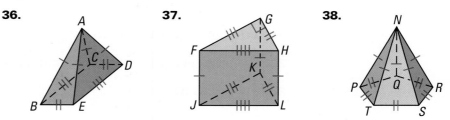

Logical Reasoning Determine whether the statement is *true* or *false*. Explain your reasoning.

39. Prisms, pyramids, cylinders, cones, and spheres are all solids.

40. Prisms, pyramids, cylinders, cones, and spheres are all polyhedra.

41. Every face of a prism is also a base of the prism.

42. Every base of a prism is also a face of the prism.

Visualize It! Copy the partial drawing. Then complete the drawing of the solid.

43. square pyramid   **44.** hexagonal prism   **45.** cylinder

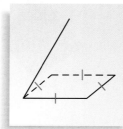
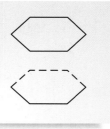

Sketching Solids Sketch the solid described.

46. rectangular prism   **47.** rectangular pyramid

48. cube   **49.** cone

50. cylinder   **51.** sphere

EXAMPLE Euler's Formula

Mathematician Leonhard Euler proved that the number of faces (*F*), vertices (*V*), and edges (*E*) of a polyhedron are related by the formula $F + V = E + 2$.

Use Euler's Formula to find the number of vertices on the *tetrahedron* shown.

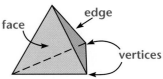

Solution

The tetrahedron has 4 faces and 6 edges.

$F + V = E + 2$	Write Euler's Formula.
$4 + V = 6 + 2$	Substitute 4 for *F* and 6 for *E*.
$4 + V = 8$	Simplify.
$V = 8 - 4$	Subtract 4 from each side.
$V = 4$	Simplify.

ANSWER ▶ The tetrahedron has 4 vertices.

Link to
History

PLATO The solids on this page are called *Platonic solids*, named after the Greek mathematician and philosopher Plato. The image of Plato above is a detail of *The School of Athens* (1509–10) by Raphael.

Platonic Solids A Platonic solid has faces that are congruent, regular polygons. Use the example above to find the number of vertices on the Platonic solid.

52. cube
6 faces, 12 edges

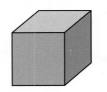

53. octahedron
8 faces, 12 edges

54. dodecahedron
12 faces, 30 edges

55. icosahedron
20 faces, 30 edges

Using Algebra Use Euler's Formula to find the number of faces, edges, or vertices. Use the example above as a model.

56. A prism has 5 faces and 6 vertices. How many edges does it have?

57. A pyramid has 12 edges and 7 vertices. How many faces does it have?

58. A prism has 8 faces and 12 vertices. How many edges does it have?

59. Multiple Choice How many faces does the prism below have?

Ⓐ 2   Ⓑ 3

Ⓒ 4   Ⓓ 5

60. Multiple Choice How many edges does the pyramid at the right have?

Ⓕ 6   Ⓖ 5

Ⓗ 4   Ⓙ 3

61. Multiple Choice How many vertices does the pyramid above have?

Ⓐ 6   Ⓑ 5   Ⓒ 4   Ⓓ 3

Mixed Review

Finding Measures of Squares and Rectangles Use the given information to find the missing measure. *(Lesson 8.3)*

62. A square has a side length of 9 centimeters. Find its area.

63. A rectangle has a height of 4 meters and a base length of 7 meters. Find its area.

64. A rectangle has an area of 60 square inches and a height of 6 inches. Find the length of its base.

65. A square has an area of 169 square feet. Find its side length.

Finding Circumference and Area of a Circle Find the circumference and the area of the circle. Round your answers to the nearest whole number. *(Lesson 8.7)*

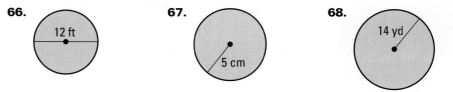

66.   67.   68.

Algebra Skills

Evaluating Expressions Evaluate the expression. *(Skills Review, p. 670)*

69. $92 - (12 + 39)$ **70.** $8 + 4 \cdot 3 - 5$ **71.** $(7 - 5) \cdot 14$

72. $10 - (5 - 2)^2 + 8$ **73.** $14 + 4^2 - 26$ **74.** $3(10 - 3)^2$

Substituting and Simplifying Expressions Evaluate the expression when $\ell = 3$, $h = 5$, and $w = 2$. Write your answer in terms of π, if appropriate. *(Skills Review, p. 674)*

75. $\ell \cdot w \cdot h$ **76.** $2\ell + 2w + 2h$ **77.** $2\pi h$

78. $\pi w^2 h$ **79.** $\pi \ell^2$ **80.** $2\ell + 2w$

Materials

- graph paper
- scissors

Question

How can you find the surface area of a solid figure?

Explore

1 The diagram below shows a pattern, or *net*, for making a solid. Copy the net on graph paper. Draw the dashed lines as shown. Then label the sections as shown.

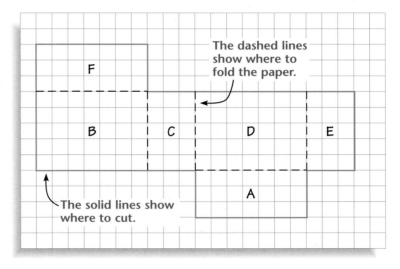

The dashed lines show where to fold the paper.

The solid lines show where to cut.

2 Cut out the net along the solid lines.

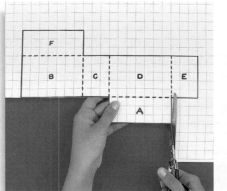

3 Fold the net along the dashed lines to form a polyhedron.

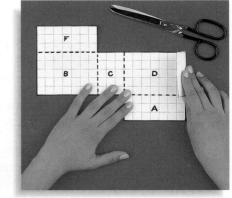

4 What is the name of the polyhedron formed in Step 3?

continued on next page

5 Use the net you made to complete the table below. Each square on the graph paper measures 1 unit by 1 unit.

Rectangle	Length	Width	Area
A	?	?	?
B	?	?	?
C	?	?	?
D	?	?	?
E	?	?	?
F	?	?	?
		Total Area	?

6 Find the following measures.

A = Area of rectangle $A = (\ell \times w) = $ __?__

P = Perimeter of rectangle $A = (2\ell + 2w) = $ __?__

h = Height of rectangles B, C, D, and $E = $ __?__

Think About It

1. Use the values for A, P, and h from Step 6 above to find the value of $2A + Ph$.

2. The *surface area* of a polyhedron is the sum of the areas of its faces. Compare the value of $2A + Ph$ to the total of the areas of all the rectangles that you found in Step 5.

3. **Make a Conjecture** Write a formula for finding the surface area of a rectangular prism.

4. **Extension** Draw the net of another rectangular prism with different dimensions. Cut out and fold the net to make sure that it forms a rectangular prism. Use the formula you wrote in *Think About It* Question 3 to calculate the surface area.

Surface Area of Prisms and Cylinders

Goal

Find the surface areas of prisms and cylinders.

Key Words

- prism
- surface area
- lateral face
- lateral area
- cylinder

A **prism** is a polyhedron with two congruent faces that lie in parallel planes.

To visualize the surface area of a prism, imagine unfolding it so that it lies flat. The flat representation of the faces is called a *net*.

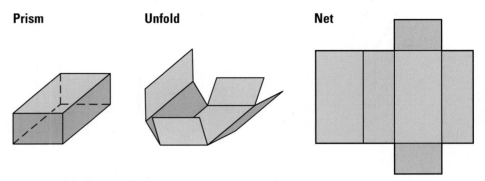

Prism   **Unfold**   **Net**

The **surface area** of a polyhedron is the sum of the areas of its faces. The surface area of a prism is equal to the area of its net.

EXAMPLE 1 Use the Net of a Prism

Find the surface area of the rectangular prism.

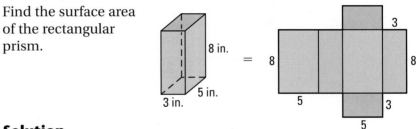

Solution

Add the areas of all the rectangles that form the faces of the prism.

Congruent Faces	Dimensions	Area of Face
Left face and right face	8 in. by 5 in.	$8 \times 5 = 40$ in.^{2}
Front face and back face	8 in. by 3 in.	$8 \times 3 = 24$ in.^{2}
Top face and bottom face	3 in. by 5 in.	$3 \times 5 = 15$ in.^{2}

Student Help

STUDY TIP
Remember that area is measured in square units, such as ft^2, m^2, and in.^{2}

Add the areas of all the faces to get the surface area.

$$S = 40 + 40 + 24 + 24 + 15 + 15 \qquad \text{Add the area of all six faces.}$$
$$= 158 \qquad\qquad\qquad\qquad\qquad \text{Simplify.}$$

ANSWER ▶ The surface area of the prism is 158 square inches.

Lateral Faces and Area The **lateral faces** of a prism are the faces of the prism that are not bases. **Lateral area** is the sum of the areas of the lateral faces.

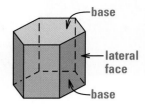

base

lateral face

base

Surface Area of a Prism One way to find the surface area of a prism is to use the method in Activity 9.2, summarized below.

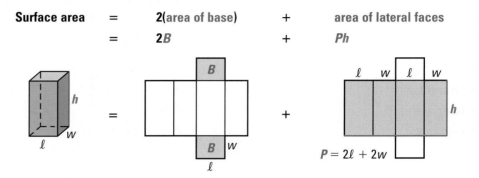

Surface area = 2(area of base) + area of lateral faces

= 2B + Ph

$P = 2\ell + 2w$

Student Help

STUDY TIP
The formula at the right works for any prism, regardless of the shape of its bases.

SURFACE AREA OF A PRISM

Words Surface area = 2(area of base) + (perimeter of base)(height)

Symbols $S = 2B + Ph$

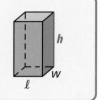

EXAMPLE **2** **Find Surface Area of a Prism**

Find the surface area of the prism.

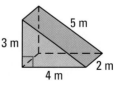

5 m
3 m
2 m
4 m

Solution

❶ Find the area of a triangular base.

$$B = \frac{1}{2} \cdot 4 \cdot 3 = 2 \cdot 3 = 6$$

❷ Find the perimeter of a base.

$$P = 3 + 4 + 5 = 12$$

❸ Find the height of the prism. In the diagram, $h = 2$.

❹ Use the formula for surface area of a prism.

$S = 2B + Ph$ Formula for the surface area of a prism

$= 2 \cdot 6 + 12 \cdot 2$ Substitute 6 for *B*, 12 for *P*, and 2 for *h*.

$= 12 + 24$ Multiply.

$= 36$ Add.

ANSWER ▶ The surface area of the prism is 36 square meters.

Visualize It!

It may help you to visualize the bases and the height if you redraw the solid in Example 2 so that it lies on a base.

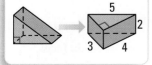

5
3 4
2

Find the surface area of the prism.

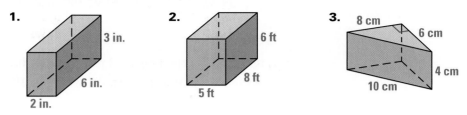

1. 3 in.
6 in.
2 in.

2. 6 ft
8 ft
5 ft

3. 8 cm
6 cm
4 cm
10 cm

Surface Area of a Cylinder A **cylinder** is a solid with two congruent circular bases that lie in parallel planes. The *lateral area* of a cylinder is the area of the curved surface.

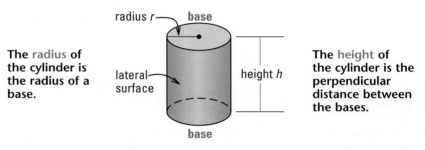

radius *r* — base

The **radius** of the cylinder is the radius of a base.

lateral surface

height *h*

The **height** of the cylinder is the perpendicular distance between the bases.

base

Visualize It!

The label below represents the lateral surface of a cylinder. When unwrapped, the label is a rectangle.

Yummy-Tummy
Vegetable
Soup

The diagram below shows how to find the surface area of a cylinder.

Surface area	=	2(area of base)	+	lateral area
	=	$2\pi r^2$	+	$(2\pi r)h$

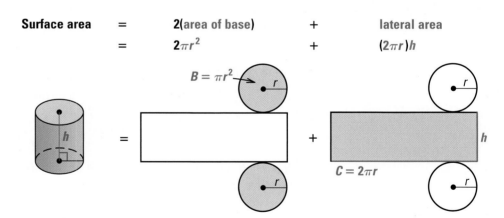

$B = \pi r^2$

$C = 2\pi r$

SURFACE AREA OF A CYLINDER

Words Surface area =
2(area of base) + (circumference of base)(height)

Symbols $S = 2B + Ch$
$= 2\pi r^2 + 2\pi rh$

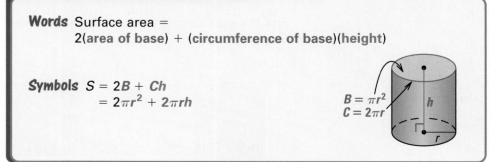

$B = \pi r^2$
$C = 2\pi r$

Student Help

LOOK BACK
See p. 452 to review
calculations with π.

EXAMPLE 3 Find Surface Area of a Cylinder

Find the surface area of the cylinder. Round
your answer to the nearest whole number.

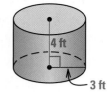

4 ft

3 ft

Solution

The radius of the base is 3 feet and the height
4 feet. Use these values in the formula for
surface area of a cylinder.

$S = 2\pi r^2 + 2\pi rh$	Write the formula for surface area.
$= 2\pi(3^2) + 2\pi(3)(4)$	Substitute 3 for r and 4 for h.
$= 18\pi + 24\pi$	Simplify.
$= 42\pi$	Add.
≈ 132	Multiply.

ANSWER ▶ The surface area is about 132 square feet.

Student Help

CLASSZONE.COM

MORE EXAMPLES
More examples at
classzone.com

EXAMPLE 4 Find Lateral Area

About how much plastic is used to make a straw that has a diameter
of 5 millimeters and a height of 195 millimeters?

Solution

The straw is a cylinder with no bases. Use the formula for the
surface area of a cylinder, but do not include the areas of the bases.

The diameter is 5 millimeters. So the radius is $5 \div 2 = 2.5$.

Lateral area $= 2\pi rh$	Surface area formula without bases.
$= 2\pi(2.5)(195)$	Substitute 2.5 for r and 195 for h.
$= 975\pi$	Simplify.
≈ 3063	Multiply.

ANSWER ▶ The straw is made with about 3063 square millimeters
of plastic.

Checkpoint ✓ **Find Surface Area of Cylinders**

**Find the area described. Round your answer to the nearest
whole number.**

4. surface area

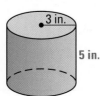

3 in.

5 in.

5. surface area

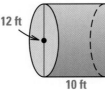

12 ft

10 ft

6. lateral area

1 m

2 m

9.2 Exercises

Guided Practice

Vocabulary Check

Tell whether the statement is *true* or *false*.

1. The solid is a triangular prism.

2. The blue face is a lateral face of the solid.

3. The red face is a lateral face of the solid.

4. The blue face is a base of the solid.

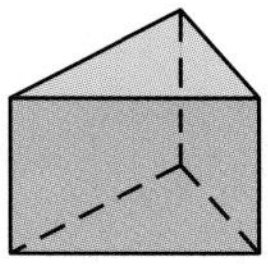

Skill Check

Find the surface area of the solid. If necessary, round your answer to the nearest whole number.

5. 10 in. 4 in. 6 in.

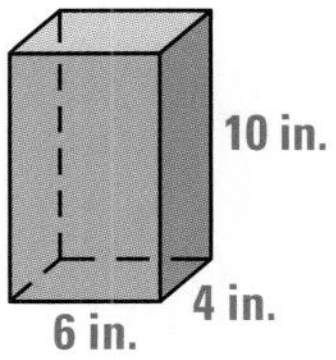

6. 6 ft 4 ft

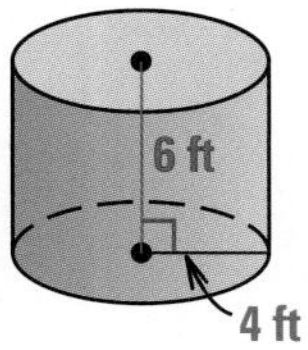

7. 4 m 2 m 3 m

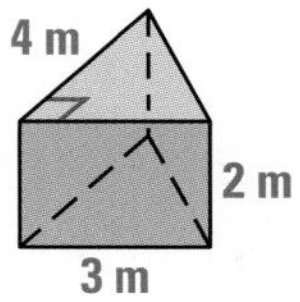

Practice and Applications

Extra Practice

See p. 691.

Identifying Parts of a Prism In Exercises 8–10, use the diagram at the right.

8. What is the height of the solid?

9. What is the area of a base?

10. What is the perimeter of a base?

5 in. 3 in. 2 in.

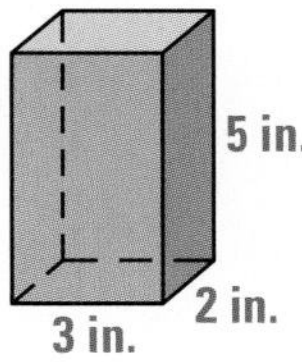

Identifying Parts of a Cylinder In Exercises 11–13, use the diagram at the right.

11. What is the height of the solid?

12. What is the area of a base?

13. What is the circumference of a base?

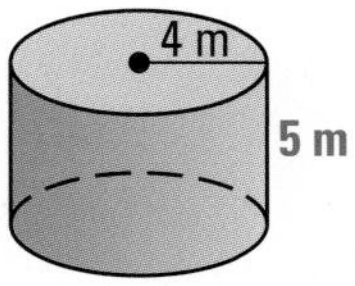

4 m 5 m

Homework Help

Example 1: Exs. 17–20, 28, 29, 31
Example 2: Exs. 17–20, 28, 29, 31
Example 3: Exs. 24–27, 30
Example 4: Exs. 39–44

Identifying Parts of a Prism In Exercises 14–16, use the diagram at the right.

14. What is the height of the solid?

15. What is the area of a base?

16. What is the perimeter of a base?

10 ft 6 ft 15 ft 8 ft

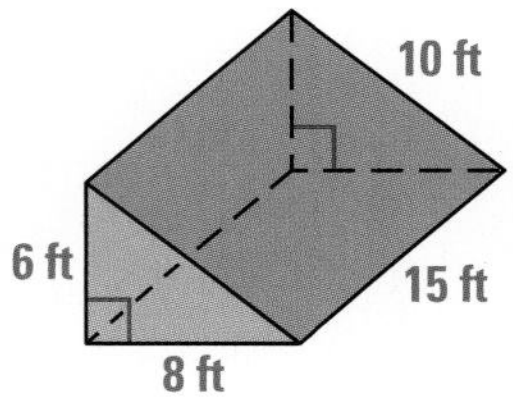

Surface Area of a Prism Find the surface area of the prism.

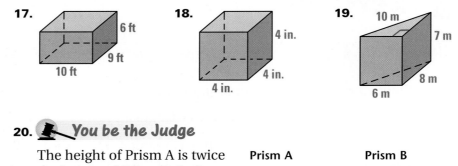

17. 6 ft, 9 ft, 10 ft

18. 4 in., 4 in., 4 in.

19. 10 m, 7 m, 8 m, 6 m

20. **You be the Judge**

The height of Prism A is twice the height of Prism B. Is the surface area of Prism A twice the surface area of Prism B? Explain.

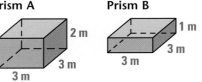

Prism A: 2 m, 3 m, 3 m   Prism B: 1 m, 3 m, 3 m

Analyzing Nets Name the solid that can be folded from the net.

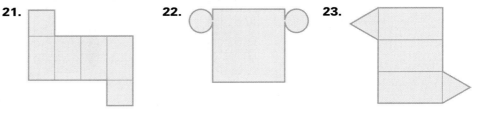

21.   **22.**   **23.**

Finding Surface Area of a Cylinder Find the surface area of the cylinder. Round your answer to the nearest whole number.

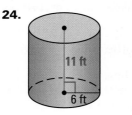   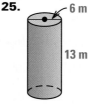   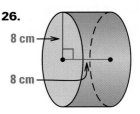

24. 11 ft, 6 ft

25. 6 m, 13 m

26. 8 cm, 8 cm

Finding Surface Area Find the surface area of the solid. Round your answer to the nearest whole number.

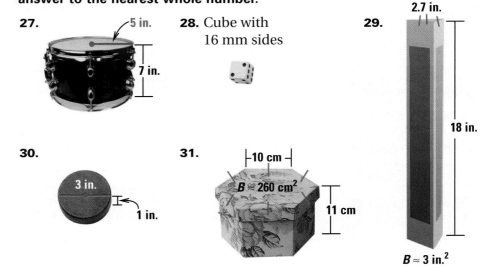

27. 5 in., 7 in.

28. Cube with 16 mm sides

29. 2.7 in., 18 in., $B \approx 3$ in.²

30. 3 in., 1 in.

31. 10 cm, $B \approx 260$ cm², 11 cm

32. Error Analysis Juanita is trying to find the surface area of the cylinder shown below. What did she do wrong?

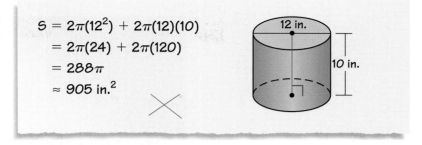

$$S = 2\pi(12^2) + 2\pi(12)(10)$$
$$= 2\pi(24) + 2\pi(120)$$
$$= 288\pi$$
$$\approx 905 \text{ in.}^2$$

12 in.

10 in.

Visualize It! Sketch the solid that results after the net has been folded. Use the shaded faces as bases.

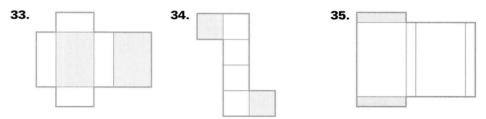

33.

34.

35.

Visualize It! Sketch the solid described and find its surface area.

36. A rectangular prism with a height of 10 feet, a length of 3 feet, and a width of 6 feet.

37. A cylinder with a radius of 3 meters and a height of 7 meters.

38. A triangular prism with a height of 5 inches and a base that is a right triangle with legs of 8 inches and 6 inches.

Finding Lateral Area Find the lateral area of the solid. If necessary, round your answer to the nearest whole number.

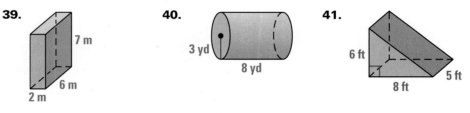

39.
7 m
6 m
2 m

40.
3 yd
8 yd

41.
6 ft
8 ft
5 ft

42. Clothes Rod Find the lateral area of a clothes rod that has a radius of 2 centimeters and a height of 90 centimeters.

43. Wax Cylinder Records In the late 1800's, a standard-sized cylinder record was about 2 inches in diameter and 4 inches long. Find the lateral area of the cylinder described.

44. Compact Discs A standard compact disc has an outer radius of 60 millimeters and a height of 1.2 millimeters. Find the lateral area of the disc.

Link to
Music

WAX CYLINDER RECORDS The first type of phonograph records were hollow wax cylinders. The cylinder is rotated on a phonograph to produce the music.

Architecture In Exercises 45 and 46 use the following information. Suppose a skyscraper is a prism that is 415 meters tall and each base is a square that measures 64 meters on a side.

45. What is the lateral area of this skyscraper?

46. Challenge What is the surface area of this skyscraper? (*Hint*: The ground is not part of the surface area of the skyscraper.)

Standardized Test Practice

47. Multiple Choice What is the approximate surface area of the cylinder shown?

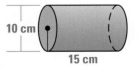

    A 502 cm^2 **B** 628 cm^2

    C 785 cm^2 **D** 1570 cm^2

48. Multiple Choice What is the height of the prism shown if the surface area is 104 square feet?

    F 4 feet   **G** 5 feet

    H 6 feet   **J** 7 feet

Mixed Review

Finding Area Find the area of the polygon made up of rectangles and triangles. *(Lessons 8.3, 8.4)*

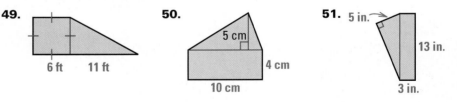

49.

50.

51.

52. A parallelogram has a height of 5 feet and an area of 70 square feet. Find the base. *(Lesson 8.5)*

Algebra Skills

Solving Proportions Solve the proportion. *(Skills Review, p. 660)*

53. $\dfrac{6}{x} = \dfrac{2}{5}$ **54.** $\dfrac{1}{10} = \dfrac{4}{x}$ **55.** $\dfrac{3}{5} = \dfrac{x}{35}$

56. $\dfrac{4}{7} = \dfrac{16}{x}$ **57.** $\dfrac{33}{x} = \dfrac{11}{13}$ **58.** $\dfrac{x}{32} = \dfrac{5}{8}$

9.3 # Surface Area of Pyramids and Cones

Goal
Find the surface areas of pyramids and cones.

Key Words
- pyramid
- height of a pyramid
- slant height of a pyramid
- cone
- height of a cone
- slant height of a cone

The Rainforest Pyramid on Galveston Island in Texas is one example of how pyramids are used in architecture.

The base of a **pyramid** is a polygon and the lateral faces are triangles with a common vertex.

This greenhouse is home to plants, butterflies, and bats.

Height

Slant height

The **height of a pyramid** is the perpendicular distance between the vertex and base.

The **slant height of a pyramid**, represented by the letter ℓ, is the height of any of its lateral faces.

Visualize It!

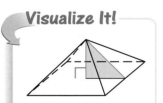

For a square pyramid, the **slant height** is the length of the hypotenuse of a right triangle formed by the height of the pyramid and half of the length of the base.

EXAMPLE 1 Find the Slant Height

Find the slant height of the Rainforest Pyramid. Round your answer to the nearest whole number.

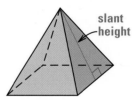
100 ft
200 ft
200 ft

Solution

To find the slant height, use the right triangle formed by the height and half of the base.

$$(\text{slant height})^2 = (\text{height})^2 + \left(\frac{1}{2}\,\text{side}\right)^2 \qquad \text{Use the Pythagorean Theorem.}$$

$$= 100^2 + \left(\frac{1}{2} \cdot 200\right)^2 \qquad \begin{array}{l}\text{Substitute 100 for height and}\\ \text{200 for base side length.}\end{array}$$

$$= 10{,}000 + 10{,}000 \qquad \text{Simplify.}$$

$$\text{slant height} = \sqrt{20{,}000} \qquad \text{Take the positive square root.}$$

$$\approx 141.42 \qquad \text{Use a calculator.}$$

ANSWER ▶ The slant height is about 141 feet.

Surface Area of a Pyramid The diagrams show the surface area of a pyramid with a square base.

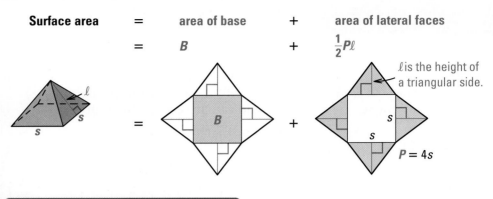

Surface area	=	area of base	+	area of lateral faces
	=	B	+	$\frac{1}{2}P\ell$

ℓ is the height of a triangular side.

$P = 4s$

Student Help

STUDY TIP
A *regular pyramid* has a regular polygon for a base. The slant height, ℓ, is the same on all of the lateral faces of a regular pyramid.

SURFACE AREA OF A PYRAMID

Words Surface area =
(area of base) + $\frac{1}{2}$(perimeter of base)(slant height)

Symbols $S = B + \frac{1}{2}P\ell$

EXAMPLE 2 Find Surface Area of a Pyramid

Find the surface area of the pyramid.

Solution

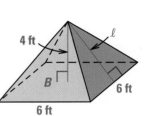

❶ Find the area of the base.

$B = 6 \times 6 = 36$

Student Help

SKILLS REVIEW
For help with area and perimeter, see p. 674.

❷ Find the perimeter of the base.

$P = 6 + 6 + 6 + 6 = \mathbf{24}$

❸ Find the slant height.

$(\text{slant height})^2 = (\text{height})^2 + (\frac{1}{2}\text{side})^2$	Use the Pythagorean Theorem.
$= 4^2 + 3^2$	Substitute. Half of 6 is 3.
$= 16 + 9$	Simplify powers.
$= 25$	Simplify.
slant height $= \sqrt{25} = 5$	Take positive square root.

❹ Substitute values into the formula for surface area of a pyramid.

$S = B + \frac{1}{2}P\ell$	Write the formula for surface area.
$= 36 + \frac{1}{2}(\mathbf{24})(5)$	Substitute.
$= 96$	Simplify.

ANSWER ▶ The surface area of the pyramid is 96 square feet.

Find the surface area of the pyramid.

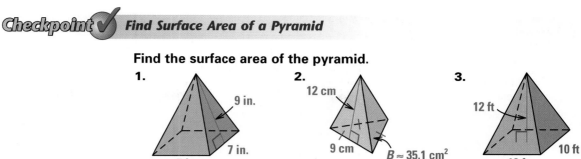

1. 9 in. 7 in. 7 in.

2. 12 cm 9 cm $B \approx 35.1$ cm²

3. 12 ft 10 ft 10 ft

Surface Area of a Cone A **cone** has a circular base and a vertex that is not in the same plane as the base. In a right cone, the height meets the base at its center. In this lesson, only right cones are shown.

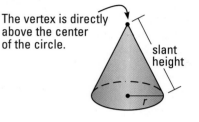

vertex
height
lateral surface
base
r

The vertex is directly above the center of the circle.
slant height
r

The **height of a cone** is the perpendicular distance between the vertex and the base.

The **slant height of a cone** is the distance between the vertex and a point on the base edge.

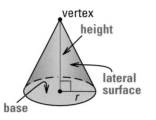

Student Help

LOOK BACK
To review how to find the area of a sector, see p. 454.

The diagrams show the surface area of a cone.

Surface area	=	area of base	+	area of sector
	=	*B*	+	$\pi r \ell$

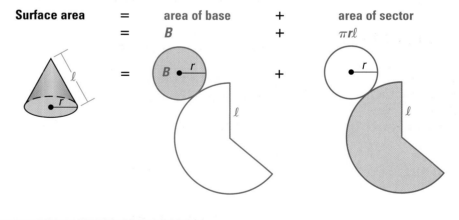

ℓ, *r* = *B*, *r* + *r*, ℓ, ℓ

SURFACE AREA OF A CONE

Words Surface area = (area of base) + (area of sector)

= (area of base) + π(radius of base)(slant height)

Symbols $S = B + \pi r \ell$

$= \pi r^2 + \pi r \ell$

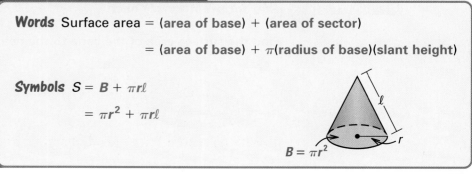

ℓ
r
$B = \pi r^2$

EXAMPLE 3 Find Surface Area of a Cone

Find the surface area of the cone to the nearest whole number.

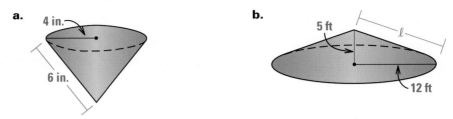

a. 4 in. 6 in.

b. 5 ft ℓ 12 ft

Solution

a. The radius of the base is 4 inches and the slant height is 6 inches.

$S = \pi r^2 + \pi r \ell$	Write the formula for surface area of a cone.
$= \pi(4)^2 + \pi(4)(6)$	Substitute 4 for r and 6 for ℓ.
$= 40\pi$	Simplify $16\pi + 24\pi$.
≈ 126	Multiply.

ANSWER ▶ The surface area is about 126 square inches.

Using Algebra

b. **First** find the slant height.

$(\textbf{slant height})^2 = r^2 + h^2$	Use the Pythagorean Theorem.
$= (12)^2 + (5)^2$	Substitute 12 for r and 5 for h.
$= 169$	Simplify $144 + 25$.
$\textbf{slant height} = \sqrt{169}$	Find the positive square root.
$= 13$	Simplify.

Next substitute 12 for r and 13 for ℓ in the formula for surface area.

$S = \pi r^2 + \pi r \ell$	Write the formula for surface area.
$= \pi(12)^2 + \pi(12)(13)$	Substitute.
$= 300\pi$	Simplify $144\pi + 156\pi$.
≈ 942	Multiply.

ANSWER ▶ The surface area is about 942 square feet.

Checkpoint ✓ **Find Surface Area of Cones**

Find the surface area of the cone to the nearest whole number.

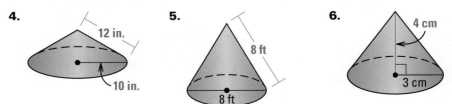

4. 12 in. 10 in.

5. 8 ft 8 ft

6. 4 cm 3 cm

Guided Practice

Vocabulary Check   **Complete the statement using *height* or *slant height*.**

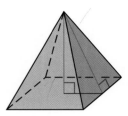

1. The red line segment is the __?__ of the pyramid.

2. The blue line segment is the __?__ of the pyramid.

3. The height of the lateral faces of the pyramid is the __?__.

4. The __?__ of a pyramid is the perpendicular distance between the vertex and base.

Skill Check   **5.** Find the slant height of the pyramid shown at the right.

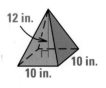

12 in.
10 in.
10 in.

Find the surface area of the solid.

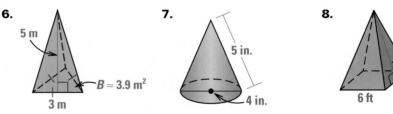

6. 5 m $B \approx 3.9$ m^2 3 m

7. 5 in.   4 in.

8. 10 ft   6 ft   6 ft

Practice and Applications

Extra Practice

See p. 691.

Recognizing Slant Height Tell whether the red line segment is the *height* or the *slant height*.

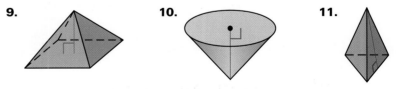

9.

10.

11.

Homework Help

Example 1: Exs. 9–14
Example 2: Exs. 15–20
Example 3: Exs. 23–28

Finding Slant Height Find the slant height of the solid.

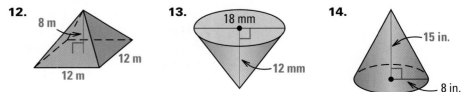

12. 8 m   12 m   12 m

13. 18 mm   12 mm

14. 15 in.   8 in.

Surface Area of a Pyramid In Exercises 15–20, find the surface area of the pyramid.

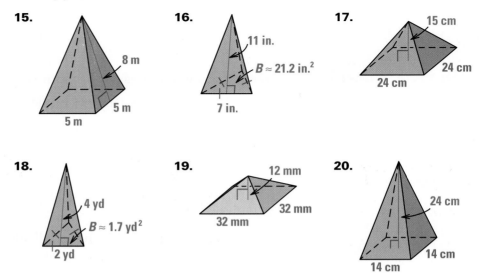

15.

8 m
5 m
5 m

16.

11 in.
B ≈ 21.2 in.²
7 in.

17.

15 cm
24 cm
24 cm

18.

4 yd
B ≈ 1.7 yd²
2 yd

19.

12 mm
32 mm
32 mm

20.

24 cm
14 cm
14 cm

21. **Logical Reasoning** Explain why the slant height of a pyramid must be greater than the height of the pyramid.

22. **Error Analysis** Jamie is trying to find the surface area of the pyramid below. His solution is shown. What did he do wrong in his calculations?

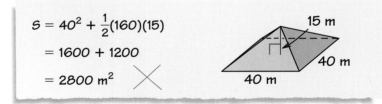

$S = 40^2 + \frac{1}{2}(160)(15)$

$= 1600 + 1200$

$= 2800 \text{ m}^2$ ✗

15 m
40 m
40 m

Surface Area of a Cone Find the surface area of the cone. Round your answer to the nearest whole number.

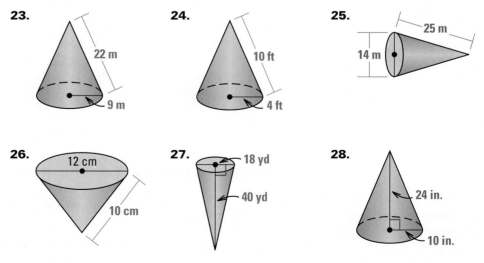

23.

22 m
9 m

24.

10 ft
4 ft

25.

25 m
14 m

26.

12 cm
10 cm

27.

18 yd
40 yd

28.

24 in.
10 in.

Finding Lateral Area Find the lateral area of the object.

29.

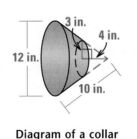

$P = 28$ cm
$\ell = 14$ cm

30.

$r = 4.3$ in.
$\ell = 22.3$ in.

31.

GO TEAM!

$d = 8$ in.
$\ell = 14$ in.

Visualize It! Sketch the described solid and find its surface area. If necessary, round your answer to the nearest whole number.

32. A pyramid has a square base with congruent edges of 12 meters and a height of 8 meters.

33. A pyramid has a triangular base with congruent edges of 8 feet and a slant height of 13 feet. The base area is 27.7 square feet.

34. A cone has a diameter of 6 yards and a slant height of 7 yards.

35. A cone has a radius of 10 inches and a height of 14 inches.

Using Nets Name the solid that can be folded from the net. Then find its surface area.

36.

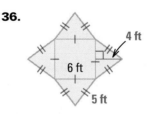

4 ft

6 ft

5 ft

37.

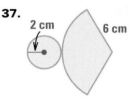

2 cm

6 cm

Veterinary Medicine A cone-shaped collar, called an Elizabethan collar, is used to prevent pets from aggravating a healing wound.

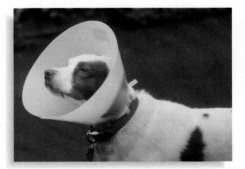

3 in.

4 in.

12 in.

10 in.

Diagram of a collar

38. Find the lateral area of the entire cone shown above.

39. Find the lateral area of the small cone that has a radius of 3 inches and a height of 4 inches.

40. Use your answers to Exercises 38 and 39 to find the amount of material needed to make the Elizabethan collar shown.

LAMPSHADES Many lampshades are shaped like cones or pyramids. This lamp was designed by architect and designer Frank Lloyd Wright.

Lampshades In Exercises 41 and 42, refer to the lampshade with a square base shown at the right.

41. Use the Pythagorean Theorem to find the slant height of the lampshade. Round your answer to the nearest whole number.

42. Estimate the amount of glass needed to make the lampshade by calculating the lateral area of the pyramid.

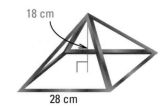

Challenge Find the surface area of the combined solids. (*Hint*: Find the surface area of each solid and add them together. In each calculation, remember to omit the surface where the solids connect.)

43.   **44.**   **45.**

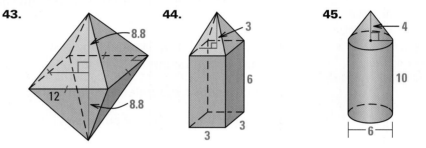

46. Multi-Step Problem Complete parts (a)–(e).

a. Find the surface area of each cone described in the table. Round your answer to the nearest whole number.

	Radius	Slant Height	Surface Area
Cone A	3 ft	6 ft	?
Cone B	3 ft	8 ft	?
Cone C	3 ft	10 ft	?

b. What measurement stayed the same in the cones in part (a)?

c. Find the surface area of each cone described in the table. Round your answer to the nearest whole number.

	Radius	Slant Height	Surface Area
Cone D	2 ft	8 ft	?
Cone E	4 ft	8 ft	?
Cone F	6 ft	8 ft	?

d. What measurement stayed the same in the cones in part (c)?

e. Compare the measurements you found in the two tables. Which measurement has a greater influence on surface area? Why?

Evaluating Expressions Evaluate the expression for the given value of the variable. *(Skills Review, p. 670)*

47. $3x^2$ when $x = 6$ **48.** $x^2 + 6$ when $x = 4$ **49.** $2x^2 - 3$ when $x = 3$

50. $4x^2 - 10$ when $x = 2$ **51.** $x^2 + 4x$ when $x = 6$ **52.** $3x^2 + 5x$ when $x = 5$

Finding Areas of Sectors Find the area of the green sector given the area of the circle. Round your answer to the nearest whole number. *(Lesson 8.7)*

53. $A = 180 \text{ m}^2$ **54.** $A = 114 \text{ ft}^2$ **55.** $A = 258 \text{ cm}^2$

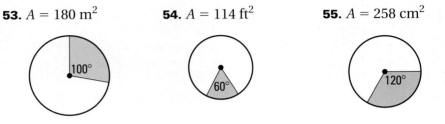

Algebra Skills

Simplifying Expressions Simplify. *(Skills Review, p. 670)*

56. $-2x + 3 + 6x$ **57.** $4y + 5 - 4y - 1$ **58.** $4 - (2x - 1) + x$

59. $7x - 2 - (3x + 2)$ **60.** $x - 9x + 6x$ **61.** $10c - (5 - 3c)$

Quiz 1

Identify the shape of the base(s) of the solid and name the solid. Then tell if the solid is a polyhedron. If so, count the number of faces of the polyhedron. *(Lesson 9.1)*

1.   **2.**   **3.**

Find the surface area of the figure. If necessary, round your answer to the nearest whole number. *(Lessons 9.2, 9.3)*

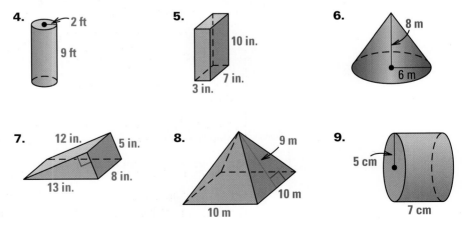

4. 2 ft, 9 ft   **5.** 10 in., 7 in., 3 in.   **6.** 8 m, 6 m

7. 12 in., 5 in., 8 in., 13 in.   **8.** 9 m, 10 m, 10 m   **9.** 5 cm, 7 cm

Volume of Prisms and Cylinders

Goal
Find the volumes of prisms and cylinders.

Key Words
- prism p. 483
- cylinder p. 485
- volume

The amount of water in an aquarium is an example of *volume.* The **volume** of a solid is the number of cubic units contained in its interior.

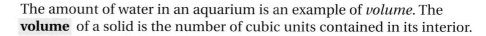

EXAMPLE 1 Find the Volume of a Rectangular Prism

Find the volume of the box by determining how many unit cubes fit in the box.

unit cube 1 1 1

Solution

The base is 5 units by 3 units. So, 3 • 5, or 15 unit cubes are needed to cover the base layer.

There are 4 layers. Each layer has 15 cubes. So, the total number of cubes is 4 • 15, or 60.

4 units
3 units
5 units

ANSWER ▶ The volume of the box is 60 cubic units.

> **Student Help**
>
> **READING TIP**
> Volume is measured in cubic units, such as ft³, read as "cubic feet."

Volume of a Prism The process used in Example 1 can be used to determine the volume of any prism.

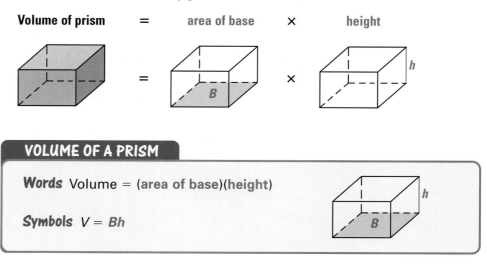

Volume of prism	=	area of base	×	height

VOLUME OF A PRISM

Words Volume = (area of base)(height)

Symbols $V = Bh$

h

B

EXAMPLE 2 **Find the Volume of a Prism**

Find the volume of the prism.

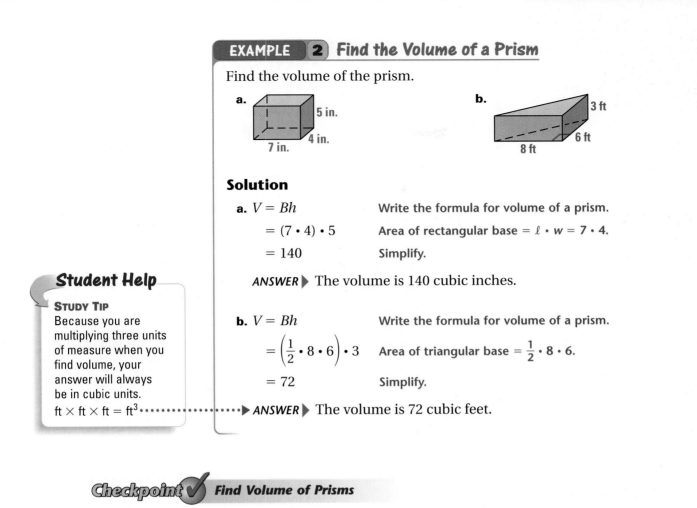

a. [5 in., 7 in., 4 in.]

b. [3 ft, 6 ft, 8 ft]

Solution

a. $V = Bh$ Write the formula for volume of a prism.

    $= (7 \cdot 4) \cdot 5$ Area of rectangular base $= \ell \cdot w = 7 \cdot 4$.

    $= 140$ Simplify.

ANSWER ▶ The volume is 140 cubic inches.

b. $V = Bh$ Write the formula for volume of a prism.

    $= \left(\dfrac{1}{2} \cdot 8 \cdot 6\right) \cdot 3$ Area of triangular base $= \dfrac{1}{2} \cdot 8 \cdot 6$.

    $= 72$ Simplify.

▶ *ANSWER* ▶ The volume is 72 cubic feet.

Student Help

STUDY TIP
Because you are multiplying three units of measure when you find volume, your answer will always be in cubic units.
$ft \times ft \times ft = ft^3$ • • • •

Checkpoint ✓ **Find Volume of Prisms**

Find the volume of the prism.

1. [6 ft, 9 ft, 4 ft]

2. [5 cm, 5 cm, 5 cm]

3. [7 in., 7 in., 10 in.]

Volume of a Cylinder The method for finding the volume of a cylinder is the same for finding the volume of a prism.

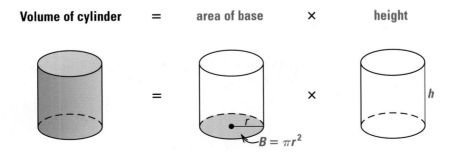

Volume of cylinder   =   area of base   ×   height

         =   × h

                     $B = \pi r^2$

VOLUME OF A CYLINDER

Words Volume = (area of base)(height)

Symbols $V = Bh$
$\quad\quad\ = \pi r^2 h$

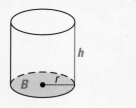

EXAMPLE **3** *Compare Volumes of Cylinders*

a. How do the radius and height of the mug compare to the radius and height of the dog bowl?

b. How many times greater is the volume of the bowl than the volume of the mug?

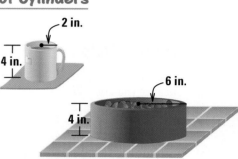

Solution

a. The radius of the mug is 2 inches and the radius of the dog bowl is 6 inches. The radius of the bowl is three times the radius of the mug. The height of the mug is the same as the height of the bowl.

b.
Volume of mug		**Volume of dog bowl**
$V = \pi r^2 h$	Write the formula for volume.	$V = \pi r^2 h$
$= \pi(2^2)(4)$	Substitute for *r* and for *h*.	$= \pi(6^2)(4)$
$= 16\pi$	Simplify.	$= 144\pi$

To compare the volume of the bowl to the volume of the mug, divide the volume of the bowl by the volume of the mug.

$$\frac{\text{Volume of bowl}}{\text{Volume of mug}} = \frac{144\pi}{16\pi} = 9$$

ANSWER ▶ The volume of the bowl is nine times the volume of the mug.

Checkpoint ✓ *Find Volume of Cylinders*

Find the volume of the cylinder. Round your answer to the nearest whole number.

4. 2 ft, 3 ft

5. 1 in., 5 in.

6. 4 m, 10 m

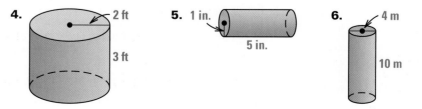

9.4 Exercises

Guided Practice

Vocabulary Check Based upon the units, tell whether the number is a measure of *surface area* or *volume*.

1. 5 ft^3 **2.** 7 yd^2 **3.** 3 m^2 **4.** 2 cm^3

Skill Check Candles Find the volume of the candle.

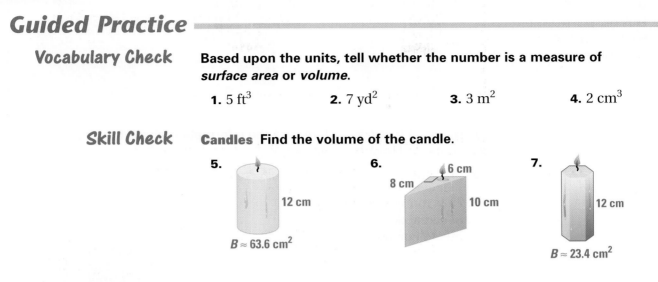

5. 12 cm $B \approx 63.6 \text{ cm}^2$

6. 6 cm, 8 cm, 10 cm

7. 12 cm $B \approx 23.4 \text{ cm}^2$

Practice and Applications

Extra Practice

See p. 692.

Using Unit Cubes Find the number of unit cubes that will fit in the box. Explain your reasoning.

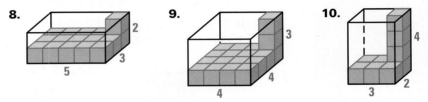

8. 2, 3, 5

9. 3, 4, 4

10. 4, 3, 2

Volume of a Prism Find the volume of the prism.

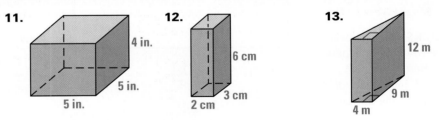

11. 4 in., 5 in., 5 in.

12. 6 cm, 2 cm, 3 cm

13. 12 m, 9 m, 4 m

Volume of a Cube In Exercises 14–16, you are given the length of each side of a cube. Sketch the cube and find its volume.

14. 3 meters   **15.** 7 feet   **16.** 10 centimeters

Visualize It! In Exercises 17 and 18, make a sketch of the solid. Then find its volume.

17. A prism has a square base with 4 meter sides and a height of 7 meters.

18. A prism has a rectangular base that is 3 feet by 6 feet and a height of 8 feet.

Homework Help

Example 1: Exs. 8–10
Example 2: Exs. 11–18
Example 3: Exs. 27–40

Finding Volume Find the volume of the combined prisms.

19.

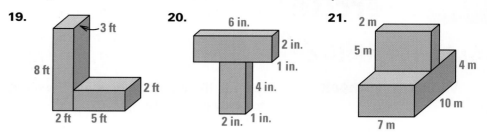

3 ft
8 ft
2 ft
2 ft   5 ft

20.

6 in.
2 in.
1 in.
4 in.
2 in.   1 in.

21.

2 m
5 m
4 m
10 m
7 m

Shopping In Exercises 22–24, use the information about the sizes of the cereal boxes shown below.

22. Find the volume of each box of cereal.

23. How many small boxes of cereal do you have to buy to equal the amount of cereal in a large box?

24. Which box gives you the most cereal for your money? Explain.

$2.00
Cereal
Part of a well balanced breakfast
10 in.
8 in.   2 in.

$6.00
Cereal
Part of a well balanced breakfast
16 in.
10 in.   4 in.

Soo Locks In Exercises 25 and 26, use the information below.
Lake Superior is about 22 feet higher than Lake Huron. In order for ships to safely pass from one lake to the other, they must go through one of the four Soo Locks.

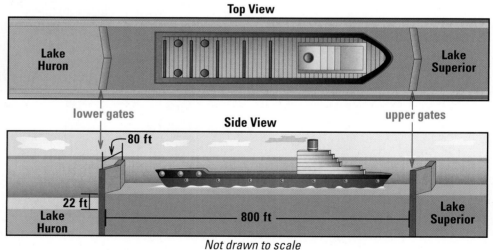

Top View

Lake Huron

Lake Superior

lower gates   upper gates

Side View

80 ft

22 ft
Lake Huron

800 ft

Lake Superior

Not drawn to scale

25. Water is added to the MacArthur Lock until the height is increased by 22 feet. To find the amount of water added to the lock, find the volume of a rectangular prism with a length of 800 feet, a width of 80 feet, and a height of 22 feet.

26. How many gallons of water are added to the MacArthur Lock to raise the ship to the level of Lake Superior? Use the fact that $1 \text{ ft}^3 \approx 7.5$ gal.

Volume of a Cylinder Find the volume of the cylinder. Round your answer to the nearest whole number.

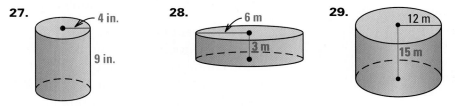

27. 4 in. 9 in.

28. 6 m 3 m

29. 12 m 15 m

Swimming Pools In Exercises 30–32, find the volume of the pool. Round your answer to the nearest whole number. Then compare the volumes of the pools to answer Exercise 33.

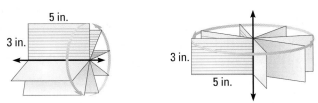

30. 20 ft 4 ft

31. 24 ft 4 ft

32. 15 ft 3 ft

33. Which pool above requires the least amount of water to fill it?

Visualize It! In Exercises 34 and 35, use the information below. Suppose that a 3-inch by 5-inch index card is rotated around a horizontal line and a vertical line to produce two different solids.

5 in.   3 in.

3 in.   5 in.

34. Find the volume of each solid.

35. Which solid has a greater volume? Explain your reasoning.

Aquariums In Exercises 36 and 37, use the information below. The Giant Ocean Tank at the New England Aquarium is a cylinder that is 23 feet deep and 40 feet in diameter as shown.

36. Find the volume of the tank.

37. How many gallons of water are needed to fill the tank? ($1 \text{ ft}^3 \approx 7.5$ gal)

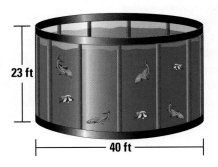

23 ft

40 ft

38. Personal Aquariums To avoid overcrowding in a personal aquarium, you should buy one fish for every gallon of water ($231 \text{ in.}^3 \approx 1$ gal). About how many fish should be in an aquarium that is a rectangular prism measuring 20 inches wide, 10 inches long, and is filled with water to a height of 11 inches?

Link to Careers

AQUARIUM DIVER In addition to feeding and taking care of the fish and the plants in an aquarium, divers make sure that the tank does not get too crowded.

You be the Judge In Exercises 39 and 40, use the cartons shown.

39. Find the volume of each carton of ice cream.

40. Terry assumes that because the dimensions doubled, the jumbo carton contains twice as much ice cream as the regular carton. Is Terry right? Explain your reasoning.

10 cm

5 cm

20 cm

10 cm

EXAMPLE **Find Volume**

Find the volume of the passenger car of the Space Spiral at Cedar Point Amusement Park in Sandusky, Ohio.

Solution

The passenger car is a cylinder with a "hole" in it. To find the volume, subtract the volume of the hole from the volume of the larger cylinder.

$$\text{Volume of larger cylinder} = \pi r^2 h$$
$$= \pi(10^2)(14)$$
$$\approx 4398$$

$$\text{Volume of "hole"} = \pi r^2 h$$
$$= \pi(4^2)(14)$$
$$\approx 704$$

14 ft

10 ft   4 ft

ANSWER ▶ The volume of the passenger car is about $4398 - 704 = 3694$ cubic feet.

Student Help
CLASSZONE.COM

HOMEWORK HELP
Extra help with problem solving in Exs. 41–43 is at classzone.com

Finding Volume In Exercises 41–43, find the volume of the solid.

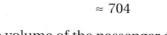

41. 2 in.   1 in.
8 in.
6 in.   2 in.

42. 8 ft
3 ft
10 ft

43. 1 m
4 m
4 m
4 m

Using Algebra Write an expression for the volume of the solid in terms of *x*.

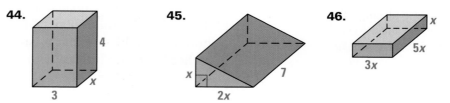

44. 4
x
3

45. x
2x
7

46. x
5x
3x

Challenge In Exercises 47–49, find the missing dimension(s). If necessary, round your answer to the nearest whole number.

47. A cylinder has a volume of 100.48 cubic inches and a diameter of 4 inches. Find the height of the cylinder.

48. A cylinder has a volume of 1538.6 cubic feet and a height of 10 feet. Find the radius of the cylinder.

49. The length of a rectangular prism is twice its width. The height of the prism equals the width. Find the dimensions of the prism, given that the volume is 54 cubic inches.

Standardized Test Practice

50. Multiple Choice What is the approximate volume of the cylinder shown at the right?

  A 100 in.^{3} **B** 785 in.^{3}

  C 1570 in.^{3} **D** 6280 in.^{3}

51. Multiple Choice The volume of the prism shown at the right is 168 cubic feet. What is the height of the prism?

  F 6 feet   **G** 7 feet

  H 8 feet   **J** 9 feet

Mixed Review

Using the Pythagorean Theorem Find the unknown side length. Round your answer to the nearest tenth. *(Lesson 4.4)*

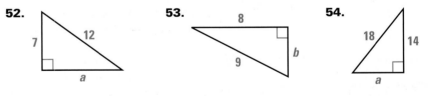

52.   **53.**   **54.**

Surface Area Find the surface area of the solid. If necessary, round your answer to the nearest whole number. *(Lessons 9.2, 9.3)*

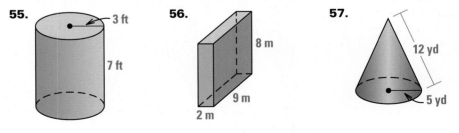

55.   **56.**   **57.**

Algebra Skills

Solving Equations Solve the equation. *(Skills Review, p. 672)*

58. $x - 7 = 0$ **59.** $m - 1 = -12$ **60.** $10 + c = -3$

61. $\frac{3}{4}b = 24$ **62.** $-14d = 2$ **63.** $6n = 102$

Question

How does the volume of a pyramid relate to the volume of a prism with the same base?

Materials

- poster board
- ruler
- scissors
- tape
- unpopped popcorn, uncooked rice, or dried beans

Explore

1 Use a ruler to draw the two nets shown below on poster board. Be sure to draw the dashed lines on the net as shown.

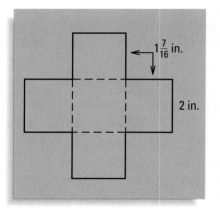

$1\frac{7}{16}$ in.

2 in.

2 in.   2 in.

2 in.

2 Cut out the nets.

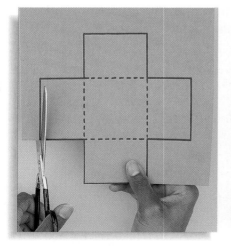

3 Fold along the dashed lines to form an open prism and an open pyramid.

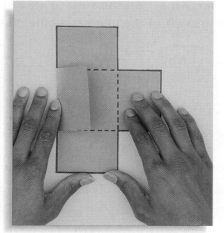

4 Tape each solid to hold it in place, making sure that the edges do not overlap.

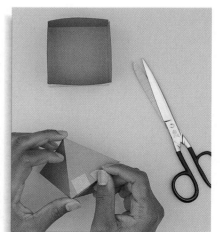

Think About It

1. Compare the area of the base of the pyramid to the area of the base of the prism. Fitting the pyramid inside the prism will help. What do you notice?

2. Compare the heights of the solids. What do you notice?

3. Which solid do you think has the greater volume? Why?

Explore

5 Fill the pyramid to the top with unpopped popcorn, uncooked rice, or dried beans. Pour the contents of the pyramid into the prism.

6 Repeat Step 5 until the prism is full. Count the number of times you empty the contents of the pyramid into the prism.

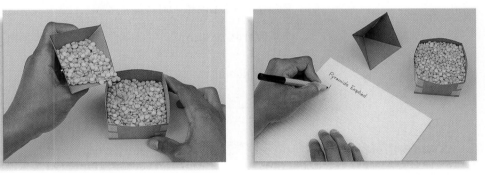

Think About It

4. How many times did you empty the contents of the pyramid into the prism? What does this tell you about the volume of the pyramid and the prism?

5. Complete each sentence with the appropriate number.

   Volume of the prism = __?__ × Volume of the pyramid

   Volume of the pyramid = __?__ × Volume of the prism

6. Use your results from Exercise 5 to write a formula for the volume of a pyramid.

   Volume of a prism: $V = Bh$

   Volume of a pyramid: $V = $ __?__ Bh

9.5 Volume of Pyramids and Cones

Goal
Find the volumes of pyramids and cones.

Key Words
- pyramid p. 491
- cone p. 493
- volume p. 500

In the puzzle below, you can see that the square prism can be made using three congruent pyramids. The volume of each pyramid is one-third the volume of the prism.

Volume Puzzle

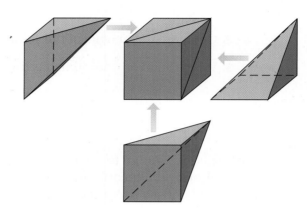

VOLUME OF A PYRAMID

Words Volume = $\frac{1}{3}$(area of base)(height)

Symbols $V = \frac{1}{3}Bh$

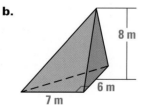

Student Help

STUDY TIP
In Example 1(b), 6 m is the height of the triangular base and 8 m is the height of the pyramid.

EXAMPLE 1 Find the Volume of a Pyramid

Find the volume of the pyramid.

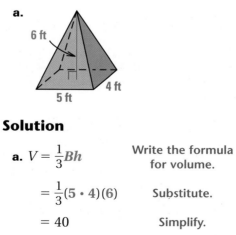

a. 6 ft, 4 ft, 5 ft

b. 8 m, 6 m, 7 m

Solution

a. $V = \frac{1}{3}Bh$ — Write the formula for volume.

$= \frac{1}{3}(5 \cdot 4)(6)$ — Substitute.

$= 40$ — Simplify.

ANSWER ▶ The volume is 40 cubic feet.

b. $V = \frac{1}{3}Bh$

$= \frac{1}{3}\left(\frac{1}{2} \cdot 7 \cdot 6\right)(8)$

$= 56$

ANSWER ▶ The volume is 56 cubic meters.

Find the volume of the pyramid.

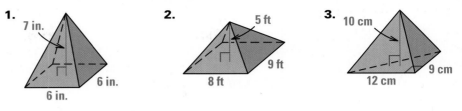

1. 7 in. 6 in. 6 in.

2. 5 ft 9 ft 8 ft

3. 10 cm 9 cm 12 cm

Student Help

LOOK BACK
For help with relating the volume of a pyramid to the volume of a prism, see p. 508.

Volume of a Cone The volume of a cone is related to the volume of a cylinder in the same way that the volume of a pyramid is related to the volume of a prism.

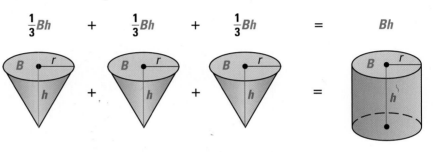

$$\frac{1}{3}Bh \quad + \quad \frac{1}{3}Bh \quad + \quad \frac{1}{3}Bh \quad = \quad Bh$$

VOLUME OF A CONE

Words Volume $= \frac{1}{3}$(area of base)(height)

Symbols $V = \frac{1}{3}Bh$

$\qquad = \frac{1}{3}\pi r^2 h$

EXAMPLE **2** **Find the Volume of a Cone**

Find the volume of the cone. Round your answer to the nearest whole number.

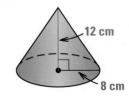

12 cm 8 cm

Solution

The radius of the cone is $r = 8$ cm.

The height of the cone is $h = 12$ cm.

$V = \frac{1}{3}\pi r^2 h$	Write the formula for volume of a cone.
$= \frac{1}{3}\pi (8^2)(12)$	Substitute 8 for r and 12 for h.
≈ 804	Multiply.

ANSWER ▶ The volume is about 804 cubic centimeters.

Using Algebra

EXAMPLE 3 Find the Volume of a Cone

What is the volume of the cone shown at the right?

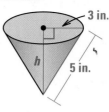

Solution

You are given the slant height of the cone. You need to find the height of the cone before you can find the volume.

❶ Find the height.

$(\text{leg})^2 + (\text{leg})^2 = (\text{hypotenuse})^2$	Use the Pythagorean Theorem.
$3^2 + h^2 = 5^2$	Substitute.
$9 + h^2 = 25$	Simplify.
$h^2 = 25 - 9$	Subtract 9 from each side.
$h^2 = 16$	Simplify.
$h = \sqrt{16}$	Take the positive square root.
$h = 4$	Simplify.

❷ Find the volume.

$V = \frac{1}{3}\pi r^2 h$	Write the formula for volume.
$= \frac{1}{3}\pi (3^2)(4)$	Substitute 3 for *r* and 4 for *h*.
≈ 38	Multiply.

ANSWER ▶ The volume is about 38 cubic inches.

Student Help

LOOK BACK
For help with the Pythagorean Theorem, see p. 192.

Checkpoint ✓ *Find the Volume of a Cone*

Find the volume of the cone. Round your answer to the nearest whole number.

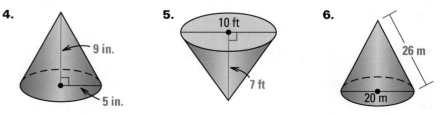

4.   9 in.   5 in.

5.   10 ft   7 ft

6.   26 m   20 m

7. Find the volume of a cone with a height of 6 inches and a diameter of 8 inches.

8. Find the volume of a cone with a slant height of 17 feet and a diameter of 16 feet.

9.5 Exercises

Guided Practice

Vocabulary Check

Match the solid with its volume formula. Use each formula once.

A. Pyramid   **B.** Cone   **C.** Prism   **D.** Cylinder

1. $V = \pi r^2 h$ **2.** $V = Bh$ **3.** $V = \frac{1}{3}\pi r^2 h$ **4.** $V = \frac{1}{3}Bh$

Skill Check

Find the volume of the solid. If necessary, round your answer to the nearest whole number.

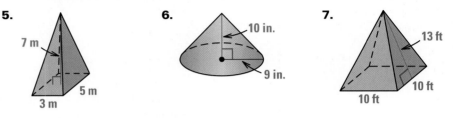

5. 7 m, 5 m, 3 m

6. 10 in., 9 in.

7. 13 ft, 10 ft, 10 ft

8. Find the volume of a cone with a slant height of 15 inches and a radius of 9 inches. Leave your answer in terms of π.

Practice and Applications

Extra Practice

See p. 692.

Find Base Areas Find the area of the base of the solid.

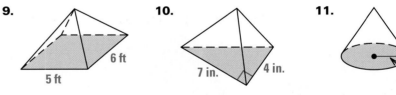

9. 6 ft, 5 ft

10. 7 in., 4 in.

11. 8 cm

Volume of a Pyramid Find the volume of the pyramid.

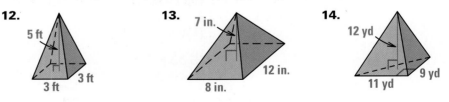

12. 5 ft, 3 ft, 3 ft

13. 7 in., 12 in., 8 in.

14. 12 yd, 11 yd, 9 yd

Homework Help

Example 1: Exs. 12–16, 20–25
Example 2: Exs. 17–19, 21, 26
Example 3: Exs. 30–32

Volume of a Pyramid Find the volume.

15. Find the volume of a pyramid with a base area of 48 square feet and a height of 5 feet.

16. Find the volume of a pyramid with a height of 3 inches and a square base with side lengths of 4 inches.

Volume of a Cone Find the volume of the cone. Round your answer to the nearest whole number.

17.

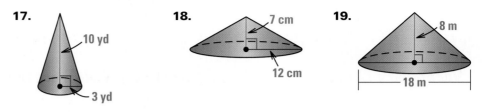

10 yd

3 yd

18.

7 cm

12 cm

19.

8 m

18 m

Finding Volume Find the volume of the object. Round your answer to the nearest whole number.

20.

3 in.

$B = 16$ in.^{2}

21.

5 cm

8 cm

22.

$h = 144$ m

$B = 46{,}535$ m^2

Logical Reasoning In Exercises 23 and 24, use a pyramid that has a height of 8 feet and a square base with a side length of 6 feet.

23. How does the volume of the pyramid change if the base stays the same and the height is doubled?

24. How does the volume of the pyramid change if the height stays the same and the side length of the base is doubled?

Error Analysis In Exercises 25 and 26, explain the student's error and correct it.

25.

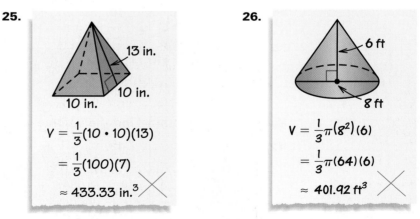

13 in.

10 in.

10 in.

$V = \frac{1}{3}(10 \cdot 10)(13)$

$= \frac{1}{3}(100)(7)$

≈ 433.33 in.^{3}

26.

6 ft

8 ft

$V = \frac{1}{3}\pi(8^2)(6)$

$= \frac{1}{3}\pi(64)(6)$

≈ 401.92 ft^3

Student Help

CLASSZONE.COM

HOMEWORK HELP

Extra help with problem solving in Exs. 27–29 is at classzone.com

Finding Dimensions Find the missing dimension.

27. A pyramid has a volume of 20 cubic inches and the area of the base is 15 square inches. What is the height of the pyramid?

28. A cone has a volume of 8π cubic feet and a height of 6 feet. What is the radius of the base?

29. A pyramid with a square base has a volume of 120 cubic meters and a height of 10 meters. What is a side length of the base?

Finding Volume with Slant Height Find the volume of the solid. If necessary, round your answer to the nearest whole number.

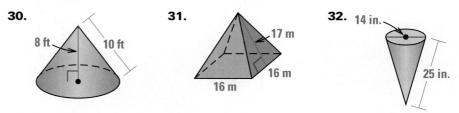

30. 8 ft 10 ft

31. 17 m 16 m 16 m

32. 14 in. 25 in.

Student Help

STUDY TIP
Recall that the radius of the sector that forms a cone is the slant height of the cone. This is shown on p. 493.

Using Nets In Exercises 33–35, use the net to sketch the solid. Then find the volume of the solid. Round your answer to the nearest whole number.

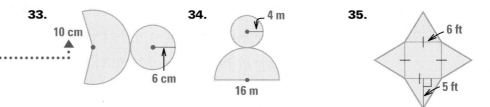

33. 10 cm 6 cm

34. 4 m 16 m

35. 6 ft 5 ft

Popcorn A movie theater serves a small size of popcorn in a conical container and a large size of popcorn in a cylindrical container.

36. What is the volume of the small container? What is the volume of the large container?

37. How many small containers of popcorn do you have to buy to equal the amount of popcorn in a large container?

38. Which container gives you more popcorn for your money? Explain your reasoning.

3 in. 6 in. POPCORN $2.00

3 in. 6 in. Butter POPCORN $4.00

Student Help
CLASSZONE.COM

HOMEWORK HELP
Extra help with problem solving in Exs. 39–41 is at classzone.com

Pet Feeder In Exercises 39–41, use the diagram of the automatic pet feeder.

39. Calculate the amount of food that can be placed in the feeder. (*Hint*: Add the volume of the cylinder and the volume of the cone.)

40. If a cat eats 1 cup of food each day, how much food does the cat eat in five days? Express your answer in cubic inches. (1 cup ≈ 14.4 in.^{3})

41. Will the feeder hold enough food for the five days described in Exercise 40? Explain.

2.5 in. 7.5 in. 4 in.

Volcanoes In Exercises 42–44, use the information below.

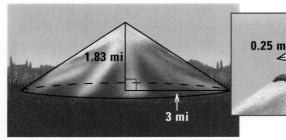

Before 1980, Mount St. Helens was a cone-shaped volcano.

In 1980, Mount St. Helens erupted, destroying the cone-shaped tip.

42. What was the volume of Mount St. Helens before 1980?

43. What was the volume of the cone-shaped tip that was destroyed?

44. What is the volume of Mount St. Helens today? (*Hint*: Subtract the volume of the tip from the volume before 1980.)

Standardized Test Practice

45. Multiple Choice A pyramid has a height of 9 yards and a volume of 96 cubic yards. Which of these are possible dimensions for its rectangular base?

    Ⓐ 4 yards by 8 yards   Ⓑ 2 yards by 8 yards

    Ⓒ 6 yards by 7 yards   Ⓓ 5 yards by 8 yards

Mixed Review

Finding Circumference and Area Find the circumference and the area of the circle. Round your answer to the nearest whole number. (*Lesson 8.7*)

46.
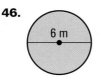
6 m

47.
14 in.

48.
12 cm

Surface Area Find the surface area of the figure. If necessary, round your answer to the nearest whole number. (*Lessons 9.2, 9.3*)

49.
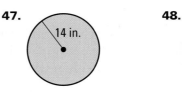
7 in.
8 in.
5 in.

50.
5 ft
9 ft

51.

12 m
9 m

Algebra Skills

Slope Plot the points and draw a line through them. Then tell if the slope is *positive, negative, zero,* or *undefined.* (*Skills Review, p. 665*)

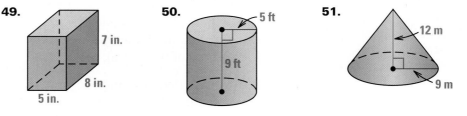

52. (0, 0) and (4, 3)   **53.** (5, 5) and (1, −2)   **54.** (−3, 2) and (6, 2)

55. (−2, −2) and (0, 4)   **56.** (−4, −1) and (−4, 7)   **57.** (−3, 5) and (4, −1)

Surface Area and Volume of Spheres

Goal
Find surface areas and volumes of spheres.

Key Words
- sphere
- hemisphere

A globe is an example of a *sphere*. A **sphere** is the set of all points in space that are the same distance from a point, the center of the sphere.

A geometric plane passing through the center of a sphere divides it into two **hemispheres** . The globe is divided into the Northern Hemisphere and the Southern Hemisphere.

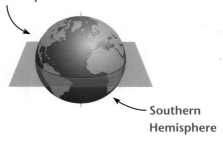

Northern Hemisphere

Southern Hemisphere

The globe is divided into two hemispheres.

SURFACE AREA OF A SPHERE

Words Surface area = $4\pi(\text{radius})^2$

Symbols $S = 4\pi r^2$

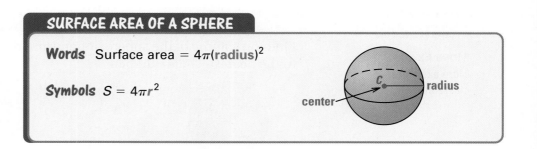

center

c

radius

Visualize It!

To sketch a sphere, draw a **circle** and its **center**. Then draw an **oval** to give the sphere dimension.

EXAMPLE **1** **Find the Surface Area of a Sphere**

Find the surface area of the sphere. Round your answer to the nearest whole number.

a.
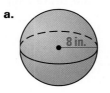
8 in.

b.
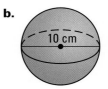
10 cm

Solution

a. The radius is 8 inches, so $r = 8$.

$$S = 4\pi r^2$$
$$= 4 \cdot \pi \cdot 8^2$$
$$\approx 804$$

The surface area is about 804 square inches.

b. The diameter is 10 cm, so the radius is $\frac{10}{2} = 5$. So, $r = 5$.

$$S = 4\pi r^2$$
$$= 4 \cdot \pi \cdot 5^2$$
$$\approx 314$$

The surface area is about 314 square centimeters.

Find the surface area of the sphere. Round your answer to the nearest whole number.

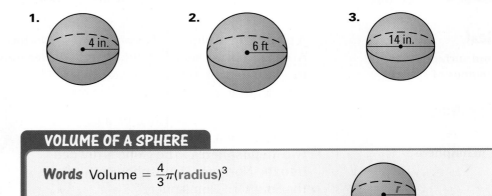

1.   4 in.

2.   6 ft

3.   14 in.

VOLUME OF A SPHERE

Words Volume = $\frac{4}{3}\pi(\text{radius})^3$

Symbols $V = \frac{4}{3}\pi r^3$

r

Student Help
CLASSZONE.COM

MORE EXAMPLES
More examples at
classzone.com

EXAMPLE 2 *Find the Volume of a Sphere*

Find the volume of the sphere or hemisphere. Round your answer to the nearest whole number.

a.

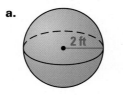

2 ft

b.

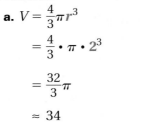

5 in.

Solution

a. $V = \frac{4}{3}\pi r^3$ Write the formula for volume of a sphere.

$\quad = \frac{4}{3} \cdot \pi \cdot 2^3$ Substitute 2 for r.

$\quad = \frac{32}{3}\pi$ Simplify. $2^3 = 2 \cdot 2 \cdot 2 = 8$

$\quad \approx 34$ Multiply.

ANSWER ▶ The volume is about 34 cubic feet.

b. A hemisphere has half the volume of a sphere.

$V = \frac{1}{2}\left(\frac{4}{3}\pi r^3\right)$ Write the formula for $\frac{1}{2}$ the volume of a sphere.

$\quad = \frac{1}{2} \cdot \left(\frac{4}{3} \cdot \pi \cdot 5^3\right)$ Substitute 5 for r.

$\quad = \frac{250}{3}\pi$ Simplify. $5^3 = 5 \cdot 5 \cdot 5 = 125$

$\quad \approx 262$ Multiply.

ANSWER ▶ The volume is about 262 cubic inches.

EXAMPLE 3 Find the Volume of a Sphere

Estimate the volume of air in a beach ball that has a 12 inch diameter. Round your answer to the nearest whole number.

Solution

$$V = \frac{4}{3}\pi r^3$$ Write volume formula.

$$= \frac{4}{3} \cdot \pi \cdot 6^3$$ Substitute $\frac{12}{2} = 6$ for r.

$$= 288\pi$$ Simplify.

$$\approx 905$$ Multiply.

ANSWER ▶ The volume of air in the ball is about 905 cubic inches.

Checkpoint ✓ **Find the Volume of a Sphere**

Find the volume to the nearest whole number.

4.
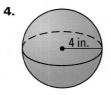
4 in.

5.

3 cm

6.
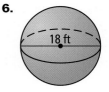
18 ft

9.6 Exercises

Guided Practice

Vocabulary Check   **1.** Explain the difference between a *sphere* and a *hemisphere*.

Skill Check   **Find the surface area to the nearest whole number.**

2.

1 in.

3.
3 ft

4.
9 m

Find the volume to the nearest whole number.

5.

3 ft

6.
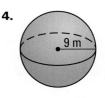
11 cm

7.
20 yd

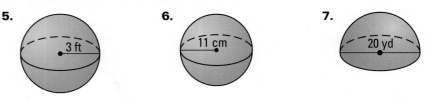

Practice and Applications

Extra Practice

See p. 692.

Find Surface Area of a Sphere Find the surface area of the sphere.
Round your answer to the nearest whole number.

8. 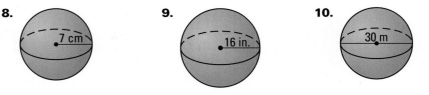 7 cm

9. 16 in.

10. 30 m

11. **Error Analysis** Bob is asked to find the surface area of a sphere
with a diameter of 10 millimeters. Explain and correct his error(s).

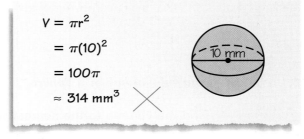

$$V = \pi r^2$$
$$= \pi(10)^2$$
$$= 100\pi$$
$$\approx 314 \text{ mm}^3 \quad \times$$

10 mm

Sports In Exercises 12–17, estimate the surface area of the ball.
Round your answer to the nearest whole number.

12. Soccer ball

$r = 4.3$ in.

13. Tennis ball

$r = 3.3$ cm

14. Bowling ball

$r = 10.9$ cm

15. Golf ball

$d = 1.7$ in.

16. Basketball

$d = 9.5$ in.

17. Softball

$d = 9.6$ cm

Homework Help

Example 1: Exs. 8–17
Example 2: Exs. 23–28,
37–39
Example 3: Exs. 23–28,
37–39

18. **You be the Judge** Julie thinks that if
you double the radius of the sphere shown at
the right, the surface area will double. Is she
right? Explain your reasoning.

3 cm

Astronomy In Exercises 19–22, use the information about Earth and its moon given in the photo.

19. Find the surface area of Earth.

20. Find the surface area of Earth's moon.

21. Compare the surface areas of Earth and its moon.

22. About 70% of Earth's surface is water. How many square miles of water are on Earth's surface?

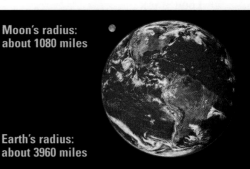

Moon's radius: about 1080 miles

Earth's radius: about 3960 miles

Finding Volume of a Sphere Find the volume of the sphere. Round your answer to the nearest whole number.

23.
8 m

24.
4 ft

25.
10 cm

26.
22 yd

27.
14 ft

28.
7 in.

Technology Use formulas to create a spreadsheet like the one shown. Then answer Exercises 29–32.

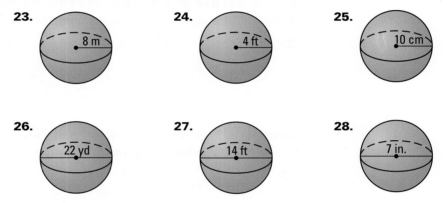

	A	B	C
	Radius, r	Surface area, $4\pi r^2$	Surface area of new sphere / Surface area of original sphere
1			
2	3	113.1	1
3	6	452.4	4
4	9	?	?
5	12	?	?

Comparing Spheres

29. How many times greater is the surface area of a sphere if the radius is doubled? tripled? quadrupled?

30. Explain why the surface area changes by a greater amount than the radius.

31. How many times greater do you think the volume of a sphere will be if the radius is doubled? tripled?

32. Create a spreadsheet for the volume of a sphere. Then answer Exercises 29 and 30 for the volume of a sphere.

Student Help

LOOK BACK
See pp. 470–471 for more information about The Rose Center for Earth and Space.

Spheres in Architecture In Exercises 33–36, refer to the information below about The Rose Center for Earth and Space at New York City's American Museum of Natural History.

The sphere has a diameter of 87 feet. The glass cube surrounding the sphere is 95 feet long on each edge.

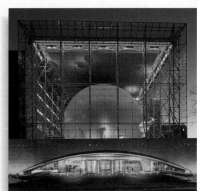

33. Find the surface area of the sphere.

34. Find the volume of the sphere.

35. Find the volume of the glass cube.

36. Find the approximate amount of glass used to make the cube. (*Hint*: Do not include the ground or roof in your calculations.)

Finding Volume of a Hemisphere Find the volume of the hemisphere. Round your answer to the nearest whole number.

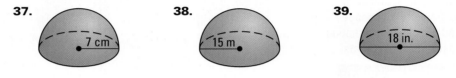

37. 7 cm   **38.** 15 m   **39.** 18 in.

Composite Solids Find the volume of the solid. Round your answer to the nearest whole number.

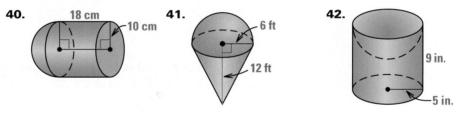

40. 18 cm, 10 cm   **41.** 6 ft, 12 ft   **42.** 9 in., 5 in.

Student Help
CLASSZONE.COM

HOMEWORK HELP
Extra help with problem solving in Exs. 43–45 is at classzone.com

Architecture The entrance to the Civil Rights Institute in Birmingham, Alabama, includes a hemisphere that has a radius of 25.3 feet.

43. Find the volume of the hemisphere.

44. Find the surface area of the hemisphere, not including its base.

45. The walls of the hemisphere are 1.3 feet thick. So, the rounded surface inside the building is a hemisphere with a radius of 24 feet. Find its surface area, not including its base.

25.3 ft

Standardized Test Practice

46. Multiple Choice What is the approximate surface area of the sphere shown?

    A 3217 in.^{2} **B** 4287 in.^{2}

    C 12,861 in.^{2} **D** 17,149 in.^{2}

32 in.

Mixed Review

Surface Area Find the surface area of the solid. If necessary, round your answer to the nearest whole number. *(Lessons 9.2, 9.3)*

47. A cone has a height of 12 meters and a base radius of 3 meters.

48. A pyramid has a slant height of 3 feet and a square base that measures 4 feet on a side.

49. A cylinder has a radius of 9 centimeters and a height of 9 centimeters.

Simplifying Radicals Evaluate. Give the exact value if possible. Otherwise, approximate to the nearest tenth. *(Skills Review, p. 668)*

50. $\sqrt{6}$ **51.** $\sqrt{18}$ **52.** $\sqrt{77}$ **53.** $\sqrt{400}$

54. $\sqrt{256}$ **55.** $\sqrt{99}$ **56.** $\sqrt{40}$ **57.** $\sqrt{120}$

Algebra Skills

Using Formulas Find the missing length using the given information. *(Skills Review, p. 674)*

58. A rectangle is 6 feet wide and 11 feet long. Find the perimeter.

59. A square has an area of 100 square inches. Find the perimeter.

60. Find the width of a rectangle with a length of 8 meters and an area of 40 square meters.

61. The perimeter of a square is 44 yards. Find the side length.

Quiz 2

Find the volume of the solid. If necessary, round your answer to the nearest whole number. *(Lessons 9.4, 9.5, 9.6)*

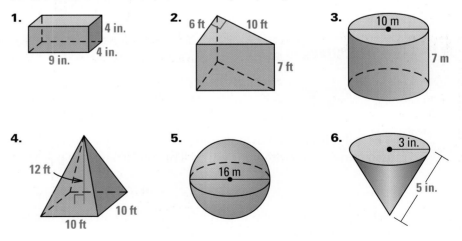

1. 4 in., 4 in., 9 in.

2. 6 ft, 10 ft, 7 ft

3. 10 m, 7 m

4. 12 ft, 10 ft, 10 ft

5. 16 m

6. 3 in., 5 in.

7. Sketch a cylinder with a radius of 4 inches and a height of 4 inches. Then find its volume. *(Lesson 9.4)*

8. Sketch a sphere with a radius of 9 centimeters. Then find its surface area. *(Lesson 9.6)*

VOCABULARY

- **solid,** *p. 473*
- **polyhedron,** *p. 473*
- **base,** *p. 473*
- **face,** *p. 474*
- **edge,** *p. 474*
- **prism,** *p. 483*
- **surface area,** *p. 483*

- **lateral face,** *p. 484*
- **lateral area,** *p. 484*
- **cylinder,** *p. 485*
- **pyramid,** *p. 491*
- **height of a pyramid,** *p. 491*
- **slant height of a pyramid,** *p. 491*

- **cone,** *p. 493*
- **height of a cone,** *p. 493*
- **slant height of a cone,** *p. 493*
- **volume,** *p. 500*
- **sphere,** *p. 517*
- **hemisphere,** *p. 517*

VOCABULARY REVIEW

Fill in the blank.

1. Polyhedra are named by the shape of their __?__.

2. The __?__ of a polyhedron is the sum of the areas of its faces.

3. A(n) __?__ is a polyhedron with two congruent faces that lie in parallel planes.

4. The __?__ of a prism are the faces of the prism that are not bases.

5. The __?__ of a solid is the number of cubic units contained in its interior.

9.1 SOLID FIGURES

Examples on pp. 473–475

EXAMPLE **Tell whether the solid is a polyhedron. If so, identify the shape of the base(s) and then name the solid.**

The solid is formed by polygons so it is a polyhedron. There are two congruent triangular bases. This is a triangular prism.

Tell whether the solid is a polyhedron. If so, identify the shape of the base(s) and then name the solid.

6.

7.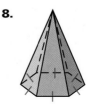

8.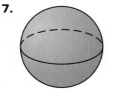

9.2 SURFACE AREA OF PRISMS AND CYLINDERS

Examples on pp. 483–486

EXAMPLES Find the surface area to the nearest whole number.

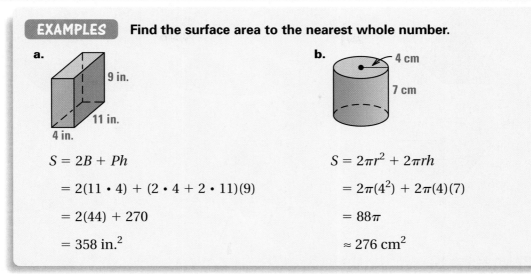

a.
9 in.
11 in.
4 in.

$$S = 2B + Ph$$
$$= 2(11 \cdot 4) + (2 \cdot 4 + 2 \cdot 11)(9)$$
$$= 2(44) + 270$$
$$= 358 \text{ in.}^2$$

b.
4 cm
7 cm

$$S = 2\pi r^2 + 2\pi rh$$
$$= 2\pi(4^2) + 2\pi(4)(7)$$
$$= 88\pi$$
$$\approx 276 \text{ cm}^2$$

Find the surface area to the nearest whole number.

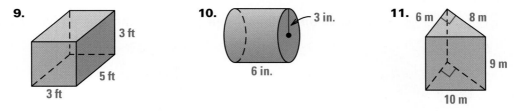

9.
3 ft
5 ft
3 ft

10.
3 in.
6 in.

11.
6 m   8 m
9 m
10 m

9.3 SURFACE AREA OF PYRAMIDS AND CONES

Examples on pp. 491–494

EXAMPLES Find the surface area to the nearest whole number.

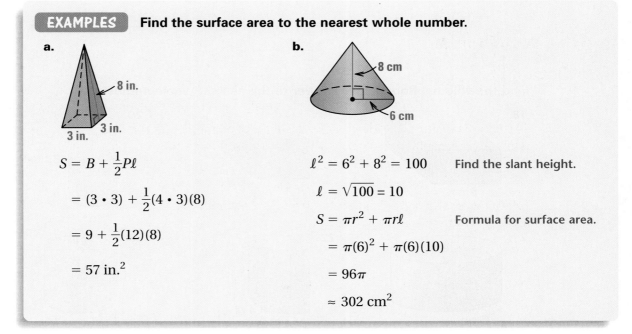

a.
8 in.
3 in.
3 in.

$$S = B + \frac{1}{2}P\ell$$
$$= (3 \cdot 3) + \frac{1}{2}(4 \cdot 3)(8)$$
$$= 9 + \frac{1}{2}(12)(8)$$
$$= 57 \text{ in.}^2$$

b.
8 cm
6 cm

$$\ell^2 = 6^2 + 8^2 = 100 \qquad \text{Find the slant height.}$$
$$\ell = \sqrt{100} = 10$$
$$S = \pi r^2 + \pi r\ell \qquad \text{Formula for surface area.}$$
$$= \pi(6)^2 + \pi(6)(10)$$
$$= 96\pi$$
$$\approx 302 \text{ cm}^2$$

Find the surface area of the solid. Round your answer to the nearest whole number.

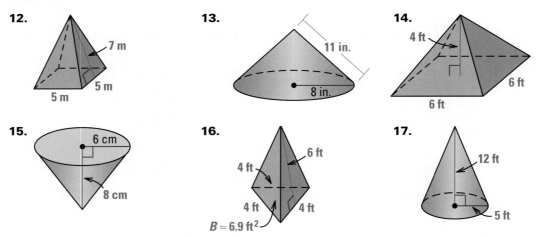

12. 7 m
     5 m
     5 m

13. 11 in.
     8 in.

14. 4 ft
     6 ft
     6 ft

15. 6 cm
     8 cm

16. 6 ft
     4 ft
     4 ft 4 ft
     $B \approx 6.9$ ft²

17. 12 ft
     5 ft

9.4 VOLUME OF PRISMS AND CYLINDERS

Examples on pp. 500–502

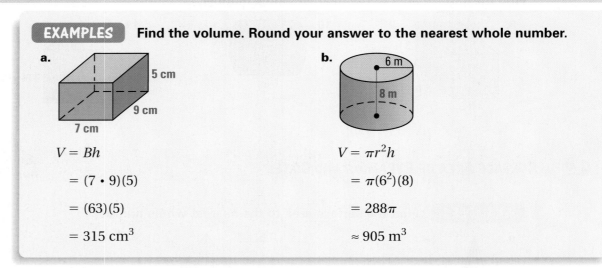

EXAMPLES Find the volume. Round your answer to the nearest whole number.

a. 5 cm
        9 cm
        7 cm

$V = Bh$

$= (7 \cdot 9)(5)$

$= (63)(5)$

$= 315$ cm³

b. 6 m
        8 m

$V = \pi r^2 h$

$= \pi(6^2)(8)$

$= 288\pi$

≈ 905 m³

Find the volume. Round your answer to the nearest whole number.

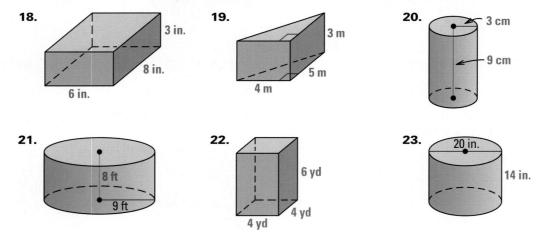

18. 3 in.
     8 in.
     6 in.

19. 3 m
     5 m
     4 m

20. 3 cm
     9 cm

21. 8 ft
     9 ft

22. 6 yd
     4 yd
     4 yd

23. 20 in.
     14 in.

9.5 VOLUME OF PYRAMIDS AND CONES

Examples on pp. 510–512

EXAMPLES Find the volume. Round your answer to the nearest whole number.

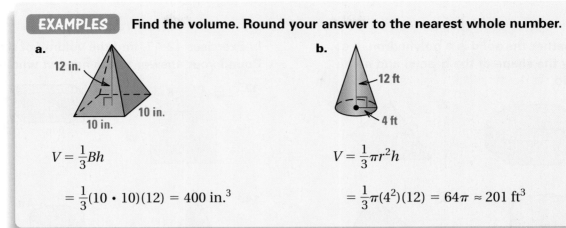

a.

12 in.

10 in.

10 in.

$$V = \frac{1}{3}Bh$$

$$= \frac{1}{3}(10 \cdot 10)(12) = 400 \text{ in.}^3$$

b.

12 ft

4 ft

$$V = \frac{1}{3}\pi r^2 h$$

$$= \frac{1}{3}\pi(4^2)(12) = 64\pi \approx 201 \text{ ft}^3$$

Find the volume. Round your answer to the nearest whole number.

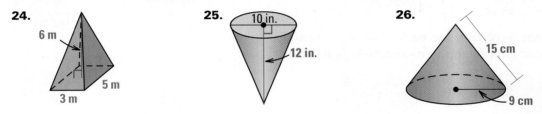

24.

6 m

5 m

3 m

25.

10 in.

12 in.

26.

15 cm

9 cm

9.6 SURFACE AREA AND VOLUME OF SPHERES

Examples on pp. 517–519

EXAMPLE Find the surface area and the volume of the sphere. Round your answer to the nearest whole number.

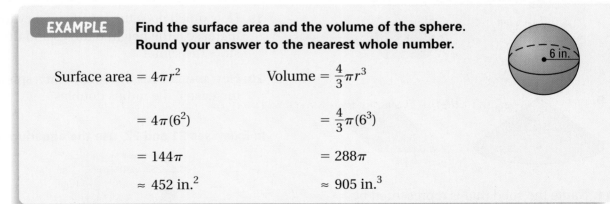

6 in.

Surface area = $4\pi r^2$

$$= 4\pi(6^2)$$

$$= 144\pi$$

$$\approx 452 \text{ in.}^2$$

Volume = $\frac{4}{3}\pi r^3$

$$= \frac{4}{3}\pi(6^3)$$

$$= 288\pi$$

$$\approx 905 \text{ in.}^3$$

Find the surface area and the volume of the sphere. Round your answer to the nearest whole number.

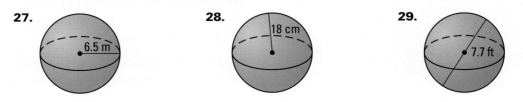

27.

6.5 m

28.

18 cm

29.

7.7 ft

Tell whether the solid is a polyhedron. If so, identify the shape of the base(s) and name the solid.

1.

2.

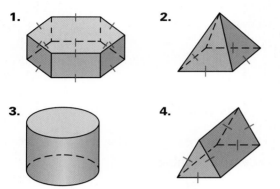

3.

4.

In Exercises 5–10, find the surface area of the solid. Round your answer to the nearest whole number.

5. 5 ft 9 ft 4 ft

6. 3 in. 3 in. 3 in.

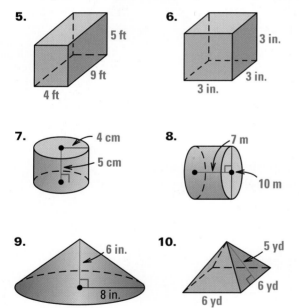

7. 4 cm 5 cm

8. 7 m 10 m

9. 6 in. 8 in.

10. 5 yd 6 yd 6 yd

11. Name the solid that is represented by the net below. Then find its surface area and volume. Round your answers to the nearest whole number.

3 ft

10 ft

In Exercises 12–17, find the volume of the solid. Round your answer to the nearest whole number.

12. 4 yd 8 yd 7 yd

13. 3 in. 2 in. 6 in.

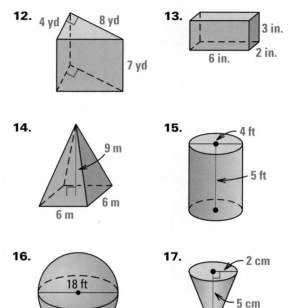

14. 9 m 6 m 6 m

15. 4 ft 5 ft

16. 18 ft

17. 2 cm 5 cm

18. How much does the volume of a cylinder increase if the radius doubles and the height stays the same?

19. How much does the volume of a cylinder increase if the height doubles and the radius stays the same?

20. How much does the volume of a sphere increase if the radius doubles?

In Exercises 21 and 22, use the aquarium below.

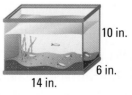

10 in.

6 in.

14 in.

21. If you fill the aquarium to a height of 8 inches, what is the volume of water in the aquarium?

22. How much glass is used to make the aquarium? (Do not include the top of the aquarium in your calculations.)

Test Tip   Read each question carefully to avoid missing preliminary steps. Do not look at the answers until you are sure you understand the question.

1. Which term correctly describes the solid shown below?

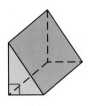

- (A) square pyramid
- (B) triangular prism
- (C) triangular pyramid
- (D) rectangular prism

2. What is the approximate surface area of the solid shown below?

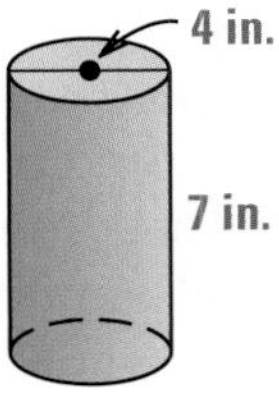

- (F) 87.9 in.^{2}
- (G) 113 in.^{2}
- (H) 276 in.^{2}
- (J) 352 in.^{2}

4 in.

7 in.

3. What is the approximate surface area of a sphere with a diameter of 8 centimeters?

- (A) 50 cm^2
- (B) 100 cm^2
- (C) 201 cm^2
- (D) 268 cm^2

4. What is the volume of the pyramid shown?

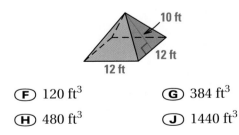

10 ft

12 ft

12 ft

- (F) 120 ft^3
- (G) 384 ft^3
- (H) 480 ft^3
- (J) 1440 ft^3

5. Suppose the length of each side of the cube is doubled. How many times larger is the surface area of the new cube?

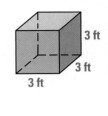

3 ft
3 ft
3 ft

- (A) 2
- (B) 3
- (C) 4
- (D) 8

6. A cone has a diameter of 12 inches and a volume of 48π cubic inches. Find the height.

- (F) 1 in.
- (G) 1.3 in.
- (H) 3 in.
- (J) 4 in.

7. What is the approximate volume of the solid shown below?

- (A) 213 ft^3
- (B) 269 ft^3
- (C) 288 ft^3
- (D) 307 ft^3

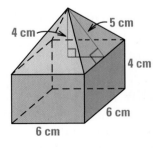

8 ft
1 ft
6 ft
6 ft

Multi-Step Problem Use the solid below.

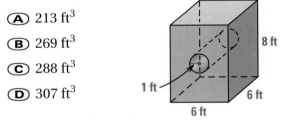

5 cm
4 cm
4 cm
6 cm
6 cm

8. Find the volume of the solid.

9. Find the surface area of the solid.

10. How does the volume of the prism section of the solid relate to the volume of the pyramid section of the solid? Explain your answer.

BraiN GaMes

Volume War

Materials

• 40 volume cards

Object of the Game

To get more cards than your opponent.

Set Up

Mix up the cards and deal them so that all players have the same number of cards. Put any extra cards aside. Each player makes a pile of their cards, face down.

How to Play

Step 1 ▶ Each player turns over the top card on his or her pile of cards.

Step 2 ▶ Compare the volume of each card. The player with the greatest volume takes all of the cards that are face up and puts them on the bottom of his or her pile of cards.

Step 3 ▶ If two or more of the cards have the same volume, the players who turned those cards over each turn a new card and the winner takes all of the face up cards.

Step 4 ▶ Continue playing until one player has all the cards or the most cards in a set amount of time.

Another Way to Play

Make a set of your own cards. None of the volumes should be greater than 36 cubic units.

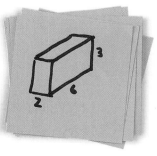

EXAMPLE 1 *Use a Calculator*

Use a calculator to evaluate $\dfrac{3}{\sqrt{2}}$. Round to the nearest tenth.

Solution

Calculator keystrokes	Display	Rounded value
3 ÷ √ 2 ENTER	2.121320344	2.1

ANSWER ▶ So, $\dfrac{3}{\sqrt{2}} \approx 2.1$.

Try These

Use a calculator to evaluate. Round to the nearest tenth.

1. $\dfrac{1}{\sqrt{5}}$

2. $\dfrac{7}{\sqrt{2}}$

3. $\dfrac{3}{\sqrt{10}}$

4. $\dfrac{9}{\sqrt{17}}$

5. $\dfrac{10}{\sqrt{7}}$

6. $\dfrac{\sqrt{5}}{\sqrt{11}}$

7. $\dfrac{\sqrt{19}}{\sqrt{3}}$

8. $\dfrac{4\sqrt{21}}{7\sqrt{5}}$

9. $6 - \dfrac{6}{\sqrt{6}}$

10. $5 + \dfrac{2}{\sqrt{3}}$

The *quotient property of radicals* states the following:

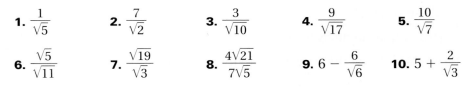

$\sqrt{\dfrac{a}{b}} = \dfrac{\sqrt{a}}{\sqrt{b}}$, where $a \geq 0$ and $b > 0$.

EXAMPLE 2 *Use the Quotient Property*

Simplify the expression.

a. $\sqrt{\dfrac{25}{4}}$

b. $\sqrt{\dfrac{45}{100}}$

Solution

a. $\sqrt{\dfrac{25}{4}} = \dfrac{\sqrt{25}}{\sqrt{4}} = \dfrac{5}{2}$

b. $\sqrt{\dfrac{45}{100}} = \dfrac{\sqrt{45}}{\sqrt{100}} = \dfrac{\sqrt{9 \cdot 5}}{\sqrt{100}} = \dfrac{\sqrt{9} \cdot \sqrt{5}}{\sqrt{100}} = \dfrac{3\sqrt{5}}{10}$

Try These

Simplify the expression.

11. $\sqrt{\dfrac{25}{49}}$

12. $\sqrt{\dfrac{9}{64}}$

13. $\sqrt{\dfrac{81}{121}}$

14. $\sqrt{\dfrac{1}{36}}$

15. $\sqrt{\dfrac{49}{16}}$

16. $\sqrt{\dfrac{7}{16}}$

17. $\sqrt{\dfrac{18}{81}}$

18. $\sqrt{\dfrac{8}{100}}$

19. $\sqrt{\dfrac{147}{400}}$

20. $\sqrt{\dfrac{128}{144}}$

1. In a coordinate plane, plot the points $A(4, 6)$, $B(-1, 3)$, and $C(5, -1)$ and sketch $\angle ABC$. Then classify the angle. (Lesson 1.6)

2. Find $m\angle 1$, $m\angle 2$, and $m\angle 3$ in the diagram shown at the right.
   (Lesson 2.4)

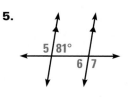

Find the measure of each numbered angle. (Lessons 3.2, 3.4)

3.

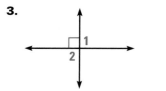

4.

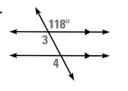

5.

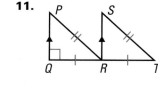

Use the triangle shown at the right. (Lesson 4.2, 4.7)

6. Find the value of x.

7. Classify the triangle by its angles.

8. Write the sides of the triangle from longest to shortest.

Is it possible to show that the triangles are congruent? If so, state the postulate or theorem you would use. Explain your reasoning.
(Lessons 5.2–5.4)

9.

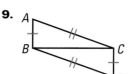

10.

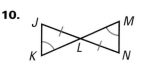

11.

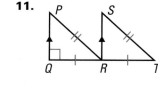

Use *always, sometimes,* or *never* to complete the statement.
(Lessons 2.3, 5.7, 6.4)

12. Two acute angles are __?__ complementary.

13. The sides of a rhombus are __?__ congruent.

14. A rectangle __?__ has exactly one line of symmetry.

15. Two squares are __?__ congruent.

Find the value of the variable(s). (Lessons 6.1, 6.4, 6.5)

16. $PQST$ is a trapezoid.

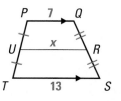

17. $ABCD$ is a rhombus.

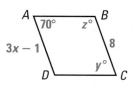

18. $JKLM$ is a rectangle.

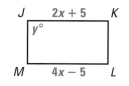

Use the diagram shown at the right. (Lessons 7.3–7.5)

19. Which theorem or postulate could you use to show that △*ABC* ~ △*ADE*?

20. Complete the proportion $\frac{DB}{DA} = \frac{?}{EA}$.

21. Find the value of *x*.

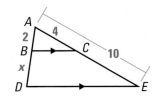

Use the polygon shown at the right. (Lessons 6.1, 8.1, 8.2)

22. Classify the polygon by its sides.

23. Is the polygon convex or concave? Explain your reasoning.

24. What is the sum of the measures of the interior angles of the polygon? What is the sum of its exterior angles, one at each vertex?

Tiles The tile pattern shown at the right contains regular octagonal tiles. (Lessons 6.6, 8.2)

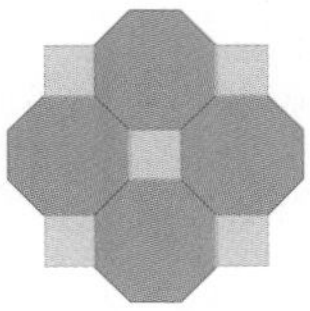

25. What is the measure of an interior angle of one of the regular octagonal tiles?

26. What type of shape are the yellow figures? Explain your reasoning.

Find the area of the polygon. (Lessons 8.3–8.6)

27.
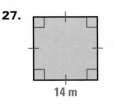
14 m

28.
17 ft
8 ft

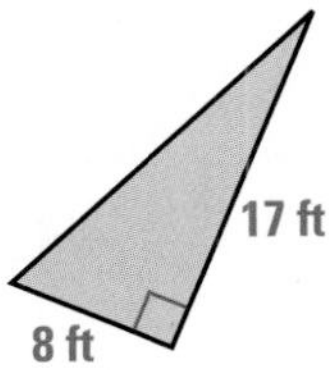

29.
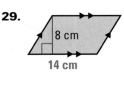
8 cm
14 cm

30.
4 in.
4 in.
9 in.

Find the surface area and the volume of the solid. If necessary, round your answer to the nearest whole number. (Lessons 9.2–9.5)

31.
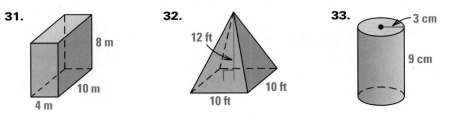
8 m
10 m
4 m

32.
12 ft
10 ft
10 ft

33.
3 cm
9 cm

34.
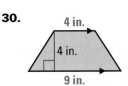
20 cm
24 cm

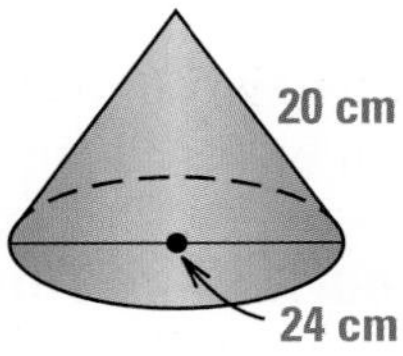

The sphere shown at the right has a diameter of 32 inches. Round your answer to the nearest whole number. (Lesson 9.6)

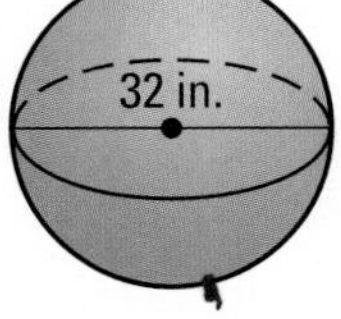

35. Find the surface area of the sphere.

36. What is half the volume of the sphere?

32 in.

10

Right Triangles and Trigonometry

At what angle does the space shuttle land?

The diagram shows the *glide angle* at which the space shuttle approaches Earth during landing.

To calculate the glide angle, you need to know the altitude, the distance to the runway, and *trigonometric ratios*, which you will study in this chapter.

Learn More About It

You will learn more about calculating glide angles in Exercise 33 on p. 574.

Who uses Right Triangles and Trigonometry?

PERSONAL TRAINER
Personal trainers develop fitness programs suited to an individual's abilities and goals. They study anatomy, nutrition, and physiology. (p. 553)

FORESTER
Foresters manage and protect forests. To determine the height of a tree, a forester may use trigonometry. (p. 559)

How will you use these ideas?

- Analyze jewelry designs. (p. 546)
- Determine correct positions for certain exercises. (p. 553)
- Measure the height of a tree. (p. 559)
- Plan a skateboard ramp. (p. 567)
- Calculate the glide angle of the space shuttle. (p. 574)

Chapter 10 Study Guide

PREVIEW

What's the chapter about?

- Simplifying **square roots**
- Finding the side lengths of **45°-45°-90°** triangles and **30°-60°-90°** triangles
- Finding the **sine**, **cosine**, and **tangent** of acute angles
- Solving right triangles

Key Words

- **radical,** *p. 537*
- **radicand,** *p. 537*
- **45°-45°-90° triangle,** *p. 542*
- **30°-60°-90° triangle,** *p. 549*
- **trigonometric ratio,** *p. 557*
- **leg opposite an angle,** *p. 557*
- **leg adjacent to an angle,** *p. 557*
- **tangent,** *p. 557*
- **sine,** *p. 563*
- **cosine,** *p. 563*
- **solve a right triangle,** *p. 569*

PREPARE

Chapter Readiness Quiz

Take this quick quiz. If you are unsure of an answer, look at the reference pages for help.

Vocabulary Check *(refer to p. 201)*

1. What type of triangle is shown at the right?

Ⓐ acute　　Ⓑ right　　Ⓒ obtuse　　Ⓓ isosceles

Skill Check *(refer to pp. 180, 192)*

2. What is the value of x in the triangle shown at the right?

Ⓕ 20　　Ⓖ 30　　Ⓗ 50　　Ⓙ 60

3. What is the approximate value of z in the triangle shown at the right?

Ⓐ 4.0　　Ⓑ 7.5　　Ⓒ 10.3　　Ⓓ 16.0

VISUAL STRATEGY

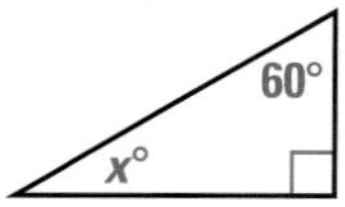

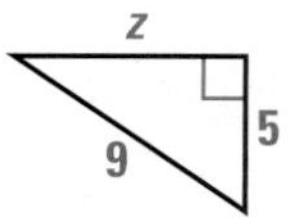

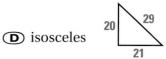

Labeling Triangles

Visualize It!

When labeling a right triangle, it may be helpful to use colored pencils. Use one color for the triangle, a second for its angle measures, and a third for its segment lengths.

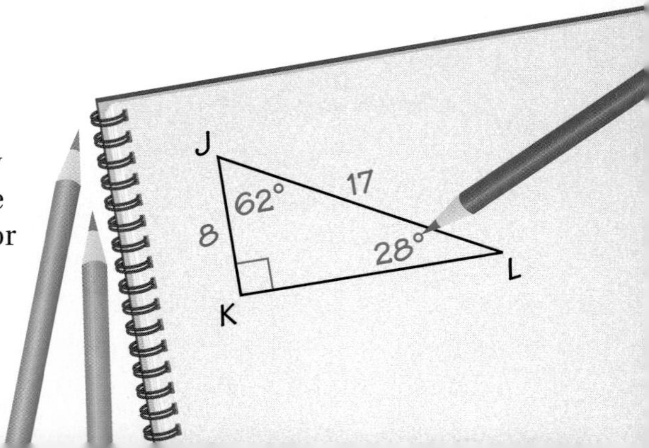

10.1 Simplifying Square Roots

Goal
Simplify square roots.

Key Words
- radical
- radicand

Square roots are written with a radical symbol $\sqrt{}$. An expression written with a radical symbol is called a *radical expression*, or **radical**. The number or expression inside the radical symbol is the **radicand**.

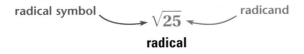

radical symbol $\longrightarrow \sqrt{25} \longleftarrow$ radicand

radical

The radical symbol always indicates the nonnegative square root of a number. For example, $\sqrt{25} = 5$ because $5^2 = 25$.

EXAMPLE 1 Use a Calculator to Find Square Roots

Find the square root of 52. Round your answer to the nearest tenth. Check that your answer is reasonable.

Solution

Calculator keystrokes	Display	Rounded value
52 $\sqrt{}$ or $\sqrt{}$ 52 ENTER	7.21110	$\sqrt{52} \approx 7.2$

This is reasonable, because 52 is between the perfect squares 49 and 64. So, $\sqrt{52}$ should be between $\sqrt{49}$ and $\sqrt{64}$, or 7 and 8. The answer 7.2 is between 7 and 8.

EXAMPLE 2 Find Side Lengths

Use the Pythagorean Theorem to find the length of the hypotenuse to the nearest tenth.

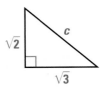

Student Help

> **STUDY TIP**
> Recall that for any number $a \geq 0$,
> $(\sqrt{a})^2 = a$.

Solution

$$a^2 + b^2 = c^2 \qquad \text{Write Pythagorean Theorem.}$$
$$(\sqrt{2})^2 + (\sqrt{3})^2 = c^2 \qquad \text{Substitute } \sqrt{2} \text{ for } a \text{ and } \sqrt{3} \text{ for } b.$$
$$2 + 3 = c^2 \qquad \text{Simplify.}$$
$$5 = c^2 \qquad \text{Add.}$$
$$\sqrt{5} = c \qquad \text{Take the square root of each side.}$$
$$2.2 \approx c \qquad \text{Use a calculator.}$$

Multiplying Radicals You can use the *Product Property of Radicals* to multiply radical expressions.

$$\sqrt{a} \cdot \sqrt{b} = \sqrt{ab}, \text{ where } a \geq 0 \text{ and } b \geq 0.$$

EXAMPLE 3 Multiply Radicals

Multiply the radicals. Then simplify if possible.

a. $\sqrt{3} \cdot \sqrt{7}$
b. $\sqrt{2} \cdot \sqrt{8}$

Solution

a. $\sqrt{3} \cdot \sqrt{7} = \sqrt{3 \cdot 7}$
$= \sqrt{21}$

b. $\sqrt{2} \cdot \sqrt{8} = \sqrt{2 \cdot 8}$
$= \sqrt{16}$
$= 4$

Simplifying Radicals You can also use the *Product Property of Radicals* to simplify radical expressions.

$$\sqrt{ab} = \sqrt{a} \cdot \sqrt{b}, \text{ where } a \geq 0 \text{ and } b \geq 0.$$

To factor the radicand, look for perfect square factors.

EXAMPLE 4 Simplify Radicals

Simplify the radical expression.

a. $\sqrt{12}$
b. $\sqrt{45}$

Solution

a. $\sqrt{12} = \sqrt{4 \cdot 3}$
$= \sqrt{4} \cdot \sqrt{3}$
$= 2\sqrt{3}$

b. $\sqrt{45} = \sqrt{9 \cdot 5}$
$= \sqrt{9} \cdot \sqrt{5}$
$= 3\sqrt{5}$

Checkpoint ✓ Evaluate, Multiply, and Simplify Radicals

Find the square root. Round your answer to the nearest tenth. Check that your answer is reasonable.

1. $\sqrt{27}$ **2.** $\sqrt{46}$ **3.** $\sqrt{8}$ **4.** $\sqrt{97}$

Multiply the radicals. Then simplify if possible.

5. $\sqrt{3} \cdot \sqrt{5}$ **6.** $\sqrt{11} \cdot \sqrt{6}$ **7.** $\sqrt{3} \cdot \sqrt{27}$ **8.** $5\sqrt{3} \cdot \sqrt{3}$

Simplify the radical expression.

9. $\sqrt{20}$ **10.** $\sqrt{8}$ **11.** $\sqrt{75}$ **12.** $\sqrt{112}$

10.1 Exercises

Guided Practice

Vocabulary Check

1. What is the *radicand* in the expression $\sqrt{25}$?

Match the radical expression with its simplified form.

2. $\sqrt{36}$ **A.** $\sqrt{6}$

3. $\sqrt{3} \cdot \sqrt{2}$ **B.** $3\sqrt{2}$

4. $\sqrt{3} \cdot \sqrt{6}$ **C.** $4\sqrt{2}$

5. $\sqrt{32}$ **D.** 6

Skill Check

Use the figure shown at the right.

6. Use the Pythagorean Theorem to find the length of the hypotenuse in radical form.

7. Use a calculator to find the length of the hypotenuse to the nearest tenth.

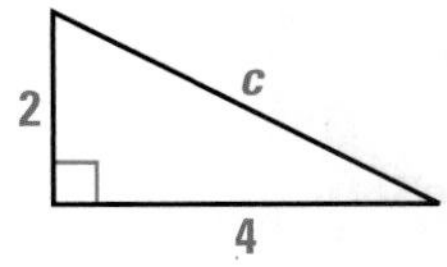

Simplify the expression.

8. $\sqrt{49}$ 9. $\sqrt{28}$ 10. $\sqrt{72}$ 11. $\sqrt{54}$

Practice and Applications

Extra Practice

See p. 693.

Finding Square Roots Find the square root. Round your answer to the nearest tenth. Check that your answer is reasonable.

12. $\sqrt{13}$ 13. $\sqrt{6}$ 14. $\sqrt{91}$ 15. $\sqrt{34}$

16. $\sqrt{106}$ 17. $\sqrt{148}$ 18. $\sqrt{62}$ 19. $\sqrt{186}$

Pythagorean Theorem Find the length of the hypotenuse. Write your answer in radical form.

20.

21.

22.

Pythagorean Theorem Find the missing side length of the right triangle. Round your answer to the nearest tenth.

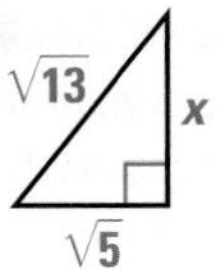

Homework Help

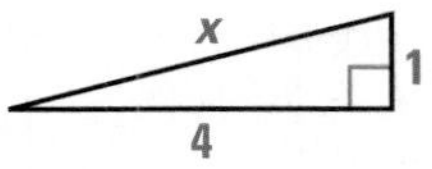

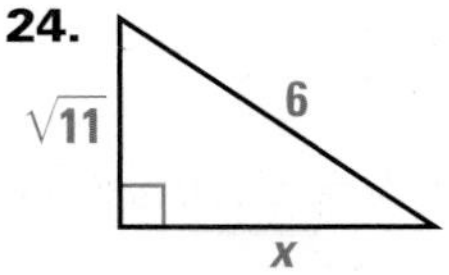

Example 1: Exs. 12–19
Example 2: Exs. 20–25
Example 3: Exs. 26–34
Example 4: Exs. 35–45

23.

24.

25.

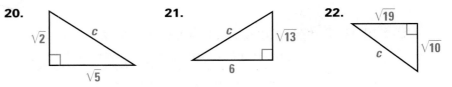

Multiplying Radicals Multiply the radicals. Then simplify if possible.

26. $\sqrt{7} \cdot \sqrt{2}$ **27.** $\sqrt{5} \cdot \sqrt{5}$ **28.** $\sqrt{3} \cdot \sqrt{11}$

29. $2\sqrt{5} \cdot \sqrt{7}$ **30.** $\sqrt{10} \cdot 4\sqrt{3}$ **31.** $\sqrt{11} \cdot \sqrt{22}$

EXAMPLE *Square a Radical*

Evaluate the expression.

a. $(3\sqrt{7})^2$ **b.** $(2\sqrt{11})^2$

Solution

a. $(3\sqrt{7})^2 = 3\sqrt{7} \cdot 3\sqrt{7}$ **b.** $(2\sqrt{11})^2 = 2\sqrt{11} \cdot 2\sqrt{11}$

            $= 3 \cdot 3 \cdot \sqrt{7} \cdot \sqrt{7}$ $= 2 \cdot 2 \cdot \sqrt{11} \cdot \sqrt{11}$

            $= 9 \cdot 7$ $= 4 \cdot 11$

            $= 63$ $= 44$

Squaring Radicals Evaluate the expression. Use the example above as a model.

32. $(6\sqrt{5})^2$ **33.** $(5\sqrt{3})^2$ **34.** $(7\sqrt{2})^2$

Simplifying Radicals Simplify the radical expression.

35. $\sqrt{18}$ **36.** $\sqrt{50}$ **37.** $\sqrt{48}$

38. $\sqrt{60}$ **39.** $\sqrt{56}$ **40.** $\sqrt{125}$

41. $\sqrt{200}$ **42.** $\sqrt{162}$ **43.** $\sqrt{44}$

You be the Judge Determine whether the expression can be simplified further. If so, explain how you would do so.

44. $\sqrt{80} = \sqrt{4 \cdot 20}$ **45.** $\sqrt{8} \cdot \sqrt{12} = \sqrt{8 \cdot 12}$

            $= \sqrt{4} \cdot \sqrt{20}$ $= \sqrt{4 \cdot 2 \cdot 4 \cdot 3}$

            $= 2\sqrt{20}$ $= 4\sqrt{6}$

Area Formula Use the area formula $A = lw$ to find the area of the rectangle. Round your answer to the nearest tenth.

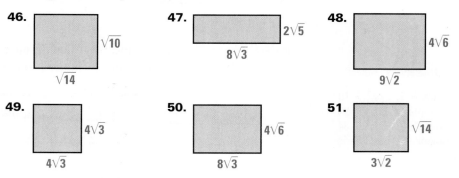

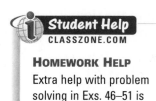

52. Area of an Equilateral Triangle The area of an
equilateral triangle with side length *s* is
given by the formula

$$A = \frac{1}{4}s^2 \sqrt{3}.$$

The flower bed shown is an equilateral triangle
with a side length of 30 feet. Find its area.

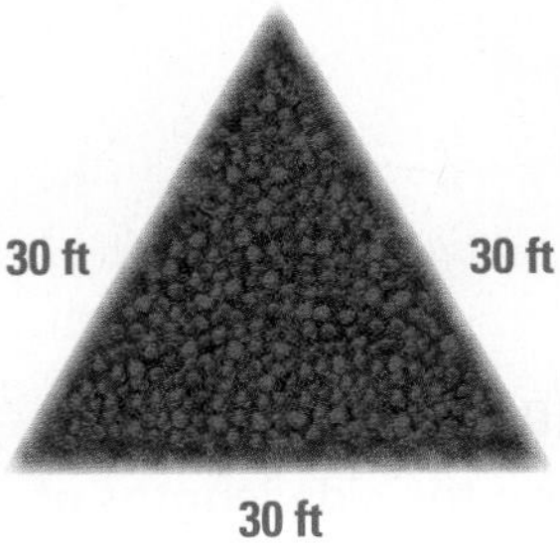

30 ft   30 ft

30 ft

53. Challenge An equilateral triangle has an area of 1 square
meter. What is the length of each side? Round your answer to
the nearest centimeter.

**Standardized Test
Practice**

54. Multiple Choice Which number is a perfect square?

(**A**) 44   (**B**) 110   (**C**) 169   (**D**) 500

55. Multiple Choice $\sqrt{220}$ is between which two integers?

(**F**) 12 and 13   (**G**) 13 and 14   (**H**) 14 and 15   (**J**) 15 and 16

56. Multiple Choice Which of the following
expressions could *not* be used to represent
the length of the hypotenuse in the triangle
shown at the right?

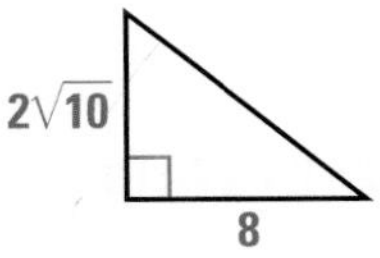

$2\sqrt{10}$

8

(**A**) $2\sqrt{26}$ (**B**) $\sqrt{104}$ (**C**) about 10.2   (**D**) $6\sqrt{10}$

Mixed Review

Finding Angle Measures Find the measure of ∠1. *(Lesson 4.2)*

57.

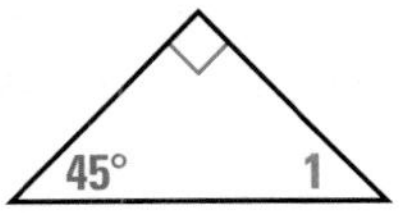

45°   1

58.

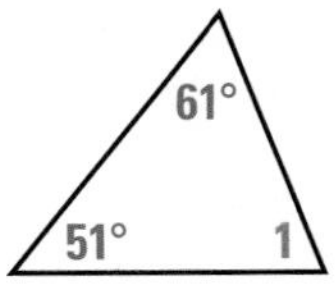

61°

51°   1

59.

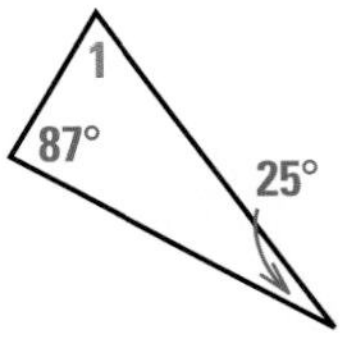

1

87°   25°

Isosceles Triangles Find the value of x. *(Lesson 4.3)*

60.

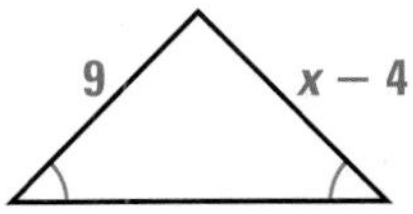

9   $x - 4$

61.

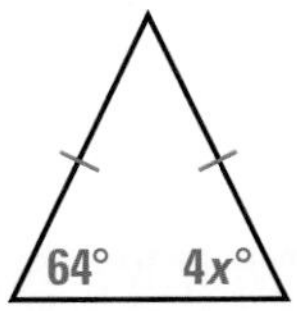

64° $4x°$

62.

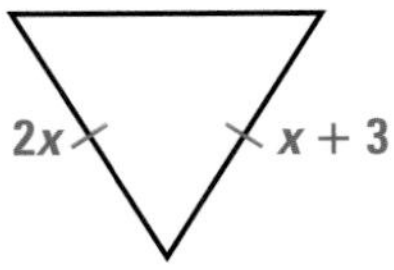

$2x$ $x + 3$

Algebra Skills

**Distributive Property Use the distributive property to rewrite the
expression without parentheses.** *(Skills Review, p. 671)*

63. $x(x + 5)$ **64.** $4(2x - 1)$ **65.** $x(3x + 4)$

66. $5x(x + 2)$ **67.** $-3(1 - x)$ **68.** $2x - (x - 6)$

10.1 *Simplifying Square Roots*   **541**

45°-45°-90° Triangles

Goal
Find the side lengths of 45°-45°-90° triangles.

Key Words
• 45°-45°-90° triangle
• isosceles triangle p. 173
• leg of a right triangle p. 192
• hypotenuse p. 192

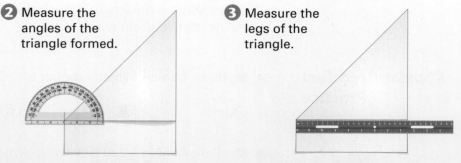

Geo-Activity ▸ **Exploring an Isosceles Right Triangle**

❶ Fold a large piece of paper so the top lines up with one side.

❷ Measure the angles of the triangle formed.

❸ Measure the legs of the triangle.

❹ Use the Pythagorean Theorem to predict the length of the hypotenuse.

❺ Measure the hypotenuse to verify your answer in Step 4.

Student Help

LOOK BACK
To review the Pythagorean Theorem, see p. 192.

A right triangle with angle measures of 45°, 45°, and 90° is called a **45°-45°-90° triangle** . You can use the Pythagorean Theorem to find the length of the hypotenuse of any 45°-45°-90° triangle.

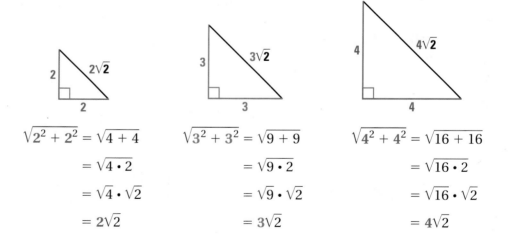

$$\sqrt{2^2 + 2^2} = \sqrt{4 + 4}$$
$$= \sqrt{4 \cdot 2}$$
$$= \sqrt{4} \cdot \sqrt{2}$$
$$= 2\sqrt{2}$$

$$\sqrt{3^2 + 3^2} = \sqrt{9 + 9}$$
$$= \sqrt{9 \cdot 2}$$
$$= \sqrt{9} \cdot \sqrt{2}$$
$$= 3\sqrt{2}$$

$$\sqrt{4^2 + 4^2} = \sqrt{16 + 16}$$
$$= \sqrt{16 \cdot 2}$$
$$= \sqrt{16} \cdot \sqrt{2}$$
$$= 4\sqrt{2}$$

THEOREM 10.1

45°-45°-90° Triangle Theorem

Words In a 45°-45°-90° triangle, the length of the hypotenuse is the length of a leg times $\sqrt{2}$.

Symbols hypotenuse = leg • $\sqrt{2}$

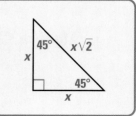

Student Help
CLASSZONE.COM
MORE EXAMPLES
More examples at classzone.com

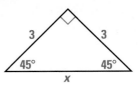

EXAMPLE 1 Find Hypotenuse Length

Find the length x of the hypotenuse in the 45°-45°-90° triangle shown at the right.

Solution

By the 45°-45°-90° Triangle Theorem, the length of the hypotenuse is the length of a leg times $\sqrt{2}$.

$\text{hypotenuse} = \text{leg} \cdot \sqrt{2}$	45°-45°-90° Triangle Theorem
$= 3 \cdot \sqrt{2}$	Substitute.

ANSWER ▶ The length of the hypotenuse is $3\sqrt{2}$.

EXAMPLE 2 Find Leg Length

Find the length x of each leg in the 45°-45°-90° triangle shown at the right.

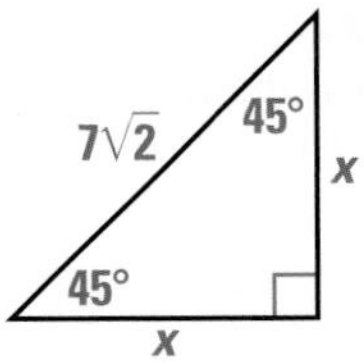

Student Help

READING TIP
The expression $x\sqrt{2}$ is equivalent to $\sqrt{2}x$.

Solution

By the 45°-45°-90° Triangle Theorem, the length of the hypotenuse is the length of a leg times $\sqrt{2}$.

$\text{hypotenuse} = \text{leg} \cdot \sqrt{2}$	45°-45°-90° Triangle Theorem
$7\sqrt{2} = x\sqrt{2}$	Substitute.
$\frac{7\sqrt{2}}{\sqrt{2}} = \frac{x\sqrt{2}}{\sqrt{2}}$	Divide each side by $\sqrt{2}$.
$7 = x$	Simplify.

ANSWER ▶ The length of each leg is 7.

Checkpoint ✓ Find Hypotenuse and Leg Lengths

Find the value of x.

1.

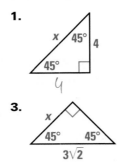

2.

3.

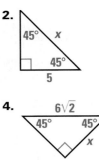

4.

Using Algebra

EXAMPLE 3 **Identify 45°-45°-90° Triangles**

Determine whether there is enough information to conclude that the triangle is a 45°-45°-90° triangle. Explain your reasoning.

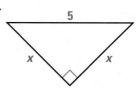

Solution

By the Triangle Sum Theorem, $x° + x° + 90° = 180°$.

So, $2x° = 90°$, and $x = 45$.

ANSWER ▶ Since the measure of each acute angle is 45°, the triangle is a 45°-45°-90° triangle.

Example 3 shows that whenever a right triangle has congruent acute angles, it is a 45°-45°-90° triangle.

Student Help

LOOK BACK
To review the Base Angles Theorem, see p. 185.

EXAMPLE 4 **Find Leg Length**

Show that the triangle is a 45°-45°-90° triangle. Then find the value of x.

Solution

The triangle is an isosceles right triangle. By the Base Angles Theorem, its acute angles are congruent. From the result of Example 3, this triangle must be a 45°-45°-90° triangle.

You can use the 45°-45°-90° Triangle Theorem to find the value of x.

hypotenuse $= $ leg $\cdot \sqrt{2}$	45°-45°-90° Triangle Theorem
$5 = x\sqrt{2}$	Substitute.
$\dfrac{5}{\sqrt{2}} = \dfrac{x\sqrt{2}}{\sqrt{2}}$	Divide each side by $\sqrt{2}$.
$\dfrac{5}{\sqrt{2}} = x$	Simplify.
$3.5 \approx x$	Use a calculator to approximate.

Checkpoint ✓ **Find Leg Lengths**

Show that the triangle is a 45°-45°-90° triangle. Then find the value of x. Round your answer to the nearest tenth.

5.

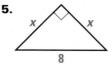

6.

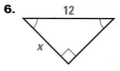

544 **Chapter 10** *Right Triangles and Trigonometry*

10.2 Exercises

Guided Practice

Vocabulary Check

1. How many congruent sides does an *isosceles right triangle* have?

2. How many congruent angles does an isosceles right triangle have? What are the measures of the three angles?

Skill Check

Find the value of *x* in the 45°-45°-90° triangle. Write your answer in radical form.

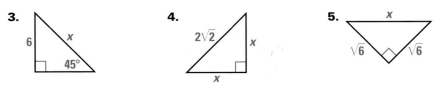

3.

4.

5.

Practice and Applications

Extra Practice

See p. 693.

Finding Hypotenuse Lengths **Find the length of the hypotenuse in the 45°-45°-90° triangle. Write your answer in radical form.**

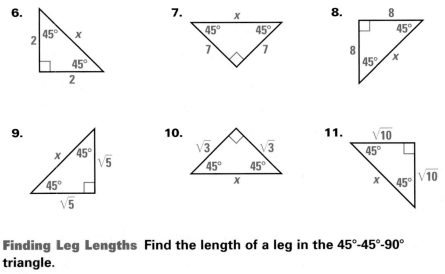

6.

7.

8.

9.

10.

11.

Finding Leg Lengths **Find the length of a leg in the 45°-45°-90° triangle.**

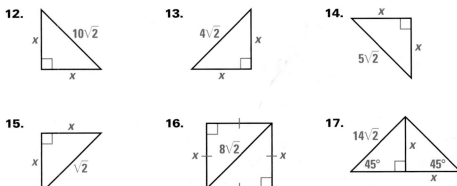

12.

13.

14.

15.

16.

17.

Homework Help

Example 1: Exs. 6–11, 18
Example 2: Exs. 12–17
Example 3: Exs. 19–27
Example 4: Exs. 22–27

18. Jewelry Use a calculator to find the length *x* of the earring shown at the right. Round your answer to the nearest tenth.

1.4 cm

1.4 cm

You be the Judge Determine whether there is enough information to conclude that the triangle is a 45°-45°-90° triangle. Explain your reasoning.

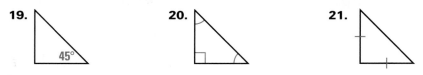

19.

45°

20.

21.

Finding Leg Lengths Show that the triangle is a 45°-45°-90° triangle. Then find the value of each variable. Round to the nearest tenth.

22.

x   4

x

23.

x

9

24.

32 / 45°

45°

x

25.

8

x°   *x*°

y

26.

20

x

27.

35

x

45°

Technology In Exercises 28–30, use geometry software.

❶ Draw $\overline{AB}$ and construct its midpoint, *C*.

❷ Construct the perpendicular bisector of $\overline{AB}$.

❸ Construct point *D* on the bisector and construct $\overline{AD}$ and $\overline{DB}$.

❹ Measure ∠*ADB*. Drag point *D* until *m*∠*ADB* = 90°.

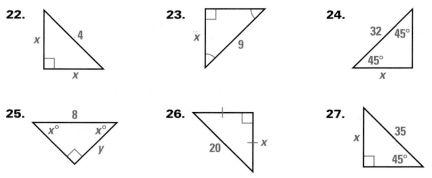

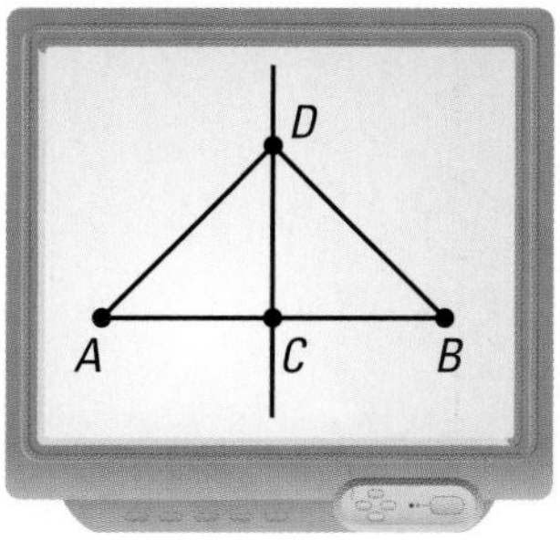

28. Name three 45°-45°-90° triangles. Explain how you know they are 45°-45°-90° triangles.

29. Measure $\overline{AC}$, $\overline{CB}$, and $\overline{CD}$. What do you notice? Explain.

30. Predict the measures of $\overline{AD}$ and $\overline{DB}$. Check your answer by measuring the segments.

31. Error Analysis A student labels a 45°-45°-90° triangle as shown. Explain and correct the error.

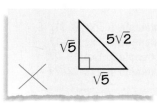

$\sqrt{5}$ $5\sqrt{2}$

$\sqrt{5}$

Quilt Design **The quilt design in the photo is based on the pattern in the diagram below. Use the diagram in Exercises 32 and 33.**

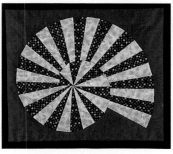

"Wheel of Theodorus,"
by Diana Venters

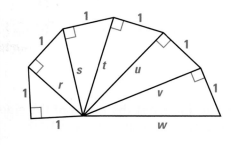

32. Working from left to right, use the Pythagorean Theorem in each right triangle to find the values of r, s, t, u, v, and w.

33. Identify any 45°-45°-90° triangles in the figure.

Standardized Test Practice

34. Multi-Step Problem Use the triangle shown below.

a. Find the value of x. Then find $m\angle A$, $m\angle B$, and $m\angle C$.

b. Find the values of b and c.

c. Use the Pythagorean Theorem or the 45°-45°-90° Triangle Theorem to justify your answers in part (b).

Mixed Review

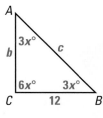

Classifying Triangles **Classify the triangle as *acute, right,* or *obtuse.*** *(Lesson 4.5)*

35.

36.

37.

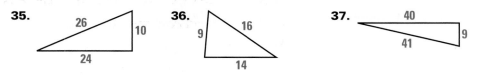

Simplifying Radicals **Simplify the radical expression.** *(Lesson 10.1)*

38. $\sqrt{24}$ **39.** $\sqrt{63}$ **40.** $\sqrt{52}$ **41.** $\sqrt{64}$

42. $\sqrt{80}$ **43.** $\sqrt{196}$ **44.** $\sqrt{250}$ **45.** $\sqrt{117}$

Algebra Skills

Writing Fractions as Decimals **Write the fraction as a decimal. For repeating decimals, also round to the nearest hundredth.** *(Skills Review, p. 657)*

46. $\frac{9}{10}$ **47.** $\frac{3}{5}$ **48.** $\frac{2}{3}$ **49.** $\frac{33}{100}$

50. $\frac{4}{9}$ **51.** $\frac{3}{20}$ **52.** $\frac{47}{50}$ **53.** $\frac{1}{6}$

Question

What is special about the ratios of the side lengths in a triangle with angle measures 30°, 60°, and 90°?

Explore

① Draw a segment at least 10 centimeters long. Label it $\overline{AB}$. Set your compass opening to AB. Draw arcs with center A and center B.

② Label the intersection of the arcs C. Draw equilateral $\triangle ABC$. Use your ruler to locate the midpoint of $\overline{AB}$. Label it D.

③ Draw $\overline{CD}$. $\triangle ACD$ has angle measures of 30°, 60°, and 90°. Measure AC, AD, and CD to the nearest millimeter.

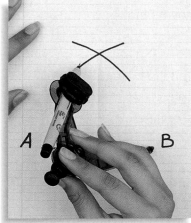

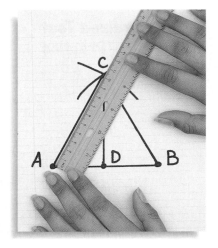

Think About It

In Exercises 1–3, AC, AD, and CD are the lengths in centimeters of the sides of triangles similar to the one you constructed. Copy and complete the table. In Exercise 4, use the values from your drawing.

Student Help

LOOK BACK
To review ratios of side lengths in similar triangles, see p. 365.

	AC	AD	CD	$\dfrac{AC}{AD}$	$\dfrac{CD}{AD}$
1.	10	5	8.7	?	?
2.	20	10	17.3	?	?
3.	50	25	43.3	?	?
4.	?	?	?	?	?

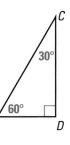

5. What do you notice about the ratios $\dfrac{AC}{AD}$ and $\dfrac{CD}{AD}$ for $\triangle ACD$ with $m\angle A = 60°$, $m\angle C = 30°$, and $m\angle D = 90°$?

30°-60°-90° Triangles

Goal
Find the side lengths of 30°-60°-90° triangles.

Key Words
• 30°-60°-90° triangle

A right triangle with angle measures of 30°, 60°, and 90° is called a **30°-60°-90° triangle**.

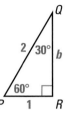

Activity 10.3 shows that the ratio of the length of the hypotenuse of a 30°-60°-90° triangle to the length of the shorter leg is 2 : 1.

EXAMPLE 1 Find Leg Length

In the diagram above, △PQR is a 30°-60°-90° triangle with $PQ = 2$ and $PR = 1$. Find the value of b.

Solution

You can use the Pythagorean Theorem to find the value of b.

$(\text{leg})^2 + (\text{leg})^2 = (\text{hypotenuse})^2$	Write the Pythagorean Theorem.
$1^2 + b^2 = 2^2$	Substitute.
$1 + b^2 = 4$	Simplify.
$b^2 = 3$	Subtract 1 from each side.
$b = \sqrt{3}$	Take the square root of each side.

Visualize It!

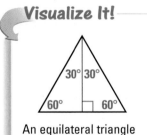

An equilateral triangle can be divided into two 30°-60°-90° triangles.

Because all 30°-60°-90° triangles are similar, the ratio of the length of the longer leg to the length of the shorter leg is always $\sqrt{3} : 1$. This result is summarized in the theorem below.

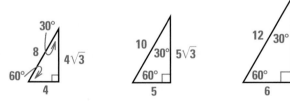

THEOREM 10.2

30°-60°-90° Triangle Theorem

Words In a 30°-60°-90° triangle, the hypotenuse is twice as long as the shorter leg, and the longer leg is the length of the shorter leg times $\sqrt{3}$.

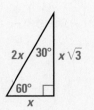

Symbols Hypotenuse = 2 • shorter leg
Longer leg = shorter leg • $\sqrt{3}$

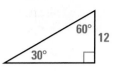

EXAMPLE 2 Find Hypotenuse Length

In the 30°-60°-90° triangle at the right, the length of the shorter leg is given. Find the length of the hypotenuse.

Solution

The hypotenuse of a 30°-60°-90° triangle is twice as long as the shorter leg.

hypotenuse	= 2 • shorter leg	30°-60°-90° Triangle Theorem
	= 2 • 12	Substitute.
	= 24	Simplify.

ANSWER ▶ The length of the hypotenuse is 24.

EXAMPLE 3 Find Longer Leg Length

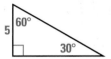

In the 30°-60°-90° triangle at the right, the length of the shorter leg is given. Find the length of the longer leg.

Solution

The length of the longer leg of a 30°-60°-90° triangle is the length of the shorter leg times $\sqrt{3}$.

| longer leg | = shorter leg • $\sqrt{3}$ | 30°-60°-90° Triangle Theorem |
| | = 5 • $\sqrt{3}$ | Substitute. |

ANSWER ▶ The length of the longer leg is $5\sqrt{3}$.

In a 30°-60°-90° triangle, the longer leg is opposite the 60° angle, and the shorter leg is opposite the 30° angle.

Checkpoint ✓ *Find Lengths in a Triangle*

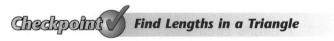

Find the value of *x*. Write your answer in radical form.

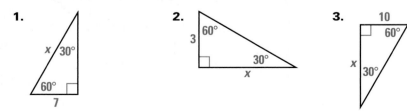

550 **Chapter 10** *Right Triangles and Trigonometry*

EXAMPLE 4 Find Shorter Leg Length

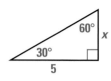

In the 30°-60°-90° triangle at the right, the length of the longer leg is given. Find the length x of the shorter leg. Round your answer to the nearest tenth.

Solution

The length of the longer leg of a 30°-60°-90° triangle is the length of the shorter leg times $\sqrt{3}$.

longer leg = shorter leg • $\sqrt{3}$	30°-60°-90° Triangle Theorem
$5 = x • \sqrt{3}$	Substitute.
$\dfrac{5}{\sqrt{3}} = x$	Divide each side by $\sqrt{3}$.
$2.9 \approx x$	Use a calculator.

ANSWER ▶ The length of the shorter leg is about 2.9.

EXAMPLE 5 Find Leg Lengths

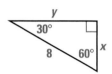

In the 30°-60°-90° triangle at the right, the length of the hypotenuse is given. Find the length x of the shorter leg and the length y of the longer leg.

Solution

Use the 30°-60°-90° Triangle Theorem to find the length of the shorter leg. Then use that value to find the length of the longer leg.

Shorter leg	*Longer leg*
hypotenuse = 2 • shorter leg	longer leg = shorter leg • $\sqrt{3}$
$8 = 2 • x$	$y = 4 • \sqrt{3}$
$4 = x$	$y = 4\sqrt{3}$

ANSWER ▶ The length of the shorter leg is 4.
The length of the longer leg is $4\sqrt{3}$.

 **Checkpoint** ✓ Find Leg Lengths

Find the value of each variable. Round your answer to the nearest tenth.

4.
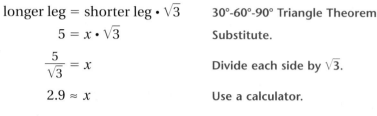

5.
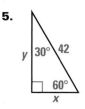

10.3 Exercises

Guided Practice

Vocabulary Check **1.** Name two special right triangles by their angle measures.

Skill Check **Use the diagram to tell whether the equation is *true* or *false*.**

2. $t = 7\sqrt{3}$ **3.** $t = \sqrt{3}h$ **4.** $h = 2t$

5. $h = 14$ **6.** $7 = \dfrac{h}{2}$ **7.** $7 = \dfrac{t}{\sqrt{3}}$

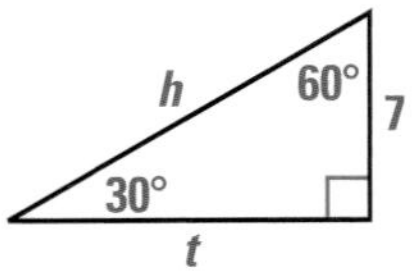

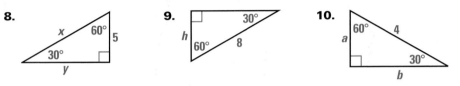

Find the value of each variable. Write your answers in radical form.

8. **9.** **10.**

Practice and Applications

Extra Practice

See p. 693.

Finding Hypotenuse Lengths Find the length of the hypotenuse.

11. **12.** 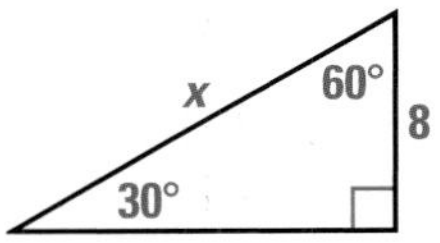 **13.** $11\sqrt{3}$

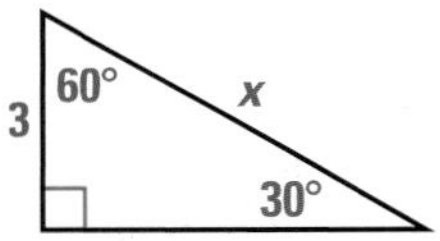

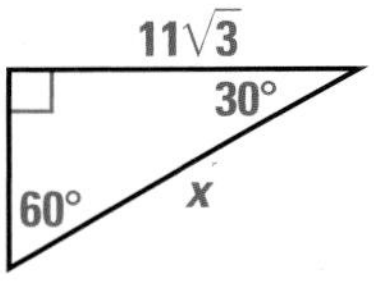

14. 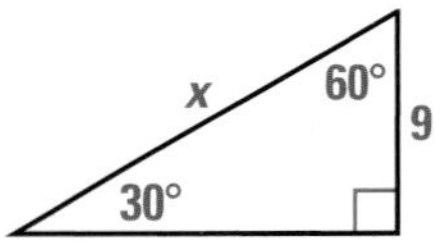 **15.** 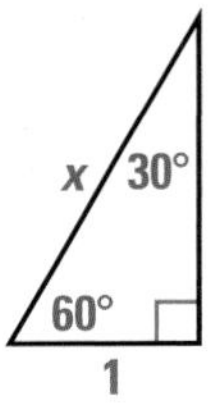 **16.** $12\sqrt{3}$

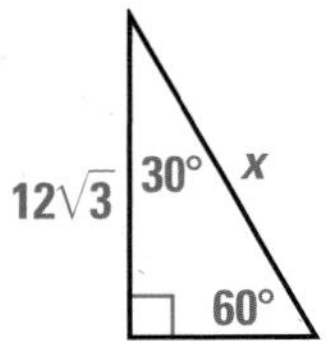

Finding Leg Lengths Find the length of the longer leg of the triangle. Write your answer in radical form.

17. **18.** **19.**

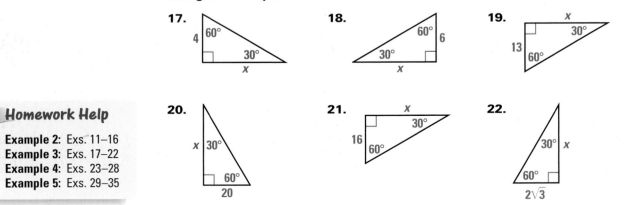

Homework Help

Example 2: Exs. 11–16
Example 3: Exs. 17–22
Example 4: Exs. 23–28
Example 5: Exs. 29–35

20. **21.** **22.**

Finding Leg Lengths **Find the length of the shorter leg of the triangle. Round your answer to the nearest tenth.**

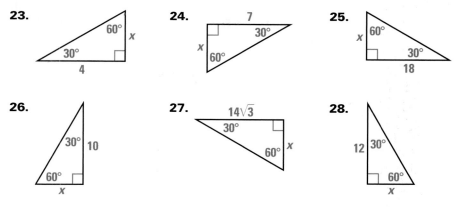

23.

60°
x
30°
4

24.

7
30°
x
60°

25.

x
60°
30°
18

26.

30°
10
60°
x

27.

14√3
30°
60°
x

28.

12
30°
60°
x

29. Tipping Platform A tipping platform is a ramp used to unload trucks as shown below. What is the height of an 60 foot ramp when it is tipped up to a 30° angle?

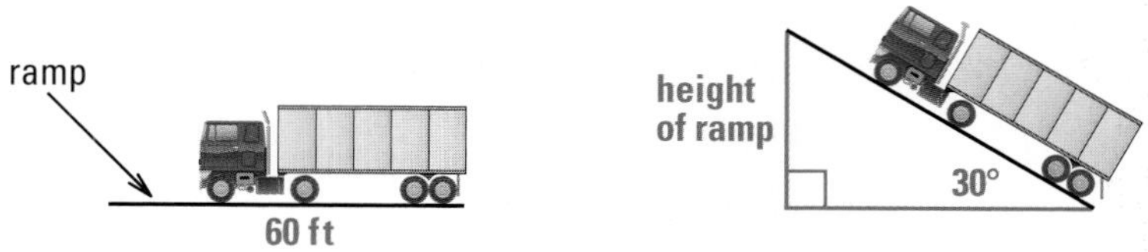

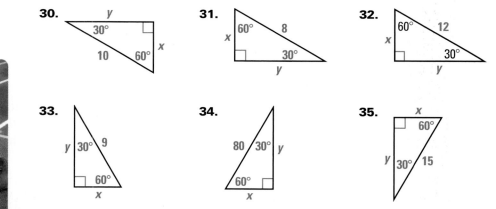

ramp
60 ft
height
of ramp
30°

Finding Leg Lengths **Find the value of each variable. Write your answers in radical form.**

30.

y
30°
10
60°
x

31.

x
60°
8
30°
y

32.

x
60°
12
30°
y

33.

y
30°
9
60°
x

34.

80
30°
y
60°
x

35.

x
60°
y
30°
15

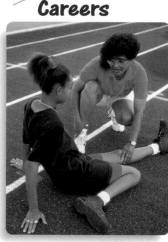

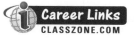

36. Fitness A "crunch" is the type of sit-up shown in the photo at the right. A personal trainer tells you that in doing a crunch, your back and shoulders should be lifted to an angle of about 30°. If your shoulder-to-waist length is 18 inches, how high should your shoulders be lifted?

Link to Careers

PERSONAL TRAINERS develop fitness programs suited to an individual's abilities and goals. They study anatomy, nutrition, and physiology.

Career Links
CLASSZONE.COM

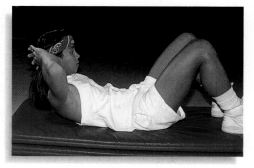

EXAMPLE · Find Area Using 30°-60°-90° Triangles

The road sign is shaped like an equilateral
triangle with side lengths of 36 inches.
Estimate the area of the sign.

Solution

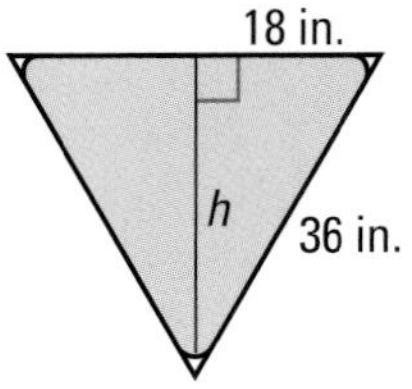

Divide the triangle into two 30°-60°-90° triangles.

The length of the shorter leg of each triangle is
18 inches. The length of the longer leg of each triangle
is $18\sqrt{3}$ inches, by the 30°-60°-90° Triangle Theorem.

Use the formula for the area of a triangle.

▶ Area $= \dfrac{1}{2}bh = \dfrac{1}{2} \cdot 36 \cdot 18\sqrt{3} \approx 561.18$

ANSWER ▶ The area of the sign is about 561 square inches.

Student Help

LOOK BACK
To review the area of a
triangle, see p. 431. · · · · · · · · · ·

Finding Area **Find the area of each triangle. Use the example above
as a model.**

37.
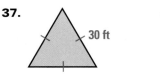
30 ft

38. 18 in.
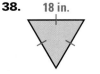

39. 7 cm

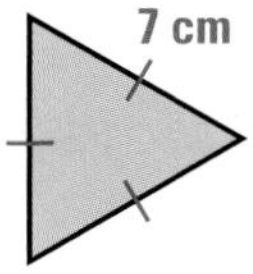

40. (x/y) **Using Algebra** Use the figure in the example above to explain
why the area A of an equilateral triangle with side length s is given
by the formula $A = \dfrac{1}{4} \cdot s^2 \cdot \sqrt{3}$.

41. Visualize It! A 30°-60°-90° triangle has a shorter leg length of
15 centimeters. Sketch the triangle and find the length of the
hypotenuse and the length of the longer leg in radical form.

42. **Challenge** The side length of the
hexagonal nut shown at the right
is 1 centimeter. Find the value of x.
(*Hint*: Use the fact that a regular
hexagon can be divided into six
congruent equilateral triangles.)

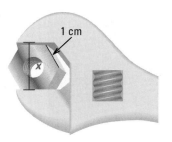

**Standardized Test
Practice**

43. **Multiple Choice** Which triangle is labeled correctly?

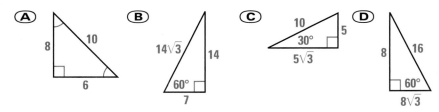

44. Multiple Choice Find the perimeter of the triangle shown below to the nearest tenth of a centimeter.

    (F) 28.4 cm   (G) 30 cm

    (H) 31.2 cm   (J) 41.6 cm

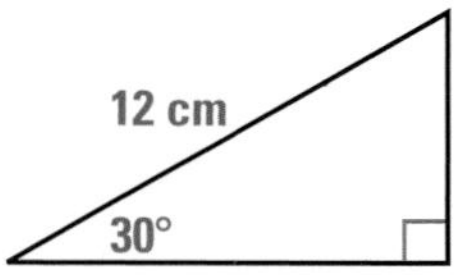

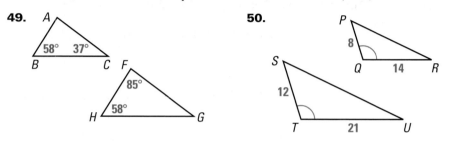

Mixed Review

Writing Ratios A football team won 10 games and lost 6 games. Find the ratio. *(Lesson 7.1)*

45. wins to losses   **46.** losses to wins

47. wins to the number of games   **48.** losses to the number of games

Similar Triangles Determine whether the triangles are similar. If they are similar, write a similarity statement. *(Lessons 7.3, 7.4)*

49.

50.

Algebra Skills

Evaluating Expressions Evaluate the expression when $x = -4$. *(Skills Review, p. 670)*

51. $5x + 4$ **52.** $10x - 1$ **53.** $x^2 - 7$

54. $(x + 3)(x - 3)$ **55.** $2x^2 - x + 1$ **56.** $5x^2 + 2x - 3$

Quiz 1

Multiply the radical expression. Then simplify if possible. *(Lesson 10.1)*

  1. $\sqrt{8} \cdot \sqrt{3}$ **2.** $\sqrt{2} \cdot \sqrt{15}$ **3.** $\sqrt{8} \cdot \sqrt{18}$ **4.** $\sqrt{80} \cdot \sqrt{5}$

Simplify the radical expression. *(Lesson 10.1)*

  5. $\sqrt{27}$ **6.** $\sqrt{176}$ **7.** $\sqrt{52}$ **8.** $\sqrt{180}$

Find the value of each variable. Write your answer in radical form. *(Lessons 10.2, 10.3)*

  9.   **10.**   **11.**

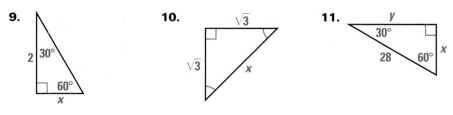

Question

Does the size of similar right triangles affect the ratio of their leg lengths?

Explore

❶ Draw a 40° angle. Mark points every 5 cm along one side.

❷ Draw perpendicular segments through four of the points.

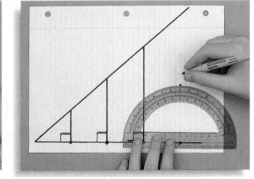

Think About It

1. There are four similar triangles in your drawing. Measure the legs and complete a table like the one below.

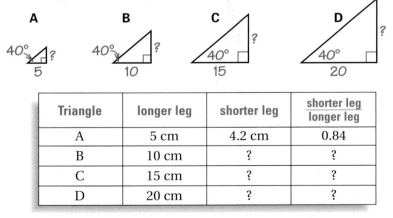

A   40° ?   5   B   40° ?   10   C   40° ?   15   D   40° ?   20

Triangle	longer leg	shorter leg	shorter leg / longer leg
A	5 cm	4.2 cm	0.84
B	10 cm	?	?
C	15 cm	?	?
D	20 cm	?	?

2. Compare the ratios of the leg lengths in the last column of your table. What do you notice?

3. Repeat using a different acute angle. Based on your results, does the ratio of leg lengths depend on the size of a right triangle or the measures of its angles?

10.4 Tangent Ratio

Goal
Find the tangent of an acute angle.

Key Words
- trigonometric ratio
- leg opposite an angle
- leg adjacent to an angle
- tangent

How can you find the height of the tree in the photograph at the right? It is too tall to be measured directly in any simple manner.

You can determine the height using a *trigonometric ratio*. A **trigonometric ratio** is a ratio of the lengths of two sides of a right triangle.

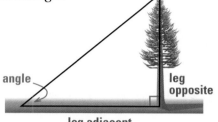

For any acute angle of a right triangle, there is a **leg opposite** the angle and a **leg adjacent** to the angle. The ratio of these legs is the **tangent** of the angle.

TANGENT RATIO

For any acute angle A of a right triangle:

$$\tan A = \frac{\text{leg opposite } \angle A}{\text{leg adjacent to } \angle A} = \frac{a}{b}$$

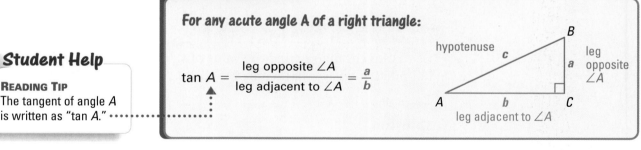

Student Help

> **READING TIP**
> The tangent of angle A is written as "tan A."

EXAMPLE 1 Find Tangent Ratio

Find tan S and tan R as fractions in simplified form and as decimals rounded to four decimal places.

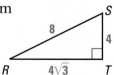

Solution

$$\tan S = \frac{\text{leg opposite } \angle S}{\text{leg adjacent to } \angle S} = \frac{4\sqrt{3}}{4} = \sqrt{3} \approx 1.7321$$

$$\tan R = \frac{\text{leg opposite } \angle R}{\text{leg adjacent to } \angle R} = \frac{4}{4\sqrt{3}} = \frac{1}{\sqrt{3}} \approx 0.5774$$

Tangent Function You can use the TAN function on a calculator to approximate the tangent of an angle. You can also use the table of trigonometric ratios on page 705.

Student Help

KEYSTROKE HELP
When calculating the tangent of an angle, be sure your calculator is in DEGREE mode.

EXAMPLE 2 Use a Calculator for Tangent

Approximate tan 74° to four decimal places.

Solution

Calculator keystrokes	Display	Rounded value
74 [TAN] *or* [TAN] 74 [ENTER]	3.487414444	3.4874

Checkpoint ✓ Find Tangent Ratio

Find tan *S* and tan *R* as fractions in simplified form and as decimals. Round to four decimal places if necessary.

1.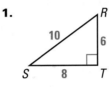

2.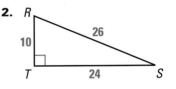

Use a calculator to approximate the value to four decimal places.

3. tan 35°   **4.** tan 85°   **5.** tan 10°

EXAMPLE 3 Find Leg Length

Use a tangent ratio to find the value of *x*. Round your answer to the nearest tenth.

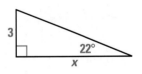

Solution

$$\tan 22° = \frac{\text{opposite leg}}{\text{adjacent leg}}$$ Write the tangent ratio.

$$\tan 22° = \frac{3}{x}$$ Substitute.

$$x \cdot \tan 22° = 3$$ Multiply each side by *x*.

$$x = \frac{3}{\tan 22°}$$ Divide each side by tan 22°.

$$x \approx \frac{3}{0.4040}$$ Use a calculator or table to approximate tan 22°.

$$x \approx 7.4$$ Simplify.

In Example 3, the unknown, *x*, was in the *denominator* of the ratio. If you prefer to use a ratio in which the unknown is in the *numerator*, use the tangent ratio for the other acute angle in the triangle.

EXAMPLE 4 Find Leg Length

Use two different tangent ratios to find the value of *x* to the nearest tenth.

Solution

▶First, find the measure of the other acute angle: $90° - 35° = 55°$.

Method 1	**Method 2**
$\tan 35° = \dfrac{\text{opposite leg}}{\text{adjacent leg}}$	$\tan 55° = \dfrac{\text{opposite leg}}{\text{adjacent leg}}$
$\tan 35° = \dfrac{4}{x}$	$\tan 55° = \dfrac{x}{4}$
$x \cdot \tan 35° = 4$	$4 \tan 55° = x$
$x = \dfrac{4}{\tan 35°}$	$4(1.4281) \approx x$
$x \approx \dfrac{4}{0.7002}$	$x \approx 5.7$
$x \approx 5.7$	

ANSWER ▶ The two methods yield the same answer: $x \approx 5.7$.

EXAMPLE 5 Estimate Height

You stand 45 feet from the base of a tree and look up at the top of the tree as shown in the diagram. Use a tangent ratio to estimate the height of the tree to the nearest foot.

Solution

$\tan 59° = \dfrac{\text{opposite leg}}{\text{adjacent leg}}$	Write ratio.
$\tan 59° = \dfrac{h}{45}$	Substitute.
$45 \tan 59° = h$	Multiply each side by 45.
$45(1.6643) \approx h$	Use a calculator or table to approximate tan 59°.
$74.9 \approx h$	Simplify.

ANSWER ▶ The tree is about 75 feet tall.

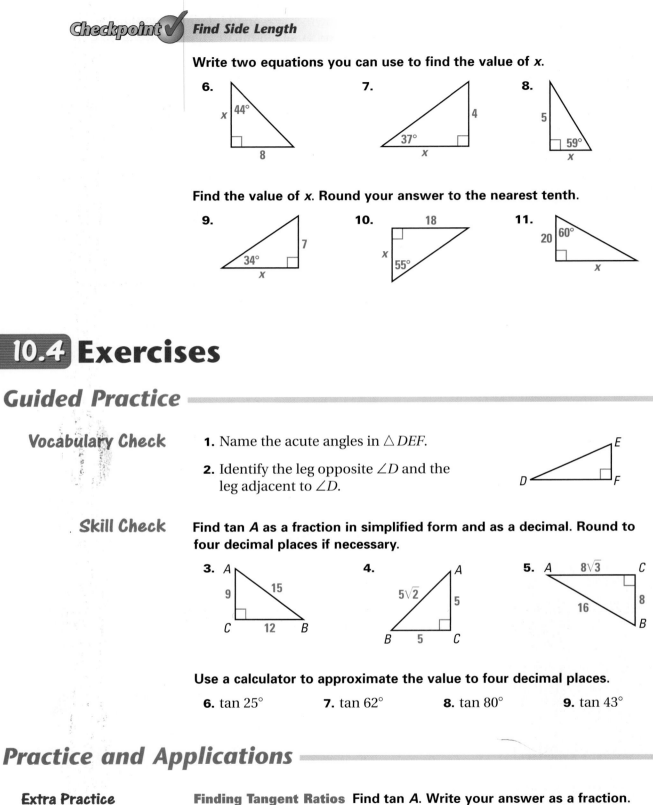

Checkpoint ✓ **Find Side Length**

Write two equations you can use to find the value of *x*.

6.

x | 44°

8

7.

4

37°

x

8.

5

59°

x

Find the value of *x*. Round your answer to the nearest tenth.

9.

7

34°

x

10.

18

x

55°

11.

20 | 60°

x

10.4 Exercises

Guided Practice

Vocabulary Check

1. Name the acute angles in △*DEF*.

2. Identify the leg opposite ∠*D* and the leg adjacent to ∠*D*.

E

D   F

Skill Check

Find tan *A* as a fraction in simplified form and as a decimal. Round to four decimal places if necessary.

3. A

9   15

C   12   B

4.

A

5√2   5

B   5   C

5. A   8√3   C

16   8

B

Use a calculator to approximate the value to four decimal places.

6. tan 25°   **7.** tan 62°   **8.** tan 80°   **9.** tan 43°

Practice and Applications

Extra Practice

See p. 693.

Finding Tangent Ratios Find tan *A*. Write your answer as a fraction.

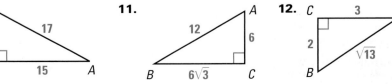

10. B

8   17

C   15   A

11.

A

12   6

B   6√3   C

12. C   3   A

2

√13

B

Homework Help

Example 1: Exs. 10–15
Example 2: Exs. 16–23
Example 3: Exs. 24–29,
32–37
Example 4: Exs. 24–29,
32–37
Example 5: Exs. 31, 38

Finding Tangent Ratios Find tan *P* and tan *R* as fractions in simplified form and as decimals rounded to four decimal places.

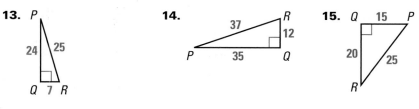

13. P, 24, 25, Q, 7, R

14. 37, R, 12, P, 35, Q

15. Q, 15, P, 20, 25, R

Using a Calculator Use a calculator to approximate the value to four decimal places.

16. tan 28°   **17.** tan 54°   **18.** tan 5°   **19.** tan 89°

20. tan 67°   **21.** tan 40°   **22.** tan 12°   **23.** tan 83°

Using Tangent Ratios Write two equations you can use to find the value of *x*. Then find the value of *x* to the nearest tenth.

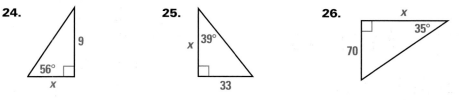

24. 9, 56°, *x*

25. *x*, 39°, 33

26. *x*, 35°, 70

Finding Leg Lengths Find the value of *x* to the nearest tenth.

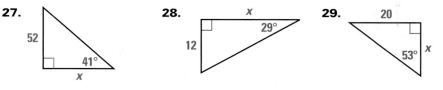

27. 52, 41°, *x*

28. *x*, 29°, 12

29. 20, 53°, *x*

30. Error Analysis To find the length of $\overline{BC}$ in the diagram at the right, a student wrote $\tan 55° = \dfrac{18}{BC}$. Explain the student's error.

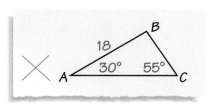

31. Water Slide A water slide makes an angle of about 13° with the ground. The slide extends horizontally about 58.2 meters as shown below. Find the height *h* of the slide to the nearest tenth of a meter.

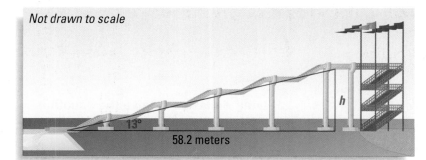

Not drawn to scale

13°

58.2 meters

Link to
Water Slides

WATER SLIDES Riders on some of the newer water slides may travel at speeds greater than 50 mi/h.

Application Links
CLASSZONE.COM

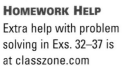
Finding Side Lengths Find the value of x to the nearest tenth.

32.

33.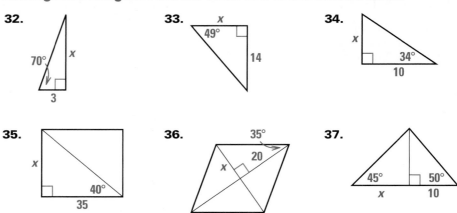

34.

35.

36.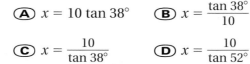

37.

38. Surveying To find the distance d
from a house on shore to a house on
an island, a surveyor measures from
the house on shore to point B, as
shown in the diagram. An instrument
called a *transit* is used to find the
measure of ∠B. Find the distance d
to the nearest tenth of a meter.

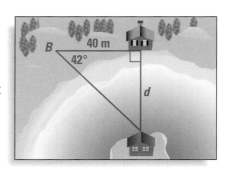

**Standardized Test
Practice**

39. Multiple Choice Which expression can be used to find the value
of x in the triangle shown?

Ⓐ $x = 10 \tan 38°$ Ⓑ $x = \dfrac{\tan 38°}{10}$

Ⓒ $x = \dfrac{10}{\tan 38°}$ Ⓓ $x = \dfrac{10}{\tan 52°}$

40. Multiple Choice What is the approximate value of y in the
triangle shown?

Ⓕ 7.2   Ⓖ 8.4

Ⓗ 9.3   Ⓙ 10.1

Mixed Review

Volume of Solids Find the volume of the solid. If necessary, round
your answer to the nearest whole number. *(Lessons 9.4, 9.5)*

41.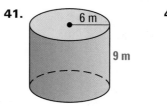

42.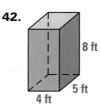

43.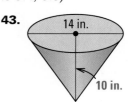

Algebra Skills

Solving Equations Solve the equation. *(Skills Review, p. 673)*

44. $8x - 10 = 3x$ **45.** $4(x + 3) = 32$ **46.** $3x - 7 - x = 11$

47. $6x + 5 = 3x - 4$ **48.** $2 - x = 4x + 22$ **49.** $5x - 18 = 2x + 21$

10.5 Sine and Cosine Ratios

Goal

Find the sine and cosine of an acute angle.

Key Words

- sine
- cosine

Two other trigonometric ratios are **sine** and **cosine**. These are abbreviated as *sin* and *cos*. Unlike the tangent ratio, these ratios involve the hypotenuse of a right triangle.

SINE AND COSINE RATIOS

For any acute angle A of a right triangle:

$$\sin A = \frac{\text{leg opposite } \angle A}{\text{hypotenuse}} = \frac{a}{c}$$

$$\cos A = \frac{\text{leg adjacent to } \angle A}{\text{hypotenuse}} = \frac{b}{c}$$

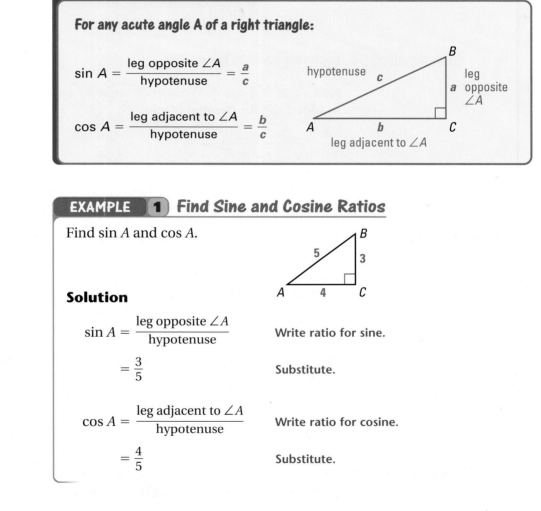

EXAMPLE 1 Find Sine and Cosine Ratios

Find sin *A* and cos *A*.

Solution

$$\sin A = \frac{\text{leg opposite } \angle A}{\text{hypotenuse}}$$ Write ratio for sine.

$$= \frac{3}{5}$$ Substitute.

$$\cos A = \frac{\text{leg adjacent to } \angle A}{\text{hypotenuse}}$$ Write ratio for cosine.

$$= \frac{4}{5}$$ Substitute.

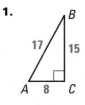 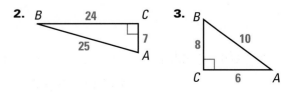 **Find Sine and Cosine Ratios**

Find sin *A* and cos *A*.

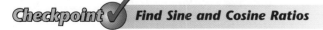

1.

2.

3.

EXAMPLE 2 Find Sine and Cosine Ratios

Find sin A and cos A. Write your answers as fractions and as decimals rounded to four decimal places.

Solution

$$\sin A = \frac{\text{leg opposite } \angle A}{\text{hypotenuse}} = \frac{5}{13} \approx 0.3846$$

$$\cos A = \frac{\text{leg adjacent to } \angle A}{\text{hypotenuse}} = \frac{12}{13} \approx 0.9231$$

Checkpoint ✓ Find Sine and Cosine Ratios

Find sin A and cos A. Write your answers as fractions and as decimals rounded to four decimal places.

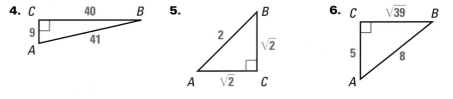

4. C   40   B
        9   41
        A

5.   B
        2   √2
        A √2 C

6. C   √39   B
        5   8
        A

Sine and Cosine Functions You can use the SIN and COS functions on a calculator to approximate the sine and cosine of an angle. You can also use the table of trigonometric ratios on page 705.

EXAMPLE 3 Use a Calculator for Sine and Cosine

Use a calculator to approximate sin 74° and cos 74°. Round your answers to four decimal places.

Solution

Calculator keystrokes	Display	Rounded value
74 SIN *or* SIN 74 ENTER	0.961261696	0.9613
74 COS *or* COS 74 ENTER	0.275637356	0.2756

Checkpoint ✓ Use a Calculator for Sine and Cosine

Use a calculator to approximate the value to four decimal places.

7. sin 43°   **8.** cos 43°   **9.** sin 15°   **10.** cos 15°

11. cos 72°   **12.** sin 72°   **13.** cos 90°   **14.** sin 90°

EXAMPLE 4 Find Leg Lengths

Find the lengths of the legs of the triangle.
Round your answers to the nearest tenth.

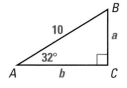

Student Help

VISUAL STRATEGY

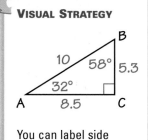

You can label side lengths and angle measures in different colors. See p. 536.

Solution

$$\sin A = \frac{\text{leg opposite } \angle A}{\text{hypotenuse}} \qquad \cos A = \frac{\text{leg adjacent to } \angle A}{\text{hypotenuse}}$$

$$\sin 32° = \frac{a}{10} \qquad\qquad \cos 32° = \frac{b}{10}$$

$$10(\sin 32°) = a \qquad\qquad 10(\cos 32°) = b$$

$$10(0.5299) \approx a \qquad\qquad 10(0.8480) \approx b$$

$$5.3 \approx a \qquad\qquad\qquad 8.5 \approx b$$

▶ **ANSWER** ▶ In the triangle, *BC* is about 5.3 and *AC* is about 8.5.

Checkpoint ✓ *Find Leg Lengths*

Find the lengths of the legs of the triangle. Round your answers to the nearest tenth.

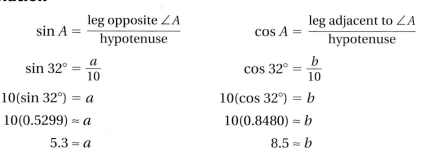

15.

16.

17.

SUMMARY **TRIGONOMETRIC RATIOS**

For any acute angle A of a right triangle:

Tangent of ∠A

$$\tan A = \frac{\text{leg opposite } \angle A}{\text{leg adjacent to } \angle A} = \frac{a}{b}$$

Sine of ∠A

$$\sin A = \frac{\text{leg opposite } \angle A}{\text{hypotenuse}} = \frac{a}{c}$$

Cosine of ∠A

$$\cos A = \frac{\text{leg adjacent to } \angle A}{\text{hypotenuse}} = \frac{b}{c}$$

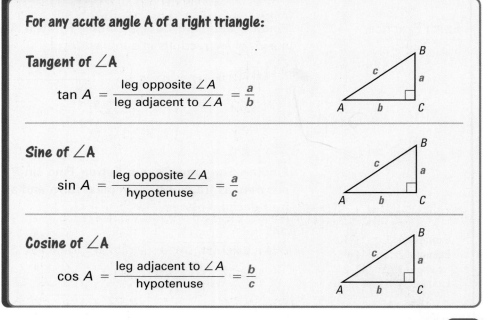

Guided Practice

Vocabulary Check   **Use the diagram shown at the right to match the trigonometric ratios.**

1. $\cos D$ **A.** $\dfrac{EF}{DE}$

2. $\sin D$ **B.** $\dfrac{DE}{DF}$

3. $\tan D$ **C.** $\dfrac{EF}{DF}$

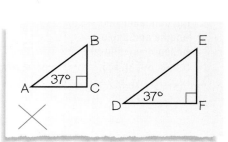

4. Error Analysis A student says that $\sin D > \sin A$ because the side lengths of $\triangle DEF$ are greater than the side lengths of $\triangle ABC$. Explain why the student is incorrect.

Skill Check   **In Exercises 5–10, use the diagram shown below to find the trigonometric ratio.**

5. $\sin A$ **6.** $\cos A$

7. $\tan A$ **8.** $\sin B$

9. $\cos B$ **10.** $\tan B$

Practice and Applications

Extra Practice
See p. 694.

Finding Sine and Cosine Ratios Find $\sin A$ and $\cos A$. Write your answers as fractions in simplest form.

11.   **12.**   **13.**

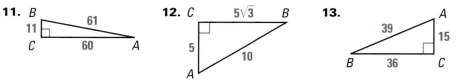

Finding Sine and Cosine Ratios Find $\sin P$ and $\cos P$. Write your answers as fractions in simplest form and as decimals rounded to four decimal places.

Homework Help
Example 1: Exs. 11–13
Example 2: Exs. 14–16
Example 3: Exs. 17–24
Example 4: Exs. 25–30

14.   **15.**   **16.**

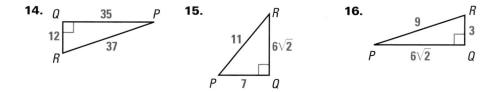

Calculator Use a calculator to approximate the value to four decimal places.

17. sin 40°   **18.** cos 23°   **19.** sin 80°   **20.** cos 5°

21. sin 59°   **22.** cos 61°   **23.** sin 90°   **24.** cos 77°

Student Help

CLASSZONE.COM

HOMEWORK HELP
Extra help with problem solving in Exs. 25–30 is at classzone.com

Finding Leg Lengths Find the lengths of the legs of the triangle. Round your answers to the nearest tenth.

25.

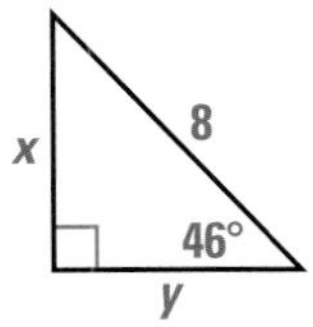

x, 8, 46°, y

26.

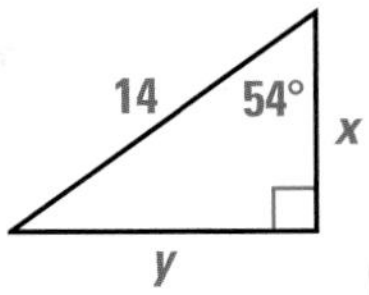

14, 54°, x, y

27.

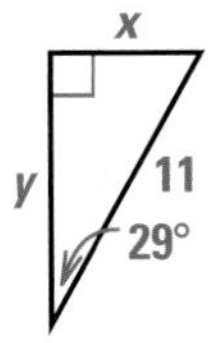

x, y, 11, 29°

28.

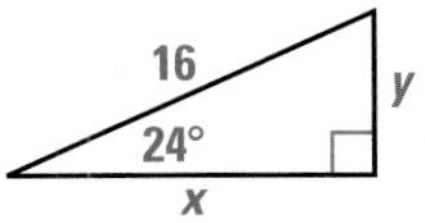

16, y, 24°, x

29.

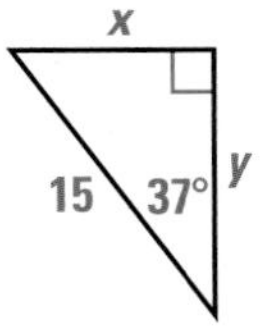

x, 15, 37°, y

30.

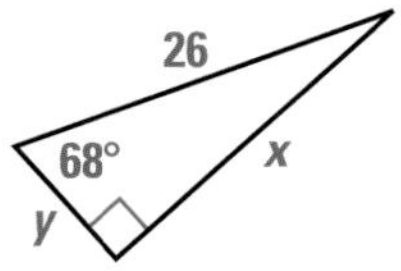

26, 68°, x, y

31. Visualize It! A ladder that is 15 feet long is leaning against a wall. The ladder makes an angle of 70° with the ground. Make a sketch. Then determine how high up the wall the ladder reaches. Round your answer to the nearest foot.

32. Skateboard Ramp You are constructing a skateboarding ramp like the one shown below. Your ramp will be 8 feet long and the ramp angle will be about 22°. Find the lengths of the legs of the triangles that support the ramp. Round your answers to the nearest inch.

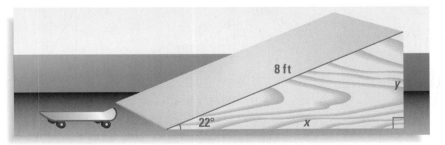

8 ft   y   22°   x

Link to
Skateboarding

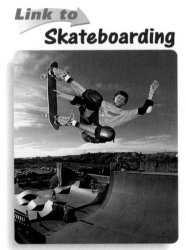

SKATEBOARD RAMPS
built with curves, called half pipes, allow freestyle skateboard riders to perform acrobatic maneuvers.

Technology In Exercises 33–35, use geometry software.

❶ Draw $\overline{AB}$.

❷ Construct a perpendicular to $\overline{AB}$ through B.

❸ Add point C on the perpendicular.

❹ Draw $\overline{AC}$.

33. Find $m\angle A$, sin A, and cos A.

34. Calculate $(\sin A)^2 + (\cos A)^2$.

35. Drag point C. What do you notice?

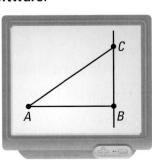

C, A, B

36. Challenge Let A be any acute angle of a right triangle. Use the definitions of sin A, cos A, and tan A to prove the following result.

$$\frac{\sin A}{\cos A} = \tan A$$

37. *You be the Judge* One student uses the ratio $\sin 42° = \frac{r}{34}$ to find the length of $\overline{ST}$. Another student uses the ratio $\cos 48° = \frac{r}{34}$. Assuming the students make no errors in calculation, who will get the correct answer?

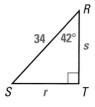

38. Multiple Choice Use the diagram below. Which expression could be used to find CD?

   Ⓐ $8(\cos 25°)$ Ⓑ $8(\sin 25°)$

   Ⓒ $\dfrac{8}{\sin 25°}$ Ⓓ $\dfrac{8}{\cos 25°}$

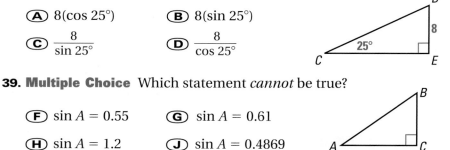

39. Multiple Choice Which statement *cannot* be true?

   Ⓕ $\sin A = 0.55$ Ⓖ $\sin A = 0.61$

   Ⓗ $\sin A = 1.2$ Ⓙ $\sin A = 0.4869$

Not drawn to scale

Finding Leg Lengths Find the value of each variable. Write your answer in radical form. *(Lesson 10.3)*

40.   **41.**   **42.**

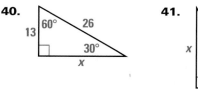 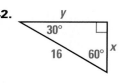

Using a Calculator Use a calculator to approximate the value to four decimal places. *(Lesson 10.4)*

43. $\tan 32°$ **44.** $\tan 88°$ **45.** $\tan 56°$

46. $\tan 24°$ **47.** $\tan 17°$ **48.** $\tan 49°$

Ordering Numbers Write the numbers in order from least to greatest. *(Skills Review, p. 662)*

49. $-0.8, 1.8, -8, 0.08, -18, 0, -1.8$

50. $2641, 2146, 2614, 2416, 2164, 2461$

51. $-0.56, -0.47, -0.61, -0.5, -0.6$

Solving Right Triangles

Goal
Solve a right triangle.

Key Words
- tangent p. 557
- sine p. 563
- cosine p. 563
- solve a right triangle
- inverse tangent
- inverse sine
- inverse cosine

To **solve a right triangle** means to find the measures of both acute angles and the lengths of all three sides. Suppose you know the lengths of the *legs* of a right triangle. How would you find the measures of the *angles*?

In the triangle at the right, the legs have lengths 7 and 10, so the tangent of $\angle A$ is $\frac{7}{10}$, or 0.7.

You can use the table of trigonometric ratios on page 705 to find the measure of $\angle A$. Or you can use the **inverse tangent** function ($\tan^{-1} x$) of a scientific calculator to find the angle measure.

Look for 0.7 in the tangent column.

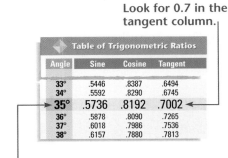

The angle with a tangent of 0.7 has a measure of about 35°.

On this calculator, you press **INV** then **TAN** to get the inverse tangent.

Student Help

READING TIP
The phrase "$\tan^{-1} z$" is read as "the inverse tangent of z."

INVERSE TANGENT

For any acute angle A of a right triangle:

If $\tan A = z$, then $\tan^{-1} z = m\angle A$.

EXAMPLE 1 Use Inverse Tangent

Use a calculator to approximate the measure of $\angle A$ to the nearest tenth of a degree.

Solution

Since $\tan A = \frac{8}{10} = 0.8$, $\tan^{-1} 0.8 = m\angle A$.

Expression	Calculator keystrokes	Display
$\tan^{-1} 0.8$	0.8 **INV** **TAN** *or* 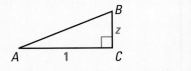	38.65980825

ANSWER ▶ Because $\tan^{-1} 0.8 \approx 38.7°$, $m\angle A \approx 38.7°$.

EXAMPLE 2 **Solve a Right Triangle**

Find each measure to the nearest tenth.

a. *c* b. *m∠B* c. *m∠A*

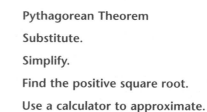

Solution

a. Use the Pythagorean Theorem to find *c*.

$$(\text{hypotenuse})^2 = (\text{leg})^2 + (\text{leg})^2 \qquad \text{Pythagorean Theorem}$$

$$c^2 = 3^2 + 2^2 \qquad \text{Substitute.}$$

$$c^2 = 13 \qquad \text{Simplify.}$$

$$c = \sqrt{13} \qquad \text{Find the positive square root.}$$

$$c \approx 3.6 \qquad \text{Use a calculator to approximate.}$$

b. Use a calculator to find *m∠B*.

Since $\tan B = \dfrac{2}{3} \approx 0.6667$, $m\angle B \approx \tan^{-1} 0.6667 \approx 33.7°$.

c. ∠A and ∠B are complementary, so $m\angle A \approx 90° - 33.7° = 56.3°$.

Checkpoint ✓ **Use Inverse Tangent**

∠**A is an acute angle. Use a calculator to approximate the measure of ∠A to the nearest tenth of a degree.**

1. $\tan A = 3.5$ **2.** $\tan A = 2$ **3.** $\tan A = 0.4402$

Find the measure of ∠A to the nearest tenth of a degree.

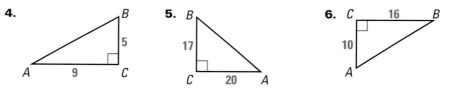

Inverse Sine and Inverse Cosine A scientific calculator has **inverse sine** ($\sin^{-1} x$) and **inverse cosine** ($\cos^{-1} x$) functions. Use these inverse functions if you are given the lengths of one leg and the hypotenuse.

On this calculator, you press
[INV] [SIN] and [INV] [COS]
to get the inverse functions.

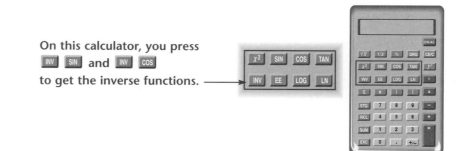

INVERSE SINE AND INVERSE COSINE

For any acute angle A of a right triangle:

If sin $A = y$, then $\sin^{-1} y = m\angle A$.

If cos $A = x$, then $\cos^{-1} x = m\angle A$.

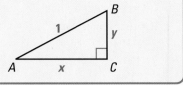

Student Help

STUDY TIP
To use the table of ratios on p. 705 to approximate $\sin^{-1} 0.55$, find the number closest to 0.55 in the sine column, then read the angle measure at its left.

EXAMPLE 3 Find the Measures of Acute Angles

$\angle A$ is an acute angle. Use a calculator to approximate the measure of $\angle A$ to the nearest tenth of a degree.

  a. sin $A = 0.55$ **b.** cos $A = 0.48$

Solution

  a. Since sin $A = 0.55$, $m\angle A = \sin^{-1} 0.55$.

     $\sin^{-1} 0.55 \approx 33.36701297$, so $m\angle A \approx 33.4°$.

  b. Since cos $A = 0.48$, $m\angle A = \cos^{-1} 0.48$.

     $\cos^{-1} 0.48 \approx 61.31459799$, so $m\angle A \approx 61.3°$.

Student Help

VISUAL STRATEGY

The triangle in Example 4 can be labeled in color, as suggested on p. 536.

EXAMPLE 4 Solve a Right Triangle

Solve $\triangle GHJ$ by finding each measure. Round decimals to the nearest tenth.

  a. $m\angle G$ **b.** $m\angle H$ **c.** g

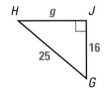

Solution

  a. Since cos $G = \dfrac{16}{25} = 0.64$, $m\angle G = \cos^{-1} 0.64$.

     $\cos^{-1} 0.64 \approx 50.2081805$, so $m\angle G \approx 50.2°$.

  b. $\angle G$ and $\angle H$ are complementary.

     $m\angle H = 90° - m\angle G \approx 90° - 50.2° = 39.8°$

  c. Use the Pythagorean Theorem to find g.

$(\text{leg})^2 + (\text{leg})^2 = (\text{hypotenuse})^2$	Pythagorean Theorem
$16^2 + g^2 = 25^2$	Substitute.
$256 + g^2 = 625$	Simplify.
$g^2 = 369$	Subtract 256 from each side.
$g = \sqrt{369}$	Find the positive square root.
$g \approx 19.2$	Use a calculator to approximate.

10.6 *Solving Right Triangles*   **571**

Checkpoint ✓ Use Inverse Sine and Inverse Cosine

$\angle A$ is an acute angle. Use a calculator to approximate the measure of $\angle A$ to the nearest tenth of a degree.

7. $\sin A = 0.5$ **8.** $\cos A = 0.92$ **9.** $\sin A = 0.1149$

10. $\cos A = 0.5$ **11.** $\sin A = 0.25$ **12.** $\cos A = 0.45$

Solve the right triangle. Round decimals to the nearest tenth.

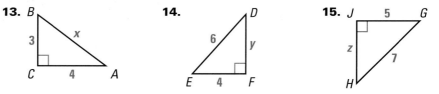

13.

14.

15.

10.6 Exercises

Guided Practice

Vocabulary Check

1. Explain what is meant by *solving a right triangle.*

Skill Check

Tell whether the statement is *true* or *false*.

2. You can solve a right triangle given only the lengths of two sides.

3. You can solve a right triangle given only the measure of one acute angle.

Find the value of x. Round your answer to the nearest tenth.

4.

5.

6.

Calculator **$\angle A$ is an acute angle. Use a calculator to approximate the measure of $\angle A$ to the nearest tenth of a degree.**

7. $\tan A = 5.4472$ **8.** $\sin A = 0.8988$ **9.** $\cos A = 0.3846$

Solve the right triangle. Round your answers to the nearest tenth.

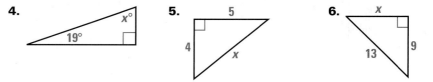

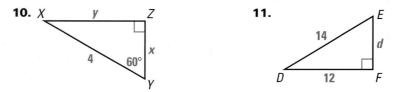

10.

11.

Practice and Applications

Extra Practice

See p. 694.

Calculator ∠A is an acute angle. Use a calculator to approximate the measure of ∠A to the nearest tenth of a degree.

12. $\tan A = 0.5$ **13.** $\tan A = 1.0$ **14.** $\tan A = 2.5$

15. $\tan A = 0.2311$ **16.** $\tan A = 1.509$ **17.** $\tan A = 4.125$

Solving a Triangle Tell what method you would use to solve for the indicated measure. Then find the measure to the nearest tenth.

18. QS **19.** $m\angle Q$ **20.** $m\angle S$

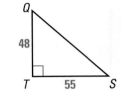

Inverse Tangent Use the Pythagorean Theorem to find the length of the hypotenuse. Then use the inverse tangent to find the measure of ∠A to the nearest tenth of a degree.

21.   **22.**   **23.**

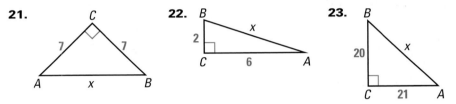

Calculator ∠A is an acute angle. Use a calculator to approximate the measure of ∠A to the nearest tenth of a degree.

24. $\sin A = 0.75$ **25.** $\cos A = 0.1518$ **26.** $\sin A = 0.6$

27. $\cos A = 0.45$ **28.** $\cos A = 0.1123$ **29.** $\sin A = 0.6364$

Ramps In Exercises 30–32, use the information about ramps.
The Uniform Federal Accessibility Standards require that the measure of the angle used in a wheelchair ramp be less than or equal to 4.76°.

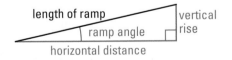

30. A ramp has a length of 20 feet and a vertical rise of 2.5 feet. Find the ramp's horizontal distance and the measure of its ramp angle. Does this ramp meet the standards?

Homework Help

Example 1: Exs. 12–17
Example 2: Exs. 18–23
Example 3: Exs. 24–29
Example 4: Exs. 34–39

31. Suppose a ramp has a vertical rise of 4 feet. Give an example of a possible length of the ramp that meets the standards.

32. Measurement Measure the horizontal distance and the vertical rise of a ramp near your home or school. Find the measure of the ramp angle. Does the ramp meet the standards? Explain.

33. Space Shuttle The glide angle of a space shuttle is the angle indicated in the photo. During the shuttle's approach to Earth, the glide angle changes. When the shuttle's altitude is about 15.7 miles, its horizontal distance to the runway is about 59 miles. Find the measure of the glide angle. Round your answer to the nearest tenth.

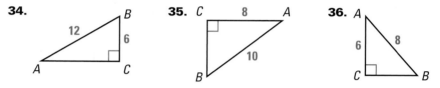

Not drawn to scale

Inverse Sine and Inverse Cosine Find the measure of ∠A to the nearest tenth of a degree.

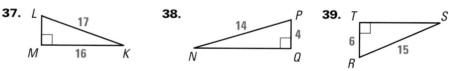

34.

35.

36.

Solving Right Triangles Solve the right triangle. Round decimals to the nearest tenth.

37.

38.

39.

40. **You be the Judge** Each of the expressions $\sin^{-1}\frac{BC}{AC}$, $\cos^{-1}\frac{AB}{AC}$, and $\tan^{-1}\frac{BC}{AB}$ can be used to approximate $m\angle A$. Which expression would you choose? Explain your choice.

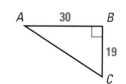

41. Multiple Choice Which additional information would *not* be enough to solve △PQR?

  (A) $m\angle P$ and PR **(B)** $m\angle P$ and $m\angle R$

  (C) PQ and PR **(D)** $m\angle P$ and PQ

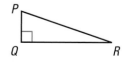

42. Multiple Choice Which expression is correct?

  (F) $\sin^{-1}\frac{JL}{JK} = m\angle J$ **(G)** $\tan^{-1}\frac{KL}{JL} = m\angle J$

  (H) $\cos^{-1}\frac{JL}{JK} = m\angle K$ **(J)** $\sin^{-1}\frac{JL}{KL} = m\angle K$

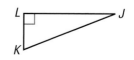

Mixed Review

Circumference and Area of Circles Find the circumference and the area of the circle. Round your answers to the nearest whole number. *(Lesson 8.7)*

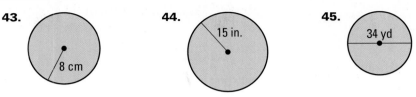

43. 8 cm

44. 15 in.

45. 34 yd

Volume of Solids Find the volume of the solid. Round your answers to the nearest whole number. *(Lesson 9.6)*

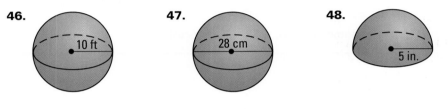

46. 10 ft

47. 28 cm

48. 5 in.

Algebra Skills

Decimal Operations Evaluate. *(Skills Review, p. 655)*

49. $0.36 + 0.194$

50. $\$8.42 - \$2.95$

51. 7×4.65

52. $55.40 \div 0.04$

53. $700 \div 0.35$

54. $\$22.50 \times 0.08$

Quiz 2

Find the value of each variable. Round the results to the nearest tenth. *(Lessons 10.4, 10.5)*

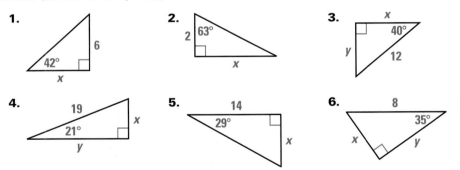

1. 6, 42°, x

2. 2, 63°, x

3. x, 40°, y, 12

4. 19, 21°, x, y

5. 14, 29°, x

6. 8, 35°, x, y

Use a calculator to approximate the value to four decimal places. *(Lessons 10.4, 10.5)*

7. $\tan 72°$

8. $\sin 52°$

9. $\cos 36°$

Solve the right triangle. Round decimals to the nearest tenth. *(Lesson 10.6)*

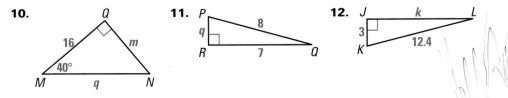

10. Q, 16, m, 40°, M, q, N

11. P, q, 8, R, 7, Q

12. J, k, L, 3, 12.4, K

VOCABULARY

- **radical,** *p. 537*
- **radicand,** *p. 537*
- **45°-45°-90° triangle,** *p. 542*
- **30°-60°-90° triangle,** *p. 549*
- **trigonometric ratio,** *p. 557*

- **leg opposite an angle,** *p. 557*
- **leg adjacent to an angle,** *p. 557*
- **tangent,** *p. 557*
- **sine,** *p. 563*
- **cosine,** *p. 563*

- **solve a right triangle,** *p. 569*
- **inverse tangent,** *p. 569*
- **inverse sine,** *p. 570*
- **inverse cosine,** *p. 570*

VOCABULARY REVIEW

Fill in the blank.

1. A(n) __?__ is an expression written with a radical symbol.

2. The number or expression inside the radical symbol is the __?__.

3. A(n) __?__ is a ratio of the lengths of two sides of a right triangle.

4. A right triangle with side lengths 9, $9\sqrt{3}$, and 18 is a(n) __?__ triangle.

5. To __?__ a right triangle means to determine the lengths of all three sides of the triangle and the measures of both acute angles.

6. A right triangle with side lengths 4, 4, and $4\sqrt{2}$ is a(n) __?__ triangle.

7. If $\angle F$ is an acute angle of a right triangle, then
$$\underline{\quad?\quad} \text{ of } \angle F = \frac{\text{leg opposite } \angle F}{\text{leg adjacent to } \angle F}.$$

8. If $\angle F$ is an acute angle of a right triangle, then
$$\underline{\quad?\quad} \text{ of } \angle F = \frac{\text{leg adjacent } \angle F}{\text{hypotenuse}}.$$

9. If $\angle F$ is an acute angle of a right triangle, then
$$\underline{\quad?\quad} \text{ of } \angle F = \frac{\text{leg opposite } \angle F}{\text{hypotenuse}}.$$

10.1 SIMPLIFYING SQUARE ROOTS

Examples on pp. 537–538

EXAMPLES Use the Product Property of Radicals to simplify the expression.

a. $\sqrt{7} \cdot \sqrt{5}$

$$\sqrt{7} \cdot \sqrt{5} = \sqrt{7 \cdot 5} = \sqrt{35}$$

b. $\sqrt{52}$

$$\sqrt{52} = \sqrt{4 \cdot 13} = 2\sqrt{13}$$

Multiply the radicals. Then simplify if possible.

10. $\sqrt{13} \cdot \sqrt{13}$ **11.** $\sqrt{2} \cdot \sqrt{72}$ **12.** $\sqrt{7} \cdot \sqrt{10}$ **13.** $(4\sqrt{7})^2$

14. $\sqrt{3} \cdot \sqrt{19}$ **15.** $\sqrt{5} \cdot \sqrt{5}$ **16.** $\sqrt{6} \cdot \sqrt{18}$ **17.** $(3\sqrt{11})^2$

Simplify the radical expression.

18. $\sqrt{27}$ **19.** $\sqrt{72}$ **20.** $\sqrt{150}$ **21.** $\sqrt{68}$

22. $\sqrt{108}$ **23.** $\sqrt{80}$ **24.** $\sqrt{7500}$ **25.** $\sqrt{507}$

Use the formula $A = \ell w$ to find the area of the rectangle. Round your answer to the nearest tenth.

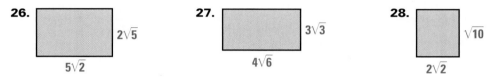

26. $2\sqrt{5}$ $5\sqrt{2}$

27. $3\sqrt{3}$ $4\sqrt{6}$

28. $\sqrt{10}$ $2\sqrt{2}$

10.2   45°-45°-90° TRIANGLES

Examples on pp. 542–544

EXAMPLES   **Find the value of x.**

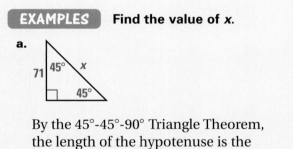

a. By the 45°-45°-90° Triangle Theorem, the length of the hypotenuse is the length of a leg times $\sqrt{2}$, so $x = 71\sqrt{2}$.

b. By the 45°-45°-90° Triangle Theorem, the length of the hypotenuse is the length of a leg times $\sqrt{2}$, so $33\sqrt{2} = x\sqrt{2}$, and $x = 33$.

Find the length of the hypotenuse in the 45°-45°-90° triangle. Write your answer in radical form.

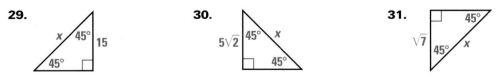

29. x, $45°$, 15, $45°$

30. $5\sqrt{2}$, $45°$, x, $45°$

31. $45°$, $\sqrt{7}$, $45°$, x

Find the length of each leg in each 45°-45°-90° triangle. Write your answer in radical form or as a decimal to the nearest tenth.

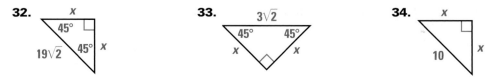

32. x, $45°$, $45°$, x, $19\sqrt{2}$

33. $3\sqrt{2}$, $45°$, $45°$, x, x

34. x, 10, x

10.3   30°-60°-90° TRIANGLES

Examples on pp. 549–551

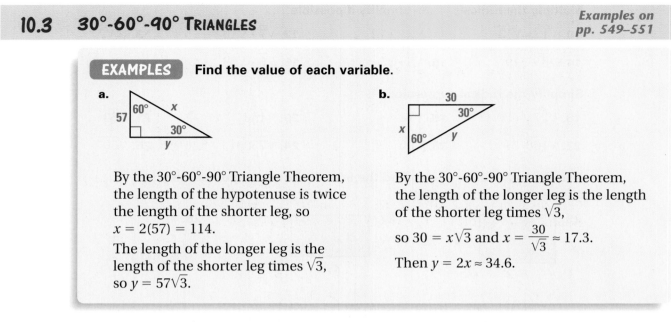

EXAMPLES   Find the value of each variable.

a.

By the 30°-60°-90° Triangle Theorem, the length of the hypotenuse is twice the length of the shorter leg, so $x = 2(57) = 114$.

The length of the longer leg is the length of the shorter leg times $\sqrt{3}$, so $y = 57\sqrt{3}$.

b.

By the 30°-60°-90° Triangle Theorem, the length of the longer leg is the length of the shorter leg times $\sqrt{3}$,

so $30 = x\sqrt{3}$ and $x = \dfrac{30}{\sqrt{3}} \approx 17.3$.

Then $y = 2x \approx 34.6$.

Find the value of each variable. Write your answers in radical form or as a decimal to the nearest tenth.

35. 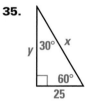   **36.** 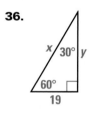   **37.** 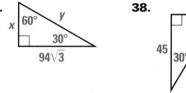   **38.**

10.4   TANGENT RATIO

Examples on pp. 557–559

EXAMPLE   Find tan A and tan B as fractions and as decimals.

$\tan A = \dfrac{\text{leg opposite to } \angle A}{\text{leg adjacent to } \angle A} = \dfrac{21}{20} = 1.05$

$\tan B = \dfrac{\text{leg opposite to } \angle B}{\text{leg adjacent to } \angle B} = \dfrac{20}{21} \approx 0.9524$

Find tan A and tan B as fractions in simplest form and as decimals. Round your answers to four decimal places if necessary.

39.   **40.**   **41.**

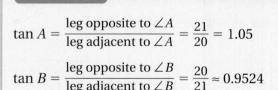

Approximate the value to four decimal places.

42. tan 17°   **43.** tan 81°   **44.** tan 36°   **45.** tan 24°

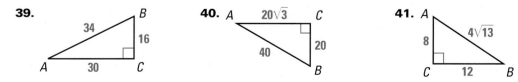

10.5 SINE AND COSINE RATIOS

Examples on pp. 563–565

EXAMPLE Find sin *A* and cos *A* as fractions and as decimals.

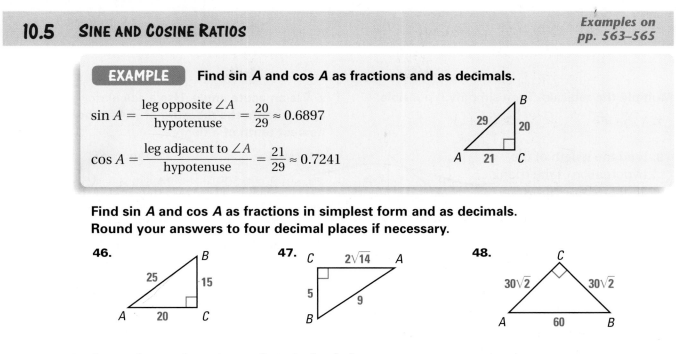

$$\sin A = \frac{\text{leg opposite } \angle A}{\text{hypotenuse}} = \frac{20}{29} \approx 0.6897$$

$$\cos A = \frac{\text{leg adjacent to } \angle A}{\text{hypotenuse}} = \frac{21}{29} \approx 0.7241$$

Find sin *A* and cos *A* as fractions in simplest form and as decimals. Round your answers to four decimal places if necessary.

46. 47. 48.

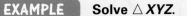

Approximate the value to four decimal places.

49. sin 57°   **50.** sin 12°   **51.** cos 31°   **52.** cos 75°

53. Find the lengths of the legs of the triangle. Round your answers to the nearest tenth.

10.6 SOLVING RIGHT TRIANGLES

Examples on pp. 569–571

EXAMPLE Solve △ *XYZ*.

By the Pythagorean Theorem, $y^2 = 5^2 + 7^2 = 25 + 49 = 74$, so $y \approx 8.6$.

$\tan X = \frac{7}{5} = 1.4$, so $m\angle X = \tan^{-1} 1.4 \approx 54.5°$.

Since $\angle X$ and $\angle Z$ are complementary,
$m\angle Z = 90° - m\angle X \approx 90° - 54.5° = 35.5°$.

∠ *A* is an acute angle. Use a calculator to approximate the measure of ∠ *A* to the nearest tenth of a degree.

54. tan *A* = 3.2145   **55.** sin *A* = 0.0888   **56.** cos *A* = 0.2243   **57.** tan *A* = 1.2067

Solve the right triangle. Round decimals to the nearest tenth.

58. 59. 60.

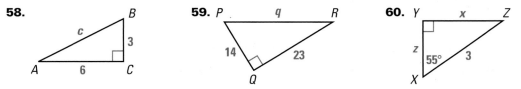

Multiply the radicals. Then simplify if possible.

1. $\sqrt{15} \cdot \sqrt{7}$ **2.** $(3\sqrt{11})^2$

3. Find the length of the hypotenuse of the triangle at the right. Write your answer in radical form.

Use the diagram below to match the segment with its length.

4. $\overline{DC}$ **A.** 12

5. $\overline{AB}$ **B.** $6\sqrt{2}$

6. $\overline{BC}$ **C.** $6\sqrt{3}$

7. $\overline{AD}$ **D.** 6

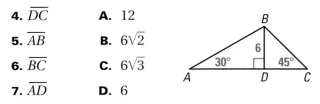

8. The hypotenuse of a 45°-45°-90° triangle has length 47. Find the length of each leg to the nearest tenth.

Find the value of each variable to the nearest tenth.

9.

10.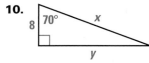

11.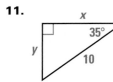

12.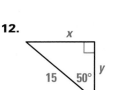

Use a calculator to approximate the value to four decimal places.

13. $\tan 70°$ **14.** $\cos 14°$

15. $\tan 31°$ **16.** $\sin 26°$

17. $\cos 30°$ **18.** $\tan 45°$

19. $\sin 5°$ **20.** $\tan 10°$

∠A is an acute angle. Use a calculator to approximate the measure of ∠A to the nearest tenth of a degree.

21. $\tan A = 5.2$ **22.** $\tan A = 7$

23. $\sin A = 0.3091$ **24.** $\sin A = 0.5318$

25. $\cos A = 0.6264$ **26.** $\cos A = 0.3751$

Solve the right triangle. Round decimals to the nearest tenth.

27.

28.

29.

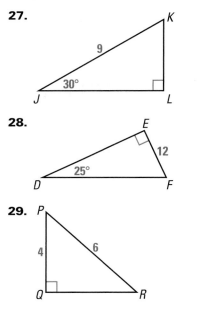

30. In the diagram of the roller coaster, $\triangle XYZ$ is a right triangle with $XZ = 320$ and $YZ = 180$. Find the measure of $\angle X$ to the nearest tenth of a degree.

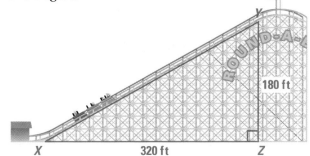

Test Tip

Ⓐ Ⓑ Ⓒ Ⓓ

Memorize important ideas like the Pythagorean Theorem, the Midpoint Theorem, and formulas for area and volume.

---

1. Simplify the expression $\sqrt{124}$.

Ⓐ $2\sqrt{31}$ Ⓑ 12

Ⓒ $2\sqrt{62}$ Ⓓ $4\sqrt{31}$

2. What is the value of x in the triangle shown below?

Ⓕ 7

Ⓖ $\sqrt{21}$

Ⓗ $2\sqrt{7}$

Ⓙ $\sqrt{14}$

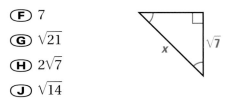

3. For $\angle J$ in the figure shown below, which statement is *true*?

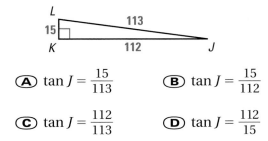

Ⓐ $\tan J = \dfrac{15}{113}$ Ⓑ $\tan J = \dfrac{15}{112}$

Ⓒ $\tan J = \dfrac{112}{113}$ Ⓓ $\tan J = \dfrac{112}{15}$

4. $\angle W$ is an acute angle and $\sin W = 0.8170$. Approximate the measure of $\angle W$.

Ⓕ $0.01°$ Ⓖ $35.2°$

Ⓗ $39.2°$ Ⓙ $54.8°$

5. Which of the following statements about the figure below is *true*?

Ⓐ $SR = 48\sqrt{2}$

Ⓑ $QR = 96$

Ⓒ $PS = 48\sqrt{3}$

Ⓓ $PQ = 96\sqrt{3}$

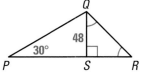

6. Find the measure of $\angle A$ to the nearest tenth of a degree.

Ⓕ $28.6°$

Ⓖ $33.1°$

Ⓗ $37.4°$

Ⓙ $56.9°$

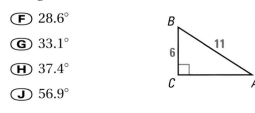

7. Which of the following statements about the triangle shown below is *true*?

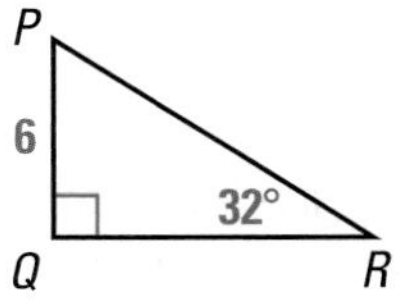

Ⓐ $m\angle P = 48°$

Ⓑ $PR \approx 11.3$

Ⓒ $RQ \approx 8.6$

Ⓓ None of these

8. The distance from a point P on the ground to a point R at the base of a cliff is 30 meters. In the figure below, the measure of $\angle P$ is $72°$. Which of the following gives the approximate height h of the cliff?

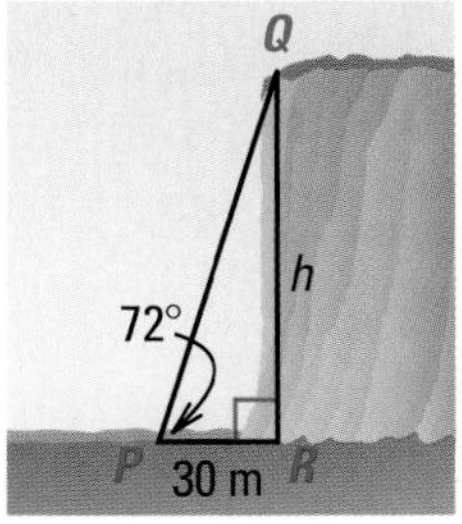

Ⓕ 60.8 m

Ⓖ 78.6 m

Ⓗ 90.4 m

Ⓙ 92.3 m

9. Which of the following gives the approximate values of x and y for the triangle shown?

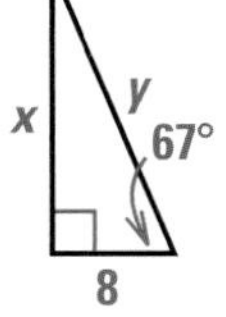

Ⓐ $x \approx 18.8$, $y \approx 20.1$

Ⓑ $x \approx 14.4$, $y \approx 19.2$

Ⓒ $x \approx 12.6$, $y \approx 18.5$

Ⓓ $x \approx 18.8$, $y \approx 20.5$

BraiN GaMes

Right Triangle Bingo

Materials
- bingo card
- chips (optional)
- calculator

Object of the Game To be the first to get 5 answers in a row.

Set Up The bingo card has a five-by-five grid and 30 answers listed. Choose 24 of the answers and use them to fill in the empty squares on the card.

Step 1 ▶ Your teacher (or a student assigned to be the caller) will read a problem.

Step 2 ▶ Solve the problem.

Step 3 ▶ If the answer is on your card, mark it with a chip or use a pencil to circle the number.

Step 4 ▶ Continue playing until someone has 5 squares in a row, column, or diagonal marked and says "BINGO."

Step 5 ▶ As a class, check that the answers marked have been called.

Another Way to Play The first one to get a T, X, or Z marked on the bingo card wins. Or use 30 questions submitted by students and write the answers on the board. Create a new bingo card and fill it in with the answers on the board. Play like above.

EXAMPLE **Solve Systems of Equations by Substitution**

Solve the linear system using substitution.

$-x + y = 8$ Equation 1

$2x + 3y = -1$ Equation 2

Solution

❶ Solve for y in Equation 1 because it is easy to isolate y.

$-x + y = 8$ Original Equation 1

$y = x + 8$ Revised Equation 1

❷ Substitute $x + 8$ for y in Equation 2 and solve for x.

$2x + 3y = -1$ Original Equation 2

$2x + 3(x + 8) = -1$ Substitute $x + 8$ for y in Equation 2.

$5x + 24 = -1$ Simplify and combine like terms.

$5x = -25$ Subtract 24 from both sides and simplify.

$x = -5$ Divide each side by 5 and simplify.

❸ Substitute -5 for x in the revised Equation 1 and solve for y.

$y = x + 8 = -5 + 8 = 3$

❹ Check that $(-5, 3)$ is a solution by substituting -5 for x and 3 for y in each of the original equations.

Equation 1: $-x + y = 8$ Equation 2: $2x + 3y = -1$

$-(-5) + 3 \stackrel{?}{=} 8$ $2(-5) + 3(3) \stackrel{?}{=} -1$

$5 + 3 = 8$ ✓ $-10 + 9 = -1$ ✓

ANSWER ▶ The solution is $(-5, 3)$.

Try These

Use the substitution method to solve the linear system.

1. $x + y = 1$
    $4x + 5y = 7$

2. $x + 2y = 9$
    $3x - y = -1$

3. $3x + y = 3$
    $7x + 2y = 1$

4. $x - y = -4$
    $x + y = 16$

5. $-x + y = 1$
    $2x + y = 4$

6. $6x - y = 2$
    $4x + 3y = -6$

7. $2x + 3y = 5$
    $x - 4y = -3$

8. $-3x - 2y = -5$
    $-x + 3y = -9$

9. $5x + 2y = 7$
    $2x - 4y = 22$

Indirect Measurement

Objective

Use indirect measurement to estimate the heights of objects.

Materials
- measuring tape
- mirror
- protractor

How to Estimate the Height of a Tall Object

You can use similar triangles to estimate the height of a tall object.

Mirror Method

Place a mirror on the ground between yourself and the object. Step backward until you can see the top of the object in the mirror. Use similar triangles to estimate the height y of the object.

Shadow Method

Stand so that the top of your shadow coincides with the top of the object's shadow. You can use this statement to find the height y.

$$\frac{x}{\text{Your shadow}} = \frac{y}{\text{Object's shadow}}$$

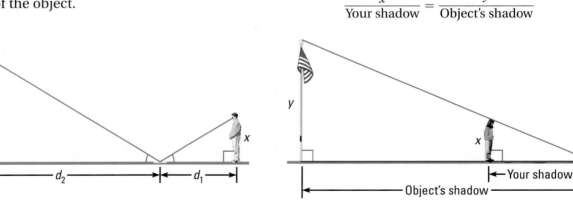

Investigation

1 Use the mirror method to estimate the heights of three objects outside, such as a tree or a building. Record your data in a table like the one below.

	Your distance from mirror, d_1	Your height, x	Distance from object to mirror, d_2	Height of object, y
Object 1	?	?	?	?
Object 2	?	?	?	?
Object 3	?	?	?	?

2 Use the shadow method to estimate the heights of the same three objects outside. Record your data in a table like the one below.

	Your height, x	Length of your shadow	Height of object, y	Length of object's shadow
Object 1	?	?	?	?
Object 2	?	?	?	?
Object 3	?	?	?	?

3 Compare the heights you found using the two methods.

Indirect Measurement

by
Jim Russsell
and
Robert Pike

Present Your Results

Write a report about the mirror and shadow methods of indirect measurement.

▶ Include your answers to Steps 1–3 of the Investigation.

▶ Use similar triangles to explain why each method works. Provide a diagram with each explanation.

▶ Compare the two methods. Which do you prefer? Describe any advantages or disadvantages of the methods.

Extension

Try another method for estimating height. Use the diagram at the right and follow the steps below.

▶ Stand and look at the top of the object.

▶ Use a protractor to estimate the value of a.

▶ Measure your distance b from the object.

▶ Use the tangent ratio to find c:

$$\tan a = \frac{\text{opposite side}}{\text{adjacent side}} = \frac{c}{b}$$

▶ Estimate the height of the object, $c + d$.

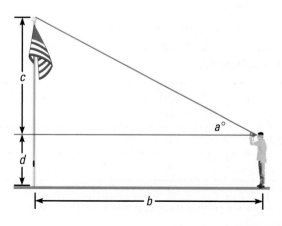

How far away can fireworks be seen?

If you watch fireworks as you sail out to sea on a clear night, the fireworks will gradually disappear over the horizon. When the ship is at point *E*, the fireworks are no longer visible.

3960 mi

Learn More About It

You will learn more about fireworks in Exercise 28 on p. 600.

Who uses Circles?

EMT
Some emergency medical technicians train for wilderness emergencies. They use the geometry of circles to find people trapped by avalanches. (p. 612)

GRAPHIC DESIGNER
Graphic designers may create symbols to represent a company or organization. These symbols often appear on packaging, stationery, and Web sites. (p. 638)

How will you use these ideas?

- Calculate how far global positioning systems can transmit signals. (p. 599)
- Find the time difference between cities. (p. 605)
- Design a logo for the Internet. (p. 624)
- Determine how cell phone towers transmit calls. (p. 631)
- Investigate patterns of rotational symmetry in art. (p. 638)

What's the chapter about?

- Identifying **parts of a circle** and studying their properties
- Writing **equations** of circles
- Identifying **rotations** in a plane

Key Words

- chord, *p. 589*
- secant, *p. 589*
- tangent, *p. 589*
- minor arc, *p. 601*
- major arc, *p. 601*

- arc length, *p. 603*
- inscribed angle, *p. 614*
- intercepted arc, *p. 614*
- rotation, *p. 633*
- rotational symmetry, *p. 634*

Chapter Readiness Quiz

Take this quick quiz. If you are unsure of an answer, look at the reference pages for help.

Vocabulary Check *(refer to p. 200)*

1. Which of the following represents side lengths of a right triangle?

(A) 5, 8, 10   (B) 12, 15, 20   (C) 4, 12, 13   (D) 16, 30, 34

Skill Check *(refer to pp. 283, 673)*

2. A segment has endpoints $C(2, 1)$ and $D(5, 4)$. What are the endpoints of the segment after it is reflected in the y-axis?

(F) $C'(-2, 1)$ (G) $C'(2, -1)$ (H) $C'(-2, -1)$ (J) $C'(-1, 2)$
     $D'(-5, 4)$ $D'(5, -4)$ $D'(-5, -4)$ $D'(-4, 5)$

3. What is the value of x in the equation $5x - 8 = 2x + 7$?

(A) $\frac{1}{3}$ (B) 2   (C) 3   (D) 5

Marking Diagrams

Visualize It! ⟹

As you solve exercises, copy diagrams and add information as you learn it.

$m\overset{\frown}{NM} = 55°$

$m\overset{\frown}{NM} = 55°$
$m\angle MQK = 180° - 55°$
$\qquad\qquad = 125°$

11.1 Parts of a Circle

Goal
Identify segments and lines related to circles.

Key Words
- chord
- diameter p. 452
- radius p. 452
- secant
- tangent
- point of tangency

The diagrams below show special segments and lines of a circle.

A **chord** is a segment whose endpoints are points on a circle.

A *diameter* is a chord that passes through the center of a circle.

A *radius* is a segment whose endpoints are the center of a circle and a point on the circle.

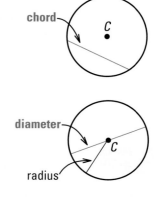

A **secant** is a line that intersects a circle in two points.

A **tangent** is a line in the plane of a circle that intersects the circle in exactly one point. The point is called a **point of tangency**.

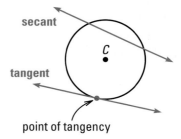

Student Help

STUDY TIP
To identify a circle, you can name the point that is the center of the circle. In Example 1, *C* is the center, so the circle is called ⊙*C*.

EXAMPLE 1 Identify Special Segments and Lines

Tell whether the line or segment is best described as a *chord*, a *secant*, a *tangent*, a *diameter*, or a *radius* of ⊙*C*.

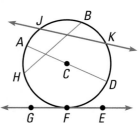

a. $\overline{AD}$ **b.** $\overline{HB}$

c. $\overleftrightarrow{EG}$ **d.** $\overleftrightarrow{JK}$

Solution

a. $\overline{AD}$ is a diameter because it passes through the center *C* and its endpoints are points on the circle.

b. $\overline{HB}$ is a chord because its endpoints are on the circle.

c. $\overleftrightarrow{EG}$ is a tangent because it intersects the circle in exactly one point.

d. $\overleftrightarrow{JK}$ is a secant because it intersects the circle in two points.

Student Help

VOCABULARY TIP
The plural of *radius* is *radii*.

EXAMPLE 2 Name Special Segments, Lines, and Points

Identify a chord, a secant, a tangent, a diameter, two radii, the center, and a point of tangency.

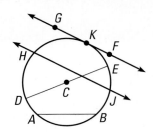

Solution

$\overline{AB}$ is a chord. $\overleftrightarrow{HJ}$ is a secant.

$\overleftrightarrow{FG}$ is a tangent. $\overline{DE}$ is a diameter.

$\overline{DC}$ is a radius. $\overline{CE}$ is a radius.

C is the center. *K* is a point of tangency.

Student Help

CLASSZONE.COM

MORE EXAMPLES
More examples at classzone.com

EXAMPLE 3 Circles in Coordinate Geometry

When a circle lies in a coordinate plane, you can use coordinates to describe particular points of the circle.

a. Name the coordinates of the center of each circle.

b. Name the coordinates of the intersection of the two circles.

c. What is the line that is tangent to both circles? Name the coordinates of the point of tangency.

d. What is the length of the diameter of ⊙*B*? What is the length of the radius of ⊙*A*?

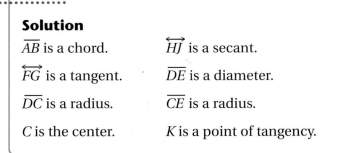

Solution

a. The center of ⊙*A* is *A*(4, 4). The center of ⊙*B* is *B*(4, 2).

b. The intersection of the two circles is the point (4, 0).

c. The *x*-axis is tangent to both circles. The point of tangency is (4, 0).

d. The diameter of ⊙*B* is 4. The radius of ⊙*A* is 4.

Checkpoint ✓ Parts of a Circle

1. Identify a chord, a secant, a tangent, a diameter, a radius, the center, and a point of tangency.

2. In Example 3, name the coordinates of the point of tangency of the *y*-axis to ⊙*A*.

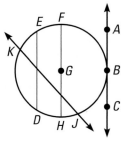

Guided Practice

Vocabulary Check

1. Sketch a circle. Then sketch and label a *radius*, a *diameter*, a *chord*, and a *tangent*.

Skill Check

Match the part of the circle with the term that best describes it.

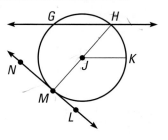

2. $\overline{GH}$ **A.** Center

3. M **B.** Chord

4. $\overline{JM}$ **C.** Diameter

5. J **D.** Radius

6. $\overline{MH}$ **E.** Point of tangency

7. $\overleftrightarrow{GH}$ **F.** Secant

Use the circle to name the coordinates of the points.

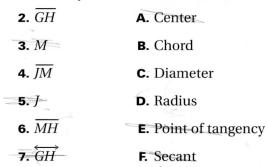

8. center

9. endpoints of a diameter

10. a point of tangency

11. endpoints of a chord that is not a diameter

12. endpoints of a radius

Practice and Applications

Extra Practice

See p. 695.

Finding Radii The diameter of a circle is given. Find the radius.

13. $d = 15$ cm   14. $d = 6.5$ in.   15. $d = 3$ ft   16. $d = 8$ m

Finding Diameters The radius of a circle is given. Find the diameter.

17. $r = 26$ in.   18. $r = 62$ ft   19. $r = 8.7$ m   20. $r = 4.4$ cm

Identifying Terms Name the term that best describes the given line, segment, or point.

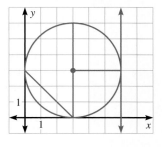

21. $\overleftrightarrow{CD}$ 22. $\overleftrightarrow{FG}$

23. $\overline{EC}$ 24. $\overline{AB}$

25. H 26. A

Homework Help

Example 1: Exs. 21–32
Example 2: Exs. 33–39
Example 3: Exs. 40–47

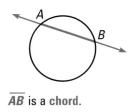

Visualize It!

A **chord** is a segment.
A **secant** is a line.

$\overline{AB}$ is a chord.

$\overleftrightarrow{AB}$ is a secant.

Identifying Terms **Tell whether the line or segment is best described as a *chord*, a *secant*, a *tangent*, a *diameter*, or a *radius*.**

27. $\overline{PZ}$ **28.** $\overline{RT}$

29. $\overline{ST}$ **30.** $\overleftrightarrow{PZ}$

31. $\overleftrightarrow{VW}$ **32.** $\overleftrightarrow{TU}$

Identifying Terms **Identify a chord, a secant, a diameter, a radius, and a point of tangency.**

33.

34.

35.

Link to Geography

MEXCALTITÁN is a tiny island located on the west coast of Mexico. Its settlement follows the circular shape of the island.

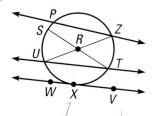

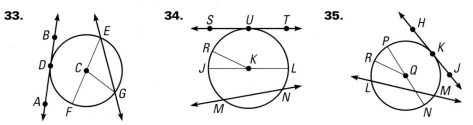

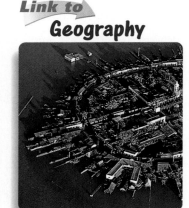

Island Map **The diagram shows the layout of the streets on Mexcaltitán Island.**

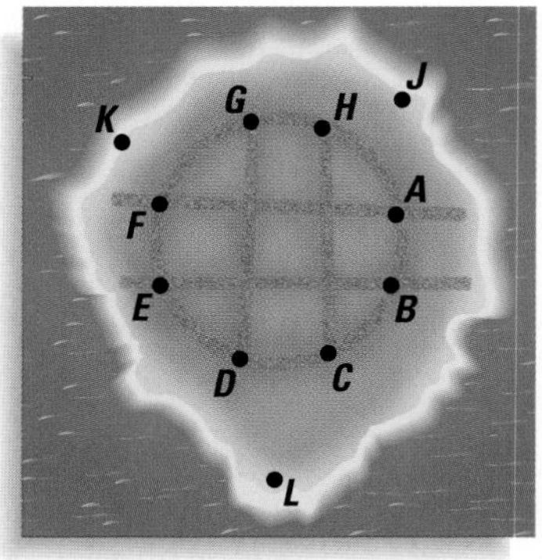

36. Name two secants.

37. Name two chords.

38. Is the diameter of the circle longer than $\overline{HC}$? Explain.

39. Can you draw a line through three of the given points that is tangent to the circle?

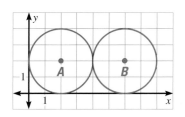

Coordinate Geometry **Use the diagram below.**

40. What are the coordinates of the center of $\odot A$? of $\odot B$?

41. What is the length of the radius of $\odot A$? of $\odot B$?

42. Name the coordinates of the intersection of the two circles.

Coordinate Geometry **Name the coordinates of the center of each circle, identify the point of intersection of the circles, and identify a line that is tangent to both circles.**

43.

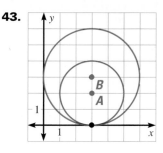

44.

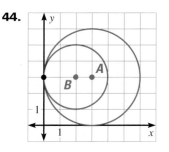

Coordinate Geometry Use the diagram below.

45. What are the lengths of the radius and the diameter of the circle?

46. Find the length of the chord $\overline{AB}$.

47. Copy the diagram and sketch a tangent that passes through A.

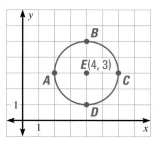

In Exercises 48 and 49, use the diagram below.

48. Multiple Choice Which of the following is a secant?

    Ⓐ $\overleftrightarrow{EF}$ Ⓑ $\overleftrightarrow{GH}$

    Ⓒ $\overline{AB}$ Ⓓ $\overrightarrow{EF}$

49. Multiple Choice Which of the following is a tangent?

    Ⓕ $\overleftrightarrow{EF}$ Ⓖ $\overleftrightarrow{GH}$

    Ⓗ $\overline{AB}$ Ⓙ $\overline{AC}$

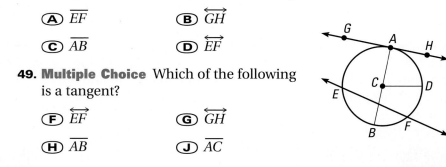

Mixed Review

Congruent Triangles Tell which theorem or postulate you can use to show that the triangles are congruent. Explain your reasoning. *(Lessons 5.2-5.4)*

50.   **51.**   **52.**

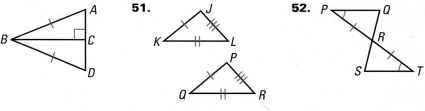

Coordinate Geometry Plot the points and draw the quadrilateral. Use the slopes of the segments to determine whether the quadrilateral is a parallelogram. *(Lesson 6.3)*

53. $A(0, 0)$, $B(1, 3)$, $C(5, 3)$, $D(4, 0)$ **54.** $P(2, 1)$, $Q(0, 5)$, $R(2, 5)$, $S(4, 1)$

Algebra Skills

Simplifying Radicals Find the square root. Round your answer to the nearest tenth. *(Lesson 10.1)*

55. $\sqrt{32}$ **56.** $\sqrt{81}$ **57.** $\sqrt{40}$ **58.** $\sqrt{104}$

59. $\sqrt{98}$ **60.** $\sqrt{192}$ **61.** $\sqrt{250}$ **62.** $\sqrt{242}$

Solving Equations Solve the equation. *(Skills Review, p. 673)*

63. $2x + 5 = 19$ **64.** $7x - 7 = 14$ **65.** $5x + 9 = 4$

66. $3x - 10 = 20$ **67.** $12 - 8x = 84$ **68.** $4x + 3 = 23$

Activity 11.2 Tangents and Circles

Question

What is the relationship between a tangent and a circle?

Materials

- compass
- ruler
- protractor

Explore

1 Use your compass to draw a circle. Label the center *C*. Draw a point outside your circle. Label this point *P*.

2 Draw two lines tangent to $\odot C$ from point *P*. Label the points of tangency *M* and *N*. Draw the radii $\overline{CM}$ and $\overline{CN}$.

3 Use a ruler to measure the *tangent segments* $\overline{MP}$ and $\overline{NP}$. Use a protractor to measure $\angle CMP$ and $\angle CNP$.

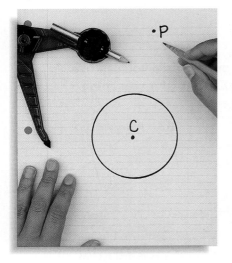

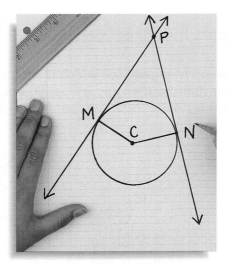

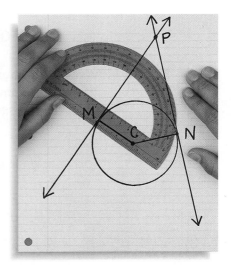

Think About It

1. Repeat Steps 1–3 for three circles of different sizes. Compare your results. Do your results depend on the size of the circle?
2. Make a conjecture about the lengths of the two tangent segments drawn to a circle from the same exterior point.
3. Make a conjecture about the angle formed by a tangent and the radius drawn to the point of tangency.

Student Help

Look Back
To review the definition of conjecture, see p. 8.

Properties of Tangents

11.2

Goal

Use properties of a tangent to a circle.

Key Words

- point of tangency p. 589
- perpendicular p. 108
- tangent segment

A discus thrower spins around in a circle one and a half times, then releases the discus. The discus forms a path tangent to the circle.

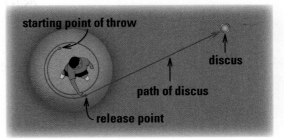

starting point of throw

discus

path of discus

release point

THEOREMS 11.1 and 11.2

Theorem 11.1

Words If a line is tangent to a circle, then it is perpendicular to the radius drawn at the point of tangency.

Symbols If ℓ is tangent to $\odot C$ at B, then $\ell \perp \overline{CB}$.

Theorem 11.2

Words In a plane, if a line is perpendicular to a radius of a circle at its endpoint on the circle, then the line is tangent to the circle.

Symbols If $\ell \perp \overline{CB}$, then ℓ is tangent to $\odot C$ at B.

Student Help

VOCABULARY TIP
Tangent is based on a Latin word meaning "to touch."

EXAMPLE 1 Use Properties of Tangents

$\overrightarrow{AC}$ is tangent to $\odot B$ at point C. Find BC.

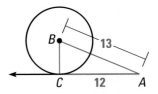

Solution

$\overline{BC}$ is a radius of $\odot B$, so you can apply Theorem 11.1 to conclude that $\overline{BC}$ and $\overrightarrow{AC}$ are perpendicular.

So, $\angle BCA$ is a right angle, and $\triangle BCA$ is a right triangle. To find BC, use the Pythagorean Theorem.

$(BA)^2 = (BC)^2 + (AC)^2$	Pythagorean Theorem
$13^2 = (BC)^2 + 12^2$	Substitute 13 for BA and 12 for AC.
$169 = (BC)^2 + 144$	Multiply.
$25 = (BC)^2$	Subtract 144 from each side.
$5 = BC$	Find the positive square root.

EXAMPLE 2 Find the Radius of a Circle

You are standing at C, 8 feet from a silo. The distance to a point of tangency is 16 feet. What is the radius of the silo?

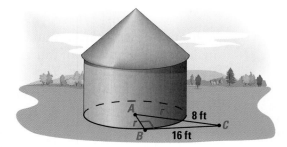

Solution

Tangent $\overleftrightarrow{BC}$ is perpendicular to radius $\overline{AB}$ at B, so $\triangle ABC$ is a right triangle. So, you can use the Pythagorean Theorem.

$(AC)^2 = (AB)^2 + (BC)^2$	Pythagorean Theorem
$(r + 8)^2 = r^2 + 16^2$	Substitute $r + 8$ for AC, r for AB, and 16 for BC.
$r^2 + 16r + 64 = r^2 + 256$	$(r + 8)(r + 8) = r^2 + 16r + 64$
$16r + 64 = 256$	Subtract r^2 from each side.
$16r = 192$	Subtract 64 from each side.
$r = 12$	Divide each side by 16.

ANSWER ▶ The radius of the silo is 12 feet.

You can use the Converse of the Pythagorean Theorem to show that a line is tangent to a circle.

EXAMPLE 3 Verify a Tangent to a Circle

How can you show that $\overleftrightarrow{EF}$ must be tangent to $\odot D$?

Student Help

LOOK BACK
To review the Converse of the Pythagorean Theorem, see p. 200.

Solution

Use the Converse of the Pythagorean Theorem to determine whether $\triangle DEF$ is a right triangle.

$(DF)^2 \stackrel{?}{=} (DE)^2 + (EF)^2$	Compare $(DF)^2$ with $(DE)^2 + (EF)^2$.
$15^2 \stackrel{?}{=} 9^2 + 12^2$	Substitute 15 for DF, 9 for DE, and 12 for EF.
$225 \stackrel{?}{=} 81 + 144$	Multiply.
$225 = 225$	Simplify.

$\triangle DEF$ is a right triangle with right angle E. So, $\overline{EF}$ is perpendicular to $\overline{DE}$. By Theorem 11.2, it follows that $\overleftrightarrow{EF}$ is tangent to $\odot D$.

VOCABULARY TIP
A tangent segment is
often simply called a
tangent.

Tangent Segment A **tangent segment** touches a circle at one of the segment's endpoints and lies in the line that is tangent to the circle at that point.

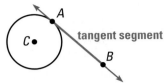

Activity 11.2, on page 594, shows that tangent segments from the same exterior point are congruent.

THEOREM 11.3

Words If two segments from the same point outside a circle are tangent to the circle, then they are congruent.

Symbols If $\overline{SR}$ and $\overline{ST}$ are tangent to $\odot P$ at points R and T, then $\overline{SR} \cong \overline{ST}$.

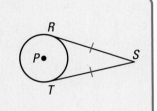

EXAMPLE 4 Use Properties of Tangents

$\overline{AB}$ is tangent to $\odot C$ at B.
$\overline{AD}$ is tangent to $\odot C$ at D.
Find the value of x.

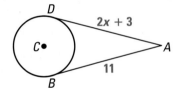

Student Help

SKILLS REVIEW
To review solving
equations, see p. 673.

Solution

$AD = AB$	Two tangent segments from the same point are congruent.
$2x + 3 = 11$	Substitute $2x + 3$ for AD and 11 for AB.
$2x = 8$	Subtract 3 from each side.
$x = 4$	Divide each side by 2.

Checkpoint ✓ **Use Properties of Tangents**

$\overline{CB}$ and $\overline{CD}$ are tangent to $\odot A$. Find the value of x.

1.

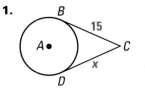

2.

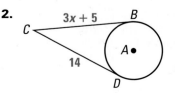

Guided Practice

Vocabulary Check

1. Complete the statement: In the diagram at the right, $\overleftrightarrow{AB}$ is __?__ to $\odot C$, and point B is the __?__.

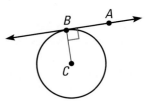

Skill Check

2. In the diagram below, $\overleftrightarrow{XY}$ is tangent to $\odot C$ at point P. What is $m\angle CPX$? Explain.

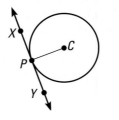

3. In the diagram below, $AB = BD = 5$ and $AD = 7$. Is $\overline{BD}$ tangent to $\odot C$? Explain.

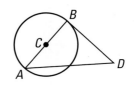

$\overline{AB}$ is tangent to $\odot C$ at A and $\overline{DB}$ is tangent to $\odot C$ at D. Find the value of x.

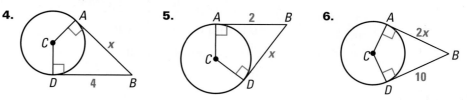

4.   **5.**   **6.**

Practice and Applications

Extra Practice
See p. 695.

Finding Segment Lengths $\overleftrightarrow{AB}$ is tangent to $\odot C$. Find the value of r.

7.   **8.**   **9.**

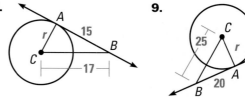

Finding Segment Lengths $\overline{AB}$ and $\overline{AD}$ are tangent to $\odot C$. Find the value of x.

Homework Help

Example 1: Exs. 7–9, 27
Example 2: Exs. 13–19
Example 3: Exs. 20–21
Example 4: Exs. 10–12, 22–26

10.   **11.**   **12.**

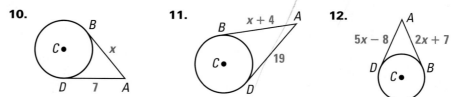
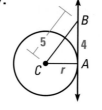

Using Algebra Square the binomial.

13. $(x + 2)^2$ **14.** $(x + 4)^2$ **15.** $(x + 7)^2$ **16.** $(x + 12)^2$

Finding the Radius of a Circle $\overline{AB}$ is tangent to $\odot C$. Find the value of r.

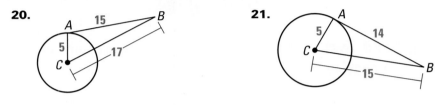

17.   **18.**   **19.**

Verifying Tangents Tell whether $\overline{AB}$ is tangent to $\odot C$. Explain your reasoning.

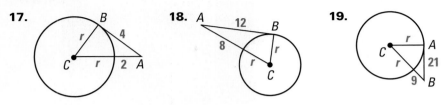

20.   **21.**

Finding Congruent Parts In Exercises 22–24, $\overline{AB}$ and $\overline{AD}$ are tangent to $\odot C$.

22. Name all congruent segments.

23. Name all congruent angles.

24. Name two congruent triangles.

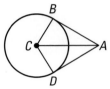

Visualize It! In Exercises 25 and 26, $\odot L$ has radii $\overline{LJ}$ and $\overline{LK}$ that are perpendicular. $\overline{KM}$ and $\overline{JM}$ are tangent to $\odot L$.

25. Sketch $\odot L$, $\overline{LJ}$, $\overline{LK}$, $\overline{KM}$, and $\overline{JM}$.

26. Is $\triangle JLM$ congruent to $\triangle KLM$? Explain your reasoning.

27. Global Positioning System GPS satellites orbit 12,500 miles above Earth. Because GPS signals can't travel through Earth, a satellite can transmit signals only as far as points A and C from point B. Find BA and BC to the nearest mile.

GPS Hikers sometimes carry navigation devices which utilize GPS technology. GPS helps hikers calculate where they are and how to get to another location.

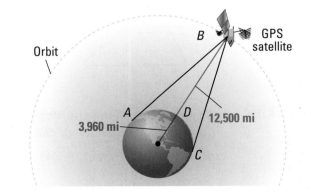

Orbit

B GPS satellite

A D 12,500 mi

3,960 mi

C

Student Help

LOOK BACK
For more about fireworks, see p. 586.

28. Challenge You are cruising away from a fireworks show over a bay at point *A*. The highest point of the fireworks is point *F*. When your ship reaches point *D*, you can no longer see the fireworks over the horizon. You are standing at point *E*. $\overline{FE}$ is tangent to Earth at *B*. Find *FE*. Round your answer to the nearest mile.

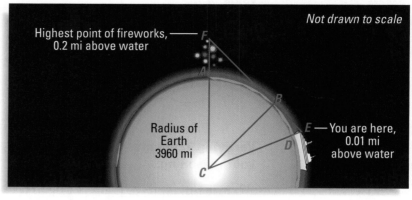

Not drawn to scale

Highest point of fireworks, — *F*
0.2 mi above water

Radius of
Earth
3960 mi

E — You are here,
0.01 mi
above water

Standardized Test Practice

29. Multiple Choice In the diagram below, $\overline{EF}$ and $\overline{EG}$ are tangent to ⊙*C*. What is the value of *x*?

Ⓐ −4   Ⓑ −1

Ⓒ 1   Ⓓ 4

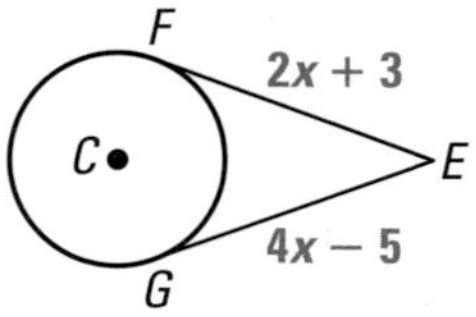

$2x + 3$

$4x - 5$

30. Multiple Choice In the diagram below, $\overline{SR}$ is tangent to ⊙*P*. Find the radius of ⊙*P*.

Ⓕ 18   Ⓖ 27

Ⓗ 36   Ⓙ 45

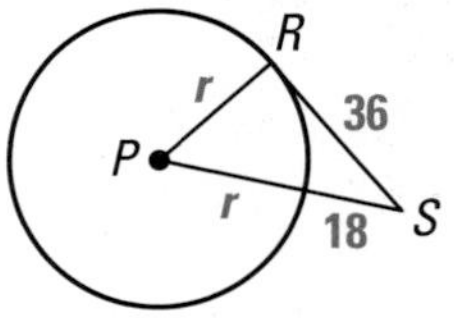

r
36
r
18

Mixed Review

Using the Triangle Inequality Can the side lengths form a triangle? Explain. *(Lesson 4.7)*

31. 5, 11, 14   **32.** 8, 14, 23   **33.** 15, 3, 13

34. 18, 25, 9   **35.** 10, 3, 7   **36.** 22, 6, 29

Using the Midsegment Theorem Find the value of *x*. *(Lesson 7.5)*

37.   **38.** 24   **39.**

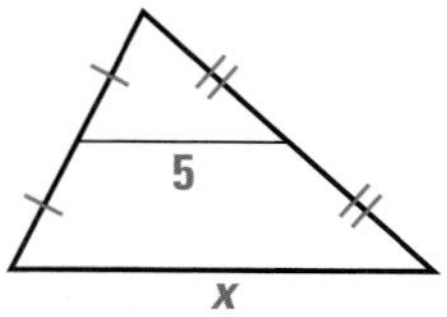

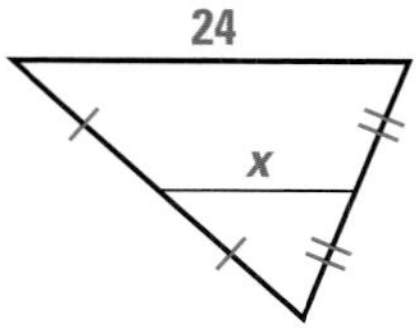

5   *x*   *x*

x   38

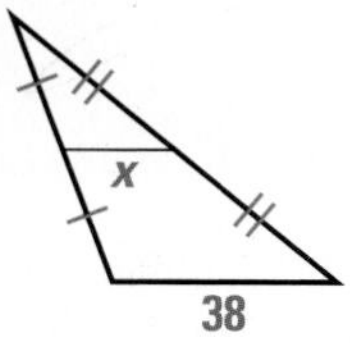

Algebra Skills

Finding Slope Find the slope of the line that passes through the points. *(Skills Review, p. 665)*

40. (0, 0) and (−3, 6)   **41.** (2, 4) and (8, 0)   **42.** (1, 5) and (−2, 1)

43. (0, −3) and (4, 7)   **44.** (−1, 6) and (4, −5)   **45.** (−7, 2) and (−1, 4)

Arcs and Central Angles

Goal
Use properties of arcs of circles.

Key Words
- minor arc
- major arc
- semicircle
- congruent circles
- congruent arcs
- arc length

Any two points *A* and *B* on a circle *C* determine a *minor arc* and a *major arc* (unless the points lie on a diameter).

If the measure of ∠*ACB* is less than 180°, then *A*, *B*, and all the points on ⊙*C* that lie in the interior of ∠*ACB* form a **minor arc**.

Points *A*, *B*, and all the points on ⊙*C* that do not lie on $\overset{\frown}{AB}$ form a **major arc**.

You name an arc by its endpoints. Use one other point on a major arc as part of its name to distinguish it from the minor arc.

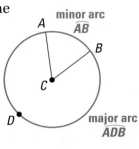

The *measures* of a minor arc and a major arc depend on the central angle of the minor arc.

Student Help

LOOK BACK
For the definition of a central angle, see p. 454.

The **measure of a minor arc** is the measure of its central angle.

The **measure of a major arc** is the difference of 360° and the measure of the related minor arc.

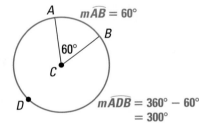

A **semicircle** is an arc whose central angle measures 180°. A semicircle is named by three points. Its measure is 180°.

EXAMPLE **1** **Name and Find Measures of Arcs**

Name the red arc and identify the type of arc. Then find its measure.

a.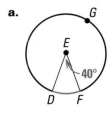

b.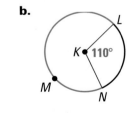

Solution

a. $\overset{\frown}{DF}$ is a minor arc. Its measure is 40°.

b. $\overset{\frown}{LMN}$ is a major arc. Its measure is 360° − 110° = 250°.

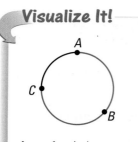

Arcs of a circle are *adjacent* if they intersect *only* at their endpoints.

$\overset{\frown}{AB}$ and $\overset{\frown}{BC}$ are adjacent.

POSTULATE 16

Arc Addition Postulate

Words The measure of an arc formed by two adjacent arcs is the sum of the measures of the two arcs.

Symbols $m\overset{\frown}{ACB} = m\overset{\frown}{AC} + m\overset{\frown}{CB}$

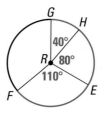

EXAMPLE 2 Find Measures of Arcs

Find the measure of $\overset{\frown}{GEF}$.

Solution

$$m\overset{\frown}{GEF} = m\overset{\frown}{GH} + m\overset{\frown}{HE} + m\overset{\frown}{EF}$$
$$= 40° + 80° + 110°$$
$$= 230°$$

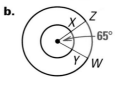

Two circles are **congruent circles** if they have the same radius. Two arcs of the same circle or of congruent circles are **congruent arcs** if they have the same measure.

EXAMPLE 3 Identify Congruent Arcs

Find the measures of the blue arcs. Are the arcs congruent?

a.
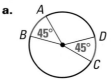

b.

Solution

a. Notice that $\overset{\frown}{AB}$ and $\overset{\frown}{DC}$ are in the same circle. Because $m\overset{\frown}{AB} = m\overset{\frown}{DC} = 45°$, $\overset{\frown}{AB} \cong \overset{\frown}{DC}$.

b. Notice that $\overset{\frown}{XY}$ and $\overset{\frown}{ZW}$ are not in the same circle or in congruent circles. Therefore, although $m\overset{\frown}{XY} = m\overset{\frown}{ZW} = 65°$, $\overset{\frown}{XY} \not\cong \overset{\frown}{ZW}$.

Checkpoint ✓ Identify Congruent Arcs

Find the measures of the arcs. Are the arcs congruent?

1. $\overset{\frown}{BC}$ and $\overset{\frown}{EF}$

2. $\overset{\frown}{BC}$ and $\overset{\frown}{CD}$

3. $\overset{\frown}{CD}$ and $\overset{\frown}{DE}$

4. $\overset{\frown}{BFE}$ and $\overset{\frown}{CBF}$

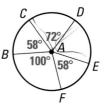

Student Help

SKILLS REVIEW
To review finding circumference of a circle, see p. 674.

Arc Length An **arc length** is a portion of the circumference of a circle. You can write a proportion to find *arc length*.

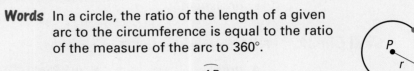

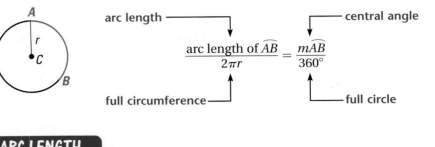

ARC LENGTH

Words In a circle, the ratio of the length of a given arc to the circumference is equal to the ratio of the measure of the arc to 360°.

Symbols Arc length of $\overset{\frown}{AB} = \dfrac{m\overset{\frown}{AB}}{360°} \cdot 2\pi r$

EXAMPLE 4 Find Arc Lengths

Find the length of the red arc.

a.
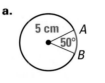

b.

c.

Student Help

STUDY TIP
You can substitute 3.14 as an approximation of π or use a calculator.

Solution

a. Arc length of $\overset{\frown}{AB} = \dfrac{50°}{360°} \cdot 2\pi(5) \approx 4.36$ centimeters

b. Arc length of $\overset{\frown}{CD} = \dfrac{50°}{360°} \cdot 2\pi(7) \approx 6.11$ centimeters

c. Arc length of $\overset{\frown}{EF} = \dfrac{98°}{360°} \cdot 2\pi(7) \approx 11.97$ centimeters

Checkpoint ✓ *Find Arc Lengths*

Find the length of the red arc. Round your answer to the nearest hundredth.

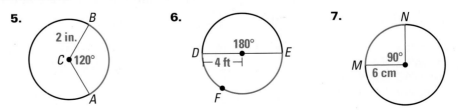

5.

6.

7.

11.3 Exercises

Guided Practice

Vocabulary Check

1. In the diagram at the right, identify a *major arc*, a *minor arc*, and a *semicircle*.

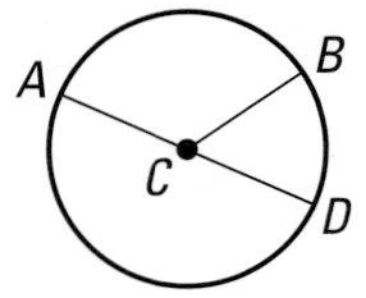

2. Draw a circle with a pair of congruent arcs.

3. What is the difference between *arc measure* and *arc length*?

Skill Check

Find the measure in ⊙T.

4. $m\widehat{RS}$

5. $m\widehat{RPS}$

6. $m\widehat{PQR}$

7. $m\widehat{QS}$

8. $m\widehat{QSP}$

9. $m\angle QTR$

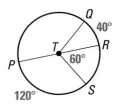

Find the blue arc length. Round your answer to the nearest hundredth.

10. Length of $\widehat{AB}$

11. Length of $\widehat{DE}$

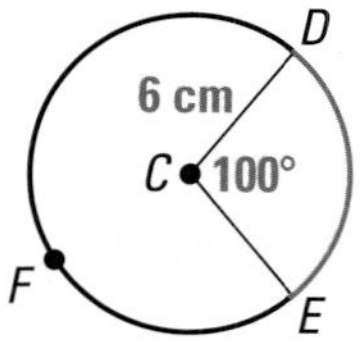

12. Length of $\widehat{FGH}$

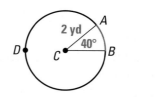

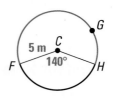

Practice and Applications

Extra Practice

See p. 695.

Naming Arcs Name the blue minor arc and find its measure.

13.

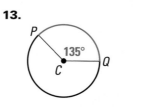

14.

15.

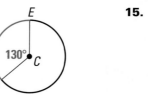

Naming Arcs Name the blue major arc and find its measure.

Homework Help

Example 1: Exs. 13–39
Example 2: Exs. 30–42
Example 3: Exs. 43–46
Example 4: Exs. 47–54

16.

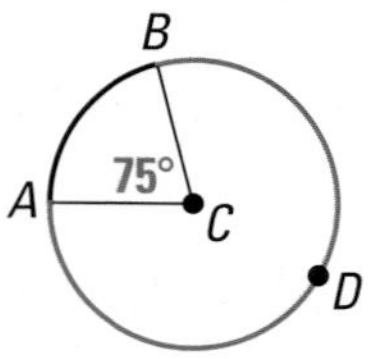

17.

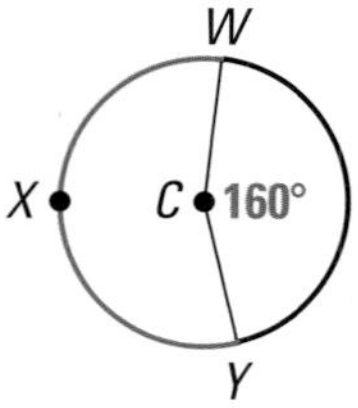

18.

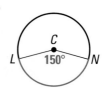

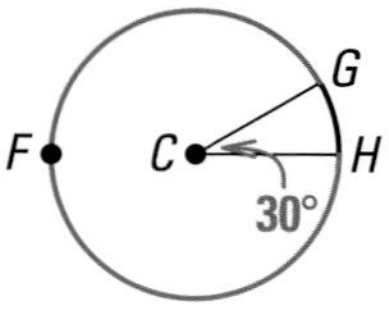

Types of Arcs Determine whether the arc is a *minor arc*, a *major arc*, or a *semicircle* of ⊙R. $\overline{PT}$ and $\overline{QU}$ are diameters.

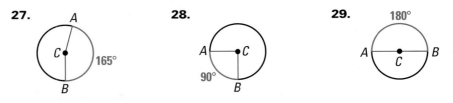

19. $\widehat{PQ}$

20. $\widehat{SU}$

21. $\widehat{PQT}$

22. $\widehat{QT}$

23. $\widehat{TUQ}$

24. $\widehat{TUP}$

25. $\widehat{QUT}$

26. $\widehat{PUQ}$

Finding the Central Angle Find the measure of ∠*ACB*.

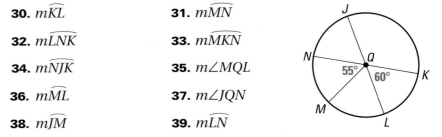

27. 165°

28. 90°

29. 180°

Student Help

VISUAL STRATEGY
In Exs. 30–39, copy the diagram and add information to it as you solve the exercises, as shown on p. 588.

Measuring Arcs and Central Angles $\overline{KN}$ and $\overline{JL}$ are diameters. Find the measure.

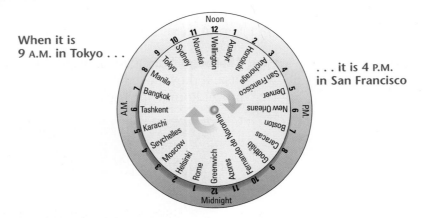

30. $m\widehat{KL}$

31. $m\widehat{MN}$

32. $m\widehat{LNK}$

33. $m\widehat{MKN}$

34. $m\widehat{NJK}$

35. $m\angle MQL$

36. $m\widehat{ML}$

37. $m\angle JQN$

38. $m\widehat{JM}$

39. $m\widehat{LN}$

Time Zone Wheel In Exercises 40–42, use the following information.
To find the time in Tokyo when it is 4 P.M. in San Francisco, rotate the small wheel until 4 P.M. and San Francisco line up as shown. Then look at Tokyo to see that it is 9 A.M. there.

When it is 9 A.M. in Tokyo . . .

. . . it is 4 P.M. in San Francisco

40. What is the arc measure for each time zone on the wheel?

41. What is the measure of the minor arc from the Tokyo zone to the Anchorage zone?

42. If two cities differ by 180° on the wheel, then it is 3:00 P.M. in one city when it is ___?___ in the other city.

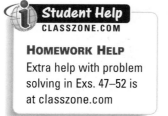
Naming Congruent Arcs Are the blue arcs congruent? Explain.

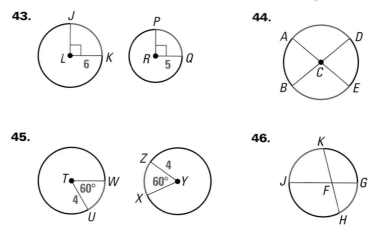

43.

44.

45.

46.

Finding Arc Length Find the length of $\overset{\frown}{AB}$. Round your answer to the nearest hundredth.

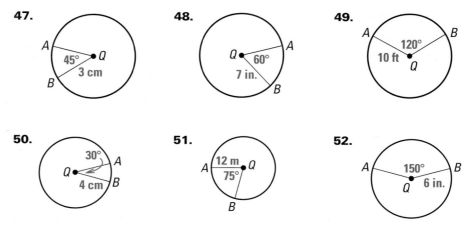

47.

48.

49.

50.

51.

52.

53. **You be the Judge** A friend tells you two arcs from different circles have the same arc length if their central angles are equal. Is your friend correct? Explain your reasoning.

54. **Challenge** Engineers reduced the lean of the Leaning Tower of Pisa. If they moved it back 0.46°, what was the arc length of the move? Round your answer to the nearest whole number.

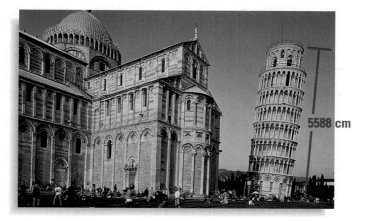

5588 cm

55. Multiple Choice What is the length of $\overset{\frown}{AC}$ in $\odot P$ shown below?

    Ⓐ 5.6 ft   **Ⓑ** 16.8 ft

    Ⓒ 19.5 ft   **Ⓓ** 25.1 ft

Mixed Review

Finding Leg Lengths Find the lengths of the legs of the triangle. Round your answers to the nearest tenth. *(Lesson 10.5)*

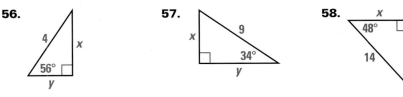

56.   **57.**   **58.**

Algebra Skills

Simplifying Ratios Simplify the ratio. *(Skills Review, p. 660)*

59. $\dfrac{2 \text{ km}}{400 \text{ km}}$ **60.** $\dfrac{5 \text{ ft}}{72 \text{ in.}}$ **61.** $\dfrac{3 \text{ yards}}{27 \text{ ft}}$ **62.** $\dfrac{4 \text{ ounces}}{8 \text{ pounds}}$

Quiz 1

Tell whether the given line, segment, or point is best described as a *chord*, a *secant*, a *tangent*, a *diameter*, a *radius*, or a *point of tangency*. *(Lesson 11.1)*

    1. $\overleftrightarrow{AB}$ **2.** $\overleftrightarrow{JH}$

    3. $\overline{GE}$ **4.** $\overline{JH}$

    5. $\overline{CE}$ **6.** D

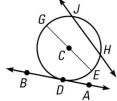

$\overline{PQ}$ and $\overline{PR}$ are tangent to $\odot C$. Find the value of *x*. *(Lesson 11.2)*

7.   **8.**   **9.**

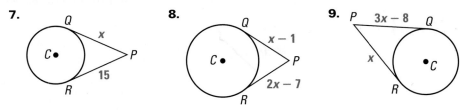

Find the length of $\overset{\frown}{AB}$. Round your answer to the nearest hundredth. *(Lesson 11.3)*

10.   **11.**   **12.**

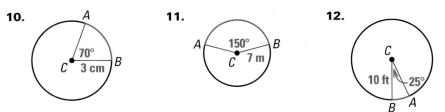

11.4 # Arcs and Chords

Goal
Use properties of chords of circles.

Key Words
- congruent arcs p. 602
- perpendicular bisector p. 274

By finding the perpendicular bisectors of two chords, an archaeologist can recreate a whole plate from just one piece.

This approach relies on Theorem 11.5, and is shown in Example 2.

THEOREM 11.4

Words If a diameter of a circle is perpendicular to a chord, then the diameter bisects the chord and its arc.

Symbols If $\overline{BG} \perp \overline{FD}$, then $\overline{DE} \cong \overline{EF}$ and $\overparen{DG} \cong \overparen{GF}$.

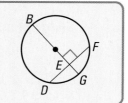

EXAMPLE 1 Find the Length of a Chord

In $\odot C$ the diameter $\overline{AF}$ is perpendicular to $\overline{BD}$. Use the diagram to find the length of $\overline{BD}$.

Solution

Because $\overline{AF}$ is a diameter that is perpendicular to $\overline{BD}$, you can use Theorem 11.4 to conclude that $\overline{AF}$ bisects $\overline{BD}$. So, $BE = ED = 5$.

$$BD = BE + ED \qquad \text{Segment Addition Postulate}$$
$$= 5 + 5 \qquad \text{Substitute 5 for } BE \text{ and } ED.$$
$$= 10 \qquad \text{Simplify.}$$

ANSWER ▶ The length of $\overline{BD}$ is 10.

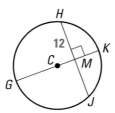 **Checkpoint** ✓ **Find the Length of a Segment**

1. Find the length of $\overline{JM}$.

2. Find the length of $\overline{SR}$.

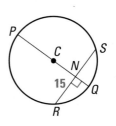

THEOREM 11.5

Words If one chord is a perpendicular bisector of another chord, then the first chord is a diameter.

Symbols If $\overline{JK} \perp \overline{ML}$ and $\overline{MP} \cong \overline{PL}$, then $\overline{JK}$ is a diameter.

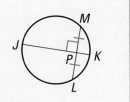

All diameters of a circle include the center of the circle. Therefore, the point where two diameters intersect is the center of the circle.

EXAMPLE 2 Find the Center of a Circle

Suppose an archaeologist finds part of a circular plate. Show how to reconstruct the original shape of the plate.

Solution

❶ Draw any two chords that are not parallel to each other.

❷ Draw the perpendicular bisector of each chord. These lines contain diameters.

❸ The diameters intersect at the circle's center. Use a compass to draw the rest of the plate.

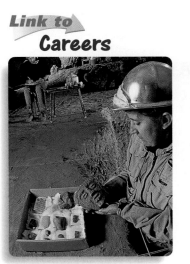

THEOREM 11.6

Words In the same circle, or in congruent circles:
- If two chords are congruent, then their corresponding minor arcs are congruent.
- If two minor arcs are congruent, then their corresponding chords are congruent.

Symbols If $\overline{AB} \cong \overline{DC}$, then $\overset{\frown}{AB} \cong \overset{\frown}{DC}$.
If $\overset{\frown}{AB} \cong \overset{\frown}{DC}$, then $\overline{AB} \cong \overline{DC}$.

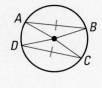

Student Help

STUDY TIP
In the same circle or in congruent circles, if two central angles are congruent then their corresponding arcs are congruent.

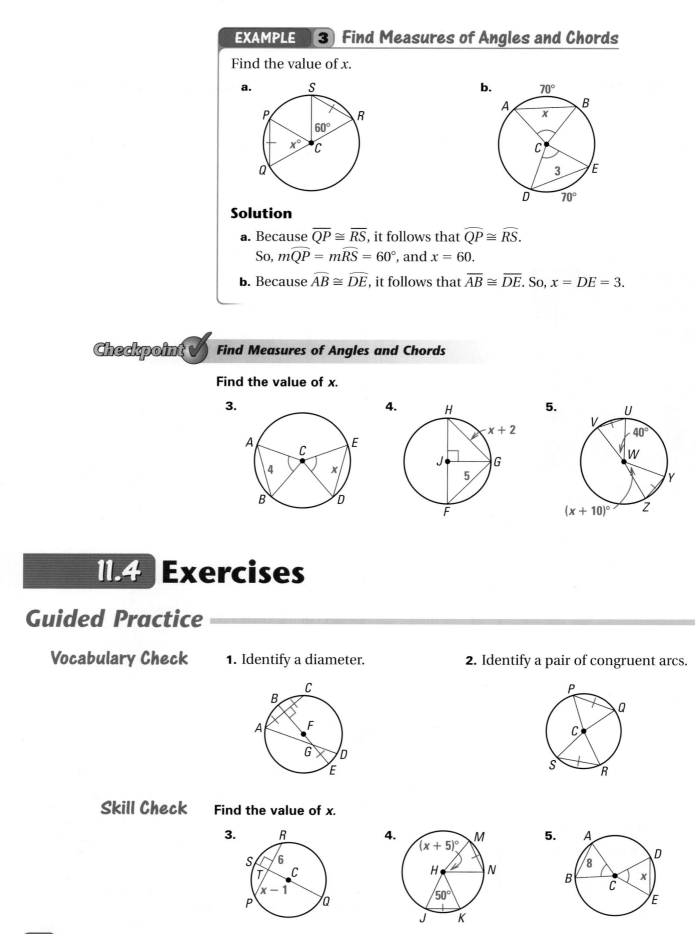

EXAMPLE 3 Find Measures of Angles and Chords

Find the value of x.

a.

S

P   R
        60°
    x° C

Q

b.

        70°
A   B
        x
    C
            3
                E
D   70°

Solution

a. Because $\overline{QP} \cong \overline{RS}$, it follows that $\overset{\frown}{QP} \cong \overset{\frown}{RS}$.
So, $m\overset{\frown}{QP} = m\overset{\frown}{RS} = 60°$, and $x = 60$.

b. Because $\overset{\frown}{AB} \cong \overset{\frown}{DE}$, it follows that $\overline{AB} \cong \overline{DE}$. So, $x = DE = 3$.

Checkpoint ✓ **Find Measures of Angles and Chords**

Find the value of x.

3.

A   E
    C
4   x
B   D

4.

        H
            x + 2
J   G
    5
F

5.

        U
V   40°
    W
            Y
(x + 10)°   Z

11.4 Exercises

Guided Practice

Vocabulary Check   **1.** Identify a diameter.

        C
    B
A   F
    G   D
        E

2. Identify a pair of congruent arcs.

        P
            Q
    C
S   R

Skill Check   **Find the value of x.**

3.

        R
S   6
    T   C
    x − 1
P   Q

4.

    (x + 5)°   M
H   N
    50°
    J   K

5.

        A
            D
    8
B   C   x
        E

Practice and Applications

Extra Practice

See p. 695.

Identifying Diameters Determine whether $\overline{AB}$ is a diameter of the circle. Explain your reasoning.

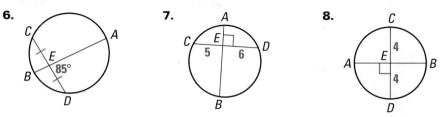

6.

7.

8.

Finding Chords and Central Angles Find the value of *x*.

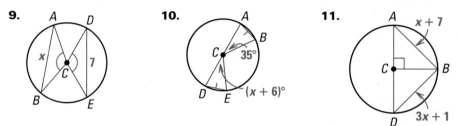

9.

10.

11.

Logical Reasoning Name any congruent arcs, chords, or angles. State a postulate or theorem that justifies your answer.

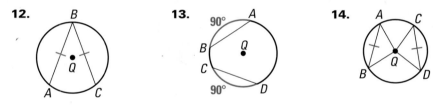

12.

13.

14.

Finding Measures Find the measure of the red segment or arc.

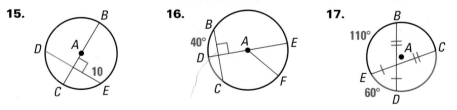

15.

16.

17.

(xy) **Using Algebra** Find the value of *x*.

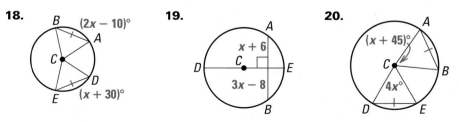

18.

19.

20.

Homework Help

Example 1: Exs. 6–8,
15–20
Example 2: Exs. 21–22
Example 3: Exs. 9–20

21. **Visualize It!** Draw a large circle and cut it out. Tear part of it off and ask another student to recreate your circle.

EMTS Some Emergency
Medical Technicians (EMTs)
train specifically for wilderness
emergencies.

Career Links
CLASSZONE.COM

22. Avalanche Rescue Beacon An avalanche rescue beacon is a device used by backcountry skiers. It gives off a signal that is detectable within a circle of a certain radius. In a practice drill, a ski patrol uses the following steps to locate a beacon buried in the snow. Explain how it works.

❶ Walk in a straight line until the signal disappears. Turn around and walk back until the signal disappears again.

❷ Walk back to the halfway point, and walk away from the line at a 90° angle until the signal disappears.

starting point

❸ Turn around and walk in a straight line until the signal disappears again.

❹ Walk back to the halfway point. You will be near the center of the circle. The beacon is under you.

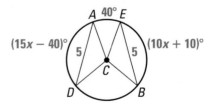

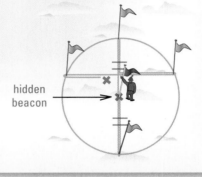

hidden beacon

Standardized Test Practice

23. Multi-Step Problem Use the diagram below.

    a. Explain why $\overarc{AD} \cong \overarc{BE}$.

    b. Find the value of x.

    c. Find $m\overarc{AD}$ and $m\overarc{BE}$.

    d. Find $m\overarc{BD}$.

A 40° E
(15x − 40)° 5   5 (10x + 10)°
C
D   B

Mixed Review

Measuring Arcs In the diagram below, $\overline{AD}$ and $\overline{BE}$ are diameters of $\odot F$. Find the measure. *(Lesson 11.3)*

24. $m\overarc{DE}$ **25.** $m\overarc{BC}$

26. $m\overarc{AE}$ **27.** $m\overarc{BCD}$

28. $m\overarc{ABC}$ **29.** $m\overarc{ADE}$

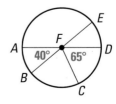

E
F
A 40° 65° D
B
C

Algebra Skills

Comparing Numbers Compare the two numbers. Write the answer using <, >, or =. *(Skills Review, p. 662)*

30. -26 and -29 **31.** $\frac{15}{20}$ and $-\frac{3}{4}$ **32.** 0.2 and $\frac{1}{5}$

Activity 11.5 Exploring Inscribed Angles

Question

How are inscribed angles related to central angles?

Materials

- compass
- straightedge
- protractor

Explore

1 Use a compass to draw a circle. Label the center *P*. Use a straightedge to draw a central angle. Label it $\angle RPS$.

2 Locate three points on $\odot P$ in the exterior of $\angle RPS$ and label them *T*, *U*, and *V*.

3 Draw $\angle RTS$, $\angle RUS$, and $\angle RVS$. These are called *inscribed angles*. Measure each angle.

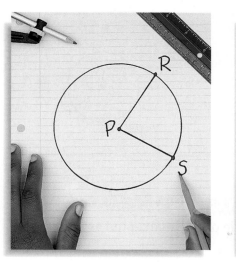

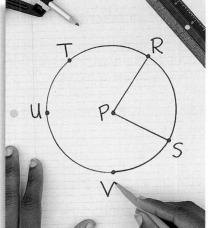

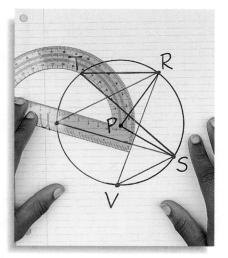

Think About It

1. Make a table similar to the one below. Record the angle measures for $\odot P$ in the table.

	Central Angle	Inscribed Angle 1	Inscribed Angle 2	Inscribed Angle 3
Name	$\angle RPS$	$\angle RTS$	$\angle RUS$	$\angle RVS$
Measure	?	?	?	?

Student Help

Look Back
To review the measures of central angles, see p. 454.

2. Draw two more circles. Repeat Steps 1–3, using different central angles. Record the measures in a table similar to the one above.

3. Use the results in your table to make a conjecture about how the measure of an inscribed angle is related to the measure of the corresponding central angle.

Inscribed Angles and Polygons

Goal
Use properties of inscribed angles.

Key Words
• inscribed angle
• intercepted arc
• inscribed
• circumscribed

An **inscribed angle** is an angle whose vertex is on a circle and whose sides contain chords of the circle.

The arc that lies in the interior of an inscribed angle and has endpoints on the angle is called the **intercepted arc** of the angle.

Activity 11.5 shows the relationship between an inscribed angle and its intercepted arc.

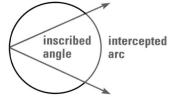

THEOREM 11.7

Measure of an Inscribed Angle

Words If an angle is inscribed in a circle, then its measure is half the measure of its intercepted arc.

Symbols $m\angle ADB = \frac{1}{2}m\widehat{AB}$

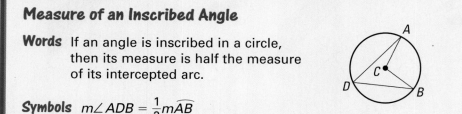

EXAMPLE 1 Find Measures of Inscribed Angles and Arcs

Find the measure of the inscribed angle or the intercepted arc.

a.

b.

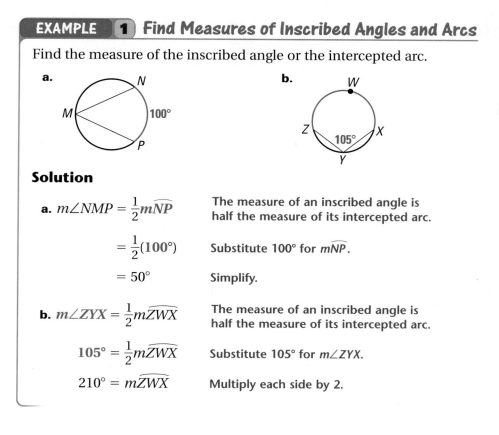

Student Help
CLASSZONE.COM

MORE EXAMPLES
More examples at classzone.com

Solution

a. $m\angle NMP = \frac{1}{2}m\widehat{NP}$ The measure of an inscribed angle is half the measure of its intercepted arc.

$= \frac{1}{2}(100°)$ Substitute 100° for $m\widehat{NP}$.

$= 50°$ Simplify.

b. $m\angle ZYX = \frac{1}{2}m\widehat{ZWX}$ The measure of an inscribed angle is half the measure of its intercepted arc.

$105° = \frac{1}{2}m\widehat{ZWX}$ Substitute 105° for $m\angle ZYX$.

$210° = m\widehat{ZWX}$ Multiply each side by 2.

Find the measure of the inscribed angle or the intercepted arc.

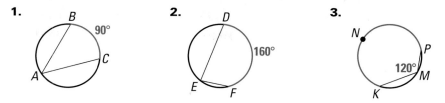

1.   **2.**   **3.**

Inscribed and Circumscribed If all the vertices of a polygon lie on a circle, the polygon is **inscribed** in the circle and the circle is **circumscribed** about the polygon. The polygon is an *inscribed polygon* and the circle is a *circumscribed circle*.

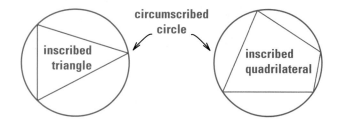

circumscribed circle

inscribed triangle

inscribed quadrilateral

THEOREM 11.8

Words If a triangle inscribed in a circle is a right triangle, then the hypotenuse is a diameter of the circle.

If a side of a triangle inscribed in a circle is a diameter of the circle, then the triangle is a right triangle.

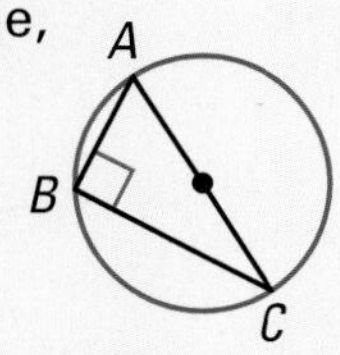

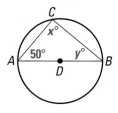

EXAMPLE 2 Find Angle Measures

Find the values of x and y.

Solution

Because $\triangle ABC$ is inscribed in a circle and $\overline{AB}$ is a diameter, it follows from Theorem 11.8 that $\triangle ABC$ is a right triangle with hypotenuse $\overline{AB}$.

Therefore, $x = 90$. Because $\angle A$ and $\angle B$ are acute angles of a right triangle, $y = 90 - 50 = 40$.

Student Help

LOOK BACK
To review the Corollary of the Triangle Sum Theorem, see p. 180.

Checkpoint ✓ Find Angle Measures

Find the values of x and y in $\odot C$.

4.

5.

6.

Visualize It!

$\angle D$ and $\angle F$ are *opposite* angles. $\angle E$ and $\angle G$ are *opposite* angles.

THEOREM 11.9

Words If a quadrilateral can be inscribed in a circle, then its opposite angles are supplementary.

If the opposite angles of a quadrilateral are supplementary, then the quadrilateral can be inscribed in a circle.

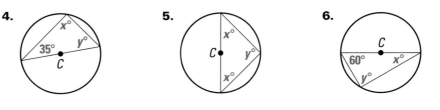

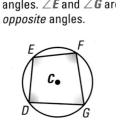

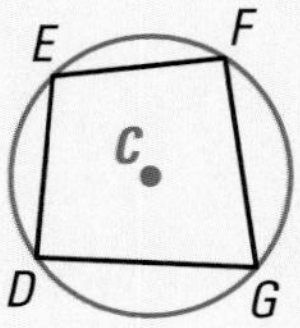

EXAMPLE 3 Find Angle Measures

Find the values of y and z.

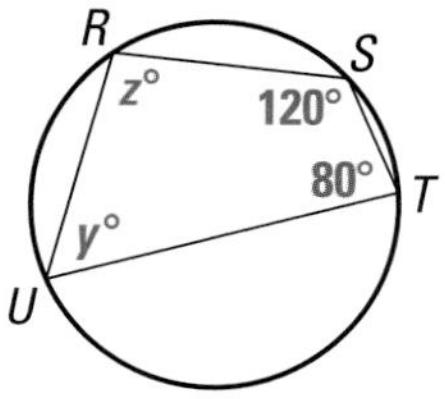

Solution

Because *RSTU* is inscribed in a circle, by Theorem 11.9 opposite angles must be supplementary.

$\angle S$ and $\angle U$ are opposite angles.

$$m\angle S + m\angle U = 180°$$
$$120° + y° = 180°$$
$$y = 60$$

$\angle R$ and $\angle T$ are opposite angles.

$$m\angle R + m\angle T = 180°$$
$$z° + 80° = 180°$$
$$z = 100$$

Checkpoint ✓ Find Angle Measures

Find the values of x and y in $\odot C$.

7.

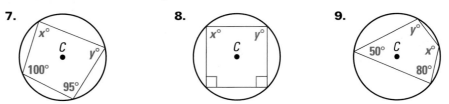

8.

9.

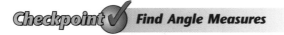

Guided Practice

Vocabulary Check

In Exercises 1 and 2, use the diagram at the right.

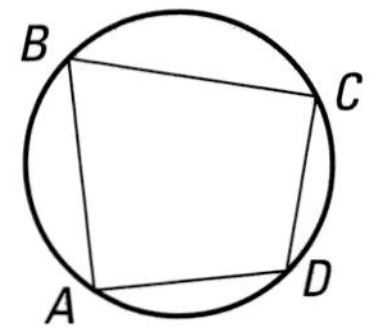

1. Name the *inscribed angles*.

2. Identify the two pairs of *opposite angles* in the inscribed quadrilateral.

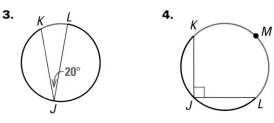

Skill Check

Find the measure of the blue intercepted arc.

3.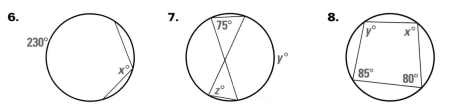

4.

5.

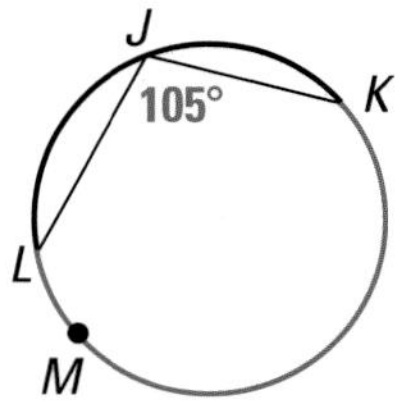

Find the value of each variable.

6.

7.

8.

Practice and Applications

Extra Practice

See p. 696.

Angle Measures Find the measure of the inscribed angle.

9.

10.

11.

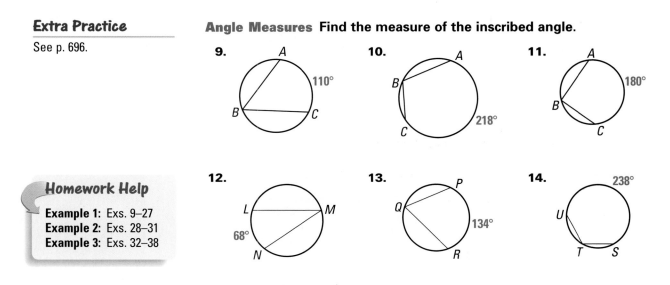

Homework Help

Example 1: Exs. 9–27
Example 2: Exs. 28–31
Example 3: Exs. 32–38

12.

13.

14.

Arc Measures Find the measure of the blue intercepted arc.

15.

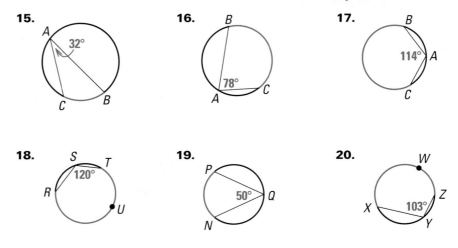

16.

17.

18.

19.

20.

Student Help

VISUAL STRATEGY
In Exs. 21–26, copy the diagram and add information to it as you solve the exercises, as shown on p. 588.

Arc and Angle Measures In Exercises 21–26, use the diagram below to find the intercepted arc or inscribed angle.

21. $m\widehat{BE}$

22. $m\angle BDE$

23. $m\angle AED$

24. $m\widehat{AD}$

25. $m\angle ABD$

26. $m\widehat{DE}$

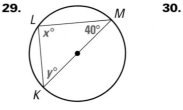

27. Are $\triangle ABC$ and $\triangle DEC$ similar? Explain your reasoning.

Inscribed Right Triangles Find the value of each variable. Explain your reasoning.

28.

29.

30.

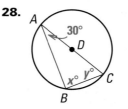

31. Carpenter's Square A carpenter's square is an L-shaped tool used to draw right angles. Suppose you are making a toy truck. To make the wheels you trace a circle on a piece of wood. How could you use a carpenter's square to find the center of the circle?

Student Help
CLASSZONE.COM

HOMEWORK HELP
Extra help with problem solving in Ex. 31 is at classzone.com

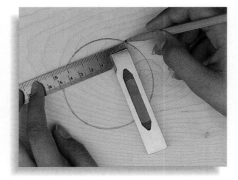

Inscribed Quadrilaterals Find the values of x and y.

32.
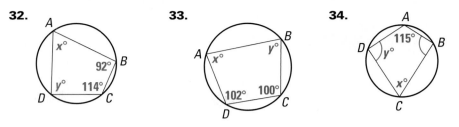

33.

34.

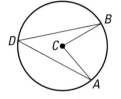 **You be the Judge** Can the quadrilateral always be inscribed in a circle? Explain your answer.

35. square

36. isosceles trapezoid

37. rhombus

38. rectangle

Standardized Test Practice

39. Multiple Choice In the diagram at the right, if ∠ACB is a central angle and m∠ACB = 80°, what is m∠ADB?

Ⓐ 20°   Ⓑ 40°

Ⓒ 80°   Ⓓ 160°

40. Multiple Choice In the diagram at the right, what are the values of x and y?

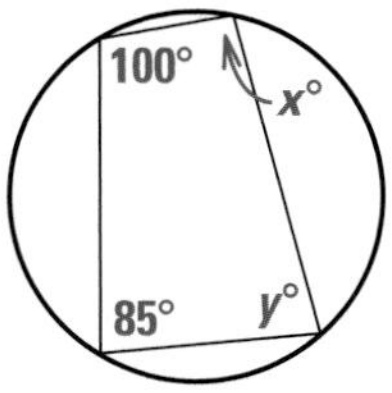

Ⓕ x = 80, y = 95   Ⓖ x = 85, y = 100

Ⓗ x = 95, y = 80   Ⓙ x = 95, y = 85

Mixed Review

Multiplying Radicals Multiply the radicals. Then simplify if possible. *(Lesson 10.1)*

41. $\sqrt{5} \cdot \sqrt{7}$

42. $\sqrt{2} \cdot \sqrt{2}$

43. $\sqrt{6} \cdot \sqrt{14}$

44. $(8\sqrt{2})^2$

45. $(3\sqrt{3})^2$

46. $2\sqrt{5} \cdot \sqrt{10}$

Solving Right Triangles Solve the right triangle. Round decimals to the nearest tenth. *(Lesson 10.6)*

47.

48.

49.

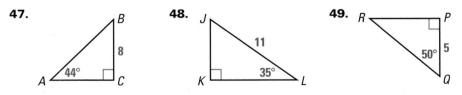

Algebra Skills

Evaluating Expressions Evaluate the expression when x = 2. *(Skills Review, p. 670)*

50. $3x + 5$

51. $8x - 7$

52. $x^2 + 9$

53. $(x + 4)(x - 4)$

54. $x^2 + 3x - 2$

55. $x^3 + x^2$

Properties of Chords

Goal

Use properties of chords in a circle.

Key Words

• chord p. 589

In Lessons 11.3 and 11.5, you saw how to find the measure of an angle formed by chords that intersect *at the center* of a circle or *on* a circle. The Geo-Activity below explores the angles formed by chords that intersect *inside* a circle.

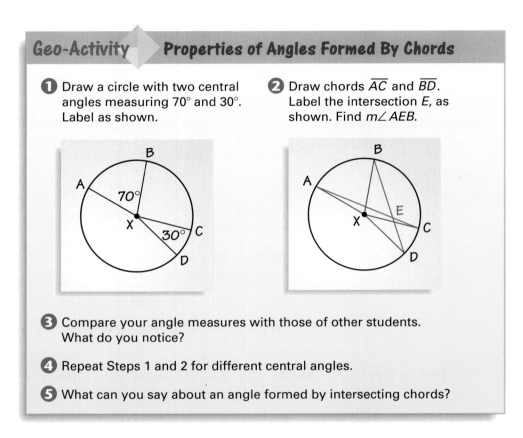

Geo-Activity — **Properties of Angles Formed By Chords**

1 Draw a circle with two central angles measuring 70° and 30°. Label as shown.

2 Draw chords $\overline{AC}$ and $\overline{BD}$. Label the intersection *E*, as shown. Find $m\angle AEB$.

3 Compare your angle measures with those of other students. What do you notice?

4 Repeat Steps 1 and 2 for different central angles.

5 What can you say about an angle formed by intersecting chords?

The result demonstrated by the Geo-Activity is summarized in the theorem below.

THEOREM 11.10

Words If two chords intersect inside a circle, then the measure of each angle formed is one half the *sum* of the measures of the arcs intercepted by the angle and its vertical angle.

Symbols $m\angle 1 = \frac{1}{2}(m\widehat{CD} + m\widehat{AB})$,

$m\angle 2 = \frac{1}{2}(m\widehat{BC} + m\widehat{AD})$

EXAMPLE 1 **Find the Measure of an Angle**

Find the value of *x*.

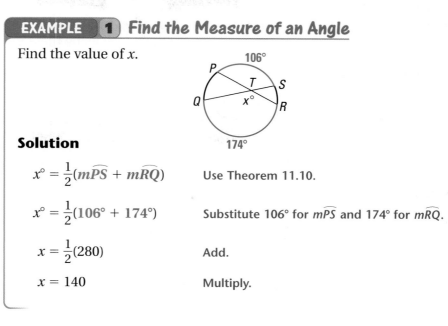

Solution

$x° = \frac{1}{2}(m\widehat{PS} + m\widehat{RQ})$ Use Theorem 11.10.

$x° = \frac{1}{2}(106° + 174°)$ Substitute 106° for $m\widehat{PS}$ and 174° for $m\widehat{RQ}$.

$x = \frac{1}{2}(280)$ Add.

$x = 140$ Multiply.

Student Help

CLASSZONE.COM

MORE EXAMPLES
More examples at classzone.com

EXAMPLE 2 **Find the Measure of an Arc**

Find the value of *x*.

Solution

$80° = \frac{1}{2}(m\widehat{AB} + m\widehat{CD})$ Use Theorem 11.10.

$80° = \frac{1}{2}(x° + 60°)$ Substitute $x°$ for $m\widehat{AB}$ and 60° for $m\widehat{CD}$.

$80 = \frac{1}{2}x + 30$ Use the distributive property.

$50 = \frac{1}{2}x$ Subtract 30 from each side.

$100 = x$ Multiply each side by 2.

Checkpoint ✓ **Find the Measure of an Angle and an Arc**

Find the value of *x*.

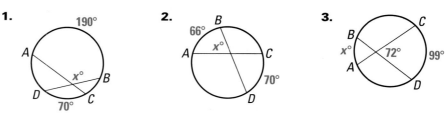

1.

2.

3.

Intersecting Chords When two chords intersect in a circle, four segments are formed. The following theorem shows the relationship among these segments.

THEOREM 11.11

Words If two chords intersect inside a circle, then the product of the lengths of the segments of one chord is equal to the product of the lengths of the segments of the other chord.

Symbols $EA \cdot EB = EC \cdot ED$

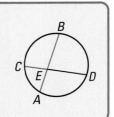

EXAMPLE 3 Find Segment Lengths

Find the value of x.

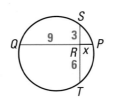

Solution

Notice that $\overline{ST}$ and $\overline{QP}$ are chords that intersect at R.

$RS \cdot RT = RQ \cdot RP$	Use Theorem 11.11.
$3 \cdot 6 = 9 \cdot x$	Substitute 3 for RS, 6 for RT, 9 for RQ, and x for RP.
$18 = 9x$	Simplify.
$2 = x$	Divide each side by 9.

Checkpoint ✓ **Find Segment Lengths**

Find the value of x.

4.

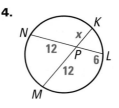

5.

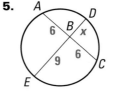

6.

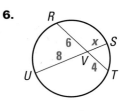

7.

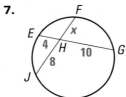

8.

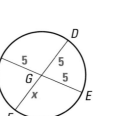

9.

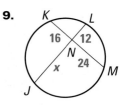

11.6 Exercises

Guided Practice

Vocabulary Check

1. In the diagram, name the points inside the circle.

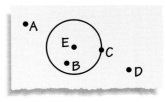

Skill Check

Find the measure of ∠1.

2.

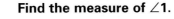

A 55° D 1 B 65° C

3.

B 92° 88° A 1 C 88° 92° D

4.

110° C B 1 A D 168°

Find the value of x.

5.

A D x 2 B 6 4 C

6.

B 14 A x 7 8 C D

7.

B x C A 18 15 10 D

Practice and Applications

Extra Practice

See p. 696.

Matching Match each angle with the correct expression you can use to find its measure.

8. $m\angle1$

9. $m\angle2$

10. $m\angle3$

11. $m\angle4$

A. $\frac{1}{2}(m\widehat{BF} + m\widehat{DE})$

B. $\frac{1}{2}(m\widehat{AB} + m\widehat{CE})$

C. $\frac{1}{2}(m\widehat{AE} + m\widehat{BC})$

D. $\frac{1}{2}(m\widehat{BD} + m\widehat{FE})$

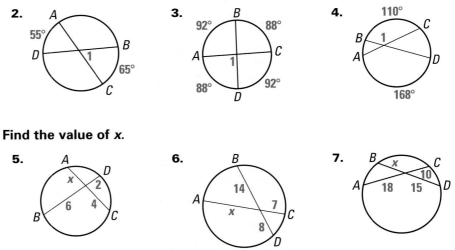

Finding Angle Measures Find the value of x.

12.

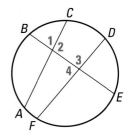

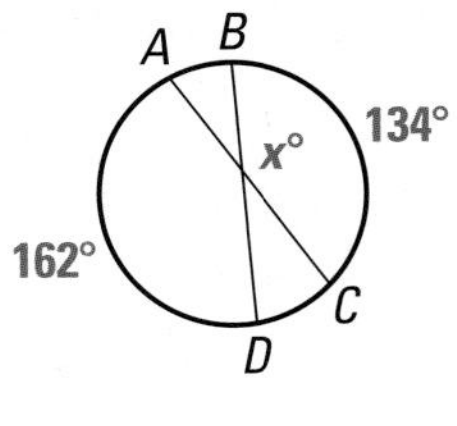

A B x° 134° 162° C D

13.

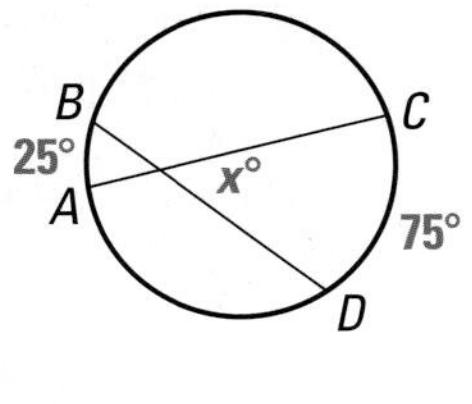

B 25° C A x° 75° D

14.

130° A x° B D 96° C

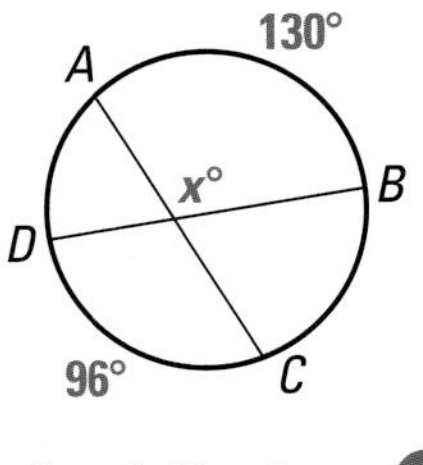

Homework Help

Example 1: Exs. 8–14
Example 2: Exs. 15–18,
Example 3: Exs. 19–26

Finding Arc Measures Find the value of *x*.

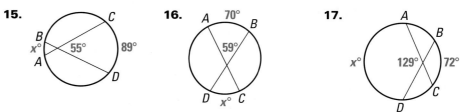

15.

16.

17.

18. **You be the Judge** A student claims if two chords intersect and the measure of each angle formed is the same as the measure of the arc intercepted by the angle, then each angle must be a central angle. Is he correct? Explain.

19. **Animation Design** You are designing an animated logo for a Web site. You want sparkles to leave point *C* and reach the circle at the same time. To find out how far each sparkle moves between frames, you need to know the distances from *C* to the circle. Three distances are shown below. Find *CN*.

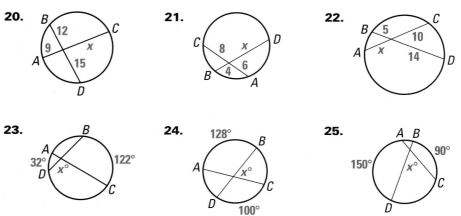

Frame 1　　Frame 2　　Frame 3

Chords in a Circle Find the value of *x*.

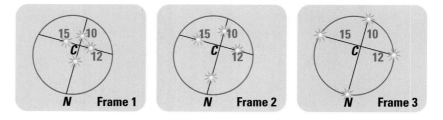

20.

21.

22.

23.

24.

25.

26. **Technology** Use geometry drawing software.

❶ Draw a circle and label points *A*, *B*, *C*, and *D* as shown.

❷ Draw lines $\overleftrightarrow{AB}$ and $\overleftrightarrow{CD}$. Label the point of intersection *E*.

❸ Measure *EA*, *EB*, *EC*, and *ED*. Then calculate *EA* · *EB* and *EC* · *ED*.

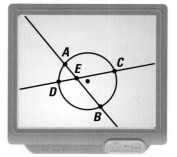

What do you notice? What theorem does this demonstrate?

27. Multi-Step Problem In the diagram, $AC = 12$, $CD = 3$, and $EC = 9$.

   a. Find BC.

   b. What is the measure of $\angle ACB$?

   c. What is the measure of $\widehat{AE}$?

   d. Is $\triangle ACB$ similar to $\triangle ECD$? Explain your reasoning.

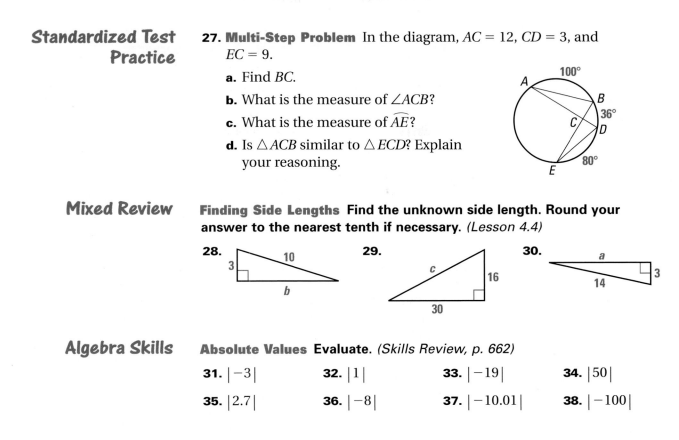

Mixed Review

Finding Side Lengths Find the unknown side length. Round your answer to the nearest tenth if necessary. *(Lesson 4.4)*

28.

29.

30.

Algebra Skills

Absolute Values Evaluate. *(Skills Review, p. 662)*

31. $|-3|$ **32.** $|1|$ **33.** $|-19|$ **34.** $|50|$

35. $|2.7|$ **36.** $|-8|$ **37.** $|-10.01|$ **38.** $|-100|$

Quiz 2

Find the value of x in $\odot C$. *(Lesson 11.4)*

1.   **2.**   **3.**

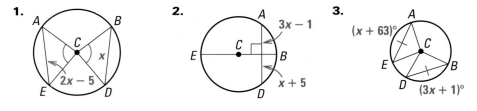

Find the value of each variable. Explain your reasoning. *(Lesson 11.5)*

4.   **5.**   **6.**

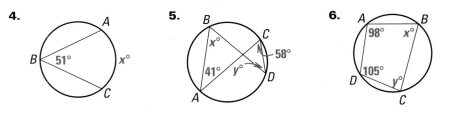

Find the value of x. *(Lesson 11.6)*

7.   **8.**   **9.**

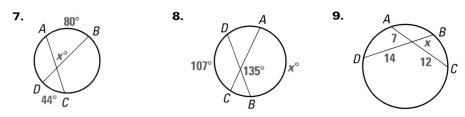

Question

What is the relationship between segments of secants that intersect?

Explore

1 Construct a circle. Then construct two secants to the circle that intersect outside the circle.

2 Label the intersections as shown.

3 Measure *JH*, *JG*, *JK*, and *JL*.

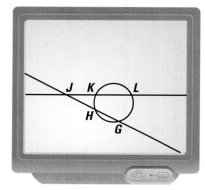

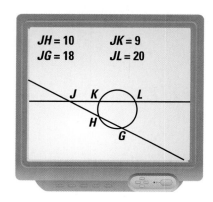

JH = 10   *JK* = 9
JG = 18   *JL* = 20

Think About It

1. Calculate *JH* · *JG* and *JK* · *JL*. What do you notice?

2. Drag point *J*. What do you notice?

3. Draw two more circles and repeat Steps 1 through 3. Are your results different?

4. Make a conjecture about the segments formed by the intersection of two secants.

5. Extension Find the measures of ∠*KJH*, $\overarc{KH}$, and $\overarc{LG}$. Compare the sum of $m\overarc{KH}$ and $m\overarc{LG}$ with *m*∠*KJH*. What do you notice? Make a conjecture about the angle formed by the intersection of two secants and the corresponding intercepted arcs.

Equations of Circles

Goal

Write and graph the equation of a circle.

Key Words

• standard equation of a circle

In the circle below, let point (x, y) represent any point on the circle whose center is at the origin. Let r represent the radius of the circle.

In the right triangle,

r = length of hypotenuse,

x = length of a leg,

y = length of a leg.

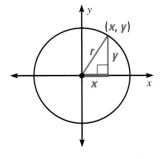

By the Pythagorean Theorem, you can write

$x^2 + y^2 = r^2$.

This is an equation of a circle with center at the origin.

EXAMPLE 1 **Write an Equation of a Circle**

Write an equation of the circle.

Solution

The radius is 4 and the center is at the origin.

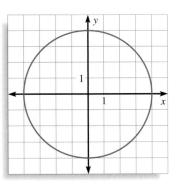

$x^2 + y^2 = r^2$ — Write an equation of a circle with center at the origin.

$x^2 + y^2 = 4^2$ — Substitute 4 for r.

$x^2 + y^2 = 16$ — Simplify.

ANSWER ▶ An equation of the circle is $x^2 + y^2 = 16$.

Checkpoint ✓ **Write an Equation of a Circle**

Write an equation of the circle.

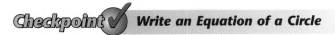

1.

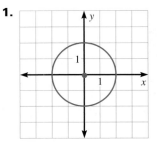

2.

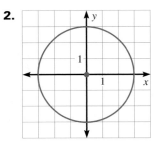

Standard Equation of a Circle If the center of a circle is not at the origin, you can use the Distance Formula to write an equation of the circle.

For example, the circle shown at the right has center (3, 5) and radius 4.

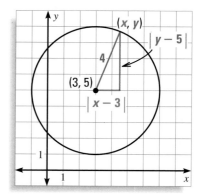

Let (x, y) represent any point on the circle. Use the Distance Formula to find the lengths of the legs.

> leg: $|x - 3|$
>
> leg: $|y - 5|$
>
> hypotenuse: 4

Use these expressions in the Pythagorean Theorem to find an equation of the circle.

$$(x - 3)^2 + (y - 5)^2 = 4^2$$

This is an example of the **standard equation of a circle**.

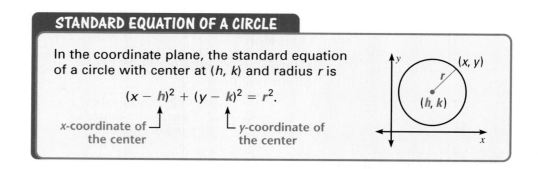

STANDARD EQUATION OF A CIRCLE

In the coordinate plane, the standard equation of a circle with center at (h, k) and radius r is

$$(x - h)^2 + (y - k)^2 = r^2.$$

x-coordinate of the center y-coordinate of the center

EXAMPLE 2   Write the Standard Equation of a Circle

Write the standard equation of the circle with center (2, −1) and radius 3.

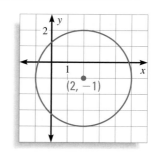

Solution

$(x - h)^2 + (y - k)^2 = r^2$	Write the standard equation of a circle.
$(x - 2)^2 + (y - (-1))^2 = 3^2$	Substitute 2 for h, −1 for k, and 3 for r.
$(x - 2)^2 + (y + 1)^2 = 9$	Simplify.

ANSWER ▸ The standard equation of the circle is $(x - 2)^2 + (y + 1)^2 = 9$.

EXAMPLE 3 Graph a Circle

Graph the given equation of the circle.

a. $(x - 1)^2 + (y - 2)^2 = 4$ **b.** $(x + 2)^2 + y^2 = 4$

Solution

a. Rewrite the equation of the circle as $(x - 1)^2 + (y - 2)^2 = 2^2$. The center is $(1, 2)$ and the radius is 2.

b. Rewrite the equation of the circle as $(x - (-2))^2 + (y - 0)^2 = 2^2$. The center is $(-2, 0)$ and the radius is 2.

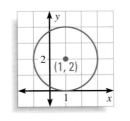

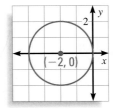

Checkpoint ✓ **Circles Not Centered at the Origin**

3. Write the standard equation of the circle with center $(-4, -6)$ and radius 5.

Graph the given equation of the circle.

4. $(x - 1)^2 + y^2 = 25$ **5.** $(x + 2)^2 + (y - 4)^2 = 16$

11.7 Exercises

Guided Practice

Vocabulary Check

1. Which of the following is a *standard equation of a circle*?

A. $(x + 2)^2 = 16y$ **B.** $(x^2 - 5) + (y^2 - 8) = 16$

C. $(x - 4)^2 + (y - 3)^2 = 16$ **D.** $2x^2 + 3y - 5 = 16$

Skill Check

Give the radius and the coordinates of the center. Write the equation of the circle in standard form.

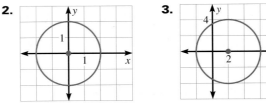

11.7 *Equations of Circles*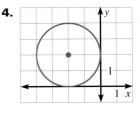

Practice and Applications

Extra Practice

See p. 696.

Matching Equations Match each graph with its equation.

A. $x^2 + y^2 = 4$ **B.** $(x - 3)^2 + y^2 = 4$ **C.** $(x + 3)^2 + y^2 = 4$

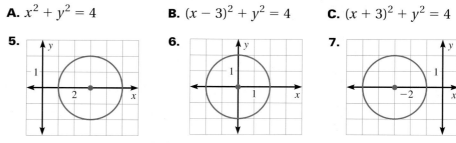

5.   **6.**   **7.**

Student Help

CLASSZONE.COM

HOMEWORK HELP

Extra help with problem solving in Exs. 8–15 is at classzone.com

Using Standard Equations Give the radius and the coordinates of the center of the circle with the given equation. Then graph the circle.

8. $x^2 + y^2 = 36$ **9.** $x^2 + y^2 = 1$

10. $(x - 2)^2 + (y - 6)^2 = 49$ **11.** $(x - 4)^2 + (y - 3)^2 = 16$

12. $(x - 5)^2 + (y - 1)^2 = 25$ **13.** $(x + 2)^2 + (y - 3)^2 = 36$

14. $(x - 2)^2 + (y + 5)^2 = 4$ **15.** $x^2 + (y - 5)^2 = 64$

Using Graphs Give the radius and the coordinates of the center of the circle. Then write the standard equation of the circle.

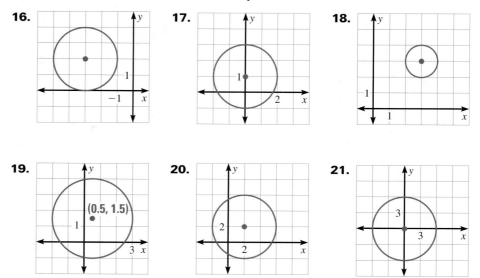

16.   **17.**   **18.**

19.   **20.**   **21.**

Homework Help

Example 1: Exs. 5–7, 21
Example 2: Exs. 5–7, 16–27
Example 3: Exs. 8–15

Writing Equations Write the standard equation of the circle with the given center and radius.

22. center $(0, 0)$, radius 10   **23.** center $(4, 0)$, radius 4

24. center $(3, -2)$, radius 2   **25.** center $(-1, -3)$, radius 6

26. center $(-3, 5)$, radius 3   **27.** center $(1, 0)$, radius 7

Use the Equation of a Circle

The equation of a circle is $(x - 5)^2 + (y - 1)^2 = 9$. Without sketching the circle, tell whether the point is *on* the circle, *inside* the circle, or *outside* the circle.

a. $(6, 0)$ **b.** $(8, 2)$

Solution

Substitute the coordinates of the point into the equation.

If the left side is *less than* the right side, the point is *inside* the circle.

If the left side is *greater than* the right side, the point is *outside* the circle.

Student Help

STUDY TIP
If the left side is *equal* to the right side, the point is *on* the circle.

a. $(x - 5)^2 + (y - 1)^2 = 9$
$(6 - 5)^2 + (0 - 1)^2 \stackrel{?}{=} 9$
$1^2 + (-1)^2 \stackrel{?}{=} 9$
$2 < 9$

Because $2 < 9$, the point $(6, 0)$ is *inside* the circle.

b. $(x - 5)^2 + (y - 1)^2 = 9$
$(8 - 5)^2 + (2 - 1)^2 \stackrel{?}{=} 9$
$3^2 + 1^2 \stackrel{?}{=} 9$
$10 > 9$

Because $10 > 9$, the point $(8, 2)$ is *outside* the circle.

Equation of a Circle The equation of a circle is $(x - 2)^2 + (y + 3)^2 = 4$. Tell whether the point is *on* the circle, *inside* the circle, or *outside* the circle. Use the example above as a model.

Link to
Communications

28. $R(0, 0)$ **29.** $A(2, -4)$ **30.** $X(0, -3)$ **31.** $K(3, -1)$

32. $M(1, -4)$ **33.** $T(2, -5)$ **34.** $D(2, 0)$ **35.** $Z(2.5, -3)$

Cell Phones In Exercises 36 and 37, use the following information.
A cellular phone network uses towers to transmit calls. Each tower transmits to a circular area. On a grid of a town, the coordinates of the towers and the circular areas covered by the towers are shown.

36. Write the equations that represent the transmission boundaries of the towers.

37. Tell which towers, if any, transmit to phones located at $J(1, 1)$, $K(4, 2)$, $L(3.5, 4.5)$, $M(2, 2.8)$, and $N(1, 6)$.

CELL PHONE towers are sometimes built to look like trees so that they blend in with their environment. Other cell phone towers have also been built to resemble farm silos and cactus plants.

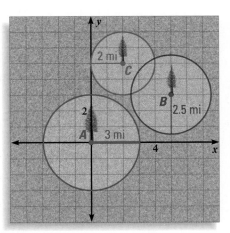

38. Error Analysis A student was asked to write the standard equation of the circle below. Why is the equation incorrect?

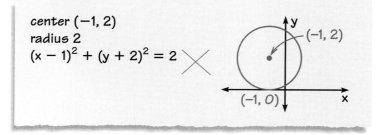

center (−1, 2)
radius 2
$(x − 1)^2 + (y + 2)^2 = 2$

(−1, 2)

(−1, 0)

Challenge Use the given information to write the standard equation of the circle.

39. The center is (1, 2). A point on the circle is (4, 6).

40. The center is (3, 2). A point on the circle is (5, 2).

41. Multiple Choice What is the standard form of the equation of a circle with center (−3, 1) and radius 2?

  Ⓐ $(x − 3)^2 + (y − 1)^2 = 2$ **Ⓑ** $(x + 3)^2 + (y − 1)^2 = 2$

  Ⓒ $(x − 3)^2 + (y − 1)^2 = 4$ **Ⓓ** $(x + 3)^2 + (y − 1)^2 = 4$

42. Multiple Choice The center of a circle is (−3, 0) and its radius is 5. Which point does *not* lie on the circle?

  Ⓕ (2, 0)   **Ⓖ** (0, 4)   **Ⓗ** (−3, 0)   **Ⓙ** (−3, −5)

Finding an Image Find the coordinates of *P′*, *Q′*, *R′*, and *S′*, using the given translation. *(Lesson 3.7)*

43. $(x, y) → (x + 2, y)$

44. $(x, y) → (x − 4, y + 1)$

45. $(x, y) → (x − 1, y − 1)$

46. $(x, y) → (x + 3, y + 6)$

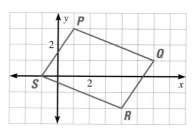

Identifying Dilations Tell whether the dilation is a *reduction* or an *enlargement*. Then find its scale factor. *(Lesson 7.6)*

47.

48.

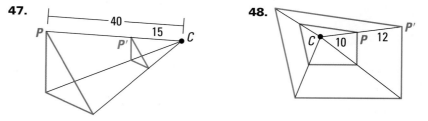

Solving Equations Solve the equation. *(Skills Review, p. 673)*

49. $14 = −3x − 7$ **50.** $11 − x = −2$ **51.** $20 = 5x − 12 − x$

11.8 Rotations

Goal
Identify rotations and rotational symmetry.

Key Words
- rotation
- center of rotation
- angle of rotation
- rotational symmetry

Geo-Activity — **Rotating a Figure**

1 Draw an equilateral triangle. Label as shown. Draw a line from the center to one of the vertices.

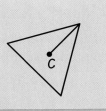

2 Copy the triangle onto a piece of tracing paper.

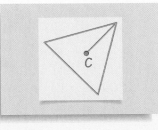

3 Place a pencil on the center point and turn the tracing paper over the original triangle until it matches up with itself.

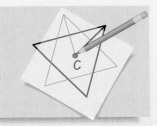

4 How many degrees did you turn the triangle? Is there more than one way to turn the triangle so that it matches up with itself?

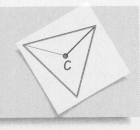

5 Draw a rectangle and a square. Repeat Steps 1 through 4. How many degrees did you turn each figure until it matched up with itself?

Visualize It!

Clockwise means to go in the direction of the hands on a clock.

Counterclockwise means to go in the opposite direction.

A **rotation** is a transformation in which a figure is turned about a fixed point. The fixed point is the **center of rotation**. In the Geo-Activity above, point C is the center of rotation. Rays drawn from the center of rotation to a point and its image form an angle called the **angle of rotation**. Rotations can be clockwise or counterclockwise.

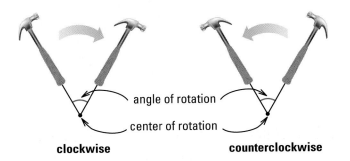

clockwise   counterclockwise

Rotational Symmetry A figure in a plane has **rotational symmetry** if the figure can be mapped onto itself by a rotation of 180° or less. For instance, the figure below has rotational symmetry because it maps onto itself by a rotation of 90°.

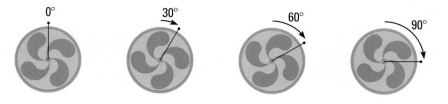

0°   30°   60°   90°

EXAMPLE 1 **Identify Rotational Symmetry**

Does the figure have rotational symmetry? If so, describe the rotations that map the figure onto itself.

a. Rectangle　　　　**b.** Regular hexagon　　　　**c.** Trapezoid

Solution

a. Yes. A rectangle can be mapped onto itself by a clockwise or counterclockwise rotation of 180° about its center.

0°　　　　　　180°

b. Yes. A regular hexagon can be mapped onto itself by a clockwise or counterclockwise rotation of 60°, 120°, or 180° about its center.

0°　　　60°　　　120°　　　180°

c. No. A trapezoid does not have rotational symmetry.

Checkpoint ✓ **Identify Rotational Symmetry**

Does the figure have rotational symmetry? If so, describe the rotations that map the figure onto itself.

1. Isosceles trapezoid　　**2.** Parallelogram　　**3.** Regular octagon

 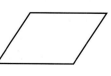

Student Help
CLASSZONE.COM

MORE EXAMPLES
More examples at classzone.com

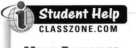

EXAMPLE 2 Rotations

Rotate $\triangle FGH$ 50° counterclockwise about point C.

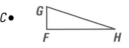

Solution

❶ To find the image of point F, draw $\overline{CF}$ and draw a 50° angle. Find F' so that $CF = CF'$.

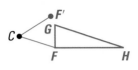

❷ To find the image of point G, draw $\overline{CG}$ and draw a 50° angle. Find G' so that $CG = CG'$.

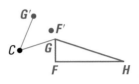

❸ To find the image of point H, draw $\overline{CH}$ and draw a 50° angle. Find H' so that $CH = CH'$. Draw $\triangle F'G'H'$.

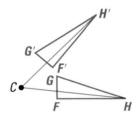

EXAMPLE 3 Rotations in a Coordinate Plane

Sketch the quadrilateral with vertices $A(2, -2)$, $B(4, 1)$, $C(5, 1)$, and $D(5, -1)$. Rotate it 90° counterclockwise about the origin and name the coordinates of the new vertices.

Solution

Plot the points, as shown in blue.

Use a protractor and a ruler to find the rotated vertices.

The coordinates of the vertices of the image are $A'(2, 2)$, $B'(-1, 4)$, $C'(-1, 5)$, and $D'(1, 5)$.

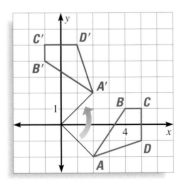

Checkpoint ✓ Rotations in a Coordinate Plane

4. Sketch the triangle with vertices $A(0, 0)$, $B(3, 0)$, and $C(3, 4)$. Rotate $\triangle ABC$ 90° counterclockwise about the origin. Name the coordinates of the new vertices A', B', and C'.

11.8 Exercises

Guided Practice

Vocabulary Check

1. What is a *center of rotation*?

2. Explain how you know if a figure has *rotational symmetry*.

Skill Check

Does the figure have rotational symmetry? If so, describe the rotations that map the figure onto itself.

3.

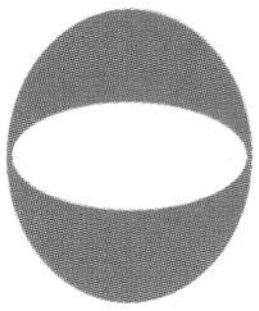

4.

5.

The diagonals of the regular hexagon shown form six equilateral triangles. Use the diagram to complete the statement.

6. A clockwise rotation of 60° about P maps R onto __?__.

7. A counterclockwise rotation of 60° about __?__ maps R onto Q.

8. A clockwise rotation of 120° about Q maps R onto __?__.

9. A counterclockwise rotation of 180° about P maps V onto __?__.

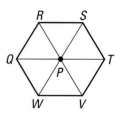

Practice and Applications

Extra Practice

See p. 696.

Rotational Symmetry Does the figure have rotational symmetry? If so, describe the rotations that map the figure onto itself.

10.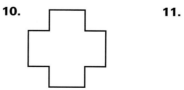

11.

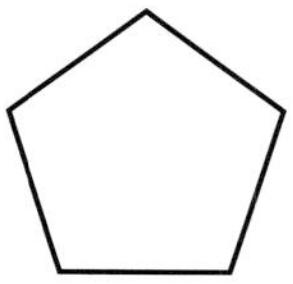

12.

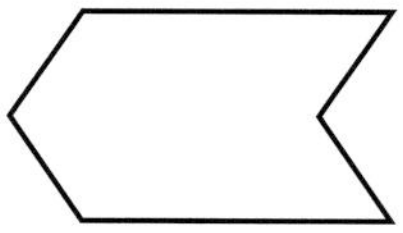

Wheel Hubs Describe the rotational symmetry of the wheel hub.

13.

14.

15.

Homework Help

Example 1: Exs. 10–15
Example 2: Exs. 16–26
Example 3: Exs. 27–30

Rotating a Figure Trace the polygon and point *P* on paper. Use a straightedge and protractor to rotate the polygon clockwise the given number of degrees about *P*.

16. 150°

17. 135°

18. 60°

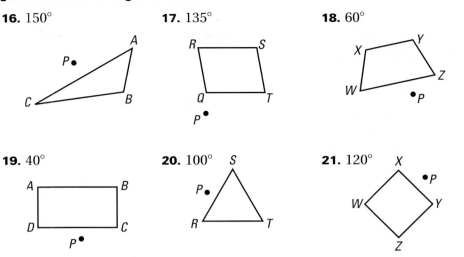

19. 40°

20. 100°

21. 120°

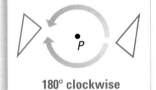

Visualize It!

Rotating a figure 180° clockwise is the same as rotating a figure 180° counterclockwise.

180° counterclockwise

180° clockwise

Describing an Image State the segment or triangle that represents the image.

22. 90° clockwise rotation of $\overline{AB}$ about *P*

23. 90° clockwise rotation of $\overline{KF}$ about *P*

24. 180° rotation of $\triangle BCJ$ about *P*

25. 180° rotation of $\triangle KEF$ about *P*

26. 90° counterclockwise rotation of $\overline{CE}$ about *E*

Finding a Pattern Use the given information to rotate the figure about the origin. Find the coordinates of the vertices of the image and compare them with the vertices of the original figure. Describe any patterns you see.

27. 90° clockwise

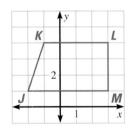

28. 90° counterclockwise

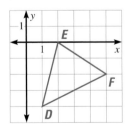

29. 90° counterclockwise

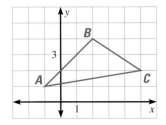

30. 180°

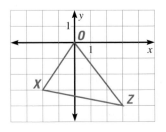

Graphic Design A music store, Ozone, is running a contest for a store logo. Two of the entries are shown. What do you notice about them?

31.

Ozone

32.

Rotations in Art In Exercises 33–36, refer to the image below by M.C. Escher. The piece is called *Circle Limit III* and was completed in 1959.

33. Does the piece have rotational symmetry? If so, describe the rotations that map the image onto itself.

34. Would your answer to Exercise 33 change if you disregard the color of the figures? Explain your reasoning.

35. Describe the center of rotation.

36. Is it possible that this piece could be hung upside down and have the same appearance? Explain.

Standardized Test Practice

37. Multiple Choice What are the coordinates of the vertices of the image of $\triangle JKL$ after a 90° clockwise rotation about the origin?

(A) $J'(1, 2)$, $K'(4, 2)$, $L'(1, 4)$

(B) $J'(2, 1)$, $K'(4, 2)$, $L'(1, 4)$

(C) $J'(4, 2)$, $K'(2, 1)$, $L'(4, -1)$

(D) $J'(2, 4)$, $K'(1, 2)$, $L'(-1, 4)$

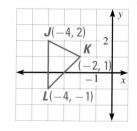

38. Multiple Choice Which of the four polygons shown below does not have rotational symmetry?

Mixed Review

Area of Polygons Find the area of the polygon. *(Lessons 8.3, 8.5, 8.6)*

39. rectangle *ABCD* **40.** parallelogram *EFGH* **41.** trapezoid *JKMN*

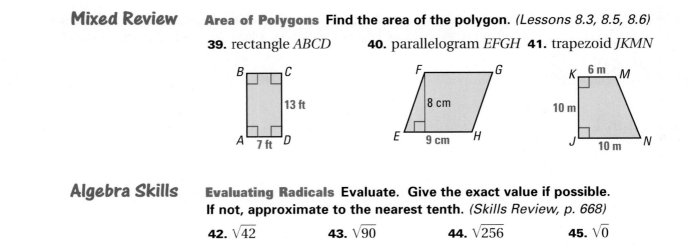

Algebra Skills

Evaluating Radicals Evaluate. Give the exact value if possible. If not, approximate to the nearest tenth. *(Skills Review, p. 668)*

42. $\sqrt{42}$ **43.** $\sqrt{90}$ **44.** $\sqrt{256}$ **45.** $\sqrt{0}$

Quiz 3

1. What are the center and the radius of the circle whose equation is $(x + 1)^2 + (y - 6)^2 = 25$? *(Lesson 11.7)*

2. Write the standard equation of the circle with center $(0, -4)$ and radius 3. *(Lesson 11.7)*

Graph the equation. *(Lesson 11.7)*

3. $x^2 + (y - 1)^2 = 36$ **4.** $(x + 2)^2 + (y - 5)^2 = 4$

5. $(x - 3)^2 + (y + 4)^2 = 9$ **6.** $(x + 1)^2 + (y + 1)^2 = 16$

Does the figure have rotational symmetry? If so, describe the rotations that map the figure onto itself. *(Lesson 11.8)*

7. **8.** **9.**

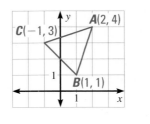
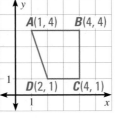

Use the given information to rotate the figure about the origin. Find the coordinates of the vertices of the image and compare them with the vertices of the original figure. Describe any patterns you see. *(Lesson 11.8)*

10. 180° **11.** 90° counterclockwise **12.** 90° clockwise

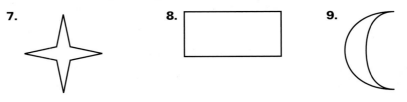
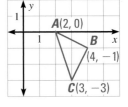

11.8 Reflections and Rotations

Question

How are reflections related to rotations?

Explore

① Draw △ABC and lines k and m. Label the intersection of k and m as point P.

② Reflect △ABC about line k.

③ Reflect △A′B′C′ about line m.

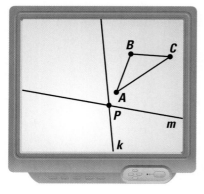

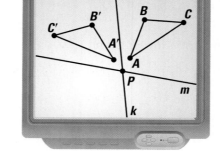

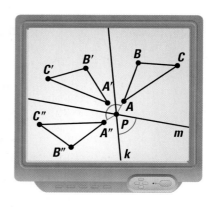

Student Help

LOOK BACK
To review reflections, see p. 282.

Think About It

1. How are △ABC and △A″B″C″ related?

2. Draw $\overline{AP}$ and $\overline{A″P}$ and measure them. What do you notice?

3. Find the measure of ∠APA″ and the measure of the acute angle formed at the intersection of the lines of reflection. What do you notice?

4. Change the positions of lines k and m so the angle formed by the lines changes. How does this affect the measure of ∠APA″?

5. Repeat Steps 1–3 and Exercises 1–4 for a different triangle. Do you get the same results?

- **chord,** *p. 589*
- **secant,** *p. 589*
- **tangent,** *p. 589*
- **point of tangency,** *p. 589*
- **tangent segment,** *p. 597*
- **minor arc,** *p. 601*
- **major arc,** *p. 601*
- **measure of a minor arc,** *p. 601*

- **measure of a major arc,** *p. 601*
- **semicircle,** *p. 601*
- **congruent circles,** *p. 602*
- **congruent arcs,** *p. 602*
- **arc length,** *p. 603*
- **inscribed angle,** *p. 614*
- **intercepted arc,** *p. 614*
- **inscribed,** *p. 615*

- **circumscribed,** *p. 615*
- **standard equation of a circle,** *p. 628*
- **rotation,** *p. 633*
- **center of rotation,** *p. 633*
- **angle of rotation,** *p. 633*
- **rotational symmetry,** *p. 634*

VOCABULARY REVIEW

Fill in the blank.

1. A __?__ is a line that intersects a circle in two points.

2. A polygon is __?__ in a circle if all of its vertices lie on the circle.

3. A line in the plane of a circle that intersects the circle in exactly one point is called a __?__.

4. If the endpoints of an arc are the endpoints of a diameter, then the arc is a __?__.

5. An __?__ is an angle whose vertex is on a circle and whose sides contain chords of the circle.

6. A __?__ is a segment whose endpoints are points on a circle.

7. A __?__ is a transformation in which a figure is turned about a fixed point.

11.1 **PARTS OF A CIRCLE**

Examples on pp. 589–590

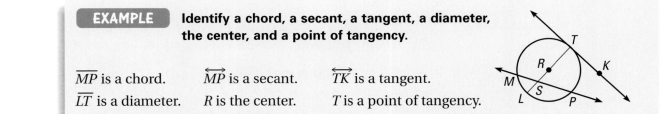

EXAMPLE Identify a chord, a secant, a tangent, a diameter, the center, and a point of tangency.

$\overline{MP}$ is a chord. $\overleftrightarrow{MP}$ is a secant. $\overleftrightarrow{TK}$ is a tangent.

$\overline{LT}$ is a diameter. R is the center. T is a point of tangency.

Tell whether the point, line, or segment is best described as a *chord*, a *secant*, a *tangent*, a *diameter*, a *radius*, the *center*, or a *point of tangency*.

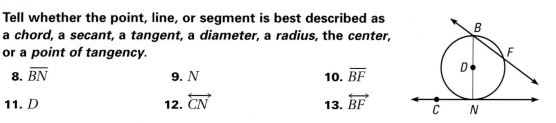

8. $\overline{BN}$　　　　**9.** N　　　　**10.** $\overline{BF}$

11. D　　　　**12.** $\overleftrightarrow{CN}$　　　　**13.** $\overleftrightarrow{BF}$

11.2　PROPERTIES OF TANGENTS

Examples on pp. 595–597

EXAMPLE　$\overleftrightarrow{AB}$ is tangent to $\odot C$. Find CB.

$(AC)^2 = (AB)^2 + (CB)^2$　　Pythagorean Theorem

$29^2 = 21^2 + (CB)^2$　　Substitute 29 for AC, and 21 for AB.

$841 = 441 + (CB)^2$　　Multiply.

$400 = (CB)^2$　　Subtract 441 from each side.

$20 = CB$　　Find the positive square root.

$\overleftrightarrow{AB}$ is tangent to $\odot C$. Find the value of *r*.

14.
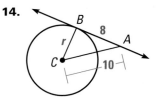

15.
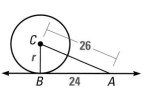

16.
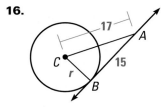

$\overline{AB}$ and $\overline{AD}$ are tangent to $\odot C$. Find the value of *x*.

17.
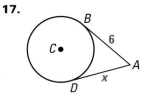

18.
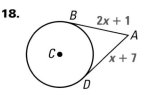

19.
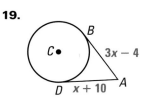

11.3　ARCS AND CENTRAL ANGLES

Examples on pp. 601–603

EXAMPLES　**Find the measure of the arc.**

a. $m\widehat{DF}$　　**b.** $m\widehat{DA}$　　**c.** $m\widehat{ABD}$

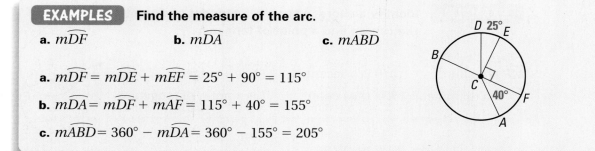

a. $m\widehat{DF} = m\widehat{DE} + m\widehat{EF} = 25° + 90° = 115°$

b. $m\widehat{DA} = m\widehat{DF} + m\widehat{AF} = 115° + 40° = 155°$

c. $m\widehat{ABD} = 360° - m\widehat{DA} = 360° - 155° = 205°$

$\overline{AD}$ is a diameter and $m\widehat{CE} = 121°$. Find the measure of the arc.

20. $\widehat{DE}$ **21.** $\widehat{AE}$ **22.** $\widehat{AEC}$

23. $\widehat{BC}$ **24.** $\widehat{BDC}$ **25.** $\widehat{BDA}$

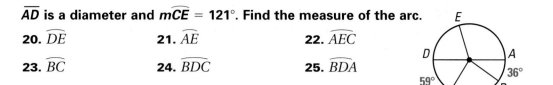

Find the length of the red arc. Round your answer to the nearest hundredth.

26.   **27.**   **28.**

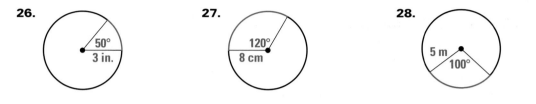

11.4   ARCS AND CHORDS

Examples on pp. 608–610

EXAMPLE   Find the value of *x*.

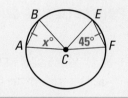

Because $\overline{AB} \cong \overline{EF}$, it follows that $\widehat{AB} \cong \widehat{EF}$.
So, $m\widehat{AB} = m\widehat{EF} = 45°$, and $x = 45$.

Find the value of *x*.

29.   **30.**   **31.**

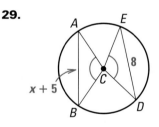

32. 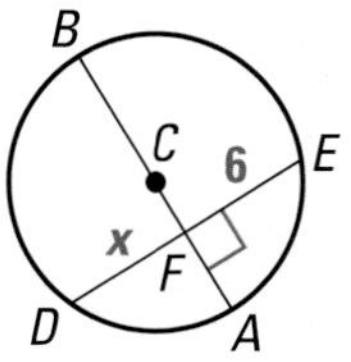   **33.** 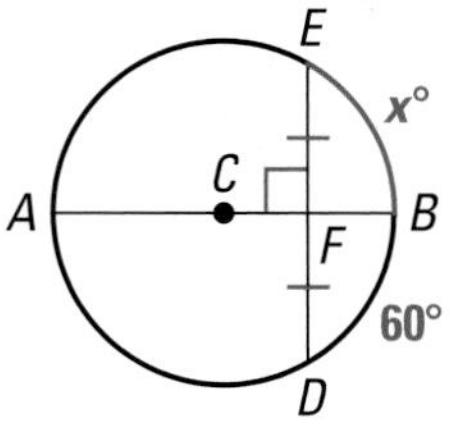   **34.**

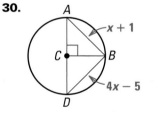
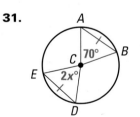

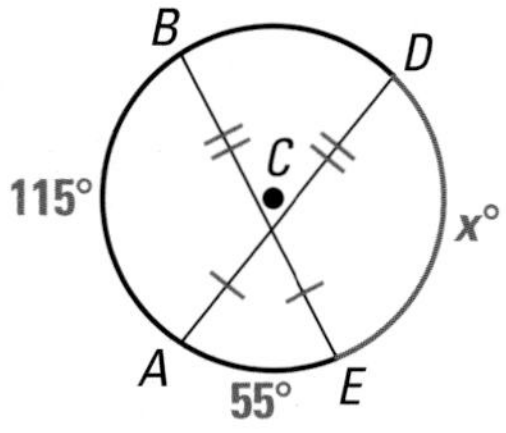

11.5   INSCRIBED ANGLES AND POLYGONS

Examples on pp. 614–616

EXAMPLE   Find the measure of the inscribed angle.

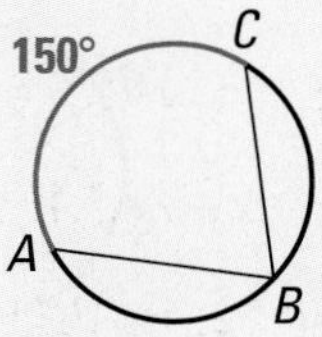

$$m\angle ABC = \frac{1}{2}m\widehat{AC} = \frac{1}{2}(150°) = 75°$$

Find the measure of the inscribed angle or intercepted arc.

35.

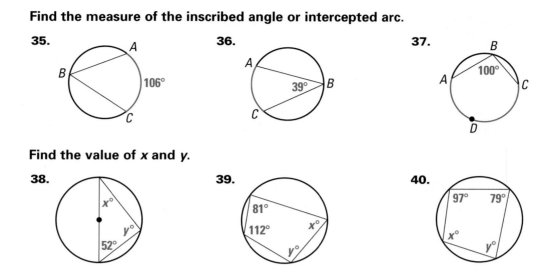

36.

37.

Find the value of *x* and *y*.

38.

39.

40.

11.6   PROPERTIES OF CHORDS

Examples on pp. 620–622

EXAMPLES   Find the value of *x*.

a.

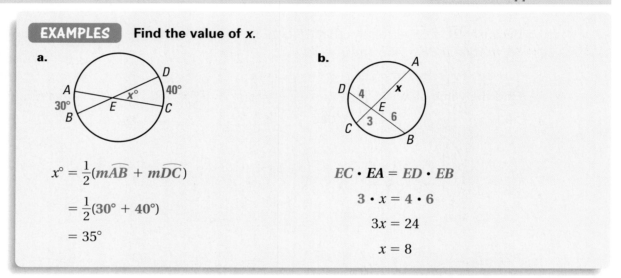

$$x° = \frac{1}{2}(m\widehat{AB} + m\widehat{DC})$$

$$= \frac{1}{2}(30° + 40°)$$

$$= 35°$$

b.

$$EC \cdot EA = ED \cdot EB$$

$$3 \cdot x = 4 \cdot 6$$

$$3x = 24$$

$$x = 8$$

Find the value of *x*.

41.

42.

43.

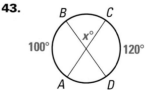

44.

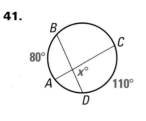

45.

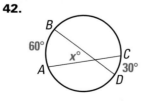

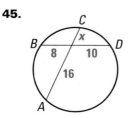

46.

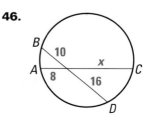

11.7 EQUATIONS OF CIRCLES

Examples on pp. 627–629

EXAMPLE **Write the standard equation of the circle.**

⊙C has center $(-3, -1)$ and radius 2. Its standard equation is

$(x - (-3))^2 + (y - (-1))^2 = 2^2$

$(x + 3)^2 + (y + 1)^2 = 4.$

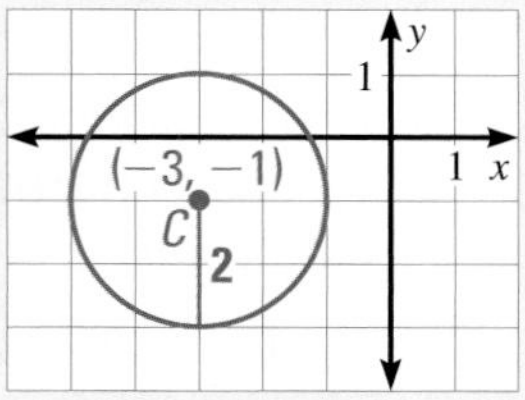

Write the standard equation of the circle with the given center and radius.

47. center $(2, 5)$, radius 3   **48.** center $(-4, -1)$, radius 4   **49.** center $(5, -2)$, radius 7

Give the radius and the coordinates of the center of the circle with the given equation. Then graph the circle.

50. $(x + 4)^2 + (y - 1)^2 = 9$ **51.** $(x - 2)^2 + (y + 3)^2 = 16$ **52.** $x^2 + y^2 = 25$

11.8 ROTATIONS

Examples on pp. 633–635

EXAMPLE **Rotate the triangle with vertices $F(-4, 1)$, $G(-3, 5)$, and $H(-1, 2)$ 90° clockwise about the origin.**

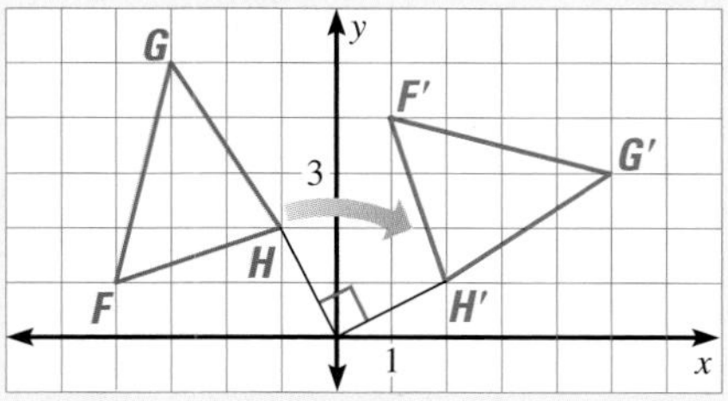

Trace the figure and point *P* on paper. Use a straightedge and protractor to rotate the figure clockwise the given number of degrees about *P*.

53. 90° counterclockwise   **54.** 90° clockwise   **55.** 180°

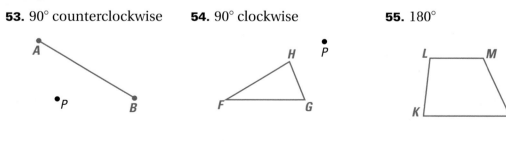

56. Does the figure shown at the right have rotational symmetry? If so, describe the rotations that map the figure onto itself.

1. Identify the center, a point of tangency, a chord, a secant, a radius, and a diameter in the circle.

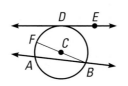

2. $\overline{CB}$ is tangent to $\odot A$. What is the length of $\overline{AB}$?

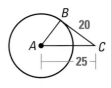

3. $\overline{RS}$ and $\overline{RV}$ are tangent to $\odot T$. What is the value of x?

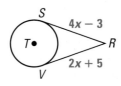

$\overline{AD}$ **is a diameter. Find the measure.**

4. $m\widehat{BC}$

5. $m\widehat{AC}$

6. $m\widehat{ABD}$

7. $m\widehat{CAE}$

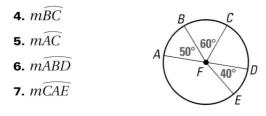

Find the length of the red arc. Round your answer to the nearest hundredth.

8. **9.**

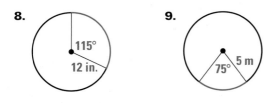

Find the value of x.

10. **11.**

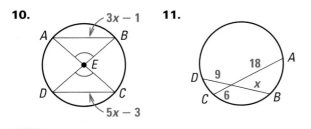

In Exercises 12 and 13, find the value of each variable.

12. **13.**

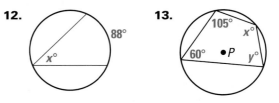

14. Write the standard equation of the circle with center $(6, -3)$ and radius 5.

15. Graph the circle with equation $(x - 3)^2 + (y - 1)^2 = 9$.

16. Graph the circle with equation $(x - 4)^2 + (y + 6)^2 = 64$.

17. Graph the circle with equation $(x - 5)^2 + y^2 = 1$.

18. Name the coordinates of the vertices of the image after rotating $\triangle ABC$ 90° counterclockwise about the origin.

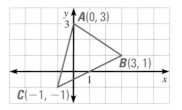

19. Rock Circle The rock circle shown below is in the Ténéré desert in the African country of Niger. The circle is about 60 feet in diameter. Suppose the center of the circle is at (30, 30) on a grid measured in units of feet. Write an equation of the circle.

Chapter 11 Standardized Test

Test Tip Write your work neatly and number it. If you have time to check your answers, it is faster to review this work rather than start over.

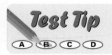

1. Which of the following is a secant in $\odot G$?

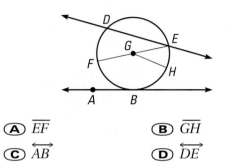

Ⓐ $\overline{EF}$ Ⓑ $\overline{GH}$

Ⓒ $\overleftrightarrow{AB}$ Ⓓ $\overleftrightarrow{DE}$

2. What is the approximate length of the blue arc?

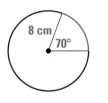

Ⓕ 8.12 cm Ⓖ 9.77 cm

Ⓗ 10.85 cm Ⓙ 11.27 cm

3. Which of the figures has rotational symmetry?

Ⓐ Ⓑ

Ⓒ Ⓓ

4. Find the value of x.

Ⓕ 4

Ⓖ 11

Ⓗ 16

Ⓙ 144

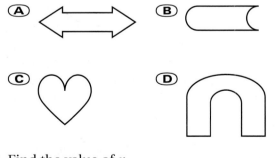

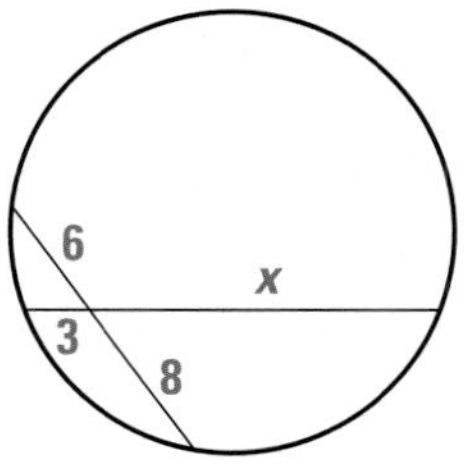

5. Find the value of x.

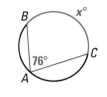

Ⓐ 38 Ⓑ 76

Ⓒ 90 Ⓓ 152

6. Find the measure of $\angle 1$.

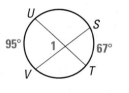

Ⓕ 67 Ⓖ 81

Ⓗ 93 Ⓙ 160

7. Which of the following is the equation of a circle with center $(7, -1)$ and radius 8?

Ⓐ $(x + 7)^2 + (y - 1)^2 = 64$

Ⓑ $(x - 7)^2 + (y + 1)^2 = 64$

Ⓒ $(x + 7)^2 + (y - 1)^2 = 8$

Ⓓ $(x - 7)^2 + (y - 1)^2 = 64$

8. Find the values of x and y.

Ⓕ $x = 83, y = 98$

Ⓖ $x = 98, y = 83$

Ⓗ $x = 83, y = 88$

Ⓙ $x = 98, y = 93$

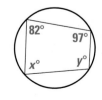

BraiN GaMes

What Did I Describe?

Materials
- circle cards
- pencil
- paper

Object of the Game To correctly draw a picture from a description.

Step 1 ▶ One player picks a card and describes the picture to the other players.

Step 2 ▶ The other players try to draw the picture described. The team gets a point for each player who draws the picture correctly.

Step 3 ▶ Continue play until each player has a turn describing a picture. The team with the most points wins.

"Draw two circles with the same radius so they touch at one point. From the point of intersection, draw a diameter for each circle..."

Another Way to Play Draw your own picture of a circle with tangents, secants, chords, inscribed angles, and central angles. Play as shown above.

"Draw a circle and a tangent line. Draw a line through the circle's center and the point of tangency..."

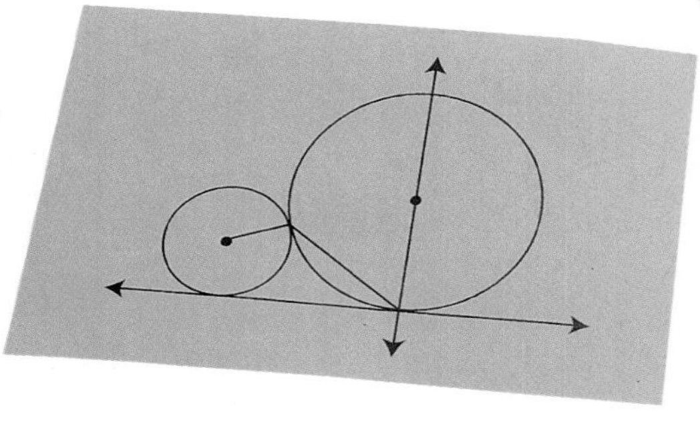

Find the measure. (Lessons 1.5, 1.6)

1. $AC = \underline{\quad ? \quad}$

2. $ST = \underline{\quad ? \quad}$

3. $m\angle STR = \underline{\quad ? \quad}$

4. $m\angle JGH = \underline{\quad ? \quad}$

In Exercises 5 and 6, $\overline{ST}$ has endpoints $S(3, 9)$ and $T(-1, 5)$.

5. Find the coordinates of the midpoint of $\overline{ST}$. (Lesson 2.1)

6. Find the distance between the points. Round your answer to the nearest tenth. (Lesson 4.4)

Find the measure of a complement and a supplement of the angle given. (Lesson 2.3)

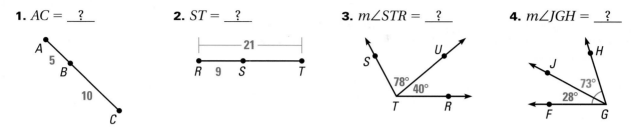

7. 70°

8. 30°

9. 48°

10. 85°

11. Find the value of x. Then use substitution to find $m\angle APB$ and $m\angle BPC$. (Lesson 2.4)

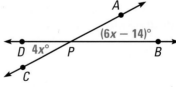

12. Show the conjecture is false by finding a counterexample: If two lines do not intersect, then the lines are parallel. (Lessons 1.2, 3.1)

Explain how you can show that $\ell \parallel m$. State any theorems or postulates that you would use. (Lessons 3.5, 3.6)

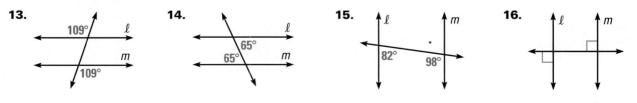

13. 109°, 109°

14. 65°, 65°

15. 82°, 98°

16.

17. An isosceles triangle has an angle of measure 124°. Find the measures of the other two angles. Explain. (Lessons 4.2, 4.3)

In Exercises 18 and 19, use △ABC.

18. Classify the triangle as *acute*, *right*, or *obtuse*. **(Lesson 4.5)**

19. Name the smallest and largest angles of △*ABC*. **(Lesson 4.7)**

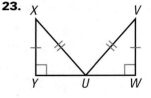

Does the diagram give enough information to show that the triangles are congruent? If so, state the postulate or theorem you would use. Explain your reasoning. (Lessons 5.2–5.4)

20.

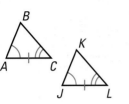

21.

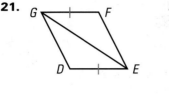

22.

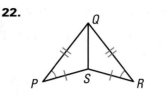

23.

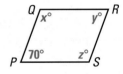

In Exercises 24–27, find the value of each variable. (Lessons 6.1, 6.2, 6.4, 6.5)

24. square *ABCD*

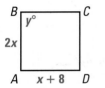

25. trapezoid *FGHJ*

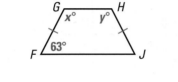

26. quadrilateral *KLMN*

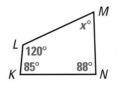

27. parallelogram *PQRS*

28. The perimeter of a rectangle is 60 centimeters. The ratio of the length to the width is 3 : 2. Sketch the rectangle. Then find the length and the width. **(Lesson 7.1)**

In Exercises 29 and 30, use the diagram at the right.

29. Show that the overlapping triangles are similar. Then write a similarity statement. **(Lesson 7.4)**

30. Find the value of *x*. **(Lesson 7.5)**

In Exercises 31–34, find the area of the figure. (Lessons 8.3, 8.5–8.7)

31. **32.** **33.** **34.**

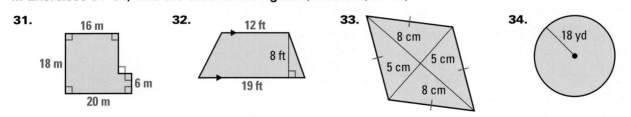

35. A parallelogram has a base of 14 meters and an area of 84 square meters. Find the height. **(Lesson 8.5)**

Find the surface area and volume of the solid. If necessary, round your answer to the nearest whole number. (Lessons 9.2–9.6)

36.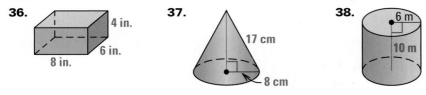

37.

38.

39.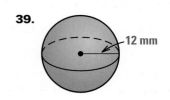

In Exercises 40 and 41, use the diagram of △RST. (Lessons 10.4–10.6)

40. Find sin *R*, cos *R* and tan *R*. Write your answers as decimals rounded to four decimal places.

41. Find the measures of ∠*R* and ∠*T* to the nearest tenth of a degree.

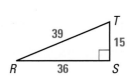

Solve the right triangle. Round decimals to the nearest tenth.
(Lessons 10.3–10.6)

42.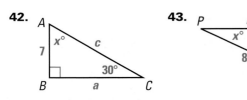

43.

44.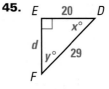

45.

In Exercises 46–48, use the diagram of ⊙O.

46. Find the area of the blue sector. (Lesson 8.7)

47. Find the measures of $\overset{\frown}{AB}$ and $\overset{\frown}{ACB}$. (Lesson 11.3)

48. Find the length of $\overset{\frown}{AB}$. (Lesson 11.3)

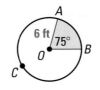

In Exercises 49–52, find the value of x. (Lessons 11.4–11.6)

49.

50.

51.

52.

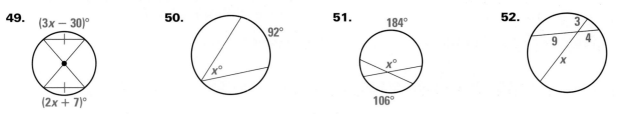

53. Write the standard equation of a circle with center $(0, -3)$ and radius 7. (Lesson 11.7)

In Exercises 54–56, copy △ABC.

54. Draw the image of △*ABC* after the translation $(x, y) \to (x - 1, y + 1)$. (Lesson 3.7)

55. Draw the reflection of △*ABC* in the *y*-axis. (Lesson 5.7)

56. Rotate △*ABC* 180° about the origin. Find the coordinates of the vertices of △*A'B'C'*. (Lesson 11.8)

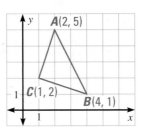

Contents of Student Resources

Skills Review Handbook — 653

Problem Solving	653	The Coordinate Plane	664
Decimals	655	Slope of a Line	665
Fraction Concepts	656	Graphing Linear Equations	666
Fractions and Decimals	657	Slope-Intercept Form	667
Adding and Subtracting Fractions	658	Powers and Square Roots	668
Multiplying and Dividing Fractions	659	Evaluating Expressions	670
		The Distributive Property	671
Ratio and Proportion	660	One-Step Equations	672
Inequalities and Absolute Value	662	Multi-Step Equations	673
Integers	663	Using Formulas	674

Extra Practice for Chapters 1–11 — 675

End-of-Course Test — 697

Tables — 701

Symbols	701	Squares and Square Roots	704
Properties and Formulas	702	Trigonometric Ratios	705

Postulates and Theorems — 706

Glossary

English-to-Spanish Glossary

Index

Selected Answers

Skills Review Handbook

PROBLEM SOLVING

One of your primary goals in mathematics should be to become a good problem solver. It helps to approach a problem with a plan.

Step ❶ Understand the problem.
Read the problem carefully. Organize the given information and decide what you need to find. Check for unnecessary or missing information. Supply missing facts, if possible.

Step ❷ Make a plan to solve the problem.
Choose a problem-solving strategy. (See the next page for a list.) Choose the correct operations. Decide if you will use a tool such as a calculator, a graph, or a spreadsheet.

Step ❸ Carry out the plan to solve the problem.
Use the strategy and any tools you have chosen. Estimate before you calculate, if possible. Do any calculations that are needed. Answer the question that the problem asks.

Step ❹ Check to see if your answer is reasonable.
Reread the problem. See if your answer agrees with the given information and with any estimate you calculated.

EXAMPLE **Eight people can be seated evenly around a rectangular table, with one person on each end. How many people can be seated around three of these tables placed end-to-end?**

Solution

❶ You know each table is rectangular, seats eight people, and can fit one person on each end. You need to find the number of people that can be seated at three tables placed end-to-end.

❷ An appropriate strategy is to draw a diagram.

❸ Draw one table, with an X for each person seated. Notice that three people can be seated at each long side of the table. Then draw three tables placed end-to-end. Draw Xs and count them.

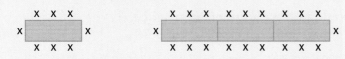

There are 20 Xs on the diagram, so 20 people can be seated.

❹ At three individual tables you can seat 24 people. Since seats are lost when tables are placed end-to-end, 20 is a reasonable answer.

In Step 2 of the problem-solving plan on the previous page you select a strategy. Here are some problem-solving strategies to consider.

Guess, check, and revise.	Use when you do not seem to have enough information.
Draw a diagram or a graph.	Use when words describe a visual representation.
Make an organized list or table.	Use when you have data or choices to organize.
Use an equation or a formula.	Use when you know a relationship between quantities.
Use a proportion.	Use when you know that two ratios are equal.
Look for a pattern.	Use when you can examine several cases.
Break into simpler parts.	Use when you have a multi-step problem.
Solve a simpler problem.	Use when smaller numbers help you understand the problem.
Work backward.	Use when you look for a fact leading to a known result.
Act out the situation.	Use when visualizing the problem is helpful.

Practice

1. During the month of May, Rosa made deposits of $128.50 and $165.19 into her checking account. She wrote checks for $25, $55.12, and $83.98. If her account balance at the end of May was $327.05, what was her balance at the beginning of May?

2. A rectangular room measures 9 feet by 15 feet. How many square yards of carpet are needed to cover the floor of this room?

3. You make 20 silk flower arrangements and plan to sell them at a craft show. Each arrangement costs $12 in materials, and your booth at the show costs $30. If you price the arrangements at $24 each, how many must you sell to make at least $100 profit?

4. A store sells sweatshirts in small, medium, large, and extra large. The color choices are red, white, blue, gray, and black. How many different kinds of sweatshirts are sold at the store?

5. If 4.26 pounds of ham cost $6.77, what would 3.75 pounds cost?

6. Roger bought some 34¢ stamps and some 20¢ stamps, and spent $2.90. How many of each type of stamp did Roger buy?

7. Abigail, Bonnie, Carla, and Dominique are competing in a race. In how many different orders can the athletes finish the race?

8. Five boys are standing in a line. Sam is before Mark and immediately after Alex. Eric is next to Charlie and Alex. List the order of the boys in line.

9. How many diagonals can be drawn on a stop sign?

DECIMALS

The steps for adding, subtracting, multiplying, and dividing with decimals are like those for computing with whole numbers.

EXAMPLES Add or subtract.

a. $15.2 - 8.65$

b. $3.8 + 0.19 + 7$

Solution Write in vertical form, lining up the decimal points. Use zeros as placeholders.

a.
$$
\begin{array}{r}
15.20 \quad \leftarrow \text{placeholder} \\
- \ 8.65 \\
\hline
6.55
\end{array}
$$

b.
$$
\begin{array}{r}
3.80 \quad \leftarrow \text{placeholder} \\
0.19 \\
+ \ 7.00 \quad \leftarrow \text{placeholders} \\
\hline
10.99
\end{array}
$$

ANSWER ▶ $15.2 - 8.65 = 6.55$

ANSWER ▶ $3.8 + 0.19 + 7 = 10.99$

EXAMPLES Multiply or divide.

a. 6.75×4.9

b. $0.068 \div 0.4$

Solution

a. Write in vertical form.

The number of decimal places in the product is equal to the sum of the number of decimal places in the factors.

$$
\begin{array}{r}
6.75 \quad \leftarrow 2 \text{ decimal places} \\
\times \ 4.9 \quad \leftarrow 1 \text{ decimal place} \\
\hline
6\ 075 \\
27\ 000 \\
\hline
33.075 \quad \leftarrow 3 \text{ decimal places}
\end{array}
$$

b. Write in long division form: $0.4\overline{)0.068}$

Move the decimal points the same number of places so that the divisor is a whole number: $0.4\overline{)0.068}$ Then divide.

$$
\begin{array}{r}
0.17 \\
4\overline{)0.68} \\
0.40 \\
\hline
28 \\
28 \\
\hline
0
\end{array}
$$

Line up the decimal point in the quotient with the decimal point in the dividend.

ANSWER ▶ $6.75 \times 4.9 = 33.075$

ANSWER ▶ $0.068 \div 0.4 = 0.17$

Practice

Evaluate.

1. $1.78 + 0.3$

2. $0.14 + 0.095$

3. $66 + 17.5 + 96.5$

4. $0.83 - 0.07$

5. $90 - 42.5$

6. $49.5 - 1.2 - 23.5$

7. 9×3.14

8. 0.15×6.2

9. 400×0.025

10. $124.2 \div 0.02$

11. $0.8 \div 0.1$

12. $600 \div 0.15$

FRACTION CONCEPTS

Multiply or divide the numerator and denominator of a fraction by the same nonzero number to write an **equivalent fraction**. To write a fraction in **simplest form**, divide the numerator and denominator by their greatest common factor. Two numbers are **reciprocals** if their product is 1.

EXAMPLE Write two fractions equivalent to $\frac{4}{10}$.

Solution

Divide the numerator and denominator by 2:

$$\frac{4}{10} = \frac{4 \div 2}{10 \div 2} = \frac{2}{5}$$

Multiply the numerator and denominator by 2:

$$\frac{4}{10} = \frac{4 \times 2}{10 \times 2} = \frac{8}{20}$$

EXAMPLE Write the fraction $\frac{8}{12}$ in simplest form.

Solution

The greatest common factor of 8 and 12 is 4.

Divide the numerator and denominator by 4: $\frac{8}{12} = \frac{8 \div 4}{12 \div 4} = \frac{2}{3}$.

EXAMPLES Find the reciprocal of the number. **a.** $\frac{4}{5}$ **b.** 10

Solution

a. Switch the numerator and the denominator. The reciprocal is $\frac{5}{4}$.

b. Write 10 as a fraction, $\frac{10}{1}$. The reciprocal is $\frac{1}{10}$.

Practice

Write two fractions equivalent to the given fraction.

1. $\frac{6}{12}$ **2.** $\frac{18}{20}$ **3.** $\frac{1}{4}$ **4.** $\frac{4}{6}$ **5.** $\frac{3}{10}$

Write the fraction in simplest form.

6. $\frac{9}{12}$ **7.** $\frac{6}{9}$ **8.** $\frac{100}{200}$ **9.** $\frac{5}{15}$ **10.** $\frac{16}{64}$

Find the reciprocal of the number.

11. $\frac{2}{5}$ **12.** $\frac{1}{8}$ **13.** $\frac{4}{3}$ **14.** 7   **15.** 1

FRACTIONS AND DECIMALS

Divide to write a fraction as a decimal. If the remainder is ever zero, the result is a **terminating decimal**. If the quotient has a digit or group of digits that repeats, the result is a **repeating decimal**.

EXAMPLES Write the fraction as a decimal.

a. $\dfrac{5}{8}$

b. $\dfrac{2}{3}$

Solution Divide the numerator by the denominator.

a.
$$\begin{array}{r} 0.625 \\ 8)\overline{5.000} \end{array}$$
terminating decimal

b.
$$\begin{array}{r} 0.666\ldots \\ 3)\overline{2.000} \end{array}$$
repeating decimal

ANSWER▸ $\dfrac{5}{8} = 0.625$

ANSWER▸ $\dfrac{2}{3} = 0.\overline{6}$ A bar indicates repeating digits.

≈ 0.67 Round for an approximation.

EXAMPLES Write the decimal as a fraction in simplest form.

a. 0.15

b. $0.8\overline{3}$

Solution

a. 0.15 is fifteen hundredths.

$$0.15 = \dfrac{15}{100} = \dfrac{3}{20}$$

Use simplest form.

ANSWER▸ $0.15 = \dfrac{3}{20}$

b.
$x = 0.8333\ldots$	Write an equation.
$10x = 8.3333\ldots$	Multiply each side by 10.
$9x = 7.5$	Find $10x - x$.
$x = \dfrac{7.5}{9} = \dfrac{75}{90} = \dfrac{5}{6}$	Solve and simplify.

ANSWER▸ $0.8\overline{3} = \dfrac{5}{6}$

Practice

Write the fraction as a decimal. For repeating decimals, also round to the nearest hundredth for an approximation.

1. $\dfrac{7}{10}$ **2.** $\dfrac{1}{4}$ **3.** $\dfrac{1}{3}$ **4.** $\dfrac{7}{8}$ **5.** $\dfrac{2}{9}$

6. $\dfrac{4}{5}$ **7.** $\dfrac{1}{8}$ **8.** $\dfrac{19}{100}$ **9.** $\dfrac{1}{2}$ **10.** $\dfrac{7}{15}$

Write the decimal as a fraction in simplest form.

11. 0.5 **12.** 0.01 **13.** 0.2 **14.** 0.75 **15.** 0.375

16. 0.24 **17.** $0.\overline{6}$ **18.** $0.5\overline{3}$ **19.** $0.1\overline{3}$ **20.** $0.\overline{4}$

ADDING AND SUBTRACTING FRACTIONS

To add or subtract two fractions with the same denominator, add or subtract the numerators. Write the result in simplest form.

EXAMPLES   **Add or subtract.**

a. $\dfrac{1}{8} + \dfrac{3}{8}$

b. $\dfrac{9}{10} - \dfrac{3}{10}$

Solution

a. $\dfrac{1}{8} + \dfrac{3}{8} = \dfrac{1+3}{8} = \dfrac{4}{8} = \dfrac{1}{2}$

b. $\dfrac{9}{10} - \dfrac{3}{10} = \dfrac{9-3}{10} = \dfrac{6}{10} = \dfrac{3}{5}$

To add or subtract two fractions with different denominators, write equivalent fractions with a common denominator. Then add or subtract and write the result in simplest form.

EXAMPLES   **Add or subtract.**

a. $\dfrac{4}{15} + \dfrac{2}{5}$

b. $\dfrac{3}{4} - \dfrac{1}{6}$

Solution

a. Write $\dfrac{2}{5}$ as $\dfrac{6}{15}$.

b. Write $\dfrac{3}{4}$ as $\dfrac{9}{12}$ and $\dfrac{1}{6}$ as $\dfrac{2}{12}$.

$\dfrac{4}{15} + \dfrac{2}{5} = \dfrac{4}{15} + \dfrac{6}{15} = \dfrac{10}{15} = \dfrac{2}{3}$

$\dfrac{3}{4} - \dfrac{1}{6} = \dfrac{9}{12} - \dfrac{2}{12} = \dfrac{7}{12}$

Practice

Add or subtract. Write the answer in simplest form.

1. $\dfrac{2}{7} + \dfrac{4}{7}$ **2.** $\dfrac{7}{12} - \dfrac{1}{12}$ **3.** $\dfrac{2}{3} - \dfrac{1}{3}$ **4.** $\dfrac{1}{6} + \dfrac{1}{6}$

5. $\dfrac{3}{4} - \dfrac{1}{4}$ **6.** $\dfrac{4}{5} + \dfrac{1}{5}$ **7.** $\dfrac{7}{20} + \dfrac{9}{20}$ **8.** $\dfrac{79}{100} - \dfrac{14}{100}$

9. $\dfrac{7}{8} - \dfrac{1}{4}$ **10.** $\dfrac{2}{3} + \dfrac{1}{6}$ **11.** $\dfrac{3}{4} + \dfrac{1}{2}$ **12.** $\dfrac{5}{12} - \dfrac{1}{3}$

13. $\dfrac{5}{7} - \dfrac{2}{5}$ **14.** $\dfrac{3}{16} + \dfrac{5}{8}$ **15.** $\dfrac{3}{8} - \dfrac{1}{12}$ **16.** $\dfrac{2}{3} + \dfrac{1}{2}$

17. $\dfrac{5}{8} + \dfrac{3}{8}$ **18.** $\dfrac{24}{25} - \dfrac{3}{5}$ **19.** $\dfrac{5}{9} + \dfrac{14}{15}$ **20.** $\dfrac{9}{10} - \dfrac{4}{5}$

21. $\dfrac{2}{3} + \dfrac{1}{5}$ **22.** $\dfrac{3}{8} - \dfrac{7}{40}$ **23.** $\dfrac{17}{20} - \dfrac{1}{5}$ **24.** $\dfrac{7}{11} + \dfrac{1}{3}$

MULTIPLYING AND DIVIDING FRACTIONS

To multiply two fractions, multiply the numerators and multiply the denominators. Then write the result in simplest form.

EXAMPLES Multiply.

a. $\dfrac{3}{4} \times \dfrac{5}{6}$

b. $20 \times \dfrac{4}{5}$

Solution

a. $\dfrac{3}{4} \times \dfrac{5}{6} = \dfrac{3 \times 5}{4 \times 6} = \dfrac{15}{24} = \dfrac{5}{8}$

b. $\dfrac{20}{1} \times \dfrac{4}{5} = \dfrac{20 \times 4}{1 \times 5} = \dfrac{80}{5} = 16$

To divide by a fraction, multiply by its reciprocal and write the product in simplest form.

EXAMPLES Divide.

a. $\dfrac{1}{5} \div \dfrac{5}{8}$

b. $9 \div \dfrac{7}{10}$

Solution

a. $\dfrac{1}{5} \div \dfrac{5}{8} = \dfrac{1}{5} \times \dfrac{8}{5} = \dfrac{1 \times 8}{5 \times 5} = \dfrac{8}{25}$

b. $9 \div \dfrac{7}{10} = \dfrac{9}{1} \times \dfrac{10}{7} = \dfrac{9 \times 10}{1 \times 7} = \dfrac{90}{7} = 12\dfrac{6}{7}$

Practice

Multiply or divide. Write the answer in simplest form.

1. $\dfrac{1}{2} \times \dfrac{3}{4}$

2. $\dfrac{2}{3} \times \dfrac{3}{11}$

3. $20 \times \dfrac{1}{8}$

4. $65 \times \dfrac{2}{5}$

5. $\dfrac{5}{12} \times \dfrac{4}{9}$

6. $\dfrac{7}{8} \times \dfrac{1}{4}$

7. $16 \times \dfrac{15}{16}$

8. $10 \times \dfrac{1}{3}$

9. $\dfrac{1}{3} \div \dfrac{1}{2}$

10. $\dfrac{3}{4} \div \dfrac{5}{6}$

11. $9 \div \dfrac{1}{7}$

12. $14 \div \dfrac{1}{2}$

13. $\dfrac{7}{8} \div \dfrac{7}{2}$

14. $\dfrac{4}{5} \div \dfrac{1}{10}$

15. $100 \div \dfrac{7}{8}$

16. $40 \div \dfrac{3}{4}$

17. $\dfrac{2}{5} \div \dfrac{1}{5}$

18. $\dfrac{1}{4} \times \dfrac{7}{10}$

19. $\dfrac{22}{7} \times 49$

20. $\dfrac{8}{9} \div 4$

21. $\dfrac{8}{3} \times \dfrac{3}{8}$

22. $\dfrac{1}{5} \div \dfrac{2}{5}$

23. $\dfrac{3}{11} \div \dfrac{3}{11}$

24. $\dfrac{5}{7} \times \dfrac{2}{15}$

25. $12 \div \dfrac{3}{2}$

26. $\dfrac{7}{2} \times \dfrac{1}{14}$

27. $\dfrac{6}{5} \div \dfrac{3}{10}$

28. $4 \times \dfrac{3}{16}$

RATIO AND PROPORTION

The **ratio of a to b** is $\frac{a}{b}$. The ratio of a to b can also be written as "a to b"

or as $a : b$. Because a ratio is a quotient, its denominator cannot be zero.

EXAMPLES A geometry class consists of 16 female students, 12 male students, and 2 teachers. Write each ratio in simplest form.

a. male students : female students   **b.** students : teachers

Solution

a. $\dfrac{12}{16} = \dfrac{3}{4}$

b. $\dfrac{16 + 12}{2} = \dfrac{28}{2} = \dfrac{14}{1}$

EXAMPLES Simplify the ratio.

a. $\dfrac{12 \text{ cm}}{4 \text{ m}}$

b. $\dfrac{6 \text{ ft}}{18 \text{ in.}}$

Solution Express both quantities in the same units of measure so that the units divide out. Write the fraction in simplest form.

a. $\dfrac{12 \text{ cm}}{4 \text{ m}} = \dfrac{\overset{3}{\cancel{12}} \text{ cm}}{\underset{1}{\cancel{4}} \cdot 100 \cancel{\text{ cm}}} = \dfrac{3}{100}$

b. $\dfrac{6 \text{ ft}}{18 \text{ in.}} = \dfrac{\overset{1}{\cancel{6}} \cdot 12 \text{ in.}}{\underset{3}{\cancel{18}} \text{ in.}} = \dfrac{12}{3} = \dfrac{4}{1}$

A **proportion** is an equation showing that two ratios are equal.

If the ratio $\frac{a}{b}$ is equal to the ratio $\frac{c}{d}$, then the following

proportion can be written:

$\dfrac{a}{b} = \dfrac{c}{d}$ where a, b, c, and d are not equal to zero

The numbers a and d are the **extremes** of the proportion.
The numbers b and c are the **means** of the proportion.

Here are two properties that are useful when solving a proportion.

Cross Product Property   The product of the extremes equals the product of the means.

If $\dfrac{a}{b} = \dfrac{c}{d}$, then $ad = bc$.

Reciprocal Property   If two ratios are equal, then their reciprocals are also equal.

If $\dfrac{a}{b} = \dfrac{c}{d}$, then $\dfrac{b}{a} = \dfrac{d}{c}$.

EXAMPLES Solve the proportion.

a. $\dfrac{x}{6} = \dfrac{5}{9}$
b. $\dfrac{3}{x} = \dfrac{4}{7}$

Solution

a. $\dfrac{x}{6} = \dfrac{5}{9}$

$9x = 6(5)$ Use cross products.

$x = \dfrac{30}{9} = \dfrac{10}{3}$ or $3\dfrac{1}{3}$

b. $\dfrac{3}{x} = \dfrac{4}{7}$

$\dfrac{x}{3} = \dfrac{7}{4}$ Use reciprocals.

$x = 3 \cdot \dfrac{7}{4} = \dfrac{21}{4}$ or $5\dfrac{1}{4}$

Practice

An algebra class consists of 10 female students, 15 male students, and 2 teachers. Write the ratio in simplest form.

1. female students : teachers
2. students : teachers
3. female students : male students

4. teachers : male students
5. teachers : students
6. male students : female students

Write the ratio of length to width for the rectangle.

7. 10 cm, 24 cm

8. 5 ft, 6 ft

9. 8 in., 8 in.

Simplify the ratio.

10. $\dfrac{3 \text{ yd}}{10 \text{ ft}}$

11. $\dfrac{4 \text{ lb}}{20 \text{ oz}}$

12. $\dfrac{40 \text{ cm}}{2 \text{ m}}$

13. $\dfrac{1 \text{ kg}}{450 \text{ g}}$

14. $\dfrac{18 \text{ in.}}{1 \text{ ft}}$

15. $\dfrac{6 \text{ mm}}{1 \text{ cm}}$

Solve the proportion.

16. $\dfrac{x}{4} = \dfrac{5}{12}$

17. $\dfrac{5}{x} = \dfrac{2}{5}$

18. $\dfrac{3}{x} = \dfrac{21}{49}$

19. $\dfrac{x}{8} = \dfrac{1}{10}$

20. $\dfrac{x}{7} = \dfrac{11}{7}$

21. $\dfrac{2}{x} = \dfrac{7}{9}$

22. $\dfrac{2}{3} = \dfrac{x}{18}$

23. $\dfrac{x}{10} = \dfrac{3}{100}$

24. $\dfrac{3}{4} = \dfrac{8}{x}$

25. $\dfrac{2}{5} = \dfrac{10}{x}$

26. $\dfrac{5}{4} = \dfrac{x}{14}$

27. $\dfrac{x}{6} = \dfrac{7}{3}$

28. $\dfrac{5}{8} = \dfrac{x}{20}$

29. $\dfrac{x}{6} = \dfrac{6}{15}$

30. $\dfrac{2}{1} = \dfrac{16}{x}$

INEQUALITIES AND ABSOLUTE VALUE

When you compare two numbers *a* and *b*, *a* must be *less than*, *equal to*, or *greater than b*. You can compare two whole numbers or positive decimals by comparing the digits of the numbers from left to right. Find the first place in which the digits are different.

a is less than *b*.	$a < b$
a is equal to *b*.	$a = b$
a is greater than *b*.	$a > b$

EXAMPLES Compare the two numbers.

a. 2.9 and 2.2

b. −4 and −1

Solution Use a number line. The numbers increase from left to right.

a.

2.9 is to the right of 2.2, so 2.9 > 2.2.
Also **9 > 2**, so 2.**9** > 2.**2**.

b.

−4 is to the left of −1, so −4 < −1.

The absolute value of a number is its distance from zero on a number line. The symbol $|a|$ represents the absolute value of *a*.

EXAMPLES Evaluate.

a. $|3|$

b. $|-2|$

Solution Use a number line.

a.

3 is 3 units from 0, so $|3| = 3$.

b.

−2 is 2 units from 0, so $|-2| = 2$.

Practice

Compare the two numbers. Write the answer using <, >, or =.

1. 6 and −6 **2.** 4108 and 4117 **3.** −2 and −8 **4.** −5 and 5

5. −7.8 and −7.6 **6.** 16 and 16.5 **7.** 0.01 and 0.1 **8.** −3.14 and −3.141

Write the numbers in order from least to greatest.

9. −2, 0, 9, −8, 4, −6, 3 **10.** −0.5, 1, 1.5, −2.5, 0.05, −2, −1.5

11. 5124, 5421, 5214, 5142, 5412 **12.** −0.39, −0.4, −0.26, −0.41, −0.32

Evaluate.

13. $|-6|$ **14.** $|4|$ **15.** $|0|$ **16.** $|-20|$ **17.** $|1.4|$

INTEGERS

You can use a number line to add two integers. Move to the right to add a positive integer. Move to the left to add a negative integer.

EXAMPLES Add. **a.** $-4 + 3$ **b.** $-2 + (-3)$

Solution Use the number lines below.

a.

$+3$

Start at -4. Go 3 units to the right.
End at -1. So, $-4 + 3 = -1$.

b.

$+(-3)$

Start at -2. Go 3 units to the left.
End at -5. So, $-2 + (-3) = -5$.

EXAMPLES Subtract. **a.** $7 - 9$ **b.** $2 - (-6)$

Solution To subtract an integer, add its opposite.

a. $7 - 9 = 7 + (-9) = -2$ **b.** $2 - (-6) = 2 + 6 = 8$

When you multiply or divide integers, use these rules.

The product or quotient of two integers with the *same* sign is positive.

The product or quotient of two integers with *opposite* signs is negative.

EXAMPLES Multiply or divide.

a. $(-3)(4)$ **b.** $-27 \div (-9)$

Solution

a. $(-3)(4) = -12 \longleftarrow$ negative product

opposite signs

b. $-27 \div (-9) = 3 \longleftarrow$ positive quotient

same signs

Practice

1. $-8 + (-2)$ **2.** $10 + (-11)$ **3.** $-4 + 6$ **4.** $3 + (-9) + (-1)$

5. $6 - (-5)$ **6.** $-1 - 8$ **7.** $-2 - (-2)$ **8.** $4 - 12$

9. $4(-4)$ **10.** $(-7)(-1)$ **11.** $(-3)(-20)$ **12.** $(-10)(5)(2)$

13. $80 \div (-2)$ **14.** $-42 \div 7$ **15.** $-16 \div (-8)$ **16.** $-81 \div (-3)$

17. $7 - (-9)$ **18.** $20 \div (-4)$ **19.** $-1 + (-5)$ **20.** $(-9)(-2)(4)$

21. $(-4)(25)$ **22.** $-5 + 8$ **23.** $-6 - 6$ **24.** $-49 \div (-7)$

25. $-13 - (-7)$ **26.** $-45 \div 15$ **27.** $(-3)(-3)$ **28.** $9 + (-12) + 2$

THE COORDINATE PLANE

A **coordinate plane** is formed by two number lines that intersect at the **origin**. The horizontal number line is the **x-axis**, and the vertical number line is the **y-axis**. Each point in a coordinate plane corresponds to an **ordered pair** of real numbers. The ordered pair for the origin is (0, 0).

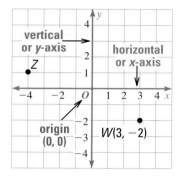

Point $W(3, -2)$, shown on the graph at the right, has an **x-coordinate** of 3 and a **y-coordinate** of -2. From the origin, point W is located 3 units to the right and 2 units down.

EXAMPLE   Use the graph above to name the coordinates of point Z.

Solution

From the origin, point Z is located 4 units to the left and 1 unit up. The coordinates of point Z are $(-4, 1)$.

EXAMPLES   Plot each point in a coordinate plane.

a. $P(-5, 2)$ **b.** $Q(3, 0)$

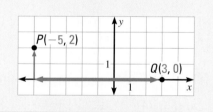

Solution

a. Start at the origin. Move 5 units left and 2 units up.

b. Start at the origin. Move 3 units right and 0 units up.

Practice

Name the coordinates of each point.

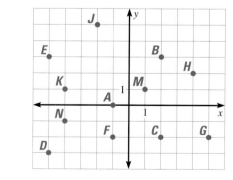

1. A **2.** B **3.** C

4. D **5.** E **6.** F

7. G **8.** H **9.** J

10. K **11.** M **12.** N

Plot the points in a coordinate plane.

13. $A(4, 6)$ **14.** $B(-3, 2)$ **15.** $C(2, -3)$ **16.** $D(0, 4)$

17. $E(-6, -6)$ **18.** $F(5, 5)$ **19.** $G(4, 0)$ **20.** $H(-2, -4)$

21. $J(0, -5)$ **22.** $K(1, -1)$ **23.** $L(-6, 1)$ **24.** $M(3, 2)$

25. $N(-4, 6)$ **26.** $P(3, -5)$ **27.** $Q(-5, -1)$ **28.** $R(-2, 0)$

SLOPE OF A LINE

The **slope** of a line is the ratio of the vertical *rise* to the horizontal *run* between any two points on the line. You subtract coordinates to find the rise and the run. If a line passes through the points (x_1, y_1) and (x_2, y_2), then

$$\text{slope} = \frac{\text{rise}}{\text{run}} = \frac{y_2 - y_1}{x_2 - x_1}.$$

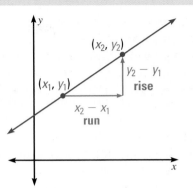

EXAMPLE   Find the slope of the line that passes through the points $(-2, 1)$ and $(5, 4)$.

Solution Let $(x_1, y_1) = (-2, 1)$ and $(x_2, y_2) = (5, 4)$.

$$\text{slope} = \frac{y_2 - y_1}{x_2 - x_1}$$

$$= \frac{4 - 1}{5 - (-2)}$$

$$= \frac{3}{7}$$

The slope of a line can be positive, negative, zero, or undefined.

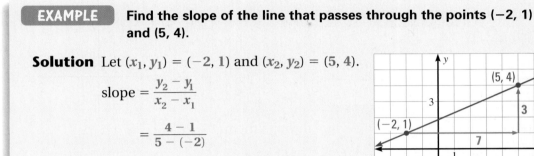

Positive slope	Negative slope	Zero slope	Undefined slope
rising line	falling line	horizontal line	vertical line

Practice

Find the slope of the line that passes through the points.

1. $(0, 3)$ and $(6, 1)$

2. $(3, 2)$ and $(8, 4)$

3. $(1, 0)$ and $(3, 4)$

4. $(1, 2)$ and $(5, 2)$

5. $(1, 1)$ and $(-4, -4)$

6. $(-3, 0)$ and $(2, -5)$

7. $(4, -1)$ and $(-2, 3)$

8. $(4, 2)$ and $(2, -6)$

9. $(-4, -5)$ and $(0, -5)$

Plot the points and draw the line that passes through them. Determine whether the slope is *positive*, *negative*, *zero*, or *undefined*.

10. $(-3, 1)$ and $(-3, -5)$

11. $(1, 4)$ and $(4, -1)$

12. $(-2, 2)$ and $(2, 4)$

13. $(0, -1)$ and $(5, -1)$

14. $(2, 0)$ and $(2, 2)$

15. $(-3, 1)$ and $(1, 2)$

GRAPHING LINEAR EQUATIONS

Equations like $2x + 3y = -6$ and $y = 5x - 1$ are **linear equations**. A **solution** of a linear equation is an ordered pair (x, y) that makes the equation true. The graph of all solutions of a linear equation is a line.

EXAMPLE Graph the equation $y - 4x = 2$.

Solution

❶ Solve the equation for y: $y - 4x = 2$, so $y = 4x + 2$.

❷ Make a table of values to graph the equation.

x	$y = 4x + 2$	(x, y)
-1	$y = 4(-1) + 2 = -2$	$(-1, -2)$
0	$y = 4(0) + 2 = 2$	$(0, 2)$
1	$y = 4(1) + 2 = 6$	$(1, 6)$

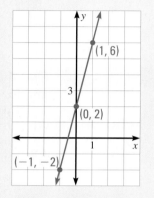

❸ Plot the points in the table and draw a line through them.

You can use **intercepts** (points where the graph crosses the x-axis and y-axis) to graph linear equations.

EXAMPLE Graph the equation $3x - 4y = 12$.

Solution

❶ To find the **x-intercept**, substitute 0 for y.

$3x - 4y = 12$

$3x - 4(0) = 12$

$x = 4$

So, $(4, 0)$ is a solution.

❷ To find the **y-intercept**, substitute 0 for x.

$3x - 4y = 12$

$3(0) - 4y = 12$

$y = -3$

So, $(0, -3)$ is a solution.

❸ Plot $(4, 0)$ and $(0, -3)$ and draw a line through them.

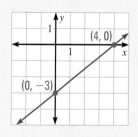

Practice

Graph the equation using a table of values or intercepts.

1. $y = x - 2$

2. $y = 3x - 5$

3. $y = -x$

4. $y = -2x + 3$

5. $y = 2.5 + x$

6. $y = 6 - x$

7. $x + y = 3$

8. $x - y = 4$

9. $2x + y = 6$

10. $2x - 3y = 12$

11. $-5x + 6y = 30$

12. $3.5x - 7y = -14$

SLOPE-INTERCEPT FORM

A linear equation $y = mx + b$ is written in **slope-intercept form**. The slope of the line is m and the y-intercept is b.

EXAMPLE Graph the equation $\frac{1}{2}x + 2y = 4$.

Solution

❶ Write the equation in slope-intercept form.

$$\frac{1}{2}x + 2y = 4$$

$$2y = -\frac{1}{2}x + 4$$

$$y = -\frac{1}{4}x + 2$$

The slope is $-\frac{1}{4}$ and the y-intercept is 2.

❷ Plot the point $(0, 2)$. Use the slope to locate other points on the line.

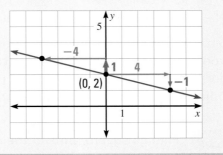

Graphs of linear equations of the form $y = b$ are horizontal lines with slope 0. Graphs of linear equations of the form $x = a$ are vertical lines with *undefined* slope.

EXAMPLES Graph the equation.

a. $y = -1$

b. $x = 3$

Solution

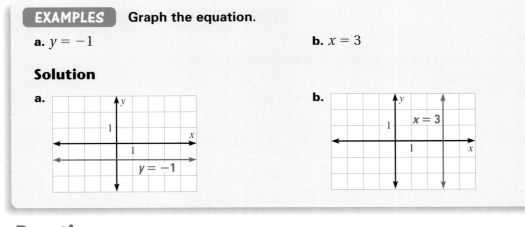

Practice

Graph the equation.

1. $y = x + 1$ **2.** $y = -2x + 5$ **3.** $y = 0.5x - 3$ **4.** $y - 3 = x$

5. $2y = 6x + 10$ **6.** $-2x + y = -6$ **7.** $y = -3$ **8.** $x = 5$

Lines with the same slope are parallel. Tell whether the graphs of the equations are *parallel* or *not parallel*.

9. $y = -3x + 2$
$\quad y = -3x - 2$

10. $y = 4 - x$
$\quad\ y = x - 4$

11. $y - 2x = 4$
$\quad\ 2y - x = 4$

12. $y = 4$
$\quad\ y = 6$

POWERS AND SQUARE ROOTS

An expression like 5^3 is called a **power.** The **exponent** 3 represents the number of times the **base** 5 is used as a factor: $5^3 = 5 \cdot 5 \cdot 5 = 125$.

EXAMPLES Evaluate.

a. 4^5

b. $(-10)^2$

Solution

a. $4^5 = 4 \cdot 4 \cdot 4 \cdot 4 \cdot 4 = 1024$

b. $(-10)^2 = (-10)(-10) = 100$

If $b^2 = a$, then b is a **square root** of a. Every positive number has two square roots, one positive and one negative. The two square roots of 16 are 4 and -4 because $4^2 = 16$ and $(-4)^2 = 16$. The radical symbol $\sqrt{}$ indicates the *nonnegative* square root, so $\sqrt{16} = 4$.

EXAMPLES Find all square roots of the number.

a. 25

b. -81

Solution

a. Since $5^2 = 25$ and $(-5)^2 = 25$, the square roots are 5 and -5.

b. Since -81 is negative, it has *no square roots*. There is no real number you can square to get -81.

The square of an integer is a **perfect square,** so the square root of a perfect square is an integer.

Integer, (n)	1	2	3	4	5	6	7	8	9	10	11	12
Perfect square, (n^2)	1	4	9	16	25	36	49	64	81	100	121	144

You can approximate the square root of a positive number that is *not* a perfect square by using a calculator and rounding.

EXAMPLES Evaluate. Give the exact value if possible. Otherwise, approximate to the nearest tenth.

a. $\sqrt{49}$

b. $\sqrt{5}$

Solution

a. Since 49 is a perfect square with $7^2 = 49$, $\sqrt{49} = 7$.

b. Since 5 is not a perfect square, use a calculator and round: $\sqrt{5} \approx 2.2$.

A number or expression inside a radical symbol is called a **radicand**. The **simplest form of a radical expression** is an expression that has no perfect square factors other than 1 in the radicand, no fractions in the radicand, and no radicals in the denominator of a fraction.

You can use the following properties to simplify radical expressions.

Product Property of Radicals $\quad \sqrt{ab} = \sqrt{a} \cdot \sqrt{b}$ where $a \geq 0$ and $b \geq 0$

Quotient Property of Radicals $\quad \sqrt{\dfrac{a}{b}} = \dfrac{\sqrt{a}}{\sqrt{b}}$ where $a \geq 0$ and $b > 0$

EXAMPLES Simplify.

a. $\sqrt{18}$
b. $\sqrt{\dfrac{9}{4}}$
c. $\dfrac{1}{\sqrt{2}}$

Solution

a. $\sqrt{18} = \sqrt{9 \cdot 2} = \sqrt{9} \cdot \sqrt{2} = 3 \cdot \sqrt{2} = 3\sqrt{2}$ Factor using perfect square factor.

b. $\sqrt{\dfrac{9}{4}} = \dfrac{\sqrt{9}}{\sqrt{4}} = \dfrac{3}{2}$ Use the quotient property and simplify.

c. $\dfrac{1}{\sqrt{2}} = \dfrac{1}{\sqrt{2}} \cdot \dfrac{\sqrt{2}}{\sqrt{2}} = \dfrac{\sqrt{2}}{2}$ Write an equivalent fraction that has no radicals in the denominator.

Practice

Evaluate.

1. 8^2
2. $(-3)^2$
3. $(-1)^3$
4. 4^3

5. 2^5
6. 10^4
7. $(-9)^2$
8. 6^3

Find all square roots of the number or write *no real square roots*.

9. 100
10. -25
11. 1
12. 49

13. -9
14. 0
15. -36
16. 64

Evaluate. Give the exact value if possible. If not, approximate to the nearest tenth.

17. $\sqrt{100}$
18. $\sqrt{2}$
19. $\sqrt{15}$
20. $\sqrt{144}$

21. $\sqrt{4}$
22. $\sqrt{87}$
23. $\sqrt{11}$
24. $\sqrt{32}$

25. $\sqrt{45}$
26. $\sqrt{36}$
27. $\sqrt{0}$
28. $\sqrt{81}$

Simplify.

29. $\sqrt{28}$
30. $\sqrt{27}$
31. $\sqrt{50}$
32. $\sqrt{48}$

33. $\sqrt{\dfrac{5}{16}}$
34. $\sqrt{\dfrac{36}{49}}$
35. $\sqrt{\dfrac{1}{9}}$
36. $\sqrt{\dfrac{3}{25}}$

37. $\dfrac{1}{\sqrt{3}}$
38. $\dfrac{10}{\sqrt{2}}$
39. $\dfrac{5}{\sqrt{2}}$
40. $\dfrac{3}{\sqrt{3}}$

EVALUATING EXPRESSIONS

To evaluate a **numerical expression** involving more than one operation, follow the **order of operations**.

❶ First do operations that occur within *grouping symbols*.

❷ Then evaluate *powers*.

❸ Then do *multiplications* and *divisions* from left to right.

❹ Finally, do *additions* and *subtractions* from left to right.

EXAMPLE Evaluate the expression $2 - (4 - 7)^2 \div (-6)$.

Solution

$2 - (4 - 7)^2 \div (-6) = 2 - (-3)^2 \div (-6)$	Evaluate within parentheses.
$= 2 - 9 \div (-6)$	Evaluate the power: $(-3)^2 = 9$.
$= 2 - (-1.5)$	Do the division $9 \div (-6)$.
$= 3.5$	Do the subtraction $2 - (-1.5)$.

To evaluate a **variable expression**, substitute a value for each variable and use the order of operations to simplify.

EXAMPLE Evaluate the expression $x^2 + x - 18$ when $x = 5$.

Solution

$x^2 + x - 18 = 5^2 + 5 - 18$	Substitute 5 for each x.
$= 25 + 5 - 18$	Evaluate the power: $5^2 = 25$.
$= 12$	Add and subtract from left to right.

Practice

Evaluate the expression.

1. $180 - (30 + 45)$

2. $(8 - 2) \cdot 180$

3. $16 + 4 \cdot 2 - 3$

4. $8^2 + (-6)^2$

5. $-7 + 2^3 - 9$

6. $9(7 - 2)^2$

7. $\frac{1}{2}(100 - 74)$

8. $\frac{5 + 7 \cdot 3}{6 + 7}$

9. $\frac{3}{4} \cdot 24 + 4^2 - 1$

Evaluate the expression when $n = 3$.

10. $-3n^2$

11. $(-3n)^2$

12. $n(n - 7)$

13. $\frac{n + 2}{n - 2}$

14. $n^2 - 7n + 6$

15. $\frac{(n - 2) \cdot 180}{n}$

16. $n^2 + 25$

17. $-2n - 18$

18. $(n + 2)(n - 2)$

THE DISTRIBUTIVE PROPERTY

Here are four forms of the **distributive property**.

$$a(b + c) = ab + ac \qquad (b + c)a = ba + ca$$

$$a(b - c) = ab - ac \qquad (b - c)a = ba - ca$$

| **EXAMPLES** | Use the distributive property to write the expression without parentheses. |

a. $x(x + 4)$

b. $5 - (n - 2)$

Solution

a. $x(x + 4) = x(x) + x(4) = x^2 + 4x$

b. $5 - (n - 2) = 5 + (-1)(n - 2) = 5 + (-1)(n) + (-1)(-2) = 5 - n + 2 = 7 - n$

When an expression is written as a sum, the parts that are added are the **terms** of the expression. **Like terms** are terms in an expression that have the same variable raised to the same power. Numbers are also considered to be like terms. You can use the distributive property to combine like terms.

| **EXAMPLES** | Simplify the expression. |

a. $-4x + 7x$

b. $2(x + y) - (4 - y)x$

Solution

a. $-4x + 7x = (-4 + 7)x = 3x$

b.
$2(x + y) - (4 - y)x = 2x + 2y - 4x + xy$	Write without parentheses.
$\qquad = (2 - 4)x + 2y + xy$	Group and combine like terms.
$\qquad = -2x + 2y + xy$	Simplify within parentheses.

Practice

Use the distributive property to write the expression without parentheses.

1. $2(a + 4)$
2. $(2k + 1)7$
3. $-(-3x + 2)$
4. $(7 - 2z)z$

5. $y(y - 9)$
6. $(j - 1)(-3)$
7. $4b(b + 3)$
8. $-2(n - 6)$

Simplify the expression.

9. $-m + 4 + 7m$
10. $6x - 9x + x$
11. $x^2 - 2x + 7x - 14$

12. $a^2 + 3a + 3a + 9$
13. $3 - (2x - 7)$
14. $8 + 3(y - 4)$

15. $6h - 3h(h + 1)$
16. $2(x + 4x) - 7$
17. $y(2y - 6) + y^2$

SOLVING ONE-STEP EQUATIONS

A **solution** of an equation is a value for the variable that makes a true statement. You can solve an equation by writing an *equivalent* equation (an equation with the same solution) that has the variable alone on one side. Here are four ways to solve a one-step equation.

- Add the same number to each side of the equation.

- Subtract the same number from each side of the equation.

- Multiply each side of the equation by the same nonzero number.

- Divide each side of the equation by the same nonzero number.

> **EXAMPLES** Solve the equation.
>
> **a.** $y - 7 = 3$ **b.** $x + 6 = -2$ **c.** $\dfrac{n}{5} = 30$ **d.** $12 = -4c$
>
> **Solution** Choose an operation to perform that will leave the variable alone on one side. Check your solution by substituting it back into the original equation.
>
> **a.** Add 7 to each side.
>
> $$y - 7 = 3$$
> $$y - 7 + 7 = 3 + 7$$
> $$y = 10$$
>
> **CHECK** ✓ $10 - 7 = 3$
>
> **b.** Subtract 6 from each side.
>
> $$x + 6 = -2$$
> $$x + 6 - 6 = -2 - 6$$
> $$x = -8$$
>
> **CHECK** ✓ $-8 + 6 = -2$
>
> **c.** Multiply each side by 5.
>
> $$\frac{n}{5} = 30$$
> $$5 \cdot \frac{n}{5} = 5 \cdot 30$$
> $$n = 150$$
>
> **CHECK** ✓ $\dfrac{150}{5} = 30$
>
> **d.** Divide each side by -4.
>
> $$12 = -4c$$
> $$\frac{12}{-4} = \frac{-4c}{-4}$$
> $$-3 = c$$
>
> **CHECK** ✓ $12 = -4(-3)$

Practice

Solve the equation.

1. $k - 6 = 0$ **2.** $19 = r - (-9)$ **3.** $w - 5 = -13$ **4.** $20 = y - 4$

5. $x + 12 = 25$ **6.** $y + 7 = -16$ **7.** $n + (-4) = -1$ **8.** $-6 = c + 4$

9. $\dfrac{1}{2}x = -14$ **10.** $\dfrac{n}{3} = 6$ **11.** $\dfrac{a}{5} = -1$ **12.** $-\dfrac{3}{4}d = 24$

13. $-36 = -9a$ **14.** $-32h = 4$ **15.** $12 = -12b$ **16.** $4z = 132$

17. $22 = x - 2$ **18.** $-\dfrac{m}{6} = -12$ **19.** $-15y = 75$ **20.** $w + 4 = 15$

SOLVING MULTI-STEP EQUATIONS

Sometimes solving an equation requires more than one step. Use the techniques for solving one-step equations given on the previous page. Simplify one or both sides of the equation first, if needed, by using the distributive property or combining like terms.

EXAMPLES **Solve the equation.**

a. $2x - 3 = 5$

b. $6y + 1 = 5y - 9$

Solution

a.

$2x - 3 = 5$	
$2x - 3 + 3 = 5 + 3$	Add 3.
$2x = 8$	Simplify.
$\dfrac{2x}{2} = \dfrac{8}{2}$	Divide by 2.
$x = 4$	Simplify.

CHECK $\checkmark 2(4) - 3 \overset{?}{=} 5$

$8 - 3 = 5$

b.

$6y + 1 = 5y - 9$	
$6y - 5y + 1 = 5y - 5y - 9$	Subtract 5y.
$y + 1 = -9$	Simplify.
$y + 1 - 1 = -9 - 1$	Subtract 1.
$y = -10$	Simplify.

CHECK $\checkmark 6(-10) + 1 \overset{?}{=} 5(-10) - 9$

$-59 = -50 - 9$

Practice

Solve the equation.

1. $2x + 3 = 11$

2. $4x - 2 = 10$

3. $7 + 2x = 17$

4. $3y - 4 = 20$

5. $\dfrac{x}{7} + 2 = 1$

6. $21 = -2z + 1$

7. $10 - x = -16$

8. $6 - \dfrac{3a}{2} = -6$

9. $8n + 2 = -30$

10. $\dfrac{3}{8}x - 6 = 18$

11. $3 = 5 + \dfrac{1}{4}x$

12. $-6m - 1 = 11$

13. $3r - (2r + 1) = 21$

14. $5(z + 3) = 30$

15. $44 = 5g - 8 - g$

16. $4(t - 7) + 6 = 30$

17. $22d - (6 + 2d) = 4$

18. $85 = \dfrac{1}{2}(226 - x)$

19. $12a - 5 = 7a$

20. $75 + 7x = 2x$

21. $5n - 9 = 3n - 1$

22. $14r + 81 = -r$

23. $4 - 6p = 2p - 12$

24. $7y - 84 = 2y + 61$

25. $1 + j = 2(2j + 1)$

26. $3(x + 1) - 6 = 9$

27. $5 - 2(r + 6) = 1$

28. $\dfrac{1}{5}y + 7 = 3$

29. $\dfrac{8 + x}{2} = 10$

30. $\dfrac{n - 2}{2} = -6$

31. $7(b - 3) = 8b + 2$

32. $12 - 23c = 7(9 - c)$

33. $4z + 2(z - 3) = 0$

USING FORMULAS

A **formula** is an algebraic equation that relates two or more real-life quantities. Here are some formulas for the perimeter P, area A, and circumference C of some common figures.

Square

side length s

$P = 4s$

$A = s^2$

Rectangle

length ℓ and width w

$P = 2\ell + 2w$

$A = \ell w$

Triangle

side lengths a, b, and c
base b and height h

$P = a + b + c$

$A = \dfrac{1}{2}bh$

Circle

radius r

$C = 2\pi r$

$A = \pi r^2$

Pi (π) is the ratio of a circle's circumference to its diameter.

EXAMPLE	**Find the length of a rectangle with perimeter 20 centimeters and width 4 centimeters.**

Solution

$P = 2\ell + 2w$	Write the appropriate formula.
$20 = 2\ell + 2(4)$	Substitute known values of the variables.
$20 = 2\ell + 8$	Simplify.
$12 = 2\ell$	Subtract 8 from each side.
$6 = \ell$	Divide each side by 2.

ANSWER ▶ The length of the rectangle is 6 centimeters.

Practice

1. The perimeter of a square is 24 meters. Find the side length.

2. Find the area of a circle with radius 1.5 centimeters. (Use $\pi \approx 3.14$.)

3. A triangle has a perimeter of 50 millimeters and two sides that measure 14 millimeters each. Find the length of the third side.

4. Find the width of a rectangle with area 32 square feet and length 8 feet.

5. The circumference of a circle is 8π inches. Find the radius.

6. Find the side length of a square with area 121 square centimeters.

7. Find the height of a triangle with area 18 square meters and base 4 meters.

8. A square has an area of 49 square units. Find the perimeter.

Chapter 1

Sketch the next figure you expect in the pattern. (Lesson 1.1)

1.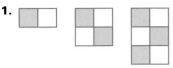

2.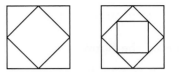

Describe a pattern in the numbers. Write the next number you expect in the pattern. (Lesson 1.1)

3. 1, 5, 25, 125, . . .

4. 1, 2, 4, 7, 11, . . .

5. $-8, -5, -2, 1, . . .$

6. 405, 135, 45, 15, . . .

7. $\dfrac{1}{1}, \dfrac{2}{3}, \dfrac{4}{9}, \dfrac{8}{27}, . . .$

8. 1, 1, 2, 6, 24, 120, . . .

9. Complete the conjecture based on the pattern you observe.
   (Lesson 1.2)

   Conjecture: The square of a negative number is a(n) __?__ number.

   $(-4)^2 = 16$ $(-1)^2 = 1$ $\left(-\dfrac{3}{4}\right)^2 = \dfrac{9}{16}$ $(-0.5)^2 = 0.25$

Show that the conjecture is false by finding a counterexample.
(Lesson 1.2)

10. Conjecture: All rectangles with an area of 12 ft^2 have the same perimeter.

11. Conjecture: The absolute value of a number is always positive.

12. Conjecture: If the sum of two numbers is positive, then the numbers must be positive.

13. Conjecture: The quotient of two positive integers is a positive integer.

Sketch the figure. (Lesson 1.3)

14. Draw three points, *A*, *B*, and *C*, that are not collinear. Then draw $\overleftrightarrow{AB}$ and $\overrightarrow{BC}$.

15. Draw two points, *P* and *Q*. Sketch $\overrightarrow{PQ}$. Then draw a point *R* that lies on $\overleftrightarrow{PQ}$ but is not on $\overline{PQ}$.

16. Draw two points *J* and *K*. Then sketch $\overleftrightarrow{JK}$. Add points *L* and *M* so that *L* is not on $\overleftrightarrow{JK}$ and *M* is between *J* and *K*. Draw $\overrightarrow{JL}$, $\overrightarrow{KL}$, and $\overline{LM}$.

Use the diagram at the right. (Lessons 1.3, 1.4)

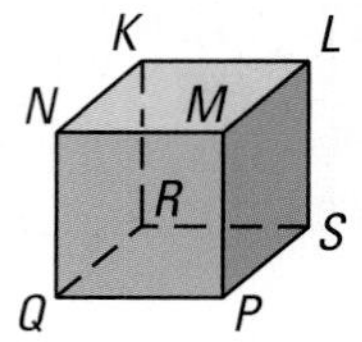

17. Name a point that is coplanar with *Q*, *N*, and *K*.

18. Are points *L*, *M*, and *N* collinear?

19. Name three segments that contain point *P*.

20. Name four lines that intersect $\overleftrightarrow{NK}$.

21. Describe the intersection of plane *KLM* and plane *QPM*.

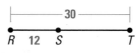

Sketch the figure. (Lesson 1.4)

22. Sketch a line and a plane that do not intersect.

23. Sketch three planes that intersect in a line.

Find the length. (Lesson 1.5)

24. Find *DF*.

25. Find *ST*.

Plot the points in a coordinate plane. Decide whether $\overline{JK}$ and $\overline{MN}$ are congruent. (Lesson 1.5)

26. *J*(−2, −3), *K*(−2, −1), *M*(0, 4), *N*(−3, 4)

27. *J*(5, 1), *K*(−1, 1), *M*(−2, 3), *N*(−2, −3)

28. *J*(3, −2), *K*(3, −5), *M*(3, 3), *N*(7, 3)

Name the vertex and the sides of the angle. Then write two names for the angle. (Lesson 1.6)

29.

30.

31.

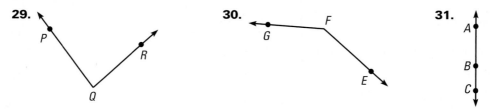

Use the Angle Addition Postulate to find the measure of the specified angle. (Lesson 1.6)

32. *m∠STR* = __?__

33. *m∠HJK* = __?__

34. *m∠DEF* = __?__

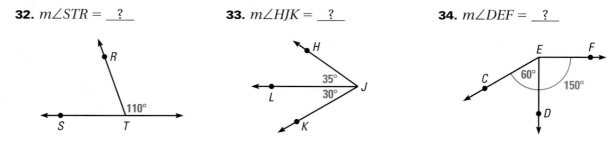

Chapter 2

M is the midpoint of $\overline{AB}$. Find the indicated segment lengths or value of the variable. (Lesson 2.1)

1. Find AB and AM.

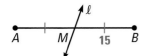

2. Find AM and MB.

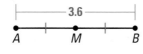

3. Find the value of x.

$$A \quad x + 6 \quad M \quad 20 \quad B$$

Find the coordinates of the midpoint of $\overline{PQ}$. (Lesson 2.1)

4. $P(-4, 2)$, $Q(8, -4)$

5. $P(-1, 5)$, $Q(7, -5)$

6. $P(-4, -6)$, $Q(-12, 4)$

7. $P(-3, 1)$, $Q(6, 5)$

8. $P(0, 4)$, $Q(-7, -5)$

9. $P(-4, -4)$, $Q(1, 1)$

$\overrightarrow{BD}$ bisects $\angle ABC$. Find the indicated angle measure or value of the variable. (Lesson 2.2)

10. Find $m\angle ABD$.

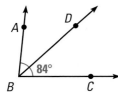

11. Find $m\angle ABC$.

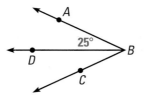

12. Find the value of x.

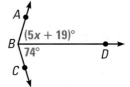

13. State whether the angles in the diagram are *complementary*, *supplementary*, or *neither*. Also state whether the angles are *adjacent* or *nonadjacent*. (Lesson 2.3)

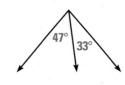

14. The measure of $\angle R$ is $12°$. Find the measures of a complement and a supplement of $\angle R$. (Lesson 2.3)

15. The measure of $\angle S$ is $53°$. Find the measures of a complement and a supplement of $\angle S$. (Lesson 2.3)

16. $\angle JKM$ and $\angle MKL$ are supplementary angles. Find the value of y. (Lesson 2.3)

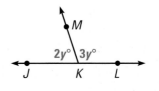

17. $\angle 1$ and $\angle 2$ are supplementary angles. Also $\angle 2$ and $\angle 3$ are supplementary angles. Name a pair of congruent angles. Explain your reasoning. (Lesson 2.3)

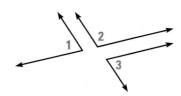

Find the measure of the numbered angle(s). (Lesson 2.4)

18.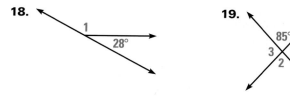

19. **20.**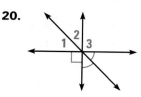

Rewrite the statement as an if-then statement. Then underline the hypothesis and circle the conclusion. (Lesson 2.5)

21. It must be true if you read it in a newspaper.

22. An apple a day keeps the doctor away.

23. The square of an odd number is odd.

24. Use the Law of Detachment to reach a conclusion from the given true statements. (Lesson 2.5)

If E is between D and F, then $DF = DE + EF$.
E is between D and F.

25. Use the Law of Syllogism to write the if-then statement that follows from the pair of true statements. (Lesson 2.5)

If it is hot today, May will go to the beach.
If May goes to the beach, I will go too.

Name the property that the statement illustrates. (Lesson 2.6)

26. $\overline{MN} \cong \overline{MN}$

27. If $ST = 4$, then $RS + ST = RS + 4$.

28. If $\angle R \cong \angle Y$, then $\angle Y \cong \angle R$.

29. If $AB = BC$ and $BC = CD$, then $AB = CD$.

30. If $m\angle P = m\angle Q$, then $2 \cdot m\angle P = 2 \cdot m\angle Q$.

31. If $AM = MB$ and $WX = XY$, then $AM - WX = MB - XY$.

32. In the diagram, $\angle 3$ and $\angle 2$ are supplementary angles. Complete the argument to show that $m\angle 3 = m\angle 1$. (Lesson 2.6)

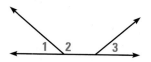

$\angle 3$ and $\angle 2$ are supplementary angles.	Given
$m\angle 3 + m\angle 2 = 180°$	__?__
$m\angle 1 + m\angle 2 = 180°$	__?__ Postulate
$m\angle 3 + m\angle 2 = m\angle 1 + m\angle 2$	__?__
$m\angle 3 = m\angle 1$	__?__

Chapter 3

**Think of each segment in the diagram as part of a line. There may be
more than one correct answer.** (Lesson 3.1)

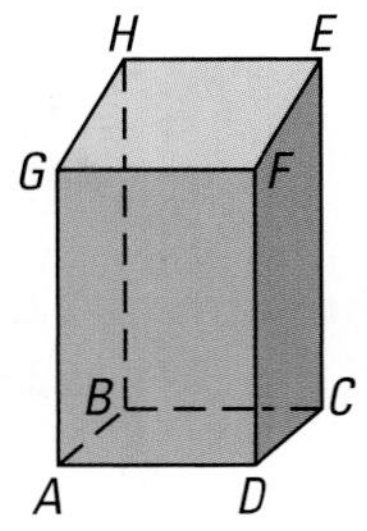

1. Name a line that appears parallel to $\overleftrightarrow{AD}$.

2. Name a line perpendicular to $\overleftrightarrow{AD}$.

3. Name a line skew to $\overleftrightarrow{AD}$.

4. Name a plane that appears parallel to plane *GAB*.

5. Name a plane perpendicular to $\overleftrightarrow{AD}$.

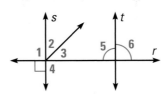

**In the diagram, $r \perp s$ and $\angle 5 \cong \angle 6$. Determine whether enough
information is given to conclude that the statement is true.** (Lesson 3.2)

6. $m\angle 5 = 90°$

7. $\angle 2 \cong \angle 3$

8. $m\angle 2 + m\angle 3 = 90°$

9. $\angle 1 \cong \angle 5$

10. $\angle 2 \cong \angle 4$

11. $r \perp t$

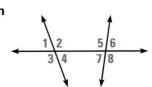

Find the value of *x*, given that $p \perp q$. (Lesson 3.2)

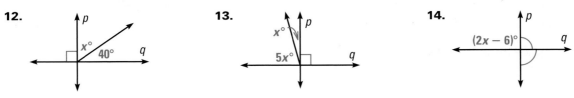

12.

13.

14.

**Use the diagram at the right to determine the relationship between
the pair of angles.** (Lesson 3.3)

15. $\angle 1$ and $\angle 8$

16. $\angle 6$ and $\angle 2$

17. $\angle 7$ and $\angle 2$

18. $\angle 1$ and $\angle 5$

19. $\angle 6$ and $\angle 3$

20. $\angle 5$ and $\angle 2$

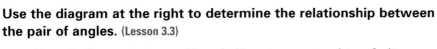

Find $m\angle 1$ and $m\angle 2$. Explain your reasoning. (Lesson 3.4)

21.

22.

23.

24.

25.

26.

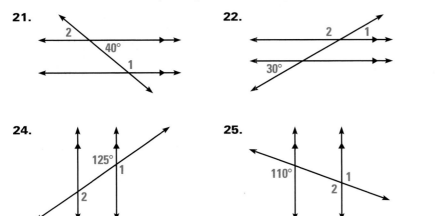

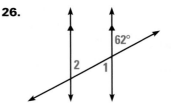

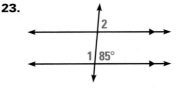

Determine whether enough information is given to conclude that
m ∥ n. (Lesson 3.5)

27.

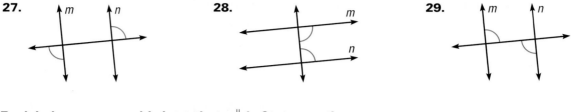

28.

29.

Explain how you would show that a ∥ b. State any theorems or
postulates that you would use. (Lesson 3.6)

30.

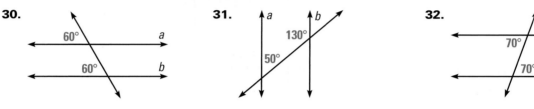

$60°$ a

$60°$ b

31. a   b

$130°$

$50°$

32.

$70°$ a

$70°$ b

Find a value of x so that p ∥ q. (Lesson 3.6)

33.

p

$(7x - 1)°$

q

34. p   q

$(3x + 28)°$ $5x°$

35.

p

$18x°$

q

36. Draw a horizontal line ℓ and choose a point A above ℓ. Construct a
line m perpendicular to ℓ through point A. **(Lesson 3.6)**

Decide whether the red figure is a translation of the blue figure.
(Lesson 3.7)

37.

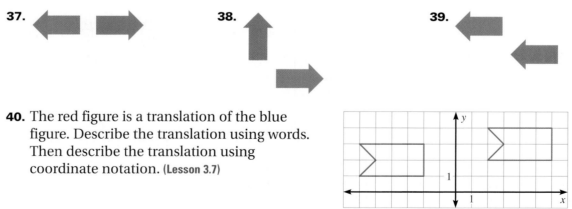

38.

39.

40. The red figure is a translation of the blue
figure. Describe the translation using words.
Then describe the translation using
coordinate notation. **(Lesson 3.7)**

Find the image of each point using the translation (x, y) → (x − 3, y + 11).
(Lesson 3.7)

41. $(0, -6)$

42. $(5, 9)$

43. $(-2, 0)$

44. $(4, -12)$

45. $(-7, -9)$

46. $(3, -11)$

Chapter 4

Classify the triangle by its sides. (Lesson 4.1)

1.
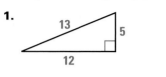

2.

3.
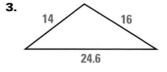

Classify the triangle by its angles. (Lesson 4.1)

4.
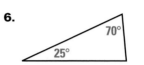

5.
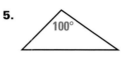

6.

Identify which side is opposite each angle. (Lesson 4.1)

7.
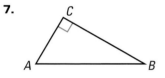

8.
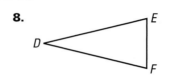

Find the measure of $\angle 1$. (Lesson 4.2)

9.
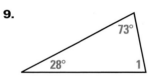

10.
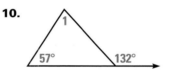

11.
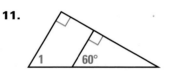

Find the value of *x*. (Lesson 4.3)

12.
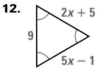

13.
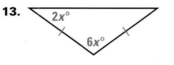

14.
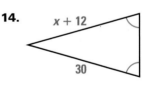

15. Use the diagram to find the measures of $\angle 1$, $\angle 2$, and $\angle 3$.
(Lesson 4.3)

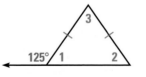

Find the unknown side length. Round your answer to the nearest tenth, if necessary. (Lesson 4.4)

16.
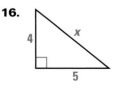

17.
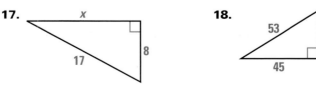

18.

Find the distance between *A* and *B*. Round your answer to the nearest tenth, if necessary. (Lesson 4.4)

19. $A(-4, 0)$
  $B(4, 6)$

20. $A(5, 7)$
  $B(0, -5)$

21. $A(2, -1)$
  $B(1, -4)$

22. $A(-7, -2)$
  $B(0, 7)$

Classify the triangle as *acute*, *right*, or *obtuse*. (Lesson 4.5)

23.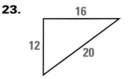

24.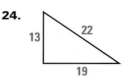

25.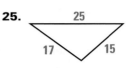

Classify the triangle with the given side lengths as *acute*, *right*, or *obtuse*. (Lesson 4.5)

26. 10, 12, 14

27. 65, 63, 16

28. 7, 9, 12

29. $\sqrt{11}$, 5, 6

30. 5, 7, 9

31. 8, 10, 12

***P* is the centroid of △*JKL*. Use the information to find the indicated lengths.** (Lesson 4.6)

32. $KN = 24$.
  Find KP and PN.

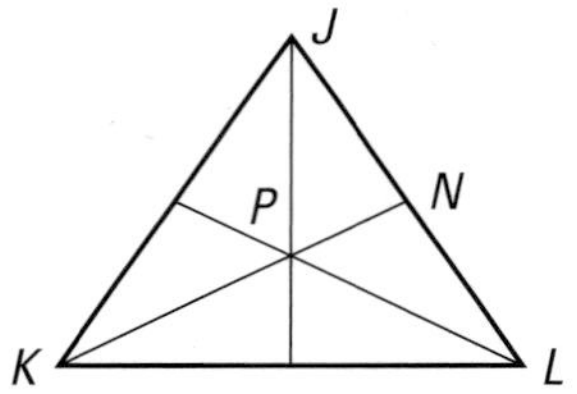

33. $PM = 7$.
  Find JP and JM.

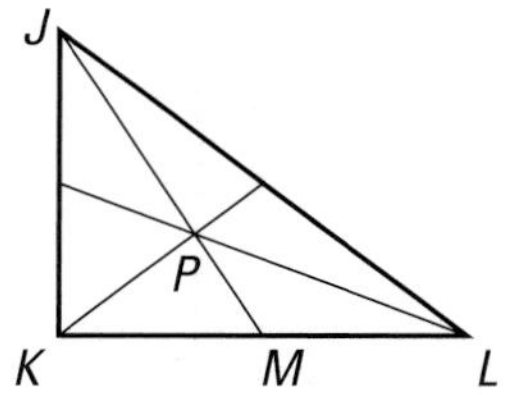

34. $LP = 10$.
  Find PR and LR.

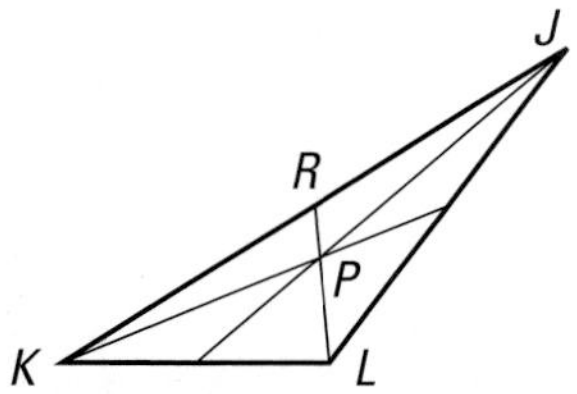

Name the angles from largest to smallest. (Lesson 4.7)

35.

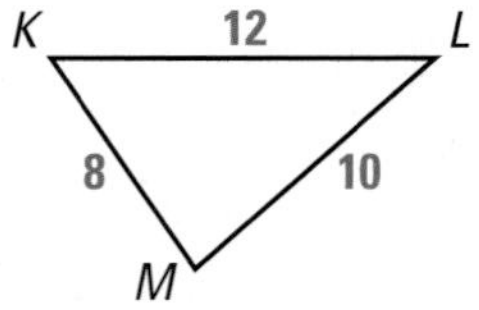

36.

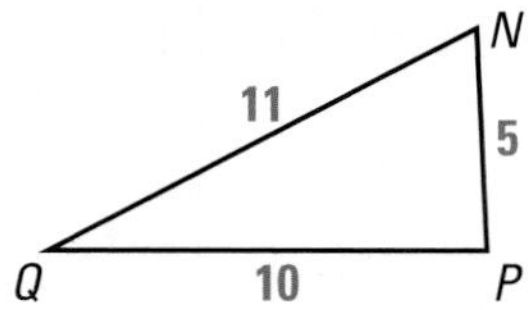

37.

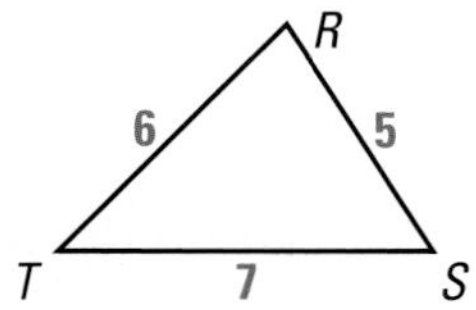

Name the sides from longest to shortest. (Lesson 4.7)

38.

39.

40.

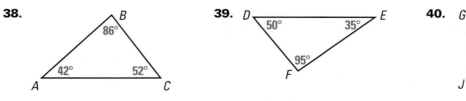

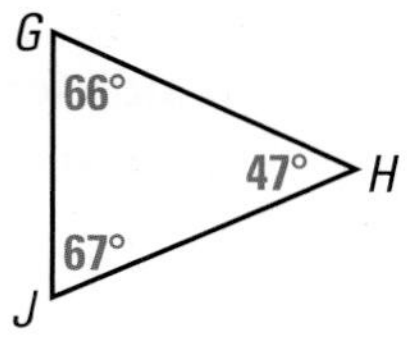

Determine whether the side lengths of the triangle are possible. Explain your reasoning. (Lesson 4.7)

41. 7, 7, 7

42. 5, 7, 12

43. 1, 2, 4

44. 10, 20, 29

Chapter 5

In Exercises 1–3, use the diagram at the right. (Lesson 5.1)

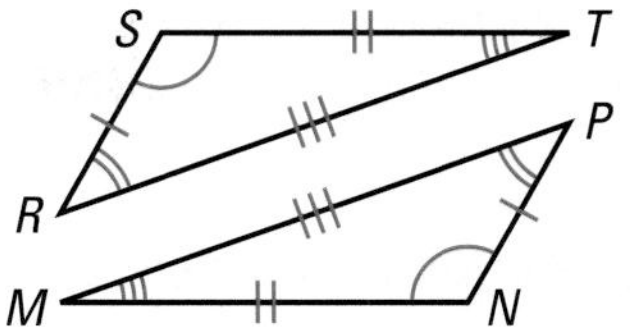

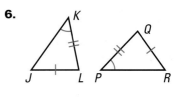

1. Name all pairs of corresponding congruent sides.

2. Name all pairs of corresponding congruent angles.

3. Write a congruence statement for the triangles.

Determine whether the triangles are congruent. If so, write a congruence statement. (Lesson 5.1)

4.

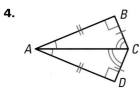

5.

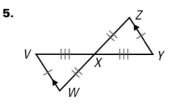

6.

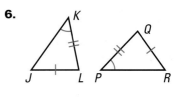

Decide whether enough information is given to show that the triangles are congruent. If so, state the congruence postulate you would use. (Lesson 5.2)

7.

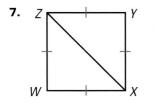

8.

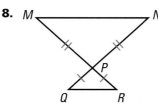

9.

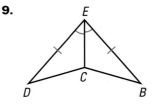

Does the diagram give enough information to show that the triangles are congruent? If so, state the postulate or theorem you would use. (Lesson 5.3)

10.

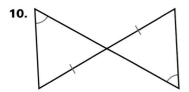

11.

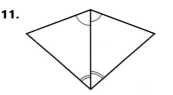

12.

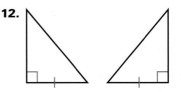

Decide whether enough information is given to show that the triangles are congruent. If so, state the postulate or theorem you would use. (Lesson 5.4)

13.

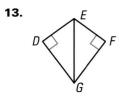

14.

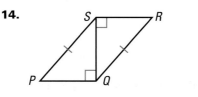

15.

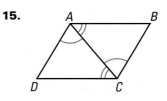

16. Sketch the overlapping triangles separately. Mark all congruent angles and sides. Then tell what theorem or postulate you could use to show that △ABC ≅ △DEF. (Lesson 5.5)

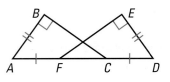

Use the information in the diagram to show that the given statement is true. (Lesson 5.5)

17. ∠GEF ≅ ∠GHJ

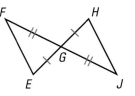

18. $\overline{AE} \cong \overline{CE}$

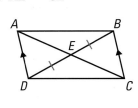

19. ∠RQT ≅ ∠RST

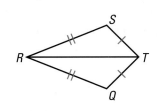

Use the diagram to find each missing measure. (Lesson 5.6)

20. Find CD.

21. Find ML.

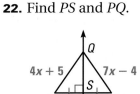

22. Find PS and PQ.

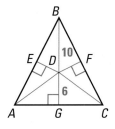

23. The perpendicular bisectors of △ABC meet at point D. Find AD. (Lesson 5.6)

Tell whether the grid shows a reflection in *the x-axis*, *the y-axis*, or *neither*. (Lesson 5.7)

24.

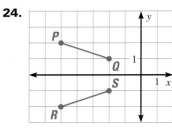

25.

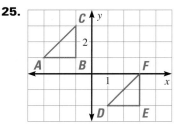

26.

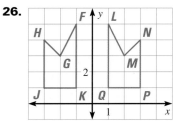

Determine the number of lines of symmetry in each figure. (Lesson 5.7)

27.

28.

29.

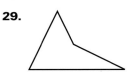

Chapter 6

Decide whether the figure is a polygon. If so, tell what type. If not, explain why. (Lesson 6.1)

1.

2.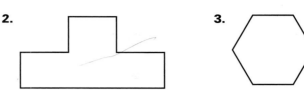

3.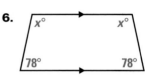

Find the value of x. (Lesson 6.1)

4.

5.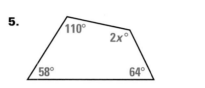

6.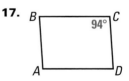

Use the diagram of ▱VWXY at the right. Complete each statement and give a reason for your answer. (Lesson 6.2)

7. $\overline{VW} \cong$ ___?___

8. $\angle VWX \cong$ ___?___

9. $\overline{XW} \cong$ ___?___

10. $\overline{VT} \cong$ ___?___

11. $\overline{WX} \parallel$ ___?___

12. $\angle XYW \cong$ ___?___

13. $\angle VYX$ is supplementary to ___?___ and ___?___.

14. Point T is the midpoint of ___?___ and ___?___.

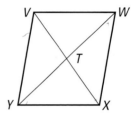

***ABCD* is a parallelogram. Find the missing angle measures.** (Lesson 6.2)

15.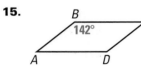

16.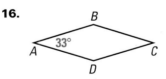

17.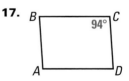

Tell whether the quadrilateral is a parallelogram. Explain your reasoning. (Lesson 6.3)

18.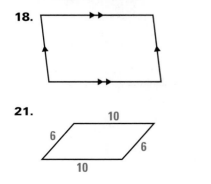

19.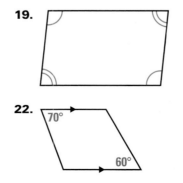

20.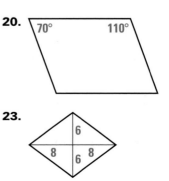

21.

22.

23.

24. In quadrilateral *EFGH*, $m\angle E = 12°$, $m\angle H = 12°$, and $m\angle F = 168°$. Is *EFGH* a parallelogram? Explain your reasoning. (Lesson 6.3)

List each quadrilateral for which the statement is true. (Lesson 6.4)

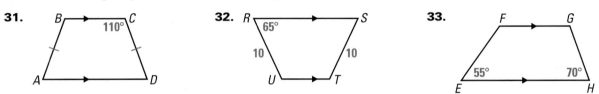

parallelogram rectangle rhombus square

25. Consecutive angles are supplementary.   **26.** Consecutive angles are congruent.

27. Consecutive sides are perpendicular.   **28.** Diagonals are congruent.

29. Consecutive sides are congruent.   **30.** Opposite sides are parallel.

Find the missing angle measures in the trapezoid. (Lesson 6.5)

31.

32.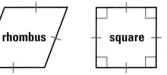

33.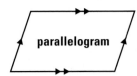

Find the value of *x* for the trapezoid. (Lesson 6.5)

34.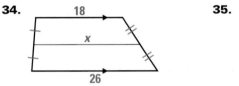

35.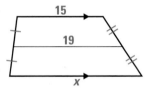

36.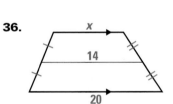

Are you given enough information to conclude that the figure is the given type of special quadrilateral? Explain your reasoning. (Lesson 6.6)

37. A parallelogram?   **38.** A rectangle?   **39.** A rhombus?

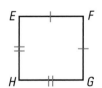   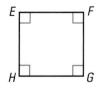   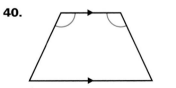

Determine whether the quadrilateral is a *trapezoid,* an *isosceles trapezoid,* a *parallelogram,* a *rectangle,* a *rhombus,* or a *square.*
(Lesson 6.6)

40.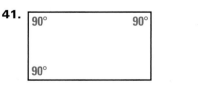

41.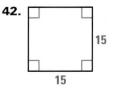

42.

Chapter 7

Simplify the ratio. (Lesson 7.1)

1. $\dfrac{50 \text{ m}}{250 \text{ cm}}$

2. $\dfrac{15 \text{ ft}}{4 \text{ yd}}$

3. $\dfrac{15 \text{ in.}}{2 \text{ ft}}$

4. $\dfrac{10 \text{ km}}{900 \text{ m}}$

Sketch the rectangle described and use ratios to label its sides. Then find the length and the width of the rectangle. (Lesson 7.1)

5. The perimeter of a rectangle is 70 feet. The ratio of the length to the width is $4 : 3$.

6. The perimeter of a rectangle is 128 meters. The ratio of the length to the width is $5 : 3$.

Solve the proportion. (Lesson 7.1)

7. $\dfrac{a}{21} = \dfrac{1}{3}$

8. $\dfrac{5}{b} = \dfrac{20}{7}$

9. $\dfrac{4}{9} = \dfrac{c}{72}$

10. $\dfrac{4}{13} = \dfrac{16}{d}$

11. $\dfrac{x+5}{24} = \dfrac{1}{2}$

12. $\dfrac{r-2}{21} = \dfrac{2}{3}$

13. $\dfrac{2y}{13} = \dfrac{12}{39}$

14. $\dfrac{3}{2z+1} = \dfrac{1}{5}$

In the diagram, *PQRS* ~ *TVWX*. (Lesson 7.2)

15. List all pairs of congruent angles.

16. Find the scale factor of *PQRS* to *TVWX*.

17. Find the value of *u*.

18. Find the value of *y*.

19. Find the value of *z*.

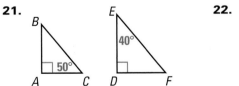

20. Find the ratio of the perimeter of *PQRS* to the perimeter of *TVWX*.

Determine whether the triangles are similar. If they are similar, write a similarity statement. (Lesson 7.3)

21.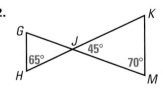

22.

23.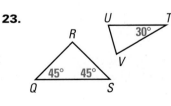

In Exercises 24 and 25, use the diagram. (Lesson 7.3)

24. Show that the triangles are similar.

25. Write a similarity statement for the triangles.

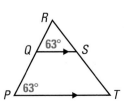

Determine whether the triangles are similar. If they are similar, state the similarity and the postulate or theorem that justifies your answer. (Lesson 7.4)

26.

27.

28.

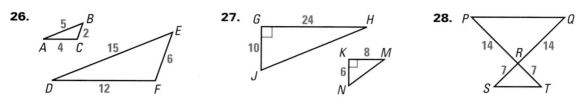

In Exercises 29 and 30, use the diagram. (Lesson 7.4)

29. Show that the overlapping triangles are similar.

30. Write a similarity statement for the triangles.

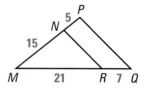

Find the value of the variable. (Lesson 7.5)

31.

32.

33.

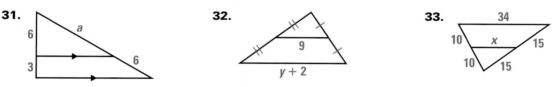

Given the diagram, determine whether $\overline{QS}$ is parallel to $\overline{PT}$. (Lesson 7.5)

34.

35.

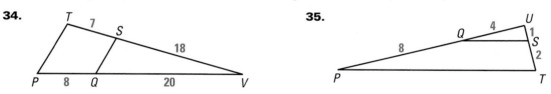

The red figure is the image of the blue figure after a dilation. Tell whether the dilation is a reduction or an enlargement. Then find the value of the variable. (Lesson 7.6)

36.

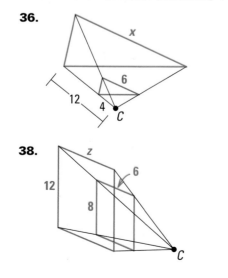

37.

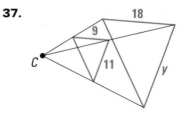

38.

39.

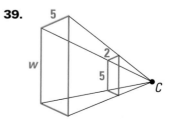

Chapter 8

Decide whether the polygon is *convex* or *concave*. (Lesson 8.1)

1.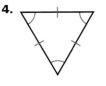

2.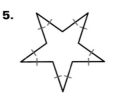

3.

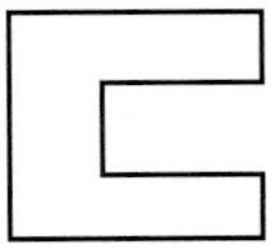

Decide whether the polygon is regular. Explain your answer. (Lesson 8.1)

4.

5.

6.

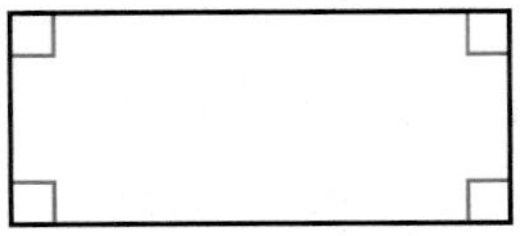

Find the sum of the measures of the interior angles of the convex polygon. (Lesson 8.2)

7. 12-gon

8. octagon

9. 18-gon

Find the value of *x*. (Lesson 8.2)

10.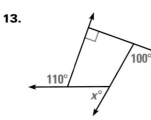

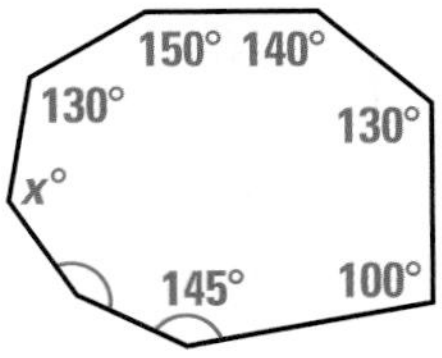

11.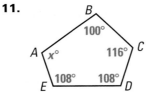

12.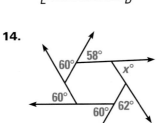

13.

14.

15.

Find the area of the polygon. (Lesson 8.3)

16.

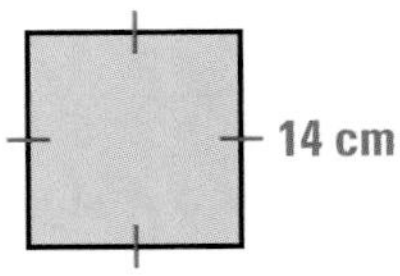

17.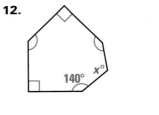

18.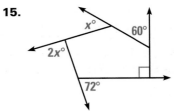

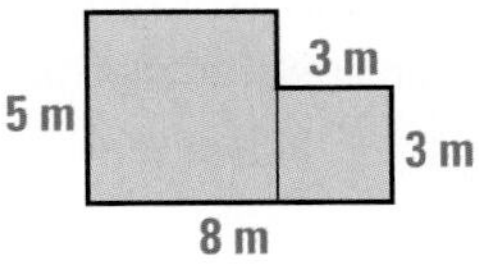

19.

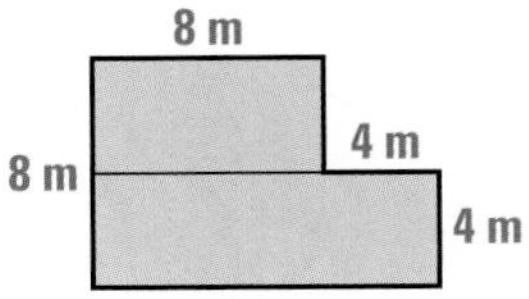

20.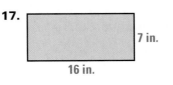

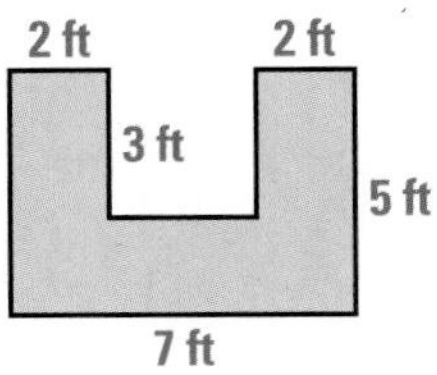

21.

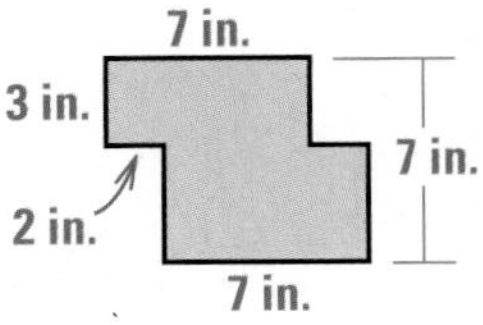

Find the area of the polygon. (Lesson 8.4)

22.

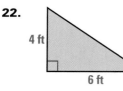

4 ft
6 ft

23.

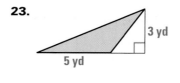

3 yd
5 yd

24.

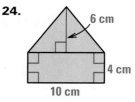

6 cm
4 cm
10 cm

25. A triangle has an area of 65 square feet and a base of 13 feet. Find the height. (Lesson 8.4)

Find the area of the quadrilateral. (Lesson 8.5)

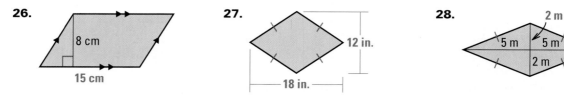

26.

8 cm
15 cm

27.

12 in.
18 in.

28.

2 m
5 m   5 m
2 m

Find the area of the trapezoid. (Lesson 8.6)

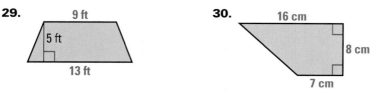

29.

9 ft
5 ft
13 ft

30.

16 cm
8 cm
7 cm

31.

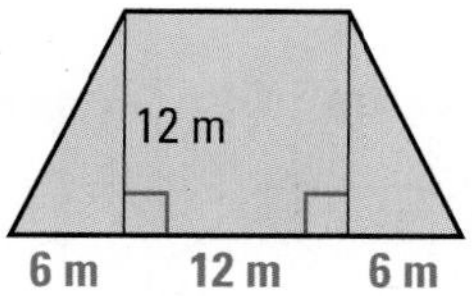

12 m
6 m   12 m   6 m

32. A trapezoid has an area of 135 square units. The lengths of the bases are 12 units and 18 units. Find the height. (Lesson 8.6)

Find the circumference and area of the circle. Round your results to the nearest whole number. (Lesson 8.7)

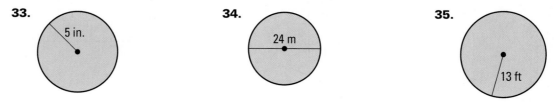

33.

5 in.

34.

24 m

35.

13 ft

Find the area of the blue sector. Start by finding the area of the circle. Round your results to the nearest whole number. (Lesson 8.7)

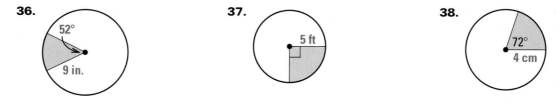

36.

52°
9 in.

37.

5 ft

38.

72°
4 cm

Chapter 9

Tell whether the solid is a polyhedron. If so, describe the shape of the base and then name the solid. (Lesson 9.1)

1.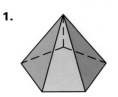

2.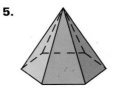

3.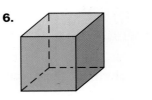

Name the polyhedron. Then count the number of faces and edges.
(Lesson 9.1)

4.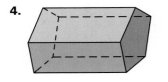

5.

6.

Find the surface area of the prism. (Lesson 9.2)

7. 4 cm, 5 cm, 10 cm

8. 11 m, 11 m, 11 m

9. 5 in., 12 in., 2 in.

Find the surface area of the cylinder. Round your answer to the nearest whole number. (Lesson 9.2)

10. 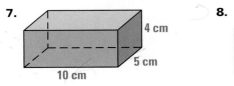 5 in., 5 in.

11. 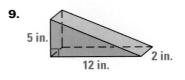 6 cm, 15 cm

12. 12 in., 6 in.

Find the surface area of the pyramid or cone. If necessary, round your answer to the nearest whole number. (Lesson 9.3)

13. 6 in., 5 in., 5 in.

14. 8 cm, Area ≈ 94 cm², 6 cm

15. 15 ft, 16 ft, 16 ft

16. 8 m, 10 m

17. 12 cm, 5 cm

18. 8 yd, 12 yd

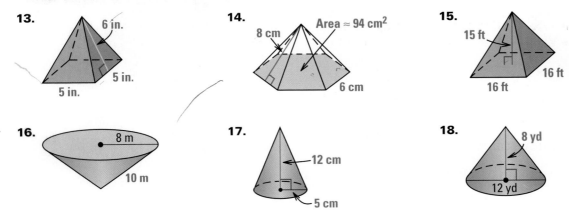

Find the volume of the prism. (Lesson 9.4)

19.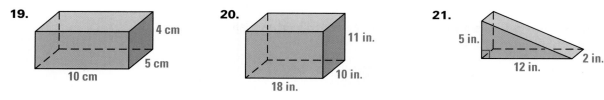
4 cm
5 cm
10 cm

20.
11 in.
10 in.
18 in.

21.
5 in.
12 in.
2 in.

Find the volume of the right cylinder. Round the result to the nearest whole number. (Lesson 9.4)

22.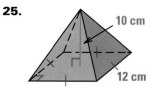
5 in.
5 in.

23.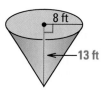
6 cm
15 cm

24.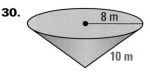
15 ft
6 ft

Find the volume of the pyramid. (Lesson 9.5)

25.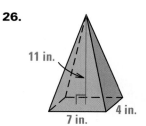
10 cm
12 cm

26.
11 in.
7 in.
4 in.

27.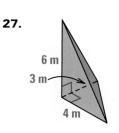
6 m
3 m
4 m

Find the volume of the cone. Round the result to the nearest whole number. (Lesson 9.5)

28.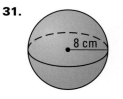
10 in.
7 in.

29.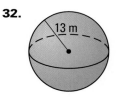
8 ft
13 ft

30.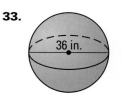
8 m
10 m

Find the surface area and volume of the sphere. Round the result to the nearest whole number. (Lesson 9.6)

31.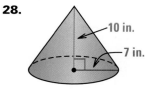
8 cm

32.
13 m

33.
36 in.

In Exercises 34 and 35, use the diagram at the right. (Lesson 9.6)

34. Find the surface areas of the spheres. What is their ratio?

35. Find the volumes of the spheres. What is their ratio?

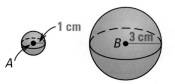
1 cm
A
B 3 cm

Chapter 10

Find the square root. Round your answer to the nearest tenth.
(Lesson 10.1)

1. $\sqrt{58}$ 2. $\sqrt{7}$ 3. $\sqrt{41}$ 4. $\sqrt{134}$ 5. $\sqrt{106}$

Multiply the radicals. Then simplify if possible. (Lesson 10.1)

6. $\sqrt{11} \cdot \sqrt{5}$ 7. $\sqrt{7} \cdot \sqrt{7}$ 8. $\sqrt{12} \cdot \sqrt{6}$ 9. $(3\sqrt{2})^2$ 10. $\sqrt{48} \cdot 2\sqrt{3}$

Simplify the radical expression. (Lesson 10.1)

11. $\sqrt{99}$ 12. $\sqrt{28}$ 13. $\sqrt{150}$ 14. $\sqrt{32}$ 15. $\sqrt{98}$

Show that the triangle is a 45°-45°-90° triangle. Then find the value of each variable. Write your answer in radical form. (Lesson 10.2)

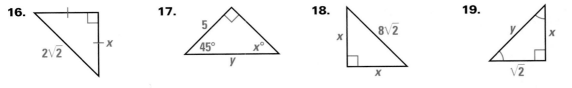

16.   17.   18.   19.

20. The hypotenuse of a 45°-45°-90° triangle has a length of 6. Sketch and label the triangle. Then find the length of each leg to the nearest tenth. (Lesson 10.2)

Find the value of each variable. Write your answer in radical form.
(Lesson 10.3)

21.   22.   23.   24.

Find tan _R_ and tan _S_. Write your answers as fractions and as decimals rounded to four decimal places. (Lesson 10.4)

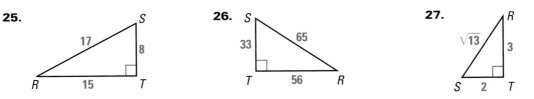

25.   26.   27.

Use a calculator to approximate the value to four decimal places.
(Lesson 10.4)

28. $\tan 15°$ 29. $\tan 72°$ 30. $\tan 60°$ 31. $\tan 9°$ 32. $\tan 37°$

33. $\tan 10°$ 34. $\tan 31°$ 35. $\tan 76°$ 36. $\tan 58°$ 37. $\tan 49°$

Find the value of _x_ to the nearest tenth. (Lesson 10.4)

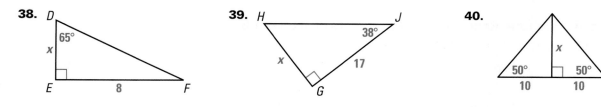

38. D, 65°, _x_, E, 8, F

39. H, J, 38°, _x_, 17, G

40. _x_, 50°, 50°, 10, 10

Find sin _R_ and cos _R_. Write your answers as fractions and as decimals rounded to four decimal places. (Lesson 10.5)

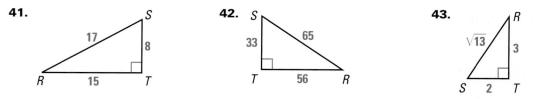

41. S, 17, 8, R, 15, T

42. S, 33, 65, T, 56, R

43. R, √13, 3, S, 2, T

Use a calculator to approximate the value to four decimal places.
(Lesson 10.5)

44. sin 33°   **45.** cos 78°   **46.** cos 8°   **47.** sin 40°   **48.** sin 57°

49. sin 43°   **50.** sin 80°   **51.** cos 20°   **52.** cos 89°   **53.** sin 12°

Find the lengths _x_ and _y_ of the legs of the triangle. Round your answers to the nearest tenth. (Lesson 10.5)

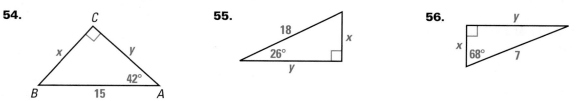

54. C, _x_, _y_, 42°, B, 15, A

55. 18, _x_, 26°, _y_

56. _y_, _x_, 68°, 7

∠_A_ is an acute angle. Use a calculator to approximate the measure of ∠_A_ to the nearest tenth of a degree. (Lesson 10.6)

57. tan _A_ = 0.8734   **58.** sin _A_ = 0.8045   **59.** cos _A_ = 0.2933   **60.** tan _A_ = 1.6

61. cos _A_ = 0.8912   **62.** sin _A_ = 0.2587   **63.** tan _A_ = 3.123   **64.** cos _A_ = 0.6789

65. sin _A_ = 0.3728   **66.** tan _A_ = 0.5726   **67.** sin _A_ = 0.9554   **68.** cos _A_ = 0.0511

Solve the right triangle. Round decimals to the nearest tenth.
(Lesson 10.6)

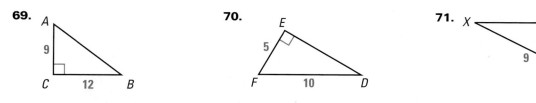

69. A, 9, C, 12, B

70. E, 5, F, 10, D

71. X, Y, 4, 9, Z

Chapter 11

Use the diagram at the right. Name the term that best describes the given line segment, line, or point. (Lesson 11.1)

1. $\overline{BF}$

2. $\overline{BD}$

3. $\overline{AC}$

4. $\overleftrightarrow{BF}$

5. $\overleftrightarrow{ED}$

6. D

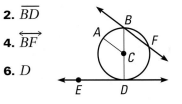

Use the diagram at the right. (Lesson 11.1)

7. Name the coordinates of the center of each circle.

8. Name the coordinates of the intersection of the two circles.

9. What is the length of the radius of $\odot C$?

10. What is the length of the diameter of $\odot D$?

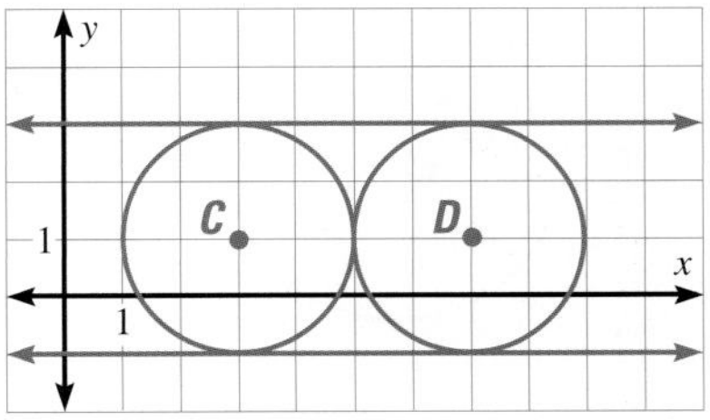

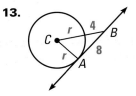

$\overleftrightarrow{AB}$, $\overline{PQ}$, and $\overline{PR}$ are tangents to the circles. Find the value of the variable. (Lesson 11.2)

11.

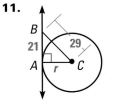

12.

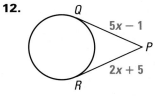

13.

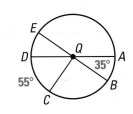

$\overline{AD}$ and $\overline{BE}$ are diameters. Copy the diagram. Find the indicated measure. (Lesson 11.3)

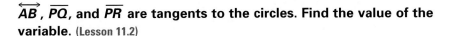

14. $m\widehat{AB}$

15. $m\angle DQC$

16. $m\widehat{BC}$

17. $m\widehat{DE}$

18. $m\angle CQE$

19. $m\angle AQE$

20. $m\widehat{AC}$

21. $m\widehat{BDC}$

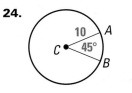

Find the length of $\widehat{AB}$. (Lesson 11.3)

22.

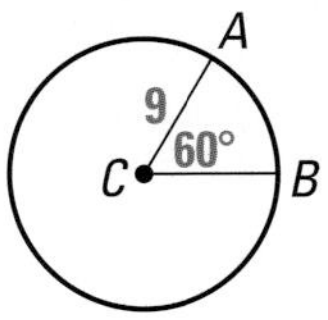

23.

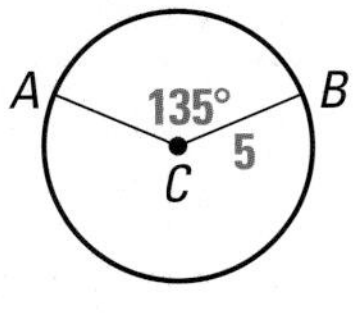

24.

Find the value of x. (Lesson 11.4)

25.

26.

27.

28.

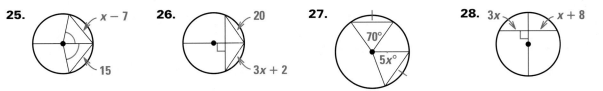

Find the value of each variable. (Lesson 11.5)

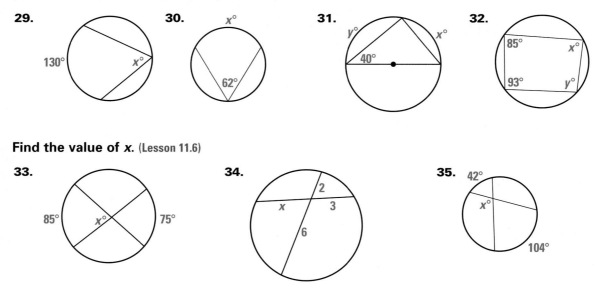

29.

30.

31.

32.

Find the value of x. (Lesson 11.6)

33.

34.

35.

Give the radius and center of the circle with the given equation. Then graph the circle. (Lesson 11.7)

36. $x^2 + y^2 = 25$

37. $(x - 1)^2 + (y + 3)^2 = 9$

38. $(x + 4)^2 + y^2 = 36$

Write the standard equation of the circle with the given center and radius. (Lesson 11.7)

39. center $(0, -1)$, radius 20

40. center $(-5, 7)$, radius 1

41. center $(3, 4)$, radius 7

Use the given information to rotate the figure about the origin. Find the coordinates of the vertices of the image and compare them with the vertices of the original figure. Describe any patterns you see. (Lesson 11.8)

42. $180°$

43. $90°$ clockwise

44. $90°$ counterclockwise

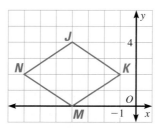

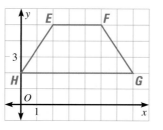

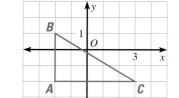

Does the figure have rotational symmetry? Is so, describe the rotations that map the figure onto itself. (Lesson 11.8)

45.

46.

47.

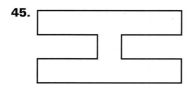

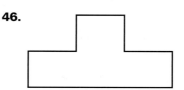

Extra Practice

End-of-Course Test

POINTS, LINES, PLANES, AND ANGLES

In Exercises 1–8, use the diagram at the right to name the following.

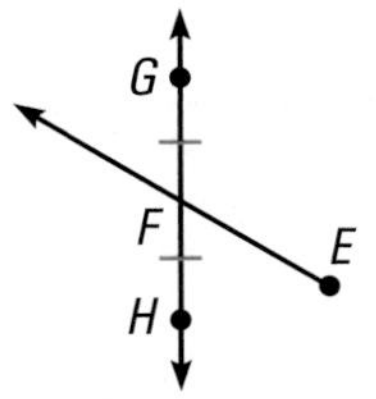

1. three collinear points

2. two rays with endpoint F

3. a segment bisector

4. a segment that is bisected

5. a straight angle

6. an acute angle

7. a linear pair

8. a point of intersection

9. Sketch three possible intersections of a line and a plane.

10. Given $P(0, 7)$ and $Q(4, -9)$, find the midpoint of $\overline{PQ}$.

11. $\angle A$ is a complement of $\angle B$, and $m\angle A = 42°$. Find $m\angle B$.

REASONING

12. Sketch the next figure you expect in the pattern at the right.

13. Show the conjecture is false by finding a counterexample.
Conjecture: A quadrilateral is always convex.

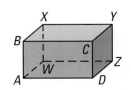

14. Write the statement as an if-then statement. Circle the conclusion.
Statement: I will buy the video if it costs less than $16.00.

15. Name the property that the statement illustrates.
If $\angle A \cong \angle B$ and $\angle B \cong \angle C$, then $\angle A \cong \angle C$.

PARALLEL AND PERPENDICULAR LINES

In the diagram at the right, think of each segment as part of a line.
Fill in the blank with *parallel, perpendicular,* or *skew*.

16. $\overleftrightarrow{AB}$ and $\overleftrightarrow{CY}$ are ___?___.

17. $\overleftrightarrow{XW}$ and $\overleftrightarrow{YZ}$ appear ___?___.

18. $\overleftrightarrow{CD}$ is ___?___ to plane ADZ.

19. Planes ABX and DCY appear ___?___.

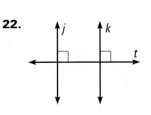

Is enough information given to conclude that $j \parallel k$? Explain.

20.

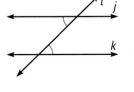

21.

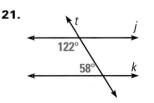

22.

TRIANGLES

Draw an example of the triangle.

23. right scalene

24. obtuse isosceles

25. equilateral

In Exercises 26–28, find the value of x.

26.

12

x

13

27.
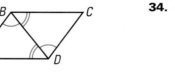
x

7

7

28.
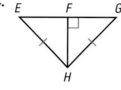
$60°$ 8

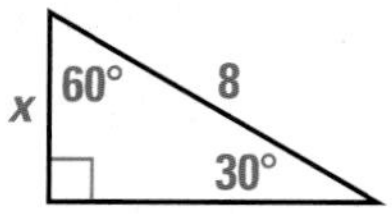

x

$30°$

29. Complete the Triangle Sum Theorem.
The sum of the measures of the angles of a triangle is __?__.

30. Find the distance between points $A(1, 4)$ and $B(9, -2)$.

31. Classify the triangle with side lengths 6, 9, and 12 as *acute, right,* or *obtuse.*

32. Can the side lengths 4, 4, and 9 form a triangle? Explain.

CONGRUENCE

In Exercises 33–35, decide whether enough information is given to show that the triangles are congruent. If so, write a congruence statement and state the theorem or postulate you would use.

33.
B   C

A   D

34.
E   F   G

H

35.
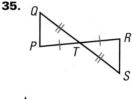
Q

P   R

T

S

36. In the diagram at the right, $\overleftrightarrow{MZ}$ is the perpendicular bisector of $\overline{PQ}$. Complete the congruence statements.

$\overline{PZ} \cong$ __?__ $\overline{PM} \cong$ __?__

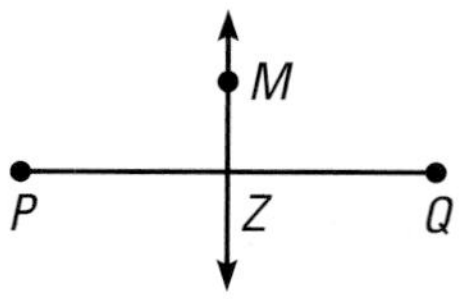

•M

P   Z   Q

Use the coordinate plane at the right.

37. Which segment is a reflection of $\overline{AB}$ in the x-axis?

38. Which segment is a reflection of $\overline{AB}$ in the y-axis?

39. Which segment is a translation of $\overline{AB}$? Describe the translation using words.

40. Determine the number of lines of symmetry in a rectangle. Draw a diagram to support your answer.

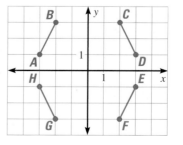

QUADRILATERALS

Name the type of polygon with the given number of sides.

41. three   **42.** four   **43.** five   **44.** six   **45.** eight

Complete each statement with _parallelogram, rectangle, rhombus, square,_ or _trapezoid._ Use each word once.

46. A ___?___ is a quadrilateral with four congruent sides.

47. A ___?___ is a quadrilateral with four right angles.

48. A ___?___ is a quadrilateral with exactly one pair of parallel sides.

49. A ___?___ is both a rectangle and a rhombus.

50. A ___?___ is a quadrilateral with both pairs of opposite sides parallel.

Tell whether the quadrilateral is a parallelogram. Explain your reasoning.

51.

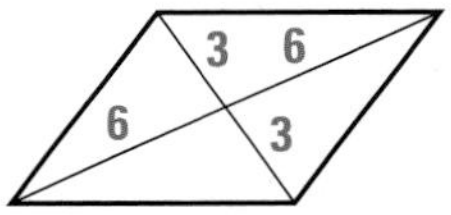

52.

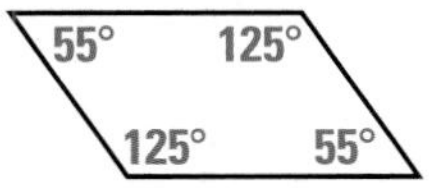

53.

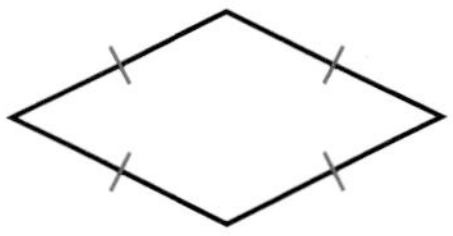

SIMILARITY

Determine whether the polygons are similar. If they are similar, write a similarity statement. Explain your reasoning.

54.

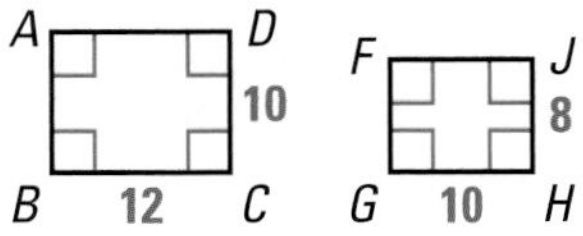

55.

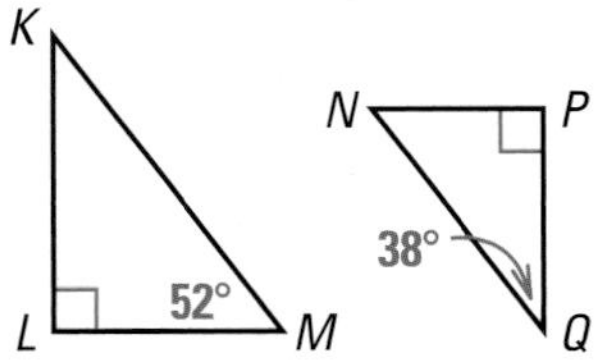

56.

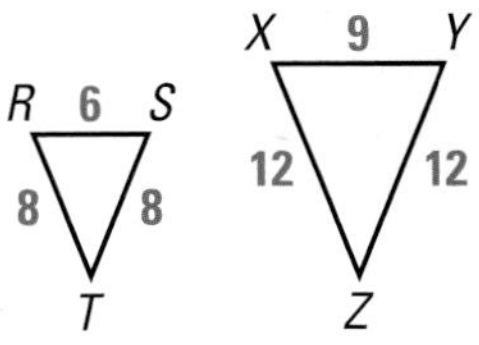

In Exercises 57–59, find the value of _x_.

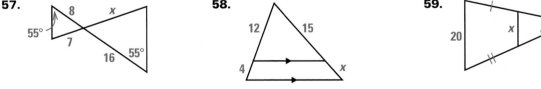

57.

58.

59.

60. What is the relationship between the original figure and its image after a dilation?

AREA AND VOLUME

Find the area of the figure. In Exercise 66, the polygon is made up of rectangles.

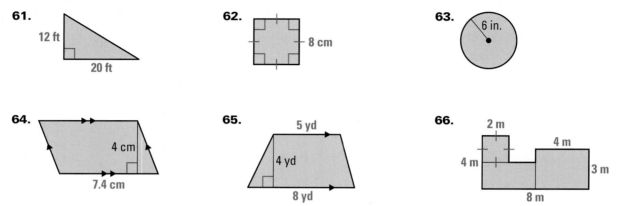

61.
12 ft
20 ft

62.
8 cm

63.
6 in.

64.
4 cm
7.4 cm

65.
5 yd
4 yd
8 yd

66.
2 m
4 m
4 m
3 m
8 m

67. Which figure in Exercises 61–66 is a regular polygon? Explain.

Name the solid. Then find its surface area and volume.

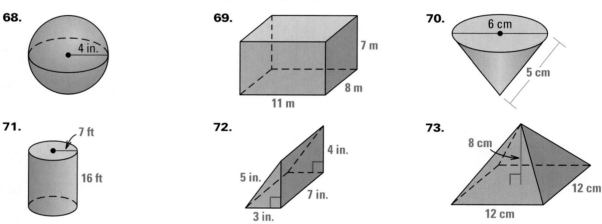

68.
4 in.

69.
7 m
8 m
11 m

70.
6 cm
5 cm

71.
7 ft
16 ft

72.
4 in.
5 in.
7 in.
3 in.

73.
8 cm
12 cm
12 cm

CIRCLES

Tell whether the point, line, or segment is best described as a *center*, a *chord*, a *secant*, a *tangent*, a *diameter*, a *radius*, or a *point of tangency*.

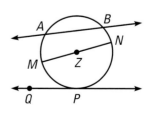

74. $\overleftrightarrow{QP}$

75. P

76. $\overline{AB}$

77. $\overleftrightarrow{AB}$

78. $\overline{MZ}$

79. $\overline{MN}$

80. What is the measure of a semicircle?

81. Write the standard equation of a circle with center at the origin and radius 5. Graph the circle in a coordinate plane.

Symbols

Symbol	Meaning	Page
$\overleftrightarrow{AB}$	line AB	16
$\overrightarrow{AB}$	ray AB	16
$\overline{AB}$	segment AB	16
AB	the length of $\overline{AB}$	28
$\parallel$	is parallel to	108
$\perp$	is perpendicular to	108
$\angle ABC$	angle ABC	35
$\triangle ABC$	triangle ABC	179
$\square ABCD$	parallelogram $ABCD$	310
n-gon	polygon with n sides	304
$\odot P$	circle P	589
$m\angle A$	measure of angle A	36
$m\overarc{AB}$	measure of minor arc AB	601
$m\overarc{ABC}$	measure of major arc ABC	601
$\cdot$	multiplication, times	9
$^{\circ}$	degrees	36
A'	A prime	153
A''	A double prime	158
π	pi	452

Symbol	Meaning	Page
$=$	is equal to	9
$\cong$	is congruent to	30
$\sim$	is similar to	365
$\approx$	is approximately equal to	193
$\neq$	is not equal to	194
$\stackrel{?}{=}$	is it equal to?	200
$<$	is less than	201
$>$	is greater than	201
$\dots$	and so on	3
$\lvert a \rvert$	absolute value of a	28
$\dfrac{a}{b}, a : b$	ratio of a to b	357
$\sqrt{a}$	square root of a	537
(x, y)	ordered pair	664
$\tan$	tangent	557
$\sin$	sine	563
$\cos$	cosine	563
$\tan^{-1}$	inverse tangent	569
$\sin^{-1}$	inverse sine	570
$\cos^{-1}$	inverse cosine	570

Properties

Properties of Equality and Congruence for Segments

	Equality	Congruence
Reflexive (p. 88)	$AB = AB$	$\overline{AB} \cong \overline{AB}$
Symmetric (p. 88)	If $AB = CD$, then $CD = AB$.	If $\overline{AB} \cong \overline{CD}$, then $\overline{CD} \cong \overline{AB}$.
Transitive (p. 88)	If $AB = CD$ and $CD = EF$, then $AB = EF$.	If $\overline{AB} \cong \overline{CD}$ and $\overline{CD} \cong \overline{EF}$, then $\overline{AB} \cong \overline{EF}$.

Properties of Equality and Congruence for Angles

	Equality	Congruence
Reflexive (p. 88)	$m\angle A = m\angle A$	$\angle A \cong \angle A$
Symmetric (p. 88)	If $m\angle A = m\angle B$, then $m\angle B = m\angle A$.	If $\angle A \cong \angle B$, then $\angle B \cong \angle A$.
Transitive (p. 88)	If $m\angle A = m\angle B$ and $m\angle B = m\angle C$, then $m\angle A = m\angle C$.	If $\angle A \cong \angle B$ and $\angle B \cong \angle C$, then $\angle A \cong \angle C$.

Algebraic Properties of Equality

	Property	Example
Addition (p. 90)	If $a = b$, then $a + c = b + c$.	If $x - 4 = 9$, then $x - 4 + 4 = 9 + 4$.
Subtraction (p. 90)	If $a = b$, then $a - c = b - c$.	If $y + 1 = 6$, then $y + 1 - 1 = 6 - 1$.
Multiplication (p. 90)	If $a = b$, then $ac = bc$.	If $z = 5$, then $z \cdot 3 = 5 \cdot 3$.
Division (p. 90)	If $a = b$ and $c \neq 0$, then $\frac{a}{c} = \frac{b}{c}$.	If $7x = 14$, then $\frac{7x}{7} = \frac{14}{7}$.
Cross Product (p. 359)	If $\frac{a}{b} = \frac{c}{d}$, then $ad = bc$.	If $\frac{3}{4} = \frac{x}{12}$, then $3 \cdot 12 = 4 \cdot x$.

Right Triangles

Pythagorean Theorem (p. 192)

$$a^2 + b^2 = c^2$$

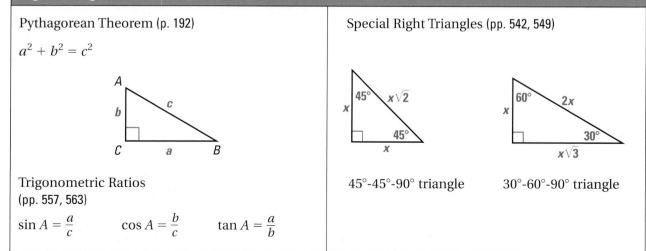

Trigonometric Ratios
(pp. 557, 563)

$$\sin A = \frac{a}{c} \qquad \cos A = \frac{b}{c} \qquad \tan A = \frac{a}{b}$$

Special Right Triangles (pp. 542, 549)

45°-45°-90° triangle   30°-60°-90° triangle

Tables

Formulas

Perimeter and Circumference

Square (p. 672)	$P = 4s$	where s = side length
Rectangle (p. 672)	$P = 2\ell + 2w$	where ℓ = length and w = width
Triangle (p. 672)	$P = a + b + c$	where a, b, c = lengths of the sides of a triangle
Circle (p. 452)	$C = \pi d$ or $C = 2\pi r$	where d = diameter and r = radius

Area

Square (p. 424)	$A = s^2$	where s = side length
Rectangle (p. 425)	$A = bh$	where b = base and h = height
Triangle (p. 431)	$A = \frac{1}{2}bh$	where b = base and h = height
Parallelogram (p. 439)	$A = bh$	where b = base and h = height
Rhombus (p. 441)	$A = \frac{1}{2}d_1 d_2$	where d_1, d_2 = diagonals
Trapezoid (p. 446)	$A = \frac{1}{2}h(b_1 + b_2)$	where h = height and b_1, b_2 = bases
Circle (p. 453)	$A = \pi r^2$	where r = radius

Surface Area

Prism (p. 484)	$S = 2B + Ph$	where B = area of base, P = perimeter, and h = height
Cylinder (p. 485)	$S = 2\pi r^2 + 2\pi rh$	where r = radius and h = height
Pyramid (p. 492)	$S = B + \frac{1}{2}P\ell$	where B = area of base, P = perimeter, and ℓ = slant height
Cone (p. 493)	$S = \pi r^2 + \pi r\ell$	where r = radius and ℓ = slant height
Sphere (p. 517)	$S = 4\pi r^2$	where r = radius

Volume

Prism (p. 500)	$V = Bh$	where B = area of base and h = height
Cylinder (p. 502)	$V = \pi r^2 h$	where r = radius and h = height
Pyramid (p. 510)	$V = \frac{1}{3}Bh$	where B = area of base and h = height
Cone (p. 511)	$V = \frac{1}{3}\pi r^2 h$	where r = radius and h = height
Sphere (p. 518)	$V = \frac{4}{3}\pi r^3$	where r = radius

Coordinate Geometry

Midpoint (p. 55)	The midpoint between $A(x_1, y_1)$ and $B(x_2, y_2)$ is $\left(\dfrac{x_1 + x_2}{2}, \dfrac{y_1 + y_2}{2}\right)$.
Distance (p. 194)	The distance between $A(x_1, y_1)$ and $B(x_2, y_2)$ is $\sqrt{(x_2 - x_1)^2 + (y_2 - y_1)^2}$.

Tables

Squares and Square Roots

No.	Square	Sq. Root	No.	Square	Sq. Root	No.	Square	Sq. Root
1	1	1.000	51	2,601	7.141	101	10,201	10.050
2	4	1.414	52	2,704	7.211	102	10,404	10.100
3	9	1.732	53	2,809	7.280	103	10,609	10.149
4	16	2.000	54	2,916	7.348	104	10,816	10.198
5	25	2.236	55	3,025	7.416	105	11,025	10.247
6	36	2.449	56	3,136	7.483	106	11,236	10.296
7	49	2.646	57	3,249	7.550	107	11,449	10.344
8	64	2.828	58	3,364	7.616	108	11,664	10.392
9	81	3.000	59	3,481	7.681	109	11,881	10.440
10	100	3.162	60	3,600	7.746	110	12,100	10.488
11	121	3.317	61	3,721	7.810	111	12,321	10.536
12	144	3.464	62	3,844	7.874	112	12,544	10.583
13	169	3.606	63	3,969	7.937	113	12,769	10.630
14	196	3.742	64	4,096	8.000	114	12,996	10.677
15	225	3.873	65	4,225	8.062	115	13,225	10.724
16	256	4.000	66	4,356	8.124	116	13,456	10.770
17	289	4.123	67	4,489	8.185	117	13,689	10.817
18	324	4.243	68	4,624	8.246	118	13,924	10.863
19	361	4.359	69	4,761	8.307	119	14,161	10.909
20	400	4.472	70	4,900	8.367	120	14,400	10.954
21	441	4.583	71	5,041	8.426	121	14,641	11.000
22	484	4.690	72	5,184	8.485	122	14,884	11.045
23	529	4.796	73	5,329	8.544	123	15,129	11.091
24	576	4.899	74	5,476	8.602	124	15,376	11.136
25	625	5.000	75	5,625	8.660	125	15,625	11.180
26	676	5.099	76	5,776	8.718	126	15,876	11.225
27	729	5.196	77	5,929	8.775	127	16,129	11.269
28	784	5.292	78	6,084	8.832	128	16,384	11.314
29	841	5.385	79	6,241	8.888	129	16,641	11.358
30	900	5.477	80	6,400	8.944	130	16,900	11.402
31	961	5.568	81	6,561	9.000	131	17,161	11.446
32	1,024	5.657	82	6,724	9.055	132	17,424	11.489
33	1,089	5.745	83	6,889	9.110	133	17,689	11.533
34	1,156	5.831	84	7,056	9.165	134	17,956	11.576
35	1,225	5.916	85	7,225	9.220	135	18,225	11.619
36	1,296	6.000	86	7,396	9.274	136	18,496	11.662
37	1,369	6.083	87	7,569	9.327	137	18,769	11.705
38	1,444	6.164	88	7,744	9.381	138	19,044	11.747
39	1,521	6.245	89	7,921	9.434	139	19,321	11.790
40	1,600	6.325	90	8,100	9.487	140	19,600	11.832
41	1,681	6.403	91	8,281	9.539	141	19,881	11.874
42	1,764	6.481	92	8,464	9.592	142	20,164	11.916
43	1,849	6.557	93	8,649	9.644	143	20,449	11.958
44	1,936	6.633	94	8,836	9.695	144	20,736	12.000
45	2,025	6.708	95	9,025	9.747	145	21,025	12.042
46	2,116	6.782	96	9,216	9.798	146	21,316	12.083
47	2,209	6.856	97	9,409	9.849	147	21,609	12.124
48	2,304	6.928	98	9,604	9.899	148	21,904	12.166
49	2,401	7.000	99	9,801	9.950	149	22,201	12.207
50	2,500	7.071	100	10,000	10.000	150	22,500	12.247

Tables

Trigonometric Ratios

Angle	Sine	Cosine	Tangent
1°	.0175	.9998	.0175
2°	.0349	.9994	.0349
3°	.0523	.9986	.0524
4°	.0698	.9976	.0699
5°	.0872	.9962	.0875
6°	.1045	.9945	.1051
7°	.1219	.9925	.1228
8°	.1392	.9903	.1405
9°	.1564	.9877	.1584
10°	.1736	.9848	.1763
11°	.1908	.9816	.1944
12°	.2079	.9781	.2126
13°	.2250	.9744	.2309
14°	.2419	.9703	.2493
15°	.2588	.9659	.2679
16°	.2756	.9613	.2867
17°	.2924	.9563	.3057
18°	.3090	.9511	.3249
19°	.3256	.9455	.3443
20°	.3420	.9397	.3640
21°	.3584	.9336	.3839
22°	.3746	.9272	.4040
23°	.3907	.9205	.4245
24°	.4067	.9135	.4452
25°	.4226	.9063	.4663
26°	.4384	.8988	.4877
27°	.4540	.8910	.5095
28°	.4695	.8829	.5317
29°	.4848	.8746	.5543
30°	.5000	.8660	.5774
31°	.5150	.8572	.6009
32°	.5299	.8480	.6249
33°	.5446	.8387	.6494
34°	.5592	.8290	.6745
35°	.5736	.8192	.7002
36°	.5878	.8090	.7265
37°	.6018	.7986	.7536
38°	.6157	.7880	.7813
39°	.6293	.7771	.8098
40°	.6428	.7660	.8391
41°	.6561	.7547	.8693
42°	.6691	.7431	.9004
43°	.6820	.7314	.9325
44°	.6947	.7193	.9657
45°	.7071	.7071	1.0000

Angle	Sine	Cosine	Tangent
46°	.7193	.6947	1.0355
47°	.7314	.6820	1.0724
48°	.7431	.6691	1.1106
49°	.7547	.6561	1.1504
50°	.7660	.6428	1.1918
51°	.7771	.6293	1.2349
52°	.7880	.6157	1.2799
53°	.7986	.6018	1.3270
54°	.8090	.5878	1.3764
55°	.8192	.5736	1.4281
56°	.8290	.5592	1.4826
57°	.8387	.5446	1.5399
58°	.8480	.5299	1.6003
59°	.8572	.5150	1.6643
60°	.8660	.5000	1.7321
61°	.8746	.4848	1.8040
62°	.8829	.4695	1.8807
63°	.8910	.4540	1.9626
64°	.8988	.4384	2.0503
65°	.9063	.4226	2.1445
66°	.9135	.4067	2.2460
67°	.9205	.3907	2.3559
68°	.9272	.3746	2.4751
69°	.9336	.3584	2.6051
70°	.9397	.3420	2.7475
71°	.9455	.3256	2.9042
72°	.9511	.3090	3.0777
73°	.9563	.2924	3.2709
74°	.9613	.2756	3.4874
75°	.9659	.2588	3.7321
76°	.9703	.2419	4.0108
77°	.9744	.2250	4.3315
78°	.9781	.2079	4.7046
79°	.9816	.1908	5.1446
80°	.9848	.1736	5.6713
81°	.9877	.1564	6.3138
82°	.9903	.1392	7.1154
83°	.9925	.1219	8.1443
84°	.9945	.1045	9.5144
85°	.9962	.0872	11.4301
86°	.9976	.0698	14.3007
87°	.9986	.0523	19.0811
88°	.9994	.0349	28.6363
89°	.9998	.0175	57.2900

Tables

Postulates

1 Two Points Determine a Line
Through any two points there is exactly one line. *(p. 14)*

2 Three Points Determine a Plane
Through any three points not on a line there is exactly one plane. *(p. 14)*

3 Intersection of Two Lines
If two lines intersect, then their intersection is a point. *(p. 22)*

4 Intersection of Two Planes
If two planes intersect, then their intersection is a line. *(p. 22)*

5 Segment Addition Postulate
If B is between A and C, then $AC = AB + BC$. If $AC = AB + BC$, then B is between A and C. *(p. 29)*

6 Angle Addition Postulate
If P is in the interior of $\angle RST$, then the measure of $\angle RST$ is the sum of the measures of $\angle RSP$ and $\angle PST$. *(p. 37)*

7 Linear Pair Postulate
If two angles form a linear pair, then they are supplementary. *(p. 75)*

8 Corresponding Angles Postulate
If two parallel lines are cut by a transversal, then corresponding angles are congruent. *(p. 128)*

9 Corresponding Angles Converse
If two lines are cut by a transversal so that corresponding angles are congruent, then the lines are parallel. *(p. 137)*

10 Parallel Postulate
If there is a line and a point not on the line, then there is exactly one line through the point parallel to the given line. *(p. 144)*

11 Perpendicular Postulate
If there is a line and a point not on the line, then there is exactly one line through the point perpendicular to the given line. *(p. 144)*

12 Side-Side-Side Congruence Postulate (SSS)
If three sides of one triangle are congruent to three sides of a second triangle, then the two triangles are congruent. *(p. 241)*

13 Side-Angle-Side Congruence Postulate (SAS)
If two sides and the included angle of one triangle are congruent to two sides and the included angle of a second triangle, then the two triangles are congruent. *(p. 242)*

14 Angle-Side-Angle Congruence Postulate (ASA)
If two angles and the included side of one triangle are congruent to two angles and the included side of a second triangle, then the two triangles are congruent. *(p. 250)*

15 Angle-Angle Similarity Postulate (AA)
If two angles of one triangle are congruent to two angles of another triangle, then the two triangles are similar. *(p. 372)*

16 Arc Addition Postulate
The measure of an arc formed by two adjacent arcs is the sum of the measures of the two arcs. *(p. 602)*

Theorems

2.1 Congruent Complements Theorem
If two angles are complementary to the same angle, then they are congruent. *(p. 69)*

2.2 Congruent Supplements Theorem
If two angles are supplementary to the same angle, then they are congruent. *(p. 69)*

2.3 Vertical Angles Theorem
Vertical angles are congruent. *(p. 76)*

3.1
All right angles are congruent. *(p. 114)*

3.2
If two lines are perpendicular, then they intersect to form four right angles. *(p. 114)*

3.3
If two lines intersect to form adjacent congruent angles, then the lines are perpendicular. *(p. 115)*

3.4
If two sides of adjacent acute angles are perpendicular, then the angles are complementary. *(p. 115)*

3.5 Alternate Interior Angles Theorem
If two parallel lines are cut by a transversal, then alternate interior angles are congruent. *(p. 129)*

3.6 Alternate Exterior Angles Theorem
If two parallel lines are cut by a transversal, then alternate exterior angles are congruent. *(p. 130)*

3.7 Same-Side Interior Angles Theorem
If two parallel lines are cut by a transversal, then same-side interior angles are supplementary. *(p. 131)*

3.8 Alternate Interior Angles Converse
If two lines are cut by a transversal so that alternate interior angles are congruent, then the lines are parallel. *(p. 138)*

3.9 Alternate Exterior Angles Converse
If two lines are cut by a transversal so that alternate exterior angles are congruent, then the lines are parallel. *(p. 138)*

3.10 Same-Side Interior Angles Converse
If two lines are cut by a transversal so that same-side interior angles are supplementary, then the lines are parallel. *(p. 138)*

3.11
If two lines are parallel to the same line, then they are parallel to each other. *(p. 145)*

3.12
In a plane, if two lines are perpendicular to the same line, then they are parallel to each other. *(p. 145)*

4.1 Triangle Sum Theorem
The sum of the measures of the angles of a triangle is 180°. *(p. 179)*

Corollary to the Triangle Sum Theorem
The acute angles of a right triangle are complementary. *(p. 180)*

4.2 Exterior Angle Theorem
The measure of an exterior angle of a triangle is equal to the sum of the measures of the two nonadjacent interior angles. *(p. 181)*

4.3 Base Angles Theorem
If two sides of a triangle are congruent, then the angles opposite them are congruent. *(p. 185)*

4.4 Converse of the Base Angles Theorem
If two angles of a triangle are congruent, then the sides opposite them are congruent. *(p. 186)*

4.5 Equilateral Theorem
If a triangle is equilateral, then it is equiangular. *(p. 187)*

4.6 Equiangular Theorem
If a triangle is equiangular, then it is equilateral. *(p. 187)*

4.7 Pythagorean Theorem
In a right triangle, the square of the length of the hypotenuse is equal to the sum of the squares of the lengths of the legs. *(p. 192)*

4.8 Converse of the Pythagorean Theorem
If the square of the length of the longest side of a triangle is equal to the sum of the squares of the lengths of the other two sides, then the triangle is a right triangle. *(p. 200)*

4.9 Intersection of Medians of a Triangle
The medians of a triangle intersect at the centroid, a point that is two thirds of the distance from each vertex to the midpoint of the opposite side. *(p. 208)*

4.10
If one side of a triangle is longer than another side, then the angle opposite the longer side is larger than the angle opposite the shorter side. *(p. 212)*

4.11
If one angle of a triangle is larger than another angle, then the side opposite the larger angle is longer than the side opposite the smaller angle. *(p. 212)*

4.12 Triangle Inequality
The sum of the lengths of any two sides of a triangle is greater than the length of the third side. *(p. 213)*

5.1 Angle-Angle-Side Congruence Theorem (AAS)
If two angles and a non-included side of one triangle are congruent to two angles and the corresponding non-included side of a second triangle, then the two triangles are congruent. *(p. 251)*

5.2 Hypotenuse-Leg Congruence Theorem (HL)
If the hypotenuse and a leg of a right triangle are congruent to the hypotenuse and a leg of a second right triangle, then the two triangles are congruent. *(p. 257)*

5.3 Angle Bisector Theorem
If a point is on the bisector of an angle, then it is equidistant from the two sides of the angle. *(p. 273)*

5.4 Perpendicular Bisector Theorem
If a point is on the perpendicular bisector of a segment, then it is equidistant from the endpoints of the segment. *(p. 274)*

6.1 Quadrilateral Interior Angles Theorem
The sum of the measures of the interior angles of a quadrilateral is 360°. *(p. 305)*

6.2
If a quadrilateral is a parallelogram, then its opposite sides are congruent. *(p. 310)*

6.3
If a quadrilateral is a parallelogram, then its opposite angles are congruent. *(p. 311)*

6.4
If a quadrilateral is a parallelogram, then its consecutive angles are supplementary. *(p. 311)*

6.5
If a quadrilateral is a parallelogram, then its diagonals bisect each other. *(p. 312)*

6.6
If both pairs of opposite sides of a quadrilateral are congruent, then the quadrilateral is a parallelogram. *(p. 316)*

6.7
If both pairs of opposite angles of a quadrilateral are congruent, then the quadrilateral is a parallelogram. *(p. 316)*

6.8
If an angle of a quadrilateral is supplementary to both of its consecutive angles, then the quadrilateral is a parallelogram. *(p. 317)*

6.9
If the diagonals of a quadrilateral bisect each other, then the quadrilateral is a parallelogram. *(p. 318)*

Rhombus Corollary
If a quadrilateral has four congruent sides, then it is a rhombus. *(p. 326)*

Rectangle Corollary
If a quadrilateral has four right angles, then it is a rectangle. *(p. 326)*

Square Corollary
If a quadrilateral has four congruent sides and four right angles, then it is a square. *(p. 326)*

6.10
The diagonals of a rhombus are perpendicular. *(p. 327)*

6.11
The diagonals of a rectangle are congruent. *(p. 327)*

6.12
If a trapezoid is isosceles, then each pair of base angles is congruent. *(p. 332)*

6.13
If a trapezoid has a pair of congruent base angles, then it is isosceles. *(p. 332)*

7.1 Perimeters of Similar Polygons
If two polygons are similar, then the ratio of their perimeters is equal to the ratio of their corresponding side lengths. *(p. 368)*

7.2 Side-Side-Side Similarity Theorem (SSS)
If the corresponding sides of two triangles are proportional, then the triangles are similar. *(p. 379)*

7.3 Side-Angle-Side Similarity Theorem (SAS)
If an angle of one triangle is congruent to an angle of a second triangle and the lengths of the sides that include these angles are proportional, then the triangles are similar. *(p. 380)*

7.4 Triangle Proportionality Theorem
If a line parallel to one side of a triangle intersects the other two sides, then it divides the two sides proportionally. *(p. 386)*

7.5 Converse of the Triangle Proportionality Theorem
If a line divides two sides of a triangle proportionally, then it is parallel to the third side. *(p. 388)*

7.6 Midsegment Theorem
The segment connecting the midpoints of two sides of a triangle is parallel to the third side and is half as long. *(p. 389)*

8.1 Polygon Interior Angles Theorem
The sum of the measures of the interior angles of a convex polygon with n sides is $(n - 2) \cdot 180°$. *(p. 417)*

8.2 Polygon Exterior Angles Theorem
The sum of the measures of the exterior angles of a convex polygon, one angle at each vertex, is 360°. *(p. 419)*

8.3 Areas of Similar Polygons
If two polygons are similar with a scale factor of $\frac{a}{b}$, then the ratio of their areas is $\frac{a^2}{b^2}$. *(p. 433)*

10.1 45°-45°-90° Triangle Theorem
In a 45°-45°-90° triangle, the length of the hypotenuse is the length of a leg times $\sqrt{2}$. *(p. 542)*

10.2 30°-60°-90° Triangle Theorem
In a 30°-60°-90° triangle, the hypotenuse is twice as long as the shorter leg, and the longer leg is the length of the shorter leg times $\sqrt{3}$. *(p. 549)*

11.1
If a line is tangent to a circle, then it is perpendicular to the radius drawn at the point of tangency. *(p. 595)*

11.2
In a plane, if a line is perpendicular to a radius of a circle at its endpoint on the circle, then the line is tangent to the circle. *(p. 595)*

11.3
If two segments from the same point outside a circle are tangent to the circle, then they are congruent. *(p. 597)*

11.4
If a diameter of a circle is perpendicular to a chord, then the diameter bisects the chord and its arc. *(p. 608)*

11.5
If one chord is a perpendicular bisector of another chord, then the first chord is a diameter. *(p. 609)*

11.6
In the same circle, or in congruent circles:

If two chords are congruent, then their corresponding minor arcs are congruent.

If two minor arcs are congruent, then their corresponding chords are congruent. *(p. 609)*

11.7 Measure of an Inscribed Angle
If an angle is inscribed in a circle, then its measure is half the measure of its intercepted arc. *(p. 614)*

11.8
If a triangle inscribed in a circle is a right triangle, then the hypotenuse is a diameter of the circle.

If a side of a triangle inscribed in a circle is a diameter of the circle, then the triangle is a right triangle. *(p. 615)*

11.9
If a quadrilateral can be inscribed in a circle, then its opposite angles are supplementary.

If the opposite angles of a quadrilateral are supplementary, then the quadrilateral can be inscribed in a circle. *(p. 616)*

11.10
If two chords intersect inside a circle, then the measure of each angle formed is one half the sum of the measures of the arcs intercepted by the angle and its vertical angle. *(p. 620)*

11.11
If two chords intersect inside a circle, then the product of the lengths of the segments of one chord is equal to the product of the lengths of the segments of the other chord. *(p. 622)*

Theorems

Appendix 1

Precision and Accuracy

Goal Determine the precision and accuracy of measurements.

All measurements are approximations. You can measure a length to a **unit of measure**, such as 1 foot or 0.1 meter. The smaller the unit of measure, the more *precise* the measurement.

The **greatest possible error** in measurement is equal to one half the unit of measure. You can use the greatest possible error to determine a range within which an exact length lies.

EXAMPLE 1 *Using Precision of a Measurement*

Bill measures Sue's height to the nearest inch. He determines that Sue is 62 inches tall. Use Bill's measurement to describe Sue's exact height.

Solution

Unit of measure = 1 inch

Greatest possible error = $\frac{1}{2}$ (unit of measure) = $\frac{1}{2}$ (1 inch) = $\frac{1}{2}$ inch

Sue's exact height is between $61\frac{1}{2}$ inches and $62\frac{1}{2}$ inches.

The **relative error** of a measurement is the ratio of the greatest possible error to the measured length. The smaller the relative error, the more accurate the measurement.

$$\text{Relative error} = \frac{\text{Greatest possible error}}{\text{Measured length}}$$

EXAMPLE 2 *Comparing Accuracy of Measurements*

A desk is 0.8 meter wide. A classroom is 12 meters wide. You can use relative error to compare the accuracy of these measurements.

DESK

Unit of measure = 0.1 m

Greatest possible error = $\frac{1}{2}$(0.1 m)

= 0.05 m

Relative error = $\frac{0.05 \text{ m}}{0.8 \text{ m}}$

= 0.0625 = 6.25%

CLASSROOM

Unit of measure = 1 m

Greatest possible error = $\frac{1}{2}$(1 m)

= 0.5 m

Relative error = $\frac{0.5 \text{ m}}{12 \text{ m}}$

≈ 0.0417 ≈ 4.17%

The classroom measurement has the smaller relative error, so it is more accurate than the desk measurement.

Appendix 1 **711**

Appendix 1 Exercises

1. Measure the segment below to the nearest inch, nearest $\frac{1}{2}$ inch, and nearest $\frac{1}{4}$ inch. Which measurement is the most precise?

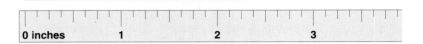

2. What is the greatest possible error you can make with the ruler above, using the smallest increments?

Find the unit of measure. Then find the greatest possible error.

3. 48 in.   4. 2.6 cm   5. 5 yd

6. 0.19 m   7. $14\frac{1}{2}$ ft   8. 81 mm

9. The length of a highway, to the nearest 10 miles, is 520 miles. Find the greatest possible error. Then copy and complete: The exact length of the highway is between ? miles and ? miles.

10. Charlie measures the height of his dog, Scout, to the nearest inch. He determines that Scout is 21 inches tall. Use Charlie's measurement to describe Scout's exact height.

Find the relative error of each measurement.

11. 8 ft   12. 35 in.   13. 141 mi

14. $\frac{1}{16}$ in.   15. 1.25 m   16. 65.4 cm

17. A piece of paper is 8.5 inches wide. A desk is 28 inches wide. Which measurement is more accurate? Explain your answer.

Find the unit of measure, the greatest possible error, and the relative error for each measurement.

18. The height of Mount Everest is *29,029 feet*.

19. Bob ran *5 kilometers* in about 20 minutes.

20. The distance between Boston and New York is *222 miles*.

21. In one minute, *3.1 centimeters* of rain fell in Maryland, on July 4, 1956.

Tell which measurement is more precise. Then tell which measurement is more accurate.

22. 15 in.; 18 in.   23. 6 ft; 4.5 ft   24. 3 mi; 5 km

25. 2 m; 2 cm   26. 1 yd; 33 in.   27. 84 mm; 9.6 cm

28. Use a real world measuring tool to explain precision and accuracy.

Appendix 2

Geometric Probability

Goal Find geometric probability using lengths and areas.

The **probability** P of an event is the number of favorable outcomes divided by the total number of outcomes. Probabilities are numbers between 0 and 1. An event that is certain to occur has a probability of 1. An event that cannot occur has a probability of 0.

A **geometric probability** requires calculating geometric measures, such as length and area. When all outcomes are equally likely, the following formulas can be used to find geometric probabilities.

PROBABILITY USING LENGTHS

$$P(\text{event}) = \frac{\text{Length of favorable segment}}{\text{Length of whole segment}}$$

PROBABILITY USING AREAS

$$P(\text{event}) = \frac{\text{Area of favorable region}}{\text{Area of whole region}}$$

EXAMPLE **1** **Using Lengths to Find a Geometric Probability**

A point is chosen at random on $\overline{AB}$. Find the probability that the point is on $\overline{XY}$.

Solution

$$P(\text{point is on } \overline{XY}) = \frac{\text{Length of } \overline{XY}}{\text{Length of } \overline{AB}}$$

$$= \frac{5 - 2}{10 - 0} = \frac{3}{10} = 0.3 = 30\%$$

The probability is 30%.

EXAMPLE **2** **Using Areas to Find a Geometric Probability**

A point is chosen at random in the square shown. Find the probability that the point is in the shaded circle.

Solution

The radius of the shaded circle is 5 inches.

$$P(\text{point is in shaded circle}) = \frac{\text{Area of shaded circle}}{\text{Area of square}}$$

$$= \frac{\pi(5)^2}{10^2} \approx 0.785 = 78.5\%$$

The probability is about 78.5%.

Appendix 2 Exercises

A point is chosen at random on $\overline{AB}$. Find the probability that the point is on the given segment.

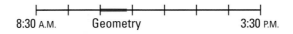

1. $\overline{VB}$ **2.** $\overline{TX}$ **3.** $\overline{ST}$ **4.** $\overline{RZ}$ **5.** $\overline{AB}$

6. Abby's school day starts at 8:30 A.M. and ends at 3:30 P.M. She has Geometry class from 10:30 A.M. to 11:20 A.M. If there is a fire drill at a random time during the school day, what is the probability it will start during Geometry class?

8:30 A.M.   Geometry   3:30 P.M.

A point is chosen at random in the figure shown. Find the probability that the point is in the shaded part of the figure.

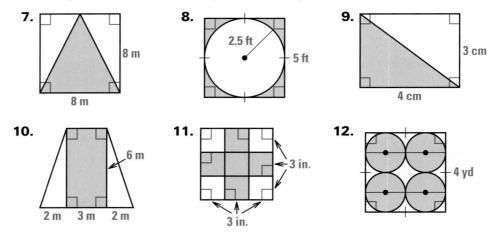

7. 8 m, 8 m   **8.** 2.5 ft, 5 ft   **9.** 3 cm, 4 cm

10. 6 m, 2 m, 3 m, 2 m   **11.** 3 in., 3 in.   **12.** 4 yd

The dartboard at the right is made up of circles that share the same center. A player randomly throws a dart, hits the dartboard, and earns the number of points shown in the region. Find the probability that a player earns the given number of points.

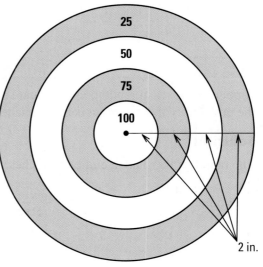

13. 100 points   **14.** 75 points

15. 50 points   **16.** 25 points

17. What should the sum be if you add all the probabilities in Exercises 13–16?

18. How many points is a player most likely to earn? least likely to earn?

Changing Dimensions of Figures

Goal Determine how changes in dimensions affect the perimeter, area, and volume of geometric figures.

EXAMPLE 1 Finding a Change in Perimeter and Area

A square has a side length of 1 inch. When the side length is doubled, the perimeter is doubled and the area is multiplied by 4. When the side length is tripled, the perimeter is tripled and the area is multiplied by 9.

	Original square	Side length doubled	Side length tripled
	$\square$ 1 in.	2 in.	3 in.
Perimeter	4(1 in.) = 4 in.	4(2 in.) = 8 in.	4(3 in.) = 12 in.
Area	$(1 \text{ in.})^2 = 1 \text{ in.}^2$	$(2 \text{ in.})^2 = 4 \text{ in.}^2$	$(3 \text{ in.})^2 = 9 \text{ in.}^2$

EXAMPLE 2 Finding a Change in Volume

A cube has an edge length of 1 cm. When the edge length is doubled, the volume is multiplied by 8. When the edge length is tripled, the volume is multiplied by 27.

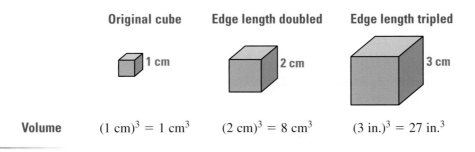

	Original cube	Edge length doubled	Edge length tripled
	1 cm	2 cm	3 cm
Volume	$(1 \text{ cm})^3 = 1 \text{ cm}^3$	$(2 \text{ cm})^3 = 8 \text{ cm}^3$	$(3 \text{ in.})^3 = 27 \text{ in.}^3$

SUMMARY

Changing Dimensions

When all lengths of a geometric figure change by a factor of c:

- perimeter changes by a factor of c
- area changes by a factor of c^2
- volume changes by a factor of c^3

Appendix 3 Exercises

1. Copy and complete the table. How do the circumference and area of a circle change when the radius is doubled? tripled?

	Original circle	Radius doubled	Radius tripled
Radius	1 in.	?	?
Circumference	?	?	?
Area	?	?	?

2. The surface area of a cube is $6s^2$, where s is the side length of an edge. How does the surface area of a cube change when the edge length is doubled? tripled?

3. A square has a side length of 3 meters. Describe the change in perimeter and area when the side length is multiplied by 5.

4. A sphere has a radius of 2 inches. Describe the change in surface area and volume when the radius is multiplied by 4.

5. A cylinder has a radius of 1 foot and a height of 5 feet. How can you change these dimensions so that the volume of the cylinder is 8 times as great?

Find the perimeter of each figure. Describe how the lengths and perimeters change from the smaller figure to the larger figure.

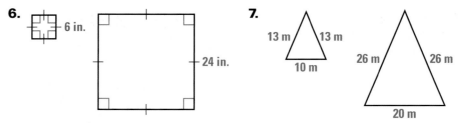

6. 6 in. 24 in.

7. 13 m 13 m 10 m 26 m 26 m 20 m

Use the rectangle at the right. Describe the change in area after the given change.

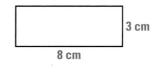

8. Double only the side lengths that measure 3 cm.

9. Double only the side lengths that measure 8 cm.

3 cm

8 cm

10. Double all the side lengths.

Find the volume of the rectangular prism or sphere. Then find the volume when all the lengths are doubled and tripled.

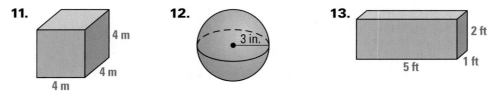

11. 4 m 4 m 4 m

12. 3 in.

13. 2 ft 5 ft 1 ft

Appendix 4

Estimating Measurements

Goal Estimate perimeter, area, surface area, and volume.

You can use rounding to estimate the perimeter, area, surface area, and volume of geometric figures. Estimation is useful when you do not need an exact answer or when you want to check the reasonableness of an exact answer.

EXAMPLE 1 **Rounding to Estimate**

Estimate the surface area and volume of the cylinder.

3.6 m
5.1 m

Solution

Round to the nearest whole number: $r \approx 4$, $h \approx 5$, $\pi \approx 3$.

$$S = 2\pi r^2 + 2\pi rh$$
$$\approx 2(3)(4)^2 + 2(3)(4)(5) = 96 + 120 = 216$$
$$V = \pi r^2 h \approx 3(4)^2(5) = 240$$

The surface area is about 216 square meters, and the volume is about 240 cubic meters.

EXAMPLE 2 **Estimating the Area of an Irregular Figure**

Estimate the area of the figure. Use square units.

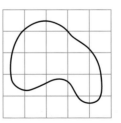

Solution

❶ First count the squares that are covered. There are 5 fully covered squares.

❷ Then group the partially covered squares so that the combined area is about 1 square unit. There are about 6 such groups.

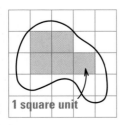
1 square unit

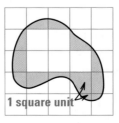
1 square unit

Add the square units you counted: $5 + 6 = 11$. The area of the figure is about 11 square units.

Appendix 4 Exercises

Estimate the perimeter and area of the figure by rounding each measurement to the nearest whole number.

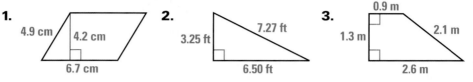

1. 4.9 cm 4.2 cm 6.7 cm

2. 3.25 ft 7.27 ft 6.50 ft

3. 0.9 m 1.3 m 2.1 m 2.6 m

4. Greg thinks that you can multiply the diameter of a circle by 3 to estimate its circumference. Do you agree or disagree? Explain.

5. The state of Wyoming is approximately a rectangle, 275 miles from north to south and 365 miles from east to west. Is 100,000 square miles a reasonable estimate for the area of Wyoming? Explain.

6. A rectangle measures 4.8 units by 8.1 units. John calculates that the perimeter of the rectangle is 12.9 units. Estimate the perimeter of the rectangle. Is John's calculation reasonable? Explain.

Estimate the surface area and volume of the solid by rounding each measurement to the nearest whole number. Use 3 for π.

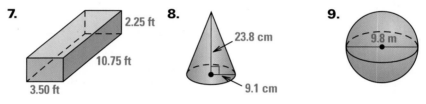

7. 2.25 ft 10.75 ft 3.50 ft

8. 23.8 cm 9.1 cm

9. 9.8 m

10. Find the volume of each cylindrical can. Estimate to check the reasonableness of your answers. Which can has the greater volume?

Tuna: $r = 4.9$ cm, $h = 4.6$ cm

Mandarin oranges: $r = 3.7$ cm, $h = 10.6$ cm

11. A cube has an edge length of 9.75 inches. Jill calculates that the surface area of the cube is 570.375 square inches. Estimate the surface area of the cube. Is Jill's calculation reasonable?

Estimate the area of the irregular figure. Use square units.

12.

13.

14.

Appendix

Glossary

A

acute angle (p. 36) An angle with measure between 0° and 90°.

acute triangle (p. 174) A triangle with three acute angles.

adjacent angles (p. 68) Two angles with a common vertex and side but no common interior points.

alternate exterior angles (p. 121) Two angles that are formed by two lines and a transversal, and lie outside the two lines on the opposite sides of the transversal. In the diagram below, ∠1 and ∠8 are alternate exterior angles.

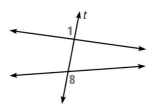

alternate interior angles (p. 121) Two angles that are formed by two lines and a transversal, and lie between the two lines on the opposite sides of the transversal. In the diagram below, ∠3 and ∠6 are alternate interior angles.

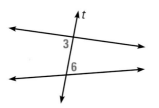

angle (p. 35) Consists of two rays with the same endpoint. The rays are the *sides* of the angle, and the endpoint is the *vertex* of the angle.

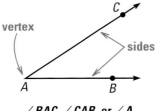

∠*BAC*, ∠*CAB*, or ∠*A*

angle bisector (p. 61) A ray that divides an angle into two angles that are congruent.

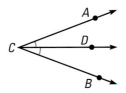

$\overrightarrow{CD}$ bisects ∠*ACB*.
m∠*ACD* = m∠*BCD*.

angle of rotation (p. 633) *See* rotation.

arc length (p. 603) A portion of the circumference of a circle.

area (p. 424) The amount of surface covered by a figure.

B

base of a cone (p. 493) *See* cone.

bases of a cylinder (p. 485) *See* cylinder.

base of an isosceles triangle (p. 185) *See* legs of an isosceles triangle.

bases of a parallelogram (p. 439) Either pair of parallel sides of a parallelogram are called the bases. *See also* height of a parallelogram.

bases of a prism (p. 473) *See* prism.

base of a pyramid (p. 491) *See* pyramid.

bases of a trapezoid (p. 332) *See* trapezoid.

base of a triangle (p. 431) *See* height of a triangle.

base angles of an isosceles triangle (p. 185) The two angles at the base of an isosceles triangle. *See also* legs of an isosceles triangle.

base angles of a trapezoid (p. 332) If trapezoid *ABCD* has bases $\overline{AB}$ and $\overline{CD}$, then there are two pairs of base angles: ∠*A* and ∠*B*, and ∠*C* and ∠*D*.

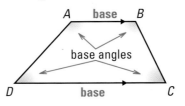

between (p. 29) When three points lie on a line, one of them is *between* the other two.

Point *B* is between points *A* and *C*.

bisect (pp. 53, 61) To divide into two congruent parts.

center of a circle (p. 452) *See* circle.

center of dilation (p. 393) *See* dilation.

center of rotation (p. 633) *See* rotation.

center of a sphere (p. 517) *See* sphere.

central angle (p. 454) An angle whose vertex is the center of a circle.

∠*PCQ* is a central angle.

centroid of a triangle (p. 208) The point at which the three medians of a triangle intersect.

chord (p. 589) A segment whose endpoints are points on a circle.

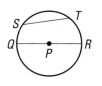

Chords: $\overline{QR}$, $\overline{ST}$

circle (pp. 452, 589) The set of all points in a plane that are the same distance from a given point, called the *center* of the circle.

Circle with center *P*, or ⊙*P*

circumference (p. 452) The distance around a circle.

circumscribed circle (p. 615) *See* inscribed polygon.

collinear points (p. 15) Points that lie on the same line.

compass (p. 143) A construction tool used to draw arcs and circles.

complement (p. 67) The sum of the measures of an angle and its *complement* is 90°.

complementary angles (p. 67) Two angles whose measures have a sum of 90°.

concave polygon (p. 411) *See* convex polygon.

conclusion (p. 82) The "then" part of an if-then statement. In the statement "If it is cold, then I will wear my coat," the conclusion is "I will wear my coat."

cone (p. 493) A solid with a circular *base* and a vertex that is not in the same plane as the base. The *height* of a cone is the perpendicular distance between the vertex and the base. The *radius* of a cone is the radius of the base. The *slant height* of a cone is the distance between the vertex and a point on the base edge.

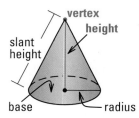

congruent angles (p. 36) Angles that have the same measure.

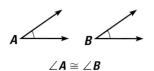

∠*A* ≅ ∠*B*

congruent arcs (p. 602) Two arcs of the same circle or of congruent circles that have the same measure.

congruent circles (p. 602) Two circles that have the same radius.

congruent figures (p. 233) Two geometric figures that have exactly the same size and shape. When two figures are congruent, all pairs of corresponding angles and corresponding sides are congruent.

congruent segments (p. 30) Segments that have the same length.

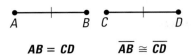

$$AB = CD \qquad \overline{AB} \cong \overline{CD}$$

conjecture (p. 8) An unproven statement that is based on a pattern or observations.

construction (p. 143) A geometric drawing that uses a limited set of tools, usually a compass and a straightedge.

converse (p. 136) The statement formed by switching the hypothesis and the conclusion of an if-then statement.

convex polygon (p. 411) A polygon is convex if no line that contains a side of the polygon passes through the interior of the polygon. A polygon that is not convex is called *concave*.

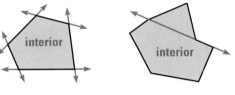

Convex polygon   **Concave polygon**

coordinate (p. 28) The real number that corresponds to a point on a line.

coplanar lines (p. 15) Lines that lie on the same plane.

coplanar points (p. 15) Points that lie on the same plane.

corollary to a theorem (p. 180) A statement that can be proved easily using the theorem.

corresponding angles (p. 121) Two angles that are formed by two lines and a transversal, and occupy corresponding positions. In the diagram below, ∠1 and ∠5 are corresponding angles.

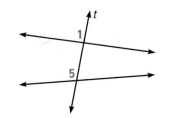

corresponding parts of congruent figures (p. 233) The corresponding sides and angles in congruent figures.

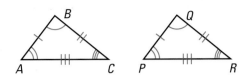

∠*B* and ∠*Q* are corresponding angles.
$\overline{BC}$ and $\overline{QR}$ are corresponding sides.

cosine (p. 563) A trigonometric ratio, abbreviated as *cos* and computed as the ratio of the length of the leg adjacent to the angle to the length of the hypotenuse.

$$\cos A = \frac{\text{leg adjacent to } \angle A}{\text{hypotenuse}} = \frac{b}{c}$$

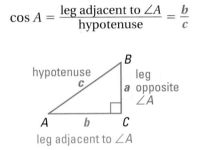

counterexample (p. 10) An example that shows that a conjecture is false.

cross product property (pp. 349, 359) If $\frac{a}{b} = \frac{c}{d}$, then $ad = bc$.

cylinder (p. 485) A solid with two congruent circular *bases* that lie in parallel planes. The *height* of a cylinder is the perpendicular distance between the bases. The *radius* of the cylinder is the radius of a base.

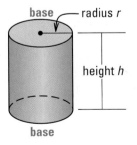

D

deductive reasoning (p. 83) Using facts, definitions, accepted properties, and the laws of logic to make a logical argument.

degrees (°) **(p. 36)** *See* measure of an angle.

diagonal of a polygon **(p. 303)** A segment that joins two nonconsecutive vertices of a polygon.

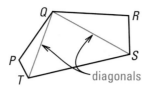

diameter **(pp. 452, 589)** The distance across the circle, through the center. The *diameter* is twice the *radius*. A chord that passes through the center of the circle is also called a *diameter*.

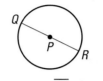

Diameter: $\overline{QR}$ or QR

dilation **(p. 393)** A transformation with center C and scale factor k that maps each point P to an image point P' so that P' lies on $\overrightarrow{CP}$ and $CP' = k \cdot CP$.

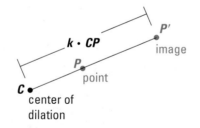

distance between two points on a line **(p. 28)** The distance AB is the absolute value of the difference of the coordinates of A and B. AB is also called the *length* of $\overline{AB}$.

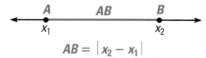

$$AB = |x_2 - x_1|$$

Distance Formula **(p. 194)** If $A(x_1, y_1)$ and $B(x_2, y_2)$ are points in a coordinate plane, then the distance between A and B is

$$\sqrt{(x_2 - x_1)^2 + (y_2 - y_1)^2}.$$

distance from a point to a line **(p. 273)** The length of the perpendicular segment from the point to the line.

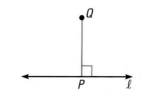

The distance from Q to line ℓ is QP.

edge of a polyhedron **(p. 474)** *See* polyhedron.

endpoint of a ray **(p. 16)** *See* ray.

endpoints of a segment **(p. 16)** *See* segment.

enlargement **(p. 394)** A dilation in which the image is larger than the original figure. The scale factor of an enlargement is greater than 1.

equiangular polygon **(p. 412)** A polygon with all of its interior angles congruent.

equiangular triangle **(p. 174)** A triangle with three congruent angles.

equidistant **(p. 273)** The same distance.

equilateral polygon **(p. 412)** A polygon with all of its sides congruent.

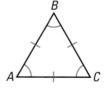

Equilateral polygon

equilateral triangle **(p. 173)** A triangle with three congruent sides.

B
A
C

Equilateral triangle

evaluate an expression **(p. 49)** Find the value of an expression by substituting values for the variables, and then simplifying the result using the order of operations.

Glossary

exponent (p. 467) *See* power.

exterior angles of a triangle (p. 181) When the sides of a triangle are extended, the angles that are adjacent to the *interior angles* of the triangle.

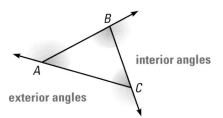

extremes of a proportion (p. 359) The extremes of the proportion $\frac{a}{b} = \frac{c}{d}$ are a and d. *See also* means of a proportion.

face (p. 474) *See* polyhedron.

H

height of a cone (p. 493) *See* cone.

height of a cylinder (p. 485) *See* cylinder.

height of a parallelogram (p. 439) The shortest distance between the bases. The segment that represents the height is perpendicular to the bases.

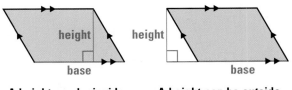

A height can be inside the parallelogram.   **A height can be outside the parallelogram.**

height of a prism (p. 484) *See* prism.

height of a pyramid (p. 491) The perpendicular distance between the vertex and base.

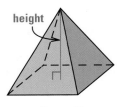

Pyramid

height of a trapezoid (p. 446) The shortest distance between the bases. The segment that represents the height is perpendicular to the bases.

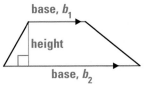

height of a triangle (p. 431) The perpendicular segment from a vertex to the line containing the opposite side, called the *base* of the triangle. The term *height* is also used to represent the length of the segment.

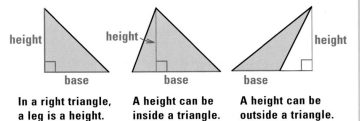

In a right triangle, a leg is a height.   **A height can be inside a triangle.**   **A height can be outside a triangle.**

hemisphere (p. 517) A geometric plane passing through the center of a sphere divides it into two *hemispheres*.

heptagon (p. 304) A polygon with seven sides.

hexagon (p. 304) A polygon with six sides.

hypotenuse (pp. 192, 257) In a right triangle, the side opposite the right angle. The hypotenuse is the longest side of a right triangle. *See also* legs of a right triangle.

hypothesis (p. 82) The "if" part of an if-then statement. In the statement "If it is cold, then I will wear my coat," the hypothesis is "it is cold."

I

if-then statement (p. 82) A statement with two parts: an "if" part that contains the hypothesis and a "then" part that contains the conclusion.

image (pp. 152, 282, 393, 633) The new figure that results from the transformation of a figure in a plane.

included angle (p. 242) An angle of a triangle whose vertex is the shared point of two sides of the triangle.

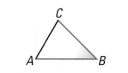

∠*B* is included between $\overline{AB}$ and $\overline{BC}$.

included side (p. 250) A side of a triangle whose endpoints are the vertices of two angles of the triangle.

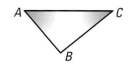

$\overline{AC}$ is included between ∠*A* and ∠*C*.

inductive reasoning (pp. 8, 83) A process that includes looking for patterns and making conjectures.

inscribed angle (p. 614) An angle whose vertex is on a circle and whose sides contain chords of the circle. The arc that lies in the interior of an inscribed angle and has endpoints on the angle is the *intercepted arc*.

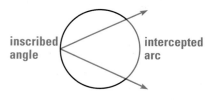

inscribed polygon (p. 615) A polygon whose vertices all lie on a circle. The circle is *circumscribed about* the polygon and is called a *circumscribed circle*.

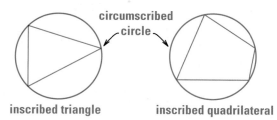

intercepted arc (p. 614) The arc that lies in the interior of an inscribed angle and has endpoints on the angle. *See also* inscribed angle.

interior of an angle (p. 37) A point is in the *interior* of an angle if it is between points that lie on each side of the angle.

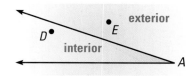

interior angles of a triangle (p. 181) *See* exterior angles of a triangle.

intersect (p. 22) Figures intersect if they have any points in common.

intersection (p. 22) The intersection of two or more figures is the point or points that the figures have in common.

inverse cosine (pp. 570, 571) A function, available on a scientific calculator as $\cos^{-1}x$, which can be used to find the measure of an angle when you know the cosine of the angle.

inverse sine (pp. 570, 571) A function, available on a scientific calculator as $\sin^{-1}x$, which can be used to find the measure of an angle when you know the sine of the angle.

inverse tangent (p. 569) A function, available on a scientific calculator as $\tan^{-1}x$, which can be used to find the measure of an angle when you know the tangent of the angle.

isosceles trapezoid (p. 332) A trapezoid with congruent legs.

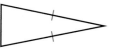

Isosceles trapezoid

isosceles triangle (p. 173) A triangle with at least two congruent sides. *See also* legs of an isosceles triangle.

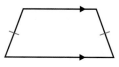

Isosceles triangle

L

lateral area of a cylinder (p. 485) The area of the curved surface of the cylinder.

lateral area of a prism (p. 484) The sum of the areas of the lateral faces.

lateral faces of a prism (p. 484) *See* prism.

lateral faces of a pyramid (p. 491) *See* pyramid.

leg adjacent to an angle (p. 557) *See* tangent of an angle.

leg opposite an angle (p. 557) *See* tangent of an angle.

legs of an isosceles triangle (p. 185) The congruent sides of an isosceles triangle. The third side is the *base*.

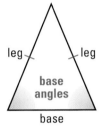

legs of a right triangle (p. 192) The sides that form the right angle.

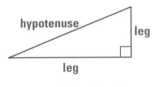

Right triangle

legs of a trapezoid (p. 332) *See* trapezoid.

length of a segment (p. 28) The distance between the endpoints of a segment. *See also* distance between two points on a line.

like terms (p. 101) Terms in an expression that have the same variable raised to the same power. Constant terms, such as 2 and −5, are also considered like terms.

line (p. 14) A line has one dimension and extends without end in two directions. It is represented by a line with two arrowheads. *See also* undefined term.

Line ℓ or $\overleftrightarrow{AB}$

line of reflection (p. 282) *See* reflection.

line of symmetry (p. 284) A figure in the plane has a line of symmetry if the figure can be reflected onto itself by a reflection in the line.

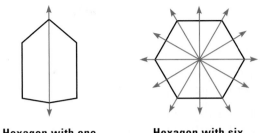

Hexagon with one line of symmetry　　　**Hexagon with six lines of symmetry**

line perpendicular to a plane (p. 109) A line that intersects a plane in a point and is perpendicular to every line in the plane that intersects it.

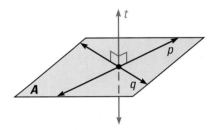

Line *t* is perpendicular to plane *A*.

linear pair (p. 75) Two adjacent angles whose noncommon sides are on the same line.

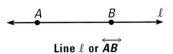

∠5 and ∠6 are a linear pair.

M

major arc (p. 601) *See* minor arc.

means of a proportion (p. 359) The means of the proportion $\frac{a}{b} = \frac{c}{d}$ are *b* and *c*. *See also* extremes of a proportion.

measure of an angle (p. 36) The size of an angle, written in units called *degrees* (°). The measure of ∠*A* is denoted by *m*∠*A*.

measure of a major arc (p. 601) The difference of 360° and the measure of the related minor arc.

measure of a minor arc (p. 601) The measure of its central angle.

Glossary

median of a triangle (p. 207) A segment from a vertex to the midpoint of the opposite side.

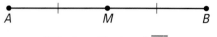

midpoint (p. 53) The point on a segment that divides it into two congruent segments.

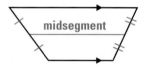

M is the midpoint of $\overline{AB}$.

Midpoint Formula (p. 55) The midpoint of the segment joining $A(x_1, y_1)$ and $B(x_2, y_2)$ is

$$M\left(\frac{x_1 + x_2}{2}, \frac{y_1 + y_2}{2}\right).$$

midsegment of a trapezoid (p. 333) The segment that connects the midpoints of the legs of a trapezoid.

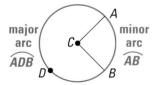

midsegment of a triangle (p. 389) A segment that connects the midpoints of two sides of a triangle.

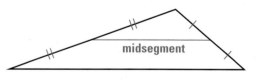

minor arc (p. 601) Points *A* and *B* on a circle *C* determine a minor arc and a major arc.

If the measure of ∠*ACB* is less than 180°, then *A*, *B*, and all the points on circle *C* that lie in the interior of ∠*ACB* form a *minor arc*.

Points *A*, *B*, and all the points of circle *C* that do not lie on $\overarc{AB}$ form a *major arc*.

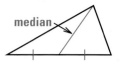

net (p. 483) A flat representation of all the faces of a polyhedron.

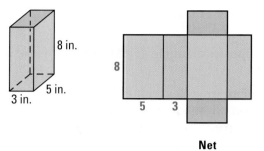

Net

_n_-gon (p. 304) A polygon with *n* sides.

obtuse angle (p. 36) An angle with measure between 90° and 180°.

obtuse triangle (p. 174) A triangle with one obtuse angle.

octagon (p. 304) A polygon with eight sides.

opposite side (p. 175) The side across from an angle of a triangle.

parallel lines (p. 108) Two lines that lie in the same plane and do not intersect. The symbol for "is parallel to" is ‖.

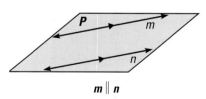

m ‖ *n*

parallel planes (p. 109) Two planes that do not intersect.

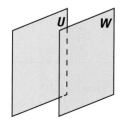

Plane *U* is parallel to plane *W*.

parallelogram (p. 310) A quadrilateral with both pairs of opposite sides parallel. The symbol for parallelogram *PQRS* is □ *PQRS*.

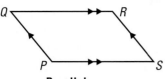

Parallelogram

pentagon (p. 304) A polygon with five sides.

perpendicular bisector (p. 274) A line that is perpendicular to a segment at its midpoint.

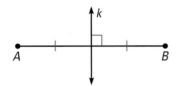

Line *k* is the perpendicular bisector of $\overline{AB}$.

perpendicular lines (p. 108) Two lines that intersect to form a right angle. The symbol for "is perpendicular to" is ⊥. The red angle mark shown below indicates a right angle.

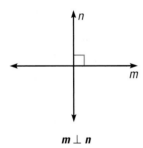

m ⊥ n

pi (p. 452) The ratio of the circumference of a circle to its diameter. Pi is an irrational number denoted by π and is approximately equal to 3.14.

plane (p. 14) A plane has two dimensions. It is represented by a shape that looks like a floor or wall. You have to imagine that it extends without end, even though the drawing of a plane appears to have edges. *See also* undefined term.

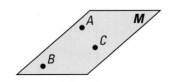

Plane *M* or plane *ABC*

point (p. 14) A point has no dimension. It is represented by a small dot. *See also* undefined term.

A.

point of tangency (p. 589) *See* tangent.

polygon (p. 303) A plane figure that is formed by three or more segments called *sides*. Each side intersects exactly two other sides at each of its endpoints. Each endpoint is a *vertex* of the polygon.

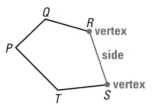

polyhedron (pp. 473, 474) A solid that is formed by polygons. The plane surfaces are called *faces* and the segments joining the vertices are called *edges*.

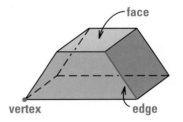

postulate (p. 14) A statement that is accepted without further justification.

power (p. 467) An expression like 7^3. The *exponent* 3 represents the number of times the *base* 7 is used as a factor: $7^3 = 7 \cdot 7 \cdot 7$.

prism (pp. 473, 475, 483) A polyhedron with two congruent faces, called *bases*, that lie in parallel planes. The other faces are called *lateral faces*. The *height* is the perpendicular distance between the bases.

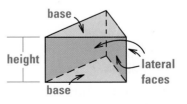

proof (p. 243) A convincing argument that shows why a statement is true.

proportion (pp. 349, 359) An equation that states that two ratios are equal. *Example:* $\frac{a}{b} = \frac{c}{d}$

pyramid (pp. 473, 475, 491) A polyhedron in which the *base* is a polygon and the *lateral faces* are triangles with a common vertex. *See also* height of a pyramid, slant height of a pyramid.

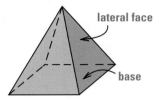

lateral face

base

Pythagorean triple (p. 196) Three positive integers *a*, *b*, and *c* that satisfy the equation $c^2 = a^2 + b^2$.

quadrilateral (p. 304) A polygon with four sides.

R

radical (p. 537) An expression written with a radical symbol $\sqrt{}$. A radical is also called a *radical expression.*

radical symbol (p. 537) The square root symbol, $\sqrt{}$, which indicates the nonnegative square root of a number. For example, $\sqrt{25} = 5$.

radicand (p. 537) The number or expression written inside a radical symbol. In the radical $\sqrt{25}$, the radicand is 25.

radius (pp. 452, 589) The distance from the center to a point on the circle. A segment whose endpoints are the center of the circle and a point on the circle is also called a *radius*. The plural of radius is *radii*.

Radius: *PQ* or $\overline{PQ}$

radius of a cone (p. 493) *See* cone.

radius of a cylinder (p. 485) *See* cylinder.

radius of a sphere (p. 517) *See* sphere.

rate of *a* to *b* (p. 227) The quotient $\frac{a}{b}$ if *a* and *b* are two quantities that have different kinds of units of measure.

ratio of *a* to *b* (pp. 227, 357) A comparison of a number *a* and a nonzero number *b* using division. The ratio of *a* to *b* can be written as the fraction $\frac{a}{b}$, as *a* : *b*, or as "*a* to *b*."

ray (p. 16) The ray $\overrightarrow{AB}$ consists of the *endpoint A* and all points on $\overleftrightarrow{AB}$ that lie on the same side of *A* as *B*.

$\overrightarrow{AB}$ **with endpoint *A***

rectangle (p. 325) A parallelogram with four right angles.

Rectangle

reduction (p. 394) A dilation in which the image is smaller than the original figure. The scale factor of a reduction is less than 1.

reflection (p. 282) A transformation that creates a mirror image. The original figure is reflected in a *line of reflection.*

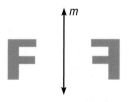

Line *m* is a line of reflection.

regular polygon (p. 412) A polygon that is both equilateral and equiangular.

rhombus (p. 325) A parallelogram with four congruent sides.

Rhombus

right angle (p. 36) An angle with measure 90°.

right triangle (p. 174) A triangle with one right angle. *See also* legs of a right triangle.

rotation (p. 633) A transformation in which a figure is turned about a fixed point, called the *center of rotation*. Rays drawn from the center of rotation to a point and its image form an angle called the *angle of rotation*.

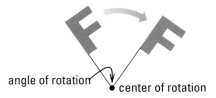

rotational symmetry (p. 634) A figure in the plane has rotational symmetry if the figure can be mapped onto itself by a rotation of 180° or less.

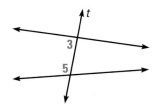

same-side interior angles (p. 121) Two angles that are formed by two lines and a transversal, and lie between the two lines on the same side of the transversal. In the diagram below, ∠3 and ∠5 are same-side interior angles.

scale factor (p. 366) The ratio of the lengths of two corresponding sides of two similar polygons.

scale factor of a dilation (p. 394) The value of k where $k = \dfrac{CP'}{CP}$. *See also* dilation.

scalene triangle (p. 173) A triangle with no congruent sides.

secant (p. 589) A line that intersects a circle in two points.

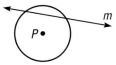

sector (p. 454) A region of a circle determined by two radii and a part of the circle.

segment (p. 16) Part of a line that consists of two points, called *endpoints*, and all points on the line that are between the endpoints.

$\overline{AB}$ with endpoints **A** and **B**

segment bisector (p. 53) A segment, ray, line, or plane that intersects a segment at its midpoint.

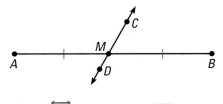

$\overleftrightarrow{CD}$ is a bisector of $\overline{AB}$.

semicircle (p. 601) An arc whose central angle measures 180°.

side of an angle (p. 35) *See* angle.

side of a polygon (p. 303) *See* polygon.

similar polygons (p. 365) Two polygons are similar polygons if corresponding angles are congruent and corresponding side lengths are proportional. The symbol for "is similar to" is ~.

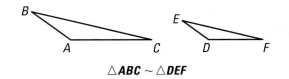

△**ABC** ~ △**DEF**

similarity statement (p. 365) A statement, such as △ABC ~ △DEF, that indicates that two polygons are similar.

sine (p. 563) A trigonometric ratio, abbreviated as *sin* and computed as the ratio of the length of the leg opposite the angle to the length of the hypotenuse.

$$\sin A = \frac{\text{leg opposite } \angle A}{\text{hypotenuse}} = \frac{a}{c}$$

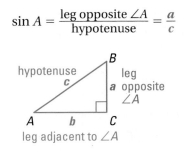

skew lines (p. 108) Two lines that do not lie in the same plane and do not intersect.

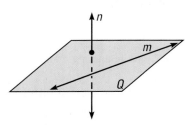

Lines *m* and *n* are skew lines.

slant height of a cone (p. 493) *See* cone.

slant height of a pyramid (p. 491) The height of a lateral face of a pyramid. The letter ℓ is used to represent the slant height.

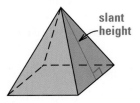

slope (pp. 150, 299, 665) The ratio of the vertical change (rise) to the horizontal change (run) between any two points on a line.

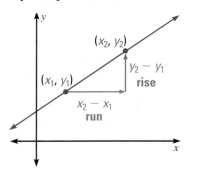

solid (p. 473) A three-dimensional shape.

solve a right triangle (p. 569) Find the measures of both acute angles and the lengths of all three sides.

sphere (p. 517) The set of all points in space that are the same distance from a point, called the *center* of the sphere. The *radius* of a sphere is the length of a segment from the center to a point on the sphere.

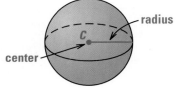

square (p. 325) A parallelogram with four congruent sides and four right angles.

square root (p. 167) If $b^2 = a$, then b is a square root of a.

standard equation of a circle (p. 628) In the coordinate plane, the standard equation of a circle with center at (h, k) and radius r is
$$(x - h)^2 + (y - k)^2 = r^2.$$

straight angle (p. 36) An angle with measure 180°.

straightedge (p. 143) A construction tool used to draw segments. A ruler without marks.

supplement (p. 67) The sum of the measures of an angle and its *supplement* is 180°.

supplementary angles (p. 67) Two angles whose measures have a sum of 180°.

surface area of a polyhedron (p. 483) The sum of the areas of the faces of a polyhedron.

T

tangent (p. 589) A line in the plane of a circle that intersects the circle in exactly one point, called a *point of tangency.*

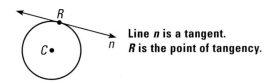

Line *n* is a tangent.
R is the point of tangency.

tangent of an angle (p. 557) A trigonometric ratio, abbreviated as *tan* and computed as the ratio of the length of the leg opposite the angle to the length of the leg adjacent to (contained in) the angle.

$$\tan A = \frac{\text{leg opposite } \angle A}{\text{leg adjacent to } \angle A} = \frac{a}{b}$$

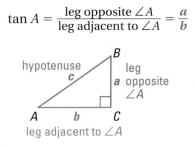

Glossary

tangent segment (p. 597) A segment that touches a circle at one of the segment's endpoints and lies in the line that is tangent to the circle at that point.

theorem (p. 69) A true statement that follows from other true statements.

transformation (p. 152) An operation that *maps*, or moves, a figure onto an image. *See also* dilation, reflection, rotation, translation.

translation (p. 152) A transformation that slides each point of a figure the same distance in the same direction.

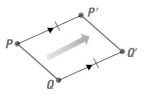

transversal (p. 121) A line that intersects two or more coplanar lines at different points.

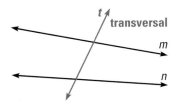

trapezoid (p. 332) A quadrilateral with exactly one pair of parallel sides, called *bases*. The nonparallel sides are the *legs*.

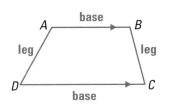

triangle (p. 173) A figure formed by three segments joining three noncollinear points, called *vertices*. The triangle symbol is △.

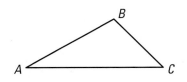

△*ABC* with vertices *A*, *B*, and *C*

trigonometric ratio (p. 557) A ratio of the lengths of two sides of a right triangle. *See also* cosine, sine, tangent of an angle.

undefined term (p. 14) A word, such as *point*, *line*, or *plane*, that is not mathematically defined using other known words, although there is a common understanding of what the word means.

vertex of an angle (p. 35) *See* angle.

vertex of a polygon (p. 303) *See* polygon.

vertex of a triangle (p. 175) A point that joins two sides of a triangle. The plural is *vertices*. *See also* triangle.

vertical angles (p. 75) Two angles that are not adjacent and whose sides are formed by two intersecting lines.

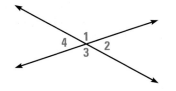

∠1 and ∠3 are vertical angles.
∠2 and ∠4 are vertical angles.

volume of a solid (p. 500) The number of cubic units contained in the interior of the solid.

English-to-Spanish Glossary

A

acute angle (p. 36) ángulo agudo Ángulo que mide entre 0° and 90°.

acute triangle (p. 174) triángulo agudo Triángulo con tres ángulos agudos.

adjacent angles (p. 68) ángulos adyacentes Dos ángulos con un vértice y un lado común pero sin puntos internos comunes.

alternate exterior angles (p. 121) ángulos exteriores alternos Dos ángulos formados por dos rectas y una transversal y situados fuera de las dos rectas en lados opuestos de la transversal. En el siguiente diagrama ∠1 y ∠8 son ángulos exteriores alternos.

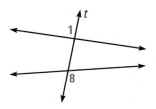

alternate interior angles (p. 121) ángulos interiores alternos Dos ángulos formados por dos rectas y una transversal y situados entre las dos rectas en lados opuestos de la transversal. En el siguiente diagrama ∠3 y ∠6 son ángulos interiores alternos.

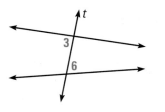

angle (p. 35) ángulo Figura formada por dos rayos que comienzan en el mismo extremo. Los rayos son los *lados* del ángulo y el extremo es el *vértice* del ángulo.

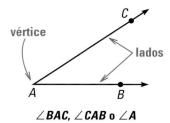

∠*BAC*, ∠*CAB* o ∠*A*

angle bisector (p. 61) bisectriz de un ángulo Rayo que divide un ángulo en dos ángulos congruentes.

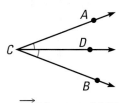

$\overrightarrow{CD}$ **biseca a** ∠*ACB*.

m∠*ACD* = *m*∠*BCD*

angle of rotation (p. 633) ángulo de rotación *Ver* rotation/rotación.

arc length (p. 603) longitud de arco Parte de la circunferencia de un círculo.

area (p. 424) área Medida de la superficie cubierta por una figura.

B

base of a cone (p. 493) base de un cono *Ver* cone/cono.

bases of a cylinder (p. 485) bases de un cilindro *Ver* cylinder/cilindro.

base of an isosceles triangle (p. 185) base de un triángulo isósceles *Ver* legs of an isosceles triangle/catetos de un triángulo isósceles.

bases of a parallelogram (p. 439) **bases de un paralelogramo** Cualquier par de lados paralelos de un paralelogramo se llama *bases*. *Ver también* height of a parallelogram/altura de un paralelogramo.

bases of a prism (p. 473) **bases de un prisma** *Ver* prism/prisma.

base of a pyramid (p. 491) **base de una pirámide** *Ver* pyramid/pirámide.

bases of a trapezoid (p. 332) **bases de un trapezoide** *Ver* trapezoid/trapezoide.

base of a triangle (p. 431) **base de un triángulo** *Ver* height of a triangle/altura de un triángulo.

base angles of an isosceles triangle (p. 185) **ángulos base de un triángulo isósceles** Los dos ángulos en la base de un triángulo isósceles. *Ver también* legs of an isosceles triangle/catetos de un triángulo isósceles.

base angles of a trapezoid (p. 332) **ángulos base de un trapezoide** Si un trapezoide $ABCD$ tiene $\overline{AB}$ y $\overline{CD}$ como bases, entonces hay dos pares de ángulos base: $\angle A$ y $\angle B$, y $\angle C$ y $\angle D$.

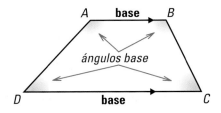

between (p. 29) **entre** Cuando tres puntos se encuentran en una recta, uno de ellos está *entre* los otros dos.

El punto **B** está entre los puntos **A** y **C**.

bisect (pp. 53, 61) **bisecar** Dividir en dos partes congruentes.

center of a circle (p. 452) **centro de un círculo** *Ver* circle/círculo.

center of dilation (p. 393) **centro de dilatación** *Ver* dilation/dilatación.

center of rotation (p. 633) **centro de rotación** *Ver* rotation/rotación.

center of a sphere (p. 517) **centro de una esfera** *Ver* sphere/esfera.

central angle (p. 454) **ángulo central** Ángulo cuyo vértice es el centro de un círculo.

∠**PCQ** es un ángulo central.

centroid of a triangle (p. 208) **centroide de un triángulo** Punto en el que se intersecan las tres medianas de un triángulo.

chord (p. 589) **cuerda** Segmento cuyos extremos son puntos de un círculo.

Cuerdas $\overline{QR}$, $\overline{ST}$

circle (pp. 452, 589) **círculo** Conjunto de todos los puntos de un plano que está a la misma distancia de un punto dado llamado *centro* del círculo.

Círculo con centro **P**, o ⊙**P**

circumference (p. 452) **circunferencia** Distancia en torno a un círculo.

circumscribed circle (p. 615) **círculo circunscrito** *Ver* inscribed polygon/polígono inscrito.

collinear points (p. 15) **puntos colineales** Puntos ubicados en la misma recta.

compass (p. 143) **compás** Instrumento de construcción utilizado para dibujar arcos y círculos.

complement (p. 67) **complemento** La suma de las medidas de un ángulo y su *complemento* es 90°.

complementary angles (p. 67) ángulos complementarios Dos ángulos cuyas medidas suman 90°.

concave polygon (p. 411) polígono cóncavo *Ver* convex polygon/polígono convexo.

conclusion (p. 82) conclusión La parte que comienza con "entonces" de un enunciado de tipo "si..., entonces...". En el enunciado "Si hace frío, entonces me pondré un abrigo", la conclusión es "me pondré un abrigo".

cone (p. 493) cono Sólido que tiene una *base* circular y un *vértice* que no pertenece al mismo plano que la base. La *altura* de un cono es la distancia perpendicular entre el vértice y la base. El *radio* de un cono es el radio de la base. La *altura inclinada* de un cono es la distancia entre el vértice y un punto del borde de la base.

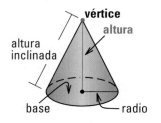

congruent angles (p. 36) ángulos congruentes Ángulos que tienen la misma medida.

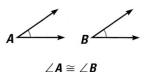

$\angle A \cong \angle B$

congruent arcs (p. 602) arcos congruentes Dos arcos del mismo círculo o de círculos congruentes que tienen la misma medida.

congruent circles (p. 602) círculos congruentes Dos círculos que tienen el mismo radio.

congruent figures (p. 233) figuras congruentes Dos figuras geométricas que tienen exactamente el mismo tamaño y la misma forma. Cuando dos figuras son congruentes, todos los pares de ángulos y lados correspondientes son congruentes.

congruent segments (p. 30) segmentos congruentes Segmentos que tienen la misma longitud.

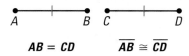

$AB = CD$ $\overline{AB} \cong \overline{CD}$

conjecture (p. 8) conjetura Enunciado no comprobado que se basa en un patrón o en observaciones.

construction (p. 143) construcción Dibujo geométrico realizado con varios instrumentos, generalmente un compás y una regla.

converse (p. 136) inverso Enunciado formado al cambiar la hipótesis y la conclusión de un enunciado de tipo "si..., entonces...".

convex polygon (p. 411) polígono convexo Un polígono es convexo si ninguna recta que contiene un lado del polígono pasa por el interior del polígono. El polígono que no es convexo se llama *cóncavo*.

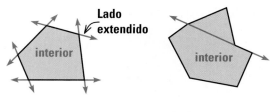

Polígono convexo   **Polígono cóncavo**

coordinate (p. 28) coordenada Número real que corresponde a un punto de una recta.

coplanar lines (p. 15) rectas coplanarias Rectas que pertenecen a un mismo plano.

coplanar points (p. 15) puntos coplanarios Puntos que pertenecen a un mismo plano.

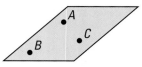

corollary to a theorem (p. 180) corolario de un teorema Enunciado que se puede probar fácilmente usando el teorema.

corresponding angles (p. 121) **ángulos correspondientes** Ángulos que están en la misma posición relativa cuando una transversal cruza dos rectas. En el siguiente diagrama, ∠1 y ∠5 son ángulos correspondientes.

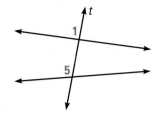

corresponding parts of congruent figures (p. 233) **partes correspondientes de figuras congruentes** Lados y ángulos correspondientes de figuras congruentes.

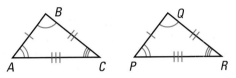

∠*B* y ∠*Q* son ángulos correspondientes.

$\overline{BC}$ y $\overline{QR}$ son lados correspondientes.

cosine (p. 563) **coseno** Razón trigonométrica que se abrevia *cos* y se calcula como la razón entre la longitud del cateto adyacente al ángulo y la longitud de la hipotenusa.

$$\cos A = \frac{\text{cateto adyacente a } \angle A}{\text{hipotenusa}} = \frac{b}{c}$$

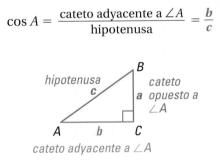

counterexample (p. 10) **contraejemplo** Ejemplo que muestra que la conjetura es falsa.

cross product property (pp. 349, 359) **propiedad de los productos cruzados** Si $\frac{a}{b} = \frac{c}{d}$, entonces $ad = bc$.

cylinder (p. 485) **cilindro** Figura sólida con dos *bases* circulares congruentes que yace sobre planos paralelos. La *altura* de un cilindro es la distancia perpendicular entre las bases. El *radio* de un cilindro es el radio de una de las bases.

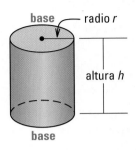

deductive reasoning (p. 83) **razonamiento deductivo** El uso de hechos, definiciones, propiedades aceptadas y las reglas de la lógica para establecer un argumento lógico.

degrees (°) (p. 36) **grados** (°) *Ver* measure of an angle/medida de un ángulo.

diagonal of a polygon (p. 303) **diagonal de un polígono** Segmento que conecta dos vértices no consecutivos de un polígono.

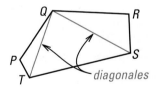

diameter (pp. 452, 589) **diámetro** Distancia a través de un círculo que pasa por su centro. La longitud del *diámetro* es el doble de la longitud del *radio*. Una cuerda que pasa por el centro del círculo también se denomina *diámetro*.

Diámetro: $\overline{QR}$ o *QR*

dilation (p. 393) **dilatación** Transformación con un centro C y un factor de escala k que refleja cada punto P en un punto de imagen P' de manera que P' se encuentra en $\overrightarrow{CP}$ y $CP' = k \cdot CP$.

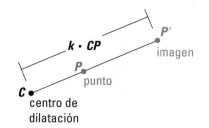

distance between two points on a line (p. 28) **distancia entre dos puntos en una recta** La distancia AB es el valor absoluto de la diferencia de las coordenadas de A y B. $\overline{AB}$ también se conoce como la longitud de $\overline{AB}$.

$$AB = |x_2 - x_1|$$

Distance Formula (p. 194) **Fórmula de distancia** Si $A(x_1, y_1)$ y $B(x_2, y_2)$ son puntos de un plano de coordenadas, la distancia entre A y B es

$$\sqrt{(x_2 - x_1)^2 + (y_2 - y_1)^2}.$$

distance from a point to a line (p. 273) **distancia de un punto a una recta** La longitud del segmento perpendicular de un punto a una recta.

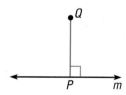

La distancia de Q a la recta m es QP.

E

edge of a polyhedron (p. 474) **arista de un poliedro** *Ver* polyhedron/poliedro.

endpoint of a ray (p. 16) **extremo de un rayo** *Ver* ray/rayo.

endpoints of a segment (p. 16) **extremos de un segmento** *Ver* segment/segmento.

enlargement (p. 394) **ampliación** Dilatación en la cual la imagen es más grande que la figura original. El factor de escala de una ampliación es mayor que 1.

equiangular polygon (p. 412) **polígono equiangular** Polígono cuyos ángulos interiores son congruentes.

equiangular triangle (p. 174) **triángulo equiangular** Triángulo en el que los tres ángulos tienen la misma medida.

equidistant (p. 273) **equidistante** La misma distancia.

equilateral polygon (p. 412) **polígono equilátero** Polígono en el que todos los lados son congruentes.

Polígono equilátero

equilateral triangle (p. 173) **triángulo equilátero** Triángulo que tiene tres lados congruentes.

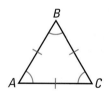

Triángulo equilátero

evaluate an expression (p. 49) **evaluar una expresión** Hallar el valor de una expresión sustituyendo valores por variables y simplificando el resultado realizando operaciones en orden.

exponent (p. 467) **exponente** *Ver* power/potencia.

exterior angles of a triangle (p. 181) **ángulos externos de un triángulo** Los ángulos adyacentes a los *ángulos internos* del triángulo cuando se amplía los lados de un triángulo.

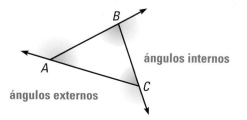

extremes of a proportion (p. 359) extremos de una proporción Los extremos de una proporción $\frac{a}{b} = \frac{c}{d}$ son *a* y *d. Ver también* means of a proportion/medias de una proporción.

face (p. 474) cara *Ver* polyhedron/poliedro.

height of a cone (p. 493) altura de un cono *Ver* cone/cono.

height of a cylinder (p. 485) altura de un cilindro *Ver* cylinder/cilindro.

height of a parallelogram (p. 439) altura de un paralelogramo La distancia más corta entre las bases. El segmento que representa la altura es perpendicular a las bases.

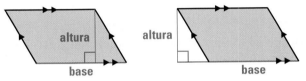

La altura puede medirse dentro del paralelogramo.   **La altura puede medirse fuera del paralelogramo.**

height of a prism (p. 484) altura de un prisma *Ver* prism/prisma.

height of a pyramid (p. 491) altura de una pirámide La distancia perpendicular entre el vértice y la base.

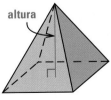

Pirámide

height of a trapezoid (p. 446) altura de un trapezoide La distancia más corta entre las bases. El segmento que representa la altura es perpendicular a las bases.

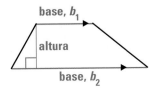

height of a triangle (p. 431) altura de un triángulo El segmento perpendicular que va de un vértice a la recta que contiene el lado opuesto, llamado *base* del triángulo. El término *altura* también se utiliza para representar la longitud del segmento.

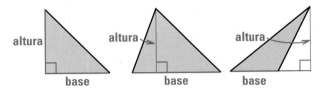

hemisphere (p. 517) hemisferio Un plano geométrico que pasa por el centro de una esfera la divide en dos *hemisferios.*

heptagon (p. 304) heptágono Polígono de siete lados.

hexagon (p. 304) hexágono Polígono de seis lados.

hypotenuse (pp. 192, 257) hipotenusa Lado de un triángulo recto que está opuesto al ángulo recto. Es el lado más largo de un triángulo recto. *Ver también* legs of a right triangle/catetos de un triángulo recto.

hypothesis (p. 82) hipótesis La parte "si" de un enunciado de tipo "si..., entonces...". En el enunciado "Si hace frío, entonces me pondré un abrigo", la hipótesis es "hace frío".

if-then statement (p. 82) enunciado de tipo "si..., entonces..." Enunciado con dos partes: una parte (si...) que expresa una hipótesis y una parte (entonces...) que expresa una conclusión.

image (pp. 152, 282, 393, 633) imagen Nueva figura formada por la transformación de una figura en un plano.

included angle (p. 242) ángulo incluido Ángulo de un triángulo cuyo vértice es el punto común de dos lados del triángulo.

$\angle B$ **está incluido entre** $\overline{AB}$ **y** $\overline{BC}$.

included side (p. 250) **lado incluido** Lado de un triángulo cuyos extremos son los vértices de dos ángulos del triángulo.

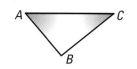

$\overline{AC}$ está incluido entre $\angle A$ y $\angle C$.

inductive reasoning (pp. 8, 83) **razonamiento inductivo** Proceso que consiste en buscar patrones para realizar conjeturas.

inscribed angle (p. 614) **ángulo inscrito** Ángulo cuyo vértice pertenece a un círculo y cuyos lados tienen cuerdas del círculo. El arco en el interior de un ángulo inscrito que tiene extremos en el ángulo es el *arco interceptado*.

ángulo inscrito

arco interceptado

inscribed polygon (p. 615) **polígono inscrito** Polígono cuyos vértices pertenecen a un círculo. El círculo *es circunscrito al* polígono y se denomina *círculo circunscrito*.

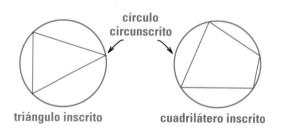

círculo circunscrito

triángulo inscrito

cuadrilátero inscrito

intercepted arc (p. 614) **arco interceptado** Arco situado en el interior de un ángulo inscrito y que tiene extremos en el ángulo. *Ver también* inscribed angle/ángulo inscrito.

interior of an angle (p. 37) **interior de un ángulo** Un punto está en el interior de un ángulo si está situado entre puntos de cada lado del ángulo.

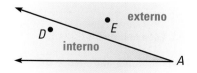

externo

interno

interior angles of a triangle (p. 181) **ángulos internos de un triángulo** *Ver* exterior angles of a triangle/ángulos externos de un triángulo.

intersect (p. 22) **intersecar** Las figuras se intersecan si tienen puntos en común.

intersection (p. 22) **intersección** La intersección de dos o más figuras es el punto o los puntos que dichas figuras tienen en común.

inverse cosine (pp. 570, 571) **coseno inverso** Función, representada en una calculadora científica por $\cos^{-1} x$, que se puede usar para hallar la medida de un ángulo si se sabe el coseno del ángulo.

inverse sine (pp. 570, 571) **seno inverso** Función, representada en una calculadora científica por $\sin^{-1} x$, que se puede usar para hallar la medida de un ángulo si se sabe el seno del ángulo.

inverse tangent (p. 569) **tangente inversa** Función, representada en una calculadora científica por $\tan^{-1} x$, que se puede usar para hallar la medida de un ángulo si se sabe la tangente del ángulo.

isosceles trapezoid (p. 332) **trapezoide isósceles** Trapezoide que tiene catetos congruentes.

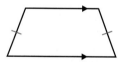

Trapezoide isósceles

isosceles triangle (p. 173) **triángulo isósceles** Triángulo que tiene al menos dos lados congruentes. *Ver también* legs of an isosceles triangle/catetos de un triángulo isósceles.

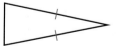

Triángulo isósceles

lateral area of a cylinder (p. 485) **área lateral de un cilindro** Área de la superficie curva de un cilindro.

lateral area of a prism (p. 484) **área lateral de un prisma** Suma de las áreas de las caras laterales.

English-to-Spanish Glossary

lateral faces of a prism (p. 484) **caras laterales de un prisma** *Ver* prism/prisma.

lateral faces of a pyramid (p. 491) **caras laterales de una pirámide** *Ver* pyramid/pirámide.

leg adjacent to an angle (p. 557) **cateto adyacente a un ángulo** *Ver* tangent of an angle/tangente de un ángulo.

leg opposite an angle (p. 557) **cateto opuesto al ángulo** *Ver* tangent of an angle/tangente de un ángulo.

legs of an isosceles triangle (p. 185) **catetos de un triángulo isósceles** Lados congruentes de un triángulo isósceles. El tercer lado es la *base*.

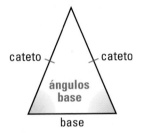

legs of a right triangle (p. 192) **catetos de un triángulo recto** Lados que forman el ángulo recto.

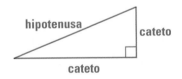

Triángulo recto

legs of a trapezoid (p. 332) **catetos de un trapezoide** *Ver* trapezoid/trapezoide.

length of a segment (p. 28) **longitud de un segmento** Distancia entre los extremos de un segmento. *Ver también* distance between two points on a line/distancia entre dos puntos en una recta.

like terms (p. 101) **términos semejantes** Términos de una expresión que tienen las mismas variables elevadas a las mismas potencias. Los términos constantes, como 2 y −5, también son considerados términos semejantes.

line (p. 14) **línea recta** o **recta** Una recta tiene una dimensión y se extiende de manera infinita en dos direcciones. Su representación es una línea recta con dos flechas. *Ver también* undefined term/término indefinido.

Recta ℓ o $\overleftrightarrow{AB}$

line of reflection (p. 282) **eje de reflexión** *Ver* reflection/reflexión.

line of symmetry (p. 284) **eje de simetría** Una figura en un plano tiene eje de simetría si se puede reflejar en sí misma a través de una reflexión en la recta.

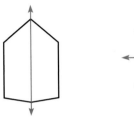

Hexágono con eje de simetría   Hexágono con seis ejes de simetría

line perpendicular to a plane (p. 109) **recta perpendicular a un plano** Recta que interseca un plano en un punto y que es perpendicular a cada recta que la interseca en el plano.

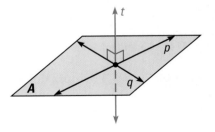

La recta *t* es perpendicular al plano *A*.

linear pair (p. 75) **par lineal** Dos ángulos adyacentes cuyos lados no comunes están en la misma recta.

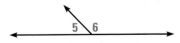

∠5 y ∠6 son un par lineal.

major arc (p. 601) **arco mayor** *Ver* minor arc/arco menor.

means of a proportion (p. 359) **medias de una proporción** Las medias de una proporción $\frac{a}{b} = \frac{c}{d}$ son b y c. *Ver también* extremes of a proportion/extremos de una proporción.

measure of an angle (p. 36) **medida de un ángulo** Tamaño de un ángulo que se expresa en unidades llamadas *grados* (°). $m\angle A$ denota la medida de $\angle A$.

measure of a major arc (p. 601) **medida de un arco mayor** La diferencia de 360° y la medida del arco menor relacionado.

measure of a minor arc (p. 601) **medida de un arco menor** Medida de su ángulo central.

median of a triangle (p. 207) **mediana de un triángulo** Segmento de un vértice al punto medio del lado opuesto.

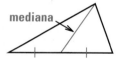

mediana

midpoint (p. 53) **punto medio** Punto de un segmento que lo divide en dos segmentos congruentes.

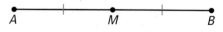

A M B

M es el punto medio de $\overline{AB}$.

Midpoint Formula (p. 55) **Fórmula del punto medio** El punto medio de un segmento que une $A(x_1, y_1)$ y $B(x_2, y_2)$ es

$$M\left(\frac{x_1 + x_2}{2}, \frac{y_1 + y_2}{2}\right).$$

midsegment of a trapezoid (p. 333) **segmento medio de un trapezoide** Segmento que une los puntos medios de los catetos de un trapezoide.

segmento medio

midsegment of a triangle (p. 389) **segmento medio de un triángulo** Segmento que une los puntos medios de dos lados de un triángulo.

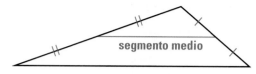

segmento medio

minor arc (p. 601) **arco menor** Los puntos A y B de un círculo C determinan un arco menor y un arco mayor.

Si la medida de $\angle ACB$ es menor que 180°, entonces A, B y todos los puntos del círculo C situados en el interior de $\angle ACB$ forman un *arco menor*.

arco mayor $\widehat{ADB}$ arco menor $\widehat{AB}$

Los puntos A, B y todos los puntos del círculo C que no están situados en $\widehat{AB}$ forman un *arco mayor*.

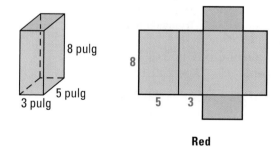

net (p. 483) **red** Representación plana de todas las caras de un poliedro.

8 pulg   5 pulg   3 pulg   8   5   3

Red

n-gon (p. 304) **n-gono** Polígono con n número de lados.

obtuse angle (p. 36) **ángulo obtuso** Ángulo que mide entre 90° y 180°.

obtuse triangle (p. 174) **triángulo obtuso** Triángulo que tiene un ángulo obtuso.

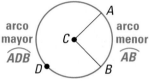

octagon (p. 304) **octágono** Polígono de ocho lados.

opposite side (p. 175) **lado opuesto** Lado situado frente a un ángulo en un triángulo.

parallel lines (p. 108) **rectas paralelas** Rectas del mismo plano que no se intersecan. El símbolo usado para representar "es paralelo a" es ∥.

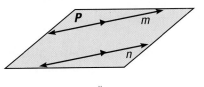

$m \parallel n$

parallel planes (p. 109) **planos paralelos** Dos planos que no se intersecan.

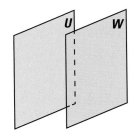

El plano *U* es paralelo al plano *W*.

parallelogram (p. 310) **paralelogramo** Cuadrilátero cuyos lados opuestos son paralelos. El símbolo ▱*PQRS* se usa para representar el paralelogramo *PQRS*.

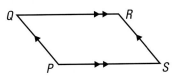

Paralelogramo

pentagon (p. 304) **pentágono** Polígono de cinco lados.

perpendicular bisector (p. 274) **bisectriz perpendicular** Recta perpendicular que pasa por el punto medio de un segmento.

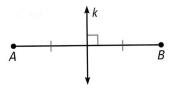

La recta *k* es la bisectriz perpendicular de $\overline{AB}$.

perpendicular lines (p. 108) **rectas perpendiculares** Dos rectas que se intersecan para formar un ángulo recto. El símbolo ⊥ representa la expresión "es perpendicular a". La marca roja del ángulo que se muestra abajo indica un ángulo recto.

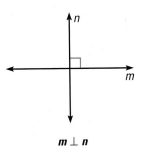

$m \perp n$

pi (p. 452) **pi** Número que representa la relación entre la circunferencia de un círculo y su diámetro. Pi es un número irracional que se denota con π y es aproximadamente igual a 3.14.

plane (p. 14) **plano** Un plano tiene dos dimensiones y se representa con una forma parecida a una pared o al piso. Es necesario imaginar que se extiende de manera infinita aunque el dibujo de un plano parezca tener bordes. *Ver también* undefined term/término indefinido.

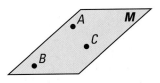

Plano *M* o plano *ABC*

point (p. 14) **punto** Un punto no tiene dimensiones. Se representa por un punto pequeño. *Ver también* undefined term/término indefinido.

A
•

point of tangency (p. 589) punto de tangencia *Ver* tangent/tangente.

polygon (p. 303) polígono Figura plana formada por tres o más segmentos llamados *lados.* Cada lado interseca otros dos lados exactamente en sus extremos. Cada extremo es un *vértice* del polígono.

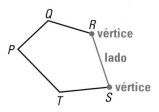

polyhedron (pp. 473, 474) poliedro Sólido formado por polígonos. Las superficies planas de un poliedro se llaman *caras* y los segmentos que unen los vértices se llaman *aristas.*

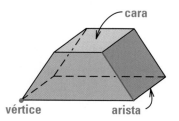

postulate (p. 14) postulado Enunciado que se admite sin ser justificado.

power (p. 467) potencia Expresión tal como 7^3. El *exponente* 3 representa el número de veces que se usa la *base* 7 como factor: $7^3 = 7 \cdot 7 \cdot 7$.

prism (p. 483) prisma Poliedro que tiene dos caras congruentes, llamadas *bases,* situadas en planos paralelos. Las otras caras se denominan *caras laterales.* La *altura* es la distancia perpendicular entre las bases.

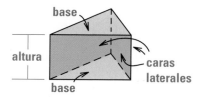

proof (p. 243) prueba Argumento convincente que muestra que un enunciado es cierto.

proportion (pp. 349, 359) proporción Ecuación que muestra que dos razones son iguales. Por ejemplo: $\frac{a}{b} = \frac{c}{d}$.

pyramid (pp. 475, 491) pirámide Poliedro cuya *base* es un polígono y cuyas *caras laterales* son triángulos que tienen un vértice común. *Ver también* height of a pyramid, slant height of a pyramid/altura de una pirámide, altura inclinada de una pirámide.

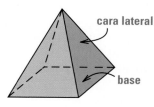

Pythagorean triple (p. 196) terna pitagórica Conjunto de tres números naturales *a, b* y *c* que cumple con la ecuación $c^2 = a^2 + b^2$.

quadrilateral (p. 304) cuadrilátero Polígono de cuatro lados.

radical (p. 537) radical Expresión escrita con un símbolo de radical $\sqrt{}$. También se llama *expresión radical.*

radical symbol (p. 537) símbolo de radical Símbolo de la raíz cuadrada, $\sqrt{}$, que indica la raíz cuadrada positiva de un número. Por ejemplo: $\sqrt{25} = 5$.

radicand (p. 537) radicando Número o expresión escrita dentro de un símbolo de radical. En el radical $\sqrt{25}$, el radicando es 25.

radius (pp. 452, 589) radio Distancia del centro a un punto de un círculo. Todo segmento cuyos extremos son el centro de un círculo y un punto del círculo también se llama *radio.*

Radio: *PQ* o $\overline{PQ}$

radius of a cone (p. 493) **radio de un cono** *Ver* cone/cono.

radius of a cylinder (p. 485) **radio de un cilindro** *Ver* cylinder/cilindro.

radius of a sphere (p. 517) **radio de una esfera** *Ver* sphere/esfera.

rate of *a* to *b* (p. 227) **tasa de *a* a *b*** El cociente $\frac{a}{b}$ si *a* y *b* son dos cantidades que se miden en diferentes unidades.

ratio of *a* to *b* (pp. 227, 357) **razón de *a* a *b*** Comparación de un número *a* y un número *b* que no es cero usando la división. La razón de *a* a *b* se puede escribir como la fracción $\frac{a}{b}$, como *a* : *b* o como "*a* a *b*".

ray (p. 16) **rayo** El rayo $\overrightarrow{AB}$ incluye el *extremo A* y todos los puntos de $\overleftrightarrow{AB}$ situados en el mismo lado de *A* como *B*.

$\overrightarrow{AB}$ **con extremo *A***

rectangle (p. 325) **rectángulo** Paralelogramo que tiene cuatro ángulos rectos.

Rectángulo

reduction (p. 394) **reducción** Dilatación en la cual la imagen es más pequeña que la figura original. El factor de escala de una reducción es menor que 1.

reflection (p. 282) **reflexión** Transformación que crea una imagen especular. La figura original se refleja en el *eje de reflexión*.

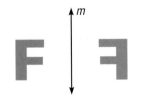

La recta *m* es un eje de reflexión.

regular polygon (p. 412) **polígono regular** Polígono equilátero y equiangular.

rhombus (p. 325) **rombo** Paralelogramo que tiene cuatro lados congruentes.

Rombo

right angle (p. 36) **ángulo recto** Ángulo que mide 90°.

right triangle (p. 174) **triángulo recto** Triángulo que tiene un ángulo recto. *Ver también* legs of a right triangle/catetos de un triángulo recto.

rotation (p. 633) **rotación** Transformación que hace girar una figura en torno a un punto fijo llamado *centro de rotación*. Los rayos que se extienden del centro de rotación a un punto y su imagen forman un ángulo llamado *ángulo de rotación*.

ángulo de rotación   centro de rotación

rotational symmetry (p. 634) **simetría rotacional** Una figura en el plano tiene simetría rotacional si coincide con sí misma luego de rotar 180° o menos en torno a un punto.

same-side interior angles (p. 121) **ángulos internos del mismo lado** Dos ángulos formados por dos rectas y una transversal y situados entre las dos rectas en el mismo lado de la transversal. En el diagrama de abajo, ∠3 y ∠5 son ángulos internos del mismo lado.

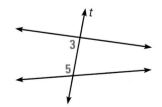

scale factor (p. 366) **factor de escala** Razón de las longitudes de dos lados correspondientes de dos polígonos semejantes.

scale factor of a dilation (pp. 392, 394) **factor de escala de dilatación** El valor de k donde $k = \dfrac{CP'}{CP}$. *Ver tambien* dilation/dilatación.

scalene triangle (p. 173) **triángulo escaleno** Triángulo que no tiene lados congruentes.

secant (p. 589) **secante** Recta que interseca un círculo en dos puntos.

sector (p. 454) **sector** Región de un círculo determinada por dos radios y una parte del círculo.

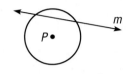

segment (p. 16) **segmento** Parte de una recta que consta de dos puntos, llamados *extremos,* y todos los puntos en la recta situados entre los extremos.

$\overline{AB}$ con extremos *A* y *B*

segment bisector (p. 53) **bisectriz de un segmento** Segmento, rayo, recta o plano que interseca un segmento en su punto medio.

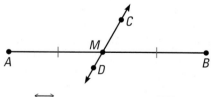

$\overleftrightarrow{CD}$ es una bisectriz de $\overline{AB}$.

semicircle (p. 601) **semicírculo** Arco cuyo ángulo central mide 180°.

side of an angle (p. 35) **lado de un ángulo** *Ver* angle/ángulo.

side of a polygon (p. 303) **lado de un polígono** *Ver* polygon/polígono.

similar polygons (p. 365) **polígonos semejantes** Dos polígonos son semejantes si sus ángulos correspondientes son congruentes y las longitudes de sus lados correspondientes son proporcionales. El símbolo ~ significa "es semejante a".

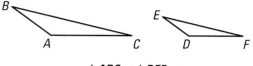

$\triangle ABC \sim \triangle DEF$

similarity statement (p. 365) **enunciado de semejanza** Enunciado tal como $\triangle ABC \sim \triangle DEF$, que indica que dos polígonos son semejantes.

sine (p. 563) **seno** Razón trigonométrica que se abrevia *sen* y que se calcula como la razón entre la longitud del cateto opuesto al ángulo y la longitud de la hipotenusa.

$$\text{sen } A = \frac{\text{cateto opuesto a } \angle A}{\text{hipotenusa}} = \frac{a}{c}$$

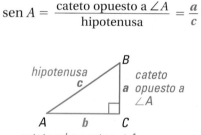

skew lines (p. 108) **rectas oblicuas** Dos rectas que no están situadas en el mismo plano y no se intersecan.

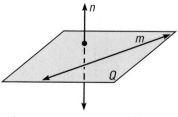

Las rectas *m* y *n* son oblicuas.

slant height of a cone (p. 493) **altura inclinada de un cono** *Ver* cone/cono.

slant height of a pyramid (p. 491) altura inclinada de una pirámide Altura de la cara lateral de una pirámide. La letra ℓ se usa para representar la altura inclinada.

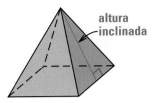

slope (pp. 150, 299, 665) inclinación Razón de la diferencia entre las coordenadas del eje vertical (elevación) y la diferencia entre las coordenadas del eje horizontal (recorrido) de dos puntos cualesquiera de una recta.

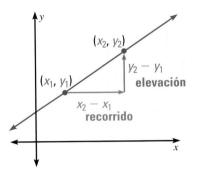

solid (p. 473) sólido Figura tridimensional.

solve a right triangle (p. 569) resolver un triángulo recto Hallar las medidas de los dos ángulos agudos y las longitudes de los tres lados.

sphere (p. 517) esfera Conjunto de puntos en el espacio que están a la misma distancia de un punto, llamado *centro* de la esfera. El *radio* de una esfera es la longitud de un segmento del centro a un punto de la esfera.

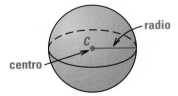

square (p. 325) cuadrado Paralelogramo que tiene cuatro lados congruentes y cuatro ángulos rectos.

square root (p. 167) raíz cuadrada Si $b^2 = a$, entonces b es la raíz cuadrada de a.

standard equation of a circle (p. 628) ecuación estándar de un círculo En el plano de coordenadas, la ecuación estándar de un círculo con centro en (h, k) y radio r es

$$(x - h)^2 + (y - k)^2 = r^2.$$

straight angle (p. 36) ángulo llano Ángulo que mide 180°.

straightedge (p. 143) regla Instrumento de construcción que se usa para dibujar segmentos; una regla sin marcas.

supplement (p. 67) suplemento La suma de las medidas de un ángulo y su *suplemento* es 90°.

supplementary angles (p. 67) ángulos suplementarios Dos ángulos cuyas medidas suman 180°.

surface area of a polyhedron (p. 483) área de la superficie de un poliedro Suma de las áreas de las caras de un poliedro.

tangent (p. 589) tangente Recta en el plano de un círculo que interseca el círculo exactamente en un punto, llamado *punto de tangencia.*

La recta **n** es una tangente. **R** es el punto de tangencia.

tangent of an angle (p. 557) tangente de un ángulo Razón trigonométrica que se abrevia *tan* y se calcula como la razón entre la longitud del cateto opuesto al ángulo y la longitud del cateto adyacente al ángulo.

$$\tan A = \frac{\text{cateto opuesto a } \angle A}{\text{cateto adyacente a } \angle A} = \frac{a}{b}$$

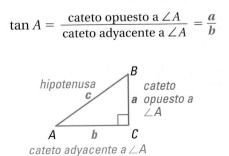

English-to-Spanish Glossary

tangent segment (p. 597) segmento tangente
Segmento que toca un círculo en uno de los extremos del segmento y que está ubicado en la recta tangente al círculo en ese punto.

theorem (p. 69) teorema Enunciado verdadero derivado de otros enunciados verdaderos.

transformation (p. 152) transformación
Operación que *desplaza,* o mueve, una figura a una imagen. *Ver también* dilation, reflection, rotation, translation/dilatación, reflexión, rotación, traslación.

translation (p. 152) traslación Transformación que desplaza cada punto de una figura la misma distancia en la misma dirección.

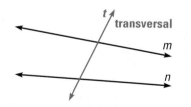

transversal (p. 121) transversal Recta que interseca dos o más rectas coplanarias en diferentes puntos.

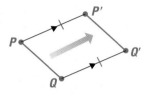

trapezoid (p. 332) trapezoide Cuadrilátero que tiene exactamente un par de lados paralelos, llamados *bases.* Los lados que no son paralelos se llaman *catetos.*

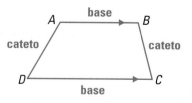

triangle (p. 173) triángulo Figura formada por tres segmentos que se unen a tres puntos no colineales, llamados *vértices.* El símbolo del triángulo es △.

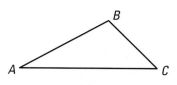

△*ABC* con vértices *A, B* y *C*

trigonometric ratio (p. 557) razón trigonométrica Razón de las longitudes de dos lados de un triángulo recto. *Ver también* cosine, sine, tangent of an angle/coseno, seno, tangente de un ángulo.

undefined term (p. 14) término indefinido
Palabra, como *punto, recta* o *plano,* que no se define matemáticamente usando otras palabras conocidas, aunque comúnmente se entiende lo que la palabra significa.

V

vertex of an angle (p. 35) vértice de un ángulo
Ver angle/ángulo.

vertex of a polygon (p. 303) vértice de un polígono *Ver* polygon/polígono.

vertex of a triangle (p. 175) vértice de un triángulo Punto en el que se unen dos puntos de un triángulo. *Ver también* triangle/triángulo.

vertical angles (p. 75) ángulos verticales Dos ángulos que no son adyacentes y cuyos lados se forman a partir de dos rectas que se intersecan.

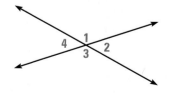

∠1 y ∠3 son ángulos verticales.

∠2 y ∠4 son ángulos verticales.

volume of a solid (p. 500) volumen de un sólido
Número de unidades cúbicas que contiene el interior del sólido.

Index

Absolute value, 662
  and distance, 28, 30, 289
Accuracy, of measurements, 711
Activities, *See also* Projects
  angle bisectors, folding, 60
  angles, kinds of, 34
  angles and intersecting lines, 74
  angles and similar triangles, 372
  angle sum of polygons, 416
  area of circles, finding, 451
  area of a parallelogram, exploring, 439
  area and right triangles, 191
  area of similar triangles, 438
  area of triangles, finding, 430
  congruence, investigating, 264
  congruent triangles, 240
    creating, 250
  conjecture, making a, 8
  conjectures about similarity, 364
  constructing a perpendicular to a line, 143
  dilation, drawing, 393
  dilations using coordinates, 399
  inscribed angles, exploring, 613
  intersecting lines, 114
  intersections, exploring, 21
  intersections of medians, 206
  isosceles right triangle, exploring, 542
  lines in space, 107
  midsegment of a trapezoid, 331
  parallel lines and angles, 126–127
  parallel lines and slope, 150–151
  parallelograms
    investigating, 309
    making, 316, 324

  perpendicular bisectors, 272
  properties of angles formed by chords, 620
  properties of isosceles triangles, 185
  proportional segments, investigating, 386
  reflections, investigating, 281
  reflections and rotations, 640
  right triangle ratio, 556
  rotating a figure, 633
  secants, segments formed by, 626
  segment bisectors, folding, 53
  special right triangles, 548
  surface area, investigating, 481
  tangents and circles, 594
  triangle, copying a, 241
  triangles, side lengths of, 199
  volume, investigating, 508–509
Act out the situation, problem solving strategy, 654
Acute angle, 34, 36
  adjacent, complementary, 115
  cosine of, 563–568
  inverse functions and, 569–574
  of a right triangle, 180
  sine of, 563–568
  tangent of, 557–562
Acute triangle, 174
Addition
  of angle measures, 37, 115
  of areas, 426
  of decimals, 655
  of fractions, 658
  of integers, 663
  order of operations and, 670
Addition Property of Equality, 90–93
Adjacent angles, 68
Adjacent arcs, 602
Adjacent leg, 557
Algebra
  angle bisectors and, 63, 66, 271, 274, 277
  angles of a polygon and, 419–421

  angles of a quadrilateral and, 307
  angles of a triangle and, 183, 184
  arcs and chords of circles and, 611
  areas and, 425, 428, 435, 440, 443, 447, 449, 453, 457, 554
  complementary angles and, 72, 116, 118, 125, 271
  coordinates and, 7, 27
  Euler's formula, 479
  $45°\text{-}45°\text{-}45°$ triangles and, 544–547
  isosceles triangles and, 186–189, 315
  medians and, 211
  midsegments and, 335
  parallel lines and, 131, 133, 134, 139, 141, 145, 148, 162
  parallelograms and, 314, 329, 330
  perpendicular bisectors and, 274, 277
  regular polygons and, 415
  segment bisector and, 54, 57
  segment lengths and, 33, 93, 362
  similar triangles and, 374, 376, 377
  supplementary angles and, 72, 118, 125, 271
  surface area and, 492, 494
  $30°\text{-}60°\text{-}90°$ triangles and, 550–553
  triangle proportionality and, 387, 388, 390
  vertical angles and, 77, 80
  volume and, 506, 512
Algebra Review, *See* Review
Algebra Skills, *See* Review
Alternate exterior angles, 121–125
  parallel lines and, 126–135
Alternate Exterior Angles Theorem, 130
  converse, 138

Alternate interior angles,
121–125
parallel lines and, 126–135
Alternate Interior Angles Theorem, 130
converse, 138
Altitude, *See* Height
Angle(s)
acute, 34, 36, 115, 180
adjacent, 68
alternate exterior, 121–125, 138
alternate interior, 121–125, 138
base
of an isosceles triangle, 185–186
of a trapezoid, 332
bisector, 60–66, 96, 273–280, 295
central, 601–606
chords and, 620–625
classifying, 34–41, 45, 62
classifying triangles by, 174–178
complementary, 67–73, 96, 115, 180
congruent, 36
consecutive, 317–319
on the coordinate plane, 39
corresponding, 121–125, 137, 233
exterior, 121–125, 181
game, 166
included, 242
inscribed, 613–619, 643–644
interior, 121–125, 181
interior of, 37
linear pairs of, 75–81
measures, 34–41, 45
adding, 37
subtracting, 37
naming, 35
obtuse, 34, 36
parallel lines and, 126–135, 137–138
of a parallelogram, 311–312, 316–319, 343
of a polygon, 416–423, 461
of a quadrilateral, 305
of a rectangle, 325
right, 34, 36, 114–119, 325–326
of rotation, 633

same-side interior, 121–125, 138
straight, 34, 36
supplementary, 67–73, 75, 96
transversals and, 121–134, 161
of a trapezoid, 332–333
of a triangle, 174, 179–184, 212, 220
vertex of, 35
vertical, 74–81, 96
Angle Addition Postulate, 37
Angle-Angle (AA) Similarity Postulate, 372–373, 401
Angle-Angle-Side (AAS) Congruence Theorem, 251, 292
Angle bisector, 60–66, 96, 273–280, 295
Angle Bisector Theorem, 273
Angle-Side-Angle Congruence (ASA), 250–251, 292
Appendices, 711–718
Applications
advertising, 86
agriculture, 596
archaeology, 609
architecture, 71, 170, 186, 192, 196, 244, 277, 411, 470, 490, 491, 522
art, 26, 27, 124, 239, 247, 354, 362, 370, 377, 379, 443, 444, 638
astronomy, 521
automobiles, 19, 122
aviation, 1, 50, 116, 254
baseball, 50, 58, 357, 362, 422
basketball, 177, 520
biking, 57, 124, 321
biology, 6
Braille, 7
carpentry, 618
construction, 118, 142, 155, 164, 190, 217, 315, 327, 329, 383, 404, 414, 422, 450
containers, 515
design, 80, 111, 122, 215, 269, 270, 335, 435, 498, 547, 624, 638
discus, 595
engineering, 504
fireworks, 586, 600
fitness, 553
fractals, 391

games, 18, 157, 520
gardening, 200, 457
geography, 40, 58, 204, 517, 592, 605
geology, 87, 408, 436, 516
history, 145, 204, 405
hockey, 374
jewelry, 546
judo, 428
kaleidoscopes, 285
kiteboarding, 141
lasers, 65
machinery, 310, 314
maps, 29, 197, 204, 217, 275, 278, 360, 363, 592
measurement, 31, 32, 573
music, 148, 489
natural resources, 183
navigation, 104, 149, 599
orienteering, 119
origami, 119, 255
photography, 314
physical therapy, 134
plants, 260, 286, 307, 456
pool, 322
race car, 122
rescue, 612
rock climbing, 189
sailing, 104
science, 6, 9, 12, 65, 133, 599
scissors lift, 300, 314
sewing, 255
shuffleboard, 384
soccer, 230, 278, 520
space shuttle, 534, 574
structures, 112, 124, 152, 198, 257, 277, 351, 405, 449, 505, 506, 553, 561, 567, 573, 580, 606
surveying, 562
tennis, 128, 520
theater, 262
Approximation, *See* Estimation
Arc(s)
adjacent, 602
central angles and, 601–606, 642–643
chords and, 608–612, 620–625, 643
theorems about, 608, 609, 620
congruent, 602
inscribed angles and, 614–619
intercepted, 614–619

length of, 603–606
major, 601
measures of, 601–606, 610, 620–625
minor, 601
naming, 601
and semicircles, 601

Arc Addition Postulate, 602

Area, *See also* Formulas; Lateral area; Surface area
changing dimensions and, 715
of a circle, 451, 453–458, 463, 674
of a circle sector, 454–455
of a complex polygon, 426–428, 458, 689
on the coordinate plane, 444
of irregular figures, 717
lateral, 484
meaning of, 424
of a parallelogram, 439–445, 462
of a rectangle, 425–429, 461, 674
of a rhombus, 441–445
of similar polygons, 433
of similar triangles, 433, 438
of a square, 424–429, 461, 674
using a 30°-60°-90° triangle, 554
of a trapezoid, 446–450, 463
of a triangle, 430–438, 462, 674
equilateral, 541

Areas of Similar Polygons Theorem, 433

Aspect ratio, 371

Assessment, *See also* Project; Review
Chapter Readiness Quiz, 2, 52, 106, 172, 232, 302, 356, 410, 472, 536, 588
Chapter Standardized Test, 47, 99, 165, 225, 297, 347, 405, 465, 529, 581, 647
Chapter Test, 46, 98, 164, 224, 296, 346, 404, 464, 528, 580, 646
End-of-Course Test, 697–700
Pre-Course Test, xx–xxi
Quiz, 20, 41, 73, 94, 120, 135, 159, 184, 198, 218, 249, 263, 290, 323, 341, 378, 398, 423, 437, 459, 499,
523, 555, 575, 607, 625, 639
Test Tip, 47, 99, 165, 225, 297, 347, 405, 465, 529, 581, 647

Axis (Axes), coordinate plane, 664

B

Base(s)
of a cone, 493
of a cylinder, 485
of an isosceles triangle, 185
of a parallelogram, 439
of a power, 467, 668
of a prism, 112, 473
of a pyramid, 473, 491
of a rectangle, 425
of a trapezoid, 332, 446
of a triangle, 431, 674

Base angle(s)
of an isosceles triangle, 185–186
of a trapezoid, 332

Base Angles Theorem, 185–186
converse of, 186

Betweenness, 29

Bisect, 53

Bisector
angle, 60–66, 96, 273–280, 295
of a chord, 608–609
construction, 272
intersecting, 275
perpendicular, 272–280, 295
segment, 53–59, 95, 272–280

Brain Games, *See* Games

Break into parts, problem solving strategy, 654

C

Calculator, *See also* Student Help; Technology
cosine function, 564
inverse, 570
exercises, 561, 567, 568, 572, 573, 575, 580
sine function, 564
inverse, 570
square root, 531, 537
tangent function, 558
inverse, 569

Careers
advertising copywriter, 86
aquarium diver, 505
archaeologist, 609
architect, 71
artist, 370
astronaut, 574
bicycle designer, 124
cake designer, 335
civil engineer, 277
emergency medical technician (EMT), 612
ergonomist, 80
facilities planner, 275
flooring installer, 414
forester, 559
furniture designer, 329
gemologist, 340
geologist, 516
graphic designer, 638
hydrologist, 183
kite designer, 62
laboratory technologist, 6
map maker, 360
personal trainer, 553
physical therapist, 134
scientist, 9
surveyor, 39
type designer, 288
veterinarian, 497

Center
of a circle, 452, 589–593
on the coordinate plane, 627–632
locating, 609
of dilation, 393
of rotation, 633
of a sphere, 517

Central angle(s)
arc length and, 603
arcs and, 601–606, 642–643
definition of, 454
semicircle, 601

Centroid, of a triangle, 208–211, 228–229

Challenge, 13, 26, 33, 59, 66, 72, 81, 93, 113, 125, 142, 149, 158, 189, 197, 205, 248, 271, 279, 315, 321, 330, 336, 341, 362, 370, 377, 391, 422, 445, 457, 490, 498, 507, 541, 554, 568, 600, 606, 632

Chapter Review, *See* Review

Chapter Standardized Test, *See* Assessment

Chapter Summary, *See* Review

Chapter Test, *See* Assessment

Chord(s), 589, 592
arcs and, 608–612, 643
intersecting, 620–625
length of, 608, 610, 620, 622
properties of, 620–625, 644
theorems about, 608, 609, 620, 622

Circle(s)
arc of, 601–606, 608–612, 642–643
area of, 451, 453–458, 463, 674
center of, 452, 589–593
on the coordinate plane, 627–632
locating, 609
central angle of, 454
chords of, 589, 608–612, 643
intersecting, 620–625, 644
circumference of, 451, 452–458, 463, 674
circumscribed, 615
congruent, 602
in coordinate geometry, 590
on a coordinate plane, 590–593, 627–632
definition of, 452
diameter of, 452, 589
equation of, 627–632, 645
standard, 628–632, 645
graphing, 629
inscribed angles and, 613–619, 643–644
inscribed polygons and, 615
major arc of, 601
minor arc of, 601
naming, 589
parts of, 589–593, 641–642
points inside, 631
points outside, 631
point of tangency, 589
radius of, 452, 589, 674
secant to, 589, 592, 626
sector of, 454–458
area, 454–458
semicircle, 601
tangent segment, 594, 597
tangent to, 589, 594–600

Circumference, of a circle, 451, 452–458, 463, 674

Circumscribed circle, 615

Classification
angle, 34–41, 45, 62
polygon, 304–308, 342–343, 411–415, 460–461
special parallelograms, 325–330
special quadrilaterals, 337–340
triangle, 173–178, 201–205, 219–220, 222

Collinear points, 15

Communication, *See* Activities;
English-to-Spanish
Glossary; Games;
Glossary; Drawing; Error
Analysis; Projects; Proof;
Student Help, Reading
Tip; Student Help,
Vocabulary Tip; Writing

Comparing, *See also*
Classification
using inequality symbols, 662
using ratio, 357–363
ratios of legs of a right
triangle, 556

Complementary angles, 67–73, 96
adjacent, 115
acute, of a right triangle, 180

Complex area, 426–428, 458

Complex polygon
area of, 426–428, 458
breaking into parts, 410, 416, 426, 428

Composite solid, 522

Concave polygon, 411

Conclusion, 82, 676

Conditional statement, 82, *See also* If-then statement

Cone, 473, 475
parts of, 493
surface area of, 493–499, 525–526
formula for, 493
volume of, 511–516, 527
formula for, 511

Congruence, *See also* Congruent
angles; Congruent arcs;
Congruent segments;
Congruent triangles
properties of, 88–93, 234–239

Congruence statement, 234

Congruent angles, 36

adjacent, 115
angle bisectors and, 61
complements and, 69
of congruent triangles, 233, 265
equilateral triangles and, 187
isosceles triangles and, 185–186
parallel lines and, 128–131
parallelograms and, 311
perpendicular lines and, 114–115
regular polygons and, 412
right angles, 114
of similar triangles, 365
supplements and, 69
vertical angles, 76

Congruent arcs, 602

Congruent circles, 602

Congruent Complements Theorem, 69

Congruent edges, of a polyhedron, 474

Congruent faces, of a polyhedron, 474

Congruent figures, 233
as bases of polyhedra, 473
reflection and, 282–289

Congruent segments, 30
equilateral polygons and, 412
tangents, 597

Congruent Supplements Theorem, 69
justification, 90

Congruent triangles, 233–239, 291, 681
Angle-Angle-Side (AAS)
Congruence Theorem
and, 251–256, 292
Angle-Side-Angle (ASA)
Congruence Postulate
and, 250–256, 292
congruence of corresponding
parts, 233–235, 265–267
on the coordinate plane, 289
Hypotenuse-Leg (HL)
Congruence Theorem
and, 257–262, 293
investigating side-side-angle
congruence, 264
overlapping, 266–271, 294
Side-Angle-Side (SAS)
Congruence Postulate
and, 242–248, 292

Side-Side-Side (SSS)
    Congruence Postulate
    and, 241–248, 292
summary of congruence
    postulates and theorems,
    258
using, 265–271, 294
Conjecture, 8–13, 43, 114, 127,
    141, 150, 158, 191, 386,
    392, 399, 439, 594, 613,
    626, 675, *See also* Logic;
    Logical reasoning
about similarity, 364
Connections, *See* Algebra;
    Applications
Consecutive angles, of a
    parallelogram, 317–319
Construction, 143, *See also*
    Paper folding
copy a triangle, 241
draw a dilation, 393
draw a triangle, 216
equilateral triangle, 187
exercises, 148, 321
midpoint of a trapezoid, 331
parallel lines, 144
perpendicular bisector, 272
perpendicular to a line, 143
tangent segments, 594
Converse
of the Alternate Exterior
    Angles Theorem, 138
of the Alternate Interior
    Angles Theorem, 138
of the Base Angles Theorem,
    186
of the Corresponding Angles
    Postulate, 137
of an if-then statement, 136
of a postulate, 137
of the Pythagorean Theorem,
    199–205, 222
of the Same-Side Interior
    Angles Theorem, 138–139
of the Triangle Proportionality
    Theorem, 388
Convex polygon, 411
Cooperative learning, *See*
    Activities; Projects;
    Technology activities
Coordinate(s)
in the coordinate plane, 28,
    664
on a line, 28

latitude-longitude, 58
Coordinate notation, 153–154
Coordinate plane
angles on, 39
area on, 444
circles on, 590–593
    equations, 627–632
defined, 664
dilations in, 399
distance on, 30–33
    formula, 194–195, 197, 221
midpoint formula and, 55–56
ordered pair, 664
origin, 664
plotting points, 664
reflection in, 283, 286–287,
    289
rotation in, 635–639
slope and parallelograms, 322
translation in, 153–159
x-axis, 664
y-axis, 664
Coplanar lines, 15
Coplanar points, 15
Corollary
definition of, 180
rectangle, 326, 344
rhombus, 326
square, 326
to the Triangle Sum Theorem,
    180
Corresponding angles
in congruent figures, 233,
    265–272
formed by lines, 121–125
parallel lines and, 126–135,
    137
similar figures and, 365–366
**Corresponding Angles
    Postulate,** 128
converse of, 137
Corresponding parts, of
    congruent figures, 233,
    265–272
Corresponding sides
of congruent figures, 233,
    265–272
of similar figures, 365–366
Cosine function, 563–568, 694,
    705
inverse, 570–574, 705
Cosine ratio, 563–568, 579
Counterexample, 10–11, 675
Counting number, 9

Critical thinking, *See* Error
    Analysis; Logic; Logical
    reasoning; Proof
Cross-curriculum connections,
    See Applications; Projects
Cross product property, 349,
    359, 660
Cube, 475, 479
Cubic unit, 500
Cumulative Practice, *See*
    Review
Cylinder, 473, 475
definition of, 485
lateral area of, 485–486
parts of, 485
surface area of, 485–490, 525
    formula for, 485
volume of, 501–507, 526
    formula for, 502

D

Decimal(s)
computing with, 655
cosine function expressed as,
    564
fractions and, 657
ordering, 662
ratios as, 357
repeating, 657
sine function expressed as,
    564
tangent function expressed
    as, 558
terminating, 657
Deductive reasoning, 82–87, 97,
    See also Logic; Logical
    reasoning; Proof
law of detachment, 83–84
law of syllogism, 83–84
logic puzzle, 100
Degree, angle measurement, 36
Detachment, law of, 83–84
Diagonal(s)
of a parallelogram, 312, 318
of a polygon, 303
polygon pattern, 12
of a quadrilateral, 305
of a rectangle, 327
of a rhombus, 327, 441
Diameter
of a circle, 452
    as hypotenuse of inscribed

right triangle, 615

perpendicular to chord, 608–609

of a sphere, 517

Dilation(s), 393–397, 399, 403, 438, 688

center of, 393

in a coordinate plane, 399

enlargement, 394–397

reduction, 394–397

Distance

on the coordinate plane, 30–33

from the endpoints of a segment, 274

from a point to a line, 273

from the sides of an angle, 273

Distance Formula, 194–195, 197, 221

Distributive property, 671

Division

of decimals, 655

of fractions, 659

of integers, 663

order of operations and, 670

Division Property of Equality, 90–93

Dodecahedron, 479

Draw a diagram or graph, problem-solving strategy, 653–654

Drawing, *See also* Technology; Transformation

angles, 39

dilations, 393

distances, 276

fractals, 391

lines, segments, rays, and planes, 16, 19, 24, 26, 31

parallel lines and transversal, 132, 140, 148

perspective, 102–103

polygons, 306, 414, 416

quadrilaterals, 306, 321, 427, 449

reflections, 287, 288

scale, 468–469

solid figures, 474, 478, 489, 497, 503

spheres, 517

tangents to a circle, 599

three-dimensional figures, 107, 472

triangles, 176, 217, 435, 567

congruent, 255, 261, 269

special, 548, 554

Venn diagram, 340

Edge(s)

Euler's Formula and, 479

of a polyhedron, 474

End-of-Course Test, 697–700

Endpoint, 16

Enlargement, 364, 394–397, 403

Equality, properties of, 88–93

Equation(s), *See also* Formulas

of a circle, 627–632, 645

standard, 628–632, 645

multi-step, 673

one-step, 672

problem solving and, 654

proportion, 660–661

systems of, 583

two-step, 49

with variables on both sides, 101

Equiangular polygon, 412

Equiangular Theorem, 187

Equiangular triangle, 174, 187

Equidistant, 273

Equilateral polygon, 412

Equilateral Theorem, 187

Equilateral triangle(s), 173

area of, 541

properties of, 185–190, 220–221

Equivalent fractions, 656

Error Analysis, 12, 33, 93, 118, 134, 176, 210, 216, 239, 248, 276, 321, 369, 443, 456, 477, 489, 496, 514, 520, 546, 561, 566, 632

Estimation

using indirect measurement, 584–585

using rounding, 717

using sine and cosine ratios, 564–568, 579

of square root, 668–669

using tangent ratio, 559–562, 578

Euler, Leonhard, 479

Euler's Formula, 479

Exponent, 467, 668

Expression(s)

combine like terms, 101

distributive property and, 671

evaluating, 49, 670

exponential, 467

radical, 407, 537–541, 668–669

simplifying, 101

square and square root, 167

variable, 670

Extended side, of a polygon, 411

Exterior angle(s), 121–125

alternate, 121–125

of a polygon, 417, 419–423

of a triangle, 181

Exterior Angle Theorem, 181

Polygon, 419

Extra Practice, 675–696

Extremes, of a proportion, 359, 660

Face(s)

Euler's Formula and, 479

lateral, 484

of a polyhedron, 474

Flip, *See* Reflection

Formula(s), 703

area

of a circle, 453, 463

of a circle sector, 454

of an equilateral triangle, 541

of a parallelogram, 439, 462

of a rectangle, 425, 461

of a rhombus, 441

of a square, 424

of a trapezoid, 446, 463

of a triangle, 431, 462

circumference of a circle, 451, 452, 455–456, 463

definition of, 674

distance, 194–195, 197, 221

Euler's, 479

geometric, 674

lateral area

of a cylinder, 485, 486

of a prism, 484

midpoint, 55–56

midsegment of a trapezoid, 333

problem solving and, 407, 654

slope, 665

Index

surface area
  of a cone, 493
  of a cylinder, 485
  of a prism, 484
  of a pyramid, 492
  of a sphere, 517
table of, 703
volume
  of a cone, 511
  of a cylinder, 502
  of a prism, 500
  of a pyramid, 510
  of a sphere, 518
45°-45°-90° triangle, 542–547, 577
45°-45°-90° Triangle Theorem, 542, 577
Fraction(s)
  adding and subtracting, 658
  concepts, 656
  cosine function as, 564
  decimals and, 657
  equivalent, 656
  multiplying and dividing, 659
  ratios as, 357
  reciprocal, 656
  simplest form, 656
  sine function as, 564
  tangent function as, 558
Function
  cosine, 563–568, 694, 705
    inverse, 570–574, 705
  sine, 563–568, 694, 705
    inverse, 570–574, 705
  tangent, 558, 705
    inverse, 569–570, 573, 574, 705

G

Games
  Geometry Scavenger Hunt, 48
  Logic Puzzle, 100
  Mirror Reflections, 298
  Picture It, 226
  Polyominoes, 348
  Right Triangle Bingo, 582
  Sum of Parts, 466
  Tangrams, 406
  Volume War, 530
  What Did I Describe, 648
  What's the Angle, 166
Geometric probability, 713

Geometry software, *See* Technology
Glossary, 719–731
  English-to-Spanish, 732–746
Graphing, *See also* Coordinate plane
  equations of circles, 629
  linear equations, 666–667
  points on the coordinate plane, 664
Graphing calculator, *See* Technology
Greatest possible error, 711
Guess, check, and revise, problem solving strategy, 654

H

Hands-on geometry, *See* Activities; Modeling; Paper cutting; Paper folding
Height
  of a cone, 493
  of a cylinder, 485
  of a parallelogram, 439
  of a pyramid, 491
  of a rectangle, 425
  slant
    of a cone, 493
    of a pyramid, 491
  of a solid figure, 474
  of a trapezoid, 446
  of a triangle, 431
Hemisphere, 517
  volume of, 522
Heptagon, 304
Hexagon, 304
Hexagonal pyramid, 474
Hypotenuse, 192, 257, *See also* Right triangle(s)
Hypotenuse-Leg (HL) **Congruence Theorem,** 257–262, 293
Hypothesis, 82

I

Icosahedron, 479
If-then statement, 22, 82–87, 97, 678

converse of, 136
law of detachment and, 83–86
law of syllogism and, 83–86
Image
  dilation, 393
  orientation, 282
  transformation, 152, 393
Included angle, 242
Included side, 250–251
Indirect measurement
  using similar triangles, 584–585
  using trigonometric ratios, 557, 585
Inductive reasoning, 8–13, 43, 83
Inequality (Inequalities)
  review of, 167, 662
  triangle, 212–217, 223
Inscribed angle
  definition of, 614
  intercepted arc and, 613–619, 643
  theorems about, 614, 615, 616
Inscribed polygon, 615
  theorems about, 615, 616
Integer, operations, 663
Integration, *See* Algebra; Trigonometric ratios
Intercept, 666
Intercepted arc, 614–619
Interior, of an angle, 37
Interior angle(s), 121–135, 138–142
  alternate, 121–125
  of a polygon, 416–423, 461
  of a quadrilateral, 305
  same side, 121–135, 138–142
  of a triangle, 181
Internet Links
  Applications, 7, 12, 40, 65, 133, 189, 196, 247, 255, 321, 377, 391, 436, 521, 561, 599
  Careers, 6, 39, 71, 80, 86, 134, 183, 275, 277, 288, 329, 340, 360, 370, 414, 516, 553, 559, 574, 609, 612, 638
  Homework Help, 12, 18, 32, 57, 72, 79, 118, 133, 148, 189, 197, 211, 238, 247, 261, 270, 278, 307, 315, 336, 363, 376, 383, 397,

421, 449, 457, 497, 504, 506, 514, 515, 522, 540, 562, 567, 599, 606, 630

More Examples, 4, 10, 24, 63, 84, 90, 137, 153, 174, 180, 202, 208, 213, 244, 258, 267, 283, 317, 326, 338, 366, 387, 412, 425, 441, 486, 494, 518, 551, 570, 590, 614, 635

Intersecting bisectors, of a triangle, 275

Intersection
  of chords, 620–625
  of lines, 22–27, 44
  of medians, 206, 208, 228–229
  of planes, 21–27, 44

Intersection of Two Lines Postulate, 22

Intersection of Two Planes Postulate, 22

Inverse cosine function, 570–574, 705

Inverse sine function, 570–574, 705

Inverse tangent function, 569–570, 573, 705

Irrational number, 452, *See also* Radical expression; Square roots
  pi, 452

Isosceles trapezoid, 332–333
  identifying, 338–340

Isosceles triangle(s), 173
  properties of, 185–190, 220–221
  right, 542–547, 577

Labeling
  images, 153
  shapes, 154

Lateral area, 484
  of a cone, 493
  of a cylinder, 485–486
  of a prism, 484
  of a pyramid, 492

Lateral face(s)
  of a prism, 484
  of a pyramid, 492

Latitude, 58

Law of detachment, 83–84

Law of syllogism, 83–84

Leg(s)
  adjacent, 557
  of an isosceles triangle, 185
  opposite, 557
  of a right triangle, 192, 257
  of a trapezoid, 332

Length
  arc, 603–606
  chord, 608, 610, 620, 622
  of a line segment, 28
  of the midsegment of a trapezoid, 333

Like terms, 101, 671

Line(s), 14–20, 44
  coplanar, 15
  graphing, 666–667
  intersecting, 22–27
  parallel, 108–113, 667, 680, *See also* Parallel lines
  perpendicular, 108–113, *See also* Perpendicular lines
  of reflection, 282
  secant, 589, 592
  skew, 108–113
  slope of, 150–151, 299, 665, 667
  of symmetry, 284–289
  tangent, 589
  transversals, 121–135, 161, 162

Linear equation(s)
  graphing, 666–667
  systems of, 583

Linear pair, 75–76

Linear Pair Postulate, 75

Line of reflection, 282

Line segment, *See* Segment(s)

Line symmetry, 284–289, 295

List, making to solve a problem, 654

Logic
  conclusion, 82
  conditional statement, 82
  conjecture, 8–13, 43, 114, 127, 141, 150, 158, 191, 386, 392, 399, 439, 594, 613, 626, 675
  converse of an if-then statement, 136
  counterexample, 10–11
  deductive reasoning, 82–87, 97, 100
  hypothesis, 82

if-then statement, 22, 82–87, 97
  inductive reasoning, 8–13, 43
  law of detachment, 83–84
  law of syllogism, 83–84
  properties of equality and congruence, 88–93
  puzzle, 100
  writing a proof, 243–244, 247–248

Logical reasoning, exercises, 87, 117, 132, 133, 140, 141, 147, 217, 256, 261, 262, 269, 270, 272, 306, 330, 336, 371, 376, 414, 422, 478, 496, 514, 611

Longitude, 58

Look for a pattern, problem solving strategy, 654

Major arc, 601
  measures of, 601–606

Make and organized list or table, problem solving strategy, 654

Mapping
  dilations, 393
  rotational symmetry and, 634–638
  translation, 152

Means, of a proportion, 359, 660

Measure(s)
  angle, 34–41, 61–66
    of an arc, 601–606, 610, 620–625
    formed by chords, 620–625
    formed by parallel lines and transversals, 128–135
    inscribed, 613–619
    of a parallelogram, 311–312
    of a quadrilateral, 305–308
    of a trapezoid, 332–333
    of a triangle, 179–184, 212–217, 220, 223
  arc length, 603–606
  chord length, 608, 610
  indirect, 557, 584–585
  of an intercepted arc, 613–619
  latitude-longitude, 58
  segment, 28–33, 45, 53–59
  of semicircles, 601

Index

Measurement
  angle, 36, 39
  estimation and, 717
  indirect, 557, 584–585
Median(s), triangle, 206–211,
  222–223, 228–229
Midpoint(s)
  of a line segment, 53
  of sides of a trapezoid, 331,
    333
  of sides of a triangle, 389
  of the diagonals of a
    parallelogram, 312
Midpoint Formula, 55
Midsegment
  of a trapezoid, 331, 333
  of a triangle, 389
Midsegment Theorem, 389
Minor arc, 601
  measures of, 601–606
Missing information, *See also*
  Error Analysis
  examples, 251
  exercises, 247, 255, 262
Mixed Review, *See* Review
Modeling, 21, 34, 53, 60, 74, 88,
  107, 114, 126–127, 143,
  150–151, 179, 185, 191,
  199, 206, 216, 240, 241,
  250, 264, 272, 281, 309,
  316, 324, 331, 372, 386,
  393, 399, 416, 419, 430,
  438, 439, 451, 481–482,
  483, 484, 485, 492, 493,
  508–509, 510, 542, 548,
  556, 594, 613, 620, 626,
  633, 640
Multiple representations, 14,
  16, 22, 29, 30, 37, 55, 69,
  75, 76, 114, 115, 128, 129,
  130, 131, 137, 138, 144,
  145, 179, 180, 181, 185,
  186, 187, 192, 200, 208,
  212, 213, 241, 242, 250,
  251, 257, 273, 274, 305,
  310, 311, 312, 316, 317,
  318, 326, 327, 332, 368,
  372, 379, 380, 386, 388,
  389, 417, 419, 433, 542,
  549, 595, 597, 602, 608,
  609, 614, 615, 616, 620
Multiplication
  of decimals, 655
  of fractions, 659
  of integers, 663
  order of operations and, 670
  of radicals, 538
**Multiplication Property of
  Equality,** 90–93
Multi-step equation, 673
Multi-Step Problem, 27, 40, 47,
  99, 149, 165, 205, 225,
  262, 297, 308, 322, 377,
  405, 429, 458, 465, 498,
  529, 547, 612, 625

Negative slope, 665
Negative square root, 668
Net, 481
  of a prism, 481–484, 508–509
  of a pyramid, 508–509
n-gon, 304
Nonadjacent angles, 74
Number(s)
  decimals, 657
  integers, 9, 663
  irrational, 452
  pi, 451, 452, 674
  positive integers, 9
  rectangular, 11
  square, 167, 668
  square of, 3, 167
  triangular, 11
  whole, 3
Number line
  absolute value and, 662
  and adding integers, 663
  inequalities on, 662
Number pattern, 3–7, 675

Obtuse angle, 34, 36
Obtuse triangle, 174
Octagon, 304, 436
Octahedron, 479
One-point perspective, 102–103
One-step equations, 672
Operations, order of, 670
Opposite angle(s)
  of an inscribed quadrilateral,
    616
  of a parallelogram, 316
Opposite leg, 557

Opposite side(s)
  of a parallelogram, 310–312,
    316–319
  in a triangle, 175
Ordered pair, 664, *See also*
  Coordinate plane
Ordering
  decimals, 662
  triangle sides and angles,
    212–217
  whole numbers, 662
Order of operations, 670
Organized list, problem solving
  strategy, 654
Orientation, image, 282
Origin, coordinate plane, 664

Paper cutting
  area of circles, 451
  intersections of planes, 21
  kinds of angles, 34
  nets, 481, 508–509
  properties of isosceles
    triangles, 185
  volume of prisms and
    pyramids, 508–509
Paper folding
  angle bisectors, 60
  angles, 40
  intersecting lines, 114
  intersections of medians, 206
  isosceles triangles, 185
  lines of symmetry, 284
  nets, 481, 508–509
  perpendicular bisectors, 272
  perpendicular lines, 114
  reflections, 281
  segment bisectors, 53
  volume of prisms and
    pyramids, 508–509
Parallel lines, 108–113, 160, 678
  alternate interior angles,
    121–125
  alternate exterior angles,
    121–125
  construction, 144
  corresponding angles,
    121–125
  determining, 388
  properties of, 128–135,
    144–149, 162–163

Index

same-side interior angles, 121–125

showing lines are parallel, 136–142, 162

slope and, 150–151, 667

transversals and, 126–135, 137–142, 162

Parallelogram(s), 309–330, *See also* Rectangle; Rhombus; Square

angle measures of, 311–312, 343

area of, 439–445, 462

bases of, 439

in the coordinate plane, 322

definition of, 310, 312

diagonals of, 312, 318, 319

height of, 439

identifying, 337–340

properties of, 309–315, 343–344, 685

special types of, 325–330

theorems, 310–312, 316–319

Parallel planes, 109–113

Parallel Postulate, 144

Patterns

interior angles of polygons, 416

number, 3–7, 43, 675

problem solving and, 654

tessellations, 352–353

visual, 3–7, 43, 675

Penrose rhombuses, 444

Pentagon, 304

Pentagonal pyramid, 475

Percent, using, 467

Perfect square, 668

Perimeter

changing dimensions and, 715

of a polygon, 415

of a rectangle, 674

of similar polygons, 367–368

of a square, 330, 674

of a triangle, 674

Perimeters of Similar Polygons Theorem, 368

Perpendicular bisector(s), 272, 274–280, 295

intersecting, 275

of a triangle, 275

Perpendicular Bisector Theorem, 274, 279

Perpendicular lines, 108–113, 160

constructing, 143

folding, 114

radius and tangent of a circle, 595

symbol for, 108

theorems about, 114–120, 145, 161

Perpendicular Postulate, 144

Perspective, one-point, 102–103

Pi, 451, 452, 674

Plane(s), 14–20, 44, *See also* Coordinate plane

intersection of, 21–27

naming, 14

parallel, 109–113

Plato, 479

Platonic solids, 479

Plotting, points on the coordinate plane, 664

Point(s), 14–20, 44

betweenness, 29

collinear, 15

coordinate, 664

coplanar, 15

distance between, 28–33

graphing, 664

on a line, 299

symbol for, 14

of tangency, 589

Polygon(s), 303–308, *See also* Area; Perimeter

angles of

exterior, 417, 419–423, 461

interior, 416–423, 461

as bases of polyhedra, 473

breaking into parts, 410, 416, 426, 428

classification, 304–308, 342–343, 411–415, 460–461

concave, 411

convex, 411

diagonal, 303

equiangular, 412

equilateral, 412

extended side of, 411

as faces of polyhedra, 474

inscribed, 615

theorems about, 615, 616

naming, 304

perimeter of, 415

puzzles, 466

regular, 412

sides, 303

similar, 365–371, 401

vertex, 303

Polygon Exterior Angles Theorem, 419

Polygon Interior Angles Theorem, 417

Polyhedron (polyhedra), 473–480

drawing, 472, 474

identifying, 473, 524

naming, 473–479

parts of, 473–474

Platonic solids, 479

surface area of, 482–485, 488, 489

Polyominoes, 348

Portfolio projects, 102–103, 228–229, 352–353, 468–469, 584–585

Positive integer, 9

Positive slope, 665

Positive square root, 668

Postulate(s), 706

Angle Addition, 37

Angle-Angle (AA) Similarity, 372–373, 401

Angle-Side-Angle (ASA) Congruence, 250–251

Arc Addition, 602

converse of, 136

Corresponding Angles, 128

converse, 137

definition of, 14

Intersection of Two Lines, 22

Intersection of Two Planes, 22

Linear Pair, 75

list of, 706

Parallel, 144

Perpendicular, 144

Segment Addition, 29

Side-Angle-Side (SAS) Congruence, 242

Side-Side-Side (SSS) Congruence, 241–242

Three Points Determine a Plane, 14

Two Points Determine a Line, 14

Power(s), 467, 668–669

order of operations and, 670

Practice, *See* Review; Test preparation

Precision, of measurements, 711

Pre-Course Practice, xxii–xxv

Index

Pre-Course Test, xx–xxi
Prediction, using patterns, 4–7
Prism
base of, 473
definition of, 483
drawing, 107, 112
lateral faces of, 484
naming, 473–479
net, 481–484
surface area of, 481–490, 525
formula for, 484
volume of, 500–509, 526
formula for, 500
Probability, geometric, 713
Problem solving, 653–654, *See also* Multi-Step Problem; Using Algebra; Visual Strategy
finding counterexamples, 10–11, 675
looking for patterns, 3–7
making conjectures, 8–13, 43
steps, 653
strategies, 654
using a table, 6, 8, 43, 127, 199, 206, 264, 272, 281, 339, 364, 416, 482, 521, 548, 556
Product Property of Radicals, 407, 538, 669
Projects
Balancing Shapes, 228–229
Creating Tessellations, 352–353
Designing a Park, 468–469
Drawing in Perspective, 102–103
Indirect Measurement, 584–585
Proof
parts of, 243
writing, 243–244, 247–248
Property (properties), 702
addition, 90–93
of chords, 620–625, 644
of congruence, 88–93, 97
cross product, 349, 660
distributive, 671
division, 90–93
of equality, 88–93, 97
of isosceles and equilateral triangles, 185–190, 220–221
multiplication, 90–93

of parallelograms, 309–315
product of radicals, 538, 669
quotient of radicals, 531, 669
reciprocal, 660
of rectangles, 325–330
reflexive, 88–93
of rhombi, 325–330
of squares, 325–330
substitution, 90–93
subtraction, 90–93
symmetric, 88–93
table of, 702
of tangents, 594–600, 642
transitive, 88–93
Proportion(s)
arc length and, 603
cross product property and, 349, 359, 660
definition of, 349, 660
dilations and, 393–397
extremes of, 359, 660
means of, 359, 660
problem solving and, 654
scale factor and, 366
similarity and, 359–363
similar triangles and, 386–392, 402–403
solving, 349, 359–363, 400, 660–661
Proportionality, 386
Proportionality Theorem, Triangle, 386
Protractor, measuring angles with, 36, 39
Pyramid
definition of, 491
naming, 473–479
net, 508
parts of, 473, 491, 492
regular, 492
surface area of, 491–499, 525–526
formula for, 492
volume of, 508–516, 527
formula for, 510
Pythagorean Theorem, 191–198, 537
converse of, 199–205, 222
for finding cone height, 512
for finding slant height, 491–492, 494
for solving right triangles, 436, 542, 547, 549, 569–574, 579

Pythagorean triples, 196

Q

Quadrilateral(s), 300–345, *See also* Parallelogram(s); Rectangle; Rhombus; Square; Trapezoid
classifying, 337–340
definition of, 304
diagonal of, 305
identifying, 337–340
inscribed, 616
interior angles of, 305–308
Quadrilateral Interior Angles Theorem, 305
Quizzes, *See* Assessment
Quotient Property of Radicals, 531, 669

R

Radical(s), 537–541
multiplying, 538
product property of, 407, 538
squaring, 540
Radical expression, 537, 668–669
simplifying, 407, 537–541, 576–577, 669
Radicand, 537
Radius
of a circle, 452, 589, 590, 674
tangents and, 595–600
of a cylinder, 485
of a sphere, 517
Rate(s), unit, 227
Ratio(s), 357–363, 400–401
arc length and, 603
aspect, 371
of circumference to diameter, 452
cosine, 563–568, 579, 694
dilations and, 393–397
45°-45°-90° triangles and, 542–547
of perimeters, 367–368
reciprocal property and, 660
scale factor and, 366
similar polygons and, 365–371
area, 433
simplifying, 227, 357, 660

sine, 563–568, 579, 694
tangent, 557–562, 578, 694
30°-60°-90° triangles and,
548–555
writing, 357, 660
Ray, 16
Reason, in a proof, 243–244,
247–248
Reasoning, *See* Logic; Logical
reasoning
Reciprocal, 656
Reciprocal property, 660
Rectangle
area of, 425–429, 461, 674
definition of, 325
identifying, 337–340
perimeter of, 674
properties, 325–330, 344
theorems about, 327
Rectangle Corollary, 326, 344
Rectangular numbers, 11
Rectangular prism, 473, 475
surface area of, 481–483
volume of, 500–509
Rectangular pyramid, 475
Reduction, 394–397, 403
Reflection, 281–289, 295
in the coordinate plane, 283,
286–287, 289
game, 298
line of, 282
properties of, 282
relationship to rotation, 640
Reflexive Property, 88–93
Regular polygon, 412
as base of a regular pyramid,
492
interior angles of, 418
Platonic solids and, 479
Regular pyramid, 492
Relative error, 711
Repeating decimal, 657
Representations, *See* Multiple
representations
Review, *See also* Assessment;
Projects; Skills Review
Handbook
Algebra Review, 49, 101, 167,
227, 299, 349, 407, 467,
531, 583
Algebra Skills, 7, 13, 20, 27, 33,
41, 59, 66, 73, 81, 87, 94,
113, 120, 125, 135, 142,
149, 159, 178, 184, 190,

198, 205, 211, 218, 239,
249, 256, 263, 271, 280,
290, 308, 315, 323, 330,
336, 341, 363, 371, 378,
385, 392, 398, 415, 423,
429, 437, 445, 450, 459,
480, 490, 499, 507, 516,
523, 541, 547, 555, 562,
568, 575, 593, 600, 607,
612, 619, 625, 632, 639
Chapter Summary and
Review, 42–45, 95–97,
160–163, 219–223,
291–295, 342–345,
400–403, 460–463,
524–527, 576–579,
641–645
Cumulative Practice, 168–169,
350–351, 532–533,
649–651
Mixed Review, 7, 13, 20, 27, 33,
41, 59, 66, 73, 81, 87, 94,
113, 120, 125, 135, 142,
149, 158, 178, 184, 190,
198, 205, 211, 218, 239,
249, 256, 263, 271, 280,
290, 308, 315, 323, 330,
336, 341, 363, 371, 378,
385, 392, 398, 415, 423,
429, 437, 445, 450, 459,
480, 490, 499, 507, 516,
523, 541, 547, 555, 562,
568, 575, 593, 600, 607,
612, 619, 625, 632, 639
Study Guide, 2, 52, 106, 172,
232, 302, 356, 410, 472,
536, 588
Rhombus
area of, 441–445
definition of, 325
diagonals of, 327, 441
identifying, 338–340
Penrose, 444
properties, 325–330, 344
theorems about, 327
Rhombus Corollary, 326, 344
Right angle(s), 34, 36
congruency theorem, 114
perpendicular lines and,
114–119
quadrilaterals and, 325–326
symbol for, 36
Right solid, 474
Right triangle(s), 174

area of, 432–433
cosine function and, 563–568,
579
inverse, 570–574
45°-45°-90°, 542–547, 577
game, 582
Hypotenuse-Leg (HL)
Congruence Theorem
and, 257–262
inscribed, 615
Pythagorean Theorem and,
191–193, 195–197
converse, 199–205
sine function and, 563–568,
579
inverse, 570–574
solving, 569–574, 579
tangent function and,
557–562, 578
inverse, 569–570, 572–574
30°-60°-90°, 548–555, 578
Rotation, 633–638, 645
angle of, 633
center of, 633
relationship to reflection, 640
Rotational symmetry, 634

S

Same-side interior angles,
121–125
parallel lines and, 126–135,
138–142
of a parallelogram, 311
Same-Side Interior Angles
Theorem, 131
converse, 138–139
Scale drawing, 468–469
Scale factor, 366
dilations and, 393–397, 403
similar polygon area and, 433
similar polygons and, 366–371
Scalene triangle, 173
Secant(s)
to a circle, 589, 592
segments formed by, 626
Sector, of a circle, 454–455
Segment(s), 16
bisecting, 53–59, 95, 272,
274–280
chords, 589, 592, 622
congruent, 30
endpoints of, 16

Index

measures of, 28–33, 45, 53–57
midpoint of, 53–57
midsegment, 389
proportional, 386
tangent, 594, 597
Segment Addition Postulate, 29
Semicircle, 601
Side(s)
of an angle, 35
classifying triangles by, 173–178
corresponding, 233
included, 250–251
of a polygon, 303
extended, 411
of a square, 424
of a triangle, 173
opposite, 175
Side-Angle-Side (SAS) Congruence Postulate, 242, 292
Side-Angle-Side (SAS) Similarity Theorem, 380–381, 402
Side-Side-Angle (SSA) Congruence, nonexistence of, 264
Side-Side-Side (SSS) Congruence Postulate, 241–242, 292
Side-Side-Side (SSS) Similarity Theorem, 379–380, 382–383, 402
Similarity, 356–405
ratio and proportion, 357–363, 400–401
scale drawings and, 468–469
similar polygons, 365–371, 401
similar triangles, 372–377, 379–392, 401–403
Similarity statement, 365
Similar polygons, 365–371, 401, 687
area of, 433
dilations and, 395
perimeters of, 367–368
Similar triangles, 372–377, 379–392, 401–403, 687–688
Angle-Angle (AA) Similarity Postulate and, 372–373
area of, 433, 438
dilations and, 395

indirect measurement and, 584–585
overlapping, 356, 381, 384
proportion and, 386–392
Side-Angle-Side (SAS) Similarity Theorem and, 380–381
Side-Side-Side Similarity Theorem (SSS) and, 379–380
Simpler problem, solving, 654
Simplest form
fraction, 656
of a radical expression, 669
of a ratio, 357
Sine function, 563–568, 694, 705
inverse, 570–574, 705
Sine ratio, 563–568, 579
Skew lines, 108–113, 160
Skills Review Handbook, 653–674
absolute value, 662
coordinate plane, 664
decimals, 655
fractions and, 657
distributive property, 671
equations
solving multi-step, 673
solving one-step, 672
evaluating expressions, 670
formulas, 674
fractions
adding and subtracting, 658
concepts, 656
decimals and, 657
multiplying and dividing, 659
graphing linear equations, 666
inequalities, 662
integers, 663
powers, 668–669
problem solving, 653–654
ratio and proportion, 660–661
slope of a line, 665
slope-intercept form, 667
solving one-step equations, 672
solving multi-step equations, 673
square roots, 668–669
Slant height
of a cone, 493
of a pyramid, 491, 492
Slide, *See* Translation

Slope
formula, 665
line, 299, 665
of a line between two points, 299
parallel lines and, 150–151, 667
undefined, 665, 667
zero, 665, 667
Slope-intercept form, 667
Solid figure(s), 473–480, 524, *See also* Cone; Cube; Cylinder; Polyhedron; Prism; Pyramid; Surface area; Volume
composite, 522
drawing, 472, 474, 478, 489, 497, 503
naming, 473–479
Platonic, 479
right, 474
types of, 475
Solution, of an equation, 672
Solve a simpler problem, problem solving strategy, 654
Spanish Glossary, 732–746
Special parallelograms, *See* Rectangle; Rhombus; Square
Special right triangles, *See* 45°-45°-90° triangle; 30°-60°-90° triangle
Sphere, 473, 475
hemisphere and, 517
parts of, 517
surface area of, 517–522
formula for, 517
volume of, 518–522, 527
formula for, 518
Square
area of, 424–429, 461, 674
definition of, 325
identifying, 338–340
perimeter of, 674
properties, 325–330, 344
Square Corollary, 326
Square prism, 475
Square roots
using a calculator to find, 537
definition of, 537, 668
estimating, 668–669
perfect squares and, 668
simplifying, 537–541, 576–577

table of, 704

Squaring
a binomial, 596
a number, 3, 167, 668
a radical, 540
Standard equation of a circle, 628–632, 645
Standardized Test, *See* Assessment
Standardized Test Practice, *See* Test preparation
Statement, in a proof, 243–248
Straight angle, 34, 36
Student Help
Homework Help, 12, 18, 32, 57, 72, 79, 118, 133, 148, 189, 197, 211, 238, 247, 261, 270, 278, 307, 315, 336, 363, 376, 383, 397, 421, 449, 457, 497, 504, 506, 514, 515, 522, 540, 562, 567, 599, 606, 618, 630
Keystroke Help, 399, 453, 531, 558
Look Back, 21, 40, 58, 60, 76, 88, 93, 115, 126, 130, 138, 149, 180, 187, 193, 200, 233, 240, 248, 265, 272, 279, 281, 289, 312, 327, 364, 380, 393, 414, 433, 436, 438, 446, 449, 486, 493, 511, 512, 522, 544, 548, 554, 594, 596, 600, 613, 615, 640
More Examples, 4, 10, 24, 63, 84, 90, 137, 153, 174, 180, 202, 208, 213, 244, 258, 267, 283, 317, 326, 338, 366, 387, 412, 425, 441, 486, 494, 518, 551, 570, 590, 614, 621, 635
Reading Tip, 9, 22, 55, 153, 154, 179, 500, 543, 557, 569
Skills Review, 28, 32, 49, 55, 150, 192, 206, 287, 322, 358, 418, 492, 597, 603, 628
Study Tip, 8, 49, 54, 68, 77, 82, 90, 101, 114, 167, 194, 201, 234, 235, 243, 244, 251, 252, 259, 270, 273, 304, 305, 316, 324, 326, 337, 349, 357, 367, 374, 380, 394, 395, 447, 452, 474, 475, 478, 483, 492, 501, 510, 515, 537, 538, 559, 571, 589, 603, 609, 631
Visual Strategy, 2, 16, 36, 52, 69, 76, 106, 112, 172, 177, 183, 232, 264, 266, 302, 314, 356, 373, 381, 384, 410, 472, 536, 571, 588, 605, 618
Vocabulary Tip, 34, 53, 58, 74, 82, 152, 173, 175, 185, 257, 303, 331, 333, 365, 451, 473, 590, 595, 597

Study Guide, *See* Review
Substitution Property of Equality, 90–93
Subtraction
of angle measures, 37
of decimals, 655
of fractions, 658
of integers, 663
order of operations and, 670
Subtraction Property of Equality, 90–93
Summaries
classification of triangles by angles, 174
classifying angles by their measures, 36
properties of parallelograms, 312
triangle congruence postulates and theorems, 258
trigonometric ratios, 565
ways to show that two lines are parallel, 146
Supplementary angles, 67–73, 96
of inscribed quadrilaterals, 616
linear pairs and, 75–76
parallelograms and, 311–312, 317, 319, 343
Surface area
changing dimensions and, 716
of a cone, 493–499, 525
formula for, 493
of a cylinder, 485–490, 525
formula for, 485
nets and, 481–482

of a polyhedron, 482
of a prism, 481–490, 525
formula for, 484
of a pyramid, 491–499, 525
formula for, 492
of a rectangular prism, 481–490
of a sphere, 517–522
formula for, 517
Syllogism, law of, 83–84
Symbol(s), 701
absolute value, 662
angle, 35
measure of, 36
arc, 601
congruent, 30
inequality, 662
line, 14
line segment, 16
parallel lines, 108
parallelogram, 310
perpendicular lines, 108
point, 14
prime, 153
radical, 537, 668
ray, 16
right angle, 36
segment, 16
similarity, 365
table of, 701
translation, 153
Symmetric Property, 88–93
Symmetry
line, 284–289, 295
rotational, 634
Systems of equations, 583

Table
of formulas, 703
of properties, 702
of squares and square roots, 704
of symbols, 701
of trigonometric ratios, 705
Tangent(s)
to a circle, 589
properties of, 594–600, 642
theorems about, 595, 597
point of tangency, 589
Tangent function, 558, 705
inverse, 569–570, 572–574, 705

Tangent ratio, 557–562, 578, 694
Tangent segment, 594–600
Tangrams, 406
Technology
    activities, 150–151, 199, 264,
        324, 331, 399, 438, 626,
        640
    exercises, 11, 19, 33, 66, 72,
        141, 158, 183, 190, 279,
        308, 340, 385, 392, 449,
        521, 546, 567, 624
Term(s)
    of an expression, 671
    undefined, 14
Terminating decimal, 657
Tessellation, 352–353
Test preparation
    Chapter Standardized Test,
        47, 99, 165, 225, 297,
        347, 405, 465, 529, 581,
        647
    Standardized Test Practice, 7,
        13, 20, 27, 33, 40, 59, 66,
        73, 81, 87, 93, 113, 119,
        125, 134, 142, 149, 158,
        178, 184, 190, 198, 205,
        211, 217, 239, 248, 256,
        262, 271, 280, 289, 308,
        315, 322, 330, 336, 341,
        363, 371, 377, 385, 392,
        397, 415, 423, 429, 437,
        445, 450, 458, 480, 490,
        507, 516, 522, 541, 554,
        562, 568, 574, 593, 600,
        607, 612, 619, 625, 632,
        638
Tetrahedron, 479
Thales, 405
Theorem(s), 707–710
    Alternate Exterior Angles, 130
        converse, 138
    Alternate Interior Angles, 129
        converse, 138
    Angle-Angle-Side (AAS)
        Congruence, 251
    Angle Bisector, 273
    Areas of Similar Polygons, 433
    Base Angles, 185–186
        converse, 186
    about chords, 608, 609, 620,
        622
    Congruent Complements, 69
    Congruent Supplements, 69
    definition of, 69

Equiangular, 187
Equilateral, 187
Exterior Angle, 181
45°-45°-90° triangle, 542, 577
Hypotenuse-Leg (HL)
    Congruence, 257–258
about inscribed angles, 614,
    615, 616
about inscribed polygons,
    615, 616
list of, 707–710
Midsegment, 389
about parallelograms,
    310–312, 316–319
Perimeters of Similar
    Polygons, 368
Perpendicular Bisector,
    274–275
about perpendicular lines,
    114–120, 145, 161
Polygon Exterior Angles, 419
Polygon Interior Angles, 417
about properties of tangents,
    595, 597
Pythagorean, 191–198
    converse, 199–205
Quadrilateral Interior Angles,
    305
Rectangle, 327
Rhombus, 327
Same-Side Interior Angles,
    131
    converse, 138–139
Side-Angle-Side (SAS)
    Similarity, 380–381, 402
Side-Side-Side (SSS)
    Similarity, 379–380, 402
about tangents to circles, 595,
    597
30°-60°-90° Triangle, 549
Trapezoid, 332
Triangle Inequality, 212–214
Triangle Proportionality, 386
    converse, 388
Triangle Sum, 179
Vertical Angles, 76
30°-60°-90° triangle, 548–555,
    578
30°-60°-90° Triangle Theorem,
    549, 578
Three-dimensional figures, *See
    also* Polyhedra; Solid
    figures
    drawing, 472

**Three Points Determine a Plane
    Postulate,** 14
Transformation
    dilation, 393–397, 399, 403
    reflection, 281–289, 295
    rotation, 633–638, 645
    translation, 152–158, 163
Transitive Property, 88–93
Translation, 152–158, 163, 680
    labeling a, 153
Transversal(s), 121–125, 161
    parallel lines and, 126–135,
        162
Trapezoid, 331–336, 345, 686
    angles of, 332–333
    area of, 446–450, 463
    base angles of, 332
    bases of, 446
    definition of, 331, 332
    height of, 446
    identifying, 338–340, 345
    isosceles, 332–333
    midsegment of, 331, 333
    theorems about, 332
Triangle(s), *See also* Right
        triangle
    angle measures of, 179–184,
        220
    area of, 430–438, 462, 674
    centroid of, 208–211, 228–229
    classifying, 173–178, 201–205,
        219–220
    congruent, 233–239, 291
        properties of, 234–239
        proving congruence,
            241–248, 250–262,
            292–293, 683
        summary of postulates and
            theorems, 258
    copying, 241
    definition of, 173, 304
    45°-45°-90°, 542–547, 577
    inequalities for, 212–217, 223
    inscribed, 615–616
    intersecting bisectors of, 275
    labeling, 536
    medians of, 206–211, 222–223,
        228–229
    midsegment of, 389
    obtuse, 174
    overlapping, 266–271, 294,
        356, 381, 384
    parts of, 175
    perimeter of, 674

properties of isosceles and equilateral, 185–190, 220–221

similar, 372–377, 379–392, 401–403

30°-60°-90°, 548–555, 578

Triangle inequality, 212–217, 223

Triangle Proportionality Theorem, 386

converse, 388

Triangle Sum Theorem, 179

corollary, 180

Triangular numbers, 11

Triangular prism, 475

Triangular pyramid, 473, 475

Trigonometric ratios, 557

cosine, 563–568

sine, 563–568

summary of, 565

table of, 705

tangent, 557–562

Two Points Determine a Line Postulate, 14

Undefined slope, 665, 667

Undefined terms, 14

Unit cube, 500

Unit rate, 227

Use an equation or formula, problem solving strategy, 654

Use a proportion, problem solving strategy, 654

Using Algebra, 6, 27, 29, 33, 54, 57, 63, 66, 72, 77, 80, 93, 118, 131, 133, 134, 135, 139, 141, 148, 183, 184, 187, 188, 189, 211, 274, 277, 289, 307, 314, 329, 335, 359, 362, 374, 390, 415, 419, 425, 428, 435, 440, 443, 449, 457, 479, 492, 494, 506, 512, 544, 554, 599, 611

Variable expression, 670

Venn diagram, using, 340

Venters, Diana, 547

Vertex (vertices)

of an angle, 35

of a cone, 493

Euler's Formula and, 479

of a polygon, 303

of a polyhedron, 474

of a pyramid, 491

of a triangle, 175

Vertical angles, 74–81, 96

Vertical Angles Theorem, 76

Visualize It!

exercises, 19, 26, 31, 39, 44, 56, 81, 111, 132, 140, 148, 178, 196, 217, 255, 261, 268, 269, 276, 287, 288, 306, 321, 336, 391, 396, 414, 422, 427, 435, 449, 478, 489, 497, 503, 505, 554, 567, 599, 611

notes, 2, 15, 23, 24, 29, 30, 36, 37, 52, 61, 62, 67, 75, 106, 107, 108, 121, 128, 129, 131, 172, 178, 181, 186, 232, 235, 242, 250, 252, 282, 284, 302, 309, 311, 332, 356, 359, 373, 394, 410, 419, 426, 428, 432, 454, 472, 484, 491, 517, 536, 549, 588, 592, 602, 616, 633, 637

Visual pattern, 3–7, 675

Visual Strategy, *See also* Student Help

breaking polygons into parts, 410

drawing quadrilaterals, 302

drawing three-dimensional figures, 472

drawing triangles, 172

labeling triangles, 536

learning vocabulary, 2

marking diagrams, 588

picturing theorems, 52

reading and drawing diagrams, 106

separating triangles, 232, 356

Vocabulary

Key Words, 2, 52, 106, 172, 232, 302, 356, 410, 472, 536, 588

Chapter Summary, 42, 95, 160, 219, 291, 342, 400, 460, 524, 576, 641

Volume

changing dimensions and, 715

of a cylinder, 501–507

formula for, 502

definition of, 500

game, 530

of a prism, 500–509

formula for, 500

of a sphere, 518–522

formula for, 518

Whole numbers, 3

Work backward, problem solving strategy, 654

Writing, 19, 21, 65, 72, 86, 93, 112, 119, 141, 148, 176, 189, 205, 217, 239, 261, 278, 287, 306, 314, 321, 329, 377, 383, 384, 392, 414, 428, 434, 456, 477, 496, 504, 515, 546, 561, 568, 574, 612, 618, 624, 638

x-axis, 664

x-coordinate, 664

of the center of a circle, 628

x-intercept, 666

y-axis, 664

y-coordinate, 664

of the center of a circle, 628

y-intercept, 666

You be the Judge, 6, 19, 32, 65, 86, 118, 141, 158, 189, 205, 217, 246, 261, 288, 314, 321, 377, 384, 428, 434, 442, 448, 456, 488, 506, 520, 540, 546, 568, 574, 606, 619, 624

Zero slope, 665, 667

Credits

Selected Answers

Pre-Course Practice

Decimals and Fractions (p. xxii) **1.** 1.715 **3.** 13.73
5. 0.37 **7.** 13.08 **9.** 20.74 **11.** 8.82 **13.** 3350
15. 10 **17–21.** Sample answers are given.
17. $\frac{4}{6}, \frac{20}{30}$ **19.** $\frac{1}{2}, \frac{5}{10}$ **21.** $\frac{8}{14}, \frac{20}{35}$ **23.** $\frac{1}{9}$ **25.** $\frac{2}{5}$
27. 1 **29.** $\frac{1}{3}$ **31.** $\frac{7}{15}$ **33.** $\frac{1}{8}$ **35.** $\frac{3}{16}$ **37.** $5\frac{5}{8}$ **39.** $\frac{1}{2}$
41. 30 **43.** 0.5 **45.** $0.\overline{4}$; 0.44 **47.** 0.75 **49.** $\frac{1}{20}$
51. $\frac{3}{10}$

Ratio and Proportion (p. xxiii) **1.** $\frac{5}{4}$ **3.** $\frac{4}{9}$ **5.** $\frac{3}{1}$
7. $\frac{17}{20}$ **9.** $2\frac{6}{7}$ **11.** $1\frac{1}{4}$ **13.** 25 **15.** $1\frac{4}{5}$

Inequalities and Absolute Value (p. xxiii)
1. $-8 > -10$ **3.** $0 > -5$ **5.** $\frac{1}{4} = 0.25$ **7.** $8.65 < 8.74$
9. $-9, -6, 0, 3, 4$ **11.** 8256, 8265, 8526, 8562, 8652
13. 9 **15.** 1 **17.** 2.5

Integers (p. xxiii) **1.** -12 **3.** -4 **5.** -11 **7.** 5
9. -56 **11.** 32 **13.** -12 **15.** -3

The Coordinate Plane (p. xxiv) **1.** (1, 3) **3.** (2, 0)
5. (−4, 2) **7.** (3, 3) **9.** (−3, −1)

Slope of a Line (p. xxiv) **1.** $\frac{1}{3}$ **3.** 0 **5.** $\frac{1}{2}$ **7.** zero
9. undefined **11.** zero

Powers and Square Roots (p. xxiv) **1.** 125 **3.** 16
5. 1 **7.** 4, −4 **9.** no real square roots **11.** 5
13. 3.2 **15.** 7 **17.** $10\sqrt{6}$ **19.** $3\sqrt{7}$ **21.** $\frac{2}{9}$
23. $\frac{\sqrt{2}}{2}$ **25.** $2\sqrt{5}$

Evaluating Expressions (p. xxv) **1.** 0 **3.** 100
5. 23 **7.** 7 **9.** 32 **11.** −8 **13.** 42 **15.** 64

The Distributive Property (p. xxv) **1.** $3y - 15$
3. $-6x - 6$ **5.** $2x + 2y$ **7.** $x^2 - 4x$ **9.** $-4x + 8$
11. $2z - 1$ **13.** $2x + 3$ **15.** $9 + x$

Solving Equations (p. xxv) **1.** 22 **3.** −7 **5.** −6
7. 1 **9.** −7 **11.** $\frac{5}{2}$ **13.** 35 **15.** −88

Using Formulas (p. xxv) **1.** 28 cm **3.** 7 m

Chapter 1

Study Guide (p. 2) **1.** A **2.** J **3.** A **4.** J

1.1 Guided Practice (p. 5)
1. 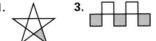 **3.**

5. Each number is 8 more than the previous
number; 35; 43. **7.** Each number is 0.5 more
than the previous number; 9.0; 9.5.
9. Each number is $\frac{1}{4}$ the previous number; 1; $\frac{1}{4}$.

1.1 Practice and Applications (pp. 5–7)
11. **13.** **15.**

17. Each number is 5 more than the previous
number; 24. **19.** Each number is $\frac{1}{4}$ the previous
number; $\frac{5}{4}$. **21.** Begin with 1 and add 2, then 3,
then 4, and so on; 21. **23.** Each point has a
y-coordinate of 3. *Sample answer:* (5, 3)
25. For each point, the y-coordinate is 2 less than
half the opposite of the x-coordinate. *Sample
answer:* (2, −3) **27.** Each distance after the first
is 4 more than the one before it. **29.** 40
31.

33. Each of the second ten letters has the same
pattern of dots as the letter above it, with an
additional dot inserted in the first column of the
third row.

35. 28 blocks **39.** *Sample answer:* 3 square feet,
8 square feet, 15 square feet, 24 square feet,
35 square feet **41.** 11.3 **43.** 1.04 **45.** 45.24
46–53.

1.2 Guided Practice (p. 11)
3. even   **5.** *Sample answer:* 6 is divisible by 2, but it is not divisible by 4.
7. *Sample answer:*

A circle cannot be drawn around any of the four-sided shapes shown.

1.2 Practice and Applications (pp. 11–13)
9. 15; 21   **11.** 121; 12,321; 1,234,321; The square of the number with n digits, all of which are 1, is the number obtained by writing the digits from 1 to n in increasing order, then the digits from $n-1$ to 1 in decreasing order. (This pattern does not continue forever.)   **13.** even   **15.** *Conjecture:* The next two shapes will have 14 diagonals and 20 diagonals.   **17.** *Sample answer:* $(-4)(-5) = 20$
19. *Sample answer:*

The triangle above shows that the conjecture is false.
25.

4
W

27. 7   **29.** -10 **31.** 14   **33.** 4
35. 2   **37.** 11   **39.** -3 **41.** 54

1.3 Guided Practice (p. 17)   **3.** false   **5.** true
7. true   **9.** true   **11.** false   **13.** false

1.3 Practice and Applications (pp. 17–20)   **15.** any four of: A, B, C, D, E **17.** plane S or plane ABC
19. false   **21.** true   **23.** true   **25.** false   **27.** K
29. M **31.** L **33.** J **35.** *Sample answers:* N, P, and R; N, Q, and R; P, Q, and R **37.** *Sample answers:* W, A, and Z; W, X, and Y **39.** G **41.** H
43. E **45.** H **47.** K, N, Q, and R **49.** P, Q, N, and M **51.** L, M, P, and S **53.** M, N, R, and S
55. *Sample answers:* A, Q, and B; A, B, and C
57. $\overleftrightarrow{BE}$, $\overleftrightarrow{CF}$, $\overleftrightarrow{RU}$, and $\overleftrightarrow{SP}$ **59.** either three of the points J, K, N, and Q, or three of the points K, L, M, and N **61.** *Sample answers:* plane LKN and plane QNM
63. *Sample answer:*

65. *Sample answer:*

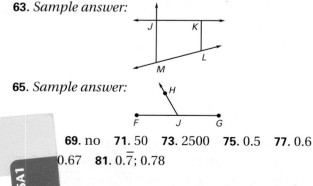

69. no   **71.** 50   **73.** 2500   **75.** 0.5   **77.** 0.6
79. 0.67   **81.** $0.\overline{7}$; 0.78

Quiz 1 (p. 20)
1. **2.** **3.** *Sample answer:* 30 is divisible by 10, but not by 20.

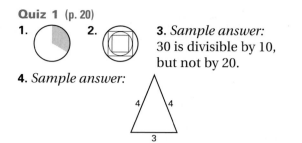

4. *Sample answer:*

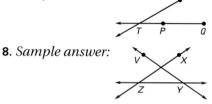

5. *Sample answer:* $2 + 0 = 2$, and 2 is not greater than 2.   **6.** If you fold the square along a line segment that joins two opposite corners and cut along the fold, you will create two triangles, not two rectangles.
7. *Sample answer:*

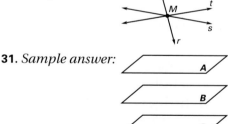

8. *Sample answer:*

1.4 Guided Practice (p. 25)   **3.** false   **5.** true

1.4 Practice and Applications (pp. 25–27)
7. intersecting lines   **9.** intersecting planes
11. They do not appear to intersect.   **13.** point T
15. $\overleftrightarrow{RS}$, $\overleftrightarrow{ST}$, or $\overleftrightarrow{RT}$ **17.** line ℓ **19.** line k
21. no intersection   **23.** point A **25.** $\overleftrightarrow{DC}$ **27.** $\overleftrightarrow{AD}$
29. *Sample answer:*

31. *Sample answer:*

35. Each point has a y-coordinate of -3. *Sample answer:* $(4, -3)$ **37.** For each point, the y-coordinate is twice the opposite of the x-coordinate. *Sample answer:* $(2, -4)$
39. *Sample answers:* B, A, and C; B, A, and D; B, C, and D **41.** 11.4   **43.** 3.7   **45.** 8.57   **47.** 7   **49.** 0
51. 2   **53.** 2

1.5 Guided Practice (p. 31)   **3.** 13   **5.** $\overline{CD}$ and $\overline{EF}$

1.5 Practice and Applications (pp. 31–33)
7. 31 mm   **9.** 25 mm   **11.** 18 mm
13. $DE + EF = DF$ **15.** $NM + MP = NP$
17. true   **19.** true   **21.** false   **23.** 21   **25.** 6
27. $\overline{CD}$, $\overline{EF}$, and $\overline{GH}$

29. yes
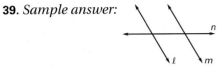

31. $8x - 1$

37. *Sample answer:* A rectangle with a length of 5 inches and a width of 3.5 inches has a perimeter of 17 inches.

39. *Sample answer:*
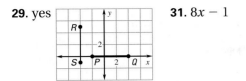

41. 26   **43.** 8   **45.** 14

1.6 Guided Practice (p. 38) **5.** E; $\overrightarrow{ED}$, $\overrightarrow{EF}$; about 35°   **7.** J; $\overrightarrow{JH}$, $\overrightarrow{JK}$; about 75°   **9.** straight
11. obtuse   **13.** yes; $m\angle DEF = m\angle FEG$

1.6 Practice and Applications (pp. 38–41)
15. X; $\overrightarrow{XF}$, $\overrightarrow{XT}$ **17.** Q; $\overrightarrow{QR}$, $\overrightarrow{QS}$ **19.** any two of $\angle C$, $\angle BCD$, $\angle DCB$ **21.** 55°   **23.** 140°   **25.** right; about 90°   **27.** 105°   **29.** 140°

31.
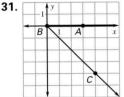
acute angle

33.
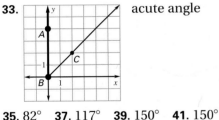
acute angle

35. 82°   **37.** 117°   **39.** 150°   **41.** 150°
43. 60°   **45. a.** $\angle AOB$, $\angle BOC$, $\angle COD$, $\angle DOE$, $\angle EOF$, $\angle FOG$, $\angle GOH$, $\angle HOA$ **b.** $\angle AOC$, $\angle BOD$, $\angle COE$, $\angle DOF$, $\angle EOG$, $\angle FOH$, $\angle GOA$, $\angle HOB$ **c.** $\angle AOD$, $\angle BOE$, $\angle COF$, $\angle DOG$, $\angle EOH$, $\angle FOA$, $\angle GOB$, $\angle HOC$ **47.** $\overrightarrow{NM}$ or $\overrightarrow{NQ}$ **49.** $XY + YZ = XZ$
51. $AB + BC = AC$ **53.** 12   **55.** 16   **57.** 12   **59.** 25

Quiz 2 (p. 41) **1.** *Sample answers:* $\overleftrightarrow{AB}$ and $\overleftrightarrow{EF}$, $\overleftrightarrow{AB}$ and $\overleftrightarrow{DE}$, $\overleftrightarrow{BC}$ and $\overleftrightarrow{DE}$, $\overleftrightarrow{BC}$ and $\overleftrightarrow{EF}$
2. two of the following: $\overleftrightarrow{AB}$, $\overleftrightarrow{BC}$, $\overleftrightarrow{BE}$
3. two of the following: $\overleftrightarrow{BE}$, $\overleftrightarrow{DE}$, $\overleftrightarrow{EF}$

4. yes
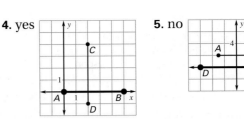

5. no
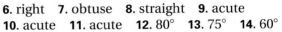

6. right   **7.** obtuse   **8.** straight   **9.** acute
10. acute   **11.** acute   **12.** 80°   **13.** 75°   **14.** 60°

Chapter Summary and Review (pp. 42–45)
1. coplanar lines   **3.** conjecture   **5.** intersect
7. collinear   **9.** congruent   **11.** obtuse   **13.** Each number is 9 more than the previous number; 41; 50.   **15.** Each number is 10 less than the previous number; 60; 50.

17.

19. *Sample answer:* $(-2)^3 = -8$ and $-8 < -2$
21. false
23.
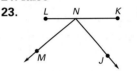
25. $\overleftrightarrow{QS}$ **27.** $\overleftrightarrow{UV}$

29. *Sample answer:*
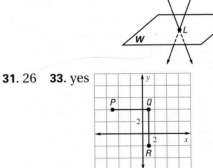

31. 26   **33.** yes

35. about 90°; right   **37.** 105°   **39.** 70°

Algebra Review (p. 49) **1.** 34   **3.** 19   **5.** 0   **7.** -11
9. 15   **11.** 6   **13.** 5   **15.** 4   **17.** -9 **19.** -7

Chapter 2

Study Guide (p. 52) **1.** C   **2.** G   **3.** C

2.1 Guided Practice (p. 56) **3.** 25; 25   **5.** 20; 40
7. 3   **9.** $\left(-\dfrac{1}{2}, -1\right)$

2.1 Practice and Applications (pp. 56–59)
11. No; M does not divide $\overline{AB}$ into two congruent segments.   **13.** No; M does not lie on $\overline{AB}$.

15. Sample answer:

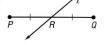

17. 41; 41   **19.** 1.35; 1.35   **21.** 15; 30   **23.** 3.6; 7.2
25. Caitlin will bike 0.95 mi and Laurie will bike
2.25 mi.   **27.** 12   **29.** −1   **31.** (5, 7)   **33.** $\left(-3, \frac{1}{2}\right)$
35. (−2, −1)   **37.** 54   **39.** (35.75°N, 118.3°W)
41. (36.1°N, 121°W)   **47.** true   **49.** true   **51.** true
53. K; $\overrightarrow{KJ}$, $\overrightarrow{KL}$; obtuse   **55.** 70   **57.** 170   **59.** 19
61. 12   **63.** −33

2.2 Guided Practice (p. 64)   **3.** 41°   **5.** 60°   **7.** 78°

2.2 Practice and Applications (pp. 64–66)
9. 54°; 54°   **11.** 33.5°; 33.5°   **13.** 45.5°; 45.5°
15. 90°; 90°   **17.** 22°; 44°; acute   **19.** 38°; 76°; acute
21. 17°; 34°; acute   **23.** ∠JRL, ∠HAM, ∠FAN,
∠DAP   **25.** 67°   **27.** Yes; *Sample answer:*
$m\angle PKR = m\angle QKR = 90°$ and $m\angle JKR = m\angle LKR$,
so $m\angle PKR - m\angle JKR = m\angle QKR - m\angle LKR$.
Therefore, $m\angle JKP = m\angle LKQ$.   **29.** 7   **31.** no; yes
35. Each number is 5 more than the previous
number; 7.   **37.** Each number is half the previous
number; 3.75.   **39.** obtuse   **41.** straight   **43.** 12
45. −7   **47.** 20

2.3 Guided Practice (p. 70)   **3.** complementary;
adjacent   **5.** supplementary; nonadjacent   **7.** 71°

2.3 Practice and Applications (pp. 70–73)
9. supplementary; adjacent   **11.** supplementary
13. complementary   **15.** 49°   **17.** 66°   **19.** 81°
21. 166°   **23.** 84°   **25.** 51°; 141°   **27.** 36°; 126°
29. ∠QPT   **31.** ∠QPS, ∠SPT   **33.** 64   **35.** 6   **37.** 16
39. Congruent Supplements Theorem   **41.** 5°
47. 12   **49.** (−2, 2)   **51.** (−2, 6)   **53.** (3, −2)
55. 3.21   **57.** 0.2318   **59.** 42.12

Quiz 1 (p. 73)   **1.** 17; 34   **2.** (4, 1)   **3.** (1, 1)
4. (−1, 0)   **5.** 41°   **6.** 22°   **7.** 116°   **8.** 79°
9. 7°; 97°

2.4 Guided Practice (p. 78)   **3.** 161°
5. $m\angle 1 = 108°$; $m\angle 2 = 72°$; $m\angle 3 = 108°$ **7.** 4

2.4 Practice and Applications (pp. 78–81)
9. neither   **11.** vertical angles   **13.** linear pair
15. 143°   **17.** 44°   **19.** 56°   **21.** 160°
23. false   **25.** true   **27.** false
29. $m\angle 1 = 98°$; $m\angle 2 = 82°$; $m\angle 3 = 98°$
31. $m\angle 1 = 125°$; $m\angle 2 = 55°$; $m\angle 3 = 125°$
33. $m\angle 1 = 40°$; $m\angle 2 = 140°$; $m\angle 3 = 40°$
35. $m\angle 1 = 90°$; $m\angle 2 = 90°$; $m\angle 3 = 90°$
37. $m\angle 1 = 95°$; $m\angle 2 = 85°$; $m\angle 3 = 95°$
39. $m\angle 1 = 30°$; $m\angle 2 = 44°$; $m\angle 3 = 106°$;
$m\angle 4 = 30°$ **41.** ∠FGE   **43.** ∠DGF   **45.** 22

47. 72   **49.** 158   **51.** 79   **53.** 58   **55.** 23; 157°
59. a. $6x = 4x + 8$ **b.** 4   **c.** 24°   **d.** 156°
61. Each number is 5 times the previous number;
1875.   **63.** Each number is 10 more than the
previous number; 444.   **65.** $\overline{LM} \cong \overline{NP} \cong \overline{QR}$
67. $7 - a$ **69.** $5b^2 + 6b$ **71.** $2w^2 + 4$

2.5 Guided Practice (p. 85)   **3.** If two angles are
adjacent angles, then they share a common side.
5. The midpoint of $\overline{AB}$ is at (2, 0).

2.5 Practice and Applications (pp. 85–87)
7. hypothesis: the car is running; conclusion: the
key is in the ignition   **9.** If <u>a number is divisible
by 6</u>, then ⎡it is also divisible by 3 and 2⎤.
11. If <u>a shape is a square</u>, then ⎡it has four sides⎤.
13. The intersection of the planes is a line.
15. The school will celebrate.   **17.** If the sun is
shining, then we will have a picnic.   **19.** If Chris
goes to the movies, then Gabriela will go to the
movies.   **21.** Answers will vary.   **23.** is
25. If <u>you want to do things</u>, then ⎡you first have
to expect things of yourself⎤.
27. If <u>a person is happy</u>, then ⎡he or she will
make others happy too⎤.   **29.** acute   **31.** right
33. straight   **35.** (−1, 3)   **37.** (3, −1)   **39.** $-\frac{5}{2}$
41. 2   **43.** 1

2.6 Guided Practice (p. 91)   **7.** Reflexive Property
of Congruence   **9.** Symmetric Property of
Congruence

2.6 Practice and Applications (pp. 91–94)
11. $m\angle Q = m\angle P$ **13.** ∠GHJ   **15.** $\overline{IJ} \cong \overline{PQ}$
17. Substitution Property of Equality
19. Substitution; Subtraction
21.

$PQ = RS$	Given
$PQ + QR = RS + QR$	Addition Property of Equality
$PQ + QR = PR$	Segment Addition Postulate
$RS + QR = QS$	Segment Addition Postulate
$PR = QS$	Substitution Property of Equality

23.

$m\angle 1 + m\angle 2 = 90°$	Definition of complementary angles
$m\angle 3 + m\angle 2 = 90°$	Definition of complementary angles
$m\angle 1 + m\angle 2 = m\angle 3 + m\angle 2$	Substitution Property of Equality
$m\angle 1 = m\angle 3$	Subtraction Property of Equality
$\angle 1 \cong \angle 3$	Definition of congruent angles

25.

$AB = BC$	Given
$BC = CD$	Given
$AB = CD$	Transitive Property of Equality
$AB = 3t + 1$	Given
$CD = 7$	Given
$3t + 1 = 7$	Substitution Property of Equality
$3t = 6$	Subtraction Property of Equality
$t = 2$	Division Property of Equality

31. D   **33.** F

35. *Sample answer:*

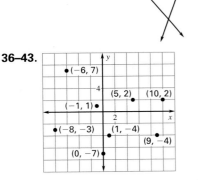

36–43.

Quiz 2 (p. 94)   **1.** $m\angle 1 = 126°$; $m\angle 2 = 54°$; $m\angle 3 = 126°$ **2.** $m\angle 4 = 40°$; $m\angle 5 = 140°$; $m\angle 6 = 40°$ **3.** $m\angle 7 = 49°$; $m\angle 8 = 90°$; $m\angle 9 = 49°$; $m\angle 10 = 41°$ **4.** If a figure is a square, then it has four sides.   **5.** If $x = 5$, then the value of x^2 is 25.   **6.** If we charter a boat, then we will be gone all day.   **7.** bisector; bisector; Transitive

Chapter Summary and Review (pp. 95–97)
1. supplementary   **3.** segment bisector

5. adjacent   **7.** 5.5; 11   **9.** $\left(2, \dfrac{3}{2}\right)$ **11.** 50°   **13.** 45°

15. $m\angle 1 = 135°$; $m\angle 2 = 45°$; $m\angle 3 = 135°$
17. $m\angle 1 = 99°$; $m\angle 2 = 81°$; $m\angle 3 = 99°$

19. If <u>a computer is in the store</u>, then the computer is on sale .   **21.** If Mike goes to the concert, then Jeannine will go to the concert.
23. A   **25.** C

Algebra Review (p. 101)   **1.** $22p$ **3.** $7q$ **5.** $3x + 3$ **7.** $19y + 40z$ **9.** 10   **11.** 6   **13.** -14 **15.** 11   **17.** 2

Chapter 3

Study Guide (p. 106)   **1.** B   **2.** H   **3.** D

3.1 Guided Practice (p. 110)   **3.** ∥   **5.** ∥   **7.** C

3.1 Practice and Applications (pp. 110–113)
9. neither   **11.** parallel   **13.** Yes; m and n do not intersect in space.   **15.** parallel   **17.** skew
19. parallel   **21.** $\overleftrightarrow{UV}$, $\overleftrightarrow{TS}$, or $\overleftrightarrow{XW}$
23. $\overleftrightarrow{SW}$, $\overleftrightarrow{TX}$, $\overleftrightarrow{VW}$, or $\overleftrightarrow{UX}$
25. *Sample answer:*

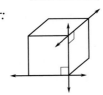

27. *Sample answer:*

29. *Sample answer:*

31. parallel   **33.** three   **35.** Yes; plane A remains parallel to the ground level for the entire time that the step is moving from ground level to the top.

37. *Sample answer:*

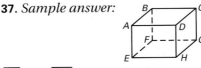

$\overline{AE}$ and $\overline{DH}$ appear parallel.
45. hypothesis: $m\angle 5 = 120°$; conclusion: $\angle 5$ is obtuse   **47.** hypothesis: we can get tickets; conclusion: we'll go to the movies   **49.** $\angle 2 \cong \angle 1$

51. $\dfrac{1}{26}$ **53.** $\dfrac{1}{10}$ **55.** 15   **57.** 11   **59.** 26   **61.** 80

3.2 Guided Practice (p. 117)   **3.** If two lines intersect to form adjacent congruent angles, then the lines are perpendicular.   **5.** $x = 90$
7. $70 + x = 90$

3.2 Practice and Applications (pp. 117–120)   **9.** no
11. Yes; perpendicular lines intersect to form 4 right angles; all right angles are congruent.

13. *Sample answers:* ∠1 and ∠2 are right angles; ∠1 ≅ ∠2.   **15.** The equation should be $(x + 4)° + 56° = 90°$.   **17.** 90   **19.** 35   **21.** 15   **23.** 10; 70°   **25.** 35; 35°   **27.** No. Since ∠1 and ∠3 are congruent and complementary, each has measure 45°. There is no information given about the measure of ∠2, so you cannot conclude that $\overrightarrow{BA} \perp \overrightarrow{BC}$.   **29.** 50°   **31.** Yes; ∠DJE and ∠EJF are adjacent acute angles and $\overline{BF} \perp \overline{HD}$, so ∠DJE and ∠EJF are complementary.   **33.** No; there is no information given about ∠AJG or the lines that form ∠AJG.   **37.** acute; about 80°   **39.** 53°   **41.** 15   **43.** 3   **45.** 11.79   **47.** 8.8   **49.** 333

Quiz 1 (p. 120) **1–4.** Sample answers are given.
1. $\overleftrightarrow{BF}, \overleftrightarrow{CG}$ **2.** $\overleftrightarrow{AD}$ **3.** $\overleftrightarrow{BC}$ **4.** $\overleftrightarrow{BC}$ **5.** 67   **6.** 11   **7.** 34

3.3 Guided Practice (p. 123) **3.** A   **5.** one of: ∠1 and ∠5, ∠2 and ∠6, ∠3 and ∠7, or ∠4 and ∠8   **7.** ∠1 and ∠7, or ∠2 and ∠8

3.3 Practice and Applications (pp. 123–125)
9. same-side interior angles   **11.** corresponding angles   **13.** *Sample answer:* ∠2 and ∠3   **15.** *Sample answer:* ∠2 and ∠4   **17.** alternate exterior   **19.** corresponding   **21.** alternate interior   **23.** alternate exterior angles   **25.** alternate exterior angles   **27.** corresponding angles   **29.** ∠5 and ∠12, ∠7 and ∠10   **31.** ∠6 and ∠11, ∠8 and ∠9   **37.** $\overleftrightarrow{AB}$, $\overleftrightarrow{GH}$, or $\overleftrightarrow{EF}$ **39.** *ABC*   **41.** 24   **43.** $\frac{2}{5}$ **45.** 1   **47.** 52   **49.** 15

3.4 Guided Practice (p. 132) **9.** Alternate Exterior Angles Theorem   **11.** Same-Side Interior Angles Theorem

3.4 Practice and Applications (pp. 132–135)
15.
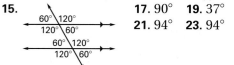
17. 90°   **19.** 37°   **21.** 94°   **23.** 94°
25. $m∠1 = 42°$ by the Alternate Interior Angles Theorem   **27.** $m∠1 = 82°$ by the Alternate Interior Angles Theorem; $m∠2 = 82°$ by the Vertical Angles Theorem.   **29.** 131°   **31.** 76°   **33.** 23   **35.** 23   **37.** 25
39.
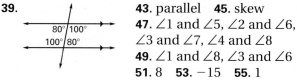
43. parallel   **45.** skew   **47.** ∠1 and ∠5, ∠2 and ∠6, ∠3 and ∠7, ∠4 and ∠8   **49.** ∠1 and ∠8, ∠3 and ∠6   **51.** 8   **53.** −15   **55.** 1

Quiz 2 (p. 135) **1.** alternate exterior angles   **2.** same-side interior angles   **3.** corresponding angles   **4.** alternate exterior angles   **5.** alternate interior angles   **6.** alternate interior angles   **7.** $m∠1 = 104°$; $m∠2 = 76°$ **8.** $m∠1 = 78°$; $m∠2 = 102°$ **9.** $m∠1 = 107°$; $m∠2 = 73°$ **10.** 21   **11.** 26   **12.** 11

3.5 Guided Practice (p. 139) **3.** C   **5.** B

3.5 Practice and Applications (pp. 140–142)
7. If $m∠1 + m∠2 = 180°$, then ∠1 and ∠2 are supplementary; true.   **9.** If ∠B is obtuse, then ∠B measures 123°; false.   **11.** yes, by the Corresponding Angles Converse   **13.** yes, by the Alternate Interior Angles Converse   **15.** No; the angles have no special relationship.
17. *Sample answer:*
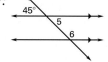
19. Yes; *Sample explanation:* $m∠ABE = 143°$ by the Vertical Angles Theorem; $143° + 37° = 180°$, so $\overleftrightarrow{AC} \parallel \overrightarrow{DF}$ by the Same-Side Interior Angles Converse.   **21.** Yes; *Sample explanation:* $m∠CBE = 115°$ by the Vertical Angles Theorem; $115° + 65° = 180°$, so $\overleftrightarrow{AC} \parallel \overrightarrow{DF}$ by the Same-Side Interior Angles Converse.   **23.** 20   **25.** 21   **27.** 11   **29.** 10   **31.** $\overleftrightarrow{HJ} \parallel \overleftrightarrow{AB}$ by the Alternate Exterior Angles Converse.   **33.** 32°   **37.** $m∠1 = m∠2 = 90°$ **39.** ∠1 and ∠2 are right angles.
41. corresponding angles   **43.** 108°   **45.** $\frac{7}{11}$ **47.** $\frac{2}{3}$

3.6 Guided Practice (p. 147) **3.** In a plane, if two lines are perpendicular to the same line, then they are parallel to each other.

3.6 Practice and Applications (pp. 147–149)
5. In a plane, if two lines are perpendicular to the same line, then they are parallel to each other.   **7.** Corresponding Angles Converse   **9.** Alternate Interior Angles Converse   **11.** In a plane, if two lines are perpendicular to the same line, then they are parallel to each other.   **13.** $p \parallel q$ by the Corresponding Angles Converse; $q \parallel r$ by the Same-Side Interior Angles Converse. Then, since $p \parallel q$ and $q \parallel r$, $p \parallel r$ (if two lines are parallel to the same line, then they are parallel to each other).   **15.** a and b are each perpendicular to d, so $a \parallel b$ (in a plane, if two lines are perpendicular to the same line, then they are parallel to each other); c and d are each perpendicular to a, so $c \parallel d$ (in a plane, if two lines are perpendicular to the same line, then they are parallel to each other).

17. The 8th fret is parallel to the 9th fret, and the 9th fret is parallel to the 10th fret. Therefore, the 8th fret is parallel to the 10th fret (if two lines are parallel to the same line, then they are parallel to each other). **19.** 11 **21.** 6

23. *Sample answer:*

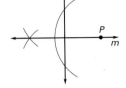

25. No; if the wind is constant, then the boats' paths will be parallel by the Corresponding Angles Converse. They will never cross.
29. true **31.** true

33–36.

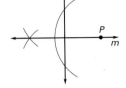

37. -32 **39.** 2 **41.** -33

3.7 Guided Practice (p. 155) **3.** yes **5.** yes
7. false; shift 3 units to the left and 2 units down

3.7 Practice and Applications (pp. 155–159) **9.** no
11. no **13.** no **15.** C **17.** B **19.** Each point is moved 2 units to the right and 3 units up.
21. Each point is moved 2 units to the left and 3 units up. **23.** $(x, y) \to (x - 4, y + 1)$ **25.** (1, 4)
27. $(8, -9)$ **29.** (0, 0) **31.** $(3, -4)$ **33.** $P'(-4, 3)$, $Q'(-1, 6)$, $R'(3, 5)$, $S'(-1, 1)$ **35.** $P'(-1, -2)$, $Q'(2, 1)$, $R'(6, 0)$, $S'(2, -4)$ **37.** Move 2 units to the right and 1 unit down.

39.

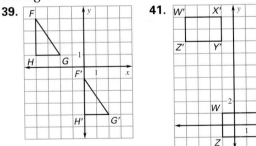

41.

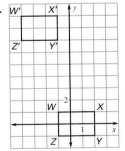

43. $(-7, 5)$ **45.** Yes; the image of $(2, -2)$ after the translation $(x, y) \to (x - 6, y + 4)$ is $(-4, 2)$. This is the point that is labeled C'. **47.** $180°$
51. acute; about $50°$ **53.** acute; about $80°$
55. 24 orders **57.** $-4, -1.5, -1.2, 0, 0.7, 1.1, 3.4$
59. $-6.8, -6.12, -6.1, 6, 6.09, 6.3$

Quiz 3 (p. 159) **1.** yes, by the Alternate Exterior Angles Converse **2.** No; there is no information about line m. **3.** yes, by the Alternate Interior Angles Converse

4. In a plane, if two lines are perpendicular to the same line, then they are parallel to each other.
5. If two lines are parallel to the same line, then they are parallel to each other. **6.** Use the Corresponding Angles Converse or Theorem 3.12 (in a plane, if two lines are perpendicular to the same line, then they are parallel to each other).

7.

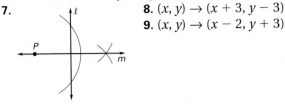

8. $(x, y) \to (x + 3, y - 3)$
9. $(x, y) \to (x - 2, y + 3)$

Chapter Summary and Review (pp. 160–163)
1. parallel **3.** perpendicular **5.** construction
7. parallel **9.** skew **11.** Yes; since $f \perp g$, $\angle 11$ is a right angle. **13.** Yes; h and j intersect to form adjacent congruent angles, so the lines are perpendicular. **15.** corresponding
17. same-side interior **19.** $99°$ **21.** $71°$
23. 20 **25.** If two lines are parallel to the same line, then they are parallel to each other.
27. Corresponding Angles Converse **29.** yes
31. Each point is moved 5 units to the right and 3 units down.

Algebra Review (p. 167) **1.** $x > 15$ **3.** $z \le -4$
5. $p \le -3$ **7.** 16 **9.** 9 **11.** 5 **13.** 9

Cumulative Practice (pp. 168–169) **1.** You begin with 10, and add 2, then 3, then 4, and so on; 30.
3. B **5.** B **7.** 16 **9.** 7
11. right

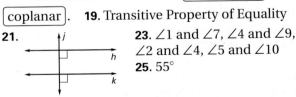

13. 17 **15.** 55

17. If <u>two lines intersect</u>, then ⟨the lines are⟩ ⟨coplanar⟩. **19.** Transitive Property of Equality
21.

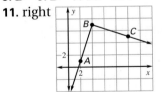

23. $\angle 1$ and $\angle 7$, $\angle 4$ and $\angle 9$, $\angle 2$ and $\angle 4$, $\angle 5$ and $\angle 10$
25. $55°$

27. yes, by the Alternate Interior Angles Converse
29. *Sample answer:* yes, by the Same-Side Interior Angles Converse **31.** $\angle 1$ **33.**

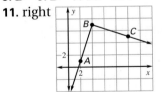

Chapter 4

Study Guide (p. 172) **1.** D **2.** H **3.** B

4.1 Guided Practice (p. 175) **3.** $\overline{PR}$ **5.** isosceles
7. scalene **9.** right

4.1 Practice and Applications (pp. 176–178)
11. scalene **13.** equilateral **15.** scalene
17. obtuse **19.** right **21.** right **23.** An acute triangle has three acute angles, so the triangle is not an acute triangle. An obtuse triangle has one obtuse angle and two acute angles. **25.** right isosceles triangle **27.** right scalene triangle
29. acute scalene triangle **31.** E **33.** D **35.** C
37. acute **39.** acute **41.** *Sample answer:* B, D, and E **43.** $\overline{DE}$ is opposite $\angle F$; $\overline{EF}$ is opposite $\angle D$; $\overline{DF}$ is opposite $\angle E$. **45.** $\overline{KL}$ is opposite $\angle M$; $\overline{LM}$ is opposite $\angle K$; $\overline{KM}$ is opposite $\angle L$.
47. $\overline{RS}$ is opposite $\angle T$; $\overline{ST}$ is opposite $\angle R$; $\overline{RT}$ is opposite $\angle S$. **49–53.** Sample answers are given.
49.　　　　**51.**

53.

57. 11 **59.** (0, 9) **61.** (−3, 6) **63.** (−6, 2)
65. (−8, 8) **67.** 39 **69.** 20 **71.** −175

4.2 Guided Practice (p. 182) **3.** 61 **5.** 35

4.2 Practice and Applications (pp. 182–184)
7. 110° **9.** 60° **11.** 45° **13.** 139° **15.** $\overline{ML}$
17. 45° to 60° **19.** 20 **21.** $x = 40$; $y = 50$
23. 77° **27.** Corresponding Angles Converse
29. Same-Side Interior Angles Converse
31. 3.5 > 3.06 **33.** 1.75 > 1.57 **35.** 2.055 < 2.1

Quiz 1 (p. 184) **1.** obtuse isosceles triangle
2. acute scalene triangle **3.** right scalene triangle
4. 30° **5.** 78° **6.** 65°

4.3 Guided Practice (p. 188) **3.** $\angle R \cong \angle T$; $\overline{RS} \cong \overline{TS}$ **5.** 50; Base Angles Theorem

4.3 Practice and Applications (pp. 188–190)
7. 55; Base Angles Theorem **9.** 45; Corollary to the Triangle Sum Theorem and the Base Angles Theorem **11.** 2 **13.** 2 **15.** 18 **17.** 120° **19.** 90°
21. 5 **23.** 5 **25.** 3 **27.** no

29.   **31.** $\triangle WXZ$, $\triangle VXW$, $\triangle YXV$, $\triangle YXZ$
35. $m\angle DBC = 42°$; $m\angle ABC = 84°$
37. $m\angle DBC = 150°$; $m\angle ABC = 75°$ **39.** 50 **41.** 7 **43.** 1

4.4 Guided Practice (p. 195) **3.** 2.2 **5.** 5.8 **7.** 6.3

4.4 Practice and Applications (pp. 195–198)
9. 41 **11.** 26 **13.** 17 **15.** 80 **17.** 4; yes
19. $\sqrt{170} \approx 13.0$; no **21.** $\sqrt{495} \approx 22.2$; no
23. yes; **25.** no **27.** 5
29. 6.1 **31.** yes
33. A to B: 115 yd; B to C: 80 yd; C to A: 65 yd
41. 1.05 **43.** 0.02 **45.** $x \geq 2$ **47.** $x \leq 0$ **49.** $\frac{2}{25}$
51. $\frac{3}{25}$ **53.** $\frac{173}{1000}$ **55.** $\frac{1}{9}$

Quiz 2 (p. 198) **1.** 6 **2.** 27 **3.** 7 **4.** $\sqrt{34} \approx 5.8$
5. $\sqrt{17} \approx 4.1$ **6.** $\sqrt{13} \approx 3.6$ **7.** $\sqrt{11} \approx 3.3$ ft

4.5 Guided Practice (p. 203)
3. obtuse **5.** C **7.** D

4.5 Practice and Applications (pp. 203–205)
9. $15^2 + 20^2 = 25^2$ **11.** $1^2 + 4^2 = (\sqrt{17})^2$
13. $4^2 + 6^2 > 7^2$ **15.** $2^2 + 6^2 < 7^2$ **17.** $13^2 + 16^2 < 22^2$ **19.** obtuse **21.** obtuse **23.** acute **25.** right
27. obtuse **29.** acute **31.** right **33.** acute
35. acute **37.** No; $714^2 < 599^2 + 403^2$, so the triangle is not a right triangle. **39.** No; the doubled side lengths will also form a right triangle. *Sample answer:* Let a, b, and c be the lengths of the sides of a right triangle with $a^2 + b^2 = c^2$. Then $(2a)^2 + (2b)^2 = 4a^2 + 4b^2 = 4(a^2 + b^2) = 4c^2 = (2c)^2$. Since $(2a)^2 + (2b)^2 = (2c)^2$, $2a$, $2b$, and $2c$ are also the side lengths of a right triangle. **43.** 67 **45.** 15 **47.** $\frac{9}{32}$ **49.** $\frac{1}{3}$
51. 14 **53.** $3\frac{1}{2}$

4.6 Guided Practice (p. 209)
5. 11 **7.** $PT = 22$; $ST = 11$

4.6 Practice and Applications (pp. 210–211)
9. 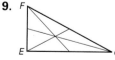 **11.** $PN = 6$; $QP = 3$
13. $PN = 20$; $QP = 10$
15. $CD = 22$; $CE = 33$

17. The equation should be $AD = \frac{2}{3}AE$, so $AD = \frac{2}{3}(18) = 12$, and $DE = 18 - 12 = 6$. **19.** $Q(5, 0)$; $R(2, 2)$; $S(8, 4)$ **21.** (5, 2) **25.** 60° **27.** 125°
29. 147° **31–41.** Sample answers are given.

31. $\dfrac{2}{10}, \dfrac{10}{50}$ **33.** $\dfrac{4}{7}, \dfrac{80}{140}$ **35.** $\dfrac{1}{10}, \dfrac{5}{50}$ **37.** $\dfrac{2}{9}, \dfrac{4}{18}$
39. $\dfrac{6}{8}, \dfrac{3}{4}$ **41.** $\dfrac{8}{11}, \dfrac{48}{66}$

4.7 Guided Practice (p. 214) **3.** $\overline{AC}$ **5.** shortest, $\overline{EF}$; longest, $\overline{DE}$ **7.** Yes; $6 + 10 > 15$, $6 + 15 > 10$, and $10 + 15 > 6$. **9.** Yes; $7 + 8 > 13$, $7 + 13 > 8$, and $8 + 13 > 7$. **11.** No; $5 + 5 = 10$.

4.7 Practice and Applications (pp. 215–218)
13. smallest, $\angle R$; largest, $\angle Q$ **15.** shortest, $\overline{RT}$; longest, $\overline{ST}$ **17.** shortest, $\overline{JK}$; longest, $\overline{JH}$ **19.** $\angle P$; $\angle Q$; $\angle N$ **21.** $\angle C$; $\angle A$; $\angle B$ **23.** $\angle D$; $\angle E$; $\angle F$ **25.** No; $3 + 5 < 9$, so the side lengths do not satisfy the Triangle Inequality. **27.** $\overline{EF}$; $\overline{DE}$; $\overline{DF}$ **29.** $\overline{AC}$; $\overline{BC}$; $\overline{AB}$ **31.** $\overline{FG}$; $\overline{GH}$; $\overline{FH}$ **33.** $3 + 10 < 14$, so the side lengths do not satisfy the Triangle Inequality. **35.** no
37.
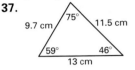

39. The diagonal and the sidewalks along Pine St. and Union St. form a triangle. The walk along the diagonal is shorter than staying on the sidewalks by the Triangle Inequality. **41.** raised **43.** Yes; when the boom is lowered and AB is greater than 100, $AB > BC$ and so $\angle ACB$ will be larger than $\angle BAC$. **45.** $\overline{RT}$ **47.** $\overline{RS}, \overline{ST}$ **49.** 58° **51.** 34° **53.** 1 **55.** 7 **57.** 70

Quiz 3 (p. 218) **1.** obtuse **2.** acute **3.** right **4.** $KN = 4$; $MN = 2$ **5.** $KN = 26$; $MN = 13$ **6.** $KN = 40$; $MN = 20$ **7.** $\overline{QM}$; $\overline{LM}$; $\overline{LQ}$ **8.** $\overline{PQ}$; $\overline{MP}$; $\overline{MQ}$ **9.** $\overline{MN}$; $\overline{NP}$; $\overline{MP}$

Chapter Summary and Review (pp. 219–223)
1. triangle **3.** corollary **5.** vertex **7.** centroid **9.** equilateral **11.** right **13.** isosceles **15.** 142° **17.** 82°, 82° **19.** 5 **21.** 4 **23.** 52 **25.** 50 **27.** 14.8 **29.** 9.8 **31.** 8.1 **33.** 12.2 **35.** 5.4 **37.** obtuse **39.** acute **41.** obtuse **43.** $KP = 28$; $PM = 14$ **45.** $CE = 12$; $DE = 4$ **47.** $CE = 42$; $DE = 14$ **49.** $\angle U$; $\angle T$; $\angle S$ **51.** $\overline{AC}$; $\overline{BC}$; $\overline{AB}$ **53.** $\overline{GH}$; $\overline{GJ}$; $\overline{HJ}$ **55.** Yes; $21 + 23 > 25$, $21 + 25 > 23$, and $23 + 25 > 21$. **57.** No; $6 + 6 = 12$. **59.** Yes; $2 + 3 > 4$, $2 + 4 > 3$, and $3 + 4 > 2$. **61.** Yes; $11 + 11 > 20$ and $11 + 20 > 11$.

Algebra Review (p. 227)
1. $\dfrac{3}{8}$ **3.** $\dfrac{1}{6}$ **5.** 7 hours/day **7.** $9.50/hour

Chapter 5

Study Guide (p. 232) **1.** D **2.** G **3.** D

5.1 Guided Practice (p. 236) **5.** $\angle F$ **7.** $\overline{ED}$ **9.** 105° **11.** 11.6 **13.** yes; *Sample answer:* $\triangle EFG \cong \triangle KLJ$

5.1 Practice and Applications (pp. 236–239)
15. neither **17.** corresponding sides **19.** corresponding angles **21.** $\angle N$ **23.** $\angle NLM$ **25.** $\triangle QRP$ **27.** yes **29.** yes **31.** no **33.** $\overline{QR} \cong \overline{TU}$; $\overline{RP} \cong \overline{US}$; $\overline{PQ} \cong \overline{ST}$; $\angle Q \cong \angle T$; $\angle R \cong \angle U$; $\angle P \cong \angle S$; *Sample answer:* $\triangle QRP \cong \triangle TUS$
35. *Sample answer:*

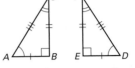

37. 5; 100° **39.** 6; 50° **41.** C **43.** yes; *Sample answer:* $\triangle JKL \cong \triangle PNM$ **45.** yes; *Sample answer:* $\triangle ABC \cong \triangle EDC$ **47.** no **49.** Base Angles Theorem **51.** Reflexive Property of Congruence **55.** Reflexive Property of Congruence **57.** Transitive Property of Equality **59.** acute **61.** 11.95 **63.** 19.33 **65.** 17.076

5.2 Guided Practice (p. 245) **7.** no

5.2 Practice and Applications (pp. 245–249)
9. $\angle ABD$ **11.** $\angle C$ **13.** $\angle BDC$ **15.** Yes; all three pairs of corresponding sides of the triangles are congruent. **17.** No; there is no information about $\overline{PS}$ and $\overline{RS}$. **19.** No; the congruent angles are not included between the congruent sides. **21.** no **23.** yes; SSS Congruence Postulate **25.** yes; SAS Congruence Postulate or SSS Congruence Postulate **27.** $\overline{AB} \cong \overline{CD}$ **29.** $\overline{BC} \cong \overline{EF}$ **31.** $\overline{PQ} \cong \overline{RQ}$ or $\angle PSQ \cong \angle RSQ$ **33.** *Sample answer:* Since $\overline{AB} \parallel \overline{CD}$, $\angle ABC \cong \angle DCB$ by the Alternate Interior Angles Theorem. $\overline{AB} \cong \overline{DC}$ is given and $\overline{BC} \cong \overline{BC}$ by the Reflexive Property. So, the triangles are congruent by the SAS Congruence Postulate.

35.

Statements	Reasons
1. $\overline{SP} \cong \overline{TP}$	1. Given
2. $\overline{PQ}$ bisects $\angle SPT$.	2. Given
3. $\angle SPQ \cong \angle TPQ$	3. Definition of angle bisector
4. $\overline{PQ} \cong \overline{PQ}$	4. Reflexive Prop. of Cong.
5. $\triangle SPQ \cong \triangle TPQ$	5. SAS Congruence Postulate

37. The congruent angles are not included between the congruent sides.   **43.** same-side interior angles   **45.** alternate interior angles   **47.** same-side interior angles   **49.** yes   **51.** 1.7   **53.** 6.3   **55.** 3.8   **57.** 1.1

Quiz 1 (p. 249)   **1.** $\angle C$ **2.** $\overline{QP}$ **3.** $\triangle PQR$ **4.** $\triangle CBA$ **5.** *Sample answer:* $\triangle EFG \cong \triangle YXZ$ **6.** No; the congruent angles are not included between the congruent sides.   **7.** Yes; *Sample answer:* the three sides of $\triangle DGF$ are congruent to the three sides of $\triangle EGF$, so $\triangle DGF \cong \triangle EGF$ by the SSS Congruence Postulate.   **8.** Yes; two sides and the included angle of $\triangle JKF$ are congruent to two sides and the included angle of $\triangle NMF$, so the triangles are congruent by the SAS Congruence Postulate.

5.3 Guided Practice (p. 253)   **5.** $\overline{AB} \cong \overline{DE}$ **7.** yes; ASA Congruence Postulate   **9.** no

5.3 Practice and Applications (pp. 254–256)   **11.** included   **13.** not included   **15.** AAS Congruence Theorem; two angles and a non-included side of $\triangle JLM$ are congruent to two angles and the corresponding non-included side of $\triangle PNM$.   **17.** Yes; SAS Congruence Postulate; two sides and the included angle of $\triangle PQR$ are congruent to two sides and the included angle of $\triangle TSM$.   **19.** Yes; ASA Congruence Postulate; vertical angles are congruent, so $\angle RVS \cong \angle UVT$; two angles and the included side of $\triangle RVS$ are congruent to two angles and the included side of $\triangle UVT$.   **21.** Yes; SSS Congruence Postulate; $\overline{XY} \cong \overline{XY}$; all three sides of $\triangle WXY$ are congruent to the three sides of $\triangle ZXY$.   **23.** AAS Congruence Theorem   **25.** $\angle K \cong \angle Q$ **27.** $\angle C \cong \angle D$ **29.** $\overline{AC} \cong \overline{AD}$ **31.** *Sample answer:*

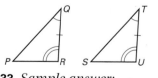

33. *Sample answer:*

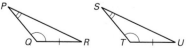

35.

Statements	Reasons
1. $\overline{BC} \cong \overline{EC}$	1. Given
2. $\overline{AB} \perp \overline{AD}$	2. Given
3. $\overline{DE} \perp \overline{AD}$	3. Given
4. $\angle A$ and $\angle D$ are right angles.	4. Perpendicular lines form right angles.
5. $\angle A \cong \angle D$	5. Right angles are congruent.
6. $\angle ACB \cong \angle DCE$	6. Vertical Angles Theorem
7. $\triangle ABC \cong \triangle DEC$	7. AAS Congruence Theorem

37. 15.0   **39.** 21.2   **41.** $\overline{ED}$ **43.** $\overline{BC}$ **45.** $\overline{FE}$ **47.** $\dfrac{1}{5}$ **49.** 2   **51.** $\dfrac{5}{8}$ **53.** $\dfrac{1}{33}$

5.4 Guided Practice (p. 260)   **7.** Yes; all three sides of $\triangle EDG$ are congruent to the three sides of $\triangle GFE$ so the triangles are congruent by the SSS Congruence Postulate.   **9.** No; both triangles are equilateral and equiangular, but there is no information about the lengths of the sides of the triangles.

5.4 Practice and Applications (pp. 260–263)   **11.** Yes; $\overline{JL} \cong \overline{JL}$, so the hypotenuse and a leg of right $\triangle JKL$ are congruent to the hypotenuse and a leg of right $\triangle JML$.   **13.** You need to know that the wires have the same length.   **15.** Yes; SAS Congruence Postulate; two sides and the included angle of $\triangle ABC$ are congruent to two sides and the included angle of $\triangle DEF$.   **17.** No; the congruent angles are not included between the congruent sides, so there is not enough information to prove the triangles congruent.   **19.** Yes; AAS Congruence Theorem; perpendicular lines form right angles and all right angles are congruent, so $\angle UTS \cong \angle UTV$; also $\overline{UT} \cong \overline{UT}$; two angles and a non-included side of $\triangle STU$ are congruent to two angles and the corresponding non-included side of $\triangle VTU$.   **21.** Yes; *Sample answer:* HL Congruence Theorem; the hypotenuse and a leg $(\overline{DB})$ of right $\triangle ABD$ are congruent to the hypotenuse and a leg $(\overline{DB})$ of right $\triangle CBD$.   **23.** Yes; *Sample answer:* SAS Congruence Postulate since $\overline{DF} \cong \overline{DF}$; two sides and the included angle of $\triangle CDF$ are congruent to two sides and the included angle of $\triangle EDF$.   **25.** *Sample answer:*

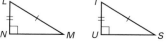

27. *Sample answer:*

29. $\angle F \cong \angle J$, ASA Congruence Postulate; or $\angle G \cong \angle L$, AAS Congruence Theorem; or $\overline{GH} \cong \overline{LK}$, SAS Congruence Postulate

31. $\overline{WX} \cong \overline{ZX}$, ASA Congruence Postulate; or $\overline{VW} \cong \overline{YZ}$, AAS Congruence Theorem; or $\overline{VX} \cong \overline{YX}$, AAS Congruence Theorem

33. a. *Sample answer:* $\overline{BD} \cong \overline{BD}$; the hypotenuse and a leg of right $\triangle ABD$ are congruent to the hypotenuse and a leg of right $\triangle CBD$, so $\triangle ABD \cong \triangle CBD$ by the HL Congruence Theorem. **b.** Yes; *Sample answer:* It is given that $\overline{AB} \cong \overline{BC}$. By the Base Angles Theorem, $\angle BAD \cong \angle BCD$. Perpendicular lines form right angles and all right angles are congruent, so $\angle BDA \cong \angle BDC$. Therefore, $\triangle ABD \cong \triangle CBD$ by the AAS Congruence Theorem. **c.** Yes; *Sample answer:* The hypotenuse and a leg of $\triangle ABD$ are congruent to the hypotenuse and a leg of $\triangle CBD$, $\triangle CEG$, and $\triangle FEG$ by the HL Congruence Theorem. **35.** $m\angle 1 = 82°$ by the Corresponding Angles Postulate; $m\angle 2 = 82°$ by the Alternate Exterior Angles Theorem (or by the Vertical Angles Theorem). **37.** Yes; AAS Congruence Theorem; two angles and a non-included side of $\triangle ABC$ are congruent to two angles and the corresponding non-included side of $\triangle DEF$. **39.** Yes; AAS Congruence Theorem; vertical angles are congruent, so $\angle JLK \cong \angle NLM$; two angles and a non-included side of $\triangle JKL$ are congruent to two angles and the corresponding non-included side of $\triangle NML$. **41.** 0 **43.** 32 **45.** 5

Quiz 2 (p. 263) **1.** yes **2.** yes **3.** no **4.** no **5.** No; only two pairs of sides are congruent. **6.** Yes; AAS Congruence Theorem; two angles and a non-included side of $\triangle JKL$ are congruent to two angles and the corresponding non-included side of $\triangle QRP$. **7.** Yes; ASA Congruence Postulate; two angles and the included side of $\triangle STU$ are congruent to two angles and the included side of $\triangle VUT$. **8.** Yes; HL Congruence Theorem; the hypotenuse and a leg of right $\triangle HEF$ are congruent to the hypotenuse and a leg of right $\triangle FGH$.

9. Yes; ASA Congruence Postulate or AAS Congruence Theorem; when two parallel lines are cut by a transversal, alternate interior angles are congruent, so $\angle R \cong \angle U$ and $\angle S \cong \angle V$; to use AAS, use congruent vertical angles $\angle RTS$ and $\angle UTV$ along with one pair of alternate interior angles. **10.** Yes; ASA Congruence Postulate or AAS Congruence Theorem; $\overline{JL} \cong \overline{JL}$; select the angles that include $\overline{JL}$ to use ASA or a pair of angles that do not include $\overline{JL}$ to use AAS.

5.5 Guided Practice (p. 268) **3.** When two parallel lines are cut by a transversal, alternate interior angles are congruent, so $\angle VSU \cong \angle TUS$ and $\angle TSU \cong \angle VUS$; also $\overline{SU} \cong \overline{SU}$; $\triangle STU \cong \triangle UVS$ by the ASA Congruence Postulate; $\angle STU \cong \angle UVS$ since corresponding parts of congruent triangles are congruent. **5.** $\overline{LN} \cong \overline{LK}$, $\angle LNM \cong \angle LKJ$, and $\angle L \cong \angle L$; $\triangle JKL \cong \triangle MNL$ by the ASA Congruence Postulate; $\angle J \cong \angle M$ since corresponding parts of congruent triangles are congruent.

5.5 Practice and Applications (pp. 268–271) **7.** $\triangle ABC \cong \triangle DBC$ **9.** $\triangle ABC \cong \triangle EDF$ **11.** Check diagrams; AAS Congruence Theorem. **13.** ASA Congruence Postulate; $\angle GJH \cong \angle KMH$, and $\overline{MH} \cong \overline{JH}$; $\angle H \cong \angle H$ by the Reflexive Property of Congruence.

15.

Statements	Reasons
1. $\overline{AD} \cong \overline{CD}$	1. Given
2. $\angle ABD$ and $\angle CBD$ are right angles.	2. Given
3. $\triangle ABD$ and $\triangle CBD$ are right triangles.	3. Def. of right triangle
4. $\overline{BD} \cong \overline{BD}$	4. Reflexive Property of Congruence
5. $\triangle ABD \cong \triangle CBD$	5. HL Congruence Theorem
6. $\angle A \cong \angle C$	6. Corresp. parts of $\cong$ triangles are $\cong$.

17. *Sample answer:*

Statements	Reasons
1. $\overline{RQ} \cong \overline{TS}$	1. Given
2. $\angle RTQ \cong \angle TRS$	2. Given
3. $\angle Q$ and $\angle S$ are right angles.	3. Given
4. $\angle Q \cong \angle S$	4. Right angles are congruent.
5. $\triangle RTQ \cong \triangle TRS$	5. AAS Congruence Theorem
6. $\overline{QT} \cong \overline{SR}$	6. Corresp. parts of $\cong$ triangles are $\cong$.

19.

Statements	Reasons
1. $\overline{BD}$ and $\overline{AE}$ bisect each other at C.	1. Given
2. $\overline{BC} \cong \overline{DC}$	2. Def. of segment bisector
3. $\overline{AC} \cong \overline{EC}$	3. Def. of segment bisector
4. $\angle BCA \cong \angle DCE$	4. Vertical Angles Theorem
5. $\triangle ABC \cong \triangle EDC$	5. SAS Congruence Postulate
6. $\angle A \cong \angle E$	6. Corresp. parts of $\cong$ triangles are $\cong$.

25. 18 **27.** 42 **29.** 11 **31.** -9 **33.** 7 **35.** 9

5.6 Guided Practice (p. 276) **3.** 16 **5.** 12

5.6 Practice and Applications (pp. 276–280)

7.

9. Paige cannot assume that $\overleftrightarrow{PC} \perp \overleftrightarrow{AC}$. **11.** 6
13. $\overline{BC} \cong \overline{BD}$ by the Angle Bisector Theorem
15. 18 **17.** 3 **19.** $AD = 12$; $BC = 16$ **21.** ℓ is the perpendicular bisector of the goal line.
23. $CG = AG = 2$ **25.** $\overline{FJ} \cong \overline{JG}$; $\overline{FK} \cong \overline{KH}$; $\overline{GL} \cong \overline{LH}$; $\overline{JM} \cong \overline{KM}$; $\overline{MG} \cong \overline{MH} \cong \overline{FM}$
26–28.

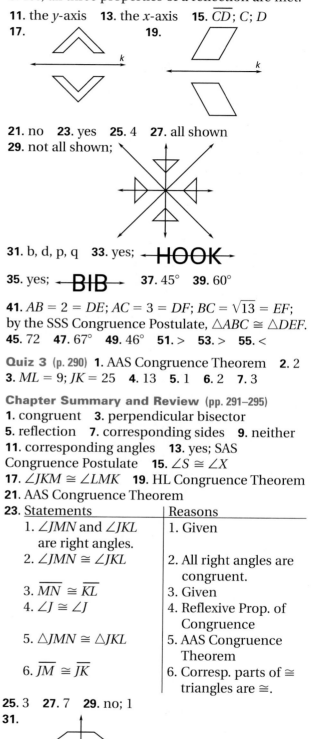

29. The fire station at A; X is in the red region, closest to station A.

31. Yes; by the Perpendicular Bisector Theorem, if D lies on the perpendicular bisector of $\overline{AB}$, then $\overline{DA}$ and $\overline{DB}$ will always be congruent segments.
37. $(8, -5)$ **39.** $(-1, -10)$ **41.** $(9, -4)$ **43.** $(13, 6)$
45. SAS Congruence Postulate; $\overline{DB} \cong \overline{DB}$ and all right angles are congruent, so two sides and the included angle of $\triangle ADB$ are congruent to two sides and the included angle of $\triangle CDB$.
47. ASA Congruence Postulate; vertical angles are congruent, so two angles and the included side of $\triangle JNK$ are congruent to two angles and the included side of $\triangle LNM$. **49.** $-1.25, -0.75,$ $-0.25, 0.25, 1, 4$ **51.** $-3.9, -3.3, -3, 3.1, 3.5, 3.8$
53. $-2.5, 1, 2.1, 3.2, 3.25, 5$ **55.** -1 **57.** 3
59. -8 **61.** 3

5.7 Guided Practice (p. 286) **3.** yes **5.** 3 **7.** 5

5.7 Practice and Applications (pp. 286–290)
9. Yes; all three properties of a reflection are met.
11. the y-axis **13.** the x-axis **15.** $\overline{CD}$; C; D
17.   **19.**

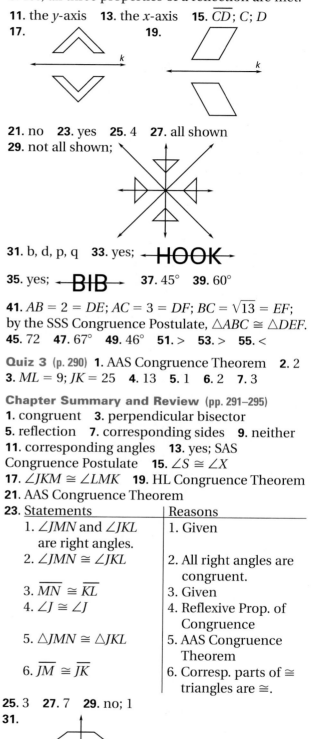

21. no **23.** yes **25.** 4 **27.** all shown
29. not all shown;

31. b, d, p, q **33.** yes; HOOK

35. yes; BIB **37.** $45°$ **39.** $60°$

41. $AB = 2 = DE$; $AC = 3 = DF$; $BC = \sqrt{13} = EF$; by the SSS Congruence Postulate, $\triangle ABC \cong \triangle DEF$.
45. 72 **47.** $67°$ **49.** $46°$ **51.** $>$ **53.** $>$ **55.** $<$

Quiz 3 (p. 290) **1.** AAS Congruence Theorem **2.** 2
3. $ML = 9$; $JK = 25$ **4.** 13 **5.** 1 **6.** 2 **7.** 3

Chapter Summary and Review (pp. 291–295)
1. congruent **3.** perpendicular bisector
5. reflection **7.** corresponding sides **9.** neither
11. corresponding angles **13.** yes; SAS Congruence Postulate **15.** $\angle S \cong \angle X$
17. $\angle JKM \cong \angle LMK$ **19.** HL Congruence Theorem
21. AAS Congruence Theorem
23.

Statements	Reasons
1. $\angle JMN$ and $\angle JKL$ are right angles.	1. Given
2. $\angle JMN \cong \angle JKL$	2. All right angles are congruent.
3. $\overline{MN} \cong \overline{KL}$	3. Given
4. $\angle J \cong \angle J$	4. Reflexive Prop. of Congruence
5. $\triangle JMN \cong \triangle JKL$	5. AAS Congruence Theorem
6. $\overline{JM} \cong \overline{JK}$	6. Corresp. parts of $\cong$ triangles are $\cong$.

25. 3 **27.** 7 **29.** no; 1
31.

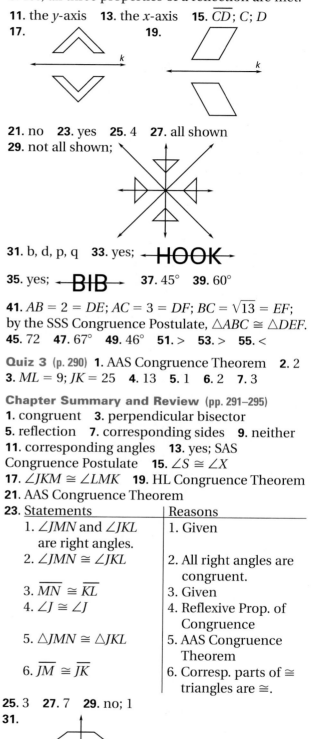

Algebra Review (p. 299) **1.** yes **3.** no **5.** no
7. $\dfrac{6}{5}$ **9.** -1 **11.** 0

Chapter 6

Study Guide (p. 302) **1.** C **2.** G **3.** C

6.1 Guided Practice (p. 306) **3.** Yes; the figure is a polygon formed by five straight lines. **5.** No; two of the sides intersect only one other side. **7.** 67°

6.1 Practice and Applications (pp. 306–308) **9.** no; not formed by segments **11.** 3; in order for each side to intersect exactly two other sides at each of its endpoints, a polygon must have at least three sides; triangle.

13. *Sample answer:*

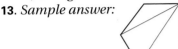

15. 71° **17.** 75° **19.** 20 **21.** 8; octagon
23. $\overline{MP}, \overline{MQ}, \overline{MR}, \overline{MS}, \overline{MT}$ **25.** 8; octagon
27. 17; 17-gon **31.** parallel **33.** neither **35.** 72°
37. $4x + 12$ **39.** $-2x + 14$ **41.** $-15x + 6$

6.2 Guided Practice (p. 313) **3.** yes **5.** $\angle KJM$; opposite $\angle$ of a parallelogram are $\cong$. **7.** $\overline{NL}$; diagonals of a parallelogram bisect each other.
9. $\overline{NK}$; diagonals of a parallelogram bisect each other. **11.** 9

6.2 Practice and Applications (pp. 313–315) **13.** B; diagonals of a parallelogram bisect each other.
15. D; diagonals of a parallelogram bisect each other. **17.** E; vertical $\angle$ are $\cong$. **19.** G; if 2 ∥ lines are cut by a transversal, then alternate interior $\angle$ are $\cong$. **21.** $\overline{HG}$; if you sketch parallelogram $EFGH$, you see that $\overline{EF}$ intersects $\overline{GF}$ and $\overline{EF}$ is parallel to $\overline{HG}$. **23.** $EF = 25$; $FG = 17$
25. $m\angle K = 129°$; $m\angle L = 51°$; $m\angle M = 129°$
27. $m\angle J = 90°$; $m\angle K = 90°$; $m\angle L = 90°$ **29.** 13
31. $x = 12$; $y = 3$ **33.** $x = 2$; $y = 7$ **35.** $m\angle B$ increases. **37.** The height increases.
39. $\angle 5$ and $\angle 8$ **45.** No; same-side interior angles are not supplementary. **47.** 31 **49.** 5 **51.** 3
53. $-\dfrac{1}{3}$ **55.** $\dfrac{3}{5}$

6.3 Guided Practice (p. 320) **5.** No; you can tell that one pair of sides must be parallel, but not both. **7.** yes, by the definition of a parallelogram

6.3 Practice and Applications (pp. 320–323)
9. Yes; both pairs of opposite sides are congruent.
11. Yes; both pairs of opposite angles are congruent. **13.** No; opposite angles are not congruent (or consecutive angles are not supplementary).

15. No; consecutive angles are not supplementary.
17. Yes; the diagonals bisect each other.
19. No; the diagonals do not bisect each other.
21. The parallel sides may not be congruent so the congruent sides may not be parallel. So the quadrilateral may not be a parallelogram.
23. The diagonals of the resulting quadrilateral were drawn to bisect each other. Therefore, the resulting quadrilateral is a parallelogram.
25. The slope of $\overline{FG}$ = slope of $\overline{JH}$ = -3, and slope of $\overline{FJ}$ = slope of $\overline{GH}$ = 0, so the opposite sides are parallel and $FGHJ$ is a parallelogram by definition. **29.** 86° **31.** 71° **33.** 14 **35.** 17
37. 22 **39.** 17 **41.** -11 **43.** 32

Quiz 1 (p. 323) **1.** yes; pentagon **2.** yes; hexagon
3. no; not formed by segments **4.** $x = 16$; $y = 15$
5. $x = 58$; $y = 122$; $z = 58$ **6.** $x = 12$; $y = 9$
7. Yes; one angle is supplementary to both of its consecutive angles. **8.** No; you can tell that one pair of sides must be parallel, but not both.
9. Yes; both pairs of opposite sides are parallel, so the quadrilateral is a parallelogram by the definition of a parallelogram.

6.4 Guided Practice (p. 328)
3. B, C, D **5.** A, B, C, D

6.4 Practice and Applications (pp. 328–330)
7. 4; 4; 4 **9.** 90; 3; 3 **11.** rhombus **13.** No, a quadrilateral with congruent diagonals does not have to be a rectangle; *Sample answer:* You need to know that the figure is a parallelogram, or that its diagonals bisect each other, or that all of its angles are right. **15.** parallelogram, rectangle, rhombus, square **17.** rhombus, square **19.** 18
21. The consecutive angles of a parallelogram are supplementary, so the two angles consecutive to $\angle J$ must also be right angles. Also, opposite angles of a parallelogram are congruent, so the fourth angle must also be a right angle. By definition, a parallelogram with four right angles is a rectangle. **29.** 90° **31.** 145° **33.** $\dfrac{2}{1}$

6.5 Guided Practice (p. 334)
3. isosceles trapezoid **5.** trapezoid **7.** 5

6.5 Practice and Applications (pp. 334–336)
9. D **11.** B **13.** A **15.** $m\angle K = 60°$; $m\angle J = 120°$; $m\angle M = 120°$ **17.** $m\angle R = 102°$; $m\angle T = 48°$
19. $m\angle Q = 90°$; $m\angle S = 30°$ **21.** 15 **23.** 6 **25.** 19

27.

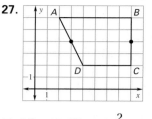

29. $\overline{AD}$ and $\overline{BC}$
31. Corresponding Angles Postulate
37. No; you can tell that one pair of sides must be parallel, but not both.
39. 10 **41.** 17 **43.** $\frac{2}{7}$ **45.** $\frac{5}{18}$

6.6 Practice and Applications (pp. 339–341)
9. trapezoid **11.** rectangle **13.** Yes; since $140° + 40° = 180°$, the top and bottom sides are parallel by the Same-Side Interior Angles Converse. Since $60° + 40° \neq 180°$, the other two sides are not parallel. The figure has exactly one pair of parallel sides, so it is a trapezoid. **15.** Yes; the four angles are congruent, so the four angles are right angles by the Quadrilateral Interior Angles Theorem. A quadrilateral with four right angles is a rectangle. **17.** Yes; both pairs of opposite sides are congruent, so the figure is a parallelogram. **19.** isosceles trapezoid **21.** true **23.** true **25.** isosceles trapezoid **27.** 1 **29.** 16 **31.** 10 **33.** 16 **35.** 0.2 **37.** 0.8333... ≈ 0.83

Quiz 2 (p. 341) **1.** 35 **2.** 6 **3.** 45 **4.** trapezoid **5.** isosceles trapezoid **6.** square, rectangle, rhombus, and parallelogram

Chapter Summary and Review (pp. 342–345)
1. parallelogram **3.** rhombus **5.** square
7. vertex **9.** legs; bases **11.** yes; hexagon
13. *Sample answer:*

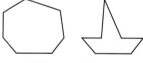

15. $BC = 4$; $DC = 8$ **17.** $PQ = 8$; $PM = 16$
19. *EFGH* is a parallelogram because both pairs of opposite sides are congruent. (If both pairs of opposite sides of a quadrilateral are congruent, then the quadrilateral is a parallelogram.)
21. $x = 8$; $y = 13$ **23.** $x = 6$; $y = 10$ **25.** true
27. true **29.** 71° **31.** No; both pairs of opposite angles are congruent, so the figure is a parallelogram. There is no information about the sides, so you cannot conclude that the figure is a rhombus. **33.** Yes; *Sample answer:* The diagonals bisect each other, so the figure is a parallelogram. One angle of the figure is given as a right angle. Consecutive angles of a parallelogram are supplementary, so the other three angles can be shown to be right angles. Because the figure is a parallelogram with four right angles, it is a rectangle by definition.

Algebra Review (p. 349) **1.** 30 **3.** 15 **5.** 2
7. $\frac{22}{7} = 3\frac{1}{7}$ **9.** $1\frac{1}{6}$ **11.** 74

Cumulative Practice (pp. 350–351) **1.** Each number is 9 more than the previous number; 38, 47.
3. $(-1, -1)$ **5.** $(1, 1)$ **7.** 9; obtuse **9.** 62°
11. same-side interior **13.** alternate interior
15. 105 **17.** 75 **19.** 58 **21.** 48 **23.** 5 **25.** 10
27. no; $3 + 6 < 12$ **29.** no **31.** yes; SAS Congruence Postulate
33. *Sample answer:*

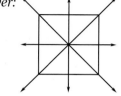

35. $x = 18$; $y = \frac{5}{2}$
37. A trapezoid; by the Quadrilateral Interior Angles Theorem, $m\angle H = 113°$; since $\angle E$ and $\angle F$ are supplementary, $\overline{EH} \parallel \overline{FG}$, but the other two sides are not parallel; a quadrilateral with exactly one pair of parallel sides is a trapezoid. **39.** Yes; $\overleftrightarrow{AB}$ and $\overleftrightarrow{DE}$ are both perpendicular to $\overleftrightarrow{AD}$ and the three lines are coplanar, so $\overleftrightarrow{AB} \parallel \overleftrightarrow{DE}$.

Chapter 7

Study Guide (p. 356) **1.** C **2.** G **3.** B

7.1 Guided Practice (p. 361)
3. $\frac{6}{5}$ **5.** $\frac{3}{1}$ **7.** $FG = 32$; $GH = 24$ **9.** 1 **11.** 15

7.1 Practice and Applications (pp. 361–363)
13. $\frac{4}{1}$ **15.** $\frac{1}{4}$ **17.** $\frac{8}{1}$ **19.** $\frac{35}{12}$ **21.** $\frac{3}{1}$ **23.** $\frac{3}{5}$
25. $\frac{20 \text{ mm}}{16 \text{ mm}}$; $\frac{5}{4}$ **27.** $\frac{2 \text{ ft}}{12 \text{ in.}}$ or $\frac{24 \text{ in.}}{12 \text{ in.}}$; $\frac{2}{1}$ **29.** $\frac{1}{1}$ **31.** $\frac{7}{2}$
33. $JK = 30$; $KL = 12$ **35.** length, 44 inches; width, 11 inches **37.** length, 48 meters; width, 18 meters
39. 15 **41.** 56 **43.** 4 **45.** 5 **47.** 1440 inches
49. about 1.0 inches **51.** about 300 miles
53. about 60 miles **57.** $\angle P$ **59.** yes; pentagon
61. yes; octagon **63.** 18.34 **65.** 19.6 **67.** 12

7.2 Guided Practice (p. 368) **3.** $\angle A \cong \angle L$; $\angle B \cong \angle M$; $\angle C \cong \angle N$ **5.** $\frac{3}{4}$ **7.** no; $\frac{7}{15} \neq \frac{4}{10}$

7.2 Practice and Applications (pp. 369–371)
9. $\angle A \cong \angle Q$; $\angle B \cong \angle R$; $\angle C \cong \angle S$; $\angle D \cong \angle T$; $\angle E \cong \angle U$; *Sample answer:* $\frac{AB}{QR} = \frac{BC}{RS} = \frac{CD}{ST} = \frac{DE}{TU} = \frac{EA}{UQ}$ **11.** yes; $\triangle GHJ \sim \triangle DEF$; $\frac{3}{4}$ **13.** yes; $JKLM \sim EFGH$; $\frac{5}{4}$ **15.** no $\left(\frac{3}{4} \neq \frac{4}{6} \right)$

17. $x = 30$; $y = 14$ **19.** $x = 8$; $y = 20$ **21.** 196 in. by 73.5 in.; 16 ft 4 in. by 6 ft $1\frac{1}{2}$ in. **23.** 80° **25.** 15 **27.** 6 : 7 **29.** No; the ratio $\frac{\text{length}}{\text{length}} = \frac{4}{16} = \frac{1}{4}$ and the ratio $\frac{\text{width}}{\text{width}} = \frac{3}{9} = \frac{1}{3}$; $\frac{1}{4} \neq \frac{1}{3}$. **31.** sometimes **33.** sometimes **35.** yes; ASA Congruence Postulate **37.** yes; HL Congruence Theorem or AAS Congruence Theorem **39.** *Sample answer:* $\frac{4}{10}, \frac{20}{50}$ **41.** *Sample answer:* $\frac{18}{8}, \frac{54}{24}$

7.3 Guided Practice (p. 375) **3.** Yes; $\angle D \cong \angle G$ and $\angle F \cong \angle H$, so $\triangle DEF \sim \triangle GJH$ by the AA Similarity Postulate. **5.** Yes; $\angle Q \cong \angle Q$ and $\angle QRT \cong \angle QSU$, so $\triangle QRT \sim \triangle QSU$ by the AA Similarity Postulate.

7.3 Practice and Applications (pp. 375–378) **7.** no **9.** yes; $\triangle ABC \sim \triangle DEF$ **11.** yes; $\triangle XYZ \sim \triangle GFH$ **13.** Yes; $\angle U \cong \angle U$ and $\angle UVW \cong \angle S$, so $\triangle UVW \sim \triangle UST$ by the AA Similarity Postulate. **15.** Yes; *Sample answer:* $\overline{DE} \parallel \overline{BA}$, so $\angle CED \cong \angle A$ and $\angle CDE \cong \angle B$; $\triangle CDE \sim \triangle CBA$ by the AA Similarity Postulate. **17.** MN **19.** 16 **21.** 14 **23.** 24 **25.** 35 **27.** true **29.** true **37.** Meredith is right; $m\angle ACB = 55°$, so $\angle ACB \cong \angle ADE$; $\angle A \cong \angle A$, so $\triangle ABC \sim \triangle AED$ by the AA Similarity Postulate. **39.** 34 **41.** $\overline{ST}$ **43.** 17 **45.** 15

46–53.

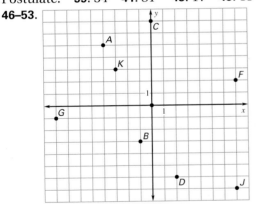

Quiz 1 (p. 378) **1.** 12 **2.** 40 **3.** 30 **4.** 10 **5.** 5 **6.** 20 **7.** Yes; $\angle A \cong \angle F$ and $\angle B \cong \angle G$, so $\triangle ABC \sim \triangle FGH$ by the AA Similarity Post. **8.** Yes; $\angle J \cong \angle R$ and $\angle K \cong \angle P$, so $\triangle JKL \sim \triangle RPQ$ by the AA Similarity Postulate. **9.** Yes; vertical angles are congruent, so $\angle SUT \cong \angle WUV$; also $\angle T \cong \angle V$, so $\triangle STU \sim \triangle WVU$ by the AA Similarity Postulate.

7.4 Guided Practice (p. 382) **3.** No; $\angle D \cong \angle R$ but $\frac{8}{6} \neq \frac{10}{8}$.

7.4 Practice and Applications (pp. 382–385) **5.** yes, $\triangle CDE \sim \triangle FGH$; $\frac{2}{3}$ **7.** no

9. yes, $\triangle UVW \sim \triangle JGH$; $\frac{3}{2}$ **11.** $\triangle RST$ is not similar to $\triangle ABC$ because the ratios of corresponding sides are not equal. $\triangle ABC \sim \triangle XYZ$ by the SSS Similarity Theorem because the ratios of corresponding sides are all equal to $\frac{3}{2}$. **13.** $\triangle RST$ is not similar to $\triangle ABC$ because the ratios of corresponding sides are not equal. $\triangle ABC \sim \triangle XYZ$ by the SSS Similarity Theorem because the ratios of corresponding sides are all equal to $\frac{3}{4}$.

15. yes; $\triangle ABC \sim \triangle DFE$ **17.** no **19.** $\angle A \cong \angle A$, $\frac{AD}{AB} = \frac{9}{30} = \frac{3}{10}$, and $\frac{AE}{AC} = \frac{6}{20} = \frac{3}{10}$; the lengths of the sides that include $\angle A$ are proportional, so $\triangle ADE \sim \triangle ABC$ by the SAS Similarity Theorem. **21.** Yes, $\triangle JKL \sim \triangle XYZ$ (or $\triangle YXZ$) by the SSS Similarity Theorem. **23.** no **25.** Yes; $\triangle PQR \sim \triangle DEF$ by the SAS Similarity Theorem. **27.** $\frac{AE}{AC} = \frac{AD}{AB}$ or $\frac{AE}{AC} = \frac{DE}{BC}$ **29.** *Sample answer:* Jon is correct. $\frac{6}{27} = \frac{4}{18}$, so the triangles are similar when $x = 6$. **31.** SAS Similarity Theorem **35.** $\angle VTS$ **37.** Yes; *Sample answer:* $\overrightarrow{TV}$ bisects $\angle STU$, so $\angle STV \cong \angle UTV$; $\angle TSV \cong \angle TUV$ and $\overline{TV} \cong \overline{TV}$, so $\triangle STV \cong \triangle UTV$ by the AAS Congruence Theorem; corresponding parts of congruent triangles are congruent, so $\angle TVS \cong \angle TVU$. **39.** 54 **41.** 24 **43.** $\frac{1}{4}$ **45.** $\frac{22}{25}$ **47.** $\frac{11}{20}$ **49.** $\frac{17}{50}$

7.5 Guided Practice (p. 390) **3.** AE **5.** AB **7.** 12 **9.** 8

7.5 Practice and Applications (pp. 390–392) **11.** $\frac{5}{6}$ **13.** 36 **15.** 18 **17.** 8 **19.** 15 **21.** yes **23.** yes **25.** 22 **27.** 10 **29.** 13.5 **33.** $\overline{BC}$ **35.** 7.5 **37.** 9.5 **39.** proportional **41.** yes; ←OHIO→ **43.** yes; ←BOOK→ **45.** 1 **47.** $-\frac{2}{3}$ **49.** $\frac{5}{2}$ **51.** 3

7.6 Guided Practice (p. 396) **3.** Enlargement; the red image is larger than the blue original figure. **5.** enlargement

7.6 Practice and Applications (pp. 396–398) **7.** enlargement; $\frac{8}{3}$ **9.** enlargement; $\frac{9}{2}$ **11.** enlargement; 21 **13.** reduction; 3 **15.** 4 **19.** 47° **21.** 3 **23.** 51 **25.** 3 **27.** 16 **29.** 26

Quiz 2 (p. 398) **1.** yes (by the SAS Similarity Theorem); $\triangle ABC \sim \triangle FGH$ **2.** yes (by the SSS Similarity Theorem); $\triangle JKL \sim \triangle PQR$ **3.** 8 **4.** 18 **5.** 44 **6.** enlargement; 2 **7.** reduction; $\frac{1}{3}$

Chapter Summary and Review (pp. 400–403)
1. $g; h; f; j$ **3.** scale factor **5.** midsegment
7. enlargement **9.** 42 **11.** 20 **13.** 20
15. $\angle P \cong \angle P$ and $\angle STP \cong \angle QRP$, so $\triangle PST \sim \triangle PQR$ by the AA Similarity Postulate.
17. $\angle B \cong \angle F$ and $\angle A \cong \angle D$, so $\triangle ABC \sim \triangle DFE$ by the AA Similarity Postulate.
19. $\angle QSR \cong \angle UST$, $\frac{QS}{US} = \frac{35}{28} = \frac{5}{4}$, and $\frac{RS}{TS} = \frac{30}{24} = \frac{5}{4}$; the lengths of the sides that include the congruent angles are proportional, so $\triangle QRS \sim \triangle UTS$ by the SAS Similarity Theorem.
21. 3 **23.** 10 **25.** enlargement; $\frac{5}{2}$

Algebra Review (p. 407) **1.** $2\sqrt{3}$ **3.** $2\sqrt{11}$ **5.** $5\sqrt{6}$
7. $4\sqrt{3}$ **9.** $h = \frac{A}{b}$ **11.** $P = \frac{S - 2B}{h}$

Chapter 8

Study Guide (p. 410) **1.** A **2.** H

8.1 Guided Practice (p. 413)
5. concave **7.** C **9.** B

8.1 Practice and Applications (pp. 413–415)
11. concave **13.** equiangular **15.** neither
17. regular (both equilateral and equiangular)
19. regular (both equilateral and equiangular)
21. not regular (equiangular but not equilateral)
23. concave **25.** C; A, B **27.** Yes. The sum of the measures of the angles of a triangle is 180°, or 3(60°). So, the missing angle measure is 60°. All three angles are congruent, so the triangle is equiangular.
29. Yes. *Sample answer:*

31. Yes. *Sample answer:*

33. 15 in. **35.** 48 ft **37.** 6 **41.** yes; pentagon
43. yes; octagon **45.** 16 **47.** 32 **49.** 1 **51.** 2.2

8.2 Guided Practice (p. 420)
3. 1260° **5.** $m\angle 1 + 66° + 130° + 100° = 360°$
7. $m\angle 1 + 85° + 59° + 57° + 117° = 360°$

8.2 Practice and Applications (pp. 421–423)
9. 1080° **11.** 1440° **13.** 3240° **15.** 9000° **17.** 99°

19. 127° **21.** 120° **23.** 60° **25.** 32 **27.** 540°
29. 108° **31.** always **33.** sometimes **41.** $BE = 4$, $ED = 2$ **43.** $BE = 34\frac{2}{3}$, $ED = 17\frac{1}{3}$ **45.** 11 **47.** 0
49. 2 **51.** 1.11

Quiz 1 (p. 423) **1.** not regular (equilateral but not equiangular) **2.** regular (both equilateral and equiangular) **3.** not regular (not equilateral and not equiangular) **4.** 140° **5.** 120° **6.** 109°
7. 101° **8.** 110°

8.3 Guided Practice (p. 427) **3.** A **5.** True; the area of the polygon is Area A + Area B + Area C.
7. True; the height is $3 + 2 = 5$ units.

8.3 Practice and Applications (pp. 427–429)
9. 144 m² **11.** 10 cm² **13.** 60.5 m² **15.** $A = 44$ m²
17. 196 m² **19.** 81 m² **21.** $b = 3$ cm **23.** Yes. Since the perimeter is 28 feet, each side measures $28 \div 4 = 7$ feet. Area $= 7^2 = 49$ square feet.
25. $b = 3$ ft, $h = 6$ ft **27.** 95 m² **29.** 116 yd²
31. 207,500 ft² **33.** about $433 **35.** C; Diagonals of a parallelogram bisect each other. **37.** D; If two parallel lines are cut by a transversal, then alternate interior angles are congruent.
39. Yes; $\triangle SUT \sim \triangle PRQ$ by the SAS Similarity Theorem. **41.** $8 > -18$ **43.** $-10 < 0$
45. $2.44 > 2.044$

8.4 Guided Practice (p. 434)
3.

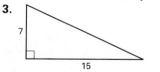

8.4 Practice and Applications (pp. 434–437)
5. 42 cm² **7.** 7.5 yd² **9.** 14 yd² **11.** 72 in.²
13. 63 ft²
15. *Sample answer:*

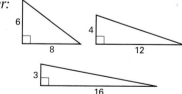

17. $h = 9$ cm **19.** 12 in. **21.** 4 in.² **23.** 42 m²
25. 68 cm² **27.** $\frac{3}{4}; \frac{9}{16}$ **29.** 8 triangles
31. 210.6 in.² **33.** 120 square units **37.** 12
39. $(-3, 3)$ **41.** $(6, 2)$ **43.** $(3, -1)$

Quiz 2 (p. 437) **1.** 144 cm² **2.** 21 in.² **3.** 46 m²
4. 154 ft² **5.** 56 mm² **6.** 96 yd² **7.** $b = 8$ in.
8. $h = 12$ m **9.** $b = 14$ cm

8.5 Guided Practice (p. 442) **3.** A **5.** 8 ft, 11 ft
7. 8 cm, 10 cm

8.5 Practice and Applications (pp. 442–445)
9. 66 square units   **11.** 8.4 square units
13. 264 square units   **15.** 192 cm^2
17. The formula is $A = bh$, not $A = \frac{1}{2}bh$. So, the
area is $(14)(11)$, or 154 square units.   **19.** $h = 6$ in.
21. 8 m   **23.** 104 square units   **25.** 40 square units
27. 234 square units   **29.** 89.49 square units
31. 4029.18 square units   **33.** 175.5 cm^2
35. 9 square units   **37.** 8 square units   **43.** 1   **45.** 8
47. concave   **49.** $2\sqrt{3}$ **51.** $2\sqrt{13}$ **53.** $10\sqrt{3}$
55. $6\sqrt{5}$

8.6 Guided Practice (p. 448)
3. $h = 12$, $b_1 = 9$, $b_2 = 19$ **5.** C   **7.** B

8.6 Practice and Applications (pp. 448–450)
9. 64 square units   **11.** 224 square units
13. 330 square units   **15.** The areas are equal.
17. Answers will vary; they are the same.
19. $h = 11$ in.   **21.** 4 units   **23.** about 3897 ft^2
25. about 4182 ft^2 **27.** 1824 in.^{2}
29. 1280 square units   **31.** 517.5 square units
35. E   **37.** B   **39.** 1   **41.** $\frac{5}{6}$

8.7 Guided Practice (p. 455)
3. 7 in.   **5.** 7 m   **7.** 8   **9.** 7

8.7 Practice and Applications (pp. 456–459)
11. 31 m   **13.** 82 yd   **15.** 50 ft^2 **17.** 113 in.^{2}
19. 201 ft^2 **21.** about 95 m^2 **23.** *Sample answer:*
Disagree. The area of the circle with radius 5 is
about 79. The area of the circle with radius 10 is
about 314. Since $314 \div 79 \approx 4$, the area is
quadrupled, not doubled.   **25.** 13 m   **27.** about
4 units   **29.** about 6 units   **31.** $\frac{x}{12} = \frac{60°}{360°}$
33. 61 m^2 **35.** 25 cm^2 **37.** 182 ft^2 **39.** 7 m^2
41. trapezoid   **43.** rhombus   **45.** 88 ft^2 **47.** 3
49. 44   **51.** -11 **53.** -16 **55.** 31

Quiz 3 (p. 459)   **1.** 63 ft^2 **2.** 31.72 cm^2 **3.** 24 m^2
4. 18 yd^2 **5.** 28 mm^2 **6.** 13 in.^{2} **7.** $h = 13$ cm
8. $b_2 = 12$ ft   **9.** $r \approx 8$ in.

Chapter Summary and Review (pp. 460–463)
1. convex   **3.** regular   **5.** height   **7.** circle
9. not regular (not equilateral and not
equiangular)   **11.** not regular (equiangular but
not equilateral)   **13.** 91°   **15.** 50°   **17.** 72 ft^2
19. 44 m^2 **21.** 58.5 cm^2 **23.** 26 ft   **25.** 56 ft^2
27. 22.5 in.^{2} **29.** 11 m   **31.** 36 ft^2 **33.** 7 m^2
35. $C \approx 82$ in.; $A \approx 531$ in.^{2} **37.** $C \approx 25$ ft; $A \approx 50$ ft^2
39. about 8 ft

Algebra Review (p. 467)   **1.** 16   **3.** -243 **5.** 1000
7. 51   **9.** 45%

Chapter 9

Study Guide (p. 472)   **1.** A   **2.** G   **3.** C

9.1 Guided Practice (p. 476)   **11.** no; cylinder
13. hexagonal prism; 8 faces and 18 edges;
congruent faces: $ABVU \cong BCWV \cong CDXW \cong$
$DEYX \cong EFZY \cong FAUZ$ and $ABCDEF \cong UVWXYZ$;
congruent edges: $\overline{AB} \cong \overline{BC} \cong \overline{CD} \cong \overline{DE} \cong \overline{EF} \cong$
$\overline{FA} \cong \overline{UV} \cong \overline{VW} \cong \overline{WX} \cong \overline{XY} \cong \overline{YZ} \cong \overline{ZU}$ and
$\overline{AU} \cong \overline{BV} \cong \overline{CW} \cong \overline{DX} \cong \overline{EY} \cong \overline{FZ}$ **15.** cube or
square prism; 6 faces and 12 edges; congruent
faces: $JKLM \cong TUVW \cong JKUT \cong KLVU \cong$
$LMWV \cong MJTW$

9.1 Practice and Applications (pp. 477–480)
17. no; cone   **19.** yes; rectangular; rectangular
pyramid   **21.** true   **23.** false   **25.** F   **27.** A   **29.** B
31. triangular prism   **33.** yes; rectangular;
rectangular pyramid   **35.** no   **37.** triangular
prism; 5 faces and 9 edges; congruent faces:
$\triangle FGH \cong \triangle JKL$; congruent edges: $\overline{FG} \cong \overline{JK}$,
$\overline{GH} \cong \overline{KL}$, $\overline{FH} \cong \overline{JL}$, $\overline{FJ} \cong \overline{GK} \cong \overline{HL}$ **39.** True;
they are all three-dimensional shapes.   **41.** False;
if a prism is not rectangular, then the bases are
the congruent faces that are not rectangular.
43. **45.**

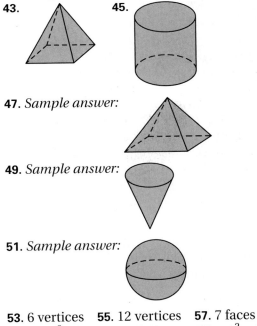

47. *Sample answer:*

49. *Sample answer:*

51. *Sample answer:*

53. 6 vertices   **55.** 12 vertices   **57.** 7 faces
63. 28 m^2 **65.** 13 ft   **67.** 31 cm; 79 cm^2 **69.** 41
71. 28   **73.** 4   **75.** 30   **77.** 10π **79.** 9π

9.2 Guided Practice (p. 487)   **5.** 248 in.^{2} **7.** 36 m^2

9.2 Practice and Applications (pp. 487–490)
9. 6 in.^{2} **11.** 5 m   **13.** about 25 m   **15.** 24 ft^2
17. 408 ft^2 **19.** 216 m^2 **21.** rectangular prism

23. triangular prism　**25.** 302 m^2　**27.** 377 in.^{2}
29. 152 in.^{2}　**31.** 1180 cm^2

33. 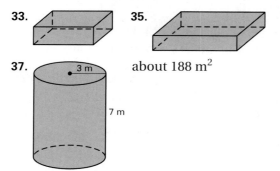　**35.**

37. about 188 m^2

39. 112 m^2　**41.** 120 ft^2　**43.** 25 in.^{2}　**45.** 106,240 m^2
49. 69 ft^2　**51.** 69 in.^{2}　**53.** 15　**55.** 21　**57.** 39

9.3 Guided Practice (p. 495)
5. 13 in.　**7.** about 44 in.^{2}

9.3 Practice and Applications (pp. 495–499)
9. height　**11.** slant height　**13.** 15 mm
15. 105 m^2　**17.** about 1498 cm^2　**19.** 2304 mm^2
21. The slant height is the hypotenuse of a right
triangle formed by the height of the pyramid and
half the length of the base. Since the hypotenuse
of a right triangle is always the longest side of the
triangle, the slant height is always greater than
the height.　**23.** 877 m^2　**25.** 704 m^2　**27.** 1414 yd^2
29. 196 cm^2　**31.** about 176 in.^{2}
33. 184 m^2

35. about 855 in.^{2}

37. right cone; about 50 cm^2　**39.** about 47 in.^{2}
41. 23 cm　**47.** 108　**49.** 15　**51.** 60　**53.** 50 m^2
55. 86 cm^2　**57.** 4　**59.** $4x - 4$　**61.** $13c - 5$

Quiz 1 (p. 499)　**1.** triangular; triangular prism; yes;
5 faces　**2.** circular; cone; no　**3.** rectangular;
rectangular pyramid; yes; 5 faces　**4.** 138 ft^2
5. 242 in.^{2}　**6.** 302 m^2　**7.** 300 in.^{2}　**8.** 280 m^2
9. 377 cm^2

9.4 Guided Practice (p. 503)
5. about 763.2 cm^3　**7.** about 280.8 cm^3

9.4 Practice and Applications (pp. 503–507)
9. 48 unit cubes; 16 unit cubes per layer and
3 layers in all　**11.** 100 in.^{3}　**13.** 216 m^3　**15.** 343 ft^3
17. 112 m^3　**19.** 78 ft^3　**21.** 350 m^3　**23.** 4 boxes
25. 1,408,000 ft^3　**27.** 452 in.^{3}　**29.** 6786 m^3

31. 1810 ft^3　**33.** the pool in Exercise 32
35. The solid on the right; the solid with the
vertical line of rotation has a volume that is
almost twice the volume of the solid with the
horizontal line of rotation.　**37.** about 216,773 gal
39. about 785 cm^3; about 6283 cm^3　**41.** 92 in.^{3}
43. 60 m^3　**45.** $7x^2$　**53.** 4.1　**55.** 188 ft^2
57. 267 yd^2　**59.** -11　**61.** 32　**63.** 17

9.5 Guided Practice (p. 513)　**5.** 35 m^3　**7.** 400 ft^3

9.5 Practice and Applications (pp. 513–516)
9. 30 ft^2　**11.** about 201 cm^2　**13.** 224 in.^{3}
15. 80 ft^3　**17.** 94 yd^3　**19.** 679 m^3　**21.** 209 cm^3
23. The volume is doubled.　**25.** The student used
the slant height instead of the height of the
pyramid. The volume should be $\frac{1}{3}(10 \cdot 10)(12) =$
400 in.^{3}　**27.** 4 in.　**29.** 6 m　**31.** 1280 m^3
33. 302 cm^3　**35.** 48 ft^3　**37.** 3　**39.** about 173.4 in.^{3}
41. Yes; the feeder holds about 173.4 in.^{3} and
only 72 in.^{3} are needed for five days.
43. about 0.04 mi^3　**47.** $C \approx 88$ in.; $A \approx 616$ in.^{2}
49. 262 in.^{2}　**51.** 679 m^2　**53.** positive
55. positive　**57.** negative

9.6 Guided Practice (p. 519)
3. 113 ft^2　**5.** 113 ft^3　**7.** 2094 yd^3

9.6 Practice and Applications (pp. 520–523)
9. 3217 in.^{2}　**11.** Bob wrote V rather than S for
surface area, used the wrong formula, used the
diameter rather than the radius, and wrote the
answer in cubic units rather than square units.
$S = 4\pi r^2 = 4\pi(5^2) = 100\pi \approx 314$ mm^2.
13. 137 cm^2　**15.** 9 in.^{2}　**17.** 290 cm^2　**19.** about
197,000,000 mi^2　**21.** The surface area of Earth is
about 13.4 times the surface area of the moon.
23. 2145 m^3　**25.** 4189 cm^3　**27.** 1437 ft^3
29. 4 times greater; 9 times greater; 16 times
greater　**31.** Answers may vary. The volume is
multiplied by 8 when the radius is doubled, and
the volume is multiplied by 27 when the radius
is tripled.　**33.** about 23,779 ft^2　**35.** 857,375 ft^3
37. 718 cm^3　**39.** 1527 in.^{3}　**41.** 905 ft^3　**43.** about
33,917 ft^3　**45.** about 3619 ft^2　**47.** 145 m^2
49. 1018 cm^2　**51.** 4.2　**53.** 20　**55.** 9.9　**57.** 11.0
59. 40 in.　**61.** 11 yd

Quiz 2 (p. 523)　**1.** 144 in.^{3}　**2.** 210 ft^3　**3.** 550 m^3
4. 400 ft^3　**5.** 2145 m^3　**6.** 38 in.^{3}　**7.** about 201 in.^{3}
8. about 1018 cm^2

Chapter Summary and Review (pp. 524–527)
1. base(s)　**3.** prism　**5.** volume　**7.** no　**9.** 78 ft^2
11. 264 m^2　**13.** 478 in.^{2}　**15.** 302 cm^2　**17.** 283 ft^2

19. 30 m^3 **21.** 2036 ft^3 **23.** 4398 in.^{3} **25.** 314 in.^{3}
27. 531 m^2; 1150 m^3 **29.** 186 ft^2; 239 ft^3

Algebra Review (p. 531) **1.** 0.4 **3.** 0.9 **5.** 3.8
7. 2.5 **9.** 3.6 **11.** $\frac{5}{7}$ **13.** $\frac{9}{11}$ **15.** $\frac{7}{4}$ **17.** $\frac{\sqrt{2}}{3}$
19. $\frac{7\sqrt{3}}{20}$

Cumulative Practice (pp. 532–533) **1.** acute
3. $m\angle 1 = m\angle 2 = 90°$ **5.** $m\angle 5 = 99°$, $m\angle 6 = 81°$,
$m\angle 7 = 99°$ **7.** acute **9.** SSS Congruence
Postulate; $\overline{AB} \cong \overline{DC}$ (Given); $\overline{BC} \cong \overline{BC}$ (Reflexive
Property of Congruence); $\overline{AC} \cong \overline{DB}$ (Given)
11. HL Congruence Theorem; $\overline{PR} \cong \overline{ST}$ (Given);
$\overline{QR} \cong \overline{RT}$ (Given) **13.** always **15.** sometimes
17. $x = 3$, $y = 70$, $z = 110$ **19.** AA Similarity
Postulate **21.** 3 **23.** Convex; *Sample answer:*
none of the extended sides pass through the
interior. **25.** 135° **27.** 196 m^2 **29.** 112 cm^2
31. 304 m^2, 320 m^3 **33.** 226 cm^2, 254 cm^3
35. 3217 in.^{2}

Chapter 10

Study Guide (p. 536) **1.** B **2.** G **3.** B

10.1 Guided Practice (p. 539)
7. 4.5 **9.** $2\sqrt{7}$ **11.** $3\sqrt{6}$

10.1 Practice and Applications (pp. 539–541)
13. 2.4; $\sqrt{4} < \sqrt{6} < \sqrt{9}$, so $2 < 2.4 < 3$. **15.** 5.8;
$\sqrt{25} < \sqrt{34} < \sqrt{36}$, so $5 < 5.8 < 6$. **17.** 12.2;
$\sqrt{144} < \sqrt{148} < \sqrt{169}$, so $12 < 12.2 < 13$. **19.** 13.6;
$\sqrt{169} < \sqrt{186} < \sqrt{196}$, so $13 < 13.6 < 14$. **21.** 7
23. 4.1 **25.** 2.8 **27.** 5 **29.** $2\sqrt{35}$ **31.** $11\sqrt{2}$
33. 75 **35.** $3\sqrt{2}$ **37.** $4\sqrt{3}$ **39.** $2\sqrt{14}$ **41.** $10\sqrt{2}$
43. $2\sqrt{11}$ **45.** no **47.** 62.0 **49.** 48 **51.** 15.9
57. 45° **59.** 68° **61.** 16 **63.** $x^2 + 5x$
65. $3x^2 + 4x$ **67.** $-3 + 3x$

10.2 Guided Practice (p. 545) **3.** $6\sqrt{2}$ **5.** $2\sqrt{3}$

10.2 Practice and Applications (pp. 545–547)
7. $7\sqrt{2}$ **9.** $\sqrt{10}$ **11.** $2\sqrt{5}$ **13.** 4 **15.** 1 **17.** 14
19. No; you cannot determine the measures of the
other two angles. **21.** No; the triangle is
isosceles, but there is no information about the
angle measures. **23.** The triangle has congruent
acute angles. By Example 3, the triangle is a
45°-45°-90° triangle. $x = \frac{9}{\sqrt{2}} \approx 6.4$. **25.** By
Example 3, $x = 45$ and the triangle is a 45°-45°-90°
triangle. $y = \frac{8}{\sqrt{2}} \approx 5.7$. **27.** By the Triangle Sum
Theorem, the third angle measures 45°. So the
triangle is a 45°-45°-90° triangle. $x = \frac{35}{\sqrt{2}} \approx 24.7$.

29. Lengths may vary, but *AC*, *CB*, and *CD* are all
equal. Since $\triangle ACD$ and $\triangle BCD$ are 45°-45°-90°
triangles, they are isosceles triangles by the
Converse of the Base Angles Theorem. Therefore,
$AC = CD$ and $CD = BC$. **31.** If the hypotenuse
has length $5\sqrt{2}$, the legs should each have length
5. If the legs have length $\sqrt{5}$, then the hypotenuse
has length $\sqrt{5} \cdot \sqrt{2}$, or $\sqrt{10}$. **33.** the right triangle
with legs of length 1 and hypotenuse of length
$r = \sqrt{2}$ **35.** right **37.** right **39.** $3\sqrt{7}$ **41.** 8
43. 14 **45.** $3\sqrt{13}$ **47.** 0.6 **49.** 0.33 **51.** 0.15
53. 0.1666... ≈ 0.17

10.3 Guided Practice (p. 552) **3.** false **5.** true
7. true **9.** 4

10.3 Practice and Applications (pp. 552–555)
11. 6 **13.** 22 **15.** 2 **17.** $4\sqrt{3}$ **19.** $13\sqrt{3}$
21. $16\sqrt{3}$ **23.** 2.3 **25.** 10.4 **27.** 14 **29.** 30 feet
31. $x = 4$; $y = 4\sqrt{3}$ **33.** $x = \frac{9}{2}$; $y = \frac{9}{2}\sqrt{3}$ **35.** $x = \frac{15}{2}$;
$y = \frac{15}{2}\sqrt{3}$ **37.** about 390 ft^2 **39.** about 21 cm^2
41. hypotenuse, 30 cm; longer leg, $15\sqrt{3}$ cm
45. $\frac{5}{3}$ **47.** $\frac{5}{8}$ **49.** yes; $\triangle ABC \sim \triangle FHG$ **51.** -16
53. 9 **55.** 37

Quiz 1 (p. 555) **1.** $2\sqrt{6}$ **2.** $\sqrt{30}$ **3.** 12 **4.** 20
5. $3\sqrt{3}$ **6.** $4\sqrt{11}$ **7.** $2\sqrt{13}$ **8.** $6\sqrt{5}$ **9.** $\frac{2}{\sqrt{3}}$ **10.** $\sqrt{6}$
11. $x = 14$; $y = 14\sqrt{3}$

10.4 Guided Practice (p. 560)
3. $\tan A = \frac{4}{3} \approx 1.3333$ **5.** $\tan A = \frac{1}{\sqrt{3}} \approx 0.5774$
7. 1.8807 **9.** 0.9325

10.4 Practice and Applications (pp. 560–562)
11. $\sqrt{3}$ **13.** $\tan P = \frac{7}{24} \approx 0.2917$; $\tan R = \frac{24}{7} \approx$
3.4286 **15.** $\tan P = \frac{4}{3} \approx 1.3333$; $\tan R = \frac{3}{4} = 0.75$
17. 1.3764 **19.** 57.2900 **21.** 0.8391 **23.** 8.1443
25. $\tan 39° = \frac{33}{x}$, $\tan 51° = \frac{x}{33}$; 40.8 **27.** 59.8
29. 15.1 **31.** 13.4 m **33.** 12.2 **35.** 29.4 **37.** 11.9
41. 1018 m^3 **43.** 513 in.^{3} **45.** 5 **47.** -3 **49.** 13

10.5 Guided Practice (p. 566)
5. $\frac{4}{5} = 0.8$ **7.** $\frac{4}{3} \approx 1.3333$ **9.** $\frac{4}{5} = 0.8$

10.5 Practice and Applications (pp. 566–568)
11. $\sin A = \frac{11}{61}$; $\cos A = \frac{60}{61}$ **13.** $\sin A = \frac{12}{13}$;
$\cos A = \frac{5}{13}$ **15.** $\sin P = \frac{6\sqrt{2}}{11} \approx 0.7714$;
$\cos P = \frac{7}{11} \approx 0.6364$ **17.** 0.6428 **19.** 0.9848
21. 0.8572 **23.** 1 **25.** $x \approx 5.8$; $y \approx 5.6$ **27.** $x \approx 5.3$;
$y \approx 9.6$ **29.** $x \approx 9.0$; $y \approx 12.0$ **31.** 14 ft

33. Answers will vary. **35.** $(\sin A)^2 + (\cos A)^2 = 1$
37. Both students will get the correct answer.
41. $x = 7\sqrt{3}$; $y = 14$ **43.** 0.6249 **45.** 1.4826
47. 0.3057 **49.** $-18, -8, -1.8, -0.8, 0, 0.08, 1.8$
51. $-0.61, -0.6, -0.56, -0.5, -0.47$

10.6 Guided Practice (p. 572) **3.** false **5.** 6.4
7. 79.6° **9.** 67.4° **11.** $d \approx 7.2$; $m\angle D \approx 31.0°$;
$m\angle E \approx 59.0°$

10.6 Practice and Applications (pp. 573–575)
13. 45° **15.** 13.0° **17.** 76.4° **19.** *Sample answer:*
Use the inverse tangent function; 48.9°.
21. $x = 7\sqrt{2} \approx 9.9$; $m\angle A = 45°$ **23.** $x = 29$;
$m\angle A \approx 43.6°$ **25.** 81.3° **27.** 63.3° **29.** 39.5°
31. *Sample answer:* 28 ft (Any length greater than
or equal to 27.6 ft will meet the standards.)
33. 14.9° **35.** 36.9° **37.** $LM \approx 5.7$; $m\angle L \approx 70.3°$;
$m\angle K \approx 19.7°$ **39.** $ST \approx 13.7$; $m\angle R \approx 66.4°$;
$m\angle S \approx 23.6°$ **43.** 50 cm; 201 cm^2 **45.** 107 yd;
908 yd^2 **47.** 11,494 cm^3 **49.** 0.554 **51.** 32.55
53. 2000

Quiz 2 (p. 575) **1.** 6.7 **2.** 3.9 **3.** $x \approx 9.2$; $y \approx 7.7$
4. $x \approx 6.8$; $y \approx 17.7$ **5.** 7.8 **6.** $x \approx 4.6$; $y \approx 6.6$
7. 3.0777 **8.** 0.7880 **9.** 0.8090 **10.** $m\angle N = 50°$;
$m \approx 13.4$; $q \approx 20.9$ **11.** $m\angle P \approx 61.0°$; $m\angle Q \approx 29.0°$;
$q \approx 3.9$ **12.** $m\angle K \approx 76.0°$; $m\angle L \approx 14.0°$; $k \approx 12.0$

Chapter Summary and Review (pp. 576–579)
1. radical **3.** trigonometric ratio **5.** solve
7. tangent **9.** sine **11.** 12 **13.** 112 **15.** 5
17. 99 **19.** $6\sqrt{2}$ **21.** $2\sqrt{17}$ **23.** $4\sqrt{5}$ **25.** $13\sqrt{3}$
27. 50.9 **29.** $15\sqrt{2}$ **31.** $\sqrt{14}$ **33.** 3 **35.** $x = 50$;
$y = 25\sqrt{3} \approx 43.3$ **37.** $x = 94$; $y = 188$
39. $\tan A = \dfrac{8}{15} \approx 0.5333$; $\tan B = \dfrac{15}{8} = 1.875$
41. $\tan A = \dfrac{3}{2} = 1.5$; $\tan B = \dfrac{2}{3} \approx 0.6667$
43. 6.3138 **45.** 0.4452 **47.** $\sin A = \dfrac{5}{9} \approx 0.5556$;
$\cos A = \dfrac{2\sqrt{14}}{9} \approx 0.8315$ **49.** 0.8387 **51.** 0.8572
53. $x \approx 5.2$; $y \approx 8.6$ **55.** 5.1° **57.** 50.4°
59. $q \approx 26.9$; $m\angle P \approx 58.7°$; $m\angle R \approx 31.3°$

Algebra Review (p. 583) **1.** $(-2, 3)$ **3.** $(-5, 18)$
5. $(1, 2)$ **7.** $(1, 1)$ **9.** $(3, -4)$

Chapter 11

Study Guide (p. 588) **1.** D **2.** F **3.** D

11.1 Guided Practice (p. 591) **3.** E **5.** A **7.** F
9. (3, 0) and (3, 6) **11.** (0, 3) and (3, 0)

11.1 Practice and Applications (pp. 591–593)
13. 7.5 cm **15.** 1.5 ft **17.** 52 in. **19.** 17.4 m
21. chord **23.** diameter **25.** point of tangency

27. chord **29.** diameter **31.** tangent **33.** $\overline{EG}$ is a
chord (as is $\overline{EF}$); $\overleftrightarrow{EG}$ is a secant; $\overline{EF}$ is a diameter;
$\overline{CE}$ is a radius (as are $\overline{CF}$ and $\overline{CG}$); D is a point of
tangency. **35.** $\overline{LM}$ is a chord (as is $\overline{PN}$); $\overleftrightarrow{LM}$ is a
secant; $\overline{PN}$ is a diameter; $\overline{QR}$ is a radius (as are
$\overline{QP}$ and $\overline{QN}$); K is a point of tangency. **37.** any
two of $\overline{GD}$, $\overline{HC}$, $\overline{FA}$, and $\overline{EB}$ **39.** Yes; $\overleftrightarrow{JK}$ is a
tangent through J, G, and K. **41.** 2; 2 **43.** $\odot A$:
(3, 2); $\odot B$: (3, 3); intersection: (3, 0); tangent line:
x-axis **45.** 2; 4

47.
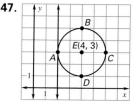

51. SSS Congruence
Postulate; three sides of
$\triangle JKL$ are congruent to
three sides of $\triangle PQR$,
so $\triangle JKL \cong \triangle PQR$ by
the SSS Congruence
Postulate.

53. yes **55.** 5.7 **57.** 6.3 **59.** 9.9 **61.** 15.8 **63.** 7
65. -1 **67.** -9

11.2 Guided Practice (p. 598) **3.** No; $5^2 + 5^2 \neq 7^2$,
so $\triangle ABD$ is not a right triangle and $\overline{AB}$ is not
perpendicular to $\overline{BD}$. Therefore, $\overline{BD}$ is not
tangent to $\odot C$. **5.** 2

11.2 Practice and Applications (pp. 598–600) **7.** 3
9. 15 **11.** 15 **13.** $x^2 + 4x + 4$ **15.** $x^2 + 14x + 49$
17. 3 **19.** 20 **21.** No; $5^2 + 14^2 \neq 15^2$, so $\triangle ABC$ is
not a right triangle and $\overline{AB}$ is not perpendicular
to $\overline{AC}$. Therefore, $\overline{AB}$ is not tangent to $\odot C$.
23. $\angle ABC \cong \angle ADC$; $\angle DAC \cong \angle BAC$;
$\angle BCA \cong \angle DCA$.

25.
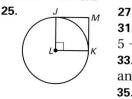

27. $BA = BC \approx 15{,}977$ miles
31. Yes; $5 + 11 > 14$,
$5 + 14 > 11$, and $11 + 14 > 5$.
33. Yes; $15 + 3 > 13$, $15 + 13 > 3$,
and $3 + 13 > 15$.
35. No; $3 + 7 = 10$.

37. 10 **39.** 19 **41.** $-\dfrac{2}{3}$ **43.** $\dfrac{5}{2}$ **45.** $\dfrac{1}{3}$

11.3 Guided Practice (p. 604) **5.** 300° **7.** 100°
9. 40° **11.** 10.47 cm

11.3 Practice and Applications (pp. 604–607)
13. $\overset{\frown}{PQ}$; 135° **15.** $\overset{\frown}{LN}$; 150° **17.** $\overset{\frown}{WXY}$; 200°
19. minor arc **21.** semicircle **23.** major arc
25. major arc **27.** 165° **29.** 180° **31.** 55°
33. 305° **35.** 65° **37.** 60° **39.** 120° **41.** 90°
43. No; the circles are not congruent. **45.** Yes;
$\overset{\frown}{UW}$ and $\overset{\frown}{XZ}$ are arcs of congruent circles with the
same measure. **47.** 2.36 cm **49.** 20.94 ft

51. 15.71 m   **53.** No; they have the same arc length only if the two circles are congruent circles.   **57.** $x \approx 5.0$; $y \approx 7.5$ **59.** $\frac{1}{200}$ **61.** $\frac{1}{3}$

Quiz 1 (p. 607)   **1.** tangent   **2.** secant   **3.** diameter   **4.** chord   **5.** radius   **6.** point of tangency   **7.** 15   **8.** 6   **9.** 4   **10.** $\frac{7}{6}\pi \approx 3.67$ cm   **11.** $\frac{35}{6}\pi \approx 18.33$ m   **12.** $\frac{25}{18}\pi \approx 4.36$ ft

11.4 Guided Practice (p. 610)   **3.** 7   **5.** 8

11.4 Practice and Applications (pp. 611–612)
7. No; $\overline{AB}$ does not bisect $\overline{CD}$, so $\overline{AB}$ is not a diameter of the circle.   **9.** 7   **11.** 3   **13.** $\overarc{AB} \cong \overarc{CD}$ (given) and $\overline{AB} \cong \overline{CD}$ (If two minor arcs are congruent, then their corresponding chords are congruent.)   **15.** 10   **17.** 170°   **19.** 7   **23. a.** In a circle, if two chords are congruent, then their corresponding minor arcs are congruent.
b. 10   **c.** $m\overarc{AD} = m\overarc{BE} = 110°$ **d.** 100°   **25.** 75°
27. 140°   **29.** 220°   **31.** $\frac{15}{20} > -\frac{3}{4}$

11.5 Guided Practice (p. 617)
3. 40°   **5.** 210°   **7.** $y = 150$; $z = 75$

11.5 Practice and Applications (pp. 617–619)
9. 55°   **11.** 90°   **13.** 67°   **15.** 64°   **17.** 228°
19. 100°   **21.** 94°   **23.** 53°   **25.** 53°   **27.** Yes. Explanations may vary; *Sample answer:* $m\angle BAC = 47° = m\angle CDE$ (from Ex. 22) and $m\angle DCE = m\angle ACB$ (vertical angles), so $\triangle ABC \sim \triangle DEC$ by the AA Similarity Postulate.
29. $\triangle KLM$ is an inscribed triangle and $\overline{KM}$ is a diameter, so $\triangle KLM$ is a right triangle with hypotenuse $\overline{KM}$; $x = 90$; $y = 90 - 40 = 50$.
31. *Sample answer:* Position the vertex of the tool on the circle and mark the two points at which the sides intersect the circle; draw a segment to connect the two points, forming a diameter of the circle. Repeat these steps, placing the vertex at a different point on the circle. The center is the point at which the two diameters intersect.
33. $x = 80$; $y = 78$ **35.** Yes; both pairs of opposite angles are right angles, which are supplementary angles.   **37.** No; if a rhombus is not a square, then the opposite angles are not supplementary.
41. $\sqrt{35}$ **43.** $2\sqrt{21}$ **45.** 27   **47.** $m\angle B = 46°$; $AC \approx 8.3$; $AB \approx 11.5$ **49.** $m\angle R = 40°$; $RP \approx 6.0$; $QR \approx 7.8$ **51.** 9   **53.** -12 **55.** 12

11.6 Guided Practice (p. 623)   **3.** 88°   **5.** 3   **7.** 12

11.6 Practice and Applications (pp. 623–625)   **9.** B
11. A   **13.** 50   **15.** 21   **17.** 186   **19.** 18   **21.** 12
23. 103   **25.** 60   **27. a.** 4   **b.** 90°   **c.** 144°   **d.** Yes. Explanations may vary. *Sample answer:* $\angle ACB \cong \angle ECD$ (vertical angles); $\frac{AC}{EC} = \frac{12}{9} = \frac{4}{3} = \frac{BC}{CD}$; by the SAS Similarity Theorem, $\triangle ACB \sim \triangle ECD$.   **29.** 34
31. 3   **33.** 19   **35.** 2.7   **37.** 10.01

Quiz 2 (p. 625)   **1.** 5   **2.** 3   **3.** 31   **4.** 102; the measure of an inscribed angle is half the measure of its intercepted arc, so $51 = \frac{1}{2}x$; $x = 102$.
5. $x = 58$ and $y = 41$; $x° = m\angle B = \frac{1}{2}m\overarc{AD} = m\angle C = 58°$; $y° = m\angle D = \frac{1}{2}m\overarc{BC} = m\angle A = 41°$.
6. $x = 75$ and $y = 82$; the opposite angles of an inscribed quadrilateral are supplementary, so $x° = 180° - 105° = 75°$ and $y° = 180° - 98° = 82°$.
7. 62   **8.** 163   **9.** 6

11.7 Guided Practice (p. 629)   **3.** radius, 4; center, $(2, 0)$; equation, $(x - 2)^2 + y^2 = 16$

11.7 Practice and Applications (pp. 630–632)
5. B   **7.** C
9. radius, 1; center, $(0, 0)$;

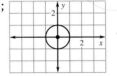

11. radius, 4; center, $(4, 3)$;

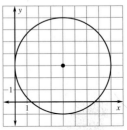

13. radius, 6; center, $(-2, 3)$;

15. radius, 8; center, $(0, 5)$;

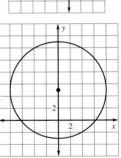

17. radius, 2; center, (0, 1); equation, $x^2 + (y - 1)^2 = 4$ **19.** radius, 2.5; center, (0.5, 1.5); equation, $(x - 0.5)^2 + (y - 1.5)^2 = 6.25$ **21.** radius, 6; center, (0, 0); equation, $x^2 + y^2 = 36$ **23.** $(x - 4)^2 + y^2 = 16$ **25.** $(x + 1)^2 + (y + 3)^2 = 36$ **27.** $(x - 1)^2 + y^2 = 49$ **29.** inside **31.** outside **33.** on **35.** inside **37.** Tower A transmits to J; tower B transmits to K; towers B and C transmit to L; no tower transmits to M; tower C transmits to N. **43.** $P'(3, 3)$; $Q'(8, 1)$; $R'(6, -2)$; $S'(1, 0)$ **45.** $P'(0, 2)$; $Q'(5, 0)$; $R'(3, -3)$; $S'(-2, -1)$ **47.** reduction; $\frac{3}{8}$ **49.** -7 **51.** 8

11.8 Guided Practice (p. 636) **3.** yes; a clockwise or counterclockwise rotation of 180° about its center **5.** no **7.** P **9.** R

11.8 Practice and Applications (pp. 636–639) **11.** yes; a clockwise or counterclockwise rotation of 72° or 144° about its center **13.** The wheel hub can be mapped onto itself by a clockwise or counterclockwise rotation of 72° or 144° about its center. **15.** The wheel hub can be mapped onto itself by a clockwise or counterclockwise rotation of 45°, 90°, 135°, or 180° about its center.

17. **19.**

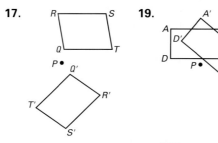

21. **23.** $\overline{LH}$ **25.** $\triangle MAB$ **27.** $J'(1, 2)$; $K'(4, 1)$; $L'(4, -3)$; $M'(1, -3)$; the coordinates of the image of the point (x, y) after a 90° clockwise rotation about the origin are $(y, -x)$.

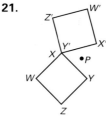

29. $A'(-1, -1)$; $B'(-4, 2)$; $C'(-2, 5)$; the coordinates of the image of the point (x, y) after a 90° counterclockwise rotation about the origin are $(-y, x)$. **31.** The design has rotational symmetry about its center; it can be mapped onto itself by a clockwise or counterclockwise rotation of 180°. **33.** Yes. The image can be mapped onto itself by a clockwise or counterclockwise rotation of 180° about its center. **35.** the center of the circle **39.** 91 ft^2 **41.** 80 m^2 **43.** 9.5 **45.** 0

Quiz 3 (p. 639) **1.** center, $(-1, 6)$; radius, 5 **2.** $x^2 + (y + 4)^2 = 9$

3. **4.**

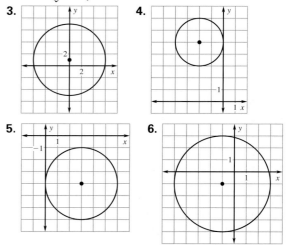

5. **6.**

7. yes; a clockwise or counterclockwise rotation of 90° or 180° about its center **8.** yes; a clockwise or counterclockwise rotation of 180° about its center **9.** no **10.** $A'(-2, -4)$; $B'(-1, -1)$; $C'(1, -3)$; the coordinates of the image of the point (x, y) after a 180° rotation about the origin are $(-x, -y)$. **11.** $A'(-4, 1)$; $B'(-4, 4)$; $C'(-1, 4)$; $D'(-1, 2)$; the coordinates of the image of the point (x, y) after a 90° counterclockwise rotation about the origin are $(-y, x)$. **12.** $A'(0, -2)$; $B'(-1, -4)$; $C'(-3, -3)$; the coordinates of the image of the point (x, y) after a 90° clockwise rotation about the origin are $(y, -x)$.

Chapter Summary and Review (pp. 641–645) **1.** secant **3.** tangent **5.** inscribed angle **7.** rotation **9.** point of tangency **11.** center **13.** secant **15.** 10 **17.** 6 **19.** 7 **21.** 118° **23.** 85° **25.** 324° **27.** 16.76 cm **29.** 3 **31.** 35 **33.** 60 **35.** 53° **37.** 200° **39.** $x = 68$; $y = 99$ **41.** 95 **43.** 70 **45.** 5 **47.** $(x - 2)^2 + (y - 5)^2 = 9$ **49.** $(x - 5)^2 + (y + 2)^2 = 49$ **51.** radius, 4; center, $(2, -3)$;

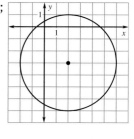

53.

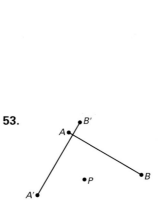

55.

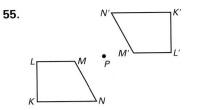

Cumulative Practice (pp. 649–651) **1.** 15 **3.** 118°
5. (1, 7) **7.** 20°; 110° **9.** 42°; 132° **11.** $x = 7$;
$m\angle APB = 28°$; $m\angle BPC = 152°$ **13.** Alternate
Exterior Angles Converse **15.** Same-Side Interior
Angles Converse **17.** 28° and 28°; Since the
triangle is isosceles, the base angles are
congruent. By the Triangle Sum Theorem, you
can show that each base angle has measure 28°.
19. smallest, $\angle A$; largest, $\angle B$ **21.** no **23.** Yes;
$\triangle XYU \cong \triangle VWU$ by the HL Congruence Theorem.
25. $x = 117$; $y = 117$ **27.** $x = 110$; $y = 70$; $z = 110$
29. *Sample answer:* $\angle CBD \cong \angle CAE$ and $\angle BCD \cong$
$\angle ACE$. Therefore, $\triangle BCD \sim \triangle ACE$ by the AA
Similarity Postulate. **31.** 312 m² **33.** 80 cm²
35. 6 m **37.** 628 cm²; 1005 cm³ **39.** 1810 mm²;
7238 mm³ **41.** $m\angle R \approx 22.6°$; $m\angle T \approx 67.4°$
43. $x = 25$; $p \approx 3.4$; $r \approx 7.3$ **45.** $d = 21$; $x \approx 46.4°$;
$y \approx 43.6°$ **47.** $m\overset{\frown}{AB} = 75°$; $m\overset{\frown}{ACB} = 285°$ **49.** 37
51. 145 **53.** $x^2 + (y + 3)^2 = 49$
55.

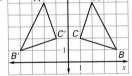

Skills Review Handbook

Problem Solving (p. 654) **1.** $197.46 **3.** at least
16 flower arrangements **5.** $5.96 **7.** 24 different
orders **9.** 20 diagonals

Decimals (p. 655)
1. 2.08 **3.** 180 **5.** 47.5 **7.** 28.26 **9.** 10 **11.** 8

Fraction Concepts (p. 656)
1–5. Sample answers are given. **1.** $\frac{1}{2}, \frac{2}{4}$ **3.** $\frac{2}{8}, \frac{3}{12}$
5. $\frac{6}{20}, \frac{15}{50}$ **7.** $\frac{2}{3}$ **9.** $\frac{1}{3}$ **11.** $\frac{5}{2}$ **13.** $\frac{3}{4}$ **15.** 1

Fractions and Decimals (p. 657)
1. 0.7 **3.** $0.\overline{3} \approx 0.33$ **5.** $0.\overline{2} \approx 0.22$ **7.** 0.125 **9.** 0.5
11. $\frac{1}{2}$ **13.** $\frac{1}{5}$ **15.** $\frac{3}{8}$ **17.** $\frac{2}{3}$ **19.** $\frac{2}{15}$

Adding and Subtracting Fractions (p. 658)
1. $\frac{6}{7}$ **3.** $\frac{1}{3}$ **5.** $\frac{1}{2}$ **7.** $\frac{4}{5}$ **9.** $\frac{5}{8}$ **11.** $1\frac{1}{4}$ **13.** $\frac{11}{35}$
15. $\frac{7}{24}$ **17.** 1 **19.** $1\frac{22}{45}$ **21.** $\frac{13}{15}$ **23.** $\frac{13}{20}$

Multiplying and Dividing Fractions (p. 659)
1. $\frac{3}{8}$ **3.** $2\frac{1}{2}$ **5.** $\frac{5}{27}$ **7.** 15 **9.** $\frac{2}{3}$ **11.** 63 **13.** $\frac{1}{4}$
15. $114\frac{2}{7}$ **17.** 2 **19.** 154 **21.** 1 **23.** 1 **25.** 8 **27.** 4

Ratio and Proportion (p. 661) **1.** $\frac{5}{1}$ **3.** $\frac{2}{3}$ **5.** $\frac{2}{25}$
7. $\frac{12}{5}$ **9.** $\frac{1}{1}$ **11.** $\frac{16}{5}$ **13.** $\frac{20}{9}$ **15.** $\frac{3}{5}$ **17.** $12\frac{1}{2}$
19. $\frac{4}{5}$ **21.** $2\frac{4}{7}$ **23.** 0.3 or $\frac{3}{10}$ **25.** 25 **27.** 14
29. $2\frac{2}{5}$

Inequalities and Absolute Value (p. 662)
1. $6 > -6$ **3.** $-2 > -8$ **5.** $-7.8 < -7.6$
7. $0.01 < 0.1$ **9.** $-8, -6, -2, 0, 3, 4, 9$ **11.** 5124,
5142, 5214, 5412, 5421 **13.** 6 **15.** 0 **17.** 1.4

Integers (p. 663) **1.** -10 **3.** 2 **5.** 11 **7.** 0 **9.** -16
11. 60 **13.** -40 **15.** 2 **17.** 16 **19.** -6 **21.** -100
23. -12 **25.** -6 **27.** 9

The Coordinate Plane (p. 664)
1. $(-1, 0)$ **3.** $(2, -2)$ **5.** $(-5, 3)$ **7.** $(5, -2)$
9. $(-2, 5)$ **11.** $(1, 1)$
13–28.

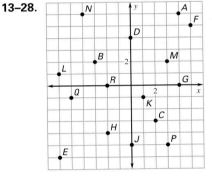

Slope of a Line (p. 665) **1.** $-\frac{1}{3}$ **3.** 2 **5.** 1 **7.** $-\frac{2}{3}$
9. 0 **11.** negative **13.** zero **15.** positive

Graphing Linear Equations (p. 666)

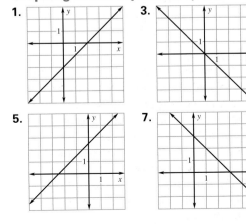

9.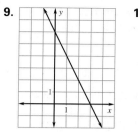

11.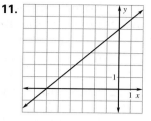

Slope-Intercept Form (p. 667)

1.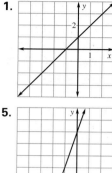

3.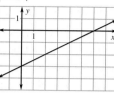

5.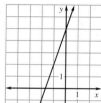

7.

9. parallel **11.** not parallel

Powers and Square Roots (p. 669)
1. 64 **3.** -1
5. 32 **7.** 81 **9.** 10, -10 **11.** 1, -1 **13.** no real square roots **15.** no real square roots **17.** 10
19. 3.9 **21.** 2 **23.** 3.3 **25.** 6.7 **27.** 0 **29.** $2\sqrt{7}$
31. $5\sqrt{2}$ **33.** $\frac{\sqrt{5}}{4}$ **35.** $\frac{1}{3}$ **37.** $\frac{\sqrt{3}}{3}$ **39.** $\frac{5\sqrt{2}}{2}$

Evaluating Expressions (p. 670)
1. 105 **3.** 21 **5.** -8 **7.** 13 **9.** 33 **11.** 81 **13.** 5 **15.** 60 **17.** -24

The Distributive Property (p. 671)
1. $2a + 8$ **3.** $3x - 2$ **5.** $y^2 - 9y$ **7.** $4b^2 + 12b$ **9.** $6m + 4$ **11.** $x^2 + 5x - 14$ **13.** $10 - 2x$ **15.** $3h - 3h^2$ **17.** $3y^2 - 6y$

Solving One-Step Equations (p. 672)
1. 6 **3.** -8 **5.** 13 **7.** 3 **9.** -28 **11.** -5 **13.** 4 **15.** -1 **17.** 24 **19.** -5

Solving Multi-Step Equations (p. 673)
1. 4 **3.** 5 **5.** -7 **7.** 26 **9.** -4 **11.** -8 **13.** 22 **15.** 13 **17.** $\frac{1}{2}$ **19.** 1 **21.** 4 **23.** 2 **25.** $-\frac{1}{3}$ **27.** -4 **29.** 12 **31.** -23 **33.** 1

Using Formulas (p. 674)
1. 6 m **3.** 22 mm **5.** 4 in. **7.** 9 m

Extra Practice

Chapter 1 (pp. 675–676)
1.   **3.** Each number is 5 times the previous number; 625. **5.** Each number is 3 more than the previous number; 4.
7. Multiply the previous number by $\frac{2}{3}$; $\frac{16}{81}$.
9. positive **11.** The absolute value of 0 is 0.
13. *Sample answer:* $2 \div 6 = \frac{1}{3}$, which is not an integer. **15.** *Sample answer:*

17. R **19.** $\overline{PQ}$, $\overline{PS}$, $\overline{PM}$ **21.** $\overleftrightarrow{NM}$

23. *Sample answer:*

25. 18 **27.** yes **29.** Q; $\overrightarrow{QP}$, $\overrightarrow{QR}$; any two of $\angle PQR$, $\angle RQP$, $\angle Q$ **31.** B; $\overrightarrow{BA}$, $\overrightarrow{BC}$; $\angle ABC$, $\angle CBA$ **33.** $65°$

Chapter 2 (pp. 677–678)
1. 30; 15 **3.** 14 **5.** $(3, 0)$ **7.** $(1.5, 3)$ **9.** $(-1.5, -1.5)$ **11.** $50°$ **13.** neither; adjacent **15.** $37°$; $127°$ **17.** $\angle 1$ and $\angle 3$; $\angle 1$ and $\angle 3$ are both supplementary to $\angle 2$, so $\angle 1 \cong \angle 3$ by the Congruent Supplements Theorem.
19. $m\angle 1 = 95°$; $m\angle 2 = 85°$; $m\angle 3 = 95°$ **21.** If <u>you read it in a newspaper</u>, then $\boxed{\text{it must be true}}$.
23. If <u>a number is odd</u>, then $\boxed{\text{its square is odd}}$.
25. If it is hot today, then I will go to the beach.
27. Addition Property of Equality **29.** Transitive Property of Equality **31.** Subtraction Property of Equality

Chapter 3 (pp. 679–680)
1–5. Sample answers are given. **1.** $\overleftrightarrow{BC}$, $\overleftrightarrow{GF}$, $\overleftrightarrow{HE}$ **3.** $\overleftrightarrow{EC}$, $\overleftrightarrow{HB}$, $\overleftrightarrow{HG}$
5. GAB, FDC **7.** no **9.** yes **11.** yes **13.** 15
15. alternate exterior angles **17.** alternate interior angles **19.** alternate exterior angles
21. $m\angle 1 = 140°$, by the Same-Side Interior Angles Theorem; $m\angle 2 = 40°$, by the Vertical Angles Theorem **23.** $m\angle 1 = 95°$, by the Linear Pair Postulate; $m\angle 2 = 85°$, by the Corresponding Angles Postulate **25.** $m\angle 1 = 110°$, by the Alternate Exterior Angles Theorem; $m\angle 2 = 110°$, by the Corresponding Angles Postulate **27.** yes
29. yes **31.** Same-Side Interior Angles Converse **33.** 13 **35.** 5 **37.** no **39.** yes **41.** $(-3, 5)$
43. $(-5, 11)$ **45.** $(-10, 2)$

Chapter 4 (pp. 681–682) **1.** scalene **3.** scalene
5. obtuse **7.** $\overline{AB}$ is opposite $\angle C$; $\overline{BC}$ is opposite $\angle A$; $\overline{AC}$ is opposite $\angle B$. **9.** 79° **11.** 60° **13.** 18
15. 55°, 55°, 70° **17.** 15 **19.** 10 **21.** 3.2 **23.** right
25. obtuse **27.** right **29.** right **31.** acute
33. $JP = 14$; $JM = 21$ **35.** $\angle M$, $\angle K$, $\angle L$ **37.** $\angle R$,
$\angle S$, $\angle T$ **39.** $\overline{DE}$, $\overline{EF}$, $\overline{DF}$ **41.** Yes; $7 + 7 > 7$.
43. No; $1 + 2 < 4$.

Chapter 5 (pp. 683–684) **1.** $\overline{RS} \cong \overline{PN}$, $\overline{ST} \cong \overline{NM}$,
$\overline{TR} \cong \overline{MP}$ **3.** $\triangle RST \cong \triangle PNM$ **5.** yes;
$\triangle XVW \cong \triangle XYZ$ **7.** yes; SSS Congruence
Postulate **9.** yes; SAS Congruence Postulate
11. yes; ASA Congruence Postulate **13.** no
15. yes; ASA Congruence Postulate

17.

Statements	Reasons
1. $\overline{EG} \cong \overline{HG}$; $\overline{GF} \cong \overline{GJ}$	1. Given
2. $\angle EGF \cong \angle HGJ$	2. Vertical $\angle$ are $\cong$.
3. $\triangle GEF \cong \triangle GHJ$	3. SAS Congruence Postulate
4. $\angle GEF \cong \angle GHJ$	4. Corresp. parts of $\cong \triangle$ are $\cong$.

19.

Statements	Reasons
1. $\overline{QT} \cong \overline{ST}$; $\overline{RQ} \cong \overline{RS}$	1. Given
2. $\overline{RT} \cong \overline{RT}$	2. Reflexive Property of Congruence
3. $\triangle RQT \cong \triangle RST$	3. SSS Congruence Postulate
4. $\angle RQT \cong \angle RST$	4. Corresp. parts of $\cong \triangle$ are $\cong$.

21. 7 **23.** 10 **25.** neither **27.** 1 **29.** 0

Chapter 6 (pp. 685–686) **1.** No; one of the sides is
not a segment. **3.** yes; hexagon **5.** 64 **7.** $\overline{XY}$;
opposite sides of a parallelogram are congruent.
9. $\overline{VY}$; opposite sides of a parallelogram are
congruent. **11.** $\overline{VY}$; by definition, a
parallelogram is a quadrilateral with both pairs
of opposite sides parallel. **13.** $\angle YVW$ and $\angle YXW$;
the consecutive angles of a parallelogram are
supplementary. **15.** $m\angle A = m\angle C = 38°$,
$m\angle D = 142°$ **17.** $m\angle B = m\angle D = 86°$, $m\angle A = 94°$
19. Yes; opposite angles are congruent. **21.** Yes;
opposite sides are congruent. **23.** Yes; the
diagonals bisect each other. **25.** parallelogram,
rectangle, rhombus, square **27.** rectangle, square
29. rhombus, square **31.** $m\angle A = 70°$; $m\angle B = 110°$;
$m\angle D = 70°$ **33.** $m\angle F = 125°$; $m\angle G = 110°$

35. 23 **37.** No; opposite sides are not congruent.
39. No; it is not given that the sides are all
congruent. **41.** rectangle

Chapter 7 (pp. 687–688) **1.** $\frac{20}{1}$ **3.** $\frac{5}{8}$ **5.** 20 ft by 15 ft
7. 7 **9.** 32 **11.** 7 **13.** 2 **15.** $\angle P \cong \angle T$; $\angle Q \cong \angle V$;
$\angle R \cong \angle W$; $\angle S \cong \angle X$ **17.** 9 **19.** 10 **21.** yes;
$\triangle ABC \sim \triangle DEF$ **23.** no **25.** $\triangle RQS \sim \triangle RPT$
27. no **29.** $\angle M \cong \angle M$ by the Reflexive Property of
Congruence. Also, $\frac{15}{15+5} = \frac{3}{4}$ and $\frac{21}{21+7} = \frac{3}{4}$.
The lengths of the sides that include $\angle M$ are
proportional. So, by the SAS Similarity Theorem,
the triangles are similar. **31.** 12 **33.** 17 **35.** Yes;
$\frac{4}{8} = \frac{1}{2}$. **37.** reduction; 22 **39.** enlargement; 12.5

Chapter 8 (pp. 689–690) **1.** concave **3.** concave
5. No; the polygon is equilateral, but it is not
equiangular. **7.** 1800° **9.** 2880° **11.** 108 **13.** 60
15. 46 **17.** 112 in.^{2} **19.** 80 m^2 **21.** 49 in.^{2}
23. 7.5 yd^2 **25.** 10 ft **27.** 108 in.^{2} **29.** 55 ft^2
31. 216 m^2 **33.** 31 in.; 79 in.^{2} **35.** 82 ft; 531 ft^2
37. 20 ft^2

Chapter 9 (pp. 691–692) **1.** yes; pentagon;
pentagonal pyramid **3.** yes; rectangle;
rectangular prism **5.** hexagonal pyramid; 7 faces;
12 edges **7.** 220 cm^2 **9.** 120 in.^{2} **11.** 339 cm^2
13. 85 in.^{2} **15.** 800 ft^2 **17.** 283 cm^2 **19.** 200 cm^3
21. 60 in.^{3} **23.** 424 cm^3 **25.** 480 cm^3 **27.** 12 m^3
29. 871 ft^3 **31.** 804 cm^2; 2145 cm^3 **33.** 4072 in.^{2};
24,429 in.^{3} **35.** $\frac{4}{3}\pi$ cm^3, 36π cm^3; 1 : 27

Chapter 10 (pp. 693–694) **1.** 7.6 **3.** 6.4 **5.** 10.3
7. 7 **9.** 18 **11.** $3\sqrt{11}$ **13.** $5\sqrt{6}$ **15.** $7\sqrt{2}$
17. $x = 45$; $y = 5\sqrt{2}$; By the Triangle Sum Theorem,
$x° + 45° + 90° = 180°$. So $x° = 45°$. Since the
measure of each acute angle is 45°, the triangle is
a 45°-45°-90° triangle. **19.** $x = \sqrt{2}$; $y = 2$; Let each
acute angle measure $d°$. By the Triangle Sum
Theorem, $d° + d° + 90° = 180°$. So, $2d° = 90°$, and
$d° = 45°$. Since the measure of each acute angle
is 45°, the triangle is a 45°-45°-90° triangle.
21. $x = 7$; $y = 7\sqrt{3}$ **23.** $x = 5\sqrt{3}$; $y = 10$
25. $\tan R = \frac{8}{15} \approx 0.5333$; $\tan S = \frac{15}{8} = 1.875$
27. $\tan R = \frac{2}{3} \approx 0.6667$; $\tan S = \frac{3}{2} = 1.5$
29. 3.0777 **31.** 0.1584 **33.** 0.1763 **35.** 4.0108
37. 1.1504 **39.** 13.3 **41.** $\sin R = \frac{8}{17} \approx 0.4706$;
$\cos R = \frac{15}{17} \approx 0.8824$ **43.** $\sin R = \frac{2}{\sqrt{13}} \approx 0.5547$;
$\cos R = \frac{3}{\sqrt{13}} \approx 0.8321$ **45.** 0.2079 **47.** 0.6428

49. 0.6820 **51.** 0.9397 **53.** 0.2079 **55.** $x \approx 7.9$; $y \approx 16.2$ **57.** 41.1° **59.** 72.9° **61.** 27.0° **63.** 72.2° **65.** 21.9° **67.** 72.8° **69.** $AB = 15$; $m\angle A \approx 53.1°$; $m\angle B \approx 36.9°$ **71.** $XY = \sqrt{65} \approx 8.1$; $m\angle X \approx 26.4°$; $m\angle Z \approx 63.6°$

Chapter 11 (pp. 695–696) **1.** chord **3.** radius **5.** tangent **7.** $\odot C$, (3, 1); $\odot D$, (7, 1) **9.** 2 **11.** 20 **13.** 6 **15.** 55° **17.** 35° **19.** 145° **21.** 270° **23.** about 11.78 **25.** 22 **27.** 14 **29.** 65 **31.** $x = 80$; $y = 100$ **33.** 80 **35.** 107 **37.** 3; (1, −3);

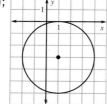

39. $x^2 + (y + 1)^2 = 400$ **41.** $(x − 3)^2 + (y − 4)^2 = 49$ **43.** $E'(5, −2)$, $F'(5, −5)$, $G'(2, −7)$, $H'(2, 0)$; $(x, y) \to (y, −x)$ **45.** yes; 180° **47.** yes; 120° clockwise or counterclockwise

Appendices

Appendix 1 Precision and Accuracy (pp. 711–712)
1. 2 in.; $2\frac{1}{2}$ in.; $2\frac{1}{4}$ in.; $2\frac{1}{4}$ in. **3.** 1 in.; $\frac{1}{2}$ in.
5. 1 yd; $\frac{1}{2}$ yd **7.** $\frac{1}{2}$ ft; $\frac{1}{4}$ ft **9.** 5 mi; The exact length of the highway is between 515 miles and 525 miles. **11.** 6.3% **13.** 0.4% **15.** 0.4% **17.** The paper measurement is more accurate because its relative error is smaller than the relative error of the desk measurement. **19.** 1 km; 0.5 km; 10% **21.** 0.1 cm; 0.05 cm; 1.6% **23.** 4.5 ft is more precise; 4.5 ft is more accurate. **25.** 2 cm is more precise; the measurements are equally accurate. **27.** the measurements are equally precise; 9.6 cm is more accurate.

Appendix 2 Geometric Probability (pp. 713–714)
1. 50% **3.** 10% **5.** 100% **7.** 50% **9.** 50% **11.** 55.6% **13.** 6.25% **15.** 31.25% **17.** 100%

Appendix 3: Changing Dimensions of Figures (pp. 715–716)
1.

	Original circle	Radius doubled	Radius tripled
Radius	1 in.	2 in.	3 in.
Circumference	2π in.	4π in.	6π in.
Area	π in.^{2}	4π in.^{2}	9π in.^{2}

When the radius is doubled, the circumference is doubled and the area is multiplied by 4. When the radius is tripled, the circumference is tripled and the area is multiplied by 9. **3.** The perimeter is multiplied by 5, and the area is multiplied by 5^2, or 25. **5.** You can double the lengths (radius and height). **7.** 36 m, 72 m; the lengths are doubled, and the perimeters are doubled. **9.** The area is doubled. **11.** 64 m^3; 512 m^3; 1728 m^3 **13.** 10 ft^3; 80 ft^3; 270 ft^3

Appendix 4: Estimating Measurements (pp. 717–718)
1. 24 cm; 28 cm^2 **3.** 7 m; 2 m^2 **5.** Answers may vary. *Sample answer:* Yes, because 300 · 400 = 120,000, which is close to 100,000. **7.** 148 ft^2; 88 ft^3 **9.** 300 m^2; 500 m^3 **11.** 600 in.^{2}; yes **13.** Estimates may vary; about 9 square units

MATHEMATICS REFERENCE SHEET

Area

Triangle $\qquad A = \frac{1}{2}bh$

Rectangle $\qquad A = lw$

Trapezoid $\qquad A = \frac{1}{2}h(b_1 + b_2)$

Parallelogram $\qquad A = bh$

Circle $\qquad A = \pi r^2$

Key

b = base

h = height

l = length

w = width

ℓ = slant height

$S.A.$ = surface area

d = diameter

r = radius

A = area

C = circumference

V = volume

Use 3.14 or $\frac{22}{7}$ for π.

Circumference

$$C = \pi d = 2\pi r$$

	Volume	Total Surface Area
Right Circular Cone	$V = \frac{1}{3}\pi r^2 h$	$S.A. = \frac{1}{2}(2\pi r)\ell + \pi r^2 = \pi r\ell + \pi r^2$
Square Pyramid	$V = \frac{1}{3}l^2 h$	$S.A. = 4\left(\frac{1}{2}l\ell\right) + l^2 = 2l\ell + l^2$
Sphere	$V = \frac{4}{3}\pi r^3$	$S.A. = 4\pi r^2$
Right Circular Cylinder	$V = \pi r^2 h$	$S.A. = 2\pi rh + 2\pi r^2$
Rectangular Solid	$V = lwh$	$S.A. = 2(lw) + 2(hw) + 2(lh)$

In the following formulas, n represents the number of sides:

In a polygon, the sum of the measures of the interior angles is equal to $180(n - 2)$.

In a regular polygon, the measure of an interior angle is equal to $\frac{180(n - 2)}{n}$.